Preface

Our goal in writing this book was to combine a strong emphasis on problem solving and software design with the study of data structures. To this end, we discuss applications of each data structure to motivate its study. After providing the specification (interface) and the implementation (a Java class) we then cover case studies that use the data structure to solve a significant problem. Examples include an ordered list, postfix expression evaluation using a stack, simulation of an airline ticket counter using a queue, and Huffman coding using a binary tree and a priority queue. In the implementation of each data structure and in the solutions of the case studies, we reinforce the message "Think, then code" by performing a thorough analysis of the problem and then carefully designing a solution (using pseudo-code and UML class diagrams) before the implementation. We also provide a performance analysis when appropriate. Readers gain an understanding of why different data structures are needed, the applications they are suited for, and the advantages and disadvantages of their possible implementations.

Intended Audience

This book was written for anyone with a curiosity or need to know about data structures, those essential elements of good programs and reliable software. We hope that the text will be useful to readers with either professional or educational interests.

It is intended as a textbook for the second programming course in a computing curriculum involving the study of data structures, especially one that emphasizes Object Oriented Design (OOD). The text could also be used in a more-advanced course in algorithms and data structures. Besides coverage of the basic data structures and algorithms (lists, stacks, queues, trees, recursion, sorting), there are chapters on sets and maps, balanced binary search trees, graphs, and an appendix on event-oriented programming. Although we expect that most readers will have completed a first programming course in Java, there is an extensive review chapter (included as an appendix) for those who may have taken a first programming course in a different object-oriented language, or for those who need a refresher in Java.

Emphasis on the Java Collections Framework

The book focuses on the interfaces and classes in the Java Collections Framework. We begin the study of a new data structure by specifying an abstract data type as an interface, which we adapt from the Java API. Readers are encouraged throughout the text to use the Java Collections Framework as a resource for their programming.

Our expectation is that readers who complete this book will be familiar with the data structures available in the Java Collections Framework and will be able to use them in their future programming. However, we also expect that they will want to know how the data structures are implemented, so we provide thorough discussions of classes that implement these data structures. Each class follows the approach taken by the Java designers where appropriate. However, when their industrial-strength solutions appear to be too complicated for beginners to understand, we have provided simpler implementations but have tried to be faithful to their approach.

Think, then Code

To help you "Think, then code" we discuss problem solving and introduce appropriate software design tools throughout the textbook. For example, Chapter 1 focuses on Object Oriented Design (OOD) and Class Hierarchies. It introduces the Uniform Modeling Language (also covered in Appendix B) to document an OOD. It introduces the use of interfaces to specify abstract data types and to facilitate contract programming and describes how to document classes using Javadoc-style comments. There is also coverage of exceptions and exception handling. Chapter 2 introduces the Java Collections Framework and focuses on the List interface, but it also discusses the use of big-O notation to analyze program efficiency. We also cover different testing strategies in some detail. (Appendix C provides further coverage of testing and debugging.) As part of our emphasis on OOD, we introduce two design patterns in Chapter 2, the object factory and delegation. We make use of them where appropriate in the textbook.

Features of Second Editions

We had two major goals in the second edition. The first was to begin the study of data structures earlier (Chapter 4 in the original edition). We accomplished this by streamlining the material formerly in the introductory chapters (Software Design, Program Correctness and Efficiency) and integrating key concepts into the study of OOD and data structures where appropriate as discussed above. This enabled us to cover Object Oriented Programming in Chapter 1 and lists in Chapter 2. It also makes the software design tools more relevant as they are taught in context rather than in isolation.

The second major goal was to update coverage of the Java Collections Framework to include new interfaces and classes in Java 6. To this end, we added discussions of new Java classes for implementing deques, priority queues, navigable sets and maps, and skip lists. We also replaced usage of the `StringTokenizer` (a legacy class) with the `String.split` method.

Case Studies

We illustrate OOD principles in the design and implementation of new data structures and in the solution of approximately 20 case studies. Case studies follow a five-step process (problem specification, analysis, design, implementation, and testing). As is done in industry, we sometimes perform these steps in an iterative fashion rather than in strict sequence. Several case studies have extensive discussions of testing and include methods that automate the testing process. Some case studies are revisited in later chapters, and solutions involving different data structures are compared. We also provide additional case studies on the Web site for the textbook (www.wiley.com/college/koffman), including one that illustrates a solution to the same problem using several different data structures.

Prerequisites

Our expectation is that the reader will be familiar with the Java primitive data types including `int`, `boolean`, `char`, and `double`; control structures including `if`, case, `while`, `for`, and `try-catch`; the `String` class; the one-dimensional array; input/output using either `JOptionPane` dialog windows or text streams (class `Scanner` or `BufferedReader`) and console input/output. For those readers who lack some of the concepts or who need some review, we provide complete coverage of these topics in Appendix A. Although labeled an Appendix, the review chapter provides full coverage of the background topics and has all the pedagogical features (discussed below) of the other chapters. We expect most readers will have some experience with Java programming, but someone who knows another object-oriented language should be able to undertake the book after careful study of the review chapter. We do not require prior knowledge of inheritance, wrapper classes, or `ArrayLists` as we cover them in the book (Chapters 1 and 2).

Pedagogy

The book contains the following pedagogical features to assist inexperienced programmers in learning the material.

- Learning objectives at the beginning of each chapter tell readers what skills they should develop.
- Introductions for each chapter help set the stage for what the chapter will cover and tie the chapter contents to other material that they have learned.
- Case Studies emphasize problem solving and provide complete and detailed solutions to real-world problems using the data structures studied in the chapter.
- Chapter Summaries review the contents of the chapter.
- Boxed Features emphasize and call attention to material designed to help readers become better programmers.

Pitfall boxes help readers identify common problems and how to avoid them.

Design Concept boxes illuminate programming design decisions and trade-offs.

Programming Style boxes discuss program features that illustrate good programming style and provide tips for writing clear and effective code.

Syntax boxes are a quick reference for the Java structures being introduced.

- Self-Check and Programming Exercises at the end of each section provide immediate feedback and practice for readers as they work through the chapter.
- Quick-Check, Review Exercises, and Programming Projects at the end of each chapter review chapter concepts and give readers a variety of skill-building activities, including longer projects that integrate chapter concepts as they exercise the use of data structures.

Theoretical Rigor

In Chapter 2, we discuss algorithm efficiency and big-O notation as a measure of algorithm efficiency. We have tried to strike a balance between pure "hand waving" and extreme rigor when determining the efficiency of algorithms. Rather than provide several paragraphs of formulas, we have provided simplified derivations of algorithm efficiency using big-O notation. We feel this will give readers an appreciation of the performance of various algorithms and methods and the process one follows to determine algorithm efficiency without bogging them down in unnecessary detail.

Overview of the book

Chapter 1 introduces Object Oriented Programming, inheritance, and class hierarchies including interfaces and abstract classes. We also introduce UML class diagrams and Javadoc-style documentation. The `Exception` class hierarchy is studied as an example of a Java class hierarchy.

Next, the Java Collections Framework is introduced as the foundation for the traditional data structures. These are covered in separate chapters: lists (Chapter 2), stacks (Chapter 3), and queues (Chapter 4). Each new data structure is introduced as an abstract data type (ADT). We provide a specification of each ADT in the form of a Java interface. Next, we implement the data structure as a class that implements the interface. Finally, we study applications of the data structure by solving sample problems and case studies.

Chapter 5 covers recursion so that readers are prepared for the study of trees, a recursive data structure. This chapter could be studied earlier. There is an optional section on list processing applications of recursion that may be skipped if the chapter is covered earlier.

Chapter 6 discusses binary trees, including binary search trees, heaps, priority queues, and Huffman trees.

Chapter 7 covers the `Set` and `Map` interfaces. It also discusses hashing and hash tables and shows how a hash table can be used in an implementation of these interfaces. The Huffman Tree case study is completed in this chapter.

Chapter 8 covers various sorting algorithms including mergesort, heapsort, and quicksort.

Chapter 9 covers self-balancing search trees, focusing on algorithms for manipulating them. Included are AVL and Red-Black trees, 2-3 trees, 2-3-4 trees, B-trees, and skip-lists.

Chapter 10 covers graphs. We provide several well-known algorithms for graphs, including Dijkstra's shortest path algorithm and Prim's minimal spanning tree algorithm. In most programs, the last few chapters would be covered in a second course in algorithms and data structures.

Supplements and Companion Web Sites

The following supplementary materials are available on the Instructor's Companion Web Site for this textbook at www.wiley.com/college/koffman. Items marked for students are accessible on the Student Companion Web Site at the same address.

- Additional homework problems with solutions
- Additional case studies, including one that illustrates a solution to the same problem using several different data structures
- Source code for all classes in the book (for students and instructors)
- PowerPoint slides
- Electronic test bank for instructors
- Solutions to end-of-section odd-numbered self-check and programming exercises (for students)
- Solutions to all exercises for instructors
- Solutions to chapter-review exercises for instructors
- Sample programming project solutions for instructors
- Additional homework problems, including cases studies and solutions

Acknowledgments

Many individuals helped us with the preparation of this book and improved it greatly. We are grateful to all of them. These include students at Temple University who have used notes that led to the preparation of this book in their coursework, and who class-tested early drafts of the book. We would like to thank Rolf Lakaemper and James Korsh, colleagues at Temple University, who used a preliminary draft in their classes. We would also like to thank a former Temple student, Michael Mayle, who provided preliminary solutions to many of the exercises.

We are especially grateful to our reviewers who provided invaluable comments that helped us correct errors in each version and helped us set our revision goals for the next version. The individuals who reviewed this book are listed below.

Reviewers of Second Edition

Mary Elaine Califf, *Illinois State University*
Adrienne Decker, *SUNY Buffalo*
Kenny Fong, *Southern Illinois University, Carbondale*
Allan M. Hart, *Minnesota State University, Mankato*
James K. Huggins, *Kettering University*
Lester McCann, *University of Arizona*
Thaddeus F. Pawlicki, *University of Rochester*
Salam N. Salloum, *California State Polytechnic University, Pomona*
Victor Shtern, *Boston University*

Reviewers of First Edition

Sheikh Iqbal Ahamed, *Marquette University*
Justin Beck, *Oklahoma State University*
John Bowles, *University of South Carolina*
Tom Cortina, *SUNY Stony Brook*
Chris Dovolis, *University of Minnesota*
Vladimir Drobot, *San Jose State University*
Ralph Grayson, *Oklahoma State University*
Chris Ingram, *University of Waterloo*
Gregory Kesden, *Carnegie Mellon University*
Sarah Matzko, *Clemson University*
Ron Metoyer, *Oregon State University*
Rich Pattis, *Carnegie Mellon University*
Sally Peterson, *University of Wisconsin—Madison*
Mike Scott, *University of Texas—Austin*
Mark Stehlik, *Carnegie Mellon University*
Ralph Tomlinson, *Iowa State University*
Frank Tompa, *University of Waterloo*
Renee Turban, *Arizona State University*
Paul Tymann, *Rochester Institute of Technology*
Karen Ward, *University of Texas—El Paso*
Jim Weir, *Marist College*
Lee Wittenberg, *Kean University*
Martin Zhao, *Mercer University*

Although all the reviewers provided invaluable suggestions, we do want to give special thanks to Chris Ingram who reviewed every version of the first edition of the manuscript, including the preliminary pages for the book. His care, attention to detail, and dedication helped us improve this book in many ways, and we are very grateful for his efforts.

Besides the principal reviewers, there were a number of faculty members who reviewed sample pages of the first edition online and made valuable comments and criticisms of its content. We would like to thank those individuals, listed below.

Content Connections Online Review

Razvan Andonie, *Central Washington University*
Antonia Boadi, *California State University Dominguez Hills*
Mikhail Brikman, *Salem State College*
Robert Burton, *Brigham Young University*
Chakib Chraibi, *Barry University*
Teresa Cole, *Boise State University*
Jose Cordova, *University of Louisiana Monroe*
Joyce Crowell, *Belmont University*
Robert Franks, *Central College*
Barabra Gannod, *Arizona State University East*
Wayne Goddard, *Clemson University*
Simon Gray, *College of Wooster*

Wei Hu, *Houghton College*
Edward Kovach, *Franciscan University of Steubenville*
Saeed Monemi, *California Polytechnic and State University*
Robert Noonan, *College of William and Mary*
Kathleen O'Brien, *Foothill College*
Rathika Rajaravivarma, *Central Connecticut State University*
Sam Rhoads, *Honolulu Community College*
Vijayakumar Shanmugasundaram, *Concordia College Moorhead*
Gene Sheppard, *Perimeter College*
Linda Sherrell, *University of Memphis*
Meena Srinivasan, *Mary Washington College*
David Weaver, *Sheperd University*
Stephen Weiss, *University of North Carolina—Chapel Hill*
Glenn Wiggins, *Mississippi College*
Bruce William, *California State University Pomona*

Finally, we want to acknowledge the participants in focus groups for the second programming course organized by John Wiley & Sons at the Annual Meeting of the SIGCSE Symposium in March 2004. They reviewed the preface, table of contents, and sample chapters and also provided valuable input on the book and future directions of the course.

Focus Group

Claude Anderson, *Rose-Human Institute*
Jay M. Anderson, *Franklin & Marshall University*
John Avitabile, *College of Saint Rose*
Cathy Bishop-Clark, *Miami University—Middletown*
Debra Burhans, *Canisius College*
Michael Clancy, *University of California—Berkeley*
Nina Cooper, *University of Nevada Las Vegas*
Kossi Edoh, *Montclair State University*
Robert Franks, *Central College*
Evan Golub, *University of Maryland*
Graciela Gonzalez, *Sam Houston State University*
Scott Grissom, *Grand Valley State University*
Jim Huggins, *Kettering University*
Lester McCann, *University of Wisconsin—Parkside*
Briana Morrison, *Southern Polytechnic State University*
Judy Mullins, *University of Missouri—Kansas City*
Roy Pargas, *Clemson University*
J.P. Pretti, *University of Waterloo*
Reza Sanati, *Utah Valley State College*
Barbara Smith, *University of Dayton*
Suzanne Smith, *East Tennessee State University*
Michael Stiber, *University of Washington, Bothell*
Jorge Vasconcelos, *University of Mexico (UNAM)*
Lee Wittenberg, *Kean University*

We would also like to acknowledge the team at John Wiley & Sons who were responsible for the inception and production of this book. Our editor, Beth Golub, was intimately involved in every detail of this book, from its origination to the final product. We are grateful to her for her confidence in us and for all the support and resources provided to help us accomplish our goal and to keep us on track. Mike Berlin assisted Beth and provided us with additional help when needed. Sujin Hong was the production editor for the book and ably managed all phases of the book's production.

We would like to acknowledge the help and support of our colleague Frank Friedman who also read an early draft of this textbook and offered suggestions for improvement. Frank and Elliot began writing textbooks together almost thirty-five years ago and Frank has had substantial influence on the format and content of these books. Frank also influenced Paul to begin his teaching career as an adjunct faculty member and then hired him as a full-time faculty member when he retired from industry. Paul is grateful for his continued support.

Finally, we would like to thank our wives who provided us with comfort and support through this arduous process. We very much appreciate their understanding and their sacrifices that enabled us to focus on this book, often during time we would normally be spending with them. In particular Elliot Koffman would like to thank

Caryn Koffman

and Paul Wolfgang would like to thank

Sharon Wolfgang

Contents

Chapter 1

Object-Oriented Programming and Class Hierarchies

Chapter Objectives

- To learn about interfaces and their role in Java
- To understand inheritance and how it facilitates code reuse
- To understand how Java determines which method to execute when there are multiple methods with the same name in a class hierarchy
- To become familiar with the Exception hierarchy and the difference between checked and unchecked exceptions
- To learn how to define and use abstract classes as base classes in a hierarchy
- To learn the role of abstract data types and how to specify them using interfaces
- To study class `Object` and its methods and to learn how to override them
- To become familiar with a class hierarchy for shapes
- To understand how to create packages and to learn more about visibility

This chapter describes important features of Java that support object-oriented programming (OOP). Object-oriented languages allow you to build and exploit hierarchies of classes in order to write code that may be more easily reused in new applications. You will learn how to extend an existing Java class to define a new class that inherits all the attributes of the original, as well as having additional attributes of its own. Because there may be many versions of the same method in a class hierarchy, we show how polymorphism enables Java to determine which version to execute at any given time.

We introduce interfaces and abstract classes and describe their relationship to each other and to actual classes. We introduce the abstract class `Number`. We also discuss class `Object`, which all classes extend, and we describe several of its methods that may be used in classes you create.

As an example of a class hierarchy and OOP, we describe the `Exception` class hierarchy and explain that the Java Virtual Machine (JVM) creates an `Exception` object whenever an error occurs during program execution. Finally, you will learn how to create packages in Java and about the different kinds of visibility for instance variables (data fields) and methods.

Inheritance and Class Hierarchies

1.1 ADTs, Interfaces, and the Java API

In earlier programming courses, you learned how to write individual classes consisting of attributes and methods (operations). You also learned how to use existing classes (for example, `String` and `Scanner`) to facilitate your programming. These classes are part of the Java Applications Programmer Interface (API).

FIGURE 1.1
Diagram of an ADT

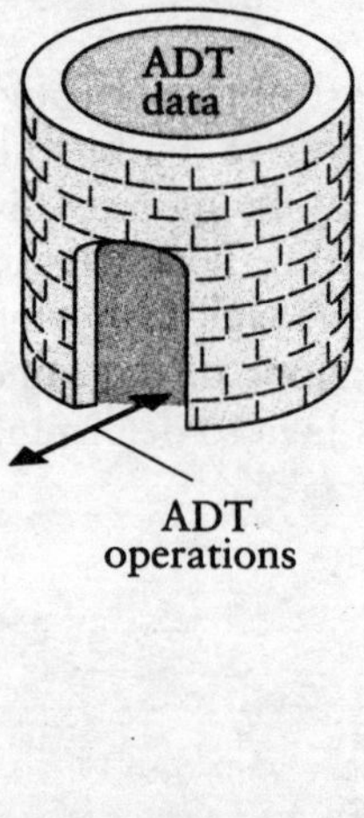

One of our goals is to write code that can be reused in many different applications. One way to make code reusable is to encapsulate the data elements together with the methods that operate on that data. A new program can then use the methods to manipulate an object's data without being concerned about details of the data representation or the method implementations. The encapsulated data together with its methods is called an abstract data type (ADT).

Figure 1.1 shows a diagram of an abstract data type. The data values stored in the ADT are hidden inside the circular wall. The bricks around this wall are used to indicate that these data values cannot be accessed except by going through the ADT's methods.

A class provides one way to implement an ADT in Java. If the data fields are private, they can be accessed only through public methods. Therefore, the methods control access to the data and determine the manner in which the data is manipulated.

Another goal of this text is to show you how to write and use ADTs in programming. As you progress through this book, you will create a large collection of ADT implementations (classes) in your own program library. You will also learn about ADTs that are available for you to use through the Java API.

Our principal focus will be on ADTs that are used for structuring data to enable you to more easily and efficiently store, organize, and process information. These ADTs are often called *data structures*. We introduce the Java Collections Framework (part of the Java API), which provides implementation of these common data structures, in Chapter 2 and study it throughout the text. Using the classes that are in the Java Collections Framework will make it much easier for you to design and implement new application programs.

Interfaces

A Java interface is a way to specify or describe an ADT to an applications programmer. An interface is like a contract that tells the applications programmer precisely what methods are available and describes the operations they perform. It also tells the applications programmer what arguments, if any, must be passed to each method and what result the method will return. Of course, in order to make use of these methods, someone else must have written a class that *implements the interface* by providing the code for these methods.

The interface tells the coder precisely what methods must be written, but it does not provide a detailed algorithm or prescription for how to write them. The coder must "program to the interface," which means he or she must develop the methods described in the interface without variation. If each coder does this job well, that ensures that other programmers can use the completed class exactly as it is written, without needing to know the details of how it was coded.

There may be more than one way to implement the methods; hence, several classes may implement the interface, but each must satisfy the contract. One class may be more efficient than the others at performing certain kinds of operations (for example, retrieving information from a database), so that class will be used if retrieval operations are more likely in a particular application. The important point is that the particular implementation that is used will not affect other classes that interact with it because every implementation satisfies the contract.

Besides providing the complete definition (implementation) of all methods declared in the interface, each implementer of an interface may declare data fields and define other methods not in the interface, including constructors. An interface cannot contain constructors because it cannot be instantiated—that is, one cannot create objects, or instances, of it. However, it can be represented by instances of classes that implement it.

EXAMPLE 1.1 An automated teller machine (ATM) enables a user to perform certain banking operations from a remote location. It must support the following operations.

1. Verify a user's Personal Identification Number (PIN).
2. Allow the user to choose a particular account.
3. Withdraw a specified amount of money.
4. Display the result of an operation.
5. Display an account balance.

A class that implements an ATM must provide a method for each operation. We can write this requirement as the interface `ATM` and save it in file `ATM.java`, shown in Listing 1.1. The keyword `interface` on the header line indicates that an interface is being declared. If you are unfamiliar with the documentation style shown in this listing, read about Java documentation in Appendix A (see Section A.7 and Table A.14).

LISTING 1.1

Interface `ATM.java`

```
/** The interface for an ATM. */
public interface ATM {

    /** Verifies a user's PIN.
        @param pin The user's PIN
    */
    boolean verifyPIN(String pin);

    /** Allows the user to select an account.
        @return a String representing the account selected
    */
    String selectAccount();

    /** Withdraws a specified amount of money
        @param account The account from which the money comes
        @param amount The amount of money withdrawn
        @return Whether or not the operation is successful
    */
    boolean withdraw(String account, double amount);

    /** Displays the result of an operation
        @param account The account for the operation
        @param amount The amount of money
        @param success Whether or not the operation was successful
    */
    void display(String account, double amount, boolean success);

    /** Displays the result of a PIN verification
        @param pin The user's pin
        @param success Whether or not the PIN was valid
    */
    void display(String pin, boolean success);
```

```
    /** Displays an account balance
        @param account The account selected
    */
    void showBalance(String account);
}
```

The interface definition shows the heading only for several methods. Because only the headings are shown, they are considered *abstract methods*. Each actual method with its body must be defined in a class that implements the interface. Therefore, a class that implements this interface must provide a `void` method called `verifyPIN` with an argument of type `String`. There are also two display methods with different signatures. The first is used to display the result of a withdrawal, and the second is used to display the result of a PIN verification. The keywords `public abstract` are optional (and usually omitted) in an interface because all interface methods are public abstract by default.

SYNTAX **Interface Definition**

FORM:

```
public interface interfaceName {
    abstract method headings
    constant declarations
}
```

EXAMPLE:

```
public interface Payable {
    public abstract double calcSalary();
    public abstract boolean salaried();
    public static final double DEDUCTIONS = 25.5;
}
```

MEANING:

Interface *interfaceName* is defined. The interface body provides headings for abstract methods and constant declarations. Each abstract method must be defined in a class that implements the interface. Constants defined in the interface (e.g., `DEDUCTIONS`) are accessible in classes that implement the interface.

NOTES:

The keywords `public` and `abstract` are implicit in each abstract method definition, and the keywords `public static final` are implicit in each constant declaration. We show them in color in the example here, but we will omit them from now on.

FIGURE 1.2

UML Diagram Showing the ATM Interface and Its Implementing Classes

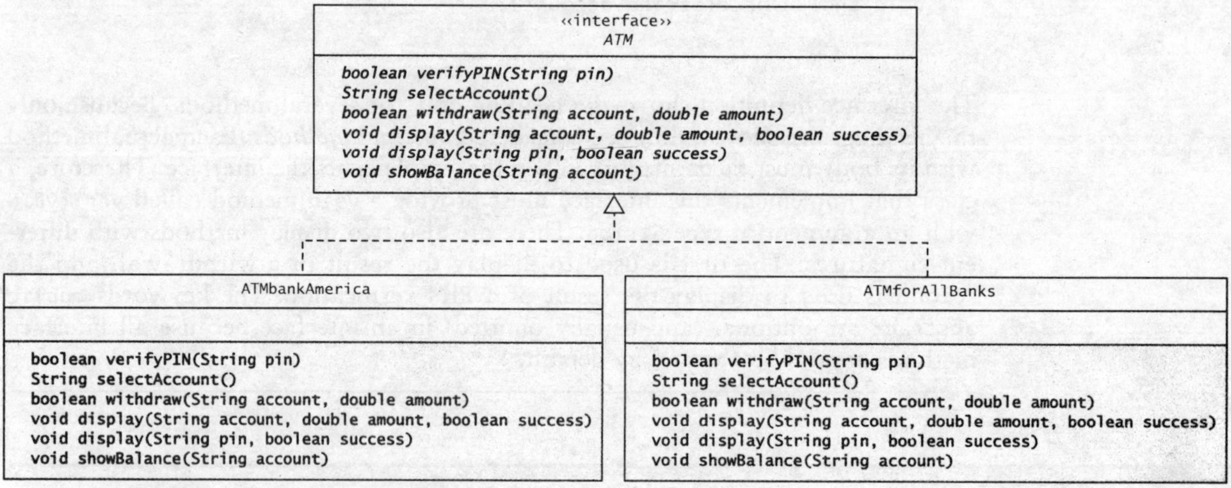

The `implements` Clause

The class headings for two classes that implement interface ATM are

```
public class ATMbankAmerica implements ATM
public class ATMforAllBanks implements ATM
```

Each class heading ends with the clause `implements ATM`. When compiling these classes, the Java compiler will verify that they define the required methods in the way specified by the interface. If a class implements more than one interface, list them all after `implements`, with commas as separators.

Figure 1.2 is a UML (Unified Modeling Language) diagram that shows the ATM interface and these two implementing classes. Note that a dashed line from the class to the interface is used to indicate that the class implements the interface. We will use UML diagrams throughout this text to show relationships between classes and interfaces. Appendix B provides detailed coverage of UML diagrams.

PITFALL

Not Properly Defining a Method to Be Implemented

If you neglect to define method `verifyPIN` in class `ATMforAllBanks` or if you use a different method signature, you will get the following syntax error:

```
class ATMforAllBanks should be declared abstract; it does not define
method verifyPIN(String) in interface ATM.
```

The above error indicates that the method `verifyPin` was not properly defined. Because it contains an abstract method that is not defined, Java incorrectly believes that ATM should be declared to be an abstract class. If you use a result type other than `boolean`, you will also get a syntax error.

PITFALL

Instantiating an Interface

An interface is not a class, so you cannot instantiate an interface. The statement

```
ATM anATM = new ATM();   // invalid statement
```

will cause the following syntax error:

```
interface ATM is abstract; cannot be instantiated.
```

Declaring a Variable of an Interface Type

In the previous programming pitfall, we mentioned that you cannot instantiate an interface. However, you may want to declare a variable that has an interface type and use it to reference an actual object. This is permitted if the variable references an object of a class type that implements the interface. After the following statements execute

```
ATM ATM1 = new ATMbankAmerica();   // valid statement
ATM ATM2 = new ATMforAllBanks();   // valid statement
```

Variable `ATM1` references an `ATMbankAmerica` object, and variable `ATM2` references an `ATMforAllBanks` object, but both `ATM1` and `ATM2` are type `ATM`.

EXERCISES FOR SECTION 1.1

SELF-CHECK

1. What are the the two parts of an ADT? Which part is accessible to a user and which is not? Explain the relationships between an ADT and a class; between an ADT and an interface; and between an interface and classes that implement the interface.
2. Assume there is an interface named `Comparable` with the following definition:
```
public interface Comparable {
    int compareTo(Object obj);
}
```
Do you think class `String` implements interface `Comparable`? Provide a reason for your answer.
3. Correct each of the following statements that is incorrect, assuming that class `PDGUI` and class `PDConsoleUI` implement interface `PDUserInterface`.
   a. `PDGUI p1 = new PDConsoleUI();`
   b. `PDGUI p2 = new PDUserInterface();`
   c. `PDUserInterface p3 = new PDUserInterface();`
   d. `PDUserInterface p4 = new PDConsoleUI();`
   e. `PDGUI p5 = new PDUserInterface();`
   `PDUserInterface p6 = p5;`

f.
```
PDUserInterface p7;
p7 = new PDConsoleUI();
```

4. Explain how an interface is like a contract.
5. What are two different uses of the term *interface* in programming?

PROGRAMMING

1. Define an interface named `Resizable` with just one abstract method, `resize`, that is a `void` method with no parameter.
2. Write a Javadoc comment for the following method of a class `Person`. Assume that class `Person` has two `String` data fields `lastName` and `firstName` with the obvious meanings. Provide preconditions and postconditions if needed.

```
public int compareTo(Person per) {
    if (lastName.equals(per.lastName))
        return firstName.compareTo(per.firstName);
    else
        return lastName.compareTo(per.lastName);
}
```

3. Write a Javadoc comment for the following method of class `Person`. Provide preconditions and postconditions if needed.

```
public void changeLastName(boolean justMarried, String newLast) {
    if (justMarried)
        lastName = newLast;
}
```

4. Write method `verifyPIN` for class `ATMbankAmerica` assuming this class has a data field `pin` (type `String`).

1.2 Introduction to Object-Oriented Programming

In this course, you will learn to use features of Java that facilitate the practice of object-oriented programming (OOP). A major reason for the popularity of OOP is that it enables programmers to reuse previously written code saved as classes, reducing the time required to code new applications. Because previously written code has already been tested and debugged, the new applications should also be more reliable and therefore easier to test and debug.

However, OOP provides additional capabilities beyond the reuse of existing classes. If an application needs a new class that is similar to an existing class but not exactly the same, the programmer can create it by extending, or inheriting from, the existing class. The new class (called the subclass) can have additional data fields and methods for increased functionality. Its objects also inherit the data fields and methods of the original class (called the superclass).

Inheritance in OOP is analogous to inheritance in humans. We all inherit genetic traits from our parents. If we are fortunate, we may even have some earlier ancestors who have left us an inheritance of monetary value. As we grow up, we benefit from our ancestors' resources, knowledge, and experiences, but our experiences will

FIGURE 1.3
Classes Mammal and Human

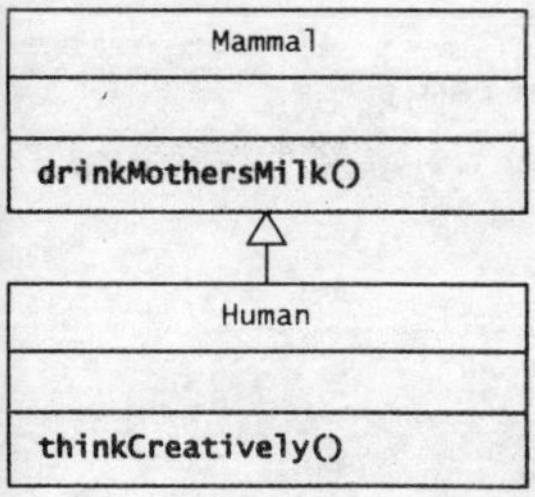

not affect how our parents or ancestors developed. Although we have two parents to inherit from, Java classes can have only one parent.

Inheritance and hierarchical organization allow you to capture the idea that one thing may be a refinement or an extension of another. For example, an object that is a `Human` is a `Mammal` (the superclass of `Human`). This means that an object of type `Human` has all the data fields and methods defined by class `Mammal` (e.g., method `drinkMothersMilk`), but it may also have more data fields and methods that are not contained in class `Mammal` (e.g., method `thinkCreatively`). Figure 1.3 shows this simple hierarchy. The solid line in the UML class diagram shows that `Human` is a subclass of `Mammal`, and, therefore, `Human` objects can use methods `drinkMothersMilk` and `thinkCreatively`. Objects farther down the hierarchy are more complex and less general than those farther up. For this reason an object that is a `Human` is a `Mammal`, but the converse is not true because every `Mammal` object does not necessarily have the additional properties of a `Human`. Although this seems counterintuitive, the subclass `Human` is actually more powerful than the superclass `Mammal` because it may have additional attributes that are not present in the superclass.

A Superclass and Subclass Example

To illustrate the concepts of inheritance and class hierarchies, let's consider a simple case of two classes: `Computer` and `Notebook`. A `Computer` object has a `manufacturer`, `processor`, `RAM`, and `disk`. A notebook computer is a kind of computer, so it has all the properties of a computer plus some additional features (screen size and weight). There may be other subclasses, such as tablet computer or game computer, but we will ignore them for now. We can define class `Notebook` as a subclass of class `Computer`. Figure 1.4 shows the class hierarchy.

FIGURE 1.4
Classes NoteBook and Computer

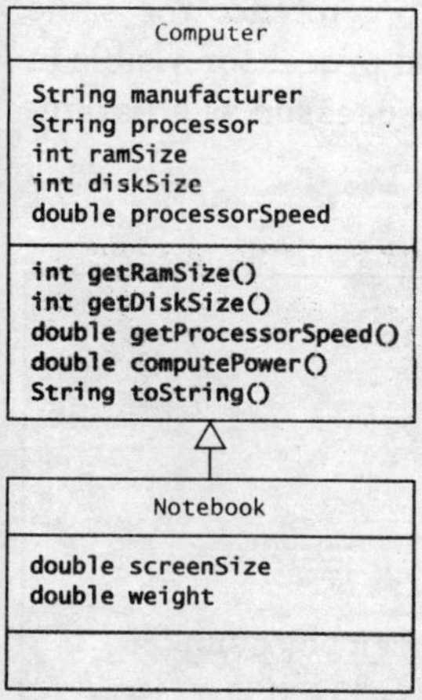

Class Computer

Listing 1.2 shows class `Computer.Java`. It is defined like any other class. It contains a constructor, several accessors, a `toString` method, and a method `computePower`, which returns the product of its RAM size and processor speed as a simple measure of its power.

LISTING 1.2
Class Computer.java

```
/** Class that represents a computer. */
public class Computer {
    // Data Fields
    private String manufacturer;
    private String processor;
    private double ramSize;
    private int diskSize;
    private double processorSpeed;

    // Methods
    /** Initializes a Computer object with all properties specified.
        @param man The computer manufacturer
```

```
        @param processor The processor type
        @param ram The RAM size
        @param disk The disk size
        @param procSpeed The processor speed
    */
    public Computer(String man, String processor, double ram,
                    int disk, double procSpeed) {
        manufacturer = man;
        this.processor = processor;
        ramSize = ram;
        diskSize = disk;
        processorSpeed = procSpeed;
    }

    public double computePower() { return ramSize * processorSpeed; }
    public double getRamSize() { return ramSize; }
    public double getProcessorSpeed() { return processorSpeed; }
    public int getDiskSize() { return diskSize; }
    // Insert other accessor and modifier methods here.

    public String toString() {
        String result = "Manufacturer: " + manufacturer +
                "\nCPU: " + processor +
                "\nRAM: " + ramSize + " megabytes" +
                "\nDisk: " + diskSize + " gigabytes" +
                "\nProcessor speed: " + processorSpeed + " gigahertz";
        return result;
    }
}
```

Use of this.

In the constructor for the Computer class, the statement

```
this.processor = processor;
```

sets data field processor in the object under construction to reference the same string as parameter processor. The prefix this. makes data field processor visible in the constructor. This is necessary because the declaration of processor as a parameter hides the data field declaration.

PITFALL

Not Using this. to Access a Hidden Data Field

If you write the preceding statement as

```
processor = processor; // Copy parameter processor to itself.
```

you will not get an error, but the data field processor in the Computer object under construction will not be initialized and will retain its default value (null). If you later attempt to use data field processor, you may get an error or just an unexpected result.

Class Notebook

In the `Notebook` class diagram in Figure 1.4, we show just the data fields declared in class `Notebook`; however, `Notebook` objects also have the data fields that are inherited from class `Computer` (`processor`, `ramSize`, and so forth). The first line in class `Notebook` (Listing 1.3),

```
public class Notebook extends Computer {
```

indicates that class `Notebook` extends class `Computer` and inherits its data and methods. Next, we define any additional data fields

```
// Data Fields
private double screenSize;
private double weight;
```

Initializing Data Fields in a Subclass

The constructor for class `Notebook` must begin by initializing the four data fields inherited from class `Computer`. Because those data fields are private to the superclass, Java requires that they be initialized by a superclass constructor. Therefore, a superclass constructor must be invoked as the first statement in the constructor body using a statement such as

```
super(man, proc, ram, disk, procSpeed);
```

This statement invokes the superclass constructor with the signature `Computer(String, String, double, int, double)`, passing the four arguments listed to the constructor. (A method signature consists of the method's name followed by its parameter types.) The following constructor for `Notebook` also initializes the data fields that are not inherited. Listing 1.3 shows class `Notebook`.

```
public Notebook(String man, String proc, double ram, int disk,
                double procSpeed, double screen, double wei) {
    super(man, proc, ram, disk, procSpeed);
    screenSize = screen;
    weight = wei;
}
```

SYNTAX super(. . .);

FORM:

`super();`
`super(`*`argumentList`*`);`

EXAMPLE:

`super(man, proc, ram, disk, procSpeed);`

MEANING:

The **`super()`** call in a class constructor invokes the superclass's constructor that has the corresponding *argumentList*. The superclass constructor initializes the inherited data fields as specified by its *argumentList*. The **`super()`** call must be the first statement in a constructor.

LISTING 1.3

Class Notebook

```
/** Class that represents a notebook computer. */
public class Notebook extends Computer {
    // Data Fields
    private double screenSize;
    private double weight;

    // Methods
    /** Initializes a Notebook object with all properties specified.
        @param man The computer manufacturer
        @param proc The processor type
        @param ram The RAM size
        @param disk The disk size
        @param procSpeed The processor speed
        @param screen The screen size
        @param wei The weight
    */
    public Notebook(String man, String proc, double ram, int disk,
                    double procSpeed, double screen, double wei) {
        super(man, proc, ram, disk, procSpeed);
        screenSize = screen;
        weight = wei;
    }
}
```

The No-Parameter Constructor

If the execution of any constructor in a subclass does not invoke a superclass constructor, Java automatically invokes the no-parameter constructor for the superclass. Java does this to initialize that part of the object inherited from the superclass before the subclass starts to initialize its part of the object. Otherwise, the part of the object that is inherited would remain uninitialized.

PITFALL

Not Defining the No-Parameter Constructor

If no constructors are defined for a class, the no-parameter constructor for that class will be provided by default. However, if any constructors are defined, the no-parameter constructor must also be defined explicitly if it needs to be invoked. Java does not provide it automatically because it may make no sense to create a new object of that type without providing initial data field values. (It was not defined in class `Notebook` or `Computer` because we want the client to specify some information about a `Computer` object when that object is created.) If the no-parameter constructor is defined in a subclass but is not defined in the superclass, you will get a syntax error `constructor not defined`. You can also get this error if a subclass constructor does not explicitly call a superclass constructor. There will be an implicit call to the no-parameter superclass constructor, so it must be defined.

Protected Visibility for Superclass Data Fields

The data fields inherited from class `Computer` have private visibility. Therefore, they can be accessed only within class `Computer`. Because it is fairly common for a subclass method to reference data fields declared in its superclass, Java provides a less restrictive form of visibility called *protected visibility*. A data field (or method) with protected visibility can be accessed in the class defining it, in any subclass of that class, or in any class in the same package. Therefore, if we had used the declaration

```
protected String manufacturer;
```

in class `Computer`, the following assignment statement would be valid in class `Notebook`:

```
manufacturer = man;
```

We will use protected visibility on occasion when we are writing a class that we intend to extend. However, in general, it is better to use private visibility because subclasses may be written by different programmers, and it is always a good practice to restrict and control access to the superclass data fields. We discuss visibility further in Section 1.7.

Is-a versus *Has-a* Relationships

One misuse of inheritance is confusing: the *has-a* relationship with the *is-a* relationship. The *is-a* relationship between classes means that one class is a subclass of the other class. For example, a game computer is a computer with specific attributes that make it suitable for gaming applications (enhanced graphics, fast processor) and is a subclass of the `Computer` class. The *is-a* relationship is achieved by extending a class.

The *has-a* relationship between classes means that one class has the second class as an attribute. For example, a game box is not really a computer (it is a kind of entertainment device), but it has a computer as a component. The *has-a* relationship is achieved by declaring a `Computer` data field in the game box class.

Another issue that sometimes arises is determining whether to define a new class in a hierarchy or whether a new object is a member of an existing class. For example, netbook computers have recently become very popular. They are smaller portable computers that can be used for general-purpose computing but are also used extensively for Web browsing. Should we define a separate class `NetBook`, or is a netbook computer a `Notebook` object with a small screen and low weight?

EXERCISES FOR SECTION 1.2

SELF-CHECK

1. Explain the effect of each valid statement in the following fragment. Indicate any invalid statements.

```
Computer c1 = new Computer();
Computer c2 = new Computer("Ace", "AMD", 1.0, 160, 2.0);
Notebook c3 = new Notebook("Ace", "AMD", 2.0, 160, 1.8);
Notebook c4 = new Notebook("Bravo", "Intel", 1.0, 160, 15.5, 7.5, 2.0);
System.out.println(c2.manufacturer + ", " + c4.processor);
System.out.println(c2.getDiskSize() + ", " + c4.getRamSize());
System.out.println(c2.toString() + "\n" + c4.toString());
```

2. Indicate where in the hierarchy you might want to add data fields for the following and the kind of data field you would add.

   Cost
   The battery identification
   Time before battery discharges
   Number of expansion slots
   Wireless Internet available

3. Can you add the following constructor to class `Notebook`? If so, what would you need to do to class `Computer`?

```
public Notebook() {}
```

PROGRAMMING

1. Write accessor and modifier methods for class `Computer`.
2. Write accessor and modifier methods for class `Notebook`.

1.3 Method Overriding, Method Overloading, and Polymorphism

In the preceding section we discussed inherited data fields. We found that we could not access an inherited data field in a subclass object if its visibility was private. Next, we consider inherited methods. Methods generally have public visibility, so we should be able to access a method that is inherited. However, what if there are multiple methods with the same name in a class hierarchy? How does Java determine which one to invoke? We answer this question next.

Method Overriding

Let's use the following main method to test our class hierarchy.

```
/** Tests classes Computer and Notebook. Creates an object of each and
    displays them.
    @param args[] No control parameters
*/
```

```
public static void main(String[] args) {
    Computer myComputer =
        new Computer("Acme", "Intel", 2, 160, 2.4);
    Notebook yourComputer =
        new Notebook("DellGate", "AMD", 4, 240,
                     1.8, 15.0, 7.5);
    System.out.println("My computer is:\n" + myComputer.toString());
    System.out.println("\nYour computer is:\n" +
                       yourComputer.toString());
}
```

In the second call to `println`, the method call

```
yourComputer.toString()
```

applies method `toString` to object `yourComputer` (type `Notebook`). Because class `Notebook` doesn't define its own `toString` method, class `Notebook` inherits the `toString` method defined in class `Computer`. Executing this method displays the following output lines:

```
My computer is:
Manufacturer: Acme
CPU: Intel
RAM: 2.0 gigabytes
Disk: 160 gigabytes
Speed: 2.4 gigahertz

Your computer is:
Manufacturer: DellGate
CPU: AMD
RAM: 4.0 gigabytes
Disk: 240 gigabytes
Speed: 1.8 gigahertz
```

Unfortunately, this output doesn't show the complete state of object `yourComputer`. To show the complete state of a notebook computer, we need to define a `toString` method for class `Notebook`. If class `Notebook` has its own `toString` method, it will override the inherited method and will be invoked by the method call `yourComputer.toString()`. We define method `toString` for class `Notebook` next.

```
public String toString() {
    String result = super.toString() +
                    "\nScreen size: " + screenSize + " inches" +
                    "\nWeight: " + weight + " pounds";
    return result;
}
```

This method `Notebook.toString` returns a string representation of the state of a `Notebook` object. The first line

```
String result = super.toString()
```

uses method call **`super`**`.toString()` to invoke the `toString` method of the superclass (method `Computer.toString`) to get the string representation of the four data fields that are inherited from the superclass. The next two lines append the data fields defined in class `Notebook` to this string.

SYNTAX **super.**

FORM:

```
super.methodName()
super.methodName(argumentList)
```

EXAMPLE:

```
super.toString()
```

MEANING:

Using the prefix **super.** in a call to method *methodName* calls the method with that name defined in the superclass of the current class.

PROGRAM STYLE

Calling Method toString() Is Optional

In the `println` statement shown earlier,

```
System.out.println("My computer is:\n" + myComputer.toString());
```

the explicit call to method `toString` is not required. The statement could be written as

```
System.out.println("My computer is:\n" + myComputer);
```

Java automatically applies the `toString` method to an object referenced in a `String` expression. Normally, we will not explicitly call `toString`.

PITFALL

Overridden Methods Must Have Compatible Return Types

If you write a method in a subclass that has the same signature as one in the superclass but a different return type, you may get the following error message: `in` *`subclass-name`* `cannot override` *`method-name`* `in` *`superclass-name`*`; attempting to use incompatible return type`. The subclass method return type must be the same as or a subclass of the superclass method's return type.

Method Overloading

Let's assume we have decided to standardize and purchase our notebook computers from only one manufacturer. We could then introduce a new constructor with one less parameter for class `Notebook`.

```
public Notebook(String proc, int ram, int disk, double procSpeed,
                double screen, double wei) {
    this(DEFAULT_NB_MAN, proc, ram, disk, procSpeed, screen, wei);
}
```

The method call

```
this(DEFAULT_NB_MAN, proc, ram, disk, procSpeed, screen, wei);
```

invokes the six-parameter constructor (see Listing 1.3), passing on the five arguments it receives and the constant string `DEFAULT_NB_MAN` (defined in class `Notebook`). The six-parameter constructor begins by calling the superclass constructor, satisfying the requirement that it be called first. We now have two constructors with different signatures in class `Notebook`. Having multiple methods with the same name but different signatures in a class is called *method overloading*.

Now we have two ways to create new `Notebook` objects. Both of the following statements are valid:

```
Notebook lTP1 = new Notebook("Intel", 2, 160, 1.8, 14, 6.5);
Notebook lTP2 = new Notebook("MicroSys", "AMD", 4, 240, 2.2, 15, 7.5);
```

The manufacturer of `lTP1` is `DEFAULT_NB_MAN`.

SYNTAX this(. . .);

FORM:

```
this(argumentList);
```

EXAMPLE:

```
this(DEFAULT_NB_MAN, proc, ram, disk, procSpeed);
```

MEANING:

The call to `this()` invokes the constructor for the current class whose parameter list matches the argument list. The constructor initializes the new object as specified by its arguments. The invocation of another constructor (through either `this()` or `super()`) must be the first statement in a constructor.

Listing 1.4 shows the complete class `Notebook`. Figure 1.5 shows the UML diagram, revised to show that `Notebook` has a `toString` method and a constant data field. The next Pitfall discusses the reason for the `@Override` annotation preceding method `toString`.

LISTING 1.4

Complete Class `Notebook` with Method `toString`

```
/** Class that represents a notebook computer. */
public class Notebook extends Computer {
    // Data Fields
    private static final String DEFAULT_NB_MAN = "MyBrand";
    private double screenSize;
    private double weight;

    /** Initializes a Notebook object with all properties specified.
    @param man The computer manufacturer
    @param proc The processor type
```

FIGURE 1.5
Revised UML Diagram for Computer Class Hierarchy

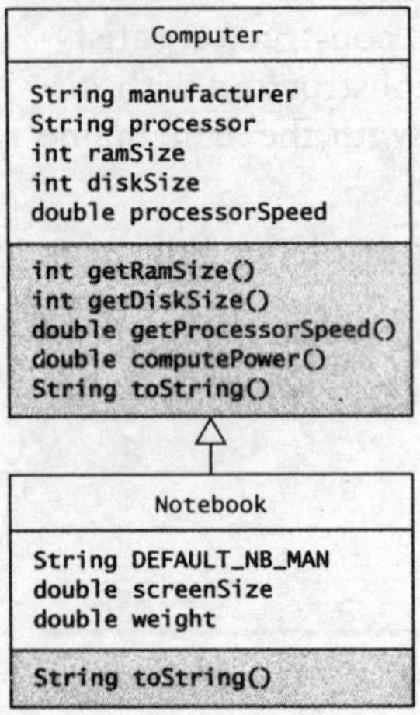


```
      @param ram The RAM size
      @param disk The disk size
      @param screen The screen size
      @param wei The weight
    */
    public Notebook(String man, String proc, int ram, int disk,
                    double procSpeed, double screen, double wei) {
      super(man, proc, ram, disk, procSpeed);
      screenSize = screen;
      weight = wei;
    }

    /** Initializes a Notebook object with 6 properties specified. */
    public Notebook(String proc, int ram, int disk,
                    double procSpeed, double screen, double wei) {
      this(DEFAULT_NB_MAN, proc, ram, disk, procSpeed, screen, wei);
    }

    @Override
    public String toString() {
      String result = super.toString() +
                      "\nScreen size: " + screenSize + " inches" +
                      "\nWeight: " + weight + " pounds";
      return result;
    }
  }
```

PITFALL

Overloading a Method When Intending to Override It

To override a method, you must use the same name and the same number and types of the parameters as the superclass method that is being overridden. If the name is the same but the number or types of the parameters are different, then the method is overloaded instead. Normally, the compiler will not detect this as an error. However, it is a sufficiently common error that a feature was added to the Java compiler so that programmers can indicate that they intend to override a method. If you precede the declaration of the method with the annotation `@Override`, the compiler will issue an error message if the method is overloaded instead of overridden.

PROGRAM STYLE

Precede an Overridden Method with the Annotation @Override

Whenever a method is overridden, we recommend preceding it with the annotation `@Override`. Some Java integrated development environments such as Netbeans and Eclipse will either issue a warning or add this annotation automatically.

Polymorphism

An important advantage of OOP is that it supports a feature called *polymorphism*, which means many forms or many shapes. Polymorphism enables the JVM to determine at run time which of the classes in a hierarchy is referenced by a superclass variable or parameter. Next we will see how this simplifies the programming process.

Suppose you are not sure whether a computer referenced in a program will be a notebook or a regular computer. If you declare the reference variable

```
Computer theComputer;
```

you can use it to reference an object of either type because a type `Notebook` object can be referenced by a type `Computer` variable. In Java, a variable of a superclass type (general) can reference an object of a subclass type (specific). `Notebook` objects are `Computer` objects with more features. When the following statements are executed,

```
theComputer = new Computer("Acme", "Intel", 2, 160, 2.6);
System.out.println(theComputer.toString());
```

you would see four output lines, representing the state of the object referenced by `theComputer`.

Now suppose you have purchased a notebook computer instead. What happens when the following statements are executed?

```
theComputer = new Notebook("Bravo", "Intel", 4, 240, 2.4. 15.0, 7.5);
System.out.println(theComputer.toString());
```

Recall that `theComputer` is type `Computer`. Will the `theComputer.toString()` method call return a string with all seven data fields or just the five data fields defined for a `Computer` object? The answer is a string with all seven data fields. The reason is that the type of the object receiving the `toString` message determines which `toString` method is called. Even though variable `theComputer` is type `Computer`, it references a type `Notebook` object, and the `Notebook` object receives the `toString` message. Therefore, the method `toString` for class `Notebook` is the one called.

This is an example of polymorphism. Variable `theComputer` references a `Computer` object at one time and a `Notebook` object another time. At compile time, the Java compiler can't determine what type of object `theComputer` will reference, but at run time, the JVM knows the type of the object that receives the `toString` message and can call the appropriate `toString` method.

EXAMPLE 1.2 If we declare the array `labComputers` as follows,

```
Computer[] labComputers = new Computer[10];
```

each subscripted variable `labComputers[i]` can reference either a `Computer` object or a `Notebook` object because `Notebook` is a subclass of `Computer`. For the method call `labComputers[i].toString()`, polymorphism ensures that the correct `toString` method is called. For each value of subscript `i`, the actual type of the object referenced by `labComputers[i]` determines which `toString` method will execute (`Computer.toString` or `Notebook.toString`).

Methods with Class Parameters

Polymorphism also simplifies programming when we write methods that have class parameters. For example, if we want to compare the power of two computers without polymorphism, we will need to write overloaded `comparePower` methods in class `Computer`, one for each subclass parameter and one with a class `Computer` parameter. However, polymorphism enables us to write just one method with a `Computer` parameter.

EXAMPLE 1.3 Method `Computer.computePowers` compares the power of the `Computer` object it is applied to with the `Computer` object passed as its argument. It returns –1, 0, or +1 depending on which computer has more power. It does not matter whether `this` or `aComputer` references a `Computer` or a `Notebook` object.

```
/** Compares power of this computer and its argument computer
    @param aComputer The computer being compared to this computer
    @return -1 if this computer has less power,
             0 if the same, and
            +1 if this computer has more power.
 */
public int comparePower(Computer aComputer) {
    if (this.computePower() < aComputer.computePower())
        return -1;
    else if (this.computePower() == aComputer.computePower())
        return 0;
    else return 1;
}
```

EXERCISES FOR SECTION 1.3

SELF-CHECK

1. Explain the effect of each of the following statements. Which one(s) would you find in class `Computer`? Which one(s) would you find in class `Notebook`?
   ```
   super(man, proc, ram, disk, procSpeed);
   this(man, proc, ram, disk, procSpeed);
   ```
2. Indicate whether methods with each of the following signatures and return types (if any) would be allowed and in what classes they would be allowed. Explain your answers.
   ```
   Computer()
   Notebook()
   int toString()
   double getRamSize()
   String getRamSize()
   String getRamSize(String)
   String getProcessor()
   double getScreenSize()
   ```

3. For the loop body in the following fragment, indicate which method is invoked for each value of `i`. What is printed?

```
Computer comp[] = new Computer[3];
comp[0] = new Computer("Ace", "AMD", 3, 160, 2.4);
comp[1] = new Notebook("Dell", "Intel", 4, 350, 2.2, 15.5, 7.5);
comp[2] = comp[1];
for (int i = 0; i < comp.length; i++) {
    System.out.println(comp[i].getRamSize() +"\n" +
                       comp[i].toString());
}
```

4. When does Java determine which `toString` method to execute for each value of `i` in the `for` statement in the preceding question: at compile time or at run time? Explain your answer.

PROGRAMMING

1. Write constructors for both classes that allow you to specify only the processor, RAM size, and disk size.
2. Complete the accessor and modifier methods for class `Computer`.
3. Complete the accessor and modifier methods for class `Notebook`.

1.4 Abstract Classes

In this section we introduce another kind of class called an *abstract class*. An abstract class is denoted by the use of the word *abstract* in its heading:

visibility `abstract class` *className*

An abstract class differs from an actual class (sometimes called a concrete class) in two respects:

- An abstract class cannot be instantiated.
- An abstract class may declare abstract methods.

Just as in an interface, an abstract method is declared through a method heading in the abstract class definition. This heading indicates the result type, method name, and parameters, thereby specifying the form that any actual method declaration must take:

visibility `abstract` *resultType methodName(parameterList)*;

However, the complete method definition, including the method body (implementation), does not appear in the abstract class definition.

In order to compile without error, an actual class that is a subclass of an abstract class must provide an implementation for each abstract method of its abstract superclass. The heading for each actual method must match the heading for the corresponding abstract method.

We introduce an abstract class in a class hierarchy when we need a base class for two or more actual classes that share some attributes. We may want to declare some of the attributes and define some of the methods that are common to these base classes. If, in addition, we want to require that the actual subclasses implement certain methods, we can accomplish this by making the base class an abstract class and declaring these methods abstract.

EXAMPLE 1.4 The Food Guide Pyramid provides a recommendation of what to eat each day based on established dietary guidelines. There are six categories of foods in the pyramid: fats, oils, and sweets; meats, poultry, fish, and nuts; milk, yogurt, and cheese; vegetables; fruits; and bread, cereal, and pasta. If we wanted to model the Food Guide Pyramid, we might have each of these as actual subclasses of an abstract class called `Food`:

```
/** Abstract class that models a kind of food. */
public abstract class Food {
    // Data Field
    private double calories;

    // Abstract Methods
    /** Calculates the percent of protein in a Food object. */
    public abstract double percentProtein();
    /** Calculates the percent of fat in a Food object. */
    public abstract double percentFat();
    /** Calculates the percent of carbohydrates in a Food object. */
    public abstract double percentCarbohydrates();

    // Actual Methods
    public double getCalories() { return calories; }
    public void setCalories(double cal) {
        calories = cal;
    }
}
```

The three abstract method declarations

```
public abstract double percentProtein();
public abstract double percentFat();
public abstract double percentCarbohydrates();
```

impose the requirement that all actual subclasses implement these three methods. We would expect a different method definition for each kind of food. The keyword **abstract** must appear in all abstract method declarations in an abstract class. Recall that this is not required for abstract method declarations in interfaces.

SYNTAX Abstract Class Definition

FORM:

```
public abstract class className {
    data field declarations
    abstract method declarations
    actual method definitions
}
```

EXAMPLE:

```
public abstract class Food {
    // Data Field
    private double calories;

    // Abstract Methods
    public abstract double percentProtein();
    public abstract double percentFat();
    public abstract double percentCarbohydrates();

    // Actual Methods
    public double getCalories() { return calories; }
    public void setCalories(double cal) {
        calories = cal;
    }
}
```

INTERPRETATION:

Abstract class *className* is defined. The class body may have declarations for data fields and abstract methods as well as actual method definitions. Each abstract method declaration consists of a method heading containing the keyword **abstract**. All of the declaration kinds shown above are optional.

PITFALL

Omitting the Definition of an Abstract Method in a Subclass

If you write class `Vegetable` and forget to define method `percentProtein`, you will get the syntax error class `Vegetable should be declared abstract, it does not define method percentProtein in class Food`. Although this error message is misleading (you did not intend `Vegetable` to be abstract), any class with undefined methods is abstract by definition. The compiler's rationale is that the undefined method is intentional, so `Vegetable` must be an abstract class, with a subclass that defines `percentProtein`.

Referencing Actual Objects

Because class `Food` is abstract, you can't create type `Food` objects. However, you can use a type `Food` variable to reference an actual object that belongs to a subclass of type `Food`. For example, an object of type `Vegetable` can be referenced by a `Vegetable` or `Food` variable because `Vegetable` is a subclass of `Food` (i.e., a `Vegetable` object is also a `Food` object).

EXAMPLE 1.5 The following statement creates a `Vegetable` object that is referenced by variable `mySnack` (type `Food`).

```
Food mySnack = new Vegetable("carrot sticks");
```

Initializing Data Fields in an Abstract Class

An abstract class can't be instantiated. However, an abstract class can have constructors that initialize its data fields when a new subclass object is created. The subclass constructor will use `super(...)` to call such a constructor.

Abstract Class Number and the Java Wrapper Classes

The abstract class `Number` is predefined in the Java class hierarchy. It has as its subclasses all the wrapper classes for primitive numeric types (e.g., `Byte`, `Double`, `Integer`, `Short`). A *wrapper class* is used to store a primitive-type value in an object type. Each wrapper class contains constructors to create an object that stores a particular primitive-type value. For example, `Integer(35)` or `Integer("35")` creates a type `Integer` object that stores the `int 35`. A wrapper class also has methods for converting the value stored to a different numeric type.

Figure 1.6 shows a portion of the class hierarchy with base class `Number`. Italicizing the class name `Number` in its class box indicates that `Number` is an abstract class and, therefore, cannot be instantiated. Listing 1.5 shows part of the definition for class `Number`. Two abstract methods are declared (`intValue` and `doubleValue`), and one actual method (`byteValue`) is defined. In the actual implementation of `Number`, the body of `byteValue` would be provided, but we just indicate its presence in Listing 1.5.

FIGURE 1.6
The Abstract Class `Number` and Selected Subclasses

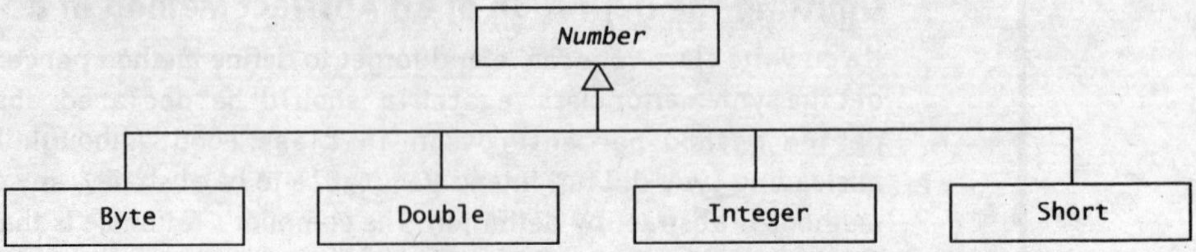

LISTING 1.5
Part of Abstract Class java.lang.Number

```
public abstract class Number {
    // Abstract Methods
    /** Returns the value of the specified number as an int.
        @return The numeric value represented by this object after
            conversion to type int
    */
    public abstract int intValue();
    /** Returns the value of the specified number as a double.
        @return The numeric value represented by this object
                after conversion to type double
    */
    public abstract double doubleValue();

    ...

    // Actual Methods
    /** Returns the value of the specified number as a byte.
        @return The numeric value represented by this object
                after conversion to type byte
    */
    public byte byteValue() {
        // Implementation not shown.
        ...
    }
}
```

Summary of Features of Actual Classes, Abstract Classes, and Interfaces

It is easy to confuse abstract classes, interfaces, and actual classes (concrete classes). Table 1.1 summarizes some important points about these constructs.

A class (abstract or actual) can extend only one other class; however, there is no restriction on the number of interfaces a class can implement. An interface cannot extend a class.

An abstract class may implement an interface just as an actual class does, but unlike an actual class, it doesn't have to define all of the methods declared in the interface. It can leave the implementation of some of the abstract methods to its subclasses.

Both abstract classes and interfaces declare abstract methods. However, unlike an interface, an abstract class can also have data fields and methods that are not abstract. You can think of an abstract class as combining the properties of an actual class, by providing inherited data fields and methods to its subclasses, and of an interface, by specifying requirements on its subclasses through its abstract method declarations.

TABLE 1.1
Comparison of Actual Classes, Abstract Classes, and Interfaces

Property	Actual Class	Abstract Class	Interface
Instances (objects) of this can be created.	Yes	No	No
This can define instance variables and methods.	Yes	Yes	No
This can define constants.	Yes	Yes	Yes
The number of these a class can extend.	0 or 1	0 or 1	0
The number of these a class can implement.	0	0	Any number
This can extend another class.	Yes	Yes	No
This can declare abstract methods.	No	Yes	Yes
Variables of this type can be declared.	Yes	Yes	Yes

Implementing Multiple Interfaces

A class can extend only one other class, but it may extend more than one interface. For example, assume interface `StudentInt` specifies methods required for student-like classes and interface `EmployeeInt` specifies methods required for employee-like classes. The following header for class `StudentWorker`

```
public class StudentWorker implements StudentInt, EmployeeInt
```

means that class `StudentWorker` must define (provide code for) all of the abstract methods declared in both interfaces. Therefore, class `StudentWorker` supports operations required for both interfaces.

Extending an Interface

Interfaces can also extend other interfaces. In Chapter 2 we will introduce the Java Collection Framework. This class hierarchy contains several interfaces and classes that manage the collection of objects. At the top of this hierarchy is the interface `Iterable`, which declares the method `iterator`. At the next lower level is interface `Collection`, which extends `Iterable`. This means that all classes that implement `Collection` must also implement `Iterable` and therefore must define the method `iterator`.

An interface can extend more than one other interface. In this case, the resulting interface includes the union of the methods defined in the superinterfaces. For example, we can define the interface `ComparableCollection`, which extends both `Comparable` and `Collection`, as follows:

```
public interface ComparableCollection extends Comparable, Collection { }
```

Note that this interface does not define any methods itself but does require any implementing class to implement all of the methods required by `Comparable` and by `Collection`.

EXERCISES FOR SECTION 1.4

SELF-CHECK

1. What are two important differences between an abstract class and an actual class? What are the similarities?
2. What do abstract methods and interfaces have in common? How do they differ?
3. Explain the effect of each statement in the following fragment and trace the loop execution for each value of `i`, indicating which `doubleValue` method executes, if any. What is the final value of x?

```
Number[] nums = new Number[5];
nums[0] = new Integer(35);
nums[1] = new Double(3.45);
nums[4] = new Double("2.45e6");
double x = 0;
for (int i = 0; i < nums.length; i++) {
    if (nums[i] != null)
        x += nums[i].doubleValue();
}
```

4. What is the purpose of the `if` statement in the loop in Question 3? What would happen if it were omitted?

PROGRAMMING

1. Write class `Vegetable`. Assume that a vegetable has three `double` constants: `VEG_PROTEIN_CAL`, `VEG_FAT_CAL`, and `VEG_CARBO_CAL`. Compute the fat percentage as `VEG_FAT_CAL` divided by the sum of all the constants.
2. Earlier we discussed a `Computer` class with a `Notebook` class as its only subclass. However, there are many different kinds of computers. An organization may have servers, mainframes, desktop PCs, and notebooks. There are also personal data assistants and game computers. So it may be more appropriate to declare class `Computer` as an abstract class that has an actual subclass for each category of computer. Write an abstract class `Computer` that defines all the methods shown earlier and declares an abstract method with the signature `costBenefit(double)` that returns the cost-benefit (type `double`) for each category of computer.

1.5 Class Object and Casting

The class `Object` is a special class in Java because it is the root of the class hierarchy, and every class has `Object` as a superclass. All classes inherit the methods defined in class `Object`; however, these methods may be overridden in the current class or in a superclass (if any). Table 1.2 shows a few of the methods of class `Object`. We discuss method `toString` next and the other `Object` methods shortly thereafter.

TABLE 1.2
The class Object

Method	Behavior
`boolean equals(Object obj)`	Compares this object to its argument.
`int hashCode()`	Returns an integer hash code value for this object.
`String toString()`	Returns a string that textually represents the object.
`Class<?> getClass()`	Returns a unique object that identifies the class of this object.

The Method toString

You should always override the `toString` method if you want to represent an object's state (information stored). If you don't override it, the `toString` method for class `Object` will execute and return a string, but not what you are expecting.

EXAMPLE 1.6 If we didn't have a `toString` method in class `Computer` or `Notebook`, the method call `aComputer.toString()` would call the `toString` method inherited from class `Object`. This method would return a string such as `Computer@ef08879`, which shows the object's class name and a special integer value that is its "hash code"—not its state. Method `hashCode` is discussed in Chapter 7.

Operations Determined by Type of Reference Variable

You have seen that a variable can reference an object whose type is a subclass of the variable type. Because `Object` is a superclass of class `Integer`, the statement

```
Object aThing = new Integer(25);
```

will compile without error, creating the object reference shown in Figure 1.7. However, even though `aThing` references a type `Integer` object, we can't process this object like other `Integer` objects. For example, the method call `aThing.intValue()` would cause the syntax error `method intValue() not found in class java.lang.Object`. The reason for this is that the type of the reference, not the type of the object referenced, determines what operations can be performed, and class `Object` doesn't have an `intValue` method. During compilation, Java can't determine what kind of object will be referenced by a type `Object` variable, so the only operations permitted are those defined for class `Object`. The type `Integer` instance methods not defined in class `Object` (e.g., `intValue`, `doubleValue`) can't be invoked.

The method call `aThing.equals(new Integer("25"))` will compile because class `Object` has an `equals` method, and a subclass object has everything that is defined in its superclass. During execution, the `equals` method for class `Integer` is invoked, not class `Object`. (Why?)

Another surprising result is that the assignment statement

```
Integer aNum = aThing;        // incompatible types
```

won't compile even though `aThing` references a type `Integer` object. The syntax error: `incompatible types: found: Java.lang.Object, required: Java.lang.Integer` indicates

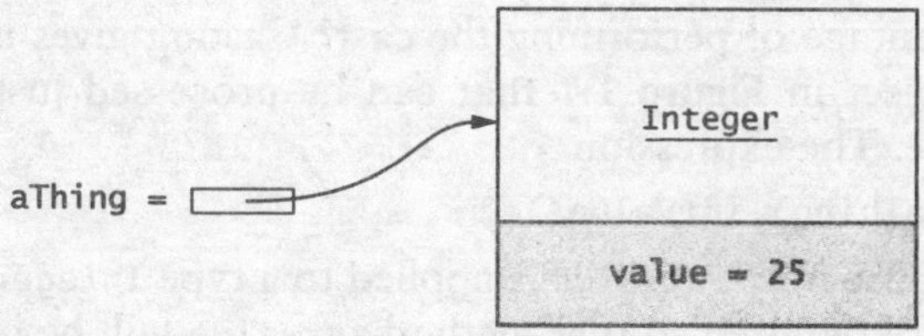

FIGURE 1.7
Type `Integer` Object Referenced by `aThing` (Type `Object`)

that the expression type is incorrect (type `Object`, not type `Integer`). The reason Java won't compile this assignment is that Java is a strongly typed language, so the Java compiler always verifies that the type of the expression (`aThing` is type `Object`) being assigned is compatible with the variable type (`aNum` is type `Integer`). We show how to use casting to accomplish this in the next section.

Strong typing is also the reason that `aThing.intValue()` won't compile; the method invoked must be an instance method for class `Object` because `aThing` is type `Object`.

> **DESIGN CONCEPT**
>
> **The Importance of Strong Typing**
>
> Suppose Java did not check the expression type and simply performed the assignment
>
> ```
> Integer aNum = aThing;      // incompatible types
> ```
>
> Farther down the line, we might attempt to apply an `Integer` method to the object referenced by `aNum`. Because `aNum` is type `Integer`, the compiler would permit this. If `aNum` were referencing a type `Integer` object, then performing this operation would do no harm. But if `aNum` was referencing an object that was not type `Integer`, performing this operation would cause either a run-time error or an undetected logic error. It is much better to have the compiler tell us that the assignment is invalid.

Casting in a Class Hierarchy

Java provides a mechanism, *casting*, that enables us to process the object referenced by `aThing` through a reference variable of its actual type, instead of through a type `Object` reference. The expression

```
(Integer) aThing
```

casts the type of the object referenced by `aThing` (type `Object`) to type `Integer`. The casting operation will succeed only if the object referenced by `aThing` is, in fact, type `Integer`; if not, a `ClassCastException` will be thrown.

What is the advantage of performing the cast? Casting gives us a type `Integer` reference to the object in Figure 1.7 that can be processed just like any other type `Integer` reference. The expression

```
((Integer) aThing).intValue()
```

will compile because now `intValue` is applied to a type `Integer` reference. Note that all parentheses are required so that method `intValue` will be invoked after the cast. Similarly, the assignment statement

```
Integer aNum = (Integer) aThing;
```

is valid because a type `Integer` reference is being assigned to `aNum` (type `Integer`).

Keep in mind that the casting operation does not change the object referenced by `aThing`; instead, it creates a type `Integer` reference to it. (This is called an *anonymous* or *unnamed reference*.) Using the type `Integer` reference, we can invoke any instance method of class `Integer` and process the object just like any other type `Integer` object. The cast

```
(Integer) aThing
```

is called a downcast because we are casting from a higher type (`Object`) to a lower type (`Integer`). It is analogous to a narrowing cast when dealing with primitive types:

```
double x = . . . ;
int count = (int) x;  // Narrowing cast, double is wider type than int
```

You can downcast from a more general type (a superclass type) to a more specific type (a subclass type) in a class hierarchy, provided that the more specific type is the same type as the object being cast (e.g., `(Integer) aThing`). You can also downcast from a more general type to a more specific type that is a superclass of the object being cast (e.g., `(Number) aThing`). *Upcasts* (casting from a more specific type to a more general type) are always valid; however, they are unnecessary and are rarely done.

PITFALL

Performing an Invalid Cast

Assume that `aThing` (type `Object`) references a type `Integer` object as before, and you want to get its string representation. The downcast

```
(String) aThing   // Invalid cast
```

is invalid and would cause a `ClassCastException` (a subclass of `RuntimeException`) because `aThing` references a type `Integer` object, and a type `Integer` object cannot be downcast to type `String` (`String` is not a superclass of `Integer`). However, the method call `aThing.toString()` is valid (and returns a string) because type `Object` has a `toString` method. (Which `toString` method would be called: `Object.toString` or `Integer.toString`?)

Using instanceof to Guard a Casting Operation

In the preceding Pitfall, we mentioned that a `ClassCastException` occurs if we attempt an invalid casting operation. Java provides the `instanceof` operator, which you can use to guard against this kind of error.

EXAMPLE 1.7 The following array `stuff` can store 10 objects of any data type because every object type is a subclass of `Object`.

```
Object[] stuff = new Object[10];
```

Assume that the array `stuff` has been loaded with data, and we want to find the sum of all numbers that are wrapped in objects. We can use the following loop to do so:

```
double sum = 0;
for (int i = 0; i < stuff.length; i++) {
    if (stuff[i] instanceof Number) {
        Number next = (Number) stuff[i];
        sum += next.doubleValue();
    }
}
```

The if condition (`stuff[i] instanceof Number`) is true if the object referenced by `stuff[i]` is a subclass of `Number`. It would be false if `stuff[i]` referenced a `String` or other nonnumeric object. The statement

```
Number next = (Number) stuff[i];
```

casts the object referenced by `stuff[i]` (type `Object`) to type `Number` and then references it through variable `next` (type `Number`). The variable `next` contains a reference to the same object as does `stuff[i]`, but the type of the reference is different (type `Number` instead of type `Object`). Then the statement

```
sum += next.doubleValue();
```

invokes the appropriate `doubleValue` method to extract the numeric value and add it to `sum`. Rather than declare variable `next`, you could write the if statement as

```
if (stuff[i] instanceof Number)
    sum += ((Number) stuff[i]).doubleValue();
```

PROGRAM STYLE

Polymorphism Eliminates Nested if Statements

If Java didn't support polymorphism, the if statement in Example 1.7 would be much more complicated. You would need to write something like the following:

```
// Inefficient code that does not take advantage of polymorphism
if (stuff[i] instanceof Integer)
    sum += ((Integer) stuff[i]).doubleValue();
else if (stuff[i] instanceof Double)
    sum += ((Double) stuff[i]).doubleValue();
else if (stuff[i] instanceof Float)
    sum += ((Float) stuff[i]).doubleValue();
...
```

Each condition here uses the instanceof operator to determine the data type of the actual object referenced by stuff[i]. Once the type is known, we cast to that type and call its doubleValue method. Obviously, this code is very cumbersome and is more likely to be flawed than the original if statement. More importantly, if a new wrapper class is defined for numbers, we would need to modify the if statement to process objects of this new class type. So be wary of selection statements like the one shown here; their presence often indicates that you are not taking advantage of polymorphism.

EXAMPLE 1.8 Suppose we have a class Employee with the following data fields:

```
public class Employee {
    // Data Fields
    private String name;
    private double hours;
    private double rate;
    private Address address;
...
```

To determine whether two Employee objects are equal, we could compare all four data fields. However, it makes more sense to determine whether two objects are the same employee by comparing their name and address data fields. Below, we show a method equals that overrides the equals method defined in class Object. By overriding this method, we ensure that the equals method for class Employee will always be called when method equals is applied to an Employee object. If we had declared the parameter type for Employee.equals as type Employee instead of Object, then the Object.equals method would be called if the argument was any data type except Employee.

```
/** Determines whether the current object matches its argument.
    @param obj The object to be compared to the current object
    @return true if the objects have the same name and address;
            otherwise, return false
*/
@Override
public boolean equals(Object obj) {
    if (obj == this) return true;
    if (obj == null) return false;
    if (this.getClass() == obj.getClass()) {
        Employee other = (Employee) obj;
```

```
            return name.equals(other.name) &&
                   address.equals(other.address);
        } else {
            return false;
        }
    }
```

If the object referenced by obj is not type Employee, we return false. If it is type Employee, we downcast that object to type Employee. After the downcast, the return statement calls method String.equals to compare the name field of the current object to the name field of object other, and method Address.equals to compare the two address data fields. Therefore, method equals must also be defined in class Address. The method result is true if both the name and address fields match, and it is false if one or both fields do not match. The method result is also false if the downcast can't be performed because the argument is an incorrect type or **null**.

The Class Class

Every class has a Class object that is automatically created when the class is loaded into an application. The Class class provides methods that are mostly beyond the scope of this text. The important point is that each Class object is unique for the class, and the getClass method (a member of Object) will return a reference to this unique object. Thus if this.getClass() == obj.getClass() in Example 1.8 is true, then we know that obj and this are both of class Employee.

EXERCISES FOR SECTION 1.5

SELF-CHECK

1. Indicate the effect of each of the following statements:

```
Object o = new String("Hello");
String s = o;
Object p = 25;
int k = p;
Number n = k;
```

2. Rewrite the invalid statements in Question 1 to remove the errors.

PROGRAMMING

1. Write an equals method for class Computer (Listing 1.2).
2. Write an equals method for class Notebook (Listing 1.4).
3. Write an equals method for the following class. What other equals methods should be defined?

```
public class Airplane {
    // Data Fields
    Engine eng;
    Rudder rud;
    Wing[] wings = new Wing[2];
    ...
}
```

1.6 A Java Inheritance Example—The `Exception` Class Hierarchy

Next we show how Java uses inheritance to build a class hierarchy that is fundamental to detecting and correcting errors during program execution (run-time errors). A run-time error occurs during program execution when the Java Virtual Machine (JVM) detects an operation that it knows to be incorrect. A run-time error will cause the JVM to *throw an exception*—that is, to create an object of an exception type that identifies the kind of incorrect operation and also interrupts normal processing. Table 1.3 shows some examples of exceptions that are run-time errors. All are subclasses of class `RuntimeException`. Following are some examples of the exceptions listed in the table.

Division by Zero

If `count` represents the number of items being processed and it is possible for `count` to be zero, then the assignment statement

```
average = sum / count;
```

can cause a division-by-zero error. If `sum` and `count` are `int` variables, this error is indicated by the JVM throwing an `ArithmeticException`. You can easily guard against such a division with an `if` statement so that the division operation will not be performed when `count` is zero:

```
if (count == 0)
    average = 0;
else
    average = sum / count;
```

Normally, you would compute an average as a `double` value, so you could cast an `int` value in `sum` to type `double` before doing the division. In this case an exception is not thrown if `count` is zero. Instead, `average` will have one of the special values `Double.POSITIVE_INFINITY`, `Double.NEGATIVE_INFINITY`, or `Double.NaN` depending on whether `sum` was positive, negative, or zero.

TABLE 1.3
Subclasses of java.lang.RuntimeException

Class	Cause/Consequence
`ArithmeticException`	An attempt to perform an integer division by zero.
`ArrayIndexOutOfBoundsException`	An attempt to access an array element using an index (subscript) less than zero or greater than or equal to the array's length.
`NumberFormatException`	An attempt to convert a string that is not numeric to a number.
`NullPointerException`	An attempt to use a `null` reference value to access an object.
`NoSuchElementException`	An attempt to get a next element after all elements were accessed.
`InputMismatchException`	The token returned by a `Scanner next . . .` method does not match the pattern for the expected data type.

Array Index Out of Bounds

An `ArrayIndexOutOfBoundsException` is thrown by the JVM when an index value (subscript) used to access an element in an array is less than zero or greater than or equal to the array's length. For example, suppose we define the array `scores` as follows:

```
int[] scores = new int[500];
```

The subscripted variable `scores[i]` uses `i` (type `int`) as the array index. An `ArrayIndexOutOfBoundsException` will be thrown if `i` is less than zero or greater than 499.

Array index out of bounds errors can be prevented by carefully checking the boundary values for an index that is also a loop control variable. A common error is using the array size as the upper limit rather than the array size minus 1.

EXAMPLE 1.9 The following loop would cause an `ArrayIndexOutOfBoundsException` on the last pass, when `i` is equal to `x.length`.

```
for (int i = 0; i <= x.length; i++)
    x[i] = i * i;
```

The loop repetition test should be `i < x.length`.

`NumberFormatException` and `InputMismatchException`

The `NumberFormatException` is thrown when a program attempts to convert a nonnumeric string (usually a data value) to a numeric value. For example, if the user types in the string `"2.6e"`, method `parseDouble`, in the following code,

```
String speedStr = JOptionPane.showInputDialog("Enter speed");
double speed = Double.parseDouble(speedStr);
```

would throw a `NumberFormatException` because `"2.6e"` is not a valid numeric string (it has no exponent after the `e`). There is no general way to avoid this exception because it is impossible to guard against all possible data entry errors the user can make.

A similar error can occur if you are using a `Scanner` object for data entry. If `scan` is a `Scanner`, the statement

```
double speed = scan.nextDouble();
```

will throw an `InputMismatchException` if the next token scanned is `"2.6e"`.

Null Pointer

The `NullPointerException` is thrown when there is an attempt to access an object that does not exist; that is, the reference variable being accessed contains a special value, known as `null`. You can guard against this by testing for `null` before invoking a method.

The Exception Class Hierarchy

The exceptions in Table 1.3 are all subclasses of `Runtime`. All Exception classes are defined within a class hierarchy that has the class `Throwable` as its superclass (see the UML diagram in Figure 1.8). The UML diagram shows that classes `Error` and `Exception` are subclasses of `Throwable`. Each of these classes has subclasses that are shown in the figure. We will focus on class `Exception` and its subclasses in this chapter. Because `RuntimeException` is a subclass of `Exception`, it is also a subclass of `Throwable` (the subclass relationship is transitive).

The Class `Throwable`

The class `Throwable` is the superclass of all exceptions. The methods that you will use from class `Throwable` are summarized in Table 1.4. Because all exception classes are subclasses of class `Throwable`, they can call any of its methods including `getMessage`, `printStackTrace`, and `toString`. If `ex` is an `Exception` object, the call

```
ex.printStackTrace();
```

displays a stack trace, discussed in Appendix A (Section A.11). The statement

```
System.err.println(ex.getMessage());
```

displays a detail message (or error message) describing the exception. The statement

```
System.err.println(ex.toString);
```

displays the name of the exception followed by the detail message.

FIGURE 1.8
Summary of `Exception` Class Hierarchy

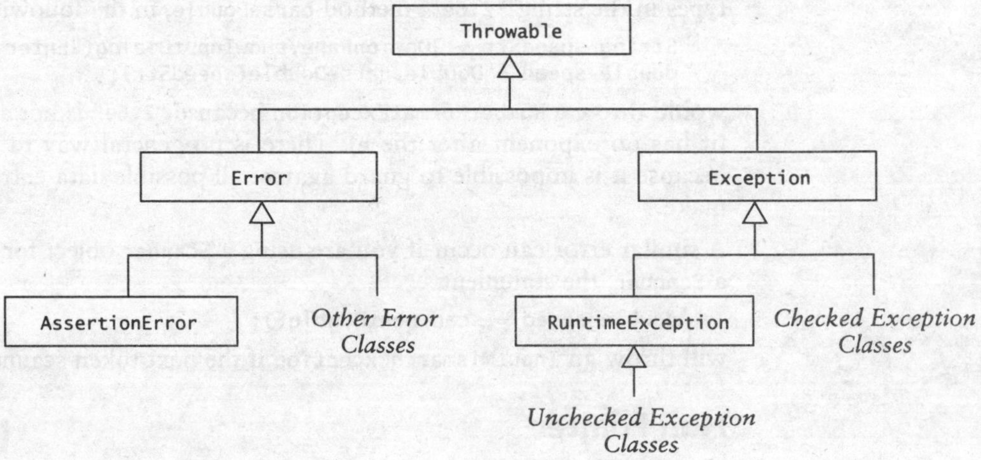

TABLE 1.4
Summary of Commonly Used Methods from the `java.lang.Throwable` Class

Method	Behavior
`String getMessage()`	Returns the detail message.
`void printStackTrace()`	Prints the stack trace to System.err.
`String toString()`	Returns the name of the exception followed by the detail message.

Checked and Unchecked Exceptions

There are two categories of exceptions: *checked* and *unchecked*. A checked exception is an error that is normally not due to programmer error and is beyond the control of the programmer. All exceptions caused by input/output errors are considered checked exceptions. For example, if the programmer attempts to access a data file that is not available because of a user or system error, a `FileNotFoundException` is thrown. The class `IOException` and its subclasses (see Table 1.5) are checked exceptions. Even though checked exceptions are beyond the control of the programmer, the programmer must be aware of them and must handle them in some way (discussed later). All checked exceptions are subclasses of `Exception`, but they are not subclasses of `RuntimeException`. Figure 1.9 is a more complete diagram of the Exception hierarchy.

The *unchecked* exceptions represent error conditions that may occur as a result of programmer error or of serious external conditions that are considered unrecoverable. For example, exceptions such as `NullPointerException` or `ArrayIndexOutOfBoundsException` are unchecked exceptions that are generally due to programmer error. These exceptions are all subclasses of `RuntimeException`. While you can sometimes prevent these exceptions via defensive programming, it is impractical to try to prevent them all or to provide exception handling for all of them. Therefore, you can handle these exceptions, but Java does not require you to do so.

The class `Error` and its subclasses represent errors that are due to serious external conditions. An example of such an error is `OutOfMemoryError`, which is thrown when there is no memory available. You can't foresee or guard against these kinds of errors. You can attempt to handle these exceptions, but you are strongly discouraged from

TABLE 1.5
Class `java.io.IOException` and Some Subclasses

Exception Class	Cause
`IOException`	Some sort of input/output error.
`EOFException`	Attempt to read beyond the end of data with a `DataInputStream`.
`FileNotFoundException`	Inability to find a file.

FIGURE 1.9

Exception Hierarchy Showing Selected Checked and Unchecked Exceptions

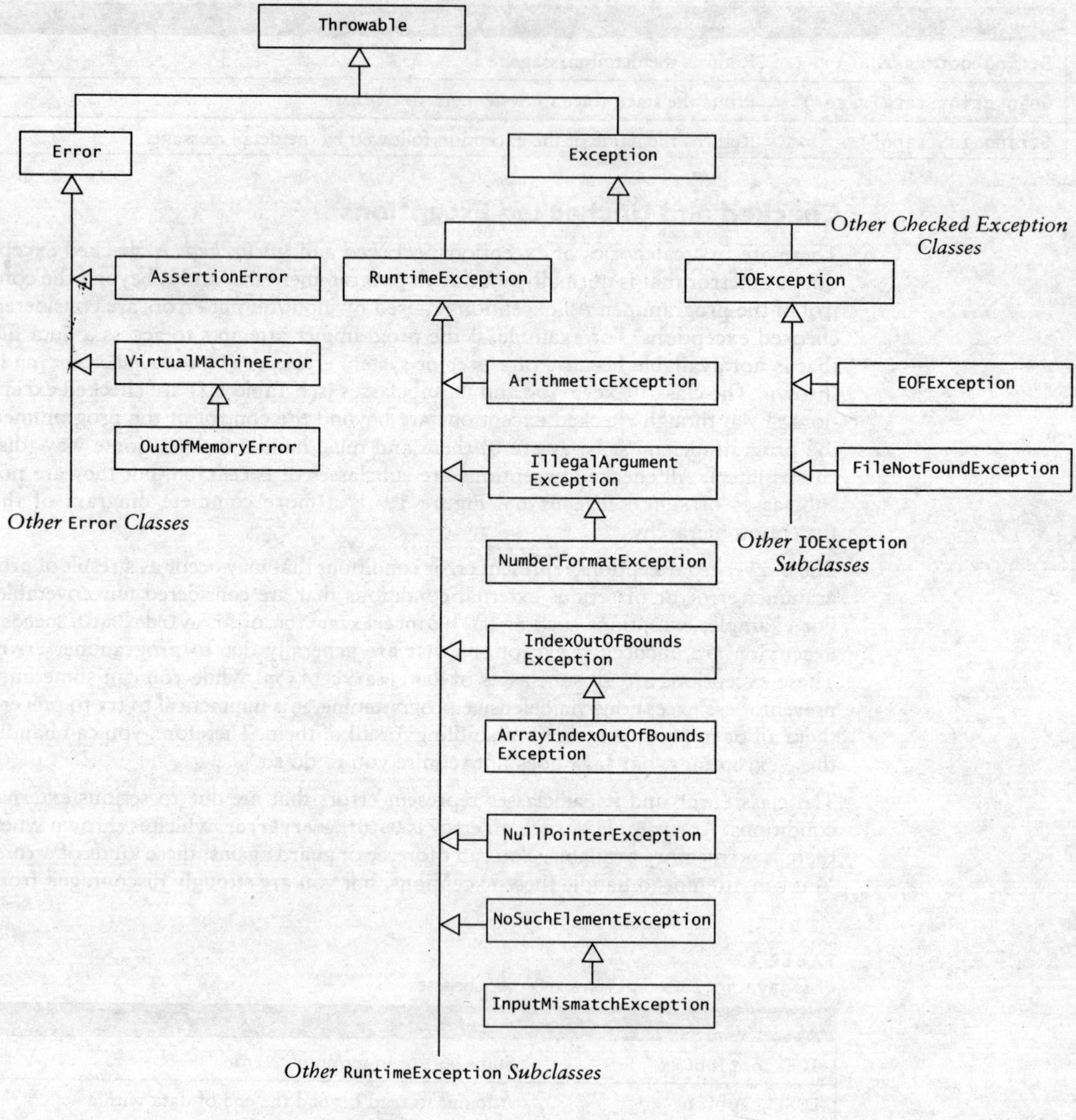

trying to do so because you probably will be unsuccessful. For example, if an `OutOfMemoryError` is thrown, there is no memory available to process the exception-handling code, so the exception would be thrown again.

How do we know which exceptions are checked and which are unchecked? Exception classes that are subclasses of `RuntimeException` and `Error` are unchecked. All other exception classes are checked exceptions.

We discuss Java exceptions further in Appendix A. Section A.11 of the Appendix describes how to use the `try-catch` statement to handle different kinds of exceptions; Section A.12 shows how to write statements that throw exceptions when your code detects an error during run time.

Handling Exceptions to Recover from Errors

Exceptions enable Java programmers to write code that can report errors and sometimes recover from them. The key to this process is the **`try-catch`** sequence. We will cover the essentials of catching and throwing exceptions in this section. A complete discussion is provided in Appendix A.11 and A.12.

The `try-catch` Sequence

The **`try-catch`** sequence is used to catch and handle exceptions. It resembles an **`if-then-else`** statement. It consists of one **`try`** block followed by one or more **`catch`** clauses. The statements in the **`try`** block are executed first. If they execute without error, the **`catch`** clauses are skipped. If a statement in the **`try`** block throws an exception, the rest of the statements in the **`try`** block are skipped and execution continues with the statements in the **`catch`** clause for that particular type of exception. If there is no **`catch`** clause for that exception type, the exception is rethrown to the calling method. If the `main` method is reached and no appropriate **`catch`** clause is located, the program terminates with an unhandled exception error. A **`try`** block with two **`catch`** clauses follows.

```
try {
    // Execute the following statements until an exception is thrown
    ...
    // Skip the catch blocks if no exceptions were thrown
} catch (ExceptionTypeA ex) {
    // Execute this catch block if an exception of type ExceptionTypeA
    // was thrown in the try block
    ...
} catch (ExceptionTypeB ex) {
    // Execute this catch block if an exception of type ExceptionTypeB
    // was thrown in the try block
    ...
}
```

A **`catch`** clause header resembles a method header. The expression in parentheses in the **`catch`** clause header is like a method parameter declaration (the parameter is ex). The statements in curly braces, the **`catch`** block, execute if the exception that was thrown is the specified exception type or is a subclass of that exception type.

PITFALL

Unreachable catch block

In the above, ExceptionTypeA cannot be a superclass of ExceptionTyeB. If it is, ExceptionTypeB is considered unreachable because its exceptions would be caught by the first catch clause.

Using try-catch to Recover from an Error

One common source of exceptions is user input. For example, the Scanner nextInt method is supposed to read a type **int** value. If an **int** is not the next item read, Java throws an InputMismatchException. Rather than have this problem terminate the program, you can read the data value in a **try** block and catch an InputMismatchException in the **catch** clause. If one is thrown, you can give the user another chance to enter an integer as shown in method getIntValue, as follows.

```
/** Reads an integer using a scanner.
    @return the first integer read.
*/
public static int getIntValue(Scanner scan) {
    int nextInt = 0;          // next int value
    boolean validInt = false; // flag for valid input
    while (!validInt) {
        try {
            System.out.println("Enter number of kids:");
            nextInt = scan.nextInt();
            validInt = true;
        } catch (InputMismatchException ex) {
            scan.nextLine();    // clear buffer
            System.out.println("Bad data -- enter an integer:");
        }
    }
    return nextInt;
}
```

The **while** loop repeats while validInt is **false** (its initial value). The **try** block attempts to read a type **int** value using Scanner scan. If the user enters an integer, validInt is set to **true** and the **try-catch** statement and **while** loop are exited. The integer data value will be returned as the method result.

If the user enters a data item that is not an integer, however, Java throws an InputMismatchException. This is caught by the **catch** clause

```
catch (InputMismatchException ex)
```

The first statement in the **catch** block clears the Scanner buffer, and the user is prompted to enter an integer. Because validInt is still false, the while loop repeats until the user successfully enters an integer.

Throwing an Exception When Recovery Is Not Obvious

In the last example, method getIntValue was able to recover from a bad data item by giving the user another chance to enter data. In some cases, you may be able to write code that detects certain kinds of errors, but there may not be an obvious way to recover from them. In these cases, the best approach is just to throw an exception reporting the error to the method that called it. The caller can then catch the exception and handle it.

Method processPositiveInteger requires a positive integer as its argument. If the argument is not positive, there is no reason to continue executing the method because the result may be meaningless, or the method execution may cause a different exception to be thrown, which could confuse the method caller. There is also no obvious way to correct this error because the method has no way of knowing what n should be, so a **try-catch** sequence would not fix the problem.

```
public static void processPositiveInteger(int n) {
    if (n < 0)
        throw new IllegalArgumentException(
                "Invalid negative argument");
    else {
        // Process n as required
        //...
        System.out.println("Finished processing" + n);
    }
}
```

If the argument n is not positive, the statement

```
        throw new IllegalArgumentException(
                "Invalid negative argument");
```

executes and throws an IllegalArgumentException object. The string in the last line is stored in the exception object's message data field, and the method is exited, returning control to the caller. The caller is then responsible for handling this exception. If possible, the caller may be able to recover from this error and would attempt to do so.

The main method, which follows, calls both getIntValue and processPositiveInteger in the **try** block. If an IllegalArgumentException is thrown, the message invalid negative argument is displayed, and the program terminates with an error indication. If no exception is thrown, the program exits normally.

```
public static void main(String[] args) {
    Scanner scan = new scanner (system.in);
    try {
        int num = getIntValue(scan);
        processPositiveInteger(num);
    } catch (IllegalArgumentException ex) {
        System.err.println(ex.getMessage());
        System.exit(1); // error indication
    }
    System.exit(0);         //normal exit
}
```

EXERCISES FOR SECTION 1.6

SELF-CHECK

1. Explain the key difference between checked and unchecked exceptions. Give an example of each kind of exception. What criterion does Java use to decide whether an exception is checked or unchecked?
2. What is the difference between the kind of unchecked exceptions in class `Error` and the kind in class `Exception`?
3. List four subclasses of `RuntimeException`.
4. List two subclasses of `IOException`.
5. What happens in the `main` method preceding the exercises if an exception of a different type occurs in method `processPositiveInteger`?
6. Trace the execution of method `getIntValue` if the following data items are entered by a careless user. What would be displayed?
```
ace
7.5
-5
```
7. Trace the execution of method `main` preceding the exercises if the data items in Question 6 were entered. What would be displayed?

1.7 Packages and Visibility

Packages

You have already seen packages. The Java API is organized into packages such as `java.lang`, `java.util`, `java.io`, and `javax.swing`. The package to which a class belongs is declared by the first statement in the file in which the class is defined using the keyword **package**, followed by the package name. For example, we could begin each class in the computer hierarchy (class `Notebook` and class `Computer`) with the line:

```
package computers;
```

All classes in the same package are stored in the same directory or folder. The directory must have the same name as the package. All the classes in the folder must declare themselves to be in the package.

Classes that are not part of a package may access only public members (data fields or methods) of classes in the package. If the application class is not in the package, it must reference the classes by their complete names. The complete name of a class is `packageName.className`. However, if the package is imported by the application class, then the prefix `packageName.` is not required. For example, we can reference the constant `GREEN` in class `java.awt.Color` as `Color.GREEN` if we import package `java.awt`. Otherwise, we would need to use the complete name `java.awt.Color.GREEN`.

The No-Package-Declared Environment

So far we have not specified packages, yet objects of one class could communicate with objects of another class. How does this work? Just as there is a default visibility, there is a default package. Files that do not specify a package are considered part of the default package. Therefore, if you don't declare packages, all your classes belong to the same package (the default package).

SYNTAX **Package Declaration**

FORM:
package *packageName*;

EXAMPLE:
```
package computers;
```

INTERPRETATION:
This declaration appears as the first line of the file in which a class is defined. The class is now considered part of the package. This file must be contained in a folder with the same name as the package.

PROGRAM STYLE

When to Package Classes

The default package facility is intended for use during the early stages of implementing classes or for small prototype programs. If you are developing an application that has several classes that are part of a hierarchy of classes, you should declare them all to be in the same package. The package declaration will keep you from accidentally referring to classes by their short names in other classes that are outside the package. It will also restrict the visibility of protected members of a class to only its subclasses outside the package (and to other classes inside the package) as intended.

Package Visibility

So far, we have discussed three layers of visibility for classes and class members (data fields and methods): private, protected, and public. There is a fourth layer, called *package visibility*, that sits between private and protected. Classes, data fields, and methods with package visibility are accessible to all other methods of the same package but are not accessible to methods outside of the package. By contrast, classes, data fields, and methods that are declared protected are visible within subclasses that are declared outside the package, in addition to being visible to all members of the package.

We have used the visibility modifiers `private`, `public`, and `protected` to specify the visibility of a class member. If we do not use one of these visibility modifiers, then the class member has package visibility and it is visible in all classes of the same package, but not outside the package. Note that there is no visibility modifier `package`; package visibility is the default if no visibility modifier is specified.

Visibility Supports Encapsulation

The rules for visibility control how encapsulation occurs in a Java program. Table 1.6 summarizes the rules in order of decreasing protection. Notice that private visibility is for members of a class that should not be accessible to anyone but the class, not even classes that extend it. Except for inner classes, it does not make sense for a class to be private. It would mean that no other class can use it.

Also notice that package visibility (the default if a visibility modifier is not given) allows the developer of a library to shield classes and class members from classes outside the package. Typically, such classes perform tasks required by the public classes within the package.

Use of protected visibility allows the package developer to give control to other programmers who want to extend classes in the package. Protected data fields are typically essential to an object. Similarly, protected methods are those that are essential to an extending class.

Table 1.6 shows that public classes and members are universally visible. Within a package, the public classes are those that are essential to communicating with objects outside the package.

TABLE 1.6
Summary of Kinds of Visibility

Visibility	Applied to Classes	Applied to Class Members
`private`	Applicable to inner classes. Accessible only to members of the class in which it is declared.	Visible only within this class.
Default or package	Visible to classes in this package.	Visible to classes in this package.
`protected`	Applicable to inner classes. Visible to classes in this package and to classes outside the package that extend the class in which it is declared.	Visible to classes in this package and to classes outside the package that extend this class.
`public`	Visible to all classes.	Visible to all classes. The class defining the member must also be public.

PITFALL

Protected Visibility Can Be Equivalent to Public Visibility

The intention of protected visibility is to enable a subclass to access a member (data field or method) of a superclass directly. However, protected members can also be accessed within any class that is in the same package. This is not a problem if the class with the protected members is declared to be in a package; however, if it is not, then it is in the default package. Protected members of a class in the default package are visible in all other classes you have defined that are not part of an actual package. This is generally not a desirable situation. You can avoid this dilemma by using protected visibility only with members of classes that are in explicitly declared packages. In all other classes, use either public or private visibility because protected visibility is virtually equivalent to public visibility.

EXERCISES FOR SECTION 1.7

SELF-CHECK

1. Consider the following declarations:

```
package pack1;
public class Class1 {
        private int v1;
        protected int v2;
        int v3;
        public int v4;
}

package pack1;
public class Class2 {...}

package pack2;
public class Class3 extends pack1.Class1 {...}

package pack2;
public class Class4 {...}
```

a. What visibility must variables declared in `pack1.Class1` have in order to be visible in `pack1.Class2`?

b. What visibility must variables declared in `pack1.Class1` have in order to be visible in `pack2.Class3`?

c. What visibility must variables declared in `pack1.Class1` have in order to be visible in `pack2.Class4`?

1.8 A Shape Class Hierarchy

In this section, we provide a case study that illustrates some of the principles in this chapter. For each case study, we will begin with a statement of the problem (Problem). Then we analyze the problem to determine exactly what is expected and to develop an initial strategy for solution (Analysis). Next, we design a solution to the problem, developing and refining an algorithm (Design). We write one or more Java classes that contain methods for the algorithm steps (Implementation). Finally, we provide a strategy for testing the completed classes and discuss special cases that should be investigated (Testing). We often provide a separate class that does the testing.

CASE STUDY Processing Geometric Figures

Problem We would like to process some standard geometric shapes. Each `figure` object will be one of three standard shapes (rectangle, circle, right triangle). We would like to be able to do standard computations, such as finding the area and perimeter, for any of these shapes.

Analysis For each of the geometric shapes we can process, we need a class that represents the shape and knows how to perform the standard computations on it (i.e., find its area and perimeter). These classes will be `Rectangle`, `Circle`, and `RtTriangle`. To ensure that these shape classes all define the required computational methods (finding area and perimeter), we will make them abstract methods in the base class for the shape hierarchy. If a shape class does not have the required methods, we will get a syntax error when we attempt to compile it.

Figure 1.10 shows the class hierarchy. We used abstract class `Shape` as the base class of the hierarchy. We didn't consider using an actual class because there are no actual objects of the base class type.The single data field `shapeName` stores the kind of shape object as a `String`.

Design We will discuss the design of the `Rectangle` class here. The design of the other classes is similar and is left as an exercise. Table 1.7 shows class `Rectangle`. Class `Rectangle` has data fields `width` and `height`. It has methods to compute area and perimeter, a method to read in the attributes of a rectangular object (`readShapeData`), and a `toString` method.

Implementation Listing 1.6 shows abstract class `Shape`.

FIGURE 1.10
Abstract class Shape and Its Three Actual Subclasses

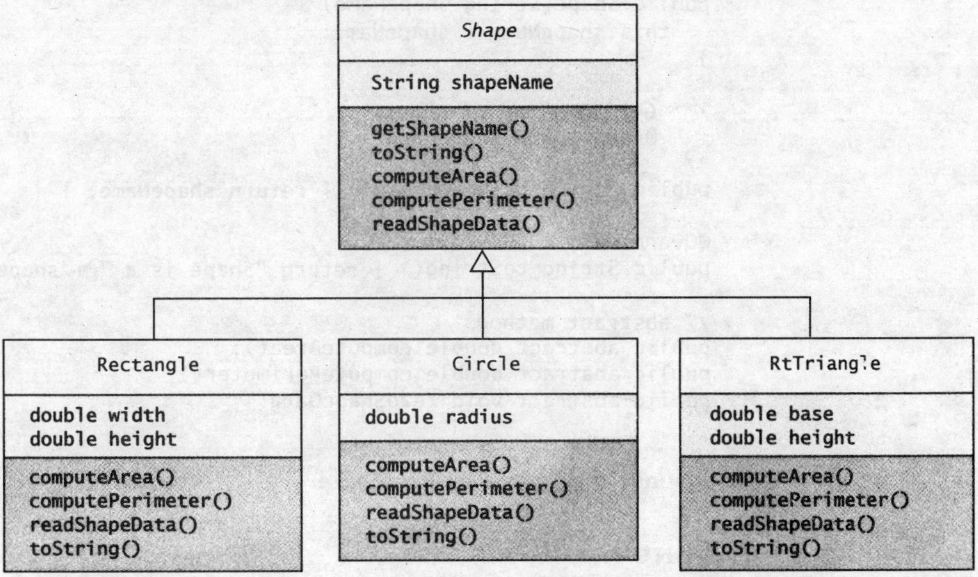

TABLE 1.7
Class Rectangle

Data Field	Attribute
`double width`	Width of a rectangle
`double height`	Height of a rectangle
Method	**Behavior**
`double computeArea()`	Computes the rectangle area (width × height)
`double computePerimeter()`	Computes the rectangle perimeter (2 × width + 2 × height)
`void readShapeData()`	Reads the width and height
`String toString()`	Returns a string representing the state

LISTING 1.6
Abstract Class Shape (Shape.java)

```
/** Abstract class for a geometric shape. */
public abstract class Shape {

  /** The name of the shape */
  private String shapeName = "";
```

```
    /** Initializes the shapeName.
        @param shapeName the kind of shape
    */
    public Shape(String shapeName) {
      this.shapeName = shapeName;
    }

    /** Get the kind of shape.
        @return the shapeName
    */
    public String getShapeName() { return shapeName; }

    @Override
    public String toString() { return "Shape is a " + shapeName; }

    // abstract methods
    public abstract double computeArea();
    public abstract double computePerimeter();
    public abstract void readShapeData();
}
```

Listing 1.7 shows class `Rectangle`.

LISTING 1.7

Class Rectangle (Rectangle.java)

```
import java.util.Scanner;

/** Represents a rectangle.
    Extends Shape.
*/
public class Rectangle extends Shape {

    // Data Fields
    /** The width of the rectangle. */
    private double width = 0;
    /** The height of the rectangle. */
    private double height = 0;

    // Constructors
    public Rectangle() {
      super("Rectangle");
    }

    /** Constructs a rectangle of the specified size.
        @param width the width
        @param height the height
    */
    public Rectangle(double width, double height) {
        super("Rectangle");
        this.width = width;
        this.height = height;
    }
```

```
    // Methods
    /** Get the width.
        @return The width
    */
    public double getWidth() {
        return width;
    }

    /** Get the height.
        @return The height
    */
    public double getHeight() {
        return height;
    }

    /** Compute the area.
        @return The area of the rectangle
    */
    @Override
    public double computeArea() {
        return height * width;
    }

    /** Compute the perimeter.
        @return The perimeter of the rectangle
    */
    @Override
    public double computePerimeter() {
        return 2 * (height + width);
    }

    /** Read the attributes of the rectangle. */
    @Override
    public void readShapeData() {
        Scanner in = new Scanner(System.in);
        System.out.println("Enter the width of the Rectangle");
        width = in.nextDouble();
        System.out.println("Enter the height of the Rectangle");
        height = in.nextDouble();
    }

    /** Create a string representation of the rectangle.
        @return A string representation of the rectangle
    */
    @Override
    public String toString() {
        return super.toString() + ": width is " + width
            + ", height is " + height;
    }

}
```

Testing

To test the shape hierarchy, we will write a program that will prompt for the kind of figure, read the parameters for that figure, and display the results. The code for `ComputeAreaAndPerimeter` is shown in Listing 1.8. The `main` method is very straightforward, and so is `displayResult`. The `main` method first calls `getShape`, which displays a list of available shapes and prompts the user for the choice. The reply is expected to be a single character. The nested `if` statement determines which shape instance to return. For example, if the user's choice is C (for Circle), the statement

```
return new Circle();
```

returns a reference to a new `Circle` object.

After the new shape instance is returned to `myShape in main`, the statement

```
myShape.readShapeData();
```

uses polymorphism to invoke the correct member function `readShapeData` to read the shape object's parameter(s). The methods `computeArea` and `computePerimeter` are then called to obtain the values of the area and perimeter. Finally, `displayResult` is called to display the result.

A sample of the output from `ComputeAreaAndPerimeter` follows.

```
Enter C for circle
Enter R for Rectangle
Enter T for Right Triangle
R
Enter the width of the Rectangle
120
Enter the height of the Rectangle
200
Shape is a Rectangle: width is 120.0, height is 200.0
The area is 24000.00
The perimeter is 640.00
```

LISTING 1.8
ComputeAreaAndPerimeter.java

```
import java.util.Scanner;

/**
    Computes the area and perimeter of selected figures.
    @author Koffman and Wolfgang
*/
public class ComputeAreaAndPerimeter {

    /** The main program performs the following steps.
        1. It asks the user for the type of figure.
        2. It asks the user for the characteristics of that figure.
        3. It computes the perimeter.
        4. It computes the area.
        5. It displays the result.
        @param args The command line arguments -- not used
```

```
    */
    public static void main(String args[]) {
      Shape myShape;
      double perimeter;
      double area;
      myShape = getShape();     // Ask for figure type
      myShape.readShapeData(); // Read the shape data
      perimeter = myShape.computePerimeter();  // Compute perimeter
      area = myShape.computeArea();            // Compute the area
      displayResult(myShape, area, perimeter); // Display the result
      System.exit(0);                         // Exit the program
    }

    /** Ask the user for the type of figure.
        @return An instance of the selected shape
    */
    public static Shape getShape() {
        Scanner in = new Scanner(System.in);
        System.out.println("Enter C for circle");
        System.out.println("Enter R for Rectangle");
        System.out.println("Enter T for Right Triangle");
        String figType = in.next();
        if (figType.equalsIgnoreCase("c")) {
            return new Circle();
        }
        else if (figType.equalsIgnoreCase("r")) {
            return new Rectangle();
        }
        else if (figType.equalsIgnoreCase("t")) {
            return new RtTriangle();
        }
        else {
            return null;
        }
    }

    /** Display the result of the computation.
        @param area The area of the figure
        @param perim The perimeter of the figure
    */
    private static void displayResult(Shape myShape,
        double area, double perim) {
        System.out.println(myShape);
        System.out.printf("The area is %.2f%nThe perimeter is %.2f%n",
                      area, perim);
    }
}
```

PROGRAM STYLE

Using Factory Methods to Return Objects

The method `getShape` is an example of a *factory method* because it creates a new object and returns a reference to it. The author of the `main` method does not need to know what kinds of shapes are available. Knowledge of the available shapes is confined to the `getShape` method. This function must present a list of available shapes to the user and decode the user's response to return an instance of the desired shape. If you add a new geometric shape class to the class hierarchy, you only need to modify the `if` statement in the factory method so that it can create and return an object of that type.

EXERCISES FOR SECTION 1.8

SELF-CHECK

1. Explain why `Shape` cannot be an actual class.
2. Explain why `Shape` cannot be an interface.

PROGRAMMING

1. Write class `Circle`.
2. Write class `RtTriangle`.

Chapter Review

- Inheritance and class hierarchies enable you to capture the idea that one thing may be a refinement or an extension of another. For example, a plant is a living thing. Such *is-a* relationships create the right balance between too much and too little structure. Think of inheritance as a means of creating a refinement of an abstraction. The entities farther down the hierarchy are more complex and less general than those higher up. The entities farther down the hierarchy may inherit data members (attributes) and methods from those farther up, but not vice versa. A class that inherits from another class **extends** that class.

- Encapsulation and inheritance impose structure on object abstractions. Polymorphism provides a degree of flexibility in defining methods. It loosens the structure a bit in order to make methods more accessible and useful. *Polymorphism* means "many forms." It captures the idea that methods may take on a variety of forms to suit different purposes.

- All exceptions in the `Exception` class hierarchy are derived from a common superclass called `Throwable`. This class provides methods for collecting and reporting the state of the program when an exception is thrown. The commonly used methods are `getMessage` and `toString`, which return a detail message describing what caused the exception to be thrown, and `printStackTrace`, which prints the exception and then shows the line where the exception occurred and the sequence of method calls leading to the exception.
- There are two categories of exceptions: checked and unchecked. Checked exceptions are generally due to an error condition external to the program. Unchecked exceptions are generally due to a programmer error or a dire event.
- The keyword **interface** defines an interface. A Java interface can be used to specify an abstract data type (ADT), and a Java class can be used to implement an ADT. A class that implements an interface must define the methods that the interface declares.
- The keyword **abstract** defines an abstract class or method. An abstract class is like an interface in that it leaves method implementations up to subclasses, but it can also have data fields and actual methods. You use an abstract class as the superclass for a group of classes in a hierarchy.
- Visibility is influenced by the package in which a class is declared. You assign classes to a package by including the statement **package** *packageName*; at the top of the file. You can refer to classes within a package by their direct names when the package is imported through an import declaration.

Java Constructs Introduced in This Chapter

`abstract`	`private`	`super(...)`
`extends`	`protected`	`this.`
`instanceof`	`public`	`this(...)`
`interface`	`super.`	
`package`		

Java API Classes Introduced in This Chapter

`java.lang.Byte`	`java.lang.Number`
`java.lang.Float`	`java.lang.Object`
`java.lang.Integer`	`java.lang.Short`

User-Defined Interfaces and Classes in This Chapter

`ComputeAreaAndPerimeter`	`Food`	`Student`
`Computer`	`Notebook`	`StudentInt`
`Employee`	`Rectangle`	`StudentWorker`
`EmployeeInt`	`Shape`	

Quick-Check Exercises

1. What does *polymorphism* mean, and how is it used in Java? What is method overriding? Method overloading?
2. What is a method signature? Describe how it is used in method overloading.
3. Describe the use of the keywords **super** and **this**.
4. Indicate whether each error or exception in the following list is checked or unchecked: `IOException`, `EOFException`, `VirtualMachineError`, `IndexOutOfBoundsException`, `OutOfMemoryError`.
5. When would you use an abstract class, and what should it contain?
6. An ______ specifies the requirements of an ADT as a contract between the ______ and ______; a ______ implements the ADT.
7. An interface can be implemented by multiple classes. (True/False)
8. Describe the difference between *is-a* and *has-a* relationships.
9. Which can have more data fields and methods: the superclass or the subclass?
10. You can reference an object of a ______ type through a variable of a ______ type.
11. You cast an object referenced by a ______ type to an object of a ______ type in order to apply methods of the ______ type to the object. This is called a ______.
12. The four kinds of visibility in order of decreasing visibility are: ______, ______, ______, and ______.

Review Questions

1. Which method is invoked in a particular class when a method definition is overridden in several classes that are part of an inheritance hierarchy? Answer the question for the case in which the class has a definition for the method and also for the case where it doesn't.
2. Explain how assignments can be made within a class hierarchy and the role of casting in a class hierarchy. What is strong typing? Why is it an important language feature?
3. If Java encounters a method call of the following form:

   ```
   superclassVar.methodName()
   ```

   where `superclassVar` is a variable of a superclass that references an object whose type is a subclass, what is necessary for this statement to compile? During run time, will method `methodName` from the class that is the type of `superclassVar` always be invoked, or is it possible that a different method `methodName` will be invoked? Explain your answer.
4. Assume the situation in Question 3, but method `methodName` is not defined in the class that is the type of `superclassVar`, though it is defined in the subclass type. Rewrite the method call so that it will compile.
5. Explain the process of initializing an object that is a subclass type in the subclass constructor. What part of the object must be initialized first? How is this done?
6. What is default or package visibility?
7. Indicate what kind of exception each of the following errors would cause. Indicate whether each error is a checked or an unchecked exception.
   a. Attempting to create a `Scanner` for a file that does not exist
   b. Attempting to call a method on a variable that has not been initialized
   c. Using −1 as an array index

8. Discuss when abstract classes are used. How do they differ from actual classes and from interfaces?
9. What is the advantage of specifying an abstract data type as an interface instead of just going ahead and implementing it as a class?
10. Define an interface to specify an ADT `Money` that has methods for arithmetic operations (addition, subtraction, multiplication, and division) on real numbers having exactly two digits to the right of the decimal point, as well as methods for representing a `Money` object as a string and as a real number. Also include methods `equals` and `compareTo` for this ADT.
11. Answer Review Question 10 for an ADT `Complex` that has methods for arithmetic operations on a complex number (a number with a real and an imaginary part). Assume that the same operations (+, –, *, /) are supported. Also provide methods `toString`, `equals`, and `compareTo` for the ADT `Complex`.
12. Like a rectangle, a parallelogram has opposite sides that are parallel, but it has a corner angle, theta, that is less than 90 degrees. Discuss how you would add parallelograms to the class hierarchy for geometric shapes (see Figure 1.10). Write a definition for class `Parallelogram`.

Programming Projects

1. A veterinary office wants to store information regarding the kinds of animals it treats. Data includes diet, whether the animal is nocturnal, whether its bite is poisonous (as for some snakes), whether it flies, and so on. Use a superclass `Pet` with abstract methods and create appropriate subclasses to support about 10 animals of your choice.
2. A student is a person, and so is an employee. Create a class `Person` that has the data attributes common to both students and employees (name, social security number, age, gender, address, and telephone number) and appropriate method definitions. A student has a grade-point average (GPA), major, and year of graduation. An employee has a department, job title, and year of hire. In addition, there are hourly employees (hourly rate, hours worked, and union dues) and salaried employees (annual salary). Define a class hierarchy and write an application class that you can use to first store the data for an array of people and then display that information in a meaningful way.
3. Create a pricing system for a company that makes individualized computers, such as you might see on a Web site. There are two kinds of computers: notebooks and desktop computers. The customer can select the processor speed, the amount of memory, and the size of the disk drive. The customer can also choose either a CD drive (CD ROM, CD-RW), a DVD drive, or both. For notebooks, there is a choice of screen size. Other options are a modem, a network card, or a wireless network. You should have an abstract class `Computer` and subclasses `DeskTop` and `Notebook`. Each subclass should have methods for calculating the price of a computer, given the base price plus the cost of the different options. You should have methods for calculating memory price, hard drive price, and so on. There should be a method to calculate shipping cost.
4. Write a banking program that simulates the operation of your local bank. You should declare the following collection of classes.

   Class `Account`

   Data fields: `customer` (type `Customer`), `balance`, `accountNumber`, `transactions` array (type `Transaction[]`). Allocate an initial `Transaction` array of a reasonable size (e.g., 20), and provide a `reallocate` method that doubles the size of the `Transaction` array when it becomes full.

   Methods: `getBalance`, `getCustomer`, `toString`, `setCustomer`

Class `SavingsAccount` extends `Account`

Methods: `deposit`, `withdraw`, `addInterest`

Class `CheckingAccount` extends `Account`

Methods: `deposit`, `withdraw`, `addInterest`

Class `Customer`

Data fields: `name`, `address`, `age`, `telephoneNumber`, `customerNumber`

Methods: Accessors and modifiers for data fields plus the additional abstract methods `getSavingsInterest`, `getCheckInterest`, and `getCheckCharge`.

Classes `Senior`, `Adult`, `Student`, all these classes extend `Customer`

Each has constant data fields `SAVINGS_INTEREST`, `CHECK_INTEREST`, `CHECK_CHARGE`, good! and `OVERDRAFT_PENALTY` that define these values for customers of that type, and each class implements the corresponding accessors.

Class `Bank`

Data field: `accounts` array (type `Account[]`). Allocate an array of a reasonable size (e.g., 100), and provide a reallocate method.

Methods: `addAccount`, `makeDeposit`, `makeWithdrawal`, `getAccount`

Class `Transaction`

Data fields: `customerNumber`, `transactionType`, `amount`, `date`, and `fees` (a string describing unusual fees)

Methods: `processTran`

You need to write all these classes and an application class that interacts with the user. In the application, you should first open several accounts and then enter several transactions.

5. You have a sizable collection of music and videos and want to develop a database for storing and processing information about this collection. You need to develop a class hierarchy for your media collection that will be helpful in designing the database. Try the class hierarchy shown in Figure 1.11, where Audio and Video are media categories. Then CDs and cassette tapes would be subclasses of `Audio`, and DVDs and VHS tapes would be subclasses of `Video`.

   If you go to the video store to get a movie, you can rent or purchase only movies that are recorded on VHS tapes or DVDs. For this reason, class `Video` (and also classes `Media` and `Audio`) should be abstract classes because there are no actual objects of these types. However, they are useful classes to help define the hierarchy.

FIGURE 1.11
Media Class Hierarchy

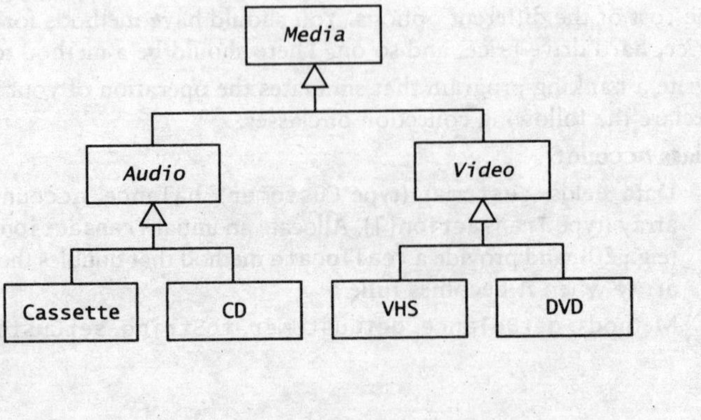

Class `Media` should have data fields and methods common to all classes in the hierarchy. Every media object has a title, major artist, distributor, playing time, price, and so on. Class `Video` should have additional data fields for information describing movies recorded on DVDs and videotapes. This would include information about the supporting actors, the producer, the director, and the movie's rating. Class DVD would have specific information about DVD movies only, such as the format of the picture and special features on the disk. Figure 1.12 shows a possible class diagram for `Media`, `Video`, and subclasses of `Video`.

Provide methods to load the media collection from a file and write it back out to a file. Also provide a method to retrieve the information for a particular item identified by its title and a method to retrieve all your items for a particular artist.

6. Add shape classes `Square` and `EquilateralTriangle` to the figures hierarchy in Section 1.7. Modify class `ComputeAreaAndPerim` (Listing 1.8) to accept the new figures.

FIGURE 1.12
Class Video and Its Supers and Subclasses

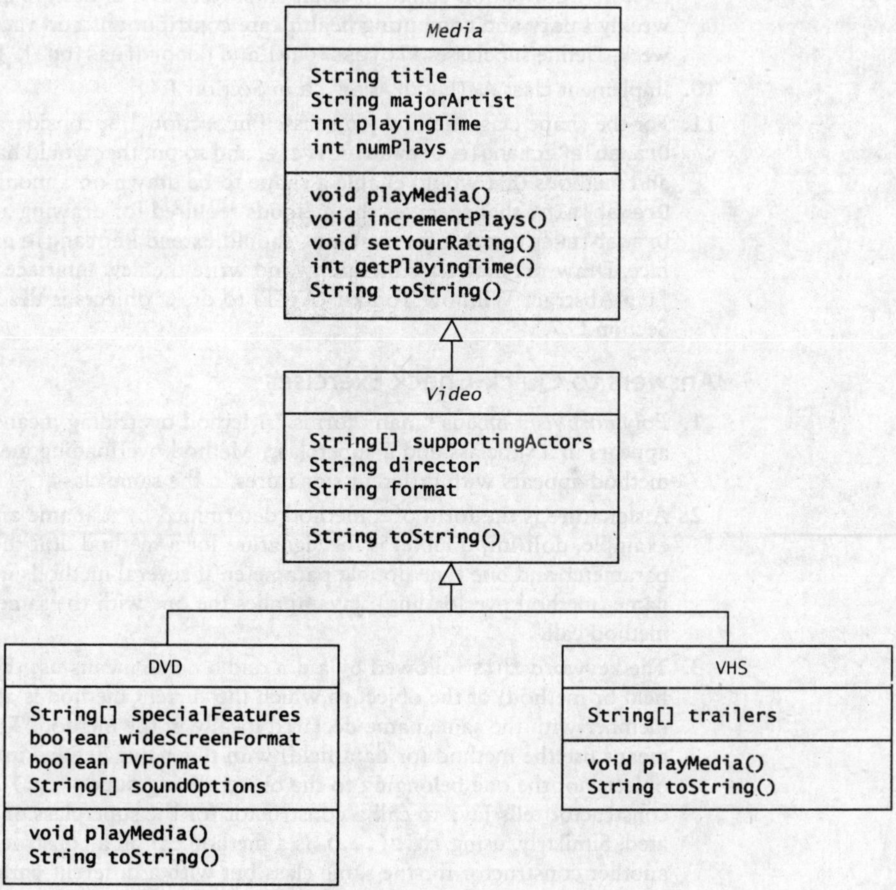

7. Complete the `Food` class hierarchy in Section 1.4. Read and store a list of your favorite foods. Show the total calories for these foods and the overall percentages of fat, protein, and carbohydrates for this list. To find the overall percentage, if an item has 200 calories and 10 percent is fat calories, then that item contributes 20 fat calories. You need to find the totals for fat calories, protein calories, and carbohydrate calories, and then calculate the percentages.
8. A hospital has different kinds of patients who require different procedures for billing and approval of procedures. Some patients have insurance and some do not. Of the insured patients, some are on Medicare, some are in HMOs, and some have other health insurance plans. Develop a collection of classes to model these different kinds of patients.
9. A company has two different kinds of employees: professional and nonprofessional. Generally, professional employees have a monthly salary, whereas nonprofessional employees are paid an hourly rate. Similarly, professional employees have a certain number of days of vacation, whereas nonprofessional employees receive vacation hours based on the number of hours they have worked. The amount contributed for health insurance is also different for each kind of employee. Use an abstract class `Employee` to store information common to all employees and to declare methods for calculating weekly salary and computing health care contributions and vacation days earned that week. Define subclasses `Professional` and `Nonprofessional`. Test your class hierarchy.
10. Implement class `AMTbandkAmerica` in Section 1.1.
11. For the shape class hierarchy discussed in Section 1.8, consider adding classes `DrawableRectangle`, `DrawableCircle`, and so on, that would have additional data fields and methods that would enable a shape to be drawn on a monitor. Provide an interface `DrawableInt` that specifies the methods required for drawing a shape. Class `DrawableRectangle`, for example, should extend `Rectangle` and implement this interface. Draw the new class hierarchy and write the new interface and classes. Using the Java Abstract Window Toolkit (AWT) to draw objects is described in Appendix Section C.7.

Answers to Quick-Check Exercises

1. *Polymorphism* means "many forms." Method overriding means that the same method appears in a subclass and a superclass. Method overloading means that the same method appears with different signatures in the same class.
2. A signature is the form of a method determined by its name and arguments. For example, doIt(int, double) is the signature for a method doIt that has one type int parameter and one type double parameter. If several methods in a class have the same name (method overloading), Java applies the one with the same signature as the method call.
3. The keyword **`this`** followed by a dot and a name means use the named member (data field or method) of the object to which the current method is applied rather than the member with the same name declared locally in the method. The keyword **`super.`** means use the method (or data field) with this name defined in the superclass of the object, not the one belonging to the object. Using **`super(...)`** as a method call in a constructor tells Java to call a constructor for the superclass of the object being created. Similarly, using **`this(...)`** as a method call in a constructor tells Java to call another constructor for the same class but with a different parameter list. The **`super(...)`** or **`this(...)`** call must be the first statement in a subclass constructor.

4. `VirtualMachineError`, `OutOfMemoryError`, and `IndexOutOfBoundsException` are unchecked; the rest are checked.
5. An abstract class is used as a parent class for a collection of related subclasses. An abstract class cannot be instantiated. The abstract methods (identified by modifier `abstract`) defined in the abstract class act as placeholders for the actual methods. Also, you should define data fields that are common to all the subclasses in the abstract class. An abstract class can have actual methods as well as abstract methods.
6. An interface specifies the requirements of an ADT as a contract between the developer and user; a class implements the ADT.
7. True.
8. An *is-a* relationship between classes means that one class is a subclass of a parent class. A *has-a* relationship means that one class has data members of the other class type.
9. Subclass.
10. You can reference an object of a subclass type through a variable of a superclass type.
11. You cast an object referenced by a superclass type to an object of a subclass type in order to apply methods of the subclass type to the object. This is called a *downcast*.
12. The four kinds of visibility in order of decreasing visibility are *public*, *protected*, *package*, and *private*.

Chapter 2

Lists and the Collections Framework

Chapter Objectives

- To become familiar with the List interface
- To understand how to write an array-based implementation of the List interface
- To study the differences between single-, double-, and circular-linked list data structures
- To understand the meaning of big-O notation and how it is used as a measure of an algorithm's efficiency
- To learn how to implement a single-linked list
- To learn how to implement the List interface using a linked list
- To understand the Iterator interface
- To learn how to implement the Iterator for a linked list
- To understand different testing strategies and when and how they are performed
- To become familiar with the Java Collections Framework

So far we have one data structure that you can use in your programming—the array. Giving a programmer an array and asking her to develop software systems is like giving a carpenter a hammer and asking him to build a house. In both cases, more tools are needed. The Java designers attempted to supply those tools by providing a rich set of data structures written as Java classes. The classes are all part of a hierarchy called the Java Collections Framework. We will discuss classes from this hierarchy in the rest of the book, starting in this chapter with the classes that are considered lists.

A list is an expandable collection of elements in which each element has a position or index. Some lists enable their elements to be accessed in arbitrary order (called *random access*) using a position value to select an element. Alternatively, you can start at the beginning and process the elements in sequence. We will also discuss iterators and their role in facilitating sequential access to lists.

In this chapter we will discuss the `ArrayList` and `Vector` classes and linked lists (class `LinkedList`) and their similarities and differences. We will show that these classes are subclasses of the abstract class `AbstractList` and that they implement the `List` interface. You will also learn about algorithm efficiency and how to characterize the efficiency of an algorithm. You will learn about big-O notation, which you can use to compare the relative efficiency of different algorithms.

The chapter discusses program testing in some detail. You will learn how to generate a proper test plan and the differences between unit and integration testing as they apply to an object-oriented design. You will also learn how to use drivers and stubs, special methods that are written to test other methods and classes.

Lists and the Collections Framework

2.1 The `List` Interface and `ArrayList` Class

An *array* is an indexed data structure, which means you can select its elements in arbitrary order as determined by the subscript value. You can also access the elements in sequence using a loop that increments the subscript. However, you can't do the following with an array object:

- Increase or decrease its length, which is fixed.
- Add an element at a specified position without shifting the other elements to make room.
- Remove an element at a specified position without shifting the other elements to fill in the resulting gap.

The classes that implement the Java `List` interface (part of Java API `java.util`) all provide methods to do these operations and more. Here are some other operations that can be performed:

- Find a specified target value.
- Add an element at either end.
- Remove an element from either end.
- Traverse the list structure without having to manage a subscript.

Although all of the classes we study in this chapter support these operations, they do not do them all with the same degree of efficiency. The kinds of operations you intend to perform in a particular application should influence your decision as to which `List` class to use.

One feature that the array data structure provides that these classes don't is the ability to store primitive-type values. The `List` classes all store references to `Objects`, so all primitive-type values must be wrapped in objects. Autoboxing facilitates this.

Figure 2.1 shows an overview of the `List` interface and the four actual classes that implement it. We will study the `ArrayList`, `Vector`, and `LinkedList` classes in this chapter; we will study the `Stack` class in the next chapter. We will briefly discuss the `RandomAccess` interface and the two abstract classes `AbstractList` and `AbstractSequentialList` in Section 2.9.

FIGURE 2.1
The `java.util.List` Interface and Its Implementers

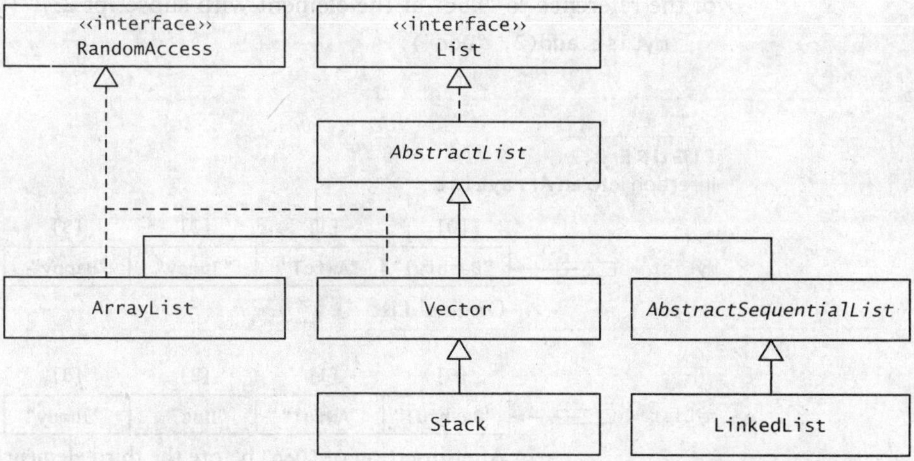

The ArrayList Class

The simplest class that implements the `List` interface is the `ArrayList` class. An `ArrayList` object is an improvement over an array object in that it supports all of the operations just listed. `ArrayList` objects are used most often when a programmer wants to be able to add new elements to the end of a list but still needs the capability to access the elements stored in the list in arbitrary order. These are the features we would need for an e-mail address book application: New entries should be added at the end, and we would also need to find e-mail addresses for entries already in the address book. The size of an `ArrayList` automatically increases as new elements are added to it, and the size decreases as elements are removed. An `ArrayList` object has an instance method `size` that returns its current size.

Each `ArrayList` object has a *capacity*, which is the number of elements it can store. When an `ArrayList`'s size is equal to its capacity, the capacity is automatically increased.

EXAMPLE 2.1 The Statement

```
List<String> myList = new ArrayList<String>();
```

declares a `List` variable `myList` whose elements will reference `String` objects. The actual list referenced by `myList` is an `ArrayList<String>` object. Initially, `myList` is empty; however, it has an initial capacity of 10 elements (the default capacity).

The statements

```
myList.add("Bashful");
myList.add("Awful");
myList.add("Jumpy");
myList.add("Happy");
```

add references to four strings as shown in the top diagram of Figure 2.2. The value of `myList.size()` is now 4.

The middle diagram of Figure 2.2 shows `ArrayList` object `myList` after the insertion of the reference to `"Doc"` at the element with subscript 2:

```
myList.add(2, "Doc");
```

FIGURE 2.2
Insertion into an `ArrayList`

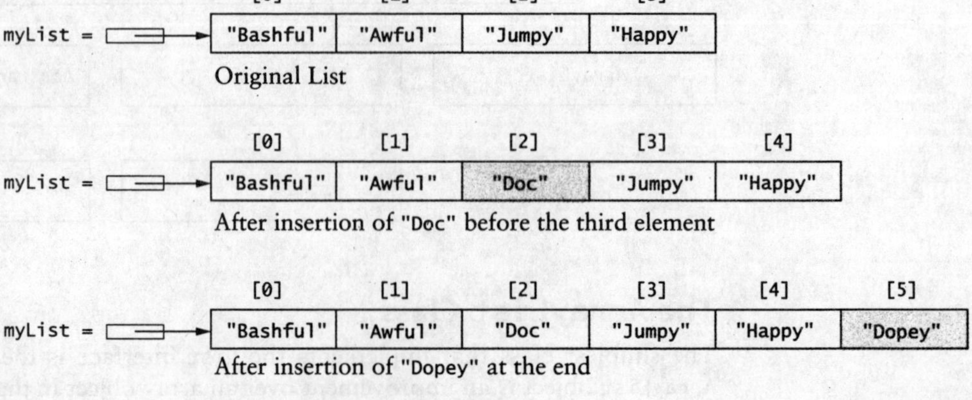

The new size is 5. The strings formerly referenced by the elements with subscripts 2 and 3 are now referenced by the elements with subscripts 3 and 4. This is the same as what happens when someone cuts into a line of people waiting to buy tickets; everyone following the person who cuts in moves back one position in the line.

The bottom diagram in Figure 2.2 shows the effect of the statement

```
myList.add("Dopey");
```

which adds a reference to `"Dopey"` at the end of the `ArrayList`. The size of `myList` is now 6.

Similarly, if you remove an element from an `ArrayList` object, the size automatically decreases, and the elements following the one removed shift over to fill the vacated space. This is the same as when someone leaves a ticket line; the people in back all move forward. Here is object `myList` after using the statement

```
myList.remove(1);
```

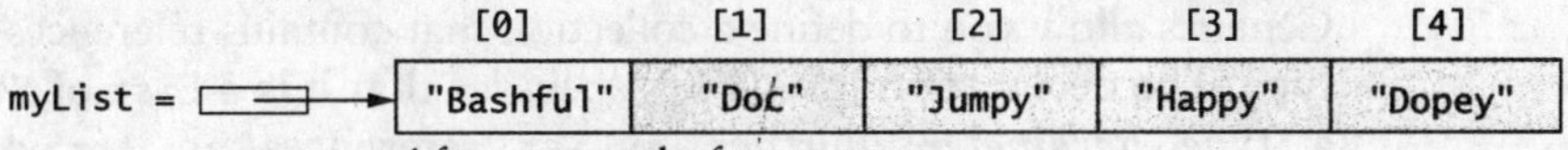

After removal of "Awful"

to remove the element with subscript 1. Notice that the strings formerly referenced by subscripts 2 through 5 are now referenced by subscripts 1 through 4 (in the darker color), and the size has decreased by 1.

Even though an `ArrayList` is an indexed collection, you can't access its elements using a subscript. Instead, you use the `get` method to access its elements. For example, the statement

```
String dwarf = myList.get(2)
```

stores a reference to the string object `"Jumpy"` in variable `dwarf`, without changing `myList`.

You use the `set` method to store a value in an `ArrayList`. The method call

```
myList.set(2, "Sneezy")
```

stores a reference to string `"Sneezy"` at index 2, replacing the reference to string `"Jumpy"`. However, variable `dwarf` would still reference the string `"Jumpy"`.

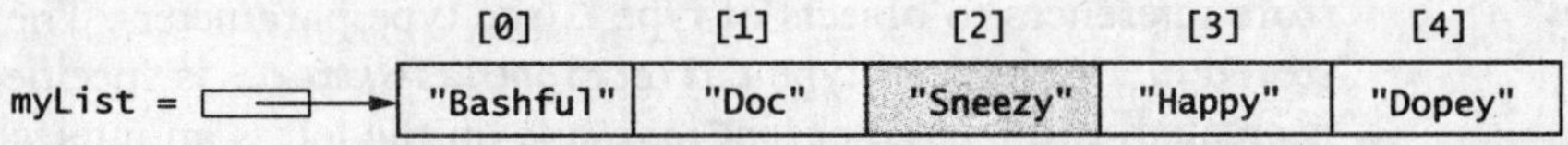

After replacing "Jumpy" with"Sneezy"

You can also search an `ArrayList.` The method call

```
myList.indexOf("Jumpy")
```

would return –1 after the reference to `"Jumpy"` was replaced, indicating an unsuccessful search. The method call

```
myList.indexOf("Sneezy")
```

would return 2.

PITFALL

Using Subscripts with an ArrayList

If you use a subscript with an `ArrayList` (e.g., `myList[i]`), you will get the syntax error `array type required for [] but ArrayList found`. This means that subscripts can be used only with arrays, not with indexed collections.

Generic Collections

The statement

```
List<String> myList = new ArrayList<String>();
```

uses a language feature introduced in Java 5.0 called *generic collections* (or *generics*). Generics allow you to define a collection that contains references to objects of a specific type. The declaration for `myList` specifies that it is a `List` of `String` where `String` is a *type parameter*. Further, `myList` references an ArrayList<String> object. Therefore, only references to objects of type `String` can be stored in `myList`, and all items retrieved would be of type `String`. A type parameter is analogous to a method parameter. In the definition of a generic collection class, the type parameter represents the data type of all objects stored in a collection. When the collection is created, the actual data type of objects it can store is specified in angle brackets.

SYNTAX Creating a Generic Collection

FORM:

```
CollectionClassName<E> variable = new CollectionClassName<E>();
```

EXAMPLE:

```
List<String> myList = new ArrayList<String>();
ArrayList<Integer> numList = new ArrayList<Integer>();
```

MEANING:

An initially empty *CollectionClassName<E>* object is created that can be used to store references to objects of type `E` (the type parameter). The actual object type stored in an object of type *CollectionClassName<E>* is specified when the object is created. If the *CollectionClassName* on the left is an interface, the *CollectionClassName* on the right must be a class that implements it. Otherwise, it must be the same class or a subclass of the one on the left.

In earlier versions of Java, generic collections were not supported. In these versions, you use the statement

```
ArrayList yourList = new ArrayList();
```

to create an initially empty `ArrayList`. Each element of `yourList` is a type `Object` reference. The data types of the actual objects referenced by elements of `yourList` are not specified, and, in fact, different elements can reference objects of different types.

Use of the adjective "generic" is a bit confusing. A nongeneric collection in Java is very general in that it can store objects of different data types. A generic collection, however, can store objects of one specified data type only. Therefore, generics enable the compiler to do more strict type checking to detect errors at compile time instead of at run time. They also eliminate downcasting from type `Object` to a specific type, as shown in the next example.

EXAMPLE 2.2 The following statements declare a nongeneric `ArrayList` object `yourList` and store references to three objects of different types.

```
ArrayList yourList = new ArrayList();
yourList.add(new Integer(35));       // Element 0 references an Integer.
yourList.add("bunny");               // Element 1 references a String.
yourList.add(new Double(3.14));      // Element 2 references a Double.
```

The programmer must keep track of the actual type of the object referenced by each element and process it accordingly. For example, the statement

```
String animal = yourList.get(1); // Invalid, incompatible types.
```

would cause the syntax error `incompatible types; found: java.lang.Object; required: java.lang.String`. In other words, it is not possible to assign a type `Object` reference to a type `String` variable. Instead, you must cast the reference to type `String` before the assignment:

```
String animal = (String) yourList.get(1);
```

Of course, this cast works only if the object referenced by element 1 is type `String`. The statement

```
String animalTwo = (String) yourList.get(2);
```

will compile, but it will cause a `ClassCastException` during run time because element 2 references a `Double` object.

PITFALL

Adding Incompatible Type Objects to a Generic ArrayList

The advantage of generics is that the compiler can ensure that all operations involving objects referenced by a generic `ArrayList` are "safe" and will not cause exceptions during run time. Any type of incompatibility will be detected during compilation. If `myList` is type `ArrayList<String>` or `ArrayList<Double>`, the statement

```
myList.add(35);
```

will not compile because 35 (type `int`) is not compatible with type `String` or `Double`. However, if `myList` is type `ArrayList<Integer>`, the `int 35` will be autoboxed and added to `myList`.

Advantages of Using Generic Collections

Generic collections have several advantages. First, as discussed in the preceding Pitfall, type incompatibilities in applications that use generic collections are detected during compilation, not during run time, because the compiler knows the data type of all objects stored in a generic collection. Also, an object retrieved from a generic collection is a specific data type, not type `Object`, so there is no need to downcast to that specific type. For these reasons, we will almost always use generic collections in this text, and we recommend that you follow this policy. The only time you should not use generics is when you need to store objects of different types in the same collection.

Specification of the `ArrayList` Class

The `ArrayList` class, part of the package `java.util`, implements the `List` interface. In the Java 5.0 documentation, the class name is `ArrayList<E>`. The suffix `<E>` indicates that a collection is generic and its instances store references to objects of type `E` (the type parameter). (All classes and interfaces in the Collections framework are generic, but we will often write the class name without the suffix `<E>` in this text.) A selected subset of the methods from this Java API is shown in Table 2.1.

TABLE 2.1
Methods of Class `java.util.ArrayList<E>`

Method	Behavior
`public E get(int index)`	Returns a reference to the element at position `index`.
`public E set(int index, E anEntry)`	Sets the element at position `index` to reference `anEntry`. Returns the previous value.
`public int size()`	Gets the current size of the `ArrayList`.
`public boolean add(E anEntry)`	Adds a reference to `anEntry` at the end of the `ArrayList`. Always returns `true`.
`public void add(int index, E anEntry)`	Adds a reference to `anEntry`, inserting it before the item at position `index`.
`int indexOf(E target)`	Searches for `target` and returns the position of the first occurrence, or –1 if it is not in the `ArrayList`.
`public E remove(int index)`	Returns and removes the item at position `index` and shifts the items that follow it to fill the vacated space.

EXERCISES FOR SECTION 2.1

SELF-CHECK

1. Describe the effect of each of the following operations on object myList as shown at the bottom of Figure 2.2. What is the value of myList.size() after each operation?

```
myList.add("Pokey");
myList.add("Campy");
int i = myList.indexOf("Happy");
myList.set(i, "Bouncy");
myList.remove(myList.size() - 2);
String temp = myList.get(1);
myList.set(1, temp.toUpperCase());
```

PROGRAMMING

1. Write the following static method:

```
/** Replaces each occurrence of oldItem in aList with newItem. */
public static void replace(ArrayList<String> aList, String oldItem,
                           String newItem)
```

2. Write the following static method:

```
/** Deletes the first occurrence of target in aList. */
public static void delete(ArrayList<String> aList, String target)
```

2.2 Applications of ArrayList

We illustrate several applications of ArrayList objects next.

EXAMPLE 2.3 The following statements create an ArrayList<Integer> object and load it with the values stored in a type int[] array. The statement

```
someInts.add(nums[i]);
```

retrieves a value from array nums (type int[]), automatically wraps it in an Integer object, and stores a reference to that object in someInts (type ArrayList<Integer>).

```
ArrayList<Integer> someInts = new ArrayList<Integer>();
int[] nums = {5, 7, 2, 15};
for (int i = 0; i < nums.length; i++) {
    someInts.add(nums[i]);
}
```

Loop exit occurs after the last Integer object is stored in someInts. The following fragment computes and displays the sum of the int values in someInts.

```
int sum = 0;
for (int i = 0; i < someInts.size(); i++) {
    sum += someInts.get(i);
}
System.out.println("sum is " + sum);
```

Although it may seem wasteful to carry out these operations when you already have an array of ints, the purpose of this example is to illustrate the steps needed to process a collection of Integer objects referenced by an ArrayList<Integer>.

A Phone Directory Application

If each entry in a phone directory consists of an object of type DirectoryEntry

```
public class DirectoryEntry {
    String name;
    String number;
}
```

you can declare an ArrayList<DirectoryEntry> object to store a phone directory (theDirectory) with your friends' names and phone numbers:

```
private ArrayList<DirectoryEntry> theDirectory =
        new ArrayList<DirectoryEntry>();
```

We can use the statement

```
theDirectory.add(new DirectoryEntry("Jane Smith", "555-549-1234"));
```

to add an entry to theDirectory. If we want to retrieve the entry for a particular name, we can use the statements

```
int index = theDirectory.indexOf(new DirectoryEntry(aName, ""));
```

to locate the entry for the person referenced by aName. Method indexOf searches theDirectory by applying the equals method for class DirectoryEntry to each element of theDirectory. We are assuming that method DirectoryEntry.equals compares the name field of each element to the name field of the argument of indexOf (an anonymous object with the desired name). If aName is found at position index, the statement

```
if (index != -1)
    dE = theDirectory.get(index);
else
    dE = null;
```

uses ArrayList.get to retrieve the desired entry (name and phone number) and stores a reference to it in dE (type DirectoryEntry). Otherwise, null is stored in dE.

EXERCISES FOR SECTION 2.2

SELF-CHECK

1. What does the following code fragment do?

```
ArrayList<Double> myList = new ArrayList<Double>();
myList.add(3.456);
myList.add(5.0);
double result = myList.get(0) + myList.get(1);
System.out.println("Result is " + result);
```

PROGRAMMING

1. Write a method `addOrChangeEntry` for a class that has a data field `theDirectory` (type `ArrayList<DirectoryEntry>`) where `class DirectoryEntry is described just before the exercises`. Assume class `DirectoryEntry` has an accessor method `getNumber` and a setter method `setNumber`.

```
/** Add an entry to theDirectory or change an existing entry.
    @param aName The name of the person being added or changed
    @param newNumber The new number to be assigned
    @return The old number, or if a new entry, null
*/
public String addOrChangeEntry(String aName, String newNumber) {
```

2. Write a `removeEntry` method for the class in programming exercise 1. Use `ArrayList` methods `indexOf` and `remove`.

```
/** Remove an entry.
    @param aName The name of the person being removed
    @return The entry removed, or null if there is no entry for aName
*/
public Entry removeEntry(String aName) {
```

2.3 Implementation of an ArrayList Class

We will implement our own version of the `ArrayList` class called `KWArrayList`. Just as Java does for an `ArrayList`, we use a Java array internally to contain the data of a `KWArrayList`, as shown in Figure 2.3. The physical size of the array is indicated by the data field `capacity`. The number of data items is indicated by the data field `size`. The elements between `size` and `capacity` are available for the storage of new items.

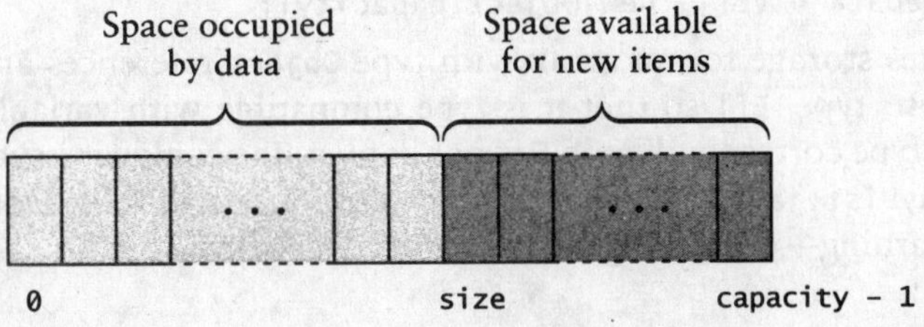

FIGURE 2.3
Internal Structure of `KWArrayList`

We are assuming the following data fields in the discussion of our `KWArrayList` class. This is not exactly how it is done in Java, but it will give you a feel for how to write the class methods. The constructor shown in the following code allocates storage for the underlying array and initializes its capacity to 10. We will not provide a complete implementation because we expect you to use the standard `ArrayList` class provided by the Java API (package `java.util`).

We show the definition of a generic class `KWArrayList<E>` where `E` is the parameter type. The actual parameter type is specified when a generic `KWArrayList` object is declared. The data type of the references stored in the underlying array `theData` (type `E[]`) is also determined when the `KWArrayList` object is declared. If no parameter type is specified, the implicit parameter type is `Object`, and the underlying data array is type `Object[]`.

```
import java.util.*;

/** This class implements some of the methods of the Java
    ArrayList class.
 */
public class KWArrayList<E> {
    // Data Fields
    /** The default initial capacity */
    private static final int INITIAL_CAPACITY = 10;

    /** The underlying data array */
    private E[] theData;

    /** The current size */
    private int size = 0;

    /** The current capacity */
    private int capacity = 0;
...
```

The Constructor for Class KWArrayList<E>

The constructor declaration follows. Because the constructor is for a generic class, the type parameter <E> is implied but it must not appear in the constructor heading.

```
public KWArrayList() {
    capacity = INITIAL_CAPACITY;
    theData = (E[]) new Object[capacity];
}
```

The statement

```
theData = (E[]) new Object[capacity];
```

allocates storage for an array with type `Object` references and then casts this array object to type `E[]` so that it is type compatible with variable `theData`. Because the actual type corresponding to `E` is not known, the compiler issues the warning message: `KWArrayList.java uses unchecked or unsafe operations`. Don't be concerned about this warning—everything is fine.

PROGRAM STYLE

Java provides an annotation that enables you to compile the constructor without an error message. If you place the statement

`@SuppressWarnings("unchecked")`

before the constructor, the compiler warning will not appear.

> **PITFALL**
>
> **Declaring a Generic Array**
>
> Rather than use the approach shown in the above constructor, you might try to create a generic array directly using the statement
>
> ```
> theData = new E[capacity]; // Invalid generic array type.
> ```
>
> However, this statement will not compile because Java does not allow you to create an array with an unspecified type. Remember, `E` is a type parameter that is not specified until a generic `ArrayList` object is created. Therefore, the constructor must create an array of type `Object[]` since `Object` is the superclass of all types and then downcast this array object to type `E[]`.

The add(E anEntry) Method

We implement two `add` methods with different signatures. The first appends an item to the end of a `KWArrayList`; the second inserts an item at a specified position. If `size` is less than `capacity`, then to append a new item:

a. Insert the new item at the position indicated by the value of `size`.

b. Increment the value of `size`.

c. Return `true` to indicate successful insertion.

This sequence of operations is illustrated in Figure 2.4. The `add` method is specified in the `Collection` interface, which is discussed in Section 2.9. The `Collection` interface is a superinterface to the `List` interface. The `add` method must return a `boolean` to indicate whether or not the insertion is successful. For an `ArrayList`, this is always true. The old value of `size` is in gray; its new value is in color.

If the `size` is already equal to the `capacity`, we must first allocate a new array to hold the data and then copy the data to this new array. The method `reallocate` (explained shortly) does this. The code for the `add` method follows.

```
public boolean add(E anEntry) {
    if (size == capacity) {
        reallocate();
    }
    theData[size] = anEntry;
    size++;
    return true;
}
```

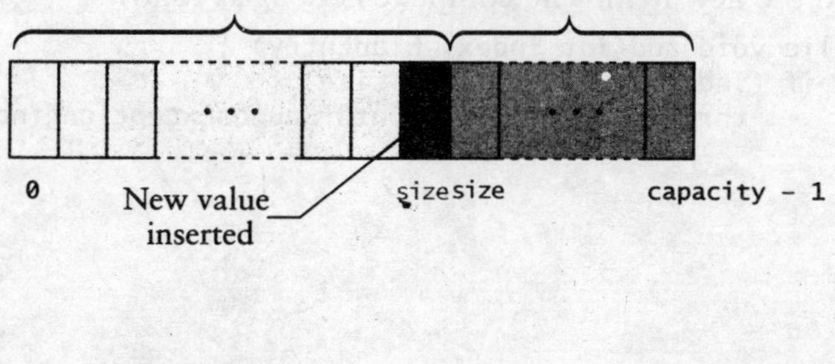

FIGURE 2.4
Adding an Element to the End of a `KWArrayList`

PROGRAM STYLE

Using the Postfix (or Prefix) Operator with a Subscript

Some programmers prefer to combine the two statements before `return` in the `add` method and write them as

```
theData[size++] = theValue;
```

This is perfectly valid. Java uses the current value of `size` as the subscript for array access and then increments it. The only difficulty is the fact that two operations are written in one statement and are carried out in a predetermined order. If you are unsure of the order, you might select prefix when you needed postfix, or vice versa.

The add(int index, E anEntry) Method

To insert an item into the middle of the array (anywhere but the end), the values that are at the insertion point and beyond must be shifted over to make room. In Figure 2.5, the arrow with label 1 shows the first element moved, the arrow with label 2 shows the next element moved, and so on. This data move is done using the following loop:

```
for (int i = size; i > index; i--) {
    theData[i] = theData[i - 1];
}
```

FIGURE 2.5
Making Room to Insert an Item into an Array

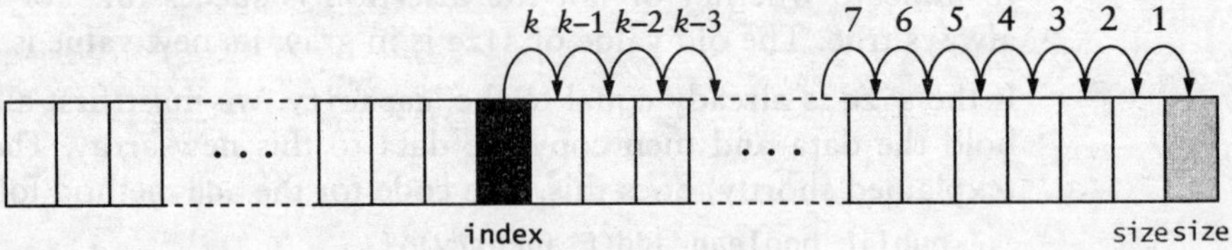

Notice that the array subscript starts at `size` and moves toward the beginning of the array (down to `index + 1`). If we had started the subscript at `index + 1` instead, we would copy the value at `index` into each element of the array with a larger subscript. Before we execute this loop, we need to be sure that `size` is not equal to `capacity`. If it is, we must call `reallocate`.

After increasing the capacity (if necessary) and moving the other elements, we can then add the new item. The complete code is as follows:

```
public void add(int index, E anEntry) {
    if (index < 0 || index > size) {
        throw new ArrayIndexOutOfBoundsException(index);
```

```
        }
        if (size == capacity) {
            reallocate();
        }
        // Shift data in elements from index to size - 1
        for (int i = size; i > index; i--) {
            theData[i] = theData[i - 1];
        }
        // Insert the new item.
        theData[index] = anEntry;
        size++;
    }
```

The set and get Methods

Methods set and get throw an exception if the array index is out of bounds; otherwise, method get returns the item at the specified index. Method set inserts the new item (parameter newValue) at the specified index and returns the value (oldValue) that was previously stored at that index.

```
public E get(int index) {
    if (index < 0 || index >= size) {
        throw new ArrayIndexOutOfBoundsException(index);
    }
    return theData[index];
}

public E set(int index, E newValue) {
    if (index < 0 || index >= size) {
        throw new ArrayIndexOutOfBoundsException(index);
    }
    E oldValue = theData[index];
    theData[index] = newValue;
    return oldValue;
}
```

The remove Method

To remove an item, the items that follow it must be moved forward to close up the space. In Figure 2.6, the arrow with label 1 shows the first element moved, the arrow with label 2 shows the next element moved, and so on. This data move is done using the for loop in method remove shown next. The item removed is returned as the method result.

```
public E remove(int index) {
    if (index < 0 || index >= size) {
        throw new ArrayIndexOutOfBoundsException(index);
    }
    E returnValue = theData[index];
    for (int i = index + 1; i < size; i++) {
        theData[i - 1] = theData[i];
    }
    size--;
    return returnValue;
}
```

FIGURE 2.6
Removing an Item from an Array

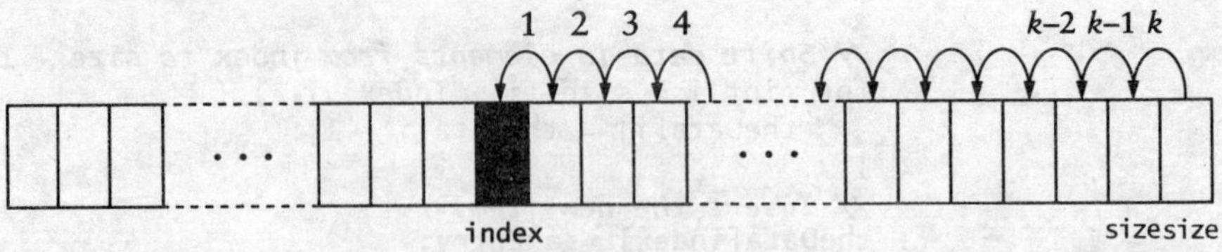

The reallocate Method

The `reallocate` method creates a new array that is twice the size of the current array and then copies the contents of the current array into the new one. The `Arrays.copyOf` method (introduced in Java 6) makes a copy of the given array truncating if the new array is shorter or padding with nulls if the new array is larger, so that the copy has the specified length. The reference variable `theData` is then set to reference this new array. The code is as follows:

```
private void reallocate() {
    capacity = 2 * capacity;
    theData = Arrays.copyOf(theData, capacity);
}
```

The reason for doubling is to spread out the cost of copying. We discuss this further in Section 2.4.

Implementing KWArrayList as a Collection of Objects

As an alternative to implementing a generic collection, you could implement an `ArrayList` that contains a collection of `Objects`. You would remove the parameter type <E> from the class heading.

```
public class KWArrayList {
    // Data Fields
    /** The default initial capacity. */
    private static final int INITIAL_CAPACITY = 10;
    /** The current size. */
    private int size = 0;
```

Each reference to data type `E` would be replaced by a reference to data type `Object`.

```
/** The underlying data array. */
private Object[] theData;
```

Also, the statement in the constructor that casts an array of type `Object[]` to type `E[]` would not be required (e.g., `theData = (E[]) new Object[capacity];`).

This is the way that class `ArrayList` and other collections were implemented in earlier versions of Java.

The Vector Class

The initial release of the Java API `java.util` contained the class `Vector`, which has similar functionality to the `ArrayList`. Because `Vector` and `ArrayList` both implement the `List` interface, they both contain all the same methods. New applications should normally use the `ArrayList` rather than the `Vector` because the `ArrayList` will generally be a little more efficient. The reason is that the `Vector` class is *synchronized,* which means that multiple threads can access a `Vector` object without conflict, whereas this is not the case for the `ArrayList`. Originally, the `Vector` class was not part of the Collections framework, but it has been retrofitted to be part of it. The class `Stack`, which we will study in the next chapter, is a subclass of `Vector`.

EXERCISES FOR SECTION 2.3

SELF-CHECK

1. Trace the execution of the following:
```
int[] anArray = {0, 1, 2, 3, 4, 5, 6, 7};
for (int i = 3; i < anArray.length - 1; i++)
    anArray[i + 1] = anArray[i];
```
and the following:
```
int[] anArray = {0, 1, 2, 3, 4, 5, 6, 7};
for (int i = anArray.length - 1; i > 3; i--)
    anArray[i] = anArray[i - 1];
```
What are the contents of `anArray` after the execution of each loop?

2. Write statements to remove the middle object from a `KWArrayList` and place it at the end.

PROGRAMMING

1. Implement the `indexOf` method of the `KWArrayList<E>` class.
2. Provide a constructor for class `KWArrayList<E>` that accepts an `int` argument that represents the initial array capacity. Use this instead of `INITIAL_CAPACITY`.

2.4 Algorithm Efficiency and Big-O

Whenever we write a new class, we will discuss the efficiency of its methods, so that you know how they compare to similar methods in other classes. You can't easily measure the amount of time it takes to run a program with modern computers. When you issue the command

```
java MyProgram
```

(or click the Run button of your integrated development environment [IDE]), the operating system first loads the Java Virtual Machine (JVM). The JVM then loads the .class file for MyProgram, it then loads other .class files that MyProgram references, and finally your program executes. (If the .class files have not yet been created, the Java IDE will compile the source file before executing the program.) Most of the time it takes to run your program is occupied with the first two steps. If you run your program a second time immediately after the first, it may seem to take less time. This is because the operating system may have kept the files in a local memory area called a cache. However, if you have a large enough or complicated enough problem, then the actual running time of your program will dominate the time required to load the JVM and .class files.

Because it is very difficult to get a precise measure of the performance of an algorithm or program, we normally try to approximate the effect of a change in the number of data items, n, that an algorithm processes. In this way, we can see how an algorithm's execution time increases with respect to n, so we can compare two algorithms by examining their growth rates.

For many problems, there are algorithms that are relatively obvious but inefficient. Although every day computers are getting faster, with larger memories, there are algorithms whose growth rate is so large that no computer, no matter how fast or with how much memory, can solve the problem above a certain size. Furthermore, if a problem that has been too large to be solved can now be solved with the latest, biggest, and fastest supercomputer, adding a few more inputs may make the problem impractical, if not impossible, again. Therefore, it is important to have some idea of the relative efficiency of different algorithms. Next, we see how we might obtain such an idea by examining three methods in the following examples.

EXAMPLE 2.4 Consider the following method, which searches an array for a value:

```
public static int search(int[] x, int target) {
    for (int i = 0; i < x.length; i++) {
        if (x[i] == target)
            return i;
    }

    // target not found
    return -1;
}
```

If the target is not present in the array, then the **for** loop body will be executed `x.length` times. If the target is present, it could be anywhere. If we consider the average over all cases where the target is present, then the loop body will execute `x.length/2` times. Therefore, the total execution time is directly proportional to `x.length`. If we doubled the size of the array, we would expect the time to double (not counting the overhead discussed earlier).

EXAMPLE 2.5 Now let us consider another problem. We want to find out whether two arrays have no common elements. We can use our `search` method to search one array for values that are in the other.

```
/** Determine whether two arrays have no common elements.
    @param x One array
```

```
        @param y The other array
        @return true if there are no common elements
    */
    public static boolean areDifferent(int[] x, int[] y) {
        for (int i = 0; i < x.length; i++) {
            if (search(y, x[i]) != -1)
                return false;
        }
        return true;
    }
```

The loop body will execute `x.length` times. But it will call `search`, whose loop body will execute `y.length` times for each of the `x.length` times it is called. Therefore, the total execution time would be proportional to the product of `x.length` and `y.length`.

EXAMPLE 2.6 Let us consider the problem of determining whether each item in an array is unique. We could write the following method:

```
    /** Determine whether the contents of an array are all unique.
        @param x The array
        @return true if all elements of x are unique
    */
    public static boolean areUnique(int[] x) {
        for (int i = 0; i < x.length; i++) {
            for (int j = 0; j < x.length; j++) {
                if (i != j && x[i] == x[j])
                    return false;
            }
        }
        return true;
    }
```

If all values are unique, the for loop with `i` as its index will execute `x.length` times. Inside this loop, the for loop with `j` as its index will also execute `x.length` times. Thus the total number of times the loop body of the innermost loop will execute is $(\texttt{x.length})^2$.

EXAMPLE 2.7 The method we showed in Example 2.5 is very inefficient because we do approximately twice as many tests as necessary. We can rewrite it as follows:

```
    /** Determine whether the contents of an array are all unique.
        @param x The array
        @return true if all elements of x are unique
    */
    public static boolean areUnique(int[] x) {
        for (int i = 0; i < x.length; i++) {
            for (int j = i + 1; j < x.length; j++) {
                if (x[i] == x[j])
                    return false;
            }
        }
```

```
        return true;
    }
```

The first time, the for loop with the `j` index will execute `x.length-1` times. The second time, it will execute `x.length-2` times, and so on. The last time, it will execute just once. The total number of times it will execute is:

```
x.length-1 + x.length-2 + ... + 2 + 1
```

The series $1 + 2 + 3 + \cdots + (n - 1)$ is a well-known series that has a value of

$$\frac{n \times (n-1)}{2}$$

Therefore, this sum is

`x.length` × (`x.length` – 1)/2 or 0.5 × (`x.length`)^2 – 0.5 × `x.length`.

Big-O Notation

Today, the type of analysis just illustrated is more important to the development of efficient software than measuring the milliseconds in which a program runs on a particular computer. Understanding how the execution time (and memory requirements) of an algorithm grow as a function of increasing input size gives programmers a tool for comparing various algorithms and how they will perform. Computer scientists have developed a useful terminology and notation for investigating and describing the relationship between input size and execution time. For example, if the time is approximately doubled when the number of inputs, n, is doubled, then the algorithm grows at a linear rate. Thus we say that the growth rate has an order of n. If, however, the time is approximately quadrupled when the number of inputs is doubled, then the algorithm grows at a quadratic rate. In this case we say that the growth rate has an order of n^2.

In the previous section we looked at four methods: one whose execution time was related to `x.length`, another whose execution time was related to `x.length` times `y.length`, one whose execution time was related to (`x.length`)^2, and one whose execution time was related to (`x.length`)^2 and `x.length`. Computer scientists use the notation $O(n)$ to represent the first case, $O(n \times m)$ to represent the second, and $O(n^2)$ to represent the third and fourth, where n is `x.length` and m is `y.length`. The symbol O (which you will see in a variety of typefaces and styles in computer science literature) can be thought of as an abbreviation for "order of magnitude." This notation is called *big-O notation.*

Often, a simple way to determine the big-O of an algorithm or program is to look at the loops and to see whether the loops are nested. Assuming that the loop body consists only of simple statements, a single loop is $O(n)$, a pair of nested loops is $O(n^2)$, a nested loop pair inside another is $O(n^3)$, and so on. However, you also must examine the number of times the loop executes.

Consider the following:

```
for (i = 1; i < x.length; i *= 2) {
    // Do something with x[i]
}
```

The loop body will execute $k - 1$ times, with `i` having the following values: 1, 2, 4, 8, 16, 32, . . . , 2^k until 2^k is greater than `x.length`. Since 2^{k-1} = `x.length` $< 2^k$ and $\log_2 2^k$ is k, we know that $k - 1 = \log_2$(`x.length`) $< k$. Thus we say that this loop is $O(\log n)$. The logarithm function grows slowly. The log to the base 2 of 1,000,000 is approximately 20. Typically, in analyzing the running time of algorithms, we use logarithms to the base 2.

Formal Definition of Big-O

Consider a program that is structured as follows:

```
for (int i = 0; i < n; i++) {
    for (int j = 0; j < n; j++) {
        Simple Statement
    }
}
for (int k = 0; i < n; k++) {
   Simple Statement 1
   Simple Statement 2
   Simple Statement 3
   Simple Statement 4
   Simple Statement 5
}
Simple Statement 6
Simple Statement 7
...
Simple Statement 30
```

Let us assume that each *Simple Statement* takes one unit of time and that the **for** statements are free. The nested loop executes a *Simple Statement* n^2 times. Then 5 *Simple Statements* are executed n times in the loop with control variable k. Finally, 25 *Simple Statements* are executed after this loop. We would then conclude that the expression

$$T(n) = n^2 + 5n + 25$$

shows the relationship between processing time and n (the number of data items processed in the loop), where $T(n)$ represents the processing time as a function of n. It should be clear that the n^2 term dominates as n becomes large.

In terms of $T(n)$, formally, the big-O notation

$$T(n) = O(f(n))$$

means that there exist two constants, n_0 and c, greater than zero, and a function, $f(n)$, such that for all $n > n_0$, $cf(n) = T(n)$. In other words, as n gets sufficiently large (larger than n_0), there is some constant c for which the processing time will always be less than or equal to $cf(n)$, so $cf(n)$ is an upper bound on the performance. The performance will never be worse than $cf(n)$ and may be better.

If we can determine how the value of $f(n)$ increases with n, we know how the processing time will increase with n. The growth rate of $f(n)$ will be determined by the growth rate of the fastest-growing term (the one with the largest exponent), which in this case is the n^2 term. This means that the algorithm in this example is an $O(n^2)$ algorithm rather than an $O(n^2 + 5n + 25)$ algorithm. In general, it is safe to ignore all constants and drop the lower-order terms when determining the order of magnitude for an algorithm.

EXAMPLE 2.8 Given $T(n) = n^2 + 5n + 25$, we want to show that this is indeed $O(n^2)$. Thus we want to show that there are constants n_0 and c such that for all $n > n_0$, $cn^2 > n^2 + 5n + 25$.

One way to do this is to find a point where

$$cn^2 = n^2 + 5n + 25$$

If we let n be n_0 and solve for c, we get

$$c = 1 + 5/n_0 + 25/n_0^2$$

We can evaluate the expression on the right easily when n_0 is $5(1 + 5/5 + 25/25)$. This gives us a c of 3. So $3n^2 > n^2 + 5n + 25$ for all n greater than 5, as shown in Figure 2.7.

FIGURE 2.7
$3n^2$ vs. $n^2 + 5n + 25$

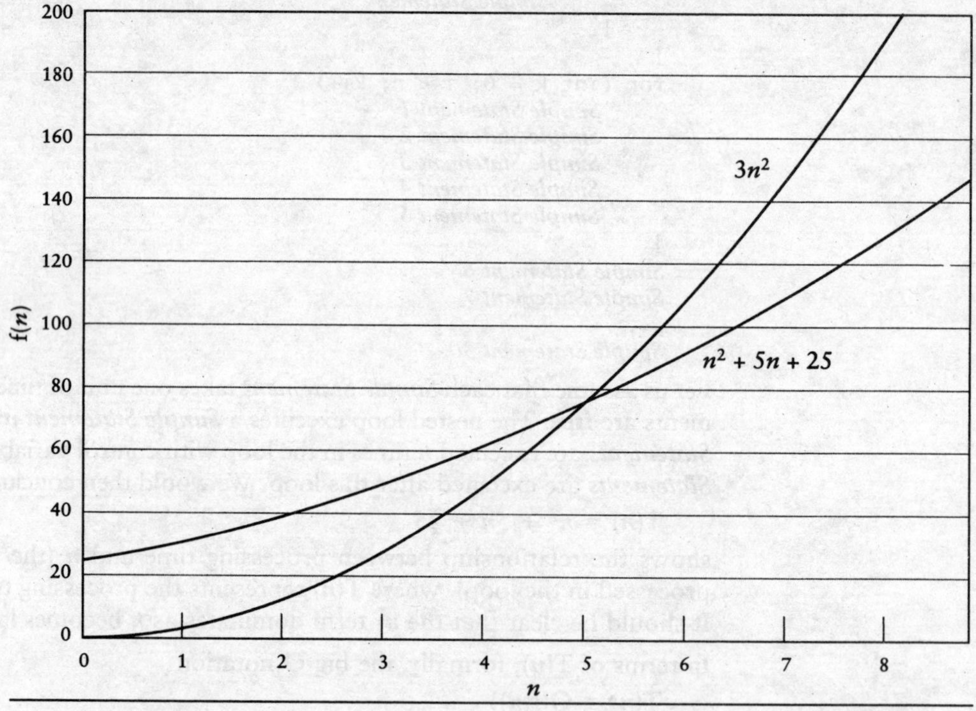

EXAMPLE 2.9 Consider the following program loop:

```
for (int i = 0; i < n - 1; i++) {
    for (int j = i + 1; j < n; j++) {
        3 simple statements
    }
}
```

The first time through the outer loop, the inner loop is executed $n - 1$ times; the next time, $n - 2$; and the last time, once. The outer loop is executed n times. So we get the following expression for $T(n)$:

$$3(n - 1) + 3(n - 2) + \cdots + 3$$

FIGURE 2.8
$1.5n^2$ versus $1.5n^2 - 1.5n$

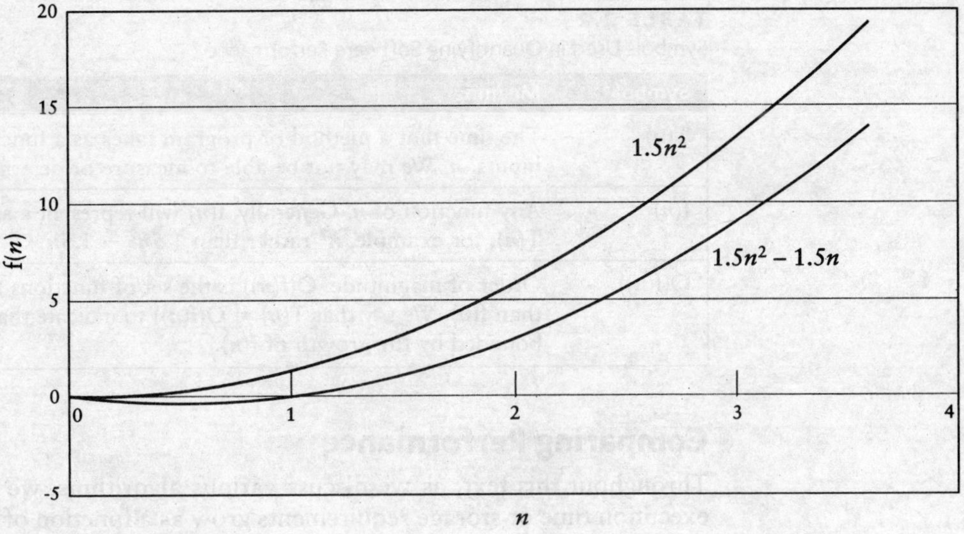

We can factor out the 3 to get

$$3(n - 1 + n - 2 + n + \cdots + 1)$$

The sum $1 + 2 + \cdots + n - 1$ (in parentheses above) is equal to

$$\frac{n \times (n-1)}{2}$$

Thus our final T(n) is

$$T(n) = 1.5n^2 - 1.5n$$

This polynomial is zero when n is 1. For values greater than 1, $1.5n^2$ is always greater than $1.5n^2 - 1.5n$. Therefore, we can use 1 for n_0 and 1.5 for c to conclude that our T(n) is O(n^2) (see Figure 2.8).

If T(n) is the form of a polynomial of degree d (the highest exponent), then it is O(n^d). A mathematically rigorous proof of this is beyond the scope of this text. An intuitive proof is demonstrated in the previous two examples. If the remaining terms have positive coefficients, find a value of n where the first term is equal to the remaining terms. As n gets bigger than this value, the n^d term will always be bigger than the remaining terms.

We use the expression O(1) to represent a constant growth rate. This is a value that doesn't change with the number of inputs. The simple steps all represent O(1). Any finite number of O(1) steps is still considered O(1).

Summary of Notation

In this section we have used the symbols T(n), f(n), and O(f(n)). Their meaning is summarized in Table 2.2.

TABLE 2.2
Symbols Used in Quantifying Software Performance

Symbol	Meaning
$T(n)$	The time that a method or program takes as a function of the number of inputs, n. We may not be able to measure or determine this exactly.
$f(n)$	Any function of n. Generally, $f(n)$ will represent a simpler function than $T(n)$, for example, n^2 rather than $1.5n^2 - 1.5n$.
$O(f(n))$	Order of magnitude. $O(f(n))$ is the set of functions that grow no faster than $f(n)$. We say that $T(n) = O(f(n))$ to indicate that the growth of $T(n)$ is bounded by the growth of $f(n)$.

Comparing Performance

Throughout this text, as we discuss various algorithms, we will discuss how their execution time or storage requirements grow as a function of the problem size using this big-O notation. Several common growth rates will be encountered and are summarized in Table 2.3.

TABLE 2.3
Common Growth Rates

Big-O	Name
$O(1)$	Constant
$O(\log n)$	Logarithmic
$O(n)$	Linear
$O(n \log n)$	Log-linear
$O(n^2)$	Quadratic
$O(n^3)$	Cubic
$O(2^n)$	Exponential
$O(n!)$	Factorial

Figure 2.9 shows the growth rate of a logarithmic, a linear, a log-linear, a quadratic, a cubic, and an exponential function by plotting $f(n)$ for a function of each type. Notice that for small values of n, the exponential function is smaller than all of the others. As shown, it is not until n reaches 20 that the linear function is smaller than the quadratic. This illustrates two points. For small values of n, the less efficient algorithm may be actually more efficient. If you know that you are going to process only a limited amount of data, the $O(n^2)$ algorithm may be much more appropriate than the $O(n \log n)$ algorithm that has a large constant factor. However, algorithms

FIGURE 2.9
Different Growth Rates

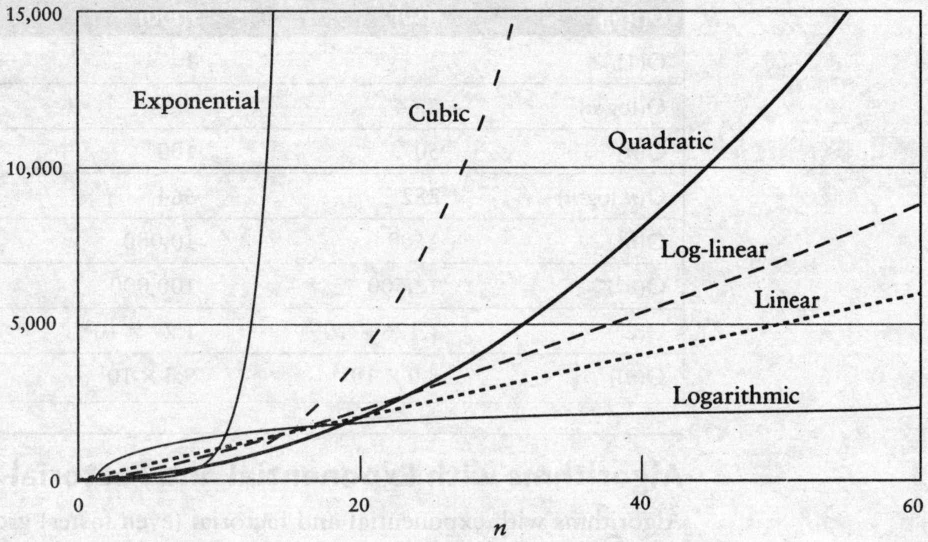

with exponential growth rates can start out small but very quickly grow to be quite large.

The raw numbers in Figure 2.9 can be deceiving. Part of the reason is that big-O notation ignores all constants. An algorithm with a logarithmic growth rate O(log *n*) may be more complicated to program, so it may actually take more time per data item than an algorithm with a linear growth rate O(*n*). For example, at $n = 25$, Figure 2.9 shows that the processing time is approximately 1800 units for an algorithm with a logarithmic growth rate and 2500 units for an algorithm with a linear growth rate. Comparisons of this sort are pretty meaningless. The logarithmic algorithm may actually take more time to execute than the linear algorithm for this relatively small data set. Again, what is important is the growth rate of these two kinds of algorithms, which tells you how performance of each kind of algorithm changes with *n*.

EXAMPLE 2.10 Let's look at how growth rates change as we double the value of *n* (say, from $n = 50$ to $n = 100$). The results are shown in Table 2.4. The third column gives the ratio of processing times for the two different data sizes. For example, it shows that it will take 2.35 times as long to process 100 numbers as it would to process 50 numbers with an O(*n* log *n*) algorithm.

TABLE 2.4
Effects of Different Growth Rates

O(f(n))	f(50)	f(100)	f(100)/f(50)
O(1)	1	1	1
O(log n)	5.64	6.64	1.18
O(n)	50	100	2
O(n log n)	282	664	2.35
O(n^2)	2500	10,000	4
O(n^3)	12,500	100,000	8
O(2^n)	1.126×10^{15}	1.27×10^{30}	1.126×10^{15}
O(n!)	3.0×10^{64}	9.3×10^{157}	3.1×10^{93}

Algorithms with Exponential and Factorial Growth Rates

Algorithms with exponential and factorial (even faster) growth rates have an effective practical upper limit on the size of problem they can be used for, even with faster and faster computers. For example, if we have an O(2^n) algorithm that takes an hour for 100 inputs, adding the 101st input will take a second hour, adding 5 more inputs will take 32 hours (more than a day!), and adding 14 inputs will take 16,384 hours, which is almost two years!

This relation is the basis for cryptographic algorithms—algorithms that *encrypt* text using a special key to make it unreadable by anyone who intercepts it and does not know the key. Encryption is used to provide security for sensitive data sent over the Internet. Some cryptographic algorithms can be broken in O(2^n) time, where n is the number of bits in the key. A key length of 40 bits is considered breakable by a modern computer, but a key length of 100 (60 bits longer) is not because the key with a length of 100 bits will take approximately a billion-billion (10^{18}) times as long as the 40-bit key to crack.

Performance of the `KWArrayList` Algorithms

The `set` and `get` methods are each a few lines of code and contain no loops. Thus we say that these methods execute in constant time, or O(1).

If we insert into (or remove from) the middle of a `KWArrayList`, then at most n items have to be shifted. Therefore, the cost of inserting or removing an element is O(n). What if we have to allocate a larger array before we can insert? Recall that when we reallocate the array, we double its size. Doubling an array of size n allows us to add n more items before we need to do another array copy. Therefore, we can add n new items after we have copied over n existing items. This averages out to 1 copy per add. Because each new array is twice the size of the previous one, it will take only about 20 `reallocate` operations to create an array that can store over a million references (2^{20} is greater than 1,000,000). Therefore, reallocation is effectively an O(1) operation, so the insertion is still O(n).

EXERCISES FOR SECTION 2.4

SELF-CHECK

1. Determine how many times the output statement is displayed in each of the following fragments. Indicate whether the algorithm is $O(n)$ or $O(n^2)$.

a.
```
for (int i = 0; i < n; i++)
  for (int j = 0; j < n; j++)
    System.out.println(i + "  " + j);
```
b.
```
for (int i = 0; i < n; i++)
  for (int j = 0; j < 2; j++)
    System.out.println(i + "  " + j);
```
c.
```
for (int i = 0; i < n; i++)
  for (int j = n - 1; j >= i; j--)
    System.out.println(i + "  " + j);
```
d.
```
for (int i = 1; i < n; i++)
  for (int j = 0; j < i; j++)
    if (j % i == 0)
      System.out.println(i + "  " + j);
```

2. For the following $T(n)$, find values of n_0 and c such that cn^3 is larger than $T(n)$ for all n larger than n_0.

$$T(n) = n^3 - 5n^2 + 20n - 10$$

3. How does the performance grow as n goes from 2000 to 4000 for the following? Answer the same question as n goes from 4000 to 8000. Provide tables similar to Table 2.4.

a. $O(\log n)$
b. $O(n)$
c. $O(n \log n)$
d. $O(n^2)$
e. $O(n^3)$

4. According to the plots in Figure 2.9, what are the processing times at $n = 20$ and at $n = 40$ for each of the growth rates shown?

PROGRAMMING

1. Write a program that compares the values of y1 and y2 in the following expressions for values of n up to 100 in increments of 10. Does the result surprise you?

```
y1 = 100 * n + 10
y2 = 5 * n * n + 2
```

2.5 Single-Linked Lists

The `ArrayList` has the limitation that the `add` and `remove` methods operate in linear ($O(n)$) time because they require a loop to shift elements in the underlying array. In this section we introduce a data structure, the linked list, that overcomes this limitation by providing the ability to add or remove items anywhere in the list in constant ($O(1)$) time. A linked list is useful when you need to insert and remove elements at arbitrary locations (not just at the end) and when you will do frequent insertions and removals.

One example would be maintaining an alphabetized list of students in a course at the beginning of a semester while students are adding and dropping courses. If you were using an `ArrayList`, you would have to shift all names that follow the new person's name down one position before you could insert a new student's name. Figure 2.10 shows this process. The names in gray were all shifted down when Barbara added the course. Similarly, if a student drops the course, the names of all students after the one who dropped (in gray in Figure 2.11) would be shifted up one position to close up the space.

FIGURE 2.10
Removing a Student from a Class List

Before adding `Browniten, Barbara`	After adding `Browniten, Barbara`
`Abidoye, Olandunni`	`Abidoye, Olandunni`
`Boado, Annabelle`	`Boado, Annabelle`
`Butler, James`	**`Browniten, Barbara`**
`Chee, Yong-Han`	`Butler, James`
`Debaggis, Tarra`	`Chee, Yong-Han`
⋮	`Debaggis, Tarra`
	⋮

FIGURE 2.11
Removing a Student from a Class List

Before dropping `Boado, Annabelle`	After dropping `Boado, Annabelle`
`Abidoye, Olandunni`	`Abidoye, Olandunni`
`Boado, Annabelle`	`Browniten, Barbara`
`Browniten, Barbara`	`Butler, James`
`Butler, James`	`Chee, Yong-Han`
`Chee, Yong-Han`	`Debaggis, Tarra`
`Debaggis, Tarra`	⋮
⋮	

Another example would be maintaining a list of students who are waiting to register for a course. Instead of having the students waiting in an actual line, you can give each student a number, which is the student's position in the line. If someone drops out of the line, everyone with a higher number gets a new number that is 1 lower than before. If someone cuts into the line because they "need the course to graduate," everyone after this person gets a new number, which is one higher than before. The person maintaining the list is responsible for giving everyone their new number after

FIGURE 2.12
Inserting into a Numbered List of Students Waiting to Register

Before inserting `Alice` at position 1	After inserting `Alice` at position 1
`0. Warner, Emily`	`0. Warner, Emily`
`1. Dang, Phong`	**`1. Franklin, Alice`**
`2. Feldman, Anna`	`2. Dang, Phong`
`3. Barnes, Aaron`	`3. Feldman, Anna`
`4. Torres, Kristopher`	`4. Barnes, Aaron`
⋮	`5. Torres, Kristopher`
	⋮

a change. Figure 2.12 illustrates what happens when Alice is inserted and given the number 1: Everyone whose number is ≥ 1 gets a new number. This process is analogous to maintaining the names in an `ArrayList`; each person's number is that person's position in the list, and some names in the list are shifted after every change.

A better way to do this would be to give each person the name of the next person in line, instead of his or her own position in the line (which can change frequently). To start the registration process, the person who is registering students calls the person who is at the head of the line. After she finishes registration, the person at the head of the line calls the next person, and so on. Now what if person A lets person B cut into the line after her? Because B will now register after A, person A must call B. Also, person B must call the person who originally followed A. Figure 2.13 illustrates what happens when Alice is inserted in the list after Emily. Only the two entries shown in color need to be changed (Emily must call Alice instead of Phong, and Alice must call Phong). Although Alice is shown at the bottom of Figure 2.13 (third column), she is really the second student in the list. The first four students in the list are Emily Warner, Alice Franklin, Phong Dang, and Anna Feldman.

FIGURE 2.13
Inserting into a List Where Each Student Knows Who Is Next

Before inserting `Alice`		After inserting `Alice`	
Person in line	*Person to call*	*Person in line*	*Person to call*
`Warner, Emily`	`Dang, Phong`	`Warner, Emily`	`Franklin, Alice`
`Dang, Phong`	`Feldman, Anna`	`Dang, Phong`	`Feldman, Anna`
`Feldman, Anna`	`Barnes, Aaron`	`Feldman, Anna`	`Barnes, Aaron`
`Barnes, Aaron`	`Torres, Kristopher`	`Barnes, Aaron`	`Torres, Kristopher`
`Torres, Kristopher`	`...`	`Torres, Kristopher`	`...`
⋮	⋮	⋮	⋮
		`Franklin, Alice`	`Dang, Phong`

What happens if someone drops out of our line? In this case, the name of the person who follows the one who drops out must be given to the person who comes before the one who drops out. Figure 2.14 illustrates this. If Aaron drops out, only one entry needs to be changed (Anna must call Kristopher instead of Aaron).

Using a linked list is analogous to the process just discussed and illustrated in Figures 2.13 and 2.14 for storing our list of student names. After we find the position of a node

FIGURE 2.14
Removing a Student from a List Where Each Student Knows Who Is Next

Before dropping Aaron		After dropping Aaron	
Person in line	*Person to call*	*Person in line*	*Person to call*
`Warner, Emily`	`Franklin, Alice`	`Warner, Emily`	`Franklin, Alice`
`Dang, Phong`	`Feldman, Anna`	`Dang, Phong`	`Feldman, Anna`
`Feldman, Anna`	`Barnes, Aaron`	`Feldman, Anna`	`Torres, Kristopher`
`Barnes, Aaron`	`Torres, Kristopher`	`Barnes, Aaron`	`Torres, Kristopher`
`Torres, Kristopher`	`...`	`Torres, Kristopher`	`...`
⋮	⋮	⋮	⋮
`Franklin, Alice`	`Dang, Phong`	`Franklin, Alice`	`Dang, Phong`

to be inserted or removed, the actual insertion or removal is done in constant time and no shifts are required. Each element in a linked list, called a node, stores information and a link to the next node in the list. For example, for our list of students in Figure 2.14, the information `"Warner, Emily"` would be stored in the first node, and the link to the next node would reference a node whose information part was `"Franklin, Alice"`. Here are the first three nodes of this list:

```
"Warner, Emily" ==> "Franklin, Alice" ==> "Dang, Phong"
```

We discuss how to represent and manipulate a linked list next.

A List Node

FIGURE 2.15
Node and Link

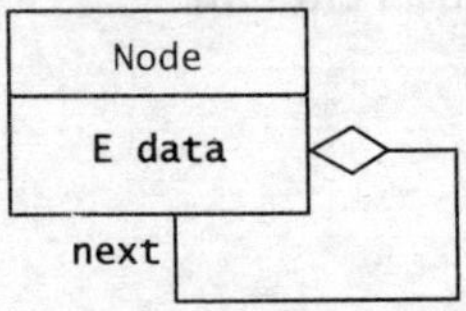

A *node* is a data structure that contains a data item and one or more links. A *link* is a reference to a node. A UML diagram of this relationship is shown in Figure 2.15. This shows that a `Node` contains a data field named `data` of type `E` and a reference (as indicated by the open diamond) to a `Node`. The name of the reference is `next`, as shown on the line from the `Node` to itself. Figure 2.16 shows four Nodes linked together to form the list `[Tom, Dick, Harry, Sam]`. In this figure we show that `data` references a `String` object. In subsequent figures we will show the string value inside the `Node`.

FIGURE 2.16
Nodes in a Linked List

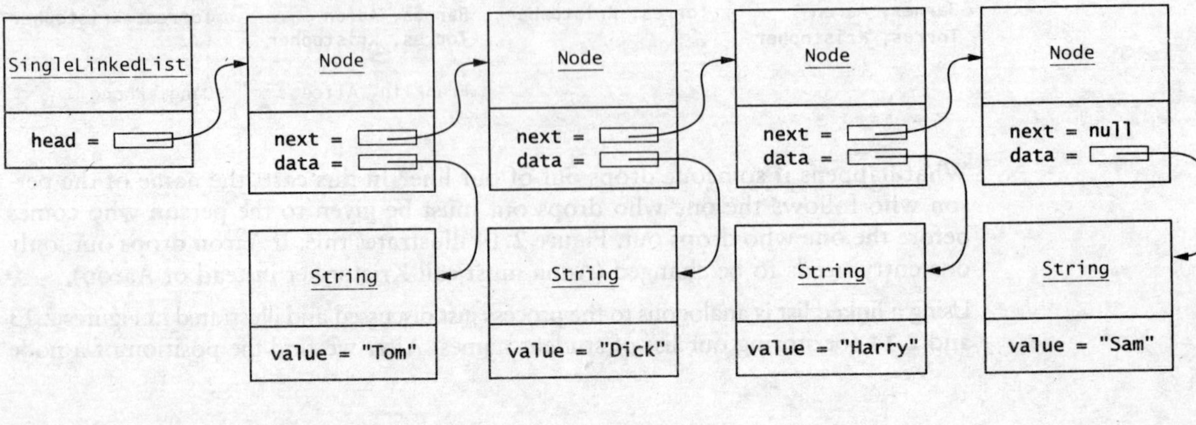

Next, we define a class `Node<E>` (see Listing 2.1) as an inner class that can be placed inside a generic list class. When each node is created, the type parameter `E` specifies the type of data stored in the node.

LISTING 2.1

An Inner Class Node

```
/** A Node is the building block for a single-linked list. */
private static class Node<E> {
    // Data Fields
    /** The reference to the data. */
    private E data;
    /** The reference to the next node. */
    private Node<E> next;

    // Constructors
    /** Creates a new node with a null next field.
        @param dataItem The data stored
    */
    private Node(E dataItem) {
        data = dataItem;
        next = null;
    }

    /** Creates a new node that references another node.
        @param dataItem The data stored
        @param nodeRef The node referenced by new node
    */
    private Node(E dataItem, Node<E> nodeRef) {
        data = dataItem;
        next = nodeRef;
    }
}
```

The keyword `static` in the class header indicates that the `Node<E>` class will not reference its outer class. (It can't because it has no methods other than constructors.) In the Java API documentation, static inner classes are also called *nested classes*.

Generally, we want to keep the details of the `Node` class private. Thus the qualifier `private` is applied to the class as well as to the data fields and constructor. However, the data fields and methods of an inner class are visible anywhere within the enclosing class (also called the *parent class*).

The first constructor stores the data passed to it in the instance variable `data` of a new node. It also sets the `next` field to `null`. The second constructor sets the `next` field to reference the same node as its second argument. We didn't define a default constructor because none is needed.

Connecting Nodes

We can construct the list shown in Figure 2.16 using the following sequence of statements:

```
Node<String> tom = new Node<String>("Tom");
Node<String> dick = new Node<String>("Dick");
Node<String> harry = new Node<String>("Harry");
Node<String> sam = new Node<String>("Sam");
tom.next = dick;
dick.next = harry;
harry.next = sam;
```

The assignment statement

```
tom.next = dick;
```

stores a reference (link) to the node with data `"Dick"` in the variable `next` of node `tom`.

A Single-Linked List Class

Generally, we do not have individual references to each node. Instead, we have a reference to the first node and work from there. Each `SingleLinkedList` object has a data field `head` that references the first list node, called the *list head*. The list head would be connected to the second node in the list, and so on. Such a list is called a *single-linked list*.

```
/** Class to represent a linked list with a link from
    each node to the next node.
*/
public class SingleLinkedList<E> {
    /** Reference to list head. */
    private Node<E> head = null;
    /** The number of items in the list */
    private int size;
    . . .
```

The initial value of `head` is `null`. Method `addFirst` below inserts one element at a time to the front of the list. In the call to the constructor for `Node`, the argument `head` references the current first list node. A new node is created, which is referenced by `head` and is linked to the previous list `head`. Variable `data` of the new list head references `item`.

```
/** Add an item to the front of the list.
    @param item The item to be added
*/
public void addFirst(E item) {
    head = new Node<E>(item, head);
    size++;
}
```

The following fragment creates a linked list `names` and builds the list shown in Figure 2.16 using method `addFirst`:

```
SingleLinkedList<String> names = new SingleLinkedList<String>();
names.addFirst("Sam");
names.addFirst("Harry");
names.addFirst("Dick");
names.addFirst("Tom");
```

Inserting a Node in a List

If we have a reference harry to node "Harry", we can insert a new node, "Bob", into the list after "Harry" as follows:

```
Node<String> bob = new Node<String>("Bob");
bob.next = harry.next; // Step 1
harry.next = bob;      // Step 2
```

The linked list now is as shown in Figure 2.17. We show the number of the step that created each link alongside it.

FIGURE 2.17
After Inserting Bob

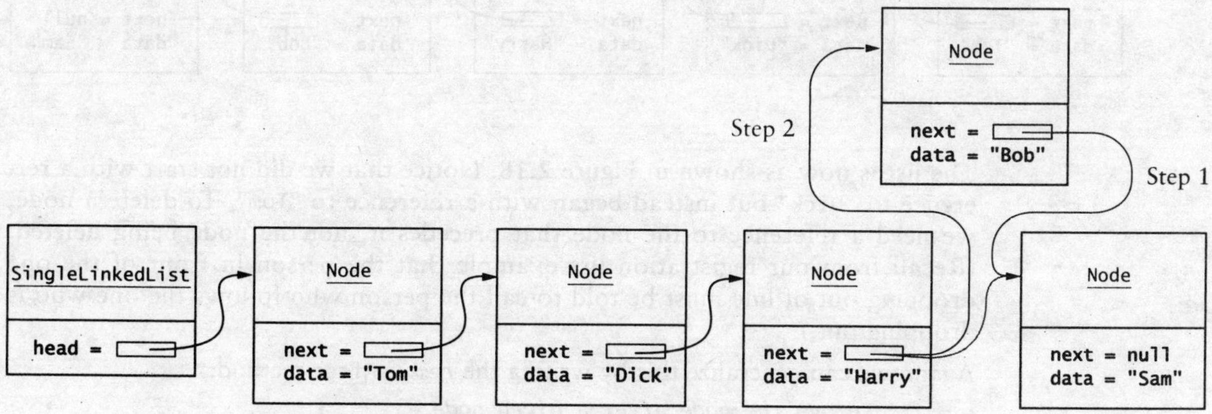

We can generalize this by writing the method addAfter as follows:

```
/** Add a node after a given node
    @param node The node preceding the new item
    @param item The item to insert
*/
private void addAfter(Node<E> node, E item) {
  node.next = new Node<E>(item, node.next);
  size++;
}
```

We declare this method private since it should not be called from outside the class. This is because we want to keep the internal structure of the class hidden. Such private methods are known as helper methods because they will help implement the public methods of the class. Later we will see how addAfter is used to implement the public add methods.

Removing a Node

If we have a reference, tom, to the node that contains "Tom", we can remove the node that follows "Tom":

```
tom.next = tom.next.next;
```

FIGURE 2.18
After Removing Node Following Tom

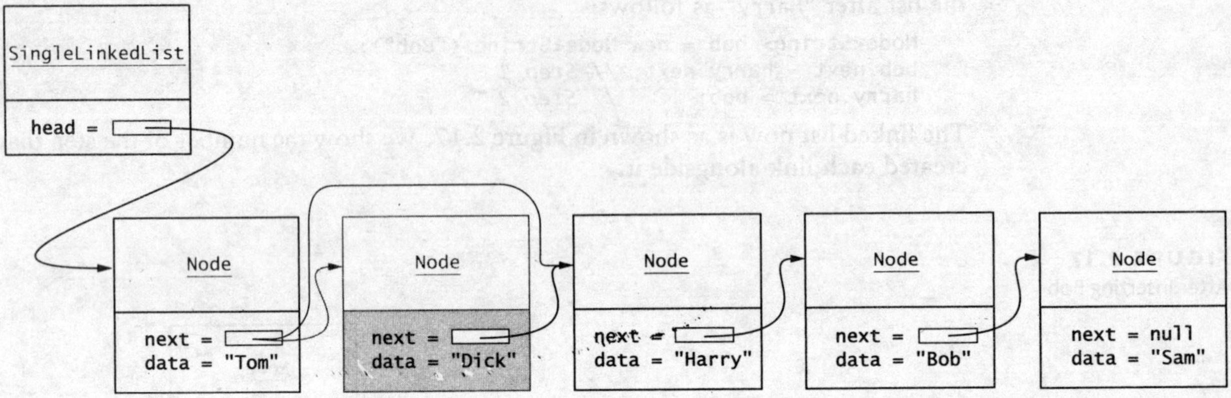

The list is now as shown in Figure 2.18. Notice that we did not start with a reference to "Dick" but instead began with a reference to "Tom". To delete a node, we need a reference to the node that precedes it, not the node being deleted. (Recall from our registration list example that the person in front of the one dropping out of line must be told to call the person who follows the one who is dropping out.)

Again, we can generalize this by writing the removeAfter method:

```
/** Remove the node after a given node
    @param node The node before the one to be removed
    @returns The data from the removed node, or null
             if there is no node to remove
 */
private E removeAfter(Node<E> node) {
  Node<E> temp = node.next;
  if (temp != null) {
    node.next = temp.next;
    size--;
    return temp.data;
  } else {
    return null;
  }
}
```

The removeAfter method works on all nodes except for the first one. For that we need a special method, removeFirst:

```
/** Remove the first node from the list
    @returns The removed node's data or null if the list is empty
 */
private E removeFirst() {
  Node<E> temp = head;
  if (head != null) {
      head = head.next;
  }
```

```
    // Return data at old head or null if list is empty
    if (temp != null) {
        size--;
        return temp.data;
    } else {
        return null;
    }
}
```

Traversing a Single-Linked List

Traversing a single-linked list is a fairly simple process.

1. Set `nodeRef` to reference the first node.
2. `while` `nodeRef` is not `null`.
3. Do something with node referenced by `nodeRef`.
4. Set `nodeRef` to `nodeRef.next`.

This is illustrated by method `toString`, which returns a string representation of a single-linked list.

```
public String toString() {
    Node<String> nodeRef = head;
    StringBuilder result = new StringBuilder();
    while (nodeRef != null) {
        result.append(nodeRef.data);
        if (nodeRef.next != null) {
            result.append (" ==> ");
        }
        nodeRef = nodeRef.next; // Advance down the list.
    }
    return result.toString();
}
```

As new values are assigned to variable `nodeRef` by the statement

```
nodeRef = nodeRef.next; // Advance down the list.
```

`nodeRef` walks down the list, referencing each of the list nodes in turn. The value of `nodeRef` is `null` when the traversal is finished.

For the list shown in Figure 2.18, method `toString` produces the following string:

```
"Tom ==> Harry ==> Bob ==> Sam"
```

Completing the SingleLinkedList Class

We conclude our illustration of the single-linked list data structure by showing how it can be used to implement a limited subset of the methods required by the List interface (see Table 2.5). Specifically we will write the `get`, `set`, `add`, and `remove` methods. Recall from the `ArrayList` that each of these methods takes an index parameter, but we showed above that the methods to add and remove a node need a reference to a node. We need an additional helper method to get a node at a given index.

TABLE 2.5
Methods of Interface `java.util.List<E>`

Method	Behavior
`public E get(int index)`	Returns a reference to the element at position `index`.
`public E set(int index, E anEntry)`	Sets the element at position `index` to reference `anEntry`. Returns the previous value.
`public int size()`	Gets the current size of the `List`.
`public boolean add(E anEntry)`	Adds a reference to `anEntry` at the end of the `List`. Always returns `true`.
`public void add(int index, E anEntry)`	Adds a reference to `anEntry`, inserting it before the item at position `index`.
`int indexOf(E target)`	Searches for `target` and returns the position of the first occurrence, or –1 if it is not in the `List`.

```
/** Find the node at a specified position
    @param index The position of the node sought
    @returns The node at index or null if it does not exist
*/
private Node<E> getNode(int index) {
  Node<E> node = head;
  for (int i = 0; i < index && node != null; i++) {
      node = node.next;
  }
  return node;
}
```

The get and set Methods

Using the `getNode` method, the `get` and `set` methods are straightforward:

```
/** Get the data value at index
    @param index The position of the element to return
    @returns The data at index
    @throws IndexOutOfBoundsException if index is out of range
*/
public E get(int index) {
  if (index < 0 || index >= size) {
      throw new IndexOutOfBoundsException(Integer.toString(index));
  }
  Node<E> node = getNode(index);
  return node.data;
}

/** Set the data value at index
    @param index The position of the item to change
    @param newValue The new value
```

```
    @returns The data value priviously at index
    @throws IndexOutOfBoundsException if index is out of range
*/
public E set(int index, E newValue) {
  if (index < 0 || index >= size) {
     throw new IndexOutOfBoundsException(Integer.toString(index));
  }
  Node<E> node = getNode(index);
  E result = node.data;
  node.data = newValue;
  return result;
}
```

The add Methods

After verifying that the index is in range, the index is checked for the special case of adding at the first element. If the index is zero, then the `addFirst` method is used to insert the new item; otherwise the `addAfter` method is used. Note that `getNode` (called before `addAfter`) returns a reference to the predecessor of the node to be inserted.

```
/** Insert the specified item at index
    @param index The position where item is to be inserted
    @param item The item to be inserted
    @throws IndexOutOfBoundsException if index is out of range
*/
public void add(int index, E item) {
    if (index < 0 || index > size) {
        throw new IndexOutOfBoundsException(Integer.toString(index));
    }
    if (index == 0) {
        addFirst(item);
    } else {
        Node<E> node = getNode(index-1);
        addAfter(node, item);
    }
}
```

The `List` interface also specifies an add method without an index that adds (appends) an item to the end of a list. It can be easily implemented by calling the `add(int index, E item)` method using `size` as the index.

```
/** Append item to the end of the list
    @param item The item to be appended
    @returns true (as specified by the Collection interface)
 */
public boolean add(E item) {
  add(size, item);
  return true;
}
```

EXERCISES FOR SECTION 2.5

SELF-CHECK

1. What is the big-O for the single-linked list `get` operation?
2. What is the big-O for the `set` operation?
3. What is the big-O for each `add` method?
4. Draw a single-linked list of `Integer` objects containing the integers 5, 10, 7, and 30 and referenced by `head`. Complete the following fragment, which adds all `Integer` objects in a list. Your fragment should walk down the list, adding all integer values to `sum`.

```
int sum = 0;
Node<Integer> nodeRef = ________________;
while (nodeRef != null) {
    int next = __________________;
    sum += next;
    nodeRef = __________________;
}
```

5. For the single-linked list in Figure 2.16, data field `head` (type `Node`) references the first node. Explain the effect of each statement in the following fragments.

a.
```
head = new Node<String>("Shakira", head.next);
```

b.
```
Node<String> nodeRef = head.next;
nodeRef.next = nodeRef.next.next;
```

c.
```
Node<String> nodeRef = head;
while (nodeRef.next != null)
    nodeRef = nodeRef.next;
nodeRef.next = new Node<String>("Tamika");
```

d.
```
Node<String> nodeRef = head;
while (nodeRef != null && !nodeRef.data.equals("Harry"))
    nodeRef = nodeRef.next;
if (nodeRef != null) {
    nodeRef.data = "Sally";
    nodeRef.next = new Node<String>("Harry", nodeRef.next.next);
}
```

PROGRAMMING

1. Write a `remove` method that removes the item at a specified index.
2. Using the single-linked list shown in Figure 2.16, and assuming that `head` references the first `Node` and `tail` references the last `Node`, write statements to do each of the following:
   a. Insert `"Bill"` before `"Tom"`.
   b. Insert `"Sue"` before `"Sam"`.
   c. Remove `"Bill"`.
   d. Remove `"Sam"`.
3. Write method `remove` for class `SingleLinkedList<E>`:

```
/** Remove the first occurrence of element item.
    @param item The item to be removed
```

```
    @return true if item is found and removed; otherwise, return false.
*/
public boolean remove(E item)
```

4. Write the following method add for class `SingleLinkedList<E>` without using any helper methods.

```
/** Insert a new item before the one at position index,
    starting at 0 for the list head. The new item is inserted between
    the one at position index - 1 and the one formerly at position
    index.
    @param index The index where the new item is to be inserted
    @param item The item to be inserted
    @throws IndexOutOfBoundsException if the index is out of range
*/
public void add(int index, E item)
```

2.6 Double-Linked Lists and Circular Lists

Our single-linked list data structure has some limitations:

- Insertion at the front of the list is O(1). Insertion at other positions is O(n), where n is the size of the list.
- We can insert a node only after a node for which we have a reference. For example, to insert "Bob" in Figure 2.17, we needed a reference to the node containing "Harry". If we wanted to insert "Bob" before "Sam" but did not have a reference to "Harry", we would have to start at the beginning of the list and search until we found a node whose next node was "Sam".
- We can remove a node only if we have a reference to its predecessor node. For example, to remove "Dick" in Figure 2.18, we needed a reference to the node containing "Tom". If we wanted to remove "Dick" without having this reference, we would have to start at the beginning of the list and search until we found a node whose next node was "Dick".
- We can traverse the list only in the forward direction, whereas with an `ArrayList` we can move forward (or backward) by incrementing (or decrementing) the index.

We can overcome these limitations by adding a reference to the previous `node` in the `Node` class, as shown in the UML class diagram in Figure 2.19. The open diamond indicates that both `prev` and `next` are references whose values can be changed. Our *double-linked list* is shown in Figure 2.20.

FIGURE 2.19
Double-Linked List Node UML Diagram

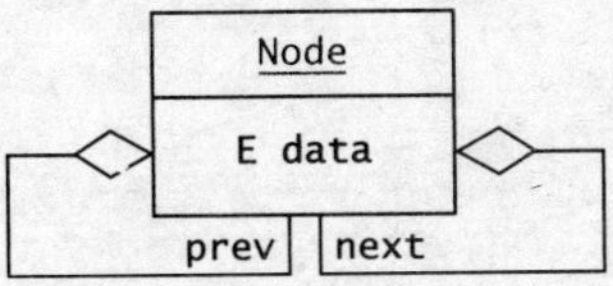

FIGURE 2.20
A Double-Linked List

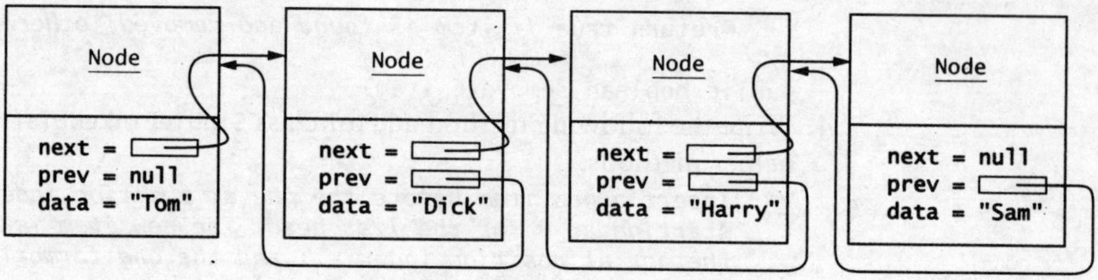

> **PITFALL**
>
> **Falling Off the End of a List**
>
> If nodeRef is at the last list element and you execute the statement
>
> `nodeRef = nodeRef.next;`
>
> nodeRef will be set to `null`, and you will have fallen off the end of the list. This is not an error. However, if you execute this statement again, you will get a `NullPointerException`, because `nodeRef.next` is undefined when nodeRef is `null`.

The Node Class

The Node class for a double-linked list has references to the data and to the next and previous nodes. The declaration of this class follows.

```
/** A Node is the building block for a double-linked list. */
private static class Node<E> {
    /** The data value. */
    private E data;
    /** The link to the next node. */
    private Node<E> next = null;
    /** The link to the previous node. */
    private Node<E> prev = null;

    /** Construct a node with the given data value.
        @param dataItem The data value
    */
    private Node(E dataItem) {
        data = dataItem;
    }
}
```

Inserting into a Double-Linked List

If `sam` is a reference to the node containing `"Sam"`, we can insert a new node containing `"Sharon"` into the list before `"Sam"` using the following statements. Before the insertion, we can refer to the predecessor of `sam` as `sam.prev`. After the insertion, this node will be referenced by `sharon.prev`.

```
Node<String> sharon = new Node<String>("Sharon");
// Link new node to its neighbors.
sharon.next = sam;         // Step 1
sharon.prev = sam.prev;    // Step 2
// Link old predecessor of sam to new predecessor.
sam.prev.next = sharon;    // Step 3
// Link to new predecessor.
sam.prev = sharon;         // Step 4
```

The three nodes affected by the insertion are shown in Figures 2.21 and 2.22. The old links are shown in gray, and the new links are shown in color. Next to each link we show the number of the step that creates it. Figure 2.21 shows the links after Steps 1 and 2, and Figure 2.22 shows the links after Steps 3 and 4.

Removing from a Double-Linked List

If we have a reference, `harry`, to the node that contains `"Harry"`, we can remove that node without having a named reference to its predecessor:

```
harry.prev.next = harry.next; // Step 1
harry.next.prev = harry.prev; // Step 2
```

The list is now as shown in Figure 2.23.

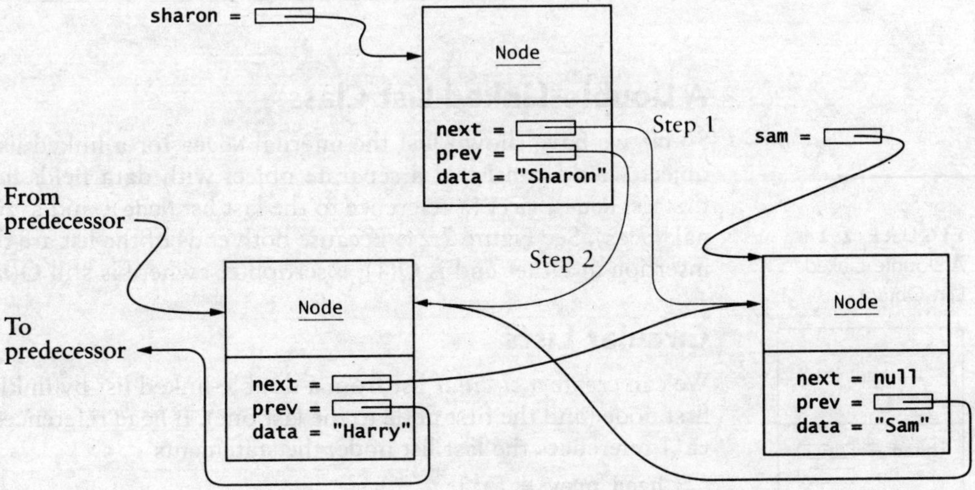

FIGURE 2.21
Steps 1 and 2 in Inserting Sharon

FIGURE 2.22
After Inserting Sharon before Sam

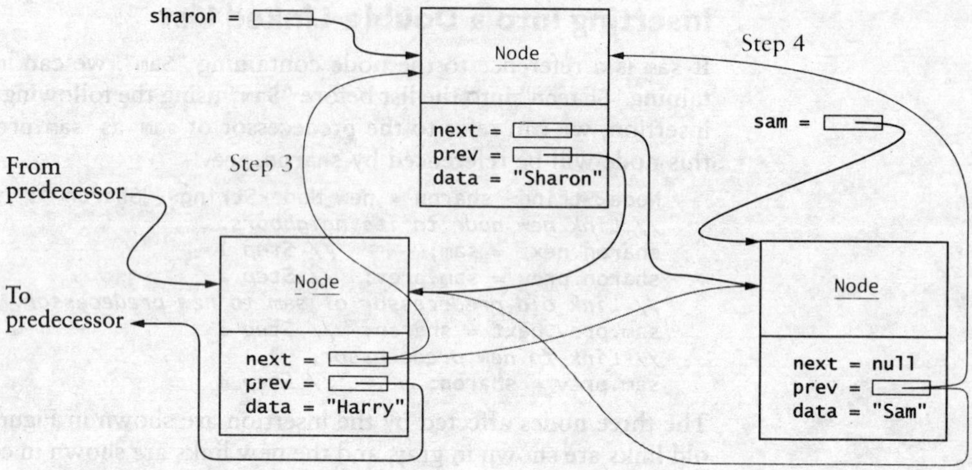

FIGURE 2.23
Removing Harry from a Double-Linked List

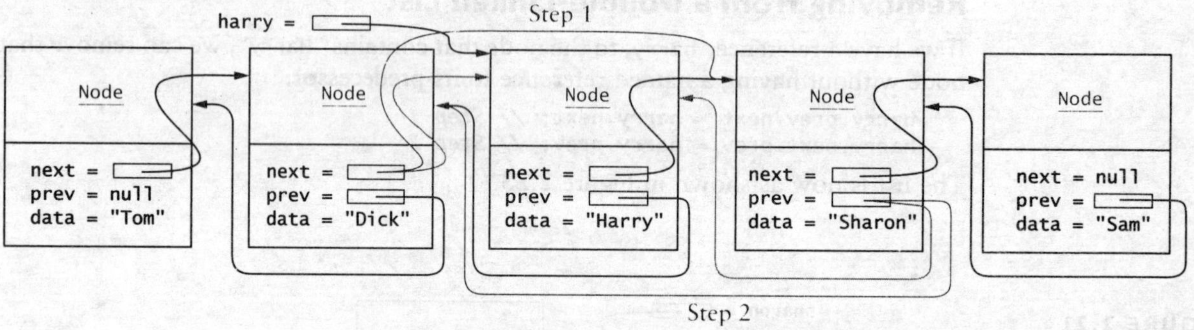

A Double-Linked List Class

So far we have shown just the internal Nodes for a linked list. A double-linked list object would consist of a separate object with data fields `head` (a reference to the first list `Node`), `tail` (a reference to the last list `Node`), and `size` (the number of internal `Node`s). See Figure 2.24. Because both ends of the list are directly accessible, now insertion at either end is O(1); insertion elsewhere is still O(n).

FIGURE 2.24
A Double-Linked List Object

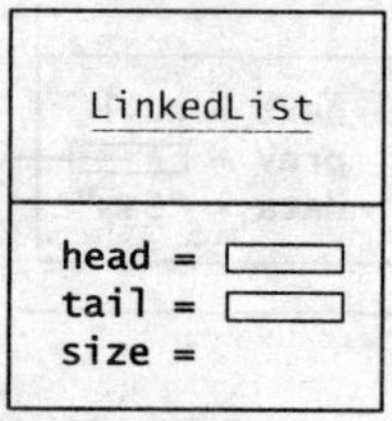

Circular Lists

We can create a *circular* list from a double-linked list by linking the last node to the first node (and the first node to the last one). If `head` references the first list node and `tail` references the last list node, the statements

```
head.prev = tail;
tail.next = head;
```

would accomplish this (see Figure 2.25).

FIGURE 2.25
A Circular Linked List

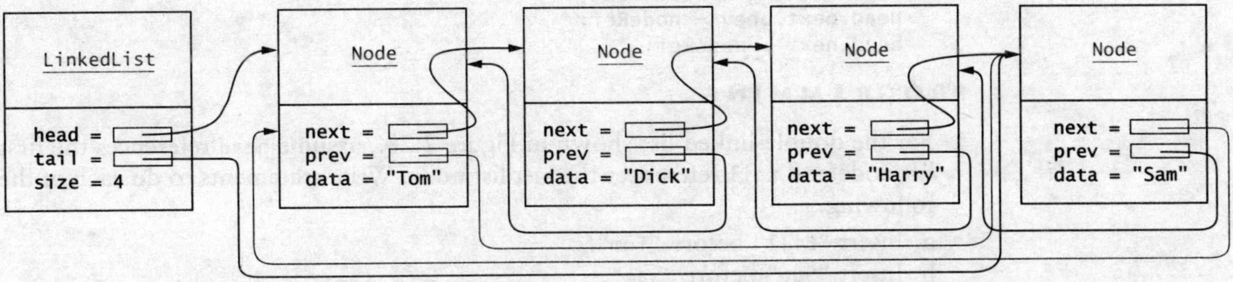

You could also create a circular list from a single-linked list by executing just the statement

```
tail.next = head;
```

This statement connects the last list element to the first list element. If you keep a reference to only the last list element, `tail`, you can access the last element and the first element (`tail.next`) in O(1) time.

One advantage of a circular list is that you can continue to traverse in the forward (or reverse) direction even after you have passed the last (or first) list node. This enables you to visit all the list elements from any starting point. In a list that is not circular, you would have to start at the beginning or at the end if you wanted to visit all the list elements. A second advantage of a circular list is that you can never fall off the end of the list. There is a disadvantage: you must be careful not to set up an infinite loop.

EXERCISES FOR SECTION 2.6

SELF-CHECK

1. Answer the following questions about lists.
   a. Each node in a single-linked list, has a reference to ______ and ______.
   b. In a double-linked list, each node has a reference to ______, ______, and ______.
   c. To remove an item from a single-linked list, you need a reference to ______.
   d. To remove an item from a double-linked list, you need a reference to ______.
2. For the double-linked list in Figure 2.20, explain the effect of each statement in the following fragments.
   a.
   ```
   Node<String> nodeRef = tail.prev;
   nodeRef.prev.next = tail;
   tail.prev = nodeRef.prev;
   ```
   b.
   ```
   Node<String> nodeRef = head;
   head = new Node<String>("Tamika");
   head.next = nodeRef;
   nodeRef.prev = head;
   ```

```
c. Node<String> nodeRef = new Node<String>("Shakira");
   nodeRef.prev = head;
   nodeRef.next = head.next;
   head.next.prev = nodeRef;
   head.next = nodeRef;
```

PROGRAMMING

1. For the double-linked list shown in Figure 2.20., assume head references the first list node and tail references the last list node. Write statements to do each of the following.
   a. Insert "Bill" before "Tom".
   b. Insert "Sue" before "Sam".
   c. Remove "Bill".
   d. Remove "Sam".

2.7 The LinkedList Class and the Iterator, ListIterator, and Iterable Interfaces

The LinkedList Class

The LinkedList<E> class, part of the Java API package java.util, implements the List<E> interface using a double-linked list. A selected subset of the methods from this Java API is shown in Table 2.6. Because the LinkedList class, like the ArrayList class, implements the List interface, it contains many of the methods found in the ArrayList class as well as some additional methods.

TABLE 2.6
Selected Methods of the java.util.LinkedList<E> Class

Method	Behavior
public void add(int index, E obj)	Inserts object obj into the list at position index.
public void addFirst(E obj)	Inserts object obj as the first element of the list.
public void addLast(E obj)	Adds object obj to the end of the list.
public E get(int index)	Returns the item at position index.
public E getFirst()	Gets the first element in the list. Throws NoSuchElementException if the list is empty.
public E getLast()	Gets the last element in the list. Throws NoSuchElementException if the list is empty.
public boolean remove(E obj)	Removes the first occurrence of object obj from the list. Returns true if the list contained object obj; otherwise, returns false.
public int size()	Returns the number of objects contained in the list.

The Iterator

Let's say we want to process each element in a LinkedList. We can use the following loop to access the list elements in sequence, starting with the one at index 0.

```
// Access each list element.
for (int index = 0; index < aList.size(); index++) {
    E nextElement = aList.get(index);
    // Do something with the element at position index (nextElement)
    . . .
}
```

The loop is executed aList.size() times; thus it is linear. During each iteration we call method get to retrieve the element at position index.

If we assume that method get begins at the first list node (head), each call to method get must advance a local reference (nodeRef) to the node at position index using a loop such as:

```
// Advance nodeRef to the element at position index.
Node<E> nodeRef = head;
for (int j = 0; j < index; j++) {
    nodeRef = nodeRef.next;
}
```

This loop (in method get) executes index times. Since index ranges from 0 to aList.size() - 1 in the outer loop, the total execution time is 1 + 2 + . . . + aList.size() - 1. The value of this series is proportional to aList.size()^2, so the loop to process the list elements is $O(n^2)$ and is, therefore, very inefficient. We would like to have an alternative way to access the elements in a linked list sequentially.

We can use the concept of an iterator to accomplish this. Think of an iterator as a moving place marker that keeps track of the current position in a particular linked list. The Iterator object for a list starts at the first element in the list. The programmer can use the Iterator object's next method to retrieve the next element. Each time it does a retrieval, the Iterator object advances to the next list element, where it waits until it is needed again. We can also ask the Iterator object to determine whether the list has more elements left to process (method hasNext). Iterator objects throw a NoSuchElementException if they are asked to retrieve the next element after all elements have been processed.

EXAMPLE 2.11 Assume iter is declared as an Iterator object for LinkedList myList. We can replace the fragment shown at the beginning of this section with the following one.

```
// Access each list element.
while (iter.hasNext()) {
    E nextElement = iter.next();
    // Do something with the next element (nextElement).
    . . .
}
```

This fragment is $O(n)$ instead of $O(n^2)$. All that remains is to determine how to declare iter as an Iterator for LinkedList object myList. We show how to do this in the next section and discuss Iterator a bit more formally.

The Iterator Interface

The interface `Iterator<E>` is defined as part of API package `java.util`. Table 2.7 summarizes the methods declared by this interface.

The `List` interface declares the method `iterator`, which returns an `Iterator` object that will iterate over the elements of that list. (The requirement for the `iterator` method is actually in the `Collection` interface, which is the superinterface for the `List` interface. We discuss the `Collection` interface in Section 2.8.)

TABLE 2.7
The `java.util.Iterator<E>` Interface

Method	Behavior
`boolean hasNext()`	Returns `true` if the `next` method returns a value.
`E next()`	Returns the next element. If there are no more elements, throws the `NoSuchElementException`.
`void remove()`	Removes the last element returned by the `next` method.

In the following loop, we process all items in `List<Integer> aList` through an `Iterator`.

```
// Obtain an Iterator to the list aList.
Iterator<Integer> itr = aList.iterator();
while (itr.hasNext() {
    int value = itr.next();
    // Do something with value.
    . . .
}
```

An `Iterator` does not refer to or point to a particular object at any given time. Rather, you should think of an `Iterator` as pointing between objects within a list. The method `hasNext` tells us whether or not calling the `next` method will succeed. If `hasNext` returns **`true`**, then a call to `next` will return the next object in the list and advance the `Iterator` (see Figure 2.26). If `hasNext` returns **`false`**, a call to `next` will cause the `NoSuchElementException` to be thrown.

You can use the `Iterator remove` method to remove elements from a list as you access them. You can remove only the element that was most recently accessed by `next`. Each call to `remove` must be preceded by a call to `next` to retrieve the next element.

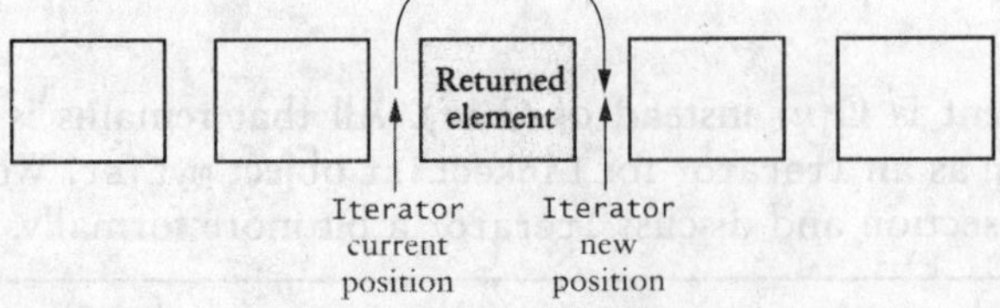

FIGURE 2.26
Advancing an `Iterator` via the next Method

EXAMPLE 2.12 We wish to remove all elements from aList (type LinkedList<Integer>) that are divisible by a particular value. The following method will accomplish this:

```
/** Remove the items divisible by div. */
    pre: LinkedList aList contains Integer objects.
    post: Elements divisible by div have been removed.
*/
public static void removeDivisibleBy(LinkedList<Integer> aList,
                                     int div) {
    Iterator<Integer> iter = aList.iterator();
    while (iter.hasNext()) {
        int nextInt = iter.next();
        if (nextInt % div == 0)
            iter.remove();
    }
}
```

The method call iter.next retrieves the next Integer in the list. Its value is unboxed, and if it is divisible by div, the statement

```
iter.remove();
```

removes the element just retrieved from the list.

PITFALL

Improper Use of remove

If a call to remove is not preceded by a call to next, remove will throw an IllegalStateException. If you want to remove two consecutive elements in a list, a separate call to next must occur before each call to remove.

PROGRAM STYLE

Removal Using Iterator.remove versus List.remove

You could also use method LinkedList.remove to remove elements from a list. However, it is more efficient to remove multiple elements from a list using Iterator.remove than it would be to use LinkedList.remove. The LinkedList.remove method removes only one element at a time, so you would need to start at the beginning of the list each time and advance down the list to each element that you wanted to remove ($O(n^2)$ process). With the Iterator.remove method, you can remove elements as they are accessed by the Iterator object without having to go back to the beginning of the list ($O(n)$ process).

The ListIterator Interface

The Iterator has some limitations. It can traverse the List only in the forward direction. It also provides only a remove method, not an add method. Also, to start an Iterator somewhere other than at first List element, you must write your own loop to advance the Iterator to the desired starting position.

The Java API also contains the ListIterator<E> interface, which is an extension of the Iterator<E> interface that overcomes these limitations. Like the Iterator, the ListIterator should be thought of as being positioned between elements of the linked list. The positions are assigned an index from 0 to size, where the position just before the first element has index 0 and the position just after the last element has index size. The next method moves the iterator forward and returns the element that was jumped over. The previous method moves the iterator backward and also returns the element that was jumped over. This is illustrated in Figure 2.27, where *i* is the current position of the iterator. The methods defined by the ListIterator interface are shown in Table 2.8.

To obtain a ListIterator, you call the listIterator method of the LinkedList class. This method has two forms, as shown in Table 2.9.

FIGURE 2.27
The ListIterator

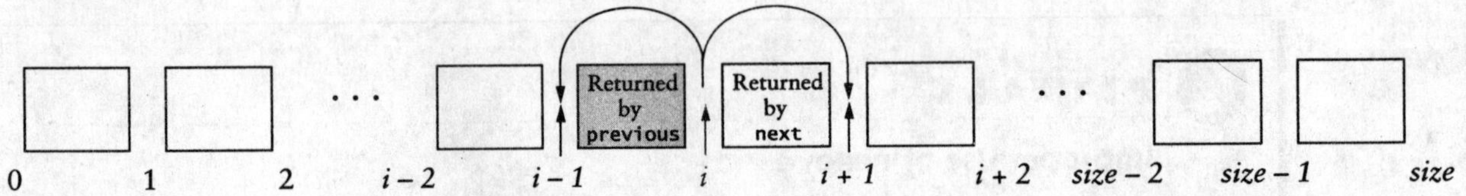

EXAMPLE 2.13 If myList is type LinkedList<String>, the statement

```
ListIterator<String> myIter = myList.listIterator(3);
```

would create a ListIterator object myIter positioned between the elements at positions 2 and 3 of the linked list. The method call

```
myIter.next()
```

would return a reference to the String object at position 3 and move the iterator forward; the method call

```
myIter.nextIndex()
```

would return 4. The method call

```
myIter.previous()
```

would return a reference to the String object at position 3 and move the iterator back to its original position. The method call

```
myIter.previousIndex()
```

would return 2. The method call

```
myIter.hasNext()
```

would return true if the list has at least four elements; the method call

```
myIter.hasPrevious()
```

would return true.

TABLE 2.8
The `java.util.ListIterator<E>` Interface

Method	Behavior
`void add(E obj)`	Inserts object `obj` into the list just before the item that would be returned by the next call to method `next` and after the item that would have been returned by method `previous`. If method `previous` is called after `add`, the newly inserted object will be returned.
`boolean hasNext()`	Returns `true` if `next` will not throw an exception.
`boolean hasPrevious()`	Returns `true` if `previous` will not throw an exception.
`E next()`	Returns the next object and moves the iterator forward. If the iterator is at the end, the `NoSuchElementException` is thrown.
`int nextIndex()`	Returns the index of the item that will be returned by the next call to `next`. If the iterator is at the end, the list size is returned.
`E previous()`	Returns the previous object and moves the iterator backward. If the iterator is at the beginning of the list, the `NoSuchElementExcepton` is thrown.
`int previousIndex()`	Returns the index of the item that will be returned by the next call to `previous`. If the iterator is at the beginning of the list, −1 is returned.
`void remove()`	Removes the last item returned from a call to `next` or `previous`. If a call to `remove` is not preceded by a call to `next` or `previous`, the `IllegalStateException` is thrown.
`void set(E obj)`	Replaces the last item returned from a call to `next` or `previous` with `obj`. If a call to `set` is not preceded by a call to `next` or `previous`, the `IllegalStateException` is thrown.

TABLE 2.9
Methods in `java.util.LinkedList<E>` that Return `ListIterators`

Method	Behavior
`public ListIterator<E> listIterator()`	Returns a `ListIterator` that begins just before the first list element.
`public ListIterator<E> listIterator(int index)`	Returns a `ListIterator` that begins just before position `index`.

EXAMPLE 2.14 The Fragment

```
ListIterator<String> myIter = myList.listIterator();
while (myIter.hasNext()) {
    if (target.equals(myIter.next())) {
        myIter.set(newItem);
        break;  // Exit loop
    }
}
```

searches for `target` in list `myList` and, if `target` is present, replaces its first occurrence with `newItem`.

Comparison of Iterator and ListIterator

Because the interface `ListIterator<E>` is a subinterface of `Iterator<E>`, classes that implement `ListIterator` must provide all of the capabilities of both. The `Iterator` interface requires fewer methods and can be used to iterate over more general data structures—that is, structures for which an index is not meaningful and ones for which traversing in only the forward direction is required. It is for this reason that the `Iterator` is required by the `Collection` interface (more general), whereas the `ListIterator` is required only by the `List` interface (more specialized). We will discuss the `Collection` interface in Section 2.9.

Conversion between a ListIterator and an Index

The `ListIterator` has the methods `nextIndex` and `previousIndex`, which return the index values associated with the items that would be returned by a call to the `next` or `previous` methods. The `LinkedList` class has the method `listIterator(int index)`, which returns a `ListIterator` whose next call to `next` will return the item at position `index`. Thus you can convert between an index and a `ListIterator`. However, remember that the `listIterator(int index)` method creates the desired `ListIterator` by creating a new `ListIterator` that starts at the beginning and then walks along the list until the desired position is found. There is a special case where `index` is equal to `size()`, but all others are an $O(n)$ operation.

The Enhanced for Statement

Java 5.0 introduced the enhanced `for` statement (also called the **for** each statement), which makes it easier to use iterators. The following loop uses the enhanced `for` statement to count the number of times that `target` occurs in `myList` (type `LinkedList<String>`).

```
count = 0;
for (String nextStr : myList) {
    if (target.equals(nextStr)) {
        count++;
    }
}
```

The enhanced **for** creates an `Iterator` object and implicitly calls its `hasNext` and `next` methods. Other `Iterator` methods, such as `remove`, are not available. In a similar way, the following loop adds all the integers in `LinkedList aList` (type

LinkedList<Integer>). Each Integer object in aList is unboxed, and its int value is stored in nextInt.

```
sum = 0;
for (int nextInt : aList) {
    sum += nextInt;
}
```

Finally, the enhanced for statement may also be used with an array. If you use the enhanced for, you can access the array elements in sequence without declaring a loop index variable. The following for loop displays on a single output line all the characters stored in array chars (type char[]).

```
for (char nextCh : chars) {
    System.out.print(nextCh);
}
System.out.println();
```

SYNTAX **The Enhanced for Statement (for each)**

FORM:

for (*formalParameter* : *expression*) { . . . }

EXAMPLE:

```
for (String nextStr : myList) { . . . }
for (int nextInt : aList) { . . . }
```

MEANING:

During each repetition of the loop, the variable specified by *formalParameter* accesses the next element of *expression*, starting with the first element and ending with the last. The *expression* must be an array or a collection that implements the Iterable interface. The Collection interface extends the Iterable interface so that all classes that implement it are implementors of the Iterable interface (see next section).

The Iterable Interface

Next we show the Iterable interface. This interface requires only that a class that implements it provide an iterator method. As mentioned above, the Collection interface extends the Iterable interface, so all classes that implement the List interface (a subinterface of Collection) must provide an iterator method.

```
public interface Iterable<E> {
    /** Returns an iterator over the elements in this collection. */
    Iterator<E> iterator();
}
```

EXERCISES FOR SECTION 2.7

SELF-CHECK

1. The method `indexOf`, part of the `List` interface, returns the index of the first occurrence of an object in a `List`. What does the following code fragment do?

```
int indexOfSam = myList.indexOf("Sam");
ListIterator<String> iteratorToSam = listIterator(indexOfSam);
iteratorToSam.previous();
iteratorToSam.remove();
```

   where the internal nodes of `myList` (type `LinkedList<String>`) are shown in the figure below:

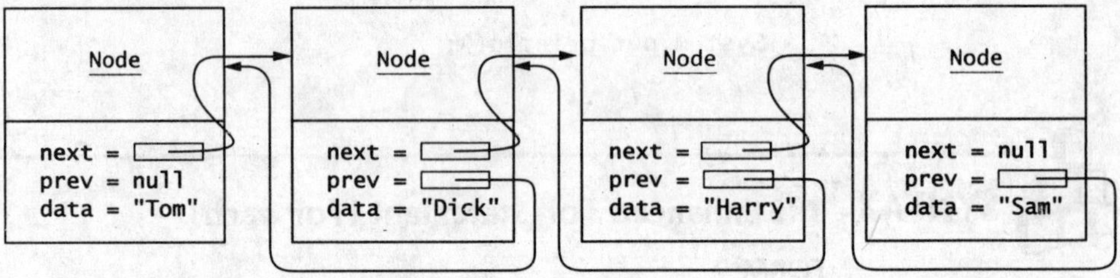

2. In Question 1, what if we change the statement

```
iteratorToSam.previous();
```

   to

```
iteratorToSam.next();
```

3. In Question 1, what if we omit the statement

```
iteratorToSam.previous();
```

PROGRAMMING

1. Write the method `indexOf` as specified in the `List` interface by adapting the code shown in Example 2.14 to return the index of the first occurrence of an object.
2. Write the method `lastIndexOf` specified in the `List` interface by adapting the code shown in Example 2.14 to return the index of the last occurrence of an object.
3. Write a method `indexOfMin` that returns the index of the minimum item in a `List`, assuming that each item in the list implements the `Comparable` interface.

2.8 Implementation of a Double-Linked List Class

In this section we will describe the class `KWLinkedList`, which implements some of the methods of the `List` interface using a double-linked list. We will not provide a complete implementation because we expect you to use the standard `LinkedList` class provided by the Java API (in package `java.util`). The data fields for the `KWLinkedList` class are shown in Table 2.10. They are declared as shown here.

```
import java.util.*;

/** Class KWLinkedList implements a double-linked list and
    a ListIterator. */
```

TABLE 2.10
Data Fields for Class KWLinkedList<E>

Data Field	Attribute
`private Node<E> head`	A reference to the first item in the list
`private Node<E> tail`	A reference to the last item in the list
`private int size`	A count of the number of items in the list

```
public class KWLinkedList<E> {
    // Data Fields
    /** A reference to the head of the list. */
    private Node<E> head = null;
    /** A reference to the end of the list. */
    private Node<E> tail = null;
    /** The size of the list. */
    private int size = 0;
    ...
```

Implementing the KWLinkedList Methods

We need to implement the methods shown earlier in Table 2.6 for the `LinkedList` class. The algorithm for the `add(int index, E obj)` method is

1. Obtain a reference, `nodeRef`, to the node at position `index`.
2. Insert a new `Node` containing `obj` before the `Node` referenced by `nodeRef`.

Similarly, the algorithm for the `get(int index)` method is

1. Obtain a reference, `nodeRef`, to the node at position `index`.
2. Return the contents of the `Node` referenced by `nodeRef`.

We also have the `listIterator(int index)` method with the following algorithm:

1. Obtain a reference, `nodeRef`, to the node at position `index`.
2. Return a `ListIterator` that is positioned just before the `Node` referenced by `nodeRef`.

These three methods all have the same first step. Therefore, we want to use a common method to perform this step.

If we look at the requirements for the `ListIterator`, we see that it has an `add` method that inserts a new item before the current position of the iterator. Thus we can refine the algorithm for the `KWLinkedList.add(int index, E obj)` method to

1. Obtain an iterator that is positioned just before the `Node` at position `index`.
2. Insert a new `Node` containing `obj` before the `Node` currently referenced by this iterator.

Thus the `KWLinkedList<E>` method `add` can be coded as

```
/** Add an item at position index.
    @param index The position at which the object is to be
           inserted
    @param obj The object to be inserted
    @throws IndexOutOfBoundsException if the index is out
           of range (i < 0 || i > size())
```

```
*/
public void add(int index, E obj) {
    listIterator(index).add(obj);
}
```

Notice that it was not necessary to declare a local `ListIterator` object in the `KWLinkedList` method `add`. The method call `listIterator(index)` returns an anonymous `ListIterator` object, to which we apply the `ListIterator.add` method.

Similarly, we can code the `get` method as

```
/** Get the element at position index.
    @param index Position of item to be retrieved
    @return The item at index
*/
public E get(int index) {
    return listIterator(index).next();
}
```

Other methods in Table 2.6 (`addFirst`, `addLast`, `getFirst`, `getLast`) can be implemented by delegation to methods `add` and `get` above.

A Class that Implements the ListIterator Interface

We can implement most of the `KWLinkedList` methods by delegation to the class `KWListIter`, which will implement the `ListIterator` interface (see Table 2.8). Because it is an inner class of `KWLinkedList`, its methods will be able to reference the data fields and members of the parent class (and also the other inner class, `Node`). The data fields for class `KWListIter` are shown in Table 2.11.

TABLE 2.11
Data Fields of Class `KWListIter`

`private Node<E> nextItem`	A reference to the next item.
`private Node<E> lastItemReturned`	A reference to the node that was last returned by `next` or `previous`.
`private int index`	The iterator is positioned just before the item at `index`.

```
/** Inner class to implement the ListIterator interface. */
private class KWListIter implements ListIterator<E> {
    /** A reference to the next item. */
    private Node<E> nextItem;
    /** A reference to the last item returned. */
    private Node<E> lastItemReturned;
    /** The index of the current item. */
    private int index = 0;
```

Figure 2.28 shows an example of a `KWLinkedList` object and a `KWListIter` object. The `next` method would return `"Harry"`, and the `previous` method would return `"Dick"`. The `nextIndex` method would return 2, and the `previousIndex` method would return 1.

The Constructor

The `KWListIter` constructor takes as a parameter the index of the `Node` at which the iteration is to begin. A test is made for the special case where the index is equal to

FIGURE 2.28
Double-Linked List with KWListIter

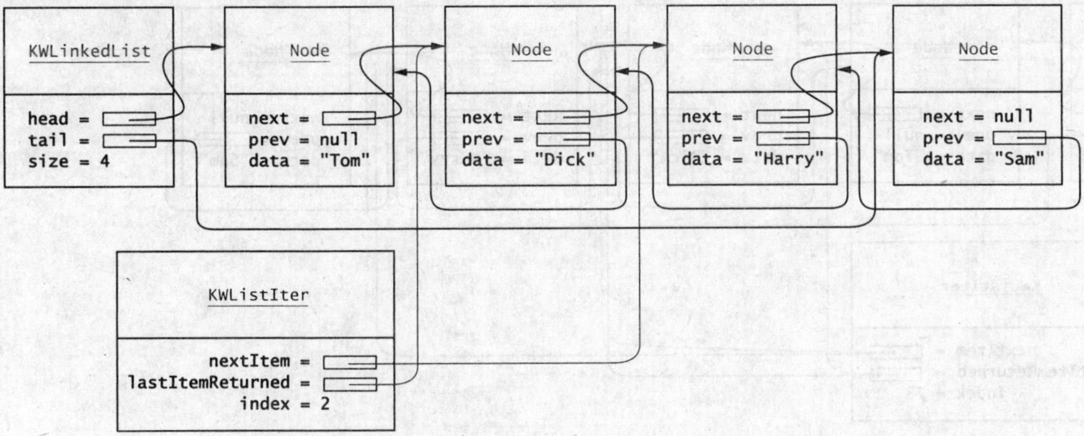

the size; in that case the iteration starts at the tail. Otherwise, a loop starting at the head walks along the list until the node at index is reached.

```
/** Construct a KWListIter that will reference the ith item.
    @param i The index of the item to be referenced
*/
public KWListIter(int i) {
    // Validate i parameter.
    if (i < 0 || i > size) {
        throw new IndexOutOfBoundsException(
            "Invalid index " + i);
    }
    lastItemReturned = null; // No item returned yet.
    // Special case of last item.
    if (i == size) {
        index = size;
        nextItem = null;
    } else { // Start at the beginning
        nextItem = head;
        for (index = 0; index < i; index++) {
            nextItem = nextItem.next;
        }
    }
}
```

The hasNext and next Methods

The data field nextItem will always reference the Node that will be returned by the next method. Therefore, the hasNext method merely tests to see whether nextItem is null.

```
/** Indicate whether movement forward is defined.
    @return true if call to next will not throw an exception
*/
public boolean hasNext() {
    return nextItem != null;
}
```

FIGURE 2.29
Advancing a KWListIter

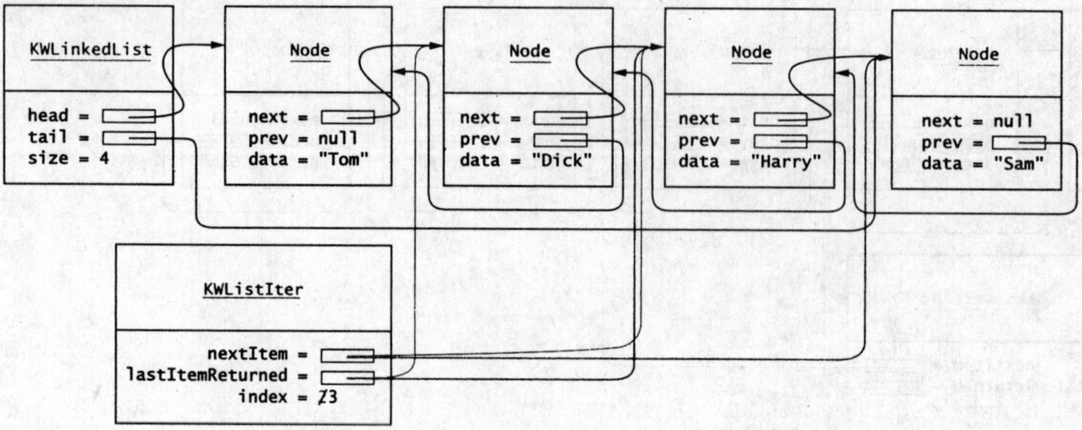

The next method begins by calling hasNext. If the result is false, the NoSuchElemenentException is thrown. Otherwise, lastItemReturned is set to nextItem; then nextItem is advanced to the next node, and index is incremented. The data field of the node referenced by lastItemReturned is returned. As shown in Figure 2.29, the previous iterator position is indicated by the gray arrows and the new position by the colored arrows.

```
/** Move the iterator forward and return the next item.
    @return The next item in the list
    @throws NoSuchElementException if there is no such object
*/
public E next() {
    if (!hasNext()) {
        throw new NoSuchElementException();
    }
    lastItemReturned = nextItem;
    nextItem = nextItem.next;
    index++;
    return lastItemReturned.data;
}
```

The hasPrevious and previous Methods

The hasPrevious method is a little trickier. When the iterator is at the end of the list, nextItem is null. In this case, we can determine that there is a previous item by checking the size—a nonempty list will have a previous item when the iterator is at the end. If the iterator is not at the end, then nextItem is not null, and we can check for a previous item by examining nextItem.prev.

```
/** Indicate whether movement backward is defined.
    @return true if call to previous will not throw an exception
*/
public boolean hasPrevious() {
    return (nextItem == null && size != 0)
            || nextItem.prev != null;
}
```

The previous method begins by calling hasPrevious. If the result is false, the NoSuchElementException is thrown. Otherwise, if nextItem is null, the iterator is past the last element, so nextItem is set to tail because the previous element must be the last list element. If nextItem is not null, nextItem is set to nextItem.prev. Either way, lastItemReturned is set to nextItem, and index is decremented. The data field of the node referenced by lastItemReturned is returned.

```
/** Move the iterator backward and return the previous item.
    @return The previous item in the list
    @throws NoSuchElementException if there is no such object
*/
public E previous() {
    if (!hasPrevious()) {
        throw new NoSuchElementException();
    }
    if (nextItem == null) { // Iterator is past the last element
        nextItem = tail;
    } else {
        nextItem = nextItem.prev;
    }
    lastItemReturned = nextItem;
    index--;
    return lastItemReturned.data;
}
```

The add Method

The add method inserts a new node before the node referenced by nextItem. There are four cases: add to an empty list, add to the head of the list, add to the tail of the list, and add to the middle of the list. We next discuss each case separately; you can combine them to write the method.

An empty list is indicated by head equal to null. In this case, a new Node is created, and both head and tail are set to reference it. This is illustrated in Figure 2.30.

FIGURE 2.30
Adding to an Empty List

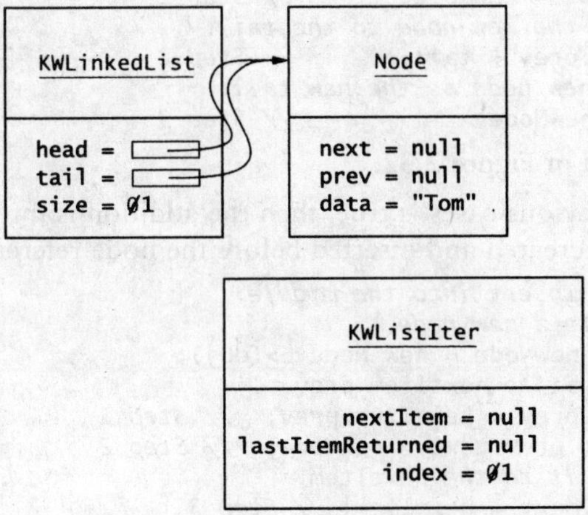

```
/** Add a new item between the item that will be returned
    by next and the item that will be returned by previous.
    If previous is called after add, the element added is
    returned.
    @param obj The item to be inserted
*/
public void add(E obj) {
    if (head == null) { // Add to an empty list.
        head = new Node<E>(obj);
        tail = head;
    ...
```

The `KWListIter` object in Figure 2.30 shows a value of `null` for `lastItemReturned` and `1` for `index`. These data fields are set at the end of the method. In all cases, data field `nextItem` is not changed by the insertion. It must reference the successor of the item that was inserted, or `null` if there is no successor.

If `nextItem` equals `head`, then the insertion is at the head. The new `Node` is created and is linked to the beginning of the list.

```
} else if (nextItem == head) { // Insert at head.
    // Create a new node.
    Node<E> newNode = new Node<E>(obj);
    // Link it to the nextItem.
    newNode.next = nextItem;    // Step 1
    // Link nextItem to the new node.
    nextItem.prev = newNode;    // Step 2
    // The new node is now the head.
    head = newNode;             // Step 3
```

This is illustrated in Figure 2.31.

If `nextItem` is `null`, then the insertion is at the tail. The new node is created and linked to the tail.

```
} else if (nextItem == null) { // Insert at tail.
    // Create a new node.
    Node<E> newNode = new Node<E>(obj);
    // Link the tail to the new node.
    tail.next = newNode;        // Step 1
    // Link the new node to the tail.
    newNode.prev = tail;        // Step 2
    // The new node is the new tail.
    tail = newNode;             // Step 3
```

This is illustrated in Figure 2.32.

If none of the previous cases is true, then the addition is into the middle of the list. The new node is created and inserted before the node referenced by `nextItem`.

```
} else { // Insert into the middle.
    // Create a new node.
    Node<E> newNode = new Node<E>(obj);
    // Link it to nextItem.prev.
    newNode.prev = nextItem.prev;  // Step 1
    nextItem.prev.next = newNode;  // Step 2
    // Link it to the nextItem.
    newNode.next = nextItem; // Step 3
    nextItem.prev = newNode; // Step 4
}
```

FIGURE 2.31
Adding to the Head of the List

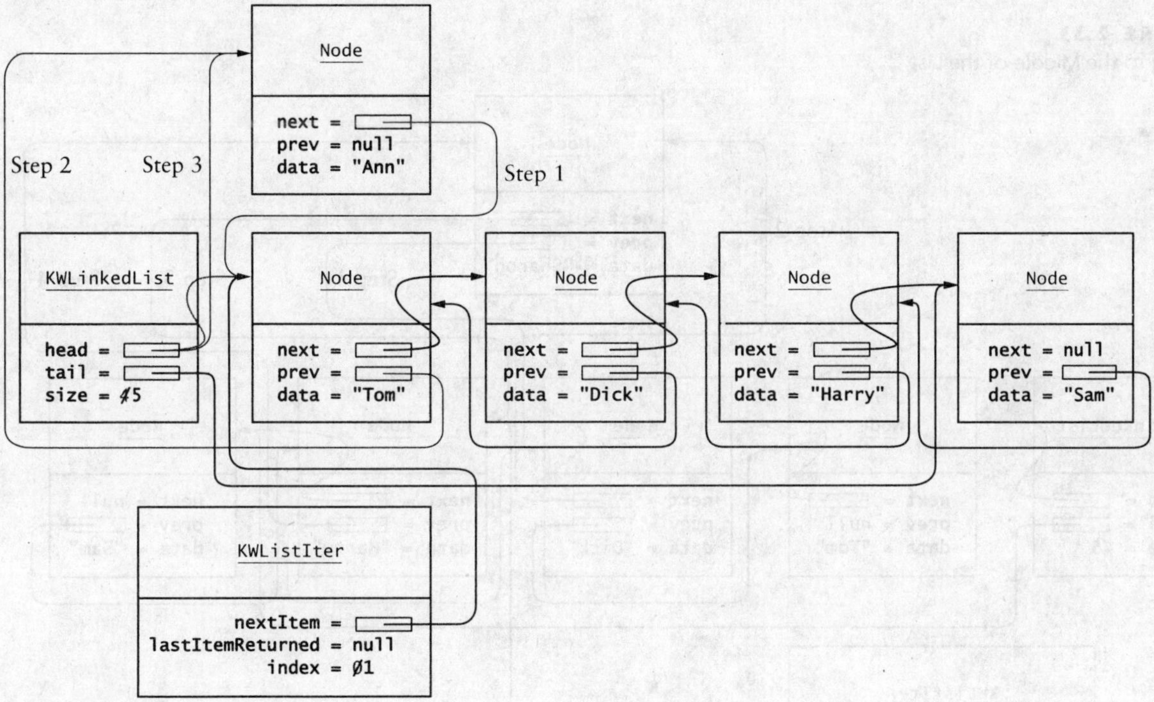

FIGURE 2.32
Adding to the Tail of the List

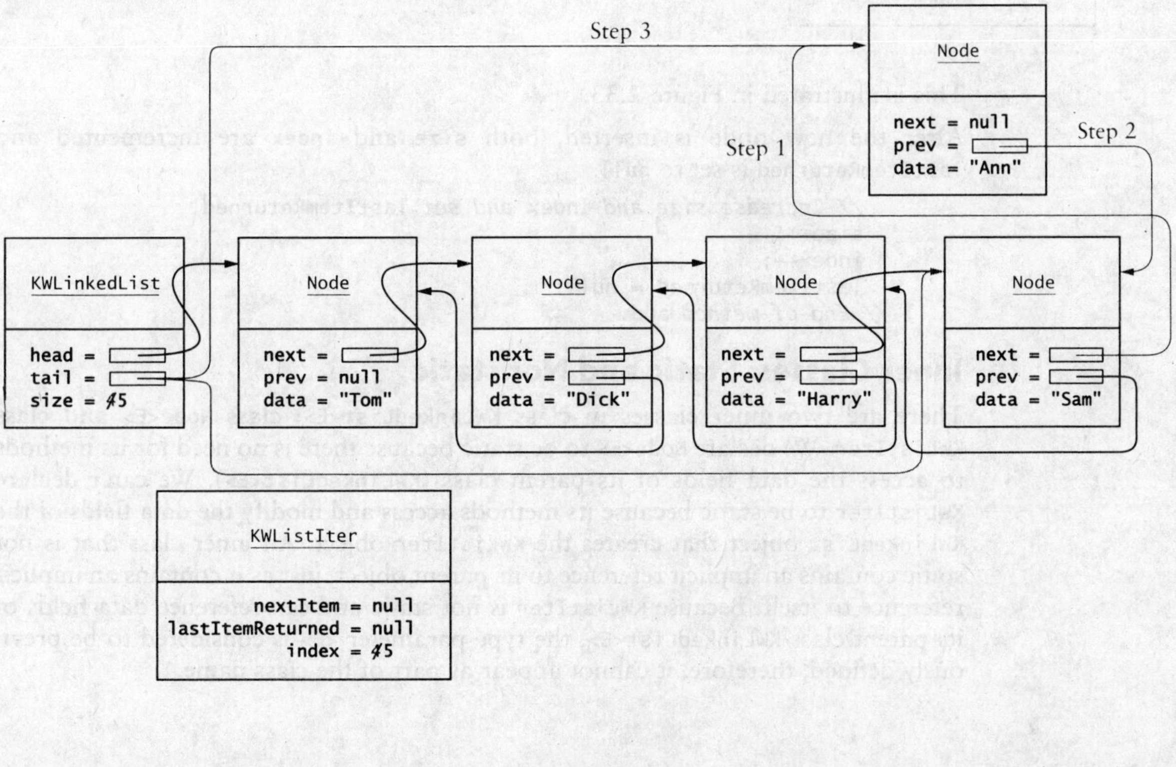

FIGURE 2.33
Adding to the Middle of the List

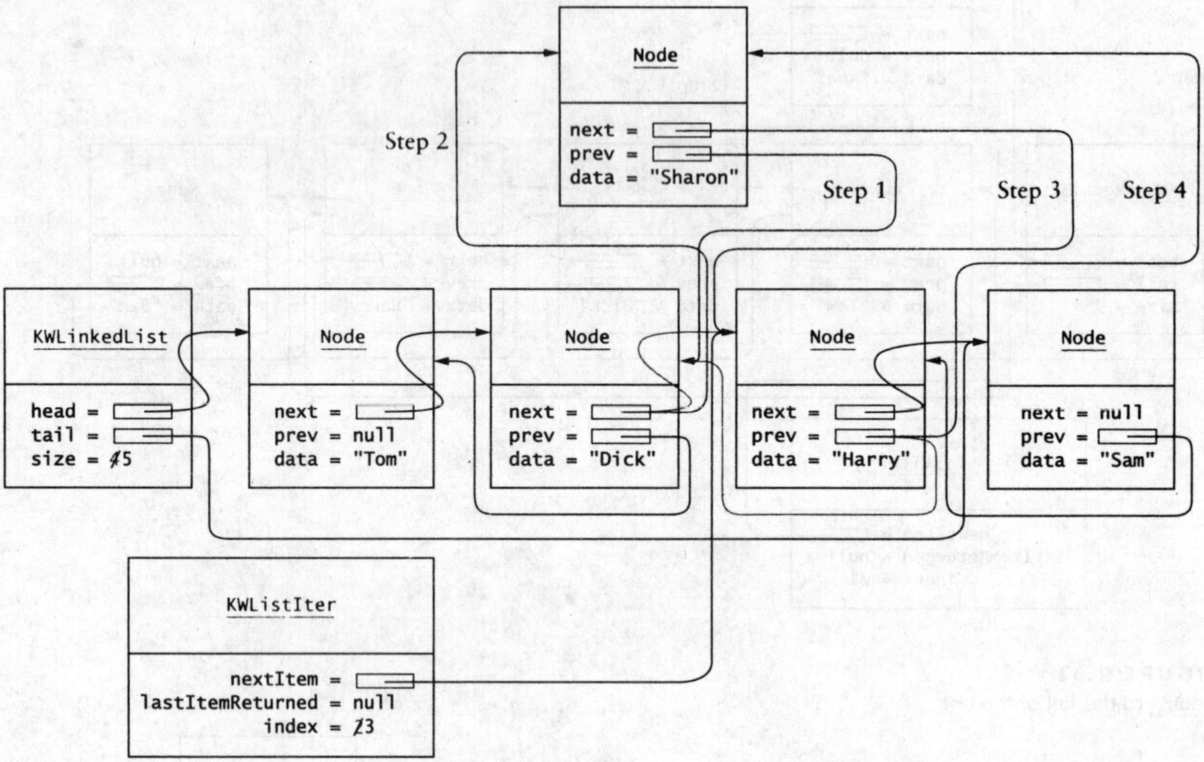

This is illustrated in Figure 2.33.

After the new node is inserted, both `size` and `index` are incremented and `lastItemReturned` is set to `null`.

```
        // Increase size and index and set lastItemReturned.
        size++;
        index++;
        lastItemReturned = null;
    } // End of method add.
```

Inner Classes: Static and Nonstatic

There are two inner classes in class `KWLinkedList<E>`: class `Node<E>` and class `KWListIter`. We declare `Node<E>` to be static because there is no need for its methods to access the data fields of its parent class (`KWLinkedList<E>`). We can't declare `KWListIter` to be static because its methods access and modify the data fields of the `KWLinkedList` object that creates the `KWListIter` object. An inner class that is not static contains an implicit reference to its parent object, just as it contains an implicit reference to itself. Because `KWListIter` is not static and can reference data fields of its parent class `KWLinkedList<E>`, the type parameter `<E>` is considered to be previously defined; therefore, it cannot appear as part of the class name.

PITFALL

Defining KWListIter as a Generic Inner Class

If you define class KWListIter as

`private class KWListIter<E>...`

you will get an `incompatible types` syntax error when you attempt to reference data field `head` or `tail` (type `Node<E>`) inside class `KWListIter`.

EXERCISES FOR SECTION 2.8

SELF-CHECK

1. Why didn't we write the `hasPrevious` method as follows?
```
public boolean hasPrevious() {
    return nextItem.prev != null
        || (nextItem == null && size != 0);
}
```
2. Why must we call `next` or `previous` before we call `remove`?
3. What happens if we call `remove` after we call `add`? What does the Java API documentation say? What does our implementation do?

PROGRAMMING

1. Implement the `KWListIter.remove` method.
2. Implement the `KWListIter.set` method.
3. Implement the `KWLinkedList listIterator` and `iterator` methods.
4. Implement the `KWLinkedList addFirst`, `addLast`, `getFirst`, and `getLast` methods.

2.9 The Collections Framework Design

The Collection Interface

The `Collection` interface specifies a subset of the methods specified in the `List` interface. Specifically, the `add(int, E)`, `get(int)`, `remove(int)`, `set(int, E)`, and related methods (all of which have an `int` parameter that represents a position) are not in the `Collection` interface, but the `add(E)` method and `remove(Object)` methods, which do not specify a position, are included. The `iterator` method is also included in the `Collection` interface. Thus, you can use an `Iterator` to access all of the items in a `Collection`, but the order in which they are retrieved is not necessarily related to the order in which they were inserted.

The `Collection` interface is part of the Collections Framework as shown in Figure 2.34. This interface has three subinterfaces: the `List` interface, the `Queue` interface (Chapter 4), and the `Set` interface (Chapter 7). The Java API does not provide any direct implementation of the `Collection` interface. The interface is used to reference collections of data in the most general way.

Common Features of Collections

Because it is the superinterface of `List`, `Queue`, and `Set`, the `Collection` interface specifies a set of common methods. If you look at the documentation for the Java API `java.util.Collection`, you will see that this is a fairly large set of methods and other requirements. A few features can be considered fundamental:

- Collections grow as needed.
- Collections hold references to objects.
- Collections have at least two constructors: one to create an empty collection and one to make a copy of another collection.

FIGURE 2.34
The Collections Framework

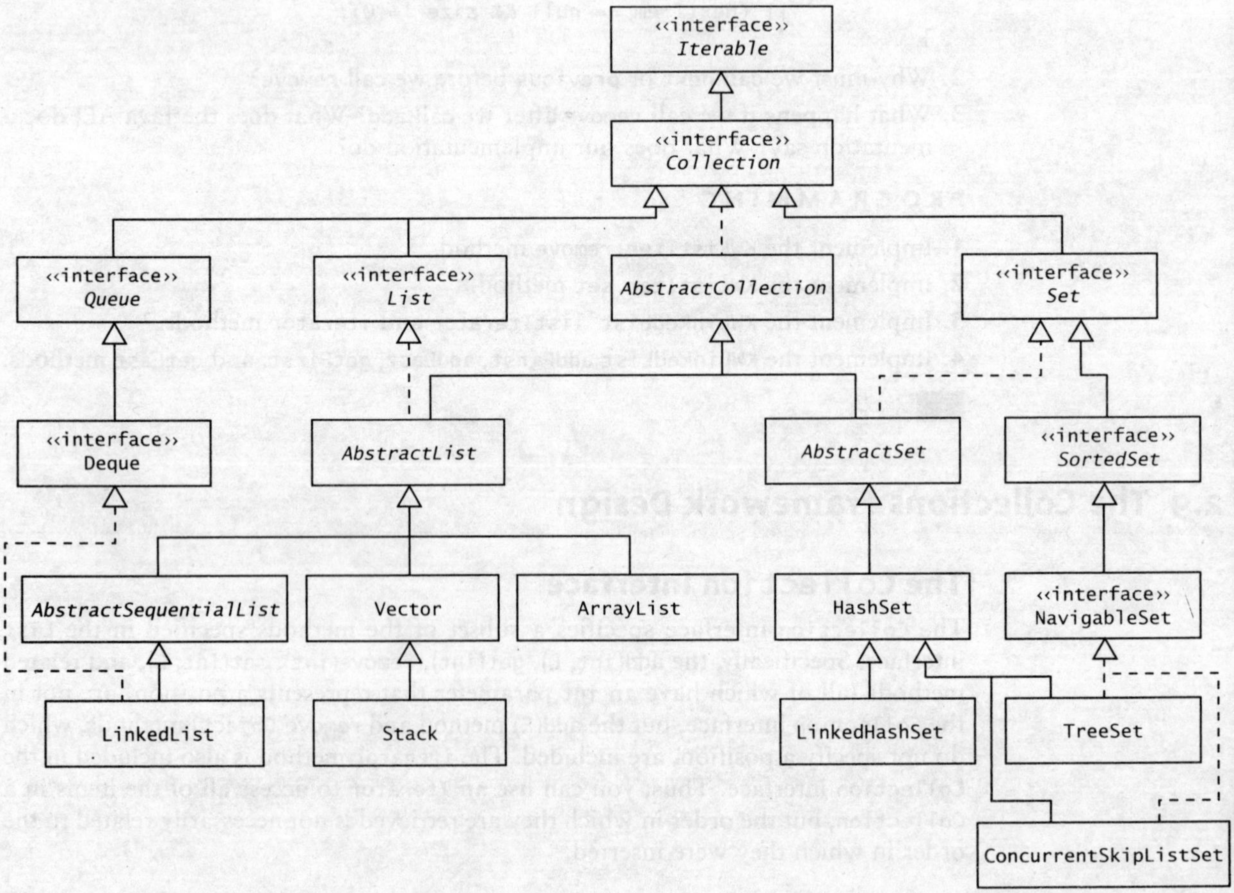

TABLE 2.12
Selected Methods of the `java.util.Collection<E>` Interface

Method	Behavior
`boolean add(E obj)`	Ensures that the collection contains the object `obj`. Returns `true` if the collection was modified.
`boolean contains(E obj)`	Returns `true` if the collection contains the object `obj`.
`Iterator<E> iterator()`	Returns an `Iterator` to the collection.
`int size()`	Returns the size of the collection.

Table 2.12 shows selected methods defined in the `Collection` interface. We have already seen and described these methods in the discussions of the `ArrayList` and `LinkedList`. The `Iterator` provides a common way to access all of the elements in a `Collection`. For collections implementing the `List` interface, the order of the elements is determined by the index of the elements. In the more general `Collection`, the order is not specified.

In the `ArrayList` and `LinkedList`, the `add(E)` method always inserts the object at the end and always returns `true`. In the more general `Collection`, the position where the object is inserted is not specified. The `Set` interface extends the `Collection` by requiring that the `add` method not insert an object that is already present; instead, in that case it returns `false`. The `Set` interface is discussed in Chapter 7.

The AbstractCollection, AbstractList, and AbstractSequentialList Classes

If you look at the Java API documentation, you will see that the `Collection` and `List` interfaces specify a large number of methods. To help implement these interfaces, the Java API includes the `AbstractCollection` and `AbstractList` classes. You can think of these classes as a kit (or as a cake mix) that can be used to build implementations of their corresponding interface. Most of the methods are provided, but you need to add a few to make it complete.

To implement the `Collection` interface completely, you need only extend the `AbstractCollection` class, provide an implementation of the `add`, `size`, and `iterator` methods, and supply an inner class to implement the `Iterator` interface. To implement the `List` interface, you can extend the `AbstractList` class and provide an implementation of the `add(int,E)`, `get(int)`, `remove(int)`, `set(int, E)`, and `size()` methods. Since we provided these methods in our `KWArrayList`, we can make it a complete implementation of the `List` interface by changing the class declaration to

```
public class KWArrayList<E> extends AbstractList<E>
                            implements List<E>
```

Note that the `AbstractList` class implements the `iterator` and `listIterator` methods using the index associated with the elements.

Another way to implement the `List` interface is to extend the `AbstractSequentialList` class, implement the `listIterator` and `size` methods, and provide an inner class that implements the `ListIterator` interface. This was the approach we took in our `KWLinkedList`. Thus, by changing the class declaration to

```
public class KWLinkedList<E> extends AbstractSequentialList<E>
                              implements List<E>
```

it becomes a complete implementation of the `List` interface. Our `KWLinkedList` class included the `add`, `get`, `remove`, and `set` methods. These are provided by the `AbstractSequentialList`, so we could remove them from our `KWLinkedList` class and still have a complete `List` implementation.

The List and RandomAccess Interfaces (Advanced)

The `ArrayList` and the `LinkedList` implement the `List` interface that we described in Section 2.1. Both the `ArrayList` and `LinkedList` represent a collection of objects that can be referenced using an index. This may not be the best design because accessing elements of a `LinkedList` using an index requires an O(n) traversal of the list until the item selected by the index is located. Unfortunately, the Java designers cannot easily change the design of the API since a lot of programs have been written and the users of Java do not want to go back and change their code. Also, there are other implementations of the `List` interface in which the indexed operations `get` and `set` are approximately O(n) instead of O(1).

The `RandomAccess` interface is applied only to those implementations in which indexed operations are efficient (e.g., `ArrayList`). An algorithm can then test to see if a parameter of type `List` is also of type `RandomAccess` and, if not, copy its contents into an `ArrayList` temporarily so that the indexed operations can proceed more efficiently. After the indexed operations are completed, the contents of the `ArrayList` are copied back to the original.

EXERCISES FOR SECTION 2.9

SELF-CHECK

1. Look at the `AbstractCollection` definition in the Java API documentation. What methods are abstract? Could we use the `KWArrayList` and extend the `AbstractCollection`, but not the `AbstractList`, to develop an implementation of the `Collection` interface? How about using the `KWLinkedList` and the `AbstractCollection`, but not the `AbstractSequentialList`?

PROGRAMMING

1. Using either the `KWArrayList` or the `KWLinkedList` as the base, develop an implementation of the `Collection` interface by extending the `AbstractCollection`. Test it by ensuring that the following statements compile:

```
Collection<String> testCollection = new KWArrayList<String>();
Collection<String> testCollection = new KWLinkedList<String>();
```

2.10 Application of the LinkedList Class

In this section, we introduce a case study that uses the Java LinkedList<E> class to solve a common problem: maintaining an ordered list. We will develop an OrderedList class. In Section 2.11, we write a class that tests it and discuss testing in general.

CASE STUDY Maintaining an Ordered List

Problem As discussed in Section 2.5, we can use a linked list to maintain a list of students who are registered for a course. We want to maintain this list so that it will be in alphabetical order even after students have added and dropped the course.

Analysis Instead of solving this problem just for a list of students, we will develop a generic OrderedList class that can be used to store any group of objects that can be compared. Java classes whose object types can be compared implement the Comparable interface, which is defined as follows:

```
/** Instances of classes that realize this interface can be compared.
*/
public interface Comparable<E> {
    /** Method to compare this object to the argument object.
        @param obj The argument object
        @return Returns a negative integer if this object < obj;
                zero if this object equals obj;
                a positive integer if this object > obj
    */
    int compareTo(E obj);
}
```

Therefore, a class that implements the Comparable interface must provide a compareTo method that returns an int value that indicates the relative ordering of two instances of that class. The result is negative if this object < argument; zero if this object equals argument; positive if this object > argument.

We can either extend the Java LinkedList class to create a new class OrderedList, or create an OrderedList class that uses a LinkedList to store the items. If we implement our OrderedList class as an extension of LinkedList, a client will be able to use methods in the List interface that can insert new elements or modify existing elements in such a way that the items are no longer in order. Therefore, we will use the LinkedList class as a component of the OrderedList class, and we will implement only those methods that preserve the order of the items.

Design The class diagram in Figure 2.35 shows the relationships among the `OrderedList` class, the `LinkedList` class, and the `Comparable` interface. The filled diamond indicates that the `LinkedList` is a component of the `OrderedList`, and the open diamond indicates that the `LinkedList` will contain `Comparable` objects. We explain the meaning of the text `E extends Comparable<E>` shortly.

FIGURE 2.35
`OrderedList` Class Diagram

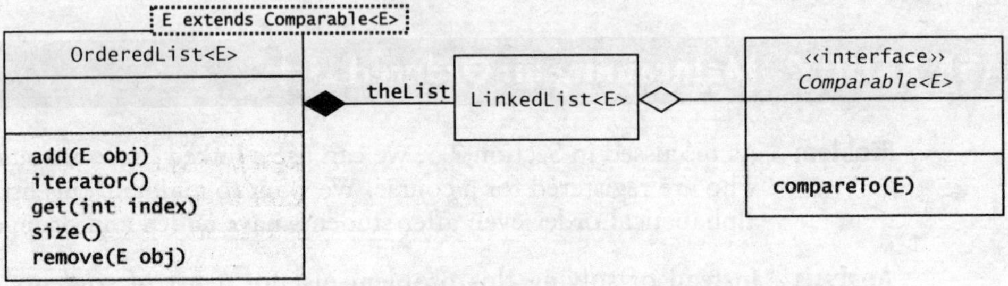

Because we want to be able to make insertions and deletions in the ordered linked list, we must implement `add` and `remove` methods. We also provide a `get` method, to access the element at a particular position, and an `iterator` method, to provide the user with the ability to access all of the elements in sequence efficiently. Table 2.13 describes the class. Although not shown in Figure 2.35, class `OrderedList<E>` implements `Iterable<E>` because it has an `iterator` method. Following is the start of its definition.

```
import java.util.*;

/** A class to represent an ordered list. The data is stored in
    a linked list data field.
*/
```

TABLE 2.13
Class `OrderedList<E extends Comparable<E>>`

Data Field	Attribute
`private LinkedList<E> theList`	A linked list to contain the data.
Method	**Behavior**
`public void add(E obj)`	Inserts `obj` into the list preserving the list's order.
`public Iterator iterator()`	Returns an `Iterator` to the list.
`public E get(int index)`	Returns the object at the specified position.
`public int size()`	Returns the size of the list.
`public E remove(E obj)`	Removes first occurrence of `obj` from the list.

```
public class OrderedList<E extends Comparable<E>>
        implements Iterable<E> {
    /** A linked list to contain the data. */
    private LinkedList<E> theList = new LinkedList<E>();
```

Because we want our ordered list to contain only objects that implement the `Comparable` interface, we need to tell the compiler that only classes that meet this criterion should be bound to the type parameter `E`. We do this by declaring our ordered list as `OrderedList<E extends Comparable<E>>`.

SYNTAX Specifying Requirements on Generic Types

FORM:

`class ClassName<TypeParameter extends ClassOrInterfaceName<TypeParameter>>`

EXAMPLE:

`class OrderedList<E extends Comparable<E>>`

MEANING:

When we declare actual objects of type *ClassName<TypeParameter>*, class *TypeParameter* must extend class *ClassOrInterfaceName* or implement interface *ClassOrInterfaceName*.

Implementation Let's say we have an ordered list that contains the data: "Alice", "Andrew", "Caryn", "Sharon" and we want to insert "Bill" (see Figure 2.36). If we start at the beginning of the list and access "Alice", we know that "Bill" must follow "Alice", but we can't insert "Bill" yet. If we access "Andrew", we know that "Bill" must follow "Andrew", but we can't insert "Bill" yet. However, when we access "Caryn", we know we must insert "Bill" before "Caryn". Therefore, to insert an element in an ordered list, we need to access the first element whose data is larger than the data in the element to be inserted. Once we have accessed the successor of our new node,

FIGURE 2.36
Inserting "Bill" before "Caryn" in an Ordered List

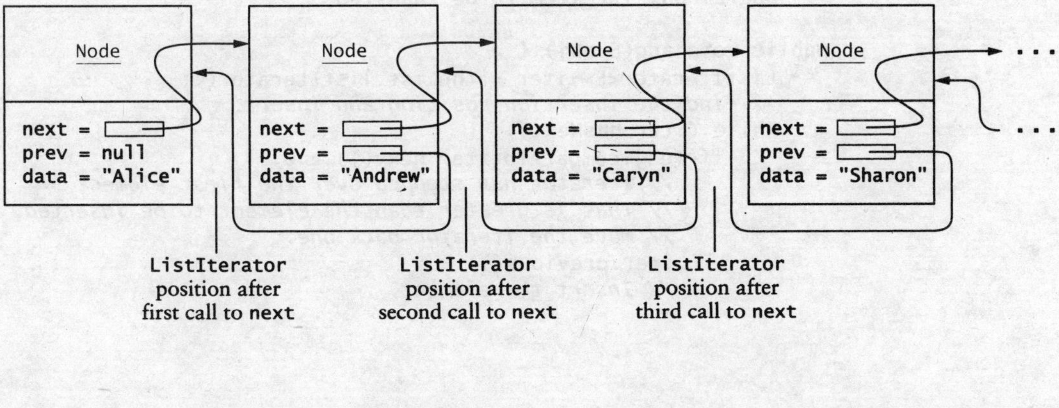

we can insert a new node just before it. (Note that in order to access "Caryn" using method next, we have advanced the iterator just past "Caryn".)

Algorithm for Insertion

The algorithm for insertion is

1. Find the first item in the list that is greater than the item to be inserted.
2. Insert the new item before this one.

We can refine this algorithm as follows:

1.1 Create a ListIterator that starts at the beginning of the list.
1.2 while the ListIterator is not at the end and the item to be inserted is greater than or equal to the next item
1.3 Advance the ListIterator.
2. Insert the new item before the current ListIterator position.

The add Method

A straightforward coding of the insertion algorithm would be the following:

```
// WARNING - THIS DOES NOT WORK.
ListIterator<E> iter = theList.listIterator();
while (iter.hasNext()
        && obj.compareTo(iter.next()) >= 0) {
    // iter was advanced - check new position.
}
iter.add(obj);
```

Unfortunately, this does not work. When the while loop terminates, either we are at the end of the list or the ListIterator has just skipped over the first item that is greater than the item to be inserted (see Figure 2.37). In the first case, the add method will insert the item at the end of the list, just as we want, but in the second case, it will insert the item just after the position where it belongs. Therefore, we must separate the two cases and code the add method as follows:

```
/** Insert obj into the list preserving the list's order.
    pre: The items in the list are ordered.
    post: obj has been inserted into the list
          such that the items are still in order.
    @param obj The item to be inserted
*/
public void add(E obj) {
    ListIterator<E> iter = theList.listIterator();
    // Find the insertion position and insert.
    while (iter.hasNext()) {
        if (obj.compareTo(iter.next()) < 0) {
            // Iterator has stepped over the first element
            // that is greater than the element to be inserted.
            // Move the iterator back one.
            iter.previous();
            // Insert the element.
```

FIGURE 2.37
Attempted Insertion into an Ordered List

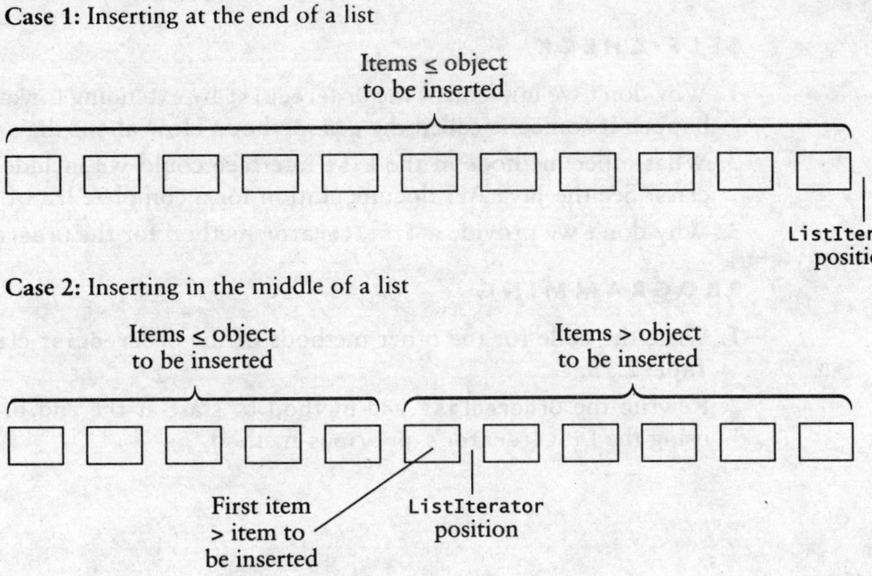


```
                iter.add(obj);
                // Exit the loop and return.
                return;
            }
        }
        // assert: All items were examined and no item is larger than
        // the element to be inserted.
        // Add the new item to the end of the list.
        iter.add(obj);
    }
```

Using Delegation to Implement the Other Methods

The other methods in Table 2.13 are implemented via delegation to the `LinkedList` class. They merely call the corresponding method in the `LinkedList`. For example, the `get` and `iterator` methods are coded as follows:

```
/** Returns the element at the specified position.
    @param index The specified position
    @return The element at position index
*/
public E get(int index) {
    return theList.get(index);
}

/** Returns an iterator to this OrderedList.
    @return The iterator, positioning it before the first element
*/
public Iterator<E> iterator() {
    return theList.iterator();
}
```

EXERCISES FOR SECTION 2.10

SELF-CHECK

1. Why don't we implement the `OrderedList` by extending `LinkedList`? What would happen if someone called the `add` method? How about the `set` method?
2. What other methods in the `List` interface could we include in the `OrderedList` class? See the Java API documentation for a complete list of methods.
3. Why don't we provide a `listIterator` method for the `OrderedList` class?

PROGRAMMING

1. Write the code for the other methods of the `OrderedList` class that are listed in Table 2.13.
2. Rewrite the `OrderedList.add` method to start at the end of the list and iterate using the `ListIterator`'s `previous` method.

2.11 Testing

Testing is the process of exercising a program (or part of a program) under controlled conditions and verifying that the results are as expected. The purpose of testing is to detect program defects after all syntax errrors have been removed and the program compiles successfully. The more thorough the testing, the greater the likelihood that the defects will be found. However, no amount of testing can guarantee the absence of defects in sufficiently complex programs. The number of test cases required to test all possible inputs and states that each method may execute in can quickly become prohibitively large. That is often why commercial software products have different versions or patches that the user must install. Version n usually corrects the errors that were still present in version $n - 1$.

Testing is generally done at the following levels:

- Unit testing refers to testing the smallest testable piece of the software. In object-oriented design (OOD), the unit will be either a method or a class. The complexity of a method determines whether it should be tested as a separate unit or whether it can be tested as part of its class.
- Integration testing involves testing the interactions among units. If the unit is the method, then integration testing includes testing interactions among methods within a class. However, generally it involves testing interactions among several classes.
- System testing is the testing of the whole program in the context in which it will be used. A program is generally part of a collection of other programs and hardware, called a *system*. Sometimes a program will work correctly until some other software is loaded onto the system, and then it will fail for no apparent reason.

- Acceptance testing is system testing designed to show that the program meets its functional requirements. It generally involves use of the system in the real environment or as close to the real environment as possible.

There are two types of testing:

- *Black-box testing* tests the item (method, class, or program) based on its interfaces and functional requirements. This is also called closed-box testing or functional testing. For testing a method, the input parameters are varied over their allowed range and the results compared against independently calculated results. In addition, values outside the allowed range are tested to ensure that the method responds as specified (e.g., throws an exception or computes a nominal value). Also, the inputs to a method are not only the parameters of the method, but also the values of the data fields and global variables that the method accesses.
- *White-box testing* tests the software element (method, class, or program) with the knowledge of its internal structure. Other terms used for this type of testing are glass-box testing, open-box testing, and coverage testing. The goal is to exercise as many paths through the element as possible or practical. There are various degrees of coverage. The simplest is statement coverage, which ensures that each statement is executed at least once. Branch coverage ensures that each choice of each branch (`if` statements, `switch` statements, and loops) is taken. For example, if there are only `if` statements, and they are not nested, then each `if` statement is tried with its condition true and with its condition false. This could possibly be done with two test cases: one with all of the `if` conditions true and one with them all false. Path coverage tests each path through a method. If there are n `if` statements, path coverage could require 2^n test cases if the `if` statements are not nested (each condition has two possible values, so there could be 2^n possible paths).

EXAMPLE 2.15 Method `testMethod` has a nested `if` statement and displays one of four messages, `path 1` through `path 4`, depending on which path is followed. The values passed to its arguments determine the path.

```
public void testMethod(char a, char b) {
    if (a < 'M') {
        if (b < 'X') {
            System.out.println("path 1");
        } else {
            System.out.println("path 2");
        }
    } else {
        if (b < 'C') {
            System.out.println("path 3");
        } else {
            System.out.println("path 4");
        }
    }
}
```

TABLE 2.14
Testing All Paths of `testMethod`

a	b	Message
'A'	'A'	path 1
'A'	'Z'	path 2
'Z'	'A'	path 3
'Z'	'Z'	path 4

To test this method, we need to pass it values for its arguments that cause it to follow the different paths. Table 2.14 shows some possible values and the corresponding path.

The values chosen for `a` and `b` in Table 2.14 are the smallest and largest uppercase letters. For a more thorough test, you should see what happens when `a` and `b` are passed values that are between A and Z. For example, what happens if the value of `a` changes from L to M? We pick those values because the condition `(a < 'M')` has different values for each of them.

Also, what happens when `a` and `b` are not uppercase letters? For example, if `a` and `b` are both digit characters (e.g., `'2'`), the `path 1` message should be displayed because the digit characters precede the uppercase letters (see Appendix A, Table A.2). If `a` and `b` are both lowercase letters, the `path 4` message should be displayed (Why?). If `a` is a digit and `b` is a lowercase letter, the `path 2` message should be displayed (Why?). As you can see, the number of test cases required to test even a simple method like `testMethod` thoroughly can become quite large.

Preparations for Testing

Although testing is usually done after each unit of the software is coded, a test plan should be developed early in the design stage. Some aspects of a test plan include deciding how the software will be tested, when the tests will occur, who will do the testing, and what test data will be used. If the test plan is developed early in the design stage, testing can take place concurrently with the design and coding. Again, the earlier an error is detected, the easier and less expensive it is to correct it.

Another advantage of deciding on the test plan early is that this will encourage programmers to prepare for testing as they write their code. A good programmer will practice defensive programming and include code that detects unexpected or invalid data values. For example, if the parameter *n* for a method is required to be greater than zero, you can place the `if` statement

```
if (n <= 0)
    throw new IllegalArgumentException("n <= 0: " + n);
```

at the beginning of the method. This `if` statement will provide a diagnostic message in the event that the parameter passed to the method is invalid.

Testing Tips for Program Systems

Most of the time, you will be testing program systems that contain collections of classes, each with several methods. Next, we provide a list of testing tips to follow in writing these methods.

1. Carefully document each method parameter and class attribute using comments as you write the code. Also describe the method operation using comments, following the Javadoc conventions discussed in Section 1.1.
2. Leave a trace of execution by displaying the method name as you enter it.
3. Display the values of all input parameters upon entry to a method. Also display the values of any class attributes that are accessed by this method. Check that these values make sense.
4. Display the values of all method outputs after returning from a method. Also, display any class attributes that are modified by this method. Verify that these values are correct by hand computation.

You should plan for testing as you write each module rather than after the fact. Include the output statements required for Steps 2 and 3 in the original Java code for the method. When you are satisfied that the method works as desired, you can "remove" the testing statements. One efficient way to remove them is to enclose them in an `if (TESTING)` block as follows:

```
if (TESTING) {
    // Code that you wish to "remove"
    . . .
}
```

You would then define `TESTING` at the beginning of the class as `true` to enable testing,

```
private static final boolean TESTING = true;
```

or as `false` to disable testing,

```
private static final boolean TESTING = false;
```

If you need to, you can define different `boolean` flags for different kinds of tests.

Developing the Test Data

The test data may be specified during the analysis and design phases. This should be done for the different levels of testing: unit, integration, and system. In black-box testing, we are concerned with the relationship between the unit inputs and outputs. There should be test data to check for all expected inputs as well as unanticipated data. The test plan should also specify the expected unit behavior and outputs for each set of input data.

In white-box testing, we are concerned with exercising alternative paths through the code. Thus the test data should be designed to ensure that all `if` statement conditions will evaluate to both `true` and `false`. For nested `if` statements, test different combinations of `true` and `false` values. For `switch` statements, make sure that the selector variable can take on all values listed as case labels and some that are not.

For loops, verify that the result is correct if an immediate exit occurs (zero repetitions). Also verify that the result is correct if only one iteration is performed and if the maximum number of iterations is performed. Finally, verify that loop repetition can always terminate.

Testing Boundary Conditions

When hand-tracing through an algorithm or performing white-box testing, you must exercise all paths through the algorithm. It is also important to check special cases called boundary conditions to make sure that the algorithm works for these cases as well as the more common ones. For example, if you are testing a method that searches for a particular target element in an array `x`, the code may contain a search loop such as

```
for (int i = 0; i < x.length; i++) {
    if (x[i] == target)
        return i;
}
```

Testing the boundary conditions means that you should make sure that the method works for all the cases in the following list. The first four cases test the boundary conditions for the loop and would be required in white-box testing. However, a program tester using black-box testing should also test these four cases. The next case (`target` in the middle) is not a boundary case, but it is a typical situation that should also be tested. The rest are boundary conditions for an array search that should be tested in either white-box or black-box testing.

- The target element is the first array element (`x[0] == target is true`).
- The target element is only in the last array element (`x[x.length - 1] == target is true`).
- The target element is not in the array (`x[i] == target` is always `false`).
- There are multiple occurrences of the target element (`x[i] == target is true` for more than one value of `i`).
- The target element is somewhere in the middle of the array.
- The array has only one element.
- The array has no elements.

To carry out the test, you can write a `main` method that creates an array to be searched. The easiest way to create such an array is to declare it using an initializer list. Listing 2.2 shows a `main` method that tests all the listed cases for an array search method. In method `search`, the array to be searched is the first parameter, and the target of the search is the second parameter.

The method `verify` is passed the array to be searched, the target value, and the expected return value. It calls the `search` method and then prints the actual and expected results.

```
int actual = search(x, target);
System.out.print("search(x, " + target + ") is "
                 + actual + ", expected " + expected);
```

It then prints either `": Pass"` or `": ****Fail"` depending on whether or not the expected value is equal to the actual value.

```
if (actual == expected)
    System.out.println (": Pass");
else
    System.out.println(": ****Fail");
```

There are calls to `verify` for each one of the test cases in the list. For example, the first call,

```
verify(x, 5, 0);
```

searches array `x` for a target 5, which is at `x[0]`. The expected result (the third argument) is therefore 0. The line displayed should be:

```
search(x, 5) is 0, expected 0: Pass
```

Figure 2.38 shows the result of a sample run. To verify that method `search` is correct, check for `Pass` at the end of each output line. For large-scale testing, you could write a program to do this.

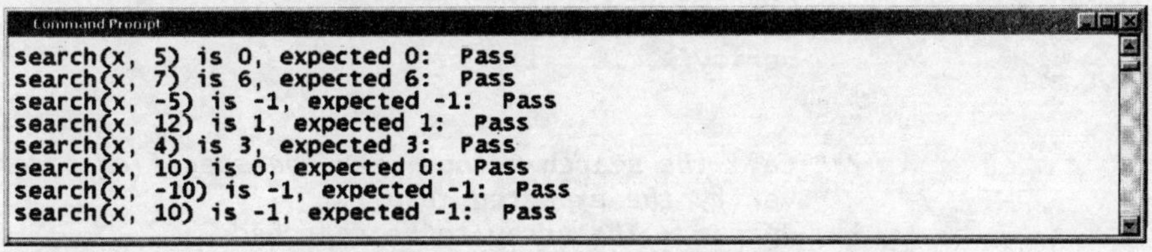

FIGURE 2.38
Testing Method `search`

LISTING 2.2
`ArraySearch.java`

```
/** Provides a static method search for searching an array. */
public class ArraySearch {

    /** Searches an array to find the first occurrence of a target.
        @param x Array to search
        @param target Target to search for
        @return The subscript of first occurrence if found;
                otherwise, return -1.
    */
    public static int search(int[] x, int target) {
        for (int i = 0; i < x.length; i++) {
            if (x[i] == target)
                return i;
        }

        // target not found
        return -1;
    }

    /** Test method.
        @param args Command line arguments. Not used.
    */
```

```
public static void main(String[] args) {
    int[] x = {5, 12, 15, 4, 8, 12, 7}; // Array to search.

    // Test for target as first element.
    verify(x, 5, 0);
    // Test for target as last element.
    verify(x, 7, 6);
    // Test for target not in array.
    verify(x, -5, -1);
    // Test for multiple occurrences of target.
    verify(x, 12, 1);
    // Test for target somewhere in middle.
    verify(x, 4, 3);

    // Test for 1-element array.
    x = new int[1];
    x[0] = 10;
    verify(x, 10, 0);
    verify(x, -10, -1);

    // Test for an empty array.
    x = new int[0];
    verify(x, 10, -1);
}

/** Call the search method with the specified parameters and
    verify the expected result.
    @param x The array to be searched
    @param target The target to be found
    @param expected The expected result
*/
private static void verify(int[] x, int target, int expected) {
    int actual = search(x, target);
    System.out.print("search(x, " + target + ") is "
                     + actual + ", expected " + expected);
    if (actual == expected)
        System.out.println(":  Pass");
    else
        System.out.println(": ****Fail");
}
}
```

Stubs

Although we want to do unit testing as soon as possible, it may be difficult to test a method or a class that interacts with other methods or classes. The problem is that not all methods and not all classes will be completed at the same time. So if a method in class A calls a method defined in class B (not yet written), the unit test for class A can't be performed without the help of a replacement method for the one in class B. The replacement for a method that has not yet been implemented or tested is called a stub. A stub has the same header as the method it replaces, but its body only displays a message indicating that the stub was called.

EXAMPLE 2.16 The following method is a stub for a void method save. The stub will enable a method that calls save to be tested even though the real method save has not been written.

```
/** Stub for method save.
    pre:  the initial directory contents are read from a data file.
    post: Writes the directory contents back to a data file.
          The flag modified is reset to false.
*/
public void save() {
    System.out.println("Stub for save has been called");
    modified = false;
}
```

Besides displaying an identification message, a stub can print out the values of the inputs and can assign predictable values (e.g., 0 or 1) to any outputs to prevent execution errors caused by undefined values. Also, if a method is supposed to change the state of a data field, the stub can do so (modified is set to false by the stub just shown). If a client program calls one or more stubs, the message printed by each stub when it is executed provides a trace of the call sequence and enables the programmer to determine whether the flow of control within the client program is correct.

Preconditions and Postconditions

In the comment for method save, the lines

```
pre:  the initial directory contents are read from a data file.
post: Writes the directory contents back to a data file.
      The flag modified is reset to false.
```

show the precondition (following *pre:*) and postcondition (following *post:*) for method save. A *precondition* is a statement of any assumptions or constraints on the method data (input parameters) before the method begins execution. A *postcondition* describes the result of executing the method. A method's preconditions and postconditions serve as a contract between a method caller and the method programmer—if a caller satisfies the precondition, the method result will satisfy the postcondition. If the precondition is not satisfied, there is no guarantee that the method will do what is expected, and it may even fail. The preconditions and postconditions allow both a method user and a method implementer to proceed without further coordination.

We will use postconditions to describe the change in object state caused by executing a mutator method. As a general rule, you should write a postcondition comment for all void methods. If a method returns a value, you do not usually need a postcondition comment because the @return comment describes the effect of executing the method.

Drivers

Another testing tool for a method is a driver program. A driver program declares any necessary object instances and variables, assigns values to any of the method's inputs (as specified in the method's preconditions), calls the method, and displays the values of any outputs returned by the method. Since each class can have a main method, you can put a `main` method in a class to serve as the test driver for that class's methods. When you run a Java program, execution begins at the `main` method in the class you designate as the one to execute; any other `main` methods are ignored. The `main` method shown in Listing 2.2 is a driver program to test method `search`.

Using JUnit and Debuggers

Appendix C describes how to use a popular program for Java projects called JUnit to help you develop testing methods. The appendix also discusses finding and correcting errors using a debugger program.

Testing Class `OrderedList`

Next, we illustrate the design of a class that tests our implementation of the `OrderedList` in Section 2.10.

CASE STUDY Maintaining an Ordered List (continued)

Testing You can test the `OrderedList` class by storing a collection of randomly generated positive integers in an `OrderedList`. You can then insert a negative integer and an integer larger than any integer in the list. This tests the two special cases of inserting at the beginning and at the end of the list. You can then create an iterator and use it to traverse the list, displaying an error message if the current integer is smaller than the previous integer, which is an indication that the list is not ordered. You can also display the list during the traversal so that you can inspect it to verify that it is in order. Finally, you can remove the first element, the last element, and an element in the middle and repeat the traversal to show that removal does not affect the ordering. Listing 2.3 shows a class with methods that performs these tests.

Method `traverseAndShow` traverses an ordered list passed as an argument using an enhanced **`for`** statement to access the list elements. Each `Integer` is stored in `thisItem`. The **`if`** statement displays an error message if the previous value is greater than the current value (`prevItem > thisItem is true`). Method `main` calls `traverseAndShow` after all elements are inserted and after the three elements are removed. In method `main`, the loop

```
for (int i = 0; i < START_SIZE; i++) {
    int anInteger = random.nextInt(MAX_INT);
    testList.add(anInteger);
}
```

fills the ordered list with randomly generated values between `0` and `MAX_INT - 1`. Variable `random` is an instance of class `Random` (in API `java.util`), which contains methods for generating pseudorandom numbers. Method `Random.nextInt` generates random integers between 0 and its argument.

LISTING 2.3

Class TestOrderedList

```
import java.util.*;

public class TestOrderedList {
    /** Traverses ordered list and displays each element.
        Displays an error message if an element is out of order.
        @param testList An ordered list of integers
    */
    public static void traverseAndShow(OrderedList<Integer> testList) {
        int prevItem = testList.get(0);

        // Traverse ordered list and display any value that
        // is out of order.
        for (int thisItem : testList) {
            System.out.println(thisItem);
            if (prevItem > thisItem)
                System.out.println("*** FAILED, value is "
                                   + thisItem);
            prevItem = thisItem;
        }
    }

    public static void main(String[] args) {
        OrderedList<Integer> testList = new OrderedList<Integer>();
        final int MAX_INT = 500;
        final int START_SIZE = 100;

        // Create a random number generator.
        Random random = new Random();
        for (int i = 0; i < START_SIZE; i++) {
            int anInteger = random.nextInt(MAX_INT);
            testList.add(anInteger);
        }

        // Add to beginning and end of list.
        testList.add(-1);
        testList.add(MAX_INT + 1);
        traverseAndShow(testList);  // Traverse and display.

        // Remove first, last, and middle elements.
        Integer first = testList.get(0);
        Integer last = testList.get(testList.size() - 1);
        Integer middle = testList.get(testList.size() / 2);
        testList.remove(first);
        testList.remove(last);
        testList.remove(middle);
        traverseAndShow(testList);  // Traverse and display.
    }
}
```

PITFALL

Omitting <E> after ListIterator<E> or Iterable<E>

If you omit <E> in the declaration for `ListIterator<E> iter` in method `add` of `OrderedList`:

```
ListIterator iter = theList.listIterator();
```

you will get a syntax error when the `if` statement

```
if (obj.compareTo(iter.next()) < 0) {
```

is compiled. The reason is that the object returned by `iter.next()` will be type `Object` instead of type `E`, so the argument of `compareTo` will not be type `E` as required.

Similarly, if you omit the <E> after `Iterable` in the header for class `OrderedList`:

```
public class OrderedList<E extends <Comparable<E>>
        implements Iterable {
```

you will get an `incompatible types` syntax error when the enhanced `for` statement

```
for (int thisItem: testList) {
```

in method `TraverseAndShow` is compiled. The reason is that the data type of the object returned by the implicit call to method `next` would be `Object`, not type `Integer` as required.

EXERCISES FOR SECTION 2.11

SELF-CHECK

1. Explain why a method that does not match its declaration in the interface would not be discovered during white-box testing.
2. During which phase of testing would each of the following tests be performed?
   a. Testing whether a method worked properly at all its boundary conditions
   b. Testing whether class `A` can use Class `B` as a component
   c. Testing whether a phone directory application and a word-processing application can run simultaneously on a personal computer
   d. Testing whether method `search` can search an array that was returned by method `buildArray`
   e. Testing whether a class with an array data field can use static method `search` defined in class `ArraySearch`

3. List two boundary conditions that should be checked when testing method `readInt` below.

```
/** Method to return an integer data value.
      @param prompt Message
      @return The data value read as an int
*/
public static int readInt(String prompt) {
    while (true) { // Repeat until valid number is read.
        try {
            String numStr = JOptionPane. showInputDialog (prompt);
            return Integer.parseInt (numStr);
        }
        catch (NumberFormatException ex) {
            JOptionPane.showMessageDialog (null,
                "Bad numeric string - Try again",
                "Error", JOptionPane.ERROR_MESSAGE);
        }
    }
}
```

4. Devise test data to test the method `readInt` using:
   a. white-box testing
   b. black-box testing

PROGRAMMING

1. Writer a driver program to test method `readInt` using the test data derived for Self-Check Exercise 4, part b.
2. Write a stub to use in place of method `readInt`.
3. Write a `search` method with four parameters: the search array, the target, the start subscript, and the finish subscript. The last two parameters indicate the part of the array that should be searched. Your method should catch or throw exceptions where warranted. Write a driver program to test this method.

Chapter Review

- The `List` is a generalization of the array. As in the array, elements of a `List` are accessed by means of an index. Unlike the array, the `List` can grow or shrink. Items may be inserted or removed from any position.
- The Java API provides the `ArrayList<E>` class, which uses an array as the underlying structure to implement the `List`. We provided an example of how this might be implemented by allocating an array that is larger than the number of items in the list. As items are inserted into the list, the items with higher indices are moved up to make room for the inserted item, and as items are removed, the items with higher indices are moved down to fill in the emptied space. When the array capacity is

reached, a new array is allocated that is twice the size and the old array is copied to the new one. By doubling the capacity, the cost of the copy is spread over each insertion, so that the copies can be considered to have a constant time contribution to the cost of each insertion.

- A linked list data structure consists of a set of nodes, each of which contains its data and a reference to the next node in the list. In a double-linked list, each node contains a reference to both the next and the previous node in the list. Insertion into and removal from a linked list is a constant-time operation.

- To access an item at a position indicated by an index in a linked list requires walking along the list from the beginning until the item at the specified index is reached. Thus, traversing a linked list using an index would be an $O(n^2)$ operation because we need to repeat the walk each time the index changes. The `Iterator` provides a general way to traverse a list so that traversing a linked list using an iterator is an $O(n)$ operation.

- An iterator provides us with the ability to access the items in a `List` sequentially. The `Iterator` interface defines the methods available to an iterator. The `List` interface defines the `iterator` method, which returns an `Iterator` to the list. The `Iterator.hasNext` method tells whether there is a next item, and the `Iterator.next` method returns the next item and advances the iterator. The `Iterator` also provides the `remove` method, which lets us remove the last item returned by the `next` method.

- The `ListIterator` interface extends the `Iterator interface`. The `ListIterator` provides us with the ability to traverse the list either forward or backward. In addition to the `hasNext` and `next` methods, the `ListIterator` has the `hasPrevious` and `previous` methods. Also, in addition to the `remove` method, it has an `add` method that inserts a new item into the list just before the current iterator position.

- The `Iterable` interface is implemented by the `Collection` interface. It imposes a requirement that its implementers (all classes that implement the `Collection` interface) provide an `iterator` method that returns an `Iterator` to an instance of that collection class. The enhanced `for` statement makes it easier to iterate through these collections without explicitly manipulating an iterator and also to iterate through an array object without manipulating an array index.

- The Java API provides the `LinkedList` class, which uses a double-linked `list` to implement the `List` interface. We show an example of how this might be implemented. Because the class that realizes the `ListIterator` interface provides the `add` and `remove` operations, the corresponding methods in the linked list class can be implemented by constructing an iterator (using the `listIterator(int)` method) that references the desired position and then calling on the iterator to perform the insertion or removal.

- We use big-O notation to describe the performance of an algorithm. Big-O notation specifies how the performance increases with the number of data items being processed by an algorithm. The best performance is $O(1)$, which means the performance is constant regardless of the number of data items processed.

- Black-box (also called closed-box) testing tests the item (unit or system) based on its functional requirements without using any knowledge of the internal structure.
- White-box (also called glass-box or open-box) testing tests the item using knowledge of its internal structure. One of the goals of white-box testing is to achieve test coverage. This can range from testing every statement at least once to testing each branch condition (`if` statements, `switch` statements, and loops) for each path, to testing each possible path through the program.
- Test drivers and stubs are tools used in testing. A test driver exercises a method or class and drives the testing. A stub stands in for a method that the unit being tested calls. This can be used to provide a test result, and it can be used to enable a caller of that method to be tested when the method being called is not yet coded.
- The `Collection` interface is the root of the `Collections Framework`. The `Collection` is more general than the `List`, because the items in a `Collection` are not indexed. The `add` method inserts an item into a `Collection` but does not specify where it is inserted. The `Iterator` is used to traverse the items in a `Collection`, but it does not specify the order of the items.
- The `Collection` interface and the `List` interface define a large number of methods that make these abstractions useful for many applications. In our discussion of both the `ArrayList` and `LinkedList`, we showed how to implement only a few key methods. The `Collections Framework` includes the `AbstractCollection`, `AbstractList`, and `AbstractSequentialList` classes. These classes implement their corresponding interface except for a few key methods; these are the same methods for which we showed implementations.

Java API Interfaces and Classes Introduced in This Chapter

```
java.util.AbstractCollection
java.util.AbstractList
java.util.AbstractSequentialList
java.util.ArrayList
java.util.Collection
java.util.Iterable
java.util.Iterator
java.util.LinkedList
java.util.List
java.util.ListIterator
java.util.RandomAccess
```

User-Defined Interfaces and Classes in This Chapter

```
KWArrayList
KWLinkedList
KWListIter
Node
OrderedList
SingleLinkedList
```

Quick-Check Exercises

1. Elements of a `List` are accessed by means of ______.
2. A `List` can ______ or ______ as items are added or removed.
3. When we allocate a new array for an `ArrayList` because the current capacity is exceeded, we make the new array at least ______. This allows us to ______.
4. Determine the order of magnitude (big-O) for an algorithm whose running time is given by the equation $T(n) = 3n^4 - 2n^2 + 100n + 37$.
5. In a single-linked list, if we want to remove a list element, which list element do we need to access? If `nodeRef` references this element, what statement removes the desired element?

6. Suppose a single-linked list contains three Nodes with data "him", "her", and "it" and head references the first element. What is the effect of the following fragment?

```
Node<String> nodeRef = head.next;
nodeRef.data = "she";
```

7. Answer Question 5 for the following fragment.

```
Node<String> nodeRef = head.next;
head.next = nodeRef.next;
```

8. Answer Question 5 for the following fragment.

```
head = new Node<String>("his", head);
```

9. An Iterator allows us to access items of a List ______.
10. A ListIterator allows us to access the elements ______.
11. The Java LinkedList class uses a ______ to implement the List interface.
12. ______ testing requires the use of test data that exercise each statement in a module.
13. ______ testing focuses on testing the functional characteristics of a module.
14. The Collection is a ______ of the List.

Review Questions

1. What is the difference between the size and the capacity of an ArrayList? Why might we have a constructor that lets us set the initial capacity?
2. What is the difference between the remove(Object obj) and remove(int index) methods?
3. When we insert an item into an ArrayList, why do we start shifting at the last element?
4. The Vector and ArrayList both provide the same methods, since they both implement the List interface. The Vector has some additional methods with the same functionality but different names. For example, the Vector addElement and add methods have the same functionality. There are some methods that are unique to Vector. Look at the Java API documentation and make a list of the methods that are in Vector that have equivalent methods in ArrayList and ones that are unique. Can the unique methods be implemented using the methods available in ArrayList?
5. If a loop processes n items and n changes from 1024 to 2048, how does that affect the running time of a loop that is $O(n^2)$? How about a loop that is $O(\log n)$? How about a loop that is $O(n \log n)$?
6. What is the advantage of a double-linked list over a single-linked list? What is the disadvantage?
7. Why is it more efficient to use an iterator to traverse a linked list?
8. What is the difference between the Iterator and ListIterator interfaces?
9. How would you make a copy of a ListIterator? Consider the following:

```
ListIterator copyOfIter =
     myList.ListIterator(otherIterator.previousIndex());
```

   Is this an efficient approach? How would you modify the KWLinkedList class to provide an efficient method to copy a ListIterator?
10. What is a Collection? Are there any classes in the Java API that completely implement the Collection interface?
11. Describe the differences between stubs and drivers.

Programming Projects

1. Develop a program to maintain a list of homework assignments. When an assignment is assigned, add it to the list, and when it is completed, remove it. You should keep track of the due date. Your program should provide the following services:
   - Add a new assignment.
   - Remove an assignment.
   - Provide a list of the assignments in the order they were assigned.
   - Find the assignment(s) with the earliest due date.
2. We can represent a polynomial as an ordered list of terms, where the terms are ordered by their exponents. To add two polynomials, you traverse both lists and examine the two terms at the current iterator position. If the exponent of one is smaller than the exponent of the other, then insert the larger one into the result and advance that list's iterator. If the exponents are equal, then create a new term with that exponent and the sum of the coefficients, and advance both iterators. For example:

   $3x^4 + 2x^2 + 3x + 7$ added to $2x^3 + 4x + 5$ is $3x^4 + 2x^3 + 2x^2 + 7x + 12$

   Write a program to read and add polynomials. You should define a class `Term` that contains the exponent and coefficient. This class should implement the `Comparable` interface by comparing the values of the exponents.
3. Write a program to manage a list of students waiting to register for a course as described in Section 2.5. Operations should include adding a new student at the end of the list, adding a new student at the beginning of the list, removing the student from the beginning of the list, and removing a student by name.
4. A circular-linked list has no need of a head or tail. Instead, you need only a reference to a current node, which is the `nextNode` returned by the `Iterator`. Implement such a `CircularList` class. For a nonempty list, the `Iterator.hasNext` method will always return `true`.
5. The Josephus problem is named after the historian Flavius Josephus, who lived between the years 37 and 100 CE. Josephus was also a reluctant leader of the Jewish revolt against the Roman Empire. When it appeared that Josephus and his band were to be captured, they resolved to kill themselves. Josephus persuaded the group by saying, "Let us commit our mutual deaths to determination by lot. He to whom the first lot falls, let him be killed by him that hath the second lot, and thus fortune shall make its progress through us all; nor shall any of us perish by his own right hand, for it would be unfair if, when the rest are gone, somebody should repent and save himself" (Flavius Josephus, *The Wars of the Jews,* Book III, Chapter 8, Verse 7, tr. William Whiston, 1737). Yet that is exactly what happened; Josephus was left for last, and he and the person he was to kill surrendered to the Romans. Although Josephus does not describe how the lots were assigned, the following approach is generally believed to be the way it was done. People form a circle and count around the circle some predetermined number. When this number is reached, that person receives a lot and leaves the circle. The count starts over with the next person. Using the circular-linked list developed in Exercise 4, simulate this problem. Your program should take two parameters: n, the number of people who start, and m, the number of counts. For example, try $n = 20$ and $m = 12$. Where does Josephus need to be in the original list so that he is the last one chosen?
6. To mimic the procedure used by Josephus and his band strictly, the person eliminated remains in the circle until the next one is chosen. Modify your program to take this into account. You may need to modify the circular-linked list class to make a copy of an iterator. Does this change affect the outcome?

7. A two-dimensional shape can be defined by its boundary-polygon, which is simply a list of all coordinates ordered by a traversal of its outline. See the following figure for an example.

The left picture shows the original shape; the middle picture, the outline of the shape. The rightmost picture shows an abstracted boundary, using only the "most important" vertices. We can assign an importance measure to a vertex P by considering its neighbors L and R. We compute the distances LP, PR, and LR. Call these distances $l1$, $l2$, and $l3$. Define the importance as $l1 + l2 - l3$.

Use the following algorithm to find the *n* most important points.

1. `while` the number of points is greater than *n*
2.   Compute the importance of each point.
3.   Remove the least significant one.

Write a program to read a set of coordinates that form an outline and reduce the list to the *n* most significant ones, where *n* is an input value. Draw the initial and resulting shapes. *Note*: This problem and the algorithm for its solution are based on the paper: L. J. Latecki and R. Lakämper, "Convexity Rule for Shape Decomposition Based on Discrete Contour Evolution," *Computer Vision and Image Understanding (CVIU)* 73(1999): 441–454.

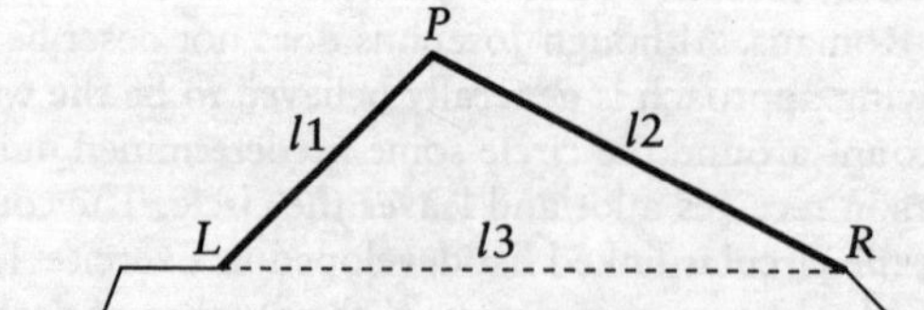

8. As an additional feature, add a slider to your application in Project 7, showing each step of the simplification. Because a slider can go back and forth, you have to store the results of each single simplification step. Consult the Java API documentation on how to use a slider.

Answers to Quick-Check Exercises

1. an index
2. grow, shrink
3. twice the size, spread out the cost of the reallocation so that it is effectively a constant-time operation.
4. $O(n^4)$
5. The predecessor of this node. `nodeRef.next = nodeRef.next.next;`
6. Replaces `"her"` with `"she"`.
7. Deletes the second list element (`"she"`).
8. Insert a new first element containing `"his"`.
9. sequentially
10. both forward and backward
11. double-linked list
12. White-box
13. Black-box
14. superinterface

Chapter 3

Stacks

Chapter Objectives

- To learn about the stack data type and how to use its four methods: push, pop, peek, and empty
- To understand how Java implements a stack
- To learn how to implement a stack using an underlying array or a linked list
- To see how to use a stack to perform various applications, including finding palindromes, testing for balanced (properly nested) parentheses, and evaluating arithmetic expressions

In this chapter we illustrate how to use and implement an abstract data type known as a stack. A stack is more restrictive than the linked list data structure that we studied in the last chapter. A client can access any element in a linked list and can insert elements at any location. However, a client can access only a single element in a stack: the one that was most recently inserted in the stack. This may seem like a serious restriction that would make stacks not very useful, but it turns out that stacks are actually one of the most commonly used data structures in computer science. For example, during program execution, a stack is used to store information about the parameters and return points for all the methods that are currently executing (you will see how this is done in Chapter 5, "Recursion"). Compilers also use stacks to store information while evaluating expressions. Part of the reason for the widespread use of stacks is that a stack is relatively easy to implement. This was an important consideration for programming in languages that did not provide the capability for implementing ADTs as classes.

We will discuss several applications of stacks in this chapter. We will also show how to implement stacks using both arrays and linked lists.

Stacks

3.1 Stack Abstract Data Type

In a cafeteria you can see stacks of dishes placed in spring-loaded containers. Usually several dishes are visible above the top of the container, and the rest are inside the container. You can access only the dish that is on top of the stack. If you want to place more dishes on the stack, you can place the dishes on top of those that are already there. The spring inside the stack container compresses under the weight of the additional dishes, adjusting the height of the stack so that only the top few dishes are always visible.

Another physical example of a stack is a Pez® dispenser (see Figure 3.1). A Pez dispenser is a toy that contains candies. There is also a spring inside the dispenser. The top of the dispenser is a character's head. When you open the dispenser, a single candy *pops* out. You can only extract one candy at a time. If you want to eat more than one candy, you have to open the dispenser multiple times.

FIGURE 3.1
A Pez Dispenser

In programming, a stack is a data structure with the property that only the top element of the stack is accessible. In a stack, the top element is the data value that was most recently stored in the stack. Sometimes this storage policy is known as Last-In, First-Out, or *LIFO*.

Next, we specify some of the operations that we might wish to perform on a stack.

Specification of the Stack Abstract Data Type

Because only the top element of a stack is visible, a stack performs just a few operations. We need to be able to inspect the top element (method `peek`), retrieve the top element (method `pop`), push a new element onto the stack (method `push`), and test for an empty stack (method `empty`). Table 3.1 shows a specification for the Stack ADT that specifies the stack operators. We will write this as interface `StackInt<E>`. We introduce this interface because we want to discuss different implementations of a stack. In the Java API, class `java.util.Stack<E>` implements a stack; there is no stack interface.

TABLE 3.1
Specification of StackInt<E>

Methods	Behavior
`boolean empty()`	Returns **true** if the stack is empty; otherwise, returns **false**.
`E peek()`	Returns the object at the top of the stack without removing it.
`E pop()`	Returns the object at the top of the stack and removes it.
`E push(E obj)`	Pushes an item onto the top of the stack and returns the item pushed.

Listing 3.1 shows the interface StackInt<E>, which declares the methods in the Stack ADT. The methods are the same as those found in class java.util.Stack<E>.

LISTING 3.1
StackInt.java

```
/** A Stack is a data structure in which objects are inserted into
    and removed from the same end (i.e., Last-In, First-Out).
*/
public interface StackInt<E> {

    /** Pushes an item onto the top of the stack and returns
        the item pushed.
        @param obj The object to be inserted
        @return The object inserted
    */
    E push(E obj);

    /** Returns the object at the top of the stack
        without removing it.
        post: The stack remains unchanged.
        @return The object at the top of the stack
        @throws EmptyStackException if stack is empty
    */
    E peek();

    /** Returns the object at the top of the stack
        and removes it.
        post: The stack is one item smaller.
        @return The object at the top of the stack
        @throws EmptyStackException if stack is empty
    */
    E pop();

    /** Returns true if the stack is empty; otherwise,
        returns false.
        @return true if the stack is empty
    */
    boolean empty();
}
```

EXAMPLE 3.1 A stack names (type Stack<String>) contains five strings as shown in Figure 3.2(a). The name "Rich" was placed on the stack before the other four names; "Jonathan" was the last element placed on the stack.

For stack names in Figure 3.2(a), the value of names.empty() is **false**. The statement

```
String last = names.peek();
```

stores "Jonathan" in last without changing names. The statement

```
String temp = names.pop();
```

removes "Jonathan" from names and stores a reference to it in temp. The stack names now contains four elements and is shown in Figure 3.2(b). The statement

```
names.push("Philip");
```

pushes "Philip" onto the stack; the stack names now contains five elements and is shown in Figure 3.2(c).

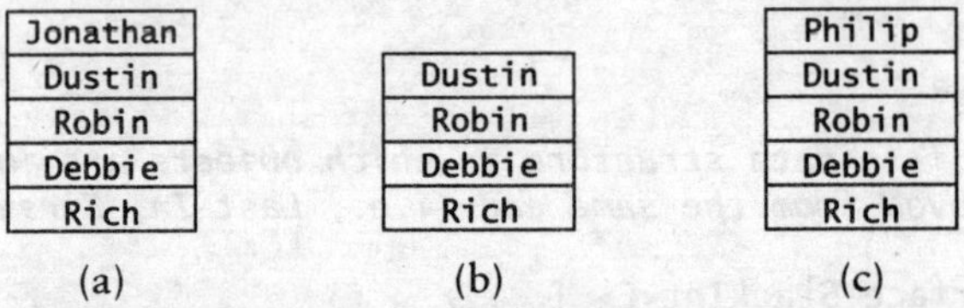

FIGURE 3.2
Stack names

EXERCISES FOR SECTION 3.1

SELF-CHECK

1. Assume that the stack names is defined as in Figure 3.2(c) and perform the following sequence of operations. Indicate the result of each operation and show the new stack if it is changed.
```
names.push("Jane");
names.push("Joseph");
String top = names.pop();
String nextTop = names.peek();
```
2. For the stack names in Figure 3.2(c), what is the effect of the following:
```
while (!names.empty()) {
    System.out.println(names.pop());
}
```
3. What would be the effect of using peek instead of pop in Question 2?

PROGRAMMING

1. Write a main function that creates three stacks of Integer objects. Store the numbers -1, 15, 23, 44, 4, 99 in the first two stacks. The top of each stack should store 99.
2. Write a loop to get each number from the first stack and store it into the third stack.
3. Write a second loop to remove a value from the second stack and from the third stack and display each pair of values on a separate output line. Continue until the stacks are empty. Show the output.

3.2 Stack Applications

In this section we will study two client programs that use stacks: a palindrome finder and a program that verifies that the parentheses in an expression are nested properly. We will use class `java.util.Stack`.

CASE STUDY Finding Palindromes

Problem A palindrome is a string that reads the same in either direction: left to right or right to left. For example, "kayak" is a palindrome, as is "I saw I was I". A well-known palindrome regarding Napoleon Bonaparte is "Able was I ere I saw Elba" (the island where he was sent in exile). We would like a program that reads a string and determines whether it is a palindrome.

Analysis This problem can be solved in many different ways. For example, you could set up a loop in which you compare the characters at each end of a string as you work toward the middle. If any pair of characters is different, the string can't be a palindrome. Another approach would be to scan a string backward (from right to left) and append each character to the end of a new string, which would become the reverse of the original string. Then you could see whether the strings were equal. The approach we will study here uses a stack to assist in forming the reverse of a string. It is not the most efficient way to solve the problem, but it makes good use of a stack.

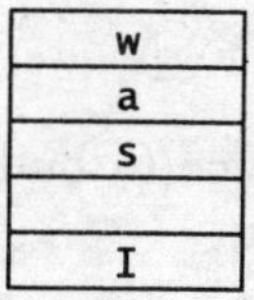

If we scan the input string from left to right and push each character in the input string onto a stack, we can form the reverse of the string by popping the characters and joining them together in the order that they come off the stack. For example, the stack at left contains the characters in the string `"I saw"`.

If we pop them off and join them together, we will get `"w" + "a" + "s" + " " + "I"`, or the string `"was I"`. When the stack is empty, we can compare the string we formed with the original. If they are the same, the original string is a palindrome. Because **char** is a primitive type, each character must be wrapped in a `Character` object before it can be pushed onto the stack.

Data Requirements

PROBLEM INPUTS

An input string to be tested

PROBLEM OUTPUTS

A message indicating whether the string is a palindrome

TABLE 3.2
Class `PalindromeFinder`

Data Fields	Attributes
`private String inputString`	The input string.
`private Stack<Character> charStack`	The stack where characters are stored.
Methods	**Behavior**
`public PalindromeFinder(String str)`	Initializes a new `PalindromeFinder` object, storing a reference to the parameter `str` in `inputString` and pushing each character onto the stack.
`private void fillStack()`	Fills the stack with the characters in `inputString`.
`private String buildReverse()`	Returns the string formed by popping each character from the stack and joining the characters. Empties the stack.
`public boolean isPalindrome()`	Returns **`true`** if `inputString` and the string built by `buildReverse` have the same contents, except for case. Otherwise, returns **`false`**.

Design We can define a class called `PalindromeFinder` (Table 3.2) with data fields for storing the input string and the stack (`Stack<Character> charStack`). The class needs methods to push all characters from the input string onto the stack (`fillStack`), to build a string by popping the characters off the stack and joining them (`buildReverse`), and to compare the strings to see whether they are palindromes (`isPalindrome`).

Implementation Listing 3.2 shows the class. The constructor calls method `fillStack` to build the stack when a new `PalindromeFinder` object is created. The statement

```
charStack.push(inputString.charAt(i));
```

autoboxes a character and pushes it onto the stack.

In method `buildReverse`, the loop

```
while (!charStack.empty()) {
    // Remove top item from stack and append it to result.
    result.append(charStack.pop());
}
```

pops each object off the stack and appends it to the result string.

Method `isPalindrome` uses the `String` method `equalsIgnoreCase` to compare the original `String` with its reverse.

```
return inputString.equalsIgnoreCase(buildReverse());
```

LISTING 3.2
PalindromeFinder.java

```
import java.util.*;

/** Class with methods to check whether a string is a palindrome. */
public class PalindromeFinder {

    /** String to store in stack. */
    private String inputString;
    /** Stack to hold characters. */
    private Stack<Character> charStack = new Stack<Character>();

    /** Store the argument string in a stack of characters.
        @param str String of characters to store in the stack
    */
    public PalindromeFinder(String str) {
        inputString = str;
        fillStack();
    }

    /** Method to fill a stack of characters from an input string. */
    private void fillStack() {
        for (int i = 0; i < inputString.length(); i++) {
            charStack.push(inputString.charAt(i));
        }
    }

    /** Method to build a string containing
        the characters in a stack.
        post: The stack is empty.
        @return The string containing the words in the stack
    */
    private String buildReverse() {
        StringBuilder result = new StringBuilder();
        while (!charStack.empty()) {
            // Remove top item from stack and append it to result.
            result.append(charStack.pop());
        }
        return result.toString();
    }

    public boolean isPalindrome() {
        return inputString.equalsIgnoreCase(buildReverse());
    }
}
```

Testing To test this class you should run it with several different strings, including both palindromes and nonpalindromes, as follows:

- A single character (always a palindrome)
- Multiple characters in one word
- Multiple words
- Different cases
- Even-length strings
- Odd-length strings
- An empty string (considered a palindrome)

CASE STUDY Testing Expressions for Balanced Parentheses

Problem When analyzing arithmetic expressions, it is important to determine whether an expression is balanced with respect to parentheses. For example, the expression

```
(w * (x + y) / z - (p / (r - q)))
```

is balanced. This problem is easy if all parentheses are the same kind—all we need to do is increment a counter each time we scan an opening parenthesis and decrement the counter when we scan a closing parenthesis. If the counter is always greater than or equal to zero, and the final counter value is zero, the expression is balanced. However, if we can have different kinds of open and closing parentheses, the problem becomes more difficult. For example,

```
(w * [x + y] / z - [p / {r - q}])
```

is balanced, but the expression

```
(w * [x + y) / z - [p / {r - q}])
```

is not, because the subexpression `[x + y)` is incorrect. In this expression, the set of opening parentheses includes the symbols `{`, `[`, `(`, and the set of closing parentheses includes the matching symbols `}`, `]`, `)`.

Analysis An expression is balanced if each subexpression that starts with the symbol `{` ends with the symbol `}`, and the same statement is true for the other symbol pairs. Another way of saying this is that an opening parenthesis at position *k* in the sequence `{[(` must be paired with the closing parenthesis at position *k* in the sequence `}])`. We can use a stack to determine whether the parentheses are balanced (or nested properly). We will scan the expression from left to right, ignoring all characters except for parentheses. We will push each open parenthesis onto a stack of characters. When we reach a closing parenthesis, we will see whether it matches the open parenthesis symbol on the top of the stack. If so, we will pop it off and continue the scan. If the characters don't match or the stack is empty, there is an error in the expression. If there are any characters left on the stack when we are finished, that also indicates an error.

Data Requirements

PROBLEM INPUTS

An expression string

PROBLEM OUTPUTS

A message indicating whether the expression has balanced parentheses

Design We will write class `ParenChecker` to check for balanced parentheses. The class should define a method `isBalanced` that returns a **`boolean`** value indicating whether the expression is balanced. We also need methods `isOpen` and `isClose` to determine whether a character is an opening or closing parenthesis. Because `isBalanced` is the only method that processes the expression, we make it a **`static`** method with the expression as a parameter. Table 3.3 shows the class methods. Method `isBalanced` implements the following algorithm.

Algorithm for Method `isBalanced`

```
1.  Create an empty stack of characters.
2.  Assume that the expression is balanced (balanced is true).
3.  Set index to 0.
4.  while balanced is true and index < the expression's length
5.      Get the next character in the data string.
6.      if the next character is an opening parenthesis
7.          Push it onto the stack.
8.      else if the next character is a closing parenthesis
9.          Pop the top of the stack.
10.         if stack was empty or its top does not match the closing
            parenthesis
11.             Set balanced to false.
12.     Increment index.
13. Return true if balanced is true and the stack is empty.
```

The **`if`** statement at Step 6 tests each character in the expression, ignoring all characters except for opening and closing parentheses. If the next character is an opening parenthesis, it is pushed onto the stack. If the next character is a closing parenthesis, the nearest unmatched opening parenthesis is retrieved (by popping the stack) and compared to the closing parenthesis.

TABLE 3.3
Methods of Class ParenChecker

Method	Behavior
`public static boolean isBalanced(String expression)`	Returns **true** if expression is balanced with respect to parentheses and **false** if it is not.
`private static boolean isOpen(char ch)`	Returns **true** if ch is an opening parenthesis.
`private static boolean isClose(char ch)`	Returns **true** if ch is a closing parenthesis.

Implementation Listing 3.3 shows the ParenChecker class. In the **try** block of method isBalanced, the **while** loop (Step 4 of the algorithm) begins by storing the next character (starting with the character at position 0) of expression in nextCh.

```
int index = 0;
while (balanced && index < expression.length()) {
    char nextCh = expression.charAt(index);
```

Method isOpen (isClose) returns **true** if its type char argument is in the string of opening parentheses, string OPEN (closing parentheses, string CLOSE). If nextCh stores an opening parenthesis, the statement

```
s.push(nextCh);
```

pushes nextCh onto the stack s (a local Stack<Character>). Java autoboxes nextCh in a Character object, because only objects can be placed on a Stack.

For each closing parenthesis, the pop method retrieves the nearest unmatched opening parenthesis from the stack:

```
char topCh = s.pop();
```

Each Character object popped off the stack is unboxed. Next, we see whether topCh is a corresponding opening parenthesis to the nextCh closing parenthesis. This is done by comparing their positions in the list of open and close parentheses using the expression

```
OPEN.indexOf(topCh) == CLOSE.indexOf(nextCh)
```

The method String.indexOf returns the position of the character argument in the string. Thus we must be careful when defining the list of opening (OPEN) and closing (CLOSE) parentheses that the corresponding parentheses are in the same position.

The **catch** block executes if an attempt is made to pop the stack of opening parentheses when it is empty. It sets balanced to **false**.

After the **try** or **catch** block finishes execution, the function result is returned. The result is **true** only when the expression is balanced and the stack is empty:

```
return balanced && s.empty();
```

LISTING 3.3

ParenChecker.java

```
import java.util.Stack;
import java.util.EmptyStackException;
import javax.swing.JOptionPane;

/** Class to check for balanced parentheses. */
public class ParenChecker {

    // Constants
    /** Set of opening parenthesis characters. */
    private static final String OPEN = "([{";
    /** Set of closing parenthesis characters, matches OPEN. */
    private static final String CLOSE = ")]}";

    /** Test the input string to see that it contains balanced
        parentheses. This method tests an input string to see
        that each type of parenthesis is balanced. '(' is matched
        with ')', '[' is matched with ']', and
        '{' is matched with '}'.
        @param expression A String containing the expression to
               be examined
        @return true if all the parentheses match
    */
    public static boolean isBalanced(String expression) {
        // Create an empty stack.
        Stack<Character> s = new Stack<Character>();
        boolean balanced = true;
        try {
            int index = 0;
            while (balanced && index < expression.length()) {
                char nextCh = expression.charAt(index);
                if (isOpen(nextCh)) {
                    s.push(nextCh);
                } else if (isClose(nextCh)) {
                    char topCh = s.pop();
                    balanced = OPEN.indexOf(topCh)
                               == CLOSE.indexOf(nextCh);
                }
                index++;
            }
        } catch (EmptyStackException ex) {
            balanced = false;
        }
        return (balanced && s.empty());
    }

    /** Method to determine whether a character is one of the
        opening parentheses.
        @param ch Character to be tested
        @return true if ch is one of the opening parentheses
    */
    private static boolean isOpen(char ch) {
        return OPEN.indexOf(ch) > -1;
    }
```

```java
    /** Method to determine whether a character is one of the
        closing parentheses.
        @param ch Character to be tested
        @return true if ch is one of the closing parentheses
    */
    private static boolean isClose(char ch) {
        return CLOSE.indexOf(ch) > -1;
    }

    /** main method. Ask the user for a string and
        call the ParenChecker to see whether the parentheses
        are balanced.
        @param args Not used
    */
    public static void main(String args[]) {
        String expression = JOptionPane.showInputDialog(
            "Enter an expression containing parentheses");
        if (ParenChecker.isBalanced(expression)) {
            JOptionPane.showMessageDialog(null, expression
                                         + " is balanced");
        } else {
            JOptionPane.showMessageDialog(null, expression
                                         + " is not balanced");
        }
        System.exit(0);
    }
}
```

PITFALL

Attempting to Pop an Empty Stack

If you attempt to pop an empty stack, your program will throw an EmptyStackException. You can guard against this error by testing for a nonempty stack before popping the stack. Alternatively, you can catch the error if it occurs and handle it as was done in method `isBalanced` (`balanced` is set to **`false`**). We chose this approach because attempting to pop an empty stack is a reasonable thing to do when an expression has more closing parentheses than opening parentheses.

PROGRAM STYLE

Declaring Constants

We declared OPEN and CLOSE as class constants instead of declaring them locally in the methods where they are used (`isOpen` and `isClose`). There are two reasons for this. First, it is a more efficient use of memory to declare them as class constants instead of having to allocate storage for these constants each time the method is called. Also, if a new kind of parenthesis is introduced, it is easier to locate and update the class constants instead of having to find their declarations inside a method.

Testing A simple test driver is included in Listing 3.3. Test this program by providing a variety of input expressions and displaying the result (`true` or `false`). You should try expressions that have several levels of nested parentheses. Also, try expressions that would be properly nested if the parentheses were all of one type, but are not properly nested because a closing parenthesis does not match a particular opening parenthesis (e.g., `{x + y]` is not balanced because `]` is not the correct closing parenthesis for `{ }`). Also check expressions that have too many opening or closing parentheses. Finally, test for some strange strings such as `"{[}]"`, which should fail. The string `"{[a * + b]}"`, which is not a valid expression, should pass because its parentheses are balanced.

EXERCISES FOR SECTION 3.2

SELF-CHECK

1. The result returned by the palindrome finder depends on all characters in a string, including spaces and punctuation. Discuss how you would modify the palindrome finder so that only the letters in the input string were used to determine whether the input string was a palindrome. You should ignore any other characters.
2. Trace the execution of method `isBalanced` for each of the following expressions. Your trace should show the stack after each `push` or `pop` operation. Also show the values of `balanced`, `isOpen`, and `isClose` after each closing parenthesis is processed.

```
(a + b * {c / [d - e]}) + (d * [e - f])
(a + b * {c / [d - e}}) + (d / e)
(w * (x + y))) - 2 * z
```

PROGRAMMING

1. Write a method that reads a line and reverses the words in the line (not the characters) using a stack. For example, given the following input:

   `The quick brown fox jumps over the lazy dog`

   you should get the following output:

   `dog lazy the over jumps fox brown quick The`
2. Three different approaches to finding palindromes are discussed in the Analysis section of that case study. Code the first approach.
3. Code the second approach to finding palindromes.

3.3 Implementing a Stack

This section discusses how to implement the Stack interface. You may have recognized that a stack is very similar to an `ArrayList`. In fact, in the Java Collections framework, the class `Stack` extends class `Vector`, which is the historical predecessor of `ArrayList`.

Implementing a Stack as an Extension of Vector

The Java API includes a `Stack` class as part of the package `java.util`. This class is declared as follows:

```
public class Stack<E> extends Vector<E>
```

The `Vector` class implements a growable array of objects. Like an `ArrayList`, it contains components that can be accessed using an integer index. Also, the size of a `Vector` can grow or shrink as needed to accommodate adding and removing items after the `Vector` has been created. Figure 3.3 shows the characters of the string `"Java"` stored in a stack `s`, represented as a `Vector` where `s[3]`, the last element of the `Vector`, references the `Character` object at the top of the stack. To implement interface `StackInt`, all we need to do is write methods that perform the required operations. We can use the methods inherited from class `Vector` to facilitate this. For example, `push` can be implemented as follows:

```
public E push(E obj) {
    add(obj);
    return obj;
}
```

FIGURE 3.3
Characters of "Java" Stored in Stack s (a Vector)

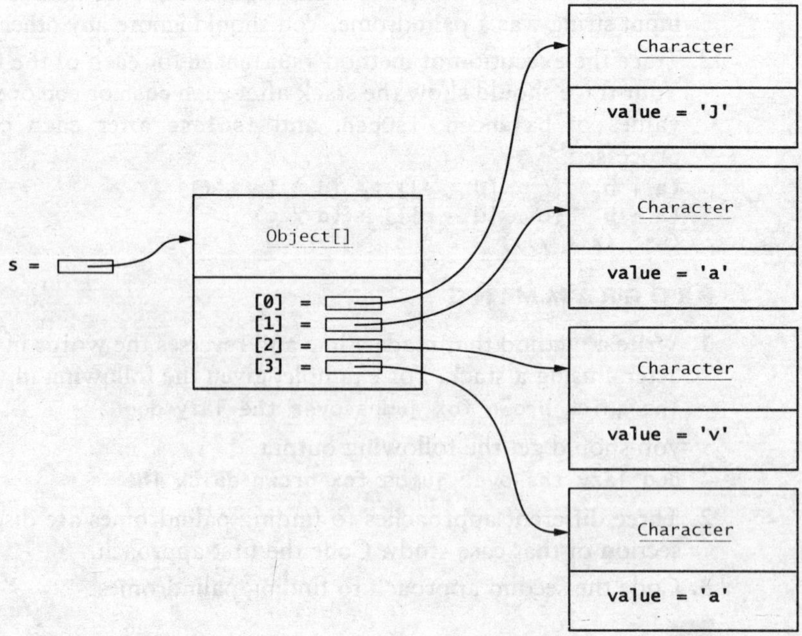

PITFALL

Accessing a Stack Element That Is Out of Bounds

Because Java implements a Stack as an extension of Vector, you can use the methods defined in the Vector class with a Stack object. This means that you may get an ArrayIndexOutOfBoundsException if you attempt to access a Vector element with an invalid index (e.g., using Vector method get). This is another reason to restrict yourself to using just the methods described in the Stack specification (push, pop, peek, empty).

Similarly, pop can be coded as:

```
public E pop() throws EmptyStackException {
    try {
        return remove(size() - 1);
    } catch (ArrayIndexOutOfBoundsException ex) {
        throw new EmptyStackException();
    }
}
```

There is a drawback to the approach taken by the Java designers, however. Because their implementation incorrectly states that a Stack *is a* Vector, all of the operations for a Vector can be applied. Therefore, the entire stack can be displayed (using Vector.toString) or searched (using Vector.indexOf or Stack.search), which violates the principle of information hiding (only the top element of a stack should be accessible). We discuss a better way to do this in the next section.

Implementing a Stack with a List Component

An alternative to implementing a stack as an extension of Vector is to write a class, which we will call ListStack, that has a List component. We can use either the ArrayList, the Vector, or the LinkedList for this component (all of them implement the List interface). We will call this component theData, and it will contain the stack data.

The code for the public methods of the ListStack<E> and java.util.Stack<E> classes are essentially the same. For example, in java.util.Stack<E>, the push method is coded as:

```
public E push(E obj) {
    add(obj);
    return obj;
}
```

and we code the ListStack<E>.push method as:

```
public E push(E obj) {
    theData.add(obj);
    return obj;
}
```

The `ListStack` class is said to be an *adapter class* because it adapts the methods available in another class (a `List`) to the interface its clients expect by giving different names to essentially the same operations (e.g., `push` instead of `add`). This is an example of *method delegation.*

Listing 3.4 shows the `ListStack` class. Note that the statements that manipulate the stack explicitly refer to data field `theData`. For example, in `ListStack push` we use the statement

```
theData.add(obj);
```

instead of the statement

```
add(obj);
```

which was used when the stack was considered an extension of `Vector`.

LISTING 3.4
ListStack.java

```
import java.util.*;

/** Class ListStack<E> implements the interface StackInt<E> as
    an adapter to the List. This implementation is functionally
    equivalent to that given in java.util.Stack<E> except that the
    underlying List<E> is not publicly exposed.
*/
public class ListStack<E> implements StackInt<E> {

    /** The List containing the data */
    private List<E> theData;

    /** Construct an empty stack using an ArrayList as the
        container. */
    public ListStack() {
        theData = new ArrayList<E>();
    }

    /** Push an object onto the stack.
        post: The object is at the top of the stack.
        @param obj The object to be pushed
        @return The object pushed
    */
    @Override
    public E push(E obj) {
        theData.add(obj);
        return obj;
    }

    /** Peek at the top object on the stack.
        @return The top object on the stack
        @throws EmptyStackException if the stack is empty
    */
    @Override
    public E peek() {
        if (empty()) {
            throw new EmptyStackException();
        }
        return theData.get(theData.size() - 1);
    }
```

```
    /** Pop the top object off the stack.
        post: The object at the top of the stack is removed.
        @return The top object, which is removed
        @throws EmptyStackException if the stack is empty
    */
    @Override
    public E pop() {
        if (empty()) {
            throw new EmptyStackException();
        }
        return theData.remove(theData.size() - 1);
    }

    /** See whether the stack is empty.
        @return true if the stack is empty
    */
    @Override
    public boolean empty() {
        return theData.size() == 0;
    }
}
```

DESIGN CONCEPT

Using an ArrayList Object as a Stack Component

In Listing 3.4 we used an `ArrayList` object to store the `ListStack` data. We could use any of the implementers of `List`, but an `ArrayList` is the best choice because a `Vector` is not recommended for new applications and a `LinkedList` would require more storage. Regardless of the container used, all stack operations would be performed in $O(1)$ time.

Implementing a Stack Using an Array

We can also use an array data field for storage of a stack instead of using Java's `ArrayList` class. In that case, however, we need to allocate storage for an array with an initial default capacity when we create a new stack object. We also need to keep track of the top of the stack (`topOfStack`), because the array size does not grow and shrink after each push and pop. Also, there is no `size` method (as there is for an `ArrayList`) to tell us how many elements are currently in the stack. The value of `topOfStack` is the subscript of the element at the top of the stack; for an empty stack, `topOfStack` should be –1. The data field declarations and constructor follow.

```
import java.util.EmptyStackException;
import java.util.Arrays;

/** Implementation of the interface StackInt<E> using
    an array.
*/
public class ArrayStack<E> implements StackInt<E> {
    // Data Fields
    /** Storage for stack. */
    private E[] theData;
```

```
        /** Index to top of stack. */
        int topOfStack = -1;      // Initially empty stack.
        private static final int INITIAL_CAPACITY = 10;

        /** Construct an empty stack with the default
            initial capacity.
        */
        @SuppressWarnings("unchecked")
        public ArrayStack() {
            theData = (E[]) new Object[INITIAL_CAPACITY];
        }
    . . .
```

Figure 3.4 shows an ArrayStack of characters after pushing the individual letters of the string "Java", where the last character in the string is at the top of the stack. The value of topOfStack is 3. If we pop a character (the 'a' at position 3), topOfStack decreases to 2; if we push a character onto the stack, topOfStack increases to 4 and the new character is stored at theData[4].

The push method needs to reallocate additional storage space when the array becomes filled, as was done for class KWArrayList in Section 2.3. Then topOfStack is incremented, and the item is inserted at the element with subscript topOfStack.

```
    /** Insert a new item on top of the stack.
        post: The new item is the top item on the stack.
              All other items are one position lower.
        @param obj The item to be inserted
        @return The item that was inserted
    */
    @Override
    public E push(E obj) {
        if (topOfStack == theData.length - 1) {
            reallocate();
        }
        topOfStack++;
        theData[topOfStack] = obj;
        return obj;
    }
```

Method pop is shown next. The return statement gets the element at the top of the stack and then decrements topOfStack. Method peek is the same, except that topOfStack is not decremented. Method empty (not shown) would return true if topOfStack is equal to –1.

```
    /** Remove and return the top item on the stack.
        pre: The stack is not empty.
        post: The top item on the stack has been
              removed and the stack is one item smaller.
        @return The top item on the stack
        @throws EmptyStackException if the stack is empty
    */
    @Override
    public E pop() {
        if (empty()) {
            throw new EmptyStackException();
        }
        return theData[topOfStack--];
    }
```

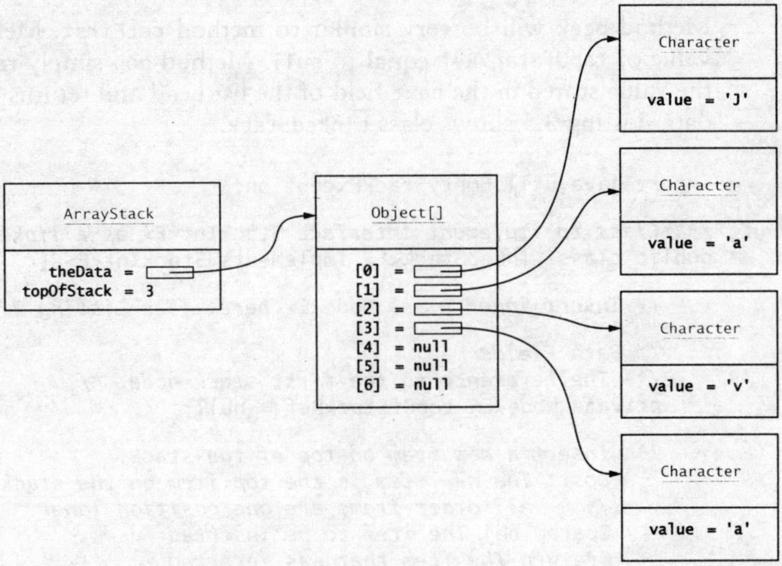

FIGURE 3.4
Stack of Character Objects in an Array

Implementing a Stack as a Linked Data Structure

We can also implement a stack using a single-linked list of nodes. We show the stack containing the characters in `"Java"` in Figure 3.5, with the last character in the string stored in the node at the top of the stack. Class `LinkedStack<E>` contains a collection of `Node<E>` objects (see Section 2.5). Recall that inner class `Node<E>` has attributes `data` (type `E`) and `next` (type `Node<E>`).

Reference variable `topOfStackRef` (type `Node<E>`) references the last element placed on the stack. Because it is easier to insert and delete from the head of a linked list, we will have `topOfStackRef` reference the node at the head of the list.

Method `push` inserts a node at the head of the list. The statement

```
topOfStackRef = new Node<E>(obj, topOfStackRef);
```

sets `topOfStackRef` to reference the new node; `topOfStackRef.next` references the old top of the stack. When the stack is empty, `topOfStackRef` is **`null`**, so the attribute `next` for the first object pushed onto the stack (the item at the bottom) will be **`null`**.

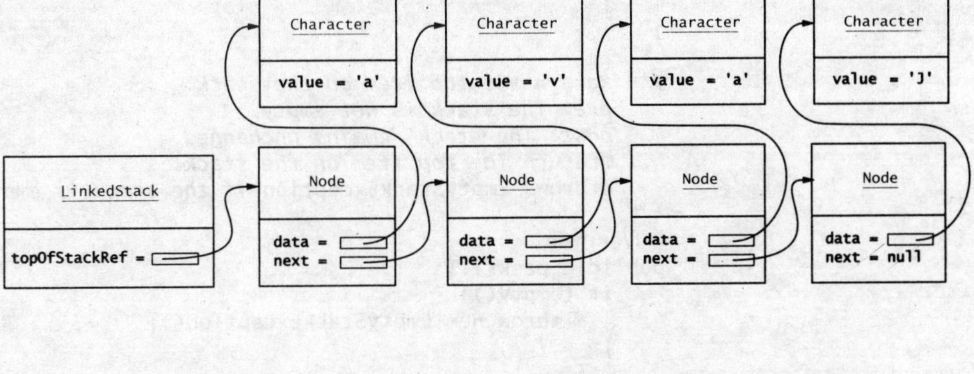

FIGURE 3.5
Stack of Character Objects in a Linked List

Method peek will be very similar to method getFirst. Method empty tests for a value of topOfStackRef equal to **null**. Method pop simply resets topOfStackRef to the value stored in the next field of the list head and returns the old topOfStackRef data. Listing 3.5 shows class LinkedStack.

LISTING 3.5
Class LinkedStack

```
import java.util.EmptyStackException;

/** Class to implement interface StackInt<E> as a linked list. */
public class LinkedStack<E> implements StackInt<E> {

    // Insert inner class Node<E> here. (See Listing 2.1)

    // Data Fields
    /** The reference to the first stack node. */
    private Node<E> topOfStackRef = null;

    /** Insert a new item on top of the stack.
        post: The new item is the top item on the stack.
              All other items are one position lower.
        @param obj The item to be inserted
        @return The item that was inserted
    */
    @Override
    public E push(E obj) {
        topOfStackRef = new Node<E>(obj, topOfStackRef);
        return obj;
    }

    /** Remove and return the top item on the stack.
        pre: The stack is not empty.
        post: The top item on the stack has been
              removed and the stack is one item smaller.
        @return The top item on the stack
        @throws EmptyStackException if the stack is empty
    */
    @Override
    public E pop() {
        if (empty()) {
            throw new EmptyStackException();
        }
        else {
            E result = topOfStackRef.data;
            topOfStackRef = topOfStackRef.next;
            return result;
        }
    }

    /** Return the top item on the stack.
        pre: The stack is not empty.
        post: The stack remains unchanged.
        @return The top item on the stack
        @throws EmptyStackException if the stack is empty
    */
    @Override
    public E peek() {
        if (empty()) {
            throw new EmptyStackException();
        }
```

```
        else {
            return topOfStackRef.data;
        }
    }

    /** See whether the stack is empty.
        @return true if the stack is empty
    */
    @Override
    public boolean empty() {
        return topOfStackRef == null;
    }
}
```

Comparison of Stack Implementations

As stated earlier, the implementation of the Stack ADT as an extension of `Vector` is a poor choice because all the `Vector` methods are accessible. The easiest approach to implementing a stack in Java would be to give it a `List` component for storing the data. Since all insertions and deletions are at one end, the stack operations would all be O(1) operations. You could use an object of any class that implements the `List` interface to store the stack data, but the `ArrayList` is the simplest.

Alternatively, you could use an underlying array data structure, but this would be slightly more difficult to implement, as you would have to update the index to the top of the stack after each insertion or deletion. You would also have to reallocate storage when the stack became filled. All stack operations using an underlying array would be O(1).

Finally, you could also use your own linked data structure. This has the advantage of using exactly as much storage as is needed for the stack. However, you would also need to allocate storage for the links. Because all insertions and deletions are at one end, the flexibility provided by a linked data structure is not utilized. All stack operations using a linked data structure would be O(1).

EXERCISES FOR SECTION 3.3

SELF-CHECK

1. For the implementation of stack `s` using an array as the underlying data structure (see Figure 3.4), show how the underlying data structure changes after each statement below executes. What is the value of `topOfStack`? Assume the initial capacity of the stack is 7 and the characters in `"Happy"` are stored on the stack (`H` pushed on first).

```
s.push('i');
s.push('s');
char ch1 = s.pop();
s.pop();
s.push(' ');
char ch2 = s.peek();
```

2. How do your answers to Question 1 change if the initial capacity is 4 instead of 7?

3. For the implementation of stack s using a linked list of nodes as the underlying data structure (see Figure 3.5), show how the underlying data structure changes after each statement in Question 1 executes. Assume the characters in "Happy" are stored on the stack (H pushed on first).

PROGRAMMING

1. Write a method size for class LinkedStack<E> that returns the number of elements currently on a LinkedStack<E>.
2. Complete the implementation of ArrayStack<E>. Write methods reallocate and empty.

3.4 Additional Stack Applications

In this section we consider two case studies that relate to evaluating arithmetic expressions. The first problem is slightly easier, and it involves evaluating expressions that are in postfix form. The second problem discusses how to convert from *infix notation* (common mathematics notation) to postfix form.

Normally we write expressions using infix notation, in which binary operators (*, +, etc.) are inserted between their operands. Infix expressions present no special problem to humans because we can easily scan left and right to find the operands of a particular operator. A calculator (or computer), however, normally scans an expression string in the order that it is input (left to right). Therefore, it is easier to evaluate an expression if the user types in the operands for each operator before typing the operator (*postfix notation*). Table 3.4 shows some examples of expressions in postfix and infix form. The braces under each postfix expression will help you visualize the operands for each operator.

The advantage of the postfix form is that there is no need to group subexpressions in parentheses or even to consider operator precedence. (We talk more about postfix in the second case study in this section.) The braces in Table 3.4 are for our convenience and are not required. The next case study develops a program that evaluates a postfix expression.

TABLE 3.4
Postfix Expressions

Postfix Expression	Infix Expression	Value
4 7 *	4 * 7	28
4 7 2 + *	4 * (7 + 2)	36
4 7 * 20 -	(4 * 7) - 20	8
3 4 7 * 2 / +	3 + ((4 * 7) / 2)	17

CASE STUDY Evaluating Postfix Expressions

Problem Write a class that evaluates a postfix expression. The postfix expression will be a string containing digit characters and operator characters from the set +, –, *, /. The space character will be used as a delimiter between tokens (integers and operators).

Analysis In a postfix expression the operands precede the operators. A stack is the perfect place to save the operands until the operator is scanned. When the operator is scanned, its operands can be popped off the stack (the last operand scanned, the right operand, will be popped first). Therefore, our program will push each integer operand onto the stack. When an operator is read, the top two operands are popped, the operation is performed on its operands, and the result is pushed back onto the stack. The final result should be the only value remaining on the stack when the end of the expression is reached.

Design We will write class `PostfixEvaluator` to evaluate postfix expressions. The class should define a method `eval`, which scans a postfix expression and processes each of its tokens, where a token is either an operand (an integer) or an operator. We also need a method `evalOp`, which evaluates each operator when it is scanned, and a method `isOperator`, which determines whether a character is an operator. Table 3.5 describes the class.

The algorithm for `eval` follows. The stack operators perform algorithm steps 1, 5, 7, 8, 10, and 11.

Table 3.6 shows the evaluation of the third expression in Table 3.4 using this algorithm. The arrow under the expression points to the character being processed; the stack diagram shows the stack after this character is processed.

TABLE 3.5
Class `PostfixEvaluator`

Data Field	Attribute
`Stack<Integer> operandStack`	The stack of operands (`Integer` objects).
Method	**Behavior**
`public int eval(String expression)`	Returns the value of `expression`.
`private int evalOp(char op)`	Pops two operands and applies operator `op` to its operands, returning the result.
`private boolean isOperator(char ch)`	Returns **`true`** if `ch` is an operator symbol.

TABLE 3.6
Evaluating a Postfix Expression

Expression	Action	Stack
`4 7 * 20 -` ↑ (at 4)	Push 4	4
`4 7 * 20 -` ↑ (at 7)	Push 7	7 4
`4 7 * 20 -` ↑ (at *)	Pop 7 and 4 Evaluate 4 * 7 Push 28	28
`4 7 * 20 -` ↑ (at 20)	Push 20	20 28
`4 7 * 20 -` ↑ (at -)	Pop 20 and 28 Evaluate 28 – 20 Push 8	8
`4 7 * 20 -` ↑ (past end)	Pop 8 Stack is empty Result is 8	

Algorithm for method `eval`

1. Create an empty stack of integers.
2. **while** there are more tokens
3.   Get the next token.
4.   **if** the first character of the token is a digit
5.   Push the integer onto the stack.
6.   **else if** the token is an operator
7.   Pop the right operand off the stack.
8.   Pop the left operand off the stack.
9.   Evaluate the operation.
10.   Push the result onto the stack.
11. Pop the stack and return the result.

Implementation Listing 3.6 shows the implementation of class `PostfixEvaluator`. The only data field is the operand stack. There is an inner class that defines the exception `SyntaxErrorException`.

Method `eval` implements the algorithm shown in the design section. To simplify the extraction of tokens, we will assume that there are spaces between operators and operands. As explained in Appendix A.5, the method call

```
String[] tokens = expression.split("\\s+");
```

stores in array `tokens` the individual tokens (operands and operators) of string `expression` where the argument string "\\s+" specifies that the delimiter is one or more white-space characters. (We will remove the requirement for spaces between tokens and consider parentheses in part 2 of the case study.)

The enhanced **for** statement

```
for (String nextToken : tokens) {
```

ensures that each of the strings in `tokens` is processed, and the **if** statement in the loop tests the first character of each token to determine its category (number or operator). Therefore, the body of method `eval` is enclosed within a **try-catch** sequence. An `EmptyStackException`, thrown either as a result of a `pop` operation in `eval` or by a `pop` operation in a method called by `eval`, will be caught by the **catch** clause. In either case, a `SyntaxErrorException` is thrown.

Private method `isOperator` determines whether a character is an operator. When an operator is encountered, private method `evalOp` is called to evaluate it. This method pops the top two operands from the stack. The first item popped is the right-hand operand, and the second is the left-hand operand.

```
int rhs = operandStack.pop();
int lhs = operandStack.pop();
```

A **switch** statement is then used to select the appropriate expression to evaluate for the given operator. For example, the following **case** processes the addition operator and saves the sum of `lhs` and `rhs` in `result`.

```
case '+' : result = lhs + rhs;
           break;
```

LISTING 3.6
PostfixEvaluator.java

```
import java.util.*;

/** Class that can evaluate a postfix expression. */
public class PostfixEvaluator {

    // Nested Class
    /** Class to report a syntax error. */
    public static class SyntaxErrorException extends Exception {
        /** Construct a SyntaxErrorException with the specified
            message.
            @param message The message
        */
        SyntaxErrorException(String message) {
            super(message);
        }
    }

    // Constant
    /** A list of operators. */
    private static final String OPERATORS = "+-*/";

    // Data Field
    /** The operand stack. */
    private Stack<Integer> operandStack;
```

```
// Methods
/** Evaluates the current operation.
    This function pops the two operands off the operand
    stack and applies the operator.
    @param op A character representing the operator
    @return The result of applying the operator
    @throws EmptyStackException if pop is attempted on
            an empty stack
*/
private int evalOp(char op) {
    // Pop the two operands off the stack.
    int rhs = operandStack.pop();
    int lhs = operandStack.pop();
    int result = 0;
    // Evaluate the operator.
    switch (op) {
        case '+' : result = lhs + rhs;
                   break;
        case '-' : result = lhs - rhs;
                   break;
        case '/' : result = lhs / rhs;
                   break;
        case '*' : result = lhs * rhs;
                   break;
    }
    return result;
}

/** Determines whether a character is an operator.
    @param op The character to be tested
    @return true if the character is an operator
*/
private boolean isOperator(char ch) {
    return OPERATORS.indexOf(ch) != -1;
}

/** Evaluates a postfix expression.
    @param expression The expression to be evaluated
    @return The value of the expression
    @throws SyntaxErrorException if a syntax error is detected
*/
public int eval(String expression) throws SyntaxErrorException {
    // Create an empty stack.
    operandStack = new Stack<Integer>();

    // Process each token.
    String[] tokens = expression.split("\\s+");
    try {
        for (String nextToken : tokens) {
            char firstChar = nextToken.charAt(0);
            // Does it start with a digit?
            if (Character.isDigit(firstChar)) {
```

```
                    // Get the integer value.
                    int value = Integer.parseInt(nextToken);
                    // Push value onto operand stack.
                    operandStack.push(value);
                } // Is it an operator?
                else if (isOperator(firstChar) {
                    // Evaluate the operator.
                    int result = evalOp(firstChar);
                    // Push result onto the operand stack.
                    operandStack.push(result);
                }
                else {
                    // Invalid character.
                    throw new SyntaxErrorException(
                        "Invalid character encountered: " + firstChar);
                }
            }   // End for.

            // No more tokens - pop result from operand stack.
            int answer = operandStack.pop();
            // Operand stack should be empty.
            if (operandStack.empty()) {
                return answer;
            } else {
                // Indicate syntax error.
                throw new SyntaxErrorException(
                    "Syntax Error: Stack should be empty");
            }
        } catch (EmptyStackException ex) {
            // Pop was attempted on an empty stack.
            throw new SyntaxErrorException(
                "Syntax Error: The stack is empty");
        }
    }
}
```

PROGRAM STYLE

Creating Your Own Exception Class

The program would work just the same if we did not bother to declare the SyntaxError Exception class and just threw a new Exception object each time an error occurred. However, we feel that this approach gives the user a more meaningful description of the cause of an error. Also, if other errors are possible in a client of this class, any SyntaxErrorException can be caught and handled in a separate **catch** clause.

Testing You will need to write a driver for the `PostfixEvaluator` class. This driver should create a `PostfixEvaluator` object, read one or more expressions, and report the result. It will also have to catch the exception `PostfixEvaluator.SyntaxErrorException`. A white-box approach to testing would lead you to consider the following test cases. First, you want to exercise each path in the `evalOp` method by entering a simple expression that uses each operator. Then you need to exercise the paths through `eval` by trying different orderings and multiple occurrences of the operators. These tests exercise the normal cases, so you next need to test for possible syntax errors. Consider the following cases: an operator without any operands, a single operand, an extra operand, an extra operator, a variable name, and finally an empty string.

CASE STUDY Converting from Infix to Postfix

We normally write expressions in infix notation. Therefore, one approach to evaluating expressions in infix notation is first to convert it to postfix and then to apply the evaluation technique just discussed. We will show in this case study how to accomplish this conversion using a stack. An infix expression can also be evaluated directly using two stacks. This is left as a programming project.

Problem To complete the design of an expression evaluator, we need a set of methods that convert infix expressions to postfix form. We will assume that the expression will consist only of spaces, operands, and operators, where the space is a delimiter character between tokens. All operands that are identifiers begin with a letter or underscore character; all operands that are numbers begin with a digit. (Although we are allowing for identifiers, our postfix evaluator can't really handle them.)

Analysis Table 3.4 showed the infix and postfix forms of four expressions. For each expression pair, the operands are in the same sequence; however, the placement of the operators changes in going from infix to postfix. For example, in converting

```
w - 5.1 / sum * 2
```

to its postfix form

```
w 5.1 sum / 2 * -
```

we see that the four operands (the tokens `w`, `5.1`, `sum`, `2`) retain their relative ordering from the infix expression, but the order of the operators is changed. The first operator in the infix expression, `-`, is the last operator in the postfix expression. Therefore, we can insert the operands in the output expression (`postfix`) as soon as they are scanned in the input expression (`infix`), but each operator should be inserted in the postfix string after its operands and in the order in which they should be evaluated, not the order in which they were scanned. For expressions without parentheses, there are two criteria that determine the order of operator evaluation:

- Operators are evaluated according to their *precedence* or rank. Higher-precedence operators are evaluated before lower-precedence operators. For example, *, /, and % (the *multiplicative* operators) are evaluated before +, -.
- Operators with the same precedence are evaluated in left-to-right order (left-associative rule).

If we temporarily store the operators on a stack, we can pop them whenever we need to and insert them in the postfix string in an order that indicates when they should be evaluated, rather than when they were scanned. For example, if we have the first two operators from the string `"w - 5.1 / sum * 2"` stored on a stack as follows,

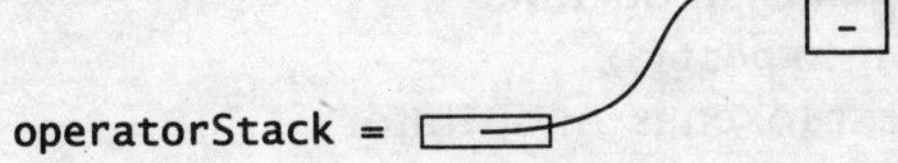

the operator / (scanned second) must come off the stack and be placed in the postfix string before the operator - (scanned first). If we have the stack as just shown and the next operator is *, we need to pop the / off the stack and insert it in the postfix string before *, because the multiplicative operator scanned earlier (/) should be evaluated before the multiplicative operator (*) scanned later (the left-associative rule).

Design Class `InfixToPostfix` contains methods needed for the conversion. The class should have a data field `operatorStack`, which stores the operators. It should also have a method `convert`, which does the initial processing of all tokens (operands and operators). Method `convert` needs to get each token and process it. Each token that is an operand should be appended to the postfix string. Method `processOperator` will process each operator token. Method `isOperator` determines whether a token is an operator, and method `precedence` returns the precedence of an operator. Table 3.7 describes class `InfixToPostfix`.

TABLE 3.7
Class `InfixToPostfix`

Data Field	Attribute
`private Stack<Character> operatorStack`	Stack of operators.
`private StringBuilder postfix`	The postfix string being formed.
Method	**Behavior**
`public String convert(String infix)`	Extracts and processes each token in `infix` and returns the equivalent postfix string.
`private void processOperator(char op)`	Processes operator `op` by updating `operatorStack`.
`private int precedence(char op)`	Returns the precedence of operator `op`.
`private boolean isOperator(char ch)`	Returns **true** if `ch` is an operator symbol.

The algorithm for method `convert` follows. The **`while`** loop extracts and processes each token, calling `processOperator` to process each operator token. After all tokens are extracted from the infix string and processed, any operators remaining on the stack should be popped and appended to the postfix string. They are appended to the end because they have lower precedence than those operators inserted earlier.

Algorithm for Method `convert`

1. Initialize `postfix` to an empty `StringBuilder`.
2. Initialize the operator stack to an empty stack.
3. **`while`** there are more tokens in the infix string
4.   Get the next token.
5.   **`if`** the next token is an operand
6.   Append it to `postfix`.
7.   **`else if`** the next token is an operator
8.   Call `processOperator` to process the operator.
9.   **`else`**
10.   Indicate a syntax error.
11. Pop remaining operators off the operator stack and append them to `postfix`.

Method `processOperator`

The real decision making happens in method `processOperator`. By pushing operators onto the stack or popping them off the stack (and into the postfix string), this method controls the order in which the operators will be evaluated.

Each operator will eventually be pushed onto the stack. However, before doing this, `processOperator` compares the operator's precedence with that of the stacked operators, starting with the operator at the top of the stack. If the current operator has higher precedence than the operator at the top of the stack, it is pushed onto the stack immediately. This will ensure that none of the stacked operators can be inserted into the postfix string before it.

However, if the operator at the top of the stack has higher precedence than the current operator, it is popped off the stack and inserted in the postfix string, because it should be performed before the current operator, according to the precedence rule. Also, if the operator at the top of the stack has the same precedence as the current operator, it is popped off the stack and inserted into the postfix string, because it should be performed before the current operator, according to the left-associative rule. After an operator is popped off the stack, we repeat the process of comparing the precedence of the operator currently at the top of the stack with the precedence of the current operator until the current operator is pushed onto the stack.

A special case is an empty operator stack. In this case, there are no stacked operators to compare with the new one, so we will simply push the current operator onto the stack. We use method `peek` to access the operator at the top of the stack without removing it.

Algorithm for Method processOperator

```
1.   if the operator stack is empty
2.        Push the current operator onto the stack.
     else
3.        Peek the operator stack and let topOp be the top operator.
4.        if the precedence of the current operator is greater than the
          precedence of topOp
5.             Push the current operator onto the stack.
          else
6.             while the stack is not empty and the precedence of the current
               operator is less than or equal to the precedence of topOp
7.                  Pop topOp off the stack and append it to postfix.
8.                  if the operator stack is not empty
9.                       Peek the operator stack and let topOp be the top
                         operator.
10.            Push the current operator onto the stack.
```

Table 3.8 traces the conversion of the infix expression `w - 5.1 / sum * 2` to the postfix expression `w 5.1 sum / 2 * -`. The final value of `postfix` shows that / is performed first (operands `5.1` and `sum`), * is performed next (operands `5.1 / sum` and `2`), and - is performed last.

TABLE 3.8
Conversion of `w - 5.1 / sum * 2`

Next Token	Action	Effect on operatorStack	Effect on postfix
w	Append w to postfix.		w
-	The stack is empty Push - onto the stack	-	w
5.1	Append 5.1 to postfix	-	w 5.1
/	precedence(/) > precedence(-), Push / onto the stack	/ -	w 5.1
sum	Append sum to postfix	/ -	w 5.1 sum
*	precedence(*) equals precedence(/) Pop / off of stack and append to postfix	-	w 5.1 sum /

TABLE 3.8 (continued)

Next Token	Action	Effect on operatorStack	Effect on postfix
*	precedence(*) > precedence(-), Push * onto the stack	* -	w 5.1 sum /
2	Append 2 to postfix	* -	w 5.1 sum / 2
End of input	Stack is not empty, Pop * off the stack and append to postfix	-	w 5.1 sum / 2 *
End of input	Stack is not empty, Pop - off the stack and append to postfix		w 5.1 sum / 2 * -

Although the algorithm will correctly convert a well-formed expression and will detect some expressions with invalid syntax, it doesn't do all the syntax checking required. For example, an expression with extra operands would not be detected. We discuss this further in the testing section.

Implementation Listing 3.7 shows the `InfixToPostfix` class. The `convert` method begins by initializing `postfix` and the `operatorStack`. The tokens are extracted using `String.split` and processed within a **try** block. The condition

```
(Character.isJavaIdentifierStart(firstChar)
        || Character.isDigit(firstChar))
```

tests the first character (`firstChar`) of the next token to see whether the next token is an operand (identifier or number). Method `isJavaIdentifierStart` returns **true** if the next token is an identifier; method `isDigit` returns **true** if the next token is a number (starts with a digit). If this condition is true, the token is appended to `postfix` followed by a space character. The next condition,

```
(isOperator(firstChar))
```

is true if `nextToken` is an operator. If so, method `processOperator` is called. If the next token is not an operand or an operator, the exception `SyntaxErrorException` is thrown.

Once the end of the expression is reached, the remaining operators are popped off the stack and appended to `postfix`. Finally, `postfix` is converted to a `String` and returned.

Method processOperator uses private method precedence to determine the precedence of an operator (2 for *, /; 1 for +, -.). If the stack is empty or the condition

```
(precedence(op) > precedence(topOp))
```

is true, the current operator, op, is pushed onto the stack. Otherwise, the **while** loop executes, popping all operators off the stack that have the same or greater precedence than op and appending them to the postfix string.

```
while (!operatorStack.empty()
       && precedence(op) <= precedence(topOp)) {
    operatorStack.pop();
    postfix.append(topOp);
    postfix.append(' ');
```

After loop exit, the statement

```
operatorStack.push(op);
```

pushes the current operator onto the stack.

In method precedence, the statement

```
return PRECEDENCE[OPERATORS.indexOf(op)];
```

returns the element of **int**[] array PRECEDENCE selected by the method call OPERATORS.indexOf(op). The precedence value returned will be 1 or 2.

LISTING 3.7

InfixToPostfix.java

```
import java.util.*;

/** Translates an infix expression to a postfix expression. */
public class InfixToPostfix {

    // Insert nested class SyntaxErrorException. See Listing 3.6.

    // Data Fields
    /** The operator stack */
    private Stack<Character> operatorStack;
    /** The operators */
    private static final String OPERATORS = "+-*/";
    /** The precedence of the operators matches order in OPERATORS. */
    private static final int[] PRECEDENCE = {1, 1, 2, 2};
    /** The postfix string */
    private StringBuilder postfix;

    /** Convert a string from infix to postfix.
        @param infix The infix expression
        @throws SyntaxErrorException
    */
    public String convert(String infix)
            throws SyntaxErrorException {
        operatorStack = new Stack<Character>();
        postfix = new StringBuilder();
```

```
        String[] tokens = infix.split("\\s+");
        try {
            // Process each token in the infix string.
            for (String nextToken : tokens) {
                char firstChar = nextToken.charAt(0);
                // Is it an operand?
                if (Character.isJavaIdentifierStart(firstChar)
                        || Character.isDigit(firstChar)) {
                    postfix.append(nextToken);
                    postfix.append(' ');
                } // Is it an operator?
                else if(isOperator(firstChar)) {
                    processOperator(firstChar);
                }
                else {
                    throw new SyntaxErrorException
                        ("Unexpected Character Encountered: "
                         + firstChar);
                }
            }   // end loop.

            // Pop any remaining operators and
            // append them to postfix.
            while (!operatorStack.empty()) {
                char op = operatorStack.pop();
                postfix.append(op);
                postfix.append(' ');
            }
            // assert: Stack is empty, return result.
            return postfix.toString();
        } catch (EmptyStackException ex) {
            throw new SyntaxErrorException
                ("Syntax Error: The stack is empty");
        }
    }

    /** Method to process operators.
        @param op The operator
        @throws EmptyStackException
    */
    private void processOperator(char op) {
        if (operatorStack.empty()) {
            operatorStack.push(op);
        } else {
            // Peek the operator stack and
            // let topOp be top operator.
            char topOp = operatorStack.peek();
            if (precedence(op) > precedence(topOp)) {
                operatorStack.push(op);
            }
```

```
                else {
                    // Pop all stacked operators with equal
                    // or higher precedence than op.
                    while (!operatorStack.empty()
                           && precedence(op) <= precedence(topOp)) {
                        operatorStack.pop();
                        postfix.append(topOp);
                        postfix.append(' ');
                        if (!operatorStack.empty()) {
                            // Reset topOp.
                            topOp = operatorStack.peek();
                        }
                    }
                    // assert: Operator stack is empty or
                    //         current operator precedence >
                    //         top of stack operator precedence.
                    operatorStack.push(op);
                }
            }
        }

        /** Determine whether a character is an operator.
            @param ch The character to be tested
            @return true if ch is an operator
        */
        private boolean isOperator(char ch) {
            return OPERATORS.indexOf(ch) != -1;
        }

        /** Determine the precedence of an operator.
            @param op The operator
            @return the precedence
        */
        private int precedence(char op) {
            return PRECEDENCE[OPERATORS.indexOf(op)] ;
        }
    }
```

PROGRAM STYLE

Updating a StringBuilder Is an Efficient Operation

We used a `StringBuilder` object for `postfix` because we knew that `postfix` was going to be continually updated. Because `String` objects are immutable, it would have been less efficient to use a `String` object for `postfix`. A new `String` object would have to be allocated each time `postfix` changed.

Testing Listing 3.8 shows a `main` method that tests the `InfixToPostfix` class. When entering a test expression, be careful to type a space character between operands and operators.

Use enough test expressions to satisfy yourself that the conversion is correct for properly formed input expressions. For example, try different orderings and multiple occurrences of the operators. You should also try infix expressions where all operators have the same precedence (e.g., all multiplicative).

If `convert` detects a syntax error, it will throw the exception `InfixToPostfix.SyntaxErrorException`. The driver will catch this exception and display an error message. If an exception is not thrown, the driver will display the result. Unfortunately, not all possible errors are detected. For example, an adjacent pair of operators or operands is not detected. To detect this error, we would need to add a **`boolean`** flag whose value indicates whether the last token was an operand. If the flag is **`true`**, the next token must be an operator; if the flag is **`false`**, the next token must be an operand. This modification is left as an exercise.

LISTING 3.8
Main Method to Test `InfixToPostfix`

```
public static void main(String args[]) {
    InfixToPostfix inToPost = new InfixToPostfix();
    String infix = JOptionPane.showInputDialog
                   ("Enter an infix expression");
    try {
        String postfix = inToPost.convert(infix);
        JOptionPane.showMessageDialog(null,
                "Infix expression " + infix +
                "\nconverts to " + postfix);
    } catch (SyntaxErrorException e) {
        JOptionPane.showMessageDialog(null, e.getMessage());
    }
    System.exit(0);
}
```

CASE STUDY Converting Expressions with Parentheses

Problem The ability to convert expressions with parentheses is an important (and necessary) addition. Parentheses are used to separate an expression into subexpressions.

Analysis We can think of an opening parenthesis on an operator stack as a boundary or fence between operators. Whenever we encounter an opening parenthesis, we want to push it onto the stack. A closing parenthesis is the terminator symbol for a subexpression. Whenever we encounter a closing parenthesis, we want to pop off all operators on the stack until we pop the matching opening parenthesis. Neither opening nor closing parentheses should appear in the postfix expression. Because operators scanned after the opening parenthesis should be evaluated before the opening parenthesis, the precedence of the opening parenthesis must be smaller than any other operator. We also give a closing parenthesis the lowest precedence. This ensures that a "(" can only be popped by a ")".

Design We should modify method `processOperator` to push each opening parenthesis onto the stack as soon as it is scanned. Therefore, the method should begin with the following new condition:

```
if (operatorStack.empty() || op == '(') {
    operatorStack.push(op);
```

When a closing parenthesis is scanned, we want to pop all operators up to and including the matching opening parenthesis, inserting all operators popped (except for the opening parenthesis) in the postfix string. This will happen automatically in the **`while`** statement if the precedence of the closing parenthesis is smaller than that of any other operator except for the opening parenthesis:

```
while (!operatorStack.empty()
        && precedence(op) <= precedence(topOp)) {
    operatorStack.pop();
    if (topOp == '(') {
        // Matching '(' popped - exit loop.
        break;
    }
    postfix.append(topOp);
```

A closing parenthesis is considered processed when an opening parenthesis is popped from the stack and the closing parenthesis is not placed on the stack. The following **`if`** statement executes after the **`while`** loop exit:

```
if (op != ')')
    operatorStack.push(op);
```

Implementation Listing 3.9 shows class `InfixToPostfixParens`, modified to handle parentheses. The additions are shown in color. We have omitted parts that do not change.

Rather than impose the requirement of spaces between delimiters, we will use the `Scanner` method `findInLine` to extract tokens. The statements

```
Scanner scan = new Scanner(infix);
while ((nextToken = scan.findInLine("
        [\\p{L}\\p{N}]+|[-+/\\*()]")) ! = null)  {
```

create a `Scanner` object to scan the characters in `infix` (see Appendix A.10). The `while` loop repetition condition calls method `findInLine` to extract the next token from `infix`. Each token can be a sequence of letter and digit characters, or a single character that is an operator or a left or right parenthesis. This character is processed in the same way that it was in Listing 3.7. Loop exit occurs after all tokens are extracted (`findInLine` returns `null`).

LISTING 3.9
InfixToPostfixParens.java

```
import java.util.*;

/** Translates an infix expression with parentheses
    to a postfix expression.
*/
public class InfixToPostfixParens {

    // Insert nested class SyntaxErrorException here. See Listing 3.6.

    // Data Fields
    /** The operator stack */
    private Stack<Character> operatorStack;
    /** The operators */
    private static final String OPERATORS = "+-*/()";
    /** The precedence of the operators, matches order of OPERATORS. */
    private static final int[] PRECEDENCE = {1, 1, 2, 2, -1, -1};
    /** The postfix string */
    private StringBuilder postfix;

    /** Convert a string from infix to postfix.
        @param infix The infix expression
        @throws SyntaxErrorException
    */
    public String convert(String infix)
            throws SyntaxErrorException {
        operatorStack = new Stack<Character>();
        postfix = new StringBuilder();
        try {
            // Process each token in the infix string.
            String nextToken;
            Scanner scan = new Scanner(infix);
            while ((nextToken = scan.findInLine(
                    "[\\p{L}\\p{N}]+|[-+/\\*()]")) != null) {
                char firstChar = nextToken.charAt(0);
                // Is it an operand?
                if (Character.isJavaIdentifierStart(firstChar)
                        || Character.isDigit(firstChar)) {
                    postfix.append(nextToken);
                    postfix.append(' ');
                } // Is it an operator?
                else if(isOperator(firstChar)) {
```

```
                processOperator(firstChar);
            }
            else {
                throw new SyntaxErrorException
                    ("Unexpected Character Encountered: "
                     + firstChar);
            }
        } // end loop.

        // Pop any remaining operators
        // and append them to postfix.
        while (!operatorStack.empty()) {
            char op = operatorStack.pop();
            // Any '(' on the stack is not matched.
            if (op) == '(')
                throw new SyntaxErrorException(
                        "Unmatched opening parenthesis");
            postfix.append(op);
            postfix.append(' ');
        }
        // assert: Stack is empty, return result.
        return postfix.toString();
    } catch (EmptyStackException ex) {
        throw new SyntaxErrorException
            ("Syntax Error: The stack is empty");
    }
}

/** Method to process operators.
    @param op The operator
    @throws EmptyStackException
*/
private void processOperator(char op) {
    if (operatorStack.empty() || op == '(') {
        operatorStack.push(op);
    } else {
        // Peek the operator stack and
        // let topOp be the top operator.
        char topOp = operatorStack.peek();
        if (precedence(op) > precedence(topOp)) {
            operatorStack.push(op);
        }
        else {
            // Pop all stacked operators with equal
            // or higher precedence than op.
            while (!operatorStack.empty()
                   && precedence(op) <= precedence(topOp)) {
                operatorStack.pop();
                if (topOp == '(') {
                    // Matching '(' popped - exit loop.
                    break;
                }
                postfix.append(topOp);
```

```
                    postfix.append(' ');
                    if (!operatorStack.empty()) {
                        // Reset topOp.
                        topOp = operatorStack.peek();
                    }
                }

                // assert: Operator stack is empty or
                //         current operator precedence >
                //         top of stack operator precedence.
                if (op != ')')
                    operatorStack.push(op);
            }
        }
    }

    // Insert isOperator and precedence here. See Listing 3.7.
}
```

Tying the Case Studies Together

You can use the classes developed for the prior case studies to evaluate infix expressions with integer operands and nested parentheses. Your driver program will need to create instances of both classes and apply method `convert` to the `InfixToPostfixParens` object. The argument for `convert` will be the infix expression. The result will be its postfix form. Next it will apply method `eval` of the `PostfixEvaluator` object. The argument for `eval` will be the postfix expression returned by `convert`.

EXERCISES FOR SECTION 3.4

SELF-CHECK

1. Trace the evaluation of the following expressions using class `PostfixEvaluator`. Show the operand stack each time it is modified.

   `13 2 * 5 / 6 2 5 * - +`

   `5 4 * 6 7 + 4 2 / - *`

2. Trace the conversion of the following expressions to postfix using class `InfixToPostfix` or `InfixToPostfixParens`. Show the operator stack each time it is modified.

   ```
   y - 7 / 35 + 4 * 6 - 10
   ( x + 15 ) * ( 3 * ( 4 - (5 + 7 / 2 ) )
   ```

PROGRAMMING

1. Modify class `InfixToPostfix` to handle the exponentiation operator, indicated by the symbol `^`. The first operand is raised to the power indicated by the second operand. Assume that a sequence of `^` operators will not occur and that `precedence('^')` is greater than `precedence('*')`.

2. Discuss how you would modify the infix-to-postfix `convert` method to detect a sequence of two operators or two operands.

Chapter Review

- A stack is a last-in, first-out data structure (*LIFO*). This means that the last item added to a stack is the first one removed.
- A stack is a simple but powerful data structure. It has only four operators: empty, peek, pop, and push.
- Stacks are useful when we want to process information in the reverse of the order that it is encountered. For this reason, a stack was used to implement the balanced parenthesis checker and the palindrome finder.
- `java.util.Stack` is implemented as an extension of the `Vector` class. The problem with this approach is that it allows a client to invoke other methods from the `Vector` class.
- We showed three different ways to implement stacks: using an object of a class that implements the `List` interface as a container, using an array as a container, and using a linked list as a container.
- Stacks can be applied in algorithms for evaluating arithmetic expressions. We showed how to evaluate postfix expressions and how to translate infix expressions with and without parentheses to postfix.

Java API Interfaces and Classes Introduced in This Chapter

```
java.util.EmptyStackException
java.util.Stack
```

User-Defined Interfaces and Classes in This Chapter

```
ArrayStack               PalindromeFinder
InfixToPostfix           ParenChecker
InfixToPostfixParens     PostfixEvaluator
IsPalindrome             StackInt
LinkedStack              SyntaxErrorException
ListStack
```

Quick-Check Exercises

1. A stack is a ______-in, ______-out data structure.
2. Draw this stack `s` as an object of type `ArrayStack<Character>`. What is the value of data field `topOfStack`?

3. What is the value of s.empty() for the stack shown in Question 2?
4. What is returned by s.pop() for the stack shown in Question 2?
5. Answer Question 2 for a stack s implemented as a linked list (type LinkedStack<Character>).
6. Why should the statement s.remove(i), where s is of type StackInt and i is an integer index, not appear in a client program? Can you use this statement with an object of the Stack class defined in java.util? Can you use it with an object of class ArrayStack or LinkedStack?
7. What would be the postfix form of the following expression?

   ```
   x + y - 24  *  zone - ace /  25 + c1
   ```

   Show the contents of the operator stack just before each operator is processed and just after all tokens are scanned using method InfixToPostfix.convert.
8. Answer Question 7 for the following expression.

   ```
   ( x + y - 24 ) * ( zone - ace / ( 25 + c1 ) )
   ```

9. The value of the expression 20 35 - 5 / 10 7 * + is ______. Show the contents of the operand stack just before each operator is processed and just after all tokens are scanned.

Review Questions

1. Show the effect of each of the following operations on stack s. Assume that y (type Character) contains the character '&'. What are the final values of x and success and the contents of the stack s?

   ```
   Stack<Character> s = new Stack<Character>();
   char x;
   s.push('+');
   try {
       x = s.pop();
       success = true;
   }
   catch (EmptyStackException e) {
       success = false;
   }
   try {
       x = s.pop();
       success = true;
   }
   catch (EmptyStackException e) {
       success = false;
   }
   s.push('(');
   s.push(y);
   try {
       x = s.pop();
       success = true;
   }
   catch (EmptyStackException e) {
       success = false;
   }
   ```

2. Write a toString method for class ArrayStack<E>.
3. Write a toString method for class LinkedStack<E>.
4. Write an infix expression that would convert to the postfix expression in Quick-Check Question 9.

5. Write a constructor for class LinkedStack<E> that loads the stack from an array parameter. The last array element should be at the top of the stack.
6. Write a client that removes all negative numbers from a stack of Integer objects. If the original stack contained the integers 30, –15, 20, –25 (top of stack), the new stack should contain the integers 30, 20.
7. Write a method peekNextToTop that allows you to retrieve the element just below the one at the top of the stack without removing it. Write this method for both ArrayStack<E> and LinkedStack<E>. It should return **null** if the stack has just one element, and it should throw an exception if the stack is empty.

Programming Projects

1. Add a method isPalindromeLettersOnly to the PalindromeFinder class that bases its findings only on the letters in a string (ignoring spaces and other characters that are not letters).
2. Provide a complete implementation of class LinkedStack and test it on each of the applications in this chapter.
3. Provide a complete implementation of class ArrayStack and test it on each of the applications in this chapter.
4. Develop an Expression Manager that can do the following operations:

   Balanced Symbols Check
   - Read a mathematical expression from the user.
   - Check and report whether the expression is balanced.
   - {, }, (,), [,] are the only symbols considered for the check. All other characters can be ignored.

   Infix to Postfix Conversion
   - Read an infix expression from the user.
   - Perform the Balanced Parentheses Check on the expression read.
   - If the expression fails the Balanced Parentheses Check, report a message to the user that the expression is invalid.
   - If the expression passes the Balanced Parentheses Check, convert the infix expression into a postfix expression and display it to the user.
   - Operators to be considered are +, –, *, /, %.

   Postfix to Infix Conversion
   - Read a postfix expression from the user.
   - Convert the postfix expression into an infix expression and display it to the user.
   - Display an appropriate message if the postfix expression is not valid.
   - Operators to be considered are +, –, *, /, %.

   Evaluating a Postfix Expression
   - Read the postfix expression from the user.
   - Evaluate the postfix expression and display the result.
   - Display an appropriate message if the postfix expression is not valid.
   - Operators to be considered are +, –, *, /, %.
   - Operands should be only integers.

   Implementation
   - Design a menu that has buttons or requests user input to select from all the aforementioned operations.

5. Write a client program that uses the Stack abstract data type to simulate a session with a bank teller. Unlike most banks, this one has decided that the last customer to arrive will always be the first to be served. Create classes that represent information about a bank customer and a transaction. For each customer, you need to store a name, current balance, and a reference to the transaction. For each transaction, you need to store the transaction type (deposit or withdrawal) and the amount of the transaction. After every five customers are processed, display the size of the stack and the name of the customer who will be served next.
6. Write a program to handle the flow of widgets into and out of a warehouse. The warehouse will have numerous deliveries of new widgets and orders for widgets. The widgets in a filled order are billed at a profit of 50 percent over their cost. Each delivery of new widgets may have a different cost associated with it. The accountants for the firm have instituted a last-in, first-out system for filling orders. This means that the newest widgets are the first ones sent out to fill an order. Also, the most recent orders are filled first. This method of inventory can be represented using two stacks: orders-to-be-filled and widgets-on-hand. When a delivery of new widgets is received, any unfilled orders (on the orders-to-be-filled stack) are processed and filled. After all orders are filled, if there are widgets remaining in the new delivery, a new element is pushed onto the widgets-on-hand stack. When an order for new widgets is received, one or more objects are popped from the widgets-on-hand stack until the order has been filled. If the order is completely filled and there are widgets left over in the last object popped, a modified object with the quantity updated is pushed onto the widgets-on-hand stack. If the order is not completely filled, the order is pushed onto the orders-to-be-filled stack with an updated quantity of widgets to be sent out later. If an order is completely filled, it is not pushed onto the stack.

   Write a class with methods to process the shipments received and to process orders. After an order is filled, display the quantity sent out and the total cost for all widgets in the order. Also indicate whether there are any widgets remaining to be sent out at a later time. After a delivery is processed, display information about each order that was filled with this delivery and indicate how many widgets, if any, were stored in the object pushed onto the widgets-on-hand stack.
7. You can combine the algorithms for converting between infix to postfix and for evaluating postfix to evaluate an infix expression directly. To do so you need two stacks: one to contain operators and the other to contain operands. When an operand is encountered, it is pushed onto the operand stack. When an operator is encountered, it is processed as described in the infix to postfix algorithm. When an operator is popped off the operator stack, it is processed as described in the postfix evaluation algorithm: The top two operands are popped off the operand stack, the operation is performed, and the result is pushed back onto the operand stack. Write a program to evaluate infix expressions directly using this combined algorithm.
8. Write a client program that uses the Stack abstract data type to compile a simple arithmetic expression without parentheses. For example, the expression

   `a + b * c - d`

   should be compiled according to the following table:

Operator	Operand 1	Operand 2	Result
*	b	c	z
+	a	z	y
–	y	d	x

The table shows the order in which the operations are performed (*, +, -) and operands for each operator. The result column gives the name of an identifier (working backward from `z`) chosen to hold each result. Assume the operands are the letters `a` through `m` and the operators are (+, -, *, /). Your program should read each character and process it as follows: If the character is blank, ignore it. If the character is neither blank nor an operand nor an operator, display an error message and terminate the program. If it is an operand, push it onto the operand stack. If it is an operator, compare its precedence to that of the operator on top of the operator stack. If the current operator has higher precedence than the one currently on top of the stack (or stack is empty), it should be pushed onto the operator stack. If the current operator has the same or lower precedence, the operator on top of the operator stack must be evaluated next. This is done by popping that operator off the operator stack along with a pair of operands from the operand stack and writing a new line in the output table. The character selected to hold the result should then be pushed onto the operand stack. Next, the current operator should be compared to the new top of the operator stack. Continue to generate output lines until the top of the operator stack has lower precedence than the current operator or until it is empty. At this point, push the current operator onto the top of the stack and examine the next character in the data string. When the end of the string is reached, pop any remaining operator along with its operand pair just described. Remember to push the result character onto the operand stack after each table line is generated.

9. Another approach to checking for palindromes would be to store the characters of the string being checked in a stack and then remove half of the characters, pushing them onto a second stack. When you are finished, if the two stacks are equal, then the string is a palindrome. This works fine if the string has an even number of characters. If the string has an odd number of characters, an additional character should be removed from the original stack before the two stacks are compared. It doesn't matter what this character is because it doesn't have to be matched. Design, code, and test a program that implements this approach.

10. Operating systems sometimes use a fixed array storage area to accommodate a pair of stacks such that one grows from the bottom (with its first item stored at index 0) and the other grows from the top (with its first item stored at the highest array index). As the stacks grow, the top of the stacks will move closer together.

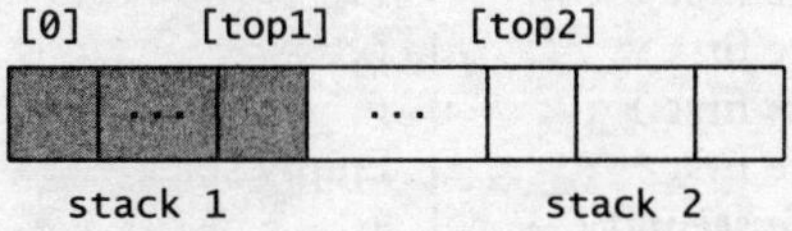

The stacks are full when the two top elements are stored in adjacent array elements (`top2 == top1 + 1`). Design, code, and test a class `DoubleStack` that implements this data structure. `DoubleStack` should support the normal stack operations (`push`, `pop`, `peek`, `empty`, etc.). Each stack method should have an additional `int` parameter that indicates which of the stacks (1 or 2) is being processed. For example, `push(1, item)` will push item onto stack 1.

Answers to Quick-Check Exercises

1. A stack is a *last*-in, *first*-out data structure.
2. Each character in array `theData` should be wrapped in a `Character` object. The value of `topOfStack` should be 2.

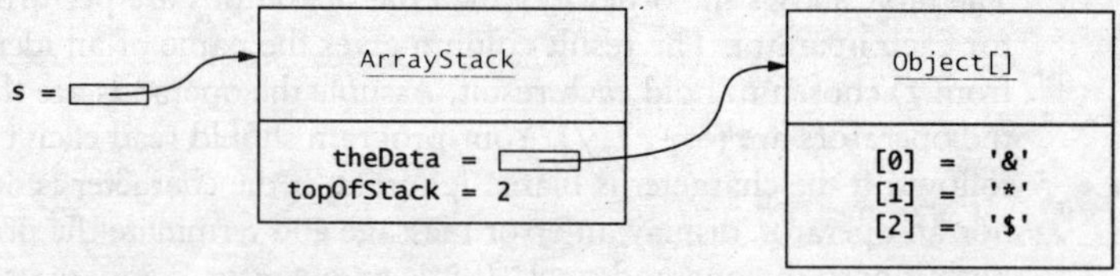

3. Method empty returns **false**.
4. pop returns a reference to the Character object that wraps '$'.
5. 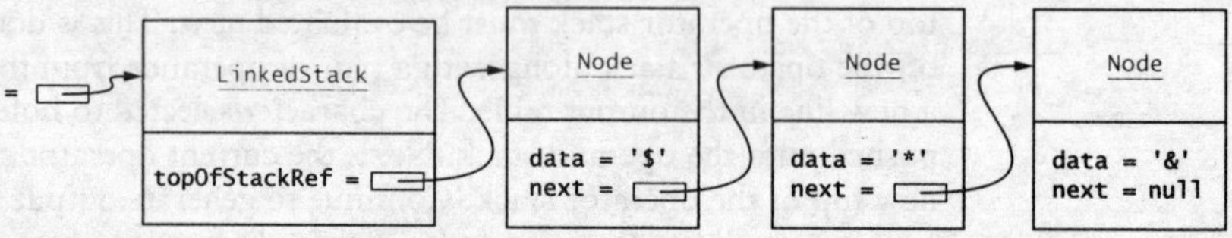

6. Method remove(int i) is not defined for classes that implement interface StackInt. The Stack class defined in API java.util would permit its use. Classes ArrayStack and LinkedStack would not.
7. Infix: x + y - 24 * zone - ace / 25 + c1
   Postfix: x y + 24 zone * - ace 25 / - c1 +
   Operator stack before first + : | Empty stack (vertical bar is bottom of stack)
   Operator stack before first - : | +
   Operator stack before first * : | -
   Operator stack before second - : | -, *
   Operator stack before first / : | -
   Operator stack before second + : | -, /
   Operator stack after all tokens scanned: | +
8. Infix: (x + y - 24) * (zone - ace / (25 + c1))
   Postfix: x y + 24 - zone ace 25 c1 + / - *
   Operator stack before first (: | Empty stack (vertical bar is bottom of stack)
   Operator stack before first + : | (
   Operator stack before first - : | (, +
   Operator stack before first) : | (, -
   Operator stack before first * : | Empty stack
   Operator stack before second (: | *
   Operator stack before second - : | *, (
   Operator stack before second / : | *, (, -
   Operator stack before third (: | *, (, -, /
   Operator stack before second + : | *, (, -, /, (
   Operator stack before second) : | *, (, -, /, (, +
   Operator stack before third) : | *, (, -, /
   Operator stack after all tokens scanned: | *
9. 20 35 - 5 / 10 7 * + is 67 (-3 + 70)
   Operand stack just before - : | 20, 35
   Operand stack just before / : | -15, 5
   Operand stack just before * : | -3, 10, 7
   Operand stack just before + : | -3, 70
   Operand stack after all tokens : | 67

Chapter 4

Queues

Chapter Objectives

- To learn how to represent a waiting line (queue) and how to use the methods in the `Queue` interface for insertion (`offer` and `add`), for removal (`remove` and `poll`), and for accessing the element at the front (`peek` and `element`)
- To understand how to implement the `Queue` interface using a single-linked list, a circular array, and a double-linked list
- To become familiar with the `Deque` interface and how to use its methods to insert and remove items from both ends of a deque
- To understand how to simulate the operation of a physical system that has one or more waiting lines using `Queues` and random number generators

In this chapter we study an abstract data type, queue, that is widely used like the stack but differs from it in one important way. A stack is a LIFO (last-in, first-out) list because the last element pushed onto a stack will be the first element popped off. A queue, on the other hand, is a FIFO (first-in, first-out) list because the first element inserted in the queue will be the first element removed.

You will learn how to use a queue to store items (e.g., customers) that will be accessed on a first-come, first-served basis. We will also show you how to implement queues. Finally, you will also learn how to use simulation to estimate the amount of time customers will spend waiting in a queue.

Queues

4.1 Queue Abstract Data Type

The easiest way to visualize a queue is to think of a line of customers waiting for service, as shown in Figure 4.1. Usually, the next person to be served is the one who has been waiting the longest, and latecomers are added to the end of the line. The Queue ADT gets its name from the fact that such a waiting line is called a queue in English-speaking countries other than the United States.

A Print Queue

In computer science, queues are used in operating systems to keep track of tasks waiting for a scarce resource and to ensure that the tasks are carried out in the order that they were generated. One example is a print queue. A Web surfer may select several pages to be printed in a few seconds. Because a printer is a relatively slow device (approximately 10 pages per minute), you will often select new pages to print faster than they can be printed. Rather than require you to wait until the current page is finished before you can select a new one, the operating system stores documents to

FIGURE 4.1
Customers Waiting in a Line or Queue

FIGURE 4.2
A Print Queue in the Windows Operating System

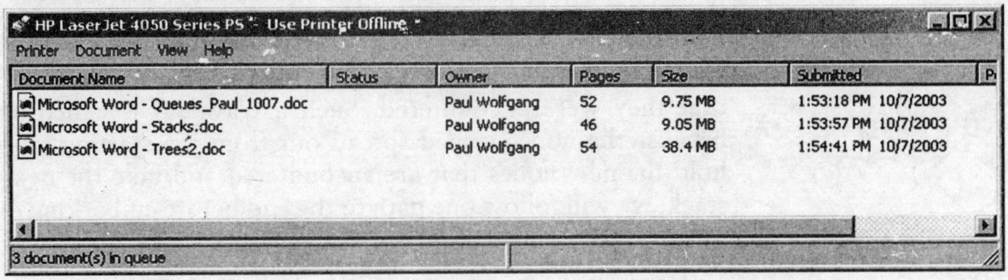

be printed in a print queue (see Figure 4.2). Because they are stored in a queue, the pages will be printed in the same order as they were selected (first-in, first-out). The document first inserted in the queue will be the first one printed.

The Unsuitability of a "Print Stack"

Suppose your operating system used a stack (last-in, first-out) instead of a queue to store documents waiting to print. Then the most recently selected Web page would be the next page to print. This may not matter if only one person is using the printer. However, if the printer is connected to a computer network, this would be a big problem. Unless the print queue was empty when you selected a page to print (and the page printed immediately), that page would not print until all pages selected after it (by yourself or any other person on the network) were printed. If you were waiting by the printer for your page to print before going to your next class, you would have no way of knowing how long your wait might be. You would also be very unhappy if people who started after you had their documents printed before yours. So a print queue is a much more sensible alternative than a print stack.

A Queue of Customers

FIGURE 4.3
A Queue of Customers

A queue of three customers waiting to buy concert tickets is shown in Figure 4.3. The name of the customer who has been waiting the longest is Thome; the name of the most recent arrival is Jones. Customer Thome will be the first customer removed from the queue (and able to buy tickets) when a ticket agent becomes available, and customer Abreu will then become the first one in the queue. Any new customers will be inserted in the queue after customer Jones.

Using a Queue for Traversing a Multi-Branch Data Structure

In Chapter 10, you will see a data structure, called a graph, that models a *network* of *nodes,* with many links connecting each node to other nodes in the network (see Figure 4.4). Unlike a linked list, in which each node has only one successor, a node in a graph may have several successors. For example, node 0 in Figure 4.4 has nodes 1 and 3 as its successors. Consequently, it is not a simple matter to visit the nodes in a systematic way and to ensure that each node is visited only once. Programmers

FIGURE 4.4
A Network of Nodes

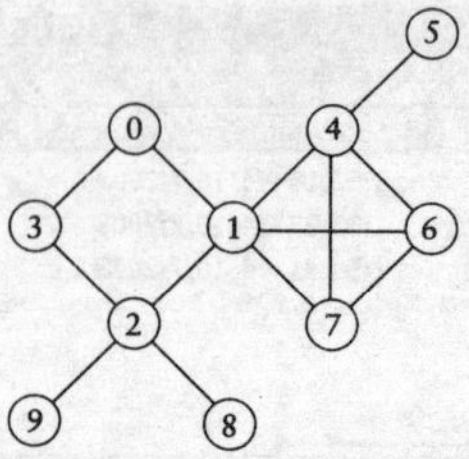

often use a queue to ensure that nodes closer to the starting point are visited before nodes that are farther away. We will not go into the details here because we cover them later, but the idea is to put nodes that have not yet been visited into the queue when they are first encountered. After visiting the current node, the next node to visit is taken from the queue. This ensures that nodes are visited in the same order that they were encountered. Such a traversal is called a *breadth-first traversal* because the nodes visited spread out from the starting point. If we use a stack to hold the new nodes that are encountered and take the next node to visit from the stack, we will follow one path to the end before embarking on a new path. This kind of traversal is called a *depth-first traversal.*

Specification for a Queue Interface

The `java.util` API provides a `Queue` interface (Table 4.1) that extends the `Collection` interface and, therefore, the `Iterable` interface (see Table 2.7). The `Queue` interface is a new feature that was added to Java 5.0.

Method `offer` inserts an element at the rear of the queue and returns **`true`** if successful and **`false`** if unsuccessful. Methods `remove` and `poll` both remove and return the element at the front of the queue. The only difference in their behavior is when the queue happens to be empty: `remove` throws an exception and `poll` just returns **`null`**. Methods `peek` and `element` both return the element at the front of the queue without removing it. The difference is that `element` throws an exception when the queue is empty.

Because interface `Queue` extends interface `Collection`, a full implementation of the `Queue` interface must implement all required methods of the `Collection` interface. Classes that implement the `Queue` interface need to code the methods in Table 4.1 as well as methods `add`, `iterator`, `isEmpty`, and `size` declared in the `Collection` interface.

TABLE 4.1
Specification of Interface Queue<E>

Method	Behavior
`boolean offer(E item)`	Inserts `item` at the rear of the queue. Returns **`true`** if successful; returns **`false`** if the item could not be inserted.
`E remove()`	Removes the entry at the front of the queue and returns it if the queue is not empty. If the queue is empty, throws a `NoSuchElementException`.
`E poll()`	Removes the entry at the front of the queue and returns it; returns **`null`** if the queue is empty.
`E peek()`	Returns the entry at the front of the queue without removing it; returns **`null`** if the queue is empty.
`E element()`	Returns the entry at the front of the queue without removing it. If the queue is empty, throws a `NoSuchElementException`.

Class LinkedList Implements the Queue Interface

Because the LinkedList class provides methods for inserting and removing elements at either end of a double-linked list, all the Queue methods can be easily implemented in class LinkedList. For this reason, the Java 5.0 LinkedList class implements the Queue interface. The statement

```
Queue<String> names = new LinkedList<String>();
```

creates a new Queue reference, names, that stores references to String objects. The actual object referenced by names is type LinkedList<String>. However, because names is a type Queue<String> reference, you can apply only the Queue methods to it.

EXAMPLE 4.1 The queue names created above contains five strings as shown in Figure 4.5(a). The name "Jonathan" was placed in the queue before the other four names; "Rich" was the last element placed in the queue.

For queue names in Figure 4.5(a), the value of names.isEmpty() is false. The statement

```
String first = names.peek();
```

or

```
String first = names.element();
```

stores "Jonathan" in first without changing names. The statement

```
String temp = names.remove();
```

or

```
String temp = names.poll();
```

removes "Jonathan" from names and stores a reference to it in temp. The queue names now contains four elements and is shown in Figure 4.5(b). The statement

```
names.offer("Philip");
```

or

```
names.add("Philip");
```

adds "Philip" to the rear of the queue; the queue names now contains five elements and is shown in Figure 4.5(c).

FIGURE 4.5
Queue names

(a)	(b)	(c)
Jonathan	Dustin	Dustin
Dustin	Robin	Robin
Robin	Debbie	Debbie
Debbie	Rich	Rich
Rich		Philip

EXERCISES FOR SECTION 4.1

SELF-CHECK

1. Draw the queue in Figure 4.3 as it will appear after the insertion of customer Harris and the removal of one customer from the queue. Which customer is removed? How many customers are left?
2. Answer Question 1 for the queue in Figure 4.5(c).

3. Assume that `myQueue` is an instance of a class that implements `Queue<String>` and `myQueue` is an empty queue. Explain the effect of each of the following operations.

```
myQueue.offer("Hello");
myQueue.offer("Bye");
System.out.println(myQueue.peek());
myQueue.remove();
myQueue.offer("Welcome");
if (!myQueue.isEmpty()) {
    System.out.println(myQueue.remove()
        + ", new size is " + myQueue.size());
    System.out.println("Item in front is " + myQueue.peek());
}
```

4. For the queue `names` in Figure. 4.3(c), what is the effect of the following?

```
while (!names.isEmpty()) {
    System.out.println(names.remove());
}
```

5. What would be the effect of using `peek` instead of `remove` in Question 4?

PROGRAMMING

1. Write a main function that creates two stacks of `Integer` objects and a queue of `Integer` objects. Store the numbers -1, 15, 23, 44, 4, 99 in the first stack. The top of the stack should store 99.
2. Write a loop to get each number from the first stack and store it in the second stack and in the queue.
3. Write a second loop to remove a value from the second stack and from the queue and display each pair of values on a separate output line. Continue until the data structures are empty. Show the output.

4.2 Maintaining a Queue of Customers

In this section we present an application that maintains a queue of `Strings` representing the names of customers waiting for service. Our goal is just to maintain the list and ensure that customers are inserted and removed properly. We will allow a user to determine the queue size, the person at the front of the queue, and how many people are ahead of a particular person in the queue.

CASE STUDY Maintaining a Queue

Problem Write a menu-driven program that maintains a list of customers waiting for service. The program user should be able to insert a new customer in the line, display the customer who is next in line, remove the customer who is next in line, display the length of the line, or determine how many people are ahead of a specified customer.

Analysis As discussed earlier, a queue is a good data structure for storing a list of customers waiting for service because they would expect to be served in the order in which they arrived. We can display the menu (using the `JOptionPane.showOptionDialog` method) and then perform the requested operation by calling the appropriate `Queue` method to update the customer list. We will use `JOptionPane` dialog windows to enter new customer names and to display results.

Problem Inputs

The operation to be performed
The name of a customer

Problem Outputs

The effect of each operation

Design We will write a class `MaintainQueue` to store the queue and control its processing. Class `MaintainQueue` has a `Queue<String>` component `customers`.

Method `processCustomers` displays a menu of choices and processes the user selection by calling the appropriate `Queue` method. Table 4.2 shows class `MaintainQueue`.

The algorithm for method `processCustomers` follows.

Algorithm for processCustomers

1. **while** the user is not finished
2. Display the menu and get the operation selected.
3. Perform the operation selected.

Each operation is performed by a call to one of the `Queue` methods, except for determining the position of a particular customer in the queue. The algorithm for this operation follows.

Algorithm for Determining the Position of a Customer

1. Get the customer name.
2. Set the count of customers ahead of this one to 0.
3. **for** each customer in the queue

TABLE 4.2
Class `MaintainQueue`

Data Field	Attribute
`private Queue<String> customers`	A queue of customers.
Method	**Behavior**
`public static void processCustomers()`	Accepts and processes each user's selection.

4. **if** this customer is not the one sought
5. Increment the count.
6. **else**
7. Display the count of customers and exit the loop.
8. **if** all customers were examined without success
9. Display a message that the customer is not in the queue.

The loop that begins at Step 3 requires us to access each element in the queue. However, only the element at the front of the queue is directly accessible using method `peek` or `element`. We will show how to get around this limitation by using an `Iterator` to access each element of the queue.

Implementation Listing 4.1 shows the data field declarations and the constructor for class `MaintainQueue`. The constructor sets `customers` to reference an instance of class `LinkedList<String>`.

LISTING 4.1

Constructor for Class `MaintainQueue`

```
import javax.swing.*;

/** Class to maintain a queue of customers. */
public class MaintainQueue {

    // Data Field
    private Queue<String> customers;

    // Constructor
    /** Create an empty queue. */
    public MaintainQueue() {
        customers = new LinkedList<String>();
    }
. . .
}
```

In method `processCustomers` (Listing 4.2), the call to method `showOptionDialog` displays the menu shown in Figure 4.6. After the selection is returned to `choiceNum`, the **`switch`** statement calls a `Queue` method to perform the selected operation. For example, if the user clicks the *insert* button, the statements

```
name = JOptionPane.showInputDialog
        ("Enter new customer name");
customers.offer(name);
```

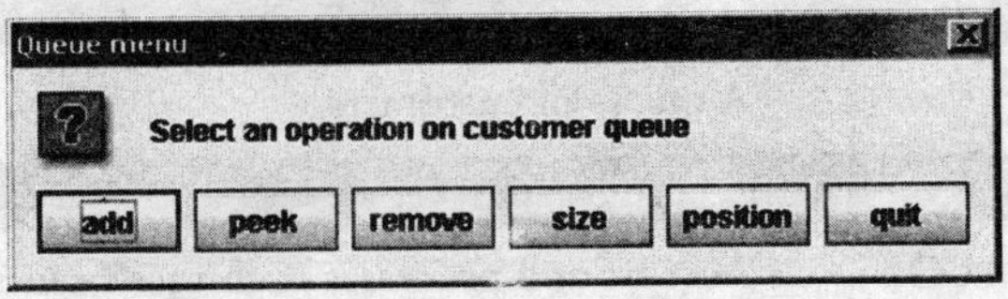

FIGURE 4.6
Menu Displayed by `MaintainQueue`

read the customer name and insert it into in the queue. The **switch** statement is inside a **try-catch** sequence that handles a NoSuchElementException (caused by an attempt to remove or retrieve an element from an empty queue) by displaying an error message window.

The implementation of each case in the **switch** statement is rather straightforward. Case 4 finds the position of a customer in the queue. The enhanced **for** statement uses an Iterator to access each element of the queue and store it in nextName. The **if** condition compares nextName to the name of the customer being sought. The variable countAhead is incremented each time this comparison is unsuccessful.

```
int countAhead = 0;
for (String nextName : customers) {
    if (!nextName.equals(name)) {
        countAhead ++;
    } else {
        JOptionPane.showMessageDialog(null,
                "The number of customers ahead of "
                + name + " is " + countAhead);
        break;          // Customer found, exit loop.
    }
}
```

If the desired name is accessed, its position is displayed and the loop is exited. If the name is not found, the loop is exited after the last name is processed. The **if** statement following the loop displays a message if the name was not found. This will be the case when countAhead is equal to the queue size.

LISTING 4.2

Method processCustomers in Class MaintainQueue

```
/** Performs the operations selected on queue customers.
    pre:  customers has been created.
    post: customers is modified based on user selections.
*/
public void processCustomers() {
    int choiceNum = 0;
    String[] choices =
        {"add", "peek", "remove", "size", "position", "quit"};

    // Perform all operations selected by user.
    while (choiceNum < choices.length - 1) {
        // Select the next operation.
        choiceNum = JOptionPane.showOptionDialog(null,
                "Select an operation on customer queue",
                "Queue menu", JOptionPane.YES_NO_CANCEL_OPTION,
                JOptionPane.QUESTION_MESSAGE, null,
                choices, choices[0]);

        // Process the current choice.
        try {
```

```
String name;
switch (choiceNum) {
    case 0 :
        name = JOptionPane.showInputDialog
                ("Enter new customer name");
        customers.offer(name);
        JOptionPane.showMessageDialog(null,
                "Customer " + name
                + " added to the queue");
        break;
    case 1 :
        JOptionPane.showMessageDialog(null,
                "Customer " + customers.element()
                + " is next in the queue");
        break;
    case 2 :
        JOptionPane.showMessageDialog(null,
                "Customer " + customers.remove()
                + " removed from the queue");
        break;
    case 3 :
        JOptionPane.showMessageDialog(null,
                "Size of queue is " + customers.size());
        break;
    case 4 :
        name = JOptionPane.showInputDialog
                ("Enter customer name");
        int countAhead = 0;
        for (String nextName : customers) {
            if (!nextName.equals(name)) {
            countAhead ++;
            } else {
                JOptionPane.showMessageDialog(null,
                        "The number of customers ahead of "
                        + name + " is " + countAhead);
                break; // Customer found, exit loop.
            }
        }
        // Check whether customer was found.
        if (countAhead == customers.size())
            JOptionPane.showMessageDialog(null,
                    name + " is not in queue");
        break;
    case 5 :
        JOptionPane.showMessageDialog(null,
                "Leaving customer queue. "
                + "\nNumber of customers in queue is "
                + customers.size());
        break;
    default :
        JOptionPane.showMessageDialog(null,
                "Invalid selection");
        break;
```

```
            }
        }
        catch (NoSuchElementException e) {
            JOptionPane.showMessageDialog(null,
                    "The Queue is empty", "",
                    JOptionPane.ERROR_MESSAGE);
        }
    }
}
```

Testing You can use class `MaintainQueue` to test each of the different `Queue` implementations discussed in the next section. You should verify that all customers are stored and retrieved in first-in, first-out order. You should also verify that a `NoSuchElementException` is thrown if you attempt to remove or retrieve a customer from an empty queue. Thoroughly test the queue by selecting different sequences of queue operations.

PROGRAM STYLE

When to Use the Different Queue Methods

For a queue of unlimited size, add and `offer` are logically equivalent. Both return `true` and will never throw an exception. For a bounded queue, add will throw an exception if the queue is full, but `offer` will return `false`.

For peek versus `element` and `poll` versus `remove`, peek and `poll` don't throw exceptions, but the user should either check for a return value of `null`, or be sure that the calls are within an `if` or `while` block that tests for a nonempty queue before they are called.

EXERCISES FOR SECTION 4.2

SELF-CHECK

1. Write an algorithm to display all the elements in a queue using just the queue operations. How would your algorithm change the queue?
2. Trace the following fragment for a `Stack<String>` s and an empty queue q (type `Queue<String>`).

```
String item;
while (!s.empty()) {
    item = s.pop();
    q.offer(item);
}
while (!q.isEmpty()) {
    item = q.remove();
    s.push(item);
}
```

a. What is stored in stack `s` after the first loop executes? What is stored in queue `q` after the first loop executes?

b. What is stored in stack `s` after the second loop executes? What is stored in queue `q` after the second loop executes?

PROGRAMMING

1. Write a `toString` method for class `MaintainQueue`.

4.3 Implementing the Queue Interface

In this section we discuss three approaches to implementing a queue: using a double-linked list, a single-linked list, and an array. We begin with a double-linked list.

Using a Double-Linked List to Implement the Queue Interface

Insertion and removal from either end of a double-linked list is O(1), so either end can be the front (or rear) of the queue. The Java designers decided to make the head of the linked list the front of the queue and the tail the rear of the queue. However, there is a problem with this approach. Because a `LinkedList` object is used as a queue, it may be possible to apply other `LinkedList` methods in addition to the ones required by the `Queue` interface. Some of them would violate the queue property that only the first element can be accessed. A better approach would be to create a new class that has a `LinkedList` component and then code, by delegation to the `LinkedList` class, only the public methods that are required by the `Queue` interface. We show some methods below; the rest are left as exercises.

```
import java.util.*;

/** Implements the Queue interface using a LinkedList component. */
public class KWQueue<E> implements Queue<E> {

    // Data Field
    private LinkedList<E> theQueue
            = new LinkedList<E>();  // LinkedList that is the queue.

    /** Inserts an item at the rear of the queue.
        @param item The element to add
        @return true (always successful)
    */
    @Override
    public boolean offer(E item) {
        theQueue.addLast(item);
        return true;
    }

    /** Removes the entry at the front of the queue and returns it.
        @return The item removed if successful, or null if not
    */
    @Override
    public E poll() {
```

```
        if (size() == 0)
            return null;
        else
            return theQueue.remove(0);
    }

    /** Returns the item at the front of the queue without removing it.
        @return The item at the front if successful; null if not
    */
    @Override
    public E peek() {
        if (size() == 0)
            return null;
        else
            return theQueue.getFirst();
    }
    . . .
```

Using a Single-Linked List to Implement the Queue Interface

We can implement a queue using a single-linked list like the one shown in Figure 4.7. Class `ListQueue` contains a collection of `Node<E>` objects (see Section 2.5). Recall that class `Node<E>` has attributes `data` (type `E`) and `next` (type `Node<E>`).

Insertions are at the rear of a queue, and removals are from the front. We need a reference to the last list node so that insertions can be performed in O(1) time; otherwise, we would have to start at the list head and traverse all the way down the list to do an insertion. There is a reference variable `front` to the first list node (the list head) and a reference variable `rear` to the last list node. There is also a data field `size`.

The number of elements in the queue is changed by methods `insert` and `remove`, so `size` must be incremented by one in `insert` and decremented by one in `remove`. The value of `size` is tested in `isEmpty` to determine the status of the queue. The method `size` simply returns the value of data field `size`.

Listing 4.3 shows class `ListQueue<E>`. Method `offer` treats insertion into an empty queue as a special case because both `front` and `rear` should reference the new node after the insertion.

```
rear = new Node<E>(item, null);
front = rear;
```

If we insert into a queue that is not empty, the new node must be linked to the old rear of the queue, but `front` is unchanged.

```
rear.next = new Node<E>(item, null);
rear = rear.next;
```

FIGURE 4.7
A Queue as a Single-Linked List

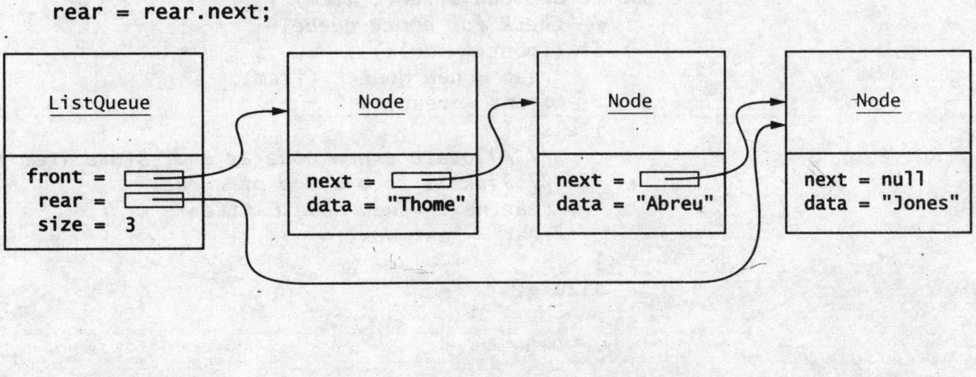

If the queue is empty, method peek returns `null`. Otherwise, it returns the element at the front of the queue:

```
return front.data;
```

Method `poll` calls method peek and returns its result. However, before returning, it disconnects the node at the front of a nonempty queue and decrements `size`.

```
front = front.next;
size--;
```

Listing 4.3 is incomplete. To finish it, you need to write methods `remove`, `element`, `size`, and `isEmpty`. You also need to code an `iterator` method and a class `Iter` with methods `next`, `hasNext`, and `remove`. This class will be similar to class `KWListIter` (see Section 2.6).

You can simplify this task by having `ListQueue<E>` extend class `java.util.AbstractQueue<E>`. This class implements `add`, `remove`, and `element` using `offer`, `poll`, and `peek`, and inherits from its superclass, `AbstractCollection<E>`, all methods needed to implement the `Collection<E>` interface (the superinterface of `Queue<E>`).

LISTING 4.3

Class `ListQueue`

```
import java.util.*;

/** Implements the Queue interface using a single-linked list. */
public class ListQueue<E> extends AbstractQueue<E>
                          implements Queue<E> {

    // Data Fields
    /** Reference to front of queue. */
    private Node<E> front;
    /** Reference to rear of queue. */
    private Node<E> rear;
    /** Size of queue. */
    private int size;

    // Insert inner class Node<E> for single-linked list here.
    // (See Listing 2.1.)

    // Methods
    /** Insert an item at the rear of the queue.
        post: item is added to the rear of the queue.
        @param item The element to add
        @return true (always successful)
    */
    @Override
    public boolean offer(E item) {
        // Check for empty queue.
        if (front == null) {
            rear = new Node<E>(item);
            front = rear;
        } else {
            // Allocate a new node at end, store item in it, and
            // link it to old end of queue.
            rear.next = new Node<E>(item);
            rear = rear.next;
        }
        size++;
```

```
        return true;
    }

    /** Remove the entry at the front of the queue and return it
        if the queue is not empty.
        post: front references item that was second in the queue.
        @return The item removed if successful, or null if not
    */
    @Override
    public E poll() {
        E item = peek();    // Retrieve item at front.
        if (item == null)
            return null;
        // Remove item at front.
        front = front.next;
        size--;
        return item;    // Return data at front of queue.
    }

    /** Return the item at the front of the queue without removing it.
        @return The item at the front of the queue if successful;
                return null if the queue is empty
    */
    @Override
    public E peek() {
        if (size == 0)
            return null;
        else
            return front.data;
    }

    // Insert class Iter and other required methods.
    . . .
}
```

Using a Circular Array to Implement the Queue Interface

While the time efficiency of using a single- or double-linked list to implement the `Queue` is acceptable, there is some space inefficiency. Each node of a single-linked list contains a reference to its successor, and each node of a double-linked list contains references to its predecessor and successor. These additional references will increase the storage space required.

An alternative is to use an array. If we use an array, we can do an insertion at the rear of the array in O(1) time. However, a removal from the front will be an O(n) process if we shift all the elements that follow the first one over to fill the space vacated. Similarly, removal from the rear is O(1), but insertion at the front is O(n). We next discuss how to avoid this inefficiency.

Overview of the Design

To represent a queue, we will use an object with four **`int`** data members (`front`, `rear`, `size`, `capacity`) and an array data member, `theData`, which provides storage for the queue elements.

```
    /** Index of the front of the queue. */
    private int front;
    /** Index of the rear of the queue. */
```

```
    private int rear;
    /** Current size of the queue. */
    private int size;
    /** Current capacity of the queue. */
    private int capacity;
    /** Default capacity of the queue. */
    private static final int DEFAULT_CAPACITY = 10;

    /** Array to hold the data. */
    private E[] theData;
```

The **int** fields front and rear are indices to the queue elements at the front and rear of the queue, respectively. The **int** field size keeps track of the actual number of items in the queue and allows us to determine easily whether the queue is empty (size is 0) or full (size is capacity).

It makes sense to store the first queue item in element 0, the second queue item in element 1, and so on. So we should set front to 0 and rear to -1 when we create an initially empty queue. Each time we do an insertion, we should increment size and rear by 1 so that front and rear will both be 0 if a queue has one element. Figure 4.8 shows an instance of a queue that is filled to its capacity (size is capacity). The queue contains the symbols &, *, +, /, –, inserted in that order.

Because the queue in Figure 4.8 is filled to capacity, we cannot insert a new character without allocating more storage. However, we can remove a queue element by decrementing size and incrementing front to 1, thereby removing theData[0] (the symbol &) from the queue. Figure 4.9 shows the queue after removing the first element (it is still in the array, but not part of the queue). The queue contains the symbols *, +, /, – in that order.

Although the queue in Figure 4.9 is no longer filled, we cannot insert a new character because rear is at its maximum value. One way to solve this problem is to

FIGURE 4.8
A Queue Filled with Characters

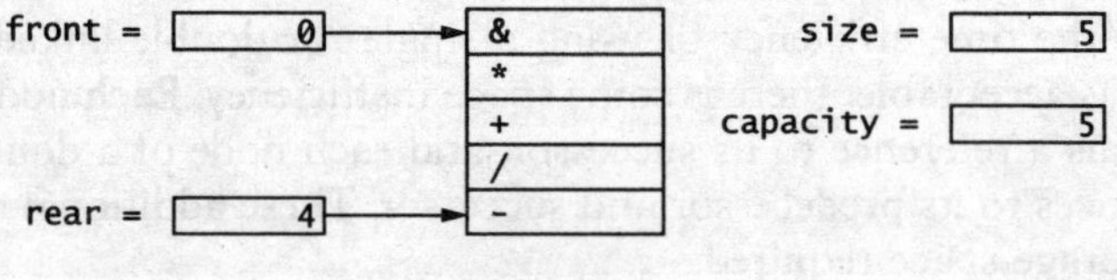

FIGURE 4.9
The Queue after Deletion of the First Element

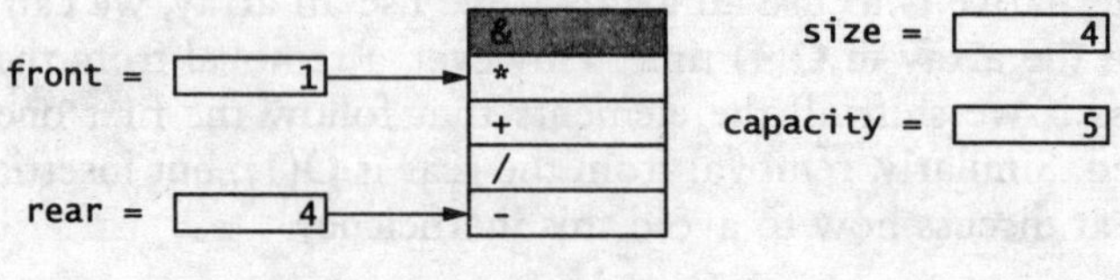

FIGURE 4.10
A Queue as a Circular Array

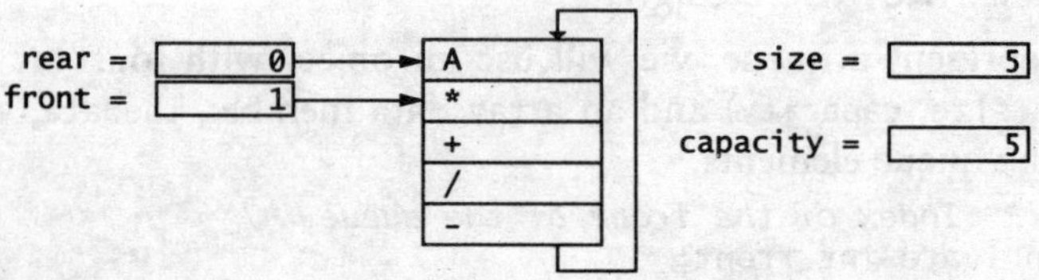

shift the elements in array `theData` so that the empty cells come after `rear` and then adjust `front` and `rear` accordingly. This array shifting must be done very carefully to avoid losing track of active array elements. It is also an O(n) operation.

A better way to solve this problem is to represent the array field `theData` as a *circular array*. In a circular array, the elements wrap around so that the first element actually follows the last. This is like counting modulo `size`; the array subscripts take on the values 0, 1, . . . , `size - 1`, 0, 1, and so on. This allows us to "increment" `rear` to 0 and store a new character in `theData[0]`. Figure 4.10 shows the queue after inserting a new element (the character `A`). After the insertion, `front` is still 1 but `rear` becomes 0. The contents of `theData[0]` change from `&` to `A`. The queue now contains the symbols `*`, `+`, `/`, `-`, `A` in that order.

EXAMPLE 4.2 The upper half of Figure 4.11 shows the effect of removing two elements from the queue just described. There are currently three characters in this queue (stored in `theData[3]`, `theData[4]`, and `theData[0]`). The queue now contains the symbols `/`, `-`, `A` in that order.

The lower half of Figure 4.11 shows the queue after insertion of a new character (`B`). The value of `rear` is incremented to 1, and the next element is inserted in `theData[1]`. This queue element follows the character `A` in `theData[0]`. The value of `front` is still 3 because the character `/` at `theData[3]` has been in the queue the longest. `theData[2]` is now the only queue element that is unused. The queue now contains the symbols `/`, `-`, `A`, `B` in that order.

FIGURE 4.11
The Effect of Two Deletions . . . and One Insertion

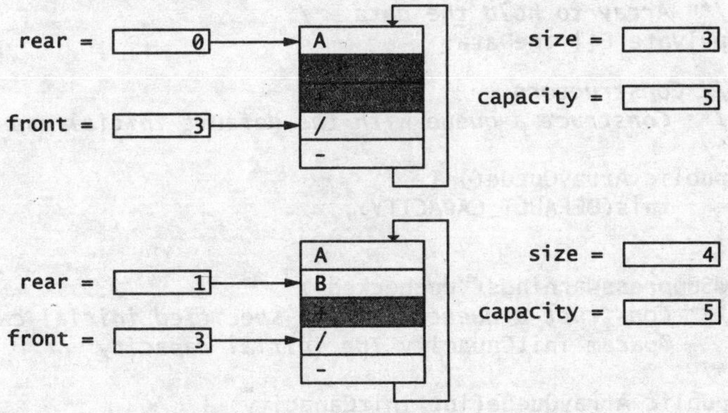

Implementing `ArrayQueue<E>`

Listing 4.4 shows the implementation of the class `ArrayQueue<E>`.

The constructors set `size` to 0 and `front` to 0 because array element `theData[0]` is considered the front of the empty queue, and `rear` is initialized to `capacity - 1` (instead of –1) because the queue is circular.

In method `offer`, the statement

```
rear = (rear + 1) % capacity;
```

is used to increment the value of rear modulo capacity. When rear is less than capacity, this statement simply increments its value by one. But when rear becomes equal to capacity - 1, the next value of rear will be 0 (capacity mod capacity is 0), thereby wrapping the last element of the queue around to the first element. Because the constructor initializes rear to capacity - 1, the first queue element will be placed in theData[0] as desired.

In method poll, the element currently stored in theData[front] is copied into result before front is incremented modulo capacity; result is then returned. In method peek, the element at theData[front] is returned, but front is not changed.

LISTING 4.4

ArrayQueue.java

```
/** Implements the Queue interface using a circular array. */
public class ArrayQueue<E> extends AbstractQueue<E>
                           implements Queue<E> {

    // Data Fields
    /** Index of the front of the queue. */
    private int front;
    /** Index of the rear of the queue. */
    private int rear;
    /** Current size of the queue. */
    private int size;
    /** Current capacity of the queue. */
    private int capacity;
    /** Default capacity of the queue. */
    private static final int DEFAULT_CAPACITY = 10;
    /** Array to hold the data. */
    private E[] theData;

    // Constructors
    /** Construct a queue with the default initial capacity.
    */
    public ArrayQueue() {
        this(DEFAULT_CAPACITY);
    }

    @SuppressWarnings("unchecked")
    /** Construct a queue with the specified initial capacity.
        @param initCapacity The initial capacity
    */
    public ArrayQueue(int initCapacity) {
        capacity = initCapacity;
        theData = (E[]) new Object[capacity];
        front = 0;
        rear = capacity - 1;
        size = 0;
    }

    // Public Methods
    /** Inserts an item at the rear of the queue.
        post: item is added to the rear of the queue.
        @param item The element to add
        @return true (always successful)
```

```
    */
    @Override
    public boolean offer(E item) {
        if (size == capacity) {
            reallocate();
        }
        size++;
        rear = (rear + 1) % capacity;
        theData[rear] = item;
        return true;
    }

    /** Returns the item at the front of the queue without removing it.
        @return The item at the front of the queue if successful;
                return null if the queue is empty
    */
    @Override
    public E peek() {
        if (size == 0)
            return null;
        else
            return theData[front];
    }

    /** Removes the entry at the front of the queue and returns it
        if the queue is not empty.
        post: front references item that was second in the queue.
        @return The item removed if successful or null if not
    */
    @Override
    public E poll() {
        if (size == 0) {
            return null;
        }
        E result = theData[front];
        front = (front + 1) % capacity;
        size--;
        return result;
    }

    // Private Methods
    /** Double the capacity and reallocate the data.
        pre: The array is filled to capacity.
        post: The capacity is doubled and the first half of the
              expanded array is filled with data.
    */
    @SuppressWarnings("unchecked")
    private void reallocate() {
        int newCapacity = 2 * capacity;
        E[] newData = (E[]) new Object[newCapacity];
        int j = front;
        for (int i = 0; i < size; i++) {
            newData[i] = theData[j];
            j = (j + 1) % capacity;
        }
        front = 0;
```

```
            rear = size - 1;
            capacity = newCapacity;
            theData = newData;
        }
    }
```

Increasing Queue Capacity

When the capacity is reached, we double the capacity and copy the array into the new one, as was done for the `ArrayList`. However, we can't simply use the `reallocate` method we developed for the `ArrayList` because of the circular nature of the array. We can't copy over elements from the original array to the first half of the expanded array, maintaining their position. We must first copy the elements from position `front` through the end of the original array to the beginning of the expanded array; then copy the elements from the beginning of the original array through `rear` to follow those in the expanded array (see Figure 4.12).

We begin by creating an array `newData`, whose capacity is double that of `theData`. The loop

```
int j = front;
for (int i = 0; i < size; i++) {
    newData[i] = theData[j];
    j = (j + 1) % capacity;
}
```

copies `size` elements over from `theData` to the first half of `newData`. In the copy operation

```
newData[i] = theData[j]
```

subscript `i` for `newData` goes from 0 to `size - 1` (the first half of `newData`). Subscript `j` for `theData` starts at `front`. The statement

```
j = (j + 1) % capacity;
```

increments the subscript for array `theData`. Therefore, subscript `j` goes from `front` to `capacity - 1` (in increments of 1) and then back to 0. So the elements are copied from `theData` in the sequence `theData[front], . . . , theData[capacity - 1],`

FIGURE 4.12
Reallocating a Circular Array

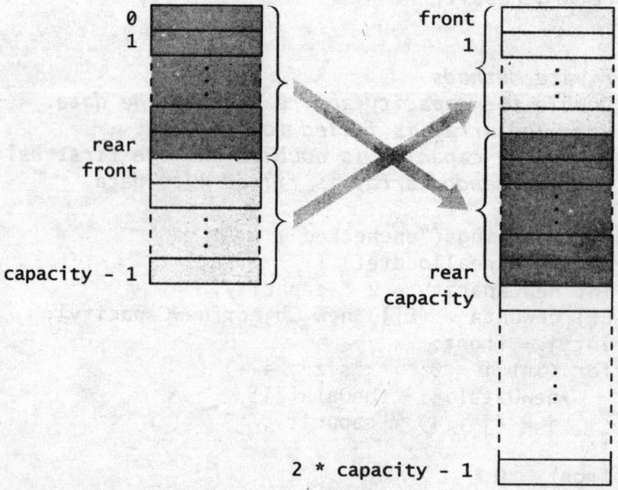

theData[0], ... , theData[rear], where theData[front] is stored in newData[0] and theData[rear] is stored in newData[size - 1]. After the copy loop, front is reset to 0 and rear is reset to size - 1 (see Figure 4.12).

By choosing a new capacity that is twice the current capacity, the cost of the reallocation is amortized across each insert, just as for an ArrayList. Thus, insertion is still considered an O(1) operation.

PITFALL

Incorrect Use of Arrays.copyOf to Expand a Circular Array

You might consider using the following method to copy all of the elements over from the original array theData to the first half of the expanded array theData.

```
private void reallocate() {
    capacity = 2 * capacity;
    theData = Arrays.copyOf(theData, capacity);
}
```

The problem is that in the circular array before expansion, element theData[0] followed the last array element. However, after expansion, the element that was formerly in the last position would now be in the middle of the array, so theData[0] would not follow it.

Implementing Class ArrayQueue<E>.Iter

Just as for class ListQueue<E>, we must implement the missing Queue methods and an inner class Iter to fully implement the Queue interface. Listing 4.5 shows inner class Iter.

Data field index stores the subscript of the next element to access. The constructor initializes index to front when a new Iter object is created. Data field count keeps track of the number of items accessed so far. Method hasNext returns **true** if count is less than the queue size. Method next returns the element at position index and increments index and count. Method Iter.remove throws an UnsupportedOperationException because it would violate the contract for a queue to remove an item other than the first one.

LISTING 4.5

Class ArrayQueue<E>.Iter

```
/** Inner class to implement the Iterator<E> interface. */
private class Iter implements Iterator<E> {
    // Data Fields
    // Index of next element */
    private int index;
    // Count of elements accessed so far */
    private int count = 0;

    // Methods
    // Constructor
```

```
        /** Initializes the Iter object to reference the first queue element.
        */
        public Iter() {
            index = front;
        }

        /** Returns true if there are more elements in the queue to access. */
        @Override
        public boolean hasNext() {
            return count < size;
        }

        /** Returns the next element in the queue.
            pre: index references the next element to access.
            post: index and count are incremented.
            @return The element with subscript index
        */
        @Override
        public E next() {
            if (!hasNext()) {
                throw new NoSuchElementException();
            }
            E returnValue = theData[index];
            index = (index + 1) % capacity;
            count++;
            return returnValue;
        }

        /** Remove the item accessed by the Iter object - not implemented. */
        @Override
        public void remove() {
            throw new UnsupportedOperationException();
        }
    }
```

Comparing the Three Implementations

As mentioned earlier, all three implementations of the Queue interface are comparable in terms of computation time. All operations are O(1) regardless of the implementation. Although reallocating an array is an $O(n)$ operation, it is amortized over n items, so the cost per item is O(1).

In terms of storage requirements, both linked-list implementations require more storage because of the extra space required for links. To perform an analysis of the storage requirements, you need to know that Java stores a reference to the data for a queue element in each node in addition to the links. Therefore, each node for a single-linked list would store a total of two references (one for the data and one for the link), a node for a double-linked list would store a total of three references, and a node for a circular array would store just one reference. Therefore, a double-linked list would require 1.5 times the storage required for a single-linked list with the same number of elements. A circular array that is filled to capacity would require half the storage of a single-linked list to store the same number of elements. However, if the array were just reallocated, half the array would be empty, so it would require the same storage as a single-linked list.

EXERCISES FOR SECTION 4.3

SELF-CHECK

1. Show the new array for the queue in Figure 4.10 after the array size is doubled.
2. Provide the algorithm for the methods in Programming Exercise 1 below.
3. Redraw the queue in Figure 4.7 so that `rear` references the list head and `front` references the list tail. Show the queue after an element is inserted and an element is removed. Explain why the approach used in the book is better.

PROGRAMMING

1. Write the missing methods required by the `Queue` interface and inner class `Iter` for class `ListQueue<E>`. Class `Iter` should have a data field `current` of type `Node<E>`. Data field `current` should be initialized to `first` when a new `Iter` object is created. Method `next` should return the value of `current` and advance `current`. Method `remove` should throw an `UnsupportedOperationException`.
2. Write the missing methods for class `KWQueue<E>` required by the `Queue` interface.
3. Write the missing methods for class `ArrayQueue<E>` required by the `Queue` interface.
4. Replace the loop in method `reallocate` with two calls to `System.arraycopy`.
5. For Self-Check Exercise 3, write methods `offer` and `poll`.

4.4 The Deque Interface

Java 6 provides the `Deque` interface. The name deque (pronounced "deck") is short for double-ended queue, which means that it is a data structure that allows insertions and removals from both ends (front and rear). Methods are provided to insert, remove, and examine elements at both ends of the deque. Method names that end in *first* access the front of the deque, and method names that end in *last* access the rear of the deque. Table 4.3 shows some of the Deque methods.

As you can see from the table, there are two pairs of methods that perform each of the insert, remove, and examine operations. One pair returns a boolean value indicating the method result, and one pair throws an exception if the operation is unsuccessful. For example, `offerFirst` and `offerLast` return a value indicating the insertion result, whereas `addFirst` and `addLast` throw an exception if the insertion is not successful. Normally, you should use a method that returns a value. Table 4.4 shows the use of these methods.

Classes that Implement Deque

The Java Collections Framework provides two implementations of the `Deque` interface, `ArrayDeque` and `LinkedList`. `ArrayDeque` utilizes a resizable circular array like our class `ArrayQueue` in Section 4.3 and is the recommended implementation because, unlike `LinkedList`, it does not support indexed operations.

TABLE 4.3
The Deque<E> Interface

Method	Behavior
`boolean offerFirst(E item)`	Inserts `item` at the front of the deque. Returns **`true`** if successful; returns **`false`** if the item could not be inserted.
`boolean offerLast(E item)`	Inserts `item` at the rear of the deque. Returns **`true`** if successful; returns **`false`** if the item could not be inserted.
`voidaddFirst(E item)`	Inserts `item` at the front of the deque. Throws an exception if the item could not be inserted.
`voidaddLast(E item)`	Inserts `item` at the rear of the deque. Throws an exception if the item could not be inserted.
`E pollFirst()`	Removes the entry at the front of the deque and returns it; returns **`null`** if the deque is empty.
`E pollLast()`	Removes the entry at the rear of the deque and returns it; returns **`null`** if the deque is empty.
`E removeFirst()`	Removes the entry at the front of the deque and returns it if the deque is not empty. If the deque is empty, throws a `NoSuchElementException`.
`E removeLast()`	Removes the item at the rear of the deque and returns it. If the deque is empty, throws a `NoSuchElementException`.
`E peekFirst()`	Returns the entry at the front of the deque without removing it; returns **`null`** if the deque is empty.
`E peekLast()`	Returns the item at the rear of the deque without removing it; returns **`null`** if the deque is empty.
`E getFirst()`	Returns the entry at the front of the deque without removing it. If the deque is empty, throws a `NoSuchElementException`.
`E getLast()`	Returns the item at the rear of the deque without removing it. If the deque is empty, throws a `NoSuchElementException`.
`boolean removeFirstOccurrence(Object item)`	Removes the first occurrence of item in the deque. Returns **`true`** if the item was removed.
`boolean removeLastOccurrence(Object item)`	Removes the last occurrence of item in the deque. Returns **`true`** if the item was removed.
`Iterator<E> iterator()`	Returns an iterator to the elements of this deque in the proper sequence.
`Iterator<E> descendingIterator()`	Returns an iterator to the elements of this deque in reverse sequential order.

TABLE 4.4
Effect of Using Deque Methods on an Initially Empty Deque<Character> d.

Deque Method	Deque d	Effect
d.offerFirst('b')	b	'b' inserted at front
d.offerLast('y')	by	'y' inserted at rear
d.addLast('z')	byz	'z' inserted at rear
d.addFirst('a')	abyz	'a' inserted at front
d.peekFirst()	abyz	Returns 'a'
d.peekLast()	abyz	Returns 'z'
d.pollLast()	aby	Removes 'z'
d.pollFirst()	by	Removes 'a'

Using a Deque as a Queue

The Deque interface extends the Queue interface, which means that a class that implements Deque also implements Queue. The Queue methods are equivalent to Deque methods as shown in Table 4.5. If elements are always inserted at the front of a deque and removed from the rear (first-in, first-out), then the deque functions as a queue.

TABLE 4.5
Equivalent Queue and Deque Methods

Queue Method	Equivalent Deque Method
add(e)	addLast(e)
offer(e)	offerLast(e)
remove()	removeFirst()
poll()	pollFirst()
element()	getFirst()
peek()	peekFirst()

Using a Deque as a Stack

Deques can also be used as stacks (last-in, first-out). When a deque is used as a stack, elements are always pushed and popped from the front of the deque. Using the Deque interface is preferable to using the legacy Stack class (based on the Vector class). Stack methods are equivalent to Deque methods, as shown in Table 4.6.

The statement

```
Deque<String> stackOfStrings = new ArrayDeque<String>();
```

TABLE 4.6
Equivalent Stack and Deque Methods

Stack Method	Equivalent Deque Method
push(e)	addFirst(e)
pop()	removeFirst()
peek()	peekFirst()
empty()	isEmpty()

creates a new Deque object called stackOfStrings. You can use Deque methods push, pop, peek, and isEmpty (instead of Stack.empty) in the normal way to manipulate stackOfStrings.

EXERCISES FOR SECTION 4.4

SELF-CHECK

1. For object stackOfStrings declared above, replace each stack operation with the appropriate Deque method and explain the effect of each statement in the following fragment.

```
stackOfStrings.push("Hello");
String one = stackOfStrings.pop();
if (!stackOfStrings.isEmpty())
   System.out.println(stackOfStrings.peek());
stackOfStrings.push("Good bye");
for (String two : stackOfStrings)
    System.out.println(two);
```

2. What would be the effect of omitting the conditional test before calling the peek method?
3. Would the following statements execute without error? If your answer is "yes," what would their effect be? If "no," why not?

```
stackOfStrings.offer("away");
String three = stackOfStrings.remove();
```

PROGRAMMING

1. Write a fragment that reads a sequence of strings and inserts each string that is not numeric at the front of a deque and each string that is numeric at the rear of a deque. Your fragment should also count the number of strings of each kind.
2. For a deque that has the form required by Programming Exercise 1, display the message "Strings that are not numeric" followed by the nonnumeric strings and then the message "Strings that are numbers" followed by the numeric strings. Do not empty the deque.
3. Write a Deque.addFirst method for class ArrayQueue.

4.5 Simulating Waiting Lines Using Queues

Simulation is a technique used to study the performance of a physical system by using a physical, mathematical, or computer model of the system. Through simulation, the designers of a new system can estimate the expected performance of the system before they actually build it. The use of simulation can lead to changes in the design that will improve the expected performance of the new system. Simulation is especially useful when the actual system would be too expensive to build or too dangerous to experiment with after its construction.

System designers often use computer models to simulate physical systems. In this section we will implement and test a computer model of an airline check-in counter in order to compare various strategies for improving service and reducing the waiting time for each passenger. We will use a queue to simulate the passenger waiting line. A special branch of mathematics called *queuing theory* has been developed to study these kinds of problems using mathematical models (systems of equations) instead of computer models.

CASE STUDY Simulate a Strategy for Serving Airline Passengers

Problem Blue Skies Airlines (BSA) is considering redesigning its ticket counters for airline passengers. The company would like to have two separate waiting lines: one for regular customers and one for frequent flyers. Assuming there is only one ticket agent available to serve all passengers, the company would like to determine the average waiting time for both types of passengers using various strategies for taking passengers from the waiting lines (see Figure 4.13).

A "democratic" strategy for serving passengers would be to take turns serving passengers from both lines (i.e., one frequent flyer, one regular passenger, one frequent flyer, etc.). Another "democratic" strategy would be to serve the passenger who has been waiting in line the longest, but this would be the same as having a single queue. (Why?) An "elitist" strategy would be to serve any frequent flyer waiting in line before serving the regular passengers.

Analysis Running a computer simulation is a good way to investigate the effect of different serving strategies. To run a computer simulation, we must keep track of the current time by maintaining a clock that is set to an initial time of zero. This clock will increase by one time unit until the simulation is finished. During each time interval, one or more of the following events may occur.

1. A new frequent flyer passenger arrives in line.
2. A new regular passenger arrives in line.
3. The ticket agent finishes serving a passenger and begins to serve a passenger from the frequent flyer line.

FIGURE 4.13
Passenger Waiting Lines

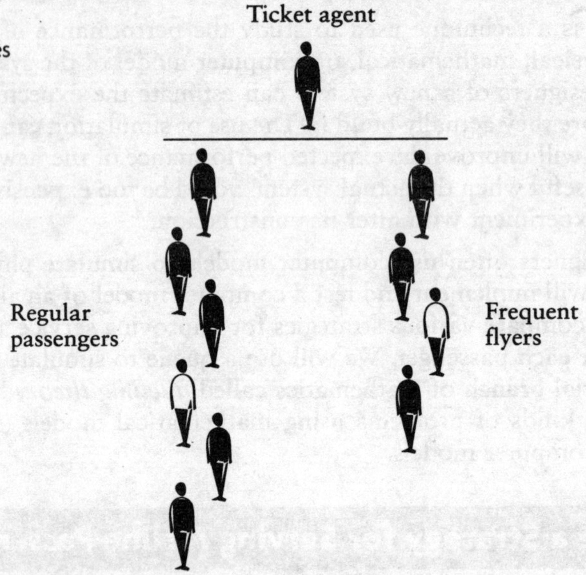

4. The ticket agent finishes serving a passenger and begins to serve a passenger from the regular passenger line.
5. The ticket agent is idle because there are no passengers in either line to serve.

The purpose of running the simulation is to determine statistics about the waiting times for frequent flyers and for regular passengers. In addition to the priority given to frequent flyers, the waiting times depend on the arrival rate of each type of passenger (number of passengers arriving per minute) and the time required to serve a passenger. There are different arrival rates for each kind of passenger. In addition to statistics on waiting times, we can display a minute-by-minute trace of events occurring during each minute of the simulation.

We can simulate different serving strategies by introducing a simulation variable `frequentFlyerMax`, which must be a positive integer. This will represent the number of consecutive frequent flyer passengers served between regular passengers. When `frequentFlyerMax` is 1, every other passenger served will be a regular passenger (the "democratic" strategy). When `frequentFlyerMax` is 2, every third passenger served will be a regular passenger. When `frequentFlyerMax` is a very large number, any frequent flyer passenger will be served before a regular passenger (the "elitist" strategy).

Design To begin an object-oriented design, we look at the problem description and identify the classes. We can use the nouns in the problem statement as a starting point. Doing this we see that we have an *agent, passengers,* and two *passenger queues.*

FIGURE 4.14
Airline Check-In Simulation: Initial UML Class Diagram

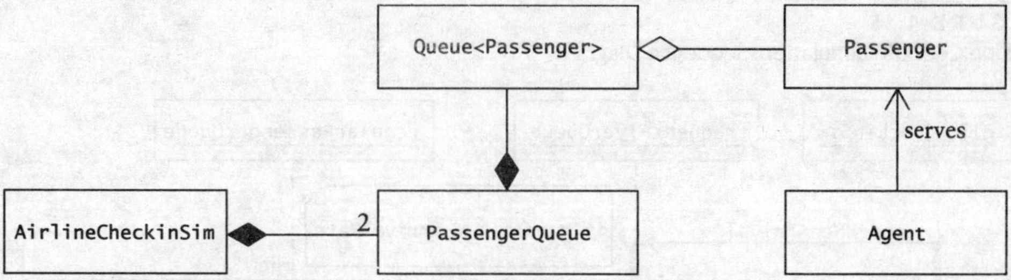

These are part of the *simulation*. This leads to the initial UML class diagram shown in Figure 4.14. The diagram shows that `PassengerQueue` has a `Queue` component and is itself a component of `AirlineCheckinSim`—the class that runs the simulation. Also, the queue stores objects of type `Passenger` (open diamond).

Next we develop a sequence diagram to see how the data flows between the objects and to identify the messages passed between them. In object-oriented design, when one object sends a message to another, this implies that the receiving object's class must have a method to respond to the message. The objects involved in the simulation are the `AirlineCheckinSim` instance, the two passenger queues, and `Passenger` objects.

Figure 4.15 is a sequence diagram that is based on the events described in the analysis section. A *sequence diagram* depicts the interaction between objects as a program executes. The diagram shows objects and classes in the horizontal direction and time in the vertical direction. The dashed line descending from each object or class (called a *lifeline*) is used to show the actions performed on that object. When a method is applied to an object, the dashed line becomes a solid-color line indicating that the method is executing. If a method call causes one object to interact with another, there will be a horizontal line from the first object's lifeline to the second object's lifeline. The method called is shown above the horizontal line. The light-color boxes show a condition that must be true in order for a particular method call to occur.

Figure 4.15 shows one clock cycle of the simulation. Class `AirlineCheckinSim` contains method `runSimulation`, which controls the simulation. Reading down the timeline for this class (on the far left), we see that each passenger queue's `checkNewArrival` method is called first. If a new arrival occurs (`random()` is less than `arrivalRate` for that queue), a new `Passenger` object of the appropriate type is created, and the `add` method for that queue is called to insert the new passenger. Next, if the agent is free (simulation clock greater than `timeDone` for the passenger being served), the `AirlineCheckinSim` `startServe` method is called. Method `startServe` calls each queue's `isEmpty` method and, based on the results, calls method `update` for either the frequent flyer queue or the regular passenger queue. Method `update` changes the value of `timeDone` and then calls the `remove` method for its queue. It then calls `Passenger` accessor methods to retrieve the arrival time and processing time for the passenger it removed.

FIGURE 4.15
Airline Check-In Simulation: Sequence Diagram

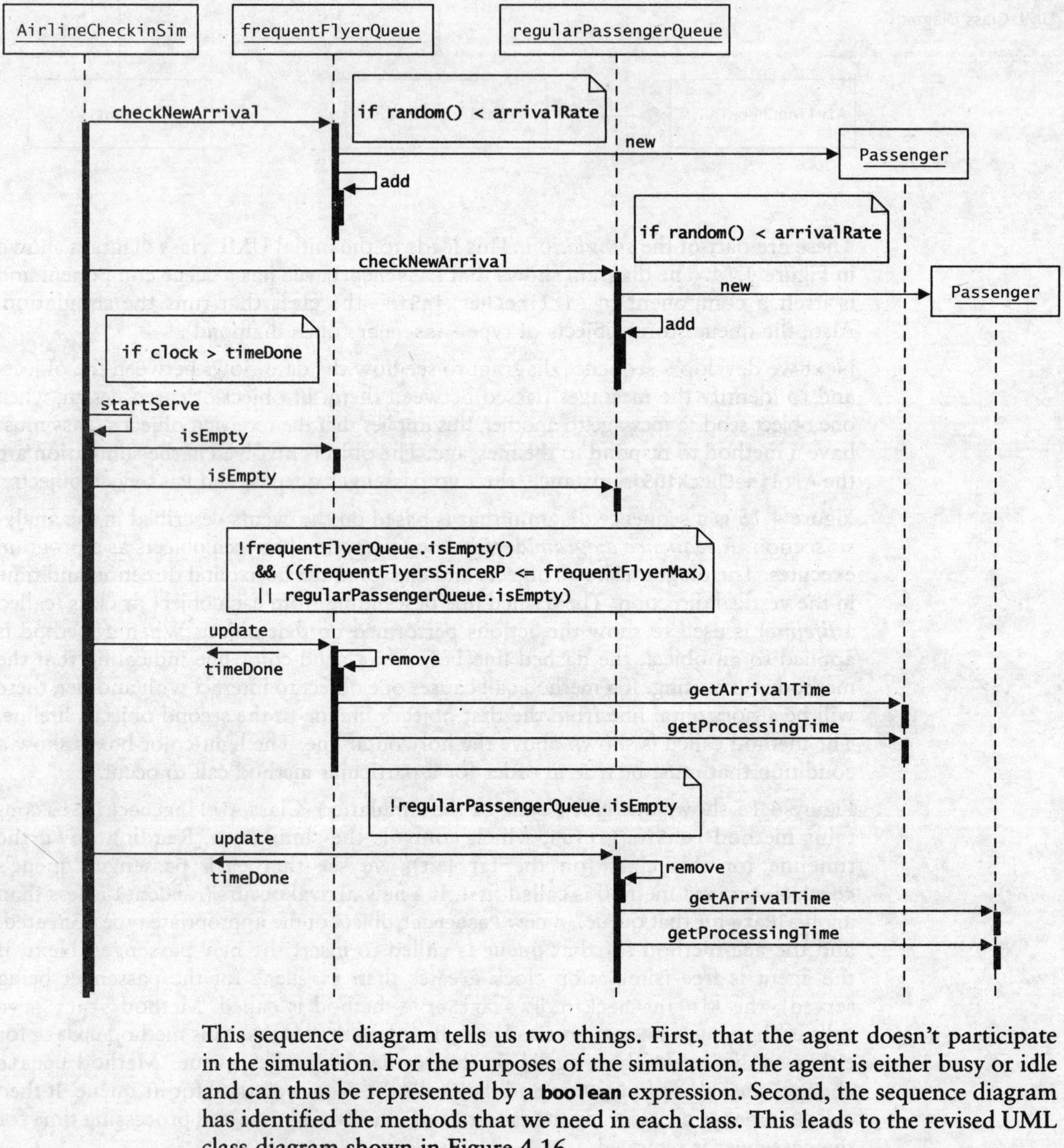

This sequence diagram tells us two things. First, that the agent doesn't participate in the simulation. For the purposes of the simulation, the agent is either busy or idle and can thus be represented by a **boolean** expression. Second, the sequence diagram has identified the methods that we need in each class. This leads to the revised UML class diagram shown in Figure 4.16.

FIGURE 4.16
Airline Check-In Simulation: Updated Class Diagram

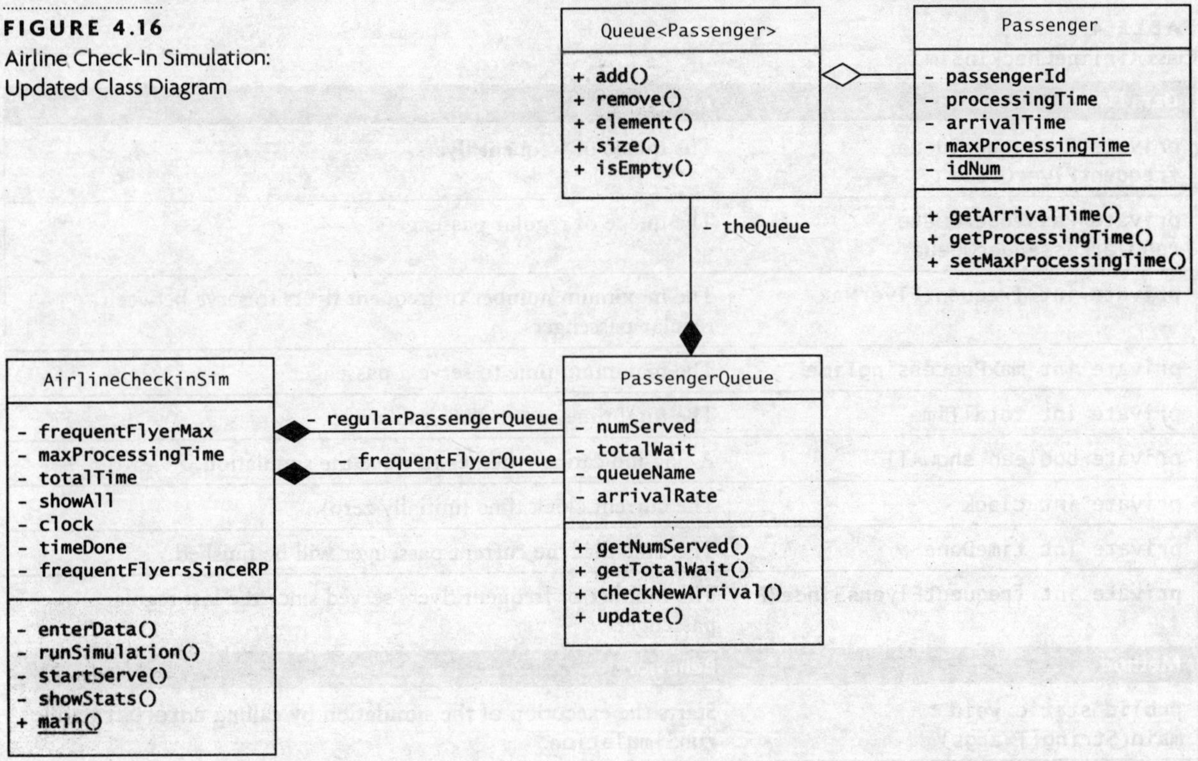

Class `AirlineCheckinSim`

Table 4.7 shows the data fields and methods for class `AirlineCheckinSim`. Methods `main`, `enterData`, and `showStats` are fairly straightforward and will be discussed briefly in the implementation. As an aid to testing our implementation, we want to have the option of printing a minute-by-minute state of the simulation and to track individual passengers. Thus, we add a `showAll` attribute to the `AirlineCheckinSim` class. If the value of `showAll` is **`true`**, we will essentially trace each action taken by the program through a call to `println`.

Class `PassengerQueue`

The `PassengerQueue` class stores the passenger queue and summary data about the queue (see Table 4.8). By encapsulating the queue within this class and having its methods manipulate both the queue and the summary data, we ensure that the summary data is always maintained. Specifically, when the method `checkNewArrival` determines that a new passenger has arrived, it inserts the passenger into the queue. When the `update` method removes a passenger, it updates the number of passengers served and the total wait time.

TABLE 4.7
Class `AirlineCheckinSim`

Data Field	Attribute
`private PassengerQueue frequentFlyerQueue`	The queue of frequent flyers.
`private PassengerQueue regularPassengerQueue`	The queue of regular passengers.
`private int frequentFlyerMax`	The maximum number of frequent flyers to serve between regular passengers.
`private int maxProcessingTime`	The maximum time to serve a passenger.
`private int totalTime`	The total time to run the simulation.
`private boolean showAll`	A flag indicating whether to trace the simulation.
`private int clock`	The current clock time (initially zero).
`private int timeDone`	The time that the current passenger will be finished.
`private int frequentFlyersSinceRP`	The number of frequent flyers served since the last regular passenger.
Method	**Behavior**
`public static void main(String[] args)`	Starts the execution of the simulation by calling `enterData` and `runSimulation`.
`private void runSimulation()`	Controls the simulation. Executes the steps shown in Figure 4.15.
`private void enterData()`	Reads in the data for the simulation.
`private void startServe()`	Initiates service for a passenger.
`private void showStats()`	Displays the summary statistics.

The `Passenger` Class

The passenger class stores the following information about a passenger:

- A unique ID number
- The time the passenger arrived
- The actual processing time
- The maximum processing time

The ID number is used to identify passengers when the simulation is traced. It starts at 0 and is incremented by 1 each time a new `Passenger` object is created. Table 4.9 shows the class methods.

TABLE 4.8
Class PassengerQueue

Data Field	Attribute
private Queue<Passenger> theQueue	The queue of passengers.
private int numServed	The number from this queue who were served.
private int totalWait	The total time spent waiting by passengers who were in this queue.
private String queueName	The name of this queue.
private double arrivalRate	The arrival rate for this queue.
Method	**Behavior**
public PassengerQueue(String queueName)	Constructs a new queue with the specified name.
private void checkNewArrival(int clock, boolean showAll)	Checks whether there was a new arrival for this queue and, if so, inserts the passenger into the queue.
private int update(int clock, boolean showAll)	Updates the total waiting time and number of passengers served when a passenger from this queue is served.
public int getTotalWait()	Returns the total waiting time for passengers in this queue.
public int getNumServed()	Returns the number of passengers served from this queue.

TABLE 4.9
Methods of the Passenger Class

Method	Behavior
public Passenger(int arrivalTime)	Constructs a new passenger, assigns it a unique ID and the specified arrival time. Computes a random processing time in the range 1 to maxProcessingTime.
public int getArrivalTime()	Returns the value of arrivalTime.
public int getProcessingTime()	Returns the value of processingTime.
public static void setMaxProcessingTime(int maxProcessingTime)	Sets the maxProcessingTime used to generate the random processing time.

Implementation Coding the **AirlineCheckinSim** Class

The class and data field declarations follow:

```
/** Simulate the check-in process of an airline.
*/
public class AirlineCheckinSim {

    // Data Fields
    /** Queue of frequent flyers. */
    private PassengerQueue frequentFlyerQueue =
            new PassengerQueue("Frequent Flyer");
    /** Queue of regular passengers. */
    private PassengerQueue regularPassengerQueue =
            new PassengerQueue("Regular Passenger");
    /** Maximum number of frequent flyers to be served
        before a regular passenger gets served. */
    private int frequentFlyerMax;
    /** Maximum time to service a passenger. */
    private int maxProcessingTime;
    /** Total simulated time. */
    private int totalTime;
    /** If set true, print additional output. */
    private boolean showAll;
    /** Simulated clock. */
    private int clock = 0;
    /** Time that the agent will be done with the current passenger.*/
    private int timeDone;
    /** Number of frequent flyers served since the
        last regular passenger was served. */
    private int frequentFlyersSinceRP;
. . .
}
```

The **main** METHOD

The main method constructs an AirlineCheckinSim object, calls enterData to read the input data, and then calls runSimulation to perform the simulation. After the simulation is complete, the showStats method displays the summary results.

```
/** Main method.
    @param args Not used
*/
public static void main(String args[]) {
    AirlineCheckinSim sim = new AirlineCheckinSim();
    sim.enterData();
    sim.runSimulation();
    sim.showStats();
    System.exit(0);
}
```

TABLE 4.10
Airline Simulation Input Parameters

Internal Variable	Attribute	Conversion
`frequentFlyerQueue.arrivalRate`	Expected number of frequent flyer arrivals per hour.	Divide input by 60 to obtain arrivals per minute.
`regularPassengerQueue.arrivalRate`	Expected number of regular passenger arrivals per hour.	Divide input by 60 to obtain arrivals per minute.
`maxProcessingTime`	Maximum service time in minutes.	None.
`totalTime`	Total simulation time in minutes.	None.
`showAll`	Flag. If **`true`**, display minute-by-minute trace of simulation.	Input beginning with `'Y'` or `'y'` will set this to **`true`**; other inputs will set it to **`false`**.

The `enterData` METHOD

The `enterData` method (not shown) gets the input values shown in Table 4.10. It could use dialog windows, a GUI, or the console. If it uses dialog windows or a GUI, it should echo the input to the console so that the trace and summary statistics can be interpreted.

The `runSimulation` METHOD

The `runSimulation` method executes a loop once for each minute of simulated time. During each iteration, it calls method `checkNewArrival` on both the `frequentFlyerQueue` and the `regularPassengerQueue` to see whether any new passengers have arrived. Variable `showAll` is passed in both method calls. If the `clock` has advanced past the value of `timeDone`, then the current passenger is finished with the ticket agent, so method `startServe` is called to start the next passenger. Data field `timeDone` is reset to the time the current passenger will be finished, which is the current clock time plus the service time.

```
private void runSimulation() {
    for (clock = 0; clock < totalTime; clock++) {
        frequentFlyerQueue.checkNewArrival(clock, showAll);
        regularPassengerQueue.checkNewArrival(clock, showAll);
        if (clock >= timeDone) {
            startServe();
        }
    }
}
```

The `startServe` METHOD

The `startServe` method selects a queue and then calls that queue's `update` method to remove the next passenger and update the simulation variables.

If the frequent flyer queue is not empty, it is selected if either of the two following conditions is true:

- The number of frequent flyers who have been served since the last regular passenger is less than or equal to `frequentFlyerMax`.
- The regular passenger queue is empty.

Otherwise, `startServe` selects the regular passenger queue. If both queues are empty and `showAll` is **`true`**, `startServe` prints a message that the agent is idle.

After selecting a queue, `startServe` increments `frequentFlyersSinceRP` or sets it to zero, depending on the passenger type being served.

```
private void startServe() {
    if (!frequentFlyerQueue.isEmpty()
            && ((frequentFlyersSinceRP <= frequentFlyerMax)
            || regularPassengerQueue.isEmpty())) {
        // Serve the next frequent flyer.
        frequentFlyersSinceRP++;
        timeDone = frequentFlyerQueue.update(clock, showAll);
    } else if (!regularPassengerQueue.isEmpty()) {
        // Serve the next regular passenger.
        frequentFlyersSinceRP = 0;
        timeDone = regularPassengerQueue.update(clock, showAll);
    } else if (showAll) {
        System.out.println("Time is " + clock
                           + " server is idle");
    }
}
```

The `showStats` METHOD

The `showStats` method displays the total number of each kind of passenger and their average waiting time. It also displays the number of passengers left in each queue at the end of the simulation.

```
/** Method to show the statistics. */
private void showStats() {
    System.out.println
            ("\nThe number of regular passengers served was "
             + regularPassengerQueue.getNumServed());
    double averageWaitingTime =
            (double) regularPassengerQueue.getTotalWait()
             / (double) regularPassengerQueue.getNumServed();
```

```
    System.out.println(" with an average waiting time of "
                       + averageWaitingTime);
    System.out.println("The number of frequent flyers served was "
                       + frequentFlyerQueue.getNumServed());
    double averageWaitingTime =
                       (double) frequentFlyerQueue.getTotalWait()
                        / (double) frequentFlyerQueue.getNumServed();
    System.out.println(" with an average waiting time of "
                       + averageWaitingTime);
    System.out.println("Passengers in frequent flyer queue: "
                       + frequentFlyerQueue.size());
    System.out.println("Passengers in regular passenger queue: "
                       + regularPassengerQueue.size());
}
```

Coding Class PassengerQueue

The data field declarations and constructor for `PassengerQueue` follow. The constructor allocates a new `LinkedList<Passenger>` for storing the queue of passengers. It also saves the name of the queue so it can be displayed when the `showAll` flag is set to show the minute-by-minute trace of the simulation.

```
/** Class to simulate a queue of passengers. */
public class PassengerQueue {
    // Data Fields
    /**  The queue of passengers. */
    private Queue<Passenger> theQueue;
    /** The number of passengers served. */
    private int numServed;
    /** The total time passengers were waiting. */
    private int totalWait;
    /** The name of this queue. */
    private String queueName;
    /** The average arrival rate. */
    private double arrivalRate;

    // Constructor
    /** Construct a PassengerQueue with the given name.
        @param queueName The name of this queue
    */
    public PassengerQueue(String queueName) {
        numServed = 0;
        totalWait = 0;
        this.queueName = queueName;
        theQueue = new LinkedList<Passenger>();
    }
  . . .
}
```

The method `checkNewArrival` is the most interesting part of the simulation program. Its purpose is to determine whether a new arrival occurs during a given time unit and, if so, to insert it in the appropriate passenger queue. During each time unit, `checkNewArrival` is applied to each passenger queue.

```
/** Check if a new arrival has occurred.
    @param clock The current simulated time
    @param showAll Flag to indicate that detailed
                   data should be output
*/
public void checkNewArrival(int clock, boolean showAll) {
    if (Math.random() < arrivalRate) {
        theQueue.add(new Passenger(clock));
        if (showAll) {
            System.out.println("Time is "
                               + clock + ": "
                               + queueName
                               + " arrival, new queue size is "
                               + theQueue.size());
        }
    }
}
```

The arrival of passengers is considered a "random event" because we cannot predict with certainty the time at which passengers arrive. The arrival rate tells us the average rate at which passengers will arrive. For example, an arrival rate of 0.25 means that on average 0.25 passengers will arrive every minute or, stated another way, one passenger will arrive every four minutes. However, this does not mean that passengers will arrive precisely at clock times 0, 4, 8, 12, and so on. A group of passengers may arrive in consecutive time units, and then we may not see another arrival for several more minutes. All we know is that if the simulation runs long enough, the number of passenger arrivals should be pretty close to the total simulation length times 0.25. In statistical terms, an arrival rate of 0.25 means that the probability of a passenger arrival in any given minute is 0.25, or 25 percent. To obtain the arrival rate, we divide the number of passengers expected per hour (a data item) by 60 because our clock increments every minute. If we expect more than 60 passengers per hour, we need to run the simulation with a smaller clock increment so that the arrival rate used by `checkNewArrival` is less than one.

We can use a pseudorandom number generator to determine whether a passenger has arrived in a given minute of the simulation. The Java API function `Math.random` is a function that generates a pseudorandom number between 0 and 1. The condition

```
Math.random() < arrivalRate
```

compares the pseudorandom number generated to the value of `arrivalRate`. Because the values being compared are in the range 0.0–1.0, the probability that this condition will be true is proportional to the value of `arrivalRate`, as desired. If `arrivalRate` is 0.25, this condition should be true 25 percent of the time.

DESIGN CONCEPT

Pseudorandom Numbers

When you need a random number, as when playing a game, you can perform some procedure, such as spinning a wheel, in which imperceptibly small variations in the physical circumstances (hand position and force, condition of the bearings) all have large enough effects on the result to make it unpredictable.

When a computer needs a random number, it uses a mathematical process that is analogous to spinning a wheel, but because the computer is a machine designed to produce consistent results regardless of variations in its physical circumstances, the "wheel" is spun a controlled number of clicks each time, so the results are not truly random. However, if the size of the "wheel" and the algorithms for determining the number of clicks are chosen properly, the results can be made to appear to be random. We say that they appear to be random because they pass statistical tests. Such numbers are *pseudorandom* numbers, though they are often called "random."

The Java API includes the Random class. Objects of this class generate random (pseudorandom) numbers in different numerical types (**`int`**, **`long`**, **`float`**, **`double`**, etc.). The class also provides a method to set the *seed* (the initial wheel position). By default, the seed is set to the date and time of day (in milliseconds). Thus, each time you run the program, you will get different random values.

When you are debugging, you can set the seed to a fixed value, thus ensuring that the same sequence of numbers will be generated for each test run. When you are finished debugging, you can remove the fixed seed.

The `Math.random` method creates a Random object when it is first called. It then uses that object's `nextDouble` method to return a random number in the range 0 to 1.

The `update` method removes a passenger from the queue, computes that passenger's waiting time (clock time – arrival time), and adds it to the total wait time. Next, `update` increments the count of passengers from this queue who have been served since the simulation began. Method `update` also computes the time that the agent will be finished with this passenger and returns the time to the method caller.

```java
/** Update statistics.
    pre: The queue is not empty.
    @param clock The current simulated time
    @param showAll Flag to indicate whether to show detail
    @return Time passenger is done being served
*/
public int update(int clock, boolean showAll) {
    Passenger nextPassenger = theQueue.remove();
    int timeStamp = nextPassenger.getArrivalTime();
    int wait = clock - timeStamp;
    totalWait += wait;
    numServed++;
    if (showAll) {
        System.out.println("Time is " + clock
                           + ": Serving "
                           + queueName
                           + " with time stamp "
                           + timeStamp);
    }
    return clock + nextPassenger.getProcessingTime();
}
```

Coding the **Passenger** Class

Data field `idNum` is the passenger sequence number. It is `static` because the same variable is used for all passengers, and we don't want it reset to zero when a new passenger is created. Since the `maxProcessingTime` applies to all instances of `Passenger`, this is a `static` attribute and the method `setMaxProcessingTime` is also `static`.

We will assume that the processing time is uniformly distributed between 1 and the `maxProcessingTime`. We call method `Random.nextInt` to generate a random `int` value between 0 and `maxProcessingTime - 1`. We compute the `processingTime` in the constructor. Listing 4.6 shows the `Passenger` class.

LISTING 4.6
`Passenger.java`

```java
/** A class to represent a passenger. */
public class Passenger {

    // Data Fields
    /** The ID number for this passenger. */
    private int passengerId;
    /** The time needed to process this passenger. */
    private int processingTime;
    /** The time this passenger arrives. */
    private int arrivalTime;
    /** The maximum time to process a passenger. */
    private static int maxProcessingTime;
    /** The sequence number for passengers. */
    private static int idNum = 0;
```

```java
    /** Create a new passenger.
        @param arrivalTime The time this passenger arrives */
    public Passenger(int arrivalTime) {
        this.arrivalTime = arrivalTime;
        processingTime = 1 + Random.nextInt(maxProcessingTime);
        passengerId = idNum++;
    }

    /** Get the arrival time.
        @return The arrival time */
    public int getArrivalTime() {
        return arrivalTime;
    }

    /** Get the processing time.
        @return The processing time */
    public int getProcessingTime() {
        return processingTime;
    }

    /** Get the passenger ID.
        @return The passenger ID */
    public int getId() {
        return passengerId;
    }

    /** Set the maximum processing time
        @param maxProcessingTime The new value */
    public static void setMaxProcessingTime(int maxProcessTime) {
        maxProcessingTime = maxProcessTime;
    }
}
```

FIGURE 4.17
Sample Run of Airline Check-In Simulation

```
Command Prompt
Expected number of frequent flyer arrivals per hour: 15
Expected number of regular passenger arrivals per hour: 30
The maximum number of frequent flyers
served between regular passengers: 5
Maximum service time in minutes: 4
The total simulation time in minutes: 10
Display minute-by-minute trace of simulation (Y or N): y
Time is 0:  Server is idle
Time is 1:  Regular Passenger arrival, new queue size is 1
Time is 1:  Serving Regular Passenger with time stamp 1, service time is 3
Time is 3:  Regular Passenger arrival, new queue size is 1
Time is 4:  Serving Regular Passenger with time stamp 3, service time is 1
Time is 5:  Frequent Flyer arrival, new queue size is 1
Time is 5:  Serving Frequent Flyer with time stamp 5, service time is 1
Time is 6:  Regular Passenger arrival, new queue size is 1
Time is 6:  Serving Regular Passenger with time stamp 6, service time is 3
Time is 7:  Regular Passenger arrival, new queue size is 1
Time is 8:  Regular Passenger arrival, new queue size is 2
Time is 9:  Frequent Flyer arrival, new queue size is 1
Time is 9:  Regular Passenger arrival, new queue size is 3
Time is 9:  Serving Frequent Flyer with time stamp 9, service time is 1

The number of regular passengers served was 3
 with an average waiting time of 0.3333333333333333
The number of frequent flyers served was 2
 with an average waiting time of 0.0
Passengers in frequent flyer queue: 0
Passengers in regular queue: 3
```

Testing Figure 4.17 shows a sample run of the simulation program with the trace turned on. To test the simulation program, you should run it a number of times with the trace turned on and verify that passengers in the frequent flyer queue have the specified priority over regular passengers. Method `enterData` should display the data values so that you can interpret the simulation results in a meaningful way. Also, make sure that the "server is idle" message is displayed only when both queues are empty. If both arrival rates are the same, check that the waiting times reflect the priority given to frequent flyers. Also see what happens when both kinds of passengers are treated equally (`frequentFlyerSinceRP` is 1).

When running the program, make sure that you use integer values for the total simulation time and for the service time. It is also a good idea to choose values for arrival rates and service time that keep the system from becoming saturated. The system will become saturated if the arrival rates are too large and passengers arrive more quickly than they can be served. This will result in very long queues and large waiting times. The system will become saturated if the total number of arrivals per minute (frequent flyer arrival rate + regular passenger arrival rate) is greater than the number of passengers being served in a minute: [`1 / (maxProcessingTime / 2)`].

After you are certain that the program runs correctly, you should turn off the trace and focus on the summary statistics. It is interesting to see how these values change for a particular set of arrival rates and service times. Remember, passenger arrivals are a random event, so the results should vary from one run to the next even if all input data stay the same.

EXERCISES FOR SECTION 4.5

SELF-CHECK

1. Show the output that would be generated by running the simulation program for 20 minutes with the following passenger arrivals when `showAll` is **true** and `frequentFlyerMax` is 1.

   A frequent flyer passenger arrives at clock = 0 and service time is 2
   A frequent flyer passenger arrives at clock = 1 and service time is 1
   A frequent flyer passenger arrives at clock = 3 and service time is 3
   A frequent flyer passenger arrives at clock = 5 and service time is 2
   A regular passenger arrives at clock = 0 and service time is 1
   A regular passenger arrives at clock = 1 and service time is 1
   A regular passenger arrives at clock = 2 and service time is 1

A regular passenger arrives at clock = 3 and service time is 1
A regular passenger arrives at clock = 4 and service time is 2

2. Answer Self-Check Exercise 1 when `frequentFlyerMax` is 2.
3. Answer Self-Check Exercise 1 when `frequentFlyerMax` is 3.
4. Method `runSimulation` begins with the statements

```
frequentFlyerQueue.checkNewArrival(clock, showAll);
regularPassengerQueue.checkNewArrival(clock, showAll);
```

Would exchanging the order of these statements change the result? Explain your answer.

PROGRAMMING

1. Run the `AirlineCheckinSim` program with a variety of inputs to determine the maximum passenger arrival rate for a given average processing time and the effect of the frequent flyer service policy.
2. Modify the `AirlineCheckinSim` program to simulate every second of simulated time. Does this affect the results?
3. Write method `enterData` using class `JOptionPane` for data entry.

Chapter Review

- The queue is an abstract data type with a first-in, first-out, or FIFO, structure. This means that the item that has been in the queue the longest will be the first one removed. Queues can be used to represent reservation lists and waiting lines (from which the data structure gets its name "queue").
- The `Queue` interface declares methods `offer`, `remove`, `poll`, `peek`, and `element`.
- We discussed three ways to implement the `Queue` interface: as a double-linked list, a single-linked list, and a circular array. All three implementations support insertion and removal in O(1) time; however, there will be a need for reallocation in the circular array implementation (amortized O(1) time). The array implementation requires the smallest amount of storage when it is close to capacity. The `LinkedList` class requires the most storage but no implementation because it is part of `java.util`.
- We discussed the `Deque` interface and showed how its methods allow insertion and removal at either end of a deque. We showed the correspondence between its methods and methods found in the `Stack` class and `Queue` interface.
- To avoid the cost of building a physical system or running an actual experiment, computer simulation can be used to evaluate the expected performance of a system or an operational strategy. We showed how to do this using a pair of queues to simulate passengers waiting for service at an airline ticket counter. We used pseudorandom numbers to determine whether a particular event occurs.

Java API Classes Introduced in This Chapter

```
java.lang.UnsupportedOperationException
java.util.AbstractQueue
java.util.ArrayDeque
java.util.Deque
java.util.NoSuchElementException
java.util.Queue
java.util.Random
```

User-Defined Interfaces and Classes in This Chapter

```
AirlineCheckinSim
ArrayQueue
ArrayQueue.Iter
KWQueue
ListQueue
MaintainQueue
Passenger
PassengerQueue
```

Quick-Check Exercises

1. A queue is a _____-in, _____-out data structure.
2. Would a compiler use a stack or a queue in a program that converts infix expressions to postfix?
3. Would an operating system use a stack or a queue to determine which print job should be handled next?
4. Assume that a queue `q` of capacity 6 (circular array representation) contains the five characters +, *, -, &, and # (all wrapped in `Character` objects), where + is the first character inserted. Assume that + is stored in the first position in the array. What is the value of `q.front`? What is the value of `q.rear`?
5. Remove the first element from the queue in Question 4 and insert the characters \ then %. Draw the new queue. What is the value of `q.front`? What is the value of `q.rear`?
6. If a single-linked list were used to implement the queue in Question 5, the character ______ would be at the head of the list and the character ______ would be at the tail of the list.
7. For a nonempty queue implemented as a single-linked list, the statement ______ would be used inside method `offer` to store a new node whose data field is referenced by `item` in the queue; the statement ______ would be used to disconnect a node after its data was retrieved from the queue.
8. Pick the queue implementation (circular array, single-linked list, double-linked list) that is most appropriate for each of the following conditions.
   a. Storage must be reallocated when the queue is full.
   b. This implementation is normally most efficient in use of storage.
   c. This is an existing class in the Java API.
9. Write an `if` statement that uses a pseudorandom number to assign `"heads"` or `"tails"` to a variable `coinFlip`. The probability of each should be 0.5.
10. Write a statement that uses a pseudorandom number to assign a value of 1 through 6 to a variable `die`, where each number is equally likely.

Review Questions

1. Show the effect of each of the following operations on queue `q`. Assume that `y` (type `Character`) contains the character `'&'`. What are the final values of `x` and `success` (type `boolean`) and the contents of queue `q`?

```
Queue<Character> q = new ArrayQueue<Character>();
boolean success = true;
char x;
q.offer('+');
try {
    x = q.remove();
    x = q.remove();
    success = true;
} catch(NoSuchElementException e) {
    success = false;
}
q.offer('(');
q.offer(y);
try {
    x = q.remove();
    success = true;
} catch(NoSuchElementException e) {
    success = false;
}
```

2. Write a new queue method called `moveToRear` that moves the element currently at the front of the queue to the rear of the queue. The element that was second in line will be the new front element. Do this using methods `Queue.offer` and `Queue.remove`.
3. Answer Question 2 without using methods `Queue.offer` or `Queue.remove` for a single-linked list implementation of `Queue`. You will need to manipulate the queue internal data fields directly.
4. Answer Question 2 without using methods `Queue.offer` or `Queue.remove` for a circular array implementation of `Queue`. You will need to manipulate the queue internal data fields directly.
5. Write a new queue method called `moveToFront` that moves the element at the rear of the queue to the front of the queue, while the other queue elements maintain their relative positions behind the old front element. Do this using methods `Queue.offer` and `Queue.remove`.
6. Answer Question 5 without using `Queue.offer` and `Queue.remove` for a single-linked list implementation of `Queue`.
7. Answer Question 5 without using methods `Queue.offer` or `Queue.remove` for a circular array implementation of `Queue`.

Programming Projects

1. Redo Programming Project 6 from Chapter 3, assuming that widgets are shipped using a first-in, first-out inventory system.
2. Write a class `MyArrayDeque` that extends class `ArrayQueue`. Class `MyArrayDeque` should implement the `Deque` interface. Test your new class by comparing its operation to that of the `ArrayDeque` class in the Java Collections Framework.
3. Write a program that reads in a sequence of characters and stores each character in a deque. Display the deque contents. Then use a second deque to store the characters in reverse order. When done, display the contents of both deques.
4. Write a program that simulates the operation of a busy airport that has only two runways to handle all takeoffs and landings. You may assume that each takeoff or landing takes 15 minutes to complete. One runway request is made during each five-minute time interval, and the likelihood of a landing request is the same as for a takeoff request.

Priority is given to planes requesting a landing. If a request cannot be honored, it is added to a takeoff or landing queue.

Your program should simulate 120 minutes of activity at the airport. Each request for runway clearance should be time-stamped and added to the appropriate queue. The output from your program should include the final queue contents, the number of takeoffs completed, the number of landings completed, and the average number of minutes spent in each queue.

5. An operating system assigns jobs to print queues based on the number of pages to be printed (less than 10 pages, less than 20 pages, or more than 20 pages but less than 50 pages). You may assume that the system printers are able to print 10 pages per minute. Smaller print jobs are printed before larger print jobs, and print jobs of the same priority are queued up in the order in which they are received. The system administrators would like to compare the time required to process a set of print jobs using one, two, or three system printers.

   Write a program that simulates processing 100 print jobs of varying lengths using one, two, or three printers. Assume that a print request is made every minute and that the number of pages to print varies from 1 to 50 pages.

   The output from your program should indicate the order in which the jobs were received, the order in which they were printed, and the time required to process the set of print jobs. If more than one printer is being used, indicate which printer each job was printed on.

6. Write a menu-driven program that uses an array of queues to keep track of a group of executives as they are transferred from one department to another, get paid, or become unemployed. Executives within a department are paid based on their seniority, with the person who has been in the department the longest receiving the most money. Each person in the department receives $1000 in salary for each person in her department having less seniority than she has. Persons who are unemployed receive no compensation.

   Your program should be able to process the following set of commands:

Join *<person>* *<department>*	*<person>* is added to *<department>*.
Quit *<person>*	*<person>* is removed from his or her department.
Change *<person>* *<department>*	*<person>* is moved from old department to *<department>*.
Payroll	Each executive's salary is computed and displayed by department in decreasing order of seniority.

   Hint: You might want to include a table that contains each executive's name and information and the location of the queue that contains his or her name, to make searching more efficient.

7. Simulate the operation of a bank. Customers enter the bank, and there are one or more tellers. If a teller is free, that teller serves the customer. Otherwise the customer enters the queue and waits until a teller is free. Your program should accept the following inputs:
   - The arrival rate for the customers
   - The average processing time
   - The number of tellers

   Use your program to determine how many tellers are required for a given arrival rate and average processing time.

8. Simulate a checkout area of a supermarket consisting of one super-express counter, two express counters, and `numStandLines` standard counters. All customers with `numSuper` or fewer items proceed to a super-express counter with the fewest customers, unless there is a free express or regular line, and those with between `numSuper` and `numExp` proceed to the express counter with the shortest line unless there is a free standard line. Customers with more than `numExp` go to the standard counter with the shortest standard line.

   The number of items bought will be a random number in the range 1 to `maxItems`. The time to process a customer is 5 seconds per item.

   Calculate the following statistics:
   - Average waiting time for each of the lines
   - Overall average waiting time
   - Maximum length of each line
   - Number of customers per hour for each line and overall
   - Number of items processed per hour for each line and overall
   - Average free time of each counter
   - Overall free time

   Note: The average waiting time for a line is the total of the customer waiting times divided by the number of customers. A customer's waiting time is the time from when he (or she) enters the queue for a given checkout line until the checkout processing begins. If the customer can find a free line, then the wait time is zero.

   Your program should read the following data:

`numSuper`	The number of items allowed in the super-express line.
`numExp`	The number of items allowed in the express line.
`numStandLines`	The number of regular lines.
`arrivalRate`	The arrival rate of customers per hour.
`maxItems`	The maximum number of items.
`maxSimTime`	The simulation time.

   It may be that some lines do not get any business. In that case you must be sure, in calculating the average, *not* to divide by zero.

9. A *randomized queue* is similar to a queue, except that the item removed is chosen at random from the items in the queue. Create a `RandomizedQueue` that contains the normal `queue` methods except that the `remove` method will delete an item chosen using a uniform distribution. You should write this class as an extension of the `ArrayQueue` class.

Answers to Quick-Check Exercises

1. *first, first*
2. stack
3. queue
4. `q.front` is 0; `q.rear` is 4

5.

`q.rear`	%
`q.front`	*
	-
	&
	#
	\

`q.front` is 1; `q.rear` is 0.

6. `'*', '%'`

7. For insertion: `rear.next = new Node<E>(item);`

   To disconnect the node removed: `front = front.next;`

8. a. circular array
   b. single-linked list
   c. double-linked list (class `LinkedList`)

9.
```
if (Math.random() < 0.5)
    coinFlip = "heads";
else
    coinFlip = "tails";
```

10. `die = 1 + (int) (6 * Math.random());`

    The expression `6 * Math.random()` generates a real number that is between 0 and 6.0 (not including 6.0). Hence the casting operation will yield an **`int`** value between 0 and 5, where each integer is equally likely.

Chapter 5

Recursion

Chapter Objectives

- To understand how to think recursively
- To learn how to trace a recursive method
- To learn how to write recursive algorithms and methods for searching arrays
- To learn about recursive data structures and recursive methods for a `LinkedList` class
- To understand how to use recursion to solve the Towers of Hanoi problem
- To understand how to use recursion to process two-dimensional images
- To learn how to apply backtracking to solve search problems such as finding a path through a maze

This chapter introduces a programming technique called recursion and shows you how to think recursively. You can use recursion to solve many kinds of programming problems that would be very difficult to conceptualize and solve without recursion. Computer scientists in the field of artificial intelligence (AI) often use recursion to write programs that exhibit intelligent behavior: playing games such as chess, proving mathematical theorems, recognizing patterns, and so on.

In the beginning of the chapter you will be introduced to recursive thinking and how to design a recursive algorithm and prove that it is correct. You will also learn how to trace a recursive method and use activation frames for this purpose.

Recursive algorithms and methods can be used to perform common mathematical operations, such as computing a factorial or a greatest common divisor. Recursion can be used to process familiar data structures, such as strings, arrays, and linked lists, and to design a very efficient array search technique called binary search. You will also see that a linked list is a recursive data structure and learn how to write recursive methods that perform common list-processing tasks.

Recursion can be used to solve a variety of other problems. The case studies in this chapter use recursion to solve a game, to search for "blobs" in a two-dimensional image, and to find a path through a maze.

Recursion

5.1 Recursive Thinking

Recursion is a problem-solving approach that can be used to generate simple solutions to certain kinds of problems that would be difficult to solve in other ways. In a recursive algorithm the original problem is split into one or more simpler versions of itself. For example, if the solution to the original problem involved n items, recursive thinking might split it into two problems: one involving $n - 1$ items and one involving just a single item. Then the problem with $n - 1$ items could be split again into one involving $n - 2$ items and one involving just a single item, and so on. If the solution to all the one-item problems is "trivial," we can build up the solution to the original problem from the solutions to the simpler problems.

As an example of how this might work, consider a collection of nested wooden figures as shown in Figure 5.1. If you wanted to write an algorithm to "process" this collection in some way (such as counting the figures or painting a face on each figure), you would have difficulty doing it because you don't know how many objects are in the nest. But you could use recursion to solve the problem in the following way.

Recursive Algorithm to Process Nested Figures

1. `if` there is one figure in the nest
2.   Do whatever is required to the figure.

   `else`
3.   Do whatever is required to the outer figure in the nest.
4.   Process the nest of figures inside the outer figure in the same way.

FIGURE 5.1
A Set of Nested Wooden Figures

In this recursive algorithm, the solution is trivial if there is only one figure: Perform Step 2. If there is more than one figure, perform Step 3 to process the outer figure. Step 4 is the recursive operation—recursively process the nest of figures inside the outer figure. This nest will, of course, have one less figure than before, so it is a simpler version of the original problem.

As another example, let's consider searching for a target value in an array. Assume that the array elements are sorted and are in increasing order. A recursive approach, which we will study in detail in Section 5.3, involves replacing the problem of searching an array of *n* elements with one of searching an array of *n*/2 elements. How do we do that? We compare the target value to the value of the element in the middle of the sorted array. If there is a match, we have found the target. If not, based on the result of the comparison, we either search the elements that come before the middle one or the elements that come after the middle one. So we have replaced the problem of searching an array with *n* elements to one that involves searching a smaller array with only *n*/2 elements. The recursive algorithm follows.

Recursive Algorithm to Search an Array

1. `if` the array is empty
2. Return –1 as the search result.

   `else if` the middle element matches the target
3. Return the subscript of the middle element as the result.

   `else if` the target is less than the middle element
4. Recursively search the array elements before the middle element and return the result.

   `else`
5. Recursively search the array elements after the middle element and return the result.

The condition in Step 1 is true when there are no elements left to search. Step 2 returns –1 to indicate that the search failed. Step 3 executes when the middle element matches the target. Otherwise, we recursively apply the search algorithm (Steps 4 and 5), thereby searching a smaller array (approximately half the size), and return the result. For each recursive search, the region of the array being searched will be different, so the middle element will also be different.

The two recursive algorithms we showed so far follow this general approach:

General Recursive Algorithm

1. `if` the problem can be solved for the current value of *n*
2. Solve it.

`else`

3. Recursively apply the algorithm to one or more problems involving smaller values of *n*.
4. Combine the solutions to the smaller problems to get the solution to the original.

Step 1 involves a test for what is called the *base case*: the value of *n* for which the problem can be solved easily. Step 3 is the *recursive case* because we recursively apply the algorithm. Because the value of *n* for each recursive case is smaller than the original value of *n*, each recursive case makes progress toward the base case. Whenever a split occurs, we revisit Step 1 for each new problem to see whether it is a base case or a recursive case.

Steps to Design a Recursive Algorithm

From what we have seen so far, we can summarize the characteristics of a recursive solution:

- There must be at least one case (the base case), for a small value of *n*, that can be solved directly.
- A problem of a given size (say, *n*) can be split into one or more smaller versions of the same problem (the recursive case).

Therefore, to design a recursive algorithm, we must

- Recognize the base case and provide a solution to it.
- Devise a strategy to split the problem into smaller versions of itself. Each recursive case must make progress toward the base case.
- Combine the solutions to the smaller problems in such a way that each larger problem is solved correctly.

Next we look at a recursive algorithm for a common programming problem. We will also provide a Java method that solves this problem. All of the methods in this section and in the next will be found in class `RecursiveMethods.java` on this textbook's Web site.

EXAMPLE 5.1 Let's see how we could write our own recursive method for finding string length. How would you go about doing this? If there is a special character that marks the end of a string, then you can count all the characters that precede this special character. But if there is no special character, you might try a recursive approach. The base case is an empty string—its length is 0. For the recursive case, consider that each string has two parts: the first character and the "rest of the string." If you can find the length of the "rest of the string," you can then add 1 (for the first character) to get the length of the larger string. For example, the length of "abcde" is 1 + the length of "bcde".

Recursive Algorithm for Finding the Length of a String

1. **if** the string is empty (has no characters)
2. The length is 0.

   else

3. The length is 1 plus the length of the string that excludes the first character.

We can implement this algorithm as a `static` method with a `String` argument. The test for the base case is a string reference of `null` or a string that contains no characters (""). In either case, the length is 0. In the recursive case,

```
return 1 + length(str.substring(1));
```

the method call `str.substring(1)` returns a reference to a string containing all characters in string `str` except for the character at position 0. Then we call method `length` again with this substring as its argument. The method result is one more than the value returned from the next call to `length`. Each time we reenter method `length`, the `if` statement executes with `str` referencing a string containing all but the first character in the previous call. Method `length` is called a *recursive method* because it calls itself.

```
/** Recursive method length (in RecursiveMethods.java).
    @param str The string
    @return The length of the string
*/
public static int length(String str) {
    if (str == null || str.equals(""))
        return 0;
    else
        return 1 + length(str.substring(1));
}
```

EXAMPLE 5.2 Method `printChars` is a recursive method that displays each character in its string argument on a separate line. In the base case (an empty or nonexistent string), the method return occurs immediately and nothing is displayed. In the recursive case, `printChars` displays the first character of its string argument and then calls itself to display the characters in the rest of the string. If the initial call is `printChars("hat")`, the method will display the lines

```
h
a
t
```

Unlike method `length` in Example 5.1, `printChars` is a **void** method. However, both methods follow the format for the general recursive algorithm shown earlier.

```
/** Recursive method printChars (in RecursiveMethods.java).
    post: The argument string is displayed, one character per line.
    @param str The string
```

```
*/
public static void printChars(String str) {
    if (str == null || str.equals("")) {
        return;
    } else {
        System.out.println(str.charAt(0));
        printChars(str.substring(1));
    }
}
```

You get an interesting result if you reverse the two statements in the recursive case.

```
/** Recursive method printCharsReverse (in RecursiveMethods.java).
    post: The argument string is displayed in reverse,
          one character per line.
    @param str The string
*/
public static void printCharsReverse(String str) {
    if (str == null || str.equals("")) {
        return;
    } else {
        printCharsReverse(str.substring(1));
        System.out.println(str.charAt(0));
    }
}
```

Method `printCharsReverse` calls itself to display the rest of the string before displaying the first character in the current string argument. The effect will be to delay displaying the first character in the current string until all characters in the rest of the string are displayed. Consequently, the characters in the string will be displayed in reverse order. If the initial call is `printCharsReverse("hat")`, the method will display the lines

```
t
a
h
```

Proving that a Recursive Method Is Correct

To prove that a recursive method is correct, you must verify that you have performed correctly the design steps listed earlier. You can use a technique that mathematicians use to prove that a theorem is true for all values of n. A *proof by induction* works the following way:

- Prove the theorem is true for the base case of (usually) $n = 0$ or $n = 1$.
- Show that if the theorem is assumed true for n, then it must be true for $n + 1$.

We can extend the notion of an inductive proof and use it as the basis for proving that a recursive algorithm is correct. To do this:

- Verify that the base case is recognized and solved correctly.
- Verify that each recursive case makes progress toward the base case.
- Verify that if all smaller problems are solved correctly, then the original problem is also solved correctly.

If you can show that your algorithm satisfies these three requirements, then your algorithm will be correct.

EXAMPLE 5.3 To prove that the `length` method is correct, we know that the base case is an empty string, and its length is correctly set at 0. The recursive case involves a call to `length` with a smaller string, so it is making progress toward the base case. Finally, if we know the length of the rest of the string, adding 1 gives us the length of the longer string consisting of the first character and the rest of the string.

Tracing a Recursive Method

Figure 5.2 traces the execution of the method call `length("ace")`. The diagram shows a sequence of recursive calls to method `length`. After returning from each call to `length`, we complete execution of the statement `return 1 + length(...);` by adding 1 to the result so far and then returning from the current call. The final result, 3, would be returned from the original call. The arrow alongside each word `return` shows which call to `length` is associated with that result. For example, `0` is the result of the method call `length("")`. After adding 1, we return 1, which is the result of the call `length("e")`, and so on. This process of returning from the recursive calls and computing the partial results is called *unwinding the recursion.*

The Run-Time Stack and Activation Frames

You can also trace a recursive method by showing what Java does when one method calls another. Java maintains a run-time stack, on which it saves new information in the form of an *activation frame*. The activation frame contains storage for the method arguments and any local variables as well as the return address of the instruction that called the method. Whenever a method is called, Java pushes a new activation frame onto the run-time stack and saves this information on the stack. This is done whether or not the method is recursive.

The left side of Figure 5.3 shows the activation frames on the run-time stack after the last recursive call (corresponding to `length("")`) resulting from an initial call to `length("ace")`. At any given time, only the frame at the top of the stack is accessible, so its argument values will be used when the method instructions execute. When the `return` statement executes, control will be passed to the instruction at the specified return address, and this frame will be popped from the stack (Figure 5.3, right).

FIGURE 5.2
Trace of `length("ace")`

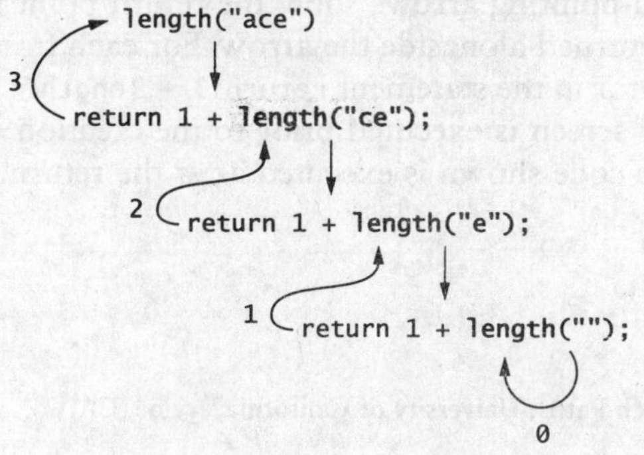

FIGURE 5.3
Run-Time Stack Before and After Removal of Frame for `length("")`

Frame for `length("")`	`str: ""` return address in `length("e")`
Frame for `length("e")`	`str: "e"` return address in `length("ce")`
Frame for `length("ce")`	`str: "ce"` return address in `length("ace")`
Frame for `length("ace")`	`str: "ace"` return address in caller

Run-time stack after all calls

Frame for `length("e")`	`str: "e"` return address in `length("ce")`
Frame for `length("ce")`	`str: "ce"` return address in `length("ace")`
Frame for `length("ace")`	`str: "ace"` return address in caller

Run-time stack after return from last call

The activation frame corresponding to the next-to-last call (`length("e")`) is now accessible.

You can think of the run-time stack for a sequence of calls to a recursive method as an office tower in which an employee on each floor has the same list of instructions.[1] The employee in the bottom office carries out part of the instructions on the list, calls the employee in the office above, and is put on hold. The employee in the office above starts to carry out the list of instructions, calls the employee in the next higher office, is put on hold, and so on. When the employee on the top floor is called, that employee carries out the list of instructions to completion and then returns an answer to the employee below. The employee below then resumes carrying out the list of instructions and returns an answer to the employee on the next lower floor, and so on, until an answer is returned to the employee in the bottom office, who then resumes carrying out the list of instructions.

To make the flow of control easier to visualize, we will draw the activation frames from the top of the page down (see Figure 5.4). For example, the activation frame at the top, which would actually be at the bottom of the run-time stack, represents the first call to the recursive method. The downward-pointing arrows connect each statement that calls a method with the frame for that particular execution of the method. The upward-pointing arrows show the return point from each lower-level call with the value returned alongside the arrow. For each frame, the return point is to the addition operator in the statement `return 1 + length(...);`. For each frame, the code in the color screen is executed prior to the creation of the next activation frame; the rest of the code shown is executed after the return.

[1] Analogy suggested by Rich Pattis, University of California, Irvine, CA.

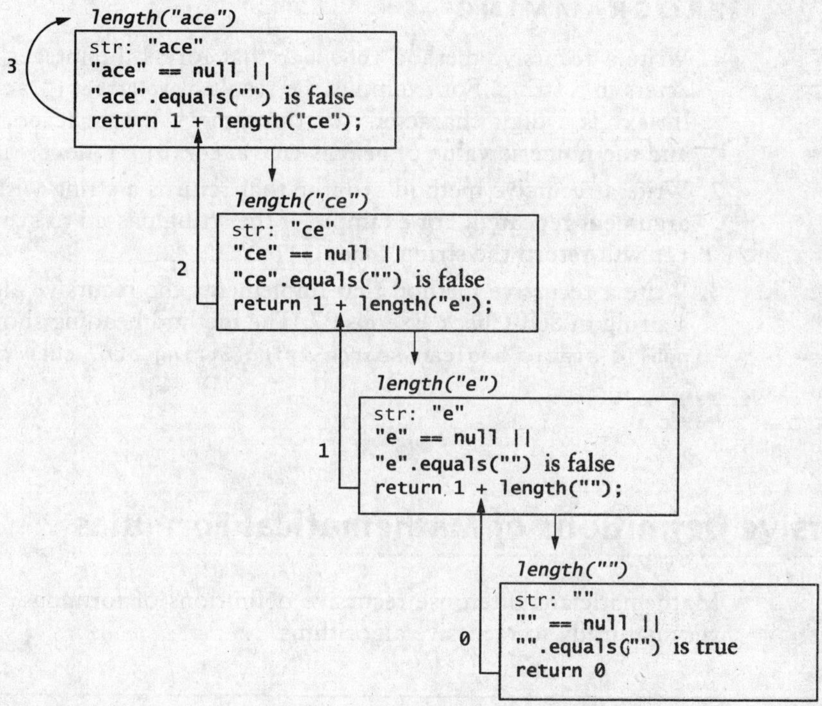

FIGURE 5.4 Trace of `length("ace")` Using Activation Frames

EXERCISES FOR SECTION 5.1

SELF-CHECK

1. Trace the execution of the call `mystery(4)` for the following recursive method using the technique shown in Figure 5.2. What does this method do?

```
public static mystery(int n) {
    if (n == 0)
        return 0;
    else
        return n * n + mystery(n - 1);
}
```

2. Answer Exercise 1 above using activation frames.
3. Trace the execution of `printChars("tic")` (Example 5.2) using activation frames.
4. Trace the execution of `printCharsReverse("toc")` using activation frames.
5. Prove that the `printChars` method is correct.
6. Trace the execution of `length("tictac")` using a diagram like Figure 5.2.
7. Write a recursive algorithm that determines whether a specified target character is present in a string. It should return `true` if the target is present and `false` if it is not. The stopping steps should be:

   a. a string reference to null or a string of length 0, the result is false

   b. the first character in the string is the target, the result is true

   The recursive step would involve searching the rest of the string.

PROGRAMMING

1. Write a recursive method `toNumber` that forms the integer sum of all digit characters in a string. For example, the result of `toNumber("3ac4")` would be 7. *Hint:* If `next` is a digit character (`'0'` through `'9'`), `Character.isDigit(next)` is true and the numeric value of `next` is `Character.digit(next, 10)`.
2. Write a recursive method `stutter` that returns a string with each character in its argument repeated. For example, if the string passed to `stutter` is `"hello"`, `stutter` will return the string `"hheelllloo"`.
3. Write a recursive method that implements the recursive algorithm for searching a string in Self-Check Exercise 7. The method heading should be:
   ```
   public static boolean searchString(String str, char ch)
   ```

5.2 Recursive Definitions of Mathematical Formulas

Mathematicians often use recursive definitions of formulas. These definitions lead very naturally to recursive algorithms.

EXAMPLE 5.4 The factorial of n, or $n!$, is defined as follows:

$$0! = 1$$
$$n! = n \times (n - 1)!$$

The first formula identifies the base case: n equal to 0. The second formula is a recursive definition. It leads to the following algorithm for computing $n!$.

Recursive Algorithm for Computing *n*!

1. `if` n equals 0
2. $n!$ is 1.
   `else`
3. $n! = n \times (n - 1)!$

To verify the correctness of this algorithm, we see that the base case is solved correctly (0! is 1). The recursive case makes progress toward the base case because it involves the calculation of a smaller factorial. Also, if we can calculate $(n - 1)!$, the recursive case gives us the correct formula for calculating $n!$.

The recursive method follows. The statement

```
return n * factorial(n - 1);
```

implements the recursive case. Each time `factorial` calls itself, the method body executes again with a different argument value. An initial method call such as `factorial(4)` will generate four recursive calls, as shown in Figure 5.5.

FIGURE 5.5
Trace of `factorial(4)`

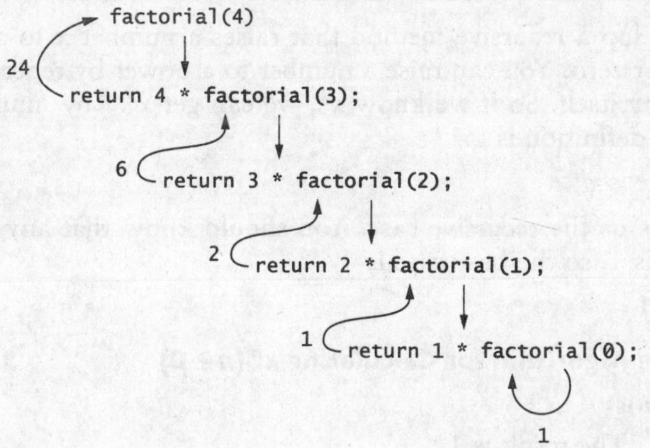


```java
/** Recursive factorial method (in RecursiveMethods.java).
    pre: n >= 0
    @param n The integer whose factorial is being computed
    @return n!
*/
public static int factorial(int n) {
    if (n == 0)
        return 1;
    else
        return n * factorial(n - 1);
}
```

PITFALL

Infinite Recursion and Stack Overflow

If you call method `factorial` with a negative argument, you will see that the recursion does not terminate. It will continue forever, because the stopping case, n equals 0, can never be reached, as n gets more negative with each call. For example, if the original value of n is –4, you will make method calls `factorial(-5)`, `factorial(-6)`, `factorial(-7)`, and so on. You should make sure that your recursive methods are constructed so that a stopping case is always reached. One way to prevent the infinite recursion in this case would be to change the terminating condition to `n <= 0`. However, this would incorrectly return a value of 1 for n! if n is negative. A better solution would be to throw an `IllegalArgumentException` if n is negative.

If your program does not terminate properly, you may see an extremely long display on the console (if the console is being used to display its results). Eventually the exception `StackOverflowError` will be thrown. This means that the memory area used to store information about method calls (the run-time stack) has been used up because there have been too many calls to the recursive method. Because there is no memory available for this purpose, your program can't execute any more method calls.

EXAMPLE 5.5 Let's develop a recursive method that raises a number x to a power n, where n is positive or zero. You can raise a number to a power by repeatedly multiplying that number by itself. So if we know x^k, we can get x^{k+1} by multiplying x^k by x. The recursive definition is

$$x^n = x \times x^{n-1}$$

This gives us the recursive case. You should know that any number raised to the power 0 is 1, so the base case is

$$x^0 = 1$$

Recursive Algorithm for Calculating x^n ($n \geq 0$)

1. **if** n is 0
2. The result is 1.

   else
3. The result is $x \times x^{n-1}$.

We show the method next.

```
/** Recursive power method (in RecursiveMethods.java).
    pre: n >= 0
    @param x The number being raised to a power
    @param n The exponent
    @return x raised to the power n
*/
public static double power(double x, int n) {
    if (n == 0)
        return 1;
    else
        return x * power(x, n - 1);
}
```

EXAMPLE 5.6 The greatest common divisor (gcd) of two numbers is the largest integer that divides both numbers. For example, the gcd of 20, 15 is 5; the gcd of 36, 24 is 12; the gcd of 36, 18 is 18. The mathematician Euclid devised an algorithm for finding the greatest common divisor of two integers, m and n, based on the following definition.

Definition of gcd(m, n) for $m > n$

gcd(m, n) = n if n is a divisor of m

gcd(m, n) = gcd(n, m % n) if n isn't a divisor of m

This definition states that gcd(m, n) is n if n divides m. This is correct because no number larger than n can divide n. Otherwise, the definition states that gcd(m, n) is the same as gcd(n, m % n), where m % n is the integer remainder of m divided by n. Therefore, gcd(20, 15) is the same as gcd(15, 5), or 5, because 5 divides 15. This recursive definition leads naturally to a recursive algorithm.

Recursive Algorithm for Calculating gcd(m, n) for $m > n$

1. **if** n is a divisor of m

2. The result is n.

```
else
```

3. The result is gcd(n, m % n).

To verify that this is correct, we need to make sure that there is a base case and that it is solved correctly. The base case is "n is a divisor of m." If so, the solution is n (n is the greatest common divisor), which is correct. Does the recursive case make progress to the base case? It must because both arguments in each recursive call are smaller than in the previous call, and the new second argument is always smaller than the new first argument (m % n must be less than n). Eventually a divisor will be found, or the second argument will become 1. Since 1 is a base case (1 divides every integer), we have verified that the recursive case makes progress toward the base case.

Next, we show method `gcd`. Notice that the method introduces a new recursive case that transposes `m` and `n` if the initial value of `n` happens to be larger than `m`:

```
else if (m < n)
    return gcd(n, m);
```

This clause allows us to handle arguments that initially are not in the correct sequence.

```
/** Recursive gcd method (in RecursiveMethods.java).
    pre: m > 0 and n > 0
    @param m The larger number
    @param n The smaller number
    @return Greatest common divisor of m and n
*/
public static double gcd(int m, int n) {
    if (m % n == 0)
        return n;
    else if (m < n)
        return gcd(n, m);   // Transpose arguments.
    else
        return gcd(n, m % n);
}
```

Recursion versus Iteration

You may have noticed that there are some similarities between recursion and iteration. Both techniques enable us to repeat a compound statement. In iteration, a loop repetition condition in the loop header determines whether we repeat the loop body or exit from the loop. We repeat the loop body while the repetition condition is true. In recursion, the condition usually tests for a base case. We stop the recursion when the base case is reached (the condition is true), and we execute the method body again when the condition is false. We can always write an iterative solution to a problem that is solvable by recursion. However, the recursive algorithm may be easier to conceptualize and may, therefore, lead to a method that is easier to write, read, and debug—all of which are very desirable attributes of code.

EXAMPLE 5.7 In Example 5.4, we wrote the recursive method.

```
public static int factorial(int n) {
    if (n == 0)
        return 1;
    else
```

```
        return n * factorial(n - 1);
}
```

It is a straightforward process to turn this method into an iterative one, replacing the `if` statement with a loop, as we show next.

```
/** Iterative factorial method.
    pre: n >= 0
    @param n The integer whose factorial is being computed
    @return n!
*/
public static int factorialIter(int n) {
    int result = 1;
    for (int k = 1; k <= n; k++)
        result = result * k;
    return result;
}
```

Efficiency of Recursion

The iterative method `factorialIter` multiplies all integers between 1 and n to compute $n!$. It may be slightly less readable than the recursive method `factorial`, but not much. In terms of efficiency, both algorithms are $O(n)$, because the number of loop repetitions or recursive calls increases linearly with n. However, the iterative version is probably faster because the overhead for a method call and return would be greater than the overhead for loop repetition (testing and incrementing the loop control variable). The difference, though, would not be significant. Generally, if it is easier to conceptualize an algorithm using recursion, then you should code it as a recursive method because the reduction in efficiency does not outweigh the advantage of readable code that is easy to debug.

EXAMPLE 5.8 The Fibonacci numbers fib_n are a sequence of numbers that were invented to model the growth of a rabbit colony. Therefore, we would expect this sequence to grow very quickly, and it does. For example, fib_{10} is 55, fib_{15} is 610, fib_{20} is 6765, and fib_{25} is 75025 (that's a lot of rabbits!). The definition of this sequence follows:

$fib_1 = 1$

$fib_2 = 1$

$fib_n = fib_{n-1} + fib_{n-2}$

Next, we show a method that calculates the nth Fibonacci number. The last line codes the recursive case.

```
/** Recursive method to calculate Fibonacci numbers
    (in RecursiveMethods.java).
    pre: n >= 1
    @param n The position of the Fibonacci number being calculated
    @return The Fibonacci number
*/
public static int fibonacci(int n) {
    if (n <= 2)
        return 1;
    else
```

```
        return fibonacci(n - 1) + fibonacci(n - 2);
}
```

Unfortunately, this solution is very inefficient because of multiple calls to `fibonacci` with the same argument. For example, calculating `fibonacci(5)` results in calls to `fibonacci(4)` and `fibonacci(3)`. Calculating `fibonacci(4)` results in calls to `fibonacci(3)` (second call) and also `fibonacci(2)`. Calculating `fibonacci(3)` twice results in two more calls to `fibonacci(2)` (three calls total), and so on (see Figure 5.6).

Because of the redundant method calls, the time required to calculate `fibonacci(n)` increases exponentially with `n`. For example, if `n` is 100, there are approximately 2^{100} activation frames. This number is approximately 10^{30}. If you could process one million activation frames per second, it would still take 10^{24} seconds, which is approximately 3×10^{16} years. However, it is possible to write recursive methods for computing Fibonacci numbers that have $O(n)$ performance. We show one such method next.

```
/** Recursive O(n) method to calculate Fibonacci numbers
    (in RecursiveMethods.java).
    pre: n >= 1
    @param fibCurrent The current Fibonacci number
    @param fibPrevious The previous Fibonacci number
    @param n The count of Fibonacci numbers left to calculate
    @return The value of the Fibonacci number calculated so far
*/
private static int fibo(int fibCurrent, int fibPrevious, int n) {
    if (n == 1)
        return fibCurrent;
    else
        return fibo(fibCurrent + fibPrevious, fibCurrent, n - 1);
}
```

Unlike method `fibonacci`, method `fibo` does not follow naturally from the recursive definition of the Fibonacci sequence. In method `fibo` the first argument is always the current Fibonacci number, and the second argument is the previous one. We update these values for each new call. When `n` is 1 (the base case), we have calculated the required Fibonacci number, so we return its value (`fibCurrent`). The recursive case,

```
return fibo(fibCurrent + fibPrevious, fibCurrent, n - 1);
```

FIGURE 5.6
Method Calls Resulting from `fibonacci(5)`

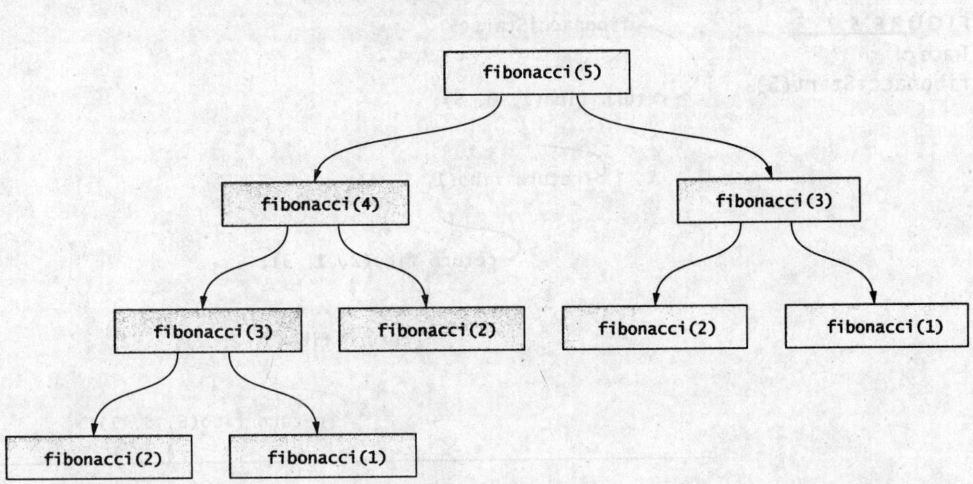

passes the sum of the current Fibonacci number and the previous Fibonacci number to the first parameter (the new value of `fibCurrent`); it passes the current Fibonacci number to the second parameter (the new value of `fibPrevious`); and it decrements `n`, making progress toward the base case.

To start this method executing, we need the following *wrapper method,* which is not recursive. This method is called a wrapper method because its only purpose is to call the recursive method and return its result. Its parameter, `n`, specifies the position in the Fibonacci sequence of the number we want to calculate. It calls the recursive method `fibo`, passing the first Fibonacci number as its first argument and `n` as its third.

```
/** Wrapper method for calculating Fibonacci numbers
    (in RecursiveMethods.java).
    pre: n >= 1
    @param n The position of the desired Fibonacci number
    @return The value of the nth Fibonacci number
*/
public static int fibonacciStart(int n) {
    return fibo(1, 0, n);
}
```

PROGRAM STYLE

Tail Recursion or Last-Line Recursion

Method `Fibo` is an example of *tail recursion or last-line recursion.* These methods have a single recursive call, and it is the last line of the method.

Figure 5.7 traces the execution of the method call `fibonacciStart(5)`. Notice that the first arguments for the method calls to `fibo` form the sequence 1, 1, 2, 3, 5, which is the Fibonacci sequence. Also notice that the result of the first return (5) is simply passed on by each successive return. That is because the recursive case does not specify any operations other than returning the result of the next call.

FIGURE 5.7
Trace of `fibonacciStart(5)`

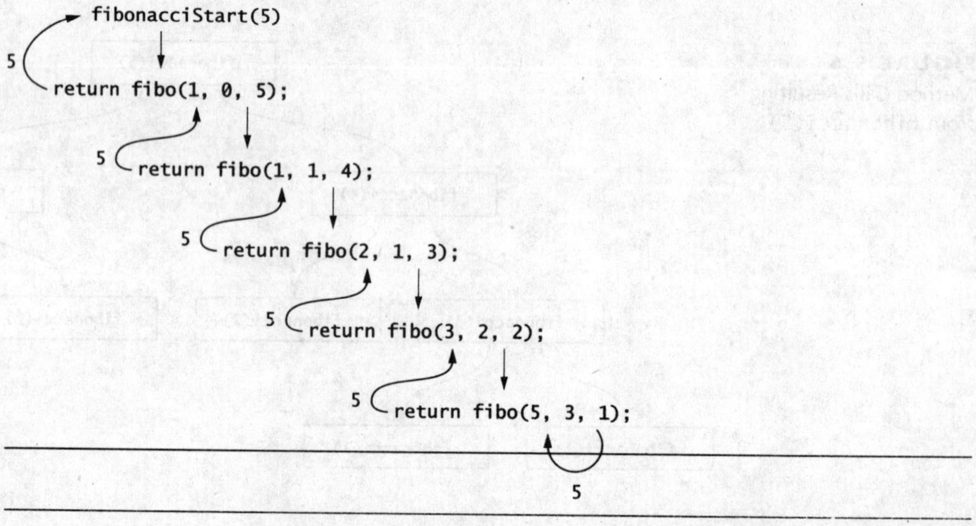

EXERCISES FOR SECTION 5.2

SELF-CHECK

1. Does the recursive algorithm for raising x to the power n work for negative values of n? Does it work for negative values of x? Indicate what happens if it is called for each of these cases.
2. Trace the execution of `fibonacciStart(5)` using activation frames.
3. Trace the execution of the following using activation frames.
```
gcd(33, 12)
gcd(12, 33)
gcd(11, 5)
```
4. For each of the following method calls, show the argument values in the activation frames that would be pushed onto the run-time stack.
   a. `gcd(6, 21)`
   b. `factorial(5)`
   c. `gcd(31, 7)`
   d. `fibonacci(6)`
   e. `fibonacciStart(7)`
5. See for what value of n method `fibonacci` begins to take a long time to run on your computer (over 1 minute). Compare the performance of `fibonacciStart` and `fibo` for this same value.

PROGRAMMING

1. Write a recursive method for raising x to the power n that works for negative n as well as positive n. Use the fact that $x^{-n} = \frac{1}{x^n}$.
2. Modify the factorial method to throw an `IllegalArgumentException` if n is negative.
3. Modify the Fibonacci method to throw an illegal argument exception if its argument is less than or equal to zero.
4. Write a class that has an iterative method for calculating Fibonacci numbers. Use an array that saves each Fibonacci number as it is calculated. Your method should take advantage of the existence of this array so that subsequent calls to the method simply retrieve the desired Fibonacci number if it has been calculated. If not, start with the largest Fibonacci number in the array rather than repeating all calculations.

5.3 Recursive Array Search

Searching an array is an activity that can be accomplished using recursion. The simplest way to search an array is a *linear search*. In a linear search, we examine one array element at a time, starting with the first element or the last element, to see whether it matches the target. The array element we are seeking may be anywhere in the array, so on average we will examine $\frac{n}{2}$ items to find the target if it is in the array. If it is not in the array, we will have to examine all n elements (the worst case). This means linear search is an $O(n)$ algorithm.

Design of a Recursive Linear Search Algorithm

Let's consider how we might write a recursive algorithm for an array search that returns the subscript of a target item.

The base case would be an empty array. If the array is empty, the target cannot be there, so the result should be –1. If the array is not empty, we will assume that we can examine just the first element of the array, so another base case would be when the first array element matches the target. If so, the result should be the subscript of the first array element.

The recursive step would be to search the rest of the array, excluding the first element. So our recursive step should search for the target starting with the current second array element, which will become the first element in the next execution of the recursive step. The algorithm follows.

Algorithm for Recursive Linear Array Search

1. **if** the array is empty
2. The result is –1.

   else if the first element matches the target

3. The result is the subscript of the first element.

   else

4. Search the array excluding the first element and return the result.

Implementation of Linear Search

The following method, `linearSearch` (part of class `RecursiveMethods`), shows the linear search algorithm.

```
/** Recursive linear search method (in RecursiveMethods.java).
    @param items The array being searched
    @param target The item being searched for
    @param posFirst The position of the current first element
    @return The subscript of target if found; otherwise -1
 */
private static int linearSearch(Object[] items,
                                Object target, int posFirst) {
    if (posFirst == items.length)
        return -1;
    else if (target.equals(items[posFirst]))
        return posFirst;
    else
        return linearSearch(items, target, posFirst + 1);
}
```

The method parameter `posFirst` represents the subscript of the current first element. The first condition tests whether the array left to search is empty. The condition `(posFirst == items.length)` is **true** when the subscript of the current first element is beyond the bounds of the array. If so, method `linearSearch` returns –1. The statement

```
return linearSearch(items, target, posFirst + 1);
```

implements the recursive step; it increments `posFirst` to exclude the current first element from the next search.

To search an array `x` for `target`, you could use the method call

```
RecursiveMethods.linearSearch(x, target, 0)
```

However, since the third argument would always be 0, we can define a nonrecursive wrapper method (also called `linearSearch`) that has just two parameters: `items` and `target`.

```
/** Wrapper for recursive linear search method (in
    RecursiveMethods.java).
    @param items The array being searched
    @param target The object being searched for
    @return The subscript of target if found; otherwise -1
*/
public static int linearSearch(Object[] items, Object target) {
    return linearSearch(items, target, 0);
}
```

The sole purpose of this method is to call the recursive method, passing on its arguments with 0 as a third argument, and return its result. This method definition overloads the previous one, which has private visibility.

Figure 5.8 traces the execution of the call to `linearSearch` in the second statement.

```
String[] greetings = {"Hi", "Hello", "Shalom"};
int posHello = linearSearch(greetings, "Hello");
```

The value returned to `posHello` will be 1.

FIGURE 5.8

Trace of `linearSearch(greetings, "Hello")`

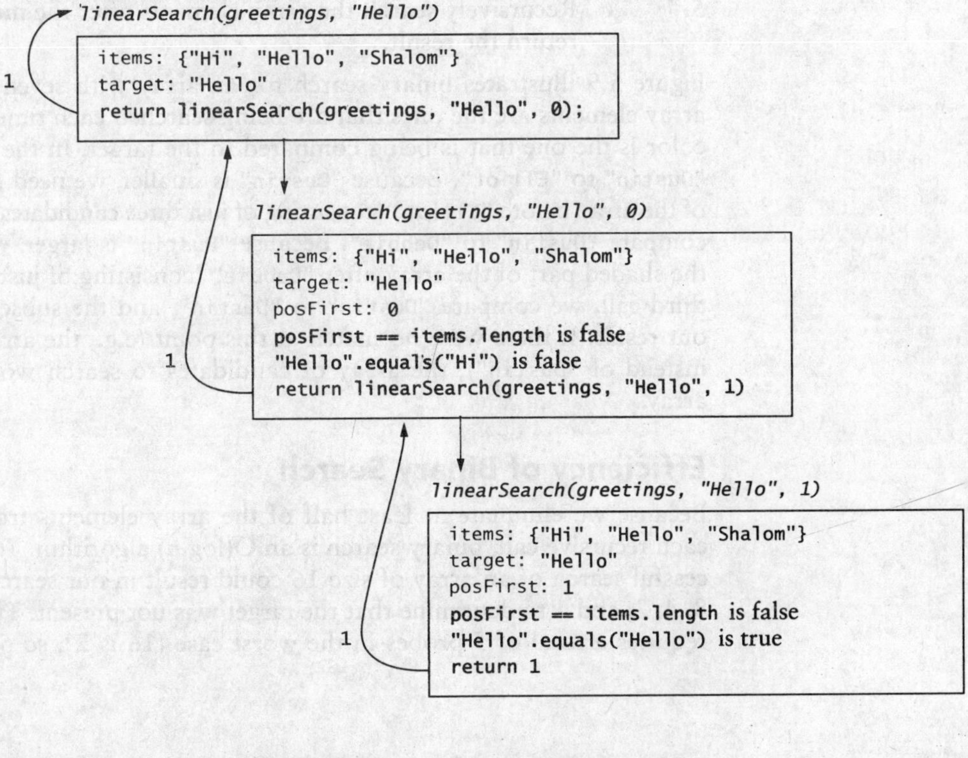

Design of a Binary Search Algorithm

A second approach to searching an array is called *binary search*. Binary search can be performed only on an array that has been sorted. In binary search, the stopping cases are the same as for linear search:

- When the array is empty
- When the array element being examined matches the target

However, rather than examining the last array element, binary search compares the "middle" element of the array to the target. If there is a match, it returns the position of the middle element. Otherwise, because the array has been sorted, we know with certainty which half of the array must be searched to find the target. We then can exclude the other half of the array (not just one element as with linear search). The binary search algorithm (first introduced in Section 5.1) follows.

Binary Search Algorithm

1. `if` the array is empty
2. Return –1 as the search result.

   `else if` the middle element matches the target
3. Return the subscript of the middle element as the result.

   `else if` the target is less than the middle element
4. Recursively search the array elements before the middle element and return the result.

   `else`
5. Recursively search the array elements after the middle element and return the result.

Figure 5.9 illustrates binary search for an array with seven elements. The shaded array elements are the ones that are being searched each time. The array element in color is the one that is being compared to the target. In the first call, we compare `"Dustin"` to `"Elliot"`. Because `"Dustin"` is smaller, we need to search only the part of the array before `"Elliot"` (consisting of just three candidates). In the second call, we compare `"Dustin"` to `"Debbie"`. Because `"Dustin"` is larger, we need to search only the shaded part of the array after `"Debbie"` (consisting of just one candidate). In the third call, we compare `"Dustin"` to `"Dustin"`, and the subscript of `"Dustin"` (2) is our result. If there were no match at this point (e.g., the array contained `"Duncan"` instead of `"Dustin"`), the array of candidates to search would become an empty array.

Efficiency of Binary Search

Because we eliminate at least half of the array elements from consideration with each recursive call, binary search is an O(log n) algorithm. To verify this, an unsuccessful search of an array of size 16 could result in our searching arrays of size 16, 8, 4, 2, and 1 to determine that the target was not present. Thus an array of size 16 requires a total of 5 probes in the worst case (16 is 2^4, so 5 is $\log_2 16 + 1$). If we

FIGURE 5.9
Binary Search for "Dustin"

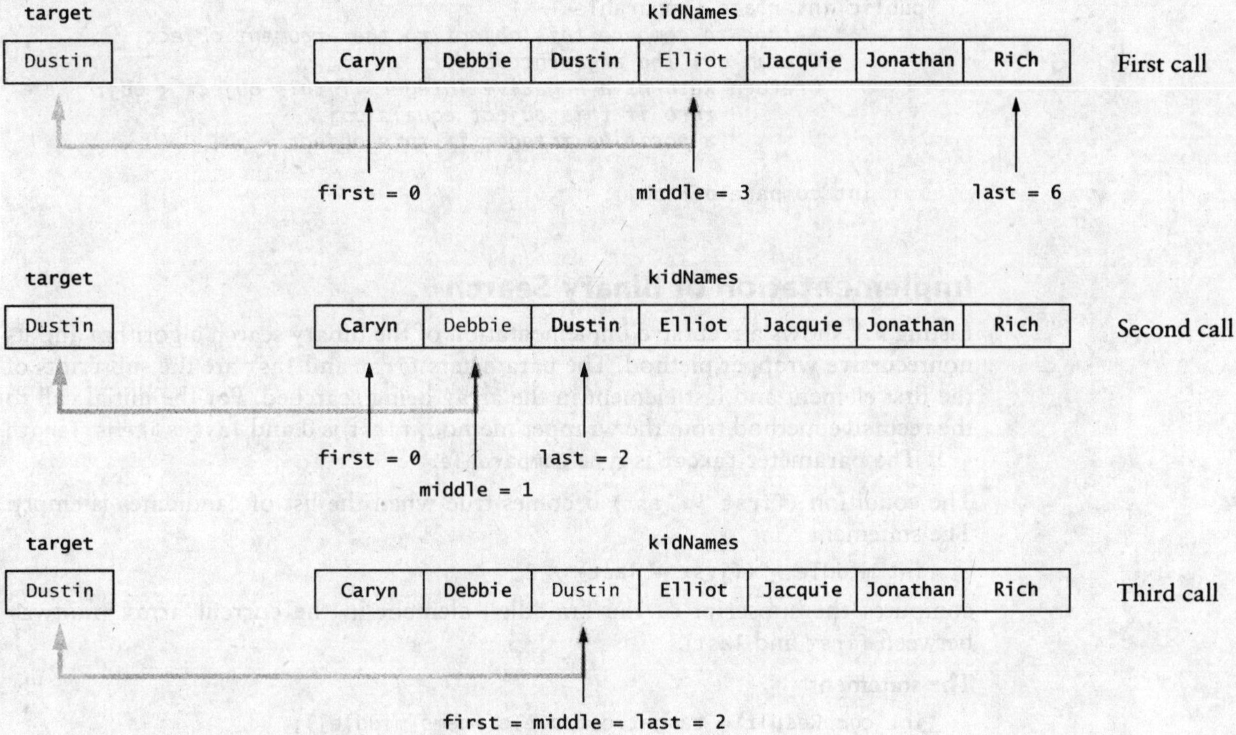

double the array size, we would need to make only 6 probes for an array of size 32 in the worst case (32 is 2^5, so 6 is $\log_2 32 + 1$). The advantages of binary search become even more apparent for larger arrays. For an array with 32,768 elements, the maximum number of probes required would be 16 ($\log_2$ 32,768 is 15), and if we expand the array to 65,536 elements, we would increase the number of probes required only to 17.

The `Comparable` Interface

We introduced the `Comparable` interface in Section 2.10. Classes that implement this interface must define a `compareTo` method that enables its objects to be compared in a standard way. Method `compareTo` returns an integer whose value indicates the relative ordering of the two objects being compared (as described in the `@return` tag below). If the target is type `Comparable`, we can apply its `compareTo` method to compare the target to the objects stored in the array. `T` represents the type of the object being compared.

```
/** Instances of classes that realize this interface can be
    compared.
*/
public interface Comparable<T> {
    /** Method to compare this object to the argument object.
        @param obj The argument object
        @return Returns a negative integer if this object < obj;
                zero if this object equals obj;
                a positive integer if this object > obj
    */
    int compareTo(T obj);
}
```

Implementation of Binary Search

Listing 5.1 shows a recursive implementation of the binary search algorithm and its nonrecursive wrapper method. The parameters `first` and `last` are the subscripts of the first element and last element in the array being searched. For the initial call to the recursive method from the wrapper method, `first` is 0 and `last` is `items.length - 1`. The parameter `target` is type `Comparable`.

The condition `(first > last)` becomes true when the list of candidates is empty. The statement

```
int middle = (first + last) / 2;
```

computes the subscript of the "middle" element in the current array (midway between `first` and `last`).

The statement

```
int compResult = target.compareTo(items[middle]);
```

saves the result of comparing the target to the middle element of the array. If the result is 0 (a match), the subscript `middle` is returned. If the result is negative, the recursive step

```
return binarySearch(items, target, first, middle - 1);
```

returns the result of searching the part of the current array before the middle item (with subscripts `first` through `middle - 1`). If the result is positive, the recursive step

```
return binarySearch(items, target, middle + 1, last);
```

returns the result of searching the part of the current array after the middle item (with subscripts `middle + 1` through `last`).

LISTING 5.1
Method `binarySearch`

```
/** Recursive binary search method (in RecursiveMethods.java).
    @param items The array being searched
    @param target The object being searched for
    @param first The subscript of the first element
    @param last The subscript of the last element
    @return The subscript of target if found; otherwise -1.
*/
```

```
private static int binarySearch(Object[] items, Comparable target,
                                int first, int last) {
    if (first > last)
        return -1;      // Base case for unsuccessful search.
    else {
        int middle = (first + last) / 2;  // Next probe index.
        int compResult = target.compareTo(items[middle]);
        if (compResult == 0)
            return middle;   // Base case for successful search.
        else if (compResult < 0)
            return binarySearch(items, target, first, middle - 1);
        else
            return binarySearch(items, target, middle + 1, last);
    }
}

/** Wrapper for recursive binary search method (in RecursiveMethods.java).
    @param items The array being searched
    @param target The object being searched for
    @return The subscript of target if found; otherwise -1.
*/
public static int binarySearch(Object[] items, Comparable target) {
    return binarySearch(items, target, 0, items.length - 1);
}
```

Figure 5.10 traces the execution of `binarySearch` for the array shown in Figure 5.9. The parameter `items` always references the same array; however, the pool of candidates changes with each call.

Testing Binary Search

To test the binary search algorithm, you must test arrays with an even number of elements and arrays with an odd number of elements. You must also test arrays that have duplicate items. Each array must be tested for the following cases:

- The target is the element at each position of the array, starting with the first position and ending with the last position.
- The target is less than the smallest array element.
- The target is greater than the largest array element.
- The target is a value between each pair of items in the array.

Method `Arrays.binarySearch`

The Java API class `Arrays` contains a `binarySearch` method. It can be called with sorted arrays of primitive types or with sorted arrays of objects. If the objects in the array are not mutually comparable or if the array is not sorted, the results are undefined. If there are multiple copies of the target value in the array, there is no guarantee as to which one will be found. This is the same as for our `binarySearch` method. The method throws a `ClassCastException` if the target is not comparable to the array elements (e.g., if the target is type `Integer` and the array elements are type `String`).

FIGURE 5.10
Trace of binarySearch(kidNames, "Dustin")

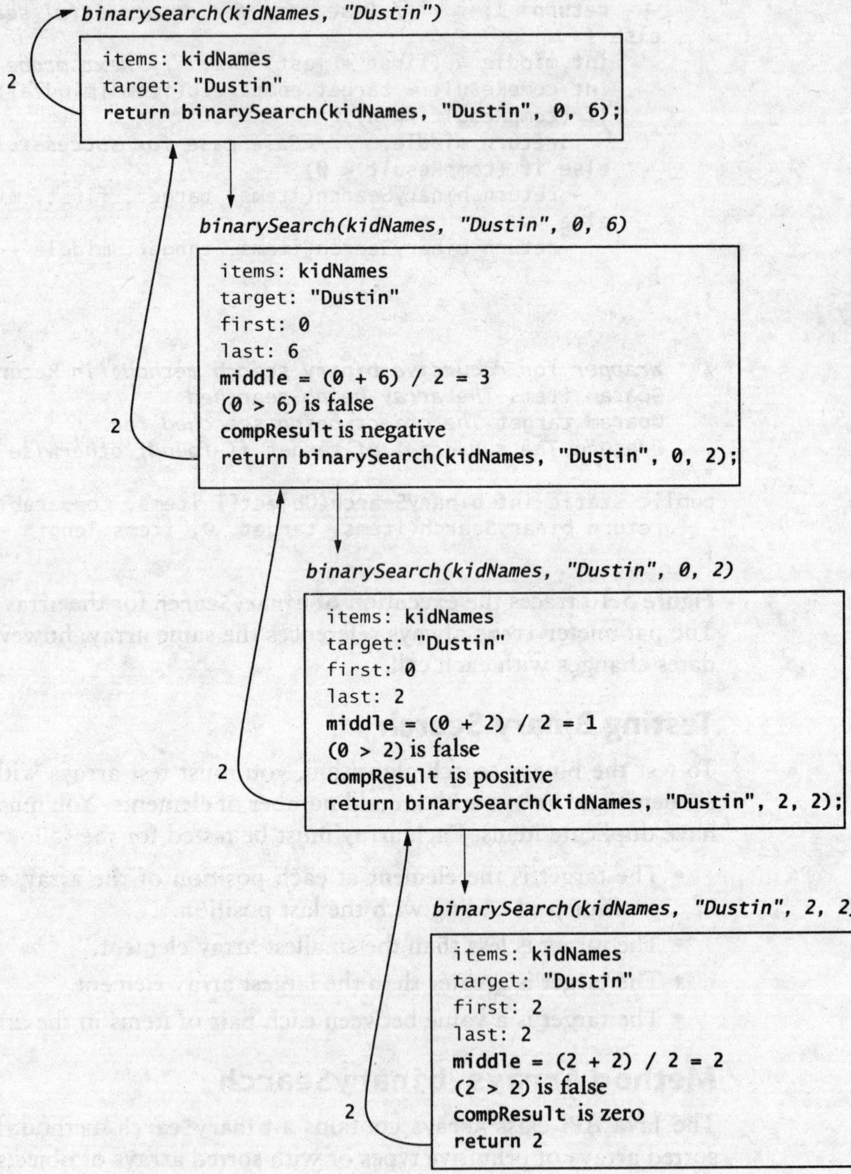

EXERCISES FOR SECTION 5.3

SELF-CHECK

1. For the array shown in Figure 5.9, show the values of `first`, `last`, `middle`, and `compResult` in successive frames when searching for a target of `"Rich"`; when searching for a target of `"Alice"`; when searching for a target of `"Daryn"`.
2. How many elements will be compared to `target` for an unsuccessful binary search in an array of 1000 items? What is the answer for 2000 items?
3. If there are multiple occurrences of the target item in an array, what can you say about the subscript value that will be returned by `linearSearch`? Answer the same question for `binarySearch`.
4. Write a recursive algorithm to find the largest value in an array of integers.
5. Write a recursive algorithm that searches a string for a target character and returns the position of its first occurrence if it is present or −1 if it is not.

PROGRAMMING

1. Write a recursive method to find the sum of all values stored in an array of integers.
2. Write a recursive linear search method with a recursive step that finds the last occurrence of a target in an array, not the first. You will need to modify the linear search method so that the last element of the array is always tested, not the first. You will need to pass the current length of the array as an argument.
3. Implement the method for Self-check Exercise 4. You will need to keep track of the largest value found so far through a method parameter.
4. Implement the method for Self-Check Exercise 5. You will need to keep track of the current position in the string through a method parameter.

5.4 Recursive Data Structures

Computer scientists often encounter data structures that are defined recursively. A *recursive data structure* is one that has another version of itself as a component. We will define the tree data structure as a recursive data structure in Chapter 6, but we can also define a linked list, described in Chapter 2, as a recursive data structure. In this section we demonstrate that recursive methods provide a very natural mechanism for processing recursive data structures. The first language developed for artificial intelligence research was a recursive language designed expressly for LISt Processing and therefore called LISP.

Recursive Definition of a Linked List

The following definition implies that a nonempty linked list is a collection of nodes such that each node references another linked list consisting of the nodes that follow it in the list. The last node references an empty list.

A linked list is empty, or it consists of a node, called the list head, that stores data and a reference to a linked list.

Class LinkedListRec

We will define a class `LinkedListRec<E>` that implements several list operations using recursive methods. The class `LinkedListRec<E>` has a private inner class called `Node<E>`, which is defined in Listing 2.1. A `Node<E>` object has attributes `data` (type `E`) and `next` (type `Node`). Class `LinkedListRec<E>` has a single data field `head` (data type `Node<E>`).

```
/** A recursive linked list class with recursive methods. */
public class LinkedListRec<E> {

    /** The list head */
    private Node<E> head;

    // Insert inner class Node<E> here. See Listing 2.1.
. . .
}
```

We will write the following recursive methods: `size` (returns the size), `toString` (represents the list contents as a string), `add` (adds an element to the end of the list), and `replace` (replaces one object in a list with another). We code each operation using a pair of methods: a public wrapper method that calls a private recursive method. To perform a list operation, you apply a wrapper method to an instance of class `LinkedListRec`.

Method size

The method `size` returns the size of a linked list and is similar to the method `length` defined earlier for a string. The recursive method returns 0 if the list is empty (`head == null` is true). Otherwise, the statement

```
return 1 + size(head.next);
```

returns 1 plus the size of the rest of the list that is referenced by `head.next`.

The wrapper method calls the recursive method, passing the list head as an argument, and returns the value returned by the recursive method. In the initial call to the recursive method, `head` will reference the first list node. In each subsequent call, `head` will reference the successor of the node that it currently references.

```
/** Finds the size of a list.
    @param head The head of the current list
    @return The size of the current list
*/
private int size(Node<E> head) {
    if (head == null)
        return 0;
    else
        return 1 + size(head.next);
}

/** Wrapper method for finding the size of a list.
    @return The size of the list
*/
public int size() {
```

```
    return size(head);
}
```

Method toString

The method toString returns a string representation of a linked list. The recursive method is very similar to method size. The statement

```
return head.data + "\n" + toString(head.next);
```

appends the data in the current list head to the string representation of the rest of the list. The line space character is inserted after each list item. If the list contains the elements "hat", "55", "dog", the string result would be "hat\n55\ndog\n".

```
/** Returns the string representation of a list.
    @param head The head of the current list
    @return The state of the current list
*/
private String toString(Node<E> head) {
    if (head == null)
        return "";
    else
        return head.data + "\n" + toString(head.next);
}

/** Wrapper method for returning the string representation of a list.
    @return The string representation of the list
*/
public String toString() {
    return toString(head);
}
```

Method replace

The method replace replaces each occurrence of an object in a list (parameter oldObj) with a different object (parameter newObj). The **if** statement in the recursive method is different from what we are used to. The method does nothing for the base case of an empty list. If the list is not empty, the **if** statement

```
if (oldObj.equals(head.data))
    head.data = newObj;
```

tests whether the item in the current list head matches oldObj. If so, it stores newObj in the current list head. Regardless of whether or not a replacement is performed, method replace is called recursively to process the rest of the list.

```
/** Replaces all occurrences of oldObj with newObj.
    post: Each occurrence of oldObj has been replaced by newObj.
    @param head The head of the current list
    @param oldObj The object being removed
    @param newObj The object being inserted
*/
private void replace(Node<E> head, E oldObj, E newObj) {
    if (head != null) {
        if (oldObj.equals(head.data))
            head.data = newObj;
        replace(head.next, oldObj, newObj);
    }
}
```

```
/*  Wrapper method for replacing oldObj with newObj.
    post: Each occurrence of oldObj has been replaced by newObj.
    @param oldObj The object being removed
    @param newObj The object being inserted
*/
public void replace(E oldObj, E newObj) {
    replace(head, oldObj, newObj);
}
```

Method add

You can use the add method to add nodes to an existing list. You can also use it to build a list by adding new nodes to the end of an initially empty list.

The add methods have two features that are different from what we have seen before. The wrapper method tests for an empty list (`head == null` is **true**), and it calls the recursive add method only if the list is not empty. If the list is empty, the wrapper add method creates a new node, which is referenced by the data field head, and stores the first list item in this node.

```
/** Adds a new node to the end of a list.
    @param head The head of the current list
    @param data The data for the new node
*/
private void add(Node<E> head, E data) {
    // If the list has just one element, add to it.
    if (head.next == null)
        head.next = new Node<E>(data);
    else
        add(head.next, data);         // Add to rest of list.
}

/** Wrapper method for adding a new node to the end of a list.
    @param data The data for the new node
*/
public void add(E data) {
    if (head == null)
        head = new Node<E>(data);  // List has 1 node.
    else
        add(head, data);
}
```

For each node referenced by argument head, the recursive method tests to see whether the node referenced by argument head is the last node in the list (`head.next` is `null`). If so, method add then resets `head.next` to reference a new node that contains the data being inserted.

PITFALL

Testing for an Empty List Instead of Testing for the Last List Node

In recursive method add, we test whether head.next is null. This condition is true when head references a list with just one node. We then reset its next field to reference a new node. If we tested whether head was null (an empty list) and then executed the statement

```
head = new Node<E>(data);
```

this would have no effect on the original list. The local reference head would be changed to reference the new node, but this node would not be connected to a node in the original list.

Removing a List Node

One of the reasons for using linked lists is that they enable easy insertion and removal of nodes. We show how to do removal next and leave insertion as an exercise. In the following recursive method remove, the first base case returns **false** if the list is empty. The second base case determines whether the list head should be removed by comparing its data field to outData. If there is a match, the assignment statement removes the list head by connecting its predecessor (referenced by pred) to the successor of the list head. For this case, method remove returns **true**. The recursive case applies remove to the rest of the list. In the next execution of the recursive method, the current list head will be referenced by pred, and the successor of the current list head will be referenced by head.

```
/** Removes a node from a list.
    post: The first occurrence of outData is removed.
    @param head The head of the current list
    @param pred The predecessor of the list head
    @param outData The data to be removed
    @return true if the item is removed
            and false otherwise
*/
private boolean remove(Node<E> head, Node<E> pred, E outData) {
    if (head == null)  // Base case - empty list.
        return false;
    else if (head.data.equals(outData)) {  // 2nd base case.
        pred.next = head.next;  // Remove head.
        return true;
    } else
        return remove(head.next, head, outData);
}
```

The following wrapper method takes care of the special case where the node to be removed is at the head of the list. The first condition returns **false** if the list is empty. The second condition removes the list head and returns **true** if the list head contains the data to be removed. The **else** clause calls the recursive remove method.

In the first execution of the recursive method, head will reference the actual second node, and pred will reference the actual first node.

```
/** Wrapper method for removing a node (in LinkedListRec).
    post: The first occurrence of outData is removed.
    @param outData The data to be removed
    @return true if the item is removed,
            and false otherwise
 */
public boolean remove(E outData) {
    if (head == null)
        return false;
    else if (head.data.equals(outData)) {
        head = head.next;
        return true;
    } else
        return remove(head.next, head, outData);
}
```

EXERCISES FOR SECTION 5.4

SELF-CHECK

1. Describe the result of executing each of the following statements:

```
LinkedListRec<String> aList = new LinkedListRec<String>();
aList.add("bye");
aList.add("hello");
System.out.println(aList.size() + ", " + aList.toString());
aList.replace("hello", "welcome");
aList.add("OK");
aList.remove("bye");
aList.remove("hello");
System.out.println(aList.size() + ", " + aList.toString());
```

2. Trace each call to a `LinkedListRec` method in Exercise 1 above.
3. Write a recursive algorithm for method `insert(E obj, int index)` where `index` is the position of the insertion.
4. Write a recursive algorithm for method `remove(int index)` where `index` is the position of the item to be removed.

PROGRAMMING

1. Write an `equals` method for the `LinkedListRec` class that compares this `LinkedListRec` object to one specified by its argument. Two lists are equal if they have the same number of nodes and store the same information at each node. Don't use the `size` method.
2. Write a `search` method that returns **`true`** if its argument is stored as the data field of a `LinkedListRec` node and returns **`false`** if its argument is not stored in any node.
3. Write a recursive method `insertBefore` that inserts a specified data object before the first occurrence of another specified data object. For example, the method call

`aList.insertBefore(target, inData)` would insert the object referenced by `inData` in a new node just before the first node of `aList` that stores a reference to `target` as its data.

4. Write a recursive method `reverse` that reverses the elements in a linked list.
5. Code method `insert` in Self-Check Exercise 3.
6. Code method `remove` in Self-Check Exercise 4.

5.5 Problem Solving with Recursion

In this section we discuss recursive solutions to two problems. Our recursive solutions will break each problem up into multiple smaller versions of the original problem. Both problems are easier to solve using recursion because recursive thinking enables us to split each problem into more manageable subproblems. They would both be much more difficult to solve without recursion.

CASE STUDY Towers of Hanoi

Problem You may be familiar with a version of this problem that is sold as a child's puzzle. There is a board with three pegs and three disks of different sizes (see Figure 5.11). The goal of the game is to move the three disks from the peg where they have been placed (largest disk on the bottom, smallest disk on the top) to one of the empty pegs, subject to the following constraints:

- Only the top disk on a peg can be moved to another peg.
- A larger disk cannot be placed on top of a smaller disk.

Analysis We can solve this problem by displaying a list of moves to be made. The problem inputs will be the number of disks to move, the starting peg, the destination peg, and the temporary peg. Table 5.1 shows the problem inputs and outputs. We will write a class `Tower` that contains a method `showMoves` that builds a string with all the moves.

FIGURE 5.11
Children's Version of Towers of Hanoi

TABLE 5.1
Inputs and Outputs for Towers of Hanoi Problem

Problem Inputs
Number of disks (an integer)
Letter of starting peg: L (left), M (middle), or R (right)
Letter of destination peg: (L, M, or R), but different from starting peg
Letter of temporary peg: (L, M, or R), but different from starting peg and destination peg
Problem Outputs
A list of moves

Design We still need to determine a strategy for making a move. If we examine the situation in Figure 5.11 (all three disks on the L peg), we can derive a strategy to solve it. If we can figure out how to move the top two disks to the M peg (a two-disk version of the original problem), we can then place the bottom disk on the R peg (see Figure 5.12). Now all we need to do is move the two disks on the M peg to the R peg. If we can solve both of these two-disk problems, then the three-disk problem is also solved:

Solution to Two-Disk Problem: Move Three Disks from Peg L to Peg R

1. Move the top two disks from peg L to peg M.
2. Move the bottom disk from peg L to peg R.
3. Move the top two disks from peg M to peg R.

FIGURE 5.12
Towers of Hanoi after the First Two Steps in Solution of the Three-Disk Problem

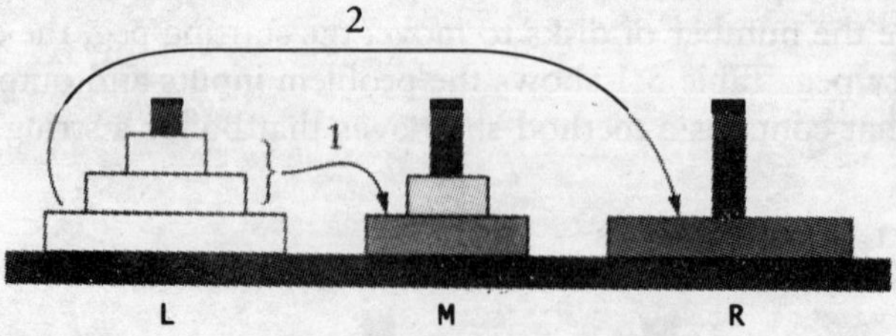

We can split the solution to each two-disk problem into three problems involving single disks. We solve the second two-disk problem next; the solution to the first one (move the top two disks from peg L to peg M) is quite similar.

Solution to Two-Disk Problem: Move Top Two Disks from Peg M to Peg R

1. Move the top disk from peg M to peg L.
2. Move the bottom disk from peg M to peg R.
3. Move the top disk from peg L to peg R.

In Figure 5.13 we show the pegs after Steps 1 and 2. When Step 3 is completed, the three pegs will be on peg R.

FIGURE 5.13
Towers of Hanoi after First Two Steps in Solution of the Two-Disk Problem

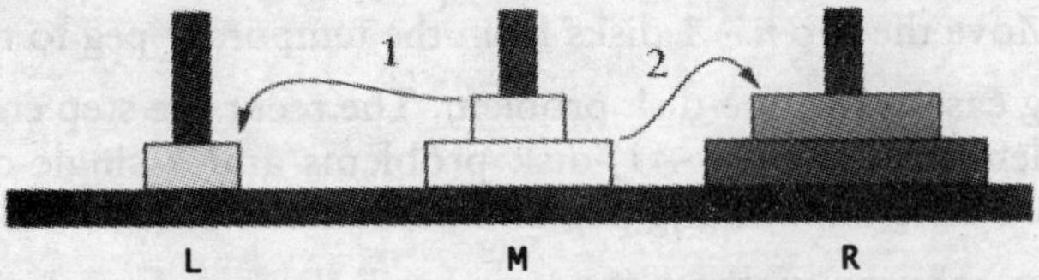

In a similar way, we can split a four-disk problem into two three-disk problems. Figure 5.14 shows the pegs after the top three disks have been moved from peg L to peg M. Because we know how to solve three-disk problems, we can also solve four-disk problems.

Solution to Four-Disk Problem: Move Four Disks from Peg L to Peg R

1. Move the top three disks from peg L to peg M.
2. Move the bottom disk from peg L to peg R.
3. Move the top three disks from peg M to peg R.

FIGURE 5.14
Towers of Hanoi after the First Two Steps in Solution of the Four-Disk Problem

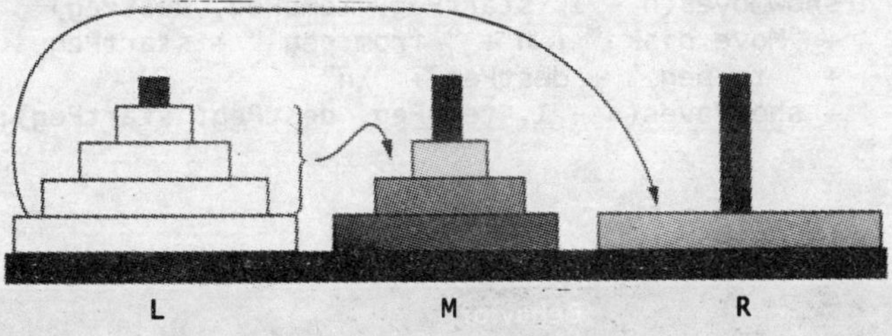

Next, we show a general recursive algorithm for moving *n* disks from one of the three pegs to a different peg.

Recursive Algorithm for *n*-Disk Problem: Move *n* Disks from the Starting Peg to the Destination Peg

1. `if` *n* is 1
2. Move disk 1 (the smallest disk) from the starting peg to the destination peg.
3. `else`
4. Move the top $n - 1$ disks from the starting peg to the temporary peg (neither starting nor destination peg).
5. Move disk *n* (the disk at the bottom) from the starting peg to the destination peg.
6. Move the top $n - 1$ disks from the temporary peg to the destination peg.

The stopping case is the one-disk problem. The recursive step enables us to split the *n*-disk problem into two $(n - 1)$-disk problems and a single-disk problem. Each problem has a different starting peg and destination peg.

Our recursive solution method `showMoves` will display the solution as a list of disk moves. For each move, we show the number of the disk being moved and its starting and destination pegs. For example, for the two-disk problem shown earlier (move two disks from the middle peg, M, to the right peg, R), the list of moves would be

```
Move disk 1 from peg M to peg L
Move disk 2 from peg M to peg R
Move disk 1 from peg L to peg R
```

The method `showMoves` must have the number of disks, the starting peg, the destination peg, and the temporary peg as its parameters. If there are *n* disks, the bottom disk has number *n* (the top disk has number 1). Table 5.2 describes the method required for class `TowersOfHanoi`.

Implementation Listing 5.2 shows class `TowersOfHanoi`. In method `showMoves`, the recursive step

```
return showMoves(n - 1, startPeg, tempPeg, destPeg)
        + "Move disk " + n + " from peg " + startPeg
        + " to peg " + destPeg + "\n"
        + showMoves(n - 1, tempPeg, destPeg, startPeg);
```

TABLE 5.2
Class `TowersOfHanoi`

Method	Behavior
`public String showMoves(int n, char startPeg, char destPeg, char tempPeg)`	Builds a string containing all moves for a game with `n` disks on `startPeg` that will be moved to `destPeg` using `tempPeg` for temporary storage of disks being moved.

returns the string formed by concatenating the list of moves for the first (n – 1)-disk problem (the recursive call after return), the move required for the bottom disk (disk n), and the list of moves for the second (n – 1)-disk problem.

LISTING 5.2

Class TowersOfHanoi

```
import javax.swing.*;

/** Class that solves Towers of Hanoi problem. */
public class TowersOfHanoi {
    /** Recursive method for "moving" disks.
        pre: startPeg, destPeg, tempPeg are different.
        @param n is the number of disks
        @param startPeg is the starting peg
        @param destPeg is the destination peg
        @param tempPeg is the temporary peg
        @return A string with all the required disk moves
    */
    public static String showMoves(int n, char startPeg,
                                   char destPeg, char tempPeg) {
        if (n == 1) {
            return "Move disk 1 from peg " + startPeg +
                " to peg " + destPeg + "\n";
        } else {  // Recursive step
            return showMoves(n - 1, startPeg, tempPeg, destPeg)
                + "Move disk " + n + " from peg " + startPeg
                + " to peg " + destPeg + "\n"
                + showMoves(n - 1, tempPeg, destPeg, startPeg);
        }
    }
}
```

Testing Figure 5.15 shows the result of executing the following main method for the data 3, L, R ("move 3 disks from peg L to peg R"). The first three lines are the solution to the problem "move 2 disks from peg L to peg M," and the last three lines are the solution to the problem "move 2 disks from peg M to peg R."

```
public static void main(String[] args) {
    String nDisks =
        JOptionPane.showInputDialog("Enter number of disks");
    String startPeg =
        JOptionPane.showInputDialog("Enter start peg (L, M, R)");
    String destPeg =
        JOptionPane.showInputDialog("Enter destination peg "
                                    + "(L, M, R), "
                                    + "but not " + startPeg);
```

```
        String tempPeg =
            JOptionPane.showInputDialog("Enter temporary peg "
                                     + "(L, M, R), "
                                     + "but not " + startPeg
                                     + " or " + destPeg);
        String moves = showMoves(Integer.parseInt(nDisks),
                                 startPeg.toUpperCase().charAt(0),
                                 destPeg.toUpperCase().charAt(0),
                                 tempPeg.toUpperCase().charAt(0));
        JOptionPane.showMessageDialog(null, moves);
    }
```

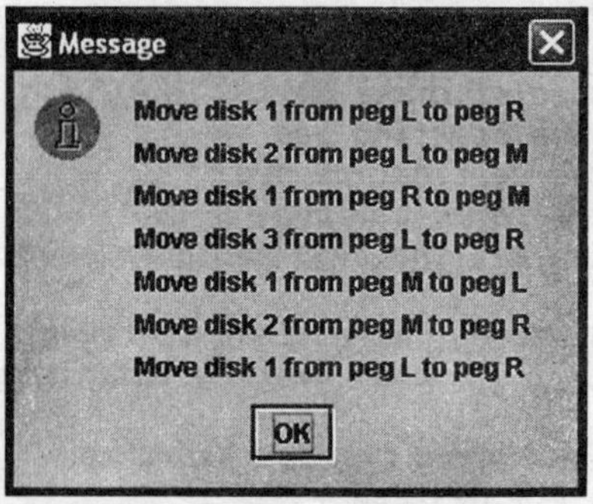

FIGURE 5.15
Solution to "Move 3 Disks from Peg L to Peg R"

Visualization of Towers of Hanoi

We have provided a graphical visualization that you can use to observe the movement of disks in a solution to the Towers of Hanoi. You can access it through the companion Web site for this book.

CASE STUDY Counting Cells in a Blob

In this case study we consider how we might process an image that is presented as a two-dimensional array of color values. The information in the two-dimensional array might come from a variety of sources. For example, it could be an image of part of a person's body that comes from an X-ray or an MRI, or it could be a picture of part of the earth's surface taken by a satellite. Our goal in this case study is to determine the size of any area in the image that is considered abnormal because of its color values.

Problem You have a two-dimensional grid of cells, and each cell contains either a normal background color or a second color, which indicates the presence of an abnormality. The user wants to know the size of a *blob*, where a blob is a collection of contiguous abnormal cells. The user will enter the x, y coordinates of a cell in the blob, and the count of all cells in that blob will be determined.

Analysis Data Requirements

PROBLEM INPUTS

- The two-dimensional grid of cells
- The coordinates of a cell in a blob

PROBLEM OUTPUTS

- The count of cells in the blob

Classes

We will have two classes. Class `TwoDimGrid` will manage the two-dimensional grid of cells. You can find the discussion of the design and implementation of this class on the Web site for this book. Here we will focus on the design of class `Blob`, which contains the recursive method that counts the number of cells in a blob.

Design Table 5.3 describes the public methods of class `TwoDimGrid`, and Table 5.4 describes class `Blob`.

Method `countCells` in class `Blob` is a recursive method that is applied to a `TwoDimGrid` object. Its parameters are the (`x`, `y`) position of a cell. The algorithm follows.

TABLE 5.3
Class `TwoDimGrid`

Method	Behavior
`void recolor(int x, int y, Color aColor)`	Resets the color of the cell at position (`x`, `y`) to `aColor`.
`Color getColor(int x, int y)`	Retrieves the color of the cell at position (`x`, `y`).
`int getNRows()`	Returns the number of cells in the y-axis.
`int getNCols()`	Returns the number of cells in the x-axis.

TABLE 5.4
Class `Blob`

Method	Behavior
`int countCells(int x, int y)`	Returns the number of cells in the blob at (`x`, `y`).

Algorithm for countCells(x, y)

1. `if` the cell at (x, y) is outside the grid
2. The result is 0.

`else if` the color of the cell at (x, y) is not the abnormal color

3. The result is 0.

`else`

4. Set the color of the cell at (x, y) to a temporary color.
5. The result is 1 plus the number of cells in each piece of the blob that includes a nearest neighbor.

The two stopping cases are reached if the coordinates of the cell are out of bounds or if the cell does not have the abnormal color and, therefore, can't be part of a blob. The recursive step involves counting 1 for a cell that has the abnormal color and adding the counts for the blobs that include each immediate neighbor cell. Each cell has eight immediate neighbors: two in the horizontal direction, two in the vertical direction, and four in the diagonal directions.

If no neighbor has the abnormal color, then the result will be just 1. If any neighbor cell has the abnormal color, then it will be counted along with all its neighbor cells that have the abnormal color, and so on until no neighboring cells with abnormal color are encountered (or the edge of the grid is reached). The reason for setting the color of the cell at (x, y) to a temporary color is to prevent it from being counted again when its neighbors' blobs are counted.

Implementation Listing 5.3 shows class `Blob`. The interface `GridColors` defines the three constants: `BACKGROUND`, `ABNORMAL`, and `TEMPORARY`. The first terminating condition,

```
(x < 0 || x >= grid.getNCols() || y < 0 || y >= grid.getNRows())
```

compares x to 0 and the value returned by `getNCols()`, the number of columns in the grid. Because x is plotted along the horizontal axis, it is compared to the number of columns, not the number of rows. The same test is applied to y and the number of rows. The second terminating condition,

```
(!grid.getColor(x, y).equals(ABNORMAL))
```

is true if the cell at (x, y) has either the background color or the temporary color.

The recursive step is implemented by the statement

```
return 1
    + countCells(x - 1, y + 1) + countCells(x, y + 1)
    + countCells(x + 1, y + 1) + countCells(x - 1, y)
    + countCells(x + 1, y) + countCells(x - 1, y - 1)
    + countCells(x, y - 1) + countCells(x + 1, y - 1);
```

Each recursive call to `countCells` has as its arguments the coordinates of a neighbor of the cell at (x, y). The value returned by each call will be the number of cells in the blob it belongs to, excluding the cell at (x, y) and any other cells that may have been counted already.

LISTING 5.3
Class Blob

```
import java.awt.*;

/** Class that solves problem of counting abnormal cells. */
public class Blob implements GridColors {

    /** The grid */
    private TwoDimGrid grid;

    /** Constructors */
    public Blob(TwoDimGrid grid) {
        this.grid = grid;
    }

    /** Finds the number of cells in the blob at (x,y).
        pre: Abnormal cells are in ABNORMAL color;
             Other cells are in BACKGROUND color.
        post: All cells in the blob are in the TEMPORARY color.
        @param x The x-coordinate of a blob cell
        @param y The y-coordinate of a blob cell
        @return The number of cells in the blob that contains (x, y)
    */
    public int countCells(int x, int y) {
        int result;

        if (x < 0 || x >= grid.getNCols()
                || y < 0 || y >= grid.getNRows())
            return 0;
        else if (!grid.getColor(x, y).equals(ABNORMAL))
            return 0;
        else {
            grid.recolor(x, y, TEMPORARY);
            return 1
                + countCells(x - 1, y + 1) + countCells(x, y + 1)
                + countCells(x + 1, y + 1) + countCells(x - 1, y)
                + countCells(x + 1, y) + countCells(x - 1, y - 1)
                + countCells(x, y - 1) + countCells(x + 1, y - 1);
        }
    }
}
```

Testing To test the recursive algorithm in this case study and the one in the next section, we will need to implement class `TwoDimGrid`. To make the program interactive and easy to use, we implemented `TwoDimGrid` as a two-dimensional grid of buttons placed in a panel. When the button panel is placed in a frame and displayed, the user can toggle the color of a button (from normal to abnormal and back to normal) by clicking it. Similarly, the program can change the color of a button by applying the `recolor` method to the button. Information about the design of class `TwoDimGrid` is on the companion Web site for this book, as is the class itself.

We also provide a class `BlobTest` on the Web site. This class allows the user to load the colors for the button panel from a file that contains a representation of the image as lines of 0s and 1s, where 0 is the background color and 1 is the abnormal color. Alternatively, the user can set the dimensions of the grid and then enter the abnormal cells by clicking on each button that represents an abnormal cell. When the grid has been finalized, the user clicks twice on one of the abnormal cells (to change its color to normal and then back to abnormal) and then clicks the button labeled Solve. This invokes method `countCells` with the coordinates of the last button clicked as its arguments. Figure 5.16 shows a sample grid of buttons with the x, y coordinate of each button shown as the button label. The background cells are dark gray, and the abnormal cells are light gray. Invoking `countCells` with a starting point of (x = 4, y = 1) should return a count of 7. Figure 5.17 shows the blob cells in the temporary color (black) after the execution of method `countCells`.

When you test this program, make sure you verify that it works for the following cases:

- A starting cell that is on the edge of the grid
- A starting cell that has no neighboring abnormal cells
- A starting cell whose only abnormal neighbor cells are diagonally connected to it
- A "bull's-eye": a starting cell whose neighbors are all normal but their neighbors are abnormal
- A starting cell that is normal
- A grid that contains all abnormal cells
- A grid that contains all normal cells

FIGURE 5.16
A Sample Grid for Counting Cells in a Blob

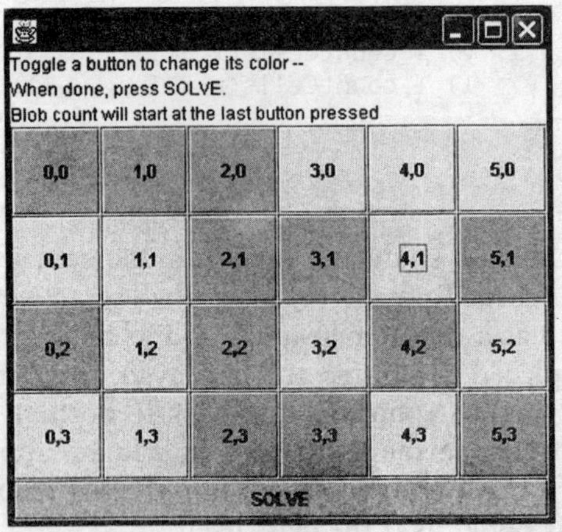

FIGURE 5.17
Blob Cells (in Black) after Execution of `countCells`

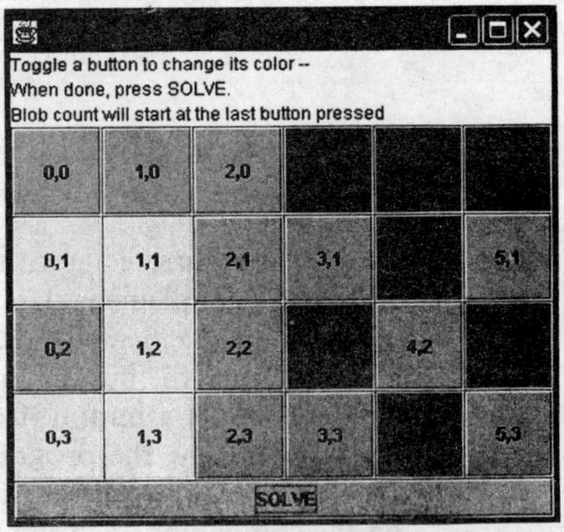

EXERCISES FOR SECTION 5.5

SELF-CHECK

1. What is the big-O for the Towers of Hanoi as a function of *n*, where *n* represents the number of disks? Compare it to the function 2^n.
2. How many moves would be required to solve the five-disk problem?
3. Provide a "trace" of the solution to a four-disk problem by showing all the calls to `showMoves` that would be generated.
4. Explain why the first condition of method `countCells` must precede the second condition.

PROGRAMMING

1. Modify method `countCells`, assuming that cells must have a common side in order to be counted in the same blob. This means that they must be connected horizontally or vertically but not diagonally. Under this condition, the value of the method call `aBlob.countCells(4, 1)` would be 4 for the grid in Figure 5.16.
2. Write a method `Blob.restore` that restores the grid to its original state. You will need to reset the color of each cell that is in the temporary color back to its original color.

5.6 Backtracking

In this section we consider the problem-solving technique called *backtracking*. Backtracking is an approach to implementing systematic trial and error in a search for a solution. An application of backtracking is finding a path through a maze.

If you are attempting to walk through a maze, you will probably follow the general approach of walking down a path as far as you can go. Eventually either you will reach your destination and exit the maze, or you won't be able to go any further. If you exit the maze, you are done. Otherwise, you need to retrace your steps (backtrack) until you reach a fork in the path. At each fork, if there is a branch you did not follow, you will follow that branch hoping to reach your destination. If not, you will retrace your steps again, and so on.

What makes backtracking different from random trial and error is that backtracking provides a systematic approach to trying alternative paths and eliminating them if they don't work out. You will never try the exact same path more than once, and you will eventually find a solution path if one exists.

Problems that are solved by backtracking can be described as a set of choices made by some method. If, at some point, it turns out that a solution is not possible with the current set of choices, the most recent choice is identified and removed. If there is an untried alternative choice, it is added to the set of choices, and search continues. If there is no untried alternative choice, then the next most recent choice is removed, and an alternative is sought for it. This process continues until either we reach a choice with an untried alternative and can continue our search for a solution, or we determine that there are no more alternative choices to try. Recursion allows us to implement backtracking in a relatively straightforward manner, because we can use each activation frame to remember the choice that was made at that particular decision point.

We will show how to use backtracking to find a path through a maze, but it can be applied to many other kinds of problems that involve a search for a solution. For example, a program that plays chess may use a kind of backtracking. If a sequence of moves it is considering does not lead to a favorable position, it will backtrack and try another sequence.

CASE STUDY Finding a Path through a Maze

Problem Use backtracking to find and display the path through a maze. From each point in a maze, you can move to the next cell in the horizontal or vertical direction, if that cell is not blocked. So there are at most four possible moves from each point.

Analysis Our maze will consist of a grid of colored cells like the grid used in the previous case study. The starting point is the cell at the top left corner (0, 0), and the exit point is the cell at the bottom right corner (`getNCols() - 1, getNRows() - 1`). All cells that can be part of a path will be in the `BACKGROUND` color. All cells that represent barriers and cannot be part of a path will be in the `ABNORMAL` color. To keep track of a cell that we have visited, we will set it to the `TEMPORARY` color. If we find a path, all cells on the path will be reset to the `PATH` color (a new color for a button defined in `GridColors`). So there are a total of four possible colors for a cell.

Design The following recursive algorithm returns **`true`** if a path is found. It changes the color of all cells that are visited but found not to be on the path to the temporary color. In the recursive algorithm, each cell `(x, y)` being tested is reachable from the starting point. We can use recursion to simplify the problem of finding a path from cell `(x, y)` to the exit. We know that we can reach any unblocked neighbor cell that is in the horizontal or vertical direction from cell `(x, y)`. So a path exists from cell `(x, y)` to the maze exit if there is a path from a neighbor cell of `(x, y)` to the maze exit. If there is no path from any neighbor cell, we must backtrack and replace `(x, y)` with an alternative that has not yet been tried. That is done automatically through recursion. If there is a path, it will eventually be found and `findMazePath` will return **`true`**.

Recursive Algorithm for `findMazePath(x, y)`

1. **`if`** the current cell is outside the maze
2. Return **`false`** (you are out of bounds).

   `else if` the current cell is part of the barrier or has already been visited
3. Return **`false`** (you are off the path or in a cycle).

   `else if` the current cell is the maze exit
4. Recolor it to the path color and return **`true`** (you have successfully completed the maze).

   `else` *// Try to find a path from the current path to the exit:*
5. Mark the current cell as on the path by recoloring it to the path color.
6. **`for`** each neighbor of the current cell
7. **`if`** a path exists from the neighbor to the maze exit
8. Return **`true`**.

   // No neighbor of the current cell is on the path.
9. Recolor the current cell to the temporary color (visited) and return **`false`**.

If no stopping case is reached (Steps 2, 3, or 4), the recursive case (the **`else`** clause) marks the current cell as being on the path and then tests whether there is a path from any neighbor of the current cell to the exit. If a path is found, we return **`true`** and begin unwinding from the recursion. During the process of unwinding from the recursion, the method will continue to return **`true`**. However, if all neighbors of the current cell are tested without finding a path, this means that the current cell cannot be on the path, so we recolor it to the temporary color and return **`false`** (Step 9). Next, we backtrack to a previous call and try to find a path through a cell that is an alternative to the cell just tested. The cell just tested will have been marked as visited (the temporary color), so we won't try using it again.

Notice there is no attempt to find the shortest path through the maze. We just show the first path that is found.

Implementation Listing 5.4 shows class `Maze` with data field `maze` (type `TwoDimGrid`). There is a wrapper method that calls recursive method `findMazePath` with its argument values set to the coordinates of the starting point (0, 0). The wrapper method returns the result of this call (**`true`** or **`false`**).

The recursive version of `findMazePath` begins with three stopping cases: two unsuccessful and one successful [(x, y) is the exit point]. The recursive case contains an **`if`** condition with four recursive calls. Because of short-circuit evaluation, if any call returns **`true`**, the rest are not executed. The arguments for each call are the coordinates of a neighbor cell. If a path exists from a neighbor to the maze exit, then the neighbor is part of the solution path, so we return **`true`**. If a neighbor cell is not on the solution path, we try the next neighbor until all four neighbors have been tested.

If there is no path from any neighbor, we recolor the current cell to the temporary color and return **false**.

LISTING 5.4
Class Maze

```
import java.awt.*;

/** Class that solves maze problems with backtracking. */
public class Maze implements GridColors {

    /** The maze */
    private TwoDimGrid maze;

    public Maze(TwoDimGrid m) {
        maze = m;
    }

    /** Wrapper method. */
    public boolean findMazePath() {
        return findMazePath(0, 0);   // (0, 0) is the start point.
    }

    /** Attempts to find a path through point (x, y).
        pre: Possible path cells are in BACKGROUND color;
             barrier cells are in ABNORMAL color.
        post: If a path is found, all cells on it are set to the
              PATH color; all cells that were visited but are
              not on the path are in the TEMPORARY color.
        @param x The x-coordinate of current point
        @param y The y-coordinate of current point
        @return If a path through (x, y) is found, true;
                otherwise, false
    */
    public boolean findMazePath(int x, int y) {
        if (x < 0 || y < 0
            || x >= maze.getNCols() || y >= maze.getNRows())
            return false;       // Cell is out of bounds.
        else if (!maze.getColor(x, y).equals(BACKGROUND))
            return false;       // Cell is on barrier or dead end.
        else if (x == maze.getNCols() - 1
                 && y == maze.getNRows() - 1) {
            maze.recolor(x, y, PATH);  // Cell is on path
            return true;               // and is maze exit.
        } else {                       // Recursive case.
            // Attempt to find a path from each neighbor.
            // Tentatively mark cell as on path.
            maze.recolor(x, y, PATH);
            if (findMazePath(x - 1, y)
                || findMazePath(x + 1, y)
                || findMazePath(x, y - 1)
```

```
                    || findMazePath(x, y + 1 ) ) {
                    return true;
                } else {
                    maze.recolor(x, y, TEMPORARY);  // Dead end.
                    return false;
                }
            }
        }
    }
```

The Effect of Marking a Cell as Visited

If a path can't be found from a neighbor of the current cell to the maze exit, the current cell is considered a "dead end" and is recolored to the temporary color. You may be wondering whether the program would still work if we just recolored it to the background color. The answer is "yes." In this case, cells that turned out to be dead ends or cells that were not visited would be in the background color after the program terminated. This would not affect the ability of the algorithm to find a path or to determine that none exists; however, it would affect the algorithm's efficiency. After backtracking, the method could try to place on the path a cell that had been found to be a dead end. The cell would be classified once again as a dead end. Marking it as a dead end (color `TEMPORARY`) the first time prevents this from happening.

To demonstrate the efficiency of this approach, we tested the program on a maze with 4 rows and 6 columns that had a single barrier cell at the maze exit. When we recolored each dead end cell in the `TEMPORARY` color, it took 93 recursive calls to `findMazePath` to determine that a path did not exist. When we recolored each tested cell in the `BACKGROUND` color, it took 177,313 recursive calls to determine that a path did not exist.

Testing We will use class `TwoDimGrid` and class `MazeTest` (from the companion Web site) to test the maze. The `MazeTest` class is very similar to `BlobTest`. The `main` method prompts for the grid dimensions and creates a new `TwoDimGrid` object with those dimensions. The class constructor builds the graphical user interface (GUI) for the maze solver, including the button panel, and registers a listener for each button. When the SOLVE button is clicked, method `MazeTest.actionPerformed` calls `findMazePath` and displays its result. Figure 5.18 shows the GUI before the SOLVE button is clicked (barrier cells are in light gray, other cells are in dark gray), and Figure 5.19 shows it after the SOLVE button is clicked and the final path is displayed. In Figure 5.19 the barrier cells are in light gray (`ABNORMAL` color), the cells on the final path are in white (`PATH` color), and the cells that were visited but then rejected (not on the path) are in black (`TEMPORARY` color).

You should test this with a variety of mazes, some that can be solved and some that can't (no path exists). You should also try a maze that has no barrier cells and one that has a single barrier cell at the exit point. In the latter case, no path exists.

FIGURE 5.18
Maze as Grid of Buttons before SOLVE Is Clicked

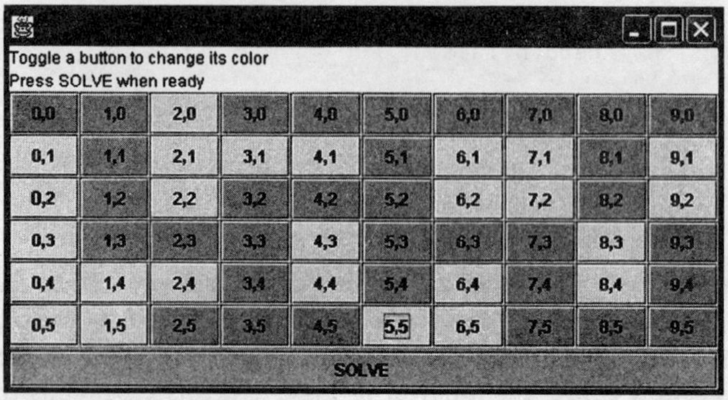

FIGURE 5.19
Maze as Grid of Buttons after SOLVE Is Clicked

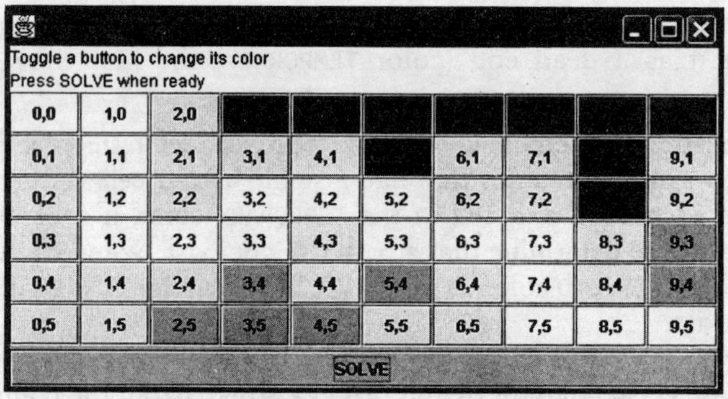

EXERCISES FOR SECTION 5.6

SELF-CHECK

1. The terminating conditions in `findMazePath` must be performed in the order specified. What could happen if the second or third condition was evaluated before the first? If the third condition was evaluated before the second condition?
2. Does it matter in which order the neighbor cells are tested in `findMazePath`? How could this order affect the path that is found?

3. Is the path shown in Figure 5.19 the shortest path to the exit? If not, list the cells on the shortest path.

PROGRAMMING

1. Show the interface `GridColors`.
2. Write a `Maze.resetTemp` method that recolors the cells that are in the TEMPORARY color to the BACKGROUND color.
3. Write a `Maze.restore` method that restores the maze to its initial state.

Chapter Review

- A recursive method has the following form, where Step 2 is the base case, and Steps 3 and 4 are the recursive case:

```
1.  if the problem can be solved for the current value of n
2.      Solve it.
    else
3.      Recursively apply the algorithm to one or more problems involving
        smaller values of n.
4.      Combine the solutions to the smaller problems to get the solution to
        the original.
```

- To prove that a recursive algorithm is correct, you must
  —Verify that the base case is recognized and solved correctly.
  —Verify that each recursive case makes progress toward the base case.
  —Verify that if all smaller problems are solved correctly, then the original problem must also be solved correctly.
- The run-time stack uses activation frames to keep track of argument values and return points during recursive method calls. Activation frames can be used to trace the execution of a sequence of recursive method calls.
- Mathematical sequences and formulas that are defined recursively can be implemented naturally as recursive methods.
- Recursive data structures are data structures that have a component that is the same data structure. A linked list can be considered a recursive data structure because each node consists of a data field and a reference to a linked list. Recursion can make it easier to write methods that process a linked list.
- Two problems that can be solved using recursion were investigated: the Towers of Hanoi problem and counting cells in a blob.
- Backtracking is a technique that enables you to write programs that can be used to explore different alternative paths in a search for a solution.

User-Defined Classes in This Chapter

`Blob`
`BlobTest`
`GridColors`
`LinkedListRec`
`Maze`
`MazeTest`
`RecursiveMethods`
`TowersOfHanoi`
`TwoDimGrid`

Quick-Check Exercises

1. A recursive method has two cases: ______ and ______.
2. Each recursive call of a recursive method must lead to a situation that is ______ to the ______ case.
3. The control statement used in a recursive method is the ______ statement.
4. What three things are stored in an activation frame? Where are the activation frames stored?
5. You can sometimes substitute ______ for recursion.
6. Explain how a recursive method might cause a stack overflow exception.
7. If you have a recursive method and an iterative method that calculate the same result, which do you think would be more efficient? Explain your answer.
8. Binary search is an O(___) algorithm, and linear search is an O(___) algorithm.
9. Towers of Hanoi is an O(___) algorithm. Explain your answer.
10. Why did you need to provide a wrapper method for recursive methods `linearSearch` and `binarySearch`?
11. Why did you need to provide a wrapper method for recursive methods in the `LinkedListRec` class?

Review Questions

1. Explain the use of the run-time stack and activation frames in processing recursive method calls.
2. What is a recursive data structure? Give an example of one.
3. For class `LinkedListRec`, write a recursive search method that returns **`true`** if its target argument is found and **`false`** otherwise. If you need a wrapper method, provide one.
4. For class `LinkedListRec`, write a recursive `replaceFirst` method that replaces the first occurrence of a reference to its first argument with a reference to its second argument. If you need a wrapper method, provide one.
5. For Towers of Hanoi, show the output string that would be created by the method call `showMoves(3, 'R', 'M', 'L')`. Also, show the sequence of method calls.
6. For the counting cells in a blob problem, show the activation frames in the first 10 recursive calls to `countCells` following `countCells(4, 1)`.
7. For the maze path found in Figure 5.19, explain why cells (3, 4), (2, 5), (3, 5), (4, 5) were never visited and why cells (5, 1) and (3, 0) through (9, 0) were visited and rejected. Show the activation frames for the first 10 recursive calls in solving the maze.

Programming Projects

1. Download and run class `BlobTest`. Try running it with a data file made up of lines consisting of 0s and 1s with no spaces between them. Also run it without a data file.
2. Download and run class `MazeTest`. Try running it with a data file made up of lines consisting of 0s and 1s with no spaces between them. Also run it without a data file.
3. Write a recursive method that converts a decimal integer to a binary string. Write a recursive method that converts a binary string to a decimal integer.
4. Write a `LinkedListRec` class that has the following methods: `size`, `empty`, `insertBefore`, `insertAfter`, `addAtHead`, `addAtEnd`, `remove`, `replace`, `peekFront`, `peekEnd`, `removeFront`, `removeEnd`, `toString`. Use recursion to implement most of these methods.
5. As discussed in Chapter 3, a palindrome is a word that reads the same left to right as right to left. Write a recursive method that determines whether its argument string is a palindrome.
6. Write a program that will read a list of numbers and a desired sum, then determine the subset of numbers in the list that yield that sum if such a subset exists.
7. Write a recursive method that will dispense change for a given amount of money. The method will display all combinations of quarters, dimes, nickels, and pennies that equal the desired amount.
8. Produce the Sierpinski fractal. Start by drawing an equilateral triangle that faces upward. Then draw an equilateral triangle inside it that faces downward.

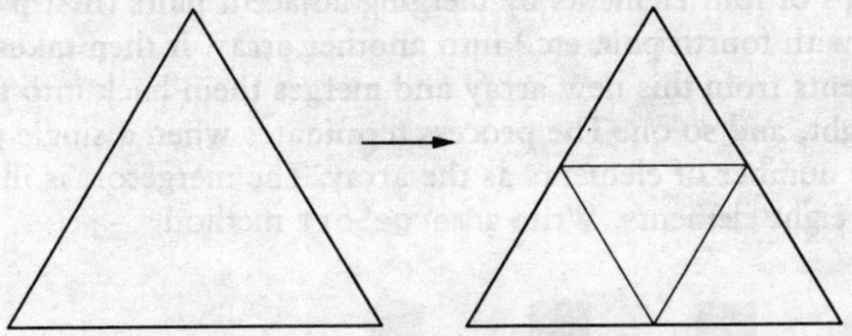

   Continue this process on each of the four smaller triangles. Stop when the side dimension for a triangle to be drawn is smaller than a specified minimum size.
9. Write a recursive method for placing eight queens on a chessboard. The eight queens should be placed so that no queen can capture another. Recall that a queen can move in the horizontal, vertical, or diagonal direction.
10. Write a recursive method that will find and list all of the one-element sequences of a letters in a `char[]` array, then all the two-element sequences, then all of the three element sequences, and so on, such that the characters in each sequence appear in the same order as they are in the array. For example, for the following array:

```
char[] letters = {'A', 'C', 'E', 'G'};
```

    the one-element sequences are "A", "C", "E", and "G"
    the two-element sequences are "AC", "AE", "AG", "CE", "CG", "EG"
    the three-element sequences are "ACE", "ACG", "AEG", "CEG"
    the four-element sequence is "ACEG"
11. One method of solving a continuous numerical function for a root implements a technique similar to the binary search. Given a numerical function, defined as f(x), and two values of x that are known to bracket one of the roots, an approximation to this root can be determined through a method of repeated division of this bracket. For a set of values

of x to bracket a root, the value of the function for one x must be negative and the other must be positive as illustrated below which plots f(x) for values of x between $x1$ and $x2$.

The algorithm requires that the midpoint between $x1$ and $x2$ be evaluated in the function, and if it equals zero the root is found; otherwise, $x1$ or $x2$ is set to this midpoint. To determine whether to replace $x1$ or $x2$, the sign of the midpoint is compared against the signs of the values f($x1$) and f($x2$). The midpoint replaces the x ($x1$ or $x2$) whose function value has the same sign as the function value at the midpoint.

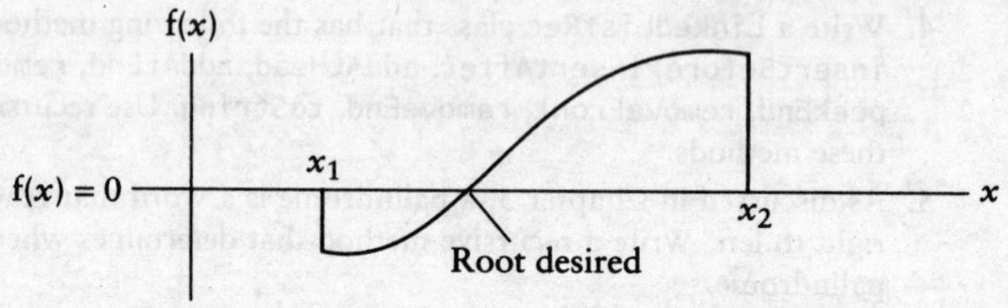

This algorithm can be written recursively. The terminating conditions are true when either the midpoint evaluated in the function is zero or the absolute value of $x1$ minus $x2$ is less than some small predetermined value (e.g., 0.0005). If the second condition occurs, then the root is said to be approximately equal to the last midpoint.

12. We can use a merge technique to sort two arrays. The *mergesort* begins by taking adjacent pairs of array values and ordering the values in each pair. It then forms groups of four elements by merging adjacent pairs (first pair with second pair, third pair with fourth pair, etc.) into another array. It then takes adjacent groups of four elements from this new array and merges them back into the original array as group of eight, and so on. The process terminates when a single group is formed that has the same number of elements as the array. The mergesort is illustrated here for an array with eight elements. Write a `mergeSort` method.

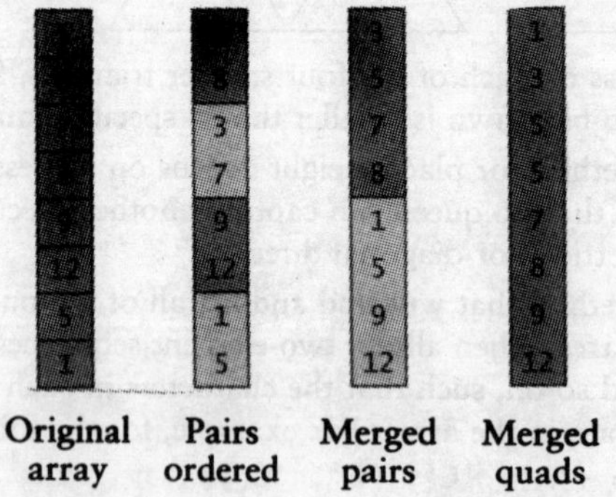

Answers to Quick-Check Exercises

1. A recursive method has two cases: *base case* and *recursive case.*
2. Each recursive call of a recursive method must lead to a situation that is *closer* to the *base* case.
3. The control statement used in a recursive method is the `if` statement.
4. An activation frame stores the following information on the run-time stack: the method argument values, the method local variable values, and the address of the return point in the caller of the method.

5. You can sometimes substitute *iteration* for recursion.
6. A recursive method that doesn't stop would continue to call itself, eventually pushing so many activation frames onto the run-time stack that a stack overflow exception would occur.
7. An *iterative* method would generally be more efficient because there is more overhead associated with multiple method calls.
8. Binary search is an $O(\log_2 n)$ algorithm, and linear search is an $O(n)$ algorithm.
9. Towers of Hanoi is an $O(2^n)$ algorithm because each problem splits into two problems at the next lower level.
10. Both search methods should be called with the array name and target as arguments. However, the recursive linear search method needs the subscript of the element to be compared to the target. The binary search method needs the search array bounds.
11. The wrapper method should be applied to a `LinkedListRec` object. The recursive method needs the current list head as an argument.

Chapter 6

Trees

Chapter Objectives

- To learn how to use a tree to represent a hierarchical organization of information
- To learn how to use recursion to process trees
- To understand the different ways of traversing a tree
- To understand the difference between binary trees, binary search trees, and heaps
- To learn how to implement binary trees, binary search trees, and heaps using linked data structures and arrays
- To learn how to use a binary search tree to store information so that it can be retrieved in an efficient manner
- To learn how to use a Huffman tree to encode characters using fewer bits than ASCII or Unicode, resulting in smaller files and reduced storage requirements

The data organizations you have studied so far are linear in that each element has only one predecessor or successor. Accessing all the elements in sequence is an O(n) process. In this chapter, we begin our discussion of a data organization that is nonlinear or hierarchical: the tree. Instead of having just one successor, a node in a tree can have multiple successors; but it has just one predecessor. A tree in computer science is like a natural tree, which has a single trunk that may split off into two or more main branches. The predecessor of each main branch is the trunk. Each main branch may spawn several secondary branches (successors of the main branches). The predecessor of each secondary branch is a main branch. In computer science, we draw a tree from the top down, so the root of the tree is at the top of the diagram instead of the bottom.

Because trees have a hierarchical structure, we use them to represent hierarchical organizations of information, such as a class hierarchy, a disk directory and its subdirectories (see Figure 6.1), or a family tree. You will see that trees are recursive data structures because they can be defined recursively. For this reason, many of the methods used to process trees are written as recursive methods.

FIGURE 6.1
Part of the Programs Directory

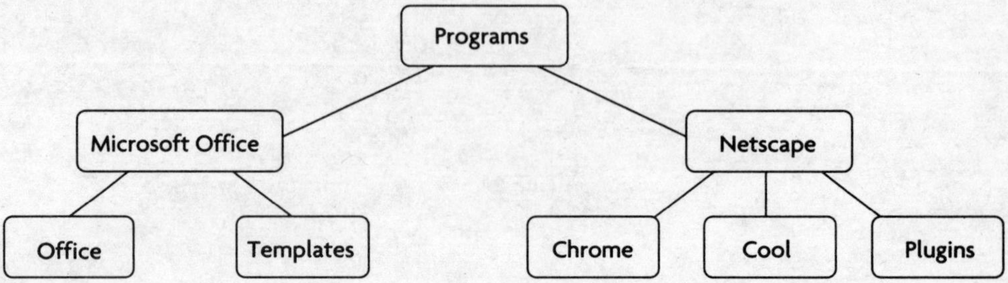

This chapter will focus on a restricted tree structure, a binary tree, in which each element has, at most, two successors. You will learn how to use linked data structures and arrays to represent binary trees. You will also learn how to use a special kind of binary tree called a binary search tree to store information (e.g., the words in a dictionary) in an ordered way. Because each element of a binary tree can have two successors, you will see that searching for an item stored in a binary search tree is much more efficient than searching for an item in a linear data structure: (generally $O(\log n)$ for a binary tree versus $O(n)$ for a list).

You also will learn about other kinds of binary trees. Expression trees are used to represent arithmetic expressions. The heap is an ordered tree structure that is used as the basis for a very efficient sorting algorithm and for a special kind of queue called the priority queue. The Huffman tree is used for encoding information and compressing files.

Trees

6.1 Tree Terminology and Applications

Tree Terminology

We use the same terminology to describe trees in computer science as we do trees in nature. A computer science tree consists of a collection of elements or nodes, with each node linked to its successors. The node at the top of a tree is called its *root* because computer science trees grow from the top down. The links from a node to its successors are called *branches*. The successors of a node are called its *children*. The predecessor of a node is called its *parent*. Each node in a tree has exactly one parent except for the root node, which has no parent. Nodes that have the same parent are *siblings*. A node that has no children is a *leaf node*. Leaf nodes are also known as *external* nodes, and nonleaf nodes are known as *internal* nodes.

A generalization of the parent-child relationship is the *ancestor-descendant relationship*. If node A is the parent of node B, which is the parent of node C, node A is node C's *ancestor*, and node C is node A's *descendant*. Sometimes we say that node A and node C are a grandparent and grandchild, respectively. The root node is an ancestor of every other node in a tree, and every other node in a tree is a descendant of the root node.

Figure 6.2 illustrates these features in a tree that stores a collection of words. The branches are the lines connecting a parent to its children. In discussing this tree, we will refer to a node by the string that it stores. For example, we will refer to the node that stores the string "dog" as node *dog*.

FIGURE 6.2
A Tree of Words

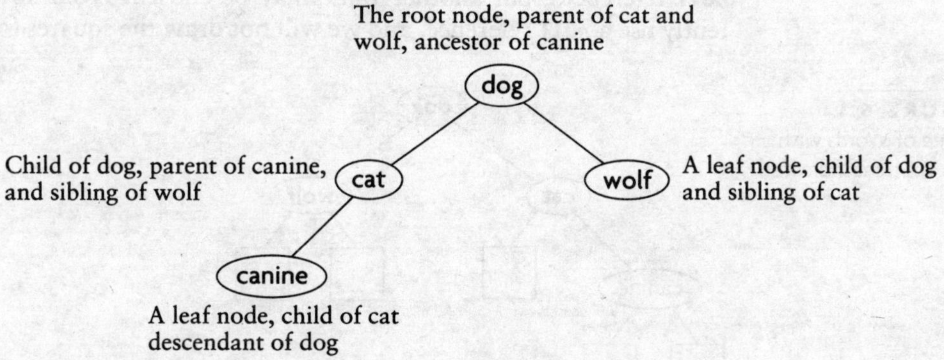

A *subtree of a node* is a tree whose root is a child of that node. For example, the nodes *cat* and *canine* and the branch connecting them are a subtree of node *dog*. The other subtree of node *dog* is the tree consisting of the single node *wolf*. The subtree consisting of the single node *canine* is a subtree of node *cat*.

The *level of a node* is a measure of its distance from the root. It is defined recursively as follows:

- If node n is the root of tree T, its level is 1.
- If node n is not the root of tree T, its level is 1 + the level of its parent.

For the tree in Figure 6.2, node *dog* is at level 1, nodes *cat* and *wolf* are at level 2, and node *canine* is at level 3. Since nodes are below the root, we sometimes use the term *depth* as an alternative term for level. The two have the same meaning.

The *height of a tree* is the number of nodes in the longest path from the root node to a leaf node. The height of the tree in Figure 6.2 is 3 (the longest path goes through the nodes *dog, cat,* and *canine*). Another way of saying this is as follows:

- If T is empty, its height is 0.
- If T is not empty, its height is the maximum depth of its nodes.

An alternate definition of the height of a tree is the number of branches in the longest path from the root node to a leaf node plus one.

Binary Trees

The tree in Figure 6.2 is a *binary tree.* Informally, this is a binary tree because each node has at most two subtrees. A more formal definition for a binary tree follows:

A set of nodes T is a binary tree if either of the following is true:

- T is empty.
- If T is not empty, its root node has two subtrees, T_L and T_R, such that T_L and T_R are binary trees.

We refer to T_L as the left subtree and T_R as the right subtree. For the tree in Figure 6.2, the right subtree of node *cat* is empty. The leaf nodes (*wolf* and *canine*) have empty left and right subtrees. This is illustrated in Figure 6.3, where the empty subtrees are indicated by the squares. Generally, the empty subtrees are represented by `null` references, but another value may be chosen. From now on, we will consistently use a `null` reference, and we will not draw the squares for the empty subtrees.

FIGURE 6.3
A Tree of Words with Null Subtrees Indicated

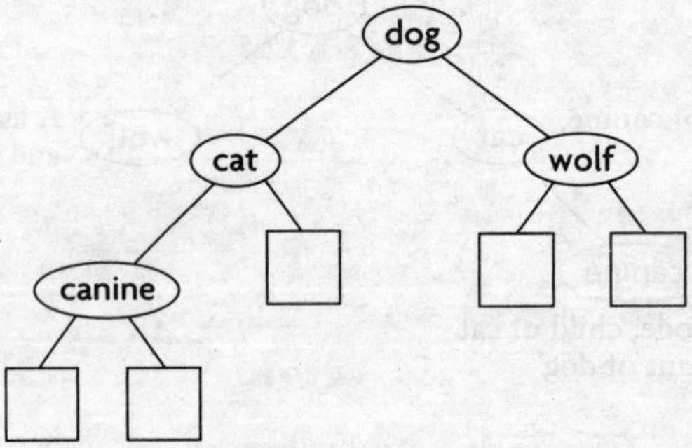

Some Types of Binary Trees

Next we discuss three different types of binary trees that are common in computer science.

An Expression Tree

Figure 6.4 shows a binary tree that stores an expression. Each node contains an operator (+, –, *, /, %) or an operand. The expression in Figure 6.4 corresponds to `(x + y) * ((a + b) / c)`. Operands are stored in leaf nodes. Parentheses are not stored in the tree because the tree structure dictates the order of operator evaluation. Operators in nodes at higher levels are evaluated after operators in nodes at lower levels, so the operator * in the root node is evaluated last. If a node contains a binary operator, its left subtree represents the operator's left operand and its right subtree represents the operator's right operand. The left subtree of the root represents the expression `x + y`, and the right subtree of the root represents the expression `(a + b) / c`.

FIGURE 6.4
Expression Tree

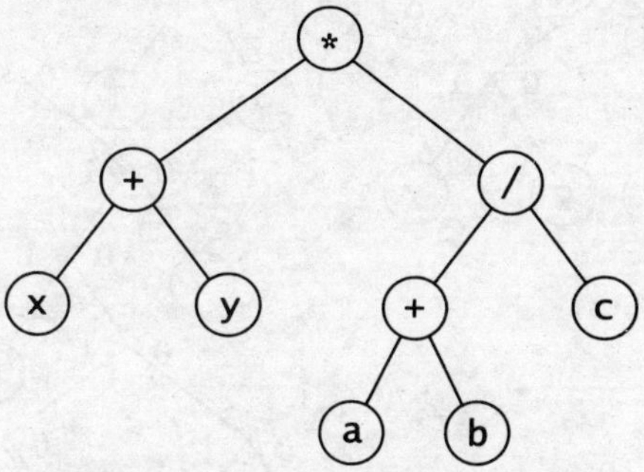

A Huffman Tree

Another use of a binary tree is to represent *Huffman codes* for characters that might appear in a text file. Unlike ASCII or Unicode encoding, which use the same number of bits to encode each character, a Huffman code uses different numbers of bits to encode the letters. It uses fewer bits for the more common letters (e.g., space, *e*, *a*, and *t*) and more bits for the less common letters (e.g., *q*, *x*, and *z*). On average, using Huffman codes to encode text files should give you files with fewer bits than you would get using other codes. Many programs that compress files use Huffman encoding to generate smaller files in order to save disk space or to reduce the time spent sending the files over the Internet.

Figure 6.5 shows the Huffman encoding tree for an alphabet consisting of the lowercase letters and the space character. All the characters are at leaf nodes. The data stored at nonleaf nodes is not shown. To determine the code for a letter, you form a binary string by tracing the path from the root node to that letter. Each time you go left, append a 0, and each time you go right, append a 1. To reach the space character, you go right three times, so the code is 111. The code for the letter *d* is 10110 (right, left, right, right, left).

The two characters shown at level 4 of the tree (space, *e*) are the most common and, therefore, have the shortest codes (111, 010). The next most common characters (*a*, *o*, *i*, etc.) are at level 5 of the tree.

You can store the code for each letter in an array. For example, the code for the space `' '` would be at position 0, the letter `'a'` would be at position 1, and the code for letter `'z'` would be at position 26. You can *encode* each letter in a file by looking up its code in the array.

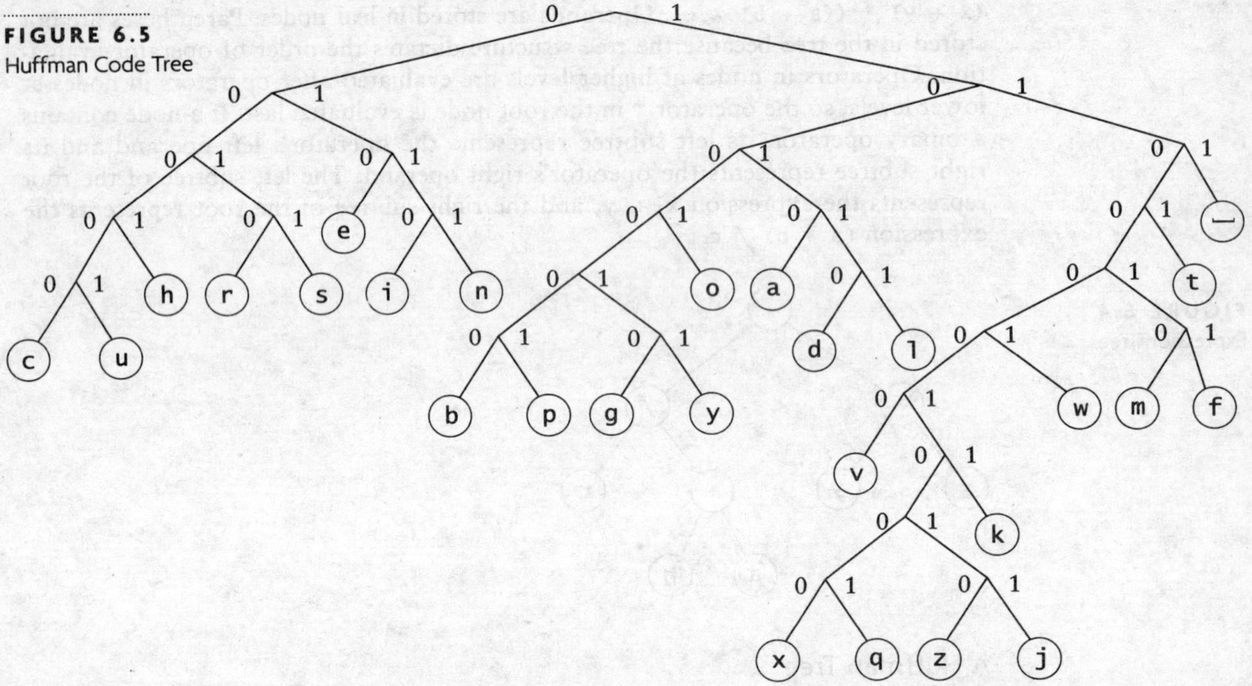

FIGURE 6.5
Huffman Code Tree

However, to *decode* a file of letters and spaces, you walk down the Huffman tree, starting at the root, until you reach a letter and then append that letter to the output text. Once you have reached a letter, go back to the root. Here is an example. The substrings that represent the individual letters are shown in alternate colors to help you follow the process. The underscore in the second line represents a space character (code is 111).

```
10001010011110101010100010101110100011
     g    o  _  e   a    g    l   e  s
```

Huffman trees are discussed further in Section 6.6.

A Binary Search Tree

The tree in Figure 6.2 is a *binary search tree* because, for each node, all words in its left subtree precede the word in that node, and all words in its right subtree follow the word in that node. For example, for the root node *dog*, all words in its left subtree (*cat, canine*) precede dog in the dictionary, and all words in its right subtree (*wolf*) follow *dog*. Similarly, for the node *cat,* the word in its left subtree (*canine*) precedes it. There are no duplicate entries in a binary search tree.

More formally, we define a binary search tree as follows:

A set of nodes T is a binary search tree if either of the following is true:

- T is empty.
- If T is not empty, its root node has two subtrees, T_L and T_R, such that T_L and T_R are binary search trees and the value in the root node of T is greater than all values in T_L and is less than all values in T_R.

The order relations in a binary search tree expedite searching the tree. A recursive algorithm for searching a binary search tree follows:

1. **if** the tree is empty
2. Return **null** *(target is not found).*
   else if the target matches the root node's data
3. Return the data stored at the root node.
   else if the target is less than the root node's data
4. Return the result of searching the left subtree of the root.
   else
5. Return the result of searching the right subtree of the root.

The first two cases are base cases and self-explanatory. In the first recursive case, if the target is less than the root node's data, we search only the left subtree (T_L) because all data items in T_R are larger than the root node's data and, therefore, larger than the target. Likewise, we execute the second recursive step (search the right subtree) if the target is greater than the root node's data.

Just as with a binary search of an array, each probe into the binary search tree has the potential of eliminating half the elements in the tree. If the binary search tree is relatively balanced (i.e., the depths of the leaves are approximately the same), searching a binary search tree is an O(log n) process, just like a binary search of an ordered array.

What is the advantage of using a binary search tree instead of just storing elements in an array and then sorting it? A binary search tree never has to be sorted because its elements always satisfy the required order relations. When new elements are inserted (or removed), the binary search tree property can be maintained. In contrast, an array must be expanded whenever new elements are added, and it must be compacted whenever elements are removed. Both expanding and contracting involve shifting items and are thus O(n) operations.

Full, Perfect, and Complete Binary Trees

The tree on the left in Figure. 6.6 is called a *full binary tree* because all nodes have either 2 children or 0 children (the leaf nodes). The tree in the middle is a *perfect binary tree,* which is defined as a full binary tree of height n (n is 3) with exactly $2^n - 1$ (7) nodes. The tree on the right is a *complete binary tree,* which is a perfect binary tree through level $n - 1$ with some extra leaf nodes at level n (the tree height), all toward the left.

General Trees

A general tree is a tree that does not have the restriction that each node of a tree has at most two subtrees. So nodes in a general tree can have any number of subtrees. Figure 6.7 shows a general tree that represents a family tree showing the descendants of King William I (the Conqueror) of England.

FIGURE 6.6
Full, Perfect, and Complete Binary Trees

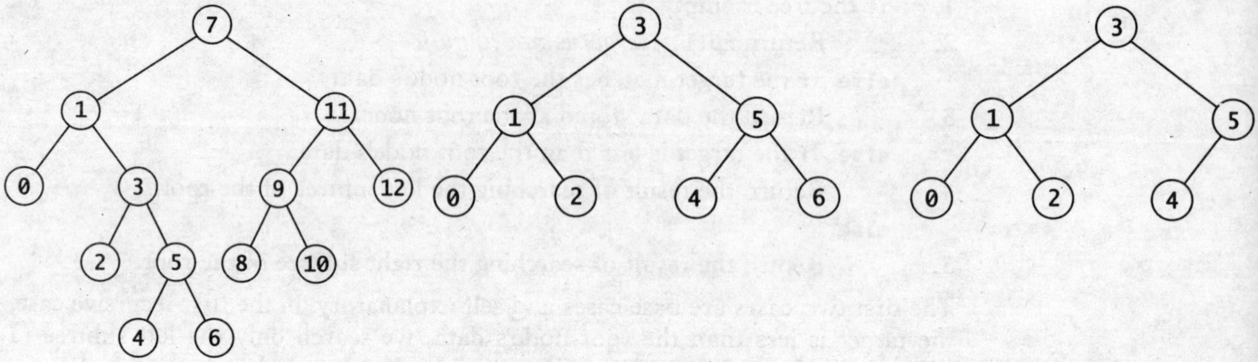

We will not discuss general trees in this chapter. However, it is worth mentioning that a general tree can be represented using a binary tree. Figure 6.8 shows a binary tree representation of the family tree in Figure 6.7. We obtained it by connecting the left branch from a node to the oldest child (if any). Each right branch from a node is connected to the next younger sibling (if any).

The names of the men who became kings are in boldface type. You would expect the eldest son to succeed his father as king; however, this would not be the case if the eldest male died before his father. For example, Robert died before William I, so William II became king instead. Starting with King John (near the bottom of the tree), the eldest son of each king did become King of England.

FIGURE 6.7
Family Tree for the Descendants of William I of England

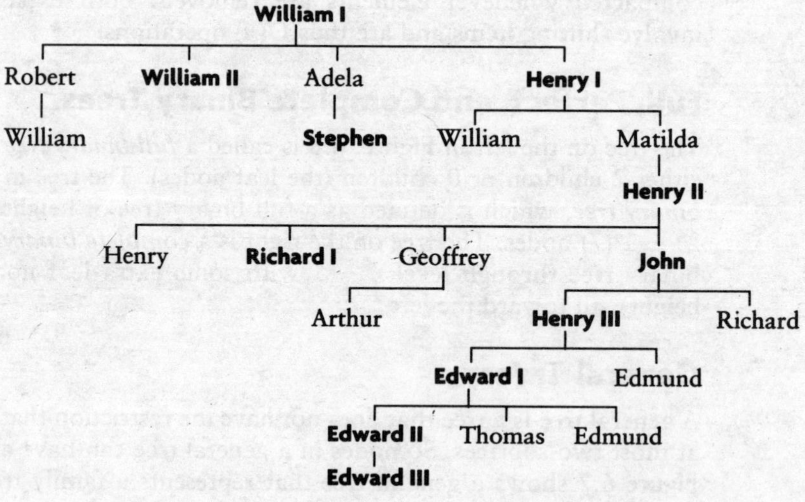

FIGURE 6.8
Binary Tree Equivalent of King William's Family Tree

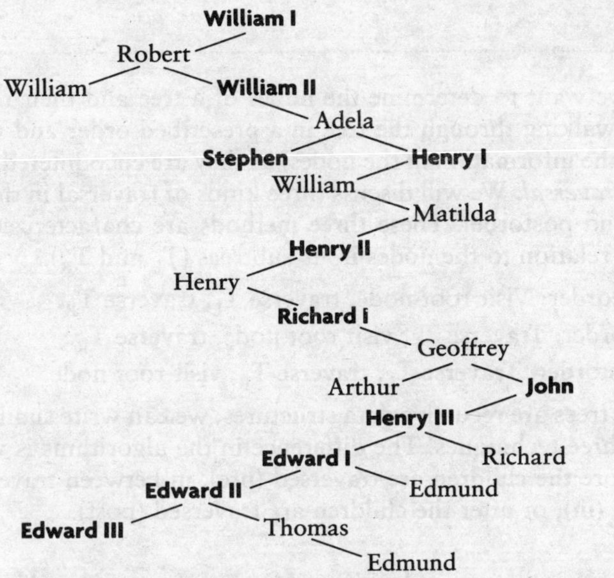

EXERCISES FOR SECTION 6.1

SELF-CHECK

1. Draw binary expression trees for the following infix expressions. Your trees should enforce the Java rules for operator evaluation (higher-precedence operators before lower-precedence operators and left associativity).
   a. `x / y + a - b * c`
   b. `(x * a) - y / b * (c + d)`
   c. `(x + (a * (b - c))/d`
2. Using the Huffman tree in Figure 6.5,
   a. Write the binary string for the message "scissors cuts paper".
   b. Decode the following binary string using the tree in Figure 6.5:
   `1100010001010001001011101100011111110001101010111101101001`
3. For each tree shown below, answer these questions. What is its height? Is it a full tree? Is it a complete tree? Is it a binary search tree? If not, make it a binary search tree.

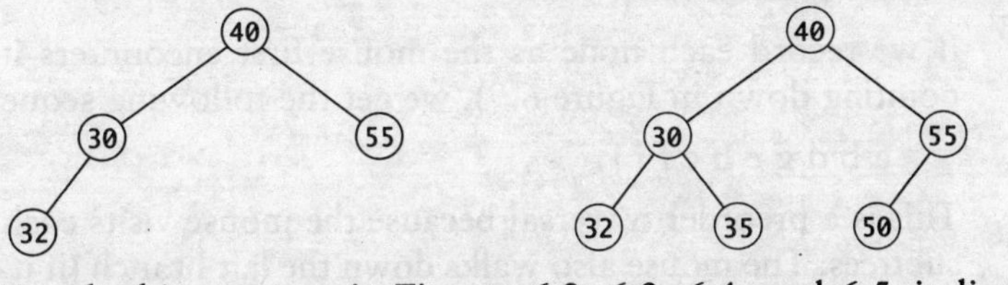

4. For the binary trees in Figures 6.2, 6.3, 6.4, and 6.5, indicate whether each tree is full, perfect, complete, or none of the above.
5. Represent the general tree in Figure 6.1 as a binary tree.

6.2 Tree Traversals

Often we want to determine the nodes of a tree and their relationship. We can do this by walking through the tree in a prescribed order and visiting the nodes (processing the information in the nodes) as they are encountered. This process is known as *tree traversal.* We will discuss three kinds of traversal in this section: inorder, preorder, and postorder. These three methods are characterized by when they visit a node in relation to the nodes in its subtrees (T_L and T_R).

- Preorder: Visit root node, traverse T_L, traverse T_R.
- Inorder: Traverse T_L, visit root node, traverse T_R.
- Postorder: Traverse T_L, traverse T_R, visit root node.

Because trees are recursive data structures, we can write similar recursive algorithms for all three techniques. The difference in the algorithms is whether the root is visited before the children are traversed (pre), in between traversing the left and right children (in), or after the children are traversed (post).

Algorithm for Preorder Traversal	**Algorithm for Inorder Traversal**	**Algorithm for Postorder Traversal**
1. `if` the tree is empty	1. `if` the tree is empty	1. `if` the tree is empty
2. Return.	2. Return.	2. Return.
`else`	`else`	`else`
3. Visit the root.	3. Inorder traverse the left subtree.	3. Postorder traverse the left subtree.
4. Preorder traverse the left subtree.	4. Visit the root.	4. Postorder traverse the right subtree.
5. Preorder traverse the right subtree.	5. Inorder traverse the right subtree.	5. Visit the root.

Visualizing Tree Traversals

You can visualize a tree traversal by imagining a mouse that walks along the edge of the tree. If the mouse always keeps the tree to the left (from the mouse's point of view), it will trace the route shown in color around the tree shown in Figure 6.9. This is known as an *Euler tour.*

If we record each node as the mouse first encounters it (indicated by the arrows pointing down in Figure 6.9), we get the following sequence:

a b d g e h c f i j

This is a preorder traversal because the mouse visits each node before traversing its subtrees. The mouse also walks down the left branch (if it exists) of each node before going down the right branch, so the mouse visits a node, traverses its left subtree, and traverses its right subtree.

If we record each node as the mouse returns from traversing its left subtree (indicated by the arrows pointing to the right in Figure 6.9), we get the following sequence:

d g b h e a i f j c

This is an inorder traversal. The mouse traverses the left subtree, visits the root, and then traverses the right subtree. Node *d* is visited first because it has no left subtree.

If we record each node as the mouse last encounters it (indicated by the arrows pointing up in Figure 6.9), we get the following sequence:

g d h e b i j f c a

This is a postorder traversal because we visit the node after traversing both its subtrees. The mouse traverses the left subtree, traverses the right subtree, and then visits the node.

FIGURE 6.9
Traversal of a Binary Tree

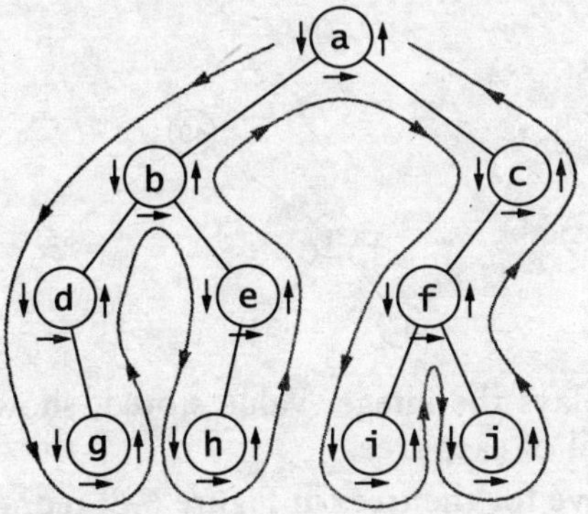

Traversals of Binary Search Trees and Expression Trees

An inorder traversal of a binary search tree results in the nodes being visited in sequence by increasing data value. For example, for the binary search tree shown earlier in Figure 6.2, the inorder traversal would visit the nodes in the sequence:

canine, cat, dog, wolf

Traversals of expression trees give interesting results. If we perform an inorder traversal of the expression tree first shown in Figure 6.4 and repeated here, we visit the nodes in the sequence `x + y * a + b / c`. If we insert parentheses where they belong, we get the infix expression

`(x + y) * ((a + b) / c)`

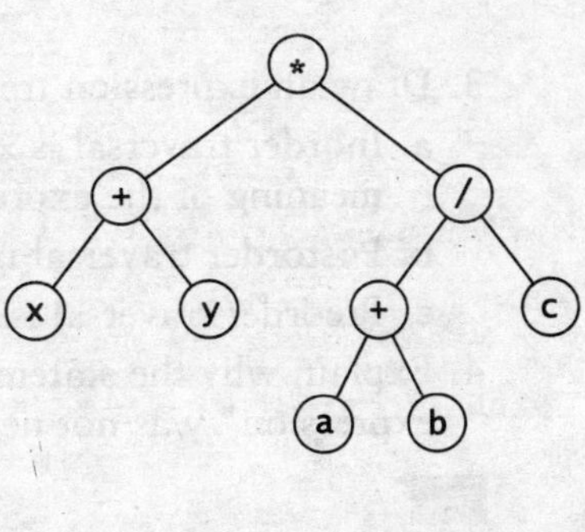

The postorder traversal of this tree would visit the nodes in the sequence

x y + a b + c / *

which is the postfix form of the expression. To illustrate this, we show the *operand-operand-operator* groupings under the expression.

The preorder traversal visits the nodes in the sequence

* + x y / + a b c

which is the prefix form of the expression. To illustrate this, we show the *operator-operand-operand* groupings under the expression.

EXERCISES FOR SECTION 6.2

SELF-CHECK

1. For the following trees:

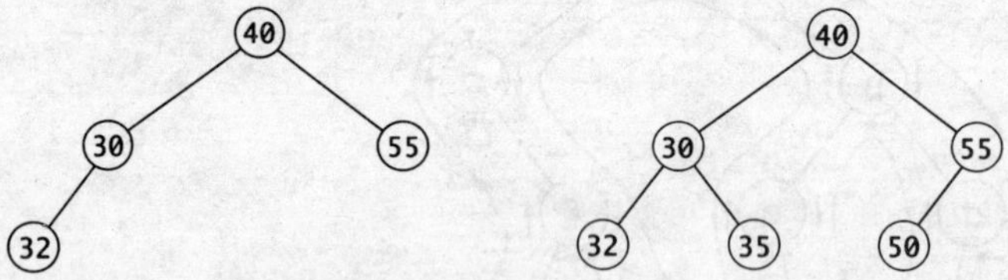

If visiting a node displays the integer value stored, show the inorder, preorder, and postorder traversal of each tree.

2. Repeat Exercise 1 above for the trees in Figure 6.6, redrawn below.

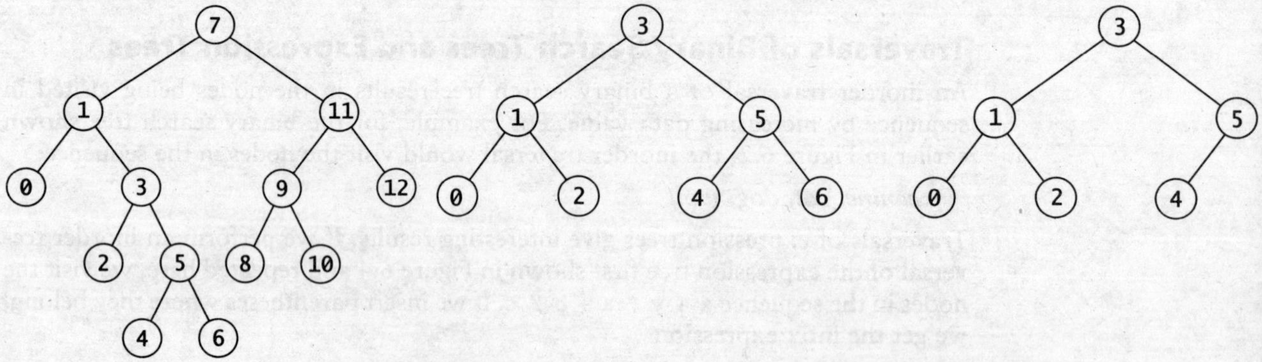

3. Draw an expression tree corresponding to each of the following:
   a. Inorder traversal is `x / y + 3 * b / c` (Your tree should represent the Java meaning of the expression.)
   b. Postorder traversal is `x y z + a b - c * / -`
   c. Preorder traversal is `* + a - x y / c d`
4. Explain why the statement "Your tree should represent the Java meaning of the expression" was not needed for parts b and c of Exercise 3 above.

6.3 Implementing a BinaryTree Class

In this section, we show how to use linked data structures to represent binary trees and binary tree nodes. We begin by focusing on the structure of a binary tree node.

The Node<E> Class

Just as for a linked list, a node consists of a data part and links (references) to successor nodes. So that we can store any kind of data in a tree node, we will make the data part a reference of type `E`. Instead of having a single link (reference) to a successor node as in a list, a binary tree node must have links (references) to both its left and right subtrees. Figure 6.10 shows the structure of a binary tree node; Listing 6.1 shows its implementation.

Class `Node<E>` is nested within class `BinaryTree<E>`. Notice that it is declared **protected** and its data fields are all **protected**. Later, we will use the `BinaryTree<E>` and `Node<E>` classes as superclasses. By declaring the nested `Node<E>` class and its data fields protected, we make them accessible in the subclasses of `BinaryTree<E>` and `Node<E>`.

The constructor for class `Node<E>` creates a leaf node (both `left` and `right` are **`null`**). The `toString` method for the class just displays the `data` part of the node.

Both the `BinaryTree<E>` class and the `Node<E>` class are declared to implement the `Serializable` interface. The `Serializable` interface defines no methods; it is used to provide a marker for classes that can be written to a binary file using the `ObjectOutputStream` and read using the `ObjectInputStream`. We clarify what this means later in the section.

FIGURE 6.10
Linked Structure to Represent a Node

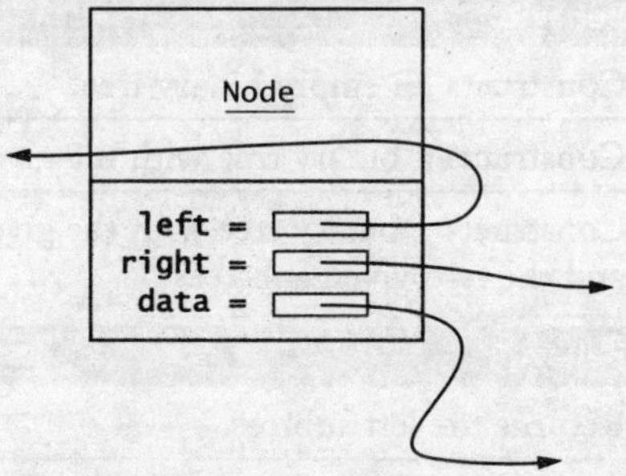

LISTING 6.1
Nested Class Node

```
/** Class to encapsulate a tree node. */
protected static class Node<E> implements Serializable {
    // Data Fields
    /** The information stored in this node. */
    protected E data;
    /** Reference to the left child. */
    protected Node<E> left;
    /** Reference to the right child. */
    protected Node<E> right;
```

```
        // Constructors
        /** Construct a node with given data and no children.
            @param data The data to store in this node
        */
        public Node(E data) {
            this.data = data;
            left = null;
            right = null;
        }

        // Methods
        /** Return a string representation of the node.
            @return A string representation of the data fields
        */
        public String toString () {
            return data.toString();
        }
    }
```

The BinaryTree<E> Class

Table 6.1 shows the design of the `BinaryTree<E>` class. The single data field root references the root node of a `BinaryTree<E>` object. It has protected visibility because we will need to access it in subclass `BinarySearchTree`, discussed later in this chapter. In

TABLE 6.1
Design of the BinaryTree<E> Class

Data Field	Attribute
`protected Node<E> root`	Reference to the root of the tree.
Constructor	**Behavior**
`public BinaryTree()`	Constructs an empty binary tree.
`protected BinaryTree(Node<E> root)`	Constructs a binary tree with the given node as the root.
`public BinaryTree(E data, BinaryTree<E> leftTree, BinaryTree<E> rightTree)`	Constructs a binary tree with the given data at the root and the two given subtrees.
Method	**Behavior**
`public BinaryTree<E> getLeftSubtree()`	Returns the left subtree.
`public BinaryTree<E> getRightSubtree()`	Returns the right subtree.
`public E getData()`	Returns the data in the root.
`public boolean isLeaf()`	Returns **`true`** if this tree is a leaf, **`false`** otherwise.
`public String toString()`	Returns a `String` representation of the tree.
`private void preOrderTraverse(Node<E> node, int depth, StringBuilder sb)`	Performs a preorder traversal of the subtree whose root is node. Appends the representation to the `StringBuilder`. Increments the value of `depth` (the current tree level).
`public static BinaryTree<E> readBinaryTree(Scanner scan)`	Constructs a binary tree by reading its data using `Scanner scan`.

FIGURE 6.11
Linked Representation of Expression Tree ((x + y) * (a / b))

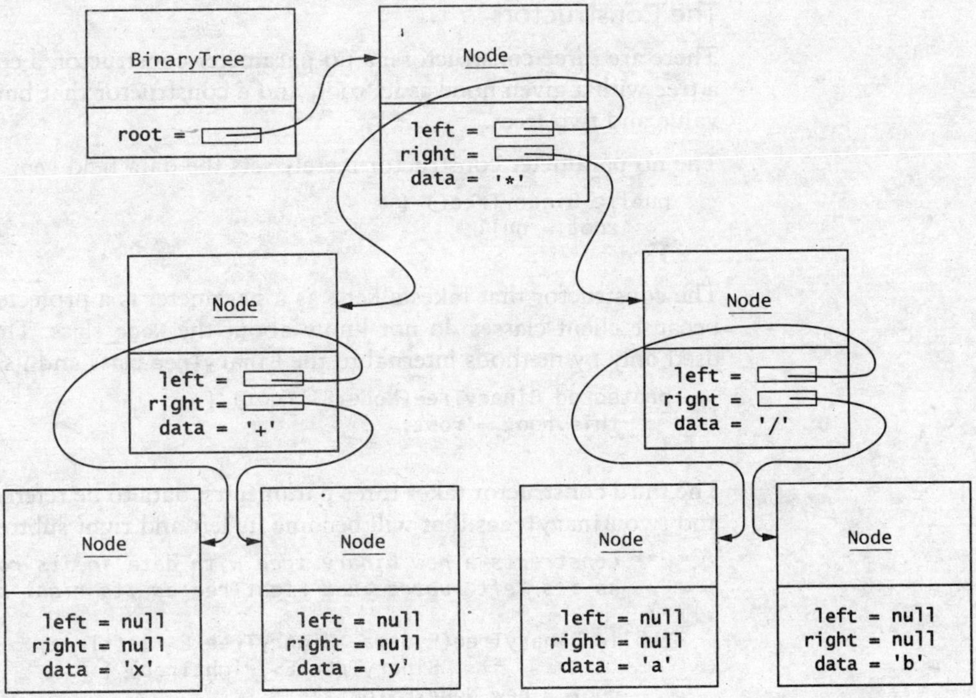

Figure 6.11, we draw the expression tree for `((x + y) * (a / b))` using our `Node` representation. Each character shown as tree data would be stored in a `Character` object.

EXAMPLE 6.1 Assume the tree drawn in Figure 6.11 is referenced by variable `bT` (type `BinaryTree`).

- `bT.root.data` references the `Character` object storing `'*'`.
- `bT.root.left` references the left subtree of the root (the root node of tree `x + y`).
- `bT.root.right` references the right subtree of the root (the root node of tree `a / b`).
- `bT.root.right.data` references the `Character` object storing `'/'`.

The class heading and data field declarations follow:

```
import java.io.*;

/** Class for a binary tree that stores type E objects. */
public class BinaryTree<E> implements Serializable {

    // Insert inner class Node<E> here.

    // Data Field
    /** The root of the binary tree */
    protected Node<E> root;
    . . .
}
```

The Constructors

There are three constructors: a no-parameter constructor, a constructor that creates a tree with a given node as its root, and a constructor that builds a tree from a data value and two trees.

The no-parameter constructor merely sets the data field `root` to **`null`**.

```
public BinaryTree() {
    root = null;
}
```

The constructor that takes a `Node` as a parameter is a protected constructor. This is because client classes do not know about the `Node` class. This constructor can be used only by methods internal to the `BinaryTree` class and its subclasses.

```
protected BinaryTree(Node<E> root) {
    this.root = root;
}
```

The third constructor takes three parameters: data to be referenced by the root node and two `BinaryTree`s that will become its left and right subtrees.

```
/** Constructs a new binary tree with data in its root leftTree
    as its left subtree and rightTree as its right subtree.
*/
public BinaryTree(E data, BinaryTree<E> leftTree,
                  BinaryTree<E> rightTree) {
    root = new Node<E>(data);
    if (leftTree != null) {
        root.left = leftTree.root;
    } else {
        root.left = null;
    }
    if (rightTree != null) {
        root.right = rightTree.root;
    } else {
        root.right = null;
    }
}
```

If `leftTree` is not **`null`**, the statement

```
root.left = leftTree.root;
```

executes. After its execution, the root node of the tree referenced by `leftTree` (`leftTree.root`) is referenced by `root.left`, making `leftTree` the left subtree of the new root node. If `lT` and `rT` are type `BinaryTree<Character>` and `lT.root` references the root node of binary tree `x + y` and `rT.root` references the root node of binary tree `a / b`, the statement

```
BinaryTree<Character> bT = new BinaryTree('*', lT, rT);
```

would cause `bT` to reference the tree shown in Figure 6.12.

The `getLeftSubtree` and `getRightSubtree` Methods

The `getLeftSubtree` method returns a binary tree whose root is the left subtree of the object on which the method is called. It uses the protected constructor discussed

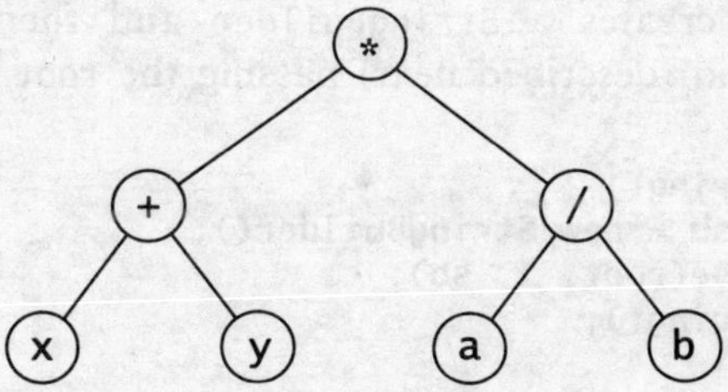

FIGURE 6.12
The Expression Tree
(x + y) * (a / b)

before to construct a new BinaryTree<E> object whose root references the left subtree of this tree. The `getRightSubtree` method is symmetric.

```
/** Return the left subtree.
@return The left subtree or null if either the root or
the left subtree is null
*/
public BinaryTree<E> getLeftSubtree() {
    if (root != null && root.left != null) {
        return new BinaryTree<E>(root.left);
    } else {
        return null;
    }
}
```

The isLeaf Method

The `isLeaf` method tests to see whether this tree has any subtrees. If there are no subtrees, then **true** is returned.

```
/** Determine whether this tree is a leaf.
    @return true if the root has no children
*/
public boolean isLeaf() {
    return (root.left == null && root.right == null);
}
```

The toString Method

The `toString` method generates a string representation of the `BinaryTree` for display purposes. The string representation is a preorder traversal in which each local root is indented a distance proportional to its depth. If a subtree is empty, the string "null" is displayed. The tree in Figure 6.12 would be displayed as follows:

```
*
 +
  x
   null
   null
  y
   null
   null
 /
  a
   null
   null
  b
   null
   null
```

The `toString` method creates a `StringBuilder` and then calls the recursive `preOrderTraverse` method (described next) passing the `root` and `1` (depth of root node) as arguments.

```
public String toString() {
    StringBuilder sb = new StringBuilder();
    preOrderTraverse(root, 1, sb);
    return sb.toString();
}
```

The preOrderTraverse Method

This method follows the preorder traversal algorithm given in Section 6.2. It begins by appending a string of spaces proportional to the level so that all nodes at a particular level will be indented to the same point in the tree display. Then, if the node is **null**, the string "null\n" is appended to the `StringBuilder`. Otherwise the string representation of the node is appended to the `StringBuilder` and the method is recursively called on the left and right subtrees.

```
/** Perform a preorder traversal.
    @param node The local root
    @param depth The depth
    @param sb The string buffer to save the output
*/
private void preOrderTraverse(Node<E> node, int depth,
                               StringBuilder sb) {
    for (int i = 1; i < depth; i++) {
        sb.append("  ");
    }
    if (node == null) {
        sb.append("null\n");
    } else {
        sb.append(node.toString());
        sb.append("\n");
        preOrderTraverse(node.left, depth + 1, sb);
        preOrderTraverse(node.right, depth + 1, sb);
    }
}
```

Reading a Binary Tree

If we use a `Scanner` to read the individual lines created by the `toString` and `preOrderTraverse` methods previously discussed, we can reconstruct the binary tree using the algorithm:

1. Read a line that represents information at the root.
2. Remove the leading and trailing spaces using the `String.trim` method.
3. **if** it is "null"
4. Return **null**.

   else

5. Recursively read the left child.
6. Recursively read the right child.
7. Return a tree consisting of the root and the two children.

The tree that is constructed will be type `BinaryTree<String>`. The code for a method that implements this algorithm is shown in Listing 6.2.

LISTING 6.2
Method to Read a Binary Tree

```
/** Method to read a binary tree.
    pre: The input consists of a preorder traversal
         of the binary tree. The line "null" indicates a null tree.
    @param scan the Scanner attached to the input file.
    @return The binary tree
*/
public static BinaryTree<String> readBinaryTree(Scanner scan) {
    // Read a line and trim leading and trailing spaces.
    String data = scan.next();
    if (data.equals("null")) {
        return null;
    } else {
        BinaryTree<String> leftTree = readBinaryTree(scan);
        BinaryTree<String> rightTree = readBinaryTree(scan);
        return new BinaryTree<String>(data, leftTree, rightTree);
    }
}
```

Using an ObjectOutputStream and ObjectInputStream

The Java API includes the class `ObjectOutputStream` that will write any object that is declared to be `Serializable`. You declare that an object is `Serializable` by adding the declaration

```
implements Serializable
```

to the class declaration. The `Serializable` interface (in `java.io`) contains no methods, but it serves to mark the class as being `Serializable`. This gives you control over whether or not you want your class to be written to an external file. Generally you will want to have this capability.

To write an object of a `Serializable` class to a file, you do the following:

```
try {
    ObjectOutputStream out =
        new ObjectOutputStream(new FileOutputStream(nameOfFile));
    out.writeObject(nameOfObject);
} catch (Exception ex) {
    ex.printStackTrace();
    System.exit(1);
}
```

The `writeObject` method performs a traversal of whatever data structure is referenced by the object being written. Thus, if the object is a binary tree, a deep copy of all of the nodes of the binary tree will be written to the file.

To read a `Serializable` class from a file, you do the following:

```
try {
    ObjectInputStream in =
        new ObjectInputStream(new FileInputStream(nameOfFile));
    objectName = (objectClass) in.readObject();
} catch (Exception ex) {
    ex.printStackTrace();
    System.exit(1);
}
```

This code will reconstruct the object that was saved to the file, including any referenced objects. Thus, if a `BinaryTree` is written to an `ObjectOutputStream`, this method will read it back and restore it completely.

PITFALL

Modifying the Class File of a Serialized Object

When an object is serialized, a unique class signature is recorded with the data. If you recompile the Java source file for the class to re-create the `.class` file, even though you did not make any changes, the resulting `.class` file will have a different class signature. When you attempt to read the object, you will get an exception.

EXERCISES FOR SECTION 6.3

SELF-CHECK

1. Draw the linked representation of the following two trees.

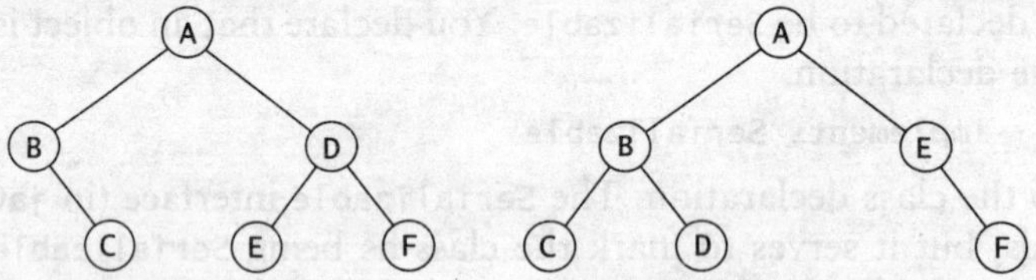

2. Show the tree that would be built by the following input string:

```
30
  15
    4
      null
      null
    20
      18
        null
        19
          null
          null
      null
  35
    32
      null
      null
    38
      null
      null
```

3. What can you say about this tree?
4. Write the strings that would be displayed for the two binary trees in Figure 6.6.

PROGRAMMING

1. Write a method for the `BinaryTree` class that returns the preorder traversal of a binary tree as a sequence of strings each separated by a space.

2. Write a method to display the postorder traversal of a binary tree in the same form as Programming Exercise 1.
3. Write a method to display the inorder traversal of a binary tree in the same form as Programming Exercise 1, except place a left parenthesis before each subtree and a right parenthesis after each subtree. Don't display anything for an empty subtree. For example, the expression tree shown in Figure 6.12 would be represented as `(((x) + (y)) * ((a) / (b)))`.

6.4 Binary Search Trees

Overview of a Binary Search Tree

In Section 6.1, we provided the following recursive definition of a binary search tree:

A set of nodes T is a binary search tree if either of the following is true:

- T is empty.
- If T is not empty, its root node has two subtrees, T_L and T_R, such that T_L and T_R are binary search trees and the value in the root node of T is greater than all values in T_L and is less than all values in T_R.

Figure 6.13 shows a binary search tree that contains the words in lowercase from the nursery rhyme "The House That Jack Built." We can use the following algorithm to find an object in a binary search tree.

FIGURE 6.13
Binary Search Tree Containing All of the Words from "The House That Jack Built"

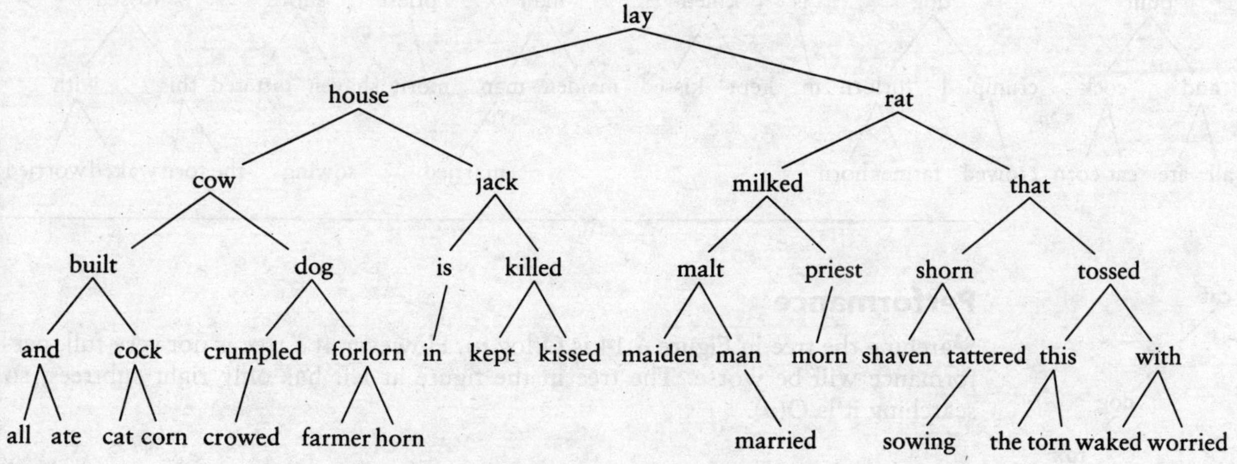

Recursive Algorithm for Searching a Binary Search Tree

1. `if` the root is `null`
2. The item is not in the tree; return `null`.
3. Compare the value of **`target`**, the item being sought, with `root.data`.
4. `if` they are equal
5. The target has been found, return the data at the root.

   `else if target` is less than `root.data`
6. Return the result of searching the left subtree.

   `else`
7. Return the result of searching the right subtree.

EXAMPLE 6.2 Suppose we wish to find *jill* in Figure 6.13. We first compare *jill* with *lay*. Because *jill* is less than *lay*, we continue the search with the left subtree and compare *jill* with *house*. Because *jill* is greater than *house*, we continue with the right subtree and compare *jill* with *jack*. Because *jill* is greater than *jack*, we continue with *killed* followed by *kept*. Now, *kept* has no left child, and *jill* is less than *kept*, so we conclude that *jill* is not in this binary search tree. (She's in a different nursery rhyme.) Follow the entire path marked in color in Figure 6.14.

FIGURE 6.14
Looking for Jill

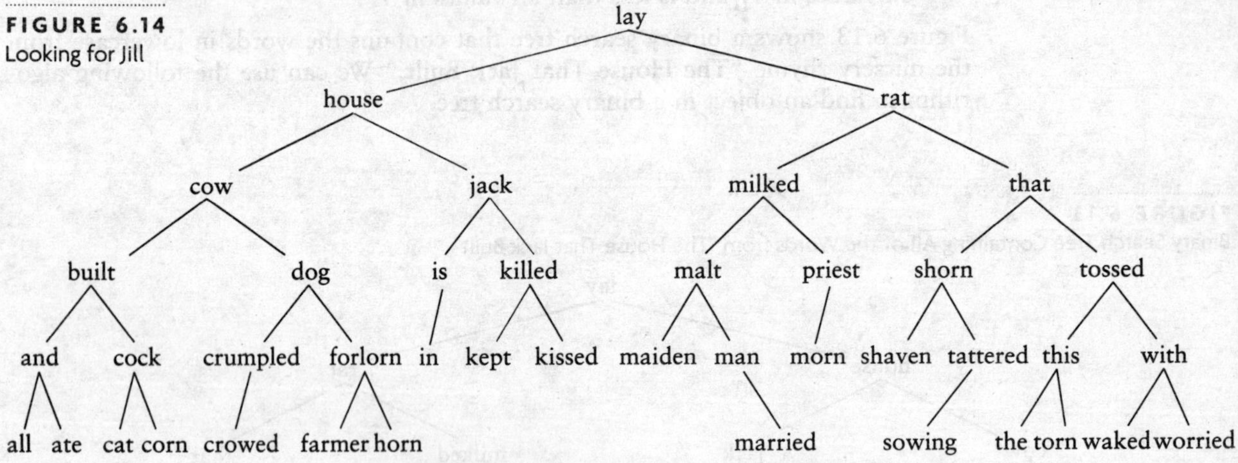

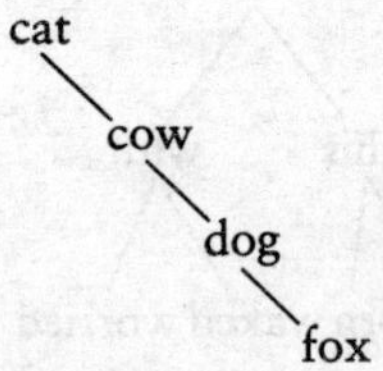

Performance

Searching the tree in Figure 6.14 is O(log n). However, if a tree is not very full, performance will be worse. The tree in the figure at left has only right subtrees, so searching it is O(n).

TABLE 6.2
The SearchTree<E> Interface

Method	Behavior
`boolean add(E item)`	Inserts `item` where it belongs in the tree. Returns **`true`** if item is inserted; **`false`** if it isn't (already in tree).
`boolean contains(E target)`	Returns **`true`** if `target` is found in the tree.
`E find(E target)`	Returns a reference to the data in the node that is equal to `target`. If no such node is found, returns **`null`**.
`E delete(E target)`	Removes `target` (if found) from tree and returns it; otherwise, returns **`null`**.
`boolean remove(E target)`	Removes `target` (if found) from tree and returns **`true`**; otherwise, returns **`false`**.

Interface SearchTree

As described, the binary search tree is a data structure that enables efficient insertion, search, and retrieval of information (best case is O(log n)). Table 6.2 shows a `SearchTree<E>` interface for a class that implements the binary search tree. The interface includes methods for insertion (`add`), search (`boolean contains` and `E find`), and removal (`E delete` and `boolean remove`). Next we discuss a class `BinarySearchTree<E>` that implements this interface.

The BinarySearchTree Class

Next we implement class `BinarySearchTree<E extends Comparable<E>>`. The type parameter specified when we create a new `BinarySearchTree` must implement the `Comparable` interface.

Table 6.3 shows the data fields declared in the class. These data fields are used to store a second result from the recursive `add` and `delete` methods that we will write for this class. Neither result can be returned directly from the recursive `add` or `delete` method because they return a reference to a tree node affected by the insertion or deletion operation. The interface for method `add` in Table 6.2 requires a **`boolean`** result (stored in `addReturn`) to indicate success or failure. Similarly, the interface for `delete` requires a type `E` result (stored in `deleteReturn`) that is either the item deleted or **`null`**.

TABLE 6.3
Data Fields of Class `BinarySearchTree<E extends Comparable<E>>`

Data Field	Attribute
`protected boolean addReturn`	Stores a second return value from the recursive `add` method that indicates whether the item has been inserted.
`protected E deleteReturn`	Stores a second return value from the recursive `delete` method that references the item that was stored in the tree.

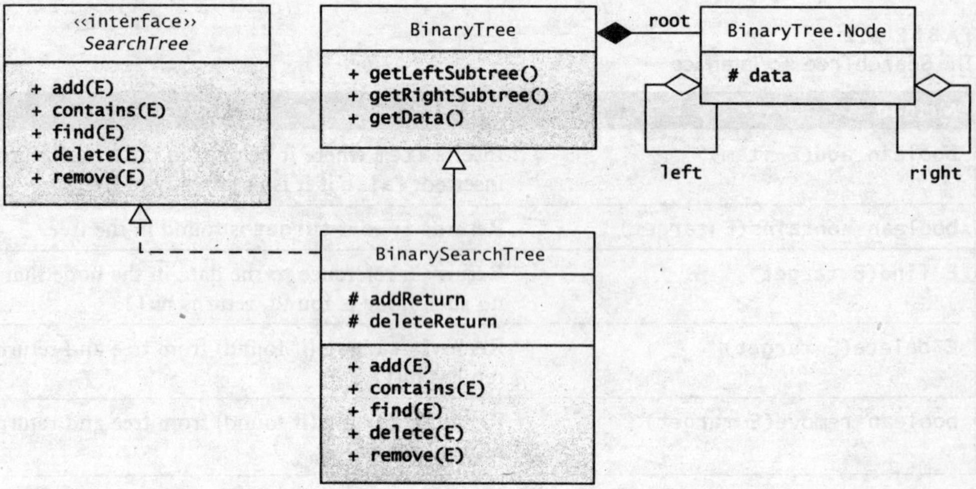

FIGURE 6.15
UML Diagram of BinarySearchTree

The class heading and data field declarations follow. Notice that class `BinarySearchTree` extends class `BinaryTree` and implements the `SearchTree` interface (see Figure 6.15). Besides the data fields shown, class `BinarySearchTree` inherits the data field `root` from class `BinaryTree` (declared as **`protected`**) and the inner class `Node<E>`.

```
public class BinarySearchTree<E extends Comparable<E>>
                          extends BinaryTree<E>
                          implements SearchTree<E> {

    // Data Fields
    /** Return value from the public add method. */
    protected boolean addReturn;
    /** Return value from the public delete method. */
    protected E deleteReturn;
    . . .
}
```

Implementing the `find` Methods

Earlier we showed a recursive algorithm for searching a binary search tree. Next we show how to implement this algorithm and a nonrecursive starter method for the algorithm. Our method `find` will return a reference to the node that contains the information we are seeking.

Listing 6.3 shows the code for method `find`. The starter method calls the recursive method with the tree root and the object being sought as its parameters. If `bST` is a reference to a `BinarySearchTree`, the method call `bST.find(target)` invokes the starter method.

The recursive method first tests the local root for **`null`**. If it is **`null`**, the object is not in the tree, so **`null`** is returned. If the local root is not **`null`**, the statement

```
int compResult = target.compareTo(localRoot.data);
```

compares target to the data at the local root. Recall that method compareTo returns an **int** value that is either negative, zero, or positive depending on whether the object (target) is less than, equal to, or greater than the argument (localRoot.data). If the objects are equal, we return the data at the local root. If target is smaller, we recursively call method find, passing the left subtree root as the parameter.

```
return find(localRoot.left, target);
```

Otherwise, we call find to search the right subtree.

```
return find(localRoot.right, target);
```

LISTING 6.3

BinarySearchTree find Method

```
/** Starter method find.
    pre: The target object must implement
         the Comparable interface.
    @param target The Comparable object being sought
    @return The object, if found, otherwise null
*/
public E find(E target) {
    return find(root, target);
}

/** Recursive find method.
    @param localRoot The local subtree's root
    @param target The object being sought
    @return The object, if found, otherwise null
*/
private E find(Node<E> localRoot, E target) {
    if (localRoot == null)
        return null;

    // Compare the target with the data field at the root.
    int compResult = target.compareTo(localRoot.data);
    if (compResult == 0)
        return localRoot.data;
    else if (compResult < 0)
        return find(localRoot.left, target);
    else
        return find(localRoot.right, target);
}
```

Insertion into a Binary Search Tree

Inserting an item into a binary search tree follows a similar algorithm as searching for the item because we are trying to find where in the tree the item would be, if it were there. In searching, a result of **null** is an indicator of failure; in inserting, we replace this **null** with a new leaf that contains the new item. If we reach a node that contains the object we are trying to insert, then we can't insert it (duplicates are not allowed), so we return **false** to indicate that we were unable to perform the insertion. The insertion algorithm follows.

Recursive Algorithm for Insertion in a Binary Search Tree

1. `if` the root is `null`
2. Replace empty tree with a new tree with the item at the root and return **`true`**.
3. `else if` the item is equal to `root.data`
4. The item is already in the tree; return **`false`**.
5. `else if` the item is less than `root.data`
6. Recursively insert the item in the left subtree.
7. `else`
8. Recursively insert the item in the right subtree.

The algorithm returns **`true`** when the new object is inserted and **`false`** if it is a duplicate (the second stopping case). The first stopping case tests for an empty tree. If so, a new `BinarySearchTree` is created and the new item is stored in its root node (Step 2).

EXAMPLE 6.3 To insert *jill* into Figure 6.13, we would follow the steps shown in Example 6.2 except that when we reached *kept*, we would insert *jill* as the left child of the node that contains *kept* (see Figure 6.16).

FIGURE 6.16
Inserting Jill

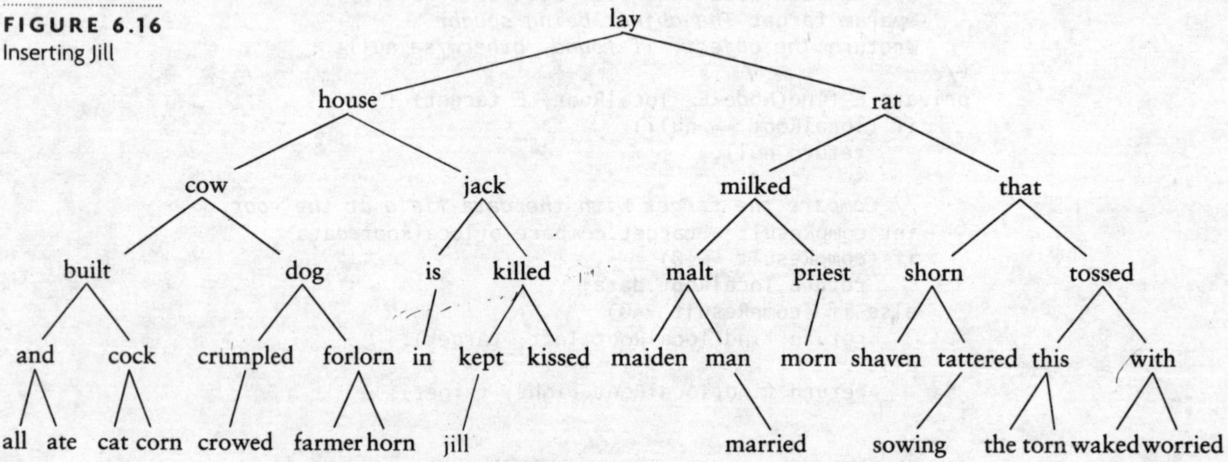

Implementing the add Methods

Listing 6.4 shows the code for the starter and recursive add methods. The recursive add follows the algorithm presented earlier, except that the return value is the new (sub)tree that contains the inserted item. The data field `addReturn` is set to **`true`** if the item is inserted and to **`false`** if the item already exists. The starter method calls the recursive method with the root as its argument. The root is set to the value returned by the recursive method (the modified tree). The value of addReturn is then returned to the caller.

In the recursive method, the statements

```
addReturn = true;
return new Node<E>(item);
```

execute when a **null** branch is reached. The first statement sets the insertion result to **true**; the second returns a new node containing item as its data.

The statements

```
addReturn = false;
return localRoot;
```

execute when item is reached. The first statement sets the insertion result to **false**; the second returns a reference to the subtree that contains item in its root.

If item is less than the root's data, the statement

```
localRoot.left = add(localRoot.left, item);
```

attempts to insert item in the left subtree of the local root. After returning from the call, this left subtree is set to reference the modified subtree, or the original subtree if there is no insertion. The statement

```
localRoot.right = add(localRoot.right, item);
```

affects the right subtree of localRoot in a similar way.

LISTING 6.4
BinarySearchTree add Methods

```
/** Starter method add.
    pre: The object to insert must implement the
        Comparable interface.
    @param item The object being inserted
    @return true if the object is inserted, false
            if the object already exists in the tree
*/
public boolean add(E item) {
    root = add(root, item);
    return addReturn;
}

/** Recursive add method.
    post: The data field addReturn is set true if the item is added to
          the tree, false if the item is already in the tree.
    @param localRoot The local root of the subtree
    @param item The object to be inserted
    @return The new local root that now contains the
            inserted item
*/
private Node<E> add(Node<E> localRoot, E item) {
    if (localRoot == null) {
        // item is not in the tree - insert it.
        addReturn = true;
        return new Node<E>(item);
```

```
        } else if (item.compareTo(localRoot.data) == 0) {
            // item is equal to localRoot.data
            addReturn = false;
            return localRoot;
        } else if (item.compareTo(localRoot.data) < 0) {
            // item is less than localRoot.data
            localRoot.left = add(localRoot.left, item);
            return localRoot;
        } else {
            // item is greater than localRoot.data
            localRoot.right = add(localRoot.right, item);
            return localRoot;
        }
    }
```

PROGRAM STYLE

Comment on Insertion Algorithm and add Methods

Notice as we return along the search path, the statement

```
localRoot.left = add(localRoot.left, item);
```

or

```
localRoot.right = add(localRoot.right, item);
```

resets each local root to reference the modified tree below it. You may wonder whether this is necessary. The answer is "No." In fact, it is only necessary to reset the reference from the parent of the new node to the new node; all references above the parent remain the same. We can modify the insertion algorithm to do this by checking for a leaf node before making the recursive call to add:

5.1. **else if** the item is less than `root.data`
5.2. **if** the local root is a leaf node.
5.3. Reset the left subtree to reference a new node with the item as its data.
else
5.4. Recursively insert the item in the left subtree.

A similar change should be made for the case where `item` is greater than the local root's data. You would also have to modify the starter add method to check for an empty tree and insert the new item in the root node if the tree is empty instead of calling the recursive add method.

One reason we did not write the algorithm this way is that we will want to be able to adjust the tree if the insertion makes it unbalanced. This involves resetting one or more branches above the insertion point. We discuss how this is done in Chapter 9.

PROGRAM STYLE

Multiple Calls to compareTo

Method add has two calls to method compareTo. We wrote it this way so that the code mirrors the algorithm. However, it would be more efficient to call compareTo once and save the result in a local variable as we did for method `find`. Depending on the number and type of data fields being compared, the extra call to method compareTo could be costly.

Removal from a Binary Search Tree

Removal also follows the search algorithm except that when the item is found, it is removed. If the item is a leaf node, then its parent's reference to it is set to **null**, thereby removing the leaf node. If the item has only a left or right child, then the grandparent references the remaining child instead of the child's parent (the node we want to remove).

EXAMPLE 6.4 If we remove *is* from Figure 6.13, we can replace it with *in*. This is accomplished by changing the left child reference in *jack* (the grandparent) to reference *in* (see Figure 6.17).

FIGURE 6.17
Removing *is*

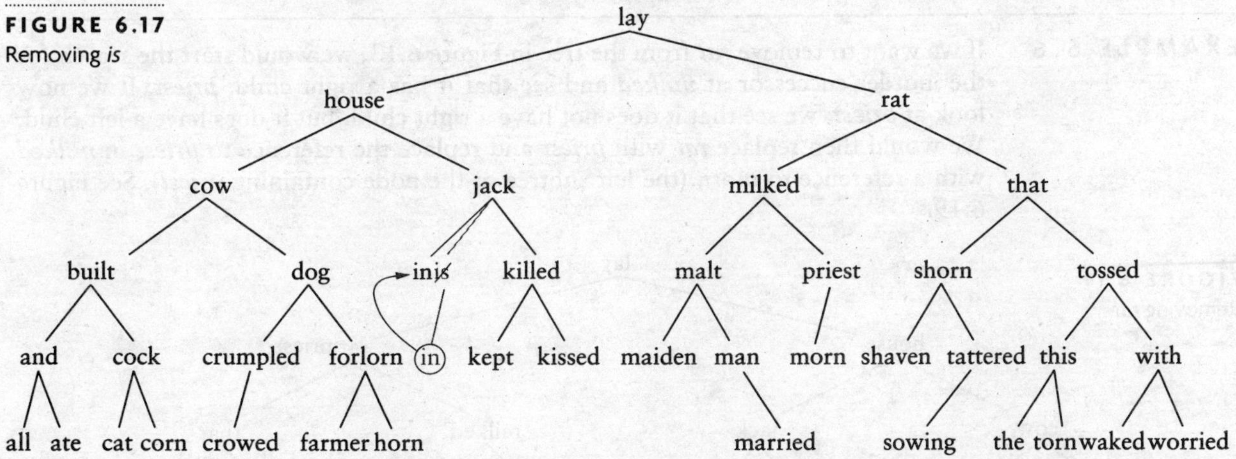

A complication arises when the item we wish to remove has two children. In this case we need to find a replacement parent for the children. Remember that the parent must be larger than all of the data fields in the left subtree and smaller than all of the data fields in the right subtree. If we take the largest item in the left subtree and promote it to be the parent, then all of the remaining items in the left subtree will be smaller. This item is also less than the items in the right subtree. This item is also known as the *inorder predecessor* of the item being removed. (We could use the inorder successor instead; this is discussed in the exercises.)

EXAMPLE 6.5 If we remove *house* from Figure 6.13, we look in the left subtree (root contains *cow*) for the largest item, *horn.* We then replace *house* with *horn* and remove the node containing *horn* (see Figure 6.18).

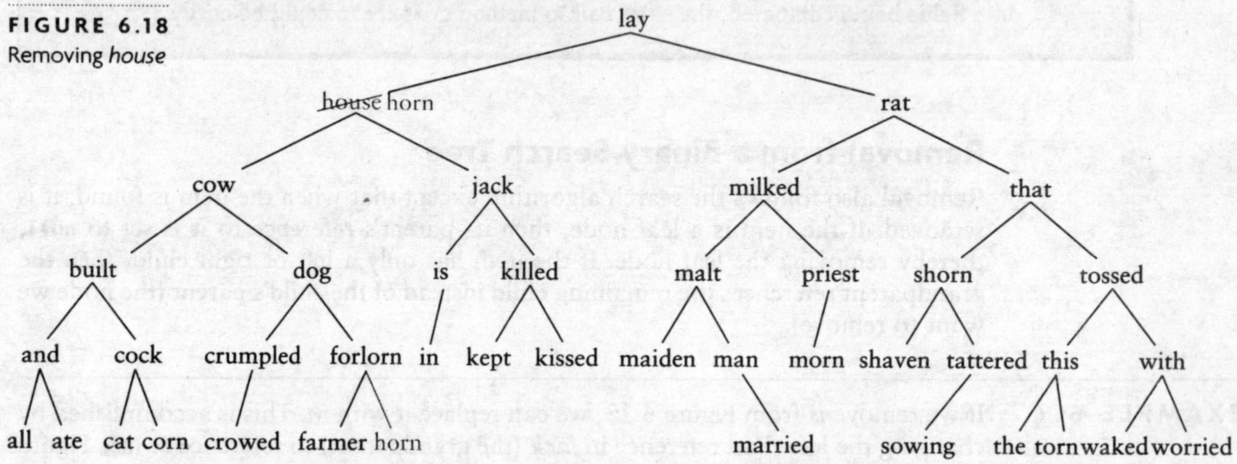

FIGURE 6.18 Removing *house*

EXAMPLE 6.6 If we want to remove *rat* from the tree in Figure 6.13, we would start the search for the inorder successor at *milked* and see that it has a right child, *priest.* If we now look at *priest,* we see that it does not have a right child, but it does have a left child. We would then replace *rat* with *priest* and replace the reference to *priest* in *milked* with a reference to *morn* (the left subtree of the node containing *priest*). See Figure 6.19.

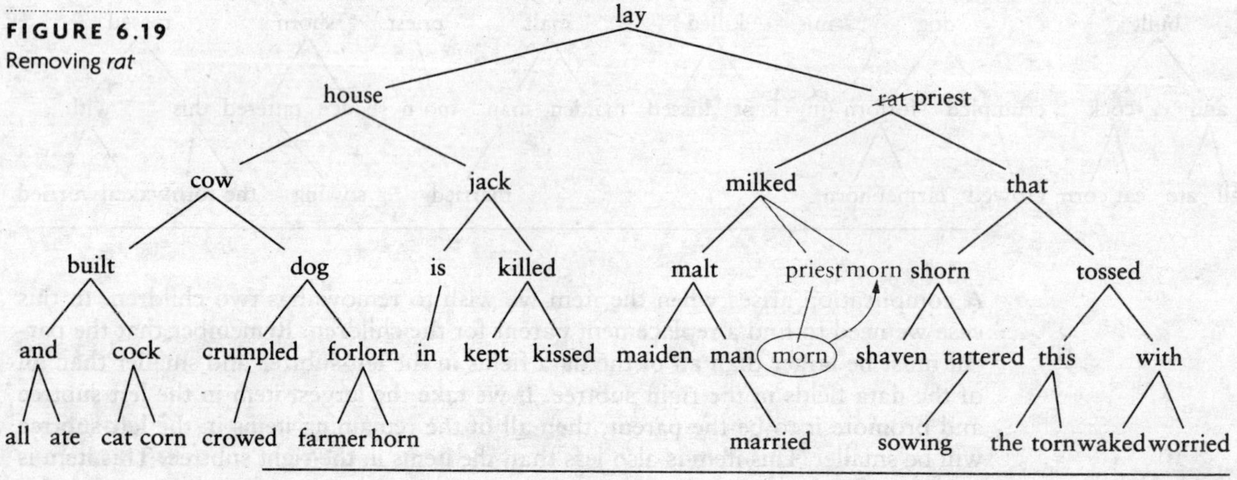

FIGURE 6.19 Removing *rat*

Recursive Algorithm for Removal from a Binary Search Tree

1. `if` the root is null
2. The item is not in tree – return `null`.
3. Compare the item to the data at the local root.
4. `if` the item is less than the data at the local root
5. Return the result of deleting from the left subtree.
6. `else if` the item is greater than the local root
7. Return the result of deleting from the right subtree.
8. `else` *// The item is in the local root*
9. Store the data in the local root in `deleteReturn`.
10. `if` the local root has no children
11. Set the parent of the local root to reference `null`.
12. `else if` the local root has one child
13. Set the parent of the local root to reference that child.
14. `else` *// Find the inorder predecessor*
15. `if` the left child has no right child it is the inorder predecessor
16. Set the parent of the local root to reference the left child.
17. `else`
18. Find the rightmost node in the right subtree of the left child.
19. Copy its data into the local root's data and remove it by setting its parent to reference its left child.

Implementing the `delete` Methods

Listing 6.5 shows both the starter and the recursive `delete` methods. As with the `add` method, the recursive `delete` method returns a reference to a modified tree that, in this case, no longer contains the item. The public starter method is expected to return the item removed. Thus the recursive method saves this value in the data field `deleteReturn` before removing it from the tree. The starter method then returns this value.

LISTING 6.5

`BinarySearchTree delete` Methods

```
/** Starter method delete.
    post: The object is not in the tree.
    @param target The object to be deleted
    @return The object deleted from the tree
            or null if the object was not in the tree
    @throws ClassCastException if target does not implement
            Comparable
*/
public E delete(E target) {
    root = delete(root, target);
    return deleteReturn;
}
```

```
/** Recursive delete method.
    post: The item is not in the tree;
          deleteReturn is equal to the deleted item
          as it was stored in the tree or null
          if the item was not found.
    @param localRoot The root of the current subtree
    @param item The item to be deleted
    @return The modified local root that does not contain
            the item
*/
private Node<E> delete(Node<E> localRoot, E item) {
    if (localRoot == null) {
        // item is not in the tree.
        deleteReturn = null;
        return localRoot;
    }

    // Search for item to delete.
    int compResult = item.compareTo(localRoot.data);
    if (compResult < 0) {
        // item is smaller than localRoot.data.
        localRoot.left = delete(localRoot.left, item);
        return localRoot;
    } else if (compResult > 0) {
        // item is larger than localRoot.data.
        localRoot.right = delete(localRoot.right, item);
        return localRoot;
    } else {
        // item is at local root.
        deleteReturn = localRoot.data;
        if (localRoot.left == null) {
            // If there is no left child, return right child
            // which can also be null.
            return localRoot.right;
        } else if (localRoot.right == null) {
            // If there is no right child, return left child.
            return localRoot.left;
        } else {
            // Node being deleted has 2 children, replace the data
            // with inorder predecessor.
            if (localRoot.left.right == null) {
                // The left child has no right child.
                // Replace the data with the data in the
                // left child.
                localRoot.data = localRoot.left.data;
                // Replace the left child with its left child.
                localRoot.left = localRoot.left.left;
                return localRoot;
            } else {
                // Search for the inorder predecessor (ip) and
                // replace deleted node's data with ip.
                localRoot.data = findLargestChild(localRoot.left);
                return localRoot;
            }
        }
    }
}
```

For the recursive method, the two stopping cases are an empty tree and a tree whose root contains the item being removed. We first test to see whether the tree is empty (local root is `null`). If so, then the item sought is not in the tree. The `deleteReturn` data field is set to `null`, and the local root is returned to the caller.

Next `localRoot.data` is compared to the item to be deleted. If the item to be deleted is less than `localRoot.data`, it must be in the left subtree if it is in the tree at all, so we set `localRoot.left` to the value returned by recursively calling this method.

```
localRoot.left = delete(localRoot.left, item);
```

If the item to be deleted is greater than `localRoot.data`, the statement

```
localRoot.right = delete(localRoot.right, item);
```

affects the right subtree of `localRoot` in a similar way.

If `localRoot.data` is the item to be deleted, we have reached the second stopping case, which begins with the lines

```
} else {
    // item is at local root.
    deleteReturn = localRoot.data;
. . .
```

The value of `localRoot.data` is saved in `deleteReturn`. If the node to be deleted has one child (or zero children), we return a reference to the only child (or `null`), so the parent of the deleted node will reference its only grandchild (or `null`).

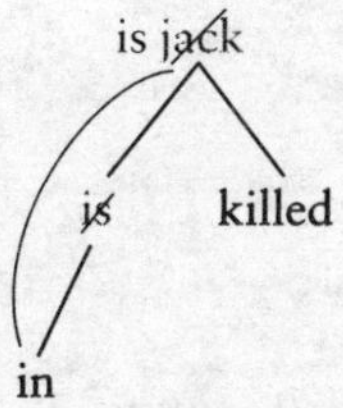

If the node to be deleted (*jack* in the figure at left) has two children, we need to find the replacement for this node. If its left child has no right subtree, the left child (*is*) is the inorder predecessor. The first statement below

```
localRoot.data = localRoot.left.data;
// Replace the left child with its left child.
localRoot.left = localRoot.left.left;
```

copies the left child's data into the local node's data (*is* to *jack*); the second resets the local node's left branch to reference its left child's left subtree (*in*).

If the left child of the node to be deleted has a right subtree, the statement

```
localRoot.data = findLargestChild(localRoot.left);
```

calls `findLargestChild` to find the largest child and to remove it. The largest child's data is referenced by `localRoot.data`. This is illustrated in Figure 6.19. The left child *milked* of the node to be deleted (*rat*) has a right child *priest*, which is its largest child. Therefore, *priest* becomes referenced by `localRoot.data` (replacing *rat*) and *morn* (the left child of *priest*) becomes the new right child of *milked*.

Method `findLargestChild`

Method `findLargestChild` (see Listing 6.6) takes the parent of a node as its argument. It then follows the chain of rightmost children until it finds a node whose right child does not itself have a right child. This is done via tail recursion.

When a parent node is found whose right child has no right child, the right child is the inorder predecessor of the node being deleted, so the data value from the right child is saved.

```
E returnValue = parent.right.data;
parent.right = parent.right.left;
```

The right child is then removed from the tree by replacing it with its left child (if any).

LISTING 6.6

BinarySearchTree findLargestChild Method

```
/** Find the node that is the
    inorder predecessor and replace it
    with its left child (if any).
    post: The inorder predecessor is removed from the tree.
    @param parent The parent of possible inorder
                  predecessor (ip)
    @return The data in the ip
*/
private E findLargestChild(Node<E> parent) {
    // If the right child has no right child, it is
    // the inorder predecessor.
    if (parent.right.right == null) {
        E returnValue = parent.right.data;
        parent.right = parent.right.left;
        return returnValue;
    } else {
        return findLargestChild(parent.right);
    }
}
```

Testing a Binary Search Tree

To test a binary search tree, you need to verify that an inorder traversal will display the tree contents in ascending order after a series of insertions (to build the tree) and deletions are performed. You can base the `main` method of your testing code on that shown in Listing 2.3 (which validates these operations for an `OrderedList<Integer>`). You need to write a `toString` method for a `BinarySearchTree` that returns the `String` built from an inorder traversal (see Programming Exercise 3).

CASE STUDY Writing an Index for a Term Paper

Problem You would like to write an index for a term paper. The index should show each word in the paper followed by the line number on which it occurred. The words should be displayed in alphabetical order. If a word occurs on multiple lines, the line numbers should be listed in ascending order. For example, the three lines

```
a, 3
a, 13
are, 3
```

show that the word *a* occurred on lines 3 and 13 and the word *are* occurred on line 3.

Analysis A binary search tree is an ideal data structure to use for storing the index entries. We can store each word and its line number as a string in a tree node. For example, the two occurrences of the word *Java* on lines 5 and 10 could be stored as the strings `"java, 005"` and `"java, 010"`. Each word will be stored in lowercase to ensure that it appears in its proper position in the index. The leading zeros are necessary so that the string `"java, 005"` is considered less than the string `"java, 010"`. If the leading zeros were removed, this would not be the case (`"java, 5"` is greater than `"java, 10"`). After all the strings are stored in the search tree, we can display them in ascending order by performing an inorder traversal. Storing each word in a search tree is an O(log n) process where n is the number of words currently in the tree. Storing each word in an ordered list would be an O(n) process.

Design We can represent the index as an instance of the `BinarySearchTree` class just discussed or as an instance of a binary search tree provided in the Java API. The Java API provides a class `TreeSet<E>` (discussed further in Section 7.1) that uses a binary search tree as its basis. Class `TreeSet<E>` provides three of the methods in interface `SearchTree`: insertion (`add`), search (`boolean contains`), and removal (`boolean remove`). It also provides an iterator that enables inorder access to the elements of a tree. Because we are only doing tree insertion and inorder access, we will use class `TreeSet<E>`.

We will write a class `IndexGenerator` (see Table 6.4) with a `TreeSet<String>` data field. Method `buildIndex` will read each word from a data file and store it in the search tree. Method `showIndex` will display the index.

Implementation Listing 6.7 shows class `IndexGenerator`. In method `buildIndex`, the repetition condition for the outer `while` loop calls method `hasNextLine`, which scans the next data line into a buffer associated with `Scanner scan` or returns `null` (causing loop exit) if all lines were scanned. If the next line is scanned, the repetition condition for the inner `while` loop below

```
while ((token = scan.findInLine("[\\p{L}\\p{N}']+")) != null) {
    token = token.toLowerCase();
    index.add(String.format("%s, %3d", token, lineNum));
}
```

TABLE 6.4
Data Fields and Methods of Class `IndexGenerator`

Data Field	Attribute
`private TreeSet<String> index`	The search tree used to store the index.
Method	**Behavior**
`public void buildIndex(Scanner scan)`	Reads each word from the file scanned by `scan` and stores it in tree `index`.
`public void showIndex()`	Performs an inorder traversal of tree `index`.

calls `Scanner` method `findInLine` to extract a token from the buffer (a sequence of letters, digits, and the apostrophe character). Next, it inserts in `index` a string consisting of the next token in lowercase followed by a comma, a space, and the current line number formatted with leading spaces so that it occupies a total of three columns. This format is prescribed by the first argument `"%s, %3d"` passed to method `String.format` (see Appendix A.5). The inner loop repeats until `findInLine` returns `null`, at which point the inner loop is exited, the buffer is emptied by the statement

```
scan.nextLine(); // Clear the scan buffer
```

and the outer loop is repeated.

LISTING 6.7
Class `IndexGenerator.java`

```
import java.io.*;
import java.util.*;

/** Class to build an index. */
public class IndexGenerator {

    // Data Fields
    /** Tree for storing the index. */
    private TreeSet<String> index;

    // Methods
    public IndexGenerator() {
        index = new TreeSet<String>();
    }

    /** Reads each word in a data file and stores it in an index
        along with its line number.
        post: Lowercase form of each word with its line
              number is stored in the index.
        @param scan A Scanner object
    */
```

```
    public void buildIndex(Scanner scan) {
        int lineNum = 0; // line number

        // Keep reading lines until done.
        while (scan.hasNextLine()) {
            lineNum++;

            // Extract each token and store it in index.
            String token;
            while ((token = scan.findInLine("[\\p{L}\\p{N}']+")) != null) {
                token = token.toLowerCase();
                index.add(String.format("%s, %3d", token, lineNum));
            }
            scan.nextLine(); // Clear the scan buffer
        }
    }

    /** Displays the index, one word per line. */
    public void showIndex() {
        // Use an iterator to access and display tree data.
        for (String next : index) {
            System.out.println(next);
        }
    }
}
```

Testing To test class IndexGenerator, write a main method that declares new Scanner and IndexGenerator<String> objects. The Scanner can reference any text file stored on your hard drive. Make sure that duplicate words are handled properly (including duplicates on the same line), that words at the end of each line are stored in the index, that empty lines are processed correctly, and that the last line of the document is also part of the index.

EXERCISES FOR SECTION 6.4

SELF-CHECK

1. Show the tree that would be formed for the following data items. Exchange the first and last items in each list, and rebuild the tree that would be formed if the items were inserted in the new order.
   a. happy, depressed, manic, sad, ecstatic
   b. 45, 30, 15, 50, 60, 20, 25, 90

2. Explain how the tree shown in Figure 6.13 would be changed if you inserted *mother*. If you inserted *jane*? Does either of these insertions change the height of the tree?
3. Show or explain the effect of removing the nodes *kept, cow* from the tree in Figure 6.13.
4. In Exercise 3 above, a replacement value must be chosen for the node *cow* because it has two children. What is the relationship between the replacement word and the word *cow*? What other word in the tree could also be used as a replacement for *cow*? What is the relationship between that word and the word *cow*?
5. The algorithm for deleting a node does not explicitly test for the situation where the node being deleted has no children. Explain why this is not necessary.
6. In Step 19 of the algorithm for deleting a node, when we replace the reference to a node that we are removing with a reference to its left child, why is it not a concern that we might lose the right subtree of the node that we are removing?

PROGRAMMING

1. Write methods `contains` and `remove` for the `BinarySearchTree` class. Use methods `find` and `delete` to do the work.
2. Self-Check Exercise 4 indicates that two items can be used to replace a data item in a binary search tree. Rewrite method `delete` so that it retrieves the leftmost element in the right subtree instead. You will also need to provide a method `findSmallestChild`.
3. Write a `main` method to test a binary search tree based on Listing 2.3. Write a `toString` method that returns the tree contents in ascending order (using an inorder traversal) with newline characters separating the tree elements.

6.5 Heaps and Priority Queues

In this section, we discuss a binary tree that is ordered but in a different way from a binary search tree. At each level of a heap, the value in a node is less than all values in its two subtrees. Figure 6.20 shows an example of a heap. Observe that 6 is the smallest value. Observe that each parent is smaller than its children and that each parent has two children, with the exception of node 39 at level 3 and the leaves. Furthermore, with the exception of 66, all leaves are at the lowest level. Also, 39 is the next-to-last node at level 3, and 66 is the last (rightmost) node at level 3.

FIGURE 6.20
Example of a Heap

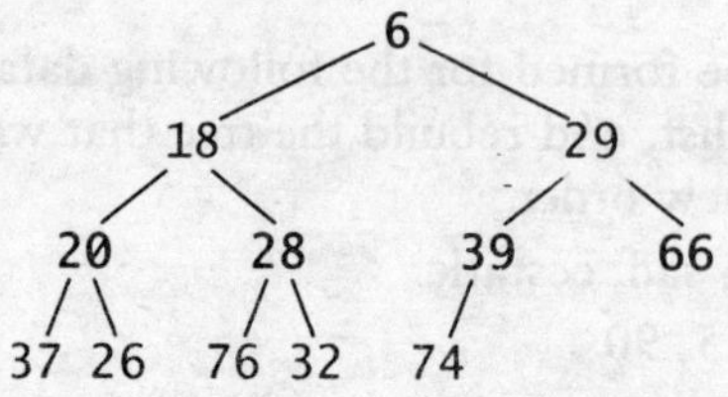

FIGURE 6.21
Inserting 8 into a Heap

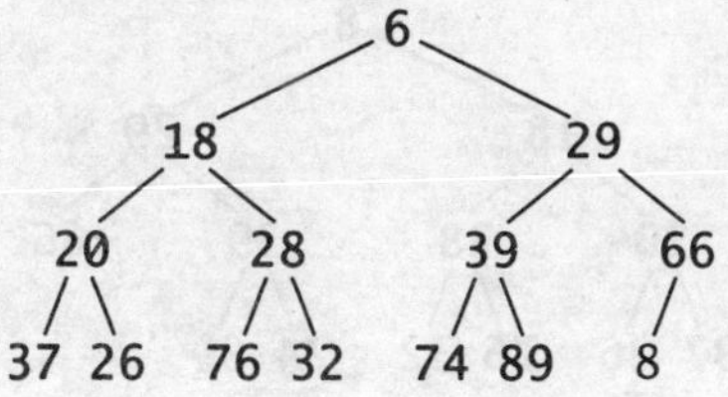

FIGURE 6.22
Swapping 8 and 66

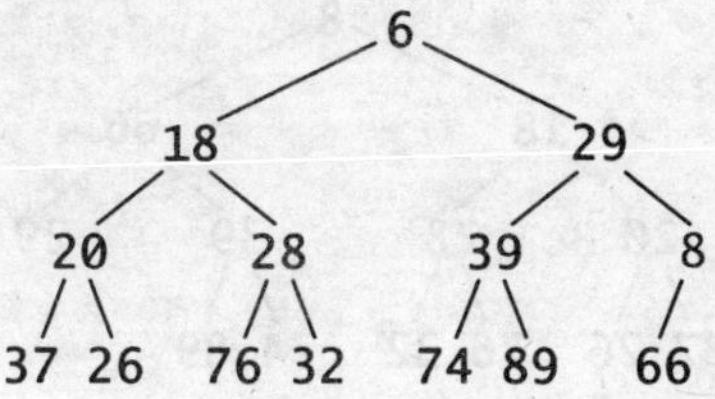

FIGURE 6.23
Swapping 8 and 29

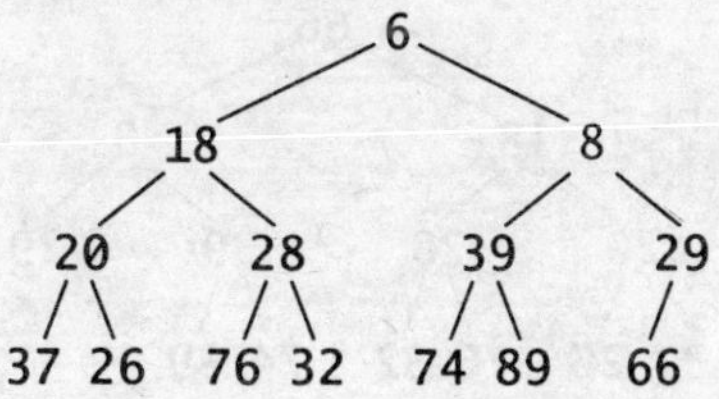

More formally, a heap is a complete binary tree with the following properties:

- The value in the root is the smallest item in the tree.
- Every subtree is a heap.

Inserting an Item into a Heap

We use the following algorithm for inserting an item into a heap. Our approach is to place each item initially in the bottom row of the heap and then move it up until it reaches the position where it belongs.

Algorithm for Inserting in a Heap

1. Insert the new item in the next position at the bottom of the heap.
2. `while` new item is not at the root and new item is smaller than its parent
3. Swap the new item with its parent, moving the new item up the heap.

New items are added to the last row (level) of a heap. If a new item is larger than or equal to its parent, nothing more need be done. If we insert 89 in the heap in Figure 6.20, 89 would become the right child of 39 and we are done. However, if the new item is smaller than its parent, the new item and its parent are swapped. This is repeated up the tree until the new item is in a position where it is no longer smaller than its parent. For example, let's add 8 to the heap shown in Figure 6.21. Since 8 is smaller than 66, these values are swapped as shown in Figure 6.22. Also, 8 is smaller than 29, so these values are swapped resulting in the updated heap shown in Figure 6.23. But 8 is greater than 6, so we are done.

Removing an Item from a Heap

Removal from a heap is always from the top. The top item is first replaced with the last item in the heap (at the lower right-hand position) so that the heap remains a complete tree. If we used any other value, there would be a "hole" in the tree where that value used to be. Then the new item at the top is moved down the heap until it is in its proper position.

FIGURE 6.24
After Removal of 6

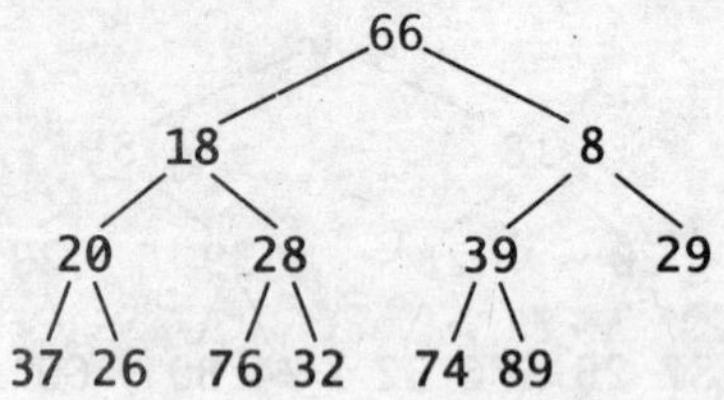

FIGURE 6.25
Swapping 66 and 8

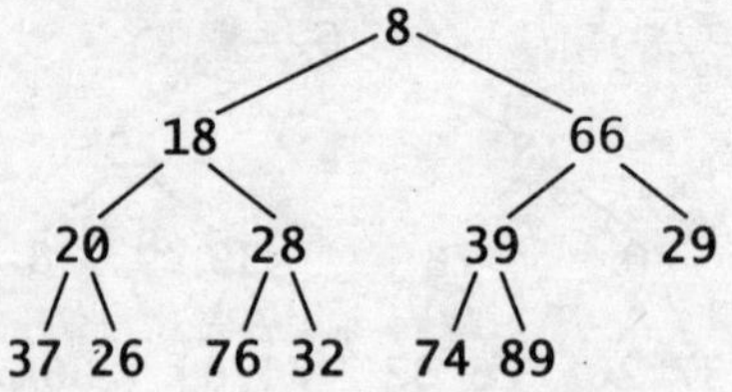

FIGURE 6.26
Swapping 66 and 29

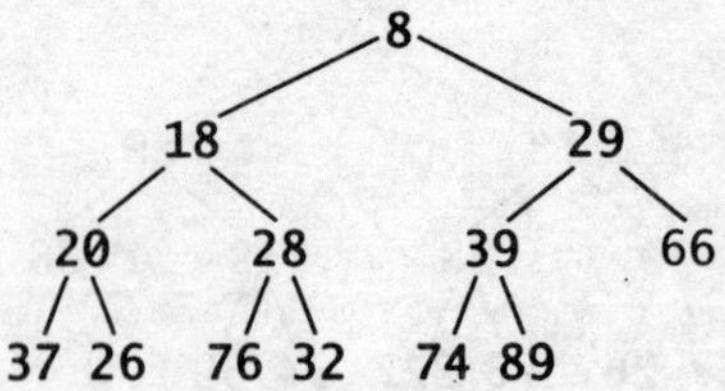

Algorithm for Removal from a Heap

1. Remove the item in the root node by replacing it with the last item in the heap (LIH).
2. **while** item LIH has children, and item LIH is larger than either of its children
3. Swap item LIH with its smaller child, moving LIH down the heap.

As an example, if we remove 6 from the heap shown in Figure 6.23, 66 replaces it as shown in Figure 6.24. Since 66 is larger than both of its children, it is swapped with the smaller of the two, 8, as shown in Figure 6.25. The result is still not a heap because 66 is larger than both its children. Swapping 66 with its smaller child, 29, restores the heap as shown in Figure 6.26.

Implementing a Heap

Because a heap is a complete binary tree, we can implement it efficiently using an array (or `ArrayList`) instead of a linked data structure. We can use the first element (subscript 0) for storing a reference to the root data. We can use the next two elements (subscripts 1 and 2) for storing the two children of the root. We can use elements with subscripts 3, 4, 5, and 6 for storing the four children of these two nodes, and so on. Therefore, we can view a heap as a sequence of rows; each row is twice as long as the previous row. The first row (the root) has one item, the second row two, the third four, and so on. All of the rows are full except for the last one (see Figure 6.27).

Observe that the root, 6, is at position 0. The root's two children, 18 and 29, are at positions 1 and 2. For a node at position p, the left child is at $2p + 1$ and the right child is at $2p + 2$. A node at position c can find its parent at $(c - 1) / 2$. Thus, as shown in Figure 6.27, children of 28 (at position 4) are at positions 9 and 10.

FIGURE 6.27
Internal Representation of the Heap

0	1	2	3	4	5	6	7	8	9	10	11	12
6	18	29	20	28	39	66	37	26	76	32	74	89

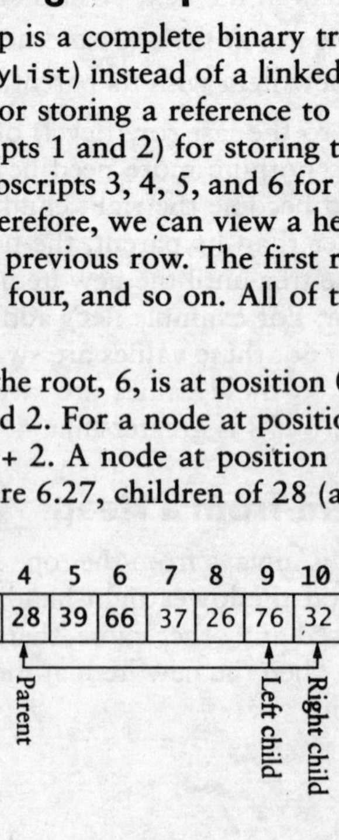

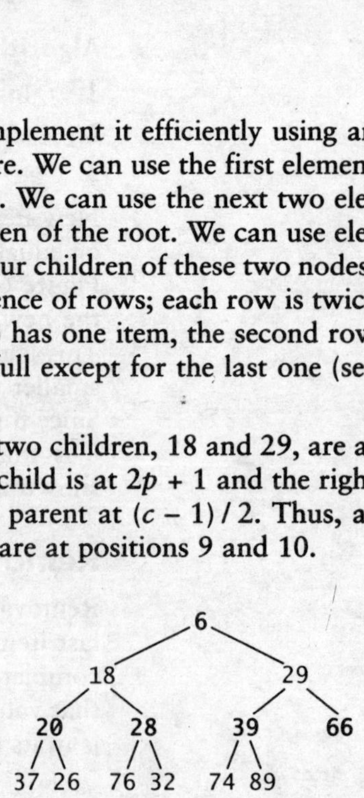

FIGURE 6.28
Internal Representation of Heap after Insertion

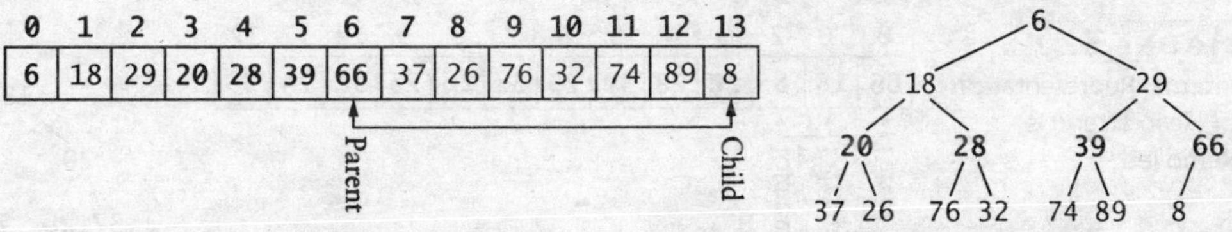

FIGURE 6.29
Internal Representation of Heap after First Swap

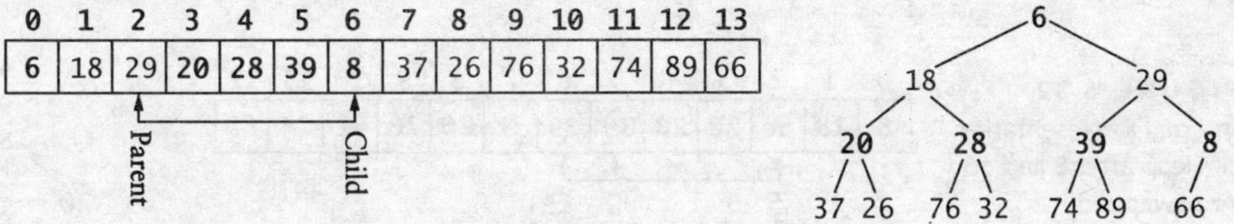

FIGURE 6.30
Internal Representation of Heap after Second Swap

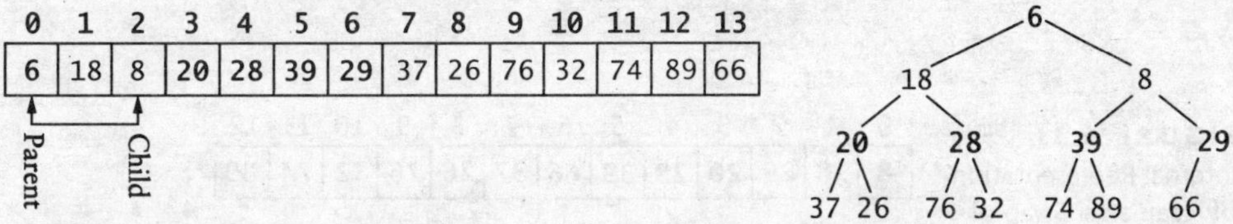

Insertion into a Heap Implemented as an `ArrayList`

We will use an `ArrayList` for storing our heap because it is easier to expand and contract than an array. Figure 6.28 shows the heap after inserting 8 into position 13. This corresponds to inserting the new value into the lower right position as shown in the figure, right. Now we need to move 8 up the heap, by comparing it to the values stored in its ancestor nodes. The parent (66) is in position 6 (13 minus 1 is 12, divided by 2 is 6). Since 66 is larger than 8, we need to swap as shown in Figure 6.29.

Now the child is at position 6 and the parent is at position 2 (6 minus 1 is 5, divided by 2 is 2). Since the parent, 29, is larger than the child, 8, we must swap again as shown in Figure 6.30.

The child is now at position 2 and the parent is at position 0. Since the parent is smaller than the child, the heap property is restored. In the heap insertion and removal algorithms that follow, we will use `table` to reference the `ArrayList` that stores the heap. We will use `table[index]` to represent the element at position `index` of `table`. In the actual code, a subscript cannot be used with an `ArrayList`.

Insertion of an Element into a Heap Implemented as an `ArrayList`

1. Insert the new element at the end of the `ArrayList` and set `child` to `table.size() - 1`.
2. Set `parent` to `(child - 1) / 2`.
3. **`while`** `(parent >= 0` and `table[parent] > table[child])`
4.   Swap `table[parent]` and `table[child]`.
5.   Set `child` equal to `parent`.
6.   Set `parent` equal to `(child - 1) / 2`.

FIGURE 6.31
Internal Representation of Heap after 6 Is Removed

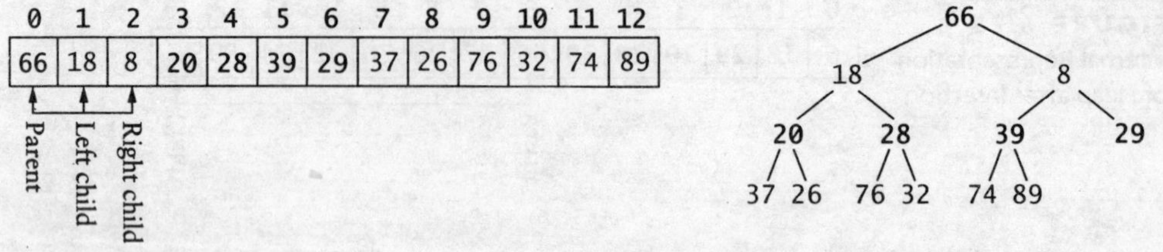

FIGURE 6.32
Internal Representation of Heap after 8 and 66 Are Swapped

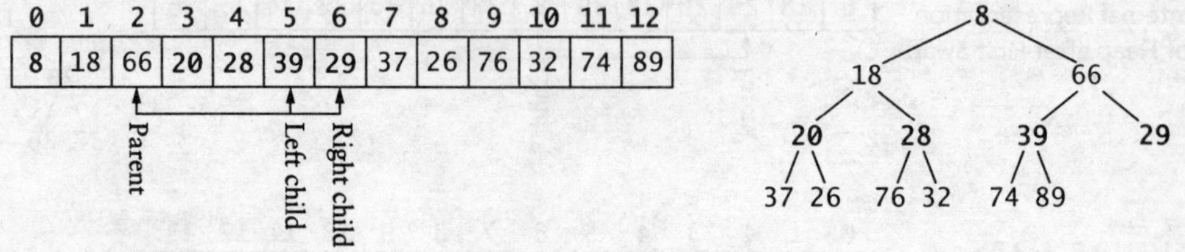

FIGURE 6.33
Internal Representation of Heap after Swap of 66 and 29

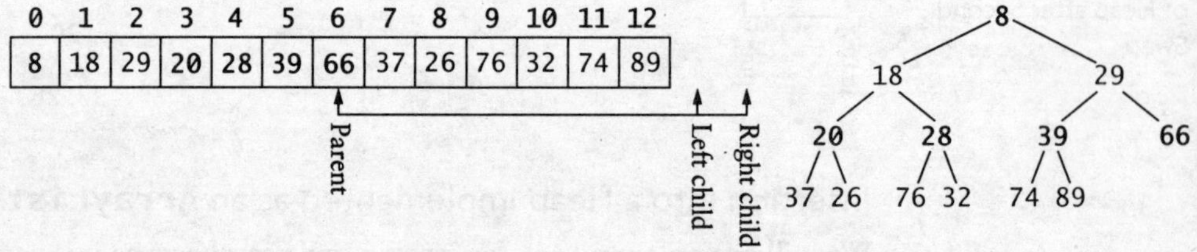

Removal from a Heap Implemented as an `ArrayList`

In removing elements from a heap, we must always remove and save the element at the top of the heap, which is the smallest element. We start with an `ArrayList` that has been organized to form a heap. To remove the first item (6), we begin by replacing the first item with the last item and then removing the last item. This is illustrated in Figure 6.31. The new value of the root (position 0) is larger than both of its children (18 in position 1, and 8 in position 2). The smaller of the two children (8 in position 2) is swapped with the parent as shown in Figure 6.32. Next, 66 is swapped with the smaller of its two new children (29), and the heap is restored (Figure 6.33).

The algorithm for removal from a heap implemented as an `ArrayList` follows.

Removing an Element from a Heap Implemented as an `ArrayList`

1. Remove the last element (i.e., the one at `size() - 1`) and set the item at 0 to this value.
2. Set `parent` to 0.
3. **`while (true)`**
4. Set `leftChild` to `(2 * parent) + 1` and `rightChild` to `leftChild + 1`.
5. **`if`** `leftChild >= table.size()`
6. Break out of loop.

```
7.         Assume minChild (the smaller child) is leftChild.
8.         if rightChild < table.size() and
           table[rightChild] < table[leftChild]
9.             Set minChild to rightChild.
10.        if table[parent] > table[minChild]
11.            Swap table[parent] and table[minChild].
12.            Set parent to minChild.
           else
13.            Break out of loop.
```

The loop (Step 3) is terminated under one of two circumstances: Either the item has moved down the tree so that it has no children (line 5 is true), or it is smaller than both its children (line 10 is false). In these cases, the loop terminates (line 6 or 13). This is shown in Figure 6.33. At this point the heap property is restored, and the next smallest item can be removed from the heap.

Performance of the Heap

Method `remove` traces a path from the root to a leaf, and method `insert` traces a path from a leaf to the root. This requires at most h steps, where h is the height of the tree. The largest heap of height h is a full tree of height h. This tree has $2^h - 1$ nodes. The smallest heap of height h is a complete tree of height h, consisting of a full tree of height $h - 1$, with a single node as the left child of the leftmost child at height $h - 1$. Thus, this tree has $2^{(h-1)}$ nodes. Therefore, both `insert` and `remove` are $O(\log n)$ where n is the number of items in the heap.

Priority Queues

In computer science, a heap is used as the basis of a very efficient algorithm for sorting arrays, called heapsort, which you will study in Chapter 8. The heap is also used to implement a special kind of queue called a priority queue. However, the heap is not very useful as an ADT on its own. Consequently, we will not create a `Heap` interface or code a class that implements it. Instead we will incorporate its algorithms when we implement a priority queue class and heapsort.

Sometimes a FIFO (First-In-First-Out) queue may not be the best way to implement a waiting line. In a print queue, you might want to print a short document before some longer documents that were ahead of the short document in the queue. For example, if you were waiting by the printer for a single page to print, it would be very frustrating to have to wait until several documents of 50 pages or more were printed just because they entered the queue before yours did. Therefore, a better way to implement a print queue would be to use a priority queue. A *priority queue* is a data structure in which only the highest priority item is accessible. During insertion, the position of an item in the queue is based on its priority relative to the priorities of other items in the queue. If a new item has higher priority than all items currently in the queue, it will be placed at the front of the queue and, therefore, will be removed before any of the other items inserted in the queue at an earlier time. This violates the FIFO property of an ordinary queue.

EXAMPLE 6.7 Figure 6.34 sketches a print queue that at first (top of diagram) contains two documents. We will assume that each document's priority is inversely proportional to its page count (priority is $\frac{1}{\text{page count}}$). The middle queue shows the effect of inserting a document three pages long. The bottom queue shows the effect of inserting a second one-page document. It follows the earlier document with that page length.

FIGURE 6.34
Insertion into a Priority Queue

`pages = 1` `title = "web page 1"`	`pages = 4` `title = "history paper"`

After inserting document with 3 pages

`pages = 1` `title = "web page 1"`	`pages = 3` `title = "Lab1"`	`pages = 4` `title = "history paper"`

After inserting document with 1 page

`pages = 1` `title = "web page 1"`	`pages = 1` `title = "receipt"`	`pages = 3` `title = "Lab1"`	`pages = 4` `title = "history paper"`

The `PriorityQueue` Class

Java provides a `PriorityQueue<E>` class that implements the `Queue<E>` interface given in Chapter 4. The differences are in the specification for the `peek`, `poll`, and `remove` methods. These are defined to return the smallest item in the queue rather than the oldest item in the queue. Table 6.5 summarizes the methods of the `PriorityQueue<E>` class.

Using a Heap as the Basis of a Priority Queue

The smallest item is always removed first from a priority queue (the smallest item has the highest priority) just as it is for a heap. Because insertion into and removal from a heap is O(log n), a heap can be the basis for an efficient implementation of a priority queue. We will call our class `KWPriorityQueue` to differentiate it from class `PriorityQueue` in the `java.util` API, which also uses a heap as the basis of its implementation.

A key difference is that class `java.util.PriorityQueue` class uses an array of type `Object[]` for heap storage. We will use an `ArrayList` for storage in `KWPriorityQueue` because the size of an `ArrayList` automatically adjusts as elements are inserted and removed. To insert an item into the priority queue, we first insert the item at the end of the `ArrayList`. Then, following the algorithm described earlier, we move this item up the heap until it is smaller than its parent.

TABLE 6.5
Methods of the `PriorityQueue<E>` Class

Method	Behavior
`boolean offer(E item)`	Inserts an item into the queue. Returns **`true`** if successful; returns **`false`** if the item could not be inserted.
`E remove()`	Removes the smallest entry and returns it if the queue is not empty. If the queue is empty, throws a `NoSuchElementException`.
`E poll()`	Removes the smallest entry and returns it. If the queue is empty, returns **`null`**.
`E peek()`	Returns the smallest entry without removing it. If the queue is empty, returns **`null`**.
`E element()`	Returns the smallest entry without removing it. If the queue is empty, throws a `NoSuchElementException`.

To remove an item from the priority queue, we take the first item from the `ArrayList`; this is the smallest item. We then remove the last item from the `ArrayList` and put it into the first position of the `ArrayList`, overwriting the value currently there. Then, following the algorithm described earlier, we move this item down until it is smaller than its children or it has no children.

Design of `KWPriorityQueue` Class

The design of the `KWPriorityQueue<E>` class is shown in Table 6.6. The data field `theData` is used to store the heap. We discuss the purpose of data field `comparator` shortly. We have added methods `compare` and `swap` to those shown earlier in Table 6.5. Method `compare` compares its two arguments and returns a type `int` value indicating their relative ordering. The class heading and data field declarations follow.

```
import java.util.*;

/** The KWPriorityQueue implements the Queue interface
    by building a heap in an ArrayList. The heap is structured
    so that the "smallest" item is at the top.
*/
public class KWPriorityQueue<E> extends AbstractQueue<E>
                                implements Queue<E> {

    // Data Fields
    /** The ArrayList to hold the data. */
    private ArrayList<E> theData;
    /** An optional reference to a Comparator object. */
    Comparator<E> comparator = null;

    // Methods
    // Constructor
    public KWPriorityQueue() {
        theData = new ArrayList<E>();
    }
. . .
```

TABLE 6.6
Design of KWPriorityQueue<E> Class

Data Field	Attribute
`ArrayList<E> theData`	An `ArrayList` to hold the data.
`Comparator<E> comparator`	An optional object that implements the `Comparator<E>` interface by providing a compare method.
Method	**Behavior**
`KWPriorityQueue()`	Constructs a heap-based priority queue that uses the elements' natural ordering.
`KWPriorityQueue (Comparator<E> comp)`	Constructs a heap-based priority queue that uses the `compare` method of `Comparator comp` to determine the ordering of the elements.
`private int compare(E left, E right)`	Compares two objects and returns a negative number if object `left` is less than object `right`, zero if they are equal, and a positive number if object `left` is greater than object `right`.
`private void swap(int i, int j)`	Exchanges the object references in `theData` at indexes `i` and `j`.

The `offer` Method

The `offer` method appends the new item to the `ArrayList theData`. It then moves this item up the heap until the `ArrayList` is restored to a heap.

```
/** Insert an item into the priority queue.
    pre: The ArrayList theData is in heap order.
    post: The item is in the priority queue and
          theData is in heap order.
    @param item The item to be inserted
    @throws NullPointerException if the item to be inserted is null.
*/
@Override
public boolean offer(E item) {
    // Add the item to the heap.
    theData.add(item);
    // child is newly inserted item.
    int child = theData.size() - 1;
    int parent = (child - 1) / 2;  // Find child's parent.
    // Reheap
    while (parent >= 0 && compare(theData.get(parent),
                                  theData.get(child)) > 0) {
        swap(parent, child);
        child = parent;
        parent = (child - 1) / 2;
    }
    return true;
}
```

The `poll` Method

The `poll` method first saves the item at the top of the heap. If there is more than one item in the heap, the method removes the last item from the heap and places it at the top. Then it moves the item at the top down the heap until the heap property is restored. Next it returns the original top of the heap.

```
/** Remove an item from the priority queue
    pre: The ArrayList theData is in heap order.
    post: Removed smallest item, theData is in heap order.
    @return The item with the smallest priority value or null if empty.
*/
@Override
public E poll() {
    if (isEmpty()) {
        return null;
    }
    // Save the top of the heap.
    E result = theData.get(0);
    // If only one item then remove it.
    if (theData.size() == 1) {
        theData.remove(0);
        return result;
    }

    /* Remove the last item from the ArrayList and place it into
       the first position. */
    theData.set(0, theData.remove(theData.size() - 1));
    // The parent starts at the top.
    int parent = 0;
    while (true) {
        int leftChild = 2 * parent + 1;
        if (leftChild >= theData.size()) {
            break; // Out of heap.
        }
        int rightChild = leftChild + 1;
        int minChild = leftChild;  // Assume leftChild is smaller.
        // See whether rightChild is smaller.
        if (rightChild < theData.size()
            && compare(theData.get(leftChild),
                       theData.get(rightChild)) > 0) {
            minChild = rightChild;
        }
        // assert: minChild is the index of the smaller child.
        // Move smaller child up heap if necessary.
        if (compare(theData.get(parent),
                    theData.get(minChild)) > 0) {
            swap(parent, minChild);
            parent = minChild;
        } else { // Heap property is restored.
            break;
        }
    }
    return result;
}
```

The Other Methods

The `iterator` and `size` methods are implemented via delegation to the corresponding `ArrayList` methods. Method `isEmpty` tests whether the result of calling method `size` is 0 and is inherited from class `AbstractCollection` (a super interface to

AbstractQueue). Methods peek and remove (based on poll) must also be implemented; they are left as exercises. Methods add and element are inherited from AbstractQueue where they are implemented by calling methods offer and peek, respectively.

Using a Comparator

How do we compare elements in a PriorityQueue? In many cases, we will insert objects that implement Comparable<E> and use their natural ordering as specified by method compareTo. However, we may need to insert objects that do not implement Comparable<E>, or we may want to specify a different ordering from that defined by the object's compareTo method. For example, files to be printed may be ordered by their name using the compareTo method, but we may want to assign priority based on their length. The Java API contains the Comparator<E> interface, which allows us to specify alternative ways to compare objects. An implementer of the Comparator<E> interface must define a compare method that is similar to compareTo except that it has two parameters (see Table 6.6).

To indicate that we want to use an ordering that is different from the natural ordering for the objects in our heap, we will provide a constructor that has a Comparator<E> parameter. The constructor will set data field comparator to reference this parameter. Otherwise, comparator will remain **null**. To match the form of this constructor in the java.util.PriorityQueue class, we provide a first parameter that specifies the initial capacity of ArrayList theData.

```
/** Creates a heap-based priority queue with the specified initial
    capacity that orders its elements according to the specified
    comparator.
    @param cap The initial capacity for this priority queue
    @param comp The comparator used to order this priority queue
    @throws IllegalArgumentException if cap is less than 1
*/
public KWPriorityQueue(Comparator<E> comp) {
    if (cap < 1)
        throw new IllegalArgumentException();
    theData = new ArrayList<E>();
    comparator = comp;
}
```

The compare Method

If data field comparator references a Comparator<E> object, method compare will delegate the task of comparing its argument objects to that object's compare method. If comparator is **null**, the natural ordering of the objects should be used, so method compare will delegate to method compareTo. Note that parameter left is cast to type Comparable<E> in this case. In the next example, we show how to write a Comparator class.

```
/** Compare two items using either a Comparator object's compare method
    or their natural ordering using method compareTo.
    pre: If comparator is null, left and right implement Comparable<E>.
    @param left One item
    @param right The other item
    @return Negative int if left less than right,
            0 if left equals right,
            positive int if left > right
```

```
        @throws ClassCastException if items are not Comparable
    */
    private int compare(E left, E right) {
        if (comparator != null) {  // A Comparator is defined.
            return comparator.compare(left, right);
        } else {                   // Use left's compareTo method.
            return ((Comparable<E>) left).compareTo(right);
        }
    }
```

EXAMPLE 6.8 The class `PrintDocument` is used to define documents to be printed on a printer. This class implements the `Comparable` interface, but the result of its `compareTo` method is based on the name of the file being printed. The class also has a `getSize` method that gives the number of bytes to be transmitted to the printer and a `getTimeStamp` method that gets the time that the print job was submitted. Instead of basing the ordering on file names, we want to order the documents by a value that is a function of both size and time submitted. If we were to use either time or size alone, small documents could be delayed while big ones are printed, or big documents would never be printed. By using a priority value that is a combination, we achieve a balanced usage of the printer.

We define the `Comparator` for our `PrintDocument` class as shown in Listing 6.8. The method `orderValue` computes the weighted sum of the size and `timeStamp` using the weighting factors `P1` and `P2`. The method `Double.compare` is defined by the Java API. It compares two `double` values and returns –1, 0, or +1 depending on whether its left argument is less than, equal to, or greater than its right argument.

In a client program, we can use the statement

```
Queue printQueue =
    new PriorityQueue(new ComparePrintDocuments());
```

to create a print queue (referenced by `printQueue`). The argument expression `new ComparePrintDocuments()` creates a new object that implements the `Comparator` interface. This object will be referenced by data field `comparator` in the priority queue.

LISTING 6.8

`ComparePrintDocuments.java`

```
import java.util.Comparator;

/** Class to compare PrintDocuments based on both
    their size and time stamp.
*/
public class ComparePrintDocuments implements Comparator<PrintDocument> {
    /** Weight factor for size. */
    private static final double P1 = 0.8;
    /** Weight factor for time. */
    private static final double P2 = 0.2;

    /** Compare two PrintDocuments.
        @param left The left-hand side of the comparison
        @param right The right-hand side of the comparison
```

```
         @return -1 if left < right; 0 if left == right;
                   and +1 if left > right
      */
     public int compare(PrintDocument left, PrintDocument right) {
         return Double.compare(orderValue(left), orderValue(right));
     }

     /** Compute the order value for a print document.
         @param pd The PrintDocument
         @return The order value based on the size and time stamp
      */
     private double orderValue(PrintDocument pd) {
         return P1 * pd.getSize() + P2 * pd.getTimeStamp();
     }
}
```

EXERCISES FOR SECTION 6.5

SELF-CHECK

1. Show the heap that would be used to store the words *this, is, the, house, that, jack, built,* assuming they are inserted in that sequence. Exchange the order of arrival of the first and last words and build the new heap.
2. Draw the heaps for Exercise 1 above as arrays.
3. Show the result of removing the number 18 from the heap in Figure 6.26. Show the new heap and its array representation.
4. The heaps in this chapter are called min heaps because the smallest key is at the top of the heap. A max heap is a heap in which each element has a key that is smaller than its parent, so the largest key is at the top of the heap. Build the max heap that would result from the numbers 15, 25, 10, 33, 55, 47, 82, 90,18 arriving in that order.
5. Show the printer queue after receipt of the following documents:

time stamp	size
1100	256
1101	512
1102	64
1103	96

PROGRAMMING

1. Complete the implementation of the `KWPriorityQueue` class. Write method `swap`. Also write methods `peek`, `remove`, `isEmpty`, and `size`.

6.6 Huffman Trees

In Section 6.1, we showed the Huffman coding tree and how it can be used to decode a message. We will now implement some of the methods needed to build a tree and decode a message. We will do this using a binary tree and a `PriorityQueue` (which also uses a binary tree).

A straight binary coding of an alphabet assigns a unique binary number k to each symbol in the alphabet a_k. An example of such a coding is Unicode, which is used by Java for the **char** data type. There are 65,536 possible characters, and they are assigned a number between 0 and 65,535, which is a string of 16 binary digit ones. Therefore, the length of a message would be $16 \times n$, where n is the total number of characters in the message. For example, the message "go eagles" contains 9 characters and would require 9×16 or 144 bits. As shown in the example in Section 6.1, a Huffman coding of this message requires just 38 bits.

Table 6.7, based on data published in Donald Knuth, *The Art of Computer Programming, Vol 3: Sorting and Searching* (Addison-Wesley, 1973), p. 441, represents the relative frequencies of the letters in English text and is the basis of the tree shown in Figure 6.35. The letter *e* occurs an average of 103 times every 1000 letters, or 10.3% of the letters are *e*'s. (This is a useful table to know if you are a fan of *Wheel of Fortune.*) We can use this Huffman tree to encode and decode a file of English text. However, files may contain other symbols or may contain these symbols in different frequencies from what is found in normal English. For this reason, you may want to build a custom Huffman tree based on the contents of the file you are encoding. You would from attach this tree to the encoded file so that it can be used to decode the file. We discuss how to build a Huffman tree in the next case study.

TABLE 6.7
Frequency of Letters in English Text

Symbol	Frequency	Symbol	Frequency	Symbol	Frequency
␣	186	h	47	g	15
e	103	d	32	p	15
t	80	l	32	b	13
a	64	u	23	v	8
o	63	c	22	k	5
i	57	f	21	j	1
n	57	m	20	q	1
s	51	w	18	x	1
r	48	y	16	z	1

FIGURE 6.35
Huffman Tree Based on Frequency of Letters in English Text

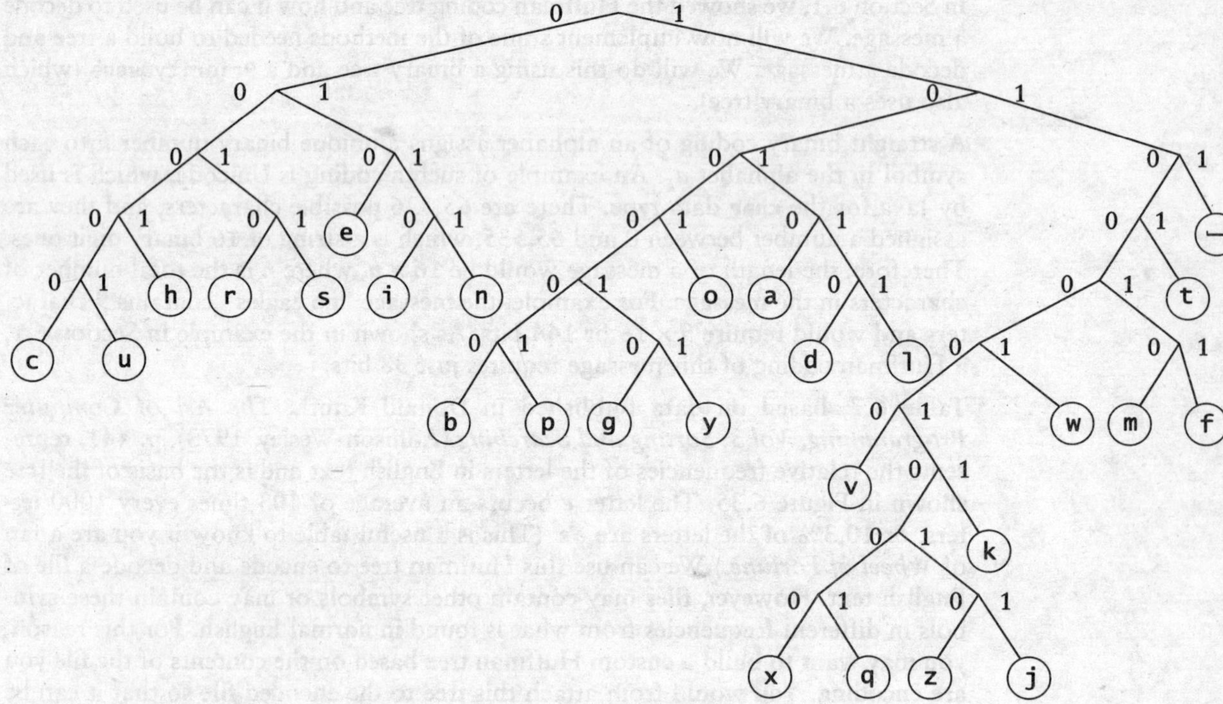

CASE STUDY Building a Custom Huffman Tree

Problem You want to build a custom Huffman tree for a particular file. Your input will consist of an array of objects such that each object contains a reference to a symbol occurring in that file and the frequency of occurrence (weight) for the symbol in that file.

Analysis Each node of a Huffman tree has storage for two data items: the weight of the node and the symbol associated with that node. All symbols will be stored at leaf nodes. For nodes that are not leaf nodes, the symbol part has no meaning. The weight of a leaf node will be the frequency of the symbol stored at that node. The weight of an interior node will be the sum of frequencies of all nodes in the subtree rooted at the interior node. For example, the interior node with leaf nodes *c* and *u* (on the left of Figure 6.35) would have a weight of 45 (22 + 23).

We will use a priority queue as the key data structure in constructing the Huffman tree. We will store individual symbols and subtrees of multiple symbols in order by their priority (frequency of occurrence). We want to remove symbols that occur less frequently first because they should be lower down in the Huffman tree we are constructing. We discuss how this is done next.

FIGURE 6.36
Priority Queue with the Symbols *a, b, c, d,* and *e*

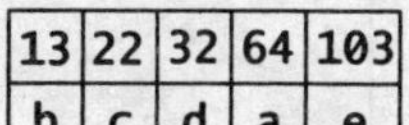

To build a Huffman tree, we start by inserting references to trees with just leaf nodes in a priority queue. Each leaf node will store a symbol and its weight. The queue elements will be ordered so that the leaf node with smallest weight (lowest frequency) is removed first. Figure 6.36 shows a priority queue, containing just the symbols *a, b, c, d, e,* that uses the weights shown in Table 6.7. The item at the front of the queue stores a reference to a tree with a root node that is a leaf node containing the symbol *b* with a weight (frequency) of 13. To represent the tree referenced by a queue element, we list the root node information for that tree. The queue elements are shown in priority order.

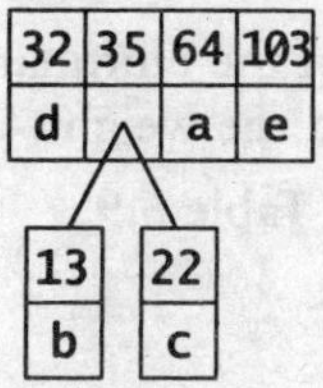

Now we start to build the Huffman tree. We build it from the bottom up. The first step is to remove the first two tree references from the priority queue and combine them to form a new tree. The weight of the root node for this tree will be the sum of the weights of its left and right subtrees. We insert the new tree back into the priority queue. The priority queue now contains references to four binary trees instead of five. The tree referenced by the second element of the queue has a combined weight of 35 (13 + 22) as shown on the left.

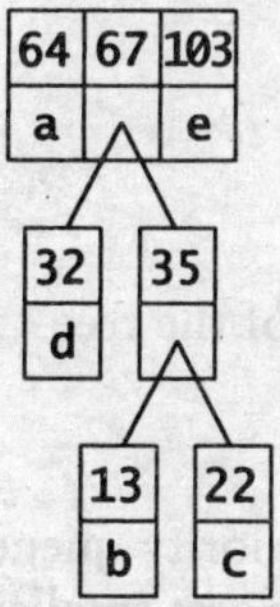

Again we remove the first two tree references and combine them. The new binary tree will have a weight of 67 in its root node. We put this tree back in the queue, and it will be referenced by the second element of the queue.

We repeat this process again. The new queue follows:

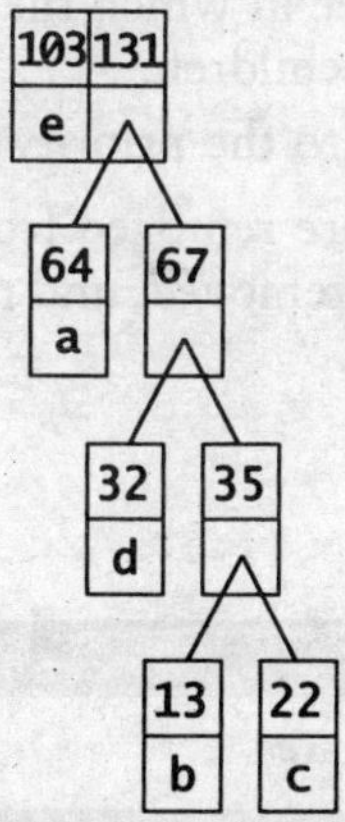

Finally, we combine the last two elements into a new tree and put a reference to it in the priority queue. Now there is only one tree in the queue, so we have finished building the Huffman tree (see Figure 6.37). Table 6.8 shows the codes for this tree.

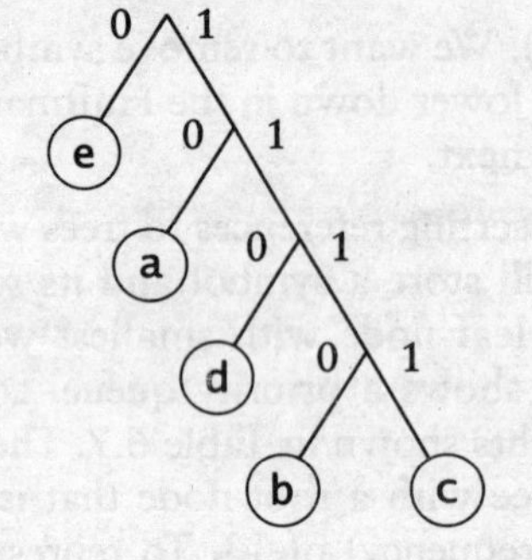

FIGURE 6.37
Huffman Tree of *a, b, c, d, e*

TABLE 6.8
Huffman Code for *a, b, c, d, e*

Symbol	Code
a	10
b	1110
c	1111
d	110
e	0

Design The class HuffData will represent the data to be stored in each node of the Huffman binary tree. For a leaf, a HuffData object will contain the symbol and the weight. Our class HuffmanTree will have the methods and attributes listed in Table 6.9.

Algorithm for Building a Huffman Tree

1. Construct a set of trees with root nodes that contain each of the individual symbols and their weights.
2. Place the set of trees into a priority queue.
3. **while** the priority queue has more than one item
4. Remove the two trees with the smallest weights.
5. Combine them into a new binary tree in which the weight of the tree root is the sum of the weights of its children.
6. Insert the newly created tree back into the priority queue.

Each time through the **while** loop, two nodes are removed from the priority queue and one is inserted. Thus, effectively one tree is removed, and the queue gets smaller with each pass through the loop.

TABLE 6.9
Data Fields and Methods of Class HuffmanTree

Data Field	Attribute
BinaryTree<HuffData> huffTree	A reference to the Huffman tree.
Method	**Behavior**
buildTree(HuffData[] input)	Builds the Huffman tree using the given alphabet and weights.
String decode(String message)	Decodes a message using the generated Huffman tree.
printCode(PrintStream out)	Outputs the resulting code.

Implementation Listing 6.9 shows the data field declarations for class HuffmanTree. The Comparator class and the methods are discussed in following subsections.

LISTING 6.9
Class HuffmanTree

```
import java.util.*;
import java.io.*;

/** Class to represent and build a Huffman tree. */
public class HuffmanTree implements Serializable {

    // Nested Classes
    /** A datum in the Huffman tree. */
    public static class HuffData implements Serializable {
        // Data Fields
        /** The weight or probability assigned to this HuffData. */
        private double weight;
        /** The alphabet symbol if this is a leaf. */
        private Character symbol;

        public HuffData(double weight, Character symbol) {
            this.weight = weight;
            this.symbol = symbol;
        }
    }

    // Data Fields
    /** A reference to the completed Huffman tree. */
    private BinaryTree<HuffData> huffTree;
```

The Comparator

Because the BinaryTree class does not implement Comparable, we need to define a Comparator for use with our PriorityQueue. The type parameter for interface Comparator indicates that the compare method will be comparing two BinaryTree<HuffData> objects, or two Huffman trees. It will compare the weights in the HuffData objects stored in the root node of each Huffman tree.

```
/** A Comparator for Huffman trees; nested class. */
private static class CompareHuffmanTrees
                implements Comparator<BinaryTree<HuffData>> {
    /** Compare two objects.
        @param treeLeft The left-hand object
        @param treeRight The right-hand object
        @return -1 if left less than right,
                0 if left equals right,
                and +1 if left greater than right
    */
```

```
        public int compare(BinaryTree<HuffData> treeLeft,
                           BinaryTree<HuffData> treeRight)
        {
            double wLeft = treeLeft.getData().weight;
            double wRight = treeRight.getData().weight;
            return Double.compare(wLeft, wRight);
        }
    }
```

The **buildTree** Method

Method buildTree (see Listing 6.10) takes an array of HuffData objects as its parameter. The statement

```
Queue<BinaryTree<HuffData>> theQueue
    = new PriorityQueue<BinaryTree<HuffData>>
      (symbols.length, new CompareHuffmanTrees());
```

creates a new priority queue for storing BinaryTree<HuffData> objects using the PriorityQueue class in the java.util API. This priority queue will use a CompareHuffmanTrees comparator.

The enhanced **for** loop loads the priority queue with trees consisting just of leaf nodes. Each leaf node contains a HuffData object with the weight and alphabet symbol.

The **while** loop builds the tree. Each time through this loop, the trees with the smallest weights are removed and referenced by left and right. The statements

```
HuffData sum = new HuffData(wl + wr, null);
BinaryTree<HuffData> newTree
    = new BinaryTree<HuffData>(sum, left, right);
```

combine them to form a new BinaryTree with a root node whose weight is the sum of the weights of its children. This new tree is then inserted into the priority queue. The number of trees in the queue decreases by 1 each time we do this. Eventually there will only be one tree in the queue, and that will be the completed Huffman tree. The last statement sets the variable huffTree to reference this tree.

LISTING 6.10
The buildTree Method (HuffmanTree.java)

```
/** Builds the Huffman tree using the given alphabet and weights.
    post:  huffTree contains a reference to the Huffman tree.
    @param symbols An array of HuffData objects
*/
public void buildTree(HuffData[] symbols) {
    Queue<BinaryTree<HuffData>> theQueue
          = new PriorityQueue<BinaryTree<HuffData>>
            (symbols.length, new CompareHuffmanTrees());
    // Load the queue with the leaves.
    for (HuffData nextSymbol : symbols) {
        BinaryTree<HuffData> aBinaryTree =
                new BinaryTree<HuffData>(nextSymbol, null, null);
```

```
        theQueue.offer(aBinaryTree);
    }

    // Build the tree.
    while (theQueue.size() > 1) {
        BinaryTree<HuffData> left = theQueue.poll();
        BinaryTree<HuffData> right = theQueue.poll();
        double wl = left.getData().weight;
        double wr = right.getData().weight;
        HuffData sum = new HuffData(wl + wr, null);
        BinaryTree<HuffData> newTree =
                new BinaryTree<HuffData>(sum, left, right);
        theQueue.offer(newTree);
    }

    // The queue should now contain only one item.
    huffTree = theQueue.poll();
}
```

Testing Methods printCode and decode can be used to test the custom Huffman tree. Method printCode displays the tree so you can examine it and verify that the Huffman tree that was built is correct based on the input data.

Method decode will decode a message that has been encoded using the code stored in the Huffman tree and displayed by printCode so you can pass it a message string that consists of binary digits only and see whether it can be transformed back to the original symbols.

We will discuss testing the Huffman tree further in the next chapter when we continue the case study.

The printCode Method

To display the code for each alphabet symbol, we perform a preorder traversal of the final tree. The code so far is passed as a parameter along with the current node. If the current node is a leaf, as indicated by the symbol not being **null**, then the code is output. Otherwise the left and right subtrees are traversed. When we traverse the left subtree, we append a 0 to the code, and when we traverse the right subtree, we append a 1 to the code. Recall that at each level in the recursion there is a new copy of the parameters and local variables.

```
/** Outputs the resulting code.
    @param out A PrintStream to write the output to
    @param code The code up to this node
    @param tree The current node in the tree
*/
private void printCode(PrintStream out, String code,
                       BinaryTree<HuffData> tree) {
    HuffData theData = tree.getData();
    if (theData.symbol != null) {
        if (theData.symbol.equals(" ")) {
            out.println("space: " + code);
```

```
            } else {
                out.println(theData.symbol + ": " + code);
            }
        } else {
            printCode(out, code + "0", tree.getLeftSubtree());
            printCode(out, code + "1", tree.getRightSubtree());
        }
    }
```

The **decode** Method

To illustrate the decode process, we will show a method that takes a `String` that contains a sequence of the digit characters `'0'` and `'1'` and decodes it into a message that is also a `String`. Method `decode` starts by setting `currentTree` to the Huffman tree. It then loops through the coded message one character at a time. If the character is a `'1'`, then `currentTree` is set to the right subtree; otherwise, it is set to the left subtree. If the `currentTree` is now a leaf, the symbol is appended to the result and `currentTree` is reset to the Huffman tree (see Listing 6.11). Note that this method is for testing purposes only. In actual usage, a message would be encoded as a string of bits (not digit characters) and would be decoded one bit at a time.

LISTING 6.11
The decode Method (`HuffmanTree.java`)

```
/** Method to decode a message that is input as a string of
    digit characters '0' and '1'.
    @param codedMessage The input message as a String of
                        zeros and ones.
    @return The decoded message as a String
*/
public String decode(String codedMessage) {
    StringBuilder result = new StringBuilder();
    BinaryTree<HuffData> currentTree = huffTree;
    for (int i = 0; i < codedMessage.length(); i++) {
        if (codedMessage.charAt(i) == '1') {
            currentTree = currentTree.getRightSubtree();
        } else {
            currentTree = currentTree.getLeftSubtree();
        }
        if (currentTree.isLeaf()) {
            HuffData theData = currentTree.getData();
            result.append(theData.symbol);
            currentTree = huffTree;
        }
    }
    return result.toString();
}
```

PROGRAM STYLE

A Generic HuffmanTree Class

We chose to implement a nongeneric HuffmanTree class to simplify the coding. However, it may be desirable to build a Huffman tree for storing Strings (e.g., to encode words in a document instead of the individual letters) or for storing groups of pixels in an image file. A generic HuffmanTree<T> class would define a generic inner class HuffData<T> where the T is the data type of data field symbol. Each parameter type <HuffData> in our class HuffmanTree would be replaced by <HuffData<T>>, which indicates that T is a type parameter for class HuffData.

EXERCISES FOR SECTION 6.6

SELF-CHECK

1. What is the Huffman code for the letters *a, j, k, l, s, t, v* using Figure 6.35?
2. Trace the execution of method printCode for the Huffman tree in Figure 6.37.
3. Trace the execution of method decode for the Huffman tree in Figure 6.37 and the encoded message string "11101011011001111".
4. Create the Huffman code tree for the following frequency table. Show the different states of the priority queue as the tree is built (see Figure 6.36).

Symbol	Frequency
*	50
+	30
–	25
/	10
%	5

5. What would the Huffman code look like if all symbols in the alphabet had equal frequency?

PROGRAMMING

1. Write a method encode for the HuffmanTree class that encodes a String of letters that is passed as its first argument. Assume that a second argument, codes (type String[]), contains the code strings (binary digits) for the symbols (space at position 0, *a* at position 1, *b* at position 2, etc.).

Chapter Review

- A tree is a recursive, nonlinear data structure that is used to represent data that is organized as a hierarchy.
- A binary tree is a collection of nodes with three components: a reference to a data object, a reference to a left subtree, and a reference to a right subtree. A binary tree object has a single data field, which references the root node of the tree.
- In a binary tree used to represent arithmetic expressions, the root node should store the operator that is evaluated last. All interior nodes store operators, and the leaf nodes store operands. An inorder traversal (traverse left subtree, visit root, traverse right subtree) of an expression tree yields an infix expression, a preorder traversal (visit root, traverse left subtree, traverse right subtree) yields a prefix expression, and a postorder traversal (traverse left subtree, traverse right subtree, visit root) yields a postfix expression.
- A binary search tree is a tree in which the data stored in the left subtree of every node is less than the data stored in the root node, and the data stored in the right subtree of every node is greater than the data stored in the root node. The performance depends on the fullness of the tree and can range from $O(n)$ (for trees that resemble linked lists) to $O(\log n)$ if the tree is full. An inorder traversal visits the nodes in increasing order.
- A heap is a complete binary tree in which the data in each node is less than the data in both its subtrees. A heap can be implemented very effectively as an array. The children of the node at subscript p are at subscripts $2p + 1$ and $2p + 2$. The parent of child c is at $(c - 1) / 2$. The item at the top of a heap is the smallest item.
- Insertion and removal in a heap are both $O(\log n)$. For this reason, a heap can be used to efficiently implement a priority queue. A priority queue is a data structure in which the item with the highest priority (indicated by the smallest value) is removed next. The item with the highest priority is at the top of a heap and is always removed next.
- A Huffman tree is a binary tree used to store a code that facilitates file compression. The length of the bit string corresponding to a symbol in the file is inversely proportional to its frequency, so the symbol with the highest frequency of occurrence has the shortest length. In building a Huffman tree, a priority queue is used to store the symbols and trees formed so far. Each step in building the Huffman tree consists of removing two items and forming a new tree with these two items as the left and right subtrees of the new tree's root node. A reference to each new tree is inserted in the priority queue.

Java API Interfaces and Classes Introduced in This Chapter

```
java.text.DecimalFormat        java.util.PriorityQueue
java.util.Comparator           java.util.TreeSet
```

User-Defined Interfaces and Classes in This Chapter

`BinarySearchTree`	`IndexGenerator`
`BinaryTree`	`KWPriorityQueue`
`CompareHuffmanTrees`	`Node`
`ComparePrintDocuments`	`PrintDocument`
`HuffData`	`PriorityQueue`
`HuffmanTree`	`SearchTree`

Quick-Check Exercises

1. For the following expression tree

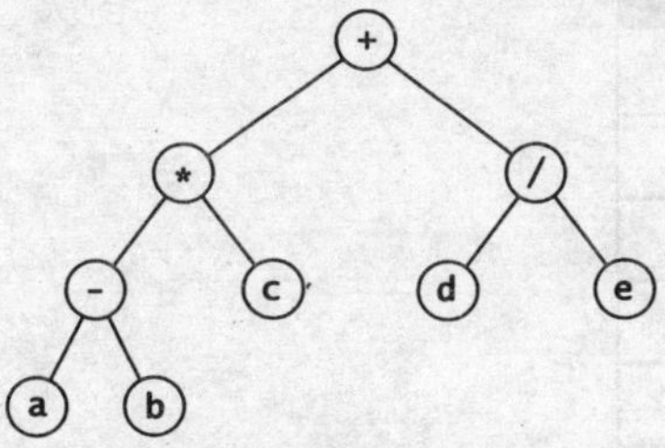

   a. Is the tree full? _____ Is the tree complete? _____
   b. List the order in which the nodes would be visited in a preorder traversal.
   c. List the order in which the nodes would be visited in an inorder traversal.
   d. List the order in which the nodes would be visited in a postorder traversal.
2. Searching a full binary search tree is O(___).
3. A heap is a binary tree that is a (full / complete) tree.
4. Show the binary search tree that would result from inserting the items 35, 20, 30, 50, 45, 60, 18, 25 in this sequence.
5. Show the binary search tree in Exercise 4 after 35 is removed.
6. Show the heap that would result from inserting the items from Exercise 4 in the order given.
7. Draw the heap from Exercise 6 as an array.
8. Show the heap in Exercise 7 after 18 is removed.
9. In a Huffman tree, the item with the highest frequency of occurrence will have the _____ code.
10. List the code for each symbol shown in the following Huffman tree.

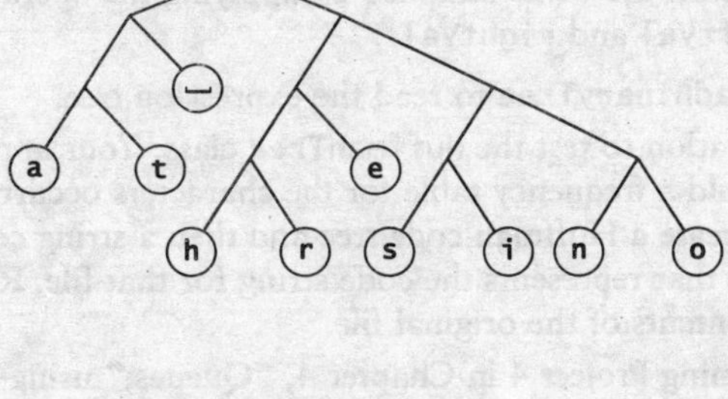

Review Questions

1. Draw the tree that would be formed by inserting the words in this question into a binary search tree. Use lowercase letters.
2. Show all three traversals of this tree.
3. Show the tree from Question 1 after removing *draw*, *by*, and *letters* in that order.
4. Answer Question 1, but store the words in a heap instead of a binary search tree.
5. Given the following frequency table, construct a Huffman code tree. Show the initial priority queue and all changes in its state as the tree is constructed.

Symbol	Frequency
x	34
y	28
w	20
a	10
b	8
c	5

Programming Projects

1. Assume that a class `ExpressionTree` has a data field that is a `BinaryTree`. Write an instance method to evaluate an expression stored in a binary tree whose nodes contain either integer values (stored in `Integer` objects) or operators (stored in `Character` objects). Your method should implement the following algorithm.

   ### Algorithm to Evaluate an Expression Tree

   1. `if` the root node is an `Integer` object
   2.   Return the integer value.
   3. `else if` the root node is a `Character` object
   4.   Let `leftVal` be the value obtained by recursively applying this algorithm to the left subtree.
   5.   Let `rightVal` be the value obtained by recursively applying this algorithm to the right subtree.
   6.   Return the value obtained by applying the operator in the root node to `leftVal` and `rightVal`.

   Use method `readBinaryTree` to read the expression tree.
2. Write an application to test the `HuffmanTree` class. Your application will need to read a text file and build a frequency table for the characters occurring in that file. Once that table is built, create a Huffman code tree and then a string consisting of `'0'` and `'1'` digit characters that represents the code string for that file. Read that string back in and re-create the contents of the original file.
3. Solve Programming Project 4 in Chapter 4, "Queues," using the class `PriorityQueue`.
4. Build a generic `HuffmanTree<T>` class such that the symbol type `T` is specified when the tree is created. Test this class by using it to encode the words in your favorite nursery rhyme.
5. Write `clone`, `size`, and `height` methods for the `BinaryTree` class.

6. In a breadth-first traversal of a binary tree, the nodes are visited in an order prescribed by their level. First visit the node at level 1, the root node. Then visit the nodes at level 2, in left-to-right order, and so on. You can use a queue to implement a breadth-first traversal of a binary tree.

Algorithm for Breadth-First Traversal of a Binary Tree

1. Insert the root node in the queue.
2. **while** the queue is not empty
3. Remove a node from the queue and visit it.
4. Place references to its left and right subtrees in the queue.

Code this algorithm and test it on several binary trees.

7. Define an `IndexTree` class such that each node has data fields to store a word, the count of occurrences of that word in a document file, and the line number for each occurrence. Use an `ArrayList` to store the line numbers. Use an `IndexTree` object to store an index of words appearing in a text file, and then display the index by performing an inorder traversal of this tree.

8. Extend the `BinaryTreeClass` to implement the `Iterable` interface by providing an iterator. The iterator should access the tree elements using an inorder traversal. The iterator is implemented as a nested private class. (Note: Unlike **Node**, this class should not be static.)

Design hints:

You will need a stack to hold the path from the current node back to the root. You will also need a reference to the current node (`current`) and a variable that stores the last item returned.

To initialize `current`, the constructor should start at the root and follow the left links until a node is reached that does not have a left child. This node is the initial current node.

The `remove` method can throw an `UnsupportedOperationException`. The **next** method should use the following algorithm:

1. Save the contents of the current node.
2. If the current node has a right child
3. push the current node onto the stack
4. set the current node to the right child
5. **while** the current node has a left child
6. push the current node onto the stack
7. set the current node to the left child
8. **else** the current node does not have a right child
9. **while** the stack is not empty and
   the top node of the stack's right child is equal to the current node
10. set the current node to the top of the stack and pop the stack
11. if the stack is empty
12. set the current node to null indicating that iteration is complete
13. else
14. set the current node to the top of the stack and pop the stack
15. return the saved contents of the initial current node

9. The Morse code (see Table 6.10) is a common code that is used to encode messages consisting of letters and digits. Each letter consists of a series of dots and dashes; for example, the code for the letter *a* is •– and the code for the letter *b* is –•••. Store each letter of the alphabet in a node of a binary tree of level 5. The root node is at level 1 and stores no letter. The left node at level 2 stores the letter *e* (code is •), and the right node stores the letter *t* (code is –). The 4 nodes at level 3 store the letters with codes (••, •–, –•, ––). To build the tree (see Figure 6.38), read a file in which each line consists of a letter followed by its code. The letters should be ordered by tree level. To find the position for a letter in the tree, scan the code and branch left for a dot and branch right for a dash. Encode a message by replacing each letter by its code symbol. Then decode the message using the Morse code tree. Make sure you use a delimiter symbol between coded letters.

TABLE 6.10
Morse Code for Letters

a	•–	b	–•••	c	–•–•	d	–••	e	•	f	••–•
g	––•	h	••••	i	••	j	•–––	k	–•–	l	•–••
m	––	n	–•	o	–––	p	•––•	q	––•–	r	•–•
s	•••	t	–	u	••–	v	•••–	w	•––	x	–••–
y	–•––	z	––••								

FIGURE 6.38
Morse Code Tree

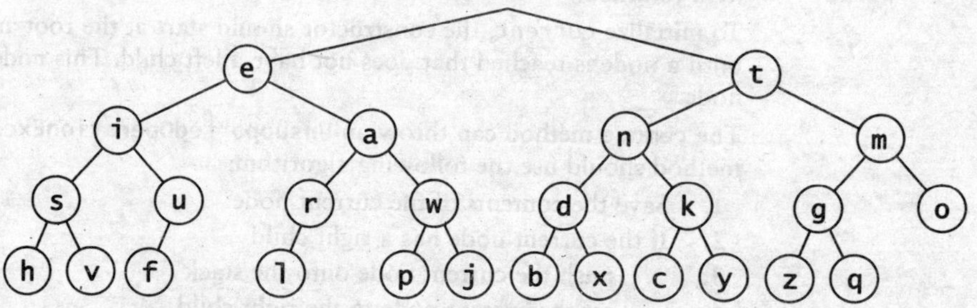

10. Create an abstract class `Heap` that has two subclasses, `MinHeap` and `MaxHeap`. Each subclass should have two constructors, one that takes no parameters and the other that takes a `Comparator` object. In the abstract class, the `compare` method should be abstract, and each subclass should define its own `compare` method to ensure that the ordering of elements corresponds to that required by the heap. For a `MinHeap`, the key in each node should be greater than the key of its parent; the ordering is reversed for a `MaxHeap`.

11. A right-threaded tree is a binary search tree in which each right link that would normally be null is a "thread" that links that node to its inorder successor. The thread enables nonrecursive algorithms to be written for search and inorder traversals that are more efficient than recursive ones. Implement a `RightThreadTree` class as an extension of a `BinarySearchTree`. You will also need an `RTNode` that extends the `Node` class to include a flag that indicates whether a node's right link is a real link or a thread.

Answers to Quick-Check Exercises

1. a. Not full, complete
   b. `+ * - a b c / d e`
   c. `a - b * c + d / e`
   d. `a b - c * d e / +`
2. O(log *n*)
3. A heap is a binary tree that is a *complete* tree.
4. 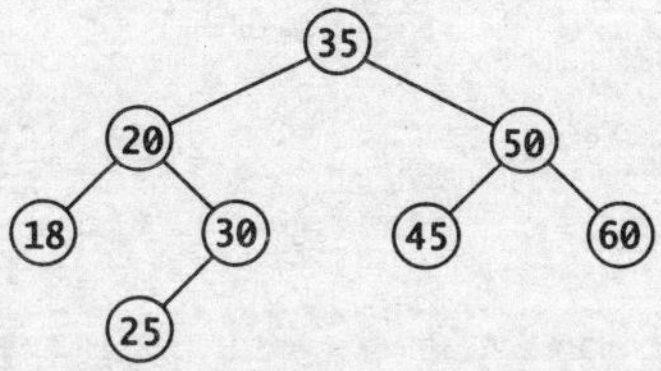

5. 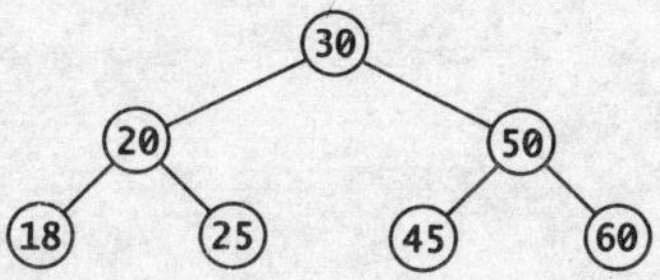

6. 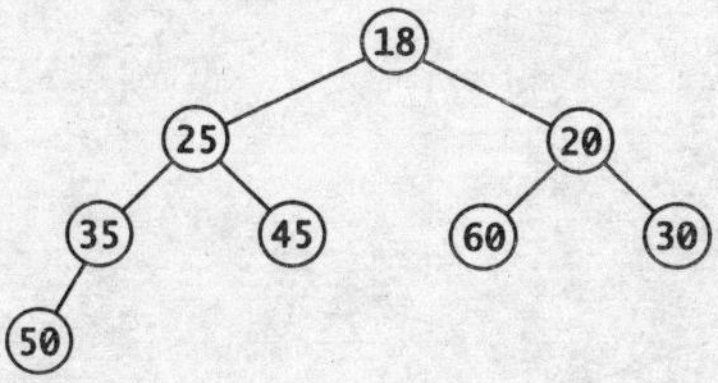

7. 18, 25, 20, 35, 45, 60, 30, 50, where 18 is at position 0 and 50 is at position 7.
8. 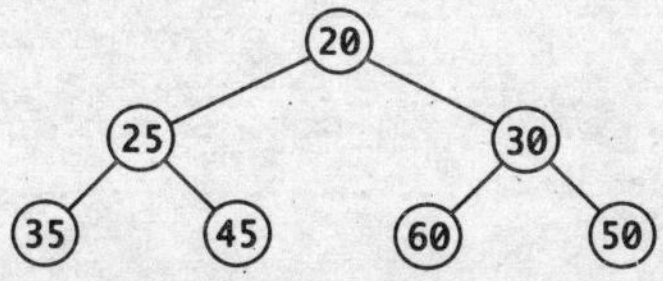

9. In a Huffman tree, the item with the highest frequency of occurrence will have the *shortest* code.
10.

Symbol	Code	Symbol	Code
Space	01	n	1110
a	000	o	1111
e	101	r	1001
h	1000	s	1100
i	1101	t	001

Chapter 7

Sets and Maps

Chapter Objectives

- To understand the Java Map and Set interfaces and how to use them
- To learn about hash coding and its use to facilitate efficient search and retrieval
- To study two forms of hash tables—open addressing and chaining—and to understand their relative benefits and performance trade-offs
- To learn how to implement both hash table forms
- To be introduced to the implementation of Maps and Sets
- To see how two earlier applications can be implemented more easily using Map objects for data storage

In Chapter 2, we introduced the Java Collections Framework, focusing on the `List` interface and the classes that implement it (`ArrayList` and `LinkedList`). The classes that implement the `List` interface are all indexed collections. That is, there is an index or a subscript associated with each member (element) of an object of these classes. Often an element's index reflects the relative order of its insertion in the `List` object. Searching for a particular value in a `List` object is generally an $O(n)$ process. The exception is a binary search of a sorted object, which is an $O(\log n)$ process.

In this chapter, we consider the other part of the `Collection` hierarchy: the `Set` interface and the classes that implement it. `Set` objects are not indexed, and the order of insertion of items is not known. Their main purpose is to enable efficient search and retrieval of information. It is also possible to remove elements from these collections without moving other elements around. By contrast, if an element is removed from the collection in an `ArrayList` object, the elements that follow it are normally shifted over to fill the vacated space.

A second, related interface is the Map. Map objects provide efficient search and retrieval of entries that consist of pairs of objects. The first object in each pair is the key (a unique value), and the second object is the information associated with that key. You retrieve an object from a Map by specifying its key.

We also study the hash table data structure. The hash table is a very important data structure that has been used very effectively in compilers and in building dictionaries. It can be used as the underlying data structure for a Map or Set implementation. It stores objects at arbitrary locations and offers an average constant time for insertion, removal, and searching.

We will see two ways to implement a hash table and how to use it as the basis for a class that implements the Map or Set. We will not show you the complete implementation of an object that implements Map or Set because we expect that you will use the ones provided by the Java API. However, we will certainly give you a head start on what you need to know to implement these interfaces.

Sets and Maps

7.1 Sets and the Set Interface

We introduced the Java Collections Framework in Chapter 2. We covered the part of that framework that focuses on the List interface and its implementers. In this section we explore the Set interface and its implementers.

Figure 7.1 shows the part of the Collections Framework that relates to sets. It includes interfaces Set, Sortedset, and Navigableset; abstract class AbstractSet; and actual classes HashSet, TreeSet, and ConcurrentSkipListSet. The HashSet is a set that is implemented using a hash table (discussed in Section 7.3). The TreeSet is implemented using a special kind of binary search tree, called the Red-Black tree (discussed in Chapter 9). The ConcurrentSkipListSet is implemented using a skip list (discussed in Chapter 9). In Section 6.4, we showed how to use a TreeSet to store an index for a term paper.

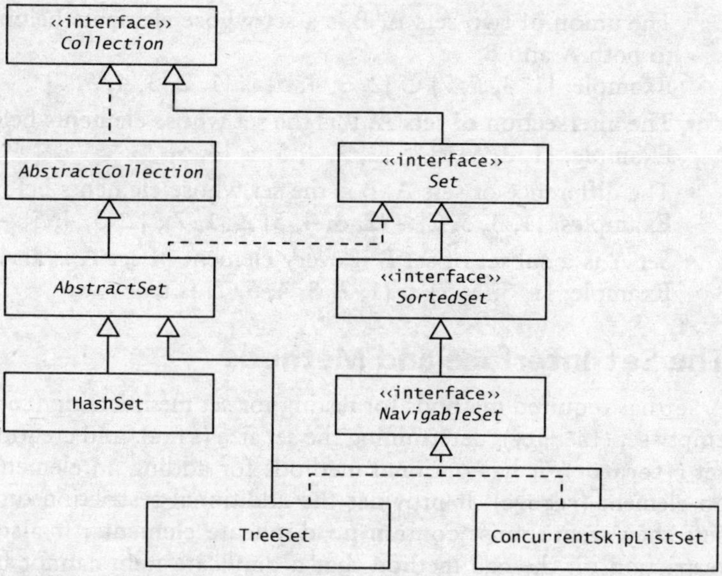

FIGURE 7.1
The Set Hierarchy

The Set Abstraction

The Java API documentation for the interface `java.util.Set` describes the `Set` as follows:

> A collection that contains no duplicate elements. More formally, sets contain no pair of elements `e1` and `e2` such that `e1.equals(e2)`, and at most one `null` element. As implied by its name, this interface models the mathematical *set* abstraction.

What mathematicians call a *set* can be thought of as a collection of objects. There is the additional requirement that the elements contained in the set are unique. For example, if we have the set of fruits {`"apples"`, `"oranges"`, and `"pineapples"`} and add `"apples"` to it, we still have the same set. Also, we usually want to know whether or not a particular object is a member of the set rather than where in the set it is located. Thus, if `s` is a set, we would be interested in the expression

```
s.contains("apples")
```

which returns the value **`true`** if `"apples"` is in set `s` and **`false`** if it is not. We would have no need to use a method such as

```
s.indexOf("apples")
```

which might return the location or position of `"apples"` in set `s`. Nor would we have a need to use the expression

```
s.get(i)
```

where `i` is the position (index) of an object in set `s`.

We assume that you are familiar with sets from a course in discrete mathematics. Just as a review, however, the operations that are performed on a mathematical set are testing for membership (method `contains`), adding elements, and removing elements. Other common operations on a mathematical set are *set union* ($A \cup B$), *set intersection* ($A \cap B$), and *set difference* ($A - B$). There is also a *subset operator* ($A \subset B$). These operations are defined as follows:

- The union of two sets A, B is a set whose elements belong either to A or B or to both A and B.
  Example: $\{1, 3, 5, 7\} \cup \{2, 3, 4, 5\}$ is $\{1, 2, 3, 4, 5, 7\}$
- The intersection of sets A, B is the set whose elements belong to both A and B.
  Example: $\{1, 3, 5, 7\} \cap \{2, 3, 4, 5\}$ is $\{3, 5\}$
- The difference of sets A, B is the set whose elements belong to A but not to B.
  Examples: $\{1, 3, 5, 7\} - \{2, 3, 4, 5\}$ is $\{1, 7\}$; $\{2, 3, 4, 5\} - \{1, 3, 5, 7\}$ is $\{2, 4\}$
- Set A is a subset of set B if every element of set A is also an element of set B.
  Example: $\{1, 3, 5, 7\} \subset \{1, 2, 3, 4, 5, 7\}$ is true

The Set Interface and Methods

A `Set` has required methods for testing for set membership (`contains`), testing for an empty set (`isEmpty`), determining the set size (`size`), and creating an iterator over the set (`iterator`). It has optional methods for adding an element (`add`) and removing an element (`remove`). It provides the additional restriction on constructors that all sets they create must contain no duplicate elements. It also puts the additional restriction on the `add` method that a duplicate item cannot be inserted. Table 7.1 shows the commonly used methods of the `Set` interface. The `Set` interface also has

TABLE 7.1
Some `java.util.Set<E>` Methods (with Mathematical Set Operations in Italics)

Method	Behavior
`boolean add(E obj)`	Adds item `obj` to this set if it is not already present (optional operation) and returns **`true`**. Returns false if `obj` is already in the set.
`boolean addAll(Collection<E> coll)`	Adds all of the elements in collection `coll` to this set if they're not already present (optional operation). Returns **`true`** if the set is changed. Implements *set union* if `coll` is a `Set`.
`boolean contains(Object obj)`	Returns **`true`** if this set contains an element that is equal to `obj`. Implements a test for *set membership*.
`boolean containsAll(Collection<E> coll)`	Returns **`true`** if this set contains all of the elements of collection `coll`. If `coll` is a set, returns **`true`** if this set is a subset of `coll`.
`boolean isEmpty()`	Returns **`true`** if this set contains no elements.
`Iterator<E> iterator()`	Returns an iterator over the elements in this set.
`boolean remove(Object obj)`	Removes the set element equal to `obj` if it is present (optional operation). Returns **`true`** if the object was removed.
`boolean removeAll(Collection<E> coll)`	Removes from this set all of its elements that are contained in collection `coll` (optional operation). Returns **`true`** if this set is changed. If `coll` is a set, performs the *set difference* operation.
`boolean retainAll(Collection<E> coll)`	Retains only the elements in this set that are contained in collection `coll` (optional operation). Returns **`true`** if this set is changed. If `coll` is a set, performs the *set intersection* operation.
`int size()`	Returns the number of elements in this set (its cardinality).

methods that support the mathematical set operations. The required method `containsAll` tests the subset relationship. There are optional methods for set union (`addAll`), set intersection (`retainAll`), and set difference (`removeAll`). We show the methods that are used to implement the mathematical set operations in italics in Table 7.1.

Calling a method "optional" means just that: An implementer of the `Set` interface is not required to provide it. However, a method that matches the signature must be provided. This method should throw the `UnsupportedOperationException` whenever it is called. This gives the class designer some flexibility. For example, if a class instance is intended to provide efficient search and retrieval of the items stored, the class designer may decide to omit the optional mathematical set operations.

EXAMPLE 7.1 Listing 7.1 contains a `main` method that creates three sets: `setA`, `setAcopy`, and `setB`. It loads these sets from two arrays and then forms their union in `setA` and their intersection in `setAcopy`, using the statements

```
setA.addAll(setB);          // Set union
setAcopy.retainAll(setB);   // Set intersection
```

Running this method generates the output lines below. The brackets and commas are inserted by method `toString`.

```
The 2 sets are:
[Jill, Ann, Sally]
[Bill, Jill, Ann, Bob]
Items in set union are: [Bill, Jill, Ann, Sally, Bob]
Items in set intersection are: [Jill, Ann]
```

LISTING 7.1

Illustrating the Use of Sets

```
public static void main(String[] args) {

    // Create the sets.
    String[] listA = {"Ann", "Sally", "Jill", "Sally"};
    String[] listB = {"Bob", "Bill", "Ann", "Jill"};
    Set<String> setA = new HashSet<String>();
    Set<String> setAcopy = new HashSet<String>();  // Copy of setA
    Set<String> setB = new HashSet<String>();

    // Load sets from arrays.
    for (int i = 0; i < listA.length; i++) {
        setA.add(listA[i]);
        setAcopy.add(listA[i]);
    }

    for (int i = 0; i < listB.length; i++) {
        setB.add(listB[i]);
    }
    System.out.println("The 2 sets are: " + "\n" + setA
                       + "\n" + setB);
```

```
    // Display the union and intersection.
    setA.addAll(setB);           // Set union
    setAcopy.retainAll(setB);    // Set intersection
    System.out.println("Items in set union are: " + setA);
    System.out.println("Items in set intersection are: "
                       + setAcopy);
}
```

Comparison of Lists and Sets

Collections implementing the `Set` interface must contain unique elements. Unlike the `List.add` method, the `Set.add` method will return **`false`** if you attempt to insert a duplicate item.

Unlike a `List`, a `Set` does not have a `get` method. Therefore, elements cannot be accessed by index. So if `setA` is a `Set` object, the method call `setA.get(0)` would cause the syntax error `method get(int) not found`.

Although you can't reference a specific element of a `Set`, you can iterate through all its elements using an `Iterator` object. The loop below accesses each element of `Set` object `setA`. However, the elements will be accessed in arbitrary order. This means that they will not necessarily be accessed in the order in which they were inserted.

```
// Create an iterator to setA.
Iterator<String> setAIter = setA.iterator();
while (setAIter.hasNext()) {
    String nextItem = setAIter.next();
    // Do something with nextItem
    . . .
}
```

We can simplify the task of accessing each element in a `Set` using the Java 5.0 enhanced **`for`** statement.

```
for (String nextItem : setA) {
    // Do something with nextItem
    . . .
}
```

EXERCISES FOR SECTION 7.1

SELF-CHECK

1. Explain the effect of the following method calls.

```
Set<String> s = new HashSet<String>();
s.add("hello");
s.add("bye");
s.addAll(s);
Set<String> t = new TreeSet<String>();
t.add("123");
s.addAll(t);
System.out.println(s.containsAll(t));
System.out.println(t.containsAll(s));
```

```
System.out.println(s.contains("ace"));
System.out.println(s.contains("123"));
s.retainAll(t);
System.out.println(s.contains("123"));
t.retainAll(s);
System.out.println(t.contains("123"));
```

2. What is the relationship between the `Set` interface and the `Collection` interface?
3. What are the differences between the `Set` interface and the `List` interface?
4. In Example 9.1, why is `setAcopy` needed? What would happen if you used the statement

   ```
   setAcopy = setA;
   ```

   to define `setAcopy`?

PROGRAMMING

1. Assume you have declared three sets `a`, `b`, and `c` and that sets `a` and `b` store objects. Write statements that use methods from the `Set` interface to perform the following operations:

   a. `c = (a ∪ b)`

   b. `c = (a ∩ b)`

   c. `c = (a – b)`

   d.
   ```
   if (a ⊂ b)
       c = a;
   else
       c = b;
   ```
2. Write a `toString` method for a class that implements the `Set` interface and displays the set elements in the form shown in Example 9.1.

7.2 Maps and the Map Interface

The `Map` is related to the `Set`. Mathematically, a `Map` is a set of ordered pairs whose elements are known as the key and the value. The key is required to be unique, as are the elements of a set, but the value is not necessarily unique. For example, the following would be a map:

{(J, Jane), (B, Bill), (S, Sam), (B1, Bob), (B2, Bill)}

The keys in this example are strings consisting of one or two characters, and each value is a person's name. The keys are unique but not the values (there are two Bills). The key is based on the first letter of the person's name. The keys **B1** and **B2** are the keys for the second and third person whose name begins with the letter B.

You can think of each key as "mapping" to a particular value (hence the name *map*). For example, the key J maps to the value Jane. The keys B and B2 map to the value Bill. You can also think of the keys as forming a set (keySet) and the values as

FIGURE 7.2
Example of Mapping

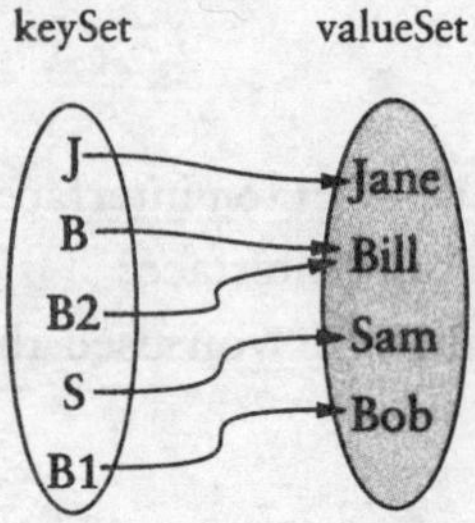

forming a set (valueSet). Each element of keySet maps to a particular element of valueSet, as shown in Figure 7.2. In mathematical set terminology, this is a *many-to-one mapping* (i.e., more than one element of keySet may map to a particular element of valueSet). For example, both keys **B** and **B2** map to the value Bill. This is also an *onto mapping* in that all elements of valueSet have a corresponding member in keySet.

A `Map` can be used to enable efficient storage and retrieval of information in a table. The key is a unique identification value associated with each item stored in a table. As you will see, each key value has an easily computed numeric code value.

EXAMPLE 7.2

When information about an item is stored in a table, the information stored may consist of a unique ID (identification code, which may or may not be a number) as well as descriptive data. The unique ID would be the key, and the rest of the information would represent the value associated with that key. Some examples follow.

Type of Item	Key	Value
University student	Student ID number	Student name, address, major, grade-point average
Customer for online store	E-mail address	Customer name, address, credit card information, shopping cart
Inventory item	Part ID	Description, quantity, manufacturer, cost, price

In the above examples, the student ID number may be assigned by the university, or it may be the student's social security number. The e-mail address is a unique address for each customer, but it is not numeric. Similarly, a part ID could consist of a combination of letters and digits.

In comparing maps to indexed collections, you can think of the keys as selecting the elements of a map, just as indexes select elements in a `List` object. The keys for a map, however, can have arbitrary values (not restricted to 0, 1, etc., as for indexes). As you will see later, an implementation of the `Map` interface should have methods of the form

```
V get(Object key)
V put(K key, V value)
```

The `get` method retrieves the value corresponding to a specified key; the `put` method stores a key-value pair in a map.

The Map Hierarchy

Figure 7.3 shows part of the `Map` hierarchy in the Java API. Although not strictly part of the `Collection` hierarchy, the `Map` interface defines a structure that relates elements in one set to elements in another set. The first set, called the *keys*, must implement the `Set` interface; that is, the *keys* are unique. The second set is not strictly a `Set` but an arbitrary `Collection` known as the *values*. These are not

FIGURE 7.3
The Map Hierarchy

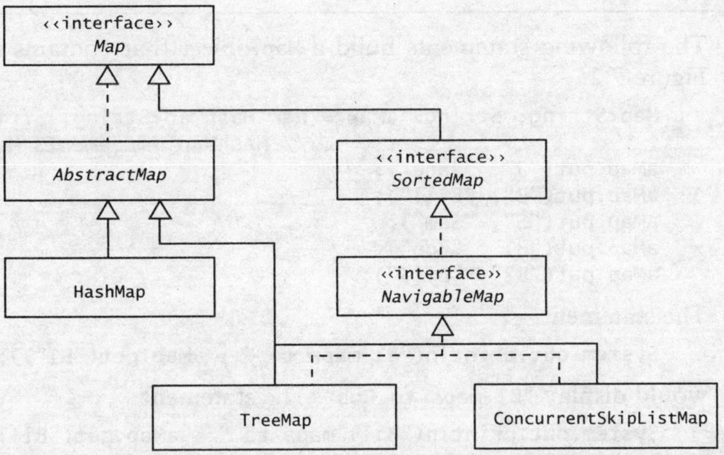

required to be unique. The `Map` is a more useful structure than the `Set`. In fact, the Java API implements the `Set` using a `Map`.

The `TreeMap` uses a Red-Black binary search tree (discussed in Chapter 9) as its underlying data structure, and the `ConcurrentSkipListMap` uses a skip list (also discussed in Chapter 9) as its underlying data structure. We will focus on the `HashMap` and show how to implement it later in the chapter.

The Map Interface

Methods of the `Map` interface (in Java API `java.util`) are shown in Table 7.2. The `put` method either inserts a new mapping or changes the value associated with an existing mapping. The `get` method returns the current value associated with a given key. The `remove` method deletes an existing mapping. Both `put` and `remove` return the previous value (or **`null`**, if there was none) of the mapping that is changed or deleted. There are two type parameters, `K` and `V`, and they represent the data type of the key and value, respectively.

TABLE 7.2
Some `java.util.Map<K, V>` Methods

Method	Behavior
`V get(Object key)`	Returns the value associated with the specified `key`. Returns **`null`** if the key is not present.
`boolean isEmpty()`	Returns **`true`** if this map contains no `key-value` mappings.
`V put(K key, V value)`	Associates the specified `value` with the specified `key` in this map (optional operation). Returns the previous `value` associated with the specified `key`, or **`null`** if there was no mapping for the `key`.
`V remove(Object key)`	Removes the mapping for this `key` from this map if it is present (optional operation). Returns the previous `value` associated with the specified `key`, or **`null`** if there was no mapping for the `key`.
`int size()`	Returns the number of `key-value` mappings in this map.

EXAMPLE 7.3 The following statements build a `Map` object that contains the mapping shown in Figure 7.2.

```
Map<String, String> aMap = new HashMap<String, String>();
                                  // HashMap implements Map
aMap.put("J", "Jane");
aMap.put("B", "Bill");
aMap.put("S", "Sam");
aMap.put("B1", "Bob");
aMap.put("B2", "Bill");
```

The statement

```
System.out.println("B1 maps to " + aMap.get("B1"));
```

would display `"B1 maps to Bob"`. The statement

```
System.out.println("Bill maps to " + aMap.get("Bill"));
```

would display `"Bill maps to null"` because `"Bill"` is a value, not a key.

EXAMPLE 7.4 In Section 6.4, we used a binary search tree to store an index of words occurring in a term paper. Each data element in the tree was a string consisting of a word followed by a three-digit line number.

Although this is one approach to storing an index, it would be more useful to store each word and all the line numbers for that word as a single index entry. We could do this by storing the index in a `Map` in which each word is a key and its associated value is a list of all the line numbers at which the word occurs. While building the index, each time a word is encountered, its list of line numbers would be retrieved (using the word as a key) and the most recent line number would be appended to this list (an `ArrayList<Integer>`). For example, if the word *fire* has already occurred on lines 4 and 8 and we encounter it again on line 20, the `ArrayList<Integer>` associated with *fire* would reference three `Integer` objects wrapping the numbers 4, 8, and 20.

Listing 7.2 shows method `buildIndex` (adapted from `buildIndex` in Listing 6.7). Data field index is a `Map` with key type `String` and value type `ArrayList<Integer>`.

```
private Map<String, ArrayList<Integer>> index;
```

The statement

```
ArrayList<Integer> lines = index.get(token);
```

retrieves the value (an `ArrayList<Integer>` or **`null`**) associated with the next `token`. The **`if`** statement sets `lines` to an empty `ArrayList` if this is the first occurrence of `token` (`lines` is **`null`**). The statements

```
lines.add(lineNum);
index.put(token, lines);                // Store the list.
```

add the new line number to the `ArrayList` and store it back in the `Map`. In Section 7.5, we show how to display the final index.

LISTING 7.2
Method `buildIndexAllLines`

```
/** Reads each word in a data file and stores it in an index
    along with a list of line numbers where it occurs.
    post: Lowercase form of each word with its line
          number is stored in the index.
    @param scan A Scanner object
*/
public void buildIndex(Scanner scan) {
    int lineNum = 0;      // Line number

    // Keep reading lines until done.
    while (scan.hasNextLine()) {
        lineNum++;

        // Extract each token and store it in index.
        String token;
        while ((token = scan.findInLine("[\\P{L}\\P{N}']+"))  != null) {
            token = token.toLowerCase();
            // Get the list of line numbers for token
            ArrayList<Integer> lines = index.get(token);
            if (lines == null) {
                lines = new ArrayList<Integer>();
            }
            lines.add(lineNum);
            index.put(token, lines);    // Store new list of line numbers
        }
        Scan.nextline();    // Clear the scan buffer
    }
}
```

EXERCISES FOR SECTION 7.2

SELF-CHECK

1. If you were using a `Map` to store the following lists of items, which data field would you select as the key, and why?
   a. textbook title, author, ISBN (International Standard Book Number), year, publisher
   b. player's name, uniform number, team, position
   c. computer manufacturer, model number, processor, memory, disk size
   d. department, course title, course ID, section number, days, time, room
2. For the `Map index` in Example 7.4, what key-value pairs would be stored for each token in the following data file?
   ```
   this line is first
   and line 2 is second
   followed by the third line
   ```
3. Explain the effect of each statement in the following fragment on the index built in Self-Check Exercise 2.

```
lines = index.get("this");
lines = index.get("that");
lines = index.get("line");
lines.add(4);
index.put("is", lines);
```

PROGRAMMING

1. Write statements to create a `Map` object that will store each word occurring in a term paper along with the number of times the word occurs.
2. Write a method `buildWordCounts` (based on `buildIndex`) that builds the `Map` object described in Programming Exercise 1.

7.3 Hash Tables

Before we discuss the details of implementing the required methods of the `Set` and `Map` interfaces, we will describe a data structure, the *hash table*, that can be used as the basis for such an implementation. The goal behind the hash table is to be able to access an entry based on its key value, not its location. In other words, we want to be able to access an element directly through its key value rather than having to determine its location first by searching for the key value in an array. (This is why the `Set` interface has method `contains(obj)` instead of `get(index)`.) Using a hash table enables us to retrieve an item in constant time (expected O(1)). We say expected O(1) rather than just O(1) because there will be some cases where the performance will be much worse than O(1) and may even be O(n), but on the average, we expect that it will be O(1). Contrast this with the time required for a linear search of an array, O(n), and the time to access an element in a binary search tree, O(log n).

Hash Codes and Index Calculation

The basis of hashing (and hash tables) is to transform the item's key value to an integer value (its *hash code*) that will then be transformed into a table index. Figure 7.4 illustrates this process for a table of size n. We discuss how this might be done in the next few examples.

EXAMPLE 7.5 Consider the Huffman code problem discussed in Section 6.6. To build the Huffman tree, you needed to know the number of occurrences of each character in the text being encoded. Let's assume that the text contained only the ASCII characters (the first 128 Unicode values starting with `\u0000`). We could use a table of size 128, one element for each possible character, and let the Unicode for each character be its location in the table. Using this approach, table element 65 would give us the number of occurrences of the letter A, table element 66 would give us the number of occurrences of the letter B, and so on. The hash code for each character is its Unicode value (a number), which is also its index in the table. In this case, we could calculate the table index for character `asciiChar` using the following assignment statement, where `asciiChar` represents the character we are seeking in the table:

```
int index = asciiChar;
```

FIGURE 7.4
Index Calculation for a Key

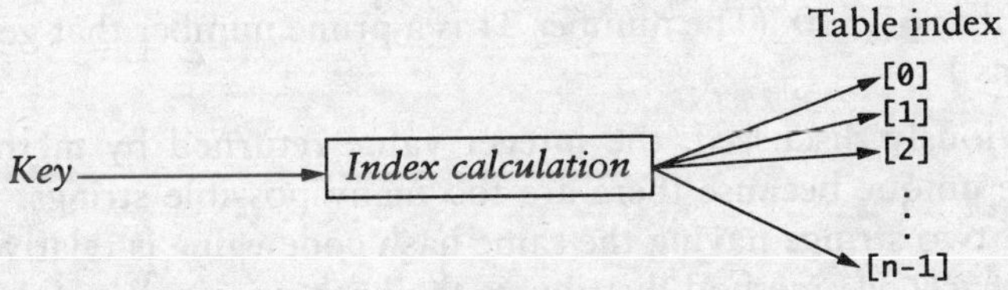

EXAMPLE 7.6 Let's consider a slightly harder problem: Assume that any of the Unicode characters can occur in the text, and we want to know the number of occurrences of each character. There are over 65,000 Unicode characters, however. For any file, let's assume that at most 100 different characters actually appear. So, rather than use a table with 65,536 elements, it would make sense to try to store these items in a much smaller table (say, 200 elements). If the hash code for each character is its Unicode value, we need to convert this value (between 0 and 65,536) to an array index between 0 and 199. We can calculate the array index for character `uniChar` as:

```
int index = uniChar % 200
```

Because the range of Unicode values (the key range) is much larger than the `index` range, it is likely that some characters in our text will have the same index value. Because we can store only one key-value pair in a given array element, a situation known as a *collision* results. We discuss how to deal with collisions shortly.

Methods for Generating Hash Codes

In most applications, the keys that we will want to store in a table will consist of strings of letters or digits rather than a single character (e.g., a social security number, a person's name, or a part ID). We need a way to map each string to a particular table index. Again, we have a situation in which the number of possible key values is much larger than the table size. For example, if a string can store up to 10 letters or digits, the number of possible strings is 36^{10} (approximately 3.7×10^{15}), assuming the English alphabet with 26 letters.

Generating good hash codes for arbitrary strings or arbitrary objects is somewhat of an experimental process. Simple algorithms tend to generate a lot of collisions. For example, simply summing the **`int`** values for all characters in a string would generate the same hash code for words that contained the same letters but in different orders, such as "sign" and "sing", which would have the same hash code using this algorithm (`'s' + 'i' + 'n' + 'g'`). The algorithm used by the Java API accounts for the position of the characters in the string as well as the character values.

The `String.hashCode()` method returns the integer calculated by the formula

$$s_0 \times 31^{(n-1)} + s_1 \times 31^{(n-2)} + \cdots + s_{n-1}$$

where s_i is the *i*th character of the string, and `n` is the length of the string. For example, the string `"Cat"` would have a hash code of `'C'` $\times\ 31^2 +$ `'a'` $\times\ 31 +$ `'t'`. This is the number 67,510. (The number 31 is a prime number that generates relatively few collisions.)

As previously discussed, the integer value returned by method `String.hashCode` can't be unique because there are too many possible strings. However, the probability of two strings having the same hash code value is relatively small because the `String.hashCode` method distributes the hash code values fairly evenly throughout the range of `int` values.

Because the hash codes are distributed evenly throughout the range of `int` values, method `String.hashCode` will appear to produce a random value, as will the expressions `s.hashCode() % table.length`, which selects the initial value of `index` for `String s`. If the object is not already present in the table, the probability that this expression does not yield an empty slot in the table is proportional to how full the table is.

One additional criterion for a good hash function, besides a random distribution for its values, is that it be relatively simple and efficient to compute. It doesn't make much sense to use a hash function whose computation is an O(n) process to avoid doing an O(n) search.

Open Addressing

Next we consider two ways to organize hash tables: open addressing and chaining. In open addressing, each hash table element (type `Object`) references a single key-value pair. We can use the following simple approach (called *linear probing*) to access an item in a hash table. If the index calculated for an item's key is occupied by an item with that key, we have found the item. If that element contains an item with a different key, we increment the index by one. We keep incrementing the index (modulo the table length) until either we find the key we are seeking or we reach a `null` entry. A `null` entry indicates that the key is not in the table.

Algorithm for Accessing an Item in a Hash Table

1. Compute the index by taking the item's `hashCode() % table.length`.
2. **if** `table[index]` is `null`
3. The item is not in the table.
4. **else if** `table[index]` is equal to the item
5. The item is in the table.
   else
6. Continue to search the table by incrementing the index until either the item is found or a `null` entry is found.

Step 1 ensures that the `index` is within the table range (0 through `table.length – 1`). If the condition in Step 2 is true, the table index does not reference an object, so the item is not in the table. The condition in Step 4 is true if the item being sought is at position `index`, in which case the item is located. Steps 1 through 5 can be done in O(1) expected time.

Step 6 is necessary for two reasons. The values returned by method `hashCode` are not unique, so the item being sought can have the same hash code as another one in the table. Also, the remainder calculated in Step 1 can yield the same index for different hash code values. Both of these cases are examples of collisions.

Table Wraparound and Search Termination

Notice that as you increment the table index, your table should wrap around (as in a circular array), so that the element with subscript 0 "follows" the element with subscript `table.length - 1`. This enables you to use the entire table, not just the part with subscripts larger than the hash code value, but it leads to the potential for an infinite loop in Step 6 of the algorithm. If the table is full and the objects examined so far do not match the one you are seeking, how do you know when to stop? One approach would be to stop when the index value for the next probe is the same as the hash code value for the object. This means that you have come full circle to the starting value for the index. A second approach would be to ensure that the table is never full by increasing its size after an insertion if its occupancy rate exceeds a specified threshold. This is the approach that we take in our implementation.

EXAMPLE 7.7 We illustrate insertion of five names in a table of size 5 and in a table of size 11. Table 7.3 shows the names, the corresponding hash code, the hash code modulo 5 (in column 3), and the hash code modulo 11 (in column 4). We picked prime numbers (5 and 11) because empirical tests have shown that hash tables with a size that is a prime number often give better results.

For a table of size 5 (an occupancy rate of 100 percent), `"Tom"`, `"Dick"`, and `"Sam"` have hash indexes of 4, and `"Harry"` and `"Pete"` have hash indexes of 3; for a table length of 11 (an occupancy rate of 45 percent), `"Dick"` and `"Sam"` have hash indexes of 5, but the others have hash indexes that are unique. We see how the insertion process works next.

For a table of size 5, if `"Tom"` and `"Dick"` are the first two entries, `"Tom"` would be stored at the element with index 4, the last element in the table. Consequently, when `"Dick"` is inserted, because element 4 is already occupied, the hash index is incremented to 0 (the table wraps around to the beginning), where `"Dick"` is stored.

TABLE 7.3
Names and `hashCode` Values for Table Sizes 5 and 11

Name	hashCode()	hashCode()%5	hashCode()%11
"Tom"	84274	4	3
"Dick"	2129869	4	5
"Harry"	69496448	3	10
"Sam"	82879	4	5
"Pete"	2484038	3	7

[0]	"Dick"
[1]	null
[2]	null
[3]	null
[4]	"Tom"

"Harry" is stored in position 3 (the hash index), and "Sam" is stored in position 1 because its hash index is 4 but the elements at 4 and 0 are already filled.

[0]	"Dick"
[1]	"Sam"
[2]	null
[3]	"Harry"
[4]	"Tom"

Finally, "Pete" is stored in position 2 because its hash index is 3 but the elements at positions 3, 4, 0, 1 are filled.

[0]	"Dick"
[1]	"Sam"
[2]	"Pete"
[3]	"Harry"
[4]	"Tom"

For the table of size 11, the entries would be stored as shown in the following table, assuming that they were inserted in the order "Tom", "Dick", "Harry", "Sam", and finally "Pete". Insertions go more smoothly for the table of size 11. The first collision occurs when "Sam" is stored, so "Sam" is stored at position 6 instead of position 5.

[0]	null
[1]	null
[2]	null
[3]	"Tom"
[4]	null
[5]	"Dick"
[6]	"Sam"
[7]	"Pete"
[8]	null
[9]	null
[10]	"Harry"

For the table of size 5, retrieval of "Tom" can be done in one step. Retrieval of all of the others would require a linear search because of collisions that occurred when they were inserted. For the table of size 11, retrieval of all but "Sam" can be done in one step, and retrieval of "Sam" requires only two steps. This example illustrates that the best way to reduce the probability of a collision is to increase the table size.

Traversing a Hash Table

One thing that you cannot do is traverse a hash table in a meaningful way. If you visit the hash table elements in sequence and display the objects stored, you would display the strings "Dick", "Sam", "Pete", "Harry", "Tom" for the table of length 5 and the strings "Tom", "Dick", "Sam", "Pete", "Harry" for a table of length 11. In either case, the list of names is in arbitrary order.

Deleting an Item Using Open Addressing

When an item is deleted, we cannot just set its table entry to `null`. If we do, then when we search for an item that may have collided with the deleted item, we may incorrectly conclude that the item is not in the table. (Because the item that collided was inserted after the deleted item, we will have stopped our search prematurely.) By storing a dummy value when an item is deleted, we force the search algorithm to keep looking until either the desired item is found or a `null` value, representing a free cell, is located.

Although the use of a dummy value solves the problem, keep in mind that it can lead to search inefficiency, particularly when there are many deletions. Removing items from the table does not reduce the search time because the dummy value is still in the table and is part of a search chain. In fact, you cannot even replace a deleted value with a new item because you still need to go to the end of the search chain to ensure that the new item is not already present in the table. So deleted items waste storage space and reduce search efficiency. In the worst case, if the table is almost full and then most of the items are deleted, you will have $O(n)$ performance when searching for the few items remaining in the table.

Reducing Collisions by Expanding the Table Size

Even with a good hashing function, it is still possible to have collisions. The first step in reducing these collisions is to use a prime number for the size of the table. In addition, the probability of a collision is proportional to how full the table is. Therefore, when the hash table becomes sufficiently full, a larger table should be allocated and the entries reinserted.

We previously saw examples of expanding the size of an array. Generally, what we did was to allocate a new array with twice the capacity of the original, copy the values in the original array to the new array, and then reference the new array instead of the original. This approach will not work with hash tables. If you use it, some search chains will be broken because the new table does not wrap around in the same way as the original table. The last element in the original table will be in the middle of the new table, and it does not wrap around to the first element of the new table. Therefore, you expand a hash table (called *rehashing*) using the following algorithm.

Algorithm for Rehashing

1. Allocate a new hash table with twice the capacity of the original.
2. Reinsert each old table entry that has not been deleted into the new hash table.
3. Reference the new table instead of the original.

Step 2 reinserts each item from the old table into the new table instead of copying it over to the same location. We illustrate this in the hash table implementation. Notice that deleted items are not reinserted into the new table, thereby saving space and reducing the length of some search chains.

FIGURE 7.5
Clustering with Linear Probing

[0]	
[1]	
[2]	
[3]	
[4]	
[5]	1st item with hash code 5
[6]	1st item with hash code 6
[7]	2nd item with hash code 5
[8]	2nd item with hash code 6
[9]	1st item with hash code 7
[10]	

Reducing Collisions Using Quadratic Probing

The problem with linear probing is that it tends to form clusters of keys in the table, causing longer search chains. For example, if the table already has keys with hash codes of 5 and 6, a new item that collides with either of these keys will be placed at index 7. An item that collides with any of these three items will be placed at index 8, and so on. Figure 7.5 shows a hash table of size 11 after inserting elements with hash codes in the sequence 5, 6, 5, 6, 7. Each new collision expands the cluster by one element, thereby increasing the length of the search chain for each element in that cluster. For example, if another element is inserted with any hash code in the range 5 through 9, it will be placed at position 10, and the search chain for items with hash codes of 5 and 6 would include the elements at indexes 7, 8, 9, and 10.

One approach to reduce the effect of clustering is to use *quadratic probing* instead of linear probing. In quadratic probing, the increments form a quadratic series ($1 + 2^2 + 3^2 + \cdots$). Therefore, the next value of `index` is calculated using the steps:

```
probeNum++;
index = (startIndex + probeNum * probeNum) % table.length
```

where `startIndex` is the index calculated using method `hashCode` and `probeNum` starts at 0. Ignoring wraparound, if an item has a hash code of 5, successive values of `index` will be 6 (5 + 1), 9 (5 + 4), 14 (5 + 9), . . . , instead of 6, 7, 8, ... Similarly, if the hash code is 6, successive values of `index` will be 7, 10, 15, and so on. Unlike linear probing, these two search chains have only one table element in common (at index 6).

Figure 7.6 illustrates the hash table after elements with hash codes in the same sequence as in the preceding table (5, 6, 5, 6, 7) have been inserted with quadratic probing. Although the cluster of elements looks similar, their search chains do not overlap as much as before. Now the search chain for an item with a hash code of 5 consists of the elements at 5, 6, and 9, and the search chain for an item with a hash code of 6 consists of the elements at positions 6 and 7.

Problems with Quadratic Probing

One disadvantage of quadratic probing is that the next index calculation is a bit time consuming as it involves a multiplication, an addition, and a modulo division. A more efficient way to calculate the next index follows:

FIGURE 7.6
Insertion with Quadratic Probing

[0]	
[1]	
[2]	
[3]	
[4]	
[5]	1st item with hash code 5
[6]	1st item with hash code 6
[7]	2nd item with hash code 6
[8]	1st item with hash code 7
[9]	2nd item with hash code 5
[10]	

```
k += 2;
index = (index + k) % table.length;
```

which replaces the multiplication with an addition. If the initial value of k is –1, successive values of k will be 1, 3, 5, 7, ... If the hash code is 5, successive values of index will be 5, 6 (5 + 1), 9 (5 + 1 + 3), 14 (5 + 1 + 3 + 5), . . . The proof of the equality of these two approaches to calculating index is based on the following mathematical series:

$$n^2 = 1 + 3 + 5 + \cdots + 2n - 1$$

A more serious problem with quadratic probing is that not all table elements are examined when looking for an insertion index, so it is possible that an item can't be inserted even when the table is not full. It is also possible that your program can get stuck in an infinite loop while searching for an empty slot. It can be proved that if the table size is a prime number and the table is never more than half full, this can't happen. However, requiring that the table be half empty at all times wastes quite a bit of memory. For these reasons, we will use linear probing in our implementation.

Chaining

An alternative to open addressing is a technique called *chaining,* in which each table element references a linked list that contains all the items that hash to the same table index. This linked list is often called a *bucket,* and this approach is sometimes called *bucket hashing*. Figure 7.7 shows the result of chaining for our earlier example with a table of size 5. Each new element with a particular hash index can be placed at the beginning or the end of the associated linked list. The algorithm for accessing such a table is the same as for open addressing, except for the step for resolving collisions. Instead of incrementing the table index to access the next item with a particular hash code value, you traverse the linked list referenced by the table element with index `hashCode() % table.length`.

One advantage of chaining is that only items that have the same value for `hashCode() % table.length` will be examined when looking for an object. In open addressing, search chains can overlap, so a search chain may include items in the table that have different starting index values.

FIGURE 7.7
Example of Chaining

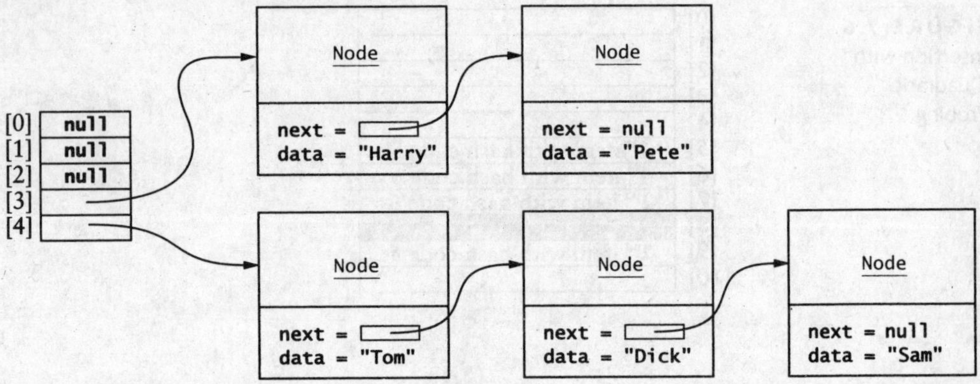

A second advantage is that you can store more elements in the table than the number of table slots (indexes), which is not the case for open addressing. If each table index already references a linked list, additional items can be inserted in an existing list without increasing the table size (number of indexes).

Once you have determined that an item is not present, you can insert it either at the beginning or at the end of the list. To delete an item, simply remove it from the list. In contrast to open addressing, removing an item actually deletes it, so it will not be part of future search chains.

Performance of Hash Tables

The *load factor* for a hash table is the number of filled cells divided by table size. The load factor has the greatest effect on hash table performance. The lower the load factor, the better the performance because there is less chance of a collision when a table is sparsely populated. If there are no collisions, the performance for search and retrieval is O(1), regardless of the table size.

Performance of Open Addressing versus Chaining

Donald E. Knuth (*Searching and Sorting,* vol. 3 of *The Art of Computer Programming,* Addison-Wesley, 1973) derived the following formula for the expected number of comparisons, c, required for finding an item that is in a hash table using open addressing with linear probing and a load factor L:

$$c = \frac{1}{2}\left(1 + \frac{1}{1-L}\right)$$

Table 7.4 (second column) shows the value of c for different values of load factor (L). It shows that if L is 0.5 (half full), the expected number of comparisons required is 1.5. If L increases to 0.75, the expected number of comparisons is 2.5, which is still very respectable. If L increases to 0.9 (90 percent full), the expected number of comparisons is 5.5. This is true regardless of the size of the table.

TABLE 7.4
Number of Probes for Different Values of Load Factor (L)

L	Number of Probes with Linear Probing	Number of Probes with Chaining
0.0	1.00	1.00
0.25	1.17	1.13
0.5	1.50	1.25
0.75	2.50	1.38
0.85	3.83	1.43
0.9	5.50	1.45
0.95	10.50	1.48

Using chaining, if an item is in the table, on average we have to examine the table element corresponding to the item's hash code and then half of the items in each list. The average number of items in a list is L, the number of items divided by the table size. Therefore, we get the formula

$$c = 1 + \frac{L}{2}$$

for a successful search. Table 7.4 (third column) shows the results for chaining. For values of L between 0.0 and 0.75, the results are similar to those of linear probing, but chaining gives better performance than linear probing for higher load factors. Quadratic probing (not shown) gives performance that is between those of linear probing and chaining.

Performance of Hash Tables versus Sorted Arrays and Binary Search Trees

If we compare hash table performance with binary search of a sorted array, the number of comparisons required by binary search is O(log n), so the number of comparisons increases with table size. A sorted array of size 128 would require up to 7 probes (2^7 is 128), which is more than for a hash table of any size that is 90 percent full. A sorted array of size 1024 would require up to 10 probes (2^{10} is 1024). A binary search tree would yield the same results.

You can insert into or remove elements from a hash table in O(1) expected time. Insertion or removal from a binary search tree is O(log n), but insertion or removal from a sorted array is O(n) (you need to shift the larger elements over). (Worst-case performance for a hash table or a binary search tree is O(n).)

Storage Requirements for Hash Tables, Sorted Arrays, and Trees

The performance of hashing is certainly preferable to that of binary search of an array (or a binary search tree), particularly if L is less than 0.75. However, the trade-off is that the lower the load factor, the more unfilled storage cells there are in a hash table, whereas there are no empty cells in a sorted array. Because a binary search tree requires three references per node (the item, the left subtree, and the right subtrees), more storage would be required for a binary search tree than for a hash table with a load factor of 0.75.

EXAMPLE 7.8 A hash table of size 100 with open addressing could store 75 items with a load factor of 0.75. This would require storage for 100 references. This would require storage for 100 references (25 references would be `null`).

Storage Requirements for Open Addressing and Chaining

Next, we consider the effect of chaining on storage requirements. For a table with a load factor of L, the number of table elements required is n (the size of the table). For open addressing, the number of references to an item (a key-value pair) is n. For chaining, the average number of nodes in a list is L. If we use the Java API `LinkedList`, there will be three references in each node (the item, the next list element, and the previous element). However, we could use our own single-linked list and eliminate the previous-element reference (at some time cost for deletions). Therefore, we will require storage for $n + 2L$ references.

EXAMPLE 7.9 If we have 60,000 items in our hash table and use open addressing, we would need a table size of 80,000 to have a load factor of 0.75 and an expected number of comparisons of 2.5. Next, we calculate the table size, n, needed to get similar performance using chaining.

$$2.5 = 1 + \frac{L}{2}$$

$$5.0 = 2 + L$$

$$3.0 = \frac{60{,}000}{n}$$

$$n = 20{,}000$$

A hash table of size 20,000 requires storage space for 20,000 references to lists. There will be 60,000 nodes in the table (one for each item). If we use linked lists of nodes, we will need storage for 140,000 references (2 references per node plus the 20,000 table references). This is almost twice the storage needed for open addressing.

EXERCISES FOR SECTION 7.3

SELF-CHECK

1. For the hash table search algorithm shown in this section, why was it unnecessary to test whether all table entries had been examined as part of Step 5?
2. For the items in the 5-element table of Table 7.3, compute `hashCode() % table.length` for lengths of 7 and 13. What would be the position of each word in tables of these sizes using open addressing and linear probing? Answer the same question for chaining.

3. The following table stores `Integer` keys with the `int` values shown. Show one sequence of insertions that would store the keys as shown. Which elements were placed in their current position because of collisions? Show the table that would be formed by chaining.

Index	Key
[0]	24
[1]	6
[2]	20
[3]	
[4]	14

4. For Table 7.3 and the table size of 5 shown in Example 7.7, discuss the effect of deleting the entry for Dick and replacing it with a `null` value. How would this affect the search for Sam, Pete, and Harry? Answer both questions if you replace the entry for Dick with the string `"deleted"` instead of `null`.
5. Explain what is wrong with the following strategy to reclaim space that is filled with deleted items in a hash table: When attempting to insert a new item in the table, if you encounter an item that has been deleted, replace the deleted item with the new item.
6. Compare the storage requirement for a hash table with open addressing, a table size of 500, and a load factor of 0.5 with a hash table that uses chaining and gives the same performance.
7. One simple hash code is to use the sum of the ASCII codes for the letters in a word. Explain why this is not a good hash code.
8. If p_i is the position of a character in a string and c_i is the code for that character, would $c_1p_1 + c_2p_2 + c_3p_3 + \ldots$ be a better hash code? Explain why or why not.
9. Use the hash code in Self-Check Exercise 7 to store the words `"cat"`, `"hat"`, `"tac"`, `"act"` in a hash table of size 10. Show this table using open hashing and chaining.

PROGRAMMING

1. Code the following algorithm for finding the location of an object as a static method. Assume a hash table array and an object to be located in the table are passed as arguments. Return the object's position if it is found; return –1 if the object is not found.

```
1.   Compute the index by taking the hashCode() % table.length.
2.   if table[index] is null
3.        The object is not in the table.
     else if table[index] is equal to the object
4.        The object is in the table.
     else
5.        Continue to search the table (by incrementing index) until either the
          object is found or a null entry is found.
```

7.4 Implementing the Hash Table

In this section, we discuss how to implement a hash table. We will show implementations for hash tables using open addressing and chaining.

Interface KWHashMap

Because we want to show more than one way to implement a hash table, we introduce an interface `KWHashMap<K, V>` in Table 7.5. The methods for interface `KWHashMap<K, V>` (`get`, `put`, `isEmpty`, `remove`, and `size`) are similar to the ones shown earlier for the `Map` interface (see Table 7.2). There is a class `Hashtable` in the Java API `java.util`; however, it has been superseded by the class `HashMap`. Our interface `KWHashMap` doesn't include all the methods of interface `Map`.

Class Entry

A hash table stores key-value pairs, so we will use an inner class `Entry` in each hash table implementation with data fields `key` and `value` (see Table 7.6). The implementation of inner class `Entry` is straightforward, and we show it in Listing 7.3.

TABLE 7.5
Interface `KWHashMap<K, V>`

Method	Behavior
`V get(Object key)`	Returns the value associated with the specified key. Returns `null` if the key is not present.
`boolean isEmpty()`	Returns `true` if this table contains no `key-value` mappings.
`V put(K key, V value)`	Associates the specified `value` with the specified `key`. Returns the previous `value` associated with the specified `key`, or `null` if there was no mapping for the `key`.
`V remove(Object key)`	Removes the mapping for this `key` from this table if it is present (optional operation). Returns the previous `value` associated with the specified `key`, or `null` if there was no mapping.
`int size()`	Returns the size of the table.

TABLE 7.6
Inner Class `Entry<K, V>`

Data Field	Attribute
`private K key`	The key.
`private V value`	The value.
Constructor	**Behavior**
`public Entry(K key, V value)`	Constructs an `Entry` with the given values.

TABLE 7.6 (continued)

Method	Behavior
`public K getKey()`	Retrieves the key.
`public V getValue()`	Retrieves the value.
`public V setValue(V val)`	Sets the value.

LISTING 7.3

Inner Class Entry

```
/** Contains key-value pairs for a hash table. */
private static class Entry<K, V> {

    /** The key */
    private K key;
    /** The value */
    private V value;

    /** Creates a new key-value pair.
        @param key The key
        @param value The value
    */
    public Entry(K key, V value) {
        this.key = key;
        this.value = value;
    }

    /** Retrieves the key.
        @return The key
    */
    public K getKey() {
        return key;
    }

    /** Retrieves the value.
        @return The value
    */
    public V getValue() {
        return value;
    }

    /** Sets the value.
        @param val The new value
        @return The old value
    */
    public V setValue(V val) {
        V oldVal = value;
        value = val;
        return oldVal;
    }
}
```

TABLE 7.7
Data Fields for Class `HashtableOpen<K, V>`

Data Field	Attribute
`private Entry<K, V>[] table`	The hash table array.
`private static final int START_CAPACITY`	The initial capacity.
`private double LOAD_THRESHOLD`	The maximum load factor.
`private int numKeys`	The number of keys in the table excluding keys that were deleted.
`private int numDeletes`	The number of deleted keys.
`private final Entry<K, V> DELETED`	A special object to indicate that an entry has been deleted.

Class `HashtableOpen`

In a hash table that uses open addressing, we represent the hash table as an array of `Entry` objects (initial size is `START_CAPACITY`). We describe the data fields in Table 7.7. The `Entry` object `DELETED` is used to indicate that the `Entry` at a particular table element has been deleted; a **`null`** reference indicates that a table element was never occupied.

The data field declarations and constructor for `HashtableOpen` follow. Because generic arrays are not permitted, the constructor creates an `Entry[]` array, which is referenced by `table` (type `Entry<K, V>[]`).

```
/** Hash table implementation using open addressing. */
public class HashtableOpen<K, V> implements KWHashMap<K, V> {
    // Data Fields
    private Entry<K, V>[] table;
    private static final int START_CAPACITY = 101;
    private double LOAD_THRESHOLD = 0.75;
    private int numKeys;
    private int numDeletes;
    private final Entry<K, V> DELETED =
            new Entry<K, V>(null, null);

    // Constructor
    public HashTableOpen() {
        table = new Entry[START_CAPACITY];
    }

    // Insert inner class Entry<K, V> here.
    . . .
```

Several methods for class `HashtableOpen` use a private method `find` that searches the table (using linear probing) until it finds either the target key or an empty slot. By expanding the table when its load factor exceeds the `LOAD_THRESHOLD`, we ensure that there will always be an empty slot in the table. Table 7.8 summarizes these private methods.

The algorithm for method `find` follows. Listing 7.4 shows the method.

TABLE 7.8
Private Methods for Class HashtableOpen

Method	Behavior
`private int find(Object key)`	Returns the index of the specified key if present in the table; otherwise, returns the index of the first available slot.
`private void rehash()`	Doubles the capacity of the table and permanently removes deleted items.

Algorithm for HashtableOpen.find(Object key)

1. Set index to key.hashCode() % table.length.
2. if index is negative, add table.length.
3. while table[index] is not empty and the key is not at table[index]
4. Increment index.
5. if index is greater than or equal to table.length
6. Set index to 0.
7. Return the index.

LISTING 7.4
Method HashtableOpen.find

```
/** Finds either the target key or the first empty slot in the
    search chain using linear probing.
    pre: The table is not full.
    @param key The key of the target object
    @return The position of the target or the first empty slot if
            the target is not in the table.
*/
private int find(Object key) {
    // Calculate the starting index.
    int index = key.hashCode() % table.length;
    if (index < 0)
        index += table.length;  // Make it positive.

    // Increment index until an empty slot is reached
    // or the key is found.
    while ((table[index] != null)
            && (!key.equals(table[index].key))) {
        index++;
        // Check for wraparound.
        if (index >= table.length)
            index = 0;    // Wrap around.
    }
    return index;
}
```

Notice that the method call key.hashCode() calls key's hashCode. The condition (!key.equals(table[index].key)) compares the key at table[index] with the key being sought (the method parameter). Notice that it is not necessary to use getKey with table[index] because the key field is defined in an inner class. Therefore, when key is used with a prefix of type Entry<K, V>, it refers to the data field key; when key is used without a prefix, it refers to the parameter key.

Next we discuss the public methods: get and put. Listing 7.5 shows the code. The get algorithm follows.

Algorithm for get(Object key)

1. Find the first table element that is empty or the table element that contains the key.
2. **if** the table element found contains the key
   Return the value at this table element.
3. **else**
4. Return **null**.

LISTING 7.5

Method HashtableOpen.get

```
/** Method get for class HashtableOpen.
    @param key The key being sought
    @return the value associated with this key if found;
            otherwise, null
*/
@Override
public V get(Object key) {
    // Find the first table element that is empty
    // or the table element that contains the key.
    int index = find(key);

    // If the search is successful, return the value.
    if (table[index] != null)
        return table[index].value;
    else
        return null;  // key not found.
}
```

Next we write the algorithm for method put. After inserting a new entry, the method checks to see whether the load factor exceeds the LOAD_THRESHOLD. If so, it calls method rehash to expand the table and reinsert the entries. Listing 7.6 shows the code for method put.

Algorithm for HashtableOpen.put(K key, V value)

1. Find the first table element that is empty or the table element that contains the key.
2. **if** an empty element was found
3. Insert the new item and increment numKeys.
4. Check for need to rehash.
5. Return **null**.
6. The key was found. Replace the value associated with this table element and return the old value.

LISTING 7.6
Method HashtableOpen.put

```
/** Method put for class HashtableOpen.
    post: This key-value pair is inserted in the
          table and numKeys is incremented. If the key is already
          in the table, its value is changed to the argument
          value and numKeys is not changed. If the LOAD_THRESHOLD
          is exceeded, the table is expanded.
    @param key The key of item being inserted
    @param value The value for this key
    @return Old value associated with this key if found;
            otherwise, null
*/
@Override
public V put(K key, V value)  {
    // Find the first table element that is empty
    // or the table element that contains the key.
    int index = find(key);

    // If an empty element was found, insert new entry.
    if (table[index] == null) {
        table[index] = new Entry<K, V>(key, value);
        numKeys++;
        // Check whether rehash is needed.
        double loadFactor =
                (double) (numKeys + numDeletes) / table.length;
        if (loadFactor > LOAD_THRESHOLD)
            rehash();
        return null;
    }

    // assert: table element that contains the key was found.
    // Replace value for this key.
    V oldVal = table[index].value;
    table[index].value = value;
    return oldVal;
}
```

PITFALL

Integer Division for Calculating Load Factor

Before calling method rehash, method put calculates the load factor by dividing the number of filled slots by the table size. This is a simple computation, but if you forget to cast the numerator or denominator to **double**, the load factor will be zero (because of integer division), and the table will not be expanded. This will slow down the performance of the table when it becomes nearly full, and it will cause an infinite loop (in method find) when the table is completely filled.

Next, we write the algorithm for method `remove`. Note that we "remove" a table element by setting it to reference object `DELETED`. We leave the implementation as an exercise.

Algorithm for `remove(Object key)`

1. Find the first table element that is empty or the table element that contains the key.
2. **`if`** an empty element was found
3.   Return **`null`**.
4. Key was found. Remove this table element by setting it to reference `DELETED`, increment `numDeletes`, and decrement `numKeys`.
5. Return the value associated with this key.

Finally, we write the algorithm for private method `rehash`. Listing 7.7 shows the method. Although we do not take the effort to make the table size a prime number, we do make it an odd number.

Algorithm for `HashtableOpen.rehash`

1. Allocate a new hash table that is double the size and has an odd length.
2. Reset the number of keys and number of deletions to 0.
3. Reinsert each table entry that has not been deleted in the new hash table.

LISTING 7.7

Method `HashtableOpen.rehash`

```
/** Expands table size when loadFactor exceeds LOAD_THRESHOLD
    post: The size of the table is doubled and is an odd integer.
          Each nondeleted entry from the original table is
          reinserted into the expanded table.
          The value of numKeys is reset to the number of items
          actually inserted; numDeletes is reset to 0.
*/
private void rehash() {
    // Save a reference to oldTable.
    Entry<K, V>[] oldTable = table;
    // Double capacity of this table.
    table = new Entry[2 * oldTable.length + 1];

    // Reinsert all items in oldTable into expanded table.
    numKeys = 0;
    numDeletes = 0;
    for (int i = 0; i < oldTable.length; i++) {
        if ((oldTable[i] != null) && (oldTable[i] != DELETED)) {
            // Insert entry in expanded table
            put(oldTable[i].key, oldTable[i].value);
        }
    }
}
```

TABLE 7.9
Data Fields for Class `HashtableChain<K, V>`

Data Field	Attribute
`private LinkedList<Entry<K, V>>[] table`	A table of references to linked lists of `Entry<K, V>` objects.
`private int numKeys`	The number of keys (entries) in the table.
`private static final int CAPACITY`	The size of the table.
`private static final int LOAD_THRESHOLD`	The maximum load factor.

Class HashtableChain

Next we turn our attention to class `HashtableChain`, which implements `KWHashMap` using chaining. We will represent the hash table as an array of linked lists as shown in Table 7.9. Even though a hash table that uses chaining can store any number of elements in the same slot, we will expand the table if the number of entries becomes three times the number of slots (`LOAD_THRESHOLD` is 3.0) to keep the performance at a reasonable level.

Listing 7.8 shows the data fields and the constructor for class `HashtableChain`.

LISTING 7.8
Data Fields and Constructor for `HashtableChain.java`

```
import java.util.*;

/** Hash table implementation using chaining. */
public class HashtableChain<K, V> implements KWHashMap<K, V> {
    /** The table */
    private LinkedList<Entry<K, V>>[] table;
    /** The number of keys */
    private int numKeys;
    /** The capacity */
    private static final int CAPACITY = 101;
    /** The maximum load factor */
    private static final double LOAD_THRESHOLD = 3.0;

    // Insert inner class Entry<K, V> here.

    // Constructor
    public HashtableChain() {
        table = new LinkedList[CAPACITY];
    }
. . .
}
```

Next we discuss the three methods `get`, `put`, and `remove`. Instead of introducing a `find` method to search a list for the key, we will include a search loop in each method. We will create a `ListIterator` object and use that object to access each list element.

We begin with the algorithm for get. Listing 7.9 shows its code. We didn't use methods getKey and getValue to access an item's key and value because those private data fields of class Entry are visible in the class that contains it.

Algorithm for HashtableChain.get(Object key)

1. Set index to key.hashCode() % table.length.
2. **if** index is negative
3. Add table.length.
4. **if** table[index] is **null**
5. key is not in the table; return **null**.
6. For each element in the list at table[index]
7. **if** that element's key matches the search key
8. Return that element's value.
9. key is not in the table; return **null**.

LISTING 7.9
Method HashtableChain.get

```
/** Method get for class HashtableChain.
    @param key The key being sought
    @return The value associated with this key if found;
            otherwise, null
*/
@Override
public V get(Object key) {
    int index = key.hashCode() % table.length;
    if (index < 0)
        index += table.length;
    if (table[index] == null)
        return null;  // key is not in the table.

    // Search the list at table[index] to find the key.
    for (Entry<K, V> nextItem : table[index]) {
        if (nextItem.key.equals(key))
            return nextItem.value;
    }

    // assert: key is not in the table.
    return null;
}
```

Next we write the algorithm for method put. Listing 7.10 shows its code.

Algorithm for HashtableChain.put(K key, V value)

1. Set index to key.hashCode() % table.length.
2. **if** index is negative, add table.length.
3. **if** table[index] is **null**
4. Create a new linked list at table[index].
5. Search the list at table[index] to find the key.

6. **if** the search is successful
7. Replace the value associated with this key.
8. Return the old value.
9. **else**
10. Insert the new key-value pair in the linked list at `table[index]`.
11. Increment `numKeys`.
12. **if** the load factor exceeds the `LOAD_THRESHOLD`
13. Rehash.
14. Return **null**.

LISTING 7.10

Method `HashtableChain.put`

```java
/** Method put for class HashtableChain.
    post: This key-value pair is inserted in the
          table and numKeys is incremented. If the key is already
          in the table, its value is changed to the argument
          value and numKeys is not changed.
    @param key The key of item being inserted
    @param value The value for this key
    @return The old value associated with this key if
            found; otherwise, null
*/
@Override
public V put(K key, V value) {
    int index = key.hashCode() % table.length;
    if (index < 0)
        index += table.length;
    if (table[index] == null) {
        // Create a new linked list at table[index].
        table[index] = new LinkedList<Entry<K, V>>();
    }

    // Search the list at table[index] to find the key.
    for (Entry<K, V> nextItem : table[index]) {
        // If the search is successful, replace the old value.
        if (nextItem.key.equals(key)) {
            // Replace value for this key.
            V oldVal = nextItem.value;
            nextItem.setValue(value);
            return oldVal;
        }
    }

    // assert: key is not in the table, add new item.
    table[index].addFirst(new Entry<K, V>(key, value));
    numKeys++;
    if (numKeys > (LOAD_THRESHOLD * table.length))
        rehash();
    return null;
}
```

Last, we write the algorithm for method `remove`. We leave the implementation of `rehash` and `remove` as an exercise.

Algorithm for `HashtableChain.remove(Object key)`

1. Set `index` to `key.hashCode() % table.length`.
2. `if` `index` is negative, add `table.length`.
3. `if` `table[index]` is `null`
4. `key` is not in the table; return `null`.
5. Search the list at `table[index]` to find the key.
6. `if` the search is successful
7. Remove the entry with this key and decrement `numKeys`.
8. `if` the list at `table[index]` is empty
9. Set `table[index]` to `null`.
10. Return the value associated with this key.
11. The `key` is not in the table; return `null`.

Testing the Hash Table Implementations

We discuss two approaches to testing the hash table implementations. One way is to create a file of key-value pairs and then read each key-value pair and insert it in the hash table, observing how the table is filled. To do this, you need to write a `toString` method for the table that captures the index of each table element that is not `null` and then the contents of that table element. For open addressing, the contents would be the string representation of the key-value pair. For chaining, you could use a list iterator to traverse the linked list at that table element and append each key-value pair to the result string (see the Programming exercises for this section).

If you use a data file, you can carefully test different situations. The following are some of the cases you should examine:

- Does the array index wrap around as it should?
- Are collisions resolved correctly?
- Are duplicate keys handled appropriately? Is the new value retrieved instead of the original value?
- Are deleted keys retained in the table but no longer accessible via a `get`?
- Does rehashing occur when the load factor reaches 0.75 (3.0 for chaining)?

By stepping through the `get` and `put` methods, you can observe how the table is probed and examine the search chain that is followed to access or retrieve a key.

An alternative to creating a data file is to insert randomly generated integers in the hash table. This will allow you to create a very large table with little effort. The following loop generates `SIZE` key-value pairs. Each key is an integer between 0 and 32,000 and is autoboxed in an `Integer` object. For each table entry, the value is the same as the key. The `Integer.hashCode` method returns the `int` value of the object to which it is applied.

```
for (int i = 0; i < SIZE; i++) {
    Integer nextInt = (int) (32000 * Math.random());
    hashTable.put(nextInt, nextInt);
}
```

Because the keys are generated randomly, you can't investigate the effect of duplicate keys as you can with a data file. However, you can build arbitrarily large tables and observe how the elements are placed in the tables. After the table is complete, you can interactively enter items to retrieve, delete, and insert and verify that they are handled properly.

If you are using open addressing, you can add statements to count the number of items probed each time an insertion is made. You can accumulate these totals and display the average search chain length. If you are using chaining, you can also count the number of probes made and display the average. After all items have been inserted, you can calculate the average length of each linked list and compare that with the number predicted by the formula provided in the discussion of performance in Section 7.3.

EXERCISES FOR SECTION 7.4

SELF-CHECK

1. The following table stores `Integer` keys with the `int` values shown. Where would each key be placed in the new table resulting from rehashing the current table?

Index	Key
0	24
1	6
2	20
3	
4	14

PROGRAMMING

1. Write a `remove` method for class `HashtableOpen`.
2. Write `rehash` and `remove` methods for class `HashtableChain`.
3. Write a `toString` method for class `HashtableOpen`.
4. Write a `toString` method for class `HashtableChain`.
5. Write a method `size` for both hash table implementations.
6. Modify method `find` to count and display the number of probes made each time it is called. Accumulate these in a data field `numProbes` and count the number of times `find` is called in another data field. Provide a method that returns the average number of probes per call to `find`.

7.5 Implementation Considerations for Maps and Sets

Methods hashCode and equals

Class `Object` implements methods `hashCode` and `equals`, so every class can access these methods unless it overrides them. Method `Object.equals` compares two objects based on their addresses, not their contents. Similarly, method `Object.hashCode` calculates an object's hash code based on its address, not its contents. If you want to compare two objects for equality, you must implement an `equals` method for that class. In doing so, you should override the `equals` method for class `Object` by providing an `equals` method with the form

```
public boolean equals(Object obj) { . . . }
```

Most predefined classes (e.g., `String` and `Integer`) override method `equals` and method `hashCode`. If you override the `equals` method, Java recommends you also override the `hashCode` method. Otherwise, your class will violate the Java contract for `hashCode`, which states:

```
If obj1.equals(obj2) is true, then obj1.hashCode() == obj2.hashCode().
```

Consequently, you should make sure that your `hashCode` method uses the same data field(s) as your `equals` method. We provide an example next.

EXAMPLE 7.10 Class `Person` has data field `IDNumber`, which is used to determine whether two `Person` objects are equal. The `equals` method returns true only if the objects' `IDNumber` fields have the same contents.

```
public boolean equals(Object obj) {
    if (obj instanceof Person)
        return IDNumber.equals(((Person) obj).IDNumber);
    else
        return false;
}
```

To satisfy its contract, method `Object.hashCode` must also be overridden as follows. Now two objects that are considered equal will also have the same hash code.

```
public int hashCode() {
    return IDNumber.hashCode();
}
```

Implementing HashSetOpen

We can modify the hash table methods from Section 7.4 to implement a hash set. Table 7.10 compares corresponding `Map` and `Set` methods.

The `Set contains` method performs a test for set membership instead of retrieving a value, so it is type **`boolean`**. Similarly, each of the other `Set` methods in Table 7.10 returns a **`boolean`** value that indicates whether the method was able to perform its task. The process of searching the hash table elements would be done the same way in each `Set` method as it is done in the corresponding `Map` method.

TABLE 7.10
Corresponding Map and Set Methods

Map Method	Set Method
`V get(Object key)`	`boolean contains(Object key)`
`V put(K key, V value)`	`boolean add(K key)`
`V remove(Object key)`	`boolean remove(Object key)`

For open addressing, method `put` uses the statement

```
table[index] = new Entry<K, V>(key, value);
```

to store a reference to a new `Entry` object in the hash table. The corresponding statement in method `add` would be

```
table[index] = new Entry<K>(key);
```

because the `key` is the only data that is stored.

Writing HashSetOpen as an Adapter Class

Instead of writing new methods from scratch, we can implement `HashSetOpen` as an adapter class with the data field

```
private KWHashMap<K, V> setMap = new HashtableOpen<K, V>();
```

We can write methods `contains`, `add`, and `remove` as follows. Because the map stores key-value pairs, we will have each set element reference an `Entry` object with the same key and value.

```
/** A hash table for storing set elements using open addressing. */
public class HashSetOpen {
    private KWHashMap<K, V> setMap = new HashtableOpen<K, V>();

    /** Adapter method contains.
        @return true if the key is found in setMap
    */
    public boolean contains(Object key) {
        // HashtableOpen.get returns null if the key is not found.
        return (setMap.get(key) != null);
    }

    /** Adapter method add.
        post: Adds a new Entry object (key, key)
              if key is not a duplicate.
        @return true if the key is not a duplicate
    */
    public boolean add(K key) {
        /* HashtableOpen.put returns null if the
           key is not a duplicate. */
        return (setMap.put(key, key) == null);
    }

    /** Adapter method remove.
        post: Removes the key-value pair (key, key).
```

```
        @return true if the key is found and removed
    */
    public boolean remove(Object key) {
        /* HashtableOpen.remove returns null if the
           key is not removed. */
        return (setMap.remove() != null);
    }
}
```

Implementing the Java Map and Set Interfaces

Our goal in this chapter was to show you how to implement the operators in our hash table interface, not to implement the `Map` or `Set` interface fully. However, the Java API uses a hash table to implement both the `Map` and `Set` interfaces (class `HashMap` and class `HashSet`). You may be wondering what additional work would be required to implement the `Map` and `Set` interfaces using the classes we have developed so far.

The task of implementing these interfaces is simplified by the inclusion of abstract classes `AbstractMap` and `AbstractSet` in the Collections framework (see Figures 7.1 and 7.3). These classes provide implementations of several methods for the `Map` and `Set` interfaces. So if class `HashtableOpen` extends class `AbstractMap`, we can reduce the amount of additional work we need to do.

The `AbstractMap` provides relatively inefficient ($O(n)$) implementations of the `get` and `put` methods. Because we overrode these methods in both our implementations (`HashtableOpen` and `HashtableChain`), we will get $O(1)$ expected performance. There are other, less critical methods that we don't need to provide because they are implemented in `AbstractMap` or its superclasses, such as `clear`, `isEmpty`, `putAll`, `equals`, `hashCode`, and `toString`.

Nested Interface `Map.Entry`

One requirement on the key-value pairs for a `Map` object is that they implement the interface `Map.Entry<K, V>`, which is an inner interface of interface `Map`. This may sound a bit confusing, but what it means is that an implementer of the `Map` interface must contain an inner class that provides code for the methods described in Table 7.11. The inner class definition would be similar to the definition of inner class `Entry<K, V>` in Listing 7.3, except it would end with the clause `implements Map.Entry<K, V>`.

TABLE 7.11
The `java.util.Map.Entry<K, V>` Interface

Method	Behavior
`K getKey()`	Returns the key corresponding to this entry.
`V getValue()`	Returns the value corresponding to this entry.
`V setValue(V val)`	Resets the value field for this entry to `val`. Returns its previous value field.

Creating a Set View of a Map

Method entrySet creates a set view of the entries in a Map. This means that method entrySet returns an object that implements the Set interface—that is, a set. The members of the set returned are the key-value pairs defined for that Map object. For example, if a key is "0123" and the corresponding value is "Jane Doe", the pair ("0123", "Jane Doe") would be an element of the set view. This is called a view because it provides an alternative way to access the contents of the Map, but there is only a single copy of the underlying Map object.

We usually call method entrySet via a statement of the form:

```
Iterator<Map.Entry<K, V>> iter = myMap.entrySet().iterator();
```

The method call myMap.entrySet() creates a set view of myMap; next, we apply method iterator to that set, thereby returning an Iterator object for it. We can access all the elements in the set through Iterator iter's methods hasNext and next, but the elements are in arbitrary order. The objects returned by the iterator's next method are Map.Entry<K, V> objects. We show an easier way to do this using the enhanced **for** statement in Example 7.11.

Method entrySet and Classes EntrySet and SetIterator

Method entrySet returns a set view of the underlying hash table (its key-value pairs) by returning an instance of inner class EntrySet. We define method entrySet next and then class EntrySet.

```
/** Creates a set view of a map.
    @return a set view of all key-value pairs in this map
*/
public Set<Map.Entry<K, V>> entrySet() {
    return new EntrySet();
}
```

We show the inner class EntrySet in Listing 7.11. This class is an extension of the AbstractSet, which provides a complete implementation of the Set interface except for the size and iterator methods. The other methods required by the Set interface are defined using these methods. Most methods are implemented by using the Iterator object that is returned by the EntrySet.iterator method to access the contents of the hash table through its set view. You can also use such an Iterator object to access the elements of the set view.

LISTING 7.11

The Inner Class EntrySet

```
/** Inner class to implement the set view. */
private class EntrySet extends AbstractSet<Map.Entry<K, V>> {

    /** Return the size of the set. */
    @Override
    public int size() {
        return numKeys;
    }
```

```java
    /** Return an iterator over the set. */
    @Override
    public Iterator<Map.Entry<K, V>> iterator() {
        return new SetIterator();
    }
}
```

The final step is to write class `SetIterator`, which implements the `Iterator` interface. The inner class `SetIterator` enables access to the entries in the hash table. The `SetIterator` class implements the `java.util.Iterator` interface and provides methods `hasNext`, `next`, and `remove`. Its implementation is left as a Programming Project (see Project 6).

Classes TreeMap and TreeSet

Besides `HashMap` and `HashSet`, the Java Collections Framework provides classes `TreeMap` and `TreeSet` that implement the `Map` and `Set` interfaces. These classes use a Red-Black tree (Section 9.3), which is a balanced binary search tree. We discussed earlier that the performances for search, retrieval, insertion, and removal operations are better for a hash table than for a binary search tree (expected O(1) versus O(log *n*)). However, the primary advantage of a binary search tree is that it can be traversed in sorted order. Hash tables, however, can't be traversed in any meaningful way. Also, subsets based on a range of key values can be selected using a `TreeMap` but not by using a `HashMap`.

EXAMPLE 7.11 In Example 7.4 we showed how to use a `Map` to build an index for a term paper. Because we want to display the words of the index in alphabetical order, we must store the index in a `TreeMap`. Method `showIndex` below displays the string representation of each index entry in the form

key = *value*

If the word *fire* appears on lines 4, 8, and 20, the corresponding output line would be

```
fire =[4, 8, 20]
```

It would be relatively easy to display this in the more common form: `fire, 4, 8, 20` (see Programming Exercise 4).

```java
/** Displays the index, one word per line. */
public void showIndex() {
    for (Map.Entry<String, ArrayList<Integer>> entry
            : index.entrySet()) {
        System.out.println(entry);
    }
}
```

In the enhanced **for** statement, `entry` is declared as a `Map.Entry` object with a `String` key and with an `ArrayList` of `Integers` as its value. During each loop iteration, the next value assigned to `entry` is determined by an implicit call to method `next` of an `Iterator` over the set view of `Map index`.

EXERCISES FOR SECTION 7.5

SELF-CHECK

1. Explain why the nested interface `Map.Entry` is needed.

PROGRAMMING

1. Write statements to display all key-value pairs in `Map` object `m`, one pair per line. You will need to create an iterator to access the map entries.
2. Assume a `Person` has data fields `lastName` and `firstName`. Write an `equals` method that returns true if two `Person` objects have the same first and last names. Write a `hashCode` method that satisfies the `hashCode` contract. Make sure that your `hashCode` method does not return the same value for Henry James and James Henry. Your `equals` method should return a value of **`false`** for these two people.
3. Assume class `HashSetOpen` is written using an array `table` for storage instead of a `HashMap` object. Write method `contains`.
4. Modify method `showIndex` so each output line displays a word followed by a comma and a list of line numbers separated by commas. You can either edit the string corresponding to each `Map` entry before displaying it or use methods `Map.Entry.getKey` and `Map.Entry.getValue` to build a different string.

7.6 Additional Applications of Maps

In this section we will consider two case studies that use a `Map` object. The first is the design of a contact list for a cell phone, and the second involves completing the Huffman Coding Case Study started in Section 6.6.

CASE STUDY Implementing a Cell Phone Contact List

Problem A cell phone manufacturer would like a Java program that maintains the list of contacts for a cell phone owner. For each contact, a person's name, there should be a list of phone numbers that can be changed. The manufacturer has provided the interface for the software (see Table 7.12).

Analysis A map is an ideal data structure for the contact list. It should associate names (which must be unique) to lists of phone numbers. Therefore, the name should be the key field, and the list of phone numbers should be the value field. A sample entry would be:

name: Jane Smith *phone numbers:* 215-555-1234, 610-555-4820

TABLE 7.12
Methods of `ContactListInterface`

Method	Behavior
`List<String> addOrChangeEntry(String name, List<String> numbers)`	Changes the numbers associated with the given name or adds a new entry with this name and list of numbers. Returns the old list of numbers or `null` if this is a new entry.
`List<String> lookupEntry(String name)`	Searches the contact list for the given name and returns its list of numbers or `null` if the name is not found.
`List<String> removeEntry(String name)`	Removes the entry with the specified name from the contact list and returns its list of numbers or `null` if the name is not in the contact list.
`void display();`	Displays the contact list in order by name.

Thus, we can implement `ContactListInterface` by using a `Map<String, List<String>>` object for the contact list. For the sample entry above, this object would contain the key-value pair ("Jane Smith", ["215-555-1234", "610-555-4820"]).

Design We need to design the class `MapContactList`, which implements `ContactListInterface`. The contact list can be stored in the data field declared as follows:

```
public class MapContactList implements ContactListInterface {

    /** The contact list */
    Map<String, List<String>> contacts =
                              new TreeMap<String, List<String>>();
```

Writing the required methods using the `Map` methods is a straightforward task.

Implementation We begin with method `addOrChangeEntry`:

```
    public List<String> addOrChangeEntry(String name,
                                         List<String> newNumbers) {
        List<String> oldNumbers = contacts.put(name, newNumbers);
        return oldNumbers;
    }
```

Method `put` inserts the new name and list of numbers (method arguments) for a `Map` entry and returns the old value for that name (the list of numbers) if it was previously stored. If an entry with the given name was not previously stored, `null` is returned.

The `lookupEntry` method uses the `Map.get` method to retrieve the directory entry. The entry key field (`name`) is passed as an argument.

```
public List<String> lookupEntry(String name) {
    return contacts.get(name);
}
```

The `removeEntry` method uses the `Map.remove` method to delete a contact list entry.

```
public List<String> removeEntry(String name) {
    return contacts.remove(name);
}
```

To display the contact list in order by name, we need to retrieve each name and its associated list of numbers from the contact list. We can use the `Map.entrySet()` method to obtain a view of the map's contents as a set of `Map.Entry<String, List<String>>` objects. We can use the **for-each** construct to write out the contents of the map as a sequence of consecutive lines containing the name-number pairs. The iterator accesses the entries in order by key field, which is what we desire.

```
public void display() {
    for (Map.Entry<String, List<String>> current :
                    contacts.entrySet()) {
        // Display the name.
        println(current.getKey());
        // Display the list of numbers.
        println(current.getValue());
    }
}
```

Each entry is stored in `current`. Then method `getKey` returns the key field (the person's name), and method `getValue` returns the value field (the person's list of phone numbers).

Testing To test class `MapContactList`, you can write a main function that creates a new `MapContacList` object. Then apply the `addOrChangeEntry` method several times to this object, using new names and phone number lists, to build the initial contact list. For example, the following sequence of statements stores two entries in `contactList`.

```
MapContactList contactList = new MapContactList();
List<String> nums = new ArrayList<String>();
nums.add("123"); nums.add("345");
contactList.addOrChangeEntry("Jones", nums);
nums = new ArrayList<String>();
nums.add("135"); nums.add("357");
contactList.addOrChangeEntry("King", nums);
```

Once you have created an initial contact list, you can display it and then update it to verify that all the methods are correct.

CASE STUDY Completing the Huffman Coding Problem

Problem In Section 6.6 we showed how to compress a file by using a Huffman tree to encode the symbols occurring in the file so that the most frequently occurring characters had the shortest binary codes. The input to method `buildTree` of class `HuffmanTree` was a `HuffData` array consisting of (weight, symbol) pairs, where the weight in each pair was the frequency of occurrence of the corresponding symbol. We need a method to build this array for any data file so that we can create the Huffman tree. Once the tree is built, we need to encode each symbol in the input file by writing the corresponding bit string for that symbol to the output file.

Analysis A `Map` is a very useful data structure for both of these tasks: creating the array of `HuffData` elements and replacing each input character by its bit string code in the output file. For either situation, we need to look up a symbol in a table. Using a `Map` ensures that the table lookup is an expected O(1) process.

To build the frequency table, we need to read a file and count the number of occurrences of each symbol in the file. The symbol will be the `key` for each entry in a `Map<Character, Integer>` object, and the corresponding `value` will be the count of occurrences so far. As each symbol is read, we retrieve its `Map` entry and increment the corresponding count. If the symbol is not yet in the frequency table, we insert it with a count of 1.

Once we have the frequency table, we can construct the Huffman tree using a priority queue as explained in Section 6.6. Then we need to build a code table that stores the bit string code associated with each symbol to facilitate encoding the data file. Storing the code table in a `Map<Character, BitString>` object makes the encoding process more efficient because we can look up the symbol and retrieve its bit string code (expected O(1) process). To build the code table, we do a preorder traversal of the Huffman tree.

Design The algorithm for building the frequency table follows. After all characters are read, we create a set view of the map and traverse it using an iterator. We retrieve each `Map.Entry` and transpose its fields to create the corresponding `HuffData` item, a (weight, symbol) pair.

Algorithm for `buildFreqTable`

1. **`while`** there are more characters in the input file
2. Read a character and retrieve its corresponding entry in `frequencies`.
3. **`if`** the `value` field is **`null`**
4. Set `value` to 1.
5. **`else`**
6. Increment `value`.
7. Create a set view of `frequencies`.

8. **for** each entry in the set view
9. Store its data as a weight-symbol pair in the `HuffData` array.
10. Return the `HuffData` array.

We can use a `Map<Character, BitString>` object that stores each symbol and its corresponding bit code string (a string of 0 and 1 bits) to encode the file. Class `BitString` may be downloaded from the Web site for this textbook. The `BitString` methods we use (the constructor and `append`) are similar to their counterparts in classes `StringBuffer` and `StringBuilder`.

Method `buildCodeTable` builds the code table by performing a preorder traversal of the Huffman tree. The code table should be declared as a data field:

```
private Map<Character, String> codeTable;
```

As we traverse the tree, we keep track of the bit code string so far. When we traverse left, we append a 0 to the bit string, and when we traverse right, we append a 1 to the bit string. If we encounter a symbol in a node, we insert that symbol along with a copy of the code so far as a new entry in the code table. Because all symbols are stored in leaf nodes, we return immediately without going deeper in the tree.

Algorithm for Method `buildCodeTable`

1. Get the data at the current root.
2. **if** a symbol is stored in the current root (reached a leaf node)
3. Insert the symbol and bit string code so far as a new code table entry.
4. **else**
5. Append a 0 to the bit string code so far.
6. Apply the method recursively to the left subtree.
7. Append a 1 to the bit string code.
8. Apply the method recursively to the right subtree.

Finally, to encode the file, we read each character, look up its bit string code in the code table `Map`, and then write it to the output file.

Algorithm for Method encode

1. **while** there are more characters in the input file
2. Read a character and get its corresponding bit string code.
3. Write its bit string to the output file.

Implementation Listing 7.12 shows the code for method `buildFreqTable`. The **while** loop inside the **try** block builds the frequency table (`Map frequencies`). Each character is stored as an `int` in `nextChar` and then cast to type `char`. Because a `Map` stores references to objects, each character is autoboxed in a `Character` object (the key) and its count in an `Integer` object (the value). Once the table is built, we use an enhanced **for** loop to traverse the set view, retrieving each entry from the map and using its data to create a new `HuffData` element for array `freqTable`. When we finish, we return `freqTable` as the method result.

LISTING 7.12
Method buildFreqTable

```
public static HuffData[] buildFreqTable(BufferedReader ins) {
    // Map of frequencies.
    Map<Character, Integer> frequencies =
            new HashMap<Character, Integer>();
    try {
        int nextChar;   // For storing the next character as an int
        while ((nextChar = ins.read()) != -1) { // Test for more data
            // Get the current count and increment it.
            Integer count = frequencies.get((char) nextChar);
            if (count == null)
                count = 1;   // First occurrence.
            else
                count++;

            // Store updated count.
            frequencies.put((char) nextChar, count);
        }
        ins.close();
    } catch (IOException ex) {
        ex.printStackTrace();
        system.exit(1);
    }
    // Copy Map entries to a HuffData[] array.
    HuffData[] freqTable = new HuffData[frequencies.size()];
    int i = 0;      // Start at beginning of array.
    // Get each map entry and store it in the array
    // as a weight-symbol pair.
    for (Map.Entry<Character, Integer> entry : frequencies.entrySet()) {
        freqTable[i] =
            new HuffData(entry.getValue().doubleValue(), entry.getKey());
        i++;
    }
    return freqTable;     // Return the array.
}
```

Next, we show method buildCodeTable. We provide a starter method that initializes codeMap to an empty HashMap and calls the recursive method that implements the algorithm discussed in the Design section.

```
/** Starter method to build the code table.
    post: The table is built.
*/
public void buildCodeTable() {
    // Initialize the code map.
    codeMap = new HashMap<Character, BitString>();
    // Call recursive method with empty bit string for code so far.
    buildCodeTable(huffTree, new BitString());
}
```

```
/** Recursive method to perform breadth-first traversal
    of the Huffman tree and build the code table.
    @param tree The current tree root
    @param code The code string so far
*/
private void buildCodeTable(BinaryTree<HuffData> tree, BitString code)
{
    // Get data at local root.
    HuffData datum = tree.getData();
    if (datum.symbol != null) {  // Test for leaf node.
        // Found a symbol, insert its code in the map.
        codeMap.put(datum.symbol, code);
    } else {
        // Append 0 to code so far and traverse left.
        BitString leftCode = (BitString) code.clone();
        leftCode.append(false); // false is 0.
        buildCodeTable(tree.getLeftSubtree(), leftCode);
        // Append 1 to code so far and traverse right.
        BitString rightCode = (BitString) code.clone();
        rightCode.append(true); // true is 1.
        buildCodeTable(tree.getRightSubtree(), rightCode);
    }
}
```

Method encode reads each character again, looks up its bit code string, and writes it to the output file. We assume that the code table is in Map codeTable (a data field).

```
/** The Map to store the code table. */
private Map<Character, BitString> codeTable
        = new HashMap<Character, BitString>();
```

Following is the encode method.

```
/** Encodes a data file by writing it in compressed bit string form.
    @param ins The input stream
    @param outs The object output stream
*/
public void encode(BufferedReader ins, ObjectOutputStream outs) {
    BitString result = new BitString();  // The complete bit string.
    try {
        int nextChar;
        while ((nextChar = ins.read()) != -1) {  // More data?
            Character next = (char) nextChar;

            // Get bit string corresponding to symbol nextChar.
            BitString nextChunk = codeMap.get(next);
            result.append(nextChunk);   // Append to result string.
        }

        // Write result to output file and close files.
        result.trimCapacity();
        outs.writeObject(result);
        ins.close();
```

```
                outs.close();
            } catch (IOException ex) {
                ex.printStackTrace();
                System.exit(1);
            }
        }
```

Testing To test these methods completely, you need to download class `BitString` (see Project 1) and write a `main` method that calls them in the proper sequence. For interim testing, you can read a data file and display the frequency table that is constructed to verify that it is correct. You can also use the `StringBuffer` or `StringBuilder` class instead of class `BitString` in methods `buildCodeTable` and `encode`. The resulting code string would consist of a sequence of digit characters `'0'` and `'1'` instead of a sequence of 0 and 1 bits. But this would enable you to verify that the program works correctly.

EXERCISES FOR SECTION 7.6

SELF-CHECK

1. Why did we make clones of the bit string code in recursive method `buildCodeTable`? What would happen if we didn't?

PROGRAMMING

1. Write a class to complete the test of the `MapContactList` class.

7.7 Navigable Sets and Maps

The `SortedSet` interface (part of Java 5.0) extends the `Set` by enabling the user to get an ordered view of the elements with the ordering defined by a `compareTo` method or by means of a `Comparator`. Because the items have an ordering, additional methods can be defined, which return the first and last elements and define subsets over a specified range. However, the ability to define subsets was limited. In particular, subsets were defined always to include the starting element and to exclude the ending element. The Java 5.0 `SortedMap` interface provides an ordered view of a map with the elements ordered by key value. Because the elements of a submap are ordered, submaps can also be defined.

In Java 6, the NavigableSet and NavigableMap interfaces were introduced as an extension to SortedSet and SortedMap. The new interfaces allow the user to specify whether the start or end items are included or excluded. They also enable the user to specify a subset or submap that is traversable in the reverse order. As they are more general, we will discuss the NavigableSet and NavigableMap interfaces. Java retains the SortedSet and SortedMap interfaces for compatibility with existing software. Table 7.13 shows some methods of the NavigableSet interface.

TABLE 7.13
NavigableSet Interface

Method	Behavior
E ceiling(E e)	Returns the smallest element in this set that is greater than or equal to e, or null if there is no such element.
Iterator<E> descendingIterator()	Returns an iterator that traverses the Set in descending order.
NavigableSet<E> descendingSet()	Returns a reverse order view of this set.
E first()	Returns the smallest element in the set.
E floor(E e)	Returns the largest element that is less than or equal to e, or null if there is no such element.
NavigableSet<E> headset(E toEl, boolean incl)	Returns a view of the subset of this set whose elements are less than toEl. If incl is true, the subset includes the element toEl if it exists.
E higher(E e)	Returns the smallest element in this set that is strictly greater than e, or null if there is no such element.
Iterator<E> iterator()	Returns an iterator to the elements in the set that traverses the set in ascending order.
E last()	Returns the largest element in the set.
E lower(E e)	Returns the largest element in this set that is strictly less than e, or null if there is no such element.
E pollFirst()	Retrieves and removes the first element. If the set is empty, returns null.
E pollLast()	Retrieves and removes the last element. If the set is empty, returns null.
NavigableSet<E> subSet(E fromEl, boolean fromIncl, E toEl, boolean toIncl)	Returns a view of the subset of this set that ranges from fromEl to toEl. If the corresponding fromIncl or toIncl is true, then the fromEl or toEl elements are included.
NavigableSet<E> tailSet(E fromEl, boolean incl)	Returns a view of the subset of this set whose elements are greater than fromEl. If incl is true, the subset includes the element fromE if it exists.

EXAMPLE 7.12 Listing 7.13 illustrates the use of a NavigableSet. The output of this program consists of the lines:

```
The original set odds is [1, 3, 5, 7, 9]
The ordered set b is [3, 5, 7]
Its first element is 3
Its smallest element >= 6 is 7
```

LISTING 7.13

Using a NavigableSet

```
public static void main(String[] args) {
    // Create and fill the sets
    NavigableSet<Integer> odds = new TreeSet<Integer>();
    odds.add(5); odds.add(3); odds.add(7); odds.add(1); odds.add(9);
    System.out.println("The original set odds is " + odds);
    NavigableSet b = odds.subSet(1, false, 7, true);
    System.out.println("The ordered set b is " + b);
    System.out.println("Its first element is " + b.first());
    System.out.println("Its smallest element >= 6 is " + b.ceiling(6));
}
```

The methods defined by the NavigableMap interface are similar to those defined in NavibableSet except that the parameters are keys and the results are either keys, Map.Entrys, or submaps. For example, the NavigableSet has a method ceiling that returns a single set element or **null** while the NavigableMap has two similar methods: ceilingEntry(K key), which returns the Map.Entry that is associated with the smallest key greater than or equal to the given key, and ceilingKey(K key), which returns just the key of that entry.

Table 7.14 shows some methods of the NavigableMap interface. Not shown are methods firstKey, firstEntry, floorKey, floorEntry, lowerKey, lowerEntry, lastKey, lastEntry, higherKey, higherEntry, which have the same relationship to their NavigableSet counterparts (methods first, floor, etc.) as do ceilingKey and ceilingEntry.

The entries in a NavigableMap can be processed in key-value order. This is sometimes a desirable feature, which is not available in a HashMap (or hash table). Class TreeMap and a new Java 6 class, ConcurrentSkipListMap, implement the NavigableMap interface. To use the class ConcurrentSkipListSet or ConcurrentSkipListMap, you must insert both of the following statements.

```
import java.util.*;
import java.util.concurrent.*;
```

Application of a NavigableMap

Listing 7.14 shows methods computeAverage and computeSpans. The method computeAverage computes the average of the values defined in a Map. Method computeSpans creates a group of submaps of a NavigableMap and passes each submap to computeAverage. Given a NavigableMap in which the keys represent years and the values some statistic for that year, we can generate a table of averages covering

TABLE 7.14
NavigableMap Inteface

Method	Behavior
`Map.Entry<K, V> ceilingEntry(K key)`	Returns a key-value mapping associated with the least key greater than or equal to the given key, or `null` if there is no such key.
`K ceilingKey(K key)`	Returns the least key greater than or equal to the given key, or `null` if there is no such key.
`NavigableSet<K> descendingKeySet()`	Returns a reverse-order `NavigableSet` view of the keys contained in this map.
`NavigableMap<K, V> descendingMap()`	Returns a reverse-order view of this map.
`NavigableMap<K, V> headMap(K toKey, boolean incl)`	Returns a view of the submap of this map whose keys are less than `toKey`. If `incl` is `true`, the submap includes the entry with key `toKey` if it exists.
`NavigableMap<K, V> subMap(K fromKey, boolean fromIncl, K toKey, boolean toIncl)`	Returns a view of the submap of this map that ranges from `fromKey` to `toKey`. If the corresponding `fromIncl` or `toIncl` is `true`, then the entries with key `fromKey` or `toKey` are included.
`NavigableSet<E> tailMap(K fromKey, boolean fromIncl)`	Returns a view of the submap of this map whose elements are greater than `fromKey`. If `fromIncl` is `true`, the submap includes the entry with key `fromKey` if it exists.
`NavigableSet<K> navigableKeySet()`	Returns a `NavigableSet` view of the keys contained in this map.

different periods. For example, if we have a map of storms that represents the number of tropical storms in a given year for the period 1960–1969, the method call

```
List<Number> stormAverage = computeSpans(storms, 2);
```

will calculate the average number of storms for the years 1960–1961, 1962–1963, and so on, and store these values in the `List` `stormAverage`. The value passed to `delta` is 2, so within method `computeSpans`, the first statement below

```
double average =
    computeAverage(valueMap.subMap(index, true,
                                   index+delta, false));
result.add(average);
```

will create a submap for a pair of years (years `index` and `index+1`) and then compute the average of the two values in this submap. The second statement appends the average to the `List` `result`. This would be repeated for each pair of years starting with the first pair (1960–1961). For the method call

```
List<Number> stormAverage = computeSpans(storms, 3);
```

a submap would be created for each nonoverlapping group of three years: 1960–1962, 1963–1965, 1966–1968, and then 1969 by itself. The average of the three values in each submap (except for the last, which contains just one entry) would be calculated and stored in List result.

LISTING 7.14

Methods computeAverage and computeSpans

```
/** Returns the average of the numbers in its Map argument.
    @param valueMap The map whose values are averaged
    @return The average of the map values
*/
public static double computeAverage(Map<Integer, Double> valueMap) {
    int count = 0;
    double sum = 0;
    for (Map.Entry<Integer, Double> entry : valueMap.entrySet()) {
        sum += entry.getValue().doubleValue();
        count++;
    }
    return (double) sum / count;
}

/** Returns a list of the averages of nonoverlapping spans of
    values in its NavigableMap argument.
    @param valueMap The map whose values are averaged
    @param delta The number of map values in each span
    @return An ArrayList of average values for each span
*/
public static List<Double> computeSpans(NavigableMap valueMap, int delta)
{
    List<Double> result = new ArrayList<Double>();
    Integer min = (Integer) valueMap.firstEntry().getKey();
    Integer max = (Integer) valueMap.lastEntry().getKey();
    for (int index = min; index <= max; index += delta) {
        double average =
            computeAverage(valueMap.subMap(index, true,
                                           index+delta, false));
        result.add(average);
    }
    return result;
}
```

EXERCISES FOR SECTION 7.7

SELF-CHECK

1. What is displayed by the execution of the following program?

```
public static void main(String[] args) {
    NavigableSet<Integer> s = new TreeSet<Integer>();
    s.add(5); s.add(6); s.add(3); s.add(2); s.add(9);
    NavigableSet<Integer> a = s.subSet(1, true, 9, false);
    NavigableSet<Integer> b = s.subSet(4, true, 9, true);
    System.out.println(a);
    System.out.println(b);
    System.out.println(s.higher(5));
    System.out.println(s.lower(5));
```

```
    System.out.println(a.first());
    System.out.println(b.lower(4));
    int sum = 0;
    for (int i : a) {
        System.out.println(i);
        sum += i;
    }
    System.out.println(sum);
}
```

2. Trace the execution of methods computeSpans and computeAverage for the call computeSpans(storms, 4) where NavigableMap<Integer, Double> storms has the following entries: {(1960, 10), (1961, 5), (1962, 20), (1963, 8), (1964, 16), (1965, 50), (1966, 25), (1967, 15), (1968, 21), (1969, 13)}.
3. Write an algorithm for method computeGaps that has two parameters like computeSpans, except the int parameter represents the number of years between entries in the NavigableMap that are being averaged together. For NavigableMap storms defined in the previous exercise, the call computeGaps(storms, 2) would first compute the average for the values in {(1960, 10), (1962, 20), (1964, 16) . . . } and then compute the average for the values in {(1961, 5), (1963, 8), (1965, 50) . . . }.

PROGRAMMING

1. Write a program fragment to display the elements of a set s in normal order and then in reverse order.
2. Write a main method that tests method computeSpans.
3. Code method computeGaps from Self-Check Exercise 2.

Chapter Review

- The Set interface describes an abstract data type that supports the same operations as a mathematical set. We use Set objects to store a collection of elements that are not ordered by position. Each element in the collection is unique. Sets are useful for determining whether a particular element is in the collection, not its position or relative order.
- The Map interface describes an abstract data type that enables a user to access information (a value) corresponding to a specified key. Each key is unique and is mapped to a value that may or may not be unique. Maps are useful for retrieving or updating the value corresponding to a given key.
- A hash table uses hashing to transform an item's key into a table index so that insertions, retrievals, and deletions can be performed in expected O(1) time. When the hashCode method is applied to a key, it should return an integer value that appears to be a random number. A good hashCode method should be easy to compute and should distribute its values evenly throughout the range of **int** values. We use modulo division to transform the hash code value to a table index. Best performance occurs when the table size is a prime number.

- A collision occurs when two keys hash to the same table index. Collisions are expected, and hash tables utilize either open addressing or chaining to resolve collisions. In open addressing, each table element references a key-value pair, or `null` if it is empty. During insertion, a new entry is stored at the table element corresponding to its hash index if it is empty; otherwise, it is stored in the next empty location following the one selected by its hash index. In chaining, each table element references a linked list of key-value pairs with that hash index or `null` if none does. During insertion, a new entry is stored in the linked list of key-value pairs for its hash index.
- In open addressing, linear probing is often used to resolve collisions. In linear probing, finding a target or an empty table location involves incrementing the table index by 1 after each probe. This approach may cause clusters of keys to occur in the table, leading to overlapping search chains and poor performance. To minimize the harmful effect of clustering, quadratic probing increments the index by the square of the probe number. Quadratic probing can, however, cause a table to appear to be full when there is still space available, and it can lead to an infinite loop.
- The best way to avoid collisions is to keep the table load factor relatively low by rehashing when the load factor reaches a value such as 0.75 (75 percent full). To rehash, you increase the table size and reinsert each table element.
- In open addressing, you can't remove an element from the table when you delete it, but you must mark it as deleted. In chaining, you can remove a table element when you delete it. In either case, traversal of a hash table visits its entries in an arbitrary order.
- A set view of a `Map` can be obtained through method `entrySet`. You can create an `Iterator` object for this set view and use it to access the elements in the set view in order by key value.
- Two Java API implementations of the `Map` (`Set`) interface are `HashMap` (`HashSet`) and `TreeMap` (`TreeSet`). The `HashMap` (and `HashSet`) implementation uses an underlying hash table; the `TreeMap` (and `TreeSet`) implementations use a Red-Black tree. Search and retrieval operations are more efficient using the underlying hash table (expected $O(1)$ versus $O(\log n)$). The tree implementation, however, enables you to traverse the key-value pairs in a meaningful way and allows for subsets based on a range of key values.
- The Java 6 `NavigableSet` and `NavigableMap` interfaces enable the creation of subsets and submaps that may or may not include specified boundary items. The elements in a `NavigableSet` (or `NavigableMap`) are in increasing order by element value (or by key value for a `NavigableMap`).
- The Java 6 `ConcurrentSkipListSet` and `ConcurrentSkipListMap` are new classes that implement these interfaces.

Java API Interfaces and Classes Introduced in This Chapter

```
java.util.AbstractMap
java.util.AbstractSet
java.util.concurrent.ConcurrentSkipListMap
java.util.concurrent.ConcurrentSkipListSet
java.util.HashMap
java.util.HashSet
java.util.Map
java.util.Map.Entry
java.util.NavigableMap
java.util.NavigableSet
java.util.Set
java.util.TreeMap
java.util.TreeSet
```

User-Defined Interfaces and Classes in This Chapter

```
BitString                  HashtableChain
ContactListInterface       HashtableOpen
Entry                      KWHashMap
EntrySet                   MapContactList
HashSetOpen                SetIterator
```

Quick-Check Exercises

1. If s is a set that contains the characters `'a'`, `'b'`, `'c'`, write a statement to insert the character `'d'`.
2. What is the effect of each of the following method calls, given the set in Exercise 1, and what does it return?

```
s.add('a');
s.add('A');
next = 'b';
s.contains(next);
```

For Questions 3–7, a `Map`, `m`, contains the following entries: `(1234, "Jane Doe")`, `(1999, "John Smith")`, `(1250, "Ace Ventura")`, `(2000, "Bill Smythe")`, `(2999, "Nomar Garciaparra")`.

3. What is the effect of the statement `m.put(1234, "Jane Smith");`? What is returned?
4. What is returned by `m.get(1234)`? What is returned by `m.get(1500)`?
5. If the entries for `Map m` are stored in a hash table of size 1000 with open addressing and linear probing, where would each of the items be stored?
6. Answer Question 5 for the case where the entries were stored using quadratic probing.
7. Answer Question 5 for the case where the entries were stored using chaining.
8. What class does the Java API provide that facilitates coding an implementer of the `Map` interface? Of the `Set` interface?
9. List two classes that the Java API provides that implement the `Map` interface. List two that implement the `Set` interface.
10. You apply method ______ to a `Map` to create a set view. You apply method ______ to this set view to get an object that facilitates sequential access to the `Map` elements.

Review Questions

1. Show where the following keys would be placed in a hash table of size 5 using open addressing: 1000, 1002, 1007, 1003. Where would these keys be after rehashing to a table of size 11?
2. Answer Question 1 for a hash table that uses chaining.
3. Write a `toString` method for class `HashtableOpen`. This method should display each table element that is not **`null`** and is not deleted.
4. Class `HashtableChain` uses the class `LinkedList`, which is implemented as a double-linked list. Write the `put` method using a single-linked list to hold elements that hash to the same index.
5. Write the `get` method for the class in Question 4.
6. Write the `remove` method for the class in Question 4.
7. Write inner class `EntrySet` for the class in Question 4 (see Listing. 7.11).

Programming Projects

1. Complete all methods of class `HuffmanTree` and test them out using a document file and a Java source file on your computer. You can download class `BitString` from the Web site for this textbook.
2. Use a `HashMap` to store the frequency counts for all the words in a large text document. When you are done, display the contents of this `HashMap`. Next, create a set view of the `Map` and store its contents in an array. Then sort the array based on key value and display it. Finally, sort the array in decreasing order by frequency and display it.
3. Solve Project 2 using a `TreeMap`. You can display the words in key sequence without performing a sort.
4. Modify Project 2 to save the line numbers for every occurrence of a word as well as the count.
5. (Based on an example in Brian W. Kernighan and Rob Pike, *The Practice of Programming,* Addison-Wesley, 1999) We want to generate "random text" in the style of another author. Your first task is to collect a group of prefix strings of two words that occur in a text file and associate them with a list of suffix strings using a `Map`. For example, the text for Charles Dickens' *A Christmas Carol* contains the four phrases:

   Marley was dead: to begin with.
   Marley was as dead as a door-nail.
   Marley was as dead as a door-nail.
   Marley was dead.

   The prefix string `"Marley was"` would be associated with the `ArrayList` containing the four suffix strings `"dead:"`, `"as"`, `"as"`, `"dead."`. You must go through the text and examine each successive pair of two-word strings to see whether that pair is already in the map as a key. If so, add the next word to the `ArrayList` that is the value for that prefix string. For example, in examining the first two sentences shown, you would first add to the entry (`"Marley was"`, `ArrayList "dead:"`). Next you would add the entry (`"was dead"`, `ArrayList "as"`). Next you would add the entry (`"dead as"`, `ArrayList "a"`), and so on. When you retrieve the prefix `"Marley was"` again, you would modify the `ArrayList` that is its value, and the entry would become (`"Marley was"`, `ArrayList "dead:", "as"`). When you are all finished, add the entry `"THE_END"` to the suffix list for the last prefix placed in the `Map`.

Once you have scanned the complete text, it is time to use the Map to begin generating new text that is in the same style as the old text. Output the first prefix you placed in the Map: "Marley was". Then retrieve the ArrayList that is the value for this prefix. Randomly select one of the suffixes and then output the suffix. For example, the output text so far might be "Marley was dead" if the suffix "dead" was selected from the ArrayList of suffixes for "Marley was". Now continue with the two-word sequence consisting of the second word from the previous prefix and the suffix (that would be the string "was dead"). Look it up in the map, randomly select one of the suffixes, and output it. Continue this process until the suffix "THE_END" is selected.

6. Complete class HashtableOpen so that it fully implements the Map interface described in Section 7.2. As part of this, write method entrySet and classes EntrySet and SetIterator as described in Section 7.5. Class SetIterator provides methods hasNext and next. Use data field index to keep track of the next value of the iterator (initially 0). Data field lastItemReturned keeps track of the index of the last item returned by next; this is used by the remove method. The remove method removes the last item returned by the next method from the Set. It may only be called once for each call to next. Thus, the remove method checks to see that lastItemReturned has a valid value (not –1) and then sets it to an invalid value (–1) just before returning to the caller.
7. Complete class HashtableChain so that it fully implements the Map interface, and test it out. Complete class SetIterator as described in Project 6.
8. Complete the implementation of class HashSetOpen, writing it as an adapter class of HashtableOpen.
9. Complete the implementation of class HashSetChain, writing it as an adapter class of HashtableChain.
10. Revise method put for HashtableOpen to place a new item into an already deleted spot in the search chain. Don't forget to check the scenario where the key has already been inserted.

Answers to Quick-Check Exercises

1. s.add('d');
2.
```
s.add('a');          // add 'a', duplicate - returns false
s.add('A');          // add 'A', returns true
next = 'b';
s.contains(next);    // 'b' is in the set, returns true
```
3. The value associated with key 1234 is changed to "Jane Smith". The string "Jane Doe" is returned.
4. The string "Jane Doe" and then **null**.
5. 1234 at 234, 1999 at 999, 1250 at 250, 2000 at 000, 3999 at 001.
6. 1234 at 234, 1999 at 999, 1250 at 250, 2000 at 000, 3999 at 003.
7. 2000 in a linked list at 000, 1234 in a linked list at 234, 1250 in a linked list at 250, 1999 and 3999 in a linked list at 999.
8. AbstractMap, AbstractSet
9. HashMap and TreeMap, HashSet and TreeSet
10. entrySet, iterator

Chapter 8

Sorting

Chapter Objectives

- To learn how to use the standard sorting methods in the Java API
- To learn how to implement the following sorting algorithms: selection sort, bubble sort, insertion sort, Shell sort, merge sort, heapsort, and quicksort
- To understand the difference in performance of these algorithms, and which to use for small arrays, which to use for medium arrays, and which to use for large arrays

Sorting is the process of rearranging the data in an array or a list so that it is in increasing (or decreasing) order. Because sorting is done so frequently, computer scientists have devoted much time and effort to developing efficient algorithms for sorting arrays. Even though many languages (including Java) provide sorting utilities, it is still very important to study these algorithms because they illustrate several well-known ways to solve the sorting problem, each with its own merits. You should know how they are written so that you can duplicate them if you need to use them with languages that don't have sorting utilities.

Another reason for studying these algorithms is that they illustrate some very creative approaches to problem solving. For example, the insertion sort algorithm adapts an approach used by card players to arrange a hand of cards; the merge sort algorithm builds on a technique used to sort external data files. Several algorithms use divide-and-conquer to break a larger problem into more manageable subproblems. The Shell sort is a very efficient sort that works by sorting many small subarrays using insertion sort, which is a relatively inefficient sort when used by itself. The merge sort and quicksort algorithms are both recursive. Method heapsort uses a heap as its underlying data structure. The final reason for studying sorting is to learn how computer scientists analyze and compare the performance of several different algorithms that perform the same operation.

We will cover three quadratic ($O(n^2)$) sorting algorithms that are fairly simple and appropriate for sorting small arrays but are not recommended for large arrays. We will also discuss three sorting algorithms that give improved performance ($O(n \log n)$) on large arrays and one that gives performance that is much better than $O(n^2)$ but not as good as $O(n \log n)$.

Our goal is to provide a sufficient selection of quadratic sorts and faster sorts. A few other sorting algorithms are described in the programming projects. Our expectation is that your instructor will select which algorithms you should study.

Sorting

8.1 Using Java Sorting Methods

The Java API `java.util` provides a class `Arrays` with several overloaded `sort` methods for different array types. In addition, the class `Collections` (also part of the API `java.util`) contains similar sorting methods for `Lists`. The methods for arrays of primitive types are based on the quicksort algorithm (Section 8.9), and the methods for arrays of `Objects` and for `Lists` are based on the merge sort algorithm (Section 8.7). Both algorithms are $O(n \log n)$.

Method `Arrays.sort` is defined as a **`public static void`** method and is overloaded (see Table 8.1). The first argument in a call can be an array of any primitive type (although we have just shown `int[]`) or an array of objects. If the first argument is an array of objects, then either the class type of the array must implement the `Comparable` interface or a `Comparator` object must be passed as the last argument (see Section 6.5). A class that implements the `Comparable` interface must define a `compareTo` method that determines the natural ordering of its objects. If a `Comparator` is passed, its `compare` method will be used to determine the ordering.

For method `Collections.sort` (see Table 8.1), the first argument must be a collection of objects that implement the `List` interface (e.g., an `ArrayList` or a `LinkedList`). If only one argument is provided, the objects in the `List` must implement the `Comparable` interface. Method `compareTo` is called by the sorting method to determine the relative ordering of two objects.

Optionally, a `Comparator` can be passed as a second argument. Using a `Comparator`, you can compare objects based on some other information rather than using their natural ordering (as determined by method `compareTo`). The `Comparator` object must be the last argument in the call to the sorting method. Rather than rearranging the elements in the `List`, method `sort` first copies the `List` elements to an array, sorts the array using `Arrays.sort`, and then copies them back to the `List`.

TABLE 8.1
Methods `sort` in Classes `java.util.Arrays` and `java.util.Collections`

Method sort in Class Arrays	Behavior
`public static void sort(int[] items)`	Sorts the array `items` in ascending order.
`public static void sort(int[] items, int fromIndex, int toIndex)`	Sorts array elements `items[fromIndex]` to `items[toIndex]` in ascending order.
`public static void sort(Object[] items)`	Sorts the objects in array `items` in ascending order using their natural ordering (defined by method `compareTo`). All objects in `items` must implement the `Comparable` interface and must be mutually comparable.
`public static void sort(Object[] items, int fromIndex, int toIndex)`	Sorts array elements `items[fromIndex]` to `items[toIndex]` in ascending order using their natural ordering (defined by method `compareTo`). All objects must implement the `Comparable` interface and must be mutually comparable.
`public static <T> void sort(T[] items, Comparator<? super T> comp)`	Sorts the objects in `items` in ascending order as defined by method `comp.compare`. All objects in `items` must be mutually comparable using method `comp.compare`.
`public static <T> void sort(T[] items, int fromIndex, int toIndex, Comparator<? super T> comp)`	Sorts the objects in `items[fromIndex]` to `items[toIndex]` in ascending order as defined by method `comp.compare`. All objects in `items` must be mutually comparable using method `comp.compare`.
Method sort in Class Collections	**Behavior**
`public static <T extends Comparable<T>> void sort(List<T> list)`	Sorts the objects in `list` in ascending order using their natural ordering (defined by method `compareTo`). All objects in `list` must implement the `Comparable` interface and must be mutually comparable.
`public static <T> void sort (List<T> list, Comparator<? super T> comp)`	Sorts the objects in `list` in ascending order as defined by method `comp.compare`. All objects must be mutually comparable.

SYNTAX Declaring a Generic Method

FORM:

methodModifiers <genericParameters> returnType methodName(methodParameters)

EXAMPLE:

```
public static <T extends Comparable<T>> int binarySearch(T[] items,
                                                          T target)
```

MEANING:

To declare a generic method, list the *genericParameters* inside the symbol pair <> and between the *methodModifiers* (e.g., public static) and the return type. The *genericParameters* can then be used in the specification of the *methodParameters*.

In class Arrays, the two methods that use a Comparator are *generic methods*. Generic methods, like generic classes, have parameters. The generic parameter(s) precede the method type. For example, in the declaration

```
public static <T> void sort(T[] items, Comparator<? super T> comp)
```

T represents the generic parameter for the sort method and should appear in the method parameter list (e.g., T[] items). For the second method parameter, the notation Comparator<? super T> means that comp must be an object that implements the Comparator interface for type T or for a superclass of type T. For example, you can define a class that implements Comparator<Number> and use it to sort an array of Integer objects or an array of Double objects.

Both methods in class Collections are generic.

```
public static <T extends Comparable<T>> void sort(List<T> list)
```

The notation <T extends Comparable<T>> means that generic parameter T must implement the interface Comparable<T>. The method parameter list (the object being sorted) is of type List<T>.

EXAMPLE 8.1 If array items stores a collection of integers, the method call

```
Arrays.sort(items, 0, items.length / 2) ;
```

sorts the integers in the first half of the array, leaving the second half of the array unchanged.

EXAMPLE 8.2 Let's assume class Person is defined as follows:

```
public class Person implements Comparable<Person> {
    // Data Fields
    /* The last name */
    private String lastName;
    /* The first name */
    private String firstName;
    /* Birthday represented by an integer from 1 to 366 */
    private int birthDay;

    // Methods
    /** Compares two Person objects based on names. The result
        is based on the last names if they are different;
        otherwise, it is based on the first names.
        @param obj The other Person
        @return A negative integer if this person's name
                precedes the other person's name;
                0 if the names are the same;
                a positive integer if this person's name follows
                the other person's name.
    */
    @Override
    public int compareTo(Person obj) {
        Person other = obj;
        // Compare this Person to other using last names.
        int result = lastName.compareTo(other.lastName);
        // Compare first names if last names are the same.
        if (result == 0)
            return firstName.compareTo(other.firstName);
        else
            return result;
    }

    // Other methods
    . . .
}
```

Method `Person.compareTo` compares two `Person` objects based on their names using the last name as the primary key and the first name as the secondary key (the natural ordering). If `people` is an array of `Person` objects, the statement

```
Arrays.sort(people);
```

places the elements in array `people` in ascending order based on their names. Although the sort operation is $O(n \log n)$, the comparison of two names is $O(k)$ where k is the length of the shorter name.

EXAMPLE 8.3 You can also use a class that implements Comparator<Person> to compare Person objects. As an example, method compare in class ComparePerson compares two Person objects based on their birthdays, not their names.

```
import java.util.Comparator;

public class ComparePerson implements Comparator<Person> {
    /** Compare two Person objects based on birth date.
        @param left The left-hand side of the comparison
        @param right The right-hand side of the comparison
        @return A negative integer if the left person's birthday
                precedes the right person's birthday;
                0 if the birthdays are the same;
                a positive integer if the left person's birthday
                follows the right person's birthday.
    */
    @Override
    public int compare(Person left, Person right) {
        return left.getBirthDay() - right.getBirthDay();
    }
}
```

If peopleList is a List of Person objects, the statement

```
Collections.sort(peopleList, new ComparePerson());
```

places the elements in peopleList in ascending order based on their birthdays. Comparing two birthdays is an O(1) operation.

EXERCISES FOR SECTION 8.1

SELF-CHECK

1. Indicate whether each of the following method calls is valid. Describe why it isn't valid or, if it is valid, describe what it does. Assume people is an array of Person objects and peopleList is a List of Person objects.
   a. `people.sort();`
   b. `Arrays.sort(people, 0, people.length - 3);`
   c. `Arrays.sort(peopleList, 0, peopleList.length - 3);`
   d. `Collections.sort(people);`
   e. `Collections.sort(peopleList, new ComparePerson());`
   f. `Collections.sort(peopleList, 0, peopleList.size() - 3);`

PROGRAMMING

1. Write a method call to sort the last half of array people using the natural ordering.
2. Write a method call to sort the last half of array people using the ordering determined by class ComparePerson.
3. Write a method call to sort peopleList using the natural ordering.

8.2 Selection Sort

Selection sort is a relatively easy-to-understand algorithm that sorts an array by making several passes through the array, *selecting* the next smallest item in the array each time, and placing it where it belongs in the array. We illustrate all sorting algorithms using an array of integer values for simplicity. However, each algorithm sorts an array of `Comparable` objects, so the `int` values must be wrapped in `Integer` objects.

We show the algorithm next, where n is the number of elements in an array with subscripts 0 through $n - 1$ and `fill` is the subscript of the element that will store the next smallest item in the array.

Selection Sort Algorithm

1. **for** `fill = 0` to `n - 2` do
2. Set `posMin` to the subscript of the smallest item in the subarray starting at subscript `fill`.
3. Exchange the item at `posMin` with the one at `fill`.

Step 2 involves a search for the smallest item in each subarray. It requires a loop in which we compare each element in the subarray, starting with the one at position `fill + 1`, with the smallest value found so far. In the refinement of Step 2 shown in the following algorithm (Steps 2.1 through 2.4), we use `posMin` to store the subscript of the smallest value found so far. We assume that its initial position is `fill`.

Refinement of Selection Sort Algorithm (Step 2)

2.1 Initialize `posMin` to `fill`.
2.2 **for** `next = fill + 1` to `n - 1`
2.3 `if` the item at `next` is less than the item at `posMin`
2.4 Reset `posMin` to `next`.

First the selection sort algorithm finds the smallest item in the array (smallest is 20) and moves it to position 0 by exchanging it with the element currently at position 0. At this point, the sorted part of the array consists of the new element at position 0. The values to be exchanged are shaded dark in all diagrams.

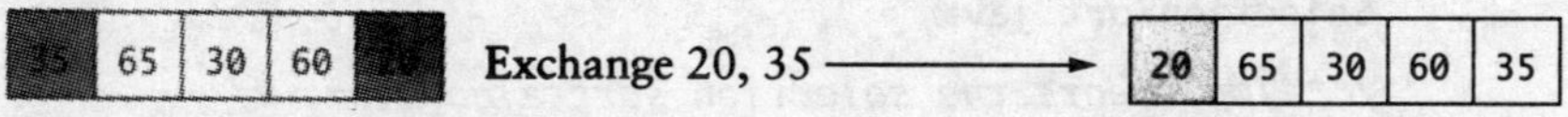

Next the algorithm finds the smallest item in the subarray starting at position 1 (next smallest is 30) and exchanges it with the element currently at position 1:

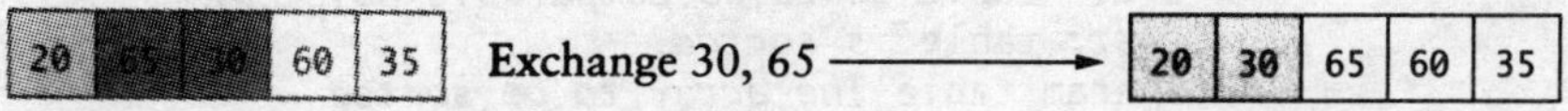

At this point, the sorted portion of the array consists of the elements at positions 0 and 1. Next the algorithm selects the smallest item in the subarray starting at position 2 (next smallest is 35) and exchanges it with the element currently at position 2:

20	30	[redacted]	60	[redacted]	Exchange 35, 65 →	20	30	35	60	65

At this point, the sorted portion of the array consists of the elements at positions 0, 1, and 2. Next the algorithm selects the smallest item in the subarray starting at position 3 (next smallest is 60) and exchanges it with the element currently at position 3:

20	30	35	[redacted]	65	Exchange 60 with itself →	20	30	35	60	65

The element at position 4, the last position in the array, must store the largest value (largest is 65), so the array is sorted.

Analysis of Selection Sort

Steps 2 and 3 are performed $n - 1$ times. Step 3 performs an exchange of items; consequently, there are $n - 1$ exchanges.

Step 2.3 involves a comparison of items and is performed $(n - 1 - \textit{fill})$ times for each value of *fill*. Since *fill* takes on all values between 0 and $n - 2$, the following series computes the number of executions of Step 2.3:

$$(n-1) + (n-2) + \cdots + 3 + 2 + 1$$

This is a well-known series that can be written in closed form as

$$\frac{n \times (n-1)}{2} = \frac{n^2}{2} - \frac{n}{2}$$

For very large n we can ignore all but the most significant term in this expression, so the number of comparisons is $O(n^2)$ and the number of exchanges is $O(n)$. Because the number of comparisons increases with the square of n, the selection sort is called a *quadratic sort*.

Code for Selection Sort

Listing 8.1 shows the code for selection sort, which follows the algorithm above.

LISTING 8.1

SelectionSort.java

```java
/** Implements the selection sort algorithm. */
public class SelectionSort {

    /** Sort the array using selection sort algorithm.
        pre:  table contains Comparable objects.
        post: table is sorted.
        @param table The array to be sorted
     */
    public static void sort(Comparable[] table) {
        int n = table.length;
        for (int fill = 0; fill < n - 1; fill++) {
            // Invariant: table[0 . . . fill - 1] is sorted.
            int posMin = fill;
```

```
            for (int next = fill + 1; next < n; next++) {
                // Invariant: table[posMin] is the smallest item in
                // table[fill . . . next - 1].
                if (table[next].compareTo(table[posMin]) < 0) {
                    posMin = next;
                }
            }
            // assert: table[posMin] is the smallest item in
            // table[fill . . . n - 1].
            // Exchange table[fill] and table[posMin].
            Comparable temp = table[fill];
            table[fill] = table[posMin];
            table[posMin] = temp;
            // assert: table[fill] is the smallest item in
            // table[fill . . . n - 1].
        }
        // assert: table[0 . . . n - 1] is sorted.
    }
}
```

PROGRAM STYLE

Making Sort Methods Generic

The code in Listing 8.1 will compile, but it will generate a warning message regarding an unchecked call to compareTo. You can eliminate this warning message by making the sort a generic sort. To accomplish this for the sort above, change the method heading to

```
public static <T extends Comparable<T>> void sort(T[] table) {
```

where the generic type parameter, T, must implement the Comparable<T> interface. Also, change the data type of variable temp from Comparable to type T, the data type of the array elements.

```
T temp = table[fill];
```

We will code the other sorting algorithms in this chapter as generic methods.

EXERCISES FOR SECTION 8.2

SELF-CHECK

1. Show the progress of each pass of the selection sort for the following array. How many passes are needed? How many comparisons are performed? How many exchanges? Show the array after each pass.

   40 35 80 75 60 90 70 75 50 22

2. How would you modify selection sort to arrange an array of values in decreasing sequence?

3. It is not necessary to perform an exchange if the next smallest element is already at position `fill`. Modify the selection sort algorithm to eliminate the exchange of an element with itself. How does this affect big-O for exchanges? Discuss whether the time saved by eliminating unnecessary exchanges would exceed the cost of these extra steps.

PROGRAMMING

1. Modify the selection sort method to sort the elements in decreasing order and to incorporate the change in Self-Check Exercise 3.
2. Add statements to trace the progress of selection sort. Display the array contents after each exchange.

8.3 Bubble Sort

The next quadratic sorting algorithm, *bubble sort,* compares adjacent array elements and exchanges their values if they are out of order. In this way the smaller values *bubble* up to the top of the array (toward the first element), while the larger values sink to the bottom of the array, hence the name.

Bubble Sort Algorithm

1. **do**
2.   **for** each pair of adjacent array elements
3.   **if** the values in a pair are out of order
4.   Exchange the values
5. **while** the array is not sorted.

As an example, we will trace through one execution of Step 2, or one pass through an array being sorted. By scanning the diagrams of Figure 8.1 from left to right, you can see the effect of each comparison. The pair of array elements being compared is shown in a darker color in each diagram. The first pair of values (`table[0]` is 60, `table[1]` is 42) is out of order, so the values are exchanged. The next pair of values (`table[1]` is now 60, `table[2]` is 75) is compared in the second array shown in Figure 8.1; this pair is in order, and so is the next pair (`table[2]` is 75, `table[3]` is 83). The last pair (`table[3]` is 83, `table[4]` is 27) is out of order, so the values are exchanged as shown in the last diagram, and 83 has sunk to the bottom of the array.

FIGURE 8.1
One Pass of Bubble Sort

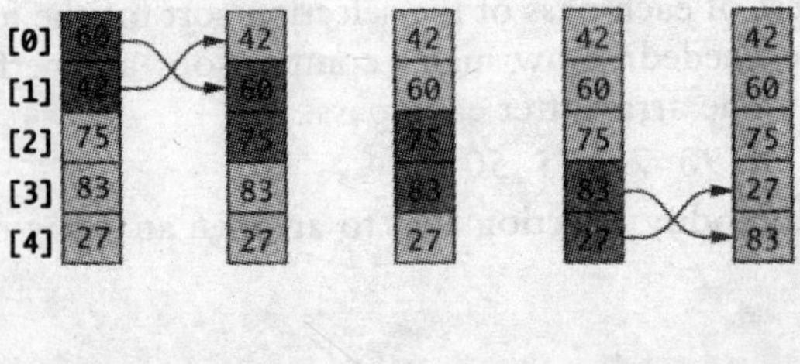

The last array shown in Figure 8.1 is closer to being sorted than is the original. The only value that is out of order is the number 27 in `table[3]`. Unfortunately, it will be necessary to complete three more passes through the array before this value bubbles up to the top of the array. In each of these passes, only one pair of values will be out of order, so only one exchange will be made. The contents of array `table` after the completion of each pass is shown in Figure 8.2; the portion that is sorted is shown in color.

FIGURE 8.2
Array after Completion of Each Pass

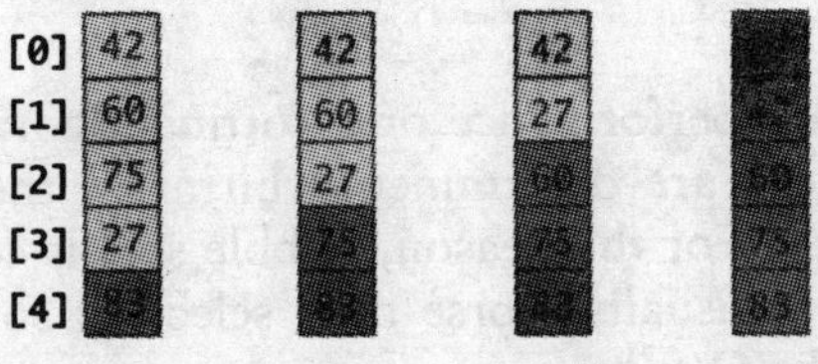

At the end of pass 1, only the last array element must be in its correct place; at the end of pass 2, the last two array elements must be in their correct places; and so on. There is no need to examine array elements that are already in place, so there is one less pair to test in the next pass. Only one pair will be tested during the last pass.

After the completion of four passes ($n - 1$ is 4), the array is now sorted. Sometimes an array will become sorted before $n - 1$ passes. This situation can be detected if a pass is made through the array without doing any exchanges. This is the reason for the **`boolean`** flag `exchanges` in the following refined bubble sort algorithm: to keep track of whether any exchanges were made during the current pass (`exchanges` is set to **`false`** when the pass begins and is reset to **`true`** after an exchange).

Refinement of Bubble Sort Algorithm (Step 2)

2.1 Initialize `exchanges` to **`false`**. // *No exchanges yet—array may be sorted*
2.2 **`for`** each pair of adjacent array elements
2.3 **`if`** the values in a pair are out of order
2.4 Exchange the values.
2.5 Set `exchanges` to **`true`**. // *Made an exchange, array not sorted*

Analysis of Bubble Sort

Because the actual numbers of comparisons and exchanges performed depend on the array being sorted, the bubble sort algorithm provides excellent performance in some cases and very poor performance in other cases. It works best when an array is nearly sorted to begin with.

Because all adjacent pairs of elements in the unsorted region are compared in each pass and there may be $n - 1$ passes, the number of comparisons is represented by the series

$$(n - 1) + (n - 2) + \cdots + 3 + 2 + 1$$

However, if the array becomes sorted early, the later phases and comparisons are not performed. In the worst case, the number of comparisons is $O(n^2)$. Unfortunately, each comparison can lead to an exchange if the array is badly out of order. The worst case occurs when the array is *inverted* (i.e., the array elements are in descending order as defined by the `compareTo` method), and the number of exchanges is $O(n^2)$.

The best case occurs when the array is already sorted. Only one pass will be required, in which there are $n - 1$ comparisons ($O(n)$ comparisons). If the array is sorted, there will be no exchanges, so the number of exchanges is 0 ($O(1)$ exchanges).

In estimating the worst-case performance of a sorting algorithm on a large array whose initial element values are determined arbitrarily, the definition of big-O requires us to be pessimistic. For this reason, bubble sort is considered a quadratic sort, and its performance is usually worse than selection sort ($O(n)$) because the number of exchanges can be $O(n^2)$.

Code for Bubble Sort

Listing 8.2 shows the code for the `BubbleSort` class. Notice that the outer **`do-while`** loop terminates when the condition (`exchanges`) is false. This indicates the array is sorted because no exchanges occurred during the pass just completed. If the array does not become sorted until all `n - 1` passes are completed, then an extra pass will be required. However, the inner loop will be exited immediately because `table.length - pass` will be equal to `0`.

The inner loop control variable, `i`, is the subscript of the first element of each pair; consequently, `i + 1` is the subscript of the second element of each pair. The initial value of `i` is 0. The final value must be one less than the last subscript in the unsorted region. For an array of `n` elements, the final value of `i` is `n - pass - 1`, where `pass` is the number of the current pass, starting at 1 for the first pass.

LISTING 8.2

`BubbleSort.java`

```
/** Implements the bubble sort algorithm. */
public class BubbleSort {

    /** Sort the array using bubble sort algorithm.
        pre:  table contains Comparable objects.
        post: table is sorted.
        @param table The array to be sorted
    */
    public static <T extends Comparable<T>> void sort(T[] table) {
        int pass = 1;
        boolean exchanges = false;
        do {
            // Invariant: Elements after table.length - pass + 1
            // are in place.
            exchanges = false;  // No exchanges yet.
```

```
            // Compare each pair of adjacent elements.
            for (int i = 0; i < table.length - pass; i++) {
                if (table[i].compareTo(table[i + 1]) > 0) {
                    // Exchange pair.
                    T temp = table[i];
                    table[i] = table[i + 1];
                    table[i + 1] = temp;
                    exchanges = true;  // Set flag.
                }
            }
            pass++;
        } while (exchanges);
        // assert: Array is sorted.
    }
}
```

EXERCISES FOR SECTION 8.3

SELF-CHECK

1. How many passes of bubble sort are needed to sort the following array of integers? How many comparisons are performed? How many exchanges? Show the array after each pass.

   40 35 80 75 60 90 70 75 50 22

2. How would you modify bubble sort to arrange an array of values in decreasing sequence?

PROGRAMMING

1. Add statements to trace the progress of bubble sort. Display the array contents after each pass is completed.

8.4 Insertion Sort

Our next quadratic sorting algorithm, *insertion sort,* is based on the technique used by card players to arrange a hand of cards. The player keeps the cards that have been picked up so far in sorted order. When the player picks up a new card, the player makes room for the new card and then *inserts* it in its proper place.

The left diagram of Figure 8.3 shows a hand of cards (ignoring suits) after three cards have been picked up. If the next card is an 8, it should be inserted between the 6 and 10, maintaining the numerical order (middle diagram). If the next card is a 7, it should be inserted between the 6 and 8 as shown on the right in Figure 8.3.

FIGURE 8.3
Picking Up a Hand of Cards

To adapt this insertion algorithm to an array that has been filled with data, we start with a sorted subarray consisting of the first element only. For example, in the leftmost array of Figure 8.4, the initial sorted subarray consists of only the first value 30 (in element 0). The array element(s) that are in order after each pass are in color, and the elements waiting to be inserted are in gray. We first *insert* the second element (25). Because it is smaller than the element in the sorted subarray, we insert it before the old first element (30), and the sorted subarray has two elements (25, 30 in second diagram). Next, we *insert* the third element (15). It is also smaller than all the elements in the sorted subarray so we insert it before the old first element (25), and the sorted subarray has three elements (15, 25, 30 in third diagram). Next, we *insert* the fourth element (20). It is smaller than the second and third elements in the sorted subarray so we insert it before the old second element (25), and the sorted subarray has four elements (15, 20, 25, 30 in the fourth diagram). Finally, we insert the last element (28). It is smaller than the last element in the sorted subarray, so we insert it before the old last element (30), and the array is sorted. The algorithm follows.

Insertion Sort Algorithm

1. **for** each array element from the second (`nextPos = 1`) to the last
2. Insert the element at `nextPos` where it belongs in the array, increasing the length of the sorted subarray by 1 element.

To accomplish Step 2, the insertion step, we need to make room for the element to be inserted (saved in `nextVal`) by shifting all values that are larger than it, starting with the last value in the sorted subarray.

FIGURE 8.4
An Insertion Sort

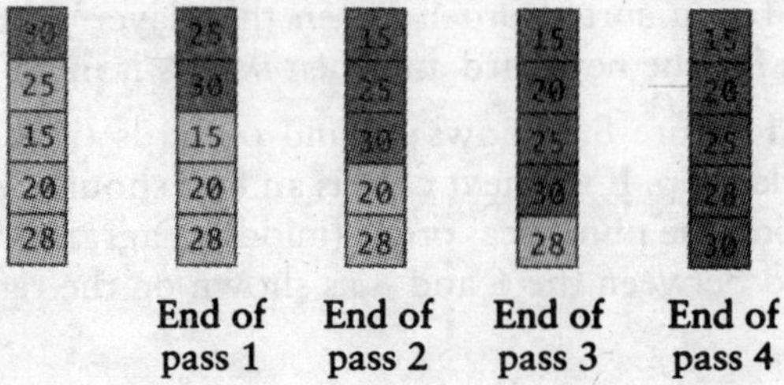

FIGURE 8.5
Inserting the Fourth Array Element

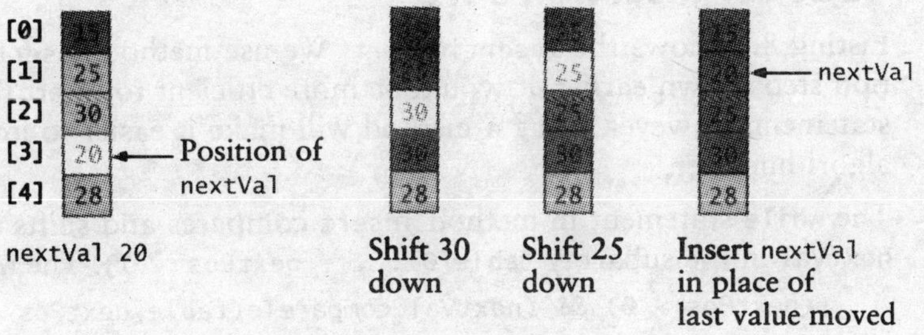

Refinement of Insertion Sort Algorithm (Step 2)

2.1 `nextPos` is the position of the element to insert.

2.2 Save the value of the element to insert in `nextVal`.

2.3 **`while`** `nextPos > 0` and the element at `nextPos - 1 > nextVal`

2.4   Shift the element at `nextPos - 1` to position `nextPos`.

2.5   Decrement `nextPos` by 1.

2.6 Insert `nextVal` at `nextPos`.

We illustrate these steps in Figure 8.5. For the array shown on the left, the first three elements (positions 0, 1, and 2) are in the sorted subarray, and the next element to insert is 20. First we save 20 in `nextVal` and 3 in `nextPos`. Then we shift the value in position 2 (30) down one position (see the second array in Figure 8.5), and then we shift the value in position 1 (25) down one position (see third array in Figure 8.5). After these shifts (third array), there will temporarily be two copies of the last value shifted (25). The first of these (shown in gray in Figure 8.5) is overwritten when the value in `nextVal` is moved into its correct position (`nextPos` is 1). The four-element sorted subarray is shown in color on the right of Figure 8.5.

Analysis of Insertion Sort

The insertion step is performed $n - 1$ times. In the worst case, all elements in the sorted subarray are compared to `nextVal` for each insertion, so the maximum number of comparisons is represented by the series

$$1 + 2 + 3 + \cdots + (n-2) + (n-1)$$

which is $O(n^2)$. In the best case (when the array is already sorted), only one comparison is required for each insertion, so the number of comparisons is $O(n)$. The number of shifts performed during an insertion is one less than the number of comparisons or, when the new value is the smallest so far, the same as the number of comparisons. However, a shift in an insertion sort requires the movement of only one item, whereas in a bubble sort or a selection sort, an exchange involves a temporary item and requires the movement of three items. A Java array of objects contains references to the actual objects, and it is these references that are changed. The actual objects remain in the physical locations where they were first created.

Code for Insertion Sort

Listing 8.3 shows the `InsertionSort`. We use method `insert` to perform the insertion step shown earlier. It would be more efficient to insert this code inside the **`for`** statement; however, using a method will make it easier to implement the Shell sort algorithm later.

The **`while`** statement in method `insert` compares and shifts all values greater than `nextVal` in the subarray `table[0 . . . nextPos - 1]`. The **`while`** condition

```
((nextPos > 0) && (nextVal.compareTo(table[nextPos - 1]) < 0))
```

causes loop exit if the first element has been moved or if `nextVal` is not less than the next element to move. It could lead to an out-of-range subscript error if the order of the conditions were reversed. Recall that Java performs short-circuit evaluation. If the left-hand operand of an && operation is false, the right-hand operand is not evaluated. If this were not the case, when `nextPos` becomes 0, the array subscript would be –1, which is outside the subscript range. Because `nextPos` is a value parameter, variable `nextPos` in `sort` is unchanged.

LISTING 8.3
InsertionSort.java

```
/** Implements the insertion sort algorithm. */
public class InsertionSort {
    /** Sort the table using insertion sort algorithm.
        pre: table contains Comparable objects.
        post: table is sorted.
        @param table The array to be sorted
     */
    public static <T extends Comparable<T>> void sort(T[] table) {
        for (int nextPos = 1; nextPos < table.length; nextPos++) {
            // Invariant: table[0 . . . nextPos - 1] is sorted.
            // Insert element at position nextPos
            // in the sorted subarray.
            insert(table, nextPos);
        } // End for.
    } // End sort.

    /** Insert the element at nextPos where it belongs
        in the array.
        pre: table[0 . . . nextPos - 1] is sorted.
        post: table[0 . . . nextPos] is sorted.
        @param table The array being sorted
        @param nextPos The position of the element to insert
     */
    private static <T extends Comparable<T>> void insert(T[] table,
                                                          int nextPos) {
        T nextVal = table[nextPos]; // Element to insert.
        while (nextPos > 0
               && nextVal.compareTo(table[nextPos - 1]) < 0) {
            table[nextPos] = table[nextPos - 1]; // Shift down.
            nextPos--;                  // Check next smaller element.
        }
        // Insert nextVal at nextPos.
        table[nextPos] = nextVal;
    }
}
```

EXERCISES FOR SECTION 8.4

SELF-CHECK

1. Sort the following array using insertion sort. How many passes are needed? How many comparisons are performed? How many exchanges? Show the array after each pass.
   40 35 80 75 60 90 70 75 50 22

PROGRAMMING

1. Eliminate method `insert` in Listing 8.3 and write its code inside the **for** statement.
2. Add statements to trace the progress of insertion sort. Display the array contents after the insertion of each value.

8.5 Comparison of Quadratic Sorts

Table 8.2 summarizes the performance of the three quadratic sorts. To give you some idea as to what these numbers mean, Table 8.3 shows some values of n and n^2. If n is small (say, 100 or less), it really doesn't matter which sorting algorithm you use. Of the three, insertion sort gives the best performance for most arrays, and bubble sort generally gives the worst performance. Insertion sort is better because it takes advantage of any partial sorting that is in the array and uses less costly shifts instead of exchanges to rearrange array elements. Unless the array is nearly sorted, bubble sort's performance usually exhibits its worst-case behavior, $O(n^2)$. For this reason, bubble sort performs much worse than the others unless the initial array is nearly sorted. In the next section, we discuss a variation on insertion sort, known as Shell sort, that has $O(n^{3/2})$ or better performance.

Since the time to sort an array of n elements is proportional to n^2, none of these algorithms is particularly good for large arrays (i.e., $n > 100$). The best sorting algorithms provide $n \log n$ average-case behavior and are considerably faster for large arrays. In fact, one of the algorithms that we will discuss has $n \log n$ worst-case behavior. You can get a feel for the difference in behavior by comparing the last column of Table 8.3 with the middle column.

TABLE 8.2
Comparison of Quadratic Sorts

	Number of Comparisons		Number of Exchanges	
	Best	Worst	Best	Worst
Selection sort	$O(n^2)$	$O(n^2)$	$O(n)$	$O(n)$
Bubble sort	$O(n)$	$O(n^2)$	$O(1)$	$O(n^2)$
Insertion sort	$O(n)$	$O(n^2)$	$O(n)$	$O(n^2)$

TABLE 8.3
Comparison of Rates of Growth

n	n^2	$n \log n$
8	64	24
16	256	64
32	1,024	160
64	4,096	384
128	16,384	896
256	65,536	2,048
512	262,144	4,608

Recall from Section 2.4 that big-O analysis ignores any constants that might be involved or any overhead that might occur from method calls needed to perform an exchange or a comparison. However, the tables give you an estimate of the relative performance of the different sorting algorithms.

We haven't talked about storage usage for these algorithms. All the quadratic sorts require storage for the array being sorted. However, there is only one copy of this array, so the array is sorted in place. There are also requirements for variables that store references to particular elements, loop control variables, and temporary variables. However, for large n, the size of the array dominates these other storage considerations, so the extra space usage is proportional to O(1).

Comparisons versus Exchanges

We have analyzed comparisons and exchanges separately, but you may be wondering whether one is more costly (in terms of computer time) than the other. In Java, an exchange requires your computer to switch two object references using a third object reference as an intermediary. A comparison requires your computer to execute a `compareTo` method. The cost of a comparison depends on its complexity, but it will probably be more costly than an exchange because of the overhead to call and execute method `compareTo`. In some programming languages (but not Java), an exchange may require physically moving the information in each object rather than simply swapping object references. For these languages, the cost of an exchange would be proportional to the size of the objects being exchanged and may be more costly than a comparison.

EXERCISES FOR SECTION 8.5

SELF-CHECK

1. Complete Table 8.3 for $n = 1024$ and $n = 2048$.
2. What do the new rows of Table 8.3 tell us about the increase in time required to process an array of 1024 elements versus an array of 2048 elements for $O(n)$, $O(n^2)$, and $O(n \log n)$ algorithms?

8.6 Shell Sort: A Better Insertion Sort

Next, we describe the *Shell sort,* which is a type of insertion sort but with $O(n^{3/2})$ or better performance. Unlike the other algorithms, Shell sort is named after its discoverer, Donald L. Shell ("A High-Speed Sorting Procedure," *Communications of the ACM,* Vol. 2, No. 7 [1959], pp. 30–32). You can think of the Shell sort as a divide-and-conquer approach to insertion sort. Instead of sorting the entire array at the start, the idea behind Shell sort is to sort many smaller subarrays using insertion sort before sorting the entire array. The initial subarrays will contain two or three elements, so the insertion sorts will go very quickly. After each collection of subarrays is sorted, a new collection of subarrays with approximately twice as many elements as before will be sorted. The last step is to perform an insertion sort on the entire array, which has been presorted by the earlier sorts.

As an example, let's sort the following array using initial subarrays with only two and three elements. We determine the elements in each subarray by setting a gap value between the subscripts in each subarray. We will explain how we pick the gap values later. We will use an initial gap of 7.

[0]	[1]	[2]	[3]	[4]	[5]	[6]	[7]	[8]	[9]	[10]	[11]	[12]	[13]	[14]	[15]
40	[illegible]	80	75	60	90	70	75	55	90	85	34	45	62	57	65

A gap of 7 means the first subarray has subscripts 0, 7, 14 (element values 40, 75, 57, shown in light blue); the second subarray has subscripts 1, 8, 15 (element values 35, 55, 65, shown in dark blue); the third subarray has subscripts 2, 9 (element values 80, 90, shown in gray); and so on. There are seven subarrays. We start the process by inserting the value at position 7 (value of gap) into its subarray (elements at 0 and 7). Next, we insert the element at position 8 into its subarray (elements at 1 and 8). We continue until we have inserted the last element (at position 15) in its subarray (elements at 1, 8, and 15). The result of performing insertion sort on all seven subarrays with two or three elements follows:

[0]	[1]	[2]	[3]	[4]	[5]	[6]	[7]	[8]	[9]	[10]	[11]	[12]	[13]	[14]	[15]
40	35	80	75	34	45	62	57	55	90	85	60	90	70	75	[illegible]

Next, we use a gap of 3. There are only three subarrays, and the longest one has six elements. The first subarray has subscripts 0, 3, 6, 9, 12, 15; the second subarray has subscripts 1, 4, 7, 10, 13; the third subarray has subscripts 2, 5, 8, 11, 14.

[0]	[1]	[2]	[3]	[4]	[5]	[6]	[7]	[8]	[9]	[10]	[11]	[12]	[13]	[14]	[15]
40	35	80	75	34	45	62	57	55	90	85	60	90	70	75	65

We start the process by inserting the element at position 3 (value of gap) into its subarray. Next, we insert the element at position 4, and so on. The result of all insertions follows:

[0]	[1]	[2]	[3]	[4]	[5]	[6]	[7]	[8]	[9]	[10]	[11]	[12]	[13]	[14]	[15]
40	[illegible]	45	62	[illegible]	55	65	[illegible]	60	75	[illegible]	75	90	[illegible]	80	90

Finally, we use a gap of 1, which performs an insertion sort on the entire array. Because of the presorting, it will require 1 comparison to insert 34, 1 comparison to insert 45 and 62, 4 comparisons to insert 35, 2 comparisons to insert 55, 1 comparison to insert 65, 3 comparisons to insert 57, 1 comparison to insert 60, and only 1 or 2 comparisons to insert each of the remaining values except for 80 (3 comparisons).

The algorithm for Shell sort follows. Steps 2 through 4 correspond to the insertion sort algorithm shown earlier. Because the elements with subscripts 0 through `gap - 1` are the first elements in their subarrays, we begin Step 4 by inserting the element at position `gap` instead of at position 1 as we did for the insertion sort. Step 1 sets the initial `gap` between subscripts to `n` / 2, where `n` is the number of array elements. To get the next `gap` value, Step 6 divides the current gap value by 2.2 (chosen by experimentation). We want the `gap` to be 1 during the last insertion sort so that the entire array will be sorted. Step 5 ensures this by resetting `gap` to 1 if it is 2.

Shell Sort Algorithm

1. Set the initial value of `gap` to `n` / 2.
2. `while` `gap > 0`
3.   `for` each array element from position `gap` to the last element
4.   Insert this element where it belongs in its subarray.
5.   `if` `gap` is 2, set it to 1.
6.   `else gap = gap` / 2.2.

Refinement of Step 4, the Insertion Step

4.1 `nextPos` is the position of the element to insert.
4.2 Save the value of the element to insert in `nextVal`.
4.3 `while` `nextPos > gap` and the element at `nextPos - gap > nextVal`
4.4   Shift the element at `nextPos - gap` to position `nextPos`.
4.5   Decrement `nextPos` by `gap`.
4.6 Insert `nextVal` at `nextPos`.

Analysis of Shell Sort

You may wonder why Shell sort is an improvement over regular insertion sort, because it ends with an insertion sort of the entire array. Each later sort (including the last one) will be performed on an array whose elements have been presorted by the earlier sorts. Because the behavior of insertion sort is closer to $O(n)$ than $O(n^2)$ when an array is nearly sorted, the presorting will make the later sorts, which involve larger subarrays, go more quickly. As a result of presorting, only 19 comparisons were required to perform an insertion sort on the last 15-element array shown in the previous section. This is critical because it is precisely for larger arrays where $O(n^2)$ behavior would have the most negative impact. For the same reason, the improvement of Shell sort over insertion sort is much more significant for large arrays.

A general analysis of Shell sort is an open research problem in computer science. The performance depends on how the decreasing sequence of values for `gap` is chosen. It is known that Shell sort is $O(n^2)$ if successive powers of 2 are used for gap (i.e., 32, 16, 8, 4, 2, 1). If successive values for gap are of the form $2^k - 1$ (i.e., 31, 15, 7, 3, 1), however, it can be proven that the performance is $O(n^{3/2})$. This sequence is known as *Hibbard's sequence.* There are other sequences that give similar or better performance.

We have presented an algorithm that selects the initial value of gap as $\frac{n}{2}$ and then divides by 2.2 and truncates to the next lowest integer. Empirical studies of this approach show that the performance is $O(n^{5/4})$ or maybe even $O(n^{7/6})$, but there is no theoretical basis for this result (M. A. Weiss, *Data Structures and Problem Solving Using Java* [Addison-Wesley, 1998], p. 230).

Code for Shell Sort

Listing 8.4 shows the code for Shell sort. Method `insert` has a third parameter, `gap`. The expression after `&&`

```
((nextPos > gap - 1)
  && (nextVal.compareTo(table[nextPos - gap]) < 0))
```

compares elements that are separated by the value of `gap` instead of by 1. The expression before `&&` is false if `nextPos` is the subscript of the first element in a subarray. The statements in the **`while`** loop shift the element at `nextPos` down by `gap` (one position in the subarray) and reset `nextPos` to the subscript of the element just moved.

LISTING 8.4
ShellSort.java

```
/** Implements the Shell sort algorithm. */
public class ShellSort {
    /** Sort the table using Shell sort algorithm.
        pre:  table contains Comparable objects.
        post: table is sorted.
        @param table The array to be sorted
     */
    public static <T extends Comparable<T>> void sort(T[] table) {
        // Gap between adjacent elements.
        int gap = table.length / 2;
        while (gap > 0) {
            for (int nextPos = gap; nextPos < table.length;
                    nextPos++) {
                // Insert element at nextPos in its subarray.
                insert(table, nextPos, gap);
            } // End for.

            // Reset gap for next pass.
            if (gap == 2) {
                gap = 1;
            } else {
                gap = (int) (gap / 2.2);
            }
        } // End while.
    } // End sort.
```

```java
    /** Inserts element at nextPos where it belongs in array.
        pre:  Elements through nextPos - gap in subarray are sorted.
        post: Elements through nextPos in subarray are sorted.
        @param table The array being sorted
        @param nextPos The position of element to insert
        @param gap The gap between elements in the subarray
    */
    private static <T extends Comparable<T>> void insert(T[] table,
                                                          int nextPos,
                                                          int gap) {
        T nextVal = table[nextPos]; // Element to insert.
        // Shift all values > nextVal in subarray down by gap.
        while ((nextPos > gap - 1)  // First element not shifted.
               && (nextVal.compareTo(table[nextPos - gap]) < 0)) {
            table[nextPos] = table[nextPos - gap];  // Shift down.
            nextPos -= gap;    // Check next position in subarray.
        }
        table[nextPos] = nextVal;  // Insert nextVal.
    }
}
```

EXERCISES FOR SECTION 8.6

SELF-CHECK

1. Trace the execution of Shell sort on the following array. Show the array after all sorts when the gap is 3 and after the final sort when the gap is 1. List the number of comparisons and exchanges required when the gap is 3 and when the gap is 1. Compare this with the number of comparisons and exchanges that would be required for a regular insertion sort.
   40 35 80 75 60 90 70 65 50 22
2. For the example of Shell sort shown in this section, determine how many comparisons and exchanges are required to insert all the elements for each gap value. Compare this with the number of comparisons and exchanges that would be required for a regular insertion sort.

PROGRAMMING

1. Eliminate method `insert` in Listing 8.4 and write its code inside the **for** statement.
2. Add statements to trace the progress of Shell sort. Display each value of `gap`, and display the array contents after all subarrays for that `gap` value have been sorted.

8.7 Merge Sort

The next algorithm that we will consider is called *merge sort*. A *merge* is a common data processing operation that is performed on two sequences of data (or data files) with the following characteristics:

- Both sequences contain items with a common `compareTo` method.
- The objects in both sequences are ordered in accordance with this `compareTo` method (i.e., both sequences are sorted).

The result of the merge operation is to create a third sequence that contains all of the objects from the first two sorted sequences. For example, if the first sequence is 3, 5, 8, 15 and the second sequence is 4, 9, 12, 20, the final sequence will be 3, 4, 5, 8, 9, 12, 15, 20. The algorithm for merging the two sequences follows.

Merge Algorithm

1. Access the first item from both sequences.
2. **`while`** not finished with either sequence
3. Compare the current items from the two sequences, copy the smaller current item to the output sequence, and access the next item from the input sequence whose item was copied.
4. Copy any remaining items from the first sequence to the output sequence.
5. Copy any remaining items from the second sequence to the output sequence.

The **`while`** loop (Step 2) merges items from both input sequences to the output sequence. The current item from each sequence is the one that has been most recently accessed but not yet copied to the output sequence. Step 3 compares the two current items and copies the smaller one to the output sequence. If input sequence A's current item is the smaller one, the next item is accessed from sequence A and becomes its current item. If input sequence B's current item is the smaller one, the next item is accessed from sequence B and becomes its current item. After the end of either sequence is reached, Step 4 or Step 5 copies the items from the other sequence to the output sequence. Note that either Step 4 or Step 5 is executed, but not both.

As an example, consider the sequences shown in Figure 8.6. Steps 2 and 3 will first copy the items from sequence A with the values **244** and **311** to the output sequence; then items from sequence B with values 324 and 415 will be copied; and then the item from sequence A with value **478** will be copied. At this point, we have copied

FIGURE 8.6
Merge Operation

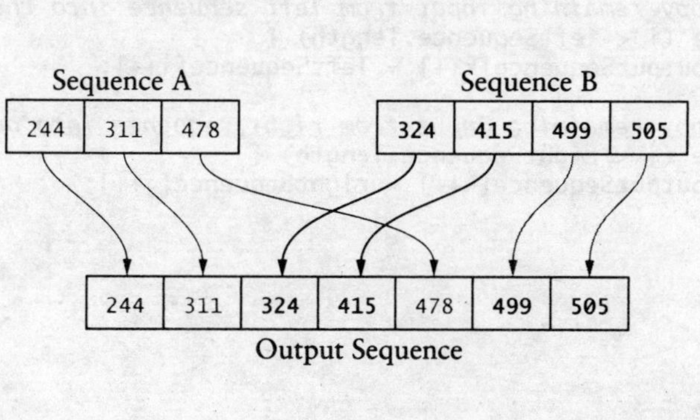

all items in sequence A, so we exit the **while** loop and copy the remaining items from sequence B (499, 505) to the output (Steps 4 and 5).

Analysis of Merge

For two input sequences that contain a total of *n* elements, we need to move each element from its input sequence to its output sequence, so the time required for a merge is O(*n*). How about the space requirements? We need to be able to store both initial sequences and the output sequence. So the array cannot be merged in place and the *additional* space usage is O(*n*).

Code for Merge

Listing 8.5 shows the merge algorithm applied to arrays of `Comparable` objects. Algorithm Steps 4 and 5 are implemented as **while** loops at the end of the method.

LISTING 8.5
Merge Method

```
/** Merge two sequences.
    pre: leftSequence and rightSequence are sorted.
    post: outputSequence is the merged result and is sorted.
    @param outputSequence The destination
    @param leftSequence The left input
    @param rightSequence The right input
*/
private static <T extends Comparable<T>> void merge(T[] outputSequence,
                                                    T[] leftSequence,
                                                    T[] rightSequence) {
    int i = 0; // Index into the left input sequence.
    int j = 0; // Index into the right input sequence.
    int k = 0; // Index into the output sequence.
    // While there is data in both input sequences
    while (i < leftSequence.length && j < rightSequence.length) {
        // Find the smaller and
        // insert it into the output sequence.
        if (leftSequence[i].compareTo(rightSequence[j]) < 0) {
            outputSequence[k++] = leftSequence[i++];
        } else {
            outputSequence[k++] = rightSequence[j++];
        }
    }
    // assert: one of the sequences has more items to copy.
    // Copy remaining input from left sequence into the output.
    while (i < leftSequence.length) {
        outputSequence[k++] = leftSequence[i++];
    }
    // Copy remaining input from right sequence into output.
    while (j < rightSequence.length) {
        outputSequence[k++] = rightSequence[j++];
    }
}
```

PROGRAM STYLE

By using the postincrement operator on the index variables, you can both extract the current item from one sequence and append it to the end of the output sequence in one statement. The statement:

```
outputSequence[k++] = leftSequence[i++];
```

is equivalent to the following three statements, executed in the order shown:

```
outputSequence[k] = leftSequence[i];
k++;
i++;
```

Both the single statement and the group of three statements maintain the invariant that the indexes reference the current item.

Algorithm for Merge Sort

We can modify merging to serve as an approach to sorting a single, unsorted array as follows:

1. Split the array into two halves.
2. Sort the left half.
3. Sort the right half.
4. Merge the two.

What sort algorithm should we use to do Steps 2 and 3? We can use the merge sort algorithm we are developing! The base case will be a table of size 1, which is already sorted, so there is nothing to do for the base case. We write the algorithm next, showing its recursive step.

Algorithm for Merge Sort

1. `if` the `tableSize` is > 1
2. Set `halfSize` to `tableSize` divided by 2.
3. Allocate a table called `leftTable` of size `halfSize`.
4. Allocate a table called `rightTable` of size `tableSize - halfSize`.
5. Copy the elements from `table[0 ... halfSize - 1]` into `leftTable`.
6. Copy the elements from `table[halfSize ... tableSize]` into `rightTable`.
7. Recursively apply the merge sort algorithm to `leftTable`.
8. Recursively apply the merge sort algorithm to `rightTable`.
9. Apply the merge method using `leftTable` and `rightTable` as the input and the original table as the output.

Trace of Merge Sort Algorithm

Each recursive call to method sort with an array argument that has more than one element splits the array argument into a left array and a right array, where each new array is approximately half the size of the array argument. We then sort each of these arrays, beginning with the left half, by recursively calling method sort with the left array and right array as arguments. After returning from the sort of the left array and right array at each level, we merge these two halves together back into the space occupied by the array that was split. Figure 8.7 illustrates this process. The left subarray in each recursive call (in gray) will be sorted before the processing of its corresponding right subarray (in color) begins. Lines 4 and 6 merge two one-element arrays to form a sorted two-element array. At line 7, the two sorted two-element arrays (50, 60 and 30, 45) are merged into a sorted four-element array. Next, the right subarray in color on line 1 will be sorted in the same way. When done, the sorted subarray (15, 20, 80, 90) will be merged with the sorted subarray on line 7.

FIGURE 8.7
Trace of Merge Sort

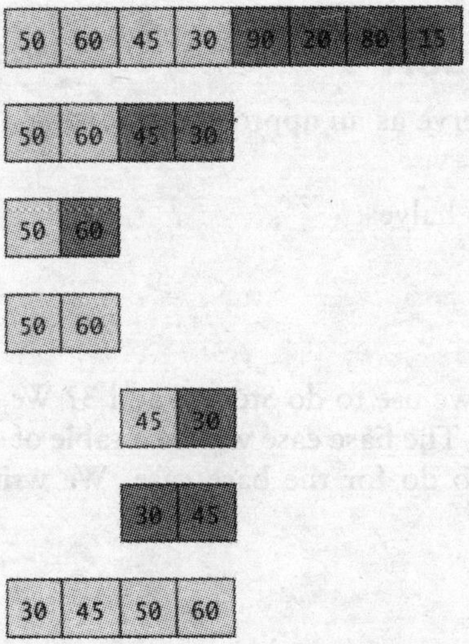

1. *Split array into two 4-element arrays.*
2. *Split left array into two 2-element arrays.*
3. *Split left array (50, 60) into two 1-element arrays.*
4. *Merge two 1-element arrays into a 2-element array.*
5. *Split right array from Step 2 into two 1-element arrays.*
6. *Merge two 1-element arrays into a 2-element array.*
7. *Merge two 2-element arrays into a 4-element array.*

Analysis of Merge Sort

In Figure 8.7, the size of the arrays being sorted decreases from 8 to 4 (line 1) to 2 (line 2) to 1 (line 3). After each pair of subarrays is sorted, the pair will be merged to form a larger sorted array. Rather than showing a time sequence of the splitting and merging operations, we summarize them as follows:

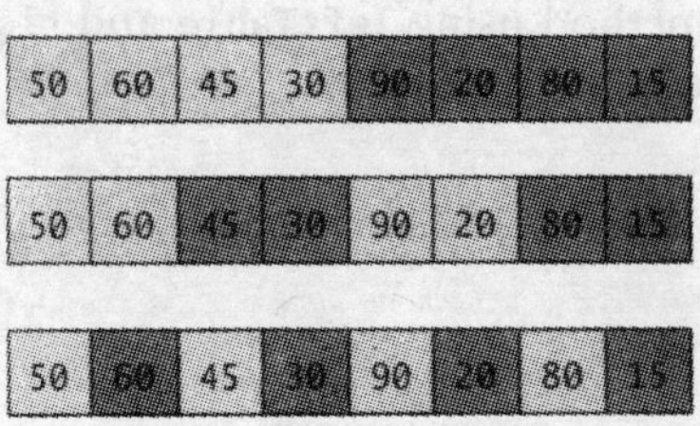

1. *Split the 8-element array.*
2. *Split the 4-element arrays.*
3. *Split the 2-element arrays.*

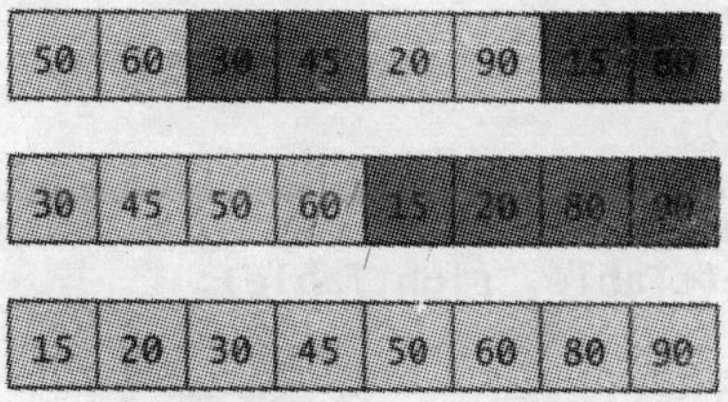

4. *Merge the 1-element arrays into 2-element arrays.*
5. *Merge the 2-element arrays into 4-element arrays.*
6. *Merge the 4-element arrays into an 8-element array.*

Lines 1 through 3 show the splitting operations, and lines 4 through 6 show the merge operations. Line 4 shows the two-element arrays formed by merging two-element pairs, line 5 shows the four-element arrays formed by merging 2-element pairs, and line 6 shows the sorted array. Because each of these lines involves a movement of n elements from smaller-size arrays to larger arrays, the effort to do each merge is $O(n)$. The number of lines that require merging (three in this case) is $\log n$ because each recursive step splits the array in half. So the total effort to reconstruct the sorted array through merging is $O(n \log n)$.

Recall from our discussion of recursion that whenever a recursive method is called, a copy of the local variables is saved on the run-time stack. Thus, as we go down the recursion chain sorting the `leftTables`, a sequence of `rightTables` of size $\frac{n}{2}$, $\frac{n}{4}, \ldots, \frac{n}{2^k}$ is allocated. Since $\frac{n}{2} + \frac{n}{4} + \ldots + 2 + 1 = n - 1$, a total of n additional storage locations are required.

Code for Merge Sort

Listing 8.6 shows the `MergeSort` class.

LISTING 8.6
MergeSort.java

```
/** Implements the recursive merge sort algorithm. In this version, copies
    of the subtables are made, sorted, and then merged.
*/
public class MergeSort {
    /** Sort the array using the merge sort algorithm.
        pre: table contains Comparable objects.
        post: table is sorted.
        @param table The array to be sorted
    */
    public static <T extends Comparable<T>> void sort(T[] table) {
        // A table with one element is sorted already.
        if (table.length > 1) {
            // Split table into halves.
            int halfSize = table.length / 2;
            T[] leftTable = (E[]) new Comparable[halfSize];
            T[] rightTable =
                    (E[]) new Comparable[table.length - halfSize];
            System.arraycopy(table, 0, leftTable, 0, halfSize);
            System.arraycopy(table, halfSize, rightTable, 0,
                             table.length - halfSize);
```

```
            // Sort the halves.
            sort(leftTable);
            sort(rightTable);

            // Merge the halves.
            merge(table, leftTable, rightTable);
        }
    }
    // See Listing 8.5 for the merge method.
    . . .
}
```

EXERCISES FOR SECTION 8.7

SELF-CHECK

1. Trace the execution of the merge sort on the following array, providing a figure similar to Figure 8.7.
   55 50 10 40 80 90 60 100 70 80 20 50 22
2. For the array in Question 1 above, show the value of `halfSize` and arrays `leftTable` and `rightTable` for each recursive call to method `sort` in Listing 8.5 and show the array elements after returning from each call to `merge`. How many times is `sort` called, and how many times is `merge` called?

PROGRAMMING

1. Add statements that trace the progress of method `sort` by displaying the array `table` after each merge operation. Also display the arrays referenced by `leftTable` and `rightTable`.

8.8 Heapsort

The merge sort algorithm has the virtue that its time is O(n log n), but it still requires, at least temporarily, n extra storage locations. This next algorithm can be implemented without requiring any additional storage. It uses a heap to store the array and so is called *heapsort*.

First Version of a Heapsort Algorithm

We introduced the heap in Section 6.5. When used as a priority queue, a heap is a data structure that maintains the smallest value at the top. The following algorithm first places an array's data into a heap. Then it removes each heap item (an O(log n) process) and moves it back into the array.

Heapsort Algorithm: First Version

1. Insert each value from the array to be sorted into a priority queue (heap).
2. Set `i` to 0.
3. **`while`** the priority queue is not empty
4. Remove an item from the queue and insert it back into the array at position `i`.
5. Increment `i`.

Although this algorithm can be shown to be $O(n \log n)$, it does require n extra storage locations (the array and heap are both size n). We address this problem next.

Revising the Heapsort Algorithm

In the heaps we have used so far, each parent node value was less than the values of its children. We can also build the heap so that each parent is larger than its children. Figure 8.8 shows an example of such a heap.

Once we have such a heap, we can remove one item at a time from the heap. The item removed is always the top element, and it will end up at the bottom of the heap. When we reheap, we move the larger of a node's two children up the heap, instead of the smaller, so the next largest item is then at the top of the heap. Figure 8.9 shows the heap after we have removed one item, and Figure 8.10 shows the heap after we have removed two items. In both figures, the items in color have been removed from the heap. As we continue to remove items from the heap, the heap size shrinks as the number of the removed items increases. Figure 8.11 shows the heap after we have emptied it.

FIGURE 8.8
Example of a Heap with Largest Value in Root

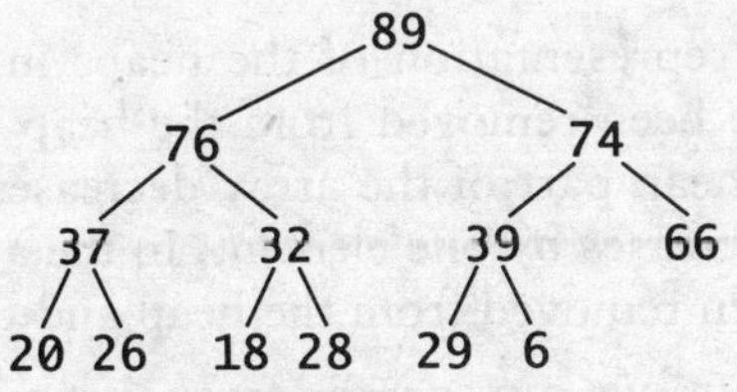

FIGURE 8.9
Heap after Removal of Largest Item

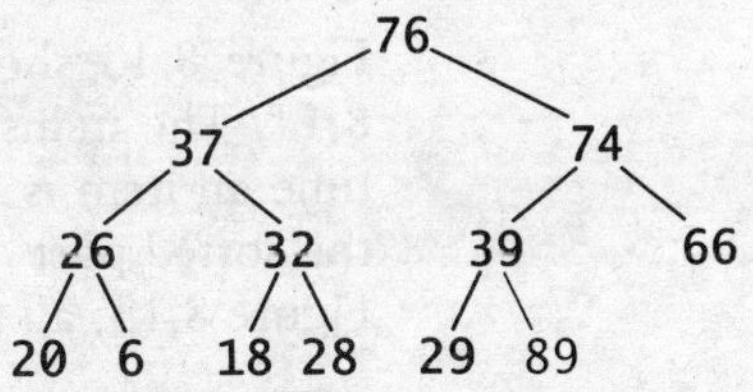

FIGURE 8.10
Heap after Removal of Two Largest Items

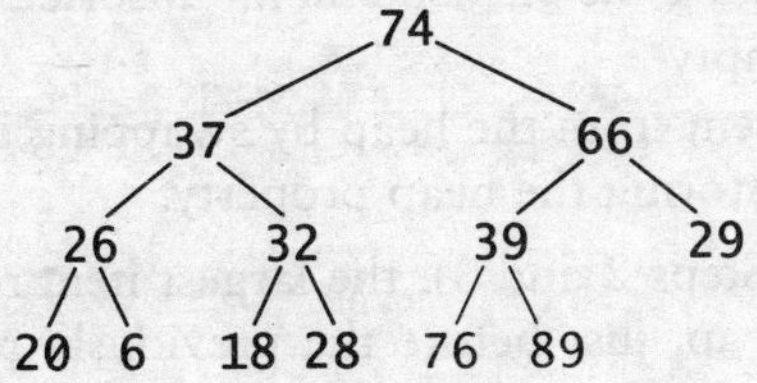

FIGURE 8.11
Heap after Removal of All Its Items

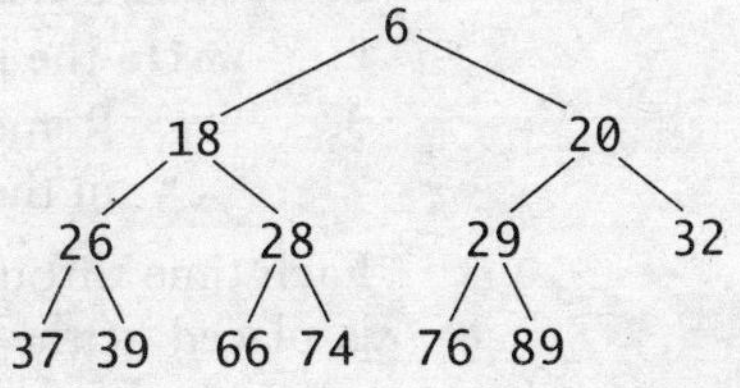

FIGURE 8.12
Internal Representation of the Heap Shown in Figure 8.8

[0]	[1]	[2]	[3]	[4]	[5]	[6]	[7]	[8]	[9]	[10]	[11]	[12]
89	76	74	37	32	39	66	20	26	18	28	29	6

FIGURE 8.13
Internal Representation of the Heaps Shown in Figures 8.9 through 8.11

[0]	[1]	[2]	[3]	[4]	[5]	[6]	[7]	[8]	[9]	[10]	[11]	[12]
76	37	74	26	32	39	66	20	6	18	28	29	89

[0]	[1]	[2]	[3]	[4]	[5]	[6]	[7]	[8]	[9]	[10]	[11]	[12]
74	37	66	26	32	39	29	20	6	18	28	76	89

⋮

[0]	[1]	[2]	[3]	[4]	[5]	[6]	[7]	[8]	[9]	[10]	[11]	[12]
6	18	20	26	28	29	32	37	39	66	74	76	89

If we implement the heap using an array, each element removed will be placed at the end of the array but in front of the elements that were removed earlier. After we remove the last element the array will be sorted. We illustrate this next.

Figure 8.12 shows the array representation of the original heap. As before, the root, 89, is at position 0. The root's two children, 76 and 74, are at positions 1 and 2. For a node at position p, the left child is at $2p + 1$ and the right child is at $2p + 2$. A node at position c can find its parent at $(c - 1) / 2$.

Figure 8.13 shows the array representation of the heaps in Figures 8.9 through 8.11. The items in color have been removed from the heap and are sorted. Each time an item is removed, the heap part of the array decreases by one element and the sorted part of the array increases by one element. In the array at the bottom of Figure 8.13, all items have been removed from the heap and the array is sorted.

From our foregoing observations, we can sort the array that represents a heap in the following way.

Algorithm for In-Place Heapsort

1. Build a heap by rearranging the elements in an unsorted array.
2. `while` the heap is not empty
3. Remove the first item from the heap by swapping it with the last item in the heap and restoring the heap property.

Each time through the loop (Steps 2 and 3), the largest item remaining in the heap is placed at the end of the heap, just before the previously removed items. Thus, when the loop terminates, the items in the array are sorted. In Section 6.5 we discussed how to remove an item from a heap and restore the heap property. We also implemented a `remove` method for a heap in an `ArrayList`.

Algorithm to Build a Heap

Step 1 of the algorithm builds a heap. If we start with an array, `table`, of length `table.length`, we can consider the first item (index 0) to be a heap of one item. We now consider the general case where the items in array `table` from `0` through `n - 1` form a heap; the items from `n` through `table.length - 1` are not in the heap. As each is inserted, we must "reheap" to restore the heap property.

Refinement of Step 1 for In-Place Heapsort

1.1 **`while`** `n` is less than `table.length`
1.2   Increment `n` by 1. This inserts a new item into the heap.
1.3   Restore the heap property.

Analysis of Revised Heapsort Algorithm

From our knowledge of binary trees, we know that a heap of size *n* has log *n* levels. Building a heap requires finding the correct location for an item in a heap with log *n* levels. Because we have *n* items to insert and each insert (or remove) is O(log *n*), the `buildHeap` operation is O(*n* log *n*). Similarly, we have *n* items to remove from the heap, so that is also O(*n* log *n*). Because we are storing the heap in the original array, no extra storage is required.

Code for Heapsort

Listing 8.7 shows the `HeapSort` class. The `sort` method merely calls the `buildHeap` method followed by the `shrinkHeap` method, which is based on the `remove` method shown in Section 6.5. Method `swap` swaps the items in the table.

LISTING 8.7
`HeapSort.java`

```
/** Implementation of the heapsort algorithm. */
public class HeapSort {
    /** Sort the array using heapsort algorithm.
        pre: table contains Comparable items.
        post: table is sorted.
        @param table The array to be sorted
    */
    public static <T extends Comparable<T>> void sort(T[] table) {
        buildHeap(table);
        shrinkHeap(table);
    }

    /** buildHeap transforms the table into a heap.
        pre:  The array contains at least one item.
        post: All items in the array are in heap order.
        @param table The array to be transformed into a heap
    */
```

```
private static <T extends Comparable<T>> void buildHeap(T[] table) {
    int n = 1;
    // Invariant: table[0 . . . n - 1] is a heap.
    while (n < table.length) {
        n++;  // Add a new item to the heap and reheap.
        int child = n - 1;
        int parent = (child - 1) / 2;  // Find parent.
        while (parent >= 0
                && table[parent].compareTo(table[child]) < 0) {
            swap(table, parent, child);
            child = parent;
            parent = (child - 1) / 2;
        }
    }
}

/** shrinkHeap transforms a heap into a sorted array.
    pre: All items in the array are in heap order.
    post: The array is sorted.
    @param table The array to be sorted
*/
private static <T extends Comparable<T>> void shrinkHeap(T[] table) {
    int n = table.length;
    // Invariant: table[0 . . . n - 1] forms a heap.
    // table[n . . . table.length - 1] is sorted.
    while (n > 0) {
        n--;
        swap(table, 0, n);
        // table[1 . . . n - 1] form a heap.
        // table[n . . . table.length - 1] is sorted.
        int parent = 0;
        while (true) {
            int leftChild = 2 * parent + 1;
            if (leftChild >= n) {
                break;      // No more children.
            }
            int rightChild = leftChild + 1;
            // Find the larger of the two children.
            int maxChild = leftChild;
            if (rightChild < n  // There is a right child.
                && table[leftChild].compareTo(table[rightChild]) < 0) {
                maxChild = rightChild;
            }
            // If the parent is smaller than the larger child,
            if (table[parent].compareTo(table[maxChild]) < 0) {
                // Swap the parent and child.
                swap(table, parent, maxChild);
                // Continue at the child level.
                parent = maxChild;
            } else {   // Heap property is restored.
                break; // Exit the loop.
            }
        }
    }
}
```

```
    /** Swap the items in table[i] and table[j].
        @param table The array that contains the items
        @param i The index of one item
        @param j The index of the other item
    */
    private static <T extends Comparable<T>> void swap(T[] table,
                                                       int i, int j) {
        T temp = table[i];
        table[i] = table[j];
        table[j] = temp;
    }
}
```

EXERCISES FOR SECTION 8.8

SELF-CHECK

1. Build the heap from the numbers in the following list. How many exchanges were required? How many comparisons?

   55 50 10 40 80 90 60 100 70 80 20 50 22

2. Shrink the heap from Question 1 to create the array in sorted order. How many exchanges were required? How many comparisons?

8.9 Quicksort

The next algorithm we will study is called *quicksort*. Developed by C. A. R. Hoare in 1962, it works in the following way: Given an array with subscripts `first . . . last` to sort, quicksort rearranges this array into two parts so that all the elements in the left subarray are less than or equal to a specified value (called the *pivot*) and all the elements in the right subarray are greater than the pivot. The pivot is placed between the two parts. Thus all of the elements on the left of the pivot value are smaller than all elements on the right of the pivot value, so the pivot value is in its correct position. By repeating this process on the two halves, the whole array becomes sorted.

As an example of this process, let's sort the following array:

44	75	23	43	55	12	64	77	33

We will assume that the first array element (44) is arbitrarily selected as the pivot value. A possible result of rearranging, or *partitioning*, the element values follows:

12	33	23	43	44	55	64	77	75

After the partitioning process, the pivot value, 44, is at its correct position. All values less than 44 are in the left subarray, and all values larger than 44 are in the right subarray, as desired. The next step would be to apply quicksort recursively to the two subarrays on either side of the pivot value, beginning with the left subarray (12, 33, 23, 43). Here is the result when 12 is the pivot value:

The pivot value is in the first position. Because the left subarray does not exist, the right subarray (33, 23, 43) is sorted next, resulting in the following situation:

The pivot value 33 is in its correct place, and the left subarray (23) and right subarray (43) have single elements, so they are sorted. At this point, we are finished sorting the left part of the original subarray, and quicksort is applied to the right subarray (55, 64, 77, 75). In the following array, all the elements that have been placed in their proper position are in dark blue.

If we use 55 for the pivot, its left subarray will be empty after the partitioning process and the right subarray 64, 77, 75 will be sorted next. If 64 is the pivot, the situation will be as follows, and we sort the right subarray (77, 75) next.

If 77 is the pivot and we move it where it belongs, we end up with the following array. Because the left subarray (75) has a single element, it is sorted and we are done.

Algorithm for Quicksort

The algorithm for quicksort follows. We will describe how to do the partitioning later. We assume that the indexes `first` and `last` are the end points of the array being sorted and that the index of the pivot after partitioning is `pivIndex`.

Algorithm for Quicksort

1. `if first < last` then
2. Partition the elements in the subarray `first . . . last` so that the pivot value is in its correct place (subscript `pivIndex`).
3. Recursively apply quicksort to the subarray `first . . . pivIndex - 1`.
4. Recursively apply quicksort to the subarray `pivIndex + 1 . . . last`.

Analysis of Quicksort

If the pivot value is a random value selected from the current subarray, then statistically it is expected that half of the items in the subarray will be less than the pivot and half will be greater than the pivot. If both subarrays always have the same number of elements (the best case), there will be log *n* levels of recursion. At each level, the partitioning process involves moving every element into its correct partition, so quicksort is O(*n* log *n*), just like merge sort.

But what if the split is not 50–50? Let us consider the case where each split is 90–10. Instead of a 100-element array being split into two 50-element arrays, there will be one array with 90 elements and one with just 10. The 90-element array may be split 50–50, or it may also be split 90–10. In the latter case, there would be one array with 81 elements and one with just 9 elements. Generally, for random input, the splits will not be exactly 50–50, but neither will they all be 90–10. An exact analysis is difficult and beyond the scope of this book, but the running time will be bound by a constant $\times$ *n* log *n*.

There is one situation, however, where quicksort gives very poor behavior. If, each time we partition the array, we end up with a subarray that is empty, the other subarray will have one less element than the one just split (only the pivot value will be removed). Therefore, we will have *n* levels of recursive calls (instead of log *n*), and the algorithm will be $O(n^2)$. Because of the overhead of recursive method calls (versus iteration), quicksort will take longer and require more extra storage on the run-time stack than any of the earlier quadratic algorithms. We will discuss a way to handle this situation later.

Code for Quicksort

Listing 8.8 shows the `QuickSort` class. The public method `sort` calls the recursive `quickSort` method, giving it the bounds of the `table` as the initial values of `first` and `last`. The two recursive calls in `quickSort` will cause the procedure to be applied to the subarrays that are separated by the value at `pivIndex`. If any subarray contains just one element (or zero elements), an immediate return will occur.

LISTING 8.8

QuickSort.java

```java
/** Implements the quicksort algorithm. */
public class QuickSort {

    /** Sort the table using the quicksort algorithm.
        pre: table contains Comparable objects.
        post: table is sorted.
        @param table The array to be sorted
    */
    public static <T extends Comparable<T>> void sort(T[] table) {
        // Sort the whole table.
        quickSort(table, 0, table.length - 1);
    }

    /** Sort a part of the table using the quicksort algorithm.
        post: The part of table from first through last is sorted.
        @param table The array to be sorted
        @param first The index of the low bound
        @param last The index of the high bound
    */
```

```
private static <T extends Comparable<T>> void quickSort(T[] table,
                                                       int first,
                                                       int last) {
    if (first < last) {  // There is data to be sorted.
        // Partition the table.
        int pivIndex = partition(table, first, last);
        // Sort the left half.
        quickSort(table, first, pivIndex - 1);
        // Sort the right half.
        quickSort(table, pivIndex + 1, last);
    }
}

// Insert partition method. See Listing 8.9
. . .
}
```

Algorithm for Partitioning

The `partition` method selects the pivot and performs the partitioning operation. When we are selecting the pivot, it does not really matter which element is the pivot value (if the arrays are randomly ordered to begin with). For simplicity we chose the element with subscript `first`. We then begin searching for the first value at the left end of the subarray that is greater than the pivot value. When we find it, we search for the first value at the right end of the subarray that is less than or equal to the pivot value. These two values are exchanged, and we repeat the search and exchange operations. This is illustrated in Figure 8.14, where up points to the first value greater than the pivot and down points to the first value less than or equal to the pivot value. The elements less than the pivot are in light blue, and the elements greater than the pivot are in gray.

The value 75 is the first value at the left end of the array that is larger than 44, and 33 is the first value at the right end that is less than or equal to 44, so these two values are exchanged. The indexes up and down are advanced again, as shown in Figure 8.15.

The value 55 is the next value at the left end that is larger than 44, and 12 is the next value at the right end that is less than or equal to 44, so these two values are exchanged, and up and down are advanced again, as shown in Figure 8.16.

After the second exchange, the first five array elements contain the pivot value and all values less than or equal to the pivot; the last four elements contain all values larger than the pivot. The value 55 is selected once again by up as the next element larger than the pivot; 12 is selected by down as the next element less than or equal to the pivot. Since up has now "passed" down, these values are not exchanged. Instead, the pivot value (subscript `first`) and the value at position down are exchanged. This puts the pivot value in its proper position (the new subscript is down) as shown in Figure 8.17.

The partition process is now complete, and the value of down is returned to the pivot index `pivIndex`. Method `quickSort` will be called recursively to sort the left subarray and the right subarray. The algorithm for `partition` follows:

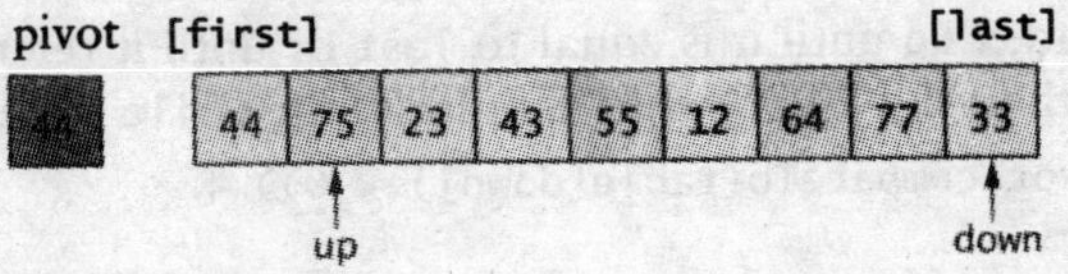

FIGURE 8.14
Locating First Values to Exchange

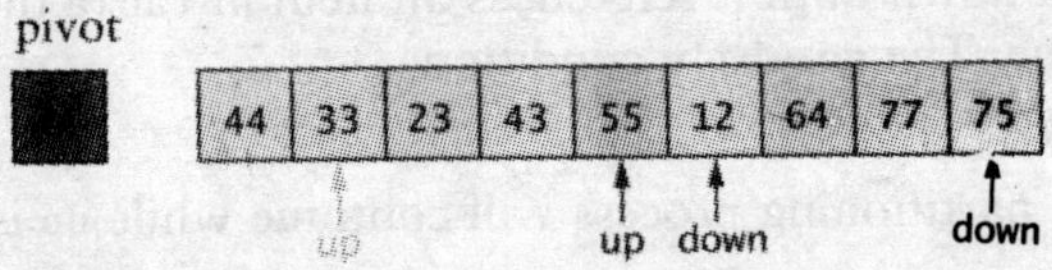

FIGURE 8.15
Array after the First Exchange

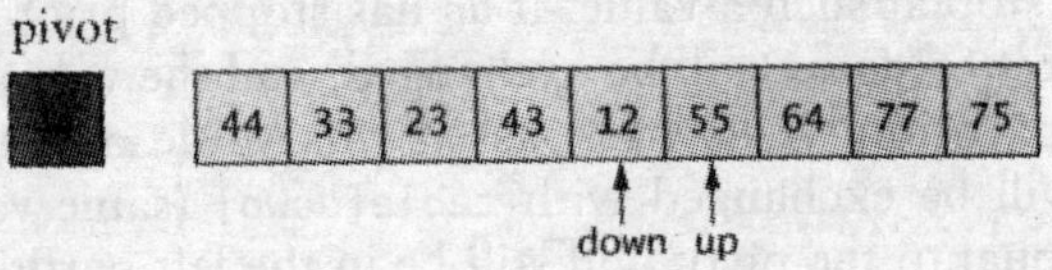

FIGURE 8.16
Array after the Second Exchange

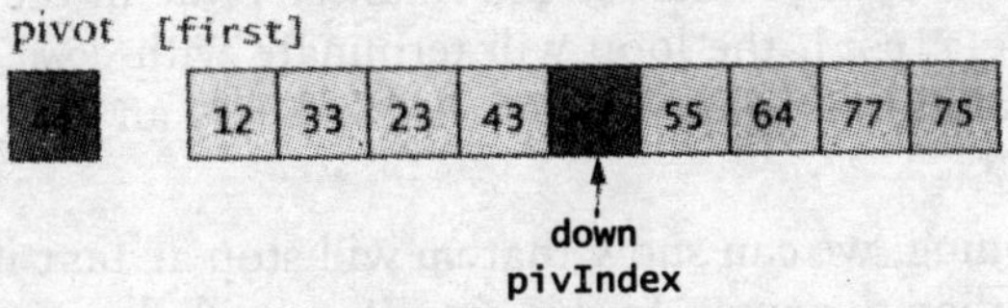

FIGURE 8.17
Array after the Pivot Is Inserted

Algorithm for `partition` Method

1. Define the pivot value as the contents of `table[first]`.
2. Initialize `up` to `first` and `down` to `last`.
3. **do**
4. Increment `up` until `up` selects the first element greater than the pivot value or `up` has reached `last`.
5. Decrement `down` until `down` selects the first element less than or equal to the pivot value or `down` has reached `first`.
6. **if** `up < down` then
7. Exchange `table[up]` and `table[down]`.
8. **while** `up` is to the left of `down`
9. Exchange `table[first]` and `table[down]`.
10. Return the value of `down` to `pivIndex`.

Code for `partition`

The code for `partition` is shown in Listing 8.9. The **`while`** statement:

```
while ((up < last) && (pivot.compareTo(table[up]) >= 0)) {
    up++;
}
```

advances the index up until it is equal to `last` or until it references an item in `table` that is greater than the pivot value. Similarly, the **`while`** statement:

```
while (pivot.compareTo(table[down]) < 0)) {
    down--;
}
```

moves the index down until it references an item in `table` that is less than or equal to the pivot value. The **`do-while`** condition

```
(up < down)
```

ensures that the partitioning process will continue while up is to the left of down.

What happens if there is a value in the array that is the same as the pivot value? The index down will stop at such a value. If up has stopped prior to reaching that value, `table[up]` and `table[down]` will be exchanged, and the value equal to the pivot will be in the left partition. If up has passed this value and therefore passed down, `table[first]` will be exchanged with `table[down]` (same value as `table[first]`), and the value equal to the pivot will still be in the left partition.

What happens if the pivot value is the smallest value in the array? Since the pivot value is at `table[first]`, the loop will terminate with down equal to `first`. In this case, the left partition is empty. Figure 8.18 shows an array for which this is the case.

By similar reasoning, we can show that up will stop at `last` if there is no element in the array larger than the pivot. In this case, down will also stay at `last`, and the pivot value (`table[first]`) will be swapped with the last value in the array, so the right partition will be empty. Figure 8.19 shows an array for which this is the case.

FIGURE 8.18
Values of up, down, and `pivIndex` If the Pivot Is the Smallest Value

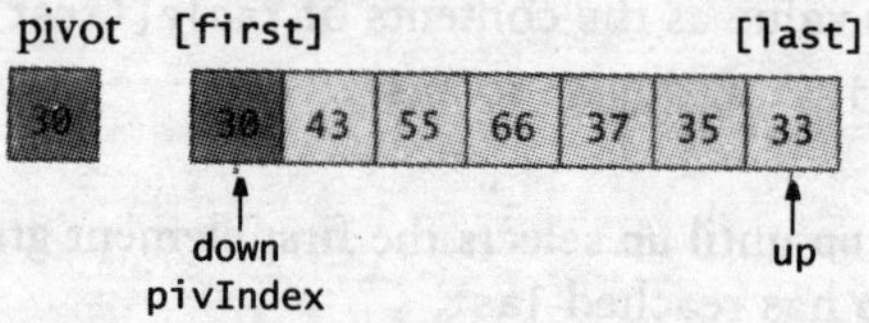

FIGURE 8.19
Values of up, down, and `pivIndex` If the Pivot Is the Largest Value

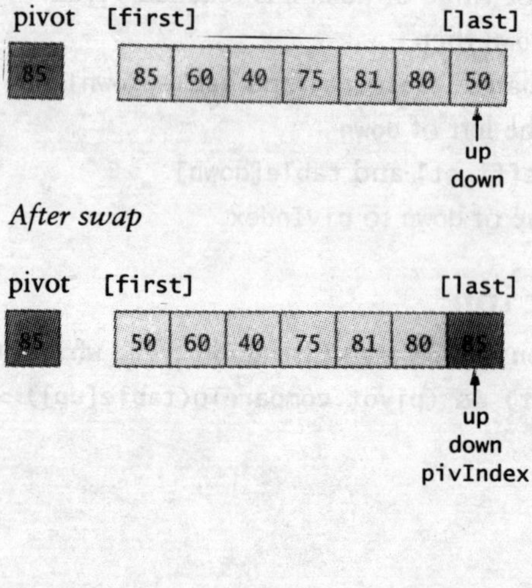

LISTING 8.9

Quicksort partition Method (First Version)

```
/** Partition the table so that values from first to pivIndex
    are less than or equal to the pivot value, and values from
    pivIndex to last are greater than the pivot value.
    @param table The table to be partitioned
    @param first The index of the low bound
    @param last  The index of the high bound
    @return The location of the pivot value
*/
private static <T extends Comparable<T>> int partition(T[] table,
                                                       int first,
                                                       int last) {
    // Select the first item as the pivot value.
    T pivot = table[first];
    int up = first;
    int down = last;
    do {
        /* Invariant:
           All items in table[first . . . up - 1] <= pivot
           All items in table[down + 1 . . . last] > pivot
        */
        while ((up < last) && (pivot.compareTo(table[up]) >= 0)) {
            up++;
        }
        // assert: up equals last or table[up] > pivot.
        while (pivot.compareTo(table[down]) < 0) {
            down--;
        }
        // assert: down equals first or table[down] <= pivot.
        if (up < down) {  // if up is to the left of down.
            // Exchange table[up] and table[down].
            swap(table, up, down);
        }
    } while (up < down); // Repeat while up is left of down.
    // Exchange table[first] and table[down] thus putting the
    // pivot value where it belongs.
    swap(table, first, down);
    // Return the index of the pivot value.
    return down;
}
```

A Revised partition Algorithm

We stated earlier that quicksort is $O(n^2)$ when each split yields one empty subarray. Unfortunately, that would be the case if the array was sorted. So the worst possible performance occurs for a sorted array, which is not very desirable.

A better solution is to pick the pivot value in a way that is less likely to lead to a bad split. One approach is to examine the first, middle, and last elements in the array and select the median of these three values as the pivot. We can do this by sorting the three-element subarray (in color in Figure 8.20). After sorting, the smallest of the three values is in position `first`, the median is in position `middle`, and the largest is in position `last`.

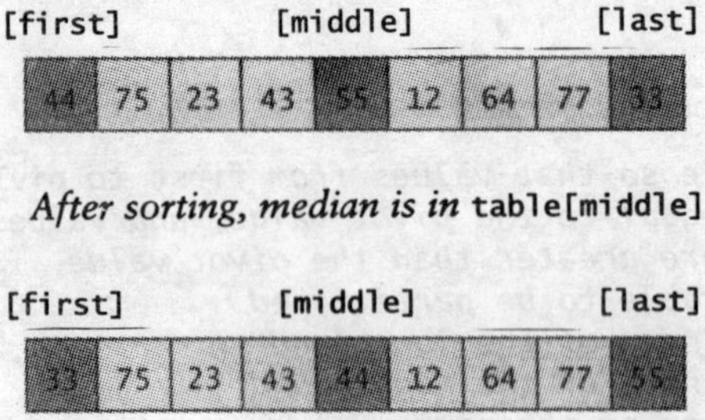

FIGURE 8.20
Sorting First, Middle, and Last Elements in Array

At this point, we can exchange the first element with the middle element (the median) and use the partition algorithm shown earlier, which uses the first element (now the median) as the pivot value. When we exit the partitioning loop, `table[first]` and `table[down]` are exchanged, moving the pivot value where it belongs (back to the middle position). This revised partition algorithm follows.

Algorithm for Revised `partition` Method

1. Sort `table[first]`, `table[middle]`, and `table[last]`.
2. Move the median value to `table[first]` (the pivot value) by exchanging `table[first]` and `table[middle]`.
3. Initialize up to `first` and down to `last`.
4. **do**
5.   Increment up until up selects the first element greater than the pivot value or up has reached `last`.
6.   Decrement down until down selects the first element less than or equal to the pivot value or down has reached `first`.
7.   **if** up < down then
8.   Exchange `table[up]` and `table[down]`.
9. **while** up is to the left of down.
10. Exchange `table[first]` and `table[down]`.
11. Return the value of down to pivIndex.

You may be wondering whether you can avoid the double shift (Steps 2 and 10) and just leave the pivot value at `table[middle]`, where it belongs. The answer is "yes," but you would also need to modify the partition algorithm further if you did this. Programming Project 6 addresses this issue and the construction of an industrial-strength quicksort method.

Code for Revised `partition` Method

Listing 8.10 shows the revised version of method `partition` with method `bubbleSort3`, which applies the bubble sort algorithm to the three selected items in `table` so that

```
table[first] <= table[middle] <= table[last]
```

Method `partition` begins with a call to method `bubbleSort3` and then calls `swap` to make the median the pivot. The rest of the method is unchanged.

LISTING 8.10

Revised `partition` Method and `bubbleSort3`

```
private static <T extends Comparable<T>> int partition(T[] table,
                                                        int first,
                                                        int last) {
    /* Put the median of table[first], table[middle], table[last]
       into table[first], and use this value as the pivot.
    */
    bubbleSort3(table, first, last);
    // Swap first element with median.
    swap(table, first, (first + last) / 2);

    // Continue as in Listing 8.9
    // . . .

/** Sort table[first], table[middle], and table[last].
    @param table The table to be sorted
    @param first Index of the first element
    @param last Index of the last element
*/
private static <T extends Comparable<T>> void bubbleSort3(T[] table,
                                                           int first,
                                                           int last) {
    int middle = (first + last) / 2;
    /* Perform bubble sort on table[first], table[middle],
       table[last]. */
    if (table[middle].compareTo(table[first]) < 0) {
        swap(table, first, middle);
    }
    // assert: table[first] <= table[middle]
    if (table[last].compareTo(table[middle]) < 0) {
        swap(table, middle, last);
    }
    // assert: table[last] is the largest value of the three.
    if (table[middle].compareTo(table[first]) < 0) {
        swap(table, first, middle);
    }
    // assert: table[first] <= table[middle] <= table[last].
}
```

PITFALL

Falling Off Either End of the Array

A common problem when incrementing up or down during the partition process is falling off either end of the array. This will be indicated by an `ArrayIndexOutOfBoundsException`. We used the condition

```
((up < last) && (pivot.compareTo(table[up]) >= 0))
```

to keep `up` from falling off the right end of the array. Self-Check Exercise 3 asks why we don't need to write similar code to avoid falling off the left end of the array.

EXERCISES FOR SECTION 8.9

SELF-CHECK

1. Trace the execution of quicksort on the following array, assuming that the first item in each subarray is the pivot value. Show the values of `first` and `last` for each recursive call and the array elements after returning from each call. Also, show the value of `pivot` during each call and the value returned through `pivIndex`. How many times is `sort` called, and how many times is `partition` called?

   55 50 10 40 80 90 60 100 70 80 20 50 22
2. Redo Question 1 above using the revised `partition` algorithm, which does a preliminary sort of three elements and selects their median as the pivot value.
3. Explain why the condition `(down > first)` is not necessary in the loop that decrements down.

PROGRAMMING

1. Insert statements to trace the quicksort algorithm. After each call to `partition`, display the values of `first`, `pivIndex`, and `last` and the array.

8.10 Testing the Sort Algorithms

To test the sorting algorithms, we need to exercise them with a variety of test cases. We want to make sure that they work, and we also want to get some idea of their relative performance when sorting the same array. We should test the methods with small arrays, large arrays, arrays whose elements are in random order, arrays that are already sorted, and arrays with duplicate copies of the same value. For performance comparisons to be meaningful, the methods must sort the same arrays.

Listing 8.11 shows a driver program that tests methods `Arrays.Sort` (from the API `java.util`) and `QuickSort.sort` on the same array of random integer values. Method `System.currentTimeMillis` returns the current time in milliseconds. This method is called just before a sort begins and just after the return from a sort. The elapsed time between calls is displayed in the console window. Although the numbers shown will not be precise, they give a good indication of the relative performance of two sorting algorithms if this is the only application currently executing.

Method `verify` verifies that the array elements are sorted by checking that each element in the array is not greater than its successor. Method `dumpTable` (not shown) should display the first 10 elements and last 10 elements of an array (or the entire array if the array has 20 or fewer elements).

LISTING 8.11
Driver to Test Sort Algorithms

```
/** Driver program to test sorting methods.
    @param args Not used
*/
public static void main(String[] args) {
    int size = Integer.parseInt(
               JOptionPane.showInputDialog("Enter Array size:"));
    Integer[] items = new Integer[size];  // Array to sort.
    Integer[] copy = new Integer[size];   // Copy of array.
    Random rInt = new Random();  // For random number generation

    // Fill the array and copy with random Integers.
    for (int i = 0; i < items.length; i++) {
        items[i] = rInt.nextInt();
        copy[i] = items[i];
    }

    // Sort with utility method.
    long startTime = System.currentTimeMillis();
    Arrays.sort(items);
    System.out.println("Utility sort time is "
                       + (System.currentTimeMillis()
                       - startTime) + "ms");
    JOptionPane.showMessageDialog(null,
            "Utility sort successful (true/false): "
            + verify(items));

    // Reload array items from array copy.
    for (int i = 0; i < items.length; i++) {
        items[i] = copy[i];
    }

    // Sort with quicksort.
    startTime = System.currentTimeMillis();
    QuickSort.sort(items);
    System.out.println("QuickSort time is "
                       + (System.currentTimeMillis()
                       - startTime) + " ms");
    JOptionPane.showMessageDialog(null,
            "QuickSort successful (true/false): "
            + verify(items));

    dumpTable(items);     // Display part of the array.
}

/** Verifies that the elements in array test are
    in increasing order.
    @param test The array to verify
    @return true if the elements are in increasing order;
            false if any 2 elements are not in increasing order
*/
private static boolean verify(Comparable[] test) {
    boolean ok = true;
    int i = 0;
    while (ok && i < test.length - 1) {
        ok = test[i].compareTo(test[i + 1]) <= 0;
        i++;
    }
    return ok;
}
```

EXERCISES FOR SECTION 8.10

SELF-CHECK

1. Explain why method `verify` will always determine whether an array is sorted. Does `verify` work if an array contains duplicate values?
2. Explain the effect of removing the second **for** statement in the `main` method.

PROGRAMMING

1. Write method `dumpTable`.
2. Modify the driver method to fill array `items` with a collection of integers read from a file when `args[0]` is not **`null`**.
3. Extend the driver to test all O(n log n) sorts and collect statistics on the different sorting algorithms. Test the sorts using an array of random numbers and also a data file processed by the solution to Programming Exercise 2.

8.11 The Dutch National Flag Problem (Optional Topic)

A variety of partitioning algorithms for quicksort have been published. Most are variations on the one presented in this text. There is another popular variation that uses a single left-to-right scan of the array (instead of scanning left and scanning right as we did). The following case study illustrates a partitioning algorithm that combines both scanning techniques to partition an array into three segments. The famous computer scientist Edsger W. Dijkstra described this problem in his book *A Discipline of Programming* (Prentice-Hall, 1976).

CASE STUDY The Problem of the Dutch National Flag

Problem The Dutch national flag consists of three stripes that are colored (from top to bottom) red, white, and blue as shown in Figure 8.21. Because we only have two colors, we use gray for red. Unfortunately, when the flag arrived, it looked like Figure 8.22; threads of each of the colors were all scrambled together! Fortunately, we have a machine that can unscramble it, but it needs software.

Analysis Our unscrambling machine has the following abilities:

- It can look at one thread in the flag and determine its color.
- It can swap the position of two threads in the flag.

Our machine can also execute **`while`** loops and **`if`** statements.

FIGURE 8.21
The Dutch National Flag

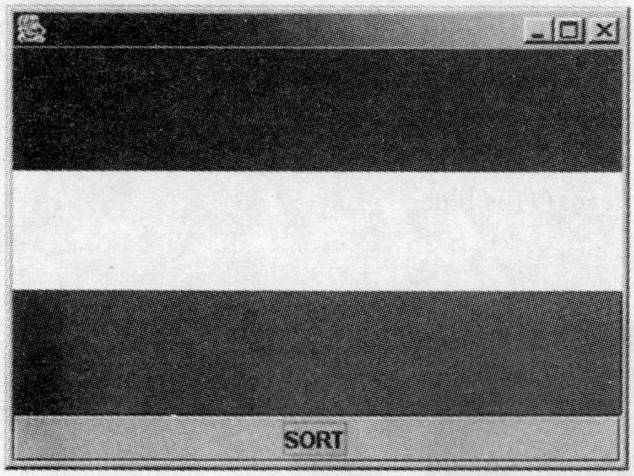

FIGURE 8.22
Scrambled Dutch National Flag

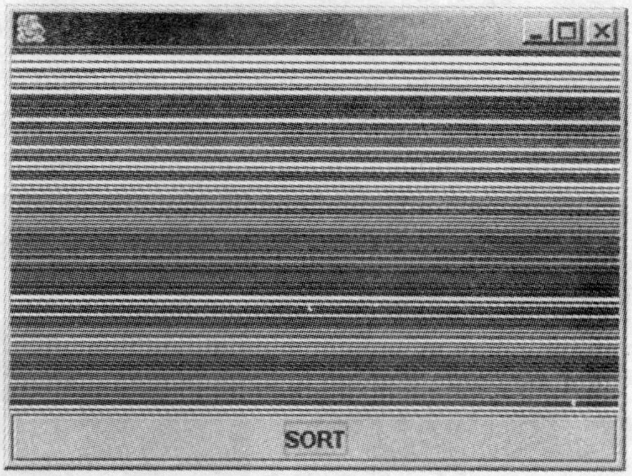

Design Loop Invariant

When we partitioned the array in quicksort, we split the array into three regions. Values between `first` and `up` were less than or equal to the pivot; values between `down` and `last` were greater than the pivot; and values between `up` and `down` were unknown. We started with the unknown region containing the whole array (`first == up`, and `down == last`). The partitioning algorithm preserves this invariant while shrinking the unknown region. The loop terminates when the unknown region becomes empty (`up > down`).

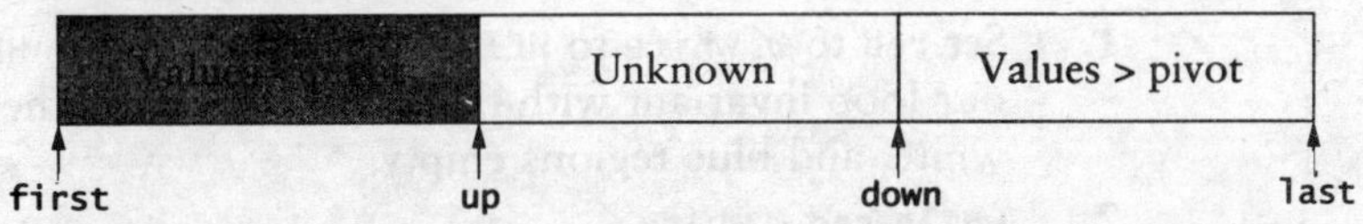

Since our goal is to have three regions when we are done, let us define four regions: the red region, the white region, the blue region, and the unknown region. Now, initially the whole flag is unknown. When we get done, however, we would like the red region on top, the white region in the middle, and the blue region on the bottom. The unknown region must be empty.

Let us assume that the threads are stored in an array `threads` and that the total number of threads is `HEIGHT`. Let us define `red` to be the upper bound of the red region, `white` to be the lower bound of the white region, and `blue` to be the lower bound of the blue region. Then, if our flag is complete, we can say the following:

- If $0 \le$ `i` < `red`, then `threads[i]` is red.
- If `white` < `i` $\le$ `blue`, then `threads[i]` is white.
- If `blue` < `i` < `HEIGHT`, then `threads[i]` is blue.

What about the case where red ≤ i ≤ white? When the flag is all sorted, red should equal white, so this region should not exist. However, when we start, everything is in this region, so a thread in that region can have any color.

Thus, we can define the following loop invariant:

- If 0 ≤ i < red, then threads[i] is red.
- If red ≤ i ≤ white, then the color is unknown.
- If white < i ≤ blue, then threads[i] is white.
- If blue < i < HEIGHT, then threads[i] is blue.

This is illustrated in Figure 8.23.

FIGURE 8.23
Dutch National Flag Loop Invariant

Algorithm We can solve our problem by establishing the loop invariant and then executing a loop that both preserves the loop invariant and shrinks the unknown region.

1. Set red to 0, white to HEIGHT - 1, and blue to HEIGHT - 1. This establishes our loop invariant with the unknown region the whole flag and the red, white, and blue regions empty.
2. **while** red < white
3. Shrink the distance between red and white while preserving the loop invariant.

Preserving the Loop Invariant

Let us assume that we now know the color of threads[white] (the thread at position white). Our goal is to either leave threads[white] where it is (in the white region if it is white) or "move it" to the region where it belongs. There are three cases to consider:

Case 1: The color of threads[white] is white. In this case we merely decrement the value of white to restore the invariant. By doing so, we increase the size of the white region by one thread.

Case 2: The color of `threads[white]` is red. We know from our invariant that the color of `threads[red]` is unknown. Therefore, if we swap the thread at `threads[red]` with the one at `threads[white]`, we can then increment the value of `red` and preserve the invariant. By doing this, we add the thread to the end of the red region and reduce the size of the unknown region by one thread.

Case 3: The color of `threads[white]` is blue. We know from our invariant that the color of `threads[blue]` is white. Thus, if we swap the thread at `threads[white]` with the thread at `threads[blue]` and then decrement both `white` and `blue`, we preserve the invariant. By doing this, we insert the thread at the beginning of the blue region and reduce the size of the unknown region by one thread.

Implementation A complete implementation of this program is left as a programming project. We show the coding of the sort algorithm in Listing 8.12.

LISTING 8.12
Dutch National Flag Sort

```
public void sort() {
    int red = 0;
    int white = height - 1;
    int blue = height - 1;
    /* Invariant:
       0 <= i < red          ==>threads[i].getColor() == Color.RED
       red <= i <= white ==>threads[i].getColor() is unknown
       white < i < blue     ==>threads[i].getColor() == Color.WHITE
       blue < i < height ==>threads[i].getColor() == Color.BLUE
    */
    while (red <= white) {
        if (threads[white].getColor() == Color.WHITE) {
            white--;
        } else if (threads[white].getColor() == Color.RED) {
            swap(red, white, g);
            red++;
        } else {  // threads[white].getColor() == Color.BLUE
            swap(white, blue, g);
            white--;
            blue--;
        }
    }
    // assert: red == white so unknown region is now empty.
}
```

EXERCISES FOR SECTION 8.11

PROGRAMMING

1. Adapt the Dutch National Flag algorithm to do the quicksort partitioning. Consider the red region to be those values less than the pivot, the white region to be those values equal to the pivot, and the blue region to be those values equal to the pivot. You should initially sort the first, middle, and last items and use the middle value as the pivot value.

Chapter Review

- We analyzed several sorting algorithms; their performance is summarized in Table 8.4.
- The three quadratic algorithms, $O(n^2)$, are selection sort, bubble sort, and insertion sort. They give satisfactory performance for small arrays (up to 100 elements). Generally, insertion sort is considered to be the best of the quadratic sorts. Bubble sort is a good choice when the array is likely to be nearly sorted but should be avoided otherwise.
- Shell sort, $O(n^{5/4})$, gives satisfactory performance for arrays up to 5000 elements.
- Quicksort has average-case performance of $O(n \log n)$, but if the pivot is picked poorly, the worst-case performance is $O(n^2)$.
- Merge sort and heapsort have $O(n \log n)$ performance.
- The Java API contains "industrial-strength" sort algorithms in the classes `java.util.Arrays` and `java.util.Collections`. The methods in `Arrays` use a mixture of quicksort and insertion sort for sorting arrays of primitive-type values and merge sort for sorting arrays of objects. For primitive types, quicksort is used until the size of the subarray reaches the point where insertion sort is quicker (7 elements or less). The sort method in `Collections` merely copies the list into an array and then calls `Arrays.sort`.

Java Classes Introduced in This Chapter

```
java.util.Arrays
java.util.Collections
```

TABLE 8.4
Comparison of Sort Algorithms

	Number of Comparisons		
	Best	Average	Worst
Selection sort	$O(n^2)$	$O(n^2)$	$O(n^2)$
Bubble sort	$O(n)$	$O(n^2)$	$O(n^2)$
Insertion sort	$O(n)$	$O(n^2)$	$O(n^2)$
Shell sort	$O(n^{7/6})$	$O(n^{5/4})$	$O(n^2)$
Merge sort	$O(n \log n)$	$O(n \log n)$	$O(n \log n)$
Heapsort	$O(n \log n)$	$O(n \log n)$	$O(n \log n)$
Quicksort	$O(n \log n)$	$O(n \log n)$	$O(n^2)$

User-Defined Interfaces and Classes in This Chapter

`BubbleSort`	`Person`
`ComparePerson`	`QuickSort`
`InsertionSort`	`SelectionSort`
`MergeSort`	`ShellSort`

Quick-Check Exercises

1. Name three quadratic sorts.
2. Name two sorts with $n \log n$ worst-case behavior.
3. Which algorithm is particularly good for an array that is already sorted? Which is particularly bad? Explain your answers.
4. What determines whether you should use a quadratic sort or a logarithmic sort?
5. Which quadratic sort's performance is least affected by the ordering of the array elements? Which is most affected?
6. What is a good all-purpose sorting algorithm for medium-size arrays?

Review Questions

1. When does quicksort work best, and when does it work worst?
2. Write a recursive procedure to implement the insertion sort algorithm.
3. What is the purpose of the pivot value in quicksort? How did we first select it in the text, and what is wrong with that approach for choosing a pivot value?
4. For the following array

   30 40 20 15 60 80 75 4 20

   show the new array after each pass of insertion sort, bubble sort, and selection sort. How many comparisons and exchanges are performed by each?
5. For the array in Question 4, trace the execution of Shell sort.

6. For the array in Question 4, trace the execution of merge sort.
7. For the array in Question 4, trace the execution of quicksort.
8. For the array in Question 4, trace the execution of heapsort.
9. The shaker sort is an adaptation of the bubble sort that alternates the direction in which the array elements are scanned during each pass. The first pass starts its scan with the first element, moving the larger element in each pair down the array. The second pass starts its scan with the next-to-last element, moving the smaller element in each pair up the array, and so on. Indicate what the advantage of the shaker sort might be.

Programming Projects

1. Use the random number function to store a list of 1000 pseudorandom integer values in an array. Apply each of the sort classes described in this chapter to the array and determine the number of comparisons and exchanges. Make sure the same array is passed to each sort method.
2. Investigate the effect of array size and initial element order on the number of comparisons and exchanges required by each of the sorting algorithms described in this chapter. Use arrays with 100 and 10,000 integers. Use three initial orderings of each array (randomly ordered, inversely ordered, and ordered). Be certain to sort the same six arrays with each sort method.
3. Implement the shaker sort algorithm described in Review Question 9.
4. A variation of the merge sort algorithm can be used to sort large sequential data files. The basic strategy is to take the initial data file, read in several (say, 10) data records, sort these records using an efficient array-sorting algorithm, and then write these sorted groups of records (runs) alternately to one of two output files. After all records from the initial data file have been distributed to the two output files, the runs on these output files are merged one pair of runs at a time and written to the original data file. After all runs from the output file have been merged, the records on the original data file are redistributed to the output files, and the merging process is repeated. Runs no longer need to be sorted after the first distribution to the temporary output files.

   Each time runs are distributed to the output files, they contain twice as many records as the time before. The process stops when the length of the runs exceeds the number of records in the data file. Write a program that implements merge sort for sequential data files. Test your program on a file with several thousand data values.
5. Write a method that sorts a linked list.
6. Write an industrial-strength quicksort method with the following enhancements:
   a. If an array segment contains 20 elements or fewer, sort it using insertion sort.
   b. After sorting the first, middle, and last elements, use the median as the pivot instead of swapping the median with the first element. Because the first and last elements are in the correct partitions, it is not necessary to test them before advancing `up` and `down`. This is also the case after each exchange, so increment `up` and decrement `down` at the beginning of the **`do-while`** loop. Also, it is not necessary to test whether `up` is less than `last` before incrementing `up` because the condition `pivot.compareTo(last) > 0` is false when `up` equals `last` (the median must be ≤ the last element in the array).
7. In the early days of data processing (before computers), data was stored on punched cards. A machine to sort these cards contained 12 bins (one for each digit value and + and –). A stack of cards was fed into the machine, and the cards were placed into the appropriate bin depending on the value of the selected column. By restacking the cards

so that all 0s were first, followed by the 1s, followed by the 2s, and so forth, and then sorting on the next column, the whole deck of cards could be sorted. This process, known as *radix sort*, requires $c \times n$ passes, where c is the number of columns and n is the number of cards.

We can simulate the action of this machine using an array of queues. During the first pass, the least-significant digit (the ones digit) of each number is examined and the number is added to the queue whose subscript matches that digit. After all numbers have been processed, the elements of each queue are added to an eleventh queue, starting with `queue[0]`, followed by `queue[1]`, and so forth. The process is then repeated for the next significant digit, taking the numbers out of the eleventh queue. After all the digits have been processed, the eleventh queue will contain the numbers in sorted order.

Write a program that implements radix sort on an array of **`int`** values. You will need to make 10 passes because an **`int`** can store numbers up to 2,147,483,648.

8. Complete the Dutch National Flag case study. You will need to develop the following classes:
   a. A main class that extends `JFrame` to contain the flag and a control button (Sort).
   b. A class to represent the flag; an extension of `JPanel` is suggested. This class will contain the array of threads and the sort method.
   c. A class to represent a thread. Each thread should have a color and a method to draw the thread.

Answers to Quick-Check Exercises

1. Selection sort, insertion sort, bubble sort
2. Merge sort, heapsort
3. Bubble sort—it requires $n - 1$ comparisons with no exchanges. Quicksort can be bad if the first element is picked as the pivot value, because the partitioning process always creates one subarray with a single element.
4. Array size
5. Selection sort, bubble sort
6. Shell sort or any O(n log n) sort

Chapter 9

Self-Balancing Search Trees

Chapter Objectives

- To understand the impact that balance has on the performance of binary search trees
- To learn about the AVL tree for storing and maintaining a binary search tree in balance
- To learn about the Red-Black tree for storing and maintaining a binary search tree in balance
- To learn about 2-3 trees, 2-3-4 trees, and B-trees and how they achieve balance
- To learn about skip-lists and how they have properties similar to balanced search trees
- To understand the process of search and insertion in each of these trees and to be introduced to removal

In Chapter 6 we introduced the binary search tree. The performance (time required to find, insert, or remove an item) of a binary search tree is proportional to the total *height of the tree,* where we define the height of a tree as the maximum number of nodes along a path from the root to a leaf. A full binary tree of height k can hold $2^k - 1$ items. Thus, if the binary search tree were full and contained n items, the expected performance would be O(log n).

Unfortunately, if we build the binary search tree as described in Chapter 6, the resulting tree is not necessarily full or close to being full. Thus the actual performance is worse than expected. In this chapter we explore two algorithms for building binary search trees so that they are as full as possible. We call these trees *self-balancing* because they attempt to achieve a balance so that the height of each left subtree and right subtree is equal or nearly equal.

Next we look at the B-tree and its specializations, the 2-3 and 2-3-4 trees. These are not binary search trees, but they achieve and maintain balance.

Finally we look at the skip-list. The skip-list is not a tree structure, but it allows for search, insertion, and removal in O(log n) time.

In this chapter we focus on algorithms and methods for search and insertion. We also discuss removing an item, but we have left the details of removal to the programming projects.

Self-Balancing Search Trees

9.1 Tree Balance and Rotation

Why Balance Is Important

Figure 9.1 shows an example of a valid, but extremely unbalanced, binary search tree. Searches or inserts into this tree would be O(n), not O(log n). Figure 9.2 shows the binary search tree resulting from inserting the words of the sentence "The quick brown fox jumps over the lazy dog". It too is not well balanced, having a height of 7 but containing only nine words. (Note that the string "The" is the smallest because it begins with an uppercase letter.)

FIGURE 9.1
Very Unbalanced Binary Search Tree

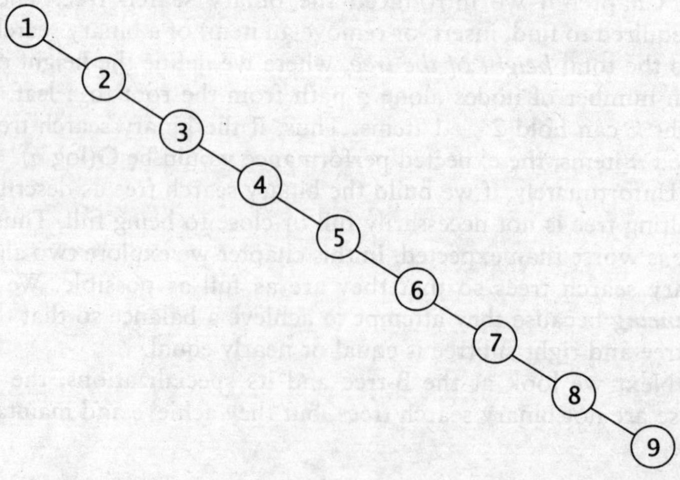

FIGURE 9.2
Realistic Example of an Unbalanced Binary Search Tree

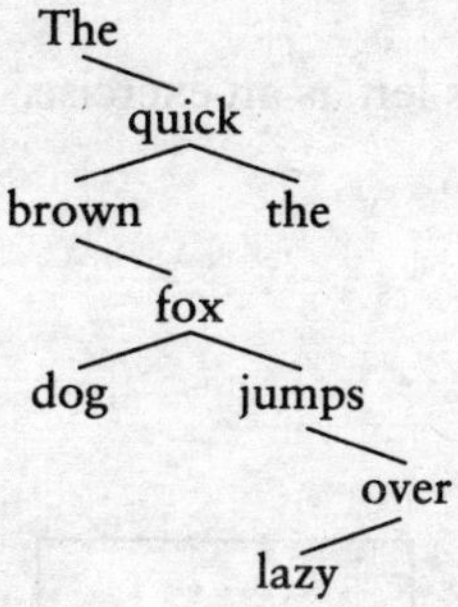

Rotation

To achieve self-adjusting capability, we need an operation on a binary search tree that will change the relative heights of left and right subtrees but preserve the binary search tree property—that is, the items in each left subtree are less than the item at the root, and the items in each right subtree are greater than the item in the root. In Figure 9.3 we show an unbalanced binary search tree with a height of 4 right after the insertion of node 7. The height of the left subtree of the root (20) is 3, and the height of the right subtree is 1.

We can transform the tree in Figure 9.3 by doing a *right rotation* around node 20, making 10 the root and 20 the root of the right subtree of the new root (10). Because 20 is now the right subtree of 10, we need to move node 10's old right subtree (root is 15). We will make it the left subtree of 20, as shown in Figure 9.4.

After these changes the new binary search tree has a height of 3 (one less than before), and the left and right subtrees of the new root (10) have a height of 2, as shown in Figure 9.5. Note that the binary search tree property is maintained for all the nodes of the tree.

This result can be generalized. If node 15 had children, its children would have to be greater than 10 and less than 20 in the original tree. The left and right subtrees of node 15 would not change when node 15 was moved, so the binary search tree property would still be maintained for all children of node 15 in the new tree (> 10 and < 20). We can make a similar statement for any of the other leaf nodes in the original tree.

Algorithm for Rotation

Figure 9.6 illustrates the internal representation of the nodes of our original binary search tree whose branches (indicated by arrows in color) will be changed by rotation. Initially, root references node 20. Rotation right is achieved by the following algorithm.

Algorithm for Rotation Right

1. Remember the value of `root.left` (`temp = root.left`).
2. Set `root.left` to the value of `temp.right`.
3. Set `temp.right` to `root`.
4. Set `root` to `temp`.

FIGURE 9.3
Unbalanced Tree before Rotation

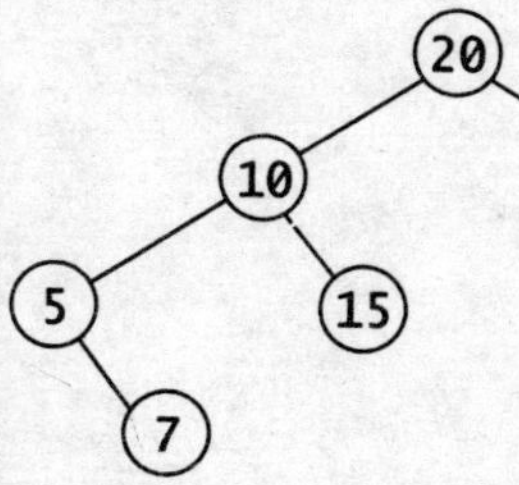

FIGURE 9.4
Right Rotation

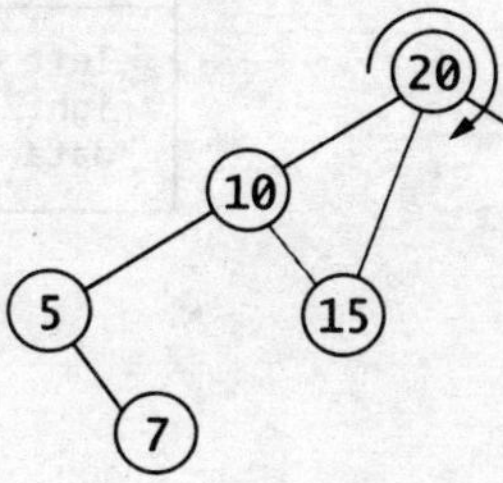

FIGURE 9.5
More Balanced Tree after Rotation

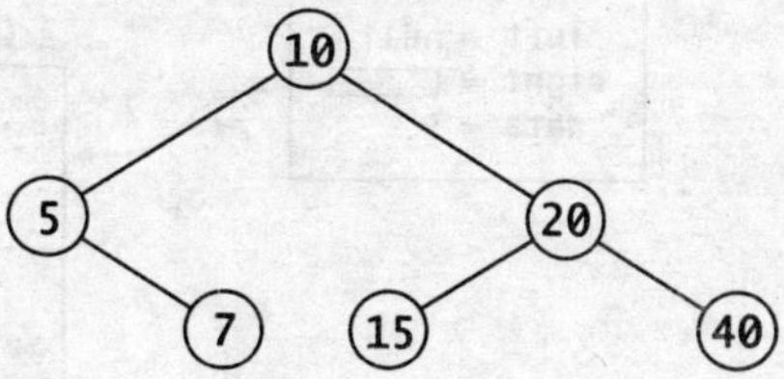

Figure 9.7 shows the rotated tree. Step 1 sets `temp` to reference the left subtree (node 10) of the original root. Step 2 resets the original root's left subtree to reference node 15. Step 3 resets node `temp`'s right subtree to reference the original root. Then Step 4 sets `root` to reference node `temp`. The internal representation corresponds to the tree shown in Figure 9.5.

The algorithm for rotation left is symmetric to rotation right and is left as an exercise.

FIGURE 9.6
Internal Representation of Binary Search Tree

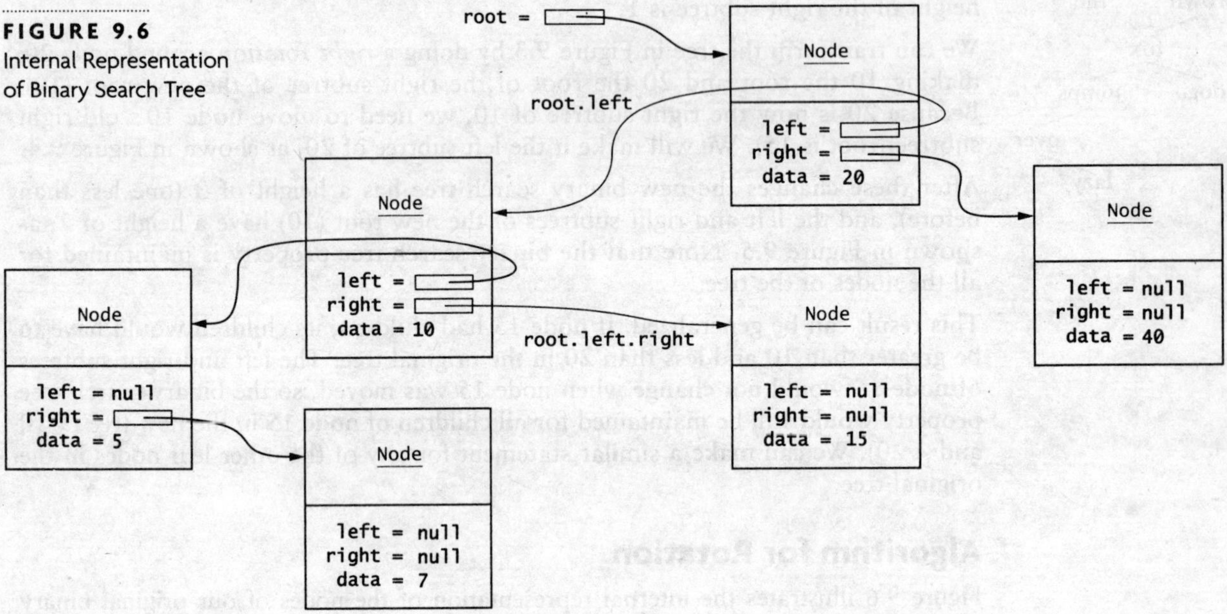

FIGURE 9.7
Effect of Rotation Right on Internal Representation

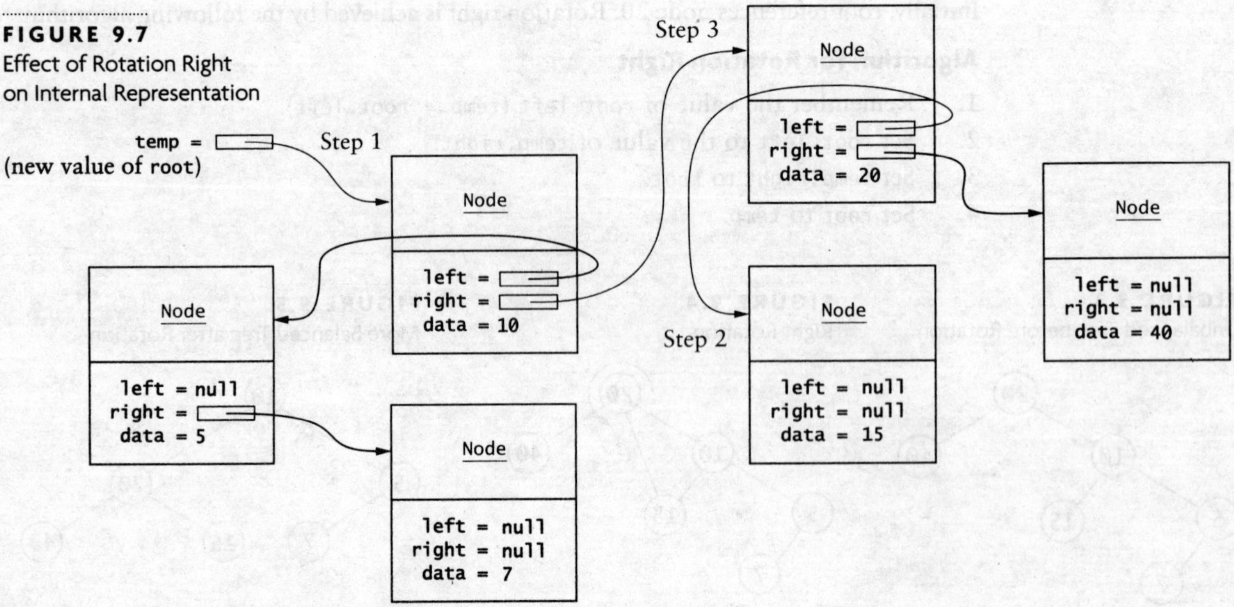

Implementing Rotation

Listing 9.1 shows class `BinarySearchTreeWithRotate`. This class is an extension of the `BinarySearchTree` class described in Chapter 6, and it will be used as the base class for the other search trees discussed in this chapter. Like class `BinarySearchTree`, class `BinarySearchTreeWithRotate` must be declared as a generic class with type parameter `<E extends Comparable<E>>`. It contains the methods `rotateLeft` and `rotateRight`. These methods take a reference to a `Node` that is the root of a subtree and return a reference to the root of the rotated tree. Figure 9.8 is a UML class diagram that shows the relationships between `BinarySearchTreeWithRotate` and the other classes in the hierarchy. `BinarySearchTreeWithRotate` is a subclass of `BinaryTree` as well as `BinarySearchTree`. Class `BinaryTree` has the static inner class `Node` and the data field `root`, which references the `Node` that is the root of the tree. The figure shows that a `Node` contains a data field named `data` and two references (as indicated by the open diamond) to a `Node`. The names of the reference are `left` and `right`, as shown on the line from the `Node` to itself.

FIGURE 9.8
UML Diagram of `BinarySearchTreeWithRotate`

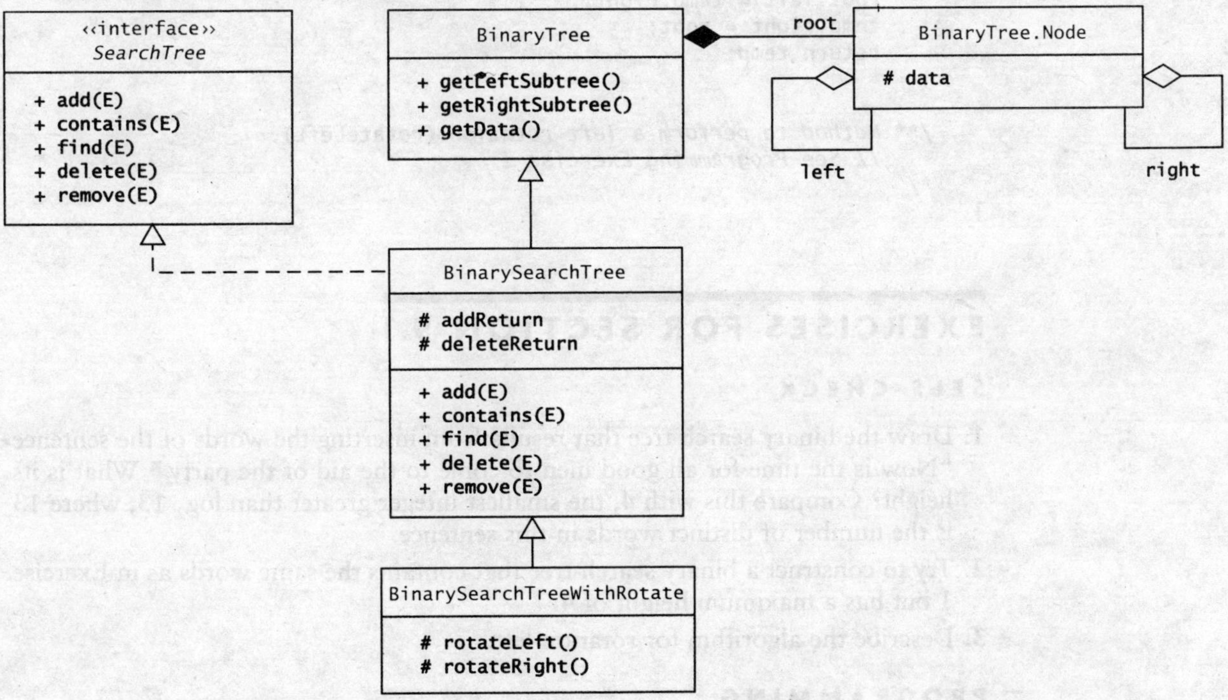

LISTING 9.1
BinarySearchTreeWithRotate.java

```
/** This class extends the BinarySearchTree by adding the rotate
    operations. Rotation will change the balance of a search
    tree while preserving the search tree property.
    Used as a common base class for self-balancing trees.
*/
public class BinarySearchTreeWithRotate<E extends Comparable<E>>
        extends BinarySearchTree<E> {
    // Methods
    /** Method to perform a right rotation.
        pre:  root is the root of a binary search tree.
        post: root.right is the root of a binary search tree,
              root.right.right is raised one level,
              root.right.left does not change levels,
              root.left is lowered one level,
              the new root is returned.
        @param root The root of the binary tree to be rotated
        @return The new root of the rotated tree
    */
    protected Node<E> rotateRight(Node<E> root) {
        Node<E> temp = root.left;
        root.left = temp.right;
        temp.right = root;
        return temp;
    }

    /** Method to perform a left rotation (rotateLeft).
        // See Programming Exercise 1
    */
}
```

EXERCISES FOR SECTION 9.1

SELF-CHECK

1. Draw the binary search tree that results from inserting the words of the sentence "Now is the time for all good men to come to the aid of the party." What is its height? Compare this with 4, the smallest integer greater than $\log_2 13$, where 13 is the number of distinct words in this sentence.
2. Try to construct a binary search tree that contains the same words as in Exercise 1 but has a maximum height of 4.
3. Describe the algorithm for rotation left.

PROGRAMMING

1. Add the `rotateLeft` method to the `BinarySearchTreeWithRotate` class.

9.2 AVL Trees

Two Russian mathematicians, G. M. Adel'son-Vel'skiî and E. M. Landis, published a paper in 1962 that describes an algorithm for maintaining overall balance of a binary search tree. Their algorithm keeps track of the difference in height of each subtree. As items are added to (or removed from) the tree, the balance (i.e., the difference in the heights of the subtrees) of each subtree from the insertion point up to the root is updated. If the balance ever gets out of the range –1 . . . +1, the subtree is rotated to bring it back into balance. Trees using this approach are known as *AVL trees* after the initials of the inventors. As before, we define the height of a tree as the number of nodes in the longest path from the root to a leaf node, including the root.

Balancing a Left-Left Tree

Figure 9.9 shows a binary search tree with a balance of –2 caused by an insert into its left-left subtree. Each white triangle with label a, b, or c represents a tree of height k; the shaded area at the bottom of the left-left triangle (tree a) indicates an insertion into this tree (its height is now $k + 1$). We use the formula

$$h_R - h_L$$

to calculate the balance for each node, where h_L and h_R are the heights of the left and right subtrees, respectively. The actual heights are not important; it is their relative difference that matters. The right subtree (b) of node 25 has a height of k; its left subtree (a) has a height of $k + 1$, so its balance is –1. The right subtree (of node 50) has a height of k; its left subtree has a height of $k + 2$, so its factor is –2. Such a tree is called a Left-Left tree because its root and the left subtree of the root are both left-heavy.

Figure 9.10 shows this same tree after a rotation right. The new tree root is node 25. Its right subtree (root 50) now has tree b as its left subtree. Notice that balance has now been achieved. Also, the overall height has not increased. Before the insertion, the tree height was $k + 2$; after the rotation, the tree height is still $k + 2$.

FIGURE 9.9
Left-Heavy Tree

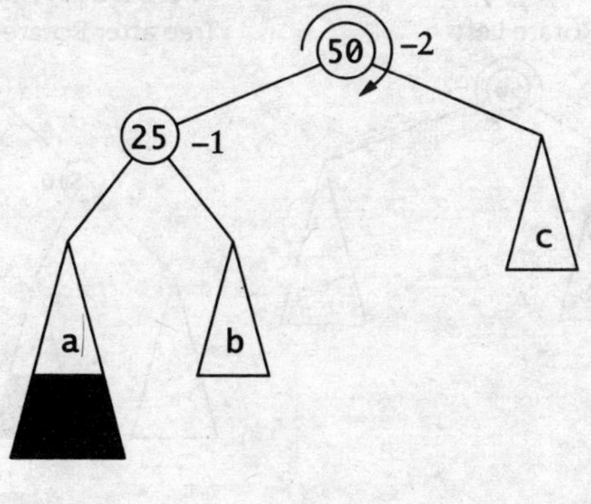

FIGURE 9.10
Left-Heavy Tree after Rotation Right

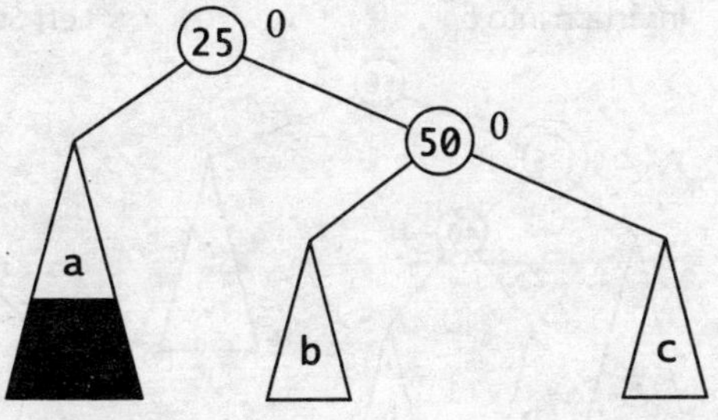

Balancing a Left-Right Tree

Figure 9.11 shows a left-heavy tree caused by an insert into the left-right subtree. This tree is called a Left-Right tree because its root is left-heavy but the left-subtree of the root is right-heavy. We cannot fix this with a simple rotation right as in the Left-Left case. (See Self-Check Exercise 2 at the end of this section.)

FIGURE 9.11
Left-Right Tree

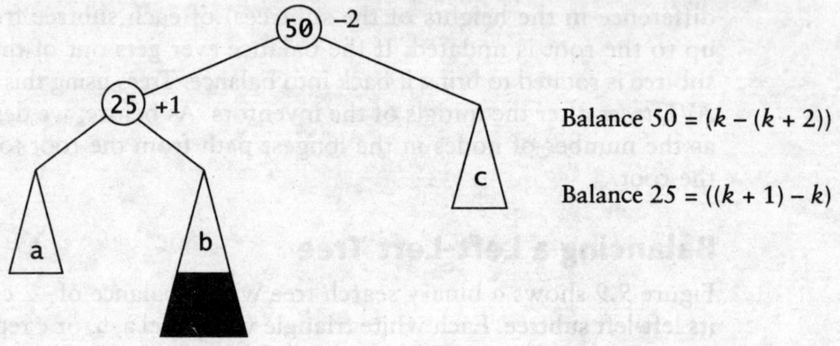

Figure 9.12 shows a general Left-Right tree. Node 40, the root of the Left-Right subtree, is expanded into its subtrees b_L and b_R. Figure 9.12 shows the effect of an insertion into b_L, making node 40 left-heavy. If the left subtree is rotated left, as shown in Figure 9.13, the overall tree is now a Left-Left tree, similar to the case of Figure 9.9. Now if the modified tree is rotated right, overall balance is achieved, as shown in Figure 9.14. Figures 9.15 to 9.17 illustrate the effect of these double rotations after insertion into b_R.

In both cases, the new tree root is 40; its left subtree has node 25 as its root, and its right subtree has node 50 as its root. The balance of the root is 0. If the critically unbalanced situation was due to an insertion into subtree b_L, the balance of the root's left child is 0, and the balance of the root's right child is +1 (Figure 9.14). For insertion into subtree b_R, the balance of the root's left child is −1, and the balance of the root's right child is 0 (Figure 9.17).

FIGURE 9.12
Insertion into b_L

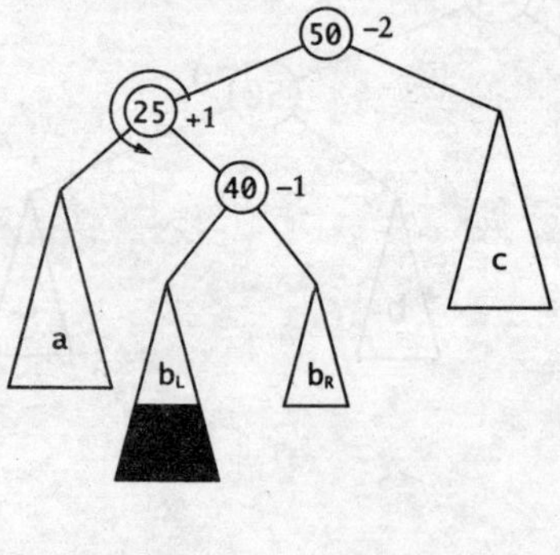

FIGURE 9.13
Left Subtree after Rotate Left

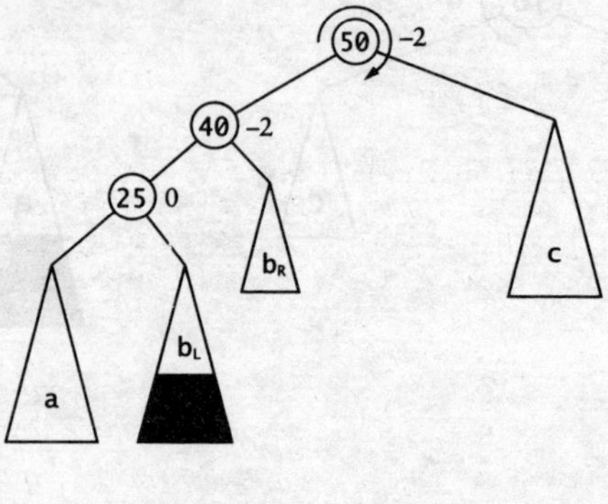

FIGURE 9.14
Tree after Rotate Right

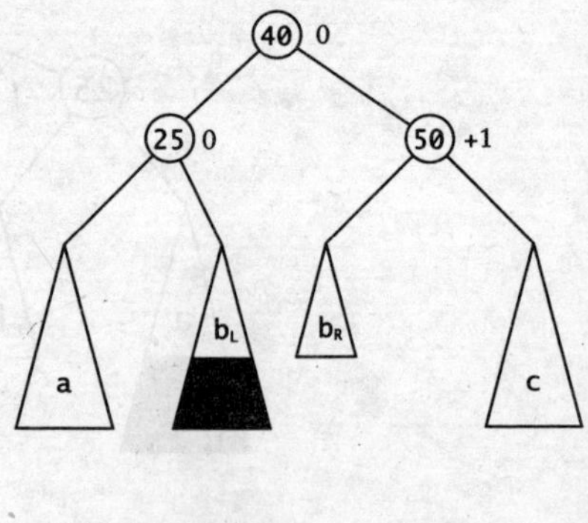

FIGURE 9.15
Insertion into b_R

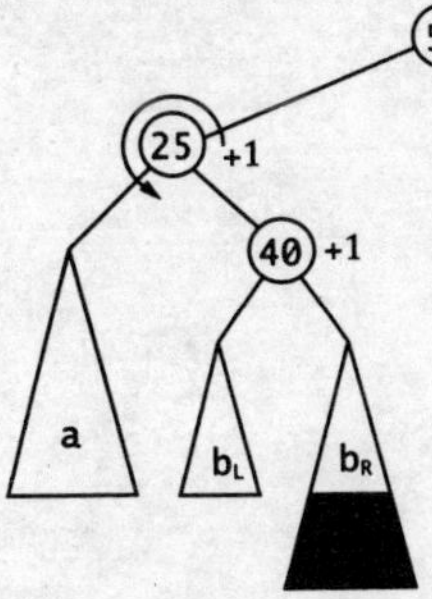

FIGURE 9.16
Left Subtree after Rotate Left

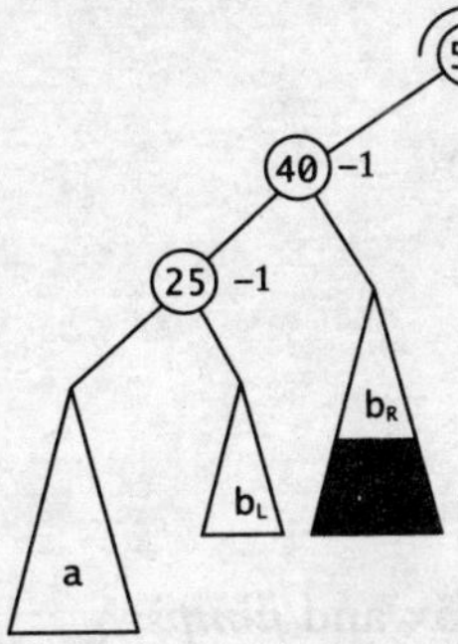

FIGURE 9.17
Tree after Rotate Right

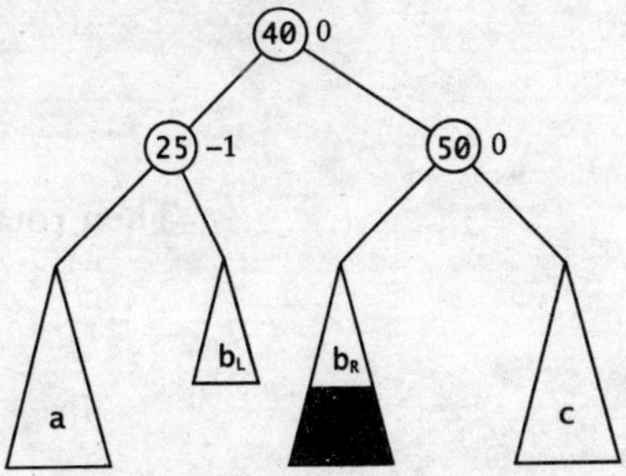

Four Kinds of Critically Unbalanced Trees

How do we recognize unbalanced trees and determine what to do to balance them? For the Left-Left tree shown in Figure 9.9 (parent and child nodes are both left-heavy, parent balance is −2, child balance is −1), the remedy is to rotate right around the parent.

For the Left-Right example shown in Figure 9.11 (parent is left-heavy with balance −2, child is right-heavy with balance +1), the remedy is to rotate left around the child and then rotate right around the parent. We list the four cases that need rebalancing and their remedies next.

- Left-Left (parent balance is −2, left child balance is −1): Rotate right around parent.
- Left-Right (parent balance is −2, left child balance is +1): Rotate left around child, then rotate right around parent.
- Right-Right (parent balance is +2, right child balance is +1): Rotate left around parent.
- Right-Left (parent balance is +2, right child balance is −1): Rotate right around child, then rotate left around parent.

EXAMPLE 9.1 We will build an AVL tree from the words in the sentence "The quick brown fox jumps over the lazy dog".

After inserting the words *The*, *quick*, and *brown*, we get the following tree.

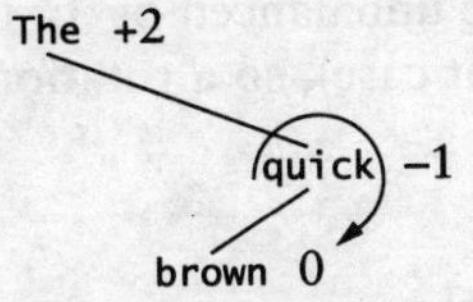

The subtree with the root *quick* is left-heavy by 1, but the overall tree with the root of *The* is right-heavy by 2 (Right-Left case). We must first rotate the subtree around *quick* to the right:

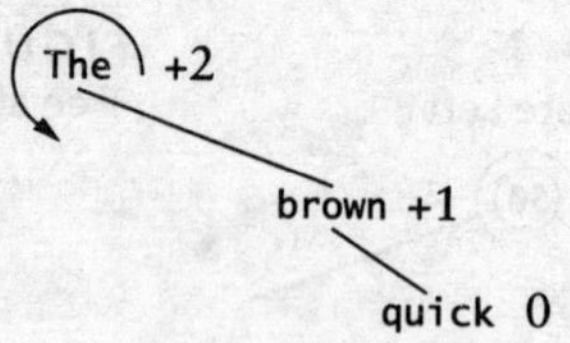

Then rotate left about *The*:

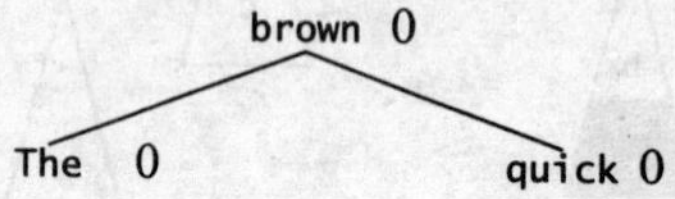

We now proceed to insert *fox* and *jumps*:

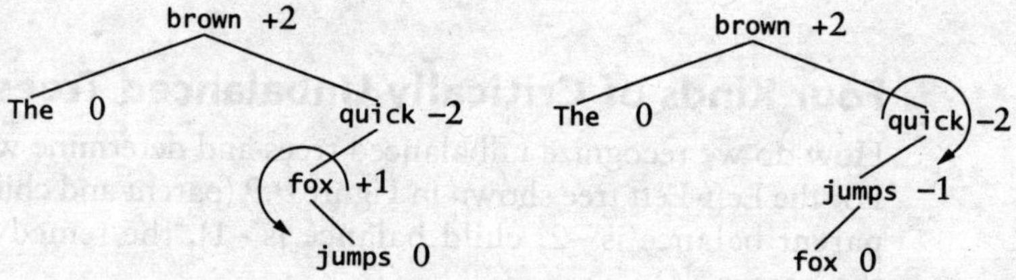

The subtree rooted about *quick* is now left-heavy by 2 (Left-Right case). Because this case is symmetric with the previous one, we rotate left about *fox* and then right about *quick*, giving the following result.

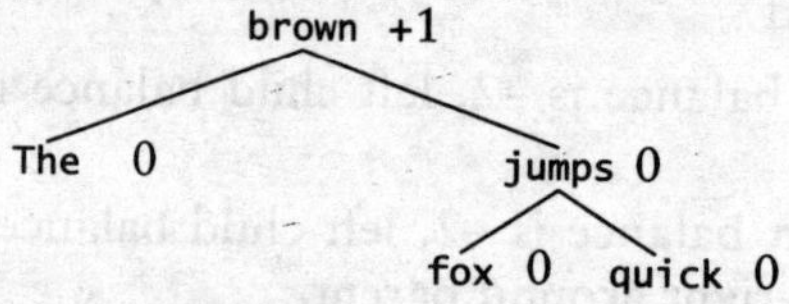

We now insert *over*.

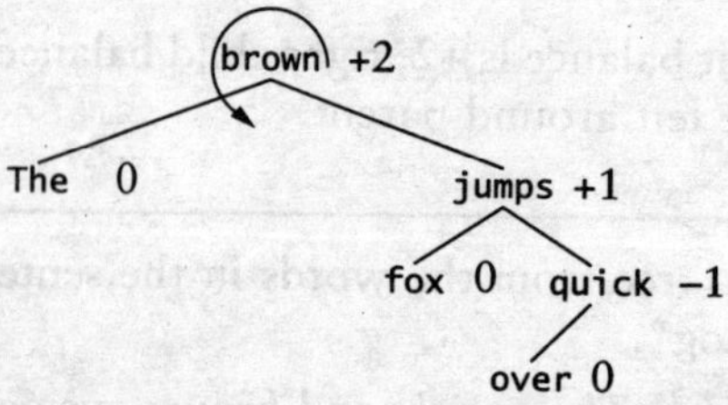

The subtrees at *quick* and *jumps* are unbalanced by 1. The subtree at *brown*, however, is right-heavy by 2 (Right-Right case), so a rotation left solves the problem.

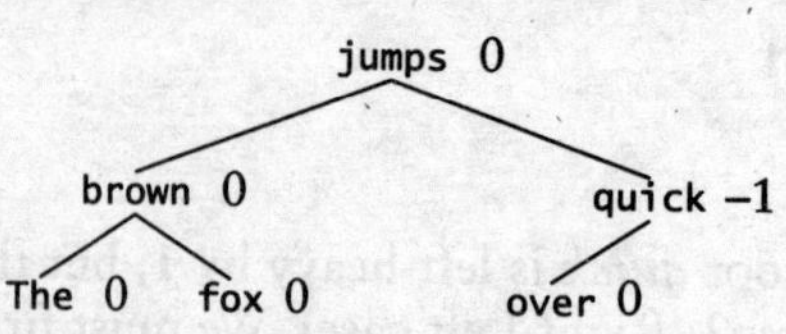

We can now insert *the, lazy,* and *dog* without any additional rotations being necessary.

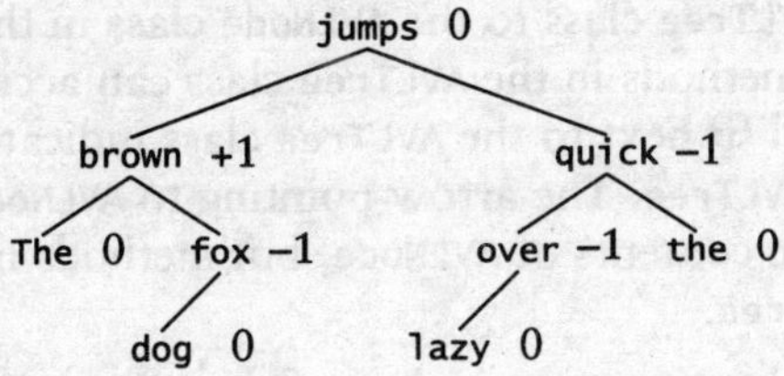

Implementing an AVL Tree

We begin by deriving the class `AVLTree` from `BinarySearchTreeWithRotate` (see Listing 9.1). Figure 9.18 is a UML class diagram showing the relationship between `AVLTree` and `BinarySearchTreeWithRotate`. The `AVLTree` class contains the **`boolean`** data field `increase`, which indicates whether the current subtree height has increased as a result of the insertion. We override the methods `add` and `delete` but inherit method `find` because searching a balanced tree is no different from searching an unbalanced tree. We also extend the inner class `BinaryTree.Node` with `AVLNode`. Within this class we add the additional field `balance`.

FIGURE 9.18
UML Class Diagram of AVLTree

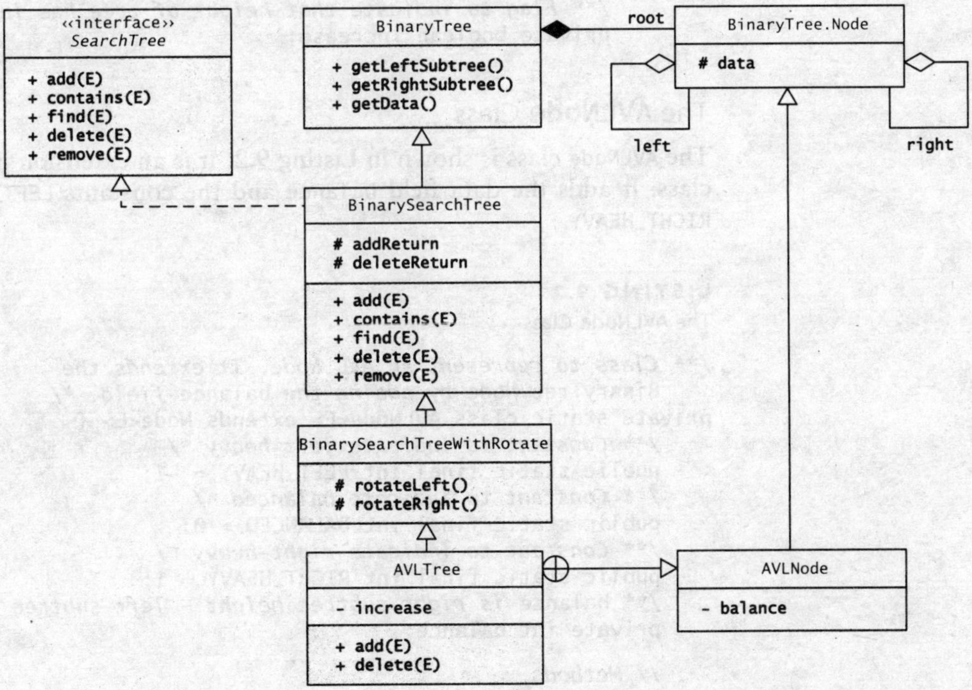

SYNTAX **UML Syntax**

The line from the AVLTree class to the AVLNode class in the diagram in Figure 9.18 indicates that methods in the AVLTree class can access the private data field balance. The symbol ⊕ next to the AVLTree class indicates that the AVLNode class is an inner class of AVLTree. The arrow pointing to AVLNode indicates that methods in AVLTree access the contents of AVLNode, but methods in AVLNode do not access the contents of AVLTree.

Note that the Node class is an inner class of the BinaryTree class, but we do not show the ⊕. This is because an object of type Node, called root, is a component of the BinaryTree class, as indicated by the filled diamond next to the BinaryTree class. Showing both the ⊕ and the filled diamond would clutter the diagram, so only the filled diamond is shown.

```
/** Self-balancing binary search tree using the algorithm defined
    by Adelson-Velskii and Landis.
*/
public class AVLTree<E extends Comparable<E>>
        extends BinarySearchTreeWithRotate<E> {

    // Insert nested class AVLNode<E> here.

    // Data Fields
    /** Flag to indicate that height of tree has increased. */
    private boolean increase;
. . .
```

The **AVLNode** Class

The AVLNode class is shown in Listing 9.2. It is an extension of the BinaryTree.Node class. It adds the data field balance and the constants LEFT_HEAVY, BALANCED, and RIGHT_HEAVY.

LISTING 9.2
The AVLNode Class

```
/** Class to represent an AVL Node. It extends the
    BinaryTree.Node by adding the balance field. */
private static class AVLNode<E> extends Node<E> {
    /** Constant to indicate left-heavy */
    public static final int LEFT_HEAVY = -1;
    /** Constant to indicate balanced */
    public static final int BALANCED = 0;
    /** Constant to indicate right-heavy */
    public static final int RIGHT_HEAVY = 1;
    /** balance is right subtree height - left subtree height */
    private int balance;

    // Methods
    /** Construct a node with the given item as the data field.
        @param item The data field
```

```
    */
    public AVLNode(E item) {
        super(item);
        balance = BALANCED;
    }

    /** Return a string representation of this object.
        The balance value is appended to the contents.
        @return String representation of this object
    */
    @Override
    public String toString() {
        return balance + ": " + super.toString();
    }
}
```

Inserting into an AVL Tree

The easiest way to keep a tree balanced is never to let it become unbalanced. If any node becomes critical and needs rebalancing, rebalance immediately. You can identify critical nodes by checking the balance at the root node of a subtree as you return to each parent node along the insertion path. If the insertion was in the left subtree and the left subtree height has increased, you must check to see whether the balance for the root node of the left subtree has become critical (–2 or +2). If so, you need to fix it by calling `rebalanceLeft` (rebalance a left-heavy tree when balance is –2) or `rebalanceRight` (rebalance a right-heavy tree when balance is +2). A symmetric strategy should be followed after returning from an insertion into the right subtree. The **`boolean`** variable `increase` is set before return from recursion to indicate to the next higher level that the height of the subtree has increased. This information is then used to adjust the balance of the next level in the tree. The following algorithm is based on the algorithm for inserting into a binary search tree, described in Chapter 6.

Algorithm for Insertion into an AVL Tree

1. **`if`** the root is **`null`**
2. Create a new tree with the item at the `root` and return **`true`**.
   `else if` the item is equal to `root.data`
3. The item is already in the tree; return **`false`**.
   `else if` the item is less than `root.data`
4. Recursively insert the item in the left subtree.
5. **`if`** the height of the left subtree has increased (`increase` is **`true`**)
6. Decrement `balance`.
7. **`if`** `balance` is zero, reset `increase` to **`false`**.
8. **`if`** `balance` is less than –1
9. Reset `increase` to **`false`**.
10. Perform a `rebalanceLeft`.
    `else if` the item is greater than `root.data`
11. The processing is symmetric to Steps 4 through 10. Note that `balance` is incremented if `increase` is true.

After returning from the recursion (Step 4), examine the global data field `increase` to see whether the left subtree has increased in height. If it did, then decrement the balance. If the balance had been +1 (current subtree was right-heavy), it is now zero, so the overall height of the current subtree is not changed. Therefore, reset `increase` to **`false`** (Steps 5–7).

If the balance was –1 (current subtree was left-heavy), it is now –2, and a `rebalanceLeft` must be performed. The rebalance operation reduces the overall height of the tree by 1, so `increase` is reset to **`false`**. Therefore, no more rebalancing operations will occur, so you can fix the tree by either a single rotation (Left-Left case) or a double rotation (Left-Right case) (Steps 8–10).

add Starter Method

We are now ready to implement the insertion algorithm. The `add` starter method merely calls the recursive `add` method with the root as its argument. The returned `AVLNode` is the new root.

```
/** add starter method.
    pre: the item to insert implements the Comparable interface.
    @param item The item being inserted.
    @return true if the object is inserted; false
            if the object already exists in the tree
    @throws ClassCastException if item is not Comparable
*/
@Override
public boolean add(E item) {
    increase = false;
    root = add((AVLNode<E>) root, item);
    return addReturn;
}
```

As for the `BinarySearchTree` in Chapter 6, the recursive `add` method will set the data field `addReturn` to **`true`** (inherited from class `BinarySearchTree`) if the item is inserted and **`false`** if the item is already in the tree.

Recursive **add** Method

The declaration for the recursive `add` method begins as follows:

```
/** Recursive add method. Inserts the given object into the tree.
    post: addReturn is set true if the item is inserted,
          false if the item is already in the tree.
    @param localRoot The local root of the subtree
    @param item The object to be inserted
    @return The new local root of the subtree with the item
            inserted
*/
private AVLNode<E> add(AVLNode<E> localRoot, E item)
```

We begin by seeing whether the `localRoot` is **`null`**. If it is, then we set `addReturn` and `increase` to **`true`** and return a new `AVLNode`, which contains the item to be inserted.

```
if (localRoot == null) {
    addReturn = true;
    increase = true;
    return new AVLNode<E>(item);
}
```

Next we compare the inserted item with the data field of the current node. If it is equal, we set addReturn and increase to **false** and return the localRoot unchanged.

```
if (item.compareTo(localRoot.data) == 0) {
    // Item is already in the tree.
    increase = false;
    addReturn = false;
    return localRoot;
}
```

If it is less than this value, we recursively call the add method (Step 4 of the insertion algorithm), passing localRoot.left as the parameter and replacing the value of localRoot.left with the returned value.

```
else if (item.compareTo(localRoot.data) < 0) {
    // item < data
    localRoot.left = add((AVLNode<E>) localRoot.left, item);
. . .
```

Upon return from the recursion, we examine the global data field increase. If increase is **true**, then the height of the left subtree has increased, so we decrement the balance by calling the decrementBalance method. If the balance is now less than –1, we reset increase to **false** and call the rebalanceLeft method. The return value from the rebalanceLeft method is the return value from this call to add. If the balance is not less than –1, or if the left subtree height did not increase, then the return from this recursive call is the same local root that was passed as the parameter.

```
if (increase) {
    decrementBalance(localRoot);
    if (localRoot.balance < AVLNode.LEFT_HEAVY) {
        increase = false;
        return rebalanceLeft(localRoot);
    }
}
return localRoot;     // Rebalance not needed.
```

If the item is not equal to localRoot.data and not less than localRoot.data, then it must be greater than localRoot.data. The processing is symmetric with the less-than case and is left as an exercise.

Initial Algorithm for rebalanceLeft

Method rebalanceLeft rebalances a left-heavy tree. Such a tree can be a Left-Left tree (fixed by a single right rotation) or a Left-Right tree (fixed by a left rotation followed by a right rotation). If its left subtree is right-heavy, we have a Left-Right case, so we first rotate left around the left subtree. Finally we rotate the tree right.

1. **if** the left subtree has positive balance (Left-Right case)
2. Rotate left around left subtree root.
3. Rotate right.

The algorithm for rebalanceRight is left as an exercise.

The Effect of Rotations on Balance

The rebalancing algorithm just presented is incomplete. So far we have focused on changes to the root reference and to the internal branches of the tree being balanced, but we have not adjusted the balances of the nodes. In the beginning of this section we showed that for a Left-Left tree, the balances of the new root node and of its right child are 0 after a right rotation; the balances of all other nodes are unchanged (see Figure 9.10).

The Left-Right case is more complicated. We made the following observation after studying the different cases.

The balance of the root is 0. If the critically unbalanced situation was due to an insertion into subtree b_L, the balance of the root's left child is 0 and the balance of the root's right child is +1 (Figure 9.14). For insertion into subtree b_R, the balance of the root's left child is –1, and the balance of the root's right child is 0 (Figure 9.17). So we need to change the balances of the new root node and both its left and right children; all other balances are unchanged. We will call insertion into subtree b_L the Left-Right-Left case and insertion into subtree b_R the Left-Right-Right case.

Revised Algorithm for `rebalanceLeft`

Based on the foregoing discussion, we can now develop the complete algorithm for `rebalanceLeft`, including the required balance changes. It is easier to store the new balance for each node before the rotation than after.

1. **if** the left subtree has a positive balance (Left-Right case)
2.   **if** the left-left subtree has a negative balance (Left-Right-Left case)
3.   Set the left subtree (new left subtree) balance to 0.
4.   Set the left-left subtree (new root) balance to 0.
5.   Set the local root (new right subtree) balance to +1.
       else (Left-Right-Right case)
6.   Set the left subtree (new left subtree) balance to –1.
7.   Set the left-left subtree (new root) balance to 0.
8.   Set the local root (new right subtree) balance to 0.
9.   Rotate the left subtree left.
   else (Left-Left case)
10.   Set the left subtree balance to 0.
11.   Set the local root balance to 0.
12. Rotate the local root right.

The algorithm for `rebalanceRight` is left as an exercise.

Method `rebalanceLeft`

The code for `rebalanceLeft` is shown in Listing 9.3. First we test to see whether the left subtree is right-heavy (Left-Right case). If so, the Left-Right subtree is examined.

Depending on its balance, the balances of the left subtree and local root are set as previously described in the algorithm. The rotations will reduce the overall height of the tree by 1, so `increase` is now set to **`false`**. The left subtree is then rotated left, and the tree is rotated right.

If the left child is LEFT_HEAVY, the rotation process will restore the balance to both the tree and its left subtree and reduce the overall height by 1; the balance for the left subtree and local root are both set to BALANCED, and `increase` is now set to **`false`**. The tree is then rotated right to correct the imbalance.

LISTING 9.3

The `rebalanceLeft` Method

```
/** Method to rebalance left.
    pre: localRoot is the root of an AVL subtree that is
         critically left-heavy.
    post: Balance is restored.
    @param localRoot Root of the AVL subtree
         that needs rebalancing
    @return a new localRoot
*/
private AVLNode<E> rebalanceLeft(AVLNode<E> localRoot) {
    // Obtain reference to left child.
    AVLNode<E> leftChild = (AVLNode<E>) localRoot.left;
    // See whether left-right heavy.
    if (leftChild.balance > AVLNode.BALANCED) {
        // Obtain reference to left-right child.
        AVLNode<E> leftRightChild = (AVLNode<E>) leftChild.right;
        /** Adjust the balances to be their new values after
            the rotations are performed.
        */
        if (leftRightChild.balance < AVLNode.BALANCED) {
            leftChild.balance = AVLNode.BALANCED;
            leftRightChild.balance = AVLNode.BALANCED;
            localRoot.balance = AVLNode.RIGHT_HEAVY;
        } else {
            leftChild.balance = AVLNode.LEFT_HEAVY;
            leftRightChild.balance = AVLNode.BALANCED;
            localRoot.balance = AVLNode.BALANCED;
        }
        // Perform left rotation.
        localRoot.left = rotateLeft(leftChild);
    } else {   Left-Left case
        /** In this case the leftChild (the new root)
            and the root (new right child) will both be balanced
            after the rotation.
        */
        leftChild.balance = AVLNode.BALANCED;
        localRoot.balance = AVLNode.BALANCED;
    }
    // Now rotate the local root right.
    return (AVLNode<E>) rotateRight(localRoot);
}
```

We also need a `rebalanceRight` method that is symmetric with `rebalanceLeft` (i.e., all `lefts` are changed to `rights` and all `rights` are changed to `lefts`). Coding of this method is left as an exercise.

The **decrementBalance** Method

As we return from an insertion into a node's left subtree, we need to decrement the balance of the node. We also need to indicate whether the subtree height at that node has not increased, by setting `increase` (currently **`true`**) to **`false`**. There are two cases to consider: a node that is balanced and a node that is right-heavy. If a node is balanced, insertion into its left subtree will cause it to become left-heavy, and its height will also increase by 1 (see Figure 9.19). If a node is right-heavy, insertion into its left subtree will cause it to become balanced, and its height will not increase (see Figure 9.20).

```
private void decrementBalance(AVLNode<E> node) {
    // Decrement the balance.
    node.balance--;
    if (node.balance == AVLNode.BALANCED) {
        /** If now balanced, overall height has not increased. */
        increase = false;
    }
}
```

Step 11 of the insertion algorithm performs insertion into a right subtree. This can cause the height of the right subtree to increase, so we will also need an `incrementBalance` method that increments the balance and resets `increase` to **`false`** if the balance changes from left-heavy to balanced. Coding this method is left as an exercise.

FIGURE 9.19
Decrement of `balance` by Insert on Left (Height Increases)

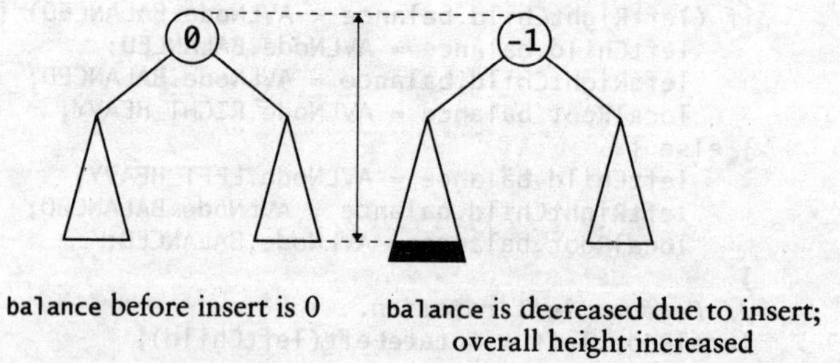

FIGURE 9.20
Decrement of `balance` by Insert on Left (Height Does Not Change)

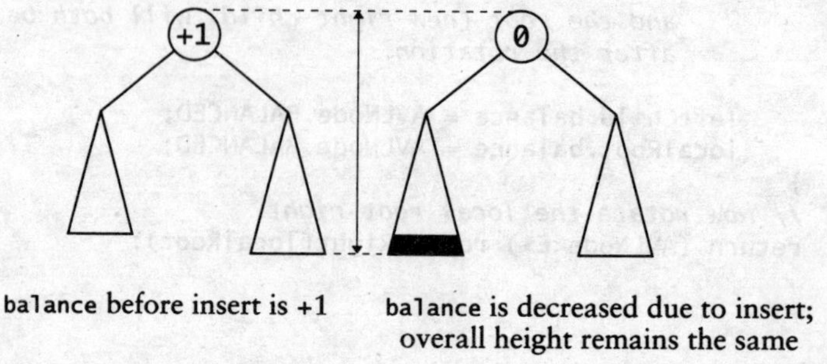

Removal from an AVL Tree

When we remove an item from a left subtree, the balance of the local root is increased, and when we remove an item from the right subtree, the balance of the local root is decreased. We can adapt the algorithm for removal from a binary search tree to become an algorithm for removal from an AVL tree. We need to maintain a data field `decrease` that tells the previous level in the recursion that there was a decrease in the height of the subtree that was just returned from. (This data field is analogous to the data field `increase`, which is used in the insertion to indicate that the height of the subtree has increased.) We can then increment or decrement the local root balance. If the balance is outside the threshold, then the rebalance methods (`rebalanceLeft` or `rebalanceRight`) are used to restore the balance.

We need to modify methods `decrementBalance`, `incrementBalance`, `rebalanceLeft`, and `rebalanceRight` so that they set the value of `decrease` (as well as `increase`) after a node's balance has been decremented. When a subtree changes from either left-heavy or right-heavy to balanced, then the height has decreased, and `decrease` should be set **`true`**; when the subtree changes from balanced to either left-heavy or right-heavy, then `decrease` should be reset to **`false`**. We also need to provide methods similar to the ones needed for removal in a binary search tree. Implementing removal is left as a programming project.

Also, observe that the effect of rotations is not only to restore balance but to decrease the height of the subtree being rotated. Thus, while only one `rebalanceLeft` or `rebalanceRight` was required for insertion, during removal each recursive return could result in a further need to rebalance.

Performance of the AVL Tree

Since each subtree is kept as close to balanced as possible, one would expect that the AVL tree provides the expected O(log *n*) performance. Each subtree is allowed to be out of balance by ±1. Thus, the tree may contain some holes.

It can be shown that in the worst case, the height of an AVL tree can be 1.44 times the height of a full binary tree that contains the same number of items. However, this would still yield O(log *n*) performance because we ignore constants.

The worst-case performance is very rare. Empirical tests (see, for example, Donald Knuth, *The Art of Computer Programming, Vol 3: Searching and Sorting* [Addison-Wesley, 1973], p. 460) show that, on the average, $\log_2 n + 0.25$ comparisons are required to insert the *n*th item into an AVL tree. Thus the average performance is very close to that of the corresponding complete binary search tree.

EXERCISES FOR SECTION 9.2

SELF-CHECK

1. Show how the final AVL tree for the "The quick brown fox" changes as you insert "apple", "cat", and "hat" in that order.

2. Show the effect of just rotating right on the tree in Figure 9.11. Why doesn't this fix the problem?
3. Build an AVL tree that inserts the integers 30, 40, 15, 25, 90, 80, 70, 85, 15, 72 in the given order.
4. Build the AVL tree from the sentence "Now is the time for all good men to come to the aid of the party".

PROGRAMMING

1. Program the `rebalanceRight` method.
2. Program the code in the `add` method for the case where `item.compareTo( localRoot.data) > 0`.
3. Program the `incrementBalance` method.

9.3 Red-Black Trees

We will now discuss another approach to keeping a tree balanced, called the *Red-Black tree.* Rudolf Bayer developed the Red-Black tree as a special case of his B-tree (the topic of Section 9.5); Leo Guibas and Robert Sedgewick refined the concept and introduced the color convention. A Red-Black tree maintains the following invariants:

1. A node is either red or black.
2. The root is always black.
3. A red node always has black children. (A **`null`** reference is considered to refer to a black node.)
4. The number of black nodes in any path from the root to a leaf is the same.

Figure 9.21 shows an example of a Red-Black tree. Invariant 4 states that a Red-Black tree is always balanced because the root node's left and right subtrees must be the same height where the height is determined by counting just black nodes. Notice that by the standards of the AVL tree, this tree is out of balance and would be considered a Left-Right tree. However, by the standards of the Red-Black tree, it is balanced because there are two black nodes (counting the root) in any path from the root to a leaf. (We have one color in this textbook other than black, so we will use that color to indicate a red node.)

FIGURE 9.21
Red-Black Tree

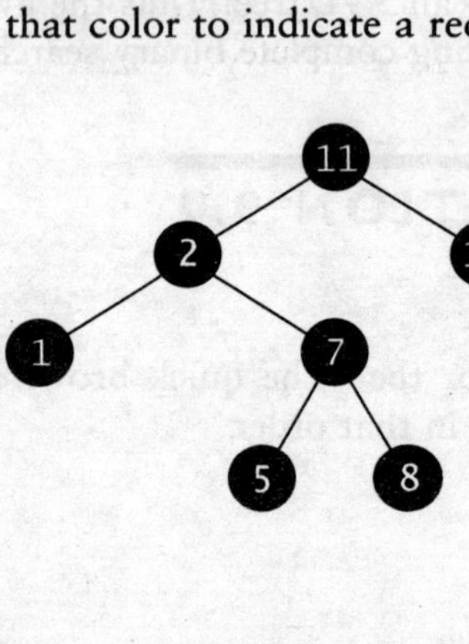

Insertion into a Red-Black Tree

The algorithm for insertion follows the same recursive search process used for all binary search trees to reach the insertion point. When a leaf is found, the new item is inserted, and it is initially given the color red, so invariant 4 will be maintained. If the parent is black, we are done.

However, if the parent is also red, then invariant 3 has been violated. Figure 9.22(a) shows the insertion of 35 as a red child of 30. If the parent's sibling is also red, then we can change the grandparent's color to red and change both the parent and parent's sibling to black. This restores invariant 3 but does not violate invariant 4. (See Figure 9.22(b).) If the root of the overall tree is now red, we can change it to black to restore invariant 2 and still maintain invariant 4 (the heights of all paths to a leaf are increased by 1). (See Figure 9.22(c).)

If we insert a value with a red parent, but that parent does not have a red sibling (see Figure 9.23(a)), then we change the color of the grandparent to red and the parent to black (see Figure 9.23(b)). Now we have violated invariant 4, as there are more black nodes on the side of the parent. We correct this by rotating about the grandparent so that the parent moves into the position where the grandparent was, thus restoring invariant 4 (see Figure 9.23(c)).

The preceding maneuver works only if the inserted value is on the same side of its parent as the parent is to the grandparent. Figure 9.24(a) shows 25 inserted as the left child of 30, which is the right child of 20. If we change the color of the grandparent (20) to red and the parent (30) to black (see Figure 9.24(b)) and then rotate (see Figure 9.24(c)), we are still left with a red parent–red child combination. Before changing the color and rotating about the grandparent level, we must first rotate about the parent so that the red child is on the same side of its parent as the parent is to the grandparent (see Figure 9.25(b)). We can then change the colors (see Figure 9.25(c)) and rotate (see Figure 9.25 (d)).

FIGURE 9.22
Insertion into a Red-Black Tree, Case 1

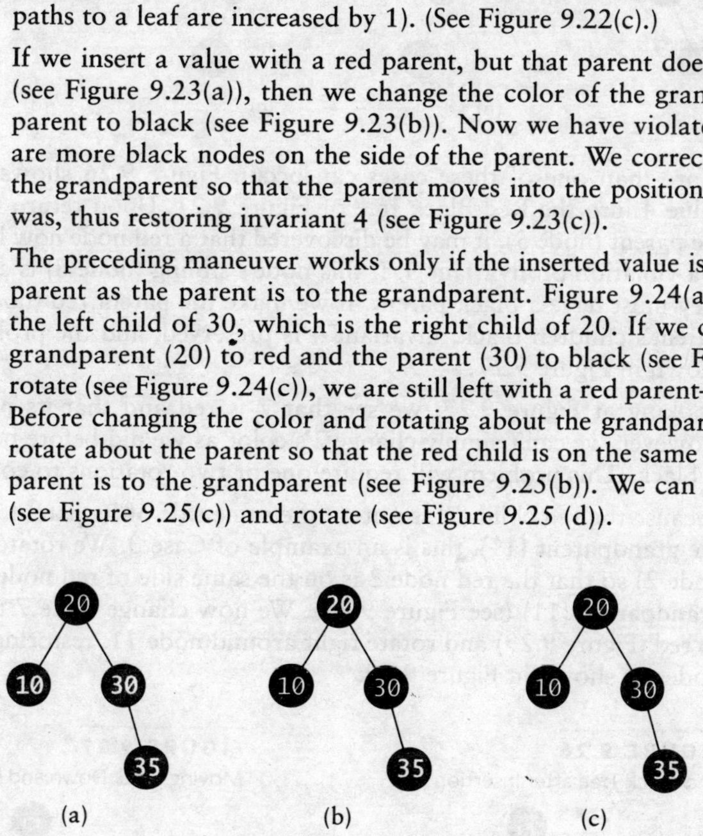

FIGURE 9.23
Insertion into a Red-Black Tree, Case 2

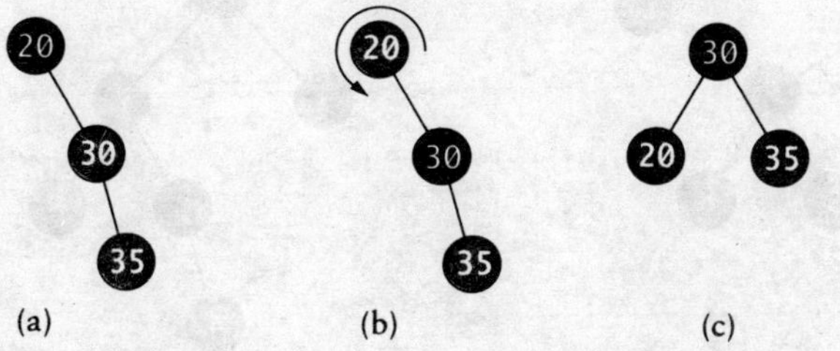

FIGURE 9.24
Insertion into a Red-Black Tree, Case 3 (Single Rotation Doesn't Work)

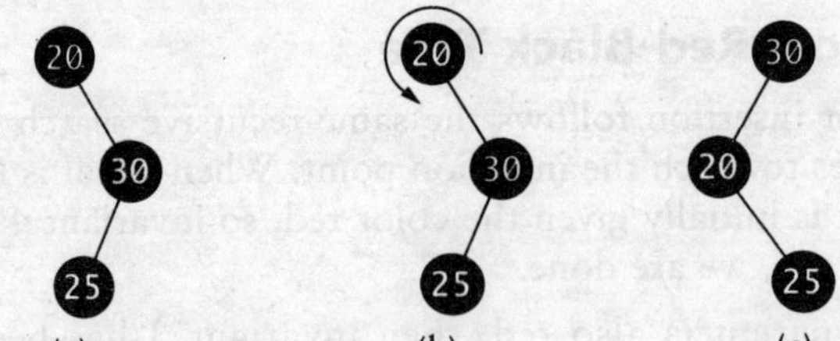

FIGURE 9.25
Insertion into a Red-Black Tree, Case 3 (Double Rotation)

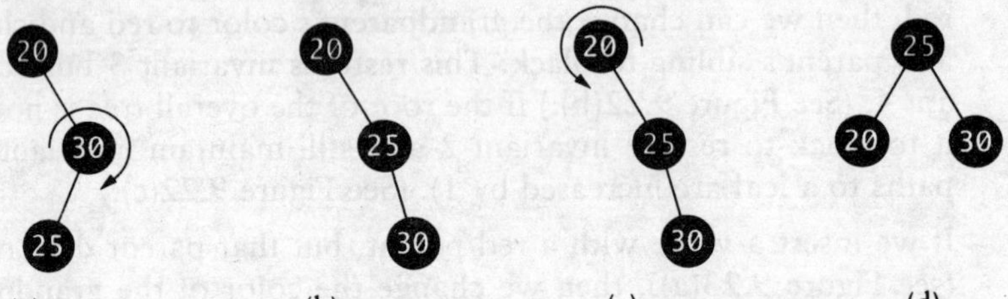

More than one of these cases can occur. Figure 9.26 shows the insertion of the value 4 into the Red-Black tree of Figure 9.21. Upon return from the insertion to the parent (node 5), it may be discovered that a red node now has a red child, which is a violation of invariant 3. If this node's sibling (node 8) is also red (case 1), then they must have a black parent. If we make the parent red (node 7) and both of the parent's children black, invariant 4 is preserved, and the problem is shifted up, as shown in Figure 9.27.

Looking at Figure 9.27, we see that 7 is red and that its parent, 2, is also red. However, we can't simply change 2's color as we did before because 2's sibling, 14, is black. This problem will require one or two rotations to correct.

Because the red child (7) is not on the same side of its parent (2) as the parent is to the grandparent (11), this is an example of Case 3. We rotate the tree left (around node 2) so that the red node 2 is on the same side of red node 7 as node 7 is to the grandparent (11) (see Figure 9.28). We now change node 7 to black and node 11 to red (Figure 9.29) and rotate right around node 11, restoring the balance of black nodes as shown in Figure 9.30.

FIGURE 9.26
Red-Black Tree after Insertion of 4

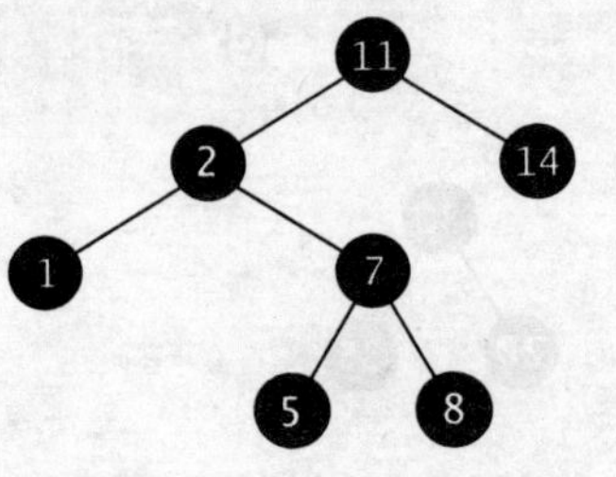

FIGURE 9.27
Moving Black Down and Red Up

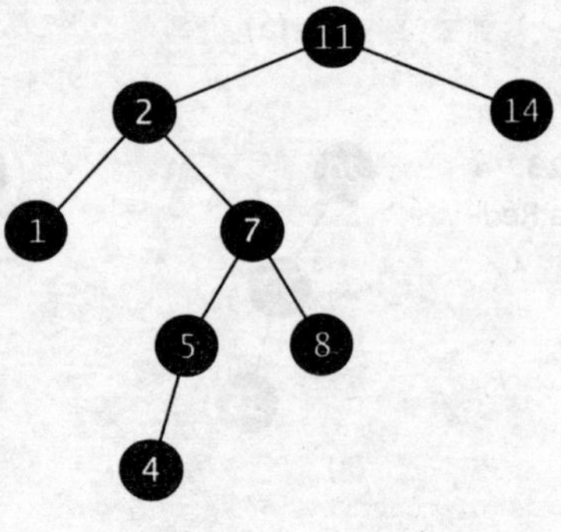

FIGURE 9.28
Rotating Red Node to Outside

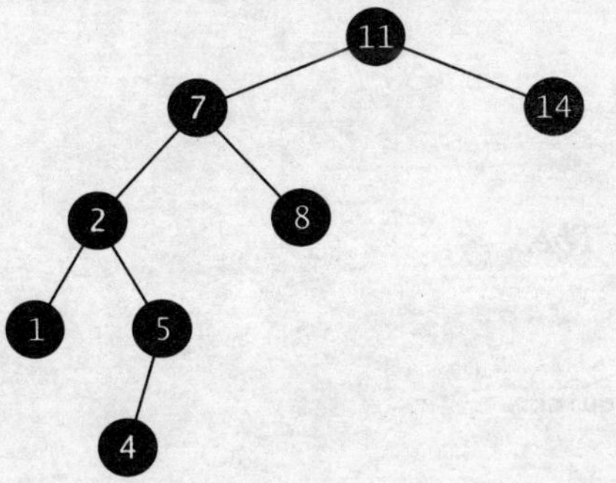

FIGURE 9.29
Changing Colors of Parent and Grandparent Nodes

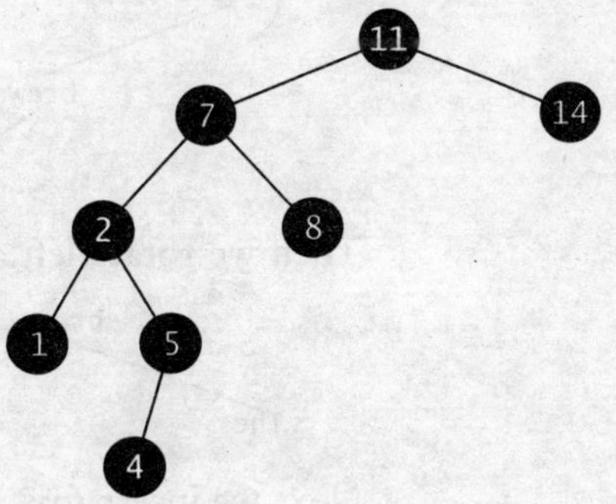

FIGURE 9.30
Final Red-Black Tree after Insert

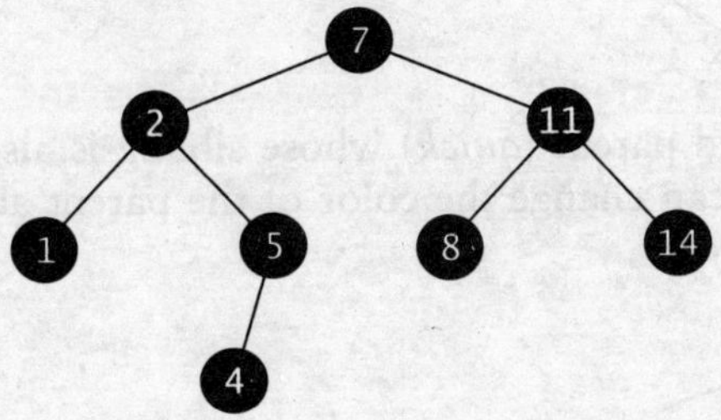

EXAMPLE 9.2 We will now build the Red-Black tree for the sentence "The quick brown fox jumps over the lazy dog".

We start by inserting *The, quick,* and *brown.*

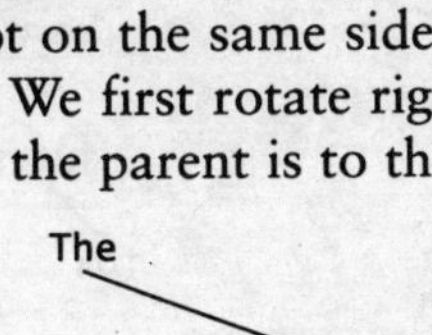

The parent of *brown* (*quick*) is red, but the sibling of *quick* is black (null nodes are considered black), so we have an example of Case 2 or Case 3. Because the child is not on the same side of the parent as the parent is to the grandparent, this is Case 3. We first rotate right about *quick* to get the child on the same side of the parent as the parent is to the grandparent.

We then change the colors of *The* and *brown.*

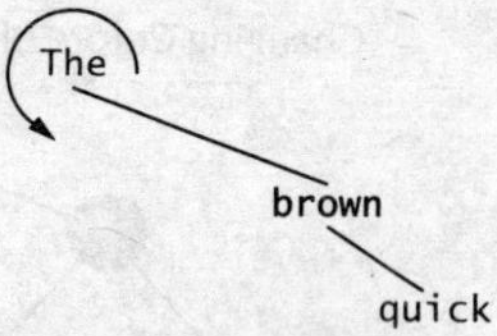

Then we rotate left about *The.*

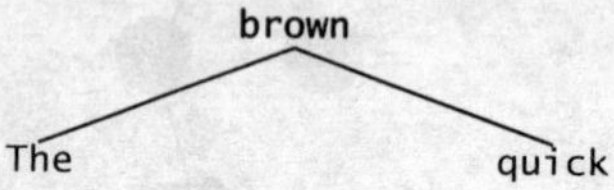

Next we insert *fox.*

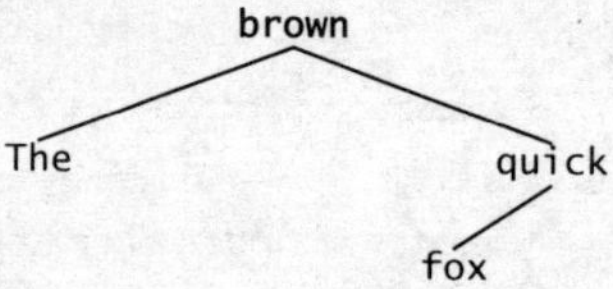

We see that *fox* has a red parent (*quick*) whose sibling is also red (*The*). This is a Case 1 insertion, so we can change the color of the parent and its sibling to black and the grandparent to red.

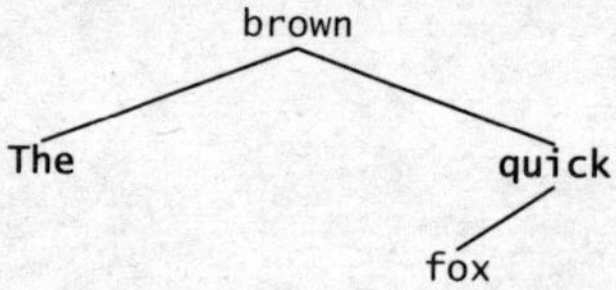

Since the root is red, we can change it to black without violating the rule of balanced black nodes.

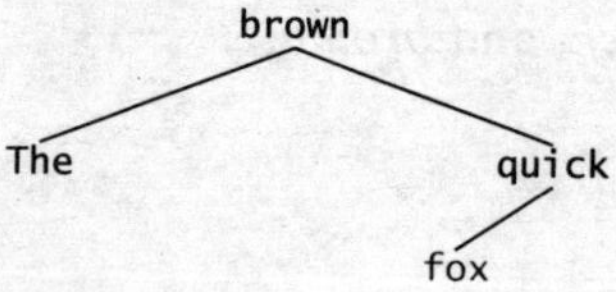

Now we add *jumps,* which gives us another Case 3 insertion.

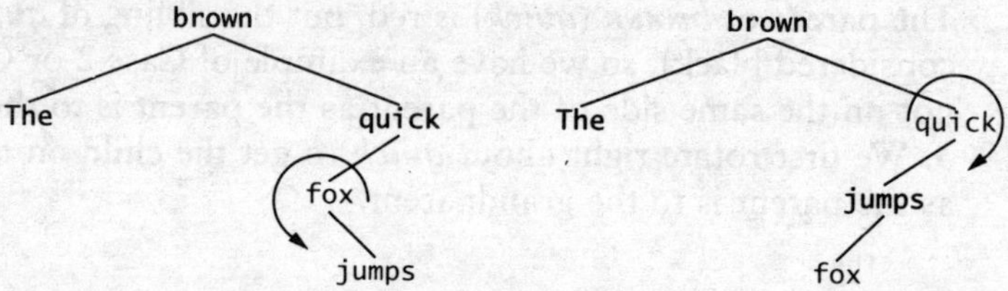

This triggers a double rotation. First rotate left about *fox* and change the color of its parent *jumps* to black and its grandparent *quick* to red. Next, rotate right about *quick*.

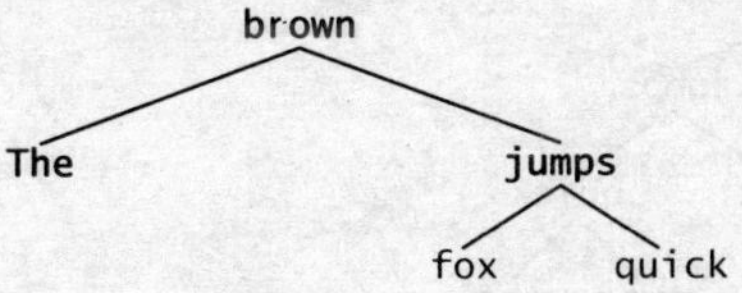

Next, we insert *over.*

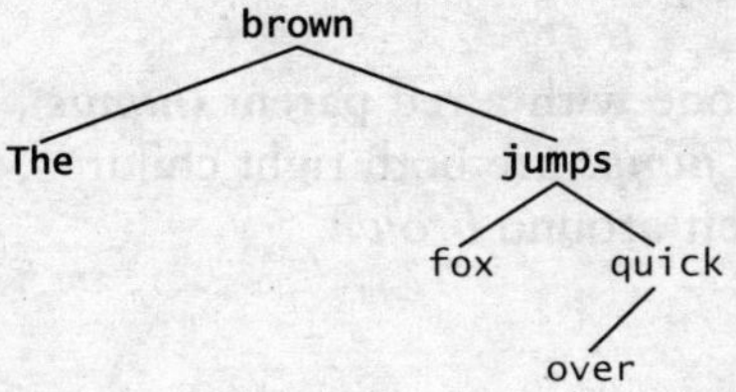

Because *quick* and *fox* are red, we have a Case 1 insertion, so we can move the black in *jumps* down, changing the color of *jumps* to red and *fox* and *quick* to black.

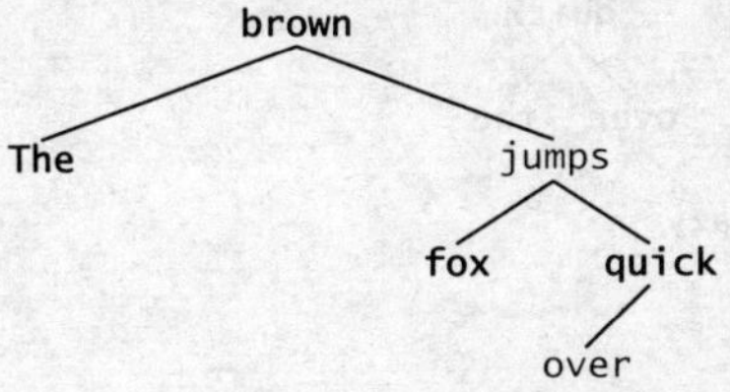

Next we add *the.* No changes are required because its parent is black.

When compared to the corresponding AVL tree, this tree looks out of balance. But the black nodes are in balance (two in each path).

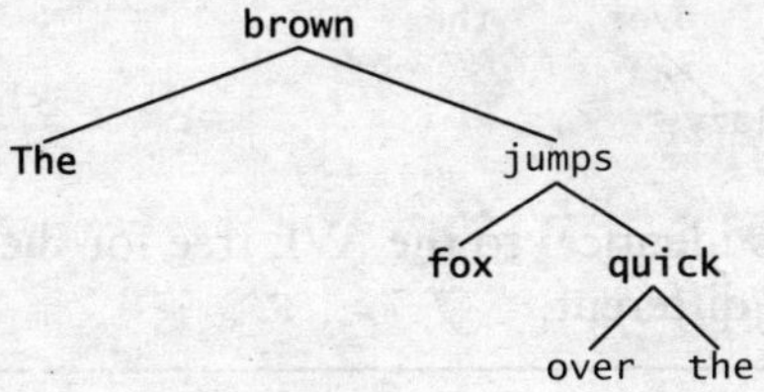

Now we insert *lazy.*

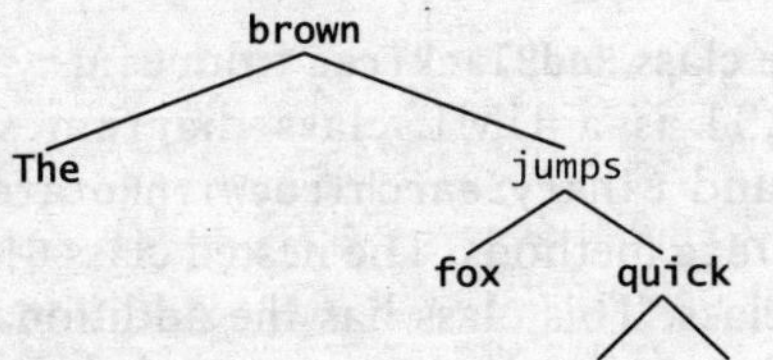

Because *over* and *the* are both red, we can move the black at *quick* down (Case 1).

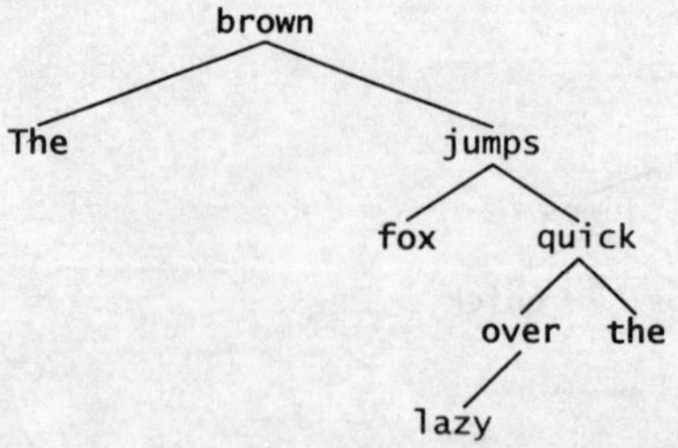

But now *quick* is a red node with a red parent (*jumps*), but whose sibling is black (*The*). Because *quick* and *jumps* are both right children, this is an example of Case 2. This triggers a rotate left around *brown*.

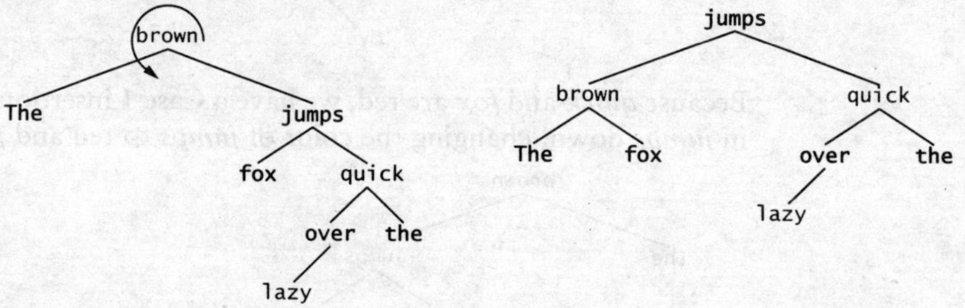

Finally we can insert *dog*.

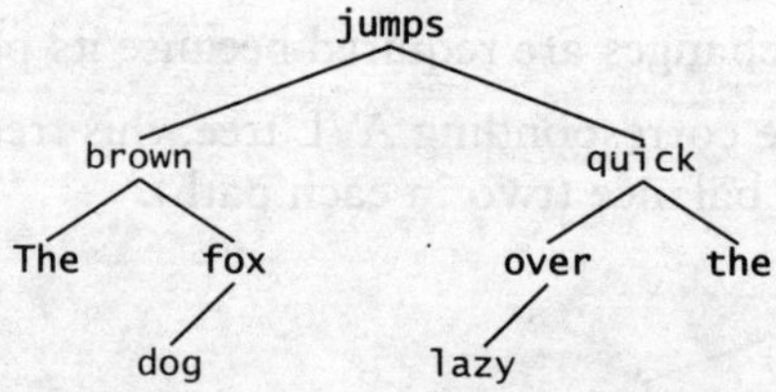

Surprisingly, the result is identical to the AVL tree for the same input, but the intermediate steps were very different.

Implementation of Red-Black Tree Class

We begin by deriving the class `RedBlackTree` from `BinarySearchTreeWithRotate` (see Listing 9.1). Figure 9.31 is a UML class diagram showing the relationship between `RedBlackTree` and `BinarySearchTreeWithRotate`. The `RedBlackTree` class overrides the `add` and `delete` methods. The nested class `BinaryTree.Node` is extended with the `RedBlackNode` class. This class has the additional data field `isRed` to indicate red nodes. Listing 9.4 shows the `RedBlackNode` class.

LISTING 9.4
The RedBlackTree and RedBlackNode Classes

```
/** Class to represent Red-Black tree. */
public class RedBlackTree<E extends Comparable<E>>
        extends BinarySearchTreeWithRotate<E> {

    /** Nested class to represent a Red-Black node. */
    private static class RedBlackNode<E> extends Node<E> {
        // Additional data members
        /** Color indicator. True if red, false if black. */
        private boolean isRed;

        // Constructor
        /** Create a RedBlackNode with the default color of red
            and the given data field.
            @param item The data field
        */
        public RedBlackNode(E item) {
            super(item);
            isRed = true;
        }

        // Methods
        /** Return a string representation of this object.
            The color (red or black) is appended to the
            node's contents.
            @return String representation of this object
        */
        @Override
        public String toString() {
            if (isRed) {
                return "Red  : " + super.toString();
            } else {
                return "Black: " + super.toString();
            }
        }
    }
    . . .
}
```

Algorithm for Red-Black Tree Insertion

Insert *over*

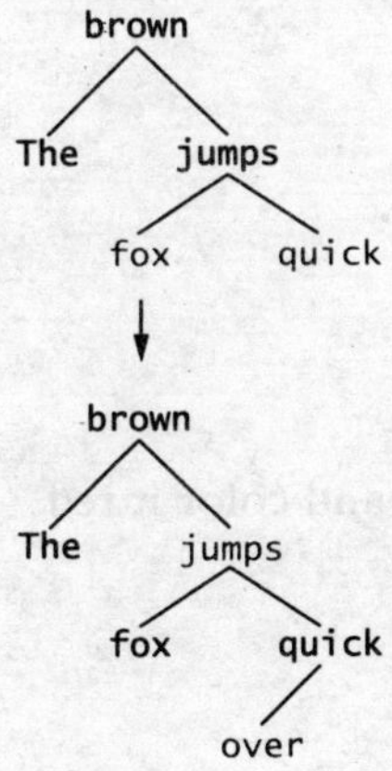

The foregoing outline of the Red-Black tree insertion algorithm is from the point of view of the node being inserted. It can be, and has been, implemented using a data structure that has a reference to the parent of each node stored in it so that, given a reference to a node, one can access the parent, grandparent, and the parent's sibling (the node's aunt or uncle).

We are going to present a recursive algorithm where the need for fix-ups is detected from the grandparent level. This algorithm has one additional difference from the algorithm as presented in the foregoing examples: Whenever a black node with two red children is detected on the way down the tree, it is changed to red and the children are changed to black (e.g., *jumps* and its children in the figure at left). If this change causes a problem, it is fixed on the way back up. This modification simplifies the logic a bit and improves the performance of the algorithm. This algorithm is also based on the algorithm for inserting into a binary search tree that was described in Chapter 6.

FIGURE 9.31
UML Class Diagram of `RedBlackTree`

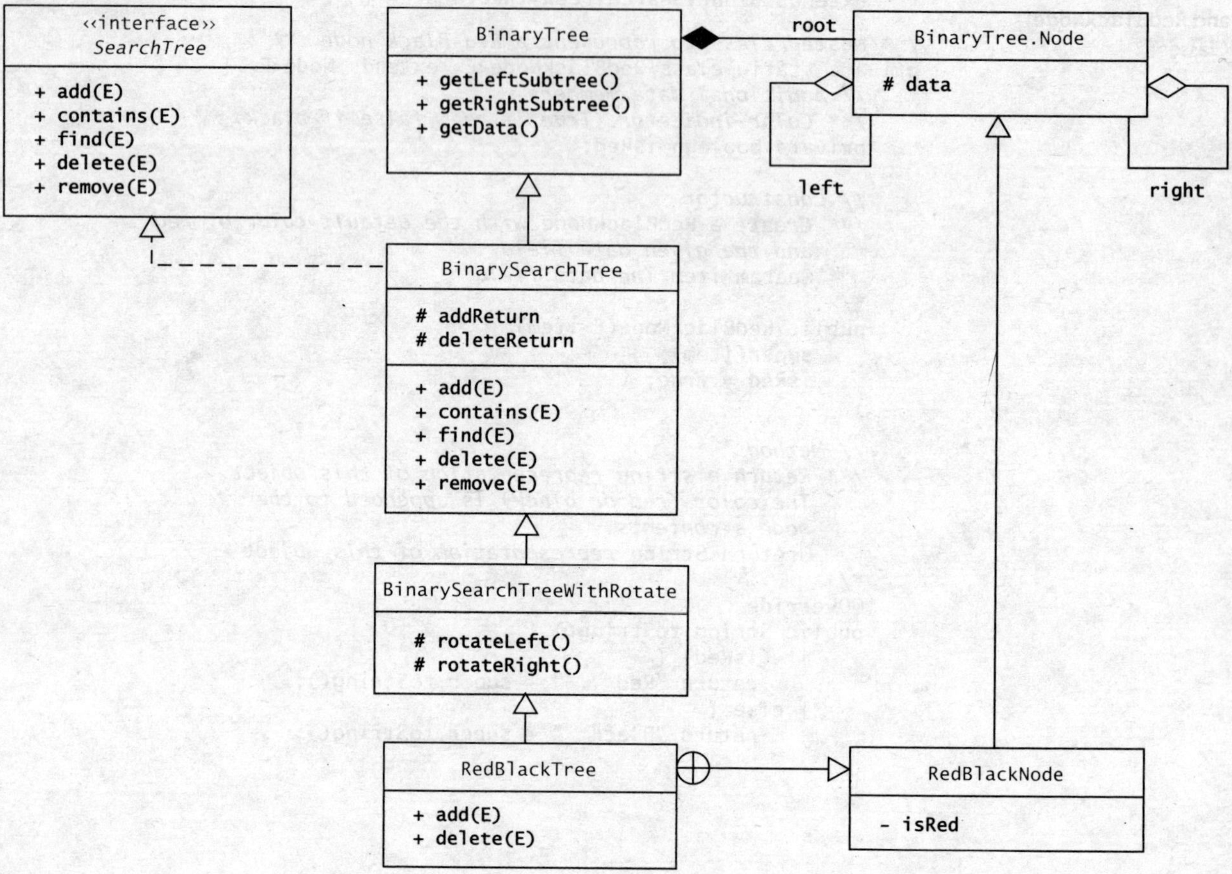

Algorithm for Red-Black Tree Insertion

1. **if** the root is **null**
2.   Insert a new Red-Black node and color it black.
3.   Return **true**.
4. **else if** the item is equal to `root.data`
5.   The item is already in the tree; return **false**.
6. **else if** the item is less than `root.data`
7.   **if** the left subtree is **null**
8.   Insert a new Red-Black node as the left subtree and color it red.
9.   Return **true**.
10.   **else**
11.   **if** both the left child and the right child are red

12. Change the color of the children to black and change local root to red.
13. Recursively insert the item into the left subtree.
14. `if` the left child is now red
15. `if` the left grandchild is now red (grandchild is an "outside" node)
16. Change the color of the left child to black and change the local root to red.
17. Rotate the local root right.
18. `else if` the right grandchild is now red (grandchild is an "inside" node)
19. Rotate the left child left.
20. Change the color of the left child to black and change the local root to red.
21. Rotate the local root right.
22. `else`
23. Item is greater than `root.data`; process is symmetric and is left as an exercise.
24. `if` the local root is the root of the tree
25. Force its color to be black.

Because Java passes the value of a reference, we have to work with a node that is a local root of a Red-Black tree. Thus, in Step 8, we replace the **`null`** reference to the left subtree with the inserted node.

If the left subtree is not **`null`** (Step 10), we recursively apply the algorithm (Step 13). But before we do so, we see whether both children are red. If they are, we change the local root to red and change the children to black (Steps 11 and 12). (If the local root's parent was red, this condition will be detected at that level during the return from the recursion.)

Upon return from the recursion (Step 14), we see whether the local root's left child is now red. If it is, we need to check its children (the local root's grandchildren). If one of them is red, then we have a red parent with a red child, and a rotation is necessary. If the left grandchild is red, a single rotation will solve the problem (Steps 15 through 17). If the right grandchild is red, a double rotation is necessary (Steps 18 through 21). Note that there may be only one grandchild or no grandchildren. However, if there are two grandchildren, they cannot both be red because they would have been changed to black by Steps 11 and 12, as described in the previous paragraph.

The **add** Starter Method

As with the other binary search trees we have studied, the `add` starter method checks for a **`null`** root and inserts a single new node. Since the root of a Red-Black tree is always black, we set the newly inserted node to black. The cast is necessary because `root` is a data field that was inherited from `BinaryTree` and is therefore of type `Node`.

```
public boolean add(E item) {
    if (root == null) {
        root = new RedBlackNode<E>(item);
        ((RedBlackNode<E>) root).isRed = false; // root is black.
        return true;
    }
    . . .
```

Otherwise the recursive add method is called. This method takes two parameters: the node that is the local root of the subtree into which the item is to be inserted and the item to be inserted. The return value is the node that is the root of the subtree that now contains the inserted item. The data field addReturn is set to **true** if the insert method succeeded and to **false** if the item is already in the subtree.

The root is replaced by the return value from the recursive add method, the color of the root is set to black, and the data field addReturn is returned to the caller of the add starter method.

```
else {
    root = add((RedBlackNode<E>) root, item);
    ((RedBlackNode<E>) root).isRed = false; // root is always black.
    return addReturn;
}
```

The Recursive **add** Method

The recursive add method begins by comparing the item to be inserted with the data field of the local root. If they are equal, then the item is already in the tree; addReturn is set to **false** and the localRoot is returned (algorithm Step 5).

```
private Node<E> add(RedBlackNode<E> localRoot, E item) {
    if (item.compareTo(localRoot.data) == 0) {
        // item already in the tree.
        addReturn = false;
        return localRoot;
    }
    . . .
```

If it is less, then localRoot.left is checked to see whether it is **null**. If so, then we insert a new node and return (Steps 7–9).

```
else if (item.compareTo(localRoot.data) < 0) {
    // item < localRoot.data.
    if (localRoot.left == null) {
        // Create new left child.
        localRoot.left = new RedBlackNode<E>(item);
        addReturn = true;
        return localRoot;
    }
    . . .
```

Otherwise, check to see whether both children are red. If so, we make them black and change the local root to red. This is done by the method moveBlackDown. Then we recursively call the add method, using root.left as the new local root (Steps 11–13).

```
else {   // Need to search.
    // Check for two red children, swap colors if found.
    moveBlackDown(localRoot);
```

```
// Recursively add on the left.
localRoot.left = add((RedBlackNode<E>) localRoot.left, item);
. . .
```

It is upon return from the recursive add that things get interesting. Upon return from the recursive call, `localRoot.left` refers to the parent of a Red-Black subtree that may be violating the rule against adjacent red nodes. Therefore, we check the left child to see whether it is red (Step 14).

```
// See whether the left child is now red
if (((RedBlackNode<E>) localRoot.left).isRed) {
  . . .
```

If the left child is red, then we need to check its two children. First we check the left grandchild (Step 15).

```
if (localRoot.left.left != null
    && ((RedBlackNode<E>) localRoot.left.left).isRed) {
    // Left-left grandchild is also red.
  . . .
```

If the left-left grandchild is red, we have detected a violation of invariant 3 (no consecutive red children), and we have a left-left case. Thus we change colors and perform a single rotation, returning the resulting local root to the caller (Steps 16–17).

```
// Single rotation is necessary.
((RedBlackNode<E>) localRoot.left).isRed = false;
localRoot.isRed = true;
return rotateRight(localRoot);
```

If the left grandchild is not red, we then check the right grandchild. If it is red, the process is symmetric to the preceding case, except that a double rotation will be required (Steps 18–21).

```
else if (localRoot.left.right != null
         && ((RedBlackNode<E>) localRoot.left.right).isRed) {
    // Left-right grandchild is also red.
    // Double rotation is necessary.
    localRoot.left = rotateLeft(localRoot.left);
    ((RedBlackNode<E>) localRoot.left).isRed = false;
    localRoot.isRed = true;
    return rotateRight(localRoot);
}
```

If upon return from the recursive call the left child is black, the return is immediate, and all of this complicated logic is skipped. Similarly, if neither the left nor the right grandchild is also red, nothing is done.

If the item is greater than `root.data`, the process is symmetric and is left as an exercise (Step 23 and Programming Exercise 1).

Removal from a Red-Black Tree

Removal follows the algorithm for a binary search tree that was described in Chapter 6. Recall that we remove a node only if it is a leaf or if it has only one child. Otherwise, the node that contains the inorder predecessor of the value being removed is the one that is removed. If the node that is removed is red, nothing further must be done because red nodes do not affect a Red-Black tree's balance. If the node to be removed is black and has a red child, then the red child takes its place, and we color it black. However, if we remove a black leaf, then the black height is now out of balance. There are several cases that must be considered. We will describe them in Programming Project 6 at the end of this chapter.

Performance of a Red-Black Tree

It can be shown that the upper limit in the height for a Red-Black tree is $2 \log_2 n + 2$, which is still $O(\log n)$. As with the AVL tree, the average performance is significantly better than the worst-case performance. Empirical studies (see Robert Sedgewick, *Algorithms in C++*, 3rd ed. [Addison-Wesley, 1998], p. 570) show that the average cost of a search in a Red-Black tree built from random values is $1.002 \log_2 n$. Thus, both the AVL and Red-Black trees give performance that is close to that of a complete binary search tree.

The `TreeMap` and `TreeSet` Classes

The Java API has a `TreeMap` class (part of the package `java.util`) that implements a Red-Black tree. The `TreeMap` class implements the `SortedMap` interface, so it defines methods `get`, `put` (a tree insertion), `remove`, and `containsKey`, among others. Because a Red-Black tree is used, these are all $O(\log n)$ operations. There is also a `TreeSet` class (introduced in Section 7.5) that implements the `SortedSet` interface. This class is implemented as an adapter of the `TreeMap` class using a technique similar to what was described in Chapter 7 to implement the `HashSet` as an adapter of the `HashMap`.

EXERCISES FOR SECTION 9.3

SELF-CHECK

1. Show how the final AVL tree for the "The quick brown fox" changes as you insert "apple", "cat", and "hat" in that order.
2. Insert the numbers 6, 3, and 0 in the Red-Black tree in Figure 9.21.
3. Build the Red-Black tree from the sentence "Now is the time for all good men to come to the aid of the party". Is it the same as the AVL tree?

PROGRAMMING

1. Program the case where the item is greater than `root.data`.

9.4 2-3 Trees

In this section we begin our discussion of three nonbinary trees. We begin with the *2-3 tree,* named for the number of possible children from each node (either 2 or 3). A 2-3 tree is made up of nodes designated as *2-nodes* and *3-nodes.* A 2-node is the same as a binary search tree node: It consists of a data field and references to two children, one child containing values less than the data field and the other child containing values greater than the data field. A 3-node contains two data fields, ordered so that the first is less than the second, and references to three children: one child containing values less than the first data field, one child containing values between the two data fields, and one child containing values greater than the second data field.

Figure 9.32 shows the general forms of a 2-node (data item is x) and a 3-node (data items are x and y). The children are represented as subtrees. Figure 9.33 shows an example of a 2-3 tree. There are only two 3-nodes in this tree (the right and right-right nodes); the rest are 2-nodes.

A 2-3 tree has the additional property that all of the leaves are at the lowest level. This is how the 2-3 tree maintains balance. This will be further explained when we study the insertion and removal algorithms.

FIGURE 9.32
2-Node and 3-Node

FIGURE 9.33
Example of a 2-3 Tree

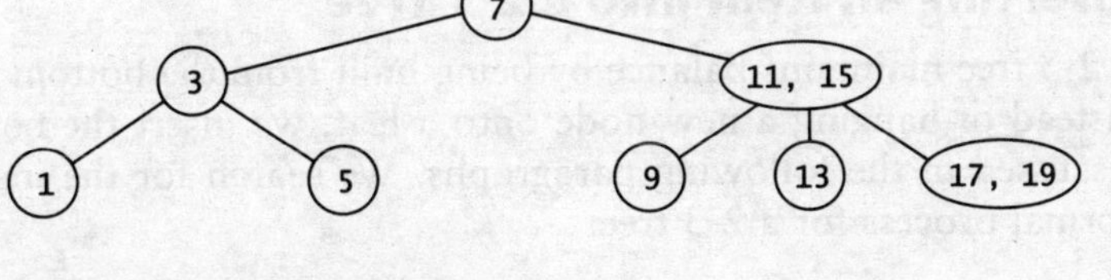

Searching a 2-3 Tree

Searching a 2-3 tree is very similar to searching a binary search tree.

1. `if` the local root is `null`
2.   Return `null`; the item is not in the tree.
3. `else if` this is a 2-node
4.   `if` the item is equal to the `data1` field
5.   Return the `data1` field.
6.   `else if` the item is less than the `data1` field
7.   Recursively search the left subtree.

```
        else
                Recursively search the right subtree.
    else // This is a 3-node
        if the item is equal to the data1 field
                Return the data1 field.
        else if the item is equal to the data2 field
                Return the data2 field.
        else if the item is less than the data1 field
                Recursively search the left subtree.
        else if the item is less than the data2 field
                Recursively search the middle subtree.
        else
                Recursively search the right subtree.
```

EXAMPLE 9.3 To search for 13 in Figure 9.33, we would compare 13 with 7 and see that it is greater than 7, so we would search the node that contains 11 and 15. Because 13 is greater than 11 but less than 15, we would next search the middle child, which contains 13: success! The search path is shown in color in Figure 9.34.

FIGURE 9.34
Searching a 2-3 Tree

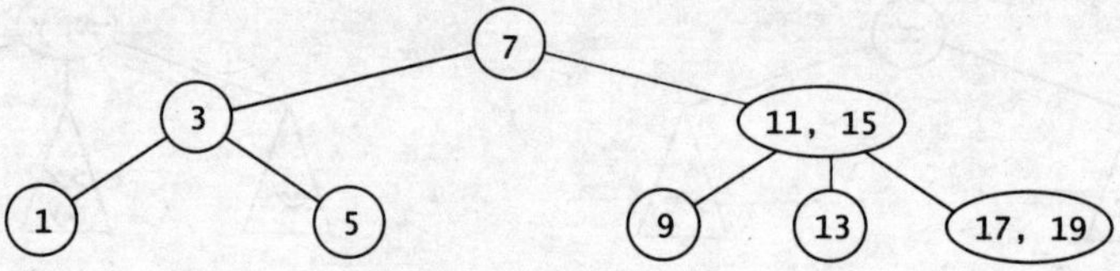

Inserting an Item into a 2-3 Tree

A 2-3 tree maintains balance by being built from the bottom up, not the top down. Instead of hanging a new node onto a leaf, we insert the new node into a leaf, as discussed in the following paragraphs. We search for the insertion node using the normal process for a 2-3 tree.

Inserting into a 2-Node Leaf

Figure 9.35 (left) shows a 2-3 tree with three 2-nodes. We want to insert 15. Because the leaf we are inserting into is a 2-node, we can insert 15 directly, creating a new 3-node (Figure 9.35 right).

FIGURE 9.35
Inserting into a Tree with All 2-Nodes

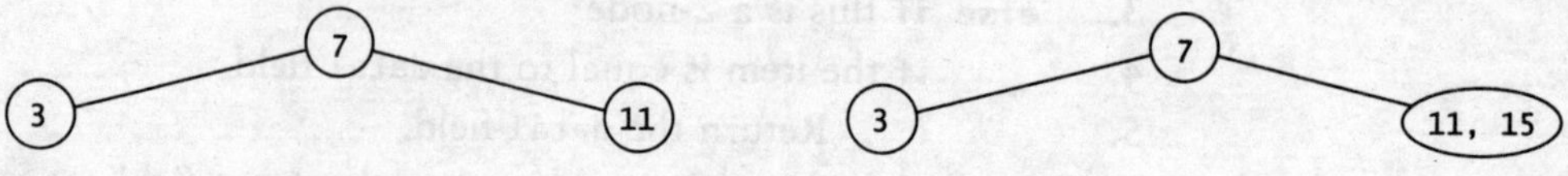

Inserting into a 3-Node Leaf with a 2-Node Parent

If we want to insert a number larger than 7 (say, 17), that number will be virtually inserted into the 3-node at the bottom right of the tree, giving the virtual node in gray in Figure 9.36. Because a node can't store three values, the middle value will propagate up to the 2-node parent, and the virtual node will be split into two new 2-nodes containing the smallest and largest values. Because the parent is a 2-node, it will be changed to a 3-node, and it will reference the three 2-nodes, as shown in Figure 9.37.

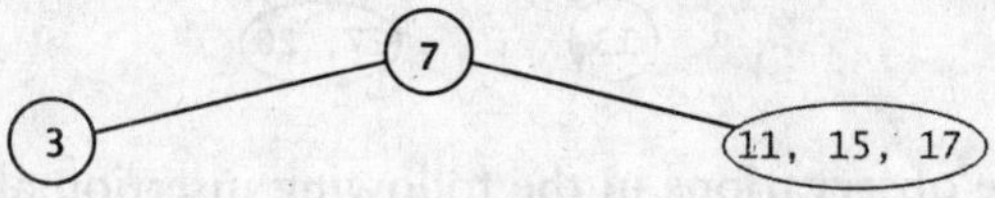

FIGURE 9.36
A Virtual Insertion

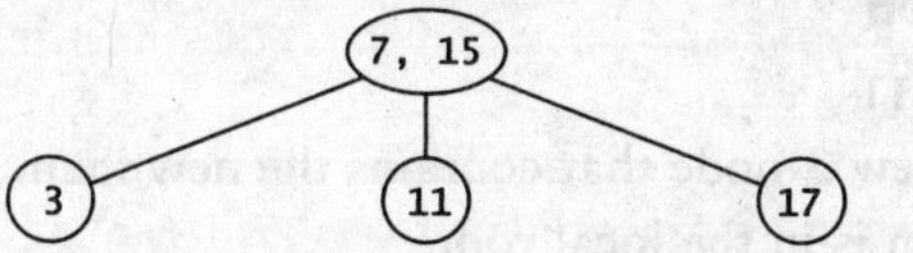

FIGURE 9.37
Result of Propagating 15 to 2-Node Parent

Let's now insert the numbers 5, 10, and 20. Each of these would go into one of the leaf nodes (all 2-nodes), changing them to 3-nodes, as shown in Figure 9.38.

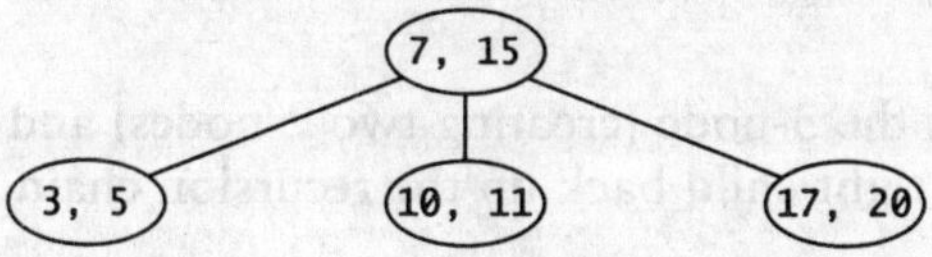

FIGURE 9.38
Inserting 5, 10, and 20

Inserting into a 3-Node Leaf with a 3-Node Parent

In the tree in Figure 9.39, all the leaf nodes are full, so if we insert any other number, one of the leaf nodes will need to be virtually split, and its middle value will propagate to the parent. Because the parent is already a 3-node, it will also need to be split.

For example, if we were to insert 13, it would be virtually inserted into the leaf node with values 10 and 11 (see Figure 9.39). This would result in two new 2-nodes with values 10 and 13, and 11 would propagate up to be virtually inserted in the 3-node at the root (see Figure 9.40). Because the root is full, it would split into two new 2-nodes with values 7 and 15, and 11 would propagate up to be inserted in a new root node. The net effect is an increase in the overall height of the tree, as shown in Figure 9.41.

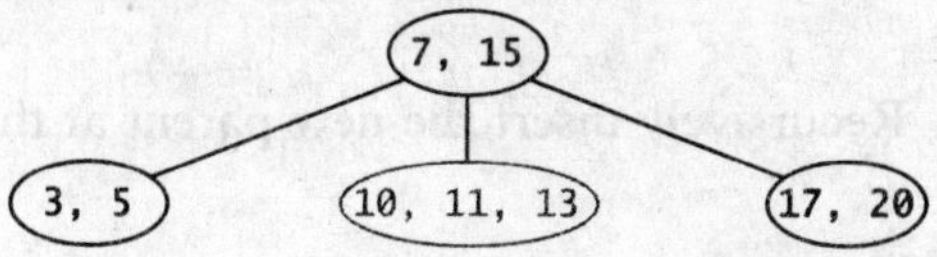

FIGURE 9.39
Virtually Inserting 13

FIGURE 9.40
Virtually Inserting 11

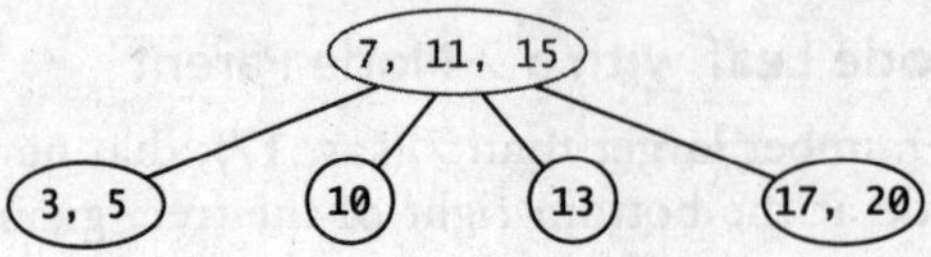

FIGURE 9.41
Result of Making 11 the New Root

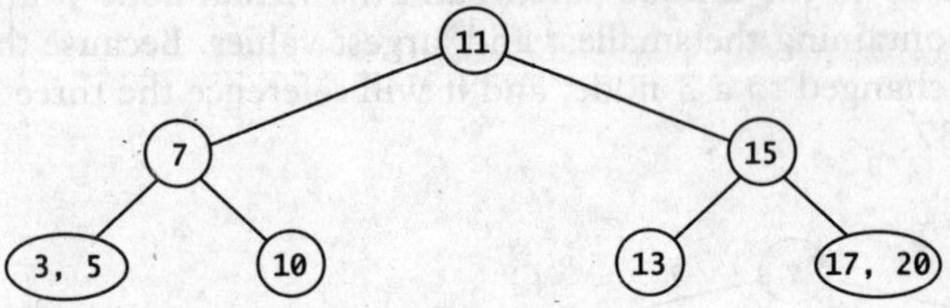

We summarize these observations in the following insertion algorithm.

Algorithm for Insertion

1. `if` the root is `null`
2.   Create a new 2-node that contains the new item.
3. `else if` the item is in the local root
4.   Return `false`.
5. `else if` the local root is a leaf
6.   `if` the local root is a 2-node
7.   Expand the 2-node to a 3-node and insert the item.
8.   `else`
9.   Split the 3-node (creating two 2-nodes) and pass the new parent and right child back up the recursion chain.
10. `else`
11.   `if` the item is less than the smaller item in the local root
12.   Recursively insert into the left child.
13.   `else if` the local root is a 2-node
14.   Recursively insert into the right child.
15.   `else if` the item is less than the larger item in the local root
16.   Recursively insert into the middle child.
17.   `else`
18.   Recursively insert into the right child.
19.   `if` a new parent was passed up from the previous level of recursion
20.   `if` the new parent will be the tree root
21.   Create a 2-node whose data item is the passed-up parent, left child is the old root, and right child is the passed-up child. This 2-node becomes the new root.
22.   `else`
23.   Recursively insert the new parent at the local root.
24. Return `true`.

EXAMPLE 9.4 We will create a 2-3 tree using "The quick brown fox jumps over the lazy dog". The initial root contains *The, quick*. If we insert *brown,* we will split the root. Because *brown* is between *The* and *quick,* it gets passed up and will become the new root.

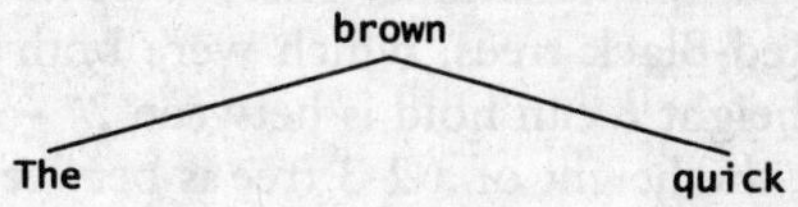

We now insert *fox* as the left neighbor of *quick,* creating a new 3-node.

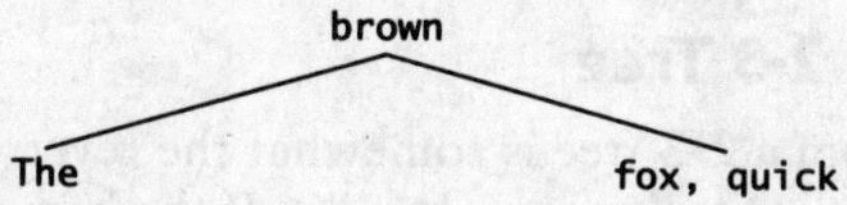

Next *jumps* is inserted between *fox* and *quick,* thus splitting this 3-node, and *jumps* gets passed up and inserted next to *brown.*

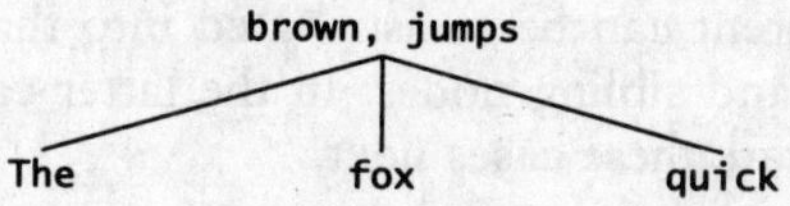

Then *over* is inserted next to *quick.*

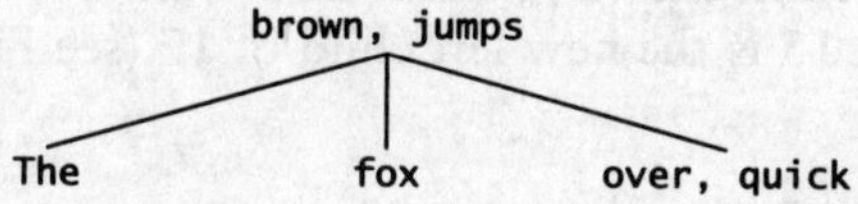

Now we insert *the*. It will be inserted to the right of *over, quick,* splitting that node, and *quick* will be passed up. It will be inserted to the right of *brown, jumps,* splitting that node as well, causing *jumps* to be passed up to the new root.

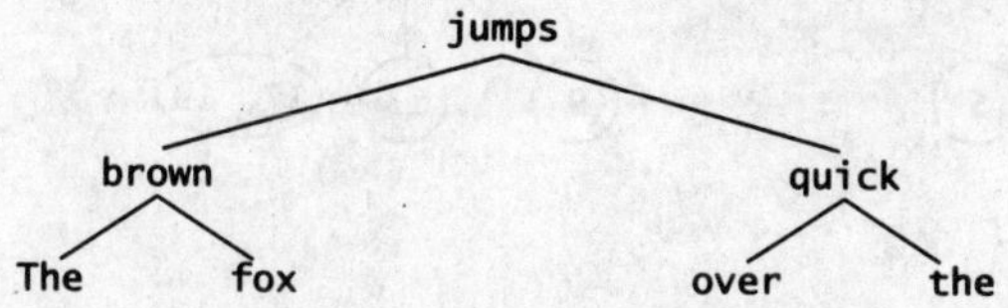

Finally, *lazy* and *dog* are inserted next to *over* and *fox,* respectively.

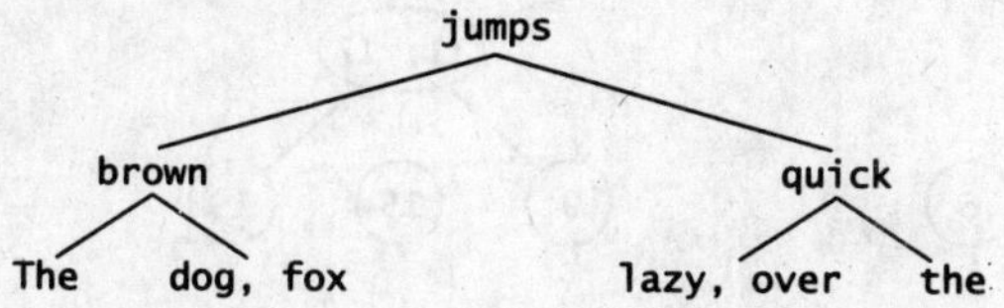

Analysis of 2-3 Trees and Comparison with Balanced Binary Trees

The 2-3 tree resulting from the preceding example is a balanced tree of height 3 that requires fewer complicated manipulations. There were no rotations, as were needed to build the AVL and Red-Black trees, which were both height 4. The number of items that a 2-3 tree of height h can hold is between $2^h - 1$ (all 2-nodes) and $3^h - 1$ (all 3-nodes). Therefore, the height of a 2-3 tree is between $\log_3 n$ and $\log_2 n$. Thus the search time is O(log n), since logarithms are all related by a constant factor, and constant factors are ignored in big-O notation.

Removal from a 2-3 Tree

Removing an item from a 2-3 tree is somewhat the reverse of the insertion process. To remove an item, we must first search for it. If the item to be removed is in a leaf, we simply delete it. However, if the item to be removed is not in a leaf, we remove it by swapping it with its inorder predecessor in a leaf node and deleting it from the leaf node. If removing a node from a leaf causes the leaf to become empty, items from the sibling and parent can be redistributed into that leaf, or the leaf can be merged with its parent and sibling nodes. In the latter case, the height of the tree may decrease. We illustrate these cases next.

If we remove item 13 from the tree shown in Figure 9.42, its node would become empty, and item 15 in the parent node would have no left child. We can merge 15 and its right child to form the virtual leaf node {15, 17, 19}. Item 17 moves up to the parent node; item 15 is the new left child of 17 (see Figure 9.43).

FIGURE 9.42
Removing 13 from a 2-3 Tree

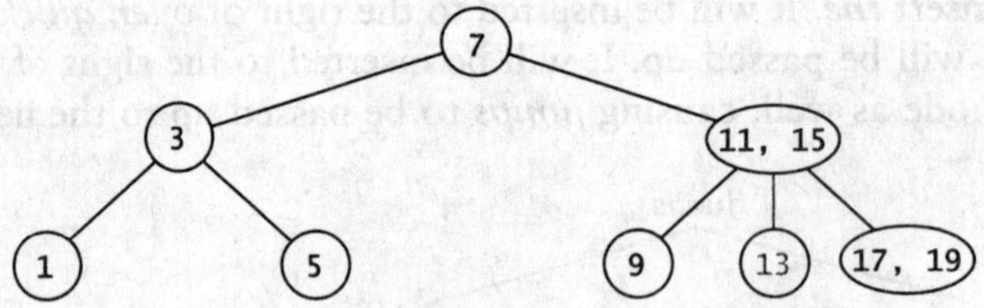

FIGURE 9.43
2-3 Tree after Redistribution of Nodes Resulting from Removal

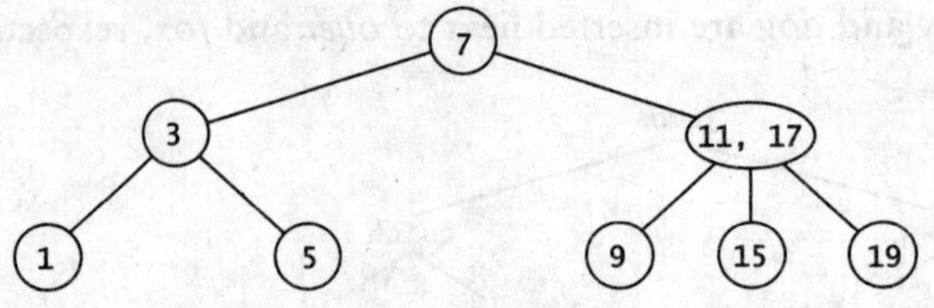

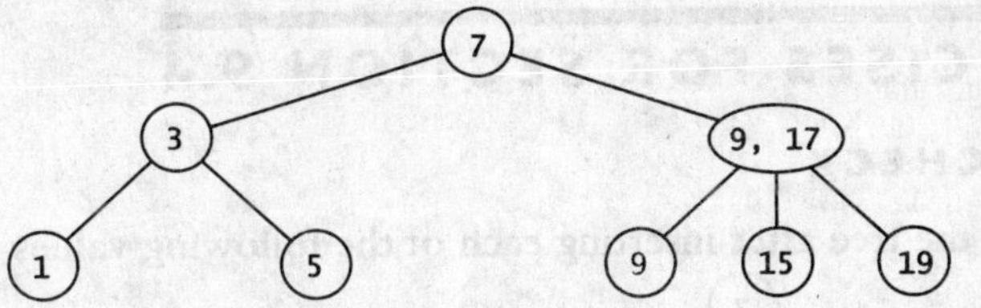

FIGURE 9.44
Removing 11 from the 2-3 Tree (Step 1)

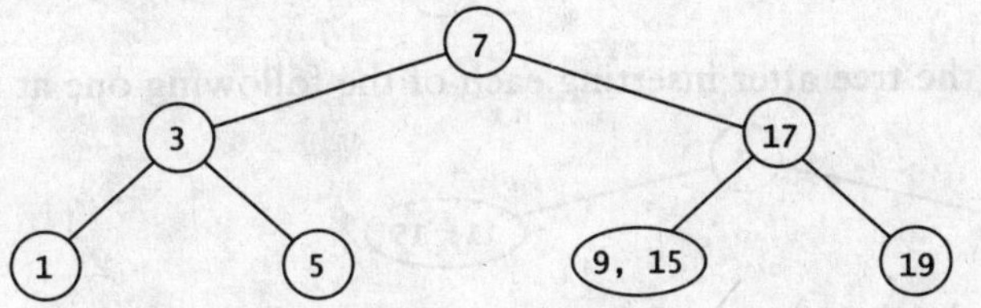

FIGURE 9.45
2-3 Tree after Removing 11

We next remove 11 from the 2-3 tree. Because this is not a leaf, we replace it with its predecessor, 9, as shown in Figure 9.44. We now have the case where the left leaf node of 9 has become empty. So we merge 9 into its right leaf node as shown in Figure 9.45.

Finally, let's consider the case in which we remove the value 1 from Figure 9.45. First, 1's parent (3) and its right sibling (5) are merged to form a 3-node, as shown in Figure 9.46. This has the effect of deleting 3 from the next higher level. Therefore, the process repeats, and 3's parent (7) and 7's right child (17) are merged, as shown in Figure 9.47. The merged node becomes the root.

The 2-3 tree served as an inspiration for the more general B-tree and 2-3-4 tree. Rather than show an implementation of the 2-3 tree, which has some rather messy complications, we will describe and implement the more general B-tree in the next section.

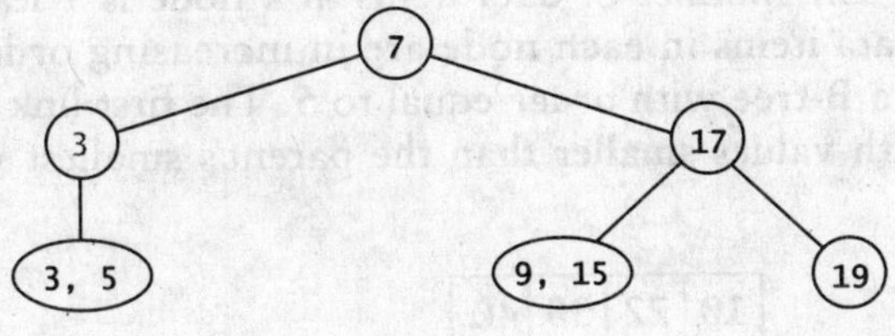

FIGURE 9.46
After Removing 1 (Intermediate Step)

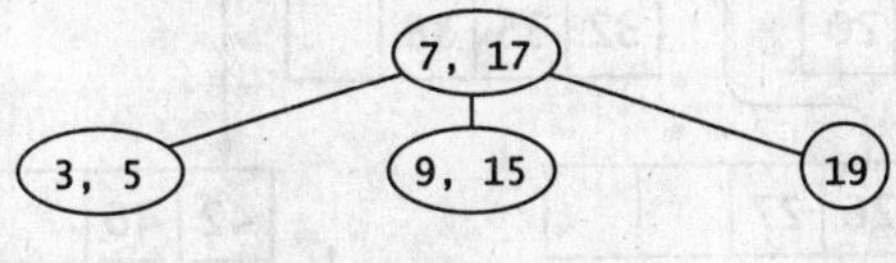

FIGURE 9.47
After Removing 1 (Final Form)

EXERCISES FOR SECTION 9.4

SELF-CHECK

1. Show the tree after inserting each of the following values one at a time: 1, 4, 9.

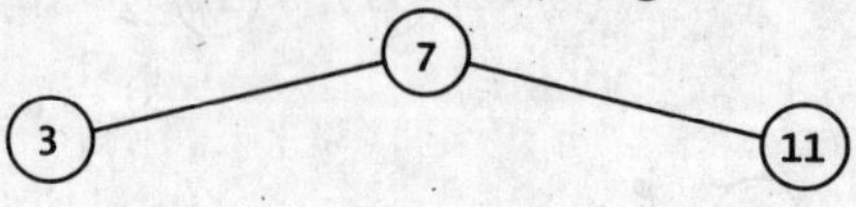

2. Show the tree after inserting each of the following one at a time: 9, 13.

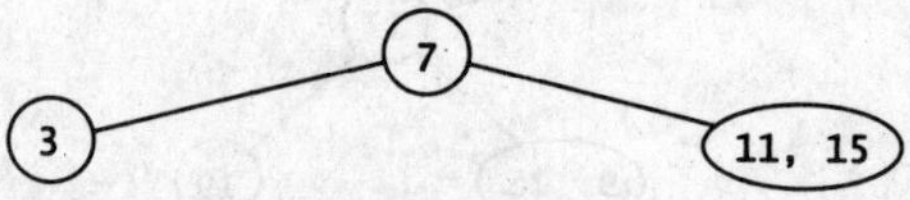

3. Show the 2-3 tree that would be built for the sentence "Now is the time for all good men to come to the aid of their party".

9.5 B-Trees and 2-3-4 Trees

The 2-3 tree was the inspiration for the more general B-tree, which allows up to *n* children per node, where *n* may be a very large number. The B-tree was designed for building indexes to very large databases stored on a hard disk. The 2-3-4 tree is a special case of a B-tree.

B-Trees

In the 2-3 tree, a 2-node has 2 children and a 3-node has 3 children. In the B-tree, the maximum number of children is the order of the B-tree, which we will represent by the variable `order`. Other than the root, each node has between `order/2` and `order` children. The number of data items in a node is 1 less than the number of children. The data items in each node are in increasing order. Figure 9.48 shows an example of a B-tree with `order` equal to 5. The first link from a node connects to a subtree with values smaller than the parent's smallest value (10 for the root

FIGURE 9.48
Example of a B-Tree

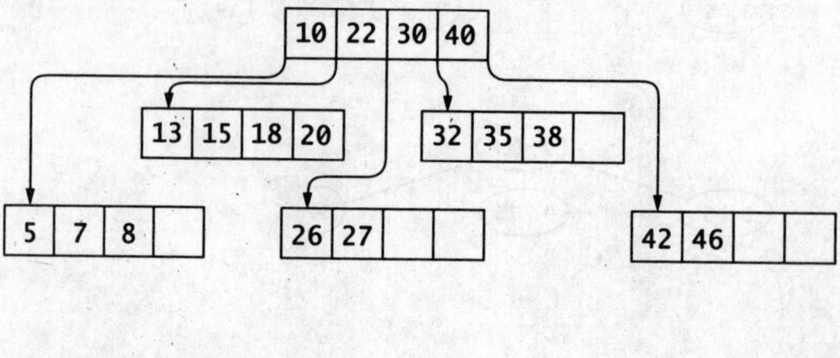

node); the last link from a node connects to a subtree with values greater than the parent's largest value (40 for the root node); the other links are to subtrees with values between each pair of consecutive values in the parent node (e.g., greater than 10 and less than 22 or greater than 22 and less than 30).

B-trees were developed to store indexes to databases on disk storage. Disk storage is broken into blocks, and the nodes of a B-tree are sized to fit in a block, so each disk access to the index retrieves exactly one B-tree node. The time to retrieve a block is large compared to the time required to process it in memory, so by making the tree nodes as large as possible, we reduce the number of disk accesses required to find an item in the index. Assuming a block can store a node for a B-tree of order 200, each node would store at least 100 items. This would enable 100^4 or 100 million items to be accessed in a B-tree of height 4.

The insertion process for a B-tree is similar to that of a 2-3 tree, and each insertion is into a leaf. For Figure 9.48, a number less than 10 would be inserted into the leftmost leaf; a number greater than 40 would be inserted into the rightmost leaf; and numbers between 11 and 39 would be inserted into one of the interior leaves. A simple case is insertion of the number 39 into the fourth child of the root node (shown in color in Figure 9.49).

FIGURE 9.49
B-tree after Inserting 39

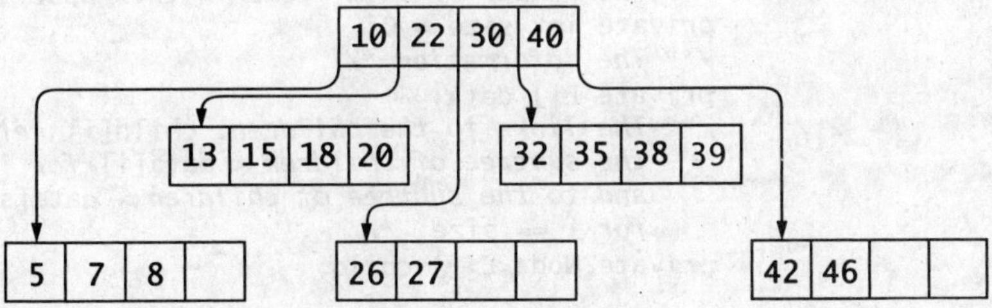

However, if the leaf being inserted into is full, it is split into two nodes, each containing approximately half the items, and the middle item is passed up to the split node's parent. If the parent is full, it is split and its middle item is passed up to its parent, and so on. If a node being split is the root of the B-tree, a new root node is created, thereby increasing the height of the B-tree. The children of the new root will be the two nodes that resulted from splitting the old root. Figure 9.50 shows the B-tree after inserting 17. Because 17 is between 10 and 22, it should be inserted into the second leaf node {13, 15, 18, 20}, with 17 as the new third or middle item {13, 15, 17, 18, 20}. However, the original leaf node was full, so it is split, and its new middle item, 17, is passed up to the root node {10, 17, 22, 30, 40}. Because the original root node was full, it is also split and its new middle item, 22, is passed up as the first item in a new root node, thereby increasing the height of the tree. It is interesting that the B-tree grows by adding nodes to the top of the tree instead of adding them at the bottom.

FIGURE 9.50
Inserting into a B-Tree

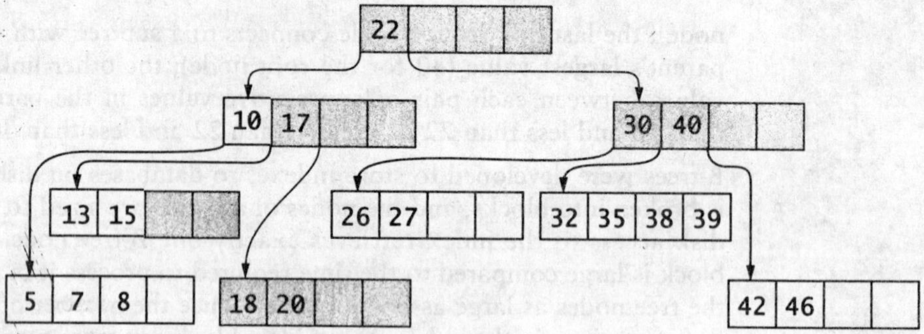

Implementing the B-Tree

The `Node` class holds up to `order-1` data items and `order` references to children. The array `data` stores the data, and the array `children` stores the references to the children. The number of data items currently stored is indicated by `size`.

```
/** A Node represents a node in a B-tree. */
private static class Node<E> {
    // Data Fields

    /** The number of data items in this node */
    private int size = 0;
    /** The information */
    private E[] data;
    /** The links to the children. child[i] refers to
        the subtree of children < data[i] for i < size
        and to the subtree of children > data[size-1]
        for i == size   */
    private Node<E>[] child;

    /** Create an empty node of size order
        @param order The size of a node
    */
    @SuppressWarnings("unchecked")
    public Node(int order) {
        data = (E[]) new Comparable[order - 1];
        child = (Node<E>[]) new Node[order];
        size = 0;
    }
}
```

The declaration for the B-tree class begins as follows:

```
/** An implementation of the B-tree. A B-tree is a
    search tree in which each node contains n data items where
    n is between (order-1)/2 and order-1. (For the root, n may be
    between 1 and order-1.) Each node not a leaf has n+1 children. The
    tree is always balanced in that all leaves are on the same level,
    i.e., the length of the path from the root to a leaf is constant.
    @author Koffman and Wolfgang
*/
```

```
public class BTree<E extends Comparable<E>>
    // Nested class
    /** A Node represents a node in a B-tree. */
    private static class Node<E> {
    . . .
    }

    /** The root node. */
    private Node<E> root = null;
    /** The maximum number of children of a node */
    private int order;

    /** Construct a B-tree with node size order
        @param order the size of a node
    */
    public BTree(int order) {
        this.order = order;
        root = null;
    }
```

The insert method is very similar to that for the 2-3 tree. Method insert searches the current node for the item. If the item is found, insertion is not possible so it returns **false**. If the item is not found in the current node, it follows the appropriate link until it reaches a leaf and then inserts the item into that leaf. If the leaf is full, it is split. In the 2-3 tree, we described this process as a virtual insertion into the full leaf, and then the middle data value is used as the parent of the split-off node. This parent value was then inserted into the parent node during the return process of the recursion.

Algorithm for insertion

1. **if** the root is **null**
2. Create a new Node that contains the inserted item
3. **else** search the local root for the item
4. **if** the item is in the local root
5. return **false**
6. **else**
7. **if** the local root is a leaf
8. **if** the local root is not full
9. insert the new item
10. return **null** as the **new_child** and **true** to indicate successful insertion
11. **else**
12. split the local root
13. return the newParent and a newChild and **true** to indicate successful insertion
14. **else**
15. recursively call the insert method
16. **if** the returned newChild is not **null**

```
17.                 if the local root is not full
18.                         insert the newParent and newChild into the
                            local root
19.                         return null as the newChild
                            and true to indicate successful insertion
20.                 else
21.                         split the local root
22.                         return the newParent and the newChild
                            and true to indicate successful insertion
23.             else
24.                 return the success/fail indicator for the insertion
```

In this algorithm we showed multiple return values. There is the `boolean` return value that indicates success or failure of the insertion. There is the `newParent` of the split-off node, and there is the split-off node, which we call the `newChild`. We implement this by using the return value from the `insert` function as the success/fail indicator, and `newParent` and `newChild` are private data fields in the `BTree` class. If there is no new child, `newChild` is set to **`null`**.

Code for the insert Method

The code for the `insert` method is shown in Listing 9.5. We use a binary search to locate the item in the local root. The `binarySearch` method returns the index of the item if it is present or the index of the position where the item should be inserted.

We need to test to see if the local root is full. If it is not full, we can insert the item into the local root; otherwise, we need to split the local root. In either case we return **`true`**.

```
if (root.size < order - 1) {
    insertIntoNode(root, index, item, null);
    newChild = null;
} else {
    splitNode(root, index, item, null);
}
return true;
```

If the local root is not a leaf, then we recursively call the `insert` method using `local.child[index]` as the root argument. Upon return from the recursion we test the value of `newChild`. If it is **`null`**, we return the result of the insertion. If it is not **`null`** and the local root is not full, we insert the `newParent` and `newChild` into the local root; otherwise, we split the local root.

```
boolean result = insert(root.child[index], item);
if (newChild != null) {
    if (root.size < order - 1) {
        insertIntoNode(root, index, newParent, newChild);
        newChild = null;
    } else {
        splitNode(root, index, newParent, newChild);
    }
}
return result;
```

The `insertIntoNode` and `splitNode` methods are described next.

LISTING 9.5

The insert Function from BTree.java

```
/** Recursively insert an item into the B-tree. Inserted
    item must implement the Comparable interface
    @param root The local root
    @param item The item to be inserted
    @return true if the item was inserted, false
    if the item is already in the tree
*/
private boolean insert(Node<E> root, E item) {
    int index = binarySearch(item, root.data, 0, root.size);
    if (index != root.size && item.compareTo(root.data[index]) == 0) {
        return false;
    }
    if (root.child[index] == null) {
        if (root.size < order - 1) {
            insertIntoNode(root, index, item, null);
            newChild = null;
        } else {
            splitNode(root, index, item, null);
        }
        return true;
    } else {
        boolean result = insert(root.child[index], item);
        if (newChild != null) {
            if (root.size < order - 1) {
                insertIntoNode(root, index, newParent, newChild);
                newChild = null;
            } else {
                splitNode(root, index, newParent, newChild);
            }
        }
        return result;
    }
}
```

The insertIntoNode Method

The insertIntoNode method shifts the data and child values to the right and inserts the new value and child at the indicated index.

```
/** Method to insert a new value into a node
    pre: node.data[index-1] < item < node.data[index];
    post: node.data[index] == item and old values are moved
          right one position
    @param node The node to insert the value into
    @param index The index where the inserted item is to be placed
    @param item The value to be inserted
    @param child The right child of the value to be inserted
*/
private void insertIntoNode(Node<E> node, int index,
                            E obj, Node<E> child) {
    for (int i = node.size; i > index; i--) {
        node.data[i] = node.data[i - 1];
        node.child[i + 1] = node.child[i];
    }
```

```
        node.data[index] = obj;
        node.child[index + 1] = child;
        node.size++;
    }
```

The splitNode Method

The `splitNode` method will perform the virtual insertion of the new item (and its child) into the node and split it so that half of the items remain in the node being split and the rest are moved to the split-off node. The middle value becomes the parent of the split-off node. The middle value is passed up to the parent node, which still links to the node that was split. This is illustrated in Figure 9.51.

FIGURE 9.51
Splitting the Node

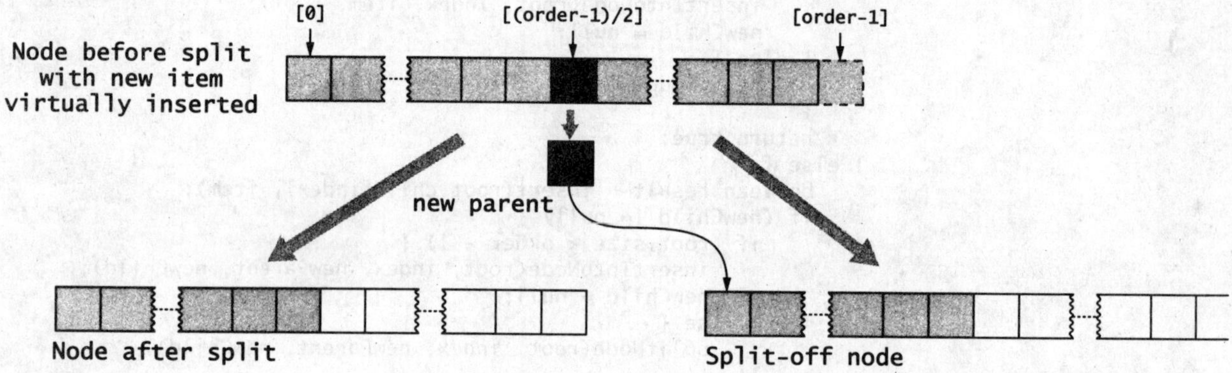

The code for the `splitNode` method is shown in Listing 9.6. Since we cannot insert the new item into the node before it is split, we need to do the split first in such a way that space is available in either the original node or the split-off node for the new item. After the split, we keep half of the items in the original node and move the other half to the split-off node. The number of items to keep is `order-1`; thus half of them is `(order-1)/2`, and the number of items to move is `(order-1) - (order-1)/2`. The reason that this is not simply `(order-1)/2` is that `order-1` may be an odd number. Thus we move `(order-1) - (order-1)/2` items, unless the new item is to be inserted into the split-off node, in which case we move one fewer item. The number of items to be moved is computed using the following statements:

```
// Determine number of items to move
int numToMove = (order - 1) - ((order - 1) / 2);
// If insertion point is in the right half, move one less item
if (index > (order - 1) / 2) {
    numToMove--;
}
```

The System.arrayCopy method is then used to move the data and the corresponding children.

```
// Move items and their children
System.arraycopy(node.data, order - numToMove - 1,
                 newChild.data, 0, numToMove);
System.arraycopy(node.child, order - numToMove,
                 newChild.child, 1, numToMove);
node.size = order - numToMove - 1;
newChild.size = numToMove;
```

Now we are ready to insert the new item and set the newChild.child[0] reference. There are three cases: the item is to be inserted as the middle item, the item is to be inserted into the original node, and the item is to be inserted into the newChild. If the item is to be inserted into the middle, then it becomes the newParent, and its child becomes newChild.child[0].

```
if (index == ((order - 1) / 2)) { // Insert as middle item
    newParent = item;
    newChild.child[0] = child;
}
```

Otherwise we can use the insertIntoNode method to insert the item into either the original node or the newChild node.

```
if (index < ((order - 1) / 2)) { // Insert into the left
    insertIntoNode(node, index, item, child);
} else {
    insertIntoNode(newChild, index - ((order - 1) / 2) - 1,
                   item, child);
}
```

In either case, after the insert, the last item in the original node becomes the newParent and its child becomes newChild.child[0]

```
// The rightmost item of the node is the new parent
newParent = node.data[node.size - 1];
// Its child is the left child of the split-off node
newChild.child[0] = node.child[node.size];
node.size--;
```

LISTING 9.6

Function splitNode from BTree.java

```
private void splitNode(Node<E> node, int index, E item, Node<E> child) {
    // Create new child
    newChild = new Node<E>(order);
    // Determine number of items to move
    int numToMove = (order - 1) - ((order - 1) / 2);
    // If insertion point is in the right half, move one less item
    if (index > (order - 1) / 2) {
        numToMove--;
    }

    // Move items and their children
    System.arraycopy(node.data, order - numToMove - 1,
                     newChild.data, 0, numToMove);
    System.arraycopy(node.child, order - numToMove,
                     newChild.child, 1, numToMove);
```

```
        node.size = order - numToMove - 1;
        newChild.size = numToMove;

        // Insert new item
        if (index == ((order - 1) / 2)) { // Insert as middle item
            newParent = item;
            newChild.child[0] = child;
        } else {
            if (index < ((order - 1) / 2)) { // Insert into the left
                insertIntoNode(node, index, item, child);
            } else {
                insertIntoNode(newChild, index - ((order - 1) / 2) - 1,
                               item, child);
            }
            // The rightmost item of the node is the new parent
            newParent = node.data[node.size - 1];
            // Its child is the left child of the split-off node
            newChild.child[0] = node.child[node.size];
            node.size--;
        }

        // Remove items and references to moved items
        for (int i = node.size; i < node.data.length; i++) {
            node.data[i] = null;
            node.child[i + 1] = null;
        }
    }
```

Removal from a B-Tree

Removing an item from a B-tree is a generalization of removing an item from a 2-3 tree. The simpler case occurs when the item to be removed is in a leaf; in this case, it is deleted from the leaf. However, if the item to be removed is in an interior node, it can't be deleted simply because that would damage the B-tree. To retain the B-tree property, the item must be replaced by its inorder predecessor (or its inorder successor), which is in a leaf. As an example, Figure 9.52 shows the tree that would be formed when 40 is removed from the tree in Figure 9.50 and is replaced with its inorder predecessor (39).

In both cases described above, if the removal of an item from a leaf results in a leaf node that is less than half full, this would violate a property of the B-tree (only the root node can be less than half full). To correct this, items from a sibling node and parent are redistributed into that leaf. However, if the sibling is itself exactly half full, the leaf, its parent item, and sibling are merged into a single node, deleting the parent item from the parent node. If the parent node is now half full, the process of node redistribution or merging is repeated during the recursive return process. The merging process may reduce the height of the B-tree.

We illustrate this process by deleting item 18 from the bottom B-tree in Figure 9.52. The leaf node that contained 18 would have only one item (20), so we merge it with its parent and left sibling into a new full node {13, 15, 17, 20} as shown in Figure 9.53.

FIGURE 9.52
Removing 40 from B-Tree of Figure 9.50

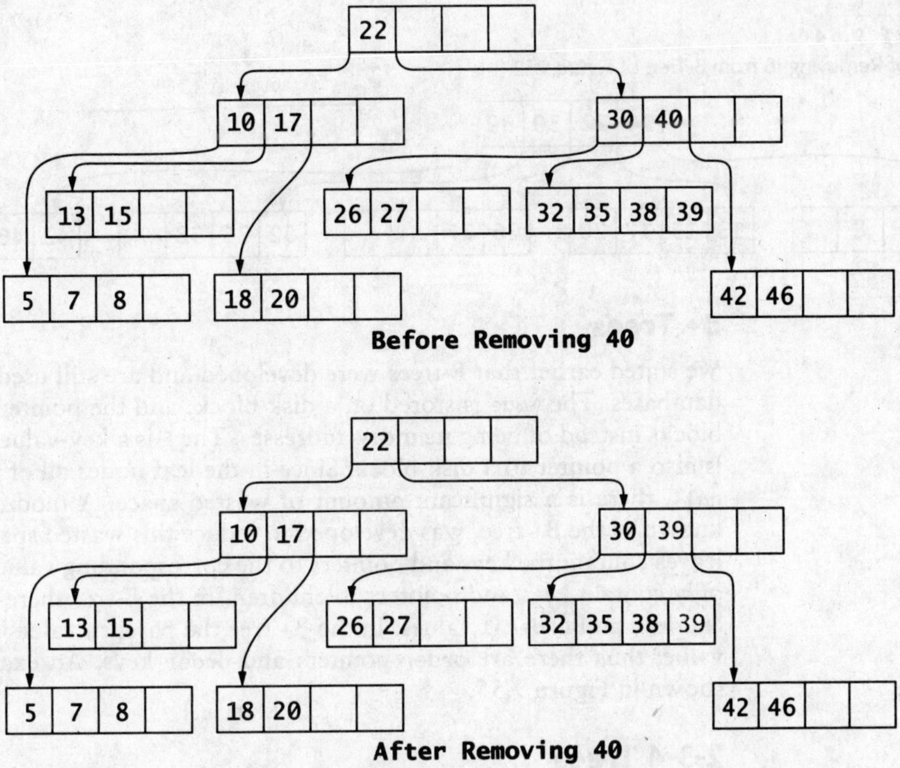

The problem is that the parent of {13, 15, 17, 20} has only one item (10), so it is merged with its parent and right sibling to form a new root node {10, 22, 30, 40} as shown in Figure 9.54. Note that the height of the resulting B-tree has also been reduced by 1.

FIGURE 9.53
Step 1 of Removing 18 from Bottom B-Tree of Figure 9.52

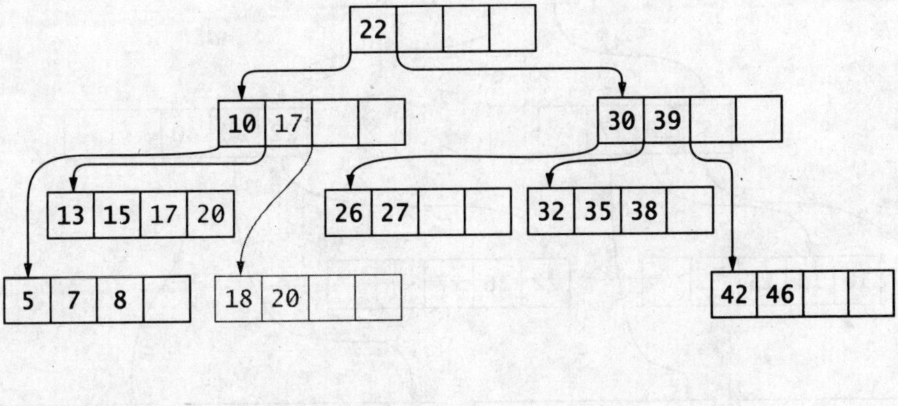

FIGURE 9.54
Step 2 of Removing 18 from B-Tree of Figure 9.52

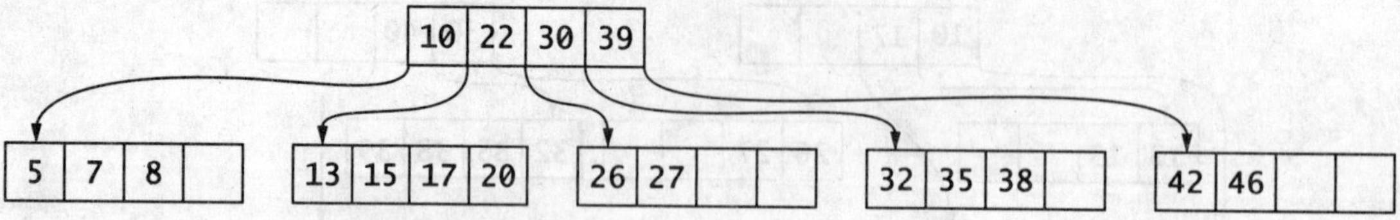

B+ Trees

We stated earlier that B-trees were developed and are still used to create indexes for databases. The `Node` is stored on a disk block, and the pointers are pointers to disk blocks instead of being memory addresses. The `E` is a key-value pair, where the value is also a pointer to a disk block. Since in the leaf nodes all of the child pointers are `null`, there is a significant amount of wasted space. A modification to the B-tree, known as the B+ tree, was developed to reduce this wasted space. In the B+ tree, the leaves contain the keys and pointers to the corresponding values. The internal nodes only contain keys and pointers to children. In the B-tree there are `order` pointers to children and `order-1` values. In the B+ tree the parent's value is repeated as the first value; thus there are `order` pointers and `order` keys. An example of a B+ tree is shown in Figure 9.55.

2-3-4 Trees

2-3-4 trees are a special case of the B-tree where `order` is fixed at 4. We refer to such a node as a 4-node (see Figure 9.56). This is a node with three data items and four children. Figure 9.57 shows an example of a 2-3-4 tree.

FIGURE 9.55
Example of a B+ Tree

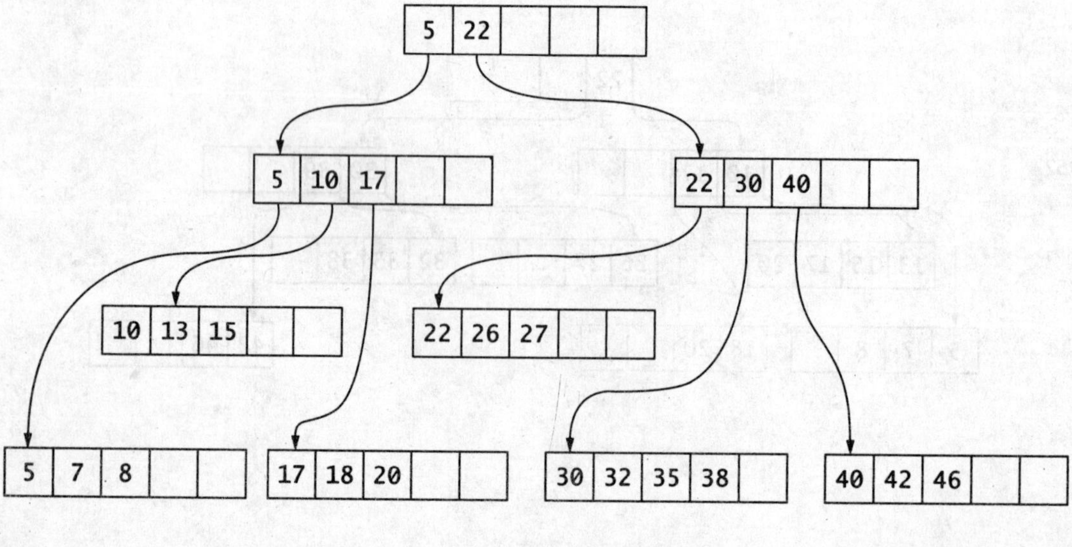

FIGURE 9.56
2-, 3-, 4- Nodes

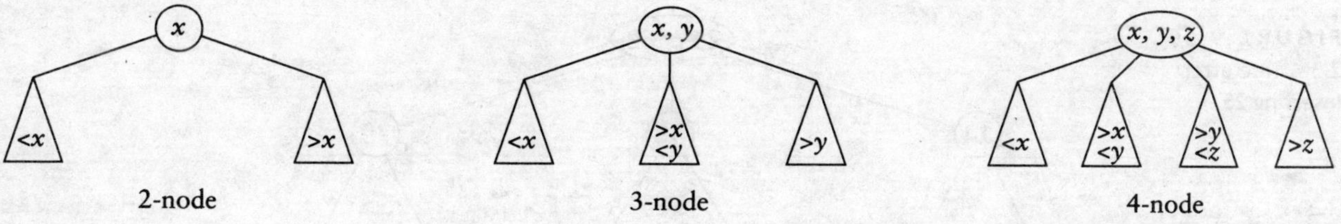

FIGURE 9.57
Example of a 2-3-4 Tree

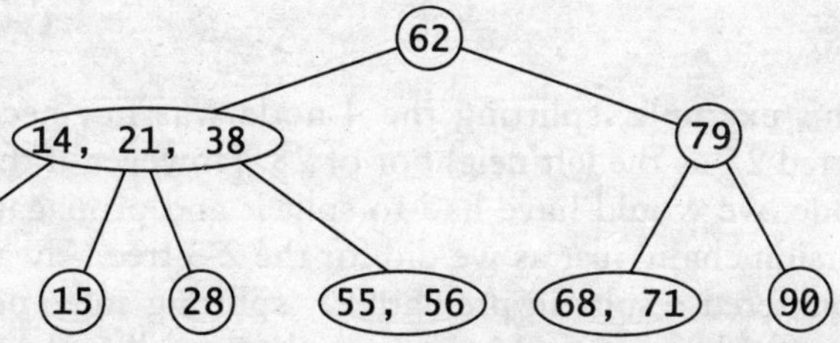

Fixing the capacity of a node at three data items simplifies the insertion logic. We can search for a leaf in the same way as for a 2-3 tree or a B-tree. If a 4-node is encountered at any point, we will split it, as discussed subsequently. Therefore, when we reach a leaf, we are guaranteed that there will be room to insert the item.

For the 2-3-4 tree shown in Figure 9.57, a number larger than 62 would be inserted in a leaf node in the right subtree. A number between 63 and 78, inclusive, would be inserted in the 3-node (68, 71), making it a 4-node. A number larger than 79 would be inserted in the 2-node (90), making it a 3-node.

When inserting a number smaller than 62 (say, 25), we would encounter the 4-node (14, 21, 38). We would immediately split it into two 2-nodes and insert the middle value (21) into the parent (62) as shown in Figure 9.58. Doing this guarantees that there will be room to insert the new item. We perform the split from the parent level and immediately insert the middle item from the split child into the parent node. Because we are guaranteed that the parent is not a 4-node, we will always have room to do this. We do not need to propagate a child or its parent back up the recursion chain. Consequently, the recursion becomes tail recursion.

FIGURE 9.58
Result of Splitting a 4-Node

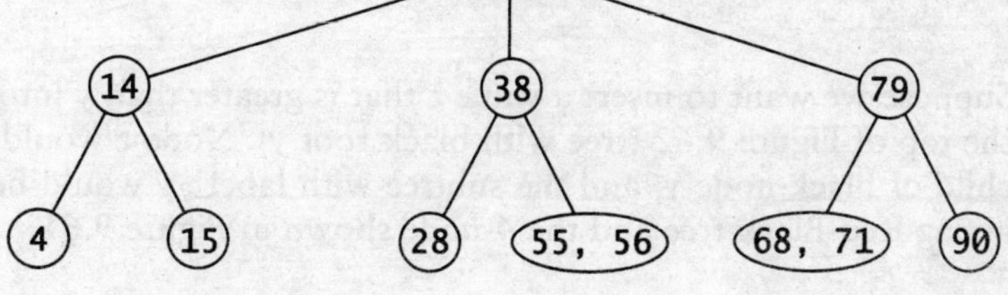

Now we can insert 25 as the left neighbor of 28 as shown in Figure 9.59.

FIGURE 9.59
2-3-4 Tree after Inserting 25

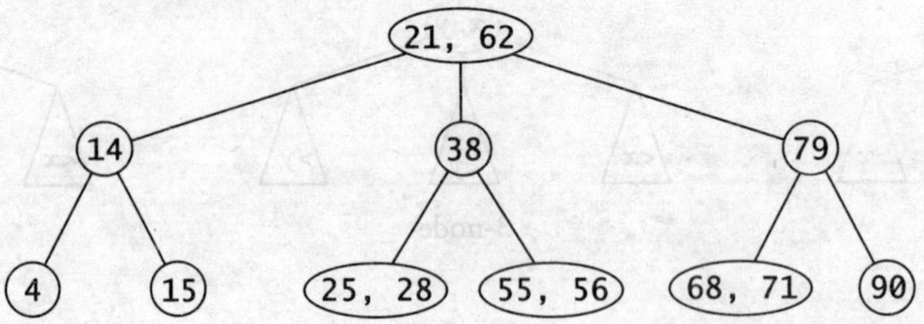

In this example, splitting the 4-node was not necessary. We could have merely inserted 25 as the left neighbor of 28. However, if the leaf being inserted into was a 4-node, we would have had to split it and propagate the middle item back up the recursion chain, just as we did for the 2-3 tree. Always splitting a 4-node when it is encountered results in prematurely splitting some nodes, but it simplifies the algorithm and has minimal impact on the overall performance.

Relating 2-3-4 Trees to Red-Black Trees

A Red-Black tree is a binary-tree equivalent of a 2-3-4 tree. A 2-node is a black node (see Figure 9.60). A 4-node is a black node with two red children (see Figure 9.61). A 3-node can be represented as either a black node with a left red child or a black node with a right red child (see Figure 9.62).

FIGURE 9.60
A 2-Node as a Black Node in a Red-Black Tree

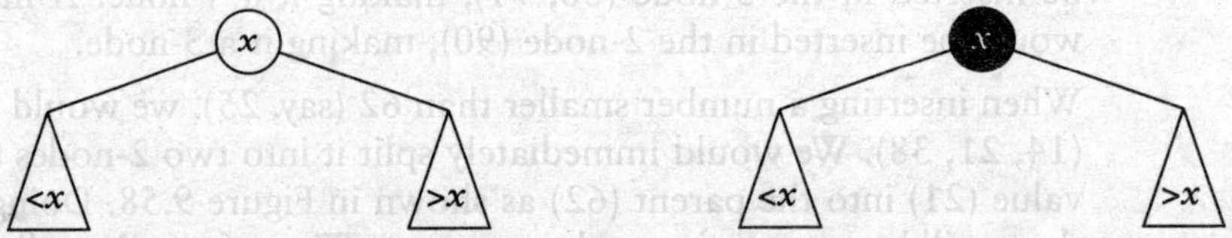

FIGURE 9.61
A 4-Node as a Black Node with Two Red Children in a Red-Black Tree

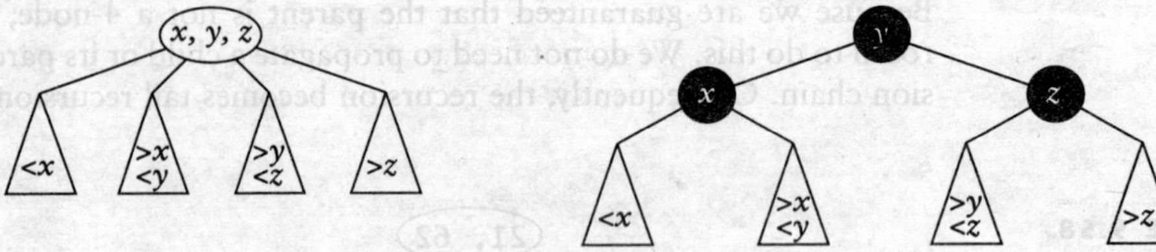

Suppose we want to insert a value *z* that is greater than *y* into the 3-node shown at the top of Figure 9.62 (tree with black root *y*). Node *z* would become the red right child of black node *y*, and the subtree with label >*y* would be split into two parts, giving Red-Black tree and the 4-node shown in Figure 9.61.

FIGURE 9.62
A 3-Node as a Black Node with One Red Child in a Red-Black Tree

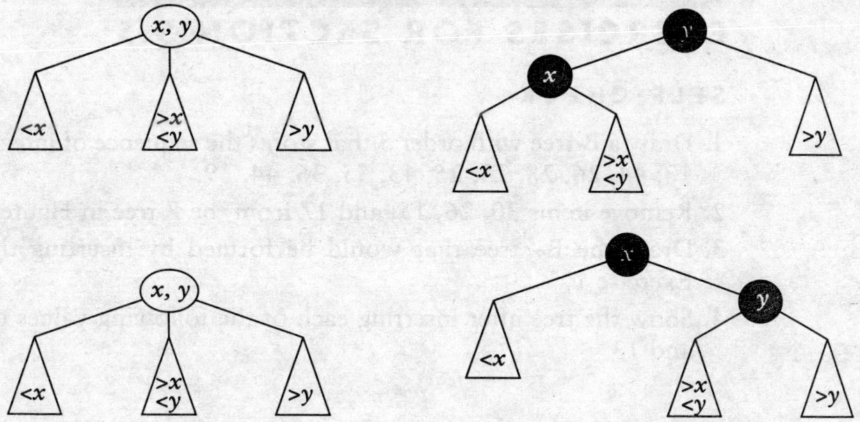

Suppose, on the other hand, we want to insert a value *z* that is between *x* and *y* into the 3-node shown at the bottom of Figure 9.62 (tree with black root *x*). Node *z* would become the red left child of red node *y* (see the left diagram in Figure 9.63), and a double rotation would be required. First rotate right around *y* (the middle diagram) and then rotate left around *x* (the right diagram). This corresponds to the situation shown in Figure 9.64 (a 4-node with *x*, *z*, *y*).

FIGURE 9.63
Inserting into the Middle of a 3-Node (Red-Black Tree Equivalent)

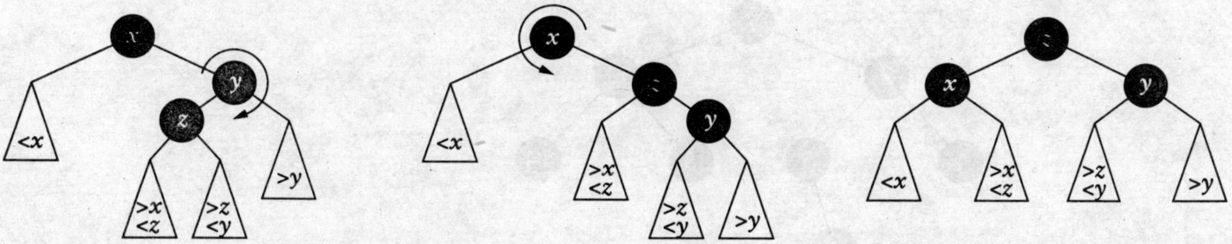

FIGURE 9.64
Inserting into the Middle of a 3-Node (2-3-4 Tree)

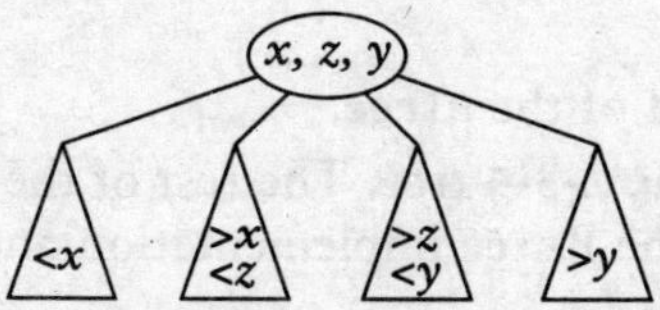

EXERCISES FOR SECTION 9.5

SELF-CHECK

1. Draw a B-tree with order 5 that stores the sequence of integers: 20, 30, 8, 10, 15, 18, 44, 26, 28, 23, 25, 43, 55, 36, 44, 39.
2. Remove items 30, 26, 15, and 17 from the B-tree in Figure 9.50.
3. Draw the B+ tree that would be formed by inserting the integers shown in Exercise 1.
4. Show the tree after inserting each of the following values one at a time: 1, 5, 9, and 13.

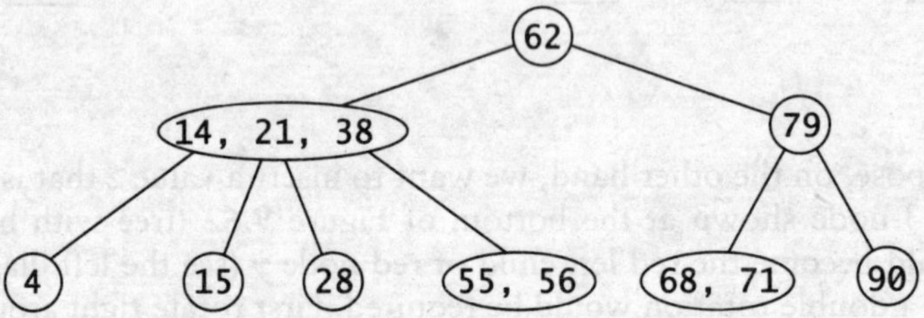

5. Build a 2-3-4 tree to store the words in the sentence "Now is the time for all good men to come to the aid of their party".
6. Draw the Red-Black tree equivalent of the 2-3-4 tree shown in Exercise 5.
7. Draw the 2-3-4 tree equivalent to the following Red-Black tree.

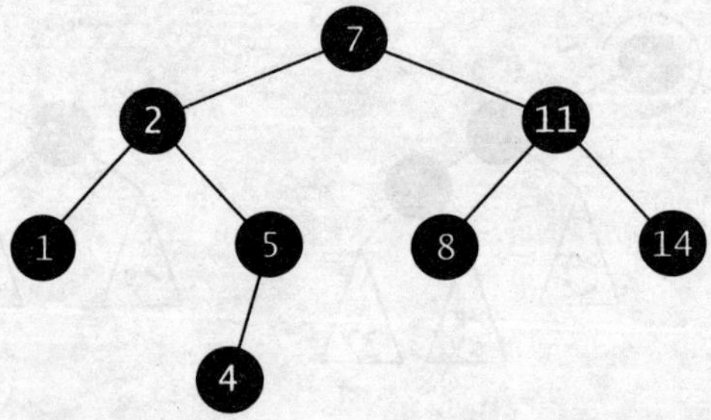

PROGRAMMING

1. Code the `binarySearch` method of the `BTree`.
2. Code the `insert` method for the 2-3-4 tree. The rest of the 2-3-4 tree implementation can be done by taking the B-tree implementation and fixing `order` at 4.

9.6 Skip-Lists

The skip-list is another data structure that can be used as the basis for the `NavigableSet` or `NavigableMap` and as a substitute for a balanced tree. Like a balanced tree, it provides for O(log n) search, insert, and remove. It has the additional advantage over the Red-Black tree–based `TreeSet` in that concurrent references are easier to achieve. With the `TreeSet` class, if two threads have iterators to the set and one thread makes a modification to the set, then the iterators are invalid and will throw the `ConcurrentModificationException` when next referenced. The `ConcurrentSkipListSet` and `ConcurrentSkipListMap` were introduced in Java 6. The concurrency features are beyond the scope of this text, but we will describe the basic structure of the skip-list and the algorithms for search, insertion, and removal.

Skip-List Structure

A skip-list is a list of lists. Each node in a list contains a data element with a key, and the elements in each list are in increasing order by key. Unlike the usual list node, which has a single forward link to the next node, the nodes in a skip list have a varying number of forward links. The number of such links is determined by the level of a node. A level-*m* node has *m* forward links. When a new data element is inserted in a skip-list, a new node is inserted to store the element. The node's level is chosen randomly in such a way that approximately 50 percent are level 1 (one forward link), 25 percent are level 2 (two forward links), 12.5 percent are level 3, and so on.

Figure 9.65 shows a skip-list with 10 data elements (only the keys are shown). In this skip-list, there are five level-1 nodes (5, 15, 25, 35, 45), three level-2 nodes (10, 30, 50), one level-3 node (20), and one level-4 node (40). If we look at node-20, we see that its level-1 link (the top one) is to node-25, its level-2 link is to node-30, and its level-3 link (the bottom one) is to node-40. The last node in the skip-list, node-50, is a level-2 node, and both links are **`null`**.

The *level* of a skip-list is defined as its highest node level, or 4 for Figure 9.65 A level-4 skip-list has individual lists of level 4, level 3, level 2, and level 1. The level-1 list consists of every node (5, 10, 15, etc.); the level-2 list (in color) consists of every other node (10, 20, 30, 40, 50); the level-3 list (in gray) consists of nodes-20 and 40; and the level-4 list consists of node-40. This is an *ideal skip-list*; most skip-lists will not have this exact structure, but their behavior will be similar.

FIGURE 9.65
Ideal Skip-List

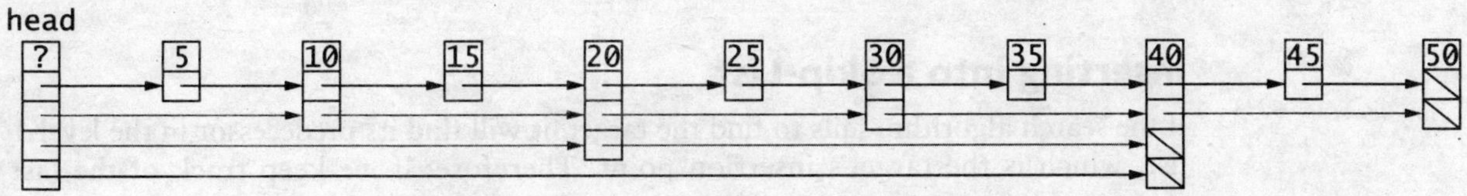

Searching a Skip-List

To search a skip-list, we start by looking for our target in the highest-level list. This list always has the fewest elements. If the target is in this list, the search is successful. If not, we stop the search in the current list at the element that is the predecessor of the target. Then we continue the search in the list with level one less than the current list, starting where we left off (the predecessor to the target). We continue this process until we either find the target or reach the level-1 list. If the target is not in the level-1 list (the list of all elements), then it is not present.

Figure 9.66 shows the search path for item 35. We start by searching the level-4 list. Its first node is 40 (>35), so we move to the level-3 list. Its first node is 20 and its second node is 40 (> 35), so we stop at node-20. We then follow node-20's level-2 link, which points to a node whose value is 30. Advancing to the 30-node, we see that its level-2 link is to 40 (> 35), so we stop at node-30. We then follow its level-1 link, which points to 35, our target. The gray links point to the predecessor of 35 in each list.

FIGURE 9.66
Searching for 35 in a Skip-List

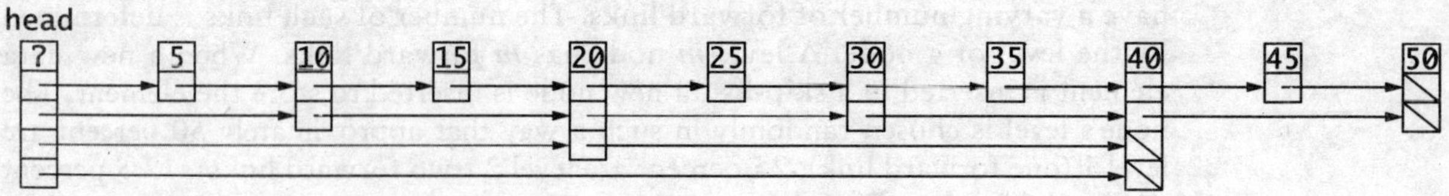

The algorithm for searching a skip-list follows:

1. Let m be the highest-level node.
2. `while` $m > 0$
3. Following the level-m links, find the node with the largest value that is less than or equal to the target.
4. If it is equal to the target, the target has been found—exit loop.
5. Set m to $m - 1$
6. If $m = 0$, the target is not in the list.

Performance of a Skip-List Search

Because the first list we search has the fewest elements (generally one or two) and each lower-level list we search has approximately half as a many elements as the current list, the search performance is similar to that of a binary search: O(log n), where n is the number of nodes in the skip-list. We discuss performance further at the end of this section.

Inserting into a Skip-List

If the search algorithm fails to find the target, it will find its predecessor in the level-1 list, which is the target's insertion point. Therefore, if we keep track of the last node we visited at each level, we know where to insert a new node containing the target. The question then is "What level should this new node be?" The answer is it is chosen at random, based on the number of items currently in the skip-list. The random number is chosen with a logarithmic distribution. Half the time a level-1 node is chosen; a quarter of the time a level-2 node is chosen, and $1/2^m$ time a level-m node is chosen. To insert 36 into the skip-list shown in Figure 9.66, we would follow the same path as to locate 35. Along the way we would have recorded the last node visited at each level: the 20 node at level 3, the 30 node at level 2, and the 35 node at level 1. If the random number generator returns a 3, the new node will be a level-3 node. The level-3 link in the 20 node will be set to point to the new 36 node, and the level-3 link in the new 36 node will be set to point to node 40. The level-2 link in the 30 node will be set to point to the new 36 node, and the level-2 link in the new 36 node will be set to point to node 40. Finally, the level-1 link in the 35 node will be set to point to the new 36 node, and the level-1 link in the new 36 node will be set to point to the 40 node. The result is shown in Figure 9.67.

FIGURE 9.67
After Insertion of 36

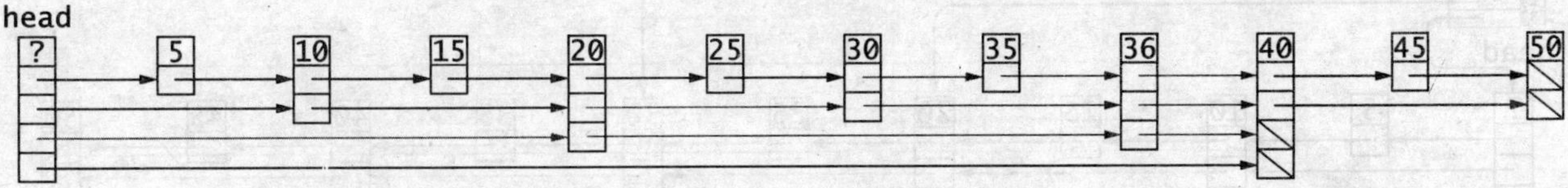

Increasing the Height of a Skip-List

The skip-list shown in the figures is a level-4 skip-list. Such a skip-list can efficiently hold up to 15 items. When a 16th item is inserted, the level is increased by 1. A level-m skip-list can hold between 2^{m-1} and $2^m - 1$ items.

Implementing a Skip-List

Next, we show how to implement a skip-list. We start with the `SLNode` class. When a new level-m node is created, the declaration for links allocates an array links with subscripts 0 through m-1. We use the same kind of node for the head node as the rest of the nodes in the skip-list. However, its data field value is not defined (indicated by ? in the figures).

```
/** Static class to contain the data and the links */
static class SLNode<E> {
    SLNode<E>[] links;
    E data;

    /** Create a node of level m */
    SLNode (int m, E data) {
        links = (SLNode<E>[]) new SLNode[m];  // create links
        this.data = data;                     // store item
    }
}
```

Searching a Skip-List

Since insertion involves the same algorithm as searching to find the insertion point, we define a common method, `search`, which will return an array `pred` of references to the `SLNodes` at each level that were last examined in the search. Because array subscripts start at 0, `pred[i]` references the predecessor in the level-(`i+1`) list of the target. The level-(`i+1`) link for the node referenced by `pred[i]` is greater than or equal to the target or is **`null`**. The result of searching for 35 is shown in Figure 9.68. Array element `pred[3]` references the head node since the level-4 link references the node 40, which is greater than 35. Array element `pred[2]` references node 20 whose level-3 link references node 40. Element `pred[1]` references node 30 whose level-2 link references 40 and whose level-1 link references 35. Finally, `pred[0]` also references node 30. By examining `links[0]` of the node referenced by `pred[0]`, we can determine whether the target is in the skip-list.

FIGURE 9.68
Result of Search for 35

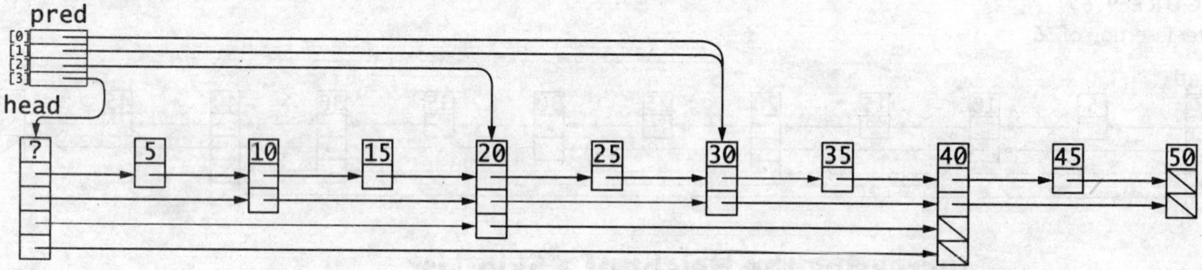

Listing 9.7 shows the code for searching a skip-list. Two methods are shown: `search` and `find`. Method `find` calls `search` to perform the search. The result returned by `search` is the array of references to the predecessor of `target` in each list. The `SkipList` data field `head` references an array of links to the first element of each list in the skip-list, where `head.links[i]` references the first node in the level-(`i+1`) list. Method `search` begins by setting `current` to `head`. The **`for`** loop ensures that each list is processed beginning with the highest-level list. The **`while`** loop advances `current` down the level-`i` list until `current` references the last node in the list or `current` references a node that is linked to either `target` or to the first element greater than `target`. The last value of `current` is saved in `pred[i]`, and the **`for`** loop sets `i` to `i-1`, causing the next list to be searched.

After `search` returns the array of predecessor references, method `find` examines the level-1 link of the predecessor saved for the level-1 list. If this link is **`null`** or if it references a node greater than the `target`, **`null`** is returned (`target` is not in the list); otherwise, the data stored in the node referenced by the level-1 link is returned as the search result.

LISTING 9.7
Methods for Searching a Skip-List

```
@SuppressWarnings("unchecked")
/** Search for an item in the list
    @param item The item being sought
```

```
        @return A SLNode array which references the predecessors
                of the target at each level.
    */
    private SLNode<E>[] search (E target) {
        SLNode<E>[] pred = (SLNode<E>[]) new SLNode[maxLevel];
        SLNode<E> current = head;
        for (int i = current.links.length-1; i >= 0; i--) {
            while (current.links[i] != null
                    && current.links[i].data.compareTo(target) < 0) {
                current = current.links[i];
            }
            pred[i] = current;
        }
        return pred;
    }

    /** Find an object in the skip-list
        @param target The item being sought
        @return A reference to the object in the skip-list that matches
                the target. If not found, null is returned.
    */
    public E find(E target) {
        SLNode<E>[] pred = search(target);
        if (pred[0].links[0] != null &&
                pred[0].links[0].data.compareTo(target) == 0) {
            return pred[0].links[0].data;
        } else {
            return null;
        }
    }
```

Insertion

The result of calling search for 36 is shown in Figure 9.69. It is the same as the search for 35 except that pred[0] references 35 since 36 will follow 35. At each level (i+1) the new node will be inserted between the node referenced by pred[i] and the node referenced by the predecessor node's links[i]. If the result of search is saved in the array pred and newNode is the new node, the code to splice newNode into the linked list is:

```
newNode.links[i] = pred[i].links[i];
pred[i].links[i] = newNode;
```

FIGURE 9.69
Result of Search for 36

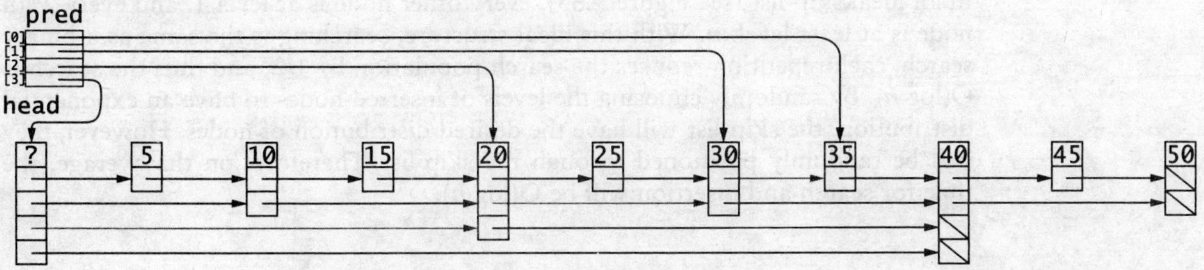

Determining the Size of the Inserted Node

We define maxCap as the smallest power of 2 that is greater than the current skip-list size. Therefore, maxLevel, the skip-list level is $\log_2$ maxCap. The random number class, Random, has a method nextInt(int n), which returns a uniformly distributed random integer from 0 up to, but not including, *n*. If we compute the $\log_2$ of this number plus 1, we get a logarithmically distributed random number between 1 and maxLevel (the skip-list level). This number has the opposite distribution of what we desire: 1/2 the numbers will be *maxLevel-1*, 1/4 of the numbers will be *maxLevel-2*, and so on. Thus we subtract the result from maxLevel.

```
/** Natural Log of 2 */
static final double LOG2 = Math.log(2.0);

/** Method to generate a logarithmic distributed integer between
    1 and maxLevel.  i.e., 1/2 of the values returned are 1, 1/4
    are 2, 1/8 are 3, etc.
    @return a random logarithmic distributed int between 1 and
            maxLevel
*/
private int logRandom() {
    int r = rand.nextInt(maxCap);
    int k = (int) (Math.log(r + 1) / LOG2);
    if (k > maxLevel - 1) {
        k = maxLevel - 1;
    }
    return maxLevel - k;
}
```

Completing the Insertion Process

Whenever a new item is inserted, the size is compared to maxCap. Recall that maxCap is $2^{maxLevel}$ - 1. If size is now greater than maxCap, maxLevel is incremented and a new value of maxCap is computed. The head node's link array needs to be expanded to accommodate nodes at the increased level.

```
if (size > maxCap) {
    maxLevel++;
    maxCap = computeMaxCap(maxLevel);
    head.links = Arrays.copyOf(head.links, maxLevel);
    pred = Arrays.copyOf(update, maxLevel);
    pred[maxLevel - 1] = head;
}
```

Performance of a Skip-List

In an ideal skip-list (see Figure 9.65), every other node is at level 1, and every 2^mth node is at least level *m*. With this ideal structure, searching is the same as a binary search; each repetition reduces the search population by 1/2, and thus the search is O(log *n*). By randomly choosing the levels of inserted nodes to have an exponential distribution, the skip-list will have the desired distribution of nodes. However, they will be randomly positioned through the skip-list. Therefore, on the average, the time for search and insertion will be O(log *n*).

EXERCISES FOR SECTION 9.6

SELF-CHECK

1. Show the skip-list after inserting the values 11, 12, 22, and 33 into the skip-list shown in Figure 9.65. Assume that the random number generator returned 2, 1, 3, and 1 for the new node levels.
2. Draw the ideal skip-list for storing the numbers 5, 10, 15, 20, 25, 30, 36, 42, 45, 50, 55, 60, 68, 72, 86, 93.

PROGRAMMING

1. Complete the code for the `add` method.
2. To remove a node from a skip-list, you need to update all references to the node being deleted to reference its successors. Code the `remove` method.

Chapter Review

- Tree balancing is necessary to ensure that a search tree has O(log *n*) behavior. Tree balancing is done as part of an insertion or removal.
- An AVL tree is a balanced binary tree in which each node has a balance value that is equal to the difference between the heights of its right and left subtrees ($h_R - h_L$). A node is balanced if it has a balance value of 0; a node is left-(right-) heavy if it has a balance of –1 (+1). Tree balancing is done when a node along the insertion (or removal) path becomes critically out of balance; that is, the absolute value of the difference of the height of its two subtrees is 2. The rebalancing is done after returning from a recursive call in the `add` or `delete` method.
- For an AVL tree, there are four kinds of imbalance and a different remedy for each.
  —Left-Left (parent balance is –2, left child balance is –1): Rotate right around parent.
  —Left-Right (parent balance is –2, left child balance is +1): Rotate left around child, then rotate right around parent.
  —Right-Right (parent balance is +2, right child balance is +1): Rotate left around parent.
  —Right-Left (parent balance is +2, right child balance is –1): Rotate right around child, then rotate left around parent.
- A Red-Black tree is a balanced tree with red and black nodes. After an insertion or removal, the following invariants must be maintained for a Red-Black tree:
  —A node is either red or black.
  —The root is always black.

—A red node always has black children. (A `null` reference is considered to refer to a black node.)

—The number of black nodes in any path from the root to a leaf is the same.

- To maintain tree balance in a Red-Black tree, it may be necessary to recolor a node and also to rotate around a node. The rebalancing is done inside the `add` or `delete` method, right after returning from a recursive call.
- Trees whose nodes have more than two children are an alternative to balanced binary search trees. These include 2-3 and 2-3-4 trees. A 2-node has two children, a 3-node has three children, and a 4-node has four children. The advantage of these trees is that keeping the trees balanced is a simpler process. Also, the tree may be less deep because a 3-node can have three children and a 4-node can have four children, but they still have O(log n) behavior.
- A B-tree of order n is a tree whose nodes can store up to n-1 items and have n children and is a generalization of a 2-3 tree. B-trees are used as indexes to large databases stored on disk. The value of n is chosen so that each node is as large as it can be and still fit in a disk block. The time to retrieve a block is large compared to the time required to process it in memory. By making the tree nodes as large as possible, we reduce the number of disk accesses required to find an item in the index.
- A 2-3-4 tree can be balanced on the way down the insertion path by splitting a 4-node into two 2-nodes before inserting a new item. This is easier than splitting nodes and rebalancing after returning from an insertion.

Java Classes Introduced in This Chapter

`java.util.TreeMap`

User-Defined Interfaces and Classes in This Chapter

`AVLTree`
`AVLTree.AVLNode`
`BinarySearchTreeWithRotate`
`RedBlackTree`
`RedBlackTree.RedBlackNode`
`TwoThreeFourTree`
`TwoThreeFourTree.Node`

Quick-Check Exercises

1. Show the following AVL tree after inserting *mouse*. What kind of imbalance occurs, and what is the remedy?

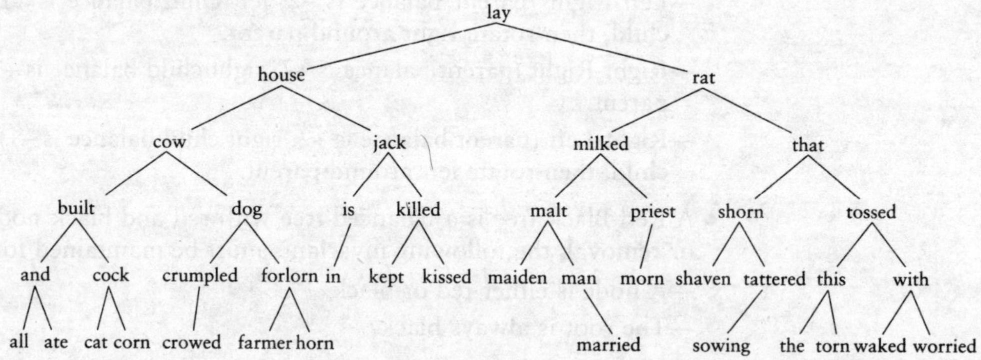

2. Show the following Red-Black tree after inserting 12 and then 13. What kind of rotation, if any, is performed?

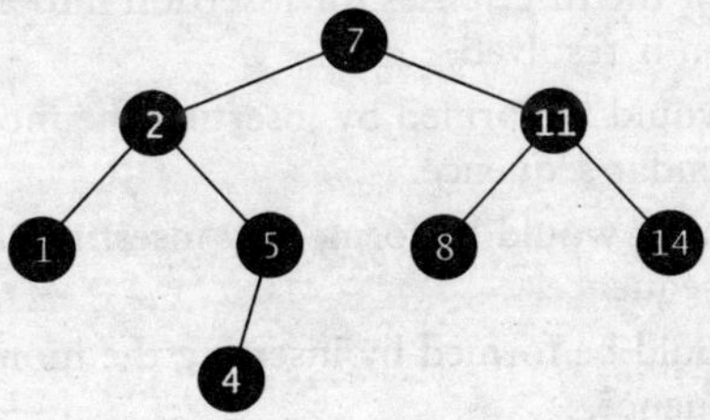

3. Show the following 2-3 tree after inserting 45 and then 20.

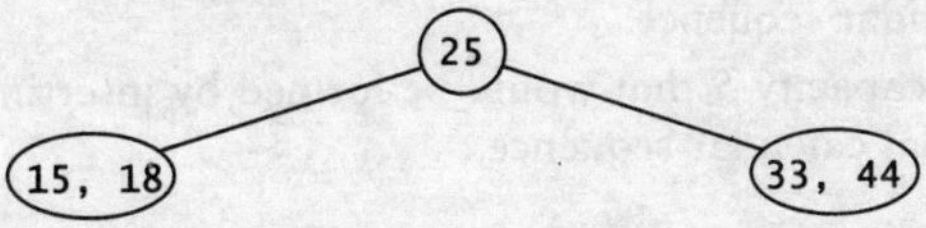

4. Show the following 2-3-4 tree after inserting 40 and then 50.

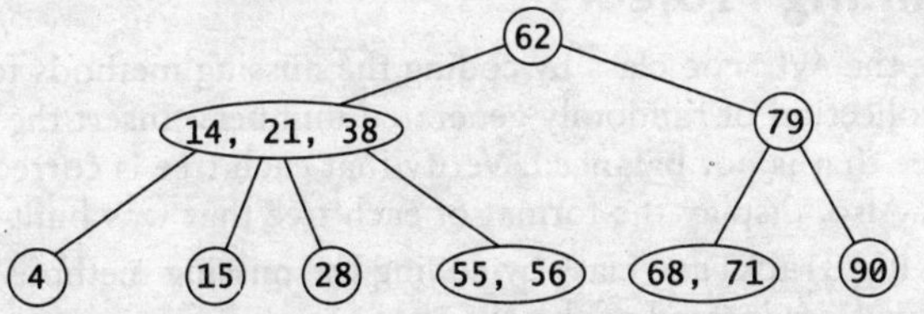

5. Draw the Red-Black tree equivalent to the following 2-3-4 tree.

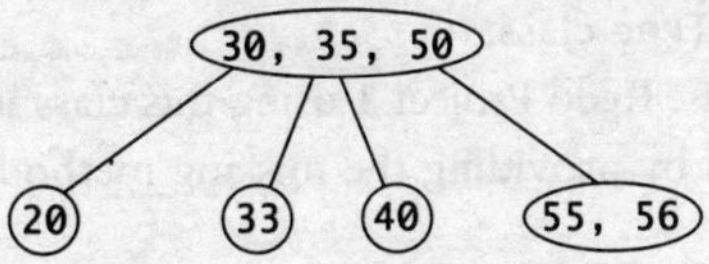

6. Draw the 2-3-4 tree equivalent to the following Red-Black tree.

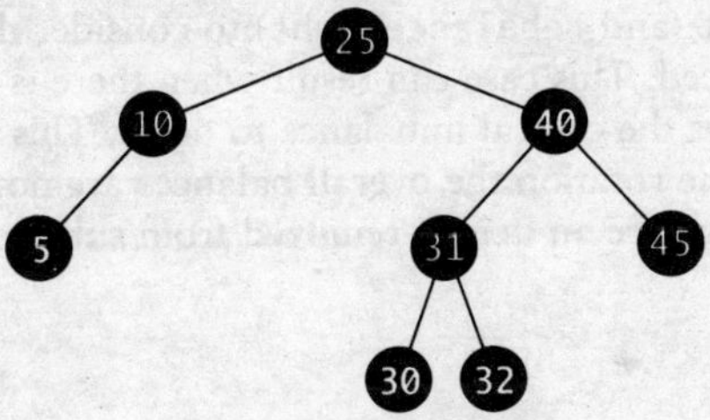

7. Show the following B-tree after inserting 45 and 21.

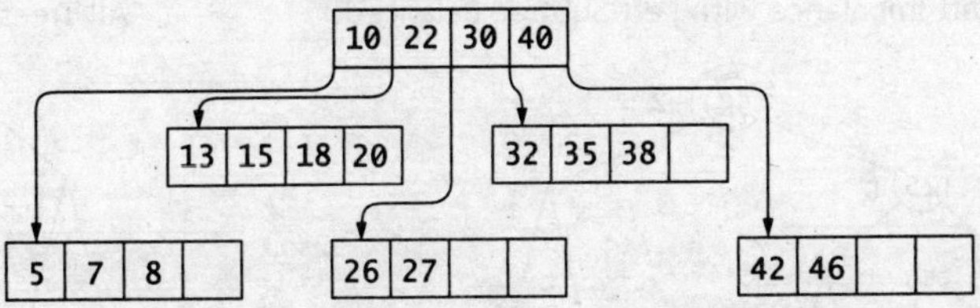

Review Questions

1. Draw the mirror images of the three cases for insertion into a Red-Black tree and explain how each situation is resolved.
2. Show the AVL tree that would be formed by inserting the month names (12 strings) into a tree in their normal calendar sequence.
3. Show the Red-Black tree that would be formed by inserting the month names into a tree in their normal calendar sequence.
4. Show the 2-3 tree that would be formed by inserting the month names into a tree in their normal calendar sequence.
5. Show the 2-3-4 tree that would be formed by inserting the month names into a tree in their normal calendar sequence.
6. Show a B-tree of capacity 5 that would be formed by inserting the month names into a tree in their normal calendar sequence.

Programming Projects

1. Complete the `AVLTree` class by coding the missing methods for insertion only. Use it to insert a collection of randomly generated numbers. Insert the same numbers in a binary search tree that is not balanced. Verify that each tree is correct by performing an inorder traversal. Also, display the format of each tree that was built and compare their heights.
2. Code the `RedBlackTree` class by coding the missing methods for insertion. Redo Project 1 using this class instead of the `AVLTree` class.
3. Code the `TwoThreeFourTree` class by coding the missing methods. Redo Project 1 using this class instead of the `AVLTree` class.
4. Code the `TwoThreeTree` class. Redo Project 1 using this class instead of the `AVLTree` class.
5. Complete the `AVLTree` class by providing the missing methods for removal. Demonstrate that these methods work.

   Review the changes required for methods `decrementBalance`, `incrementBalance`, `rebalanceLeft`, and `rebalanceRight` discussed at the end of Section 9.2. Also, modify `rebalanceLeft` (and `rebalanceRight`) to consider the cases where the left (right) subtree is balanced. This case can result when there is a removal from the right (left) subtree that causes the critical imbalance to occur. This is still a Left-Left (Right-Right) case, but after the rotation the overall balances are not zero. This is illustrated in Figures 9.70 and 9.71 where an item is removed from subtree `c`.

FIGURE 9.70
Left-Left Imbalance with Left Subtree Balanced

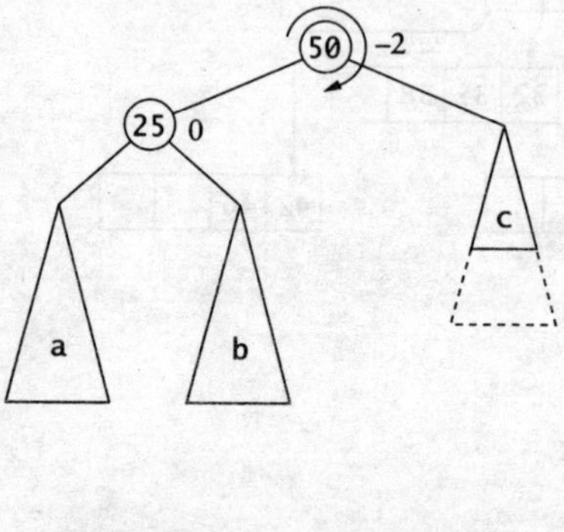

FIGURE 9.71
All Trees Unbalanced after Rotation

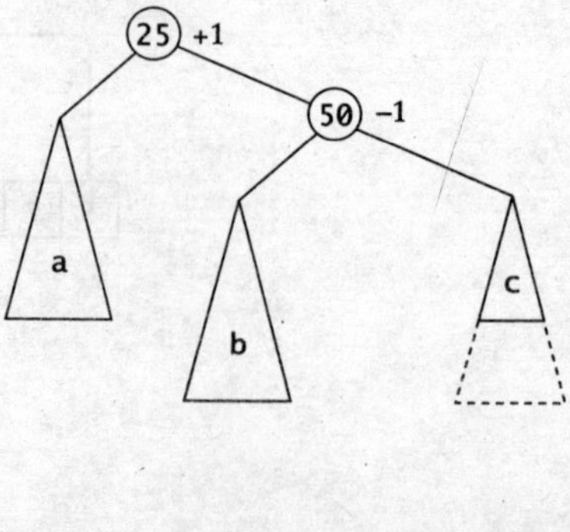

In addition, the Left-Right (or Right-Left) case can have a case in which the Left-Right (Right-Left) subtree is balanced. In this case, after the double rotation is performed, all balances are zero. This is illustrated in Figures 9.72 through 9.74.

FIGURE 9.72
Left-Right Case with Left-Right Subtree Balanced

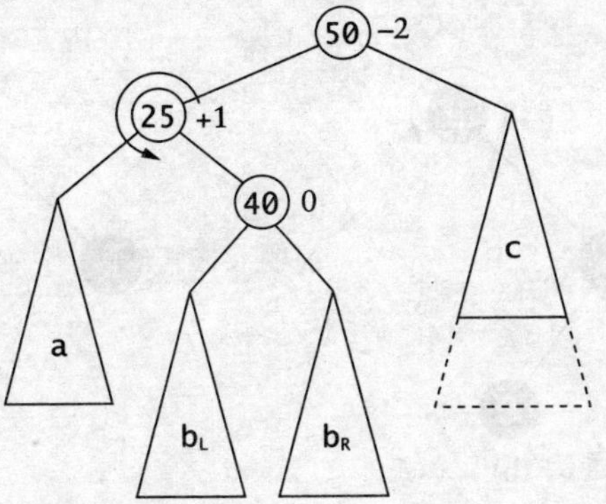

FIGURE 9.73
Imbalance after Single Rotation

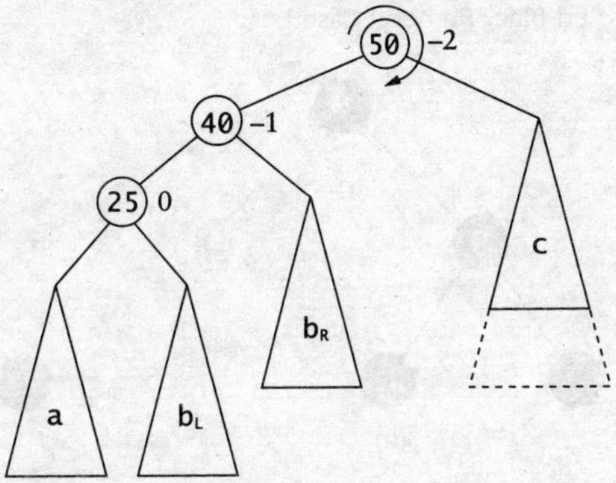

FIGURE 9.74
Complete Balance after Double Rotation

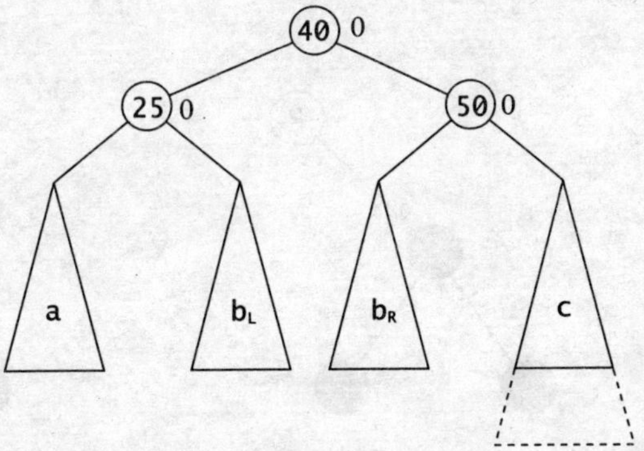

6. Complete the `RedBlackTree` class by coding the missing methods for removal. The methods `delete` and `findLargestChild` are adapted from the corresponding functions of the `BinarySearchTree` class. These adaptations are similar to those done for the AVL tree. A data field `fixupRequired` performs the role analogous to the `decrease` data field in the AVL tree. It is set when a black node is removed. Upon return from a method that can remove a node, this variable is tested. If the removal is from the right, then a new function `fixupRight` is called. If the removal is from the left, then a new method `fixupLeft` is called.

The method `fixupRight` is called with a reference to the local root of the subtree whose right subtree's black height is 1 less than the left subtree. This local root is designated P in the figures that illustrate the various cases that must be considered. The right subtree is indicated by X in a dotted circle and with a dotted line. This node X represents a back leaf that has been deleted, or it represents the root of the subtree whose black height has been reduced as shown in Figures 9.75 through 9.78.

If the node X is red, then the black height can be easily restored by setting it black. Otherwise, the `fixupRight` method must consider four cases, as follows:

- **Case 1:** The sibling of X (designated S in Figure 9.75(a)) is red. The parent (P) must be black, and S has children that must be two black nodes (L and R). We change the color of P to red and S to black (Figure 9.75(b)) and then rotate right about P (Figure 9.75(c)). Now we have a case where X has a black sibling (R). Recall that null trees are considered black. This transforms the problem into one of the other cases where R is now the sibling of X.

FIGURE 9.75
Red-Black Removal Case 1

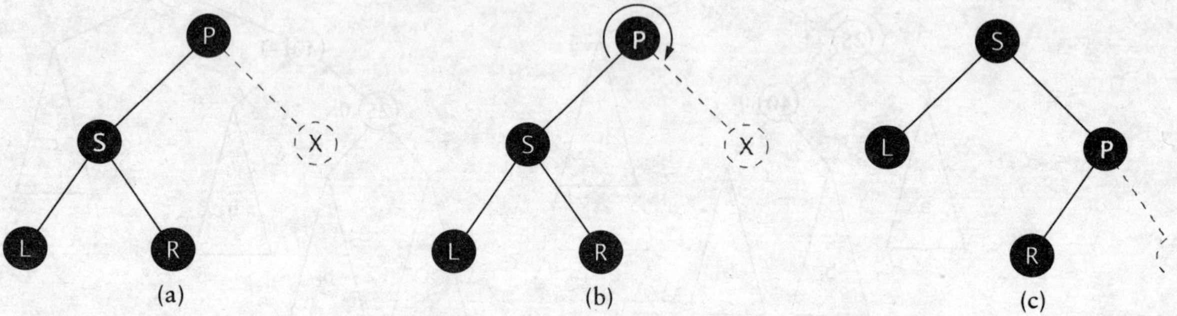

FIGURE 9.76
Red-Black Removal Case 2

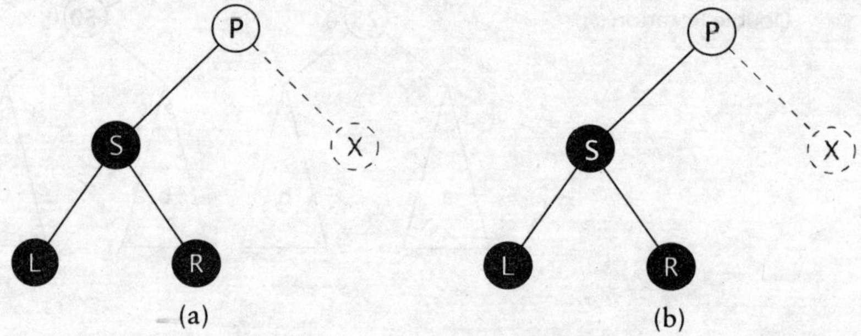

- **Case 2:** The sibling of X (designated S in Figure 9.76(a)) is black, and it is either a leaf or it has two black children. Note that we do not care what color P has, so we show it in a white circle. We change the color of S to red (Figure 9.76(b)). This reduces the black height of the subtree whose root is S, so it is now equal to the black height of the tree whose root is X. The overall black height of P has been reduced by 1, so we repeat the process at the next level (P's parent).
- **Case 3:** The sibling of X (designated S in Figure 9.77 (a)) is black, and it has a red right child (R). S may also have a left child L, but we do not care what its color is, so it is not shown. We change the color of S to red and the color of R to black (Figure 9.77(b)). Then we rotate left about S (Figure 9.77(c)). This transforms the problem into Case 4.

Note that before making this transformation, S was the root of a valid Red-Black tree. Therefore, if L (not shown) is a black node, then R must have two black children (also not shown). After performing the rotate, R is still the root of a valid Red-Black subtree. On the other hand, if L is a red node, then after the rotate, R's left child (S) is red and has a red left child (L). This will be fixed when we consider Case 4. However, the black heights of R's subtrees remain balanced.

FIGURE 9.77
Red-Black Removal Case 3

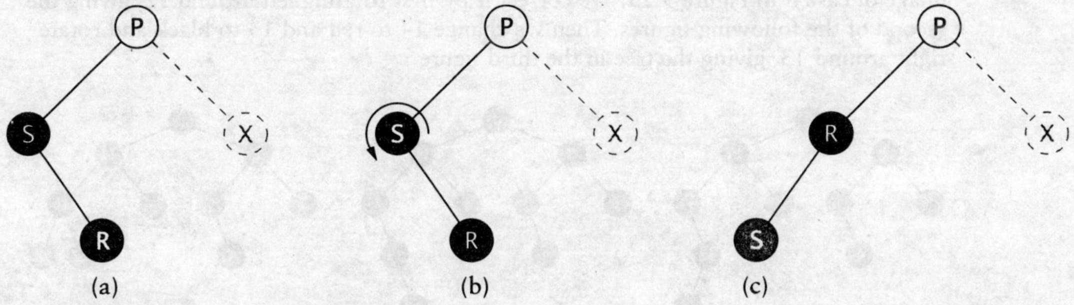

- **Case 4:** The sibling of X (designated S in Figure 9.78(a)) is black, and it has a red left child (L). S is the root of a Red-Black subtree whose black height is balanced and is 1 greater than the black height of X. We change the color of L to black. (If we got here from Case 3, the red-red problem is now fixed.) This increases the black height of L. We also change S to be the same color as P, and then we change the color of P to black (Figure 9.78(b)). By rotating right about P, we restore the black balance (Figure 9.78(c)).

FIGURE 9.78
Red-Black Removal Case 4

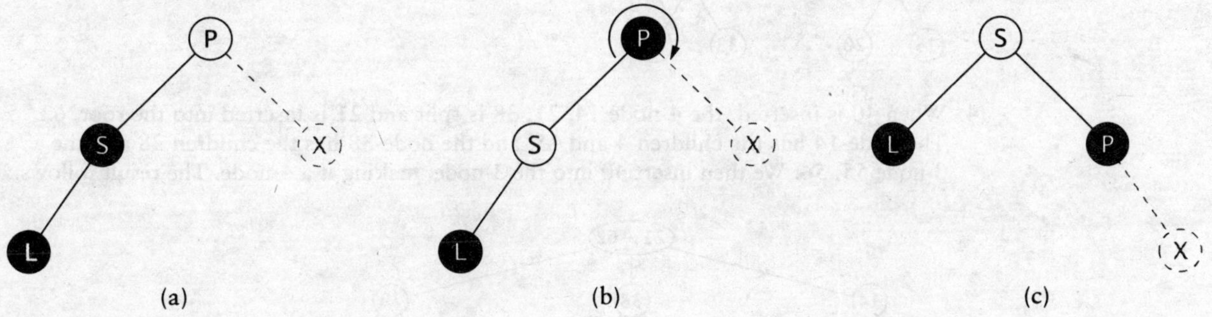

Answers to Quick-Check Exercises

1. When *mouse* is inserted (to the right of *morn*), node *morn* has a balance of +1, and node *priest* has a balance of –2. This is a case of Left-Right imbalance. Rotate left around *morn* and right around *priest*. Node *mouse* will have *morn* (*priest*) as its left (right) subtree.

2. When we insert 12 as a red node, it has a black parent, so we are done. When we insert 13, we have the situation shown in the first of the following figures. This is the mirror image of case 3 in Figure 9.25. We correct it by first rotating left around 12, giving the second of the following figures. Then we change 14 to red and 13 to black and rotate right around 13, giving the tree in the third figure.

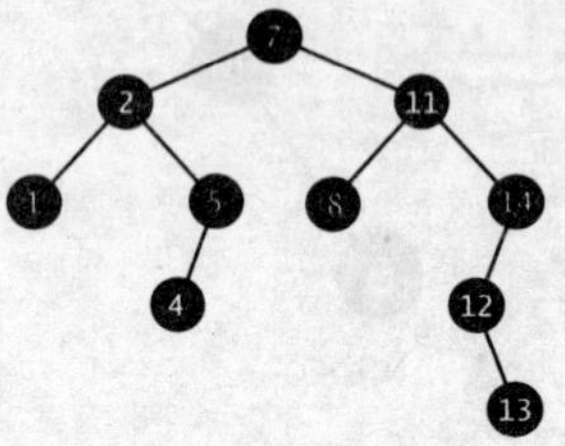

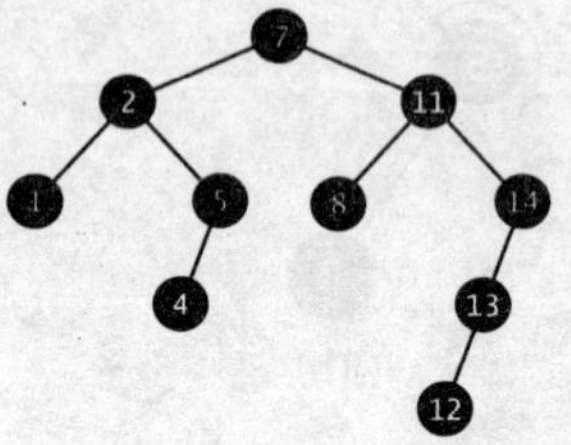

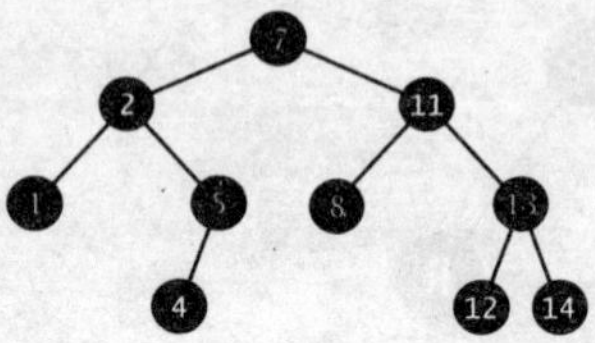

3. The 2-3 tree after inserting 45 is as follows.

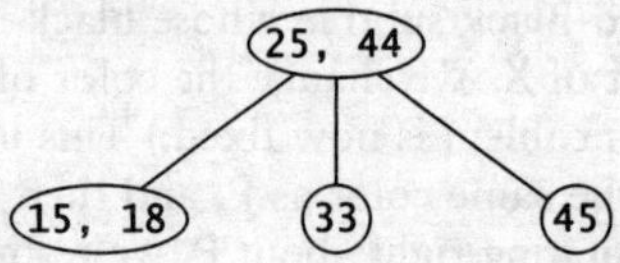

The 2-3 tree after inserting 20 is as follows.

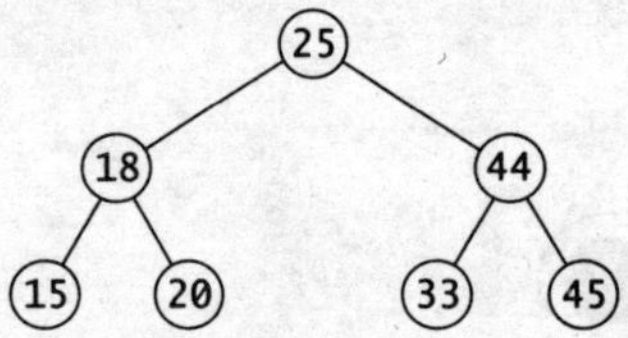

4. When 40 is inserted, the 4-node 14, 21, 38 is split and 21 is inserted into the root, 62. The node-14 has the children 4 and 15, and the node-38 has the children 28 and the 3-node 55, 56. We then insert 40 into the 3-node, making it a 4-node. The result follows.

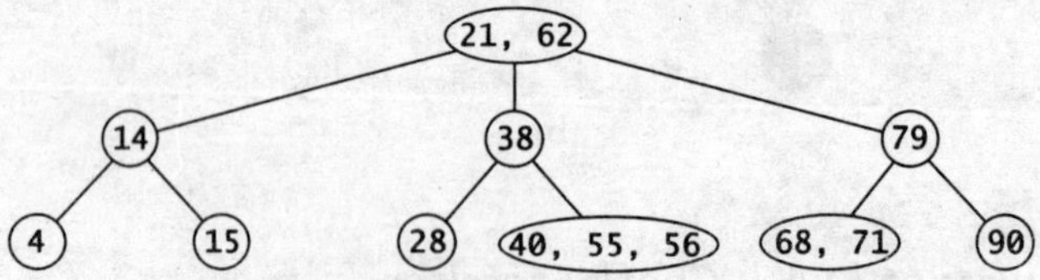

When we insert 50, the 4-node 40, 55, 56 is split and the 55 is inserted into the 2-node 38. Then 50 is inserted into the resulting 2-node, 40, making it a 3-node, as follows.

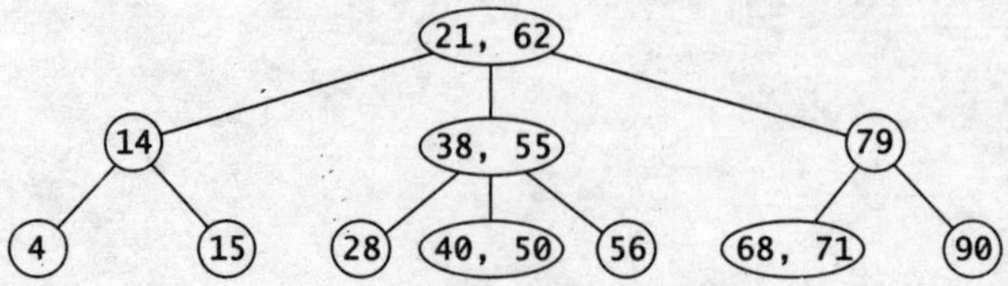

5. The equivalent Red-Black tree follows.

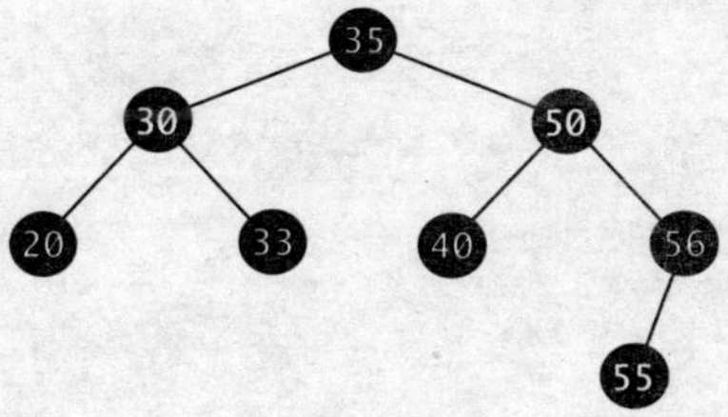

6. The equivalent 2-3-4 tree follows.

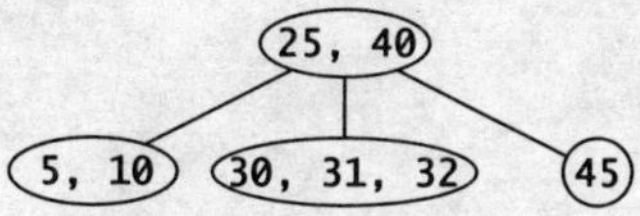

7. Insert 45 in a leaf.

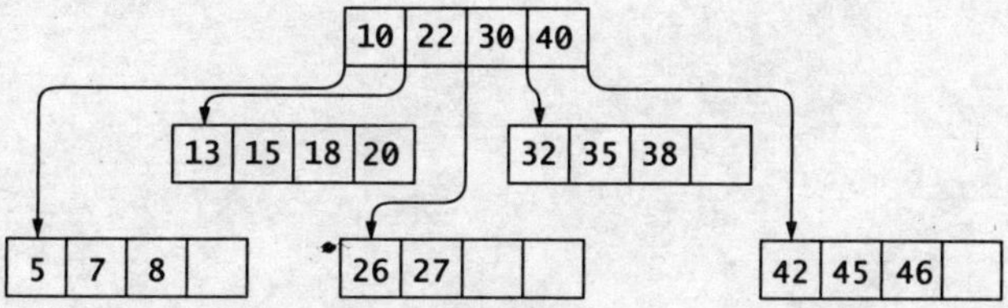

To insert 21, we need to split node {13, 15, 18, 20} and pass 18 up. Then we split the root and pass 22 up to the new root.

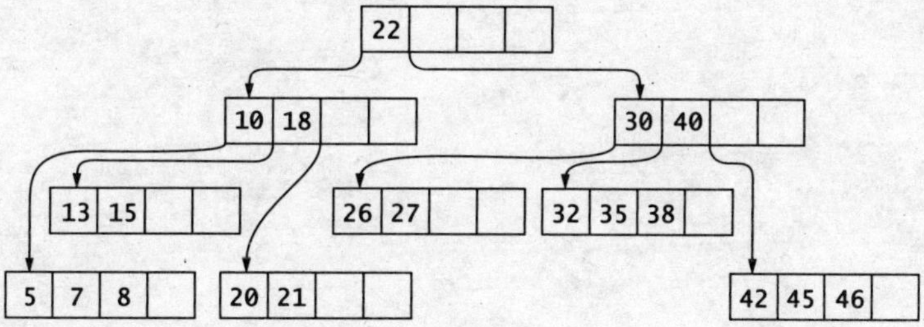

Chapter 10

Graphs

Chapter Objectives

- To become familiar with graph terminology and the different types of graphs
- To study a Graph ADT and different implementations of the Graph ADT
- To learn the breadth-first and depth-first search traversal algorithms
- To learn some algorithms involving weighted graphs
- To study some applications of graphs and graph algorithms

One of the limitations of trees is that they cannot represent information structures in which a data item has more than one parent. In this chapter we introduce a data structure known as a *graph* that will allow us to overcome this limitation.

Graphs and graph algorithms were being studied long before computers were invented. The advent of the computer made the application of graph algorithms to real-world problems possible. Graphs are especially useful in analyzing networks. Thus it is not surprising that much of modern graph theory and application was developed at Bell Laboratories, which needed to analyze the very large communications network that is the telephone system. Graph algorithms are also incorporated into the software that makes the Internet function. You can also use graphs to describe a road map, airline routes, or course prerequisites. Computer chip designers use graph algorithms to determine the optimal placement of components on a silicon chip.

You will learn how to represent a graph, determine the shortest path through a graph, and find the minimum subset of a graph.

Graphs

10.1 Graph Terminology

A graph is a data structure that consists of a set of *vertices* (or nodes) and a set of *edges* (relations) between the pairs of vertices. The edges represent paths or connections between the vertices. Both the set of vertices and the set of edges must be finite, and either set may be empty. If the set of vertices is empty, naturally the set of edges must also be empty. We restrict our discussion to simple graphs in which there is at most one edge from a given vertex to another vertex.

EXAMPLE 10.1 The following set of vertices, *V*, and set of edges, *E*, define a graph that has five vertices, with labels A through E, and four edges.

$V = \{A, B, C, D, E\}$

$E = \{\{A, B\}, \{A, D\}, \{C, E\}, \{D, E\}\}$

Each edge is a set of two vertices. There is an edge between A and B (the edge {A, B}), between A and D, between C and E, and between D and E. If there is an edge between any pair of vertices x, y, this means there is a path from vertex x to vertex y and vice versa. We discuss the significance of this shortly.

Visual Representation of Graphs

Visually we represent vertices as points or labeled circles and the edges as lines joining the vertices. Figure 10.1 shows the graph from Example 10.1.

There are many ways to draw any given graph. The physical layout of the vertices, and even their labeling, are not relevant. Figure 10.2 shows two ways to draw the same graph.

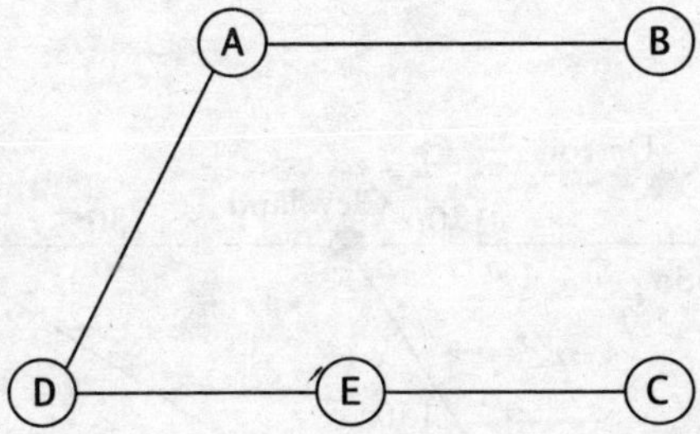

FIGURE 10.1
Graph Given in Example 10.1

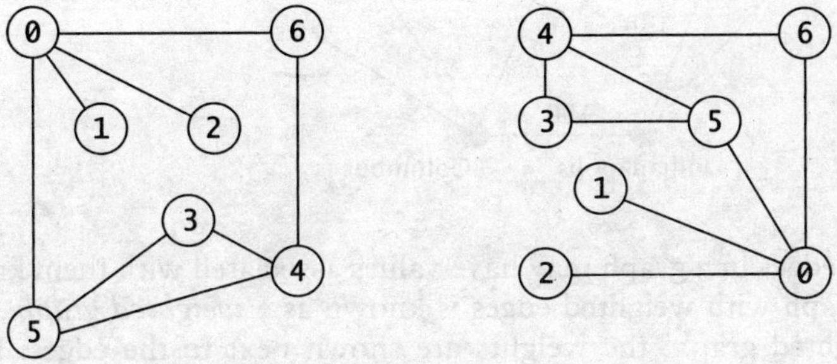

FIGURE 10.2
Two Representations of the Same Graph

Directed and Undirected Graphs

The edges of a graph are *directed* if the existence of an edge from A to B does not necessarily guarantee that there is a path in both directions. A graph that contains directed edges is known as a *directed graph* or *digraph,* and a graph that contains undirected edges is known as an *undirected graph* or simply a graph. A directed edge is like a one-way street; you can travel on it in only one direction. Directed edges are represented as lines with an arrow on one end, whereas undirected edges are represented as single lines. The graph in Figure 10.1 is undirected; Figure 10.3 shows a directed graph. The set of edges for the directed graph follows:

$$E = \{(A, B), (B, A), (B, E), (D, A), (E, A), (E, C), (E, D)\}$$

Each edge above is an ordered pair of vertices instead of a set as in an undirected graph. The edge (A, B) means there is a path from A to B. Observe that there is a path from both A to B and from B to A, but these are the only two vertices in which there is an edge in both directions. Our convention will be to denote an edge for a directed graph as an ordered pair (u, v) where this notation means that v (the destination) is adjacent to u (the source). We denote an edge in an undirected graph as the set $\{u, v\}$, which means that u is adjacent to v and v is adjacent to u. Therefore, you can create a directed graph that is equivalent to an undirected graph by substituting for each edge $\{u, v\}$ the ordered pairs (u, v) and (v, u). In general, when we describe graph algorithms in this chapter, we will use the ordered pair notation (u, v) for an edge.

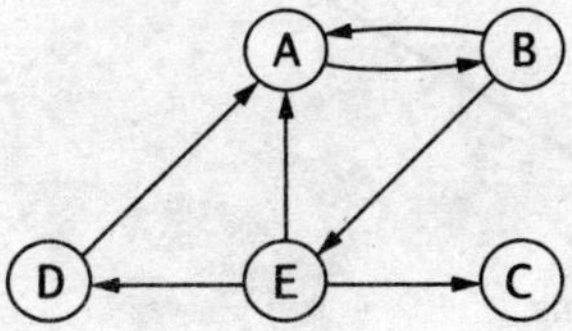

FIGURE 10.3
Example of a Directed Graph

FIGURE 10.4
Example of a Weighted Graph

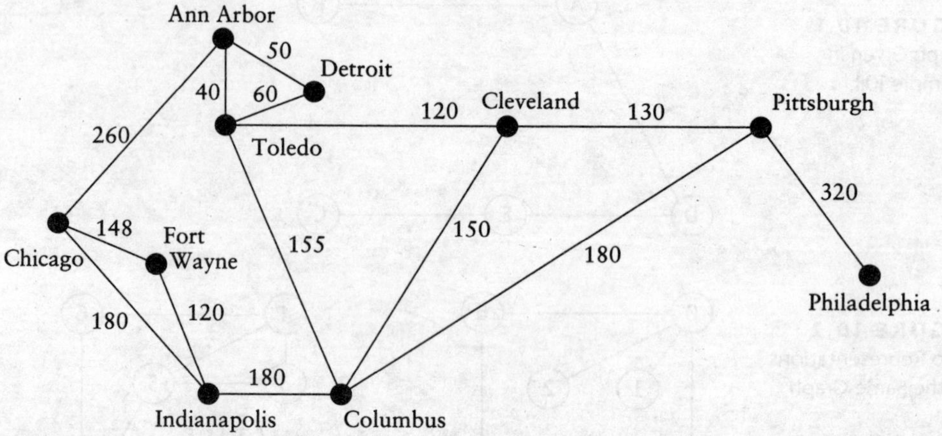

The edges in a graph may have values associated with them known as their *weights*. A graph with weighted edges is known as a *weighted graph*. In an illustration of a weighted graph, the weights are shown next to the edges. Figure 10.4 shows an example of a weighted graph. Each weight is the distance between the two cities (vertices) connected by the edge. Generally the weights are nonnegative, but there are graph problems and graph algorithms that deal with negative weighted edges.

Paths and Cycles

One reason we study graphs is to find pathways between vertices. We use the following definitions to describe pathways between vertices.

- A vertex is *adjacent* to another vertex if there is an edge to it from that other vertex. In Figure 10.4, Philadelphia is adjacent to Pittsburgh. In Figure 10.3, A is adjacent to D, but since this is a directed graph, D is not adjacent to A.
- A *path* is a sequence of vertices in which each successive vertex is adjacent to its predecessor. In Figure 10.5, the following sequence of vertices is a path: Philadelphia → Pittsburgh → Columbus → Indianapolis → Chicago.

FIGURE 10.5
A Simple Path

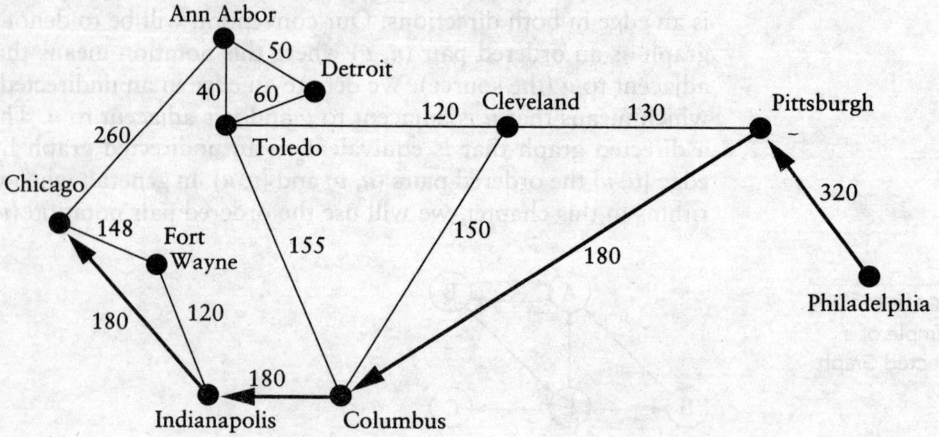

- In a *simple path*, the vertices and edges are distinct, except that the first and last vertex may be the same. In Figure 10.5, the path Philadelphia → Pittsburgh → Columbus → Indianapolis → Chicago is a simple path. The path Philadelphia → Pittsburgh → Columbus → Indianapolis → Chicago → Fort Wayne → Indianapolis is a path but not a simple path. (See Figure 10.6)

FIGURE 10.6
Not a Simple Path

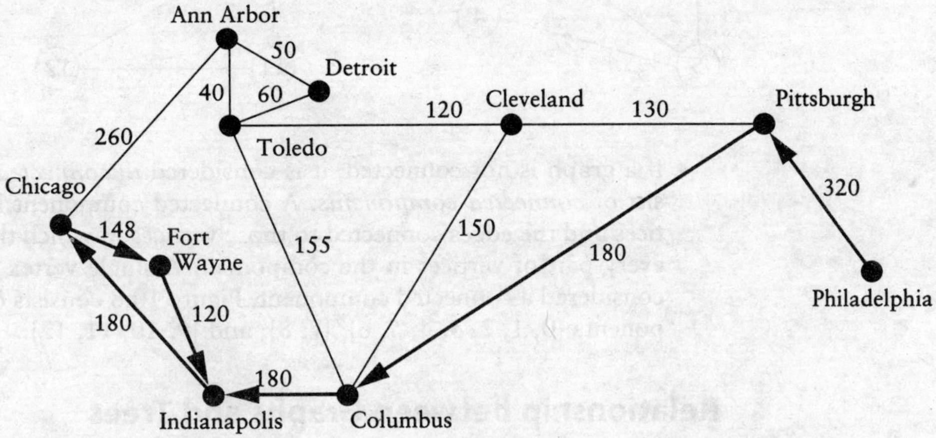

- A *cycle* is a simple path in which only the first and final vertices are the same. In Figure 10.7, the path Pittsburgh → Columbus → Toledo → Cleveland → Pittsburgh is a cycle. For an undirected graph, a cycle must contain at least three distinct vertices. Thus Pittsburgh → Columbus → Pittsburgh is not considered a cycle.

FIGURE 10.7
A Cycle

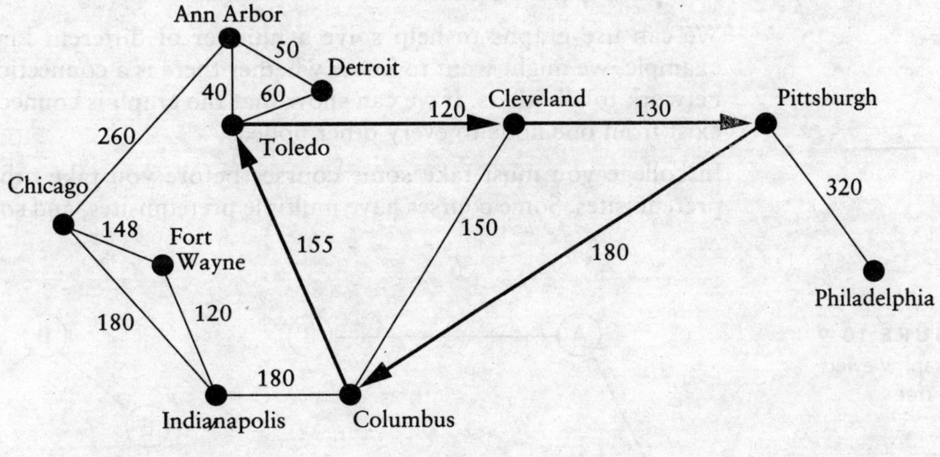

- An undirected graph is called a *connected graph* if there is a path from every vertex to every other vertex. Figure 10.7 is a connected graph, whereas Figure 10.8 is not.

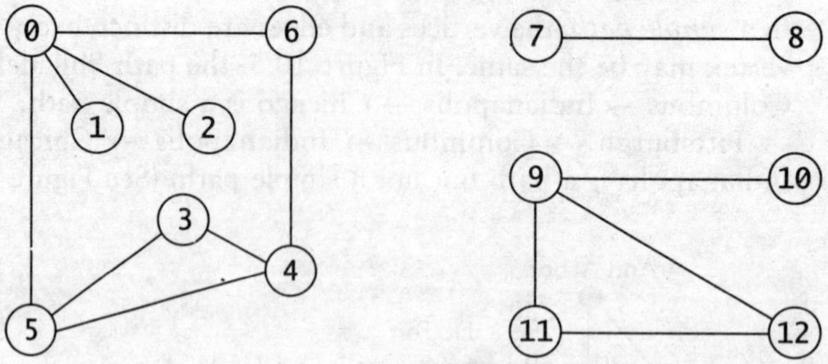

FIGURE 10.8
Example of an Unconnected Graph

- If a graph is not connected, it is considered *unconnected,* but it will still consist of *connected components.* A connected component is a subset of the vertices and the edges connected to those vertices in which there is a path between every pair of vertices in the component. A single vertex with no edges is also considered a connected component. Figure 10.8 consists of the connected components {0, 1, 2, 3, 4, 5, 6}, {7, 8}, and {9, 10, 11, 12}.

Relationship between Graphs and Trees

The graph is the most general of the data structures we have studied. It allows for any conceivable relationship among the data elements (the vertices). A tree is actually a special case of a graph. Any graph that is connected and contains no cycles can be viewed as a tree by picking one of its vertices (nodes) as the root. For example, the graph shown in Figure 10.1 can be viewed as a tree if we consider the node labeled *D* to be the root. (See Figure 10.9.)

Graph Applications

We can use graphs to help solve a number of different kinds of problems. For example, we might want to know whether there is a connection from one node in a network to all others. If we can show that the graph is connected, then a path must exist from one node to every other node.

In college you must take some courses before you take others. These are called prerequisites. Some courses have multiple prerequisites, and some prerequisites have

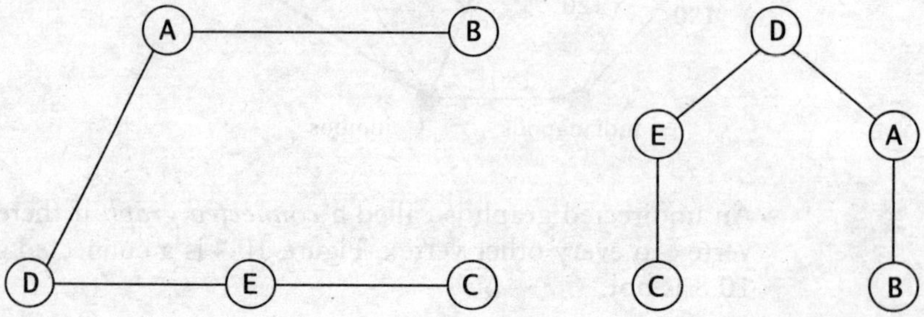

FIGURE 10.9
A Graph Viewed as a Tree

prerequisites of their own. It can be quite confusing. You may even feel that there is a loop in the maze of prerequisites and that it is impossible to schedule your classes to meet the prerequisites. We can represent the set of prerequisites by a directed graph. If the graph has no cycles, then we can find a solution. We can also find the cycles.

Another application would be finding the least-cost path or shortest path from each vertex to all other vertices in a weighted graph. For example, in Figure 10.4, we might want to find the shortest path from Philadelphia to Chicago. Or we might want to create a table showing the distance (miles in the shortest route) between each pair of cities.

EXERCISES FOR SECTION 10.1

SELF-CHECK

1. In the graph shown in Figure 10.1, what vertices are adjacent to D? In Figure 10.3?
2. In Figure 10.3, is it possible to get from A to all other vertices? How about from C?
3. In Figure 10.4, what is the shortest path from Philadelphia to Chicago?

10.2 The Graph ADT and Edge Class

Java does not provide a Graph ADT, so we have the freedom to design our own. To write programs for the applications mentioned at the end of the previous section, we need to be able to navigate through a graph or traverse it (visit all its vertices). To accomplish this, we need to be able to advance from one vertex in a graph to all its adjacent vertices. Therefore, we need to be able to do the following:

1. Create a graph with the specified number of vertices.
2. Iterate through all of the vertices in the graph.
3. Iterate through the vertices that are adjacent to a specified vertex.
4. Determine whether an edge exists between two vertices.
5. Determine the weight of an edge between two vertices.
6. Insert an edge into the graph.

With the exception of item 1, we can specify these requirements in a Java interface. Since a Java interface cannot include a constructor, the requirements for item 1 can only be specified in the comment at the beginning of the interface.

Listing 10.1 gives the declaration of the `Graph` interface.

LISTING 10.1
Graph.java

```
import java.util.*;

/** Interface to specify a Graph ADT. A graph is a set
    of vertices and a set of edges. Vertices are
    represented by integers from 0 to n - 1. Edges
    are ordered pairs of vertices. Each implementation
    of the Graph interface should provide a constructor
    that specifies the number of vertices and whether
    or not the graph is directed.
*/
public interface Graph {

    // Accessor Methods
    /** Return the number of vertices.
        @return The number of vertices
    */
    int getNumV();

    /** Determine whether this is a directed graph.
        @return true if this is a directed graph
    */
    boolean isDirected();

    /** Insert a new edge into the graph.
        @param edge The new edge
    */
    void insert(Edge edge);

    /** Determine whether an edge exists.
        @param source The source vertex
        @param dest The destination vertex
        @return true if there is an edge from source to dest
    */
    boolean isEdge(int source, int dest);

    /** Get the edge between two vertices.
        @param source The source vertex
        @param dest The destination vertex
        @return The Edge between these two vertices
                or an Edge with a weight of
                Double.POSITIVE_INFINITY if there is no edge
    */
    Edge getEdge(int source, int dest);

    /** Return an iterator to the edges connected
        to a given vertex.
        @param source The source vertex
        @return An Iterator<Edge> to the vertices
                connected to source
    */
    Iterator<Edge> edgeIterator(int source);
}
```

TABLE 10.1
The Edge Class

Data Field	Attribute
`private int dest`	The destination vertex for an edge.
`private int source`	The source vertex for an edge.
`private double weight`	The weight.
Constructor	**Purpose**
`public Edge(int source, int dest)`	Constructs an `Edge` from `source` to `dest`. Sets the `weight` to 1.0.
`public Edge(int source, int dest, double w)`	Constructs an `Edge` from `source` to `dest`. Sets the `weight` to `w`.
Method	**Behavior**
`public boolean equals(Object o)`	Compares two edges for equality. Edges are equal if their source and destination vertices are the same. The weight is not considered.
`public int getDest()`	Returns the destination vertex.
`public int getSource()`	Returns the source vertex.
`public double getWeight()`	Returns the weight.
`public int hashCode()`	Returns the hash code for an edge. The hash code depends only on the source and destination.
`public String toString()`	Returns a string representation of the edge.

Representing Vertices and Edges

Before we can implement this interface, we must decide how to represent the vertices and edges of a graph. We can represent the vertices by integers from 0 up to, but not including, $|V|$. ($|V|$ means the *cardinality of V*, or the number of vertices in set V.) For edges we will define the class `Edge` that will contain the source vertex, the destination vertex, and the weight. For unweighted edges we will use the default value of 1.0. Table 10.1 shows the `Edge` class. Observe that an `Edge` is directed. For undirected graphs we will always have two `Edge` objects: one in each direction for each pair of vertices that has an edge between them. A vertex is represented by a type `int` variable.

EXERCISES FOR SECTION 10.2

SELF-CHECK

1. Use the constructors in Table 10.1 to create the `Edge` objects connecting vertices 9 through 12 for the graph in Figure 10.8.

PROGRAMMING

1. Implement the `Edge` class.

10.3 Implementing the Graph ADT

Because graph algorithms have been studied and implemented throughout the history of computer science, many of the original publications of graph algorithms and their implementations did not use an object-oriented approach and did not even use abstract data types. The implementation of the graph was done in terms of fundamental data structures that were used directly in the algorithm. Different algorithms would use different representations.

Two representations of graphs are most common:

- Edges are represented by an array of lists called *adjacency lists,* where each list stores the vertices adjacent to a particular vertex.
- Edges are represented by a two-dimensional array, called an *adjacency matrix,* with $|V|$ rows and $|V|$ columns.

Adjacency List

An adjacency list representation of a graph uses an array of lists. There is one list for each vertex. Figure 10.10 shows an adjacency list representation of a directed graph. The list referenced by array element 0 shows the vertices (1 and 3) that are adjacent to vertex 0. The vertices are in no particular order. For simplicity, we are showing just the destination vertex as the value field in each node of the adjacency list, but in the actual implementation the entire `Edge` will be stored. Instead of storing `value = 1` (the destination vertex) in the first vertex adjacent to 0, we will store a reference to the `Edge (0, 1, 1.0)` where `0` is the source, `1` is the destination, and `1.0` is the weight. The `Edge` must be stored (not just the destination) because weighted graphs can have different values for weights.

For an undirected graph (or simply a "graph"), symmetric entries are required. Thus, if $\{u, v\}$ is an edge, then v will appear on the adjacency list for u and u will appear on the adjacency list for v. Figure 10.11 shows the adjacency list representation for an undirected graph. The actual lists will store references to `Edges`.

Adjacency Matrix

The adjacency matrix uses a two-dimensional array to represent the graph. For an unweighted graph the entries in this matrix can be **`boolean`** values, where **`true`** represents the presence of an edge and **`false`** its absence. Another popular method is to use the value 1 for an edge and 0 for no edge. The integer coding has benefits over the **`boolean`** approach for some graph algorithms that use matrix multiplication.

FIGURE 10.10
Adjacency List Representation of a Directed Graph

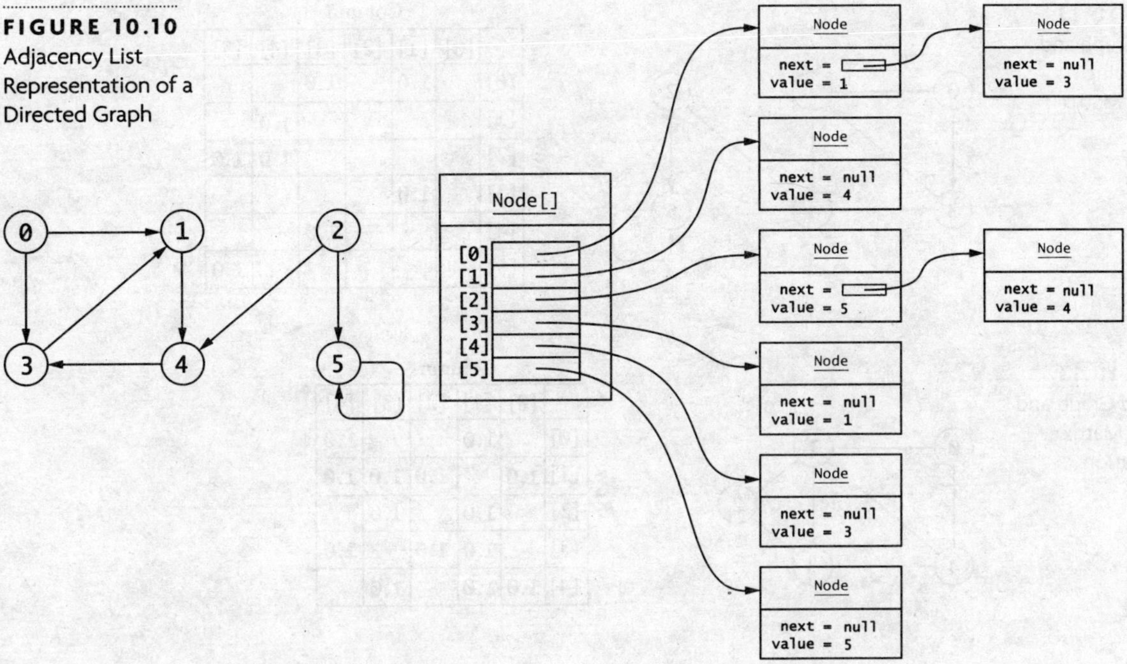

FIGURE 10.11
Adjacency List Representation of an Undirected Graph

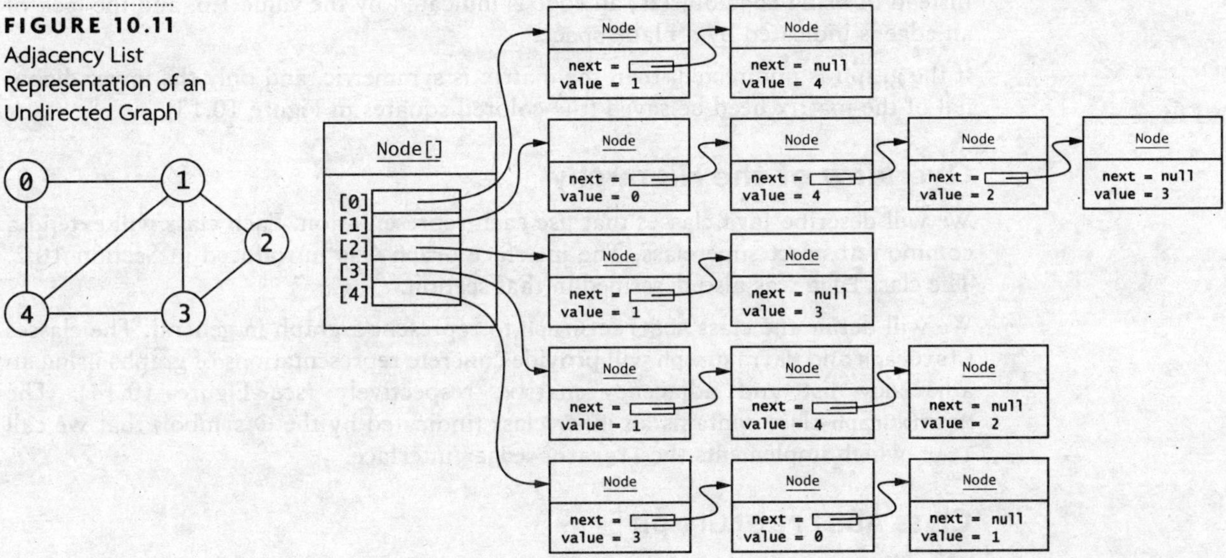

For a weighted graph the matrix would contain the weights. Since 0 is a valid weight, we will use `Double.POSITIVE_INFINITY` (a special **`double`** value in Java that approximates the mathematical behavior of infinity) to indicate the absence of an edge, and in an unweighted graph we will use a weight of 1.0 to indicate the presence of an edge.

FIGURE 10.12
Directed Graph and Corresponding Adjacency Matrix

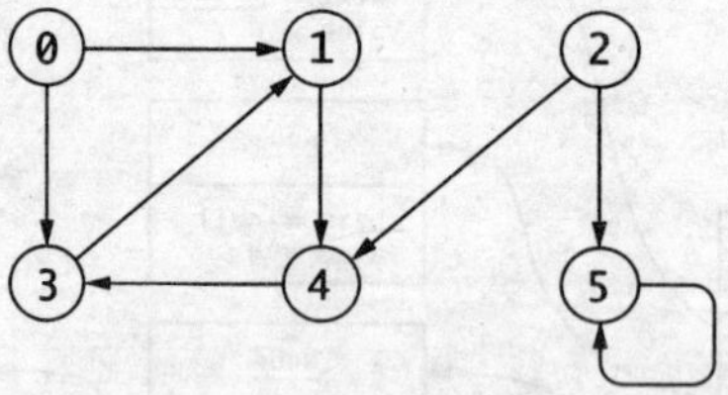

Column

Row	[0]	[1]	[2]	[3]	[4]	[5]
[0]		1.0		1.0		
[1]					1.0	
[2]					1.0	1.0
[3]		1.0				
[4]				1.0		
[5]						1.0

FIGURE 10.13
Undirected Graph and Adjacency Matrix Representation

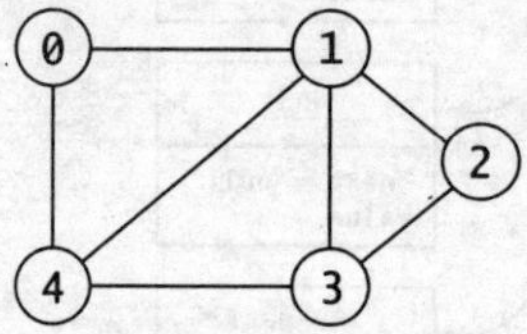

Column

Row	[0]	[1]	[2]	[3]	[4]
[0]		1.0			1.0
[1]	1.0		1.0	1.0	1.0
[2]		1.0		1.0	
[3]		1.0	1.0		1.0
[4]	1.0	1.0		1.0	

Figure 10.12 shows a directed graph and the corresponding adjacency matrix. Instead of using `Edge` objects, an edge is indicated by the value 1.0, and the lack of an edge is indicated by a blank space.

If the graph is undirected, then the matrix is symmetric, and only the lower diagonal of the matrix need be saved (the colored squares in Figure 10.13).

Overview of the Hierarchy

We will describe Java classes that use each representation. Each class will extend a common abstract superclass. The interface `Graph` was introduced in Section 10.2. The class `Edge` was also described in that section.

We will define the class `AbstractGraph` to represent a graph in general. The classes `ListGraph` and `MatrixGraph` will provide concrete representations of graphs using an adjacency list and adjacency matrix, respectively (see Figure 10.14). The `MatrixGraph` class contains an inner class (indicated by the ⊕ symbol) that we call `Iter`, which implements the `Iterator<Edge>` interface.

Class `AbstractGraph`

We will use an abstract class, `AbstractGraph`, as the common superclass for graph implementations. This will enable us to implement some of the methods for the `Graph` interface in the abstract superclass and leave other methods that are implementation specific to its subclasses. Graph algorithms will be designed to work on objects that meet the requirements defined by this abstract class. This class is

FIGURE 10.14
UML Class Diagram of Graph Class Hierarchy

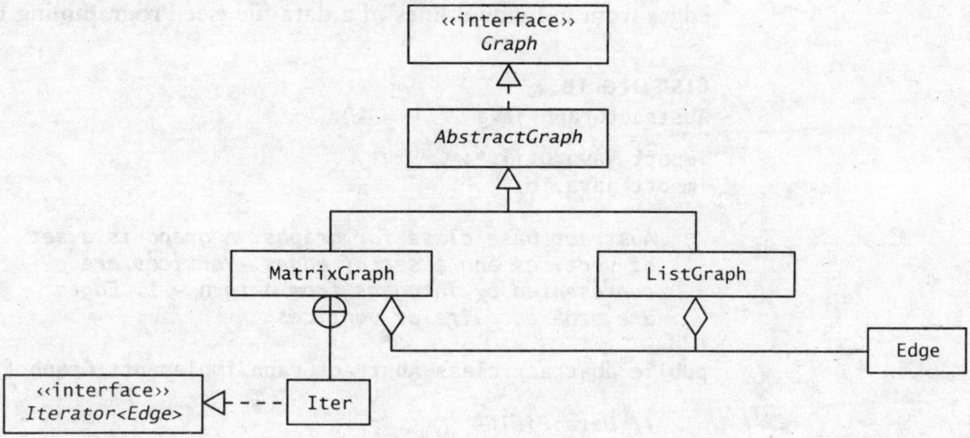

summarized in Table 10.2. Note that the methods `edgeIterator`, `getEdge`, `insert`, and `isEdge`, which are required by the `Graph` interface (see Listing 10.1), are implicitly declared abstract and must be declared in the concrete subclasses.

TABLE 10.2
The Abstract Class `AbstractGraph`

Data Field	Attribute
`private boolean directed`	**`true`** if this is a directed graph.
`private int numV`	The number of vertices.
Constructor	**Purpose**
`public AbstractGraph(int numV, boolean directed)`	Constructs an empty graph with the specified number of vertices and with the specified `directed` flag. If `directed` is **`true`**, this is a directed graph.
Method	**Behavior**
`public int getNumV()`	Gets the number of vertices.
`public boolean isDirected()`	Returns **`true`** if the graph is a directed graph.
`public void loadEdgesFromFile(Scanner scan)`	Loads edges from a data file.
`public static Graph createGraph (Scanner scan, boolean isDirected, String type)`	Factory method to create a graph and load the data from an input file.

Implementation

The implementation is shown in Listing 10.2. Method `loadEdgesFromFile` reads edges from individual lines of a data file (see Programming Exercise 1).

LISTING 10.2

AbstractGraph.java

```
import java.util.*;
import java.io.*;

/** Abstract base class for graphs. A graph is a set
    of vertices and a set of edges. Vertices are
    represented by integers from 0 to n - 1. Edges
    are ordered pairs of vertices.
*/
public abstract class AbstractGraph implements Graph {

    // Data Fields
    /** The number of vertices */
    private int numV;
    /** Flag to indicate whether this is a directed graph */
    private boolean directed;

    // Constructor
    /** Construct a graph with the specified number of vertices
        and the directed flag. If the directed flag is true,
        this is a directed graph.
        @param numV The number of vertices
        @param directed The directed flag
    */
    public AbstractGraph(int numV, boolean directed) {
        this.numV = numV;
        this.directed = directed;
    }

    // Accessor Methods
    /** Return the number of vertices.
        @return The number of vertices
    */
    public int getNumV() {
        return numV;
    }

    /** Return whether this is a directed graph.
        @return true if this is a directed graph
    */
    public boolean isDirected() {
        return directed;
    }
```

```
    // Other Methods
    /** Load the edges of a graph from the data in an input file.
        The file should contain a series of lines, each line
        with two or three data values. The first is the source,
        the second is the destination, and the optional third
        is the weight.
        @param scan The Scanner connected to the data file
    */
    public void loadEdgesFromFile(Scanner scan)
        // Programming Exercise 1
    }

    /** Factory method to create a graph and load the data from an input
        file. The first line of the input file should contain the number
        of vertices. The remaining lines should contain the edge data as
        described under loadEdgesFromFile.
        @param scan The Scanner connected to the data file
        @param isDirected true if this is a directed graph,
                          false otherwise
        @param type The string "Matrix" if an adjacency matrix is to be
                    created, and the string "List" if an adjacency list
                    is to be created
        @throws IllegalArgumentException if type is neither "Matrix"
                                         nor "List"
    */
    public static Graph createGraph(Scanner scan,
                                    boolean isDirected,
                                    String type) {
        int numV = scan.nextInt();
        AbstractGraph returnValue = null;
        if (type.equalsIgnoreCase("Matrix"))
            returnValue = new MatrixGraph(numV, isDirected);
        else if (type.equalsIgnoreCase("List"))
            returnValue = new ListGraph(numV, isDirected);
        else
            throw new IllegalArgumentException();
        returnValue.loadEdgesFromFile(scan);
        return returnValue;
    }
}
```

The ListGraph Class

The ListGraph class extends the AbstractGraph class by providing an internal representation using an array of lists. Table 10.3 describes the ListGraph class.

TABLE 10.3
The `ListGraph` Class

Data Field	Attribute
`private List<Edge>[] edges`	An array of `List`s to contain the edges that originate with each vertex.
Constructor	**Purpose**
`public ListGraph(int numV, boolean directed)`	Constructs a graph with the specified number of vertices and directionality.
Method	**Behavior**
`public Iterator<Edge> edgeIterator(int source)`	Returns an iterator to the edges that originate from a given vertex.
`public Edge getEdge(int source, int dest)`	Gets the edge between two vertices.
`public void insert(Edge e)`	Inserts a new edge into the graph.
`public boolean isEdge(int source, int dest)`	Determines whether an edge exists from vertex **source** to **dest**.

The Data Fields

The class begins as follows:

```
import java.util.*;

/** A ListGraph is an extension of the AbstractGraph abstract class
    that uses an array of lists to represent the edges.
*/
public class ListGraph extends AbstractGraph {

    // Data Field
    /** An array of Lists to contain the edges that
        originate with each vertex. */
    private List<Edge>[] edges;
. . .
```

The Constructor

The constructor allocates an array of `LinkedList`s, one for each vertex.

```
/** Construct a graph with the specified number of
    vertices and directionality.
    @param numV The number of vertices
    @param directed The directionality flag
*/
public ListGraph(int numV, boolean directed) {
    super(numV, directed);
    edges = new List[numV];
    for (int i = 0; i < numV; i++) {
        edges[i] = new LinkedList<Edge>();
    }
}
```

The isEdge Method

Method isEdge determines whether an edge exists by searching the list associated with the source vertex for an entry. This is done by calling the contains method for the List.

```
/** Determine whether an edge exists.
    @param source The source vertex
    @param dest The destination vertex
    @return true if there is an edge from source to dest
*/
public boolean isEdge(int source, int dest) {
    return edges[source].contains(new Edge(source, dest));
}
```

Observe that we had to create a dummy Edge object for the contains method to search for. The Edge.equals method does not check the edge weights, so the weight parameter is not needed.

The insert Method

The insert method inserts a new edge (source, destination, weight) into the graph by adding that edge's data to the list of adjacent vertices for that edge's source. If the graph is not directed, it adds a new edge in the opposite direction (destination, source, weight) to the list of adjacent vertices for that edge's destination.

```
/** Insert a new edge into the graph.
    @param edge The new edge
*/
public void insert(Edge edge) {
    edges[edge.getSource()].add(edge);
    if (!isDirected()) {
        edges[edge.getDest()].add(new Edge(edge.getDest(),
                                           edge.getSource(),
                                           edge.getWeight()));

    }
}
```

The edgeIterator Method

The edgeIterator method will return an Iterator<Edge> object that can be used to iterate through the edges adjacent to a given vertex. Because each LinkedList entry in the array edges is a List<Edge>, its iterator method will provide the desired object. Thus, the edgeIterator merely calls the corresponding iterator method for the specified vertex.

```
public Iterator<Edge> edgeIterator(int source) {
    return edges[source].iterator();
}
```

The getEdge Method

Similar to the isEdge method, the getEdge method also requires a search. However, we need to program the search directly. We will use the enhanced **for** statement to access all edges in the list for vertex source. We compare each edge to a target object with source and destination set to the method arguments. The equals method does not compare edge weights, only the vertices.

```
/** Get the edge between two vertices. If an
    edge does not exist, an Edge with a weight
    of Double.POSITIVE_INFINITY is returned.
    @param source The source
    @param dest The destination
    @return the edge between these two vertices
*/
public Edge getEdge(int source, int dest) {
    Edge target =
        new Edge(source, dest, Double.POSITIVE_INFINITY);
    for (Edge edge : edges[source]) {
        if (edge.equals(target))
            return edge;  // Desired edge found, return it.
    }
    // Assert: All edges for source checked.
    return target;    // Desired edge not found.
}
```

The MatrixGraph Class

The `MatrixGraph` class extends the `AbstractGraph` class by providing an internal representation using a two-dimensional array for storing the edge weights

```
double[][] edges;
```

When a new `MatrixGraph` object is created, the constructor sets the number of rows (vertices) in this array. It implements the same methods as class `ListGraph` and also has an inner iterator class `Iter`. It needs its own iterator class because there is no `Iterator` class associated with an array. The implementation is left as a project (Programming Project 1).

Comparing Implementations

Time Efficiency

The two implementations present a trade-off. Which is best depends on the algorithm and the density of the graph. The density of a graph is the ratio of $|E|$ to $|V|^2$. A *dense graph* is one in which $|E|$ is close to but less than $|V|^2$, and a *sparse graph* is one in which $|E|$ is much less than $|V|^2$. Therefore, for a dense graph we can assume that $|E|$ is $O(|V|^2)$, and for a sparse graph we can assume that $|E|$ is $O(|V|)$.

Many graph algorithms are of the form:

1. **for** each vertex u in the graph
2. **for** each vertex v adjacent to u
3. Do something with edge (u, v).

For an adjacency list representation, Step 1 is $O(|V|)$ and Step 2 is $O(|E_u|)$, where $|E_u|$ is the number of edges that originate at vertex u. Thus, the combination of Steps 1 and 2 will represent examining each edge in the graph, giving $O(|E|)$. For an adjacency matrix representation, Step 2 is also $O(|V|)$, and thus the overall algorithm is $O(|V|^2)$. Thus, for a sparse graph, the adjacency list gives better performance for this type of algorithm, whereas for a dense graph, the performance is the same for either representation.

Some graph algorithms are of the form

1. **for** each vertex u in some subset of the vertices
2. **for** each vertex v in some subset of the vertices
3. `if` (u, v) is an edge
4. Do something with edge (u, v).

For an adjacency matrix representation, Step 3 tests a matrix value and is O(1), so the overall algorithm is $O(|V|^2)$. However, for an adjacency list representation, Step 3 searches a list and is $O(|E_u|)$, so the combination of Steps 2 and 3 is $O(|E|)$ and the overall algorithm is $O(|V||E|)$. For a dense graph, the adjacency matrix gives the best performance for this type of algorithm, and for a sparse graph, the performance is the same for both representations.

Thus, if a graph is dense, the adjacency matrix representation is best, and if a graph is sparse, the adjacency list representation is best. Intuitively, this makes sense because a sparse graph will lead to a sparse matrix, or one in which most entries are `POSITIVE_INFINITY`. These entries are not included in a list representation, so they will have no effect on processing time. However, they are included in a matrix representation and will have an undesirable impact on processing time.

Storage Efficiency

Notice that storage is allocated for all vertex combinations (or at least half of them) in an adjacency matrix. So the storage required is proportional to $|V|^2$. If the graph is sparse (not many edges), there will be a lot of wasted space in the adjacency matrix. In an adjacency list, only the adjacent edges are stored.

On the other hand, in an adjacency list, each edge is represented by a reference to an `Edge` object containing data about the source, destination, and weight. There is also a reference to the next edge in the list. In a matrix representation, only the weight associated with an edge is stored. So each element in an adjacency list requires approximately four times the storage of an element in an adjacency matrix.

Based on this we can conclude that the break-even point in terms of storage efficiency occurs when approximately 25 percent of the adjacency matrix is filled with meaningful data. That is, the adjacency list uses less (more) storage when less than (more than) 25 percent of the adjacency matrix would be filled.

EXERCISES FOR SECTION 10.3

SELF-CHECK

1. Represent the following graphs using adjacency lists.

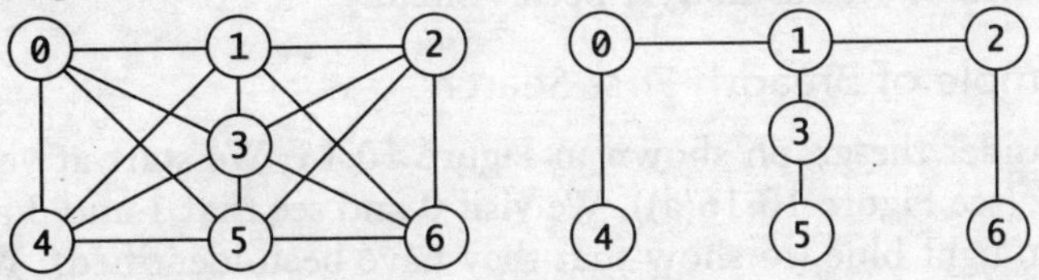

2. Represent the graphs in Exercise 1 above using an adjacency matrix.

3. For each graph in Exercise 1, what are the $|V|$, the $|E|$, and the density? Which representation is best for each graph? Explain your answers.

PROGRAMMING

1. Implement the `loadEdgesFromFile` method for class `AbstractGraph`. If there are two values on a line, an edge with the default weight of 1.0 is inserted; if there are three values, the third value is the weight.

10.4 Traversals of Graphs

Most graph algorithms involve visiting each vertex in a systematic order. Just as with trees, there are different ways to do this. The two most common traversal algorithms are breadth first and depth first. Although these are graph traversals, they are more commonly called *breadth-first* and *depth-first search.*

Breadth-First Search

In a breadth-first search, we visit the start node first, then all nodes that are adjacent to it next, then all nodes that can be reached by a path from the start node containing two edges, three edges, and so on. The requirement for a breadth-first search is that we must visit all nodes for which the shortest path from the start node is length k before we visit any node for which the shortest path from the start node is length $k + 1$. You can visualize a breadth-first traversal by "picking up" the graph at the vertex that is the start node, so the start node will be the highest node and the rest of the nodes will be suspended underneath it, connected by their edges. In a breadth-first search, the nodes that are higher up in the picked-up graph are visited before nodes that are lower in the graph.

Breadth-first search starts at some vertex. Unlike the case of a tree, there is no special start vertex, so we will arbitrarily pick the vertex with label 0. We then visit it by identifying all vertices that are adjacent to the start vertex. Then we visit each of these vertices, identifying all of the vertices adjacent to them. This process continues until all vertices are visited. If the graph is not a connected graph, then the process is repeated with one of the unidentified vertices. In the discussion that follows, we use color to distinguish among three states for a node: identified (light blue), visited (dark blue), and not identified (white). Initially, all nodes are not identified. If a node is in the identified state, that node was encountered while visiting another, but it has not yet been visited.

Example of Breadth-First Search

Consider the graph shown in Figure 10.15. We start at vertex 0 and color it light blue (see Figure 10.16(a)). We visit 0 and see that 1 and 3 are adjacent, so we color them light blue (to show that they have been identified). We are finished visiting 0 and now color it dark blue (see Figure 10.16(b)). So far we have visited node 0.

FIGURE 10.15
Graph to Be Traversed Breadth First

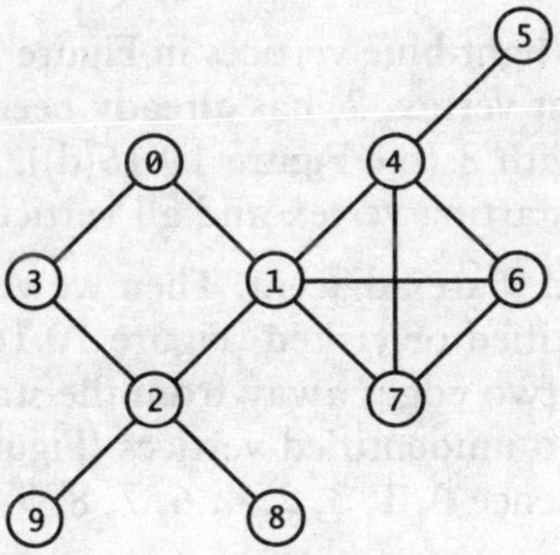

FIGURE 10.16
Example of a Breadth-First Search

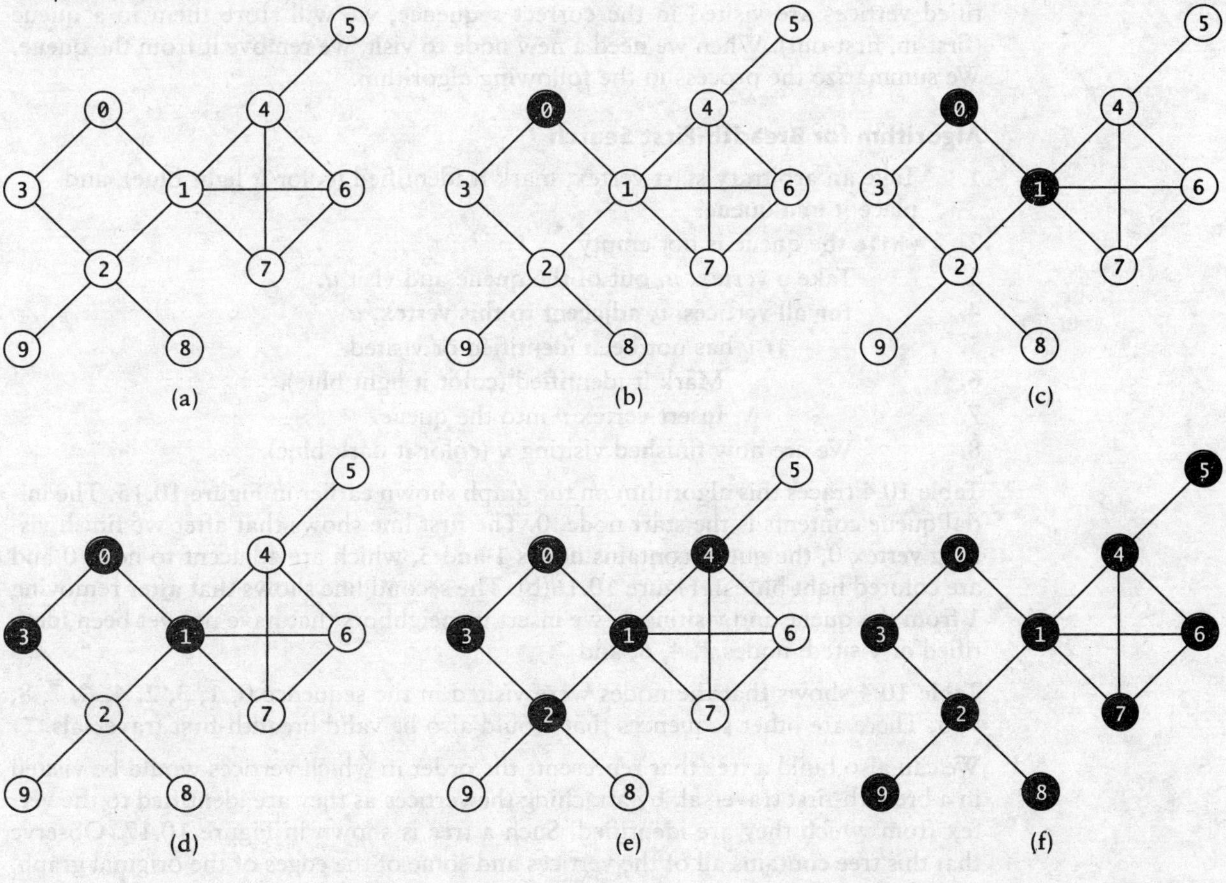

We always select the first node that was identified (light blue) but not yet visited and visit it next. Therefore, we visit 1 and look at its adjacent vertices: 0, 2, 4, 6, and 7. We skip 0 because it is not colored white, and we color the others light blue. Then we color 1 dark blue (see Figure 10.16(c)). Now we have visited nodes 0 and 1.

Then we look at 3 (the first of the light blue vertices in Figure 10.16(c) to have been identified) and see that its adjacent vertex, 2, has already been identified and 0 has been visited, so we are finished with 3 (see Figure 10.16(d)). Now we have visited nodes 0, 1, and 3, which are the starting vertex and all vertices adjacent to it.

Now we visit 2 and see that 8 and 9 are adjacent. Then we visit 4 and see that 5 is the only adjacent vertex not identified or visited (Figure 10.16(e)). Finally, we visit 6 and 7 (the last vertices that are two edges away from the starting vertex), then 8, 9, and 5, and see that there are no unidentified vertices (Figure 10.16(f)). The vertices have been visited in the sequence 0, 1, 3, 2, 4, 6, 7, 8, 9, 5.

Algorithm for Breadth-First Search

To implement breadth-first search, we need to be able to determine the first identified vertex that has not been visited, so that we can visit it. To ensure that the identified vertices are visited in the correct sequence, we will store them in a queue (first-in, first-out). When we need a new node to visit, we remove it from the queue. We summarize the process in the following algorithm.

Algorithm for Breadth-First Search

1. Take an arbitrary start vertex, mark it identified (color it light blue), and place it in a queue.
2. **while** the queue is not empty
3.   Take a vertex, *u*, out of the queue and visit *u*.
4.   **for** all vertices, *v*, adjacent to this vertex, *u*
5.   **if** *v* has not been identified or visited
6.   Mark it identified (color it light blue).
7.   Insert vertex *v* into the queue.
8.   We are now finished visiting *u* (color it dark blue).

Table 10.4 traces this algorithm on the graph shown earlier in Figure 10.15. The initial queue contents is the start node, 0. The first line shows that after we finish visiting vertex 0, the queue contains nodes 1 and 3, which are adjacent to node 0 and are colored light blue in Figure 10.16(b). The second line shows that after removing 1 from the queue and visiting 1, we insert its neighbors that have not yet been identified or visited: nodes 2, 4, 6, and 7.

Table 10.4 shows that the nodes were visited in the sequence 0, 1, 3, 2, 4, 6, 7, 8, 9, 5. There are other sequences that would also be valid breadth-first traversals.

We can also build a tree that represents the order in which vertices would be visited in a breadth-first traversal, by attaching the vertices as they are identified to the vertex from which they are identified. Such a tree is shown in Figure 10.17. Observe that this tree contains all of the vertices and some of the edges of the original graph. A path starting at the root to any vertex in the tree is the shortest path in the original graph from the start vertex to that vertex, where we consider all edges to have the same weight. Therefore, the *shortest path* is the one that goes through the smallest number of vertices. We can save the information we need to represent this tree by storing the parent of each vertex when we identify it (Step 7 of the breadth-first algorithm).

TABLE 10.4
Trace of Breadth-First Search of Graph in Figure 10.15

Vertex Being Visited	Queue Contents after Visit	Visit Sequence
0	1 3	0
1	3 2 4 6 7	0 1
3	2 4 6 7	0 1 3
2	4 6 7 8 9	0 1 3 2
4	6 7 8 9 5	0 1 3 2 4
6	7 8 9 5	0 1 3 2 4 6
7	8 9 5	0 1 3 2 4 6 7
8	9 5	0 1 3 2 4 6 7 8
9	5	0 1 3 2 4 6 7 8 9
5	empty	0 1 3 2 4 6 7 8 9 5

FIGURE 10.17
Breadth-First Search Tree of Graph in Figure 10.15

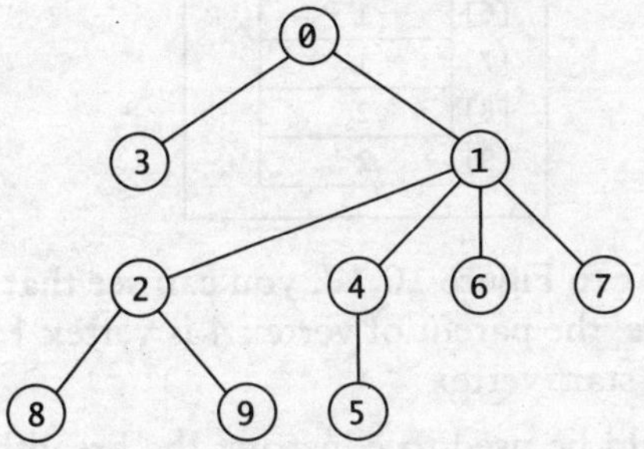

Refinement of Step 7 of Breadth-First Search Algorithm

7.1 Insert vertex v into the queue.
7.2 Set the parent of v to u.

Performance Analysis of Breadth-First Search

The loop at Step 2 will be performed for each vertex. The inner loop at Step 4 is performed for $|E_v|$ (the number of edges that originate at that vertex). The total number of steps is the sum of the edges that originate at each vertex, which is the total number of edges. Thus the algorithm is $O(|E|)$.

Implementing Breadth-First Search

Listing 10.3 shows method `breadthFirstSearch`. Notice that nothing is done when we have finished visiting a vertex (algorithm Step 8).

This method declares three data structures: `int[] parent`, `boolean[] identified`, and `Queue theQueue`. The array `identified` is used to keep track of the nodes that have been previously encountered, and `theQueue` is used to store nodes that are waiting to be visited.

The method returns array `parent`, which could be used to construct the breadth-first search tree. The element `parent[v]` contains the parent of vertex `v` in the tree. The statement

```
parent[neighbor] = current;
```

is used to "insert an edge into the breadth-first search tree". It does this by setting the parent of a newly identified node (`neighbor`) as the node being visited (`current`). If we run the `breadthFirstSearch` method on the graph shown in Figure 10.15, then the array `parent` will be defined as follows:

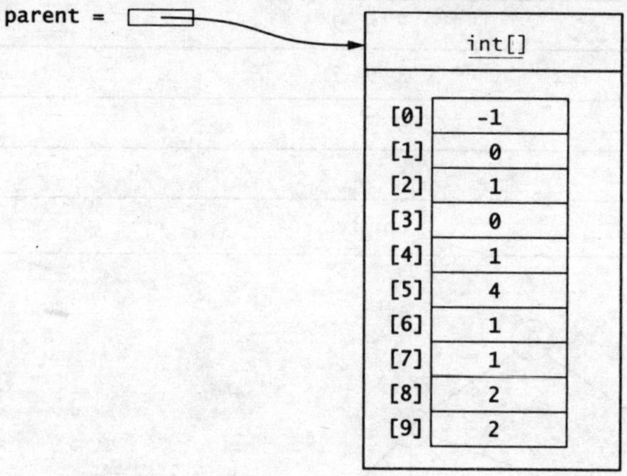

If you compare array `parent` to Figure 10.17, you can see that `parent[i]` is the parent of vertex `i`. For example, the parent of vertex 4 is vertex 1. The entry `parent[0]` is –1 because node 0 is the start vertex.

Although array `parent` could be used to construct the breadth-first search tree, we are generally not interested in the complete tree but rather in the path from the root to a given vertex. Using array `parent` to trace the path from that vertex back to the root would give you the reverse of the desired path. For example, the path derived from `parent` for vertex 4 to the root would be 4 to 1 to 0. If you place these vertices in a stack and then pop the stack until it is empty, you will get the path from the root: 0 to 1 to 4.

LISTING 10.3
Class `BreadthFirstSearch.java`

```
/** Class to implement the breadth-first search algorithm. */
public class BreadthFirstSearch {

    /** Perform a breadth-first search of a graph.
        post: The array parent will contain the predecessor
              of each vertex in the breadth-first
              search tree.
        @param graph The graph to be searched
        @param start The start vertex
        @return The array of parents
```

```
 */
public static int[] breadthFirstSearch(Graph graph, int start) {
    Queue<Integer> theQueue = new LinkedList<Integer>();
    // Declare array parent and initialize its elements to -1.
    int[] parent = new int[graph.getNumV()];
    for (int i = 0; i < graph.getNumV(); i++) {
        parent[i] = -1;
    }

    // Declare array identified and
    // initialize its elements to false.
    boolean[] identified = new boolean[graph.getNumV()];
    /* Mark the start vertex as identified and insert it
       into the queue */
    identified[start] = true;
    theQueue.offer(start);

    /* Perform breadth-first search until done */
    while (!theQueue.isEmpty()) {
        /* Take a vertex, current, out of the queue.
         (Begin visiting current). */
        int current = theQueue.remove();
        /* Examine each vertex, neighbor, adjacent to current. */
        Iterator<Edge> itr = graph.edgeIterator(current);
        while (itr.hasNext()) {
            Edge edge = itr.next();
            int neighbor = edge.getDest();
            // If neighbor has not been identified
            if (!identified[neighbor]) {
                // Mark it identified.
                identified[neighbor] = true;
                // Place it into the queue.
                theQueue.offer(neighbor);
                /* Insert the edge (current, neighbor)
                   into the tree. */
                parent[neighbor] = current;
            }
        }
        // Finished visiting current.
    }
    return parent;
  }
}
```

Depth-First Search

Another way to traverse a graph is depth-first search. In depth-first search you start at a vertex, visit it, and choose one adjacent vertex to visit. Then choose a vertex adjacent to that vertex to visit, and so on until you go no further. Then back up and see whether a new vertex (one not previously visited) can be found. In the discussion that follows, we use color to distinguish among three states for a node: being visited (light blue), finished visiting (dark blue), and not yet visited (white). Initially, of course, all nodes are not yet visited. Note that the color light blue is used in depth-first search to indicate that a vertex is in the process of being visited, whereas it was used in our discussion of breadth-first search to indicate that the vertex was identified.

Example of Depth-First Search

Consider the graph shown in Figure 10.18. We can start at any vertex, but for simplicity we will start at 0. The vertices adjacent to 0 are 1, 2, 3, and 4. We mark 0 as being visited (color it light blue; see Figure 10.19(a)). Next we consider 1. We mark 1 as being visited (see Figure 10.19(b)). The vertices adjacent to 1 are 0, 3, and 4. But 0 is being visited, so we recursively apply the algorithm with 3 as the start vertex. We mark 3 as being visited (see Figure 10.19(c)). The vertices adjacent to 3 are 0, 1, and 4. Because 0 and 1 are already being visited, we recursively apply the algorithm with 4 as the start vertex. We mark 4 as being visited (see Figure 10.19(d)). The vertices adjacent to 4 are 0, 1, and 3. All of these are being visited, so we mark 4 as finished (see Figure 10.19(e)) and return from the recursion. Now all of the vertices adjacent to 3 have been visited, so we mark 3 as finished and return from the recursion. Now all of the vertices adjacent to 1 have been visited, so we mark 1 as finished and return from the recursion to the original start vertex, 0. The order in which we started to visit vertices is 0, 1, 3, 4; the order in which vertices have become finished so far is 4, 3, 1.

We now consider vertex 2, which is adjacent to 0 but has not been visited. We mark 2 as being visited (see Figure 10.19(f)) and consider the vertices adjacent to it: 5 and 6. We mark 5 as being visited (see Figure 10.19(g)) and consider the vertices adjacent to it: 2 and 6. Because 2 is already being visited, we next visit 6. We mark 6 as being visited (see Figure 10.19(h)). The vertices adjacent to 6 (2 and 5) are already being visited. Thus we mark 6 as finished and recursively return. The vertices adjacent to 5 have all been visited, so we mark 5 as finished and return from the recursion. All of the vertices adjacent to 2 have been visited, so we mark 2 as finished and return from the recursion.

Finally, we come back to 0. Because all of the vertices adjacent to it have also been visited, we mark 0 as finished and we are done (see Figure 10.19(i)). The order in which we started to visit all vertices is 0, 1, 3, 4, 2, 5, 6; the order in which we finished visiting all vertices is 4, 3, 1, 6, 5, 2, 0. The *discovery order* is the order in which the vertices are discovered. The *finish order* is the order in which the vertices are finished. We consider a vertex to be finished when we return to it after finishing all its successors.

Figure 10.20 shows the depth-first search tree for the graph in Figure 10.18. A preorder traversal of this tree yields the sequence in which the vertices were visited: 0, 1, 3, 4, 2, 5, 6. The dashed lines are the other edges in the graph that are not part of the depth-first search tree. These edges are called *back edges* because they connect a vertex with its ancestors in the depth-first search tree. Observe that vertex 4 has two ancestors in addition to its parent, 3: 1 and 0. Vertex 1 is a grandparent, and vertex 0 is a great-grandparent.

FIGURE 10.18
Graph to Be Traversed Depth First

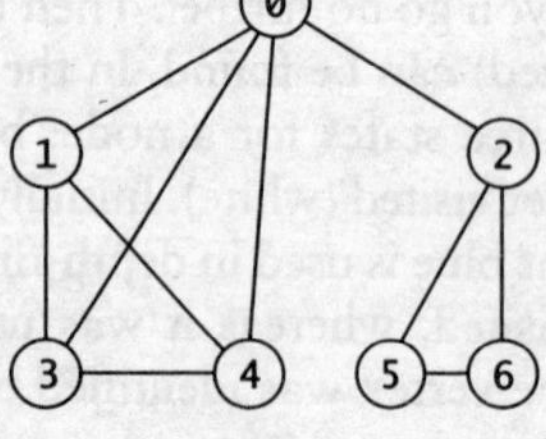

FIGURE 10.19
Example of Depth-First Search

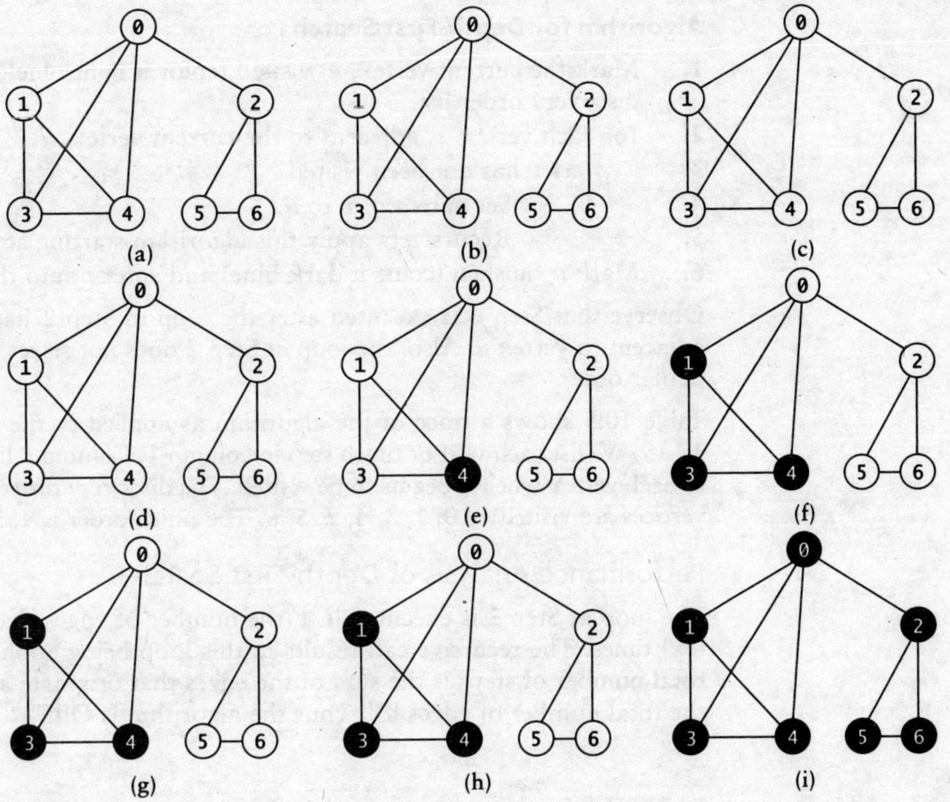

FIGURE 10.20
Depth-First Search Tree of Figure 10.18

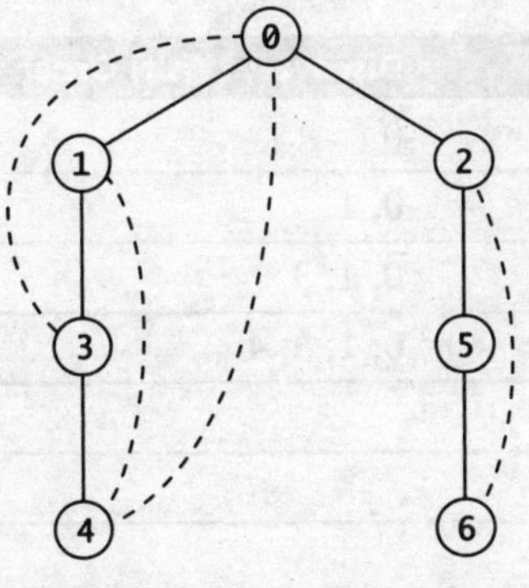

Algorithm for Depth-First Search

Depth-first search is used as the basis of other graph algorithms. However, rather than embedding the depth-first search algorithm into these other algorithms, we will implement the depth-first search algorithm to collect information about the vertices, which we can then use in these other algorithms. The information we will collect is the discovery order (or the visit order) and the finish order.

The depth-first search algorithm follows. Step 5 recursively applies this algorithm to each vertex as it is discovered.

Algorithm for Depth-First Search

1. Mark the current vertex, *u*, visited (color it light blue), and enter it in the discovery order list.
2. **for** each vertex, *v*, adjacent to the current vertex, *u*
3.   **if** *v* has not been visited
4.   Set parent of *v* to *u*.
5.   Recursively apply this algorithm starting at *v*.
6. Mark *u* finished (color it dark blue) and enter *u* into the finish order list.

Observe that Step 6 is executed after the loop in Step 2 has examined all vertices adjacent to vertex *u*. Also, the loop at Step 2 does not select the vertices in any particular order.

Table 10.5 shows a trace of the algorithm as applied to the graph shown in Figure 10.19. We list each visit or finish step in column 1. Column 2 lists the vertices adjacent to each vertex when it begins to be visited. The discovery order (the order in which the vertices are visited) is 0, 1, 3, 4, 2, 5, 6. The finish order is 4, 3, 1, 6, 5, 2, and 0.

Performance Analysis of Depth-First Search

The loop at Step 2 is executed $|E_v|$ (the number of edges that originate at that vertex) times. The recursive call results in this loop being applied to each vertex. The total number of steps is the sum of the edges that originate at each vertex, which is the total number of edges $|E|$. Thus the algorithm is $O(|E|)$.

TABLE 10.5
Trace of Depth-First Search of Figure 10.19

Operation	Adjacent Vertices	Discovery (Visit) Order	Finish Order
Visit 0	1, 2, 3, 4	0	
Visit 1	0, 3, 4	0, 1	
Visit 3	0, 1, 4	0, 1, 3	
Visit 4	0, 1, 3	0, 1, 3, 4	
Finish 4			4
Finish 3			4, 3
Finish 1			4, 3, 1
Visit 2	0, 5, 6	0, 1, 3, 4, 2	
Visit 5	2, 6	0, 1, 3, 4, 2, 5	
Visit 6	2, 5	0, 1, 3, 4, 2, 5, 6	
Finish 6			4, 3, 1, 6
Finish 5			4, 3, 1, 6, 5
Finish 2			4, 3, 1, 6, 5, 2
Finish 0			4, 3, 1, 6, 5, 2, 0

There is an implicit Step 0 to the algorithm that colors all of the vertices white. This is O(|V|); thus the total running time of the algorithm is O(|V|+|E|).

Implementing Depth-First Search

The class `DepthFirstSearch` is designed to be used as a building block for other algorithms. When constructed, this class performs a depth-first search on a graph and records the start time, finish time, start order, and finish order. For an unconnected graph or for a directed graph (whether connected or not), a depth-first search may not visit each vertex in the graph. Thus, once the recursive method returns, the vertices need to be examined to see whether they all have been visited; if not, the recursive process repeats, starting with the next unvisited vertex. Thus, the depth-first search can generate more than one tree. We will call this collection of trees a *forest*. Also, it may be important that we control the order in which the vertices are examined to form the forest. Thus, one of the constructors for the `DepthFirstSearch` class enables its caller to specify the order in which vertices are examined to select a new start vertex. The default is normal ascending order. The class is described in Table 10.6, and part of the code is shown in Listing 10.4.

TABLE 10.6
Class `DepthFirstSearch`

Data Field	Attribute
`private int discoverIndex`	The index that indicates the discovery order.
`private int[] discoveryOrder`	The array that contains the vertices in discovery order.
`private int finishIndex`	The index that indicates the finish order.
`private int[] finishOrder`	The array that contains the vertices in finish order.
`private Graph graph`	A reference to the graph being searched.
`private int[] parent`	The array of predecessors in the depth-first search tree.
`private boolean[] visited`	An array of **`boolean`** values to indicate whether or not a vertex has been visited.
Constructor	**Purpose**
`public DepthFirstSearch(Graph graph)`	Constructs the depth-first search of the specified graph selecting the start vertices in ascending vertex order.
`public DepthFirstSearch(Graph graph, int[] order)`	Constructs the depth-first search of the specified graph selecting the start vertices in the specified order. The first vertex visited is `order[0]`.
Method	**Behavior**
`public void depthFirstSearch(int s)`	Recursively searches the graph starting at vertex `s`.
`public int[] getDiscoveryOrder()`	Gets the discovery order.
`public int[] getFinishOrder()`	Gets the finish order.
`public int[] getParent()`	Gets the parents in the depth-first search tree.

Each constructor allocates storage for the arrays `parent`, `visited`, `discoveryOrder`, and `finishOrder` and initializes all elements of `parent` to `-1` (no parent). In the constructor in Listing 10.4, the **for** statement

```
for (int i = 0; i < n; i++) {
    if (!visited[i])
        depthFirstSearch(i);
}
```

calls the recursive depth-first search method. Method `depthFirstSearch` follows the algorithm shown earlier. If the graph is connected, all vertices will be visited after the return from the initial call to `depthFirstSearch`. If the graph is not connected, additional calls will be made using a start vertex that has not been visited.

In the constructor (not shown) that allows the client to control the order of selection for start vertices, the parameter `int[] order` specifies this sequence. To code this constructor, change the **if** statement just shown to

```
if (!visited[order[i]])
    depthFirstSearch(order[i]);
```

The rest of the code is the same.

LISTING 10.4

DepthFirstSearch.java

```
/** Class to implement the depth-first search algorithm. */
public class DepthFirstSearch {

    // Data Fields
    /** A reference to the graph being searched. */
    private Graph graph;
    /** Array of parents in the depth-first search tree. */
    private int[] parent;
    /** Flag to indicate whether this vertex has been visited. */
    private boolean[] visited;
    /** The array that contains each vertex in discovery order. */
    private int[] discoveryOrder;
    /** The array that contains each vertex in finish order. */
    private int[] finishOrder;
    /** The index that indicates the discovery order. */
    private int discoverIndex = 0;
    /** The index that indicates the finish order. */
    private int finishIndex = 0;

    // Constructors
    /** Construct the depth-first search of a Graph
        starting at vertex 0 and visiting the start vertices in
        ascending order.
        @param graph The graph
```

```
    */
    public DepthFirstSearch(Graph graph) {
        this.graph = graph;
        int n = graph.getNumV();
        parent = new int[n];
        visited = new boolean[n];
        discoveryOrder = new int[n];
        finishOrder = new int[n];
        for (int i = 0; i < n; i++) {
            parent[i] = -1;
        }
        for (int i = 0; i < n; i++) {
            if (!visited[i])
                depthFirstSearch(i);
        }
    }

    /** Construct the depth-first search of a Graph
        selecting the start vertices in the specified order.
        The first vertex visited is order[0].
        @param graph The graph
        @param order The array giving the order
                     in which the start vertices should be selected
    */
    public DepthFirstSearch(Graph graph, int[] order) {
        // Same as constructor above except for the if statement.
    }

    /** Recursively depth-first search the graph
        starting at vertex current.
        @param current The start vertex
    */
    public void depthFirstSearch(int current) {
        /* Mark the current vertex visited. */
        visited[current] = true;
        discoveryOrder[discoverIndex++] = current;
        /* Examine each vertex adjacent to the current vertex */
        Iterator<Edge> itr = graph.edgeIterator(current);
        while (itr.hasNext()) {
            int neighbor = itr.next().getDest();
            /* Process a neighbor that has not been visited */
            if (!visited[neighbor]) {
                /* Insert (current, neighbor) into the depth-
                   first search tree. */
                parent[neighbor] = current;
                /* Recursively apply the algorithm
                   starting at neighbor. */
                depthFirstSearch(neighbor);
            }
        }
        /* Mark current finished. */
        finishOrder[finishIndex++] = current;
    }
}
```

Testing Method depthFirstSearch

Next, we show a main method that tests the class. It is a simple driver program that can be used to read a graph and then initiate a depth-first traversal. After the traversal, the driver program displays the arrays that represent the search results.

```
/** Main method to test depth-first search method
    pre: args[0] is the name of the input file.
    @param args The command line arguments
*/
public static void main(String[] args) {
    Graph g = null;
    int n = 0;
    try {
        Scanner scan =
            new Scanner(new File(args[0]));
        g = AbstractGraph.createGraph(scan, true, "List");
        n = g.getNumV();
    } catch (IOException ex) {
        ex.printStackTrace();
        System.exit(1);   // Error
    }

    // Perform depth-first search.
    DepthFirstSearch dfs = new DepthFirstSearch(g);
    int[] dOrder = dfs.getDiscoveryOrder();
    int[] fOrder = dfs.getFinishOrder();
    System.out.println("Discovery and finish order");
    for (int i = 0; i < n; i++) {
        System.out.println(dOrder[i] + "   " + fOrder[i]);
    }
}
```

EXERCISES FOR SECTION 10.4

SELF-CHECK

1. Show the breadth-first search trees for the following graphs.

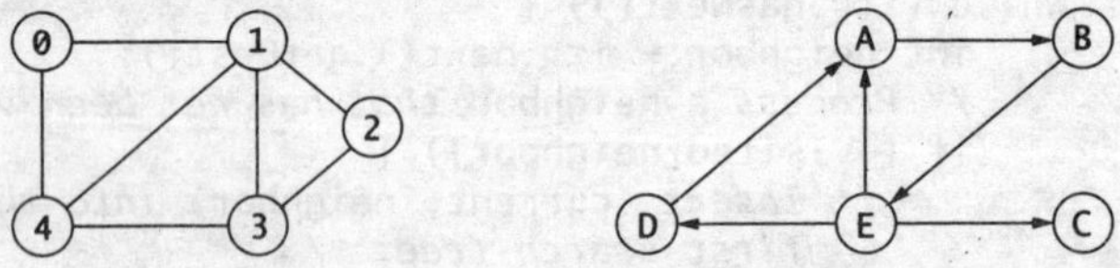

2. Show the depth-first search trees for the graphs in Exercise 1 above.

PROGRAMMING

1. Provide all accessor methods for class DepthFirstSearch and the constructor that specifies the order of start vertices.
2. Implement method depthFirstSearch without using recursion. *Hint:* Use a stack to save the parent of the current vertex when you start to search one of its adjacent vertices.

10.5 Applications of Graph Traversals

CASE STUDY Shortest Path through a Maze

Problem We want to design a program that will find the shortest path through a maze. In Chapter 5 we showed how to write a recursive program that found a solution to a maze. This program used a backtracking algorithm that visited alternate paths. When it found a dead end, it backed up and tried another path, and eventually it found a solution.

Figure 10.21 shows a maze solution generated by this recursive program. The light gray cells are barriers in the maze. The white squares show the solution path, the black squares show the squares that were visited but rejected, and the dark gray squares were not visited. As you can see, the program did not find an optimal solution. (This is a consequence of the program advancing the solution path to the south before attempting to advance it to the east.) We want to find the shortest path, defined as the one with the fewest decision points in it.

FIGURE 10.21
Recursive Solution to a Maze

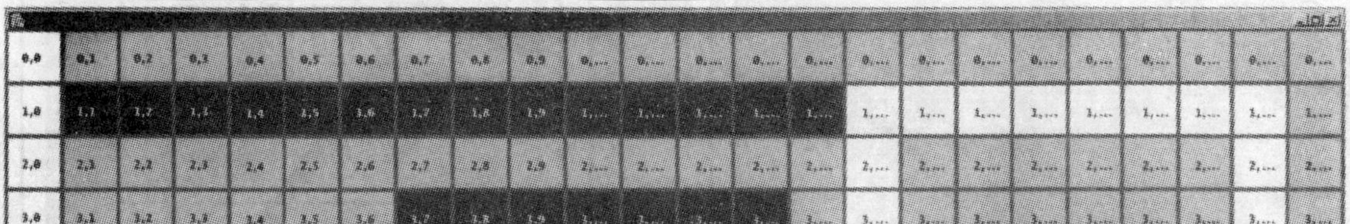

Analysis We can represent the maze shown in Figure 10.21 by a graph, where we place a node at each decision point and at each dead end, as shown in Figure 10.22.

Now that we have the maze represented as a graph, we need to find the shortest path from the start point (vertex 0) to the end point (vertex 12). The breadth-first search method will return the shortest path from each vertex to its parent (the array of parent vertices), and we can use this array to find the shortest path to the end point. Recall that our shortest path will contain the smallest number of vertices, but not necessarily the smallest number of cells, in the path.

FIGURE 10.22
Graph Representation of the Maze in Figure 10.21

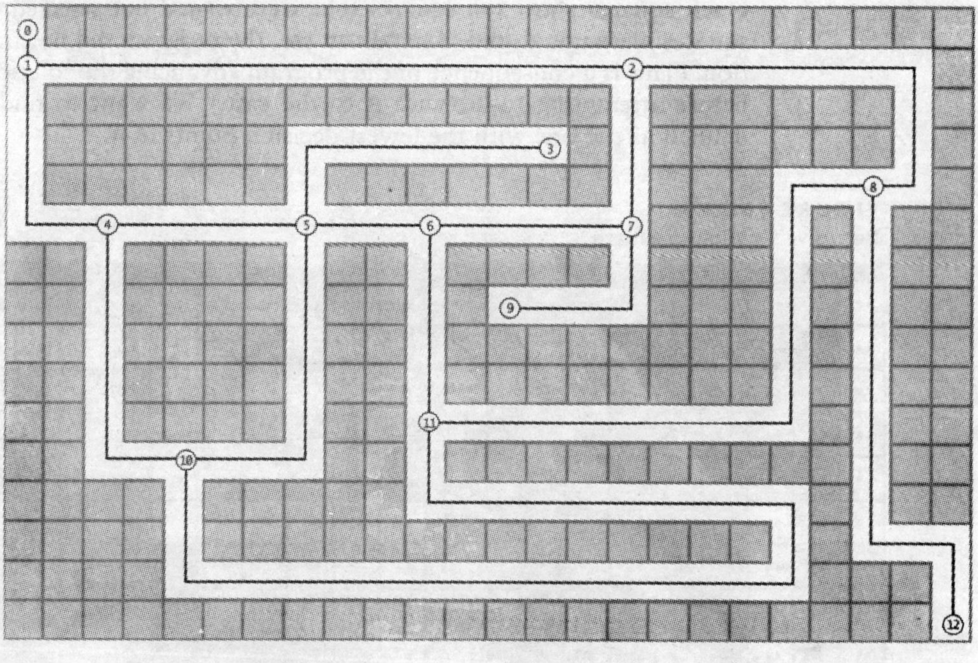

Design Your program will need the following data structures:

- An external representation of the maze, consisting of the number of vertices and the edges
- An object of a class that implements the `Graph` interface
- An array to hold the predecessors returned from the `breadthFirstSearch` method
- A stack to reverse the path

The algorithm is as follows:

1. Read in the number of vertices and create the graph object.
2. Read in the edges and insert the edges into the graph.
3. Call the `breadthFirstSearch` method with this graph and the starting vertex as its argument. The method returns the array `parent`.
4. Start at *v*, the end vertex.
5. **while** *v* is not –1
6.   Push *v* onto the stack.
7.   Set *v* to `parent[`*v*`]`.
8. **while** the stack is not empty
9.   Pop a vertex off the stack and output it.

Implementation Listing 10.5 shows the program. We assume that the graph that represents the maze is stored in a text file. The first line of this file contains the number of vertices. The edges are on subsequent lines. The method `loadEdgesFromFile` reads the source and destination vertices and inserts the edge into the graph. The rest of the code follows the algorithm.

LISTING 10.5
Program to Solve a Maze Using a Breadth-First Search

```
import java.io.*;
import java.util.*;

/** Program to solve a maze represented as a graph.
    This program performs a breadth-first search of the graph
    to find the "shortest" path from the start vertex to the
    end. It is assumed that the start vertex is 0, and the
    end vertex is numV-1.
*/
public class Maze {

    /** Main method to solve the maze.
        pre: args[0] contains the name of the input file.
        @param args Command line argument
    */
    public static void main(String[] args) {
        int numV = 0;    // The number of vertices.
        Graph theMaze = null;
        // Load the graph data from a file.
        try {
            Scanner scan =
                new Scanner(new File(args[0]));
            theMaze = AbstractGraph.createGraph(scan, false, "List");
            numV = theMaze.getNumV();
```

```
            } catch (IOException ex) {
                System.err.println("IO Error while reading graph");
                System.err.println(ex.toString());
                System.exit(1);
            }
            // Perform breadth-first search.
            int parent[] =
                BreadthFirstSearch.breadthFirstSearch(theMaze, 0);
            // Construct the path.
            Stack thePath = new Stack();
            int v = numV - 1;
            while (parent[v] != -1) {
                thePath.push(new Integer(v));
                v = parent[v];
            }
            // Output the path.
            System.out.println("The Shortest path is:");
            while (!thePath.empty()) {
                System.out.println(thePath.pop());
            }
        }
    }
```

Testing Test this program with a variety of mazes. Use mazes for which the original program finds the shortest path and mazes for which it does not. For the graph shown in Figure 10.23, the shortest path from 0 to 12 is $0 \rightarrow 1 \rightarrow 2 \rightarrow 8 \rightarrow 12$.

FIGURE 10.23
Solution to Maze in Figure 10.21

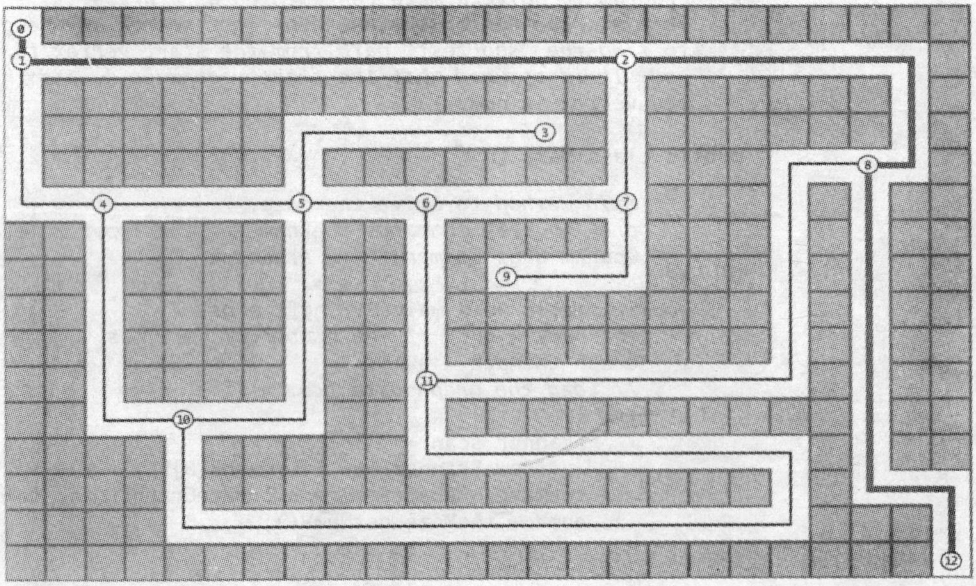

CASE STUDY Topological Sort of a Graph

Problem There are many problems in which one activity cannot be started before another one has been completed. One that you may have already encountered is determining the order in which you can take courses. Some courses have prerequisites. Some have more than one prerequisite. Furthermore, the prerequisites may have prerequisites. Figure 10.24 shows the courses and prerequisites of a Computer Science program at the authors' university.

FIGURE 10.24
Prerequisites for a Computer Science Program

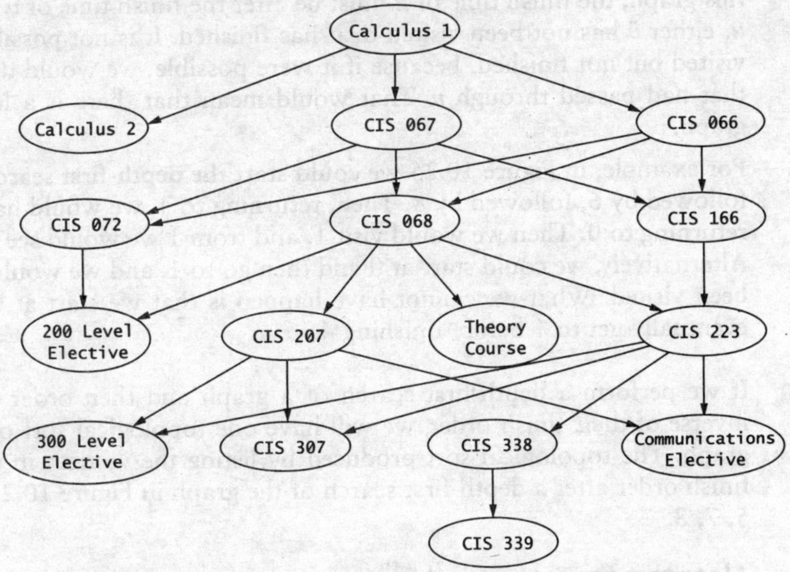

Graphs such as the one shown in Figure 10.24 are known as *directed acyclic graphs* (*DAGs*). They are directed graphs that contain no cycles; that is, there are no loops, so once you pass through a vertex, there is no path back to that vertex. Figure 10.25 shows another example of a DAG.

FIGURE 10.25
Example of a Directed Acyclic Graph

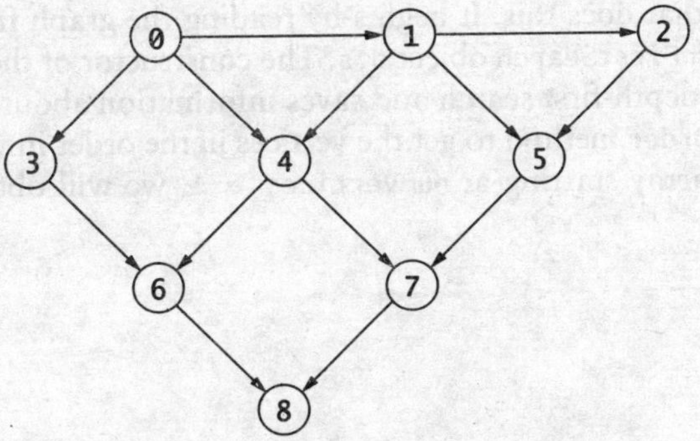

A *topological sort* of the vertices of a DAG is an ordering of the vertices such that if (u, v) is an edge, then u appears before v. This must be true for all edges. For example, 0, 1, 2, 3, 4, 5, 6, 7, 8 is a valid topological sort of the graph in Figure 10.25, but 0, 1, 5, 3, 4, 2, 6, 7, 8 is not because $2 \rightarrow 5$ is an edge, but 5 appears before 2. There are many valid paths through the prerequisite graph and many valid topological sorts. Another valid topological sort is 0, 3, 1, 4, 6, 2, 5, 7, 8.

Analysis If there is an edge from u to v in a DAG, then if we perform a depth-first search of this graph, the finish time of u must be after the finish time of v. When we return to u, either v has not been visited or it has finished. It is not possible that v would be visited but not finished, because if it were possible, we would discover u on a path that had passed through v. That would mean that there is a loop or cycle in the graph.

For example, in Figure 10.25 we could start the depth-first search at 0, then visit 4, followed by 6, followed by 8. Then, returning to 4, we would have to visit 7 before returning to 0. Then we would visit 1, and from 1 we would see that 4 has finished. Alternatively, we could start at 0 and then go to 1, and we would see that 4 has not been visited. What we cannot have happen is that we start at 0, then visit 4, and eventually get to 1 before finishing 4.

Design If we perform a depth-first search of a graph and then order the vertices by the inverse of their finish order, we will have one topological sort of a directed acyclic graph. The topological sort produced by listing the vertices in the inverse of their finish order after a depth-first search of the graph in Figure 10.25 is 0, 3, 1, 4, 6, 2, 5, 7, 8.

Algorithm for Topological Sort

1. Read the graph from a data file.
2. Perform a depth-first search of the graph.
3. List the vertices in reverse of their finish order.

Implementation We can use our `DepthFirstSearch` class to implement this algorithm. Listing 10.6 shows a program that does this. It begins by reading the graph from an input file. It then creates a `DepthFirstSearch` object `dfs`. The constructor of the `DepthFirstSearch` class performs the depth-first search and saves information about the graph. We then call the `getFinishOrder` method to get the vertices in the order in which they finished. If we output this array starting at `numVertices - 1`, we will obtain the topological sort of the graph.

LISTING 10.6

TopologicalSort.java

```
import java.util.*;

/** This program outputs the topological sort of a directed graph
    that contains no cycles.
*/
public class TopologicalSort {

    /** The main method that performs the topological sort.
        pre: arg[0] contains the name of the file
             that contains the graph. It has no cycles.
        @param args The command line arguments
    */
    public static void main(String[] args) {
        Graph theGraph = null;
        int numVertices = 0;
        try {
            // Connect Scanner to input file.
            Scanner scan =
                new Scanner(new File(args[0]));
            // Load the graph data from a file.
            theGraph = AbstractGraph.createGraph(scan, true, "List");
            numVertices = theGraph.getNumV();
        } catch (Exception ex) {
            ex.printStackTrace();
            System.exit(1); // Error exit.
        }
        // Perform the depth-first search.
        DepthFirstSearch dfs = new DepthFirstSearch(theGraph);
        // Obtain the finish order.
        int[] finishOrder = dfs.getFinishOrder();
        // Print the vertices in reverse finish order.
        System.out.println("The Topological Sort is");
        for (int i = numVertices - 1; i >= 0; i--) {
            System.out.println(finishOrder[i]);
        }
    }
}
```

Testing Test this program using several different graphs. Use sparse graphs and dense graphs. Make sure that each graph you try has no loops or cycles. If it does, the algorithm may display an invalid output.

EXERCISES FOR SECTION 10.5

SELF-CHECK

1. Draw the depth-first search tree of the graph in Figure 10.24 and then list the vertices in reverse finish order.
2. List some alternative topological sorts for the graph in Figure 10.24.

10.6 Algorithms Using Weighted Graphs

Finding the Shortest Path from a Vertex to All Other Vertices

The breadth-first search discussed in Section 10.4 found the shortest path from the start vertex to all other vertices, assuming that the length of each edge was the same. We now consider the problem of finding the shortest path where the length of each edge may be different—that is, in a weighted directed graph such as that shown in Figure 10.26. The computer scientist Edsger W. Dijkstra developed an algorithm, now called Dijkstra's algorithm ("A Note on Two Problems in Connection with Graphs," *Numerische Mathematik,* Vol. 1 [1959], pp. 269–271), to solve this problem. This algorithm makes the assumption that all of the edge values are positive.

For Dijkstra's algorithm we need two sets, *S* and *V–S,* and two arrays, d and p. *S* will contain the vertices for which we have computed the shortest distance, and *V–S* will contain the vertices that we still need to process. The entry d[*v*] will contain the shortest distance from *s* to *v,* and p[*v*] will contain the predecessor of *v* in the path from *s* to *v.*

We initialize *S* by placing the start vertex, *s,* into it. We initialize *V–S* by placing the remaining vertices into it. For each *v* in *V–S,* we initialize d by setting d[*v*] equal to the weight of the edge *w*(*s, v*) for each vertex, *v,* adjacent to *s* and to ∞ for each vertex that is not adjacent to *s.* We initialize p[*v*] to *s* for each *v* in *V–S.*

FIGURE 10.26
Weighted Directed Graph

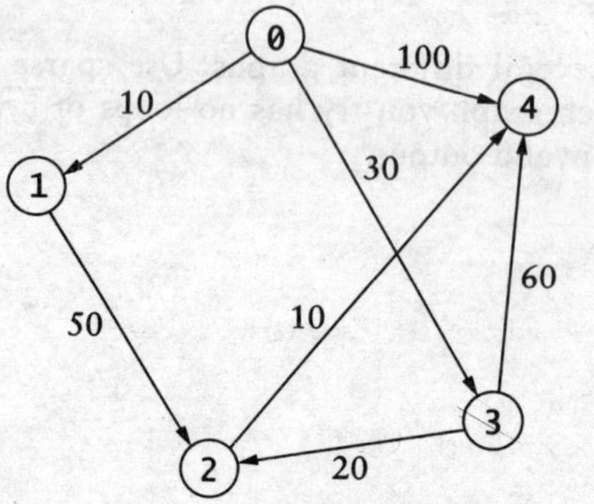

For example, given the graph shown in Figure 10.26, the set *S* would initially be {0}, and *V–S* would be {1, 2, 3, 4}. The arrays d and p would be defined as follows.

v	d[*v*]	p[*v*]
1	10	0
2	∞	0
3	30	0
4	100	0

The first row shows that the distance from vertex 0 to vertex 1 is 10 and that vertex 0 is the predecessor of vertex 1. The second row shows that vertex 2 is not adjacent to vertex 0.

We now find the vertex *u* in *V–S* that has the smallest value of d[*u*]. Using our example, this is 1. We now consider the vertices *v* that are adjacent to *u*. If the distance from *s* to *u* (d[*u*]) plus the distance from *u* to *v* (i.e., *w*(*u*, *v*)) is smaller than the known distance from *s* to *v*, d[*v*], then we update d[*v*] to be d[*u*] + *w*(*u*, *v*), and we set p[*v*] to *u*. In our example the value of d[1] is 10, and *w*(1, 2) is 50. Since 10 + 50 = 60 is less than ∞, we set d[2] to 60 and p[2] to 1. We remove 1 from *V–S* and place it into *S*. We repeat this until *V–S* is empty.

After the first pass through this loop, *S* is {0, 1}, *V–S* is {2, 3, 4}, and d and p are as follows:

v	d[*v*]	p[*v*]
1	10	0
2	60	1
3	30	0
4	100	0

We again select *u* from *V–S* with the smallest d[*u*]. This is now 3. The adjacent vertices to 3 are 2 and 4. The distance from 0 to 3, d[3], is 30. The distance from 3 to 2 is 20. Because 30 + 20 = 50 is less than the current value of d[2], 60, we update d[2] to 50 and change p[2] to 3. Also, because 30 + 60 = 90 is less than 100, we update d[4] to 90 and set p[4] to 3.

Now *S* is {0, 1, 3}, and *V–S* is {2, 4}. The arrays d and p are as follows:

v	d[*v*]	p[*v*]
1	10	0
2	50	3
3	30	0
4	90	3

Next we select vertex 2 from *V–S*. The only vertex adjacent to 2 is 4. Since d[2] + *w*(2, 4) = 50 + 10 = 60 is less than d[4], 90, we update d[4] to 60 and p[4] to 2. Now *S* is {0, 1, 2, 3}, *V–S* is {4}, and d and p are as follows:

v	d[*v*]	p[*v*]
1	10	0
2	50	3
3	30	0
4	60	2

Finally, we remove 4 from *V–S* and find that it has no adjacent vertices. We are now done. The array d shows the shortest distances from the start vertex to all other vertices, and the array p can be used to determine the corresponding paths. For example, the path from vertex 0 to vertex 4 has a length of 60, and it is the reverse of 4, 2, 3, 0; therefore, the shortest path is 0 → 3 → 2 → 4.

Dijkstra's Algorithm

```
1.   Initialize S with the start vertex, s, and V–S with the remaining vertices.
2.   for all v in V–S
3.       Set p[v] to s.
4.       if there is an edge (s, v)
5.           Set d[v] to w(s, v).
         else
6.           Set d[v] to ∞.
7.   while V–S is not empty
8.       for all u in V–S, find the smallest d[u].
9.       Remove u from V–S and add u to S.
10.      for all v adjacent to u in V–S
11.          if d[u] + w(u, v) is less than d[v].
12.              Set d[v] to d[u] + w(u, v).
13.              Set p[v] to u.
```

Analysis of Dijkstra's Algorithm

Step 1 requires |*V*| steps.

The loop at Step 2 will be executed |*V* – 1| times.

The loop at Step 7 will also be executed |*V* – 1| times.

Within the loop at Step 7 we have to consider Steps 8 and 9. For these steps we will have to search each value in *V–S*. This decreases each time through the loop at Step 7, so we will have |*V*| – 1 + |*V*| – 2 + · · · 1. This is O(|*V*|^2). Therefore, Dijkstra's algorithm as stated is O|*V*|^2). We will look at possible improvements to this for sparse graphs when we discuss a similar algorithm in the next subsection.

Implementation

Listing 10.7 provides a straightforward implementation of Dijkstra's algorithm using `HashSet vMinusS` to represent set *V–S*. We chose to implement the algorithm as a **`static`** method with the inputs (the graph and starting point) and outputs (predecessor and distance array) passed through parameters. An alternative approach would be to make them data fields in a class that contained this method. We use iterators to traverse `vMinusS`.

If we used an adjacency list representation for the graph (i.e., class `ListGraph`, described earlier), then we would code Step 10 (update the distances) to iterate through the edges adjacent to vertex `u`, and then update the distance if the destination vertex was in `vMinusS`. The modified code follows:

```
// Update the distances.
Iterator<Edge> edgeIter = graph.edgeIterator(u);
while (edgeIter.hasNext()) {
    Edge edge = edgeIter.next();
    int v = edge.getDest();
    if (vMinusS.contains(new Integer(v));
        double weight = edge.getWeight();
        if (dist[u] + weight < dist[v]) {
            dist[v] = dist[u] + weight;
            pred[v] = u;
        }
    }
}
```

LISTING 10.7
Dijkstra's Shortest-Path Algorithm

```
/** Dijkstra's Shortest-Path algorithm.
    @param graph The weighted graph to be searched
    @param start The start vertex
    @param pred Output array to contain the predecessors
                in the shortest path
    @param dist Output array to contain the distance
                in the shortest path
*/
public static void dijkstrasAlgorithm(Graph graph,
                                      int start,
                                      int[] pred,
                                      double[] dist) {
    int numV = graph.getNumV();
    HashSet<Integer> vMinusS = new HashSet<Integer>(numV);
    // Initialize V-S.
    for (int i = 0; i < numV; i++) {
        if (i != start) {
            vMinusS.add(i);
        }
    }
    // Initialize pred and dist.
    for (int v : vMinusS) {
        pred[v] = start;
        dist[v] = graph.getEdge(start, v).getWeight();
    }
```

```
    // Main loop
    while (vMinusS.size() != 0) {
        // Find the value u in V-S with the smallest dist[u].
        double minDist = Double.POSITIVE_INFINITY;
        int u = -1;
        for (int v : vMinusS) {
            if (dist[v] < minDist) {
                minDist = dist[v];
                u = v;
            }
        }
        // Remove u from vMinusS.
        vMinusS.remove(u);
        // Update the distances.
        for (int v : vMinusS) {
            if (graph.isEdge(u, v)) {
                double weight = graph.getEdge(u, v).getWeight();
                if (dist[u] + weight < dist[v]) {
                    dist[v] = dist[u] + weight;
                    pred[v] = u;
                }
            }
        }
    }
}
```

Minimum Spanning Trees

A *spanning tree* is a subset of the edges of a graph such that there is only one edge between each vertex, and all of the vertices are connected. If we have a spanning tree for a graph, then we can access all the vertices of the graph from the start node. The *cost of a spanning tree* is the sum of the weights of the edges. We want to find the *minimum spanning tree* or the spanning tree with the smallest cost. For example, if we want to start up our own long-distance phone company and need to connect the cities shown in Figure 10.4, finding the minimum spanning tree would allow us to build the cheapest network.

We will discuss the algorithm published by R. C. Prim ("Shortest Connection Networks and Some Generalizations," *Bell System Technical Journal,* Vol. 36 [1957], pp. 1389–1401) for finding the minimum spanning tree of a graph. It is very similar to Dijkstra's algorithm, but Prim published his algorithm in 1957, two years before Dijkstra's paper that contains an algorithm for finding the minimum spanning tree that is essentially the same as Prim's as well as the previously discussed algorithm for finding the shortest paths.

Overview of Prim's Algorithm

The vertices are divided into two sets: *S,* the set of vertices in the spanning tree, and *V–S,* the remaining vertices. As in Dijkstra's algorithm, we maintain two arrays: d[*v*] will contain the length of the shortest edge from a vertex in *S* to the vertex *v* that is in *V–S,* and p[*v*] will contain the source vertex for that edge. The only difference between the algorithm to find the shortest path and the algorithm to find the minimum spanning tree is the contents of d[v]. In the algorithm to find the shortest path, d[v] contains the total length of the path from the starting vertex. In the algorithm to find the minimum spanning tree, d[v] contains only the length of the final edge. We show the essentials of Prim's algorithm next.

Prim's Algorithm for Finding the Minimum Spanning Tree

```
1.  Initialize S with the start vertex, s, and V–S with the remaining vertices.
2.  for all v in V–S
3.      Set p[v] to s.
4.      if there is an edge (s, v)
5.          Set d[v] to w(s, v).
        else
6.          Set d[v] to ∞.
7.  while V–S is not empty
8.      for all u in V–S, find the smallest d[u].
9.      Remove u from V–S and add it to S.
10.     Insert the edge (u, p[u]) into the spanning tree.
11.     for all v in V–S
12.         if w(u, v) < d[v]
13.             Set d[v] to w(u, v).
14.             Set p[v] to u.
```

In the array d, d[v] contains the length of the shortest known (previously examined) edge from a vertex in S to the vertex v, while v is a member of V–S. In the array p, the value p[v] is the source vertex of this shortest edge. When v is removed from V–S, we no longer update these entries in d and p.

EXAMPLE 10.2 Consider the graph shown in Figure 10.27. We initialize S to {0} and V–S to {1, 2, 3, 4, 5}. The smallest edge from u to v, where u is in S and v is in V–S, is the edge (0, 2). We add this edge to the spanning tree and add 2 to S (see Figure 10.28(a)). The set S is now {0, 2} and V–S is {1, 3, 4, 5}. We now have to consider all of the edges (u, v), where u is either 0 or 2, and v is 1, 3, 4, or 5 (there are eight possible edges). The smallest one is (2, 5). We add this to the spanning tree, and S now is {0,

FIGURE 10.27
Graph for Example 10.2

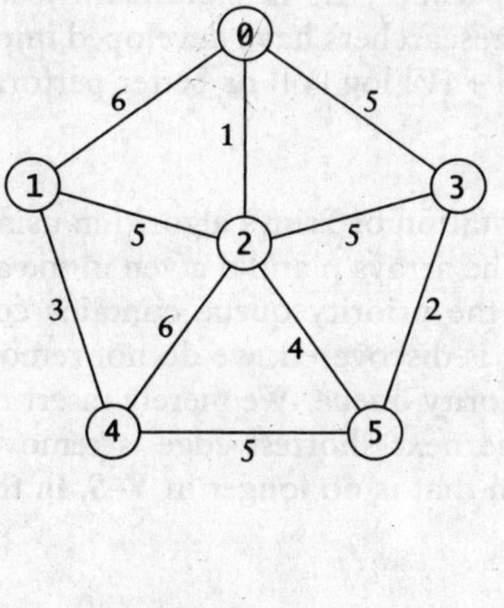

2, 5} and $V-S$ is {1, 3, 4} (see Figure 10.28(b)). The next smallest edge is (5, 3). We insert that into the tree and add 3 to S (see Figure 10.28(c)). Now $V-S$ is {1, 4}. The smallest edge is (2, 1). After adding this edge (see Figure 10.28(d)), we are left with $V-S$ being {4}. The smallest edge to 4 is (1, 4). This is added to the tree, and the spanning tree is complete (see Figure 10.28(e)).

FIGURE 10.28
Building a Minimum Spanning Tree Using Prim's Algorithm

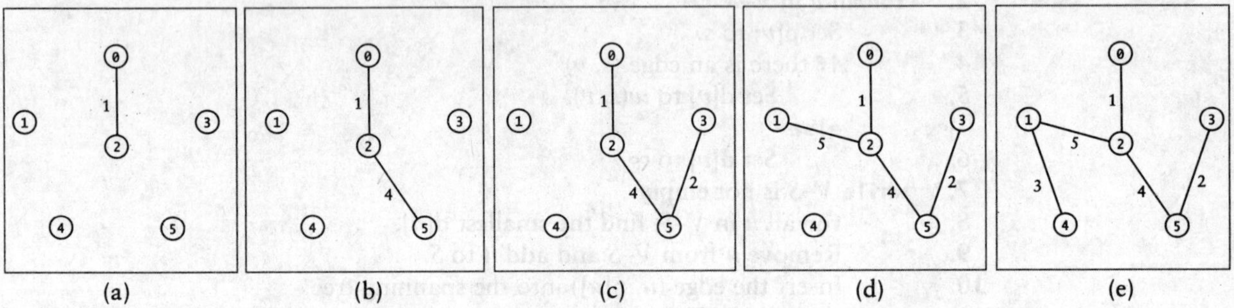

Analysis of Prim's Algorithm

Step 8 is $O(|V|)$. Because this is within the loop at Step 7, it will be executed $O(|V|)$ times for a total time of $O(|V|^2)$. Step 11 is $O(|E_u|)$, the number of edges that originate at u. Because Step 11 is inside the loop of Step 7, it will be executed for all vertices; thus, the total is $O(|E|)$. Because $|V|^2$ is greater than $|E|$, the overall cost of the algorithm is $O(|V|^2)$.

By using a priority queue to hold the edges from S to $V-S$, we can improve on this algorithm. Then Step 8 is $O(\log n)$, where n is the size of the priority queue. In the worst case, all of the edges are inserted into the priority queue, and the overall cost of the algorithm is then $O(|E| \log |V|)$. We say that the algorithm is $O(|E| \log |V|)$ instead of saying that it is $O(|E| \log |E|)$, even though the maximum size of the priority queue is $|E|$, because $|E|$ is bounded by $|V|^2$ and $\log |V|^2$ is $2 \times \log |V|$.

For a dense graph, where $|E|$ is approximately $|V|^2$, this is not an improvement; however, for a sparse graph, where $|E|$ is significantly less than $|V|^2$, it is. Furthermore, computer science researchers have developed improved priority queue implementations that give $O(|E| + |V| \log |V|)$ or better performance.

Implementation

Listing 10.8 shows an implementation of Prim's algorithm using a priority queue to hold the edges from S to $V-S$. The arrays p and d given in the algorithm description above are not needed because the priority queue contains complete edges. For a given vertex d, if a shorter edge is discovered, we do not remove the entry containing the longer edge from the priority queue. We merely insert new edges as they are discovered. Therefore, when the next shortest edge is removed from the priority queue, it may have a destination that is no longer in $V-S$. In that case, we continue to remove edges from the priority queue until we find one with a destination that is still in *V–S*. This is done with the following loop:

```
do {
    edge = pQ.remove();
    dest = edge.getDest();
} while(!vMinusS.contains(dest));
```

LISTING 10.8

Prim's Minimum Spanning Tree Algorithm

```
/** Prim's Minimum Spanning Tree algorithm.
    @param graph The weighted graph to be searched
    @param start The start vertex
    @return An ArrayList of edges that forms the MST
*/
public static ArrayList<Edge> primsAlgorithm(Graph graph,
                                             int start) {
    ArrayList<Edge> result = new ArrayList<Edge>();
    int numV = graph.getNumV();
    // Use a HashSet to represent V-S.
    Set<Integer> vMinusS = new HashSet<Integer>(numV);
    // Declare the priority queue.
    Queue<Edge> pQ =
        new PriorityQueue<Edge>(numV, new CompareEdges());
    // Initialize V-S.
    for (int i = 0; i < numV; i++) {
        if (i != start) {
            vMinusS.add(i);
        }
    }
    int current = start;
    // Main loop
    while (vMinusS.size() != 0) {
        // Update priority queue.
        Iterator<Edge> iter = graph.edgeIterator(current);
        while (iter.hasNext()) {
            Edge edge = iter.next();
            int dest = edge.getDest();
            if (vMinusS.contains(dest)) {
                pQ.add(edge);
            }
        }
        // Find the shortest edge whose source is in S and
        // destination is in V-S.
        int dest = -1;
        Edge edge = null;
        do {
            edge = pQ.remove();
            dest = edge.getDest();
        } while(!vMinusS.contains(dest));
        // Take dest out of vMinusS.
        vMinusS.remove(dest);
        // Add edge to result.
        result.add(edge);
```

```
            // Make this the current vertex.
            current = dest;
        }
        return result;
    }
```

EXERCISES FOR SECTION 10.6

SELF-CHECK

1. Trace the execution of Dijkstra's algorithm to find the shortest path from Philadelphia to the other cities shown in the following graph.

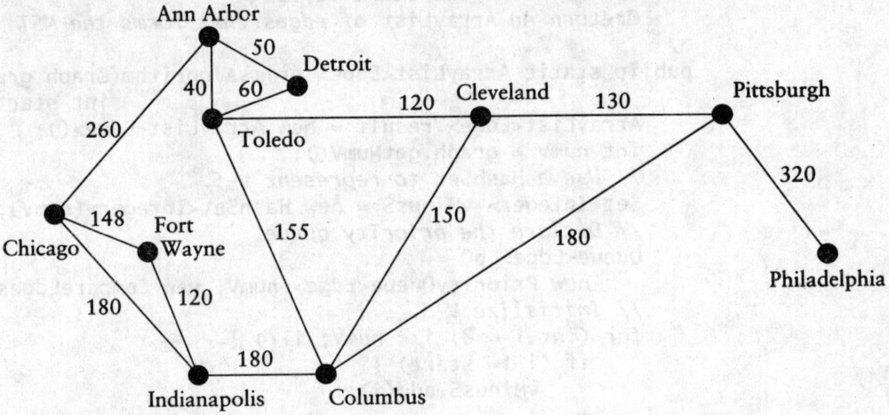

2. Trace the execution of Dijkstra's algorithm to find the shortest paths from vertex 0 to the other vertices in the following graph.

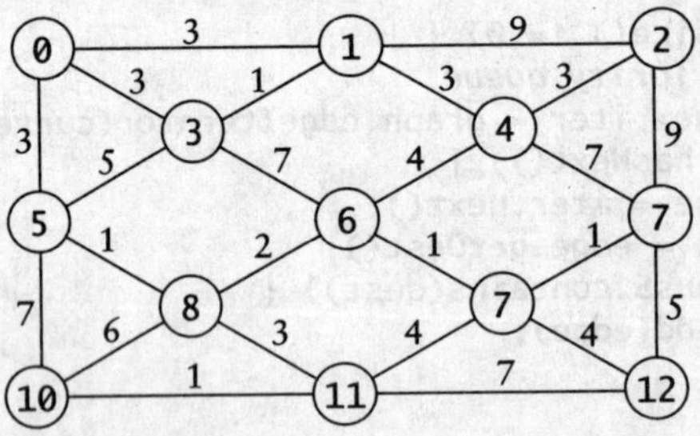

3. Trace the execution of Prim's algorithm to find the minimum spanning tree for the graph shown in Exercise 2.
4. Trace the execution of Prim's algorithm to find the minimum spanning tree for the graph shown in Exercise 1.

Chapter Review

- A graph consists of a set of vertices and a set of edges. An edge is a pair of vertices. Graphs may be either undirected or directed. Edges may have a value associated with them known as the weight.
- In an undirected graph, if {*u*, *v*} is an edge, then there is a path from vertex *u* to vertex *v*, and vice versa.
- In a directed graph, if (*u*, *v*) is an edge, then (*v*, *u*) is not necessarily an edge.
- If there is an edge from one vertex to another, then the second vertex is adjacent to the first. A path is a sequence of adjacent vertices. A path is simple if the vertices in the path are distinct except, perhaps, for the first and last vertex, which may be the same. A cycle is a path in which the first and last vertexes are the same.
- A graph is considered connected if there is a path from each vertex to every other vertex.
- A tree is a special case of a graph. Specifically, a tree is a connected graph that contains no cycles.
- Graphs may be represented by an array of adjacency lists. There is one list for each vertex, and the list contains the edges that originate at this vertex.
- Graphs may be represented by a two-dimensional square array called an adjacency matrix. The entry [*u*][*v*] will contain a value to indicate that an edge from *u* to *v* is present or absent.
- A breadth-first search of a graph finds all vertices reachable from a given vertex via the shortest path, where the length of the path is based on the number of vertices in the path.
- A depth-first search of a graph starts at a given vertex and then follows a path of unvisited vertices until it reaches a point where there are no unvisited vertices that are reachable. It then backtracks until it finds an unvisited vertex, and then continues along the path to that vertex.
- A topological sort determines an order for starting activities that are dependent on the completion of other activities (prerequisites). The finish order derived from a depth-first traversal represents a topological sort.
- Dijkstra's algorithm finds the shortest path from a start vertex to all other vertices, where the distance from one vertex to another is determined by the weight of the edge between them.
- Prim's algorithm finds the minimum spanning tree for a graph. This consists of the subset of the edges of a connected graph whose sum of weights is the minimum and the graph consisting of only the edges in the subset is still connected.

User-Defined Classes and Interfaces in This Chapter

`AbstractGraph`
`BreadthFirstSearch`
`DepthFirstSearch`
`Edge`
`Graph`
`ListGraph`
`MatrixGraph`
`MatrixGraph.Iter`
`Maze`
`TopologicalSort`

Quick-Check Exercises

1. For the following graph:
   a. List the vertices and edges.
   b. True or false: The path 0, 1, 4, 6, 3 is a simple path.
   c. True or false: The path 0, 3, 1, 4, 6, 3, 2 is a simple path.
   d. True or false: The path 3, 1, 2, 4, 7, 6, 3 is a cycle.

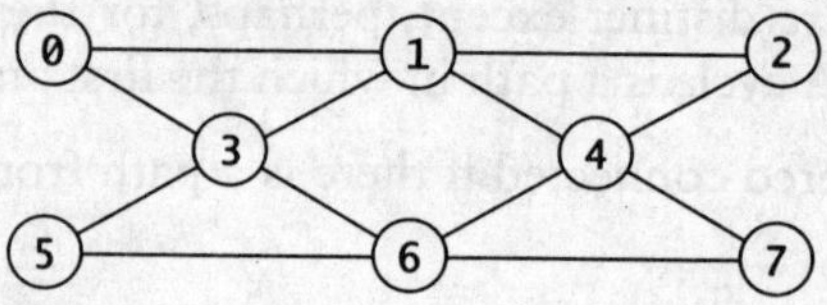

2. Identify the connected components in the following graph.

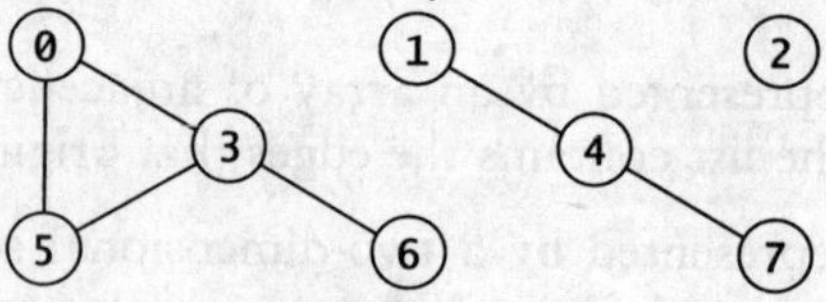

3. For the following graph:
   a. List the vertices and edges.
   b. Does this graph contain any cycles?

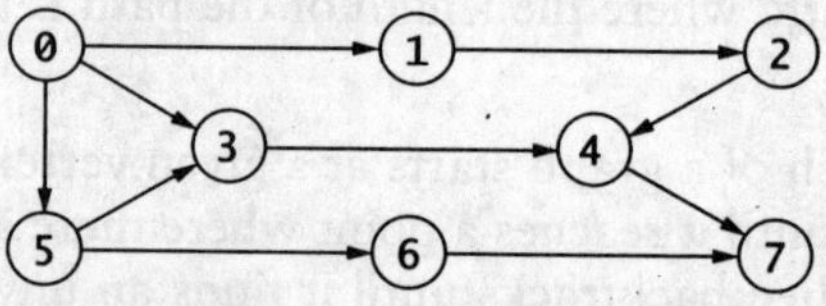

4. Show the adjacency matrices for the graphs shown in Questions 1, 2, and 3.
5. Show the adjacency lists for the graphs shown in Questions 1, 2, and 3.
6. Show the breadth-first search tree for the graph shown in Question 1, starting at vertex 0.
7. Show the depth-first search tree for the graph shown in Question 3, starting at vertex 0.
8. Show a topological sort of the vertices in the graph shown in Question 3.
9. In the following graph, find the shortest path from 0 to all other vertices.

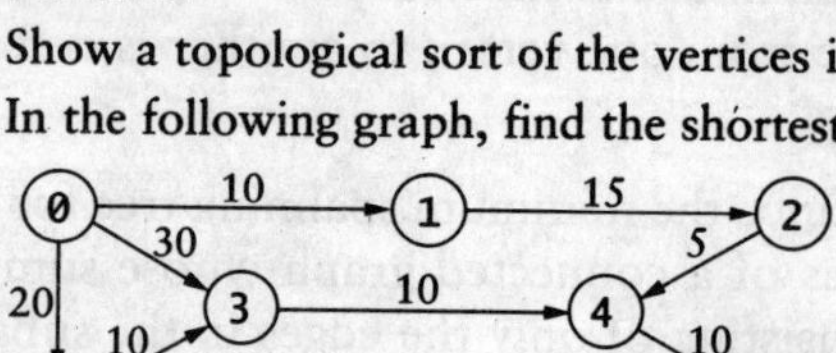

10. In the following graph, find the minimum spanning tree.

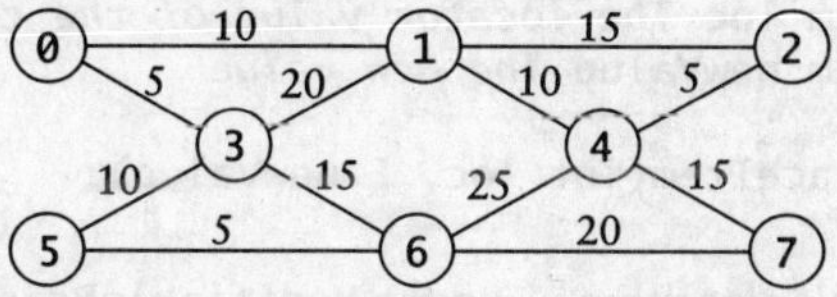

Review Questions

1. What are the different types of graphs?
2. What are the different types of paths?
3. What are two common methods for representing graphs? Can you think of other methods?
4. What is a breadth-first search? What can it be used for?
5. What is a depth-first search? What can it be used for?
6. Under what circumstances are the paths found by Dijkstra's algorithm not unique?
7. Under what circumstances is the minimum spanning tree unique?
8. What is a topological sort?

Programming Projects

1. Design and implement the `MatrixGraph` class.
2. Rewrite method `dijkstrasAlgorithm` to use a priority queue as we did for method `primsAlgorithm`. When inserting edges into the priority queue, the weight is replaced by the total distance from the source vertex to the destination vertex. The source vertex, however, remains unchanged as it is the predecessor in the shortest path.
3. In both Prim's algorithm and Dijkstra's algorithm, edges are retained in the priority queue even though a shorter edge to a given destination vertex has been found. This can be avoided, and thus performance improved, by using a `ModifiablePriorityQueue`. Extend the `PriorityQueue` class described in Chapter 6 as follows:

```
/** A ModifiablePriorityQueue stores Comparable objects. Items
    may be inserted in any order. They are removed in priority
    order, with the smallest being removed first, based on the
    compareTo method. The insert method will return a value
    known as a locator. The locator may be used to replace a
    value in the priority queue.
*/

public class ModifiablePriorityQueue<E extends Comparable<E>>
                              extends PriorityQueue<E> {
    /** Insert an item into the priority queue.
        @param obj The item to be inserted
        @return A locator to the item
    */
    int insert(E obj);

    /** Remove the smallest item in the priority queue.
        @return The smallest item in the priority queue
    */
    E poll();
```

```
    /** Replace the item at the specified location.
        @param loc The locator value of the current item
        @param newValue The new value
    */
    void replaceItem(int loc, E newValue);
    . . .
```

4. Implement Dijkstra's algorithm using the `ModifiablePriorityQueue`.
5. Implement Prim's algorithm using the `ModifiablePriortyQueue`.
6. A maze can be constructed from a series of concentric circles. Between the circles there are walls placed, and around the circles there are doors. The walls divide the areas between the circles into chambers, and the doors permit movement between chambers. The positions of the doors and walls are given in degrees measured counterclockwise from the horizontal. For example, the maze shown on the left can be described as follows:

Number of circles	4	
Position of doors	Outer circle	85–90
	Next inner circle	26–40, 135–146, 198–215, 305–319
	Next inner circle	67–90, 161–180, 243–256, 342–360
	Innermost circle	251–288
Position of walls	Outer ring	45, 135, 300
	Middle ring	0, 100, 225, 270
	Inner ring	65, 180

Write a program that inputs a description of a maze in this format and finds the shortest path from the outside to the innermost circle. The shortest path is the one that goes through the smallest number of chambers.

7. In Chapter 5 we discussed the class `MazeTest`, which reads a rectangular maze as a sequence of lines consisting of 0s and 1s, where a 0 represents an open square and a 1 represents a closed one. For example, the maze shown in Figure 10.21 and reproduced here has the following input file:

```
011111111111111111111111
000000000000000000000001
011111111111111011111101
011111100000001011111101
011111101111111011000001
000000000000000011011011
110111101101111011011011
110111101101111011011011
110111101101000011011011
110111101101111111011011
110111101100000000011011
110000001101111111111011
111101111100000000001011
111101111111111111101000
111100000000000000001110
111111111111111111111110
```

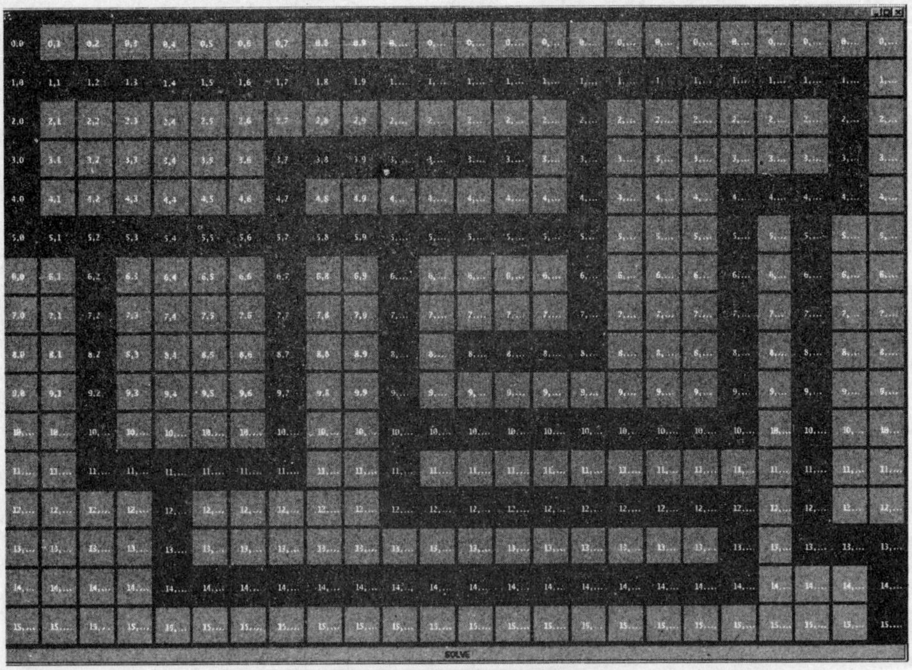

Write a program that reads input in this format and finds the shortest path, where the distance along a path is defined by the number of squares covered.

8. A third possible representation of a graph is to use the `TreeSet` class to contain the edges. By defining a comparator that compares first on the source vertex and then the destination vertex, we can use the `subSet` method to create a view that contains only edges originating at a specified vertex and then use the iterator of that view to iterate through edges. Design and implement a class that meets the requirements of the `Graph` interface and uses a `TreeSet` to hold the edges.

Answers to Quick-Check Exercises

1. **a.** Vertices: {0, 1, 2, 3, 4, 5, 6, 7}
   Edges: {{0, 1}, {0, 3}, {1, 2}, {1, 3}, {1, 4}, {2, 4}, {3, 5}, {3, 6}, {4, 6}, {4, 7}, {5, 6}, {6, 7}}

   b. True

   c. False

   d. True

2. The connected components are {0, 3, 5, 6}, {1, 4, 7}, and {2}.

3. **a.** Vertices: {0, 1, 2, 3, 4, 5, 6, 7}
   Edges: {(0, 1), (0, 3), (0, 5), (1, 2), (2, 4), (3, 4), (4, 7), (5, 3), (5, 6), (6, 7)}

   b. The graph contains no cycles.

4. For the graph shown in Question 1:

Column (Row labels at left)

	[0]	[1]	[2]	[3]	[4]	[5]	[6]	[7]
[0]		1		1				
[1]	1		1	1	1			
[2]		1			1			
[3]	1	1				1	1	
[4]		1	1				1	1
[5]				1			1	
[6]				1	1	1		1
[7]					1		1	

For Question 2:

Column (Row labels at left)

	[0]	[1]	[2]	[3]	[4]	[5]	[6]	[7]
[0]				1		1		
[1]					1			
[2]								
[3]	1					1	1	
[4]		1						1
[5]	1			1				
[6]				1				
[7]					1			

For Question 3:

Column (Row labels at left)

	[0]	[1]	[2]	[3]	[4]	[5]	[6]	[7]
[0]		1		1		1		
[1]			1					
[2]					1			
[3]					1			
[4]								1
[5]				1			1	
[6]								1
[7]								

5. For Question 1:

```
[0]   →   1 → 3
[1]   →   0 → 2 → 3 → 4
[2]   →   1 → 4
[3]   →   0 → 1 → 5 → 6
[4]   →   1 → 2 → 6 → 7
[5]   →   3 → 6
[6]   →   3 → 4 → 5 → 7
[7]   →   4 → 6
```

For Question 2:

```
[0]   →   3 → 5
[1]   →   4
[2]   →
[3]   →   0 → 5 → 6
[4]   →   1 → 7
[5]   →   0 → 3
[6]   →   3
[7]   →   4
```

For Question 3:

```
[0]   →   1 → 3 → 5
[1]   →   2
[2]   →   4
[3]   →   4
[4]   →   7
[5]   →   3 → 6
[6]   →   7
[7]   →
```

6.

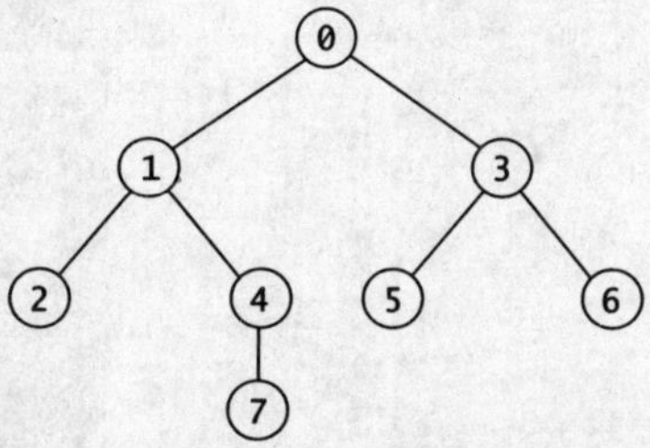

7.

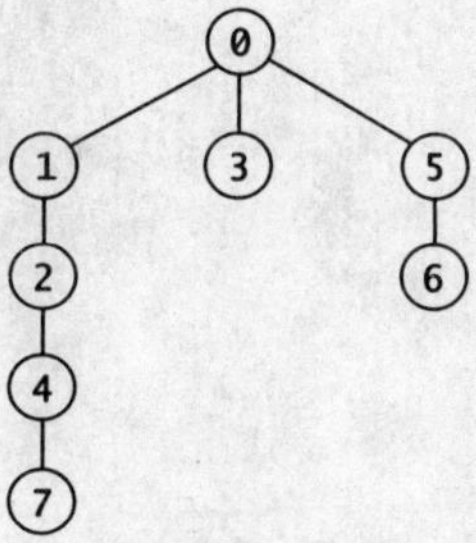

8. 0, 5, 6, 3, 1, 2, 4, 7

9.

Vertex	Distance	Path
1	10	$0 \rightarrow 1$
2	25	$0 \rightarrow 1 \rightarrow 2$
3	30	$0 \rightarrow 3$ (or $0 \rightarrow 5 \rightarrow 3$)
4	30	$0 \rightarrow 1 \rightarrow 2 \rightarrow 4$
5	20	$0 \rightarrow 5$
6	25	$0 \rightarrow 5 \rightarrow 6$
7	40	$0 \rightarrow 5 \rightarrow 6 \rightarrow 7$ (or $0 \rightarrow 1 \rightarrow 2 \rightarrow 4 \rightarrow 7$)

10.

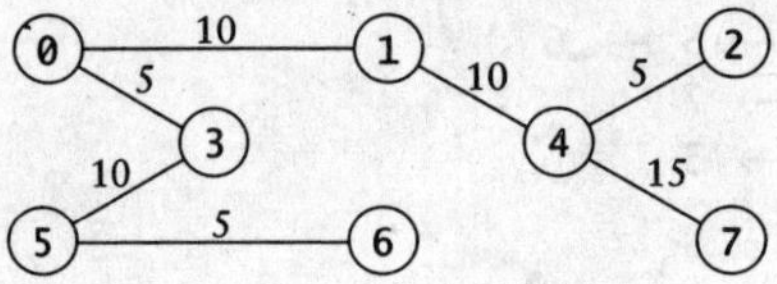

Appendix **A**

Introduction to Java

Appendix Objectives

- To understand the essentials of object-oriented programming in Java
- To learn about the primitive data types of Java
- To understand how to use the control structures of Java
- To learn how to use predefined classes such as `Math`, `String`, `StringBuilder`, and `StringBuffer`
- To introduce regular expressions and Pattern and Matcher classes
- To learn how to write and document your own Java classes
- To understand how to use arrays in Java
- To learn how to perform I/O in Java using simple dialog windows
- To introduce the `Scanner` class for input and the `Formatter` class for output
- To learn how to perform I/O in Java using streams
- To learn how to use the **`try-catch-finally`** sequence to catch and process exceptions
- To understand what it means to throw an exception and how to throw an exception in a method

This appendix reviews object-oriented programming in Java. It is oriented to a student who has had a first course in programming in Java or another language and who, therefore, is familiar with control statements for selection and repetition, basic data types, arrays, and methods or functions. If your first course was in Java, you can skim this chapter for review or just use it as a reference as needed. However, you should read it more carefully if your Java course did not emphasize object-oriented design.

If your first course was not in Java, you should read this appendix carefully. If your first course followed an object-oriented approach but was in another language, you should concentrate on the differences between Java syntax and the language that you know. If you have programmed only in a language that was not object-oriented, you will need to concentrate on aspects of object-oriented programming and classes as well as Java syntax.

The appendix begins with an introduction to the Java environment and the Java Virtual Machine (JVM). Next it covers the basic data types of Java, called primitive data types, and provides an introduction to objects and classes. Control structures and methods are then discussed.

The Java Application Programming Interface (API) provides a rich collection of classes that simplify programming in Java. The first Java classes that we cover are the `String`, `StringBuilder`, `StringBuffer`, and `Math` classes. The `String` class provides several methods and an operator + (concatenation) that process sequences of characters (strings). The `Math` class provides many methods for performing standard mathematical computations.

Next we show you how to design and write your own classes consisting of data fields and methods. We also discuss the Java wrapper classes, which enable a programmer to create and process objects that contain primitive-type values.

We describe a specific format for comments in classes. Using this commenting style enables you to generate HTML pages with clear and complete documentation for classes in the same form as the Java documentation provided on the Sun Web site.

We also review array objects in Java. We cover both one- and two-dimensional arrays.

Next we discuss input/output. We show how to use the `JOptionPane` class (part of package `javax.swing`) to create dialog windows for data entry and for output. We also show how to use streams and the console for input/output.

Finally, we discuss how to handle exceptions and to throw exceptions.

Introduction to Java

A.1 The Java Environment and Classes

Before we talk about the Java language, we will briefly discuss the Java environment and how Java programs are executed. Java, developed by Sun Microsystems Corporation, enjoys its popularity because it is a platform-independent, object-oriented

FIGURE A.1
Compiling and Executing a Java Program

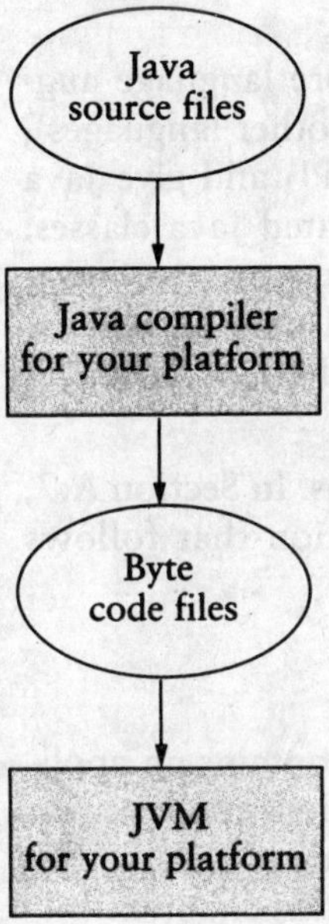

language and because certain kinds of Java programs, called *applets*, can be embedded in Web pages. Being platform independent means that a Java program will run on any kind of computer. Although platform independence is a goal for all high-level language programs, it is not always achieved. Java comes closer to achieving this goal than most by providing implementations of the Java Virtual Machine (discussed next) for many platforms.

The Java Virtual Machine

Java is platform independent because the Java designers utilize the concept of a Java Virtual Machine (JVM), which is a software "computer" that runs inside an actual computer. Before you can execute a Java program, the classes in the Java program must first be translated from the Java language in which they were written into an executable form in the traditional way by a compiler program. Instead of a file of platform-dependent machine-language instructions, however, which is the normal output from a compiler, the Java compiler generates a file of platform-independent Java *byte code* instructions. When you execute the program, your computer's JVM *interprets* each byte code instruction and carries it out. The JVM for machines running Microsoft Windows is different from the JVM for UNIX or Apple machines, but they all process byte code instructions in the same way (see Figure A.1).

The Java Compiler

The Java compiler is also platform specific even though it produces the same byte code file for a given Java source program on all platforms. It must be platform specific because it executes machine-language instructions for a particular platform, and these instructions are not the same for all platforms.

Classes and Objects

In Java and object-oriented programming in general, the class is the fundamental programming unit. Every program is written as a collection of classes, and all code that you write must be part of a class. In Java, class definitions are stored in separate files with the extension `.java`; the file name must be the same as the class name defined within.

A *class* is a named description for a group of entities (called *objects* or *instances* of the class) that have the same characteristics. These characteristics are the attributes (*data fields*) for each object and the operations (*methods*) that can be performed on these objects.

If you are new to object-oriented design, you may be confused about the differences between a class and an object. A class is a general description of a group of entities that all have the same characteristics—that is, they can all perform the same kinds of actions, and the same pieces of information are meaningful for all of them. The individual entities are objects. For example, the class `House` would describe a collection of entities that each have a number of bedrooms, a number of bathrooms, a kind of roof, and so on (but not a horsepower rating or mileage); they can all be built, remodeled, assessed for property tax, and so on (but not have their transmission fluid changed). The house where you live and the house where your best friend lives can be represented by two objects of class `House`.

Classes extend Java by providing additional data types. For example, the class `String` is a predefined class that enables the programmer to process sequences of characters easily. We will discuss the `String` class in detail in Section A.5.

The Java API

The Java programming language consists of a relatively small core language augmented by an extensive collection of *packages* (called libraries in other languages), which constitute the Java Application Programming Interface (API) and give Java additional capabilities. Each package contains a collection of related Java classes. We will use several of these packages in this textbook. Among them are the Swing package, the AWT package, and the `util` package. You can find out about these packages by accessing the Java Web site maintained by Sun Microsystems at `http://java.sun.com`.

Java documentation is provided as a linked collection of Web pages. In Section A.7, we will discuss how you can write your own Java documentation that follows this style.

The `import` Statement

Next, we show a sample Java source file (`HelloWorld.java`) that contains an application program (class `HelloWorld`). Our goal in the rest of this section is to give you an overview of the process of creating and executing an application program. The statements in this program will be covered in more detail later in this chapter.

```
import javax.swing.*;

public class HelloWorld {
    public static void main(String[] args) {
        String name = JOptionPane.showInputDialog("Enter your name");
        JOptionPane.showMessageDialog(null, "Hello " + name
                                          + ", welcome to Java!");
    }
}
```

The Java source file begins with the statement

```
import javax.swing.*;
```

This statement tells the Java compiler to make the names defined in the Swing package accessible to this file. The semicolon at the end of the line is used to terminate a Java statement.

Class `HelloWorld` begins with the line

```
public class HelloWorld {
```

which identifies `HelloWorld` as a public class and makes it visible to other classes (or the JVM).

Method `main`

The line

```
public static void main(String[] args) {
```

identifies the start of the definition for method `main`. This is the place where the JVM begins the execution of an application program. The words **`public static void`** tell the compiler that `main` is accessible outside of the class (**`public`**), it is a **`static`** method (explained in Section A.4), and it does not return a value (**`void`**). The part in parentheses after `main` describes the method's parameters, an array of `String`s. We always write the heading for method `main` in this way.

Method `main` contains two statements that call methods in class `JOptionPane`, a class in Swing that displays dialog windows (Section A.9). The statement

```
String name = JOptionPane.showInputDialog("Enter your name");
```

displays the following dialog window. The user has typed in the characters **`Katherine`**.

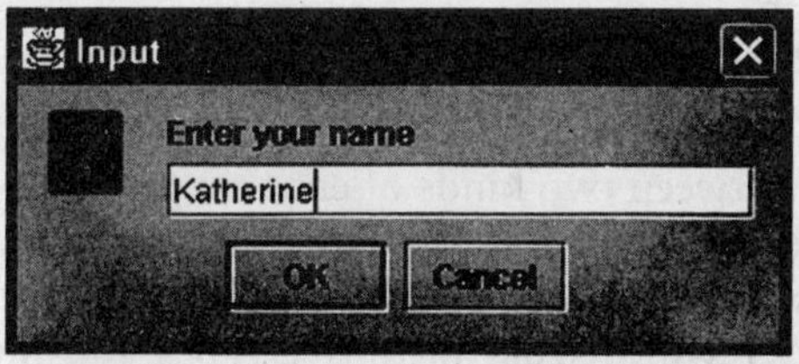

The characters typed in by the user are stored in a memory cell referenced by the variable `name`. Later, they may be displayed in a message window by the following statement, which is written on two lines. The message window follows the statement.

```
JOptionPane.showMessageDialog(null, "Hello " + name
                              + ", welcome to Java!");
```

Execution of a Java Program

You can compile and run class `HelloWorld` using an Integrated Development Environment (IDE) or the Java Development Kit (JDK). If you are using an IDE, type this class into the edit window for class `HelloWorld.java` and select **Run**. If you are not using an IDE, you must create this file using an editor program and save it as file `HelloWorld.java`. Then you can use the command

```
javac HelloWorld.java
```

to get the Java compiler to compile it. This will create the Java byte code file called `HelloWorld.class`.

The command

```
java HelloWorld
```

starts the JVM and causes it to execute the byte code instructions in file `HelloWorld.class`. It begins execution with the byte code instructions for method `main`.

EXERCISES FOR SECTION A.1

SELF-CHECK

1. What is the Java Virtual Machine? Is it hardware or software? How does its role differ from that of the Java compiler?
2. Explain the statement: You can write a Java program once and run it anywhere.
3. Explain the relationship between a class and an object. Which is general and which is specific?

A.2 Primitive Data Types and Reference Variables

Java distinguishes between two kinds of entities: primitive types (numbers, characters) and objects. Values associated with primitive-type data are stored in primitive-type variables. Objects, however, are associated with reference variables, which store an object's address. We will discuss primitive types and introduce objects in this section; we describe objects in more detail throughout the chapter.

Primitive Data Types

The primitive data types for Java represent numbers, characters, and boolean values (**`true`**, **`false`**) (see Table A.1). Integers are represented by data types **`byte`**, **`short`**, **`int`**, and **`long`**; real numbers are represented by **`float`** and **`double`**. The range of values for the data types is in increasing order in Table A.1.

Type **`char`** is used in Java to represent characters. Java uses the Unicode character set (two bytes per character), which provides a much richer set of characters than the ASCII character set (one byte per character) used by many earlier languages. Table A.2 shows the first 128 Unicode characters, which correspond to the ASCII characters. These include the control characters and the Basic Latin alphabet. The

TABLE A.1
Java Primitive Data Types in Increasing Order of Range

Data Type	Range of Values
`byte`	–128 through 127
`short`	–32,768 through 32,767
`int`	–2,147,483,648 through 2,147,483,647
`long`	–9,223,372,036,854,775,808 through 9,223,372,036,854,775,807
`float`	Approximately $\pm 10^{-38}$ through $\pm 10^{38}$ and 0 with 6 digits precision
`double`	Approximately $\pm 10^{-308}$ through $\pm 10^{308}$ and 0 with 15 digits precision
`char`	The Unicode character set
`boolean`	**`true`, `false`**

TABLE A.2
The First 128 Unicode Symbols

	000	001	002	003	004	005	006	007
0	Null		Space	0	@	P	`	p
1			!	1	A	Q	a	q
2			"	2	B	R	b	r
3			#	3	C	S	c	s
4			$	4	D	T	d	t
5			%	5	E	U	e	u
6			&	6	F	V	f	v
7	Bell		'	7	G	W	g	w
8	Backspace		(	8	H	X	h	x
9	Tab		)	9	I	Y	I	y
A	Line feed		*	:	J	Z	j	z
B		Escape	+	;	K	[	k	{
C	Form feed		,	<	L	\	l	|
D	Return		-	=	M	]	m	}
E			.	>	N	^	n	~
F			/	?	O	_	o	delete

Unicode for each character, expressed as a hexadecimal number, consists of the three-digit column number (000 through 007) followed by the row number (0 through F). For example, the Unicode for the letter `Q` is 0051, and the Unicode for the letter `q` is 0071. The characters in the first two columns of Table A.2 and the Unicode character 007F (delete) are control characters. The hexadecimal digits A through F are equivalent to the decimal values 10 through 15. The hexadecimal number 007F is equivalent to the decimal number $7 \times 16 + 15$.

Java uses type **boolean** to represent logical data. The **boolean** data type has only two values: **true** and **false**. Some languages allow you to represent type **boolean** values using the integers 0 and 1, but Java does not allow you to do this.

Primitive-Type Variables

Java uses declaration statements to declare and initialize primitive-type variables.

```
int countItems;
double sum = 0.0;
char star = '*';
boolean moreData;
```

The second and third of the preceding statements initialize variables `sum` and `star` to the values after the operator =. As shown, you can use primitive-type values (such as `0.0` and `'*'`) as *literals* in Java statements. A literal is a constant value that appears directly in a statement.

Identifiers, such as variable names in Java, must consist of some combination of letters, digits, the underscore character, and the $ character, beginning with a letter. Identifiers can't begin with a digit.

PROGRAM STYLE

Java Convention for Identifiers

Many Java programmers use "camel notation" for variable names. All letters are in lowercase except for identifiers that are made up of more than one word. The first letter of each word, starting with the second word, is in uppercase (e.g., `thisLongIdentifier`). Camel notation gets its name from the appearance of the identifier, with the uppercase letters in the interior forming "humps."

Primitive-Type Constants

Java programmers usually use all uppercase letters for constant identifiers, with an underscore symbol between words. The keywords **`static final`** identify a constant value that is **`static`** (more on this later) and **`final`**—that is, can't be changed.

```
static final int MAX_SCORE = 999;
static final double G = 3.82;
```

Operators

Table A.3 shows the Java operators in decreasing precedence. We will not use any of the bitwise operators, shifting operators, or conditional operator. The arithmetic operators (`*`, `/`, `+`, `-`) can be used with any of the primitive numeric types or type **`char`**, but not with type **`boolean`**. This is also the case for the Java remainder operator (`%`) and the increment (`++`) and decrement (`--`) operators.

Postfix and Prefix Increment

In Java you can write statements such as

```
i = i + 1;
```

using the *increment operator*:

```
i++;
```

This form is the *postfix increment*. You can also use the *prefix increment*

```
++i;
```

but the postfix increment (or decrement) is more common.

TABLE A.3
Operator Precedence

Rank	Operator	Operation	Associativity
1	[]	Array subscript	Left
	()	Method call	
	.	Member access	
	++	Postfix increment	
	--	Postfix decrement	
2	++	Prefix increment	Right
	--	Prefix decrement	
	+ -	Unary plus or minus	
	!	Complement	
	~	Bitwise complement	
	(*type*)	Type cast	
	new	Object creation	
3	*, /, %	Multiply, divide, remainder	Left
4	+	Addition or string concatenation	Left
	-	Subtraction	
5	<<	Signed bit shift left	Left
	>>	Signed bit shift right	
	>>>	Unsigned bit shift right	
6	<, <=	Less than, less than or equal	Left
	>, >=	Greater than, greater than or equal	
	instanceof	Reference test	
7	==	Equal to	Left
	!=	Not equal to	
8	&	Bitwise and	Left
9	^	Bitwise exclusive or	Left
10	|	Bitwise or	Left
11	&&	Logical and	Left
12	||	Logical or	Left
13	?:	Conditional	Left
14	=	Assignment	Right
	*=, /=, %=, +=, -=, <<=, >>=, >>>=, &=, |=	Compound assignment	

When the postfix form is used in an expression (e.g., `x * i++`), the variable `i` is evaluated and then incremented. When the prefix form is used in an expression (e.g., `x * ++i`), the variable `i` is incremented before it is evaluated.

EXAMPLE A.1 In the assignment

```
z = i++;
```

`i` is incremented, but `z` gets the value `i` had before it was incremented. So if `i` is `3` before the assignment statement, `z` would be `3` and `i` would be `4` after the assignment. In the assignment statement

```
z = ++i;
```

`i` is incremented and `z` gets its new value, so if `i` is `3` before the assignment, `z` and `i` would both be `4` after the assignment statement.

PITFALL

Using Increment and Decrement in Expressions with Other Operators

In the preceding example, the increment operator is used with the assignment operator in the same statement. Similarly, the expression `x * i++` uses the multiplication and postfix increment operators. In this expression, the variable `i` is evaluated and then incremented. When the prefix form is used in an expression (e.g., `x * ++i`), the variable `i` is incremented before it is evaluated. However, you should avoid writing expressions like these, which could easily be interpreted incorrectly by the human reader.

Type Compatibility and Conversion

In operations involving mixed-type operands, the numeric type of the smaller range is converted to the numeric type of the larger range. This means that if an operation involves a type **`int`** and a type **`double`** operand, the type **`int`** operand is automatically converted to type **`double`**. This is called a *widening conversion*.

In an assignment operation, a numeric type of a smaller range can be assigned to a numeric type of a larger range; for example, a type **`int`** expression can be assigned to a type **`float`** or **`double`** variable. Java performs the widening conversion automatically.

```
int item = . . . ;
double realItem = item;     // Valid - automatic widening
```

However, the converse is not true.

```
double y = . . . ;
int x = y;   // Invalid assignment
```

This statement is invalid because it attempts to store a real value in an integer variable. It would cause the syntax error `possible loss of precision; double,` required: int. This means that a type **int** expression is required for the assignment. You can use explicit *type cast* operations to perform a *narrowing conversion* and ensure that the assignment statement will be valid. In the following statement, the expression (int) instructs the compiler to cast the value of y to type **int** before assigning the integer value to x.

```
int x = (int) y;   // Cast to int before assignment
```

Referencing Objects

In Java, you can declare reference variables that can reference objects of specified types. For example, the statement

```
String greeting;
```

declares a reference variable named greeting that can reference a String object. The statement

```
greeting = "hello";
```

specifies the particular String object to be referenced by greeting: the one that contains the characters in the string literal "hello". What is actually stored in the memory cell allocated to greeting is the *address* of the area in memory where this particular object of type String is stored. We illustrate this in Figure A.2 by drawing an arrow from variable greeting to the object that it references (type String, value is "hello"). In contrast, the memory cell allocated to a primitive-type variable stores a value, not an address. Just as with the primitive variable declarations shown earlier, these two statements can be combined into one.

```
String greeting = "hello";
```

String objects are the only ones that can be created by assignment operations such as this one. We describe how to create other kinds of objects in the next section.

Two reference variables can reference the same object. The statement

```
String welcome = greeting;
```

copies the address in greeting to welcome, so String variable welcome also references the object shown in Figure A.2.

Creating Objects

The Java **new** *operator* can be used to create an instance of a class. The expression

```
new String("qwerty")
```

creates a new String instance (object) that stores the character sequence consisting of the first six characters of the top row of letters on the standard keyboard (called a "qwerty" keyboard). The expression new String("qwerty") invokes a special method for the String class called a *constructor*. A constructor executes whenever

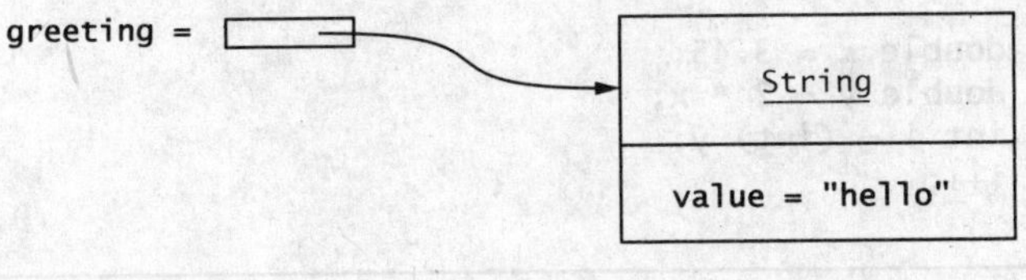

FIGURE A.2
Variable greeting References a String Object

a new object of any type is created; in this case, it initializes the contents of a `String` object to the character sequence `"qwerty"`.

The object created by the expression `new String("qwerty")` is an *anonymous* or unnamed object. Normally we want to be able to refer to objects that we create. We can declare a reference variable of type `String` and assign this object to the reference variable:

```
String keyboard = new String("qwerty");
```

EXERCISES FOR SECTION A.2

SELF-CHECK

1. For the following assignment statement, assume that `x`, `y` are type **`double`** and `m`, `n` are type **`int`**. List the order in which the operations would be performed. Include any widening and narrowing conversions that would occur.
```
m = (int) (x * y + m / n / y * (m + x));
```
2. What is the value assigned to `m` in Exercise 1 when `m` is 5, `n` is 3, `x` is 2.5, and `y` is 2.0?
3. What is the difference between a reference variable and a primitive-type variable?
4. Draw a diagram similar to Figure A.2 that shows the effect of the following statements.
```
String y = new String("abc");
String z = "def";
String w = z;
```

A.3 Java Control Statements

The control statements of a programming language determine the flow of execution through a program. They fall into three categories: sequence, selection, and repetition.

Sequence and Compound Statements

A group of statements that is executed in sequence is written as a *compound statement* delimited (enclosed) by braces. The statements execute in the order in which they are listed.

EXAMPLE A.2 The following statements constitute a compound statement:

```
{
    double x = 3.45;
    double y = 2 * x;
    int i = (int) y;
    i++;
}
```

Selection and Repetition Control

Table A.4 shows the Java control statements for selection and repetition. (Java uses the same syntax for control structures as do C and C++.) We assume that you are familiar with basic programming control structures from your first course, so we won't dwell on them here. We will introduce a looping construct that is new to Java 5.0—the enhanced `for` statement—in Chapter 4.

In Table A.3, each *condition* is a **`boolean`** expression in parentheses. Type **`boolean`** expressions often involve comparisons written using equality (==, !=) and relational operators (<, <=, >, >=). For example, the condition `(x + y > x - y)` is true if the sum of the two variables shown is larger than their difference. The logical operators ! (not, or complement), && (and), and || (or) are used to combine **`boolean`** expressions. For example, the condition `(n >= 0 && n <= 10)` is true if `n` has a value between zero and 10, inclusive.

Java uses short-circuit evaluation, which means that evaluation of a **`boolean`** expression terminates when its value can be determined. For example, if in the expression *bool1* || *bool2*, *bool1* is true, the expression must be true, so *bool2* is not evaluated. Similarly, in the expression *bool3* && *bool4*, if *bool3* is false, the expression must be false, so *bool4* is not evaluated.

EXAMPLE A.3 In the condition

```
(num != 0 && sum / num)
```

if `num` is 0, the expression following && is not evaluated. This prevents a division by zero.

TABLE A.4
Java Control Statements

Control Structure	Purpose	Syntax

`if ... else`	Used to write a decision with *conditions* that select the alternative to be executed. Executes the first (second) alternative if the *condition* is true (false).	`if (`*condition*`) {`
		`. . .`
		`} else {`
		`. . .`
		`}`

`switch`	Used to write a decision with scalar values (integers, characters) that select the alternative to be executed. Executes the *statements* following the *label* that is the *selector* value. Execution falls through to the next **`case`** if there is no **`return`** or **`break`**. Executes the statements following **`default`** if the *selector* value does not match any *label*.	`switch (`*selector*`) {`
		`case `*label*` : `*statements*`; break;`
		`case `*label*` : `*statements*`; break;`
		`. . .`
		`default : `*statements*`;`
		`}`

TABLE A.4 (continued)

Control Structure	Purpose	Syntax

`while`	Used to write a loop that specifies the repetition *condition* in the loop header. The *condition* is tested before each iteration of the loop and, if it is true, the loop body executes; otherwise, the loop is exited.	`while (`*condition*`) {`
		`. . .`
		`}`

`do ... while`	Used to write a loop that executes at least once. The repetition *condition* is at the end of the loop. The *condition* is tested after each iteration of the loop, and, if it is true, the loop body executes again; otherwise, the loop is exited.	`do {`
		`. . .`
		`} while (`*condition*`);`

`for`	Used to write a loop that specifies the *initialization*, repetition *condition*, and *update* steps in the loop header. The *initialization* statements execute before loop repetition begins; the *condition* is tested before each iteration of the loop and, if it is true, the loop body executes; otherwise, the loop is exited. The *update* statements execute after each iteration.	`for (`*initialization*`;` *condition*`;` *update*`)`
		`{`
		`. . .`
		`}`

EXAMPLE A.4 The operator `%` in the condition `(nextInt % 2 == 0)` gives the remainder after an integer division, so the condition is true if `nextInt` is an even number. If `maxVal` has been defined, the following loops (`for` loop on the left, `while` loop on the right) store the sum of the even integers from 1 to `maxVal` in variable `sum` (initial value 0), and they store the product of the odd integers in variable `prod` (initial value 1).

```
for (int nextInt = 1;
         nextInt <= maxVal;
         nextInt++) {
     if (nextInt % 2 == 0) {
         sum += nextInt;
     } else {
         prod *= nextInt;
     }
}
```

```
int nextInt = 1;
while (nextInt <= maxVal) {
     if (nextInt % 2 == 0) {
         sum += nextInt;
     } else {
         prod *= nextInt;
     }
     nextInt++
}
```

Nested `if` Statements

You can write `if` statements that select among more than two alternatives by nesting one `if` statement inside another. Often each inner `if` statement will follow the keyword `else` of its corresponding outer `if` statement.

EXAMPLE A.5 The following nested `if` statement has four alternatives. The conditions are evaluated in sequence until one evaluates to `true`. The compound statement following the first true condition then executes.

```
if (operator == '+') {
    result = x + y;
    addOp++;
}
else
    if (operator == '-') {
        result = x - y;
        subtractOp++;
    }
    else
        if (operator == '*') {
            result = x * y;
            multiplyOp++;
        }
        else
            if (operator == '/') {
                result = x / y;
                divideOp++;
            }
```

PROGRAM STYLE

Braces and Indentation in Control Statements

Java programmers often place the opening brace { on the same line as the control statement header. The closing brace } aligns with the first word in the control statement header. We will always indent the statements inside a control structure to clarify the meaning of the control statement.

Although we write the symbols } **else** { on one line, another popular style convention is to place the word **else** under the symbol } and aligned with **if**:

```
if (nextInt % 2 == 0) {
    sum += nextInt;
}
else {
    prod *= nextInt;
}
```

Some programmers omit the braces when a true task or false task or a loop body consists of a single statement. Others prefer to include them always, both for clarity and because having the braces will permit them to insert additional statements later if needed.

PITFALL

Omitting Braces around a Compound Statement

The braces in the preceding example delimit compound statements. Each compound statement consists of two statements. If you omit a brace, you will get the syntax error `'else' without 'if'`.

PROGRAM STYLE

Writing `if` Statements with Multiple Alternatives

Java programmers often write nested **if** statements like those in the preceding example without indenting each nested **if**. The following multiple-alternative decision has the same meaning but is easier to write and read.

```
if (operator == '+') {
    result = x + y;
    addOp++;
} else if (operator == '-') {
    result = x - y;
    subtractOp++;
} else if (operator == '*') {
    result = x * y;
    multiplyOp++;
} else if (operator == '/') {
    result = x / y;
    divideOp++;
}
```

The `switch` Statement

The **if** statement in Example A.5 could also be written as the following **switch** statement. Each **case** label (e.g., '+') indicates a possible value of the selector expression operator. The statements that follow a particular label execute if the selector has that value. The **break** statements cause an exit from the **switch** statement. Without them, execution would continue on to the statements in the next case. The last case, with label default, executes if the selector value doesn't match any case label. (Note that the compound statements for each case are not surrounded by braces.)

```
switch (operator) {
    case '+':
        result = x + y;
        addOp++;
        break;
    case '-':
        result = x - y;
        subtractOp++;
        break;
    case '*':
        result = x * y;
        multiplyOp++;
        break;
    case '/':
        result = x / y;
        divideOp++;
        break;
    default:
        // Do nothing
}
```

EXERCISES FOR SECTION A.3

SELF-CHECK

1. What is the purpose of the **break** statement in the preceding **switch** statement? List the statements that would execute when operator is '-' with the **break** statements in place and if they were removed.
2. What is the difference between a **while** loop and a **do ... while** loop? What is the minimum number of repetitions of the loop body with each kind of loop?

PROGRAMMING

1. Rewrite the **for** statement in Example A.4 using a **do ... while** loop.

A.4 Methods and Class Math

Java programmers can use methods to define a group of statements that perform a particular operation. Methods are very similar to functions in other programming languages such as C and C++. The Java method minChar that follows returns the character with the smaller Unicode value. The statements beginning with keyword **return** cause an exit from the method; the expression following **return** is the method result.

```
static char minChar(char ch1, char ch2) {
    if (ch1 <= ch2)
        return ch1;
    else
        return ch2;
}
```

The modifier **static** indicates that minChar is a *static method* or *class method*. A static method must be called by listing the name of the class in which it is defined, followed by a dot, followed by the method name and any arguments. This is called *dot notation*. For example, the statement

```
char ch = ClassName.minChar('a', 'A');
```

would store the letter A in ch because uppercase letters have smaller codes than lowercase letters. (If method minChar is called within the class that defines it, the prefix *ClassName.* is not needed.) If the modifier **static** does not appear in a method header, the method is an *instance method*. We describe how to invoke instance methods next and show how to define them afterward.

The Instance Methods println and print

Methods that are not preceded by the modifier **static** are instance methods. To call or invoke an instance method, you need to apply it to an object using dot notation:

object.method(arguments)

One instance method that is useful for output operations is the method `println` (defined in class `PrintStream`). It can be applied to the `PrintStream` object `System.out` (the console window), which is defined in the `System` class. It has a single argument of any data type. If `x` is a type **`double`** variable, the statement

```
System.out.println(x);
```

displays the value of `x` in the console window. The statement

```
System.out.println("Value of x is " + x);
```

has a `String` expression as its argument (+ means concatenate, or join, strings). The string consists of the character sequence `Value of x is` followed by the characters that represent the value of variable `x`. If `x` is 123.45, the output line will be

```
Value of x is 123.45
```

You would get the same effect using the statement pair

```
System.out.print("Value of x is ");
System.out.println(x);
```

The method `print` also displays its argument in the console window. However, it does not follow this information with the *newline* character, so the next execution of `print` or `println` will display information on the same output line.

PITFALL

Static Methods Can't Call Instance Methods

A static method can call other static methods directly. Also, an instance method can call a static method. However, a static method, including method `main`, can't call an instance method without first creating an object and applying the instance method to that object.

Call-by-Value Arguments

In Java, all method arguments are call-by-value. This means that if the argument is a primitive type, its value (not its address) is passed to the method, so the method can't modify the argument value and have the modification remain after return from the method. Some other programming languages provide a call-by-reference or call-by-address mechanism so that a method can modify a primitive-type argument.

If the argument is of a class type, the value that is passed to the method is the value of the reference variable, not the value of the object itself (see Section A.2). The reference variable value points to the object, allowing the method to access the object itself using the methods of the object's own class. Any modification to the object will remain after the return from the method. This will be discussed in Section A.7.

The Class Math

Class `Math` is part of the Java language, and it provides a collection of methods that are useful for performing common mathematical operations. These are all **`static`** methods, so the prefix `Math.` is required in order to invoke a method of this class.

Table A.5 shows some of these methods. The first column shows the result type for each method followed by its *signature* (the method name and the argument types). For example, for method `ceil`, the first column shows that the method returns a type **`double`** result and has a type **`double`** argument. The data type *numeric* means that any of the numeric types can be used.

TABLE A.5
Class Math Methods

Method	Behavior
`static` *numeric* `abs(`*numeric*`)`	Returns the absolute value of its *numeric* argument (the result type is the same as the argument type).
`static double ceil(double)`	Returns the smallest whole number that is not less than its argument.
`static double cos(double)`	Returns the trigonometric cosine of its argument (an angle in radians).
`static double exp(double)`	Returns the exponential number *e* (i.e., 2.718 . . .) raised to the power of its argument.
`static double floor(double)`	Returns the largest whole number that is not greater than its argument.
`static double log(double)`	Returns the natural logarithm of its argument.
`static` *numeric* `max(`*numeric*`,` *numeric*`)`	Returns the larger of its *numeric* arguments (the result type is the same as the argument types).
`static` *numeric* `min(`*numeric*`,` *numeric*`)`	Returns the smaller of its *numeric* arguments (the result type is the same as the argument type).
`static double pow(double, double)`	Returns the value of the first argument raised to the power of the second argument.
`static double random()`	Returns a random number greater than or equal to 0.0 and less than 1.0.
`static double rint(double)`	Returns the closest whole number to its argument.
`static long round(double)`	Returns the closest **`long`** to its argument.
`static int round(float)`	Returns the closest **`int`** to its argument.
`static double sin(double)`	Returns the trigonometric sine of its argument (an angle in radians).
`static double sqrt(double)`	Returns the square root of its argument.
`static double tan(double)`	Returns the trigonometric tangent of its argument (an angle in radians).
`static double toDegrees(double)`	Converts its argument (in radians) to degrees.
`static double toRadians(double)`	Converts its argument (in degrees) to radians.

Escape Sequences

The `main` method in the following `SquareRoots` class contains a loop that displays the first 10 integers and their square roots (see Figure A.3).

```
public class SquareRoots {
    public static void main(String[] args) {
        System.out.println("n \tsquare root");
        for (int n = 1; n <= 10; n++) {
            System.out.println(n + "\t" + Math.sqrt(n));
        }
    }
}
```

The `println` statements use the *escape sequence* \t, the tab character, to align the column label "square root" with the numbers in the second output column (see Figure A.3). An escape sequence is a sequence of two characters beginning with the character \. Some escape sequences are used for special output control characters. Others are used to represent characters or symbols that have a special meaning in Java. For example, a double quote character by itself is a string delimiter, so we need to use the sequence \" to represent the double quote character in a string. Table A.6 lists some common escape sequences and their meaning.

The escape sequence that starts with \u represents a Unicode character. The character code uses four hexadecimal digits, where a hexadecimal digit is formed using four binary bits and ranges from 0 (all bits 0) to F (all four bits 1). The hexadecimal digit A corresponds to a decimal value of 10, and the hexadecimal digit F corresponds to a decimal value of 15.

TABLE A.6
Escape Sequences

Sequence	Meaning
\n	Start a new output line
\t	Tab character
\\	Backslash character
\"	Double quote
\'	Single quote or apostrophe
\u*dddd*	The Unicode character whose code is *dddd* where each digit *d* is a hexadecimal digit in the range `0` to `F` (`0–9`, `A–F`)

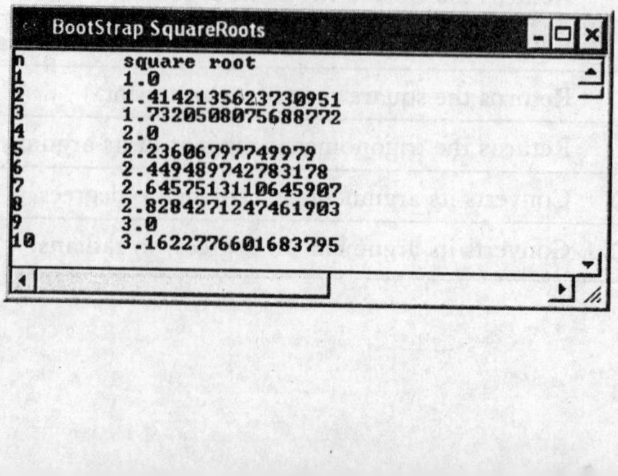

FIGURE A.3
Sample Run of Class SquareRoots

EXERCISES FOR SECTION A.4

SELF-CHECK

1. Identify the escape sequences in the following string. Show how this line would be displayed. Which of the escape sequences could be replaced by the second character of the pair without changing the effect?

```
System.out.println(
    "Jane\'s  motto is \n\"semper fi\"\n, according to Jim");
```

PROGRAMMING

1. Write a Java program that displays all odd powers of 2 between 1 and 29. Display the power that 2 is being raised to, as well as the result, on each line. Use tab characters between numbers.
2. Write a Java program that displays `n` and the natural log of `n` for values of `n` of 1000, 2000, 4000, 8000, and so on. Display the first 20 lines for this sequence. Use tab characters between numbers.

A.5 The String, StringBuilder, and StringBuffer Classes

In this section we discuss three Java classes that are used to process sequences of characters.We begin with the `String` class.

The String Class

The `String` class defines a data type that is used to store a sequence of characters. Table A.7 describes some `String` class methods. The first column shows the result type for each method followed by its signature. For example, for method `charAt`, the first column shows that the method returns a type `char` result and has a type `int` argument. The second column describes what the method does. The phrase "this string" means the string to which the method is applied by the dot notation. If type `Object` is listed as an argument type in column 1, any kind of object can be an argument. (We discuss type `Object` in Chapter 1.)

TABLE A.7
String Methods in `java.lang.String`

Method	Behavior
`char charAt(int pos)`	Returns the character at position pos.
`int compareTo(String)`	Returns a negative integer if this string's contents precede the argument string's contents in the dictionary; returns 0 if this string and the argument string have the same contents; returns a positive integer if this string's contents follow those of the argument string. This comparison is case sensitive.
`int compareToIgnoreCase(String)`	Returns a negative, zero, or positive integer according to whether this string's contents precede, match, or follow the argument string's contents in the dictionary, ignoring case.
`boolean equals(Object)`	Returns `true` if this string's contents are the same as its argument string's contents.
`boolean equalsIgnoreCase(String)`	Returns `true` if this string's contents are the same as the argument string's contents, ignoring case.
`int indexOf(char)` `int indexOf(String)`	Returns the index within this string of the first occurrence of its character or string argument, or –1 if the argument is not found.
`int indexOf(char, int index)` `int indexOf(String, int index)`	Returns the index within this string of the first occurrence of its first character or string argument, starting at the specified `index`.
`int lastIndexOf(char)` `int lastIndexOf(String)`	Returns the index within this string of the rightmost occurrence of its character or string argument.
`int lastIndexOf(char, int index)` `int lastIndexOf(String, int index)`	Returns the index within this string of the last occurrence of its first character or string argument, searching backward and stopping at the specified `index`.
`int length()`	Returns the length of this string.
`String replace(char oldChar, char newChar)`	Returns a new string resulting from replacing all occurrences of `oldChar` in this string with `newChar`.
`String substring(int start)`	Returns a new string that is a substring of this string, starting at position `start` and going to the end of the string.
`String substring(int start, int end)`	Returns a new string that is a substring of this string, starting with the character at position `start` and ending with the character at position `end - 1`.
`String toLowerCase()`	Returns a new string in which all of the letters in this string are converted to lowercase.
`String toUpperCase()`	Returns a new string in which all of the letters in this string are converted to uppercase.
`String trim()`	Returns a new string in which all the white space is removed from both ends of this string.
`static String format (String format, Object... args)`	Returns a new string with the arguments `args` formatted as prescribed by the string `format`.
`String[] split(String pattern)`	Separates the string into an array of tokens, where each token is delimited by a string that matches the regular expression `pattern`.

EXAMPLE A.6 Assume that keyboard (type String) contains "qwerty". We evaluate several expressions:

- keyboard.charAt(0) is 'q'.
- keyboard.length() is 6.
- keyboard.indexOf('o') is −1.
- keyboard.indexOf('y') is 5.

The statement

```
String upper = keyboard.toUpperCase();
```

creates a new String object, referenced by the variable upper, that stores the character sequence "QWERTY", but the String object referenced by keyboard is unchanged, as shown here.

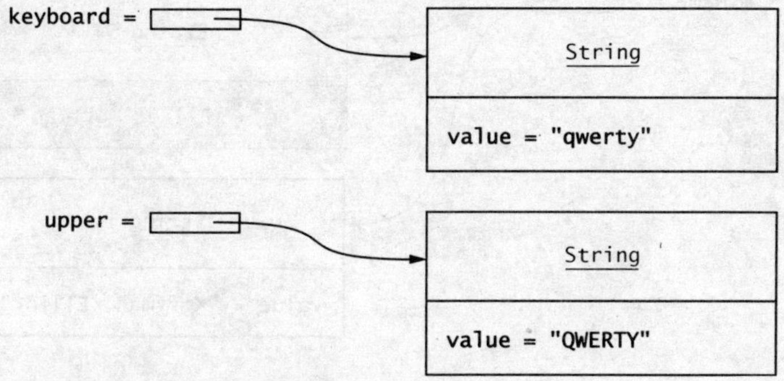

Finally, the expression

```
keyboard.charAt(keyboard.length() - 1)
```

applies two instance methods to keyboard. The inner call, to method length, returns the value 6; the outer call, to method charAt, returns y, the last character in the string (at position 5).

The method substring returns a new string containing a portion of the String object to which it is applied. If it is called with just one argument, the contents of the string returned will be all characters from its argument position to the end of the string. If it is called with two arguments, the contents of the string returned will be all characters from its first argument position up to, but excluding, the character at its second argument position. However, the string to which method substring is applied is not changed.

EXAMPLE A.7 The expression

```
keyboard.substring(0, keyboard.length() - 1)
```

returns a new string "qwert" consisting of all characters except for the last character in the string referenced by keyboard. The contents of keyboard are unchanged.

Strings Are Immutable

Strings are different from most other Java objects in that they are *immutable*. What this means is that you cannot modify a `String` object. If you attempt to do so, Java will create a new object that contains the modified character sequence. The following statements create a new `String` object storing the character sequence `"Koffman, Elliot"` that is referenced by `myName` (indicated by the blue arrow in Figure A.4). The original `String` object still exists (at least temporarily) and contains the character sequence `"Elliot Koffman"`, but it is no longer referenced by `myName` (indicated by the gray arrow in Figure A.4).

```
String myName = "Elliot Koffman";
myName = myName.substring(7) + ", " + myName.substring(0, 6);
```

FIGURE A.4
Old and New Strings Referenced by myName

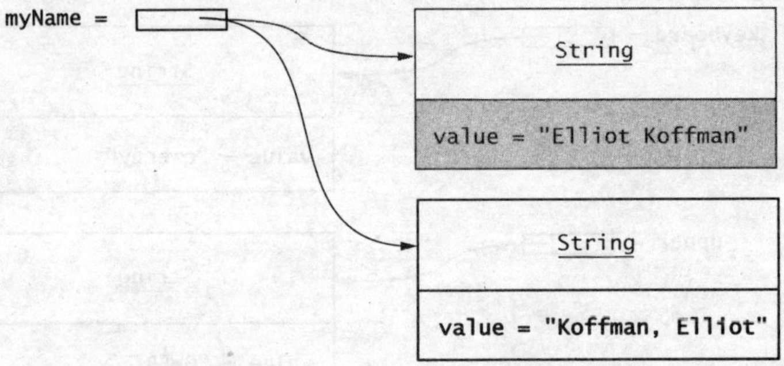

PITFALL

Attempting to Change a Character in a String

You might try to change the first character in `myName` using either of the following statements:

```
myName.charAt(0) = 'X'; // Invalid attempt to change character at
                           position 0
myName[0] = 'X';        // Invalid attempt to treat string as array
```

Both statements cause syntax errors. The first statement will not work because method `charAt` returns a value, but a variable must precede the assignment operator. The second statement attempts to change the first character in a string by treating it as an array of characters. You can do this in some programming languages, but not in Java.

The Garbage Collector

Storage space for objects that are no longer referenced is automatically reclaimed by the Java *garbage collector* so that the storage space can be reallocated and reused. The storage space occupied by the first `String` object in Figure A.4 will be reclaimed by the garbage collector. In other programming languages, the programmer is responsible for reclaiming any storage space that is no longer needed.

Comparing Objects

You can't use the relational (<, <=, >, >=) or equality operators (==, !=) to compare the values stored in strings or other objects. After the assignment

```
String anyName = new String(myName);
```

the condition `(anyName == myName)` would be **`false`** even though these variables have the same contents. The reason is that the == operator compares the *addresses* stored in `anyName` and `myName`, and the `String` objects that are referenced by these variables have different addresses (see Figure A.5).

FIGURE A.5
Two `String` Objects at Different Addresses with the Same Contents

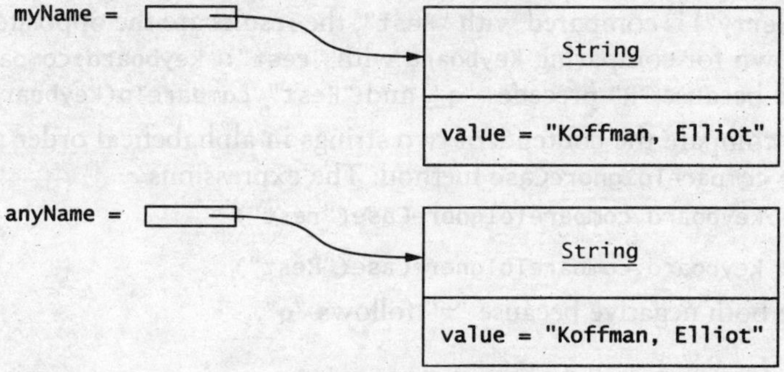

After `String anyName = new String(myName);`

To compare the character sequences stored in two `String` objects, you need to use one of the Java `String` comparison methods: `equals`, `equalsIgnoreCase`, `compareTo`, or `compareToIgnoreCase`. In general, if you want to compare instances of classes that you write, you will need to write at least an `equals` and a `compareTo` method for that class.

EXAMPLE A.8 If you execute the statement

```
String otherName = anyName;
```

the variables `anyName` and `otherName` reference the same `String` object:

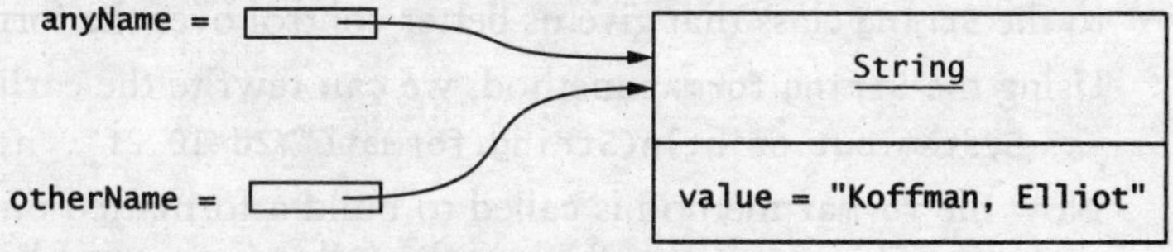

All of the following conditions are then **`true`**.

```
(anyName == otherName)
(anyName.equals(otherName))
(anyName.compareTo(otherName) == 0)
(anyName.equalsIgnoreCase(otherName))
```

If they had referenced different strings with the same contents, only the first condition would be **`false`** because of the address comparison. If they referenced different strings that contained the same words but one's contents were in uppercase and the other's contents were in lowercase, only the last condition would be **`true`**.

The compareTo and compareToIgnoreCase operators return negative or positive values according to whether the argument, in dictionary order, follows or precedes the string to which the method is applied. If keyboard contains the string "qwerty", the expression

```
keyboard.compareTo("rest")
```

is negative because "r" follows "q". For the same reason, the expression

```
"rest".compareTo(keyboard)
```

is positive.

The compareTo method performs a case-sensitive comparison, in which all of the uppercase letters precede all of the lowercase letters. If keyboard (containing "qwerty") is compared with "Rest", the results are the opposite of what we have just shown for comparing keyboard with "rest": keyboard.compareTo("Rest") is positive because "R" precedes "q", and "Rest".compareTo(keyboard) is negative.

To compare the contents of two strings in alphabetical order regardless of case, use the compareToIgnoreCase method: The expressions

```
keyboard.compareToIgnoreCase("rest")

keyboard.compareToIgnoreCase("Rest")
```

are both negative because "r" follows "q".

The String.format Method

Java uses a default format for converting the primitive types to Strings. This default formatting is applied when you output a primitive value using System.out.print or System.out.println. For example, the output lines displayed by the statement

```
System.out.println(n + "\t" + Math.sqrt(n));
```

for n = 1 and n = 2 are:

```
1       1.0
2       1.4142135623730951
```

Notice that the numbers in each column are left-justified and that a large number of significant digits is shown for the square root of 2, but only one zero is shown for the square root of 1. Java 5.0 introduced the Formatter class and the format method to the String class that give us better control over the formatting of numeric values.

Using the String format method, we can rewrite the earlier println statement as

```
System.out.println(String.format("%2d%10.2f", n, Math.sqrt(n)));
```

Now the format method is called to build a formatted output string before println executes. This statement displays the following output lines for n = 1 and n = 2:

```
 1      1.00
 2      1.41
```

The format method is unusual in that it takes a variable number of arguments. The first argument is a format string that specifies how the output string should be formed. The format string above contains a sequence of two format codes, %2d and %10.2f. Each format code describes how its corresponding argument should be formatted.

A format code begins with a % character and is optionally followed by an integer for width, a decimal point and an integer for precision (optional), and a type conversion specification (e.g., d for integer, f for real number, and s for string). The format code `%2d` means use 2 characters to represent the integer value of its corresponding argument (`n`); the format code `%10.2f` means use a total of 10 characters and 2 decimal places of precision to represent the real value of its corresponding argument (`Math.sqrt(n)`).

The width specifier gives the minimum number of characters that are used to represent a value. If more are required, then they will be inserted, but if fewer are required, then leading spaces are used to fill the character count (to achieve right-justification). If the width specifier is omitted, then the exact number of characters required to represent the value with the prescribed precision will be used.

The precision specifier (e.g., `.2`) is optional and applies only to the `f` type conversion specification. It indicates the number of digits following the decimal point. If omitted, 6 digits are displayed following the decimal point.

You can also have characters other than format codes inside a format string. The arguments to be formatted are inserted in the formatted string exactly where their format specifiers appear. For example, when `n` is 2, the statement

```
String.format("Value of square root of %d is %.3f", n, Math.sqrt(n))
```

creates the `String`

```
Value of square root of 2 is 1.414
```

The value 2 and the square root of 2 replace their format specifiers in the formatted string. Because the width specifiers are omitted, the exact number of characters required to represent the values to the desired precision is used.

Other format conversion characters used in this text are `s` (for string) and `n` for newline. The format code `%10s` causes its corresponding string argument to be formatted using 10 characters. Like numbers, strings are displayed right-justified. The format code `%-10s` will cause the string to be displayed left-justified. The format code `%n` will cause an operating system specific newline sequence to be generated. On some operating systems the newline is indicated by the `\n` character, or by the sequence `\r\n`, and on others by `\r`. The `println` method always terminates its output with the correct sequence for the operating system on which the program is executing. Using `%n` achieves the same result when using method `format`.

The Formatter Class

You can also use the `java.util.Formatter` class to create `Formatter` objects for writing formatted output to the console (or elsewhere). The statement

```
Formatter fOut = new Formatter(System.out);
```

creates a `Formatter` object `fOut` associated with the console. The statements

```
fOut.format("%2d%10.2f\n", 1, Math.sqrt(1));
fOut.format("%2d%10.2f\n", 2, Math.sqrt(2));
```

write to object `fOut` the pair of formatted strings shown earlier, each ending with a newline character (`'\n'`). Each string written to `fOut` will be displayed in the console window. You can actually apply the `format` method or the new `printf` method directly to `System.out` without wrapping `System.out` in a `Formatter` object.

```
System.out.printf("%2d%10.2f\n", 1, Math.sqrt(1));
System.out.format("%2d%10.2f\n", 2, Math.sqrt(2));
```

The `String.split` Method

Often we want to process individual pieces, or tokens, in a string. For example, in the string `"Doe, John 5/15/65"`, we are likely to be interested in one or more of the particular pieces `"Doe"`, `"John"`, `"5"`, `"15"`, and `"65"`. These pieces would have to be extracted from the string as *tokens*. You can retrieve tokens from a `String` object using the `String.split` method.

Introduction to Regular Expressions

The argument to the split method is a special kind of string known as a *regular expression*. A regular expression is a string that describes another string or family of strings. The simplest regular expression is a string that does not include any special characters, which matches itself. For example, the string `" "` represents a single space, and the string `", "` represents a comma followed by a space. For the statements

```
String personData = "Doe, John 5/15/65";
String[] tokens = personData.split(", ");
```

the string `", "` matches the two characters following the letter `e`, so `tokens[0]` is `"Doe"` and `tokens[1]` is `"John 5/15/65"`. This is not quite what we desire, as `tokens[1]` needs to be split further. The string `personData` is not changed by this operation. The character sequence comma followed by space is often called a *delimiter* because it separates the tokens.

Matching One of a Group of Characters

A string enclosed in brackets (`[` and `]`) matches any one of the characters in the string, unless the first character in the string is `^`, in which case the match is to any character not in the string that follows the `^`. For example, the string `"[, /]"` will match a comma, a space, or a slash, and the string `"[^abc]"` will match any character that is not `a`, `b`, or `c`. To match a range of characters, separate the start and end character of the range with a '–'. For example, `"[a-z]"` will match any lowercase letter. For the statement

```
tokens = personData.split("[, /]");
```

`tokens[0]` is `"Doe"`, `tokens[1]` is an empty string because the space character in `personData` is matched immediately by the space in the delimiter string, `tokens[2]` is `"John"`, `tokens[3]` is `"5"`, `tokens[4]` is `"15"`, and `tokens[5]` is `"65"`, so we are closer to what we desire.

Qualifiers

Character groups match a single character. Qualifiers are applied to regular expressions to define a new regular expression that conditionally performs a match. These qualifiers are shown in Table A.8.

In the statement

```
String[] tokens = personData.split("[, /]+");
```

the argument `"[, /]+"` will match a string of one or more space, comma, and slash characters. Therefore, `tokens[0]` is `"Doe"`, `tokens[1]` is `"John"`, `tokens[2]` is `"5"`, and so on. This is what we desire.

TABLE A.8
Regular Expression Qualifiers

Qualifier	Meaning
X?	Optionally matches the regular expression *X*.
*X**	Matches zero or more occurrences of regular expression *X*.
X+	Matches one or more occurrences of regular expression *X*.

PITFALL

Not Using the + Qualifier to Define a Delimiter Regular Expression

As we explained above, if we had omitted the + qualifier from the delimiter string `"[, /]"`, there would have been an empty string in the array of tokens. The reason for this is that the comma after Doe would match the comma in the delimiter. The `split` method would then save Doe in `tokens[0]` and search for another match to the delimiter. It would immediately find the space, and since there were no characters between the previously found delimiter and this one, an empty string would be stored. Using the + qualifier ensures that the comma and space in `personData` are treated as a single delimiter, not as two separate delimiters.

Defined Character Groups

Several character groups are defined and are indicated by a letter preceded by two backslash characters. The defined groups are shown in Table A.9.

TABLE A.9
Defined Character Groups

Regular Expression	Equivalent Regular Expression	Description
`\\d`	`[0-9]`	A digit
`\\D`	`[^0-9]`	Not a digit
`\\s`	`[ \t\n\f\r]`	A whitespace character (space, tab, newline, formfeed, or return)
`\\S`	`[^\\s]`	Not a whitespace character
`\\w`	`[a-zA-Z_0-9]`	A word character (letter, underscore, or digit)
`\\W`	`[^\\w]`	Not a word character

EXAMPLE A.9 We want to extract the symbols from an expression. We define a symbol as a string of letter or digit characters. The symbols are separated by one or more whitespace characters. The statement

```
String[] symbols = expression.split("\\s+");
```

will split the string `expression` into an array of symbols separated by whitespace characters.

EXAMPLE A.10 We want to extract the words from a text. We define a word as a string of letter or digit characters. The characters can be in any language. Thus the delimiters are any string that consists of one or more characters that are not letters or digits (e.g., whitespace, punctuation symbols, parentheses). The regular expression `"[^\\P{L}\\P{N}]+"` represents a string consisting of one or more characters that are not letters or digits. The statement

```
String[] words = line.split("[^\\p{L}\\p{N}]+");
```

will split the string `line` consisting of letters, digits, special characters, and punctuation symbols into an array of words. The meaning of `\\p{L}` and `\\p{N}` is discussed next.

Unicode Character Class Support

The groups shown in Table A.9 apply only to the first 128 Unicode characters, which is adequate for processing English text. However, Java uses the Unicode characters that can be used to represent languages other than English. In these other languages, a–z do not represent all of the letters or may not be letters at all. For example, French includes the letters à, á, and â, which are distinct from a. Greek uses characters such as α, β, and γ. Selected character groups based on the Unicode character category are shown in Table A.10.

TABLE A.10
Regular Expressions for Selected Unicode Character Categories

Regular Expression	Description
`\\p{L}`	Letter
`\\p{Lu}`	Uppercase letter
`\\p{Ll}`	Lowercase letter
`\\p{Lt}`	Titlecase letter
`\\p{N}`	Numbers
`\\p{P}`	Punctuation
`\\p{S}`	Symbols
`\\p{Zs}`	Spaces

The StringBuilder and StringBuffer Classes

Java provides a class called StringBuilder that, like String, also stores character sequences. However, unlike a String object, the contents of a StringBuilder object can be changed. Use a StringBuilder object to store a string that you plan to change; otherwise, use a String object to store that string. Table A.11 describes the methods of class StringBuilder. In Table A.11, "this StringBuilder" means the StringBuilder object to which the method is applied through the dot notation. Methods append, delete, insert, and replace modify this StringBuilder object.

The StringBuilder class was introduced in Java 5.0 as a replacement for the StringBuffer. The StringBuffer has the same methods as the StringBuilder, but is designed for programs that have multiple threads of execution. All programs presented in this text, except for those in Appendix C, are single-thread.

TABLE A.11
StringBuilder Methods in java.lang.StringBuilder

Method	Behavior
void StringBuilder append(*anyType*)	Appends the string representation of the argument to this StringBuilder. The argument can be of any data type.
int capacity()	Returns the current capacity of this StringBuilder.
void StringBuilder delete(int start, int end)	Removes the characters in a substring of this StringBuilder, starting at position start and ending with the character at position end - 1.
void StringBuilder insert(int offset, *anyType* data)	Inserts the argument data (any data type) into this StringBuilder at position offset, shifting the characters that started at offset to the right.
int length()	Returns the length (character count) of this StringBuilder.
StringBuilder replace(int start, int end, String str)	Replaces the characters in a substring of this StringBuilder (from position start through position end - 1) with characters in the argument str. Returns this StringBuilder.
String substring(int start)	Returns a new string containing the substring that begins at the specified index start and extends to the end of this StringBuilder.
String substring(int start, int end)	Return a new string containing the substring in this StringBuilder from position start through position end - 1.
String toString()	Returns a new string that contains the same characters as this StringBuilder object.

EXAMPLE A.11 The following statements declare three `StringBuilder` objects using three different constructors. The default capacity of an empty `StringBuilder` object is 16 characters. The capacity of a `StringBuilder` object is automatically doubled as required to accommodate the character sequence that is stored.

```
StringBuilder sB1 = new StringBuilder();        // Capacity is 16
StringBuilder sB2 = new StringBuilder(30);      // Capacity is 30
StringBuilder sB3 = new StringBuilder("happy"); // Stores "happy"
                                                // Capacity 16
```

The following statements result in the character sequence `"happy birthday to you"` being stored in `sB3`.

```
sB3.append("day me");          // "happyday me"
sB3.insert(9, "to ");          // "happyday to me"
sB3.insert(5, " birth");       // "happy birthday to me"
sB3.replace(18, 20, "you");    // "happy birthday to you"
```

PITFALL

String Index Out of Bounds

If an index supplied to any `String`, `StringBuilder`, or `StringBuffer` method is outside the valid range of character positions for the string object (i.e., if the index is less than `0` or greater than or equal to the string length), a `StringIndexOutOfBoundsException` will occur. This is a run-time error and will terminate program execution. We will discuss exceptions in more detail in Section A.11.

EXERCISES FOR SECTION A.5

SELF-CHECK

1. Evaluate each of these expressions.

```
"happy".equals("Happy")
"happy".compareTo("Happy")
"happy".equalsIgnoreCase("Happy")
"happy".equals("happy".charAt(0) + "Happy".substring(1))
"happy" == "happy".charAt(0) + "Happy".substring(1)
```

2. You want to extract the words in the string `"Nancy* has thirty-three*** fine!! teeth."` using the `split` method. What are the delimiter characters, and what should you use as the argument string?
3. Rewrite the following statements using `StringBuilder` objects:

```
String myName = "Elliot Koffman";
String myNameFirstLast = myName;
myName = myName.substring(7) + ", " + myName.substring(0, 6);
```

4. What is stored in `result` after the following statements execute?

```
StringBuilder result = new StringBuilder();
String sentence = "Let's all learn how to program in Java";
String[] tokens = sentence.split(\\s+);
for (String token : tokens) {
    result.append(token);
}
```

5. Revise Exercise 4 to insert a newline character between the words in `result`.

PROGRAMMING

1. Write statements to extract the individual tokens in a string of the form `"Doe, John 5/15/65"`. Use the `indexOf` method to find the string `", "` and the symbol `/` and use the substring method to extract the substrings between these delimiters.
2. Write statements to extract the words in Self-Check Exercise 2 and then create a new `String` object with all the words separated by commas. Use `StringBuilder` to build the new string.
3. For Self-Check Exercise 4, write a loop to display all the tokens that are extracted.

A.6 Wrapper Classes for Primitive Types

We have seen that the primitive numeric types are not objects, but sometimes we need to process primitive-type data as objects. For example, we may want to pass a numeric value to a method that requires an object as its argument. Java provides a set of classes called *wrapper classes* whose objects contain primitive-type values: `Float`, `Double`, `Integer`, `Boolean`, `Character`, and so on. These classes provide constructor methods to create new objects that "wrap" a specified value. They also provide methods to "unwrap," or extract, an object's value and methods to compare two objects. Table A.12 shows some methods for wrapper class `Integer` (part of `java.lang`). The other numeric wrapper classes also provide these methods, except that method `parseInt` is replaced by a method `parse`*ClassType*, where *ClassType* is the data type wrapped by that class.

In earlier versions of Java, a programmer could not mix type **int** values and type `Integer` objects in an expression. If you wanted to increment the value stored in `Integer` object `nInt`, you would have to unwrap the value, increment it, and then wrap the value in a new `Integer` object:

```
int n = nInt.intValue();
nInt = new Integer(n++);
```

Java 5.0 introduced a feature known as autoboxing/unboxing for primitive types. This enables programmers to use a primitive type in contexts where an `Object` is needed or to use a wrapper object in contexts where a primitive type is needed. Using autoboxing/unboxing, you can rewrite the statements above as:

```
int n = nInt;
nInt = n++;
```

or even as the single statement:

```
nInt++;
```

TABLE A.12
Methods for Class Integer

Method	Behavior
`int compareTo(Integer anInt)`	Compares two `Integer`s numerically.
`double doubleValue()`	Returns the value of this `Integer` as a **`double`**.
`boolean equals(Object obj)`	Returns **`true`** if the value of this `Integer` is equal to its argument's value; returns **`false`** otherwise.
`int intValue()`	Returns the value of this `Integer` as an **`int`**.
`static int parseInt(String s)`	Parses the string argument as a signed integer.
`String toString()`	Returns a `String` object representing this `Integer`'s value.

EXAMPLE A.12 The first pair of the following statements creates two `Integer` objects. The next pair unboxes the **`int`** value contained in each object. The next-to-last statement calls the static method `parseInt` to parse its string argument to an **`int`** (not `Integer`) value. The last statement displays the value (35) wrapped in `Integer` object `i1`.

```
Integer i1 = 35;                          // Autoboxes 35.
Integer i2 = 1234;                        // Autoboxes 1234.
Integer i3 = i1 + i2;                     // Unboxes i1 and i2, autoboxes
                                          // their sum 1269, and assigns
                                          // it to i3.
int i2Val = i2++;                         // Unboxes i2, increments it to
                                          // 1235 and autoboxes it, and
                                          // assigns 1234 to i2Val.
int i3Val = Integer.parseInt("-357");     // Parses "-357" to -357 and
                                          // assigns it to i3Val.
Integer i4 = new Integer("753");          // Autoboxes 753 and assigns
                                          // it to i4.
System.out.println(i1);                   // Automatically calls
                                          // toString() and displays 35.
```

EXERCISES FOR SECTION A.6

SELF-CHECK

1. Do you think objects of a wrapper type are immutable or not? Explain your answer.
2. For objects `i1`, `i2` in Example A.12, what do the following two statements display?

```
System.out.println(i1 + i2);
System.out.println(i1.toString() + i2.toString());
```

PROGRAMMING

1. Write statements that double the value stored in the `Integer` object referenced by `i1`. Draw a diagram showing the objects referenced by `i1` before and after these statements execute.
2. There is no * (multiply) operator for type `Integer` objects. Suppose you have `Integer` objects `i1`, `i2`, `i3`. Write a statement to multiply the three type **`int`** values in these objects and store the product in an `Integer` object `i4`. Show how you would do this without using autoboxing/unboxing.

A.7 Defining Your Own Classes

We mentioned earlier that a Java program is a collection of classes; consequently, when you write a Java program, you will develop one or more classes. We will show you how to write a Java class next.

A class `Person` might describe a group of objects, each of which is a particular human being. For example, instances of class `Person` would be yourself, your mother, and your father. A `Person` object could store the following data:

- Given name
- Family name
- ID number
- Year of birth

The following are a few of the operations that can be performed on a `Person` object:

- Calculate the person's age
- Test whether two `Person` objects refer to the same person
- Determine whether the person is old enough to vote
- Determine whether the person is a senior citizen
- Get one or more of the data fields for the `Person` object
- Set one or more of the data fields for the `Person` object

Figure A.6 shows a diagram of class `Person`. This figure uses the *Unified Modeling Language*™ (*UML*) to represent the class. UML diagrams are a standard means of documenting class relationships that is widely used in industry. The class is represented by a box. The top compartment of the box contains the class name. The data fields are shown in the middle compartment, and some of the methods are shown in the bottom compartment. Data fields are also called *instance variables* because each class instance (object) has its own storage for them. We discuss UML further in Appendix B.

Figure A.7 shows how two objects or instances of the class `Person` (`author1` and `author2`) are represented in UML. A curved arrow from the reference variable for each object (`author1`, `author2`) points to the object, as we have shown in previous figures. Each object is represented by a box in which the top compartment contains the class name (`Person`), underlined, and the bottom compartment contains the data

FIGURE A.6
Class Diagram for Person

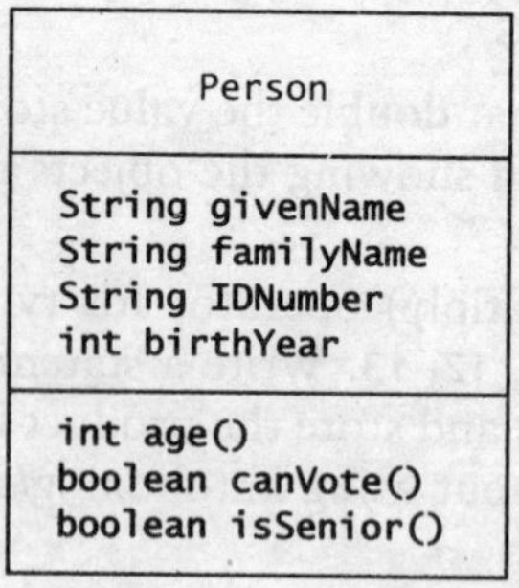

FIGURE A.7
Object Diagrams of Two Instances of Class Person

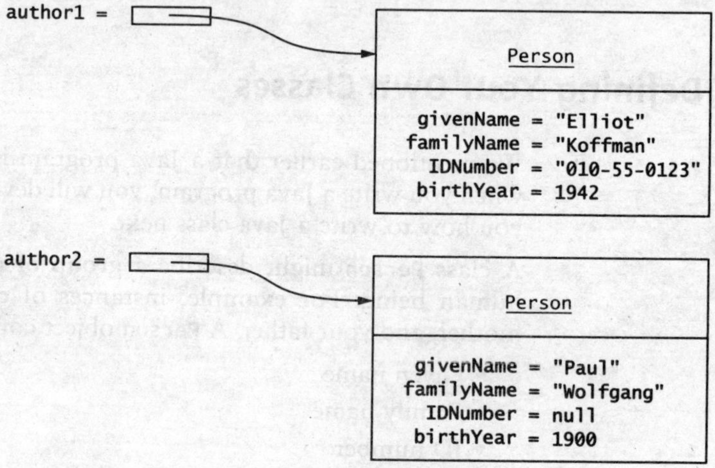

fields and their values. (For simplicity, we show the value of each `String` data field instead of a reference to a `String` object.)

Listing A.1 shows class `Person` and the instance methods for this class. The lines that are delimited by `/**` and `*/` are comments. They are program documentation, extremely important for human programmers but ignored by the compiler. We discuss the form of the comments used in class `Person` at the end of this section.

We declare four data fields and two constants (all uppercase letters) before the methods (although many Java programmers prefer to declare methods before data fields). In the constant declarations, the modifier **`final`** indicates that the constant value may not be changed. The modifier **`static`** indicates that the constant is being defined for the class and does not have to be replicated in each instance. In other words, storage for the constant VOTE_AGE is allocated once, regardless of how many instances of `Person` are created.

LISTING A.1
Class Person

```
/** Person is a class that represents a human being. */
public class Person {
    // Data Fields
    /** The given name */
    private String givenName;
    /** The family name */
```

```
    private String familyName;
    /** The ID number */
    private String IDNumber;
    /** The birth year */
    private int birthYear = 1900;

    // Constants
    /** The age at which a person can vote */
    private static final int VOTE_AGE = 18;
    /** The age at which a person is considered a senior citizen */
    private static final int SENIOR_AGE = 65;

    // Constructors
    /** Construct a person with given values
        @param first The given name
        @param family The family name
        @param ID The ID number
        @param birth The birth year
    */
    public Person(String first, String family, String ID, int birth) {
        givenName = first;
        familyName = family;
        IDNumber = ID;
        birthYear = birth;
    }

    /** Construct a person with only an IDNumber specified.
        @param ID The ID number
    */
    public Person(String ID) {
        IDNumber = ID;
    }

    // Modifier Methods
    /** Sets the givenName field.
        @param given The given name
    */
    public void setGivenName(String given) {
        givenName = given;
    }

    /** Sets the familyName field.
        @param family The family name
    */
    public void setFamilyName(String family) {
        familyName = family;
    }

    /** Sets the birthYear field.
        @param birthYear The year of birth
    */
    public void setBirthYear(int birthYear) {
        this.birthYear = birthYear;
    }

    // Accessor Methods
    /** Gets the person's given name.
```

```
    @return the given name as a String
*/
public String getGivenName() { return givenName; }

/** Gets the person's family name.
    @return the family name as a String
*/
public String getFamilyName() { return familyName; }

/** Gets the person's ID number.
    @return the ID number as a String
*/
public String getIDNumber() { return IDNumber; }

/** Gets the person's year of birth.
    @return the year of birth as an int value
*/
public int getBirthYear() { return birthYear; }

// Other Methods
/**  Calculates a person's age at this year's birthday.
     @param year The current year
     @return the year minus the birth year
*/
public int age(int year) {
    return year - birthYear;
}

/** Determines whether a person can vote.
    @param year The current year
    @return true if the person's age is greater than or
            equal to the voting age
*/
public boolean canVote(int year) {
    int theAge = age(year);
    return theAge >= VOTE_AGE;
}

/** Determines whether a person is a senior citizen.
    @param year the current year
    @return true if person's age is greater than or
            equal to the age at which a person is
            considered to be a senior citizen
*/
public boolean isSenior(int year) {
    return age(year) >= SENIOR_AGE;
}

/** Retrieves the information in a Person object.
    @return the object state as a string
*/
public String toString() {
    return "Given name: " + givenName + "\n"
        + "Family name: " + familyName + "\n"
        + "ID number: " + IDNumber + "\n"
        + "Year of birth: " + birthYear + "\n";
}
```

```
/** Compares two Person objects for equality.
    @param per The second Person object
    @return true if the Person objects have same
            ID number; false if they don't
*/
public boolean equals(Person per) {
    if (per == null)
        return false;
    else
        return IDNumber.equals(per.IDNumber);
    }
}
```

Private Data Fields, Public Methods

The modifier **private** sets the visibility of each variable or constant to *private visibility.* This means that these data fields can be accessed only within the class definition. Only class members with *public visibility* can be accessed outside of the class.

The reason for having private visibility for data fields is to control access to an object's data and to prevent improper use and processing of an object's data. If a data field is private, it can be processed outside of the class only by invoking one of the public methods that are part of the class. Therefore, the programmer who writes the public methods controls how the data field is processed. Also, the details of how the private data are represented and stored can be changed at a later time by the programmer who implements the class, and the other programs that use the class (called the class's *clients*) will not need to be changed.

Constructors

In Listing A.1, the two methods that begin with `public Person` are constructors. One of these methods is invoked when a new class instance is created. The constructor with four parameters is called if the values of all data fields are known before the object is created. For example, the statement

```
Person author1 = new Person("Elliot", "Koffman",
                            "010-055-0123", 1942);
```

creates the first object shown in Figure A.7, initializing its data fields to the values passed as arguments.

The second constructor is called when only the value of data field `IDNumber` is known at the time the object is created.

```
Person author2 = new Person("030-555-5555");
```

In this case, data field `IDNumber` is set to `"030-555-5555"`, but all the other data fields are initialized to the default values for their data type (see Table A.13) unless a different initial value is specified (1900 for `birthYear`). The `String` data fields are initialized to **`null`**, which means that no `String` object is referenced. You can use the modifier methods at a later time to set the values of the other data fields. The statement

```
author2.setGivenName("Paul");
```

TABLE A.13
Default Values for Data Fields

Data Field Type	Default Value
`int` (or other integer type)	`0`
`double` (or other real type)	`0.0`
`boolean`	`false`
`char`	`\u0000` (the smallest Unicode character: the null character)
Any reference type	`null`

sets the data field `givenName` to reference the `String` object `"Paul"`. Note that there is no `setIDNumber` method, so this data field value can't be assigned or changed at a later time.

The No-Parameter Constructor

A constructor with no parameters is called the *no-parameter constructor* (or *no-argument constructor*). This constructor is sometimes called the default constructor because Java automatically defines this constructor with an empty body for a class that has no constructor definitions. However, if you define one or more constructors for a class, you must also explicitly define the no-parameter constructor, or it will be undefined for that class. Because two constructors are defined for class `Person`, but the no-parameter constructor is not, the statement

```
Person p = new Person();    // Invalid call to no-parameter constructor.
```

will not compile.

Modifier and Accessor Methods

Because the data fields have private visibility, we need to provide public methods to access them. Normally, we want to be able to get or retrieve the value of a data field, so each data field in class `Person` has an accessor method (also called getter) that begins with the word `get` and ends with the name of the data field (e.g., `getFamilyName`). If we want to allow a class user to update or modify the value of a data field, we provide a modifier method (also called mutator or setter) beginning with the word `set` and ending with the name of the data field (e.g., `setGivenName`). Currently, there is an accessor for each data field in this example and a modifier for all but the `IDNumber` data field. The reason for this is to deny a client the ability to change a person's ID number.

The modifier methods are type `void` because they are executed for their effect (to update a data field), not to return a value. In the method `setBirthYear`,

```
public void setBirthYear(int birthYear) {
    this.birthYear = birthYear;
}
```

the assignment statement stores the integer value passed as an argument in data field birthYear. (We explain the reason for **this.** in the next subsection.)

The accessor method for data field givenName,

```
public String getGivenName() { return givenName; }
```

is type String because it returns the String object referenced by givenName. If the class designer does not want other users (clients) of the class to be able to access or change the data field values, these methods can be given private visibility.

Use of this. in a Method

Method setBirthYear uses the statement

```
this.birthYear = birthYear;
```

to store a value in data field birthYear. We can use **this.***aDataField* in a method to access a data field of the current object. Because we used birthYear as a parameter in method setBirthYear, the Java compiler will translate birthYear without the prefix **this.** as referring to the parameter birthYear, not to the data field. The reason is the declaration of birthYear as a parameter is local to the method and, therefore, hides the data field declaration.

The Method toString

The last two methods, toString and equals, are found in most Java classes. The method toString creates a String object that represents the information stored in an object (the *state* of an object). The escape sequence \n is the newline character, and it terminates an output line when the string is displayed. A client of class Person could use the statement

```
System.out.println(author1.toString());
```

to display the state of author1. In fact, the statement

```
System.out.println(author1);
```

would also display the state of author1, because System.out.println and System.out.print automatically apply method toString to an object that appears in their argument list. The following lines would be displayed by this statement.

```
Given name: Elliot
Family name: Koffman
ID number: 010-055-0123
Year of birth: 1942
```

The Method equals

The method equals compares the object to which it is applied (*this* object) to the object that is passed as an argument. It returns **true** if the objects are determined to be the same based on the data they store. It returns **false** if the argument is **null** or if the objects are not the same. We will assume that two Persons are the same if they have the same ID number.

PROGRAM STYLE

Using toString Instead of Displaying Data Fields

Java programmers use method `toString` to build a string that represents the object state. This string can then be displayed at the console, written to a file, displayed in a dialog window, or displayed in a Graphical User Interface (GUI). This is more flexible than the approach taken in many programming languages, in which each data field is displayed or written to a file.

```
public boolean equals(Person per) {
    if (per == null)
        return false;
    else
        return IDNumber.equals(per.IDNumber);
}
```

The second return statement returns the result of the method call

```
IDNumber.equals(per.IDNumber)
```

Notice that we can look at parameter `per`'s private `IDNumber` because `per` references an object of this class (type `Person`). Because `IDNumber` is type `String`, the `equals` method of class `String` is invoked with the `IDNumber` of the second object as an argument. If the two `IDNumber` data fields have the same contents, the `String equals` method will return **`true`**; otherwise, it will return **`false`**. The `Person equals` method returns the result of the `String equals` method. In Section 3.5, we discuss the `equals` method in more detail and show you a better way to write this method.

PROGRAM STYLE

Returning a Boolean Value

Some programmers unnecessarily write **`if`** statements to return a **`boolean`** value. For example, instead of writing

```
return IDNumber.equals(per.IDNumber);
```

they write

```
if (IDNumber.equals(per.IDNumber))
    return true;
else
    return false;
```

Resist this temptation. The **`return`** statement by itself returns the value of the **`if`** statement condition, which must be **`true`** or **`false`**. It does this in a clear and succinct manner using one line instead of four.

Declaring Local Variables in Class Person

There are three other methods declared in class `Person`. Methods `age`, `canVote`, and `isSenior` are all passed the current year as an argument. Method `canVote` calls method `age` to determine the person's age. The result is stored in local variable `theAge`. The result of calling method `canVote` is the value of the Boolean expression following the keyword **return**.

```
public boolean canVote(int year) {
    int theAge = age(year);      // Local variable
    return theAge >= VOTE_AGE;
}
```

It really was not necessary to introduce local variable `theAge`; the call to method age could have been placed directly in the **return** statement (as it is in method `isSenior`). We wanted, however, to show you how to declare local variables in a Java method. The scope of the local variable `theAge` and the parameter `year` is the body of method `canVote`.

PITFALL

Referencing a Data Field or Parameter Hidden by a Local Declaration

If you happen to declare a local variable (or parameter) with the same name as a data field, the Java compiler will translate the use of that name in a method as meaning the local variable (or parameter), not the data field. So if `theAge` was also declared as a data field in class `Person`, the statement

```
theAge++;
```

would increment the local variable, but the data field value would not change. To access the data field instead of the local variable, use the prefix **this.**, just as we did earlier when a parameter had the same name as a data field.

PITFALL

Using Visibility Modifiers with Local Variables

Using a visibility modifier with a local variable would cause a syntax error, because a local variable is visible only within the method that declares it. Therefore, it makes no sense to give it public or private visibility.

An Application that Uses Class Person

To test class `Person` we need to write a Java application program that contains a `main` method. The `main` method should create one or more instances of class `Person` and display the results of applying the class methods. Listing A.2 shows a class

TestPerson that does this. To execute the main method, you must compile and run class TestPerson. As long as Person and TestPerson are in the same folder (directory), the application program will run. Figure A.8 shows a sample run.

LISTING A.2
Class TestPerson

```
/** TestPerson is an application that tests class Person. */
public class TestPerson {
    public static void main(String[] args) {
        Person p1 = new Person("Sam", "Jones", "1234", 1930);
        Person p2 = new Person("Jane", "Jones", "5678", 1990);
        System.out.println("Age of " + p1.getGivenName() +
                           " is " + p1.age(2004));
        if (p1.isSenior(2004))
            System.out.println(p1.getGivenName() +
                               " can ride the subway for free");
        else
            System.out.println(p1.getGivenName() +
                               " must pay to ride the subway");

        System.out.println("Age of " + p2.getGivenName() +
                           " is " + p2.age(2004));
        if (p2.canVote(2004))
            System.out.println(p2.getGivenName() + " can vote");
        else
            System.out.println(p2.getGivenName() + " can't vote");
    }
}
```

FIGURE A.8
Sample Run of Class TestPerson

Although we will generally write separate application classes such as TestPerson, you could also insert the main method directly in class Person and then compile and run class Person. Program execution will start at the main method, and the result will be the same. If you use separate classes, make sure that you put them in the same folder (directory).

Objects as Arguments

We stated earlier that Java arguments are passed by value. For primitive-type arguments, this protects the value of a method's argument and ensures that its value can't be changed by the method. However, this is not the case for arguments that are objects. If an argument is an object, its address is passed to the method, so the method parameter will reference the same object as the method argument. If the method happens to change a data field of its object parameter, that change will be made to the object argument. We illustrate this next.

EXAMPLE A.13 Suppose method changeGivenName is defined as follows:

```
public void changeGivenName(Person per) {
    per.givenName = this.givenName;
}
```

Also suppose a client program declares firstMan and firstWoman as reference variables of type Person. After the method call

```
firstMan.changeGivenName(firstWoman)
```

parameter per (declared in method changeGivenName) and reference variable firstWoman (declared in the client) will reference the same object. The statement

```
per.givenName = this.givenName;
```

will set the givenName data field of the object referenced by per (and firstWoman) to reference the same string as the givenName field of this object (the object referenced by firstMan). Figure A.9 shows the givenName data field of the objects referenced by firstMan and firstWoman after the foregoing statement executes.

FIGURE A.9
Reference Variables firstMan and firstWoman

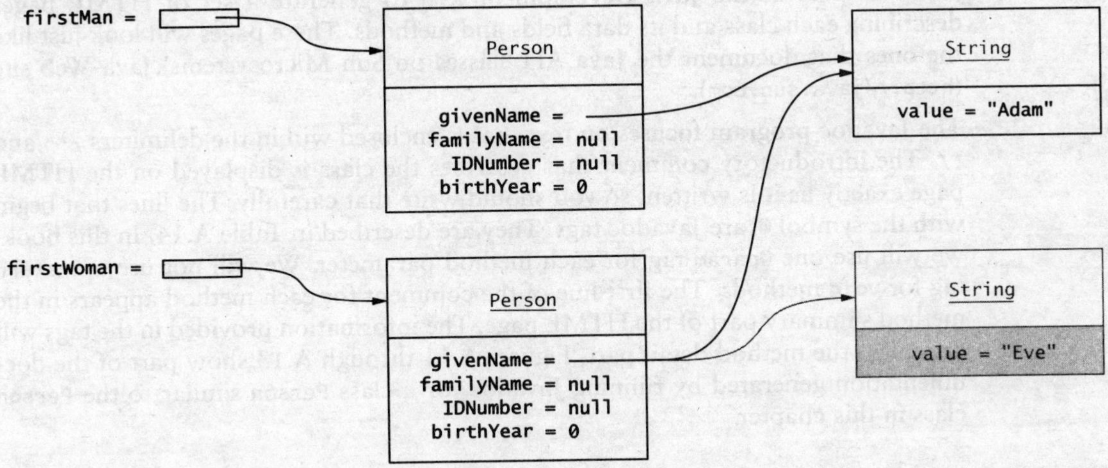

Classes as Components of Other Classes

Class Person has three data fields that are type String, so String objects are *components* of a Person object. In Figure A.10 this component relationship is indicated by the solid diamond symbol at the end of the line drawn from the box representing class String to the box representing class Person. Like the class diagram in Figure A.6 and the object diagrams in Figure A.7, Figure A.10 is a UML diagram, this one showing the relationships between classes. We will follow UML's set of conventions for documenting class relationships in this book.

FIGURE A.10
UML Diagram Showing that String Objects Are Components of Class Person

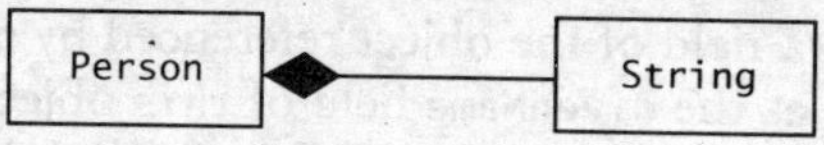

Java Documentation Style for Classes and Methods

Java provides a standard form for writing comments and documenting classes, which we will use in this book. If you use this form, you can run a program called *Javadoc* (part of the Java Development Kit) to generate a set of HTML pages describing each class and its data fields and methods. These pages will look just like the ones that document the Java API classes on Sun Microsystems' Java Web site (http://java.sun.com).

The Javadoc program focuses on text that is enclosed within the delimiters /** and */. The introductory comment that describes the class is displayed on the HTML page exactly as it is written, so you should write that carefully. The lines that begin with the symbol @ are Javadoc tags. They are described in Table A.14. In this book, we will use one @param tag for each method parameter. We will not use a @return tag for **void** methods. The first line of the comment for each method appears in the method summary part of the HTML page. The information provided in the tags will appear in the method detail part. Figures A.11 through A.13 show part of the documentation generated by running Javadoc for a class Person similar to the Person class in this chapter.

TABLE A.14
Javadoc Tags

Javadoc Tag and Example of Use	Purpose
@author *Koffman and Wolfgang*	Identifies the class author.
@param first *The given name*	Identifies a method parameter.
@return *The person's age*	Identifies a method return value.

FIGURE A.11
Field Summary for Class Person

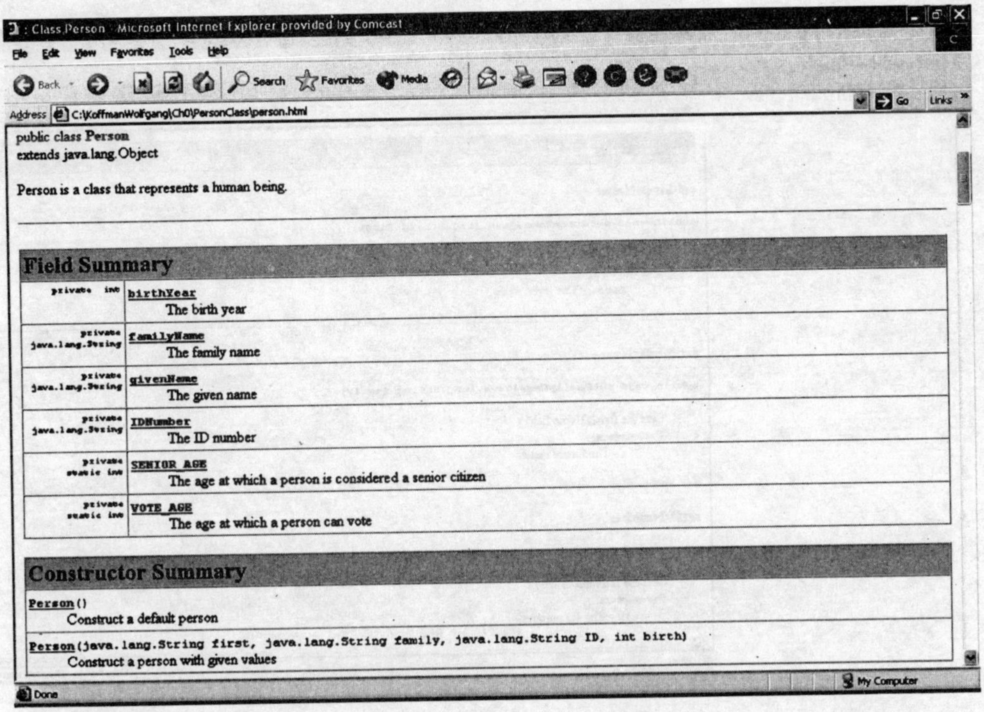

FIGURE A.12
Method Summary for Class Person

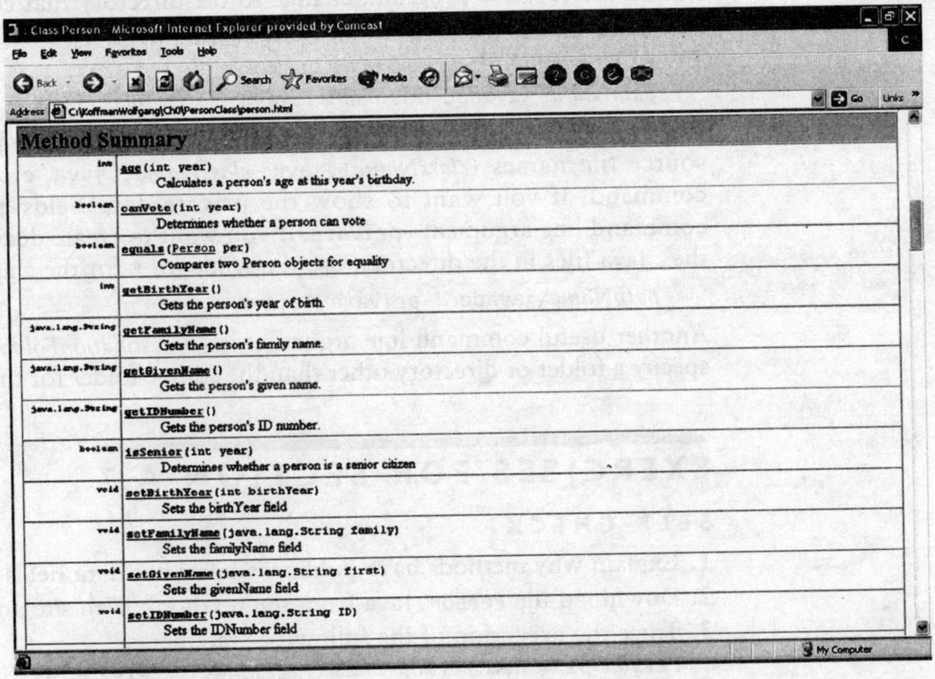

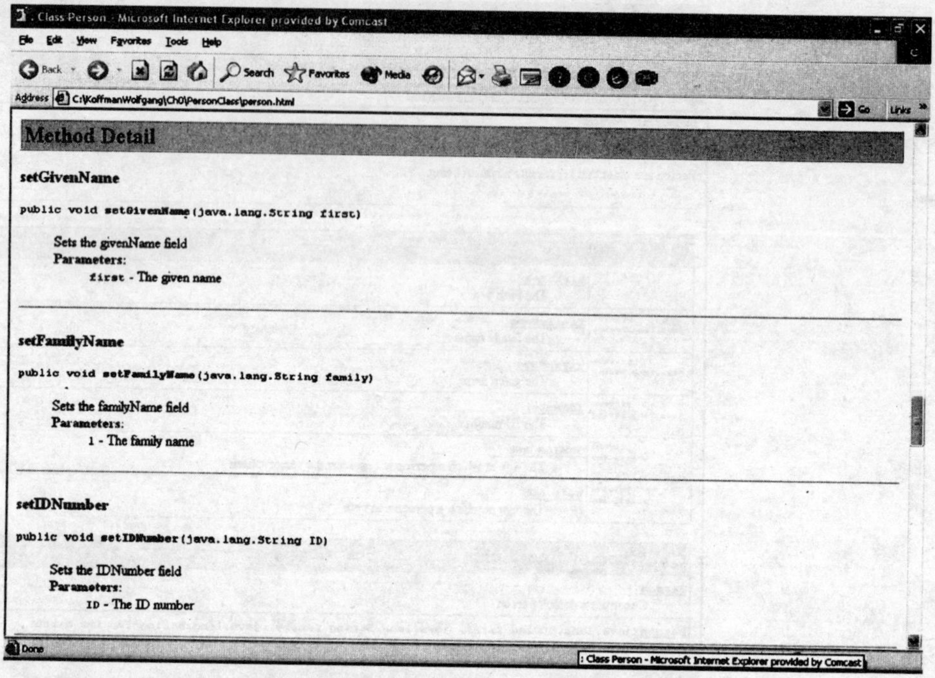

FIGURE A.13
Method Detail for Class Person

To run the Javadoc program, change to the directory that contains the source files that you would like to process. Then, to create the HTML documentation files, enter the command

pathName`\javadoc` *className1*`.java` *className2*`.java`

where *pathName* is the directory that contains the Javadoc program, and the Java source file names (*className1*`.java`, *className2*`.java`, etc.) follow the `javadoc` command. If you want to show the private data fields and methods, add the command line argument `-private`. If you want to create documentation files for all the `.java` files in the directory, use the wildcard `*` for the class name.

pathName`\javadoc -private *.java`

Another useful command line argument is `-d` *destinationFolder*, which allows you to specify a folder or directory other than the source folder for the Javadoc HTML files.

EXERCISES FOR SECTION A.7

SELF-CHECK

1. Explain why methods have public visibility but data fields have private visibility.
2. Download file `Person.java` from the textbook Web site and run `javadoc` on it.
3. Trace the execution of the following statements.

```
Person p1 = new Person("Adam", "Jones", "wxyz", 0);
p1.setBirthYear(1990);
Person p2 = new Person();
```

```
p2.setGivenName("Eve");
p2.setFamilyName(p1.getFamilyName());
p2.setBirthYear(p1.getBirthYear() + 10);
if (p1.equals(p2))
    System.out.println(p1 + "\nis same person as\n\n" + p2);
else
    System.out.println(p1 + "\nis not the same person as\n\n" + p2);
```

PROGRAMMING

1. Write a method `getInitials` that returns a string representing a `Person` object's initials. There should be a period after each initial. Write Javadoc tags for the method.
2. Add a data field `motherMaidenName` to `Person`. Write an accessor and a modifier method for this data field. Modify class `toString` and class `equals` to include this data field. Assume two `Person` objects are equal if they have the same ID number and mother's maiden name. Write Javadoc tags for the method.
3. Write a method `compareTo` that compares two `Person` objects and returns an appropriate result based on a comparison of the ID numbers. That is, if the ID number of the object that `compareTo` is applied to is less than (is greater than) the ID number of the argument object, the result should be negative (positive). The result should be 0 if they have the same ID numbers. Write Javadoc tags for the method.
4. Write a method `switchNames` that exchanges a `Person` object's given and family names. Write Javadoc tags for the method.

A.8 Arrays

In Java, an array is also an object. The elements of an array are indexed and are referenced using a subscripted variable of the form:

`arrayName[`*`subscript`*`]`

Next, we show some different ways to declare arrays and allocate storage for arrays.

EXAMPLE A.14 The following statement declares a variable `scores` that references a new array object that can store five type **int** values (subscripts 0 through 4) as shown. Each element is initialized to 0.

```
int[] scores = new int[5];  // An array with 5 type int values
```

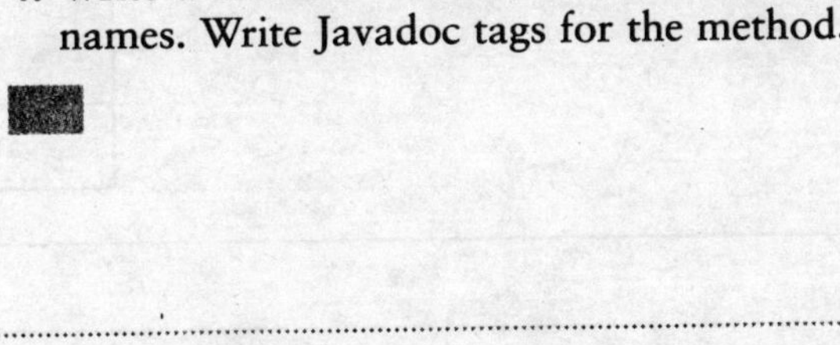

EXAMPLE A.15 The following statement declares a variable names that references a new array object that can store four type String objects. The values stored are specified in the *initializer list.*

```
String[] names = {"Sally", "Jill", "Hal", "Rick"};
```

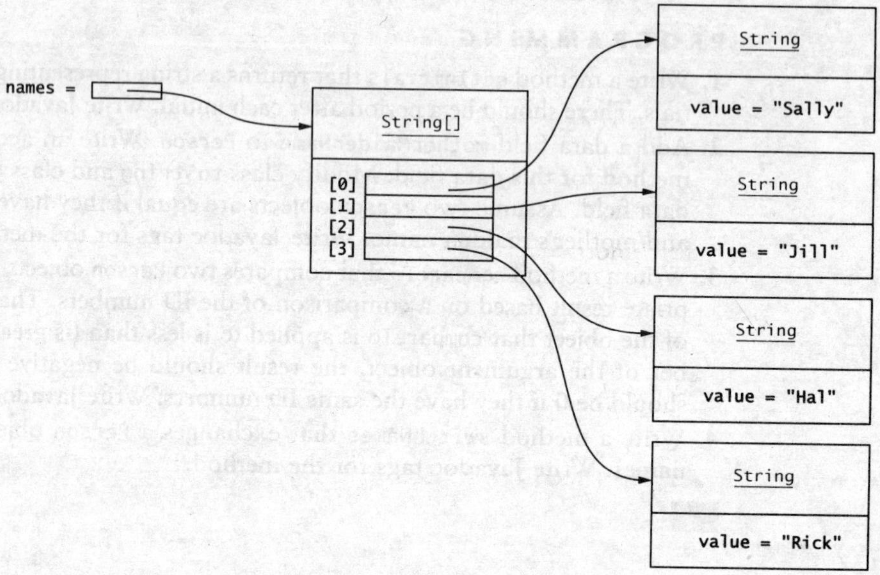

PITFALL

Out-of-Bounds Subscripts

Some programming languages allow you to use an array subscript that is outside of the array bounds. For example, if you attempt to reference scores[5], a C or C++ compiler would access the first memory cell following the array scores. This is considered an error, but it is not detected by the run-time system and will probably lead to another error that will be detected farther down the road (before it does too much damage, you hope). Java, however, verifies that the current value of each array subscript is within the array bounds. If it isn't, you will get an ArrayIndexOutOfBoundsException error.

EXAMPLE A.16 The first of the following statements declares a variable people that can reference an array object for storing type Person objects. Storage has not yet been allocated for the array object (or for the Person objects). The second statement assumes that n is defined, possibly through an input operation. The last statement allocates storage for an array object with n elements. Each array element can reference a type Person object, but initially each element has the value **null** (no object referenced).

```
// Declare people as type Person[].
Person[] people;
// Define n in some way.
int n = . . .
// Allocate storage for the array.
people = new Person[n];
```

We can create some `Person` objects and store them in the array. The following statements store two `Person` objects in array `people`.

```
people[0] = new Person("Elliot", "Koffman", "010-055-0123", 1942);
people[1] = new Person("Paul", "Wolfgang", "015-023-4567", 1945);
```

PITFALL

Forgetting to Declare Storage for an Array

As just shown, you can separate the declaration of variable `people` (the array reference variable) from the step that actually allocates storage (`people = new ...`). However, you can't reference the array elements before you allocate storage for the array. Similarly, if the array elements reference objects, you must separately allocate storage for each object.

Data Field `length`

A Java array has a `length` data field that can be used to determine the array's size. The value of `names.length` is 4; the value of `people.length` is the same as the value of `n` when storage was allocated for the array. The subscripted variable `people[people.length - 1]` references the last element in array `people`. The following **for** statement can be used to display all the `Person` objects stored in array `people`, regardless of the array size.

```
for (int i = 0; i < people.length; i++ )
    if (people[i] != null)
        System.out.println(people[i] + "\n");
```

PITFALL

Using `length` Incorrectly

The value of data field `length` is set when storage is allocated for the array, and it is `final`. Therefore, it can't be changed by the programmer. A statement such as

```
people.length++;    // invalid attempt to increment length
```

would cause a syntax error.

Another common error is using parentheses with `length`. The expression `people.length()` causes a syntax error because `length` is a data field, not a method, of an array.

Method `Arrays.copyOf`

Although you can't change the length of a particular array object, you can copy the values stored in one array object to another array object using method `Arrays.copyOf`. This method returns a copy of a given array and either truncates or pads the copy to a new length. The method is overloaded for arrays of each primitive type, and there is a generic form for copying arrays of class types.

EXAMPLE A.17 The following statements create a new array `tempScores` that is twice the size of array `scores` and contains a copy of elements in array `scores` to the first half of array `tempScores`. The remaining entries of `tempScores` are set to zero. Finally, we reset variable `scores` to reference the same array as `tempScores` (see Figure A.14). The storage originally allocated to store the elements of array `scores` can now be reclaimed by the garbage collector.

```
int[] tempScores = Arrays.copyOf(scores, 2 * scores.length);
scores = tempScores;
```

FIGURE A.14
Doubling the Size of the Array Referenced by Scores

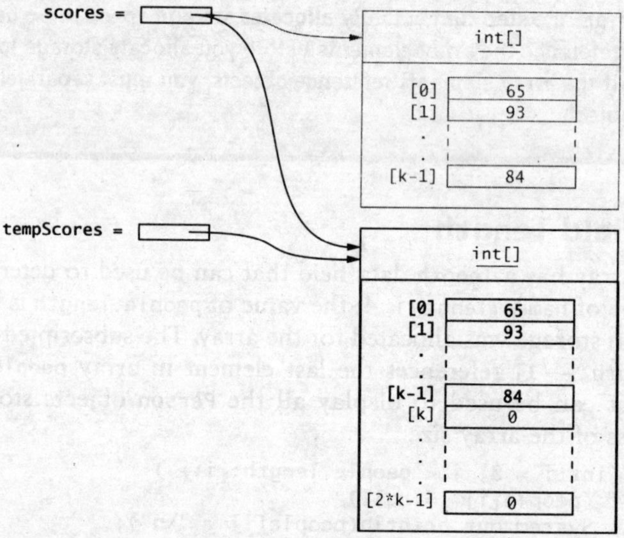

Method `System.arrayCopy`

The method `Arrays.copyOf` makes a copy of the whole array. There is also the method `Arrays.copyOfRange`, which makes a copy of a part of an array returning the selected part as a new array. A general method that will copy a selected portion of an array into another array is `System.arrayCopy`, which has the general form

`System.arraycopy(`*source, sourcePos, destination, destPos, numElements*`);`

The parameters *sourcePos* and *destPos* specify the starting positions in the *source* and *destination* arrays, respectively. The parameter *numElements* specifies the number of elements to copy. If this number is too large, an `ArrayIndexOutOfBoundsException` error occurs.

System.arraycopy is effectively the following:

```
for (int k = 0; k < numElements; k++) {
    destination[destPos + k] = source[sourcePos + k];
}
```

but is implemented within the JVM using native machine code instructions that efficiently copy a block of data from one location to another.

Array Data Fields

It is very common in Java to encapsulate an array, together with the methods that process it, within a class. Rather than allocate storage for a fixed-size array, we would like the client to be able to specify the array size when an object is created. Therefore, we should define a constructor with the array size as a parameter and have the constructor allocate storage for the array. Class Company in Listing A.3 has a data field employees that references an array of Person objects. Both constructors allocate storage for a new array when a Company object is created. The client of this class can specify the size of the array by passing a type **int** value to the constructor parameter size. If no argument is passed, the no-parameter constructor sets the array size to DEFAULT_SIZE.

LISTING A.3
Class Company

```
/** Company is a class that represents a company.
    The data field employees provides storage for
    an array of Person objects.
*/
public class Company {
    // Data Fields
    /** The array of employees */
    private Person[] employees;

    /** The default size of the array */
    private static final int DEFAULT_SIZE = 100;

    // Methods
    /** Creates a new array of Person objects.
        @param size The size of array employees
    */
    public Company(int size) {
        employees = new Person[size];
    }

    public Company() {
        employees = new Person[DEFAULT_SIZE];
    }

    /** Sets field employees.
        @param emp The array of employees
    */
    public void setEmployees(Person[] emp) {
        employees = emp;
    }
```

```
    /** Gets field employees.
        @return employees array
    */
    public Person[] getEmployees() {
        return employees;
    }

    /** Sets an element of employees.
        @param index The position of the employee
        @param emp The employee
    */
    public void setEmployee(int index, Person emp) {
        if (index >= 0 && index < employees.length)
            employees[index] = emp;
    }

    /** Gets an employee.
        @param index The position of the employee
        @return The employee object or null if not defined
    */
    public Person getEmployee(int index) {
        if (index >= 0 && index < employees.length)
            return employees[index];
        else
            return null;
    }

    /** Builds a string consisting of all employee's
        data, with newline characters between employees.
        @return The object's state
    */
    public String toString() {
        StringBuilder result = new StringBuilder();
        for (int i = 0; i < employees.length; i++)
            result.append(employees[i] + "\n");
        return result.toString();
    }
}
```

There are modifier and accessor methods that process individual elements of array `Company` (`setEmployee` and `getEmployee`). Method `getEmployee` returns the type `Person` object at position `index`, or **`null`** if the value of `index` is out of bounds.

The `toString` method returns a string representing the contents of array `employees`. In the **for** loop, the argument in each call to method `append` is the string returned by applying method `Person.toString` to the current employee. This string is appended to the string representing the data for all employees with smaller subscripts.

The following `main` method illustrates the use of class `Company` and displays the state of object `comp`.

```
public static void main(String[] args) {
    Company comp = new Company(2);
    comp.setEmployee(0, new Person("Elliot", "K", "123", 1942));
    comp.setEmployee(1, new Person("Paul", "W", "234", 1945));
    System.out.println(comp);
}
```

Array Results and Arguments

Method `setEmployees` in class `Company` takes a single argument `emp` that is type `Person[]`. The assignment statement

```
employees = emp;
```

resets array `employees` to reference the array argument. Storage allocated to the array previously referenced by `employees` can then be reclaimed by the garbage collector.

The return value of method `getEmployees` is type `Person[]`. The statement

```
return employees;
```

returns a reference to the array `employees`.

Arrays of Arrays

A Java array can have other arrays as its elements. If all these arrays are the same size, then the array of arrays is a two-dimensional array.

EXAMPLE A.18 The declaration

```
double[][] matrix = new double[5][10];
```

allocates storage for a two-dimensional array, `matrix`, that stores 50 real numbers in 5 rows and 10 columns. The variable `matrix[i][j]` references the number with row subscript `i` and column subscript `j`. You can also declare arrays with more than two dimensions.

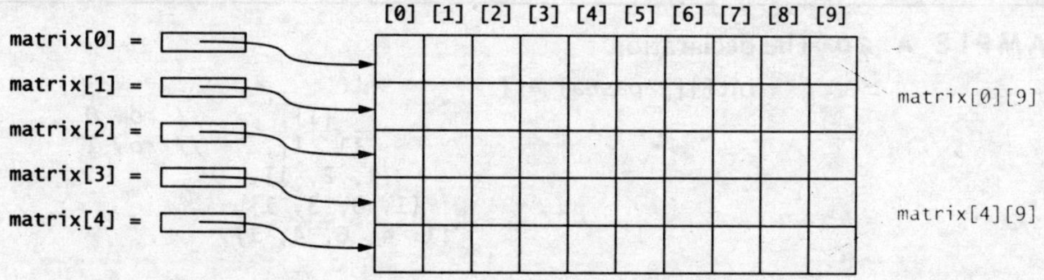

In Java you can have two-dimensional arrays with rows of different sizes. We illustrate this in the next two examples.

EXAMPLE A.19 The declaration

```
char[][] letters = new char[5][];
```

allocates storage for a two-dimensional array of characters with five rows, but the number of columns in each row is not specified. The statements

```
letters[0] = new char[4];
letters[1] = new char[10];
```

define the size of the first two rows and allocate storage for them. The subscripted variable `letters[0]` references the first row; `letters.length` is 5, the number of rows in the array; `letters[1].length` is 10, the number of elements in the row with subscript 1.

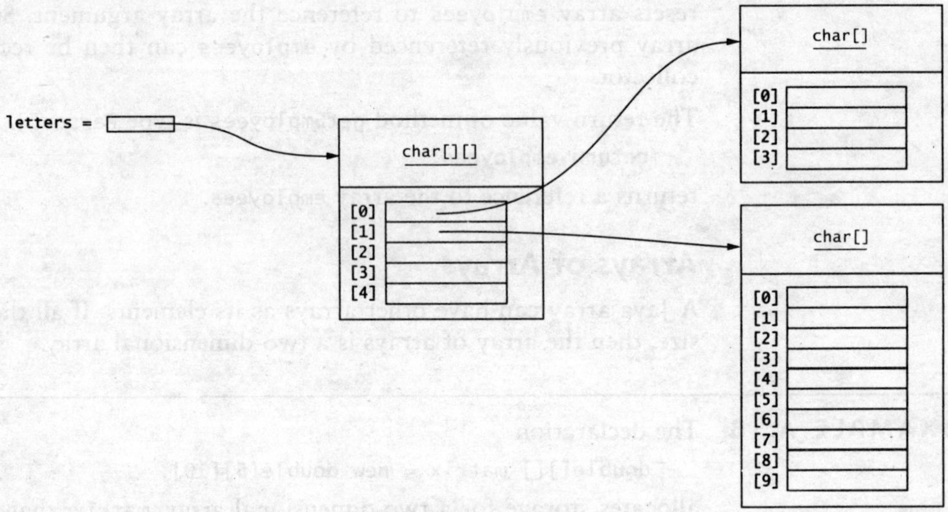

EXAMPLE A.20 The declaration

```
int[][] pascal = {
                          {1},        // row 0
                        {1, 1},       // row 1
                      {1, 2, 1},
                    {1, 3, 3, 1},
                  {1, 4, 6, 4, 1},
                 };
```

allocates storage for an array of arrays with 5 rows. The initializer list provides the values for each row, starting with row 0. The subscripted variable `pascal[0]` references the one-element array `{1}`, and `pascal[4]` references the array `{1, 4, 6, 4, 1}`. Each row has one more element than the previous one. The values shown above form a well-known mathematical entity called Pascal's triangle. Each element in a row, except for the first and last elements, is the sum of the two elements on either side of it in the previous row. For example, the number 6 in the last row is the sum of the numbers 3, 3 in the previous row. In mathematical notation,

```
pascal[i + 1][j] = pascal[i][j - 1] + pascal[i][j].
```

The first and last elements in each row are 1.

The following nested **for** statements sum all values in the Pascal triangle. In the outer **for** loop header, the expression `pascal.length` is the number of rows in the triangle. In the inner **for** loop header, the expression `pascal[row].length` is the number of columns in the array with subscript `row`.

```
int sum = 0;
for (int row = 0; row < pascal.length; row++)
    for (int col = 0; col < pascal[row].length; col++)
        sum += pascal[row][col];
```

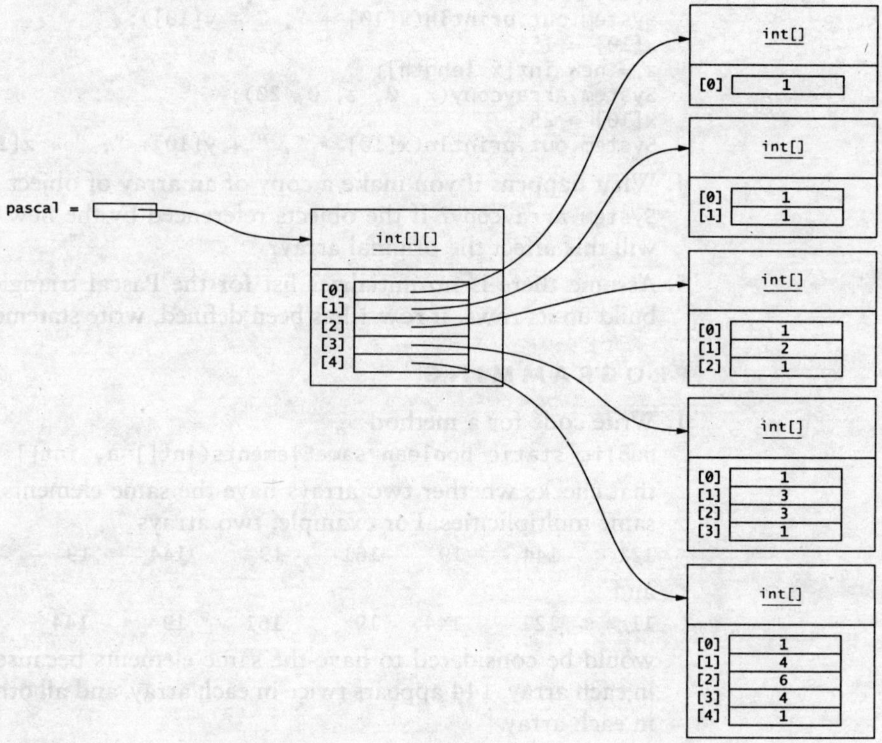

EXERCISES FOR SECTION A.8

SELF-CHECK

1. Show the output that would be displayed by method `main` following Listing A.3.
2. Show that the formula for the interior elements of a Pascal triangle row is correct by evaluating it for each interior element of the last row.

3. What is the output of the following sample code fragment?

```
int[] x;
int[] y;
int[] z;
x = new int[20];
x[10] = 0;
y = x;
x[10] = 5;
System.out.println(x[10] + ", " + y[10]);
x[10] = 15;
z = new int[x.length];
System.arraycopy(x, 0, z, 0, 20);
x[10] = 25;
System.out.println(x[10] + ", " + y[10]+ ", " + z[10]);
```

4. What happens if you make a copy of an array of object references using method `System.arraycopy`? If the objects referenced by the new array are changed, how will this affect the original array?
5. Assume there is no initializer list for the Pascal triangle and you are trying to build up its rows. If row `i` has been defined, write statements to create row `i + 1`.

PROGRAMMING

1. Write code for a method

   ```
   public static boolean sameElements(int[] a, int[] b)
   ```

   that checks whether two arrays have the same elements in some order, with the same multiplicities. For example, two arrays

   `121 144 19 161 19 144 19 11`

   and

   `11 121 144 19 161 19 144 19`

   would be considered to have the same elements because 19 appears three times in each array, 144 appears twice in each array, and all other elements appear once in each array.
2. Write an `equals` method for class `Company`. The result should be **`true`** if the employees of one company match element for element with the employees of a different company. Assume that the objects referenced by each array `employees` are in order by ID number.
3. For the two-dimensional array `letters` in Example A.19, assume `letters[i]` is going to be used to store an array that contains the individual characters in `String` object `next`. Allocate storage for `letters[i]` based on the length of `next` and write a loop that stores each character of `next` in the corresponding element of `letters[i]`. For example, the first character in `next` should be stored in `letters[i][0]`.

A.9 Input/Output Using Class JOptionPane

Prior to Java 2, it was fairly difficult to perform input/output operations (I/O) in Java. You had to either use the console for I/O, use streams (external files), or build GUIs. Java 2 provided class `JOptionPane` (part of the Swing package), which facilitates the display of dialog windows for input and message windows for output. We describe two static methods from class `JOptionPane` in Table A.15. (We discuss more Swing classes in Appendix C.) To use class `JOptionPane`, you should place the line

```
import javax.swing.JOptionPane;    // Import class JOptionPane
```

or

```
import javax.swing.*;              // Import entire Swing package
```

before the class definition in your source file.

TABLE A.15
Methods from Class `JOptionPane`

Method	Behavior
`static String showInputDialog(String prompt)`	Displays a dialog window that shows the argument as a prompt and returns the character sequence typed by the user.
`static void showMessageDialog(Object parent, String message)`	Displays a window containing a `message` string (the second argument) inside the specified container (the first argument).

EXAMPLE A.21 The statement

```
String name = JOptionPane.showInputDialog("Enter your name");
```

displays the dialog window shown on the left in Figure A.15. After the OK button is clicked or the Enter key is pressed, variable `name` references a `String` object that stores the character sequence `"Jane Doe"`. If Cancel is clicked, variable `name` stores **`null`**. The statement

```
JOptionPane.showMessageDialog(null, "Your name is " + name);
```

displays the message window shown on the right in Figure A.15. The first argument specifies the parent container in which this window will be placed. When the argument is **`null`**, the dialog window is placed in the middle of the screen (the window in which the program is executing).

FIGURE A.15
A Dialog Window (Left) and Message Window (Right)

Converting Numeric Strings to Numbers

A dialog window always returns a reference to a string. How can we convert numeric strings to numbers? Fortunately, as shown in Table A.16, class `Integer` provides a static method, `parseInt`, for converting strings consisting only of digit characters to numbers, and class `Double` provides a static method, `parseDouble`, for converting strings consisting of the characters for a real number (or integer) to a type `double` value.

TABLE A.16
Methods for Converting Strings to Numbers

Method	Behavior
`static int parseInt(String)`	Returns an **`int`** value corresponding to its argument string. A `NumberFormatException` occurs if its argument string contains characters other than digits.
`static double parseDouble(String)`	Returns a `double` value corresponding to its argument string. A `NumberFormatException` occurs if its argument string does not represent a real number.

EXAMPLE A.22 The next pair of statements stores a type **`int`** value in `numStu` if `answer` references a `String` object that contains digit characters only.

```
String answer =
    JOptionPane.showInputDialog("Enter number of students");
int numStu = Integer.parseInt(answer);
```

PITFALL

Using Nonnumeric Strings with parseInt, parseDouble

If you pass to `parseInt` a `String` that contains characters that are not digit characters, you will get a `NumberFormatException` error. If you pass to `parseDouble` a `String` that contains characters that can't be in a number, you will also get a `NumberFormatException` error.

GUI Menus Using Method showOptionDialog

Another useful method from class `JOptionPane` is method `showOptionDialog`. This method displays a menu of choices with a button for each choice (see Figure A.16). When a button is clicked, the method returns the index of the button pressed (0 for the first button, etc.). The index value can be used in a **switch** statement to select an alternative.

EXAMPLE A.23 The statements

```
String[] choices = {"insert", "delete", "add", "display"};
int selection = JOptionPane.showOptionDialog(null,
                         "Select an operation",
                         "Operation menu",
                         JOptionPane.YES_NO_CANCEL_OPTION,
                         JOptionPane.QUESTION_MESSAGE, null,
                         choices, choices[0]);
```

display the menu shown in Figure A.16. The array `choices` defines the button labels. After a button is clicked, the value stored in `selection` will be the index of that button, an integer from 0 to 3.

FIGURE A.16
Displaying a Menu

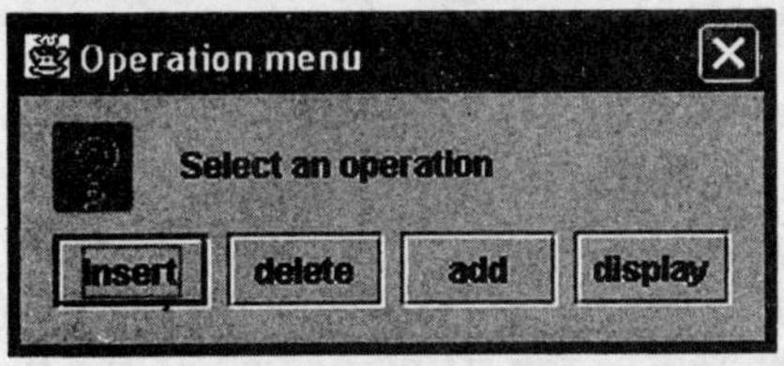

EXERCISES FOR SECTION A.9

SELF-CHECK

1. Show the statements that would be required, using Swing, to read and store the data for a `Person` object prior to calling the constructor with four parameters.

PROGRAMMING

1. Write a `main` method that reads the data for two `Person` objects, creates the objects, and displays the objects and a message indicating whether they represent the same `Person`.

A.10 Input/Output Using Streams and the Scanner Class

In this section we will show you the basics of using streams for I/O in Java. An input stream is a sequence of characters representing program data. An output stream is a sequence of characters representing program output. You can store program data in the stream associated with the console, `System.in`. When you type data characters at the console keyboard, they are appended to `System.in`. The console window is associated with `System.out`, the standard output stream. We have used methods `print` and `println` to write information to this stream.

Besides using the console for I/O, you can create and save a text file (using a word processor or editor) and then use it as an input stream for a program. Similarly, a program can write characters to an output stream and save it as a disk file.

Input Streams

To use input streams, a class file must import `java.io`:

```
import java.io.*;
```

You also need to create a `BufferedReader` object:

```
String fileName = args[0];  // The first main parameter
BufferedReader ins =
        new BufferedReader(new FileReader(fileName));
```

Although this looks fairly complicated, you can think of it as "boilerplate" (or a template for creating a `BufferedReader`). The only part of this code that can change is the `String` argument passed to the `FileReader` constructor (`fileName` in this example). Variable `fileName` references the string passed as the first parameter (`args[0]`) to method `main`. This should be the name of a data file.

The `BufferedReader` constructor needs a parameter that is type `FileReader` (or type `InputStreamReader`). The `BufferedReader` class defines a method `readLine` that can be used to read the next data line in a file (or typed at the console); the method returns a `String` object that contains the characters in that data line.

Console Input

To enable console input, you also must create a `BufferedReader` object:

```
BufferedReader con =
    new BufferedReader(new InputStreamReader(System.in));
```

The `BufferedReader` object `con` is associated with the standard input stream `System.in`, so you can invoke method `readLine` to read the next data line typed at the keyboard.

Output Streams

To create an output stream, use statements such as:

```
String outFileName = args[1];  // The second main parameter
PrintWriter outs = new PrintWriter(new FileWriter(outFileName));
```

You can apply method `print` or `println` to the `PrintWriter` object `outs`. Variable `outFileName` references the same string as `args[1]`, the string passed as the second parameter to method `main`. This should be the external name of a file. When object `outs` is created, the stream it references is always empty. Any information previously stored in the file whose name is passed to `args[1]` will be lost.

Passing Arguments to Method `main`

Earlier we set the variable `fileName` to reference the same string as `args[0]`, the first parameter for method `main`. You must specify the `main` method parameters before you run an application. When you are using the JDK and therefore running your applications from the console command line (such as an "MS-DOS Prompt" window in Windows), you list the parameters after the name of the class you are executing. For example, if you are running application `FileTest.java` with parameters `indata.txt` and `output.txt`, use the command line

```
java FileTest indata.txt output.txt
```

When you are using an IDE, you can also specify parameters before running an application. (For example, Borland JBuilder provides an option Parameters . . . on the Run menu. Selecting this option brings up a window that has a text field with label Parameters. You can type the parameters into this text field. Do not use quotes when typing in parameter names.)

Closing Streams

After processing streams, you must disconnect them from the application. The statement

```
outs.close();
```

does this for stream `outs`. Data to be written to a file is stored in an *output buffer* in memory before it is written to the disk. The `close` statement ensures that any data in the output buffer is written to disk.

PITFALL

Neglecting to Close an Output Stream

If you do not close a stream, it is not considered an error. However, you may find that not all the information written to the stream is actually stored in the corresponding disk file unless you close it.

Exceptions

Exceptions are program errors that occur during the execution of a program. We will discuss exceptions in great detail in Section A.11. In this section, we will tell you just enough about them to enable you to use streams for I/O.

When you process streams, there is a reasonable chance that a system error will occur. For example, the system may not be able to locate your file, or an error could occur during a file read operation. For this reason, Java requires you to perform all file-processing operations within the **try** block of a **try-catch** sequence, as follows:

```
try {
    // Statements that perform file-processing operations
}
catch (IOException ex) {
    ex.printStackTrace(System.err);   // Display stack trace
    System.exit(1);    // Exit with an error indication
}
```

If all operations in the **try** block execute without error, the **catch** block is skipped. If an `IOException` or error occurs, the **try** block is exited and the **catch** block executes. This **catch** block simply displays the sequence of method calls that led to the error (starting with the most recent one and working backward) in the console window (`System.err`—the standard error stream) and then exits with an error indication. If we did not exit the **catch** block after catching an error, the program would continue with the first statement following the **catch** block.

A Complete File-Processing Application

We put all these pieces together in this example. In Listing A.4, the `main` method in class `FileTest` consists of a **try-catch** sequence. The **try** block creates two `BufferedReader` objects: `ins` (associated with a data file) and `con` (associated with `System.in`). It also creates a `PrintWriter` object `outs` (associated with an output file). The **while** loop invokes method `readLine` to read data lines from stream `ins`, storing the information read in the `String` object `first`. When the end of the data file is reached, `first` will contain **null**. If `first` is not **null** (the normal situation when a data line is read), the user sees a console prompt asking for more data. The data entered by the user is read into the `String` object `second`.

```
System.out.print("Type in data to follow " + first + ": ");
String second = con.readLine();         // Read from console
```

Next, the contents of `second` are appended to `first`, and the new string is written to the output file.

```
outs.println(first + ", " + second);  // Append and write
```

This process continues until the end of the data file is reached, loop exit occurs, and the files are closed.

LISTING A.4
Class `FileTest`

```
/** FileTest is an application that illustrates stream operations. */

import java.io.*;
```

```
public class FileTest {
    /** Reads a line from an input file and a line from the console.
        Concatenates the two lines and writes them to an output file.
        Does this until all input lines have been read.
        @param args[0] The input file name
        @param args[1] The output file name
    */
    public static void main(String[] args) {
        try {
            String inFileName = args[0];    // First main parameter
            String outFileName = args[1];   // Second main parameter
            BufferedReader ins =
                new BufferedReader(new FileReader(inFileName));
            BufferedReader con =
                new BufferedReader(new InputStreamReader(System.in));
            PrintWriter outs =
                new PrintWriter(new FileWriter(outFileName));

            // Reads words and writes them to the output file until done.
            String first = ins.readLine();          // Read from file
            while (first != null) {
                System.out.print("Type in a word to follow "
                                 + first + ": ");
                String second = con.readLine();  // Read from console
                // Append and write
                outs.println(first + ", " + second);
                first = ins.readLine();              // Read from file
            }

            // Close files.
            ins.close();
            outs.close();
        }
        catch (IOException ex) {
            ex.printStackTrace(System.err);    // Display stack trace
            System.exit(1);       // Exit with an error indication
        }
    }
}
```

Figure A.17 shows a sample run. The input file contains the three lines

```
apple
cat
John
```

and the output file contains three lines consisting of a word read from the data file, a comma, and a word typed in at the console.

```
apple, butter
cat, dog
John, Doe
```

FIGURE A.17
Sample Run of Class FileTest

The Scanner

The Scanner was introduced as part of Java 5.0. The Scanner greatly simplifies the process of reading data from the console or an input file because it enables you to process a data line as a sequence of tokens. For console input, the next and hasNext methods suspend execution until input is provided. Table A.17 summarizes selected methods of this class.

To use a Scanner (part of Java.util) to read from the console, you need to create a new Scanner object and connect it the console (System.in):

```
Scanner scanConsole = new Scanner(Sytem.in);
```

To use a Scanner to read from a file, you need to create a new Scanner object and connect it to the file.

TABLE A.17
Selected Methods of the java.util.Scanner Class

Constructor	Behavior
`Scanner(File source)`	Constructs a Scanner that reads from the specified file.
`Scanner(InputStream source)`	Constructs a Scanner that reads from the specified InputStream.
`Scanner(Readable source)`	Constructs a Scanner that reads from the specified Readable object. The interface Readable is the superclass for Readers.
`Scanner(String source)`	Constructs a Scanner that reads from the specified String object.
Method	**Behavior**
`boolean hasNext()`	Returns **true** if there is another token available for input.
`boolean hasNextDouble()`	Returns **true** if the next token can be interpreted as a **double** value.
`boolean hasNextInt()`	Returns **true** if the next token can be interpreted as an **int** value.
`boolean hasNextLine()`	Returns **true** if there is another line available for input.
`IOException ioException()`	Returns the IOException last thrown by the Readable object that is used to read the input. (The other constructors create a Readable object to perform the actual input.)
`String next()`	Returns the next token.
`double nextDouble()`	Returns the next token as a **double** value. Throws InputMismatchException if the input is not in the correct format.
`int nextInt()`	Returns the next token as a **int** value. Throws InputMismatchException if the input is not in the correct format.
`String nextLine()`	Returns the next line of input as a string. A line is a sequence of characters ending with the newline character (\n). It may contain several tokens. The newline character is processed, but it is not included in the string.
`String findInLine(String pattern)`	Attempts to find the next occurrence of a substring that matches the regular expression defined by pattern returns the substring if found or **null** if not found.

```
Scanner scanFile = null;
String fileName = "dataFile.txt";              // data file name
try {
    scanFile = new Scanner(new File(fileName));
} catch (FileNotFoundException ex) {
    System.err.println(filename + " not found");
    System.exit(1);
}
```

`Scanner scanFile` is connected to a data file; the name of the data file is stored in `String fileName`. The file name is passed as an argument to the `File` constructor. Class `File` is in `java.util.io` , which must be imported (as well as `java.util` for Scanner).

You do not need to use a `try-catch` block when reading data since `IOExceptions` are captured. You do need a `try-catch` block as shown above when attaching a Scanner to a File. Also, an `InputMismatchExcepton` can occur when reading if the input does not match the requested type.

EXAMPLE A.24 The program in Listing A.5 prompts the user for a name, an integer value, another name, and another integer value. It displays the sum of the two integer values read. A sample interaction follows:

```
For your blended family,
enter the wife's name: Teresa Heinz
Enter the number of her children: 3
Enter the husband's name: John Kerry
Enter the number of his children: 2
Teresa Heinz and John Kerry have 5 children.
```

LISTING A.5

A Program for Counting Children in a Blended Family

```
import java.util.*;

/** A class to count and display children in a blended family. */
public class BlendedFamily {
    public static void main(String[] args) {
        Scanner sc = new Scanner(System.in);
        System.out.print(
            "For your blended family, \nenter the wife's name: ");
        String wife = sc.nextLine();
        System.out.print("Enter the number of her children: ");
        int herKids = sc.nextInt();

        System.out.print("Enter the husband's name: ");
        sc.nextLine();   // Skip over trailing newline character.
        String husband = sc.nextLine();
        System.out.print("Enter the number of his children: ");
        int hisKids = sc.nextInt();

        System.out.println(wife + " and " + husband + " have "
                          + (herKids + hisKids) + " children.");
    }
}
```

PITFALL

Not Skipping the Newline Character before Reading a String

In the preceding example, we used the statement pair

```
sc.nextLine();    // Skip over trailing newline character.
String husband = sc.nextLine();
```

to read a string into husband. The purpose of the first statement is to process the newline character at the end of the line containing the data value 3. If we did not include the first statement, the newline character following the data value 3 would terminate the scanning process immediately, storing an empty string in husband. Because data entry for husband was completed without the need for typing in additional data, the line

```
Enter the husband's name: Enter the number of his children:
```

would be displayed. At this point, if you enter the husband's name, you will get an `InputMismatchException`. If you enter an integer, you will get the incomplete output line:

```
Teresa Heinz and  have 5 children.
```

Tokenized Input

Often a data line will consist of a group of data items separated by spaces. In Section A.5, we discussed how to extract the individual items (tokens) from each line in order to process them. You can also use a `Scanner`. The following loop adds all the numbers read from input stream `ins`.

```
double sum = 0.0;
Scanner sc = new Scanner(ins);
while (sc.hasNextDouble()) {
    nextNum = sc.nextDouble();
    sum += nextNum;
}
```

Extracting Tokens Using Scanner.findInLine

You can use a `Scanner` to scan the characters in a string as well as the data in a file. The statement

```
Scanner scan = new Scanner(line);
```

creates a `Scanner` object to scan, or process the characters, in string `line`.

You can also extract substrings that match a specified pattern using `Scanner` method `findInLine`. If method `findInLine` is applied to `scan`, it will extract each sequence of characters in `line` matched by its regular expression argument. When there are no characters remaining that match the regular expression, `findInLine` will return **`null`**. The statements below store in `token` each sequence of digit and letter characters and display the tokens. Note that this regular expression is the same as the one used with method `split` with the ^ (not) symbol removed because we are extracting sequences of letters and digits instead of looking for delimiter characters that are not letters or digits.

```
String token;
while ((token = scan.findInLine("[\\p{L}\\p{N}]+")) != null) {
     System.out.println(token);
}
```

EXERCISES FOR SECTION A.10

SELF-CHECK

1. Show the statements that would be required, using the console for input, to read and store the data for a `Person` object prior to calling the constructor with four parameters.
2. Answer Exercise 1 above using a data file instead of the console.
3. What would happen if the output file name matched the name of a file already saved on disk? What could happen if the user forgets to close an output file?
4. When does the **`catch`** block in a **`try-catch`** sequence execute?

PROGRAMMING

1. Write a method for class `Person` that reads the data for a single employee from a `BufferedReader` object (the method argument). Assume there is one data item per line.
2. Write a method for class `Company` that reads the data for the `employees` array. This method should call the one needed for Programming Exercise 1.

A.11 Catching Exceptions

When an exception is thrown, the normal sequence of execution is interrupted because the execution of subsequent statements would most likely be erroneous. The default behavior is for the JVM to halt program execution and to display an error message indicating which type of exception was thrown and where in the program it was thrown. The JVM also displays a stack trace that shows the sequence of method calls, starting at the method that threw the exception, then showing the method that called that method, and so on, all the way back to the `main` method.

The stack trace in Figure A.18 shows that an exception occurred during the execution of class `ExceptionDemo`. The exception was a `NullPointerException`. The exception was thrown in method `doSomethingElse` (at line 18 of class `ExceptionDemo`). Method `doSomethingElse` was called from method `doSomething` (at line 13). Method `doSomething` was called from method `main` (at line 7).

FIGURE A.18
Example of a Stack Trace for an Uncaught Exception

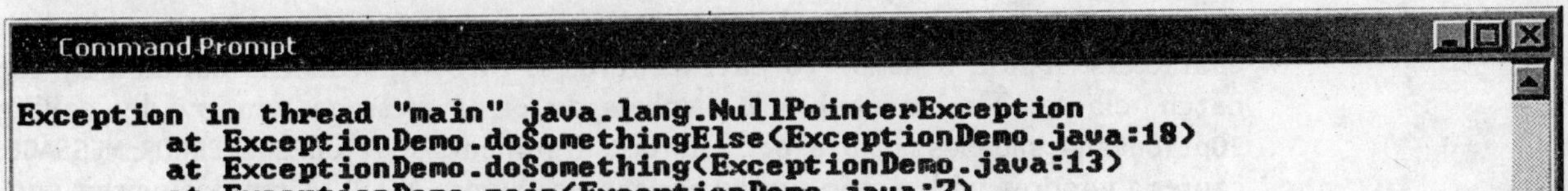

Catching and Handling Exceptions

In the next few subsections you will see how to avoid the default behavior when you write a method that may throw an exception. You will also see why it is advantageous to do this.

The Try–Catch–Finally Sequence

One way to avoid uncaught exceptions is to write a `try-catch` sequence that actually "catches" an exception and "handles it" rather than relying on the JVM to do this.

```
try {
    // Statements that perform file-processing operations.
}
catch (IOException ex) {
    ex.printStackTrace();   // Display stack trace.
    System.exit(1);     // Exit with an error indication.
}
```

If all statements in the `try` block execute without error, the `catch` block is skipped. If an `IOException` occurs, the `try` block is exited and the `catch` block executes. This particular `catch` block simply displays the sequence of method calls that led to the error (starting with the most recent one and working backward) in the console window (`System.err` – the standard error stream) and then exits with an error indication.

Although this handles the exception, it basically duplicates the default behavior for uncaught exceptions. Next, we show you how to use the `try-catch` sequence to recover from errors and continue execution of your program.

Handling Exceptions to Recover from Errors

In addition to reporting errors, exceptions provide us with the opportunity to recover from errors. One common source of exceptions is user input. For example, the method `JOptionPane.showInputDialog` displays a dialog window and allows the user to enter input. After the user enters input and presses the Enter key, the method will return a string containing the input characters. If we are expecting an integer value, we need to convert this string to an integer. The conversion is performed by method `parseInt`, which can cause a `NumberFormatException` to be thrown.

EXAMPLE A.25 Method `readInt` (Listing A.6) returns the integer value that was typed into a dialog window by the program user. The method argument is the dialog window prompt.

The `while` loop repetition condition (`true`) ensures that the `try-catch` sequence will execute "forever" or until the user enters a correct data item. The statements

```
String numStr = JOptionPane.showInputDialog(prompt);
return Integer.parseInt(numStr);
```

display the dialog window and return an integer value if `numStr` contains only digit characters. If not, a `NumberFormatException` is thrown, which is handled by the `catch` clause. The `catch` block displays an error message window by calling `JOptionPane.showMessageDialog`. The last argument, `JOptionPane.ERROR_MESSAGE`, causes a window with a stop sign to appear (see Figure A.19). After closing this window, the user has another opportunity to enter a valid numeric string.

FIGURE A.19
Bad Numeric String Error

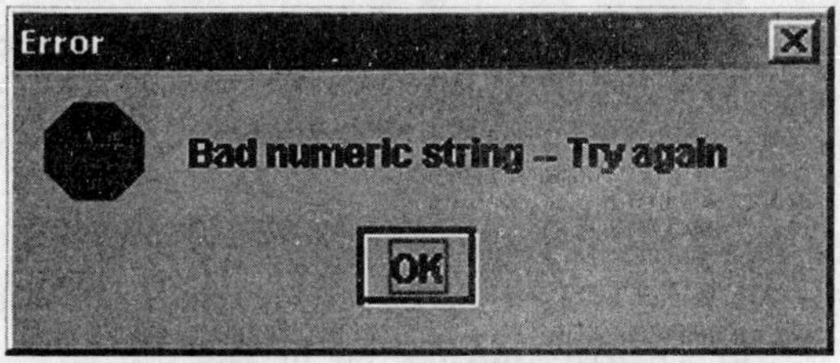

LISTING A.6
Method readInt

```
/** Method to return an integer data value.
    @param prompt Message
    @return The data value read as an int
*/
public static int readInt(String prompt) {
    while (true) {   // Loop until valid number is read.
        try {
            String numStr = JOptionPane.showInputDialog(prompt);
            return Integer.parseInt(numStr);
        }
        catch (NumberFormatException ex) {
            JOptionPane.showMessageDialog(
                null,
                "Bad numeric string - Try again",
                "Error", JOptionPane.ERROR_MESSAGE);
        }
    }
}
```

The `try` Block

The syntax for the `try` block is as follows:

```
try {
    Code that may throw an exception
}
```

The `catch` Clauses and Blocks

Exceptions are caught by what is appropriately called a `catch` clause. A `catch` clause resembles a method and has the following syntax.

```
catch (ExceptionClass exceptionArgument) {
    Code to handle the exception
}
```

The code within the brackets is called the catch block. The `catch` clause(s) must follow a `try` block. There may be multiple `catch` clauses, one for each exception class that you wish to handle.

An exception matches a `catch` clause if the type of the exception is the same as the argument of the `catch` clause or is a subclass of the argument type. When an exception is thrown from within a `try` block, the associated `catch` clause(s) is (are) examined to see whether there is a match in the exception class for any `catch` clause. If so, that `catch` block executes. If not, a search is made back through the chain of method calls to see whether any of them occurs in a `try` block with an appropriate `catch`. If so, that `catch` block executes. We illustrate this next.

EXAMPLE A.26 The body of method `readIntTwo` below contains just the statements in the `try` block of method `readInt` (Listing A.6), but the `catch` clause is omitted.

```
public static int readIntTwo(String prompt) {
    String numStr = JOptionPane.showInputDialog(prompt);
    return Integer.parseInt(numStr);
}
```

In this case, if a `NumberFormatException` is thrown by method `parseInt`, method `readIntTwo` will not be able to handle it, so `readIntTwo` is exited and a search is made for an appropriate `catch` clause in the caller of method `readIntTwo`. If method `readIntTwo` is called to read a value into age by the following `try` block:

```
try {
    // Enter a value for age.
    age = readIntTwo("Enter your age");
} catch (Exception ex) {
    System.err.println("Error occurred in call to readIntTwo");
    age = DEFAULT_AGE;
}
```

the `catch` clause will handle the `NumberFormatException` (because `NumberFormatException` is a subclass of `Exception`) and assign the value of `DEFAULT_AGE` to age. It will also display an error message on the console, and program execution will continue with the statement that follows this `try-catch` sequence.

Note that a `catch` clause is like a method, and the `catch` block is like a method body. The term `catch` clause refers to both the header and the body, whereas the term `catch` block refers to the body alone. This distinction is not generally that important, and you may see the terms used interchangeably in other texts and documentation.

EXAMPLE A.27 `EOFException` is a subclass of `IOException`. The two `catch` clauses in the following code must appear in the sequence shown to avoid a `catch is unreachable` syntax error. The first `catch` block handles an `EOFException` that occurs when all the data in the file was processed (not an error). This `catch` block tells the program user so and then exits the program normally (`System.exit(0)`). The second `catch` clause processes any other input/output exception by calling method `printStackTrace` to display a stack trace like the one shown in Figure A.18. It exits the program with an error indication (`System.exit(1)`). (*Note:* The method `printStackTrace` is defined in the `Throwable` class and is inherited by all exception objects.)

```
catch (EOFException ex) {
    System.out.print("End of file reached ")
    System.out.println(" - processing complete");
    System.exit(0);
}
catch (IOException ex) {
    System.err.println("Input/Output Error:");
    ex.printStackTrace();
    System.exit(1);
}
```

PITFALL

Unreachable catch Block

Note that only the catch block within the first catch clause having an appropriate exception class executes. All other catch blocks are skipped. If a catch clause exception type is a subclass of an exception type in an earlier catch clause, the catch block in the later catch clause cannot execute, so the Java compiler will display a catch is unreachable syntax error. To correct this error, switch the order of the catch clauses so that the catch clause whose exception class is the subclass comes first.

The finally Block

When an exception is thrown, the flow of execution is suspended and continues at the appropriate catch clause. There is no return to the try block. Instead, processing continues at the first statement after all of the catch clauses associated with the try from which the exception was thrown.

In some situations, allowing the program to continue after an exception without executing all the statements in the try block could cause problems. For example, if some calculations needed to be performed before returning from the method, these calculations would have to be duplicated in both the try block and every catch clause. To avoid such a duplication (which can be error-prone), the finally block can be used. The code in the finally block is executed either after the try block is exited or after a catch clause is exited (if one is executed). The finally block is optional. We show an example in the following syntax summary.

SYNTAX **try-catch-finally Sequence**

FORM:

try {
    Statements that may throw an exception
}
catch (*ExceptionClass*$_1$ *exceptionArgument*$_1$) {
    Statements to process ExceptionClass$_1$
}
catch (*ExceptionClass*$_2$ *exceptionArgument*$_2$) {
    Statements to process ExceptionClass$_2$
}
catch (*ExceptionClass*$_n$ *exceptionArgument*$_n$) {
    Statements to process ExceptionClass$_n$
}
finally {
    Statements to be executed after the try *block or the* exception *block exits*
}

EXAMPLE:

```
try {
    String sizeStr = JOptionPane.showInputDialog("Enter new size");
    size = Integer.parseInt(sizeStr);
}
catch (NumberFormatException ex) {
    size = DEFAULT_SIZE;  // Use default value if input error.
}
finally {
    if (size > MAX_CAPACITY)
        size = MAX_CAPACITY;
}
```

MEANING:

The statements in the `try` block execute through to completion unless an exception is thrown. If there is a `catch` clause to handle the exception, its `catch` block executes to completion. After the `try` block or `catch` block executes, the `finally` block executes to completion.

If there is no `catch` clause to handle the exception thrown in the `try` block, the `finally` block is executed, and then the exception is passed up the call chain until either it is caught by some other method in the call chain or it is processed by the JVM as an uncaught exception.

Reporting the Error and Exiting

There are many cases in which an exception is thrown but there is no obvious way to recover. For example, reading from a file or the system console can result in an `IOException` being thrown. In this case the `catch` clause should print the stack trace and exit, as follows:

```
catch (IOException ex) {
    ex.printStackTrace();
    System.exit(1);
}
```

The method call `System.exit(1)` causes a return to the operating system with an error indication.

Checked and Unchecked Exceptions

There are two categories of exceptions: checked and unchecked. A *checked exception* is caused by an error that is beyond the programmer's control, such as an input/output error (`IOException`). An *unchecked exception* is caused by a program error. An example is an `IndexOutOfBoundsException`. Checked exceptions must always be handled in some way (discussed next). There is no requirement to handle unchecked exceptions.

PITFALL

Ignoring Exceptions

Exceptions are designed to make the programmer aware of possible error conditions and to provide a way to handle them. Some programmers do not appreciate this feature and do the following:

```
catch (Exception e){}
```

Although this clause is syntactically correct and eliminates a lot of pesky error messages, it is almost always a bad idea. The program continues execution after the try–catch sequence with no indication that there was a problem. The statement that caused the exception to be thrown did not execute properly. The statements that follow it in the `try` block were not executed at all. The program will have hidden defects that will make its users very unhappy and could have even more serious consequences.

PROGRAM STYLE

Using Exceptions to Enable Straightforward Code

In computer languages that did not provide exceptions, programmers had to incorporate error-checking logic throughout their code to check for many possibilities, some of which were of low probability. The result was sometimes messy, as follows:

```
Step A
if (Step A successful) {
    Step B
    if (Step B successful) {
        Step C
    } else {
        Report error in Step B
        Cleanup after Step A
    }
} else {
    Report error in Step A
}
```

With exceptions this becomes much cleaner, as follows:

```
try {
    Step A
    Step B
    Step C
} catch (exception indicating Step B failed) {
    Report error in step B
    Cleanup after step A
} catch (exception indicating Step A failed) {
    Report error in step A
}
```

EXERCISES FOR SECTION A.11

SELF-CHECK

1. Assume that method `main` calls method `first` at line 10 of class `MyApp`, method `first` calls method `second` at line 10 of class `Others`, and method `second` calls method `parseInt` at line 20 of class `Other`. These calls result in a `NumberFormatException` at line 430 of class `Integer`. Show the stack trace.
2. Assume that you have `catch` clauses for exception classes `Exception`, `NumberFormatException`, and `RuntimeException` following a `try` block. Show the required sequence of `catch` clauses.

PROGRAMMING

1. For the `try` block

```
try {
    numStr = in.readLine();
    num = Integer.parseInt(numStr);
    average = total / num;
}
```

write a `try-catch-finally` sequence with `catch` clauses for `ArithmeticException`, `NumberFormatException`, and `IOException`. For class `ArithmeticException`, set `average` to zero and display an error message indicating the kind of exception, display the stack trace, and exit with an error indication. After exiting the `try` block or the `catch` block for `ArithmeticException`, display the message "`That's all folks`" in the finally block.

A.12 Throwing Exceptions

In the last section we showed how to catch and handle exceptions using the `try-catch` sequence. As an alternative to catching an exception in a lower-level method, you can allow it to be caught and handled by a higher-level method. You can do this in one of two ways:

1. You declare that the lower-level method may throw a checked exception by adding a `throws` clause to the method header.
2. You throw the exception in the lower-level method, using a `throw` statement, when the exception is detected.

The throws Clause

The next example illustrates the use of the `throws` clause to declare that a method may throw a particular kind of checked exception. This is a useful approach if a higher-level module already contains a `catch` clause for this exception type. If you don't use the `throws` clause, you must duplicate the `catch` clause in the lower-level method to avoid an unreported exception syntax error.

EXAMPLE A.28 Method readData reads two strings from the BufferedReader object console associated with System.in (the system console) and stores them in data fields firstName and lastName. Each call to method readLine may throw a checked IOException, so method readData cannot compile without the throws clause. If you omit it, you will get the syntax error unreported exception: Java.io.IOException; must be caught or declared to be thrown.

```
public void readData() throws IOException {
        BufferedReader console = new BufferedReader(
            new InputStreamReader(System.in));
        System.out.print("Enter first name: ");
        firstName = console.readLine();
        System.out.print("Enter last name: ");
        lastName = console.readLine();
}
```

If method readData is called by method setNewPerson, method setNewPerson must have a catch block that handles exceptions of type IOException.

```
public void setNewPerson() {
    try {
        readData();
        // Process the data read.
        . . .
    }
    catch (IOException iOEx) {
        System.err.println("Call to readLine failed in readData");
        iOEx.printStackTrace();
        System.exit(1);
    }
}
```

If a method can throw more than one exception type, list them all after throws with comma delimiters. You will get an unreported exception syntax error if you omit any checked exception type. The compiler verifies that all class names listed are exception classes.

PROGRAM STYLE

Using Javadoc @throws for Unchecked Exceptions

Listing unchecked exceptions in the throws clause is legal syntax but is considered poor programming practice. Instead you should use the Javadoc @throws tag to document any unchecked exceptions that may reasonably be expected to occur but are not caught in the method.

The throw Statement

You can use a throw statement in a lower-level method to indicate that an error condition has been detected. When the throw statement executes, the lower-level method stops executing immediately, and the JVM begins the search for an exception handler as described earlier. This approach is usually taken if the exception is unchecked and is likely to be caught in a higher-level method. If the exception thrown is a checked exception, this exception must be declared in the throws clause of the method containing the throw statement.

EXAMPLE A.29 The method addOrChangeEntry takes two String parameters: name and number. The number parameter is intended to represent a valid phone number. Therefore, we wish to validate its format to ensure that only validly formatted numbers are entered. Assuming that we have a method isPhoneNumberFormat that checks for a valid phone number, we could code the addOrChangeEntry method as follows:

```
public String addOrChangeEntry(String name, String number) {
    if (!isPhoneNumberFormat(number)) {
        throw new IllegalArgumentException
            ("Invalid phone number: " + number);
    }
    // Add/change the number.
    . . .
}
```

The throw statement creates and throws a new IllegalArgumentException, which can be handled farther back in the call chain or by the JVM if it is uncaught. The constructor argument ("Invalid phone number: " + number) for the new exception object is a message that describes the cause of the error.

If we call this method using the following try-catch sequence:

```
try {
    addOrChangeEntry(myName, myNumber);
} catch (IllegalArgumentException ex) {
    System.err.println(ex.getMessage());
}
```

and myNumber references the string "1xx1", which is not a valid phone number, the console output would be:

```
Invalid phone number: 1xx1
```

SYNTAX throw Statement

FORM:

```
throw new ExceptionClass();
throw new ExceptionClass(detailMessage);
```

EXAMPLE:

```
throw new FileNotFoundException("File " + fileSource
                                + " not found");
```

MEANING:

A new exception of type *ExceptionClass* is created and thrown. The optional `String` parameter *detailMessage* is used to specify an error message associated with this exception. If the higher-level method that catches this exception has the `catch` clause

```
catch (ExceptionClass ex) {
    System.err.println(ex.getMessage());
    System.exit(1);
}
```

the *detailMessage* will be written to the system error stream before system exit occurs.

EXAMPLE A.30 Listing A.7 shows a second method `readInt` that has three arguments. As in method `readInt` in Listing A.6, the first argument is a prompt. The second and third arguments represent the end points for a range of integer numbers. The method returns the first integer value entered by the program user that is between the end points.

The `if` statement tests whether the end points define an empty range (`minN > maxN`). If so, the statement

```
throw new IllegalArgumentException(
    "In readInt, minN " + minN
    + " not <= maxN " + maxN);
```

throws an `IllegalArgumentException`, creating an instance of this class. The message passed to the constructor gives the cause of the exception. This message would be displayed by `printStackTrace` or returned by `getMessage` or `toString`.

If the range is not empty, the `while` loop executes. Its repetition condition (`!inRange`) is true as long as the user has not yet entered a value that is within the range defined by the end points. The `try` block displays a dialog window with a prompt that shows the valid range of values. The statement

```
inRange = (minN <= n && n <= maxN);
```

sets `inRange` to true when the value assigned to `n` is within this range. If so, the loop is exited and this value is returned. However, if the user enters a string that is not numeric, the `catch` block displays an error message. If the string is not numeric or its value is not in range, `inRange` remains false, so (`!inRange`) is true and the loop repeats, giving the user another opportunity to enter a valid number.

LISTING A.7

Method readInt (part of MyInput.java) with Three Parameters

```
/** Method to return an integer data value between two
    specified end points.
    pre: minN <= maxN.
    @param prompt Message
    @param minN Smallest value in range
    @param maxN Largest value in range
    @throws IllegalArgumentException
    @return The first data value that is in range
*/
public static int readInt(String prompt, int minN, int maxN) {
    if (minN > maxN) {
        throw new IllegalArgumentException(
            "In readInt, minN " + minN
            + " not <= maxN " + maxN);
    }
    // Arguments are valid, read a number.
    boolean inRange = false; // Assume no valid number read.
    int n = 0;
    while (!inRange) {  // Repeat until valid number read.
        try {
            String line = JOptionPane.showInputDialog(
                    prompt + "\nEnter an integer between "
                    + minN + " and " + maxN);
            n = Integer.parseInt(line);
            inRange = (minN <= n && n <= maxN);
        } catch (NumberFormatException ex) {
            JOptionPane.showMessageDialog(
                null,
                "Bad numeric string - Try again",
                "Error", JOptionPane.ERROR_MESSAGE);
        }
    }   // End while
    return n;  // n is in range
}
```

PROGRAM STYLE

Reasons for Throwing Exceptions

You might wonder what is gained by intentionally throwing an exception. If it is not caught farther back in the call chain, it will go uncaught and will cause your program to terminate. However, in the examples in this section, it would not make any sense to continue with either an empty range (in `readInt`) or an invalid phone number (in `addOrChangeEntry`). In fact, the loop in method `readInt` would execute forever if the range of acceptable values was empty. Because the boundary parameters `minN` and `maxN` are defined in a higher-level method, it would also make no sense to try to get new values in `readInt`. However, if the exception is passed back and caught at the point where the boundary points are defined, the programmer can get new boundary values and call method `readInt` again instead of terminating the program.

Catching versus Throwing Exceptions

You can always avoid handling exceptions where they occur by declaring that they are thrown or by throwing them and letting them be handled farther back in the call chain. In general, though, it is better to handle an exception where it occurs rather than to pass it back. This gives you the opportunity to recover from the error and to continue on with the execution of the current method. We did this, for example, for `NumberFormatExceptions` in both `readInt` methods (see Listings A.6 and A.7). If an error is a nonrecoverable error, however, and is also likely to occur farther back in the call chain, you might as well allow the exception to be handled at the farthest point back in the call chain rather than duplicate the error-handling code in several methods. We recommend the following guidelines:

- If an exception is recoverable in the current method, handle the exception in the current method.
- If a checked exception is likely to be caught in a higher-level method, declare that it can occur using a `throws` clause, and use a `@throws` tag to document this in the Javadoc comment for this method.
- If an unchecked exception is likely to be caught in a higher-level method, use a `@throws` tag to document this fact in the Javadoc comment for the method. However, it is not necessary to use a `throws` clause with unchecked exceptions.

EXERCISES FOR SECTION A.12

SELF-CHECK

1. Explain the difference between the `throws` clause and the `throw` statement.
2. When would it be better to declare an exception rather than catch it in a method?
3. When would it be better to throw an exception rather than catch it in a method?
4. What kind of exceptions should appear in a `throws` clause?
5. For the following situations, indicate whether it would be better to catch an exception, declare an exception, or throw an exception in the lower-level method. Explain your answer and show the code required for the lower-level method to do it.
   a. A lower-level method contains a call to method `readLine`; the higher-level method that calls it contains a `catch` clause for class `IOException`.
   b. A method contains a call to method `readLine` to enter a value that is passed as an argument to a lower-level method. The lower-level method's argument must be a positive number.
   c. A lower-level method contains a call to method `readLine`, but the higher-level method that calls it does not have a `catch` clause for class `IOException`.
   d. A lower-level method reads a data string and converts it to type `int`. The higher-level method contains a `catch` clause for class `NumberFormatException`.
   e. A lower-level method detects an unrecoverable error that is an unchecked exception.

PROGRAMMING

1. The syntax display for the `throw` statement had the following example:
```
throw new FileNotFoundException("File " + fileSource
                                + " not found");
```
   Write a `catch` clause for a method farther back in the call chain that handles this exception.
2. Method `setElementOfX` shown below validates that the parameters `index` and `val` are in bounds before accessing array `x`. Rewrite this method so that it throws exceptions during array access if `val` is out of bounds if `index` is out of bounds. Pass an appropriate detail message to the new exception object. Your modified method should be type **`void`** because there is no longer a reason to return a **`boolean`** error indicator. Show `catch` blocks for a higher-level method that would handle these exceptions.
```
public boolean setElementOfX(int index, int val) {
    if (index >= 0 && index < x.length
        && val >= MIN_VAL && val <= MAX_VAL) {
        x[index] = val;
        return true;
    } else {
        return false;
    }
}
```

Appendix Review

- A Java program is a collection of classes. A programmer can use classes defined in the Java Application Programming Interface (API) to simplify the task of writing new programs and can define new classes to use as building blocks in future programs. Use

  ```
  import packageName.*;
  ```

  or

  ```
  import packageName.ClassName;
  ```

  to make the public names defined in a package or class accessible to the current file.

- The Java Virtual Machine (JVM) enables a Java program written for one machine to execute on any other machine that has a JVM. The JVM is able to execute instructions that are written in Java byte code. The byte code instructions are found in the `.class` file that is created when a Java source file is compiled.

- Java defines a set of primitive data types that are used to represent numbers (**`int`**, **`double`**, **`float`**, etc.), characters (**`char`**), and **`boolean`** data. Characters are represented using Unicode. Primitive-type variables are used to store primitive data. The Java programmer can use reference variables to reference objects. Wrapper classes can be used to encapsulate (wrap) a primitive-type value in an object.

- The control structures of Java are similar to those found in other languages: sequence (a compound statement), selection (**`if`** and **`switch`**), and repetition (**`while`**, **`for`**, **`do ... while`**).

- There are two kinds of methods: static (or class) methods and instance methods. Static methods are called using

  ClassName.methodName(arguments)

  but instance methods must be applied to objects:

  objectReference.methodName(arguments)

- The Java `String`, `StringBuilder`, and `StringBuffer` classes are used to reference objects that store character strings. `String` objects are immutable, which means they can't be changed, whereas `StringBuilder` and `StringBuffer` objects can be modified. `StringTokenizer` objects can be created for `String` objects. A `StringTokenizer` object is used to extract the individual tokens from a `String` object.

- Make sure you use methods such as `equals` and `compareTo` to compare the contents of two `String` objects (or any objects). The operator `==` compares the addresses of two objects, not their contents.

- You can use the `String.format` method or `Formatter` objects to create and display formatted strings.

- You can declare your own Java classes and create objects (instances) of these classes using the **new** operator. A constructor call must follow the **new** operator. A constructor has the same name as its class, and a class can define multiple constructors. The no-parameter constructor is defined by default if no constructors are explicitly defined.

- A class has data fields (instance variables) and instance methods. The default values for data fields are 0 or 0.0 for numbers, `\u0000` for characters, **false** for **boolean**, and **null** for reference variables. A constructor initializes data fields to values specified by its arguments. Generally, data fields have private visibility (accessible only within the class), whereas methods have public visibility (accessible outside the class).

- Array variables can reference array objects. You must use the **new** operator to allocate storage for the array object.

  ```
  int[] anArray = new int[mySize];
  ```

  The elements of an array can store primitive-type values or references to other objects. Arrays of arrays (multidimensional arrays) are permitted. The data field `length` represents the size of an array and is always accessible, but `length` can't be changed by the programmer. However, an array variable can be reset to reference a different array object with a different size.

- Class `JOptionPane` (part of Swing) can be used to display dialog windows for data entry (method `showInputDialog`) and message windows for output (method `showMessageDialog`).

- The `Scanner` class in `java.util` can be used to read numbers and strings from the console (`System.in`) using methods `nextInt`, `nextDouble`, and `nextLine`.

- The stream classes in `java.io` can enable you to read data from input files and write data to output files. Use statements like

  ```
  Scanner ins =
              new Scanner (new File(inputFileName));
  PrintWriter outs =
              new PrintWriter(new FileWriter(outFileName));
  ```

  to associate the input stream `ins` and the output stream `outs` with specified files. Many file operations must be performed within a **try-catch** sequence that catches `IOException` exceptions. You must close an output file when you have finished writing all information to it.

- The default behavior for exceptions is for the JVM to catch them by printing an error message and a call stack trace and then terminating the program. You can use the **try-catch-finally** sequence to catch and handle exceptions, possibly to recover from the error and continue, thereby avoiding the default behavior.

- There are two categories of exceptions: checked and unchecked. Checked exceptions are generally due to an error condition external to the program. Unchecked exceptions are generally due to a programmer error or a dire event.

- A method that can throw a checked exception must either catch it or declare that it is thrown using the `throws` declaration. If you throw it, you must catch it further back in the call sequence. Methods do not have to catch unchecked exceptions, and they should not be declared in the `throws` clause.
- Use the `throw` statement to throw an unchecked exception when you detect one in a method. You should catch this exception farther back in the call sequence, or it will be processed by the JVM as an uncaught exception.

Java Constructs Introduced in This Appendix

```
boolean       main
catch         new
char          private
class         public
double        static
final         throw
finally       throws
int           try
```

Java API Classes Introduced in This Appendix

```
java.io.BufferedReader          java.lang.Integer
java.io.FileReader              java.lang.Math
java.io.InputStreamReader       java.lang.NumberFormatException
java.io.IOException             java.lang.Object
java.io.OutputStreamWriter      java.lang.String
java.io.PrintWriter             java.lang.StringBuffer
java.lang.Boolean               java.lang.StringBuilder
java.lang.Character             java.util.Formatter
java.lang.Double                java.util.InputMismatchException
java.lang.Exception             java.util.Scanner
java.lang.FileWriter            javax.swing.JOptionPane
```

User-Defined Interfaces and Classes in This Appendix

```
Company      HelloWorld    SquareRoots
FileTest     Person        TestPerson
```

Quick-Check Exercises

1. The Java compiler translates Java source code to _______, which are executed by the _______.
2. Java _______ are embedded in _______, whereas Java _______ are stand-alone programs.
3. A Java program is a collection of _______. Execution of a Java application begins at method _______.
4. Java classes declare _______ and _______. Generally, the _______ have public visibility and the _______ have private visibility.
5. An _______ method is invoked by applying it to an _______; a _______ method is not.

6. If you use the operator == with objects, you are comparing their ______, not their ______.
7. To associate an input stream with the console, you must wrap an ______ object in a ______ object.
8. To associate an output stream with the console, you must wrap a ______ object in a ______ object.
9. To associate an input stream with a text file, you must wrap a ______ object in a ______ object.
10. Method ______ of class `JOptionPane` normally has ______ as its first argument and a ______ as its second argument.

Review Questions

1. Discuss how a Java source file is processed prior to execution and why this approach makes Java platform independent.
2. Declare storage for an array of arrays that will store a list of integers in its first row, the squares of all but the last integer in its second row, and the cubes of all but the last two integers in its third row. Assume that the size of the first row and its integer values are entered by the program user. Read this data into the array and store the required squares and cubes in the array.
3. Draw diagrams that illustrate the effect of each of the following statements.

```
String s1 = "woops";
String s2 = new String(s1);
String s3 = s1;
s1 = new String("Oops!");
```

   What are the values of `s1 == s2`, `s1 == s3`, and `s2 == s3`? What are the values of `s1.equals(s2)`, `s1.equals(s3)`, `s2.equals(s3)`? What are the values of `s1.compareTo(s2)`, `s1.compareTo(s3)`, `s2.compareTo(s3)`?
4. Write a class `Fraction` with integer `numerator` and `denominator` data fields. The default value of `denominator` should be 1. Define a constructor with two arguments for this class and one with just one argument (the value of the numerator). Define a method `multiply` that multiplies this `Fraction` object with the one specified by its argument and returns a new `Fraction` object as its result. Define a method `toDecimal` that returns the value of the fraction as a decimal number (be careful about integer division). Define a `toString` method for this class that represents a `Fraction` object as a string of the form *numerator / denominator.*
5. Write a `main` method that reads two `Fraction` objects using class `JOptionPane`. Multiply them and display their result as a fraction and as a decimal number using the instance methods defined in Review Question 4. Use class `JOptionPane` to display the results.
6. Write a `main` method that reads two `Fraction` objects from the console. Multiply them and display their result as a fraction and as a decimal number using the instance methods defined in Review Question 4. Use the console to display the results.

Programming Projects

1. Complete the definition of the `Fraction` class described in Review Question 4. Provide all the methods listed in that question and methods to add, subtract, and divide two fractions. Also, provide methods `equals` and `compareTo` to compare two `Fraction` objects.

2. Provide a class `MatrixOps` that has a two-dimensional array of **`double`** values as its data field. Provide the following methods:

```
MatrixOps() // Default constructor
MatrixOps(int numNows)  // Sets the number of rows
MatrixOps(int numRows, int numCols)
                       // Sets the number of rows and columns
MatrixOps(double[][] mat) // Stores the specified array
void setMatrix(double[][] mat) // Stores the specified array
double[][] getMatrix()  // Gets the array
void setRow(int row, double[] rowVals)
                       // Stores the array of rowVals in row
double[] getRow(int row)  // Returns the specified row
void setElement(int row, int col) // Sets the specified element
double getElement(int row, int col) // Returns the specified element
double sum() // Returns sum of the values in the array
double findMax() // Returns the largest value in the array
double findMin() // Returns the smallest value in the array
double[][] transpose() // Returns the transpose of the matrix
double[] multiply(double[][] mat2)
                       // Returns the product of two matrices
String toString() // Returns a string representing the array
```

3. Modify class `Person` to include a person's hours worked and hourly rate as data fields. Provide modifier and accessor methods for the new data fields and a method `calcSalary` that returns a person's salary. Also, modify method `toString`. Provide a method `calcPayroll` for class `Company` that returns the weekly payroll amount for a company (gross payroll only; don't be concerned about withholding, payroll taxes, etc.). Write a `main` method that reads the employee data for a `Company` object from a data file. Display the data stored and the calculated payroll in a message window using class `JOptionPane`. Also, write this information to an output file.
4. Write a class that stores a collection of exam scores in an array. Provide methods to find the average score, to assign a letter grade based on a standard scale, to sort the scores so they are in increasing order, and to display the scores. Test the methods of this class.
5. Write a class `Student` that stores a person's name, an array of scores for each person, an average exam score, and a letter grade. Write a class `Gradebook` that stores an instructor's name, a section ID, a course name, and an array of `Student` records. Write the following methods to process this array.
   - Load the array of `Student` records with data read from a text file.
   - Write all information stored to an output file.
   - Calculate and store each student's average exam score in that student's record.
   - Calculate and store the average score for each student in that student's record.
   - Assign a letter grade to each student based on that student's average exam score.
   - Sort the array of student records so that all information is in increasing order by student.
   - Sort the array of student records so that all information is in decreasing order by exam score.

   Write a client program that reads the data for a class and performs all the operations in the list above. Display the information in a `Gradebook` object after all the data is stored and again after all student information been calculated and stored. Also, display the information after sorting it by name and after sorting it by exam score.

Answers to Quick-Check Exercises

1. The Java compiler translates Java source code to *byte code instructions,* which are executed by the *Java Virtual Machine (JVM).*
2. Java *applets* are embedded in Web pages, whereas Java *applications* are stand-alone programs.
3. A Java program is a collection of *classes*. Execution of a Java application begins at method `main`.
4. Java classes declare *data fields* and *methods*. Generally, the *methods* have public visibility and the *data fields* have private visibility.
5. An *instance* method is invoked by applying it to an *object*; a *static* (or *class*) method is not.
6. If you use the operator == with objects, you are comparing their *addresses,* not their *contents.*
7. To associate an input stream with the console, you must wrap an `InputStreamReader` object in a `BufferedReader` object.
8. To associate an output stream with the console, you must wrap a `FileWriter` object in a `PrintWriter` object.
9. To associate an input stream with a text file, you must wrap a `FileReader` object in a `BufferedReader` object.
10. Method `showMessageDialog` of class `JOptionPane` normally has **`null`** as its first argument and a *prompt string* as its second argument.

Appendix B

Overview of UMI

The Unified Modeling Language (UML) represents the unification of earlier object-oriented design modeling techniques. Specifically, notations developed by Grady Booch, Ivar Jacobson, and James Rumbaugh were adapted to form the initial version. This version was submitted to the Object Modeling Group for formal standardization. Since that initial submission, the UML standard has undergone several revisions and continues to be revised.

We call UML a modeling *language* much in the same way we call Java a programming language. There is a formal definition of the syntax and semantics. There are software tools that are used both to draw the diagrams and to capture the underlying design information. These tools can then be used to analyze the resulting model, verify the model's consistency, and generate code.

UML defines 12 types of diagrams. In this text we use only 2 of them: the class diagram and the sequence diagram. Throughout the text, where we use these diagrams, we provide brief explanations of the diagram and the meaning of the notations used. The purpose of this appendix is to provide a more complete reference to the diagrams as they are used in this text.

In this text, we use a notation that has been adapted from the UML standard to match the syntax of Java more closely. Other books may use slightly different versions of these diagrams that follow the standard syntax, but the principles are the same.

Overview of UML

B.1 The Class Diagram

The *class diagram* shows the classes and their relationships. It is a static diagram that represents the structure of the program. The classes (including interfaces) are represented by rectangles, and lines between the classes represent the relationships. The style of a line, symbols on the ends of the lines, and text placed near the line are used to indicate the kind of relationship being modeled.

A large amount of information about the structure of a program can be represented in a class diagram. If all of the possible information were presented, the diagram would become quite cluttered. Therefore, the practice is to show only the essential information. For example, in a class diagram, the complete method declaration can show the method's visibility, return type, name, and parameter types. Sometimes only the method's name is necessary, in which case you would elect to suppress the other information. Also, some methods may not be significant to the discussion, so those methods need not be shown. Sometimes only the class's name is the essential item, and thus the methods and attributes are not shown.

Representing Classes and Interfaces

FIGURE B.1
General Representation of a Class

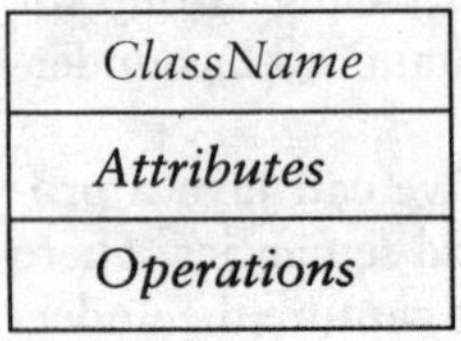

A class is represented by a rectangle divided into three segments as shown in Figure B.1.

The Class Name

Every class has a name that distinguishes it from other classes. In Java a class may be (and usually is) a member of a package, in which case we may show the complete name including the package name (e.g., `java.util.Stack`). In other cases we just show the class name (e.g., `Node`). Italics indicate abstract classes. The class name is centered in the box representing the class. For example, Figure B.2 shows the abstract class `Number` and the concrete classes derived from it.

FIGURE B.2
The Abstract Class `Number` and Concrete Subclasses

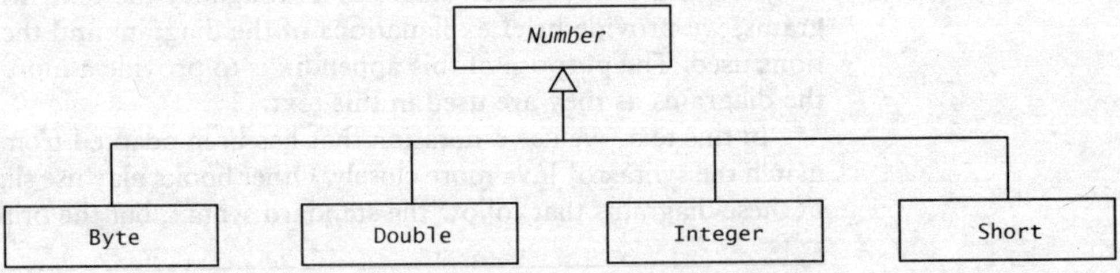

Interfaces

FIGURE B.3
The Interface `List`

The word *interface* enclosed in double angle brackets (« and », called guillemets) placed before the class name is used to indicate that this class is an interface. Because interfaces, like abstract classes, cannot be instantiated, the name is shown in italics. See Figure B.3.

FIGURE B.4
Alternative Syntax for Indicating an Abstract Class

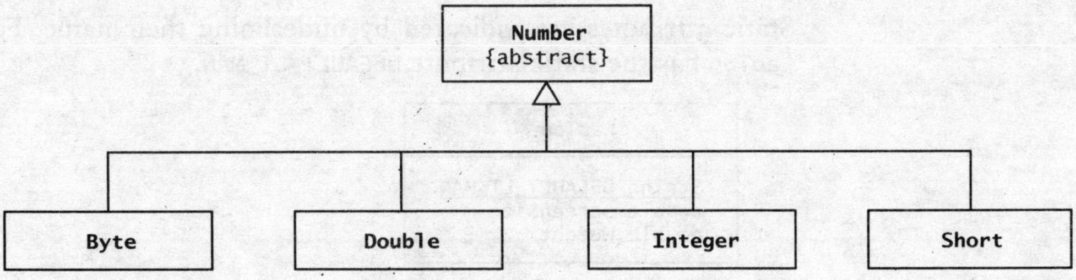

Alternative UML Syntax for Class Names

In other texts you may see the class name in a bold sans-serif font. Also, abstract classes may be indicated by `{abstract}`, as shown in Figure B.4.

The Attributes

The *attributes* of a class are the data fields. As a minimum we show the name. Optionally we can also show the visibility and type. The visibility is indicated by the symbols shown in Table B.1.

TABLE B.1
Visibility Specifiers

Symbol	Visibility
+	public
-	private
#	protected
~	package

In this text we use the Java language syntax to indicate the type of an attribute by placing the type name before the attribute name. For example, the class `Person` could have the attributes `familyName`, `givenName`, and `address`, as shown in the following figure:

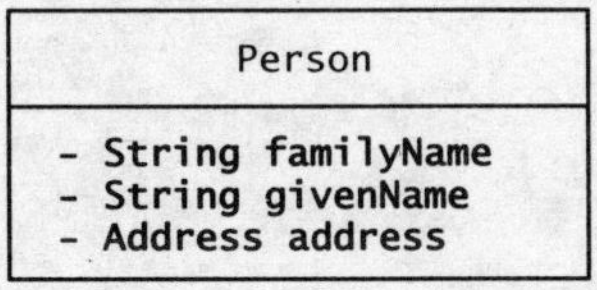

Where they are not essential to the current discussion, we will omit the visibility indicator, the type, or both, as shown in the following figure:

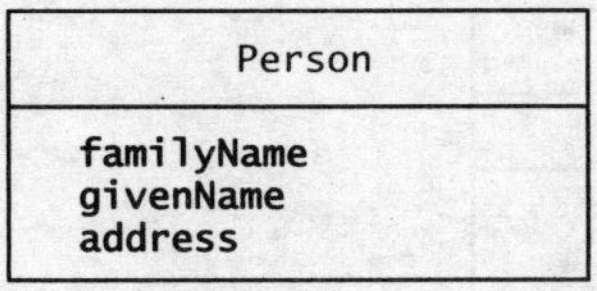

Static attributes are indicated by underlining their name. For example, the class LapTop has the static attribute DEFAULT_LT_MAN.

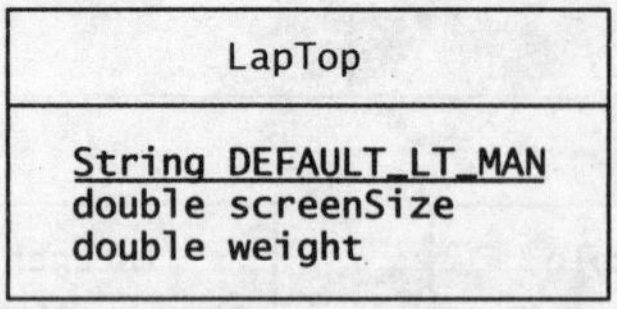

Standard UML Syntax for Attribute Types

In other texts you may see a different syntax for showing the attribute type. The UML standard specifies that the attribute type be specified following the name and separated by a colon.

The Operations

The *operations* are the methods of the class. At a minimum, we show the method name followed by a pair of parentheses. An empty set of parentheses does not necessarily indicate that this method takes no parameters. Italics are used to indicate an abstract method, and underlining is used to indicate a static method. For example, Figure B.5 shows the class Passenger with the static method setMaxProcessingTime and the nonstatic methods getArrivalTime and getProcessingTime. The attributes are not shown.

We may also show the visibility, the parameter types, and the return type. The visibility is shown using the same symbols as used for the attributes (see Table B.1). In this text we use the Java method declaration syntax, as shown in Figure B.6, to show the parameter types and return type. A return type of **void**, however, will not be shown.

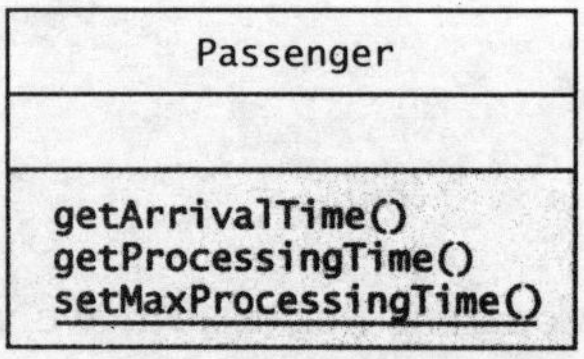

FIGURE B.5
The Class Passenger

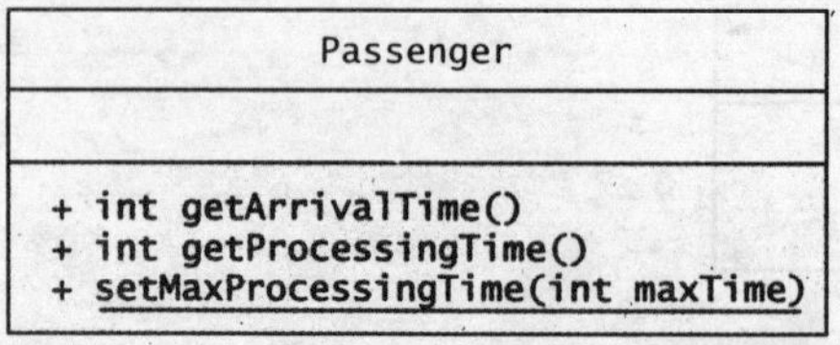

FIGURE B.6
Class Passenger Showing the Return and Parameter Types of Its Operations

Standard UML Syntax for Operations

In other texts you may see a different syntax for showing the parameter types and return type. The UML standard specifies that the parameter type be preceded by a colon and shown following the parameter name and that the return type be shown following the operation name, also preceded by a colon. The class `Passenger` using this syntax is shown in the following figure:

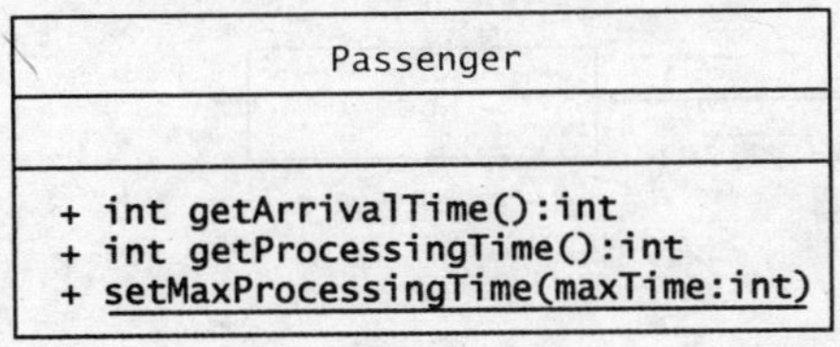

Generalization

UML uses the term *generalization* to describe the relationship between a superclass and its subclasses. Drawing a solid line with a large open arrowhead pointing to the superclass shows generalization. Figure B.7 shows the class `LapTop` as a subclass of `Computer`.

FIGURE B.7
Class LapTop as a Subclass of Computer

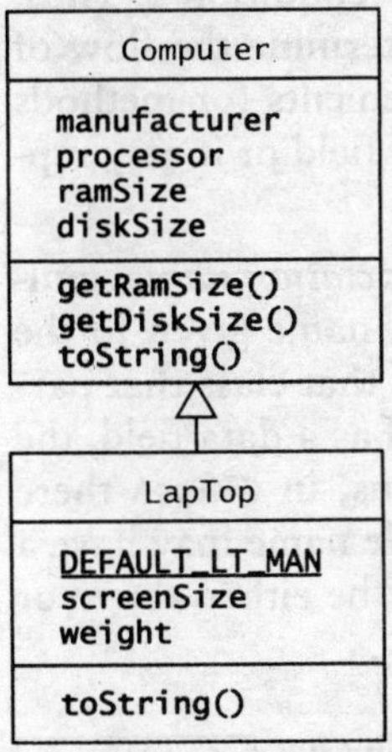

A dashed line with a large open arrowhead is used to show that a class implements an interface. Figure B.8 shows that the abstract class `AbstractList` implements the `List` interface and that the classes `ArrayList`, `Vector`, and `AbstractSequentialList` are subclasses of `AbstractList`. `Stack` is a subclass of `Vector`, and `LinkedList` is a subclass of `AbstractSequentialList`.

FIGURE B.8
The `List` Interface and Classes that Implement It

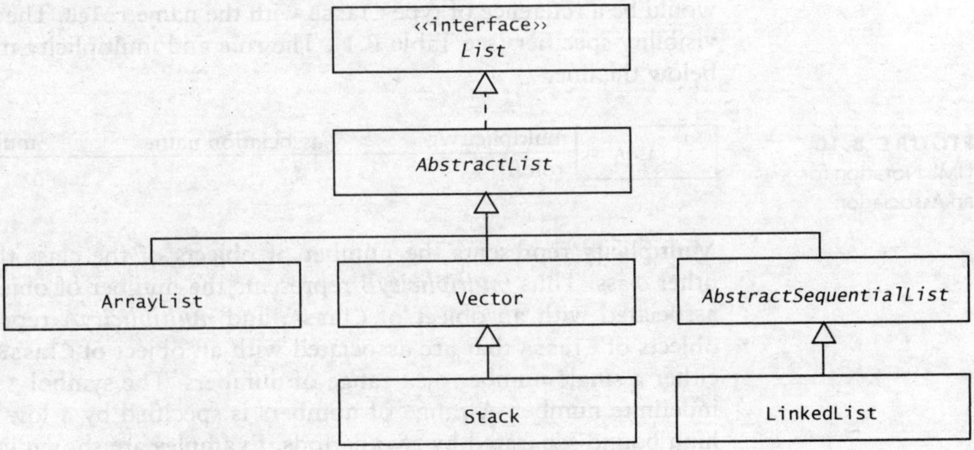

Inner or Nested Classes

A class that is declared within the body of another class is called an inner or nested class. In UML this relationship is indicated by a solid line between the two classes, with what the UML standard calls an *anchor* on the end connected to the enclosing class. The anchor is a cross inside a circle. For example, in Figure B.9 the class `Node` is declared as an inner class of the class `KWLinkedList`.

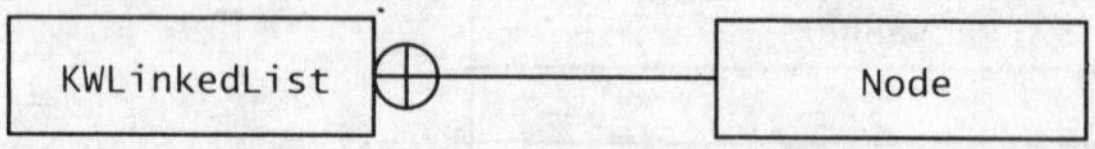

FIGURE B.9
Node as an Inner Class

Association

An *association* between classes represents a relationship between objects of those classes. In object-oriented terminology we say that "object A sends a message to object B." This statement implies two things:

1. There is a method in class B that will receive the message.
2. There must be a reference within class A that references object B.

An association indicates the presence of the reference required by condition 2. Thus, in the analysis process in which we examine a use case and determine the flow of information from one object to another, we identify the requirements for methods and associations. Note that the association may represent a data field or it may represent a parameter.

Figure B.10 shows the UML notation for an association. The *association name,* multiplicities, and roles are all optional. The association name is a name given to the association. The *multiplicity* represents the number of objects of that class that participate in the association. Where the association is implemented as a data field, the *role name* is generally used as the name of the data field. Thus, in `ClassA` there would be a reference of type `ClassB` with the name `roleB`. The role name may have a visibility specifier (see Table B.1). The role and multiplicity may be either above or below the line.

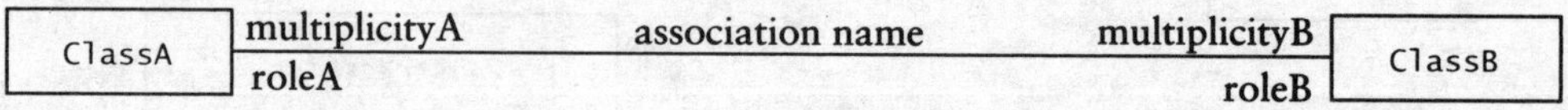

FIGURE B.10
UML Notation for an Association

Multiplicity represents the number of objects of the class that are related to the other class. Thus *multiplicityB* represents the number of objects of `ClassB` that are associated with an object of `ClassA`, and *multiplicityA* represents the number of objects of `ClassA` that are associated with an object of `ClassB`. Multiplicity may be either a single number or a range of numbers. The symbol `*` is used to indicate an indefinite number. A range of numbers is specified by a low bound followed by a high bound separated by two periods. Examples are shown in Table B.2.

In addition, an arrow can be placed at one or both ends of the line. The presence of an arrow indicates the navigation direction. Thus, if there is an arrow on the `ClassB` end, then objects of `ClassA` can send messages to objects of `ClassB`, but objects of

TABLE B.2
Multiplicity Examples

Multiplicity	Meaning
1	There is only 1.
1..5	There is at least 1, and there may be as many as 5.
3..*	There are at least 3.
*	There could be any number, including 0.

`ClassB` cannot send messages to objects of `ClassA`. The absence of arrows generally represents that navigation in both directions is possible, but it may also mean that the navigation is not being shown.

Aggregation and Composition

In those cases where we wish to show that an association definitely is represented by a data field, we place a diamond on the end of the line next to the class that will contain the data field. This represents the *has-a* relationship. If the diamond is open, this is called an *aggregation,* and if the diamond is filled, this is called a *composition.* The difference is that in a composition, the component objects are not considered to have an independent existence. For example, an `Airplane` is composed of two wings, a body, and a tail, none of which would exist unless it was a component of an `Airplane`. This would be modeled as shown in Figure B.11.

However, a `Node` in either a linked list or a tree has references to other `Node`s, but these other nodes are independent entities, and the value of the reference can be changed. Thus we use the open diamond as shown in Figure B.12. Observe that the references are to the same class (`Node`).

Aggregation is also used to indicate that one class is a collection of objects of another class. For example, the `Directory` and `File` classes are collections of `Entry` objects, as shown in Figure B.13.

FIGURE B.11
Airplane Composed of Wing, Tail, and Body

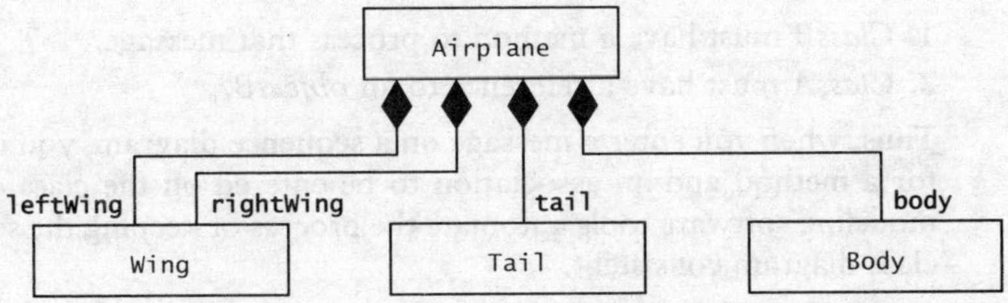

FIGURE B.12
A Node in a Double-Linked List

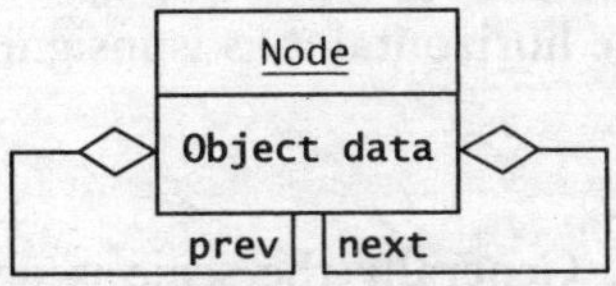

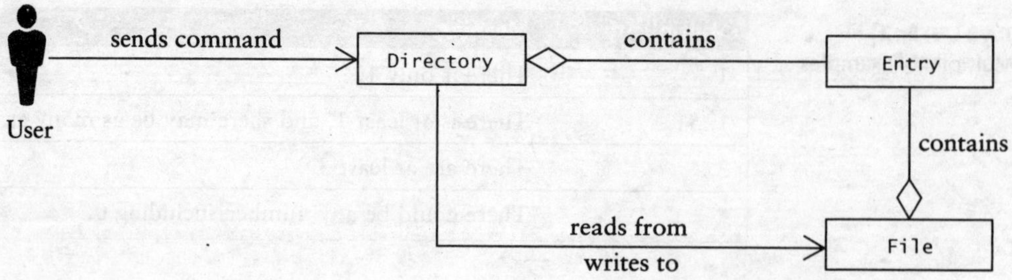

FIGURE B.13
The Directory and File Classes as Aggregations of Entrys

Generic Classes

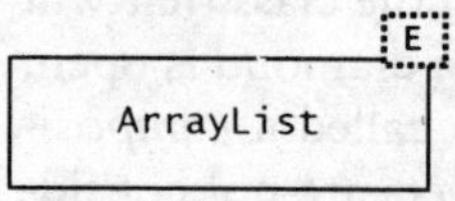

FIGURE B.14
Generic Class Representation

We will indicate a generic class by placing the generic parameter(s) in a dotted rectangle in the upper right corner of the rectangle that models the class. Thus the generic class `ArrayList<E>` is modeled by the diagram shown in Figure B.14. Alternatively, you can just write the class name as `ArrayList<E>`.

An invocation of a generic class is indicated by including the actual parameters inside a pair of less than and greater than symbols following the name. This is the same notation used by the Java language. Thus an `ArrayList` of `Strings` would be written `ArrayList<String>`.

B.2 Sequence Diagrams

Sequence diagrams are used to show the flow of information through the program. Sequence diagrams are generally developed on a use case basis and show the message sequence associated with a particular use case. The purpose of developing a sequence diagram is to identify the messages that are passed from one object to another. This then identifies the requirements for the corresponding classes. Recall that if *objectA* sends a message to *objectB*, then

1. *ClassB* must have a method to process that message.
2. *ClassA* must have a reference to an *objectB*.

Thus, when you enter a message on a sequence diagram, you identify a requirement for a method and an association to be entered on the class diagram. Many UML modeling software tools automate the process of keeping the sequence diagrams and class diagram consistent.

Figure B.15 shows an example of a sequence diagram. This is a two-dimensional diagram with time running down the vertical axis and objects listed across the horizontal axis. The ordering across the horizontal axis is insignificant.

Time Axis

Time flows down the vertical axis. Generally the scale is not significant, but for some applications, where timing is critical, a precise timing scale can be used. The sequence along the time axis is significant.

FIGURE B.15
Sequence Diagram Example

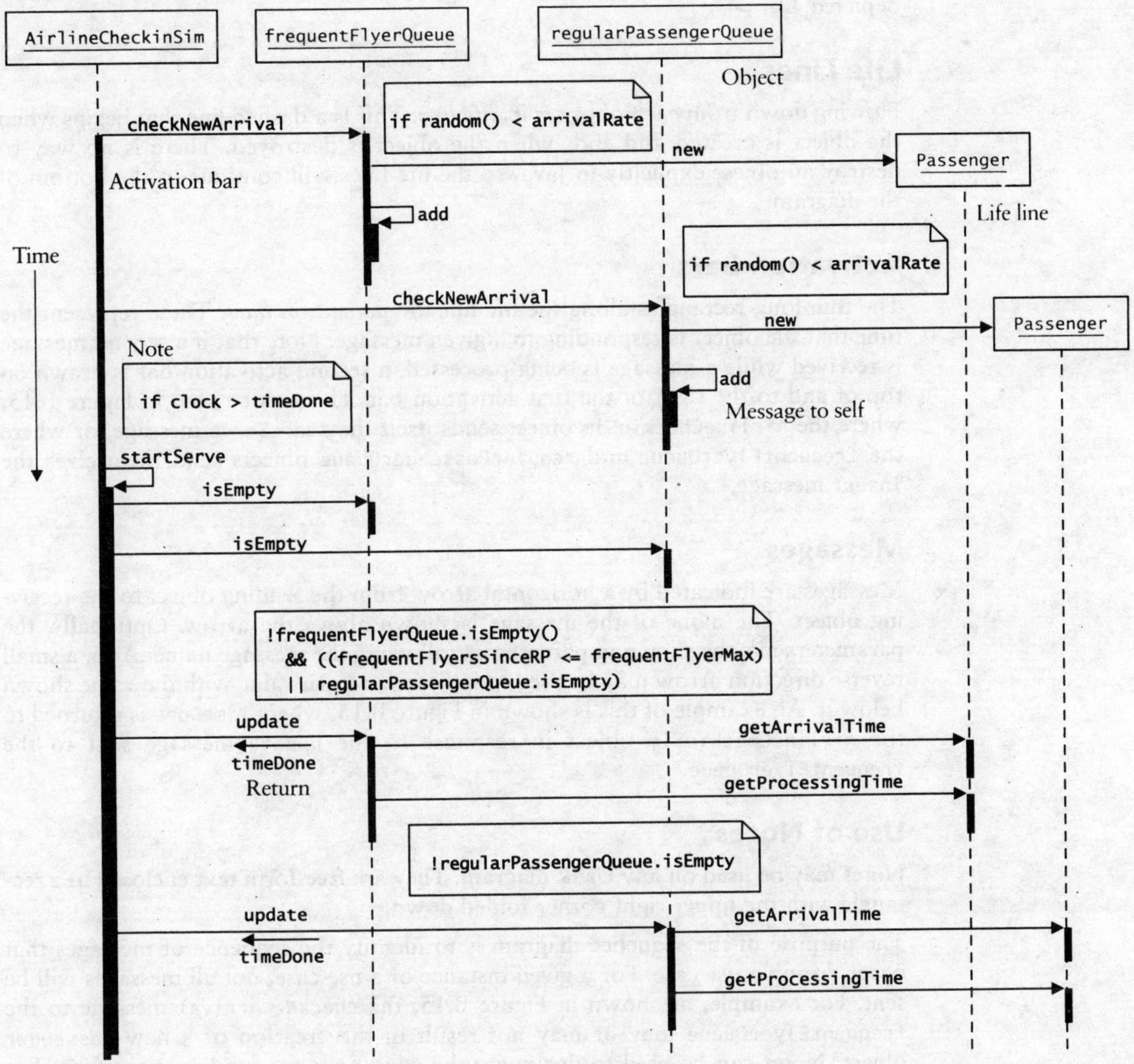

Objects

Objects are listed across the horizontal axis. Their order is insignificant. An object is represented by a rectangle with the name of the object underlined. For anonymous objects, the name of the class is given.

Objects are listed across the top of the sequence diagram unless they are created during the time period represented by the sequence diagram. If an object is created, then it is shown lower in the diagram, at the point at which it is created. As shown in Figure B.15, two `Passenger` objects are created during the sequence of events depicted.

Life Lines

Flowing down from each object is its *life line*. This is a dashed line that begins when the object is created and ends when the object is destroyed. There is no way to destroy an object explicitly in Java, so the life lines will continue to the bottom of the diagram.

Activation Bars

The thin long rectangles along the life line are *activation bars*. These represent the time that the object is responding to a given message. Note that if a second message is received while a message is being processed, a second activation bar is drawn on top of and to the right of the first activation bar. This can be seen in Figure B.15, where the `AirlineCheckinSim` object sends itself the `startServe` message, or where the `frequentFlyerQueue` and `regularPassengerQueue` objects send themselves the `insert` message.

Messages

Messages are indicated by a horizontal arrow from the sending object to the receiving object. The name of the message is shown above the arrow. Optionally, the parameters may be shown in parentheses following the message name. Also, a small reverse direction arrow may be used to indicate a return value with the value shown below it. An example of this is shown in Figure B.15, where `timeDone` is returned to the `AirlineCheckinSim` object in response to the `update` message sent to the `frequentFlyerQueue`.

Use of Notes

Notes may be used on any UML diagram. They are free-form text enclosed in a rectangle with the upper right corner folded down.

The purpose of the sequence diagram is to identify the sequence of messages that occur during a use case. For a given instance of a use case, not all messages will be sent. For example, as shown in Figure B.15, the `checkNewArrival` message to the `frequentFlyerQueue` may or may not result in the creation of a new `Passenger` object. Notes can be used to document the conditions for sending a message. For example, the `checkNewArrival` message is sent when the result of the random number generator is less than `arrivalRate`.

Appendix C

Event-Oriented Programming

Appendix Objectives

- To understand how event-driven programming differs from request-response programming
- To learn how to design and write event-driven programs using the Java graphics API
- To learn about different kinds of events that can occur
- To become familiar with the structure of the Java Swing API, including the class hierarchy, user interaction components, and ways to arrange the components
- To learn about mouse events and how to draw figures using the mouse

You are accustomed to using an operating system that has a graphical user interface (GUI) for interacting with your computer. The operating system constantly receives inputs from the keyboard, mouse, and communications network. You control the computer's operation by moving the mouse, clicking on icons, or typing information at the keyboard. However, it wasn't always that way. Initially, computers had little direct interaction with human users. Users prepared their programs and data on external media such as magnetic tape, punched paper tape, or punched cards. These were then fed directly to the computer or copied to magnetic tape by another computer whose task was to create batches of programs to be run by the main computer. (We get the term *batch processing* from this practice.) With the development of minicomputers and, later, personal computers, programmers and users were able to interact directly with their programs. With these smaller computers the *request-response* style was developed. The computer prompted the user for input, and the user supplied it.

Batch processing and request-response were not the only ways in which computers were used. Interactive systems, such as airline reservations, bank automated tellers, and military command and control systems provided real-time interaction between many users and a single program, but the request-response model is totally unworkable for these kinds of systems. In the request-response model the logic that requests the data, the logic that processes the data, and the logic that displays the results are all intertwined. Developing logic that can manage numerous different transactions in this model is all but impossible.

Thus the designers of these large, interactive systems separated requesting input, displaying data, and processing data into independent processes that could be considered as executing in parallel. The input process would constantly be ready to receive input. As each individual input was received, a processing process would be activated to process these data. The processing process would then update information that the display process would use to update the display(s).

This model has been adapted to modern personal-computer operating systems through their GUI environments. Each input represents an event. By writing and registering event listeners (methods that listen for and respond to events), we can develop very sophisticated applications that are easier to use. In this chapter we will show how to develop such programs using the Java API's which provide a GUI environment that is operating system independent.

Event-Oriented Programming

C.1 Elements of an Event-Oriented Application

This section will introduce you to event-driven programming. We will write an interface for a phone directory application that processes events that are generated by clicking buttons.

Method `JOptionPane.showOptionDialog` displays a dialog window consisting of a "menu" or a list of buttons. (See Figure C.1.) When the user clicks a button, a number is returned to the calling program. The calling program then uses this number in a **`switch`** statement to select the appropriate processing routine.

FIGURE C.1
Button Menu Displayed by PDGUI

The code for the main loop is as follows:

```
do {
    choice = JOptionPane.showOptionDialog(
        null,                              // No parent
        "Select a Command",                // Prompt message
        "PhoneDirectory",                  // Window title
        JOptionPane.YES_NO_CANCEL_OPTION,  // Option type
        JOptionPane.QUESTION_MESSAGE,      // Message type
        null,                              // Icon
        commands,                          // List of commands
        commands[commands.length - 1]);    // Default choice
    switch (choice) {
        case 0: doAddChangeEntry(); break;
        case 1: doLookupEntry(); break;
        case 2: doRemoveEntry(); break;
        case 3: doSave(); break;
        case 4: doSaveAndClose(); break;
    }
} while (choice < commands.length - 1);
```

Although this code appears to be fairly straightforward, it presents some potential maintenance issues. The labels for the buttons are given in the array `commands`, which is defined as follows:

```
String[] commands = {"Add/Change Entry",
                     "Look Up Entry",
                     "Remove Entry",
                     "Save Directory",
                     "Exit"};
```

If we were to decide to change the list of options, we would have to change the array `commands` and the **`switch`** statement. We would have to make sure that `commands[i]` corresponds to **`case`** `i` and its associated code after we make the changes.

Instead, it would be more desirable to link the processing routine directly to the button. Thus, when the button is clicked, the processing routine is called with no intervening logic to determine which button was clicked and which routine should process it. We will next describe how to write a class, `PDButtonUI`, that links the processing routines directly to the buttons.

Components and Events

The Java API documentation uses the term *component* to represent the objects that are displayed on the screen and can interact with the user. A button is a type of component. Placing the cursor over the button and clicking the mouse button triggers an *event*.

In the first few sections of the chapter, we will focus on action events (type `ActionEvent`). We will study action events that are triggered by clicking a mouse button over a GUI component and action events that are triggered by pressing the Enter key on the keyboard after typing in text. Class `ActionEvent` is a subclass of the abstract class `AWTEvent`. Both classes are defined in API `java.awt.event`. Another subclass of `AWTEvent` is `ItemEvent`. `ItemEvents` are triggered by making a selection from a list of items. A third subclass of `AWTEvent` is `MouseEvent`. `MouseEvents` are triggered by pressing and releasing mouse buttons or by dragging the mouse.

Event Listeners

When an event occurs, the button clicked will call each of the *event listeners* that are registered for the event. An action listener is a method that is to be called when an action event occurs. We need to be able to pass the name of this method to the button so that it will know whom to call, just as you need to leave your name and phone number on someone's answering machine if that person is to call you back when available. In the Java programming language, however, we can't treat methods like objects—we can't pass them to other methods as parameters, and other methods can't store them in data fields for later use. Therefore, we enclose the method in a class and pass an object of the class to the button. By defining a common interface for the classes that will enclose action listener methods, we ensure that all button objects have a common way of registering their action listeners and then calling them when the event triggered by clicking that button occurs.

The process by which an event listener is associated with an event is called *registering* the listener for the event. This is done by a method named `add`*EventType*`Listener`, where *EventType* is the type of the event. For example, action listeners are registered by calling the method `addActionListener`. The component object (e.g., a button) maintains lists of the event listeners that are registered for each of its events. When the component determines that an event has occurred, it then calls the event listeners that are registered for that event. This is called *firing an event*. The component does this by calling the `fire`*EventType* method.

The `ActionListener` Interface

The `ActionListener` interface (defined in API `java.awt.event`) declares just one method, `actionPerformed`, as follows:

```
interface ActionListener extends EventListener {
    void actionPerformed(ActionEvent e);
}
```

The interface `EventListener` (defined in `java.util`) has no methods. Such interfaces are known as *markers*. Marker interfaces are used to give a common name to a family of interfaces and classes.

EXAMPLE C.1 In the menu of Figure C.1, when the Look Up Entry button is clicked, the loop shown after the figure invokes the method `doLookupEntry`. Since the `ActionListener` interface requires a method named `actionPerformed`, we write method `doLookupEntry` as method `actionPerformed` for the class `DoLookupEntry`, as shown next:

```
/** Class to respond to the Look Up Entry Button. */
private class DoLookupEntry implements ActionListener {
    /** Method to look up an entry.
        pre:  The directory has been loaded with data.
        post: No changes made to the directory.
    */
    public void actionPerformed(ActionEvent e) {
        // Request the name.
        String theName =
            JOptionPane.showInputDialog("Enter name");
        if (theName == null) return; // Dialog was canceled.
        // Look up the name.
        String theNumber = theDirectory.lookupEntry(theName);
        String message = null;
        if (theNumber != null) { // Name was found.
            message =
                "The number for " + theName + " is " + theNumber;
        } else { // Name was not found.
            message =
                theName + " is not listed in the directory";
        }
        // Display the result.
        JOptionPane.showMessageDialog(null, message);
    }
}
```

Class `DoLookupEntry` implements the `ActionListener` interface. It is an *inner class* because it is wholly contained in class `PDButtonUI`. All private members of the outer class (e.g., `theDirectory`) are visible in an inner class. Listing C.1, in a later subsection, shows the `PDButtonUI` class with the `DoLookupEntry` class as an inner class.

Registering an Event Listener

A button is an object of the class `JButton`. This class provides the method `addActionListener` through the superclass `AbstractButton` (see Figure C.2 for the button class hierarchy; we will discuss other subclasses of `AbstractButton` later). We use this method to register the action listener as follows:

```
lookupEntryButton.addActionListener(new DoLookupEntry());
```

We can call this method at any time after the object `lookupEntryButton` is created, but generally we call it right after invoking the constructor to create this `JButton` object:

```
JButton lookupEntryButton = new JButton("Look Up Entry");
lookupEntryButton.addActionListener(new DoLookupEntry());
```

Creating a User Interface

All user interfaces are displayed within a *window*. The Java GUI API defines three kinds of windows: *frames, dialogs,* and *applets*. Of these, only a frame can stand alone. Frames are implemented by the class `Frame` and its subclass `JFrame`. The class `Frame` is part of the original Java Abstract Window Toolkit (AWT–`java.awt`), and `JFrame` is part of the more flexible Swing graphics API (`javax.swing`). In this text we will use the Swing classes wherever possible.

Therefore, we begin our definition of `PDButtonUI` as follows:

```
/** Class to display and modify a phone directory. */
public class PDButtonUI extends JFrame {
```

This states that our class inherits from `JFrame`.

The Constructor

The constructor will then build the contents of the frame. First we place a title on our frame as follows:

```
// Set the title on the top of the frame.
super("Phone Directory");
```

By default, when a frame is closed by clicking on the window close box () or by some other external command, the program that owns it is still running. We can change that default behavior by calling the `setDefaultCloseOperation`. However, we need to ensure that the phone directory data is written back to the data file. Therefore, we need to respond to the `WindowClosing` event. We register the event listener for this event as follows:

```
// Define the window close action.
addWindowListener(new WindowClosing());
```

The visible part of the frame is known as the *content pane*. Since we want to display several buttons, these are placed into another *container* that is then placed into the content pane. This container is known as a *panel* and is defined by the class `JPanel`. We create a panel to hold the buttons as follows:

```
// Create a panel to hold the buttons.
JPanel panel = new JPanel();
```

Now we can create the buttons, register their action listeners, and add them to the the panel. The code to do this for the Look Up Entry button is as follows:

```
// Look Up Entry
JButton lookupEntryButton = new JButton("Look Up Entry");
lookupEntryButton.addActionListener(new DoLookupEntry());
panel.add(lookupEntryButton);
```

These lines are repeated for each button. Finally, the panel is added to the content pane and the frame size set to hold the panel using the statements

```
// Put the panel into the frame.
getContentPane().add(panel);
// Size the frame to hold the panel.
pack();
```

The **processCommands** Method

We also provide a method processCommands as follows:

```
public void processCommands(PhoneDirectory thePhoneDirectory) {
    theDirectory = thePhoneDirectory;
    setVisible(true);
}
```

It merely saves the reference to the PhoneDirectory object and shows the frame (see Figure C.2).

FIGURE C.2
Button-Based Phone Directory User Interface

Unlike the code for the JOptionPane-based menu in Figure C.1, this method does not contain a loop that waits for input to be entered and then calls the processing routines. Instead, it displays the frame and then releases the processor to perform other tasks. When a button is clicked, the processor executes the instructions in method actionPerformed for that button's listener object.

A main method would use the statements

```
PhoneDirectory pD = new PhoneDirectory();
PDButtonUI gUI = new PDButtonUI();
gUI.processCommands(pD);
```

to display the menu and start processing commands. Class PhoneDirectory is not shown.

Listing C.1 shows the classes required for the button-based interface. The constructor creates the GUI window (a frame) as described earlier. Next comes the processCommands method. Then there are five private *inner classes* with methods that respond to different button events. They are similar to class DoLookupEntry shown in Example C.1. We will just show the listener class that responds to the window closing event.

LISTING C.1
PDButtonUI.java

```
import java.util.*;
import java.io.*;
import javax.swing.*;
import java.awt.event.*;

/** Class to display and modify a simple phone directory. */
public class PDButtonUI extends JFrame {

    // Data Field
    private PhoneDirectory theDirectory;

    // Constructor
    public PDButtonUI() {
        // Set the title on the top of the frame.
        super("Phone Directory");
```

```
        // Define the window close action.
        addWindowListener(new WindowClosing());
        // Create a panel to hold the buttons.
        JPanel panel = new JPanel();
        // Create buttons and add them to the panel.
        // Add/Change Entry
        JButton addEntryButton = new JButton("Add/Change Entry");
        addEntryButton.addActionListener(new DoAddChangeEntry());
        panel.add(addEntryButton);
        // Look Up Entry
        JButton lookupEntryButton = new JButton("Look Up Entry");
        lookupEntryButton.addActionListener(new DoLookupEntry());
        panel.add(lookupEntryButton);
        // Remove Entry
        JButton removeEntryButton = new JButton("Remove Entry");
        removeEntryButton.addActionListener(new DoRemoveEntry());
        panel.add(removeEntryButton);
        // Save Directory
        JButton saveDirectoryButton = new JButton("Save Directory");
        saveDirectoryButton.addActionListener(new DoSave());
        panel.add(saveDirectoryButton);
        // Exit
        JButton exitButton = new JButton("Exit");
        exitButton.addActionListener(new DoSaveAndExit());
        panel.add(exitButton);
        // Put the panel into the frame.
        getContentPane().add(panel);
        // Size the frame to hold the panel.
        pack();
    }

    public void processCommands(PhoneDirectory thePhoneDirectory) {
        theDirectory = thePhoneDirectory;
        setVisible(true);
    }

    // Action Event Listener Classes
    /** Class to respond to the Look Up Entry button. */
    private class DoLookupEntry implements ActionListener {
        ...
    }
    // Insert listener classes for other buttons.

    /** Class to respond to the WindowClosing event. */
    private class WindowClosing extends WindowAdapter {
        /** Method to save the directory to the data file and close
            the data file.
            pre:  The directory has been loaded with data.
            post: The current contents of the directory have been
            saved to the data file, and the data file is closed.
        */
        public void windowClosing(WindowEvent e) {
            theDirectory.save();
            System.exit(0);
        }
    }
}
```

PITFALL

Not Registering a Listener

If you forget to register an event listener for a GUI component, the component will still be displayed, but clicking on that component will have no effect. This will not cause a syntax error or exception.

EXERCISES FOR SECTION C.1

SELF-CHECK

1. What is an event, and how are events generated? What does it mean to register for an event?
2. What is an action listener? How does Java determine which `actionPerformed` method to execute when an action event is generated?
3. What is a `Container`? A `Panel`? The `contentPane`?
4. What does the `Container` method `add` do?
5. Explain the effect of executing each of the following statements. What can you say about class `HelloMonitor`?

```
JButton aButton = new JButton("Hello");
aButton.addActionListener(new HelloMonitor());
panel.add(aButton);
// Put the panel into the frame.
getContentPane().add(panel);
```

PROGRAMMING

1. Write statements to create a button with label Submit, and register class `DoSubmit` as an action listener for this button.
2. Write class `DoSubmit` and include an `actionPerformed` method that displays a message window showing the message "Thanks for the submission" when button Submit is clicked.
3. Write class `DoSave` for the phone directory problem.

C.2 Overview of the AWT and Swing Hierarchy

Whole books have been written on the Abstract Window Toolkit (AWT) and Swing. In this section we give a brief overview of the class hierarchy and discuss how the different classes interact. Figure C.3 shows the Swing and AWT class hierarchy. The Swing classes are extensions of the AWT classes.

A `Component` is a graphics object that can be displayed on a screen and can interact with a user. A `Container` is a component that can contain other components. The `JComponent` is the base class for all other Swing components except the top-level containers `JFrame`, `JDialog`, `JApplet`, and `JWindow`. Objects of class `JComponent` and its subclasses must be placed in a containment hierarchy that is rooted in one of the top-level containers. Therefore, all applications we develop will begin with a `JFrame` that will contain the other components either directly or indirectly. For more information about the various classes in AWT and Swing, you can consult the online documentation of the Java API provided at the Sun Java Web site (`www.java.sun.com`).

FIGURE C.3
Swing and AWT Class Hierarchy

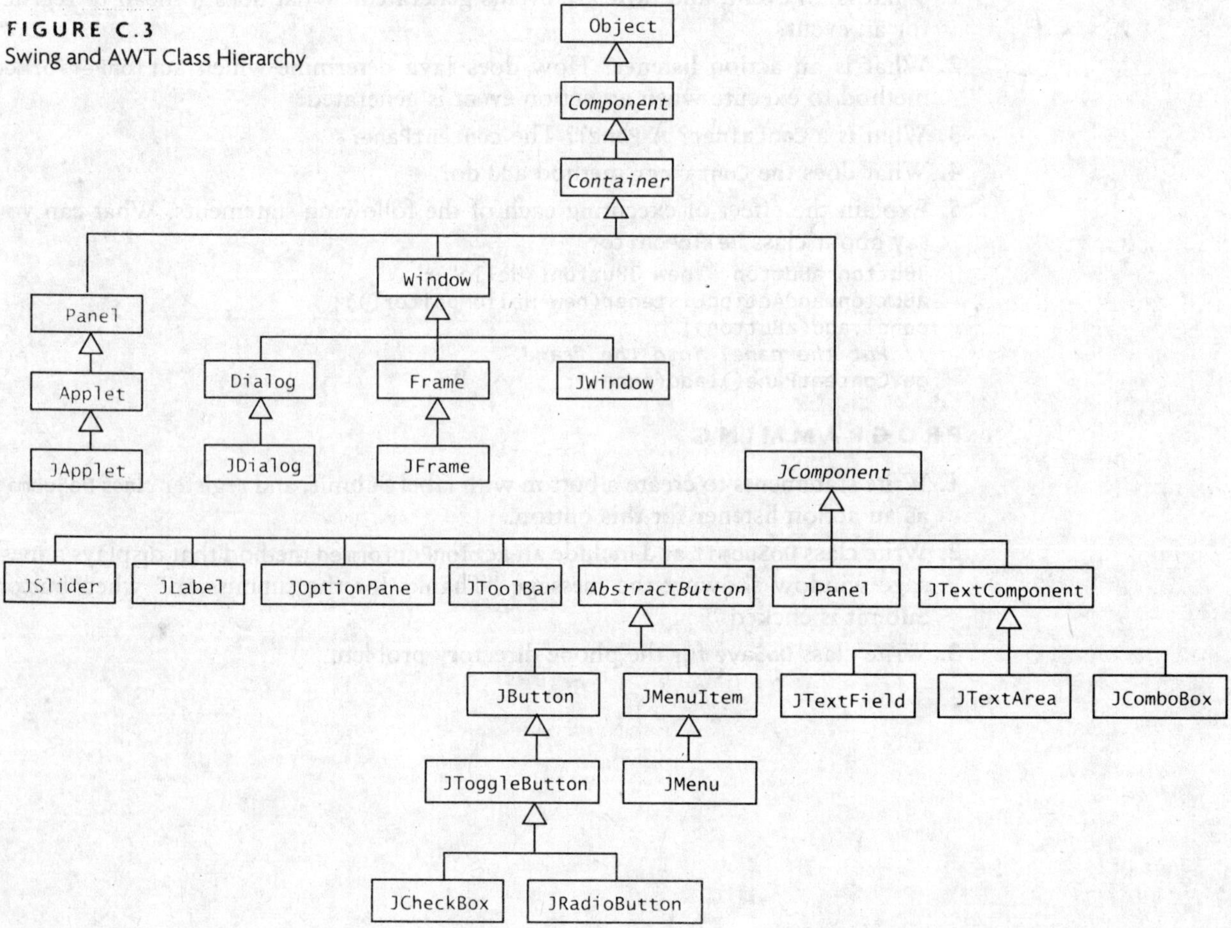

EXAMPLE C.2 Figure C.4 shows an empty `JFrame`. Other components are not directly added to a `JFrame` but rather are added to the `JFrame`'s content pane, shown in Figure C.4.

FIGURE C.4
Empty Frame Demo

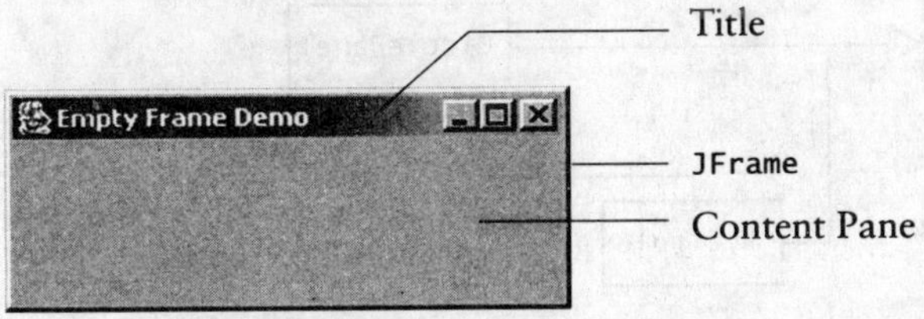

The `JPanel` is a generic container that can be used to contain other components or as a painting surface. We will use `JPanel` as the base class for customized components in our GUI examples, and we will use `JPanels` as building blocks to lay out the components of our applications.

Example and Overview: TwoCircles

Figure C.5 shows a `JFrame` whose content pane contains two `CirclePanels`, which are extensions of `JPanel`, which is in turn an extension of `JComponent`. Each of these components contains two other components: a `MyCircle` and a `JButton`. The containment hierarchy is shown in Figure C.6. The containment hierarchy is a UML diagram. A filled-in diamond shows containment. The containment hierarchy shows that objects of `MyCircle` and `JButton` are contained in an object of class `CirclePanel` that is, in turn, contained in an object of class `TwoCircles`. The classes are shown in Listings C.2, C.3, and C.4. A `CirclePanel` object is a panel containing a button and a `MyCircle` object. A `MyCircle` object is a panel in which a green rectangle is drawn. A red circle may or may not be drawn over the rectangle. The constructor for class `CirclePanel` creates a `MyCircle` object and registers an instance of `ToggleState` as the listener for events generated by clicking the button in this panel. It also adds the button and `MyCircle` object to the panel.

```
theCircle = new MyCircle();
onOffButton = new JButton("On / Off");
onOffButton.addActionListener(new ToggleState());
add(theCircle, BorderLayout.CENTER);
// Section C.3 discusses Layouts.
add(onOffButton, BorderLayout.SOUTH);
```

FIGURE C.5
TwoCircles

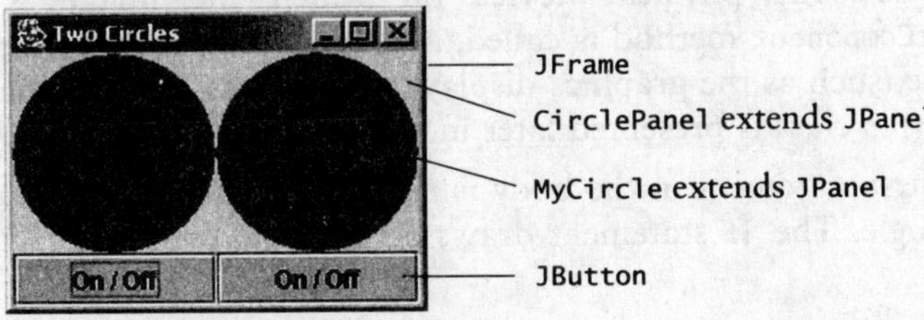

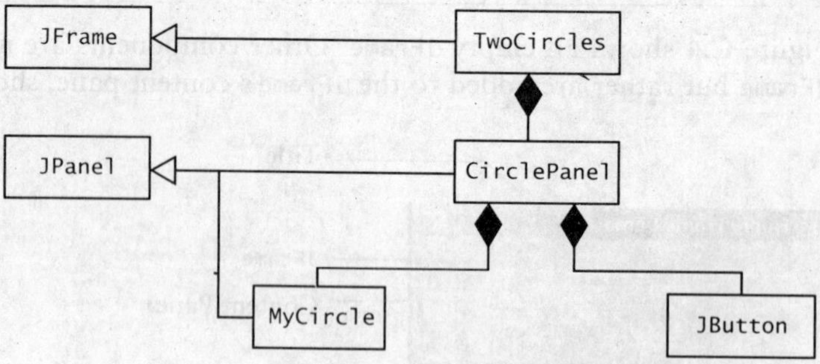

FIGURE C.6
TwoCircles Containment Hierarchy

Method `main` creates a new `TwoCircles` object (a subclass of `JFrame`). Its constructor puts two `CirclePanel` objects in a row in this object using a Grid layout (explained in Section C.3).

```
getContentPane().setLayout(new GridLayout(1,2));
getContentPane().add(new CirclePanel());
getContentPane().add(new CirclePanel());
```

Clicking the button in either of these panels generates an action event that invokes method `actionPerformed` (a member of inner class `ToggleState`) for that panel.

```
public void actionPerformed(ActionEvent e) {
    theCircle.toggleState();
}
```

The method `actionPerformed` invokes `toggleState`, which complements the **`boolean`** flag `showCircle` for that panel and causes the panel to be repainted.

```
public void toggleState() {
    showCircle = !showCircle;
    repaint();
}
```

Invoking method `repaint` causes the `paintComponent` method to execute.

```
public void paintComponent(Graphics g) {
    super.paintComponent(g);
    g.setColor(Color.GREEN);
    g.fillRect(0, 0, size, size);
    if (showCircle) {
        g.setColor(Color.RED);
        g.fillOval(0, 0, size, size);
    }
}
```

The `Graphics` class is an abstract class that provides the interface between the Java API and the physical device on which the image is created. When the `paintComponent` method is called, a concrete object that is specific for the physical device (such as the graphics display) is passed as this parameter. A summary of the `Graphics` class is presented later in this section.

The first statement in the body is required. The next two statements draw a green rectangle. The **`if`** statement draws a red circle over this rectangle if `showCircle` is true.

PITFALL

You shouldn't call the method `paintComponent` directly. It should always be invoked indirectly by calling `repaint`. The actual painting is done in a separate execution thread under the control of what is known as the window manager. A call to `repaint` tells the window manager to schedule the component for repainting as soon as possible. Also, `paintComponent` needs a `Graphics` object, which is obtained by the window manager.

LISTING C.2
TwoCircles.java

```
import java.awt.*;
import java.awt.event.*;
import javax.swing.*;

/** TwoCircles is a simple event-oriented application that
    displays two circles and two buttons. The buttons are
    placed below the circles. The buttons are labeled on/off.
    When a button is clicked, the state of the circle is toggled.
*/
public class TwoCircles extends JFrame {

    // Constructor
    /** Construct a TwoCircles object. Set the title and
        default close operation. Using a grid layout add
        two CirclePanel objects. Finally, pack the frame
        and set it visible.
    */
    public TwoCircles() {
        super("Two Circles");
        setDefaultCloseOperation(JFrame.EXIT_ON_CLOSE);
        getContentPane().setLayout(new GridLayout(1,2));
        getContentPane().add(new CirclePanel(100));
        getContentPane().add(new CirclePanel(100));
        pack();
        setVisible(true);   // Show the JFrame.
    }

    // Main Method
    /** Instantiate a TwoCircles object.
        @param args Not used. */
    public static void main(String[] args) {
        TwoCircles tc = new TwoCircles();
    }
}
```

LISTING C.3
CirclePanel.java

```
import java.awt.*;
import java.awt.event.*;
import javax.swing.*;

/** A CirclePanel will contain a circle and a button. */
public class CirclePanel extends JPanel {

    // Data Fields
    /** The button object */
    JButton onOffButton;
    /** The Circle object */
    MyCircle theCircle;

    // Constructor
    /** Construct a CirclePanel object. */
    public CirclePanel(int size) {
        setLayout(new BorderLayout());
        theCircle = new MyCircle(size);
        onOffButton = new JButton("On / Off");
        onOffButton.addActionListener(new ToggleState());
        add(theCircle, BorderLayout.CENTER);
        add(onOffButton, BorderLayout.SOUTH);
    }

    // Inner Class
    /** The action listener for the button. */
    private class ToggleState implements ActionListener {
        public void actionPerformed(ActionEvent e) {
            theCircle.toggleState();
        }
    }
}
```

LISTING C.4
MyCircle.java

```
import javax.swing.*;
import java.awt.*;
import java.awt.event.*;

/** Class MyCircle is a JPanel that consists of a circle enclosed
    in a square. The square is always displayed, but the circle can
    be turned on and off.
*/
public class MyCircle extends JPanel {

    // Data Fields
    /** The size */
    private int size;
    /** Display state for the circle */
    private boolean showCircle = true;
```

```
    // Constructors
    /** Construct a MyCircle object of the specified size.
        @param size The size of the circle in pixels
    */
    public MyCircle(int size) {
        this.size = size;
        // Encapsulate the object's dimensions in a Dimension object.
        Dimension dims = new Dimension(size, size);
        // Set the object's dimensions.
        setPreferredSize(dims);
        setMaximumSize(dims);
        setMinimumSize(dims);
    }

    /** Toggle the state of the circle. */
    public void toggleState() {
        showCircle = !showCircle;
        repaint();   // Calls paint to redraw the object.
    }

    /** Paint the component when it changes. This method is called
        by the Swing API.
        @param g The graphics object used for painting. */
    public void paintComponent(Graphics g) {
        super.paintComponent(g);
        g.setColor(Color.GREEN);
        g.fillRect(0, 0, size, size);
        if (showCircle) {
            g.setColor(Color.RED);
            g.fillOval(0, 0, size, size);
        }
    }
}
```

JFrame

The class JFrame will be the top-level container for our GUI applications. Generally our application main class will be derived from JFrame, which the main method will instantiate. Table C.1 gives a summary of selected members of the JFrame class and its superclasses.

TABLE C.1
Summary of JFrame

Constant	Usage
EXIT_ON_CLOSE	Argument to setDefaultCloseOperation.
Constructor	**Behavior**
JFrame()	Constructs a new JFrame with no title and initially invisible.
JFrame(String title)	Constructs a new JFrame with the specified title and initially invisible.

TABLE C.1 (continued)

Method	Behavior
`Container getContentPane()`	Returns the content pane object, which can then be manipulated by adding components and changing its layout manager.
`void setDefaultCloseOperation(int operation)`	Sets the operation that will happen when the user initiates a close on this frame.
`void setContentPane(Container contentPane)`	Replaces the current content pane with the specified one. Generally a `JPanel` is used as the content pane.
`void setTitle(String title)`	Sets the title.
`void setMenuBar(MenuBar bm)`	Sets the menu bar for this frame.
`void setSize(int width, int height)`	Sets the window size to the number of pixels specified by its arguments.
`void pack()`	Causes the window to be sized to fit the preferred size and layout of its subcomponents.
`void setVisible(boolean b)`	Makes the window visible, if its argument is true. Otherwise, hides the window.

JPanel

A `JPanel` is a general-purpose intermediate component. It is used to organize the other components. It can also be used as the basis for a customized component and as a drawing surface. Table C.2 shows the different constructor options for `JPanel`. The default is *double buffering* and flow layout. The choice of double buffering allows for flicker-free updates at the cost of additional memory. (Actual drawing is done in one buffer, while the other buffer is being displayed. When the drawing updates are complete, the buffers are swapped very quickly so that the change is not noticeable to the human eye.) The default layout for the panel is flow layout, which results in a left-to-right placement of the components in the order in which they were added. If not all components fit, later components will be inserted below the earlier ones, in left-to-right order. The different layout managers will be discussed in Section C.3.

The methods unique to `JPanel` are minimal and are used to change the "look and feel," a subject beyond the scope of this text. Instead, you are more likely to use the methods inherited from `JComponent`, `Container`, and `Component`. These methods are summarized in Table C.3.

TABLE C.2
Constructors for `JPanel`

Constructor	Behavior
`JPanel()`	Constructs a `JPanel` with double buffering and flow layout.
`JPanel(LayoutManager layout)`	Constructs a `JPanel` with double buffering and the specified layout manager.

TABLE C.3
Summary of `JPanel` Inherited Methods

Method	Behavior
`void add(Component c)`	Adds the specified component to the panel at the next position.
`void add(Component c, Object pos)`	Adds the specified component to the panel and notifies the layout manager to add it to the position indiated by the second argument.
`void paintComponent(Graphics g)`	Paints the component.
`void repaint()`	Schedules repainting of this component. This method is called by client programs whenever the content of the component is changed and should be repainted. Client programs should call this method only and should never call `paintComponent` directly.

Graphics

The `Graphics` class provides the ability to do the actual drawing (called image rendering) in a device-independent manner. The `Graphics` class is an abstract class. The Java API provides the correct concrete class when the `paintComponent` method is called. A summary of selected methods of this class is given in Table C.4.

TABLE C.4
Selected Methods of the `Graphics` Class

Method	Behavior
`void drawLine(int x1, int y1, int x2, int y2)`	Draws a line, using the current color, from (`x1`, `y1`) to (`x2`, `y2`).
`void drawOval(int x, int y, int width, int height)`	Draws the outline of an oval that is tangent to the bounding rectangle specified by `x`, `y`, `width`, and `height`. (See Figure C.7.)
`void drawPolygon(Polygon p)`	Draws the outline of a polygon defined by the `Polygon` object.
`void drawRect(int x, int y, int width, int height)`	Draws the outline of the specified rectangle.
`void fillOval(int x, int y, int width, int height)`	Fills an oval bounded by the specified rectangle. (See Figure C.7.)
`void fillPolygon(Polygon p)`	Fills a closed polygon defined by the specified `Polygon` object.
`void fillRect(int x, int y, int width, int height)`	Fills the specified rectangle.
`Color getColor()`	Returns the current color.
`void setColor(Color c)`	Sets this graphics context current color to the specified color.
`void setPaintMode()`	Sets the painting mode to overwrite the destination with the current color.
`void setXORMode(Color c)`	Sets the painting mode such that if the same figure is drawn twice, all pixels are restored to their original values.

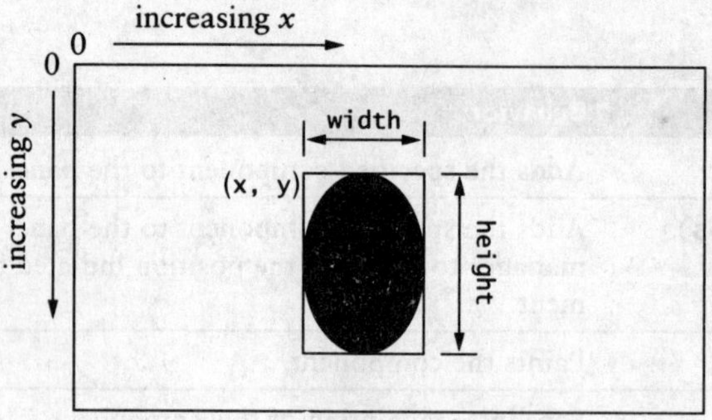

FIGURE C.7
Graphics Coordinates and Bounding Rectangle of an Oval

Graphics Coordinates

All graphics coordinates are in units of pixels. The size of a pixel is dependent on the actual output device. The origin is the upper left corner. Increasing x moves to the right. Increasing y moves down. (See Figure C.7.)

EXERCISES FOR SECTION C.2

SELF-CHECK

1. ________ is the top-level container for GUI applications.
2. A ________ is a general-purpose intermediate component used to organize the other components.
3. A `JPanel` can also be used to ________.

PROGRAMMING

1. Create a modified version of `TwoCircles` to show just the outline of a circle in green.
2. Create a modified version of `TwoCircles` to display a dialog that asks "Do you really want to do this?" *Hint:* Use `JOptionPane` to display the dialog. Try clicking on the button for the other circle when the dialog is displayed. What happens?

C.3 Layout Managers

The Java API provides different *layout managers* to position components within the display area of a container component. This frees the user from having to manipulate the graphics coordinates, although this option is still available. The layout managers we use are listed in Table C.5.

TABLE C.5
Layout Managers

Layout Manager	Description
`BorderLayout`	Arranges objects in five areas of the container: `north`, `west`, `center`, `east`, and `south`.
`FlowLayout`	Arranges objects in left-to-right order across the container, flowing down to the next row when a row is filled.
`BoxLayout`	Arranges objects in a single row or column.
`GridLayout`	Arranges objects in a two-dimensional grid.

The layout manager can be specified as an argument of the `JPanel` constructor, or it can be set in any `Container` by calling the method `setLayoutManager`. In this section we will describe the `BorderLayout`, `FlowLayout`, `BoxLayout`, and `GridLayout`.

Border Layout

The default layout for the `JFrame`'s content pane is Border Layout. This layout defines five areas: north, south, east, west, and center. These are shown in Figure C.8. Notice that the north and south areas extend across the width of the container.

The following code fragment shows how components are added to each of the areas. It is not necessary to fill each of the layout areas, however.

```
// Add the labels to the content pane.
Container contentPane = getContentPane();
contentPane.add(north, BorderLayout.NORTH);
contentPane.add(south, BorderLayout.SOUTH);
contentPane.add(east, BorderLayout.EAST);
contentPane.add(west, BorderLayout.WEST);
contentPane.add(center, BorderLayout.CENTER);
```

The program to draw Figure C.8 is shown in Listing C.5.

FIGURE C.8
Border Layout

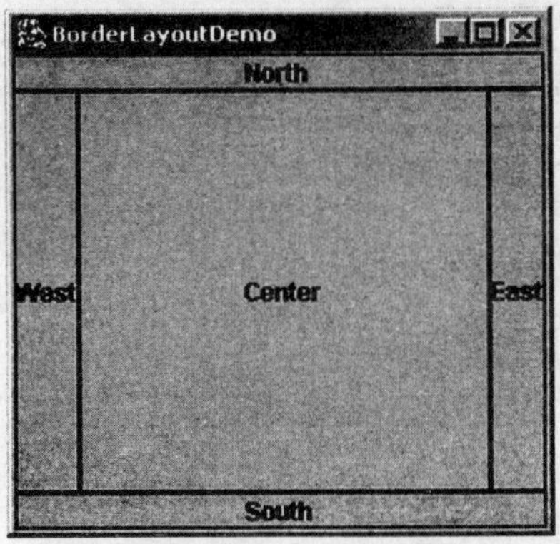

LISTING C.5
BorderLayoutDemo.java

```
import java.awt.*;
import javax.swing.*;
import javax.swing.border.*;

/** BorderLayoutDemo generates a simple frame that shows the positions
    available in a BorderLayout. */
public class BorderLayoutDemo extends JFrame {

    // Main Method
    public static void main(String args[]) {
        // Construct a BorderLayoutDemo object.
        JFrame frame = new BorderLayoutDemo();
        // Display the frame.
        frame.setVisible(true);
    }

    // Constructor
    public BorderLayoutDemo() {
        // Set the title.
        setTitle("BorderLayoutDemo");
        // Set the default close operation to exit on close.
        setDefaultCloseOperation(JFrame.EXIT_ON_CLOSE);
        // Create five labels: "North", "South", "East", "West",
        // and "Center".
        JLabel north = new JLabel("North", JLabel.CENTER);
        JLabel south = new JLabel("South", JLabel.CENTER);
        JLabel east = new JLabel("East", JLabel.CENTER);
        JLabel west = new JLabel("West", JLabel.CENTER);
        JLabel center = new JLabel("Center", JLabel.CENTER);
        // Place a black border around each label.
        Border blackBorder =
            BorderFactory.createLineBorder(Color.BLACK);
        north.setBorder(blackBorder);
        south.setBorder(blackBorder);
        east.setBorder(blackBorder);
        west.setBorder(blackBorder);
        center.setBorder(blackBorder);
        center.setPreferredSize(new Dimension(200,200));
        // Add the labels to the content pane.
        Container contentPane = getContentPane();
        contentPane.add(north, BorderLayout.NORTH);
        contentPane.add(south, BorderLayout.SOUTH);
        contentPane.add(east, BorderLayout.EAST);
        contentPane.add(west, BorderLayout.WEST);
        contentPane.add(center, BorderLayout.CENTER);
        // Size the frame to fit.
        pack();
    }
}
```

Flow Layout

The default layout manager for JPanel is Flow Layout. This is the simplest layout; items are placed left to right until the maximum width is filled, then they are placed on successive rows, much as words are placed in a paragraph. Figures C.9 and C.10 show examples of flow layout.

FIGURE C.9
Flow Layout with No Width Constraint

FIGURE C.10
Flow Layout with a Width Constraint

Figure C.9 shows the original output of the program that places 25 labels into a JPanel. Figure C.10 shows the frame after it has been resized using the mouse. Notice that by constraining the width, components are placed on successive lines. Also notice that because the components on the last line do not fill the full width, they are centered. This is the default behavior; the method setAlignment can be used to change it. Listing C.6 shows the program that generated these figures.

LISTING C.6
FlowLayoutDemo.java

```
import java.awt.*;
import javax.swing.*;
import javax.swing.border.*;

/** FlowLayoutDemo generates a simple frame that shows how components
    are arranged using FlowLayout. */
public class FlowLayoutDemo extends JFrame {

    // Main Method
    public static void main(String args[]) {
        // Construct a FlowLayoutDemo object.
        JFrame frame = new FlowLayoutDemo();
        // Display the frame.
        frame.setVisible(true);
    }

    // Constructor
    public FlowLayoutDemo() {
        setTitle("FlowLayoutDemo");
        setDefaultCloseOperation(JFrame.EXIT_ON_CLOSE);
```

```
        // Create a JPanel to hold some labels.
        JPanel aPanel = new JPanel();
        // Define the preferred size for the labels.
        Dimension preferredSize = new Dimension(20, 20);
        Border blackBorder =
            BorderFactory.createLineBorder(Color.BLACK);
        // Create some labels and add them to the panel.
        for (int i = 0; i < 25; i++) {
            JLabel aLabel =
                new JLabel(Integer.toString(i), JLabel.CENTER);
            aLabel.setPreferredSize(preferredSize);
            aLabel.setBorder(blackBorder);
            aPanel.add(aLabel);
        }
        setContentPane(aPanel);
        pack();
    }
}
```

Box Layout

Box Layout places components in either a horizontal or vertical arrangement. In contrast to Flow Layout, components do not wrap to the next line.

The `BoxLayout` constructor requires a reference to the container as one of its arguments. Therefore, to set a vertical layout, the following sequence of code is required:

```
JPanel panel = new JPanel();
panel.setLayout(new BoxLayout(panel, BoxLayout.Y_AXIS));
```

To set a horizontal layout, replace `Y_AXIS` with `X_AXIS`. Listing C.7 shows the program that creates the GUI in Figure C.11 for the button-based phone directory user interface.

FIGURE C.11
Box Layout

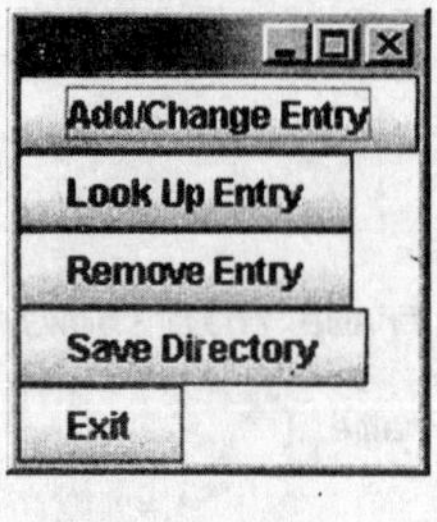

LISTING C.7
`BuildBoxLayout.java`

```
import java.awt.*;
import java.awt.event.*;
import javax.swing.*;

/** Demonstration of the Box Layout. */
public class BuildBoxLayout extends JFrame {
    public static void main(String[] args) {
        JFrame frame = new BuildBoxLayout();
    }
```

```
    public BuildBoxLayout () {
        setDefaultCloseOperation(EXIT_ON_CLOSE);
        // Create a panel to hold the buttons.
        JPanel panel = new JPanel();
        panel.setLayout(new BoxLayout(panel, BoxLayout.Y_AXIS));
        // Create buttons and add them to the panel.
        // Add/Change Entry
        JButton addEntryButton = new JButton("Add/Change Entry");
        panel.add(addEntryButton);
        // Look Up Entry
        JButton lookupEntryButton = new JButton("Look Up Entry");
        panel.add(lookupEntryButton);
        // Remove Entry
        JButton removeEntryButton = new JButton("Remove Entry");
        panel.add(removeEntryButton);
        // Save Directory
        JButton saveDirectoryButton =
            new JButton("Save Directory");
        panel.add(saveDirectoryButton);
        // Exit
        JButton exitButton = new JButton("Exit");
        panel.add(exitButton);
        // Put the panel into the frame.
        getContentPane().add(panel);
        // Size the frame to hold the panel.
        pack();
        setVisible(true);
    }
}
```

Grid Layout

Grid Layout places components in a rectangular grid. The container is divided into equal-sized rectangles, and one component is placed in each rectangle. Figure C.12 shows a grid that consists of 5 rows and 10 columns. Listing C.8 shows the program that generated Figure C.12.

FIGURE C.12
Grid Layout Demonstration

LISTING C.8
GridLayoutDemo.java

```
import java.awt.*;
import javax.swing.*;
import javax.swing.border.*;

/** GridLayoutDemo generates a simple frame that shows how components
    are arranged using Grid Layout. */
public class GridLayoutDemo extends JFrame {
```

```
    // Main Method
    public static void main(String args[]) {
        // Construct a GridLayoutDemo object.
        JFrame frame = new GridLayoutDemo();
        // Display the frame.
        frame.setVisible(true);
    }

    // Constructor
    public GridLayoutDemo() {
        setTitle("GridLayoutDemo");
        setDefaultCloseOperation(JFrame.EXIT_ON_CLOSE);
        // Create a JPanel to hold a grid.
        JPanel thePanel = new JPanel();
        thePanel.setLayout(new GridLayout(5,10));
        Border blackBorder =
            BorderFactory.createLineBorder(Color.BLACK);
        // Create some labels and add them to the panel.
        for (int i = 0; i < 5; i++) {
            for (int j = 0; j < 10; j++) {
                JLabel aLabel = new JLabel
                    (Integer.toString(i) + ", "
                     + Integer.toString(j),
                     JLabel.CENTER);
                aLabel.setBorder(blackBorder);
                thePanel.add(aLabel);
            }
        }
        setContentPane(thePanel);
        pack();
    }
}
```

Combining Layouts

By combining layouts, you can make more complicated arrangements. You can place panels within panels, each with different layout managers. The layout shown in Figure C.13 can be made by placing one panel set to Border Layout into the "center" of the content pane and placing another panel set to Grid Layout into the "south" of the content pane. You could also create the grid layout shown in Figure C.12 by creating a panel with a vertical Box Layout, each component of which is a panel with a horizontal Box Layout containing 10 components. The code for each nested layout is left as an exercise.

FIGURE C.13
Combined Layout Demo

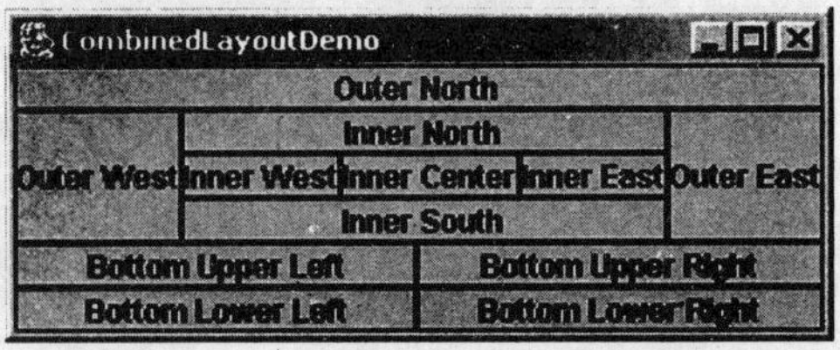

EXERCISES FOR SECTION C.3

SELF-CHECK

1. Describe the characteristics of the following layout managers:
   Border Layout
   Box Layout
   Grid Layout
   Flow Layout
2. What is the default layout for class `JFrame`? for class `JPanel`?
3. Why are layout managers useful?

PROGRAMMING

1. Create a frame that has a grid of labels that looks like this:

yellow		white		blue
		green		
	orange		purple	
green		red		blue
yellow			orange	

2. Create a frame that has a grid of labels that looks like Figure C.13.
3. Create a frame that looks like Figure C.12 using nested `BoxLayout` managers.

C.4 Components for Data Entry

A primary purpose of the Swing API is to enable a programmer to develop a GUI for a Java application. A GUI has several purposes:

1. To enable the user to provide input data to an application
2. To enable the user to control the action of the application
3. To display information or results to the user

We have shown how to control actions using buttons. In this section, we describe Swing components that enable the user to enter data; these include the `JCheckBox`, `JRadioButton`, and `JComboBox` for indicating choices, and the `JTextField` for entry of text. To display information, Swing uses `JLabel`, `JTextField`, and `JTextArea`. In this section we will describe each of them individually and demonstrate their use in very simple applications. In the next section we will then use some of them to build a more complicated application in which changes to input in one are reflected in the values displayed by the others.

Check Box

FIGURE C.14
Check Box Demo

A *check box* (JCheckBox) is a type of button. It is displayed with a label or icon next to a small square box. When the check box is selected, a check mark appears in the box. Also, when the user selects or deselects the check box (either way, by clicking it), its registered ActionListener is called. Figure C.14 shows a pair of check boxes. Listing C.9 shows the program to generate Figure C.14.

LISTING C.9
CheckBoxDemo.java

```
import java.awt.*;
import java.awt.event.*;
import javax.swing.*;
import javax.swing.event.*;
import java.io.*;

/** CheckBoxDemo generates a simple demonstration of check boxes. */
public class CheckBoxDemo extends JFrame {

    // Data Fields
    JCheckBox greenEggs;
    JCheckBox ham;

    // Main Method
    public static void main(String args[]) {
        // Create a CheckBoxDemo object.
        JFrame aFrame = new CheckBoxDemo();
        // Show it.
        aFrame.setVisible(true);
    }

    // Constructor
    public CheckBoxDemo() {
        setTitle("CheckBoxDemo");
        setDefaultCloseOperation(JFrame.EXIT_ON_CLOSE);
        // Create a JPanel to be used as the content pane.
        JPanel aPanel = new JPanel();
        aPanel.setLayout(new BoxLayout(aPanel, BoxLayout.Y_AXIS));
        // Create two check boxes and add them to the panel.
        greenEggs = new JCheckBox("Green Eggs");
        greenEggs.addActionListener(new GreenEggsChanged());
        aPanel.add(greenEggs);
        ham = new JCheckBox("Ham");
        ham.addActionListener(new HamChanged());
        aPanel.add(ham);
        setContentPane(aPanel);
        pack();
    }
```

```
    // Action Listener Classes
    private class GreenEggsChanged implements ActionListener {
        public void actionPerformed(ActionEvent e) {
            if (greenEggs.isSelected()) {
                System.out.println("Green Eggs is selected");
            }
            else {
                System.out.println("Green Eggs not selected");
            }
        }
    }

    private class HamChanged implements ActionListener {
        public void actionPerformed(ActionEvent e) {
            if (ham.isSelected()) {
                System.out.println("Ham is selected");
            }
            else {
                System.out.println("Ham not selected");
            }
        }
    }
}
```

Radio Button

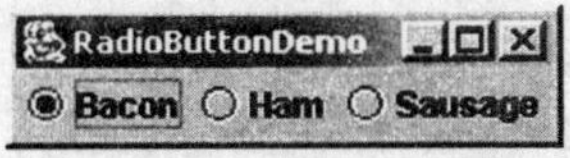

FIGURE C.15
Radio Button Demo

A *radio button* (`JRadioButton`) is similar to a check box in that it can be selected or deselected. There are two differences: Selection is indicated by having a small circle appear filled in rather than a square containing a check mark, and, more importantly, only one of a group of radio buttons may be selected at a time. Figure C.15 shows three radio buttons.

To facilitate the mutual exclusion, radio buttons are placed into a `ButtonGroup`. When one object in a `ButtonGroup` is selected, the others are automatically deselected. A `ButtonGroup` is not a `Component`. It is not displayed, and event listeners cannot be registered to it. The event listeners are registered to the individual buttons. Listing C.10 shows the program that created Figure C.15. Notice that a common `ActionListener` is registered for each of the buttons. When the buttons are created, the name of the selection is set as the *action command* of the associated `ButtonModel` using the statement:

```
radioButtons[i].getModel().setActionCommand(selections[i]);
```

The method `getSelection` in the class `ButtonGroup` returns the `ButtonModel` of the selected button, not the button itself. We can then use the method `getActionCommand` to retrieve the selected item using the statement:

```
String choice = buttonGroup.getSelection().getActionCommand();
```

LISTING C.10
RadioButtonDemo.java

```java
import java.awt.*;
import java.awt.event.*;
import javax.swing.*;
import javax.swing.event.*;
import java.io.*;

/** RadioButtonDemo generates a simple demonstration of
    radio buttons. */
public class RadioButtonDemo extends JFrame {

    // Data Fields
    String[] selections = {"Bacon", "Ham", "Sausage"};
    JRadioButton[] radioButtons =
        new JRadioButton[selections.length];
    ButtonGroup buttonGroup;

    // Main Method
    public static void main(String args[]) {
        // Create a RadioButtonDemo object.
        JFrame aFrame = new RadioButtonDemo();
        // Show it.
        aFrame.setVisible(true);
    }

    // Constructor
    public RadioButtonDemo() {
        setTitle("RadioButtonDemo");
        setDefaultCloseOperation(JFrame.EXIT_ON_CLOSE);
        // Create a JPanel to be used as the content pane.
        JPanel aPanel = new JPanel();
        aPanel.setLayout(new BoxLayout(aPanel, BoxLayout.X_AXIS));
        // Create a button group for the buttons.
        buttonGroup = new ButtonGroup();
        // Create radio buttons and add them to the panel.
        // Also add them to the button group.
        ActionListener newSelection = new SelectionChangeMade();
        for (int i = 0; i < selections.length; i++) {
            radioButtons[i] = new JRadioButton(selections[i]);
            radioButtons[i].getModel().setActionCommand(selections[i]);
            radioButtons[i].addActionListener(newSelection);
            buttonGroup.add(radioButtons[i]);
            aPanel.add(radioButtons[i]);
        }
        setContentPane(aPanel);
        pack();
    }

    // Action Listener Classes
    private class SelectionChangeMade implements ActionListener {
        public void actionPerformed(ActionEvent e) {
            String choice =
                buttonGroup.getSelection().getActionCommand();
            System.out.println(choice + " is selected");
        }
    }
}
```

Combo Box

A *combo box* combines a button or editable field and a drop-down list. Normally the current selection is displayed, as shown in Figure C.16. When the button is clicked, a menu of choices is displayed, as shown in Figure C.17. A combo box is created using the statement:

```
comboBox = new JComboBox(selections);
```

where *selections* is an array of objects that define the set of choices. Items can be added to the list of choices using the method `addItem` and removed using the method `removeItem`. The selected item can be retrieved using `getSelectedItem` (return type is `Object`) and can be reset using `setSelectedItem` (argument type is `Object`). Listing C.11 shows the program that generated Figures C.16 and C.17.

FIGURE C.16
Combo Box Showing Selected Item

FIGURE C.17
Combo Box Showing Selections Available

LISTING C.11
ComboBoxDemo.java

```
import java.awt.*;
import java.awt.event.*;
import javax.swing.*;
import javax.swing.event.*;
import java.io.*;

/** ComboBoxDemo generates a simple demonstration of a combo box. */
public class ComboBoxDemo extends JFrame {

    // Data Fields
    String[] selections = {"Bacon", "Ham", "Sausage"};
    JComboBox comboBox;

    // Main Method
    public static void main(String args[]) {
        // Create a ComboBoxDemo object.
        JFrame aFrame = new ComboBoxDemo();
        // Show it.
        aFrame.setVisible(true);
    }
```

```
    // Constructor
    public ComboBoxDemo() {
        setTitle("ComboBoxDemo");
        setDefaultCloseOperation(JFrame.EXIT_ON_CLOSE);
        // Create a JPanel to be used as the content pane.
        JPanel aPanel = new JPanel();
        // Create the combo box.
        comboBox = new JComboBox(selections);
        comboBox.addActionListener(new SelectionChangeMade());
        aPanel.add(comboBox);
        setContentPane(aPanel);
        pack();
    }

    // Action Listener Classes
    private class SelectionChangeMade implements ActionListener {
        public void actionPerformed(ActionEvent e) {
            String choice = (String)comboBox.getSelectedItem();
            System.out.println(choice + " is selected");
        }
    }
}
```

Text Field

A *text field* (`JTextField`) is a component that allows for the display and editing of a single line of text. The Java API also provides components for display and editing of multiple lines. A summary of selected constructors and methods of `JTextField` and its superclasses is shown in Table C.6.

Figure C.18 shows a simple text field with 10 columns that was generated by the program shown in Listing C.12. Pressing the Enter key generates an action event.

TABLE C.6
Summary of `JTextField`

Constructor	Behavior
`JTextField()`	Constructs a new `JTextField`.
`JTextField(int columns)`	Constructs a new empty `JTextField` with the specified number of columns.
`JTextField(String text)`	Constructs a new `JTextField` with the specified text.
`JTextField(String text, int columns)`	Constructs a new `JTextField` with the specified text and number of columns.
Method	**Behavior**
`void addActionListener(ActionListener l)`	Adds the specified action listener to receive action events from this text field.
`String getText()`	Returns the text contained in the text field.
`void setText(String t)`	Sets the text of the text field.

FIGURE C.18
Text Field Demo

LISTING C.12
TextFieldDemo.java

```
import java.awt.*;
import java.awt.event.*;
import javax.swing.*;

/** TextFieldDemo provides a simple demonstration of data input
    from a JTextField. */
public class TextFieldDemo extends JFrame {

    // Data Field
    JTextField textField;

    // Main Method
    public static void main(String[] args) {
        JFrame aFrame = new TextFieldDemo();
        aFrame.setVisible(true);
    }

    // Constructor
    private TextFieldDemo() {
        setTitle("Text Field Demo");
        setDefaultCloseOperation(JFrame.EXIT_ON_CLOSE);
        // Create a panel for the content pane.
        JPanel aPanel = new JPanel();
        // Add a label.
        aPanel.add(new JLabel("Enter a number"));
        // Create a text field.
        textField = new JTextField(10);
        // Register action listener.
        textField.addActionListener(new NumberEntered());
        // Add it to the panel.
        aPanel.add(textField);
        // Set the panel to be the content pane.
        setContentPane(aPanel);
        // Size the frame.
        pack();
    }

    // Inner Action Listener Class
    private class NumberEntered implements ActionListener {
        public void actionPerformed(ActionEvent e) {
            String text = textField.getText();
            int value = 0;
            try {
                value = Integer.parseInt(text);
                System.out.println("Number entered: " + value);
            }
```

```
            catch (NumberFormatException ex) {
                System.err.println("Invalid entry " + text);
            }
        }
    }
}
```

Label

In Listing C.12 the statement

```
aPanel.add(new JLabel("Enter a number"));
```

adds a label to the panel. As its name implies, a label is a string of characters. You can specify the string when you create the label, as shown here, or you can specify it later using method `setText`. You can retrieve the text in a label using method `getText` (returns a `String`). If you declare data field `result` as a label

```
private JLabel result = new JLabel();
```

and add `result` to `aPanel`, you can use the following statement in the **`try`**-clause (as a replacement for the call to `println`) to display the result as a label under the text field:

```
result.setText("Number entered: " + value);
```

Text Area

A text area is another component that can be used to enter data or to display information to the user. The statement

```
JTextArea textArea = new JTextArea(2, 20);
```

declares a text area with 2 lines and 20 columns. A text area is like a text field except that it can show more than one line of information. You can use methods `setText` and `getText` with a text area just as you use them with a text field (or label). You can use them in combination to append information to what is already in a text area:

```
textArea.setText(textArea.getText() + newInformation);
```

The user can also edit information that is typed into a text area or a text field prior to pressing the Enter key. The edited text is what is retrieved by the `getText` method.

EXERCISES FOR SECTION C.4

SELF-CHECK

1. Which of the data entry components (check box, radio button, combo box, or text field) is appropriate for the following situations?
   - **a.** Recording answers in a multiple-choice exam
   - **b.** Entering the state or province in a data entry form that is collecting address information
   - **c.** Entering the city in a data entry form that is collecting address information
   - **d.** Allow the user to select several different breakfast items from a menu

PROGRAMMING

1. A GUI that displays three button groups, containing radio buttons and a text area, is shown in Figure C.19. Whenever one of the radio buttons is changed, the text should be updated. Write the program.

FIGURE C.19
Radio Button Exercise

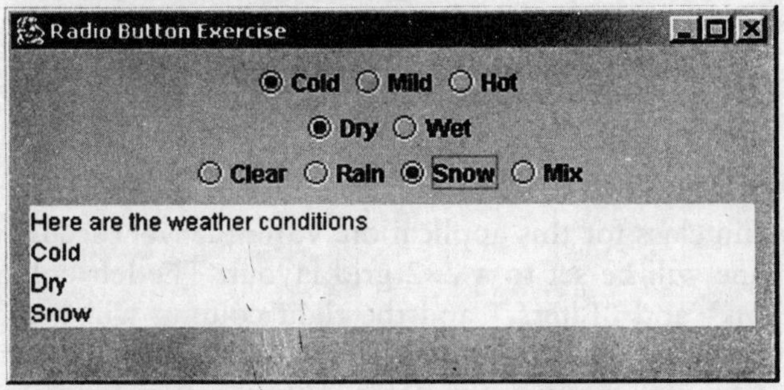

2. Revise the program written in Programming Exercise 1 to use check boxes rather than radio buttons in the third row. Eliminate the "mix" option, but let the user select both rain and snow. If clear is selected, then deselect rain and snow.

C.5 Using Data Entry Components in a GUI

In this section we will show how to use some of the data entry components to build an application in which changes entered in one component are reflected in the values displayed by the others.

CASE STUDY Liquid Volume Converter

Problem In Europe and Canada gasoline is measured in liters, whereas in the United States it is measured in (U.S.) gallons. We want to write an application that will take a value in one unit and display it in the other.

Analysis Based on the problem statement, we can identify two use cases:

- User enters a value in gallons
- User enters a value in liters

These are further expanded in Table C.7:

TABLE C.7
Use Cases for Liquid Volume Converter

User Action	System Response
User enters a value in gallons.	The system updates the corresponding value in liters. If the value entered is not a valid number, an error message is displayed.
User enters a value in liters.	The system updates the corresponding value in gallons. If the value entered is not a valid number, an error message is displayed.

Design Class `VolumeConverterGUI`

The main class for this application, `VolumeConverterGUI`, will be a `JFrame`. The content pane will be set to a 2×2 grid layout. The left column will contain the labels "Gallons" and "Liters," and the right column will contain two text boxes corresponding to the adjacent labels (see Figure C.20). `ActionListener` classes will be registered to each of the text fields. When a text field is changed, its contents are converted to a `double` value. This value is then converted to the opposite liquid volume unit, and the result is displayed in the other text field. We will also need to develop a class to perform the conversions.

FIGURE C.20
`JFrame VolumeConverterGUI`

Class `VolumeConverter`

This class provides the conversion from gallons to liters. Its design is summarized in Table C.8.

TABLE C.8
`VolumeConverter` Class Design

Data Field	Attribute
`private static final double LITERS_PER_GALLON`	The conversion factor.
Method	**Behavior**
`double toGallons(double value)`	Converts input value from liters to gallons.
`double toLiters(double value)`	Converts input value from gallons to liters.

Implementation Class `VolumeConverterGUI`

Listing C.13 shows the code for the main class. The constructor lays out the four components: two `JLabels` and two `JTextFields`. The `JTextField` objects are data fields so that the inner classes can access them.

The two inner classes are very similar. One converts from gallons to liters, and the other converts from liters to gallons. Objects of these inner classes are registered to the corresponding text fields using the statements:

```
gallonsField.addActionListener(new NewGallonsValue());
litersField.addActionListener(new NewLitersValue());
```

In the listener class `NewGallonsValue`, the statements

```
double gallonsValue = Double.parseDouble(gallonsField.getText());
double litersValue = VolumeConverter.toLiters(gallonsValue);
litersField.setText(Double.toString(litersValue));
```

retrieve the value in `gallonsField`, convert it to liters, and then place that value in `litersField`.

LISTING C.13

`VolumeConverterGUI.java`

```
import java.awt.*;
import java.awt.event.*;
import javax.swing.*;

/** VolumeConverterGUI is a GUI application that converts
    values in gallons to liters and vice versa.
*/
public class VolumeConverterGUI extends JFrame {

    // Data Fields
    /** Text field to hold gallons value */
    private JTextField gallonsField;
    /** Text field to hold liters value */
    private JTextField litersField;

    // Main Method
    /** Create an instance of the application and show it.
        @param args Command Line Arguments - not used
    */
    public static void main (String[] args) {
        JFrame frame = new VolumeConverterGUI();
        frame.setVisible(true);
    }

    // Constructor
    /** Construct the components and add them to the frame. */
    public VolumeConverterGUI() {
        super("Liquid Volume Converter");
        setDefaultCloseOperation(EXIT_ON_CLOSE);
        // Get a reference to the content pane.
        Container contentPane = getContentPane();
```

```
        // Set the layout manager to grid layout.
        contentPane.setLayout(new GridLayout(2, 2));
        contentPane.add(new JLabel("Gallons"));
        gallonsField = new JTextField(15);
        gallonsField.addActionListener(new NewGallonsValue());
        contentPane.add(gallonsField);
        contentPane.add(new JLabel("Liters"));
        litersField = new JTextField(15);
        litersField.addActionListener(new NewLitersValue());
        contentPane.add(litersField);
        // Size the frame to fit.
        pack();
    }

    // Inner Classes
    /** Class to respond to new gallons value. */
    private class NewGallonsValue implements ActionListener {
        /** Convert the gallons value to corresponding liters value.
            @param e ActionEvent object - not used
        */
        public void actionPerformed(ActionEvent e) {
            try {
                double gallonsValue = Double.parseDouble
                    (gallonsField.getText());
                double litersValue =
                    VolumeConverter.toLiters(gallonsValue);
                litersField.setText(Double.toString(litersValue));
            } catch (NumberFormatException ex) {
                JOptionPane.showMessageDialog(null,
                                              "Invalid Number Format",
                                              "",
                                              JOptionPane.ERROR_MESSAGE);
            }
        }
    }

    /** Class to respond to new liters value. */
    private class NewLitersValue implements ActionListener {
        /** Convert the liters value to corresponding gallons value.
            @param e ActionEvent object - not used
        */
        public void actionPerformed(ActionEvent e) {
            try {
                double litersValue = Double.parseDouble
                    (litersField.getText());
                double gallonsValue =
                    VolumeConverter.toGallons(litersValue);
                gallonsField.setText(Double.toString(gallonsValue));
            } catch (NumberFormatException ex) {
                JOptionPane.showMessageDialog(null,
                                              "Invalid Number Format",
                                              "",
                                              JOptionPane.ERROR_MESSAGE);
            }
        }
    }
}
```

Class VolumeConverter

The implementation of the VolumeConverter class is shown in Listing C.14. The two methods toGallons and toLiters either multiply or divide by the conversion factor as appropriate.

LISTING C.14
VolumeConverter.java

```
/** VolumeConverter is a class with static methods
    that convert between gallons and liters.
*/
public class VolumeConverter {

    /** The number of liters in a gallon.
    */
    private static final double LITERS_PER_GALLON = 3.785411784;

    /** Convert a value in liters to gallons.
        @param liters The value in liters
        @return The value in gallons
    */
    public static double toGallons(double liters) {
        return liters / LITERS_PER_GALLON;
    }

    /** Convert a value in gallons to liters.
        @param gallons The value in gallons
        @return The value in liters
    */
    public static double toLiters(double gallons) {
        return gallons * LITERS_PER_GALLON;
    }
}
```

Testing Figure C.21 shows two examples of running the VolumeConverterGUI: one in which the value for gallons is entered and the other in which the value for liters is entered. We know that the conversion factor is 3.785411784. By entering 10 as the number of gallons, we can see that the conversion factor is being multiplied correctly. By entering 37.85 as the number of liters, we can see that the conversion factor is being divided correctly as well. If we enter all 10 digits, the gallons display will be 10 exactly. You should also test this with invalidly formatted numbers to verify that an appropriate error message is displayed.

FIGURE C.21
Test of Liquid Volume Converter

TABLE C.9
The NumberFormat Class

Method	Behavior
`String format(double number)`	Formats a **double** value.
`static NumberFormat getCurrencyInstance()`	Returns a `NumberFormat` object that is configured to convert numbers to the currency format of the default locale.
`static NumberFormat getNumberInstance()`	Returns a `NumberFormat` object that is configured to convert numbers to ordinary numbers (with a fraction part) in the format of the default locale.
`static NumberFormat getPercentageInstance()`	Returns a `NumberFormat` object that is configured to convert numbers to percentages (i.e., fractions are multiplied by 100, and a percentage indicator is provided) in the format of the default locale.
`void setMaximumFractionDigits(int newValue)`	Sets the maximum number of digits allowed in the fraction portion.

Limiting the Number of Significant Digits

Some of the numbers in Figure C.21 have many more decimal places than needed. The Java API `java.text` contains the class `NumberFormat`, which can be used to format numbers either as pure numbers or as currency values. The formatting depends on the `Locale`, a class that encapsulates culture and language differences. Your computer is probably configured so that the default locale is appropriate for where you are. For example, if you live in the United States, then the default locale is appropriate for the United States. If you live in the United Kingdom, then the default locale is appropriate for the United Kingdom. To use the `NumberFormat` class, you must first create an instance. The `NumberFormat` class itself is an abstract class. It includes factory methods to create appropriate concrete instances. It also has modifiers that allow you to set the number of integer and fraction digits. The methods in this class are summarized in Table C.9.

All of the `get`*`Xxxxx`*`Instance` methods also have a form that takes a `Locale` object as a parameter. This allows you to create a `NumberFormat` object for a specific locale. We show how to use the `Number` instance and the `format` method in the following example.

EXAMPLE C.3 We can modify the `VolumeConverterGUI` to display only two fraction digits as follows:

1. We add a declaration for a `NumberFormat` to the data fields:

```
NumberFormat numberForm;
```

2. We initialize this data field in the constructor as follows:

```
numberForm = NumberFormat.getNumberInstance();
numberForm.setMaximumFractionDigits(2);
```

3. In the `NewGallonsValue` class we change the statement that sets the `litersField` to

   ```
   litersField.setText(numberForm.format(litersValue));
   ```

4. In the `NewLitersValue` class we change the statement that sets the `gallonsField` to

   ```
   gallonsField.setText(numberForm.format(gallonsValue));
   ```

The modified display is shown in Figure C.22. Notice that an input value of 37.85 liters produces a display of "10" gallons instead of "9.998912181755918". Also notice that an input of 1000 gallons gives a value of "3,785.41"

FIGURE C.22
Modified Liquid Volume Converter

Formatting Currency for Different Locales

You can obtain `NumberFormat` instances that are configured to convert numbers to local currency representation using the statement

```
NumberFormat format = getCurrencyInstance(locale);
```

where `locale` is a `Locale` object. You can consult the Java documentation on how to specify the locale and how to obtain a list of locales that are available on your computer. There are also defined constants in the API `java.util` that map to some locales. For example, `Locale.US` is a locale for the United States.

EXAMPLE C.4 Figure C.23 shows the value 12345.67 formatted as currency in different locales. Notice that both Germany and France use the comma to separate the integer portion from the fraction, whereas in both the United States and the United Kingdom, the period is used. Also notice that in Germany the period is used to group thousands, in France the space is used to group thousands, and in the United States and the United Kingom the comma is used. Listing C.15 shows the code to generate this figure.

FIGURE C.23
Currency Display Demonstration

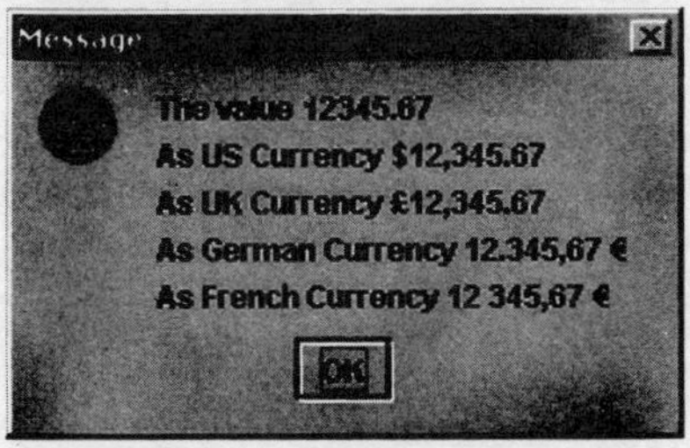

LISTING C.15
CurrencyDemo.java

```
import java.util.*;
import java.text.*;
import javax.swing.*;

/** Program to demonstrate different currency formats. */
public class CurrencyDemo {

    public static void main(String[] args) {
        NumberFormat usa =
            NumberFormat.getCurrencyInstance(Locale.US);
        NumberFormat uk =
            NumberFormat.getCurrencyInstance(Locale.UK);
        NumberFormat de =
            NumberFormat.getCurrencyInstance(Locale.GERMANY);
        NumberFormat fr =
            NumberFormat.getCurrencyInstance(Locale.FRANCE);

        double value = 12345.67;

        String result = "The value " + value
                        + "\nAs US Currency " + usa.format(value)
                        + "\nAs UK Currency " + uk.format(value)
                        + "\nAs German Currency " + de.format(value)
                        + "\nAs French Currency " + fr.format(value);

        JOptionPane.showMessageDialog(null, result);
        System.exit(0);
    }
}
```

EXERCISES FOR SECTION C.5

SELF-CHECK

1. How can you obtain a formatting with three decimal places?
2. How can you obtain currency formatting that is appropriate to the location in which the user is using the program?

PROGRAMMING

1. Write a distance converter that converts from miles to kilometers. There are 1.609344 kilometers in a mile. Display the result with only one fraction digit.

C.6 Menus and Toolbars

Menus and toolbars are another way for a user to indicate choices or initiate actions in a GUI application. Menus may be hierarchical; that is, selecting a menu choice can bring up a submenu. Generally the top level of a menu is placed on a menu bar that sits at the top of the window, just under the frame border. With Java Swing, the menu bar may be positioned like any other component. Menus can also be made to "pop up" in response an event such as a mouse click. In addition to the `JMenuItem`, most Swing components may be used as menu items. Other features of menu items are the following:

- Icons can augment or replace menu items.
- Keyboard accelerators (shortcuts) and mnemonics may be assigned.

A toolbar is a group of buttons, combo boxes, and other components together in a repositionable panel. The toolbar may be dragged into its own child window or anchored along the edge of a frame. In many GUI applications toolbars duplicate the functionality of menus. For example, the toolbar icon showing a folder opening ( ) duplicates the effect of selecting Open from the File menu. This duplication is accomplished by assigning the same `ActionListener` to the menu item and to the button in the toolbar.

The Classes `JMenuItem`, `JMenu`, and `JMenuBar`

Because `JMenuItem` is an extension of `AbstractButton`, a `JMenuItem` object can display text or an icon. It also fires action events when activated. Figure C.24 shows an example menu with five menu items. The first item consists only of an icon that represents the "new" action (the blank, dog-eared page). The second item contains both an "open" icon (the opening folder) and text "Open . . ." The third contains text and an accelerator (or shortcut), "Ctrl+S"; the fourth, only text; and the final item, a mnemonic, indicated by the underscore under the *x*. Table C.10 shows a subset of the constructors and methods of the `JMenuItem` class.

Note that an accelerator is a key combination that invokes the menu item's action listeners. A mnemonic is a key that, when pressed while the menu is displayed, will activate the action listeners without the user having to select the menu item with the mouse.

FIGURE C.24
Example of a Menu

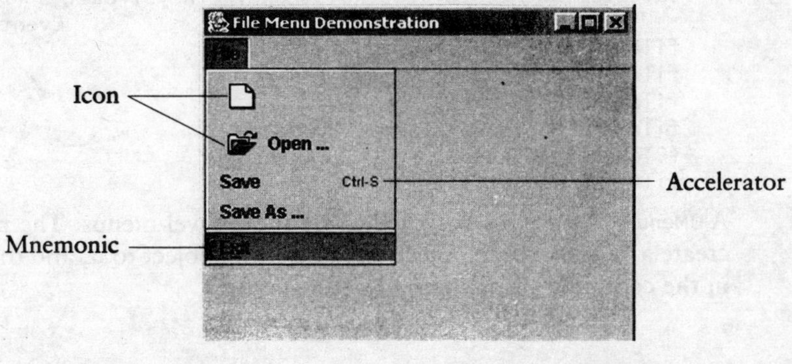

TABLE C.10
Constructors and Methods of `JMenuItem`

Constructor	Behavior
`JMenuItem()`	Creates a `JMenuItem` with no set text or icon.
`JMenuItem(Icon icon)`	Creates a `JMenuItem` with the specified icon.
`JMenuItem(String text)`	Creates a `JMenuItem` with the specified text.
`JMenuItem(String text, Icon icon)`	Creates a `JMenuItem` with the specified text and icon.
`JMenuItem(String text, int mnemonic)`	Creates a `JMenuItem` with the specified text and keyboard mnemonic. The `int` value is the key code, defined by the class `KeyEvent`.
Method	**Behavior**
`void setAccelerator(KeyStroke keystroke)`	Sets the key combination that invokes the menu item's action listeners without the user navigating the menu hierarchy.
Methods Inherited from `AbstractButton`	**Behavior**
`void setIcon(Icon icon)`	Sets the default icon.
`void setText(String text)`	Sets the text.
`setMnemonic(int mnemonic)`	Sets the mnemonic. The `int` value is the key code, defined by the class `KeyEvent`.
`void addActionListener(ActionListener l)`	Adds an `ActionListener` to this menu item.

You create a menu as a new `JMenu` object, passing the menu name as an argument. Then you create each individual menu item (type `JMenuItem`) and add it to the `JMenu` object (using method `add`). The File menu in Figure C.24 was constructed with the following sequence of Java statements:

```
JMenu fileMenu = new JMenu("File");
JMenuItem newItem = new JMenuItem(newIcon);
JMenuItem openItem = new JMenuItem("Open ...", openIcon);
JMenuItem saveItem = new JMenuItem("Save");
JMenuItem saveAsItem = new JMenuItem("Save As ...");
JMenuItem exitItem = new JMenuItem("Exit", KeyEvent.VK_X);
saveItem.setAccelerator(KeyStroke.getKeyStroke('S',
                                            Event.CTRL_MASK));
fileMenu.add(newItem);
fileMenu.add(openItem);
fileMenu.add(saveItem);
fileMenu.add(saveAsItem);
fileMenu.addSeparator();
fileMenu.add(exitItem);
```

A `JMenuBar` is a class designed to hold top-level menus. The next step would be to create a new `JMenuBar` object, add the `JMenu` object to it, and then place the `JMenuBar` in the container using method `setJMenuBar`.

```
JMenuBar menuBar = new JMenuBar();
menuBar.add(fileMenu);
setJMenuBar(menuBar);
```

Icons

An icon is a small fixed-size picture. It is used to decorate buttons and other components. Icons must implement the `Icon` interface as defined in Table C.11.

TABLE C.11
The Interface `Icon`

Method	Behavior
`int getIconHeight()`	Returns the icon's height.
`int getIconWidth()`	Returns the icon's width.
`void paintIcon(Component c, Graphics g, int x, int y)`	Draws the icon at the specified location using the given graphics context.

The class `ImageIcon` implements the `Icon` interface. It uses an image file (such as a GIF or JPEG file) to create the icon. The image file must be created by a drawing or paint program. You don't have to create all your own image files, because there are many predefined image files available in libraries. Table C.12 gives a subset of the `ImageIcon` class constructors.

TABLE C.12
A Subset of the `ImageIcon` Constructors

Constructor	Behavior
`ImageIcon()`	Creates an uninitialized image icon.
`ImageIcon(String filename)`	Creates an image icon from the specified file.
`ImageIcon(String filename, String description)`	Creates an image icon from the specified file and with the specified description that is meant to be a brief textual description of the object.

Toolbars

The `JToolBar` class is a container that can be oriented either horizontally or vertically. A toolbar contains icons that can be selected by a mouse click. Often a toolbar is used as an alternative to a menu. The toolbar shown in Figure C.25 has icons for creating a new document, opening a document, and saving a document (the diskette). The mouse can drag the toolbar to any of the four sides of a container or into its own window (see the figure).

FIGURE C.25
Examples of Different Toolbar Positions

The icons shown in Figure C.25 are created using the following statements:

```
Icon newIcon = new ImageIcon("new.gif",
                             "Create a new document");
Icon openIcon = new ImageIcon("open.gif",
                              "Open an existing document");
Icon saveIcon = new ImageIcon("disk.gif",
                              "Save file to disk");
```

Each GIF file above displays an icon for the specified button (new, open, or save) when painted. `JButton`s with these icons are then created:

```
JButton newButton = new JButton(newIcon);
JButton openButton = new JButton(openIcon);
JButton saveButton = new JButton(saveIcon);
```

`ActionListeners` must be registered for the buttons in the normal way. Generally the same action listener object is registered for each button as was registered for the corresponding menu item. Finally, the buttons are added to the toolbar, and the toolbar is added to the content pane.

```
JToolBar toolBar = new JToolBar();
toolBar.add(newButton);
toolBar.add(openButton);
toolBar.add(saveButton);
getContentPane().add(toolBar, BorderLayout.NORTH);
```

This code added the toolbar to the `NORTH` position of the content pane. The other positions shown in Figure C.25 are the result of using the mouse to drag the toolbar to different positions. You can place the toolbar in any one of the four `BorderLayout` edge positions.

CASE STUDY A Drawing Application

Problem We want to write an application that will let us draw different shapes of different sizes. The shape to be drawn is to be selected either from a menu or from a toolbar. A menu to specify the color of the shape and the color of the border should also be provided. The list of available figures should be variable. The user specifies the names of the classes that draw the figures on the command line when the application is started.

Analysis In this case study we will be concerned with initializing the application and building the menus and toolbar. The case study in the next section will complete the design of the application by including the drawing of the figures.

When the program is started, the `JFrame` should include two menus and a toolbar. One menu offers the choice of setting the interior color or setting the border color, as shown in Figure C.26. The other should offer the choice of shapes to be drawn, as shown in Figure C.27. The choice of shapes should also be provided by a toolbar.

FIGURE C.26 DrawApp Showing Color Menu and Toolbar

FIGURE C.27 DrawApp Showing Drawing Tool Menu and Toolbar

Design The `DrawApp` class will be an extension of the `JFrame` class. The constructor will perform the following steps:

1. Build a list of prototype figures based on the list of class names provided as input.
2. Build a list of icons, one for each figure kind.
3. Build the drawing tool menu that is used to select which figure is to be drawn.

4. Build the drawing tool toolbar.
5. Build the color chooser menu.
6. Create a menu bar and add the drawing tool menu and the color chooser menu to it.
7. Add the menu bar to the frame.
8. Add the toolbar to the frame.
9. Create a panel for the drawing objects and add it to the frame.

In Section 1.11, we described a `Shape` class hierarchy (see Figure 1.10) and a test application that calculated the areas and perimeters of several figures (Listing 1.8). We would like to be able to draw figure objects of different colors at various positions in a window. To accomplish this, we need a more robust class hierarchy. One such hierarchy is shown in Figure C.28. Abstract class `Drawable` declares data field `pos` (type `Point`) that represents a `Drawable` object's position and data fields `interiorColor` and `borderColor` (type `awt.Color`) that represent its color. A `DrawableRectangle` object extends class `Drawable` and contains a `Rectangle` as a component (data field `drawable`). A `Drawable` subclass must provide a `drawMe` method that contains code to draw the figure. In addition, a `Drawable` subclass must implement the methods in Table C.13. We provide more explanation of the class hierarchy and a full implementation of the `Drawable` subclasses on the textbook web site. Next, we focus on the classes needed to draw the menu.

TABLE C.13
Abstract Methods to Be Added to `Drawable`

Method	Behavior
`int getWidth()`	Returns the width.
`int getHeight()`	Returns the height.
`String getName()`	Returns the name to be used in the menu.
`DrawableIcon getIcon(int size)`	Creates an icon for this figure to be used in the toolbar.

Rather than creating images of each figure for the icons, we take advantage of the fact that our figures can draw themselves. Thus, we can create a class `DrawableIcon` (see Table C.14) that implements the `Icon` interface. The only tricky part about this is that the `paintIcon` method is passed the coordinates of the upper left corner, but each of the figures we implemented has a different origin (the rectangle's origin is the upper left corner, the circle's is the center, and the triangle's is the lower left corner). Each `DrawableIcon` class will set the position of the object that will draw the figure in the icon as needed. The `DrawableRectangle` will use an origin of (0, 0), the `DrawableCircle` will position itself to (`size/2`, `size/2`), and the `DrawableTriangle` will position itself to (0, `size`). The parameter `size` is the size of the square in which the icon image is drawn. Setting these origins will result in the figures appearing inside the square as shown in Figure C.27.

FIGURE C.28
Drawable Shapes Class Hierarchy

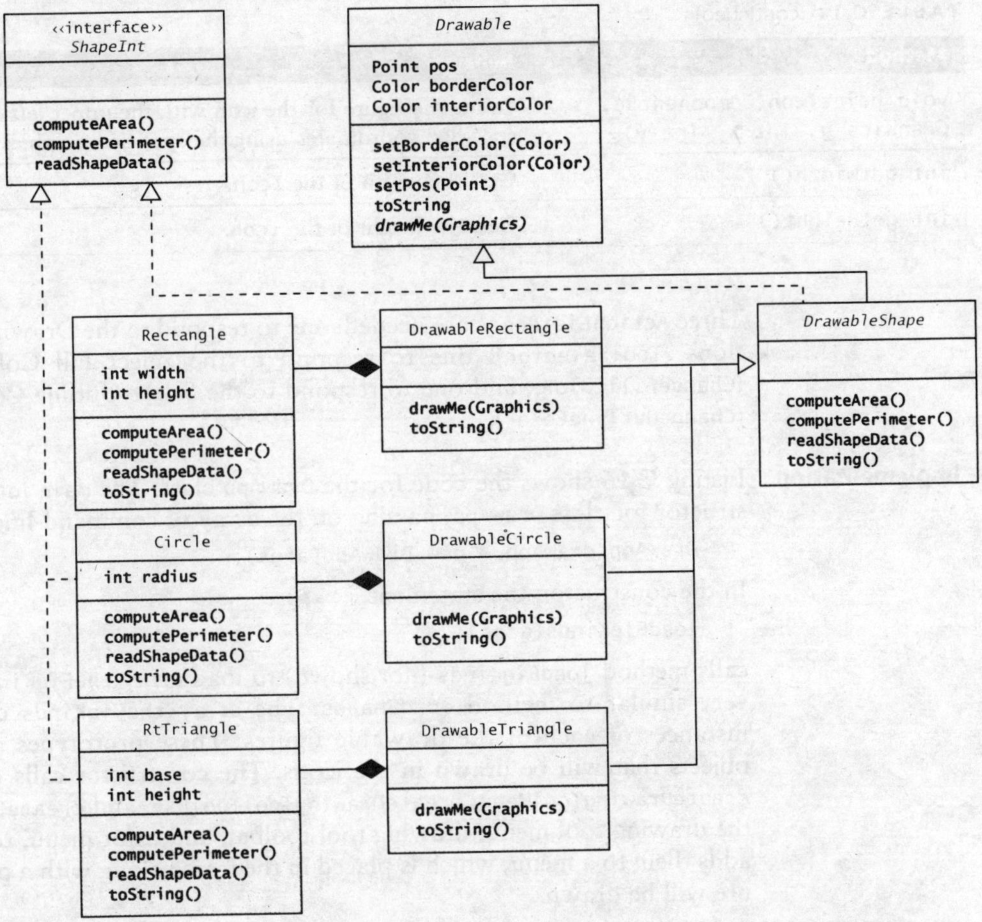

TABLE C.14
The `DrawableIcon` Class

Data Field	Attribute
`Drawable theFig`	Reference to the figure that is to be drawn in this icon.
`int x0`	The *x*-coordinate of the origin relative to the upper left corner.
`int y0`	The *y*-coordinate of the orgin relative to the upper left corner.
Constructor	**Behavior**
`DrawableIcon(Drawable f)`	Creates an icon based on the supplied `Drawable`. The figure will be placed so that the upper left corner is at (0, 0).

TABLE C.14 (continued)

Method	Behavior
`void paintIcon(Component c, Graphics g, int x, int y)`	Paints the figure for the icon with the upper left corner at the specified coordinates using the specified graphics environment.
`int getWidth()`	Gets the width of the `Icon`.
`int getHeight()`	Gets the height of the `Icon`.

Three `ActionListeners` are needed: one to respond to the Drawing Tool menu selections (`ToolSelector`), one to respond to the Select Fill Color menu selection (`ChangeFillColor`), and one to respond to the Select Outline Color menu selection (`ChangeOutlineColor`).

Implementation Listing C.16 shows the code for the `DrawApp` class. The `main` method calls the constructor for class `DrawApp`, passing on the array of command-line parameters:

```
DrawApp drawApp = new DrawApp(args);
```

In the constructor, the statement

```
loadFigKinds(args);
```

calls method `loadFigKinds` (not shown) to load array `theFigKinds`. This method is very similar to method `loadShapes`. The array `theFigKinds` contains prototype instances of each of the drawable figures. These prototypes are also the figure objects that will be drawn in the icons. The constructor calls on helper methods `createDrawingToolMenu`, `createDrawingToolToolBar`, and `createColorMenu` to create the drawing tool menu, drawing tool toolbar, and color menu, respectively. Then it adds them to a menu, which is placed in the frame along with a panel where the figure will be drawn.

The method `createDrawingToolMenu` registers action listeners for each menu item (a figure kind) using the statement

```
item.addActionListener(new ToolSelector(theFigKinds[i]));
```

and method `createDrawingToolToolBar` does the same using the statement

```
aButton.addActionListener(new ToolSelector(theFigKinds[i]));
```

These statements instantiate listener class `ToolSelector`. The statement

```
this.desiredFig = desiredFig;
```

stores a reference to the appropriate figure kind prototype (`theFigKinds[i]`) in each listener object.

When the user makes a selection from the toolbar or the drawing tool menu, an event is fired, which is processed by the `actionPerformed` method for the corresponding listener object. The method `ToolSelector.actionPerformed` copies the figure prototype referenced by this object into the `DrawApp`'s `selectedFigure` data field.

```
selectedFig = desiredFig;
```

For the two choices in the color menu—Set Interior Color and Set Border Color (method not shown)—the `JColorChooser` class is used to present a color chooser dialog. The return value from the `showDialog` method is saved in either the `currentInteriorColor` or the `currentBorderColor` data field. We cycle through array `theFigKind` to set the color values in the figure prototypes. This has two effects: The selected color will then be used in a new figure to be drawn, and the icon colors are updated. Thus the icons always display the user's most recently selected colors.

The actual drawing of the figures is handled by the `DrawingPanel` class, which we will describe in Section C.7.

LISTING C.16

DrawApp.java

```
import javax.swing.*;
import java.util.*;
import java.awt.*;
import java.awt.event.*;

/** Simple Drawing Application. This program draws selected
    figures. The list of available figures is provided as a command-line
    argument. The figure to be drawn is selected via a menu or a
    toolbar button. The interior and border colors are selected by
    a menu choice.
*/
public class DrawApp extends JFrame {

    // Data Fields
    /** Currently selected figure kind to be drawn. */
    private Drawable selectedFig = null;
    /** Currently selected border color. */
    private Color currentBorderColor = Color.BLACK;
    /** Currently selected interior color. */
    private Color currentInteriorColor = Color.WHITE;
    /** Array of figure prototypes. */
    private Drawable[] theFigKinds;

    // Constructor
    /** Construct a DrawApp object.
        @param args An array of strings containing Drawable class
        names.
    */
    private DrawApp(String args[]) {
        // Set title.
        super("Draw App");
        // Set frame size.
        setSize(750, 750);
        // Set default close operation.
        setDefaultCloseOperation(JFrame.EXIT_ON_CLOSE);
        // Load the figure kinds.
        loadFigKinds(args);
```

```
        // Create drawingToolMenu.
        JMenu drawingToolMenu = createDrawingToolMenu();
        // Create drawingToolToolBar.
        JToolBar drawingToolToolBar = createDrawingToolToolBar();
        selectedFig = theFigKinds[0];
        // Create the color choice menu.
        JMenu colorMenu = createColorMenu();
        // Create a menu bar to hold the menu.
        JMenuBar menuBar = new JMenuBar();
        menuBar.add(colorMenu);
        menuBar.add(drawingToolMenu);
        // Set the menu bar in the frame.
        setJMenuBar(menuBar);
        // Add the toolbar to the frame.
        getContentPane().add(drawingToolToolBar, BorderLayout.EAST);
        // Add the DrawPanel to the frame.
        getContentPane().add(new DrawPanel(this),
                             BorderLayout.CENTER);
    }

    /** Load and instantiate the figure prototypes based on the names
        of the Drawable classes listed in the command-line argument.
        @param args An array of strings containing Drawable class
               names
    */
    // Insert loadFigKinds here.

    /** Method to create the drawing tool menu. This method loops
        through array theFigKinds and creates a menu item for each
        entry. It then creates an action listener that will select
        this figure when the actionPerformed method is called.
        @return A reference to the JMenu object that is created
    */
    private JMenu createDrawingToolMenu() {
        JMenu drawingToolMenu = new JMenu("Drawing Tool");
        for (int i = 0; i < theFigKinds.length; i++) {
            // Create a menu item for this figure kind.
            JMenuItem item = new JMenuItem(theFigKinds[i].getName());
            // Set the action listener.
            item.addActionListener(new ToolSelector(theFigKinds[i]));
            // Add the item to the menu.
            drawingToolMenu.add(item);
        }
        return drawingToolMenu;
    }

    /** Method to create the toolbar. This method loops through
        array theFigKinds and creates a button for each entry, using that
        figure kind to construct an icon. It then creates an action
        listener that will select this figure when the actionPerformed
        method is called.
        @return A reference to the JToolBar object that is created
```

```
     */
     JToolBar createDrawingToolToolBar() {
          JToolBar drawingToolToolBar = new JToolBar(JToolBar.VERTICAL);
          for (int i = 0; i < theFigKinds.length; i++) {
               JButton aButton = new JButton(theFigKinds[i].getIcon(16));
               aButton.addActionListener
                    (new ToolSelector(theFigKinds[i]));
               drawingToolToolBar.add(aButton);
          }
          return drawingToolToolBar;
     }

     /** Method to create the color menu. The menu will contain two
          commands: Set Interior Color and Set Border Color. For each
          command a JColorChooser dialog is displayed, and the user's
          choice is saved in the appropriate attribute for each of the
          figures in array theFigKinds.
          @return A reference to the JMenu object that is created
     */
     private JMenu createColorMenu() {
          JMenu colorMenu = new JMenu("Colors");
          JMenuItem setInteriorColor =
               new JMenuItem("Set Interior Color");
          setInteriorColor.addActionListener(new SetInteriorColor());
          colorMenu.add(setInteriorColor);
          JMenuItem setBorderColor = new JMenuItem("Set Border Color");
          setBorderColor.addActionListener(new SetBorderColor());
          colorMenu.add(setBorderColor);
          return colorMenu;
     }

     /** Access the currently selected figure.
          @return The currently selected figure
     */
     public Drawable getSelectedFig() {
          return selectedFig;
     }

     /** Main method. This method instantiates a DrawApp object
          and shows it.
          @param args An array of Drawable class names
     */
     public static void main(String args[]) {
          DrawApp drawApp = new DrawApp(args);
          drawApp.setVisible(true);
     }

     // Inner Classes
     /** Common ActionListener for the figures menu and the
          figures toolbar.
     */
     private class ToolSelector implements ActionListener {
```

```
        // Data Fields
        /** Figure prototype to be selected when this action
            listener is fired. */
        private Drawable desiredFig;

        // Constructor
        /** Construct a ToolSelector object with the specified
            figure prototype.
            @param desiredFig The figure prototype to be selected
        */
        public ToolSelector(Drawable desiredFig) {
            this.desiredFig = desiredFig;
        }

        // Methods
        /** Set the selected figure to the desired figure when
            the action is performed.
            @param e Not used
        */
        public void actionPerformed(ActionEvent e) {
            selectedFig = desiredFig;
        }
    }

    /** ActionListener class for the Set Interior Color command. */
    private class SetInteriorColor implements ActionListener {
        /** Method actionPerformed displays the color chooser
            dialog and then sets the interior color of each of the
            figure prototypes. The display is then repainted
            @param e - Not used
        */
        public void actionPerformed(ActionEvent e) {
            currentInteriorColor =
                JColorChooser.showDialog(DrawApp.this,
                                         "Select Interior Color",
                                         currentInteriorColor);
            for (int i = 0; i < theFigKinds.length; i++) {
                theFigKinds[i].setInteriorColor
                    (currentInteriorColor);
            }
            repaint();
        }
    }

    /** ActionListener class for the Set Border Color command */
    // Insert setBorderColor similar to setInteriorColor

}
```

EXERCISES FOR SECTION C.6

SELF-CHECK

1. Why must we extend the abstract class `Drawable` to include the methods `getName`, `getMnemonic`, `getShortcut`, and `getIcon`?
2. Why must we extend the abstract class `Drawable` to include the methods `getWidth` and `getHeight`?

PROGRAMMING

1. Code the methods `getWidth`, `getHeight`, `getName`, `getMnemonic`, `getShortCut`, and `getIcon` for the `DrawableShape` classes.
2. Code method `loadFigKinds`.
3. Code method `setBorderColor`.

C.7 Processing Mouse Events

A commonly used input device for GUI applications is the mouse. We have seen how clicking a button on the screen triggers the `ActionListener` associated with that button. All of these examples have involved mouse-clicked events, but there are other possible mouse events. These are listed in Table C.15. Because Java is designed to be platform independent, there are no specific events for the different buttons on a two- or three-button mouse. The mouse button that caused the event is obtained from the `getButton` method of the `MouseEvent` and may have the value `BUTTON1`, `BUTTON2`, or `BUTTON3`. Table C.16 shows the methods defined in the `MouseEvent` class.

TABLE C.15
Mouse Events

Mouse Event	Cause
`MOUSE_CLICKED`	A mouse button is pressed and released.
`MOUSE_PRESSED`	A mouse button is pressed.
`MOUSE_RELEASED`	A mouse button is released.
`MOUSE_MOVED`	The mouse position has changed.
`MOUSE_DRAGGED`	The mouse position has changed while a button is pressed.
`MOUSE_ENTERED`	The mouse cursor enters the visible part of the component's geometry. If one component is on top of another, then only the top component receives the event.
`MOUSE_EXITED`	The mouse cursor exits the visible part of the component's geometry.

TABLE C.16
MouseEvent Class (Selected Methods)

Method	Behavior
`Point getPoint()`	Returns the x, y position of the event relative to the component that receives the event.
`int getButton()`	Returns which, if any, of the mouse buttons has changed state. Possible values are BUTTON1, BUTTON2, BUTTON3, or NOBUTTON.

Two interfaces are defined for event listeners for these events: `MouseMotionListener` (see Table C.17), which responds to the `MOUSE_MOVED` and `MOUSE_DRAGGED` events, and `MouseListener` (see Table C.18), which responds to all others. There is also the `MouseInputListener` interface, which combines these two (multiple inheritance is allowed for interfaces). All methods take as an argument the `MouseEvent` object that caused the method to be invoked.

TABLE C.17
`MouseMotionListener` Interface

Method	Behavior
`void mouseDragged(MouseEvent e)`	Invoked when the mouse is moved while a button is pressed.
`void mouseMoved(MouseEvent e)`	Invoked when the mouse is moved while no button is pressed.

TABLE C.18
`MouseListener` Interface

Method	Behavior
`void mouseClicked(MouseEvent e)`	Invoked when the mouse button has been clicked (pressed and released) on a component.
`void mouseEntered(MouseEvent e)`	Invoked when the mouse enters a component.
`void mouseExited(MouseEvent e)`	Invoked when the mouse exits a component.
`void mousePressed(MouseEvent e)`	Invoked when the mouse button is pressed.
`void mouseReleased(MouseEvent e)`	Invoked when the mouse button is released.

MouseAdapter and MouseMotionAdapter

The `MouseAdapter` and `MouseMotionAdapter` classes are abstract classes that facilitate writing mouse listeners. They implement the `MouseListener` and `MouseMotionListener` interfaces by providing required methods that do nothing. The user can then extend these classes by overriding only those methods for mouse events that are being used by the application, instead of having to implement all of the methods specified in the interfaces.

CASE STUDY A Drawing Application (continued)

Problem In Section C.6 we introduced an application that will let us draw different shapes of different sizes. We specified how the shape to be drawn and its color were determined. However, we did not specify how to draw the figures themselves.

We will specify the origin of the selected figure by pressing the mouse button at the desired point. Then, as the mouse is dragged, the shape outline should expand by following the current mouse position. When the mouse button is released, the shape should be filled with the selected interior color and permanently placed on the drawing canvas.

Analysis We will need to respond to the `MOUSE_PRESSED`, `MOUSE_DRAGGED`, and `MOUSE_RELEASED` events. We will also need a method to draw the shape outline continuously to represent the current mouse position. This is known as *rubber banding* because the shape seems to stretch like a rubber band. (See Figure C.29.)

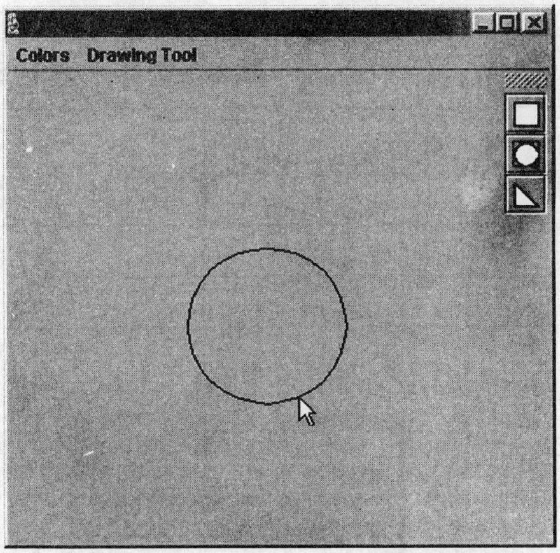

FIGURE C.29
Example of Rubber Banding

As the mouse is dragged, we need to erase the previously drawn shape outline, calculate the new size, and then draw a new outline. To support this, the `Graphics` class has a special mode known as *exclusive or* (XOR). When an image is drawn in XOR mode, it is drawn in such a way that if it is drawn again, the old image is erased and the original canvas is restored.

Design To provide a container for the `DrawableFigures` and to respond to the mouse events, we create a class `DrawPanel` as an extension to `JPanel`. This class has data fields and methods shown in Table C.19.

TABLE C.19
Design of the DrawPanel Class

Data Field	Contents
`DrawApp parent`	A reference to the parent `DrawApp` so that the method `getSelectedFig` can be accessed.
`Drawable[] figsList`	The array of figures that have been drawn.
`int numFigs`	The number of figures that have been drawn.
`Drawable currentFig`	The figure currently being drawn or **`null`**.
Constructor	**Behavior**
`DrawPanel(DrawApp p)`	Registers the `MouseListener` and `MouseMotionListener`.
Method	**Behavior**
`void paintComponent(Graphics g)`	Paints all of the figures in the `figsList`.

FIGURE C.30
Sequence Diagram for Adding a New Figure

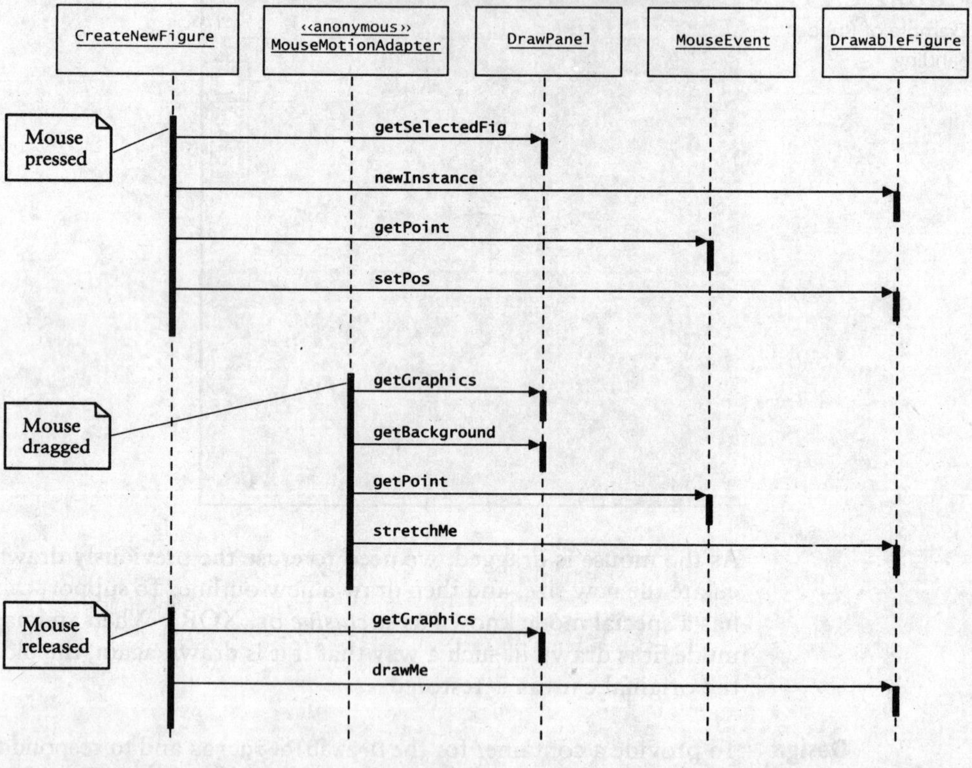

Figure C.30 shows the sequence diagram for the process of adding a new figure. The mouse pressed event is passed to the `CreateNewFigure` object. The class

CreateNewFigure is an extension of the AbstractMouseListener and is registered as the mouse listener for the DrawPanel. It then obtains the selected figure from the DrawPanel using the getSelectedFig method. Next it gets a new instance of the selected figure by calling the newInstance method. The new figure is positioned at the current mouse position by passing the result of the MouseEvent.getPoint method to the new figure's setPos method.

As the mouse is dragged, the mouseDragged method of an anonymous MouseMotionListener is called. This method gets the current graphics context and current background color from the DrawPanel via the getGraphics and getBackground methods. It then gets the current mouse position using the MouseEvent.getPoint method. These values are then passed to the figure's stretchMe method.

When the mouse is released, the figure is added to the figure list, and it is permanently drawn using the drawMe method.

The stretchMe Method

To facilitate rubber banding, we add method stretchMe to the DrawableShape class and its subclasses. This method sets the paint mode to XOR and performs the following steps:

Algorithm for stretchMe Method

1. If the outline was previously drawn in XOR mode, draw the current figure's outline in XOR mode. This erases the old figure.
2. Set the size based on the new mouse position.
3. Draw the outline in XOR mode.
4. Set a flag to indicate that the figure's outline has been drawn.

Implementation The code for the stretchMe method of the DrawableCircle class follows. This method is called by the MouseMotionListener.mouseDragged method whenever the mouse position changes. The code for this method first sets the drawing color to the figure's borderColor and then sets the drawing mode to XOR using the provided background color. If an outline was previously drawn, it is redrawn so that the previous version is erased. Then the new radius is calculated based on the figure's center and current mouse position. Then the figure's outline is drawn in XOR mode.

```
public void stretchMe(Graphics g, Point stretchPoint,
                      Color background) {
    g.setColor(drawable.borderColor);
    g.setXORMode(background);
    if (drawable.stretchableOutlineDrawn) {
        g.drawOval(drawable.pos.x - circle.radius,
                   drawable.pos.y - circle.radius,
                   2 * circle.radius,
                   2 * circle.radius);
    }
```

```
    double deltaX = drawable.pos.x - stretchPoint.x;
    double deltaY = drawable.pos.y - stretchPoint.y;
    circle.radius = (int) Math.sqrt(deltaX * deltaX
                                  + deltaY * deltaY);
    g.drawOval(drawable.pos.x - circle.radius,
               drawable.pos.y - circle.radius,
               2 * circle.radius,
               2 * circle.radius);
    drawable.stretchableOutlineDrawn = true;
    g.setPaintMode();
}
```

The code for the `stretchMe` methods of other figure kinds is left as an exercise. There is one complication, however. If the mouse is moved to the left of or above its starting position, the resulting width or height is negative. In this case the origin `x` or `y` coordinate must be set to the mouse position coordinate and the sign of the width or height reversed.

Listing C.17 shows the code for the `DrawPanel` class. The mouse event listeners do most of the work. The class `CreateNewFigure` is an extension of the `MouseAdapter`. This class overrides the methods `mousePressed` and `mouseReleased`.

The current `Graphics` object and `background` color for the `DrawPanel` are obtained by the `getGraphics` and `getBackground` methods of `JComponent`. These are callable from the `MouseMotionListener` because it is nested within the `DrawPanel` class.

When the mouse button is pressed (responded to by method `CreateNewFigure.mousePressed`), a copy of the selected figure is created by calling the figure's `newInstance` method, and the figure's origin (position of the mouse click) is saved with the new figure in data field `currentFig`:

```
currentFig = parent.getSelectedFig().newInstance();
currentFig.setPoint(e.getPoint());
```

When the mouse button is released (responded to by method `CreateNewFigure.mouseReleased`), the `currentFig` is added to the `figsList`, and the `drawMe` method is invoked to draw it.

```
figsList[numFigs++] = currentFig;
currentFig.drawMe(getGraphics());
```

We register the mouse motion listener using the following code:

```
addMouseMotionListener(new MouseMotionAdapter() {
    public void mouseDragged(MouseEvent e) {
        if (currentFig != null) {
            currentFig.stretchMe(getGraphics(),
                                 e.getPoint(),
                                 getBackground());
        }
    }
});
```

This is an example of using an anonymous inner class as an event listener. This syntax is discussed below. When the mouse is dragged, the listener object created by this code is invoked and the `currentFig`'s `stretchMe` method is called.

Whenever the window is resized or moved, the `paintComponent` method is called (by Swing). This method first calls its parent `paintComponent` to repaint the background and then loops through the `figsList` and paints each figure by calling its `drawMe` method.

Testing Figure C.31 shows an example of the `DrawApp` with several different figures drawn.

PITFALL

Forgetting to Call super.paintComponent

The first statement of `paintComponent` should always be

```
super.paintComponent(g);
```

This results in the component's background being drawn and, as a side effect, what was previously drawn is erased. If you forget to do it, the results can be quite surprising.

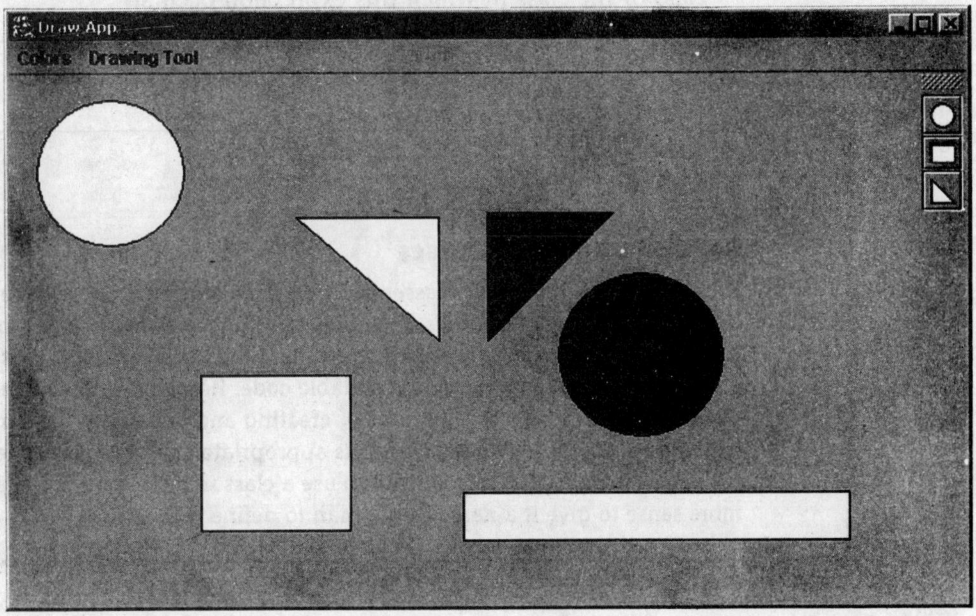

FIGURE C.31
Sample Run of DrawApp

SYNTAX Anonymous Classes

FORM

new *Base*() {*class body*}

EXAMPLE

```
new ActionListener() {
    ActionPerformed(ActionEvent e) {
        theCircle.toggleState();
    }
}
```

We can then use this expression in a statement to register an action listener as follows:

```
onOffButton.addActionListener(new ActionListener() {
    public void actionPerformed(ActionEvent e) {
        theCircle.toggleState();
    }
});
```

INTERPRETATION

An anonymous class that is either an implementation of *Base* (if *Base* is an interface) or an extension of *Base* is created with the methods defined in the class body implementing or overriding the corresponding methods in *Base*. Then an instance of this class is created. The class that is created is an inner class of the class in which this expression occurs.

PROGRAM STYLE

Use of Anonymous Classes

The syntax for anonymous classes can be quite confusing, so we have avoided it so far in the text. However, its use is quite common in Java event-oriented programs. Its proponents say that placing the code for an action listener right where it is registered to the component leads to more understandable code. However, if the processing is several lines of code long, the overall logic of creating and laying out the components can be lost. Thus, using anonymous classes is appropriate only for event listeners that require a few lines of code. Also, if you need to use a class in more than one place, it would make more sense to give it a name rather than to define it each time.

LISTING C.17
DrawPanel.java

```
import java.awt.*;
import java.awt.event.*;
import javax.swing.*;
import java.util.*;

/** The DrawPanel is the canvas on which the figures are drawn. */
public class DrawPanel extends JPanel {

    /** The maximum number of figures */
    private static final int MAX_FIG = 25;
    /** The list of figures */
    private Drawable[] figsList = new Drawable[MAX_FIG];
    /** The number of figures that have been drawn */
    private int numFigs = 0;
    /** Currently selected figure prototype */
    private Drawable currentFig = null;
    /** Reference to parent frame to access selectedFigure */
    private DrawApp parent;

    /** Construct a DrawPanel object. The constructor registers
        the mouse listeners.
        @param p Reference to parent DrawApp
    */
    public DrawPanel(DrawApp p) {
        // Save reference to parent.
        parent = p;
        // Add the mouse listeners.
        addMouseListener(new CreateNewFigure());
        addMouseMotionListener (new MouseMotionAdapter() {
                public void mouseDragged(MouseEvent e) {
                    if (currentFig != null) {
                        currentFig.stretchMe(getGraphics(),
                                             e.getPoint(),
                                             getBackground());
                    }
                }
        });
    }

    /** Method to paint the component. This method is called
        by Swing and should not be called directly.
        @param g The graphics object to do the painting
```

```
    */
    public void paintComponent(Graphics g) {
        // Always call super.paintComponent first.
        super.paintComponent(g);
        // Draw the figures.
        for (int i = 0; i < numFigs; i++) {
            figsList[i].drawMe(g);
        }
    }

    // Inner Class
    /** Class to create a new figure when the mouse button is pressed
        and released. */
    private class CreateNewFigure extends MouseAdapter {
        /** When the mouse is pressed and the figures array
            is not full, a new figure is created
            with its orgin at the current point.
            @param e MouseEvent
        */
        public void mousePressed(MouseEvent e) {
            if (parent.getSelectedFig() != null && numFigs < MAX_FIG) {
                currentFig =
                    parent.getSelectedFig().newInstance();
                currentFig.setPoint(e.getPoint());
            } else {
                currentFig = null;
            }
        }

        /** When the mouse is released, the current figure is
            redrawn as a final figure by calling its drawMe method.
            @param e MouseEvent
        */
        public void mouseReleased(MouseEvent e) {
            if (currentFig != null) {
                figsList[numFigs++] = currentFig;
                currentFig.drawMe(getGraphics());
                currentFig = null;
            } else {
                JOptionPane.showMessageDialog
                    (null, "Sorry too many figures");
            }
        }
    }
}
```

EXERCISES FOR SECTION C.7

PROGRAMMING

1. Code the `stretchMe` method for the `DrawableShape` classes.
2. Add a new figure, the rhombus (diamond), as shown, to the set of `DrawableShapes`.

3. Create an anonymous listener class for class `ComboBoxDemo` shown in Listing C.11.

Appendix Review

- In event-oriented programming the computer responds to the actions of the user or other external events. This is distinguished from the action-response mode of interacting with a program, in which the user responds to requests (prompts) from the computer. Event-oriented programming allows for much more complicated interactions between the computer and user and for simultaneous response to multiple users and other interfacing systems.
- An event is an occurrence that is initiated either by the user or by an external system or program. An event may also be internally initiated by another event. In event-oriented programming, the program responds to events. You write methods to respond to events that are encapsulated into classes that implement a listener interface that is specific to the event type. Objects of these classes are known as event listeners, and event listeners are registered with the component that recognizes the occurrence of the event. For example, a Swing `JButton` object recognizes that the mouse is clicked while the cursor is inside the `JButton`'s graphic representation. The `JButton` object will then call the `actionPerformed` method of any `ActionListener` objects that have registered with the `JButton` object.
- Event-oriented programming is used for coding graphical user interfaces (GUIs). Events are triggered by the motion of the mouse, the pressing of mouse buttons, and the pressing of keyboard keys.
- Java has an extensive framework of GUI components in the AWT and Swing packages. The AWT package was part of the original Java release, and Swing represents an extension of this framework. A GUI component is an object that has a graphical representation on the screen and that interacts with the user. Components that can contain other components are called containers.

- The `JFrame` is the Swing top-level container that is used to build GUI applications. The `JPanel` is a general-purpose container that can be used to group other components. The `Graphics` class provides the methods to create the displayed image on the screen or on another graphics device. The `Graphics` class has both a paint mode, in which image elements (pixels) are set permanently on the display canvas, and an XOR mode, in which image elements are set in such a way that if they are redrawn, the image is erased.
- A `LayoutManager` arranges the components in a container for display on the screen. Java provides several layout managers, including Border Layout, Flow Layout, Box Layout, and Grid Layout.
- Java components for interacting with the user include check boxes, radio buttons, and combo boxes for selecting from a set of choices, and text fields and text areas for entry and display of text.
- The `Locale` class encapsulates different language and cultural variations. The `NumberFormat` class enables formatting of numbers as ordinary numbers, currency, or percentages in accordance with the conventions of the default locale. A `Locale` for other languages and countries can be created and used to initialize the `NumberFormat` for that language and culture.
- You can also issue commands to a GUI application through menus and toolbars. Menu selections can have a shortcut or accelerator key associated with them, so that the command can be activated without the menu being displayed. Menu selections can also have a mnemonic, a key that will activate the menu selection when the menu is displayed. Both menu selections and toolbar buttons may have icons associated with them. An icon is a small picture that is representative of the action being selected.
- Whenever the cursor that is driven by the mouse is displayed in a portion of a component, one or more mouse events are triggered. Mouse events include the mouse entering a component, leaving a component, moving inside a component, and the mouse button pressed, released, or clicked (pressed and released quickly).

Java API Classes Introduced in This Appendix

```
java.awt.event.ActionEvent
java.awt.event.ActionListener
java.awt.event.KeyEvent
java.awt.event.MouseAdapter
java.awt.event.MouseEvent
java.awt.event.MouseListener
java.awt.event.MouseMotionAdapter
java.awt.event.MouseMotionListener
java.awt.event.WindowAdapter
java.awt.Graphics
java.text.NumberFormat
java.util.EventListener
java.util.Lacale
Javax.swing.ButtonGroup
javax.swing.Icon
javax.swing.ImageIcon
javax.swing.JButton
javax.swing.JColorChooser
javax.swing.JFrame
javax.swing.JMenu
javax.swing.JMenuBar
javax.swing.JMenuItem
javax.swing.JPanel
javax.swing.JRadioButton
javax.swing.JTextArea
javax.swing.JTextField
javax.swing.JToolBar
```

User-Defined Interfaces and Classes in This Appendix

BorderLayoutDemo
BuildBoxLayout
CheckBoxDemo
CirclePanel
ComboBoxDemo
CurrencyDemo
DoLookupEntry
DrawableIcon
DrawApp
DrawPanel
FlowLayoutDemo
GridLayoutDemo
MyCircle
PDButtonUI
RadioButtonDemo
TextFieldDemo
TwoCircles
VolumeConverter
VolumeConverterGUI

Quick-Check Exercises

1. How does the event-oriented model differ from the query-response model?
2. When a GUI button is pressed, an ________ object is fired, which invokes its ________ method, passing the ________ object as an argument.
3. The method ________ is used to register an `ActionListener` for an ________.
4. Can more than one ratio button be selected at a time? If yes, how is this done?
5. What does the grid layout do?
6. What are the names of the areas in the border layout?
7. How do you combine layouts?
8. How is the number ten thousand formatted in the United States? In Germany?
9. How do you specify that you want only two fractional digits in the display of a number?
10. The ________ responds to events generated by the movement of the mouse, and the ________ responds to other mouse events.

Review Questions

1. Write an action listener class that will increment the variables `count1` and `count2` when buttons `button1` and `button2` are clicked, respectively.
2. Assume `button1` and `button2` are variables of type `JButton`. Write statements to register action listeners for them.
3. Assume that you have an array of type `JRadioButton[]`. Write a loop that adds each radio button to a `JPanel` and a `ButtonGroup` and register an action listener for each button.
4. Write code to create a grid of buttons that represents a calculator. Provide the 10 digits, the decimal point, and the operations +, –, ×, ÷, C, and CE.
5. Write code to create a `JPanel` that contains a `JTextField` at the top and a set of radio buttons at the bottom.
6. Write code that contains a grid of `JPanel`s, all gray. When the mouse enters a panel, change its color to green, and when it leaves, reset the color to gray.

Programming Projects

1. Modify `PDButtonUI` to make the changes discussed at the beginning of this appendix. Specifically:
   - Provide separate buttons for "Add Entry" and "Change Entry"

- Remove the buttons "Save Directory" and "Exit".
- The file should be automatically saved whenever the window is closed.

2. Write a program that is a simple calculator that contains a `JTextField` and a grid of buttons. Provide the 10 digits, the decimal point, and the operations +, −, ×, ÷, C, and CE. C will completely reset the calculator, and CE will reset the current entry. Clicking one of the arithmetic operators will perform the selected operation, using the currently displayed value as the right-hand operand and the previously displayed value as the left-hand operand, and then display the result. When a number or the decimal point key is pressed after an operator key or C is pressed, the currently displayed value will be saved to become the left-hand operand, and the value associated with this key will be displayed. Additional numbers (and decimal point) will be entered to the right of the display. The decimal point may be entered only once. Pressing CE will clear the display, but the saved value will be retained.
3. Write a GUI program to convert between dollars and euros. The program should allow the amount to be specified either in dollars per euro or euros per dollar using radio buttons. The user enters the amount to be converted in a text field. The converted currency should be displayed in a second text field in the format appropriate for the locale: dollars in the U.S. locale, and euros in a European locale such as Germany.
4. Write a program to convert the price of fuel expressed in dollars per gallon to euros per liter. The currency conversion factor should be expressed either in dollars per euro or euros per dollar. Use a text field to input the price of fuel.
5. Write a program to illustrate the Towers of Hanoi game. The Towers of Hanoi consists of a board with three pegs. At the beginning of the game, a set of rings ranging from the largest on the bottom to the smallest on the top is on one of the pegs, as shown in Figure C.32. As the game is played, rings are moved from peg to peg, but the rings on each peg are always in order of size, with the smallest on top and the largest on the bottom. This program does not have to play the game; it just has to illustrate the board. Your program should have a menu command that lets the user select the number of rings. The display should fit within the frame, as shown in Figure C.32. Whenever the frame is resized, the board should be resized and redrawn.

FIGURE C.32
Design of the Towers of Hanoi Board

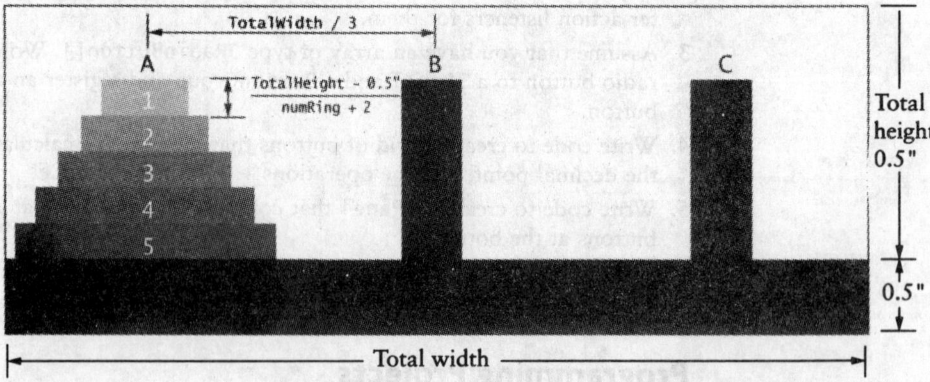

6. Write a GUI that you could use in a hotel room to order breakfast. Each item description and price appears as a label alongside a check box. You will select each item you want to order by setting its check box. When you are done, click the submit button, and the items you selected should be listed in a text area along with the total cost.
7. Write a GUI that could be used by a Web-based company to receive billing information. Use a set of radio buttons to enter the person's title (Mr., Ms., Dr.), a text box for name, a text field for the street address, a text field for city, a text field for ZIP code, a combo box for state, a combo box for the user's credit card type, a text field for the credit card number, a combo box for expiration month, and a combo box for expiration year. After the user clicks a Submit button, if some information is missing, display in a text area the names of any fields that are not set. Otherwise, display a summary of the information that was entered in the text area.
8. Write a GUI that could be used with the `Media` hierarchy project in Chapter 1 (Project 5). Use a combo box to select the operation that the user wishes to perform: add an item, retrieve an item's stored information given its title, display all items for a particular artist, display all items for a particular kind of media. When adding an item, use a set of radio buttons to designate its type and use check boxes and text fields to enter other kinds of information.
9. Redo Project 7 using a menu for the different user choices. Based on the user's choice, display an appropriate GUI in a panel. For example, if the user selects "Add an Item" from the menu, the GUI should allow the user to enter the desired information using radio buttons, check boxes, text fields, and other such components. If the user selects "Retrieve an Item", the GUI displayed should have a text field in which the user can enter the title, and it should have a text area for displaying the information retrieved.

Answers to Quick-Check Exercises

1. In the event-oriented model, the program responds to external events generated by the user. In the query-response model, the program prompts the user for inputs.
2. `ActionEvent`, `actionPerformed`, `ActionEvent`
3. `addActionListener`, `ActionEvent`
4. Yes; they must be placed within different `ButtonGroups`. Buttons in the same `ButtonGroup` are mutually exclusive.
5. It arranges components in a rectangular grid with a specified number of rows and columns.
6. `NORTH`, `SOUTH`, `EAST`, `WEST`, and `CENTER`.
7. You can combine layouts by creating `JPanel` objects, placing them into the frame's content pane using the top-level layout, and setting this layout using the desired layout manager. Each `JPanel` can then have its own layout manager assigned. If necessary, this can be repeated by placing `JPanels` within the `JPanels`.
8. In the United States: `10,000`. In Germany: `10.000`.
9. Create a `NumberFormat` object using the `getNumberInstance` method. Then apply method `setMaximumFractionDigits(2)` to the `NumberFormat` object. Finally, use the `NumberFormat` object's `format` method to format the number.
10. `MouseMotionListener`, `MouseListener`.

Appendix D

Testing and Debugging

Appendix Objectives

- To introduce testing using the JUnit Test Framework
- To illustrate how to use a debugger within a Java IDE
- To illustrate a data visualization tool

This appendix introduces and illustrates some testing and debugging techniques and tools that expand on the discussion of testing introduced in Section 2.10. We begin by describing the JUnit Test Framework, which has become a commonly used tool for creating and running unit tests. We then illustrate two tools to assist in isolating errors (commonly called *debugging*). The first tool is the debugger, which allows you to suspend the program execution at a specified point and examine the value of variables. The second tool is a data visualization tool that is valuable in understanding programs that manipulate data structures.

Testing and Debugging

D.1 Testing Using the JUnit Framework

The test driver for the ArraySearch class (see Section 2.10) showed the expected and actual results of each test and an indication of pass or fail. This test driver contained several test cases. A *test case* is an individual test. A collection of test cases is known as a *test suite*. A program that executes a series of tests and reports the results is known as a *test harness*. Thus the test driver for the ArraySearch class was both a test harness and a test suite.

A *test framework* is a software product that facilitates writing test cases, organizing the test cases into test suites, running the test suites, and reporting the results. One test framework often used for Java projects is JUnit, an open-source product that can be used in a stand-alone mode and is available from junit.org. It is also bundled with at least two popular IDEs (NetBeans and Eclipse). Below we show a test suite for the ArraySearch class constructed using the JUnit framework.

```
import org.junit.Test;
import static org.junit.Assert.*;

/**
 *
 * @author Paul Wolfgang
 */
public class ArraySearchTest {

    private int[] x = {5, 12, 15, 4, 8, 12, 7};          // Array to search.
```

We then write a series of test cases by writing methods each of which is preceded by the annotation @Test. Annotations are directions to the compiler and other language-processing tools; they do not affect the execution of the program. The JUnit main method (called the *test runner*) searches the classes on the classpath for methods with the @Test annotation and then executes them and keeps track of the pass/fail results.

The following is the test to see if the target is in the first item in the array:

```
@Test
public void firstElementTest() {
   // Test for target as first element.
   assertEquals(0, ArraySearch.search(x, 5));
}
```

The method assertEquals will report an error if its arguments are not equal, indicating that the results of search are not as expected. The various assert*Xxxxx* methods are specific to JUnit. Table D.1 shows some of the methods defined in the org.junit.Assert class.

Listing D.1 shows a complete test suite for ArraySearch.search with eight test cases. Figure D.1 shows the results of running this test suite under the control of the test harness that is integrated with NetBeans. It shows that all of the test cases passed. The number next to the "passed" indicates how long the test took to execute. If any of them had failed, there would have been an indication of which test failed and the line number of the assert*Xxxxx* method call that failed.

TABLE D.1
Methods Defined in `org.junit.Assert`

Method	Parameters	Description
`assertArrayEquals`	*[message,] expected, actual*	Tests to see if the contents of the two array parameters *expected* and *actual* are equal. This method is overloaded for arrays of the primitive types and `Object`. Arrays of `Objects` are tested with the `.equals` method applied to the corresponding elements. If an unequal pair is found, an `AssertionError` is thrown. If the optional message is included, the `AssertionError` is thrown with this message; otherwise the `AssertionError` message identified the discrepancy.
`assertEquals`	*[message,] expected, actual*	Tests to see if *expected* and *actual* are equal. This method is overloaded for the primitive types and `Object`. To test `Objects`, the `.equals` method is used.
`assertFalse`	*[message,] condition*	Tests to see if the `boolean` expression *condition* is false.
`assertNotNull`	*[message,] object*	Tests to see if the *object* is not `null`.
`assertNotSame`	*[message,] expected, actual*	Tests to see if *expected* and *actual* are not the same object. (Applies the != operator).
`assertNull`	*[message,] object*	Tests to see if the *object* is `null`.
`assertSame`	*[message,] expected, actual*	Tests to see if *expected* and *actual* are the same object. (Applies the == operator.)
`assertTrue`	*[message,] condition*	Tests to see if the `boolean` expression *condition* is true.
`fail`	*[message]*	Always throws `AssertionError`.

LISTING D.1
JUnit Test of `ArraySearch.search`

```
import org.junit.Test;
import static org.junit.Assert.*;

/**
 *
```

```
        @author Paul Wolfgang
    */

    public class ArraySearchTest {

        private int[] x = {5, 12, 15, 4, 8, 12, 7};   // Array to search.

        @Test
        public void firstElementTest() {
            // Test for target as first element.
            assertEquals(0, ArraySearch.search(x, 5));
        }

        @Test
        public void lastElementTest() {
            // Test for target as last element.
            assertEquals(6, ArraySearch.search(x, 7));
        }

        @Test
        public void notInArrayTest() {
            // Test for target not in array.
            assertEquals(-1, ArraySearch.search(x, -5));
        }

        @Test
        public void multipleOccurrencesTest() {
            // Test for multiple occurrences of target.
            assertEquals(1, ArraySearch.search(x, 12));
        }

        @Test
        public void inMiddleTest() {
            // Test for target somewhere in middle.
            assertEquals(3, ArraySearch.search(x, 4));
        }

        @Test
        public void oneElementArrayTest() {
            // Test for 1-element array
            int[] y = {10};
            assertEquals(0, ArraySearch.search(y, 10));
            assertEquals(-1, ArraySearch.search(y, -10));
        }

        @Test
        public void emptyArrayTest() {
            // Test for an empty array
            int[] y = new int[0];
            assertEquals(-1, ArraySearch.search(y, 10));
        }

        @Test(expected=NullPointerException.class)
        public void nullArrayTest() {
            int[] y = null;
            int i = ArraySearch.search(y, 10);
            fail();
        }
```

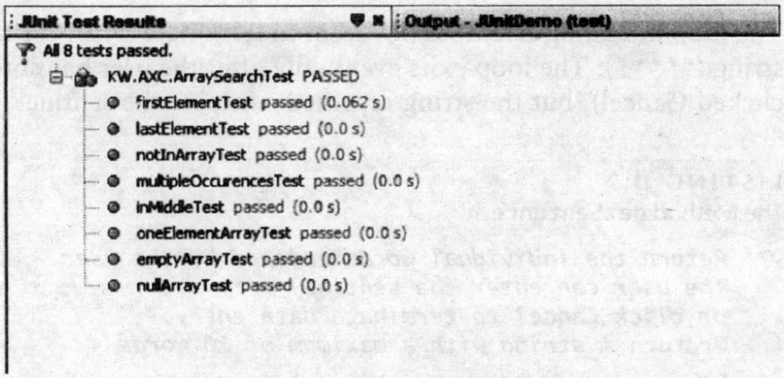

FIGURE D.1
JUnit Test of `ArraySearch.search`

The last test case in Listing D.1 differs from the others because it calls JUnit method `fail`, which causes it to throw an `AssertionException`. To tell JUnit that a test is expected to throw an exception, we added the parameter `expected=`*exception-class* to the `@Test` attribute. This parameter tells JUnit that the test should cause a `NullPointerException` (the result of calling `ArraySearch` with a `null` array). Without this parameter, JUnit would have indicated that the test case did not pass but caused an error instead.

```
@Test(expected=NullPointerException.class)
public void nullArrayTest() {
    int[] y = null;
    int i = ArraySearch.search(y, 10);
    fail();
}
```

D.2 Debugging a Program

In this section we will discuss the process of debugging (removing errors) both with and without the use of a debugger program. Debugging is the major activity performed by programmers during the testing phase. Testing determines whether you have an error; during debugging you determine the cause of run-time and logic errors and correct them, without introducing new ones. If you have followed the suggestions for testing described in the previous section, you will be well prepared to debug your program.

Debugging is like detective work. To debug a program, you must inspect carefully the information displayed by your program, starting at the beginning, to determine whether what you see is what you expect. For example, if the result returned by a method is incorrect but the arguments (if any) passed to the method had the correct values, then there is a problem inside the method. You can try to trace through the method to see whether you can find the source of the error and correct it. If you can't, you may need more information. One way to get that information is to insert additional diagnostic output statements in the method. For example, if the method contains a loop, you may want to display the values of loop control variables during loop execution.

EXAMPLE D.1 The loop in Listing D.2 does not seem to terminate when the user enters the sentinel string ("***"). The loop exits eventually after the user has entered 10 data items (or clicked Cancel), but the string returned contains the sentinel.

LISTING D.2

The Method getSentence

```
/** Return the individual words entered by the user.
    The user can enter the sentinel ***
    or click Cancel to terminate data entry.
    @return A string with a maximum of 10 words
*/
public static String getSentence() {
    String sentence = "";
    int count = 0;
    String word =
        JOptionPane.showInputDialog("Enter a word or *** to quit");
    while (word != "***" && word != null && count < 10) {
        // Append word to sentence.
        sentence = sentence + word + " ";
        count++;
        word =
            JOptionPane.showInputDialog("Enter a word or *** to quit");
    }
    return sentence;
}
```

To determine the source of the problem, you should insert a diagnostic output statement that displays the values of word and count to make sure that word is receiving the sentinel string ("***"). You could insert the line

```
System.out.println("!!! Next word is " + word + ", count is " + count);
```

as the first statement in the loop body. If the third data item you enter is the sentinel string, you will get the output line:

```
!!! next word is ***, count is 2
```

This will show you that word does indeed receive the sentinel string, but the loop body continues to execute. Therefore, there must be something wrong with the loop repetition condition. In fact, the loop header must be changed to

```
while (word != null && !word.equals("***") && count < 10) {
```

because word != "***" compares the address of the string stored in word with the address of the literal string "***", not the contents of the two strings as intended. The strings' addresses will always be different, even when their contents are the same. To compare their contents, the equals method must be used. Note that we needed to do the test word != null first because we would get a NullPointerException if equals was called when word was null.

Using a Debugger

If you are using an Integrated Development Environment (IDE), you will most likely have a debugger program as part of the IDE. A debugger can execute your program incrementally rather than all at once. After each increment of the program executes, the debugger pauses, and you can view the contents of variables to determine whether the statement(s) executed as expected. You can inspect all the program variables without needing to insert diagnostic output statements. When you have finished examining the program variables, you direct the debugger to execute the next increment.

You can choose to execute in increments as small as one program statement (called *single-step execution*) to see the effect of each statement's execution. Another possibility is to set breakpoints in your program to divide it into sections. The debugger can execute all the statements from one breakpoint to the next as a group. For example, if you wanted to see the effects of a loop's execution but did not want to step through every iteration, you could set breakpoints at the statements just before and just after the loop.

When your program pauses, if the next statement contains a call to a method, you can select single-step execution in the method being called (i.e., **step into** the method). Alternatively, you can execute all the method statements as a group and pause after the return from the method execution (i.e., **step over** the method).

The actual mechanics of using a debugger depends on the IDE that you are using. However, the process that you follow is similar among IDEs, and if you understand the process for one, you should be able to use any debugger. In this section we demonstrate how to use the debugger in NetBeans, the IDE that is distributed by Sun along with the Software Development Kit (SDK).

Figure D.2 is the display produced by this debugger at the beginning of debugging the `GetSentence` class. The source editor window displays the code to be debugged. The Debug pull-down menu shows the options for executing the code. The selected item, Step Into, is a common technique for starting single-step execution, as we have just described. A window (such as window Local Variables in the center left) typically shows the values of data fields and local variables. In this case there is one local variable for method `main`: the `String array args`, which is empty. The arrow to the left of the highlighted line in the source editor window indicates the next step to execute (the call to method `getSentence`). Select Step Into again to execute the individual statements of method `getSentence`.

Figure D.3 shows the editor and Local Variables windows after we have entered `"Hello"`, `"world"`, and `"***"`. The contents of `sentence` is `"Hello world"`, the value of `count` is 2, and the contents of `word` is `"***"`. The next statement to execute is highlighted. It is the loop header, which tests the loop repetition condition. Although we expect the condition to be false, it is true (why?), so the loop continues to execute and `"***"` will be appended to `sentence`.

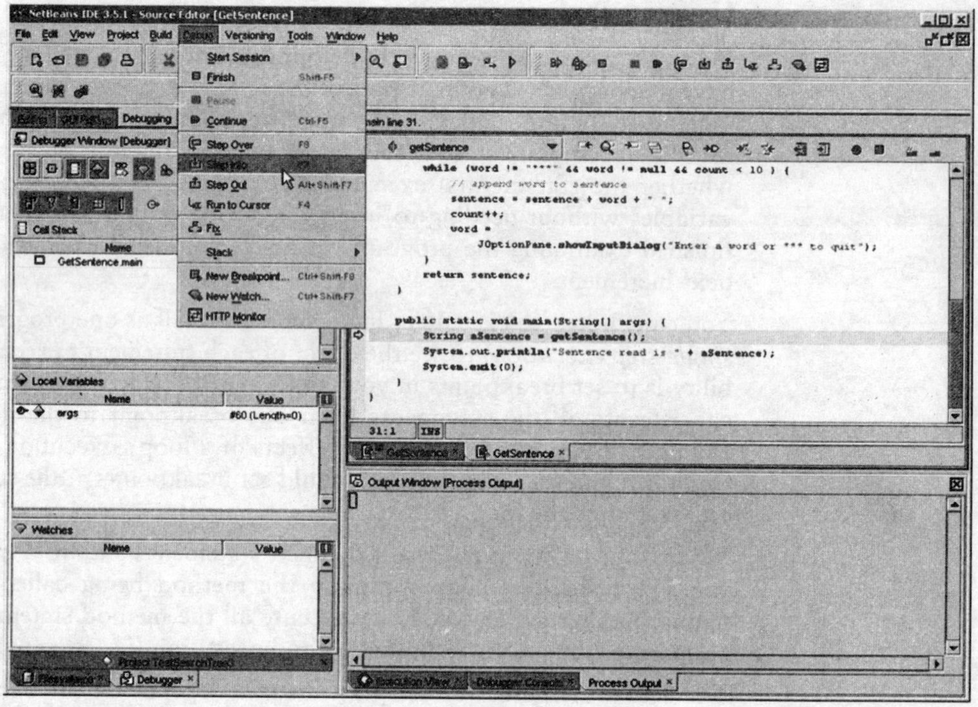

FIGURE D.2
Using the Debugger for NetBeans

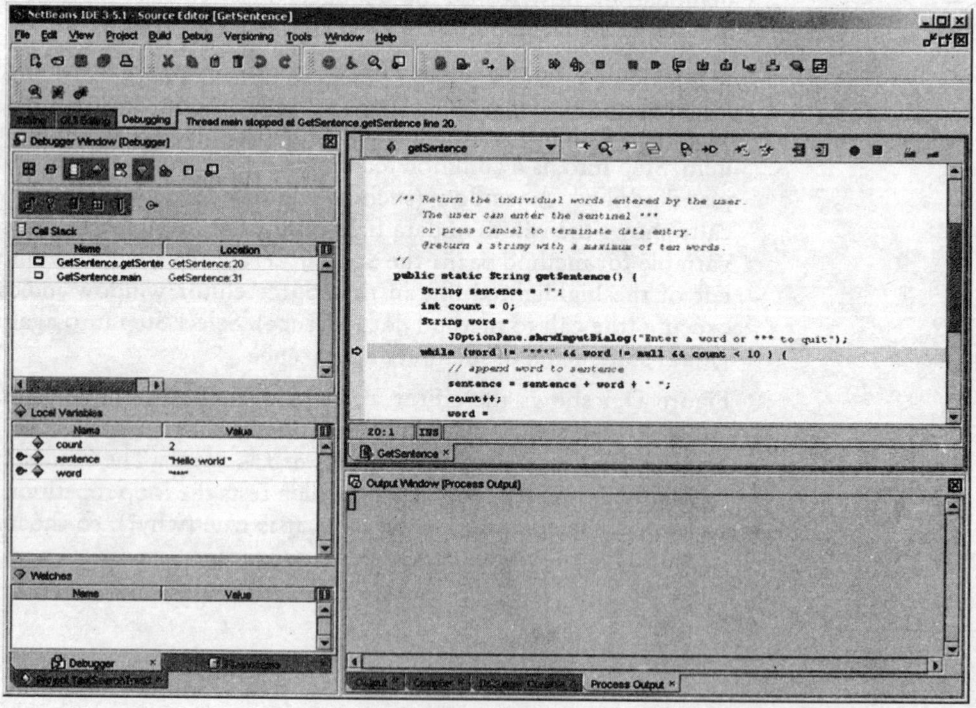

FIGURE D.3
Editor and Debugging Windows

Next we illustrate the use of breakpoints. Figure D.4 shows the Source Editor window with two breakpoints set before we begin execution: one at the loop header and one after the loop. In NetBeans you set a breakpoint by clicking in the vertical bar just to the left of the statement that you want to select as a breakpoint. The small squares and highlighted bars indicate the breakpoints. You can click again on a small square to remove the breakpoint. We selected Step Into and then Continue, so the program displayed a dialog window (where we entered "Hello") and paused at the first breakpoint (Figure D.5). If we select Continue again, the program will display another dialog window and then pause at the next breakpoint. In this case, it will pause again at the loop header. If we select Continue and click the Cancel button in the dialog window, the program will pause again at the loop header. If we select Continue again, the program will exit the loop and pause at the breakpoint following the loop.

FIGURE D.4
Two Breakpoints Selected

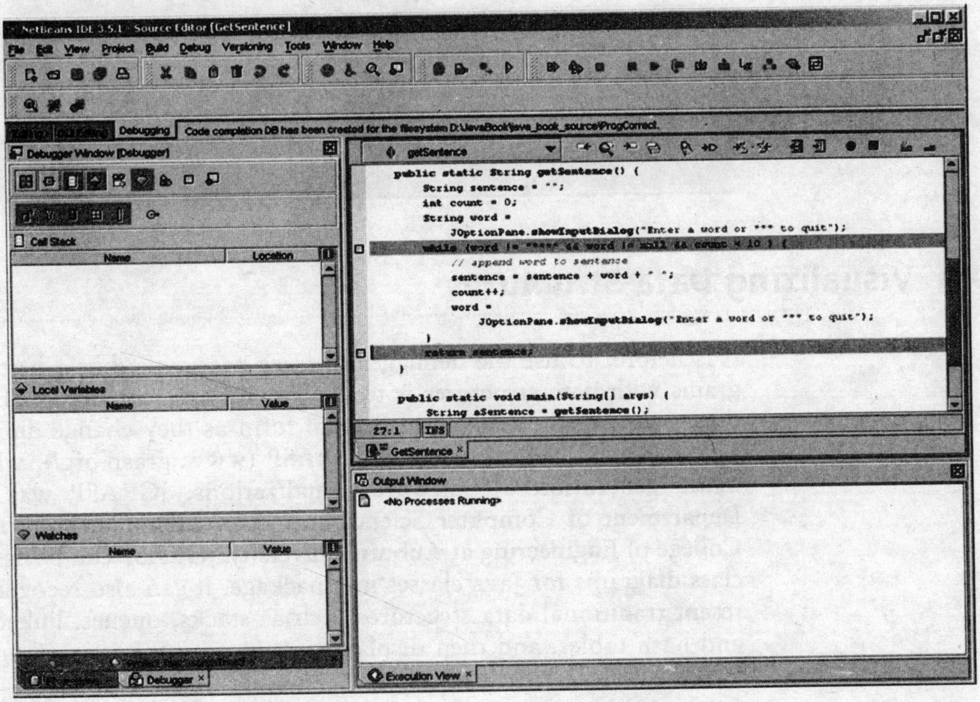

FIGURE D.5
Stop at Breakpoint

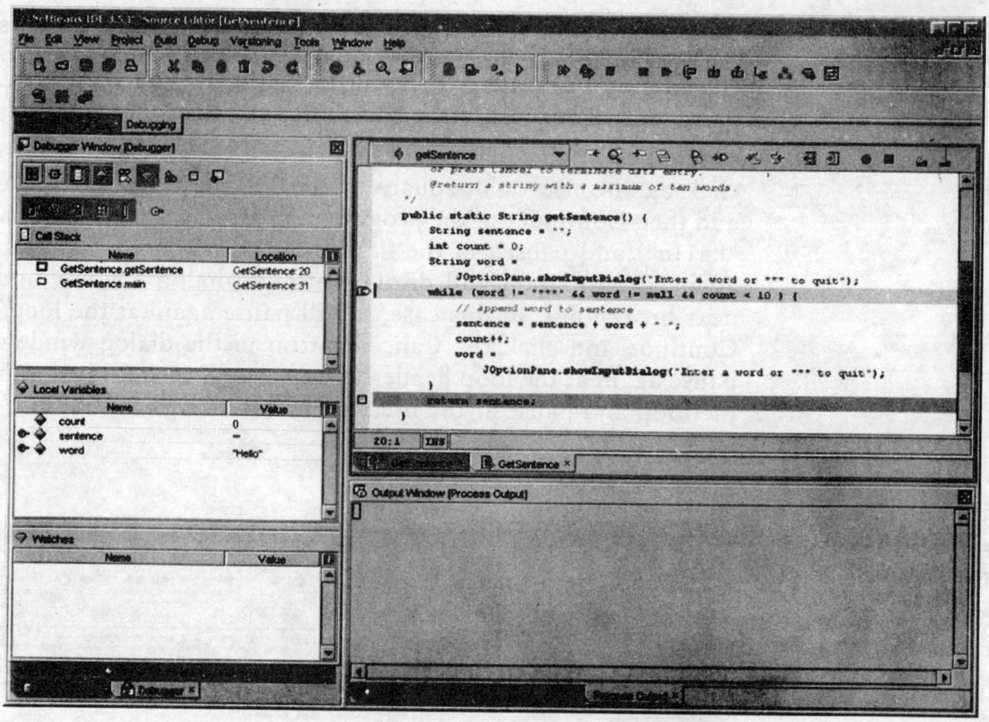

D.3 Visualizing Data Structures

It is helpful to use the debugger to trace programs, but a better solution for programs with data structures is to use an environment that enables you to visualize data structures in a two-dimensional form as they change during program execution. One such environment is jGRASP (www.jgrasp.org/), which provides automatic generation of software visualizations. jGRASP was developed by the Department of Computer Science and Software Engineering in the Samuel Ginn College of Engineering at Auburn University. jGRASP can be used to generate UML class diagrams for Java classes in a package. It can also recognize objects that represent traditional data structures such as stacks, queues, linked lists, binary trees, and hash tables, and then display them in an intuitive textbook-like presentation view.

As an illustration, consider the method `removeAfter` from the `SingleLinkedList` class shown in Section 2.5.

```
/** Remove the node after a given node
 * @param node The node before the one to be removed
 * @returns The data from the removed node, or null
 *          if there is no node to remove
 */
private E removeAfter(Node<E> node) {
  Node<E> temp = node.next;
  if (temp != null) {
    node.next = temp.next;
    size--;
    return temp.data;
  } else {
    return null;
  }
}
```

Figure D.6(a) shows the state just before the execution of the statement

```
node.next = temp.next;
```

It shows that `node` references the node `"tom"` and `temp` references `"dick"`, which is the node to be removed.

After the execution of this statement, the link from `"tom"` to `"dick"` is replaced by a link from `"tom"` to `"harry"`, and `temp` still references `"dick"` as shown in Figure D.6(b). We cannot show it in the book, but when the statement is executed within the jGRASP debugger, the node `"dick"` moves down and the node `"harry"` moves to the left.

FIGURE D.6
Executing the Statement
`node.next = temp.next`

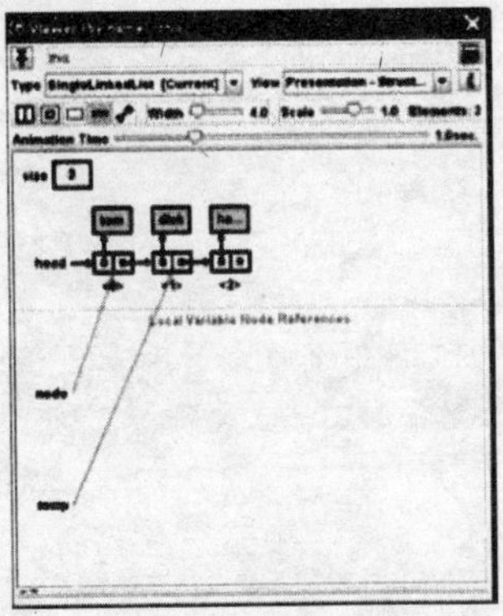

(a) Before

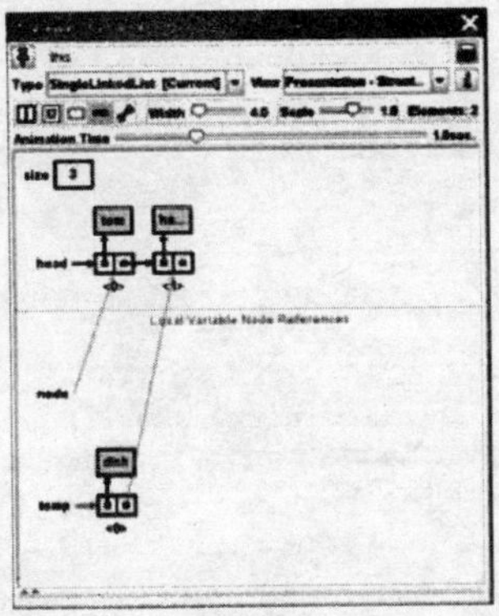

(b) After

Glossary

2-3 tree A search tree in which each node may have two or three children.

2-3-4 tree A search tree in which each node may have two, three, or four children.

2-node A node in a 2-3 or 2-3-4 tree with two children.

3-node A node in a 2-3 or 2-3-4 tree with three children.

abstract class A class that contains at least one abstract method.

abstract data type An implementation-independent specification of a set of data items and the operations performed on those data items.

abstraction A model of a physical entity or activity.

abstract method The specification of the signature of a method without its implementation. Abstract methods are declared in interfaces and abstract classes. A concrete class that is a subclass of an abstract class or an implementation of an interface must implement each abstract method declared in the abstract superclass or interface.

accelerator A key combination that invokes a menu item's action listeners without requiring the user to navigate the menu hierarchy.

acceptance testing A sequence of tests that demonstrates to the customer that a software product meets all of its requirements. Acceptance testing generally is observed by a customer representative.

action event An event caused by a user's action, such as pressing a key or clicking a GUI button.

action listener An object that contains a method that responds to an action event. An action listener is an event listener for an action event. See also *event listener*.

activation bar The thick line along the lifeline in a sequence diagram that indicates the time that a method is executing in response to the receipt of a message.

activation frame An area of memory allocated to store the actual parameters and local variables for a particular call to a method. In Java, references to activation frames are stored on the run-time stack. When a method is called, a new activation frame is pushed onto the stack, and when a method exits, the activation frame is popped.

actor An entity that is external to a given software system. In many cases an actor is a human user of the software system, but an actor may be another system.

adapter class A class that provides the same or very similar functionality as another class but with different method signatures. The actual work is performed by delegation to the methods in the other class.

address A number that represents an object's location in memory.

adjacency lists A representation of a graph in which the vertices (the destinations) adjacent to a given vertex (the source) are stored in a list associated with that vertex. The actual edge (source, destination, weight) from the source vertex to the destination may be stored.

adjacency matrix A representation of a graph in which the presence or absence of an edge is indicated by a value in a matrix that is indexed by the two vertices. The value stored is 0 for no edge, 1 for an edge in an unweighted graph, and the weight itself for a weighted graph.

adjacent [vertex] In a directed graph, a vertex, v, is adjacent to another vertex, u, if there is an edge, (u, v), from vertex u to vertex v. In an undirected graph, v is adjacent to u if there is an edge, $\{u, v\}$, between them.

aggregation An association between two classes in which one class is composed of a collection of objects of the other class.

analysis In the waterfall model, the phase of the software life cycle (workflow in the Unified Model) during which the requirements are clarified and the overall architecture of the solution is determined.

ancestor A node in a tree that is at a higher level than a given node and from which there is a path to that node (the descendant).

ancestor-descendant relationship A generalization of the parent-child relationship. (See *ancestor* and *descendant*.)

anchor The symbol ⊕ that is used in a UML class diagram to indicate that a class is an inner class of another class.

anonymous object An object for which there is no named reference. The Java **new** operator returns a reference to an anonymous object.

anonymous reference A reference to an object that itself has no name. Anonymous references are the result of a cast operation.

applet A top-level Java GUI class that is intended to be displayed in a frame that is under the control of a web browser.

assertion A statement about the current value of one or more variables.

association A relationship between two classes.

attributes The set of data values that determine the state of an object. Generally the attributes of a class are represented by data fields within the class.

auto-boxing A new Java feature (in Java 1.5) that performs automatic conversion between the primitive types and their corresponding wrapper classes.

AVL tree A self-balancing binary search tree in which the difference between the heights of the subtrees is stored in each tree node. The insertion and removal algorithms use rotations to maintain this difference within the range –1 to +1.

back edges An edge that is discovered during a depth-first search that leads to an ancestor in the depth-first search tree.

backtracking An approach to implementing a systematic trial-and-error search for a solution. When a dead end is reached, the algorithm follows a path back to the decision point that leads to the dead end, then moves forward along a different path.

balanced binary search tree A binary search tree in which the height of each pair of subtrees is approximately the same.

base case The case in a recursive algorithm that can be solved directly.

batch processing A way of using a computer in which a series of jobs (individual programs) are collected together and then executed sequentially.

big-O notation The specification of a set of functions that represent the upper bound of a given function. Formally the function $f(n)$ is said to be $O(g(n))$ if there are constants $c > 0$ and $n_0 > 0$ such that for all $n > n_0$, $cg(n) \geq f(n)$.

binary search The process of searching a sorted sequence that begins by examining the middle element. If the middle element is greater than the target, then the search is applied recursively to the lower half; if it is less than the target, the search is applied recursively to the upper half.

binary search tree A binary tree in which the items in the left subtree of a node are all less than that node, and the items in the right subtree are all greater than that node.

binary tree A tree in which each node has 0, 1, or 2 children. The children are distinguished by the names left and right. If a node has one child, that child is distinguished as being a left child or a right child.

black-box testing A testing approach in which the internal structure of the item being tested is not known or taken into account in the design of the test cases. The test cases are based only on the functional requirements for the item being tested.

block A compound statement that may contain local variables and class declarations.

bottom-up design A design process in which the lower-level methods are designed first. A lowest-level method is one that does not depend on other methods to perform its function.

boundary condition A value of a variable that causes a different path to be taken. For example, in the statement `if (x > C) { ... } else { ... }`, the value of C is a boundary condition.

branch In a tree, the link between a parent node and one of its children.

branch coverage A measure of testing thoroughness. Each alternative from a decision point (**`if`**, **`switch`**, or **`while`** statement) is considered a branch. If a test exercises a branch, then that branch is considered covered. The ratio of the covered branches to the total number of branches is the branch coverage. See also *path coverage* and *statement coverage*.

breadth-first search A way of searching through a graph in which the vertices adjacent to a given vertex are all examined and placed into a queue. Once all the adjacent vertices are examined, the next vertex is removed from the queue. Thus vertices are examined in increasing distance (as measured by the number of edges) from the starting vertex.

breadth-first traversal See *breadth-first search.*

breakpoint A point in a program at which the debugger is instructed to suspend execution when it is reached. This allows for examination of the value of variables at a given point before execution is resumed.

B-tree A balanced search tree in which each node is a leaf or may have up to n children and n–1 data items. The leaves are all at the bottom level. Each node (except for the root) is kept at least half full. That is, each node has between (n–1)/2 and n–1 data items. The root is either a single node (leaf) or it has at least one data item and two children.

bubble sort A sort algorithm that makes several passes through the sequence being sorted. During each pass, adjacent items are examined and, if out of order, swapped. If there are no exchanges on a given pass, then the process is complete. The effect of each pass is that the largest item in the unsorted part of the sequence is moved to (bubbles to) the end of the sequence.

bucket The list of keys stored in a hash table entry that uses chaining. All the keys in the list map to the index of that table entry.

bucket hashing See *chaining.*

byte code The platform-independent representation of a Java program that is the output of the Java compiler and is the input to the Java Virtual Machine (JVM). The JVM then interprets this input to execute the program.

casting When applied to a reference to an object, casting reinterprets that reference to refer to an object of a different type. The object must be of the target type (or a subclass of the target type) for the cast to be valid. When applied to a primitive numeric value, a cast represents a conversion to an equivalent value of the target primitive numeric type.

`catch` block The sequence of statements that will be executed when an exception is caught by a **`catch`** clause.

`catch` clause The specification of an exception type and the statements to be executed when an exception of that type is caught. One or more **`catch`** clauses follow a **`try`** block and will catch the exceptions thrown from that **`try`** block.

chaining An approach to hashing in which all keys that are mapped to a given entry in the hash table are placed into a list. The list is called a bucket.

check box A GUI component that may be either selected or deselected. The component is generally shown as a small square box, and the selected state is indicated by a check-mark symbol. Several check boxes may be presented to give the user the choice of one or more from a group of possible values See also *combo box* and *radio button.*

checked exception An exception that either must be declared in a throws declaration or caught by a **`try-catch`** sequence.

child A node in a tree that is the immediate descendant of another node.

class The fundamental programming unit in a Java program. A class consists of a collection of zero or more data fields (instance variables) and zero or more methods that operate on those data fields.

class diagram A UML diagram that shows a number of classes and the relationships between them.

class method See *static method.*

client A class or method that uses a given class.

cloning The process of making a deep copy of an object.

closed-box testing See *black-box testing.*

collection hierarchy The hierarchy of classes in the Java API that consists of classes designed to represent collections of other object.

collision The mapping of two or more keys into the same position in a hash table.

combo box A GUI component that is a combination of a button or editable field and a drop-down list. The drop-down list is a set (or menu) of choices, only one of which may be selected at a time. The current selection is displayed in the button of field, but when selected by a mouse click, the drop-down list is displayed, allowing the selection of one of the other choices. See also *check box* and *radio button.*

complete binary tree A binary tree in which each node is a leaf or has two children.

component In a GUI application, an object displayed on the screen that can interact with the user.

component class A class whose objects are part of another object. See *composition.*

component testing The testing of an individual part of a program by itself. In a Java program, a component may be a method or a class.

composition The association between two classes in which objects of one class are part of another class. The parts generally do not have an independent existence but are created when the parent object is created. For example, an `Airplane` object is composed of a `Body` object, two `Wing` objects, and a `Tail` object.

compound statement Zero or more statements enclosed within braces `{ ... }`.

concrete class (actual class) A class for which objects can be instantiated.

connected components A set of vertices within a graph for which there is a path between every pair of vertices.

connected graph A graph that consists of a single connected component.

construction phase The phase of the Unified Model of the software life cycle during which most of the activity is devoted to writing the software.

constructor A method that initializes an object when it is first created.

container In a GUI application, a component that contains other components.

content pane In a Swing GUI application, the component of a frame in which the application places the components to be displayed.

contract The specification of the pre- and postconditions of a method.

cost of a spanning tree The sum of the weights of the edges.

coverage testing See *branch coverage.*

cycle A path in a graph in which the first and final vertices are the same.

data abstraction The specification of the data items of a problem and the operations to be performed on these data items that does not specify how the data items will be represented and stored in memory. See also *abstract data type.*

data field (instance variable) A variable that is part of a class.

debugging The process of finding and removing defects (bugs) from a program.

deep copy A copy of an object in which data field values and references to immutable objects are simply duplicated, but each reference to a mutable object references a copy of that object. If there are mutuable references in any object that is copied, these also reference a copy of that object. The effect is that you can change any value in a deep copy of an object without modifiying the original object.

default constructor The no-parameter constructor that is generated by the Java compiler if no constructors are defined.

default visibility The same as *package visibility.*

defensive programming An approach to designing a program that builds in statements to test the values of variables that might result in an exception or run-time error (to be sure that they are valid) before statements that use the variables are executed.

delegation The implementation of a method in one class that merely calls a method in another class.

delimiter characters Characters that are defined to separate a string into tokens.

depth (level) The number of nodes in a path from the root to a node.

depth-first search A method of searching a graph in which adjacent vertices are examined along a path until a dead end is reached. The search then backtracks until an unexamined vertex is found, and the search continues with that vertex.

depth-first traversal See *depth-first search*.

deque A data structure that combines the features of a stack and queue. Items may be inserted in one end and removed from either.

descendant In a tree, a lower node that can be reached by following a path from a given node.

design The process by which classes and methods are identified and defined to create a program that satisfies a given set of requirements.

detail message An optional string to be displayed when an exception is thrown that provides additional information about the conditions that led to the exception.

dialog In a GUI application, a window that provides information or asks for data entry.

digraph See *directed graph*.

directed acyclic graph A directed graph that contains no cycles.

directed edge An edge in a directed graph.

directed graph A graph in which every edge is considered to have a direction. If *u* and *v* are vertices in a graph, then the presence of the edge (*u*, *v*) indicates that *v* is adjacent to *u*, but *u* may not be adjacent to *v*. Contrast with *undirected graph*.

discovery order The order in which vertices are discovered in a depth-first search.

double buffering In a GUI application, updates to the image are made in one area of memory while the image being displayed is based on another area of memory. When all of the updates are complete, the memory areas are swapped and the new image is displayed.

downcast A reinterpretation of a reference from a superclass to a subclass. In Java, downcasts are tested for validity. See also *casting*.

driver A method whose purpose is to call a method being tested and provide it with appropriate argument values. Usually the result of executing the method is displayed immediately to the user.

edges In a graph, the links between pairs of vertices.

elaboration phase The phase in the Unified Model of the software life cycle during which the software architecture is defined.

escape sequence A sequence of characters beginning with the backslash (\) which is used to indicate another character that cannot be directly entered. For example, the sequence \n represents the newline character.

Euler tour A path around a tree, starting and ending with the root. The tree is always kept to the left of the path when viewed from the direction of travel along the path.

event The occurrence of an external input or an internal state change.

event listener An object that is registered to respond to an event. The object's class contains a method that is called when the event occurs.

exclusive or (XOR) A graphics drawing mode in which drawing a shape twice has the effect of erasing the original shape from the image.

extending The process of adding functionality by defining a new class that adds data fields and/or adds or overrides methods of an existing class.

external node See *leaf*.

Extreme Programming A software development process in which programmers work in pairs. One programmer writes methods while the other designs tests for those methods. The programmers alternate roles. The programmers also share a workstation so that when one programmer is using the workstation, the other is observing.

factory method A method that is responsible for creating objects of a class. Generally a factory method will be associated with an abstract class or interface and will choose an appropriate concrete class that extends the abstract class or implements the interface based on parameters passed to the factory method and/or system parameters. Returns a reference to a new object of this concrete class.

`finally` block A block preceded by the key word **`finally`**. Part of the **`try-catch-finally`** sequence.

finish order The order in which the vertices are finished in a depth-first search. A vertex is considered finished when all of the paths to adjacent vertices have been finished.

firing an event The process of indicating that an event has occurred.

forest A collection of trees that may result from a depth-first search of a directed graph or an unconnected graph.

frame A top-level container in a GUI application. A frame consists of a window with a border around it.

full binary tree A binary tree in which the nodes at all but the deepest level contain two children. At the deepest level, all nodes that have two children are to the left of those that have no children, and there is at most one node with a left child that is between these two groups.

functional testing Testing that concentrates on verifying that software meets its functional requirements.

garbage collector The process of reclaiming memory that no longer has a reference to it. This process generally runs in the background.

generalization The relationship between two classes in which one class is the superclass and the other is a subclass. The superclass is a generalization of the subclass.

generic class A class with type parameters that are specified when instances are created. These parameters specify the actual data type for the internal data fields of the object that is created.

generic method A method with type parameters that are used to represent the data type of its formal parameters. The type parameters are specified when the method is called and enable the method to process actual parameters of different data types.

generic type A type that is defined in terms of another type where that other type may be specified as a parameter. For example, the class `List<E>` is a `List` designed to hold objects of type `E`, where `E` may be any other class and is specified when the object is created.

glass-box testing Testing that takes the internal structure of the unit being tested into account.

graph A mathematical structure consisting of a set of vertices and edges. The edges represent a relationship between the vertices.

hash code A function that transforms an object into an integer value that may be used as an index into a hash table.

heapsort A sort algorithm in which the items being sorted are inserted into a heap, then removed one at a time.

height of a tree The number of nodes in a path from the root to the deepest leaf.

Huffman code A varying-length binary code in which each symbol is assigned a code whose length is inversely proportional to the frequency with which that symbol appears (or is expected to appear) in a message. The resulting coded message is the minimum possible length.

image rendering The process of creating an image in a device-dependent form for display on that device. During this process, the values of individual pixels are determined.

immutable A class that is immutable has no methods to change the value of its data fields. An immutable object can't be changed.

implement (an interface) To provide in a class an implementation of all of the methods specified by an interface.

inception phase In the Unified model of the software life cycle, the initial phase of a project in which the requirements are first identified.

increment operator The operator that has the side effect of adding 1 to its operand.

index A value that specifies a position within an array.

infix notation Mathematical notation in which the operators are between the operands.

information hiding The design principle that states that the internal data representations of a class cannot be used or directly modified by clients.

inherit To receive from an ancestor. In an object-oriented language, a subclass inherits the visible methods and data fields from its superclass. These inherited methods and data fields appear to clients of the subclass as if they were members of that class.

initializer list A list of values, enclosed in braces, that initializes the values in an array.

inner class A class that is defined within another class. Methods of inner classes have access to the data fields and methods of the outer class in which they are defined and vice versa.

inorder predecessor For a binary search tree, the inorder predecessor of an item is the largest item that is less than this item. The node containing an item's inorder predecessor would be visited just prior to that item in an inorder traversal.

insertion sort A sorting algorithm in which each item is inserted into its proper place in the sorted region.

instance See *object*.

instance method A method that is associated with an object. Contrast with *static method*.

`instanceof` operator The Java operator that returns true if a reference variable references an instance of a specified class or interface.

instance variables A variable of a class that is associated with an object (i.e., a data field of an object). Contrast with *static variable*.

integration testing Testing in which the interaction of the components or units of a software program is validated.

interface The external view of a class. In Java, an interface is a class that defines nothing more than public abstract methods and constants.

internal node A node in a tree that has one or more children. Contrast with *leaf*.

interpret To translate or understand the meaning of. The Java Virtual Machine interprets the machine-independent byte code in terms of specific machine-language instructions for the computer on which it is executing.

iteration In a loop, a complete execution of the loop body. In the Unified model of the software life cycle, a sequence of activities that results in the release of a set of software artifacts.

iterator An object that accesses the objects contained in a collection one at a time.

Javadoc The commenting convention defined for Java programs. Also, the program that generates documentation from the comments that follow this convention in a program.

key A value or reference that is unique to a particular object and thereby identifies that object (e.g., a social security number).

Last In, First Out (LIFO) An organization of data such that the most recently inserted item is the one that is removed first.

last-line recursion A recursive algorithm or method in which the recursive call is the last executable statement.

layout manager An object in a GUI application that manages the visual arrangement of components in a container.

leaf (node) A node in a tree that has no children. Contrast with *internal node*.

left rotation The transformation of a binary search tree in which the right child of the current root becomes the new root and the old root becomes the left child of the new root.

level of a node The number of nodes in a path from the root to this node.

life line The dotted vertical line in a UML sequence diagram that indicates the lifetime of an object.

linear probing A collision resolution method in which sequential locations in a hash table are searched to find the item sought or an empty location.

linear search A search algorithm in which items in a sequence are examined sequentially.

link A reference from one node to another.

literal A constant value that appears directly in a statement.

logic error An error in the design of an algorithm or program. Contrast with *syntax error*.

logical view A description of the data stored in an object that does not specify the physical layout of the data in memory.

loop invariant An assertion that is true before each execution of the loop body and is true when the loop exits.

many-to-one mapping An association among items in which more than one item (a key) is associated with a single item (a value).

marker An interface that is defined with no methods or constants. It is used to give a common name to a family of interfaces or classes.

merge The process of combining two sorted sequences into a single sorted sequence.

merge sort A sorting algorithm in which sorted subsequences are merged to form larger sorted sequences.

message In an object-oriented design, a message represents an occurrence of a method call.

message to self A message that is passed from an object to itself. It represents a method calling another method within the same class.

method A sequence of statements that can be invoked (or called) passing a fixed number of values as arguments and optionally returning a value.

method declaration The specification of the name, parameters, and return type of a method. See also *signature*.

method overloading The presence of multiple methods in a class with the same name but different signatures.

method overriding The replacement of an inherited method with a different implementation in a subclass.

minimum spanning tree A subset of the edges of a connected graph such that the graph remains connected and the sum of the weights of the edges is the minimum.

mnemonic A character that can be used to select a menu item from the keyboard when the menu is displayed.

multiple inheritance Inheriting from more than one superclass.

multiplicity An indication of the number of objects in an association.

narrowing conversion A conversion from a type that has a larger range of values to a type that has a smaller one.

nested class See *inner class*.

network A system consisting of interconnected entities.

newline The special character that indicates the end of a line of input or output.

new operator The Java operator that creates objects (or instances) of a class.

node An object to store data in a linked list or tree. This object will also contain references to other nodes.

object An example or instance of a class. Internally, it is an area of memory that is structured as defined by a class. The methods of that class operate on the values defined within this memory area.

object-oriented design A design approach that identifies the entities, or objects, that participate in a problem or system and then designs classes to model these objects within a program.

onto mapping A mapping in which each value in the value set is mapped to by at least one member of the key set.

open-box testing See *glass-box testing*.

operations The methods defined in a class.

operator For classes, operator is another name for *method*. For primitive types, it represents a predefined function on one or two values (e.g., addition).

output buffer A memory area in which information written to an output stream is stored prior to being written to disk.

override Replace a method inherited from a superclass by one defined in a subclass.

package A grouping of classes under a common package name.

package visibility A level of visibility whereby variables and methods are visible to methods defined in classes within the same package.

panel A general-purpose GUI component that can be used as a drawing surface or to contain other GUI components.

parent The node that is directly above a node within a tree.

partitioning The process of separating a sequence into two sequences; used in quicksort.

path In a graph, a sequence of vertices in which each vertex is adjacent to its predecessor.

path coverage A measure of testing thoroughness. If a test exercises a path, then that path is considered covered. The ratio of the covered paths to the total number of paths is the path coverage. See also *branch coverage* and *statement coverage*.

phase In the Unified Model of the software life cycle, the span of time between two major milestones.

physical view A view of an object that considers its actual representation in computer memory.

pivot In the quicksort algorithm, a value in the sequence being sorted that is used to partition the sequence. The sequence is partitioned into values that are less than or equal to the pivot and values that are greater than the pivot.

polymorphism Many forms or many shapes. In a Java program, a method defined in a superclass (or interface) may be called through a reference to that superclass (or interface). The actual method executed is the one that overrides that method and is defined in the concrete subclass object that is referenced by the superclass (or interface) variable.

pop Remove the top element of a stack.

postcondition An assertion that will be true after a method is executed, assuming that the preconditions were true before the method is executed.

postfix increment The increment operator (e.g., `i++`) that has the side effect of incrementing the variable to which it is applied, but its current value is the value of the variable before the increment takes place (e.g., `i`).

postfix notation A mathematical notation in which the operators appear after their operands.

precedence The degree of binding of infix operators. Operators of higher precedence are evaluated before operators of lower precedence.

precondition An assertion that must be true before a method is executed for the method to perform as specified.

prefix increment The increment operator (e.g., `++i`) that has the side effect of incrementing the variable to which it is applied, and its current value is the value of the variable after the increment takes place (e.g., `i + 1`).

private visibility A level of visibility whereby variables and methods are visible only to methods defined in the same class.

procedural abstraction The philosophy that procedure (method) development should separate the concern of *what* is to be achieved by a procedure (or method) from the details of *how* it is to be achieved.

proof by induction A proof method which demonstrates that a proposition is true for a base case (usually 0) and then demonstrates that if the proposition is true for an arbitrary value (k), it is then true for the successor of that value ($k + 1$).

protected visibility A level of visibility whereby variables and methods are visible to methods defined in the same class, subclasses of that class, or the same package.

pseudocode A description of an algorithm that is structured similar to a programming language implementation but lacks the formal syntax and notation of a programming language. Generally pseudocode will use common programming language decision and looping constructs.

pseudorandom A computer-generated sequence of values that appear to be random because they pass various statistical tests that are consistent with those that would be produced by a truly random sequence.

public visibility A level of visibility whereby variables and methods are visible to all methods regardless of which class or package they are defined in.

quadratic probing In a hash table, a collision resolution technique in which the sequence of locations that are examined increases as the square of the number of probes made.

queuing theory The branch of mathematics developed to solve problems associated with queues by developing mathematical models for these problems.

quicksort A sorting algorithm in which a sequence is partitioned into two subsequences, one that is less than or equal to a pivot value and the other that is greater than the pivot value. The process is then recursively applied to the subsequences until a subsequence with one item is reached.

radio button A GUI component that may be either selected or deselected. The component is generally shown as a small open circle, and the selected state is indicated by a filled-in circle. Radio buttons are grouped into a button group so that only one item in the group may be selected at a time. See also *check box* and *combo box*.

random access The ability to access any object in a collection by means of an index.

recursive case A case in a recursive algorithm that is solved by applying the algorithm to a transformed version of its parameter.

recursive data structure A data structure that is defined in terms of itself.

recursive method A method that calls itself.

Red-Black tree A self-balancing binary search tree that maintains balance by distinguishing the nodes by one of two states: "red" or "black." Algorithms for insertion and deletion maintain balance by ensuring that the number of black nodes in any path from the root to a leaf is the same.

reference variable A variable that references an object.

registering (listener for event) The process by which a listener object is associated with an event. This is done by calling a method defined by the component that recognizes the event and passing a reference to the listener object.

regression testing Testing that ensures that changes to the item being tested do not invalidate previously verified functions.

rehashing The process of moving the items in one hash table to a larger hash table using hashing to find each item's new location.

request-response A program that issues a request to the user and then waits for input.

requirements specification A document that specifies what a program or system is to do without specifying how it is done.

reusable code Code written for one program that can be used in another.

right rotation The transformation of a binary search tree in which the left child of the current root becomes the new root and the old root becomes the right child of the new root.

root The node in a tree that has no parent and is at the top level.

rubber banding Continuously erasing and redrawing a shape so that it follows the mouse position.

run-time error An error that is detected when the program executes. In Java, run-time errors are detected by the Java Virtual Machine.

starter method See *wrapper method.*

seed The initial value in a pseudorandom number sequence. Changing the seed causes a different sequence to be generated by the pseudorandom number generator.

selection sort A sort algorithm in which the smallest item is selected from the unsorted portion of the sequence and placed into the next position in the sorted portion.

self-balancing search tree A search tree with insertion and removal algorithms that maintain the tree in balance. See *2-3 tree, 2-3-4 tree, AVL tree, balanced binary search tree,* and *Red-Black tree.*

sequence diagram A UML diagram that shows the sequence of messages between objects that are required to perform a given function or realize a use case.

set difference For sets A and B, A–B is the subset of a set, A, that does not contain elements of some other set, B.

set intersection A set of the elements that are common to two sets.

set union A set of the elements that are in one set or the other.

shallow copy A copy of an object that copies only the values of the data fields. If a data field is a reference, the original and the copy reference the same target object.

Shell sort A variation on insertion sort in which elements separated by a value known as the gap are sorted using the insertion sort algorithm. This process repeats using a decreasing sequence of values for the gap.

sibling One of two or more nodes in a tree that have a common parent.

signature A method's name and the types of its parameters. The return type is not part of the signature because it is illegal to have two methods with the same signature and different return types.

simple path A path that contains no cycles.

simulation The process of modeling a physical system using a computer program.

single-step execution In debugging, the process of executing one statement at a time so that the user may examine the values of variables after each statement is executed.

skip-list A randomized variant of an ordered linked list with additional parallel lists. Parallel lists at higher levels skip geometrically more items. Searching begins at the highest level to quickly get to the right part of the list, then uses progressively lower level lists. A new item is added by randomly selecting a level, then inserting it in order in the lists for that and all lower levels. With enough levels, searching is O(log *n*).

software life cycle The sequence of phases that a software product goes through as it is developed.

spanning tree A minimum subset of the vertices of a connected graph that still results in a connected graph.

stack trace A listing of the sequence of method calls that starts where an error is detected and ends at the program invocation.

state The current value of all of the data fields in an object.

statement coverage A measure of testing thoroughness. If a test exercises a statement, then the statement is considered covered. The ratio of the covered statements to the total number of statements is the statement coverage. See also *branch coverage* and *path coverage.*

static method A method defined within a class but not associated with any particular object of that class.

static variable A variable defined in a class that is not a member of any particular object but is shared by all objects of the class.

step into When debugging in single-step mode, setting the next statement to be executed to be the first statement of the method. Each individual statement in the method is executed in sequence.

step over When debugging in single-step mode, setting the method call to be treated as a single statement.

stepwise refinement The process of breaking a complicated problem into simpler problems. This process is repeated with the smaller problems until a problem of solvable size is reached.

strongly typed language A programming language in which the type of objects is verified when arguments are bound to parameters and when values are assigned to variables. A syntax error occurs if the types are not compatible.

structure chart A diagram that represents the relationship between problems and their subproblems.

structured walkthrough A design or code review following a defined process in which the author of a program leads the review team through the design and implementation, and the reviewers follow a checklist of common defects to verify that these defects are not present.

stub A dummy method that is used to test another method. A stub takes the place of a method that the method being tested calls. A stub typically will return a known result.

subclass A class that is an extension of another class. A subclass inherits the members of its superclass.

subset A set that contains only elements that are in some other set. A subset may contain any or all of the elements of the other set, or it may be the empty set.

subtree of a node The tree that consists of this node as its root.

superclass A class that has a subclass. See *subclass*.

syntax error An error that violates the syntax rules of the language. Syntax errors are generally the result of a mistake in entering the program into the computer (typographical error) or a misunderstanding of the language syntax. Syntax errors are detected by the compiler.

system analyst A person who analyses a problem to determine the requirements for a software program.

system testing Testing of a complete program or solution to a problem.

tail recursion See *last-line recursion*.

test case An individual test.

test framework A set of classes and procedures used to design and conduct tests.

test harness A method that executes the individual test cases of a test suite and records the results.

test suite A collection of test cases.

throw an exception Indicate that the situation that causes an exception has been detected.

token A character or string extracted from a larger string. Tokens are separated by *delimiter characters*.

top-down design A design process that represents the solution to a higher module in terms of the solution to one or more lower-level modules.

topological sort An ordering of a sequence of items for which a partial order is defined that does not violate the partial order. For example, if a is defined to be before b (a is a prerequisite of b) by the partial order, then a will not appear later in the sequence than b. A partial order is defined by a directed acylic graph.

transition phase In the Unified Model of the software life cycle, the phase in which the software product is turned over to the end users.

tree traversal The process of systematically visiting each node in a tree.

try block A block preceded by the reserved word `try`. Part of the `try-catch-finally` sequence.

`try-catch-finally` sequence A sequence consisting of a `try` block followed by one or more `catch` clauses and optionally followed by a `finally` block. Or a `try` block followed by a `finally` block. Exceptions that are thrown by the `try` block are handled by the `catch` clauses that follow it. Statements in the `finally` block are executed either after the `try` block exits normally or when a `catch` block that handles an exception exits.

type cast The process of converting from one type to another.

unchecked exception An exception that does not have to be declared in a `throws` statement or have the statements that might throw it enclosed within a `try` block.

undirected edge An edge in an undirected graph.

undirected graph A graph in which no edge has a direction. If u and v are vertices in a graph, then the presence of the edge $\{u, v\}$ indicates that v is adjacent to u and u is adjacent to v. Contrast with *directed graph*.

Unified Model A software development life cycle model that is defined in terms of a sequence of phases and workflows. The workflows are exercised during each iteration of each phase, but the distribution of the amount of effort for each workflow varies from iteration to iteration.

Unified Modeling Language (UML) A language to describe the modeling of an object-oriented design that is the unification of several previous modeling systems. Specifically, the modeling techniques developed by Booch, Jacobson, and Rumbaugh were combined to form the initial version. UML has since evolved and is defined by a standard issued by the Object Modeling Group.

unit testing Testing of an individual unit of a software program. In Java, a unit is generally a method or class.

unnamed reference See *anonymous reference*.

unwinding the recursion The process of returning from a sequence of method calls and forming the result.

upcast Casting a reference to a superclass or interface type.

user interface (UI) The way in which the user and a program interact, or the class that provides this interaction.

version control The process of keeping track of the various changes that are made to a program as it is developed or maintained.

vertices The set of items that are part of a graph. The vertices are related to one another by edges.

waterfall model A software development model in which all of the activities of one workflow are completed before the next one is started.

weight A value associated with an edge in a weighted graph.

weighted graph A graph in which each edge is assigned a value.

widening conversion A conversion from a type that has a smaller set of values to one that has a larger set of values.

window A top-level container in a GUI application. Generally a window is a rectangular area on the display surface. See also *frame*.

wrapper class A class that encapsulates a primitive data type.

wrapper method A method whose only purpose is to call a recursive method, perhaps providing initial values for some parameters and returning the result. Also called a starter method.

Index